T0180651

Lecture Notes in Computer Science 11746

More information about this series at http://www.springer.com/series/7409

David Lamas · Fernando Loizides ·
Lennart Nacke · Helen Petrie ·
Marco Winckler · Panayiotis Zaphiris (Eds.)

Human-Computer Interaction – INTERACT 2019

17th IFIP TC 13 International Conference
Paphos, Cyprus, September 2–6, 2019
Proceedings, Part I

 Springer

Editors
David Lamas 🆔
Tallinn University
Tartu, Estonia

Fernando Loizides 🆔
Cardiff University
Cardiff, UK

Lennart Nacke 🆔
University of Waterloo
Waterloo, ON, Canada

Helen Petrie 🆔
University of York
York, UK

Marco Winckler 🆔
Nice Sophia Antipolis University
Sophia Antipolis, France

Panayiotis Zaphiris 🆔
Cyprus University of Technology
Limassol, Cyprus

ISSN 0302-9743   ISSN 1611-3349   (electronic)
Lecture Notes in Computer Science
ISBN 978-3-030-29380-2   ISBN 978-3-030-29381-9   (eBook)
https://doi.org/10.1007/978-3-030-29381-9

LNCS Sublibrary: SL3 – Information Systems and Applications, incl. Internet/Web, and HCI

This Springer imprint is published by the registered company Springer Nature Switzerland AG
The registered company address is: Gewerbestrasse 11, 6330 Cham, Switzerland

Foreword

The 17th IFIP TC13 International Conference on Human-Computer Interaction, INTERACT 2019, took place during September 2–6, 2019, in Paphos, Cyprus. This conference was held at the Coral Beach Hotel & Resort. The conference was co-sponsored by the Cyprus University of Technology and Tallinn University, in cooperation with ACM and ACM SIGCHI.

The International Federation for Information Processing (IFIP) was created in 1960 under the auspices of UNESCO. The Technical Committee 13 (TC13) of the IFIP aims at developing the science and technology of human-computer interaction (HCI). TC13 has representatives from 32 countries, 2 international organizations, apart from 14 expert members and observers. TC13 started the series of INTERACT conferences in 1984. These conferences have been an important showcase for researchers and practitioners in the field of HCI. Situated under the open, inclusive umbrella of the IFIP, INTERACT has been a truly international in its spirit and has attracted researchers from several countries and cultures. The venues of the INTERACT conferences over the years bear a testimony to this inclusiveness.

INTERACT 2019 continued the INTERACT conscious efforts to lower barriers that prevent people from developing countries to participate in conferences. Thinkers and optimists believe that all regions of the world can achieve human development goals. Information and communication technologies (ICTs) can support this process and empower people to achieve their full potential. Today ICT products have many new users and many new uses, but also present new challenges and provide new opportunities. It is no surprise that HCI researchers are showing great interest in these emergent users. INTERACT 2019 provided a platform to explore these challenges and opportunities, but also made it easier for people from developing countries to participate.

Furthermore, hosting INTERACT 2019 in a small country with a small HCI community presented an opportunity to expose the local industry and academia to the concepts of HCI and user-centered design. The rich history and culture of the island of Cyprus provided a strong networking atmosphere and collaboration opportunities.

Students represent the future of our community. They bring in new energy, enthusiasm, and fresh ideas. However, it is often hard for students to participate in international conferences. INTERACT 2019 made special efforts to bring students to the conference. The conference had low registration costs, and thanks to our sponsors, we could provide several travel grants.

Finally, great research is the heart of a good conference. Like its predecessors, INTERACT 2019 aimed to bring together high-quality research. As a multidisciplinary field, HCI requires interaction and discussion among diverse people with different interests and backgrounds. The beginners and the experienced, theoreticians and practitioners, and people from diverse disciplines and different countries gathered together in Paphos to learn from each other and to contribute to each other's growth.

We thank all the authors who chose INTERACT 2019 as the venue to publish their research.

We received a total of 669 submissions distributed in 2 peer reviewed tracks, 4 curated tracks, and 4 juried tracks. Of these, the following contributions were accepted:

- 111 Full Papers (peer reviewed)
- 55 Short Papers (peer reviewed)
- 7 Industry Case Studies (curated)
- 3 Courses (curated)
- 9 Demonstrations (curated)
- 18 Interactive Posters (juried)
- 2 Panels (curated)
- 9 Workshops (juried)
- 1 Field Trips (juried)
- 17 Doctoral Consortium (juried)

The acceptance rate for contributions received in the peer-reviewed tracks was 29% for full papers and 28% for short papers. In addition to full papers and short papers, the present proceedings feature contributions accepted in the form of industry case studies, courses, demonstrations, interactive posters, panels, and description of accepted workshops. The contributions submitted to workshops were published in adjunct proceedings.

INTERACT 2019 innovated the reviewing process with the introduction of sub-committees. Each subcommittee had a chair and set of associated chairs who were in charge of coordinating the reviewing process with the help of expert reviewers. Hereafter we list the ten subcommittees of INTERACT 2019:

- Accessibility and Assistive Technologies
- Design for Business and Safety/Critical Interactive Systems
- Design of Interactive Entertainment Systems
- HCI Education and Curriculum
- Information Visualization
- Interaction Design for Culture and Development
- Interactive Systems Technologies and Engineering
- Methodologies for User-Centred Design
- Social Interaction and Mobile HCI
- Understanding Human Aspects of HCI

The final decision on acceptance or rejection of full papers was taken in a Program Committee meeting held in London, United Kingdom in March 2019. The full papers chairs, the subcommittee chairs, and the associate chairs participated in this meeting. The meeting discussed a consistent set of criteria to deal with inevitable differences among the large number of reviewers. The final decisions on other tracks were made by the corresponding track chairs and reviewers, often after electronic meetings and discussions.

INTERACT 2019 was made possible by the persistent efforts across several months by 10 subcommittees chairs, 62 associated chairs, 28 track chairs, and 510 reviewers. We thank them all.

September 2019

Panayiotis Zaphiris
David Lamas

IFIP TC13 (http://ifip-tc13.org/)

Established in 1989, the International Federation for Information Processing Technical Committee on Human–Computer Interaction (IFIP TC 13) is an international committee of 32 member national societies and 10 Working Groups, representing specialists of the various disciplines contributing to the field of human-computer interaction. This includes (among others) human factors, ergonomics, cognitive science, computer science, and design. INTERACT is its flagship conference of IFIP TC 13, staged biennially in different countries around the world. The first INTERACT conference was held in 1984 running triennially and became a biennial event in 1993.

IFIP TC 13 aims to develop the science, technology, and societal aspects of HCI by encouraging empirical research; promoting the use of knowledge and methods from the human sciences in design and evaluation of computer systems; promoting a better understanding of the relation between formal design methods and system usability and acceptability; developing guidelines, models, and methods by which designers may provide better human-oriented computer systems; and, cooperating with other groups, inside and outside IFIP, to promote user-orientation and humanization in systems design. Thus, TC 13 seeks to improve interactions between people and computers, to encourage the growth of HCI research and its practice in industry and to disseminate these benefits worldwide.

The main orientation is to place the users at the center of the development process. Areas of study include: the problems people face when interacting with computers; the impact of technology deployment on people in individual and organizational contexts; the determinants of utility, usability, acceptability, learnability, and user experience; the appropriate allocation of tasks between computers and users especially in the case of automation; modeling the user, their tasks, and the interactive system to aid better system design; and harmonizing the computer to user characteristics and needs.

While the scope is thus set wide, with a tendency toward general principles rather than particular systems, it is recognized that progress will only be achieved through both general studies to advance theoretical understanding and specific studies on practical issues (e.g., interface design standards, software system resilience, documentation, training material, appropriateness of alternative interaction technologies, design guidelines, the problems of integrating interactive systems to match system needs, and organizational practices, etc.).

In 2015, TC13 approved the creation of a Steering Committee (SC) for the INTERACT conference. The SC is now in place, chaired by Anirudha Joshi and is responsible for:

- Promoting and maintaining the INTERACT conference as the premiere venue for researchers and practitioners interested in the topics of the conference (this requires a refinement of the topics above)
- Ensuring the highest quality for the contents of the event

- Setting up the bidding process to handle the future INTERACT conferences (decision is made up at TC 13 level)
- Providing advice to the current and future chairs and organizers of the INTERACT conference
- Providing data, tools, and documents about previous conferences to the future conference organizers
- Selecting the reviewing system to be used throughout the conference (as this impacts the entire set of reviewers)
- Resolving general issues involved with the INTERACT conference
- Capitalizing history (good and bad practices)

In 1999, TC 13 initiated a special IFIP Award, the Brian Shackel Award, for the most outstanding contribution in the form of a refereed paper submitted to and delivered at each INTERACT. The award draws attention to the need for a comprehensive human-centered approach in the design and use of information technology in which the human and social implications have been taken into account. In 2007, IFIP TC 13 launched an Accessibility Award to recognize an outstanding contribution in HCI with international impact dedicated to the field of accessibility for disabled users. In 2013, IFIP TC 13 launched the Interaction Design for International Development (IDID) Award that recognizes the most outstanding contribution to the application of interactive systems for social and economic development of people in developing countries. Since the process to decide the award takes place after papers are sent to the publisher for publication, the awards are not identified in the proceedings.

This year a special agreement has been made with the *International Journal of Behaviour and Information Technology* (published by Taylor and Francis) with Panos Markopoulos as editor in chief. In this agreement, authors of BIT whose papers are within the field of HCI are offered the opportunity to present their work at the INTERACT conference. Reciprocally, a selection of papers submitted and accepted for presentation at INTERACT are offered the opportunity to extend their contribution to be published in BIT.

IFIP TC 13 also recognizes pioneers in the area of HCI. An IFIP TC 13 pioneer is one who, through active participation in IFIP Technical Committees or related IFIP groups, has made outstanding contributions to the educational, theoretical, technical, commercial, or professional aspects of analysis, design, construction, evaluation, and use of interactive systems. IFIP TC 13 pioneers are appointed annually and awards are handed over at the INTERACT conference.

IFIP TC 13 stimulates working events and activities through its Working Groups (WGs). Working Groups consist of HCI experts from many countries, who seek to expand knowledge and find solutions to HCI issues and concerns within their domains. The list of Working Groups and their area of interest is given below.

WG13.1 (Education in HCI and HCI Curricula) aims to improve HCI education at all levels of higher education, coordinate and unite efforts to develop HCI curricula, and promote HCI teaching.

WG13.2 (Methodology for User-Centered System Design) aims to foster research, dissemination of information and good practice in the methodical application of HCI to software engineering.

WG13.3 (HCI and Disability) aims to make HCI designers aware of the needs of people with disabilities and encourage the development of information systems and tools permitting adaptation of interfaces to specific users.

WG13.4 (also WG2.7) (User Interface Engineering) investigates the nature, concepts, and construction of user interfaces for software systems, using a framework for reasoning about interactive systems and an engineering model for developing user interfaces.

WG 13.5 (Human Error, Resilience, Reliability, Safety and System Development) seeks a framework for studying human factors relating to systems failure, develops leading-edge techniques in hazard analysis and safety engineering of computer-based systems, and guides international accreditation activities for safety-critical systems.

WG13.6 (Human-Work Interaction Design) aims at establishing relationships between extensive empirical work-domain studies and HCI design. It will promote the use of knowledge, concepts, methods, and techniques that enable user studies to procure a better apprehension of the complex interplay between individual, social, and organizational contexts and thereby a better understanding of how and why people work in the ways that they do.

WG13.7 (Human–Computer Interaction and Visualization) aims to establish a study and research program that will combine both scientific work and practical applications in the fields of HCI and Visualization. It integrates several additional aspects of further research areas, such as scientific visualization, data mining, information design, computer graphics, cognition sciences, perception theory, or psychology, into this approach.

WG13.8 (Interaction Design and International Development) is currently working to reformulate its aims and scope.

WG13.9 (Interaction Design and Children) aims to support practitioners, regulators, and researchers to develop the study of interaction design and children across international contexts.

WG13.10 (Human-Centered Technology for Sustainability) aims to promote research, design, development, evaluation, and deployment of human-centered technology to encourage sustainable use of resources in various domains.

New Working Groups are formed as areas of significance in HCI arise. Further information is available on the IFIP TC13 website: http://ifip-tc13.org/.

IFIP TC13 Members

Officers

Chair

Philippe Palanque, France

Vice-chair for Awards

Paula Kotze, South Africa

Vice-chair for Communications

Helen Petrie, UK

Vice-chair for Growth and Reach Out INTERACT Steering Committee Chair

Jan Gulliksen, Sweden

Vice-chair for Working Groups

Simone D. J. Barbosa, Brazil

Treasurer

Virpi Roto, Finland

Secretary

Marco Winckler, France

INTERACT Steering Committee Chair

Anirudha Joshi

Country Representatives

Australia
Henry B. L. Duh
Australian Computer Society

Austria
Geraldine Fitzpatrick
Austrian Computer Society

Belgium
Bruno Dumas
Interuniversity Micro-Electronics Center
(IMEC)

Brazil
Milene Selbach Silveira
Brazilian Computer Society (SBC)

Bulgaria
Stoyan Georgiev Dentchev
Bulgarian Academy of Sciences

Canada
Lu Xiao
Canadian Information Processing Society

Croatia
Andrina Granic
Croatian Information Technology
Association (CITA)

Cyprus
Panayiotis Zaphiris
Cyprus Computer Society

Czech Republic
Zdeněk Míkovec
Czech Society for Cybernetics
and Informatics

Finland
Virpi Roto
Finnish Information Processing
  Association

France
Philippe Palanque
Société informatique de France (SIF)

Germany
Tom Gross
Gesellschaft fur Informatik e.V.

Hungary
Cecilia Sik Lanyi
John V. Neumann Computer Society

India
Anirudha Joshi
Computer Society of India (CSI)

Ireland
Liam J. Bannon
Irish Computer Society

Italy
Fabio Paternò
Italian Computer Society

Japan
Yoshifumi Kitamura
Information Processing Society of Japan

The Netherlands
Regina Bernhaupt
Nederlands Genootschap voor
  Informatica

New Zealand
Mark Apperley
New Zealand Computer Society

Norway
Frode Eika Sandnes
Norwegian Computer Society

Poland
Marcin Sikorski
Poland Academy of Sciences

Portugal
Pedro Campos
Associacão Portuguesa para o
  Desenvolvimento da Sociedade da
  Informação (APDSI)

Serbia
Aleksandar Jevremovic
Informatics Association of Serbia

Singapore
Shengdong Zhao
Singapore Computer Society

Slovakia
Wanda Benešová
The Slovak Society for Computer
  Science

Slovenia
Matjaž Debevc
The Slovenian Computer Society
  Informatika

South Africa
Janet L. Wesson and Paula Kotze
The Computer Society of South Africa

Sweden
Jan Gulliksen
Swedish Interdisciplinary Society for
  Human-Computer Interaction
Swedish Computer Society

Switzerland
Denis Lalanne
Swiss Federation for Information
  Processing

Tunisia
Mona Laroussi
Ecole Supérieure des Communications
  De Tunis (SUP'COM)

UK
José Abdelnour Nocera
British Computer Society (BCS)

UAE
Ghassan Al-Qaimari
UAE Computer Society

International Association Members

ACM
Gerrit van der Veer
Association for Computing Machinery
(ACM)

CLEI
Jaime Sánchez
Centro Latinoamericano de Estudios en
Informatica

Expert Members

Carmelo Ardito, Italy
Orwa, Kenya
David Lamas, Estonia
Dorian Gorgan, Romania
Eunice Sari, Australia/Indonesia
Fernando Loizides, UK/Cyprus
Ivan Burmistrov, Russia

Julio Abascal, Spain
Kaveh Bazargan, Iran
Marta Kristin Larusdottir, Iceland
Nikolaos Avouris, Greece
Peter Forbrig, Germany
Torkil Clemmensen, Denmark
Zhengjie Liu, China

Working Group Chairpersons

WG 13.1 (Education in HCI and HCI Curricula)

Konrad Baumann, Austria

WG 13.2 (Methodologies for User-Centered System Design)

Regina Bernhaupt, The Netherlands

WG 13.3 (HCI and Disability)

Helen Petrie, UK

WG 13.4/2.7 (User Interface Engineering)

José Creissac Campos, Portugal

WG 13.5 (Human Error, Resilience, Reliability, Safety and System Development)

Chris Johnson, UK

WG13.6 (Human-Work Interaction Design)

Barbara Rita Barricelli, Italy

WG13.7 (HCI and Visualization)

Peter Dannenmann, Germany

WG 13.8 (Interaction Design and International Development)

José Adbelnour Nocera, UK

WG 13.9 (Interaction Design and Children)

Janet Read, UK

WG 13.10 (Human-Centred Technology for Sustainability)

Masood Masoodian, Finland

Conference Organizing Committee

General Conference Chairs

David Lamas, Estonia
Panayiotis Zaphiris, Cyprus

Technical Program Chairs

Fernando Loizides, UK
Marco Winckler, France

Full Papers Co-chairs

Helen Petrie, UK
Lennart Nacke, Canada

Short Papers Co-chairs

Evangelos Karapanos, Cyprus
Jim CS Ang, UK

Interactive Posters Co-chairs

Carmelo Ardito, Italy
Zhengjie Liu, China

Panels Co-chairs

Darelle van Greunen, South Africa
Jahna Otterbacher, Cyprus

Demonstrations and Installations Co-chairs

Giuseppe Desolda, Italy
Vaso Constantinou, Cyprus

Courses Co-chairs

Parisa Eslambolchilar, UK
Regina Bernhaupt, The Netherlands

Workshops Co-chairs

Antigoni Parmaxi, Cyprus
Jose Abdelnour Nocera, UK

Doctoral Consortium Co-chairs

Andri Ioannou, Cyprus
Nikolaos Avouris, Greece

Student Design Consortium Co-chairs

Andreas Papallas, Cyprus
Eva Korae, Cyprus

Field Trips Chairs

Andreas Papallas, Cyprus
Anirudha Joshi, India
Panayiotis Zaphiris, Cyprus

Industry Case Studies Co-chairs

Aimilia Tzanavari, USA
Panagiotis Germanakos, Germany

Proceedings Chairs

Fernando Loizides, UK
Marco Winckler, France

Sponsorship Chair

Andreas Papallas, Cyprus

Student Volunteers Chair

Vaso Constantinou, Cyprus

Web and Social Media Chair

Aekaterini Mavri, Cyprus

Program Committee

Sub-committee Chairs

Elisa Mekler, Switzerland
Fabio Paterno, Italy
Gerhard Weber, Germany
Jan Gulliksen, Sweden
Jo Lumsden, UK

Laurence Nigay, France
Nikolaos Avouris, Greece
Philippe Palanque, France
Regina Bernhaupt, The Netherlands
Torkil Clemmensen, Denmark

Associated Chairs

Adrian Bussone, UK
Anirudha Joshi, India
Antonio Piccinno, Italy
Bridget Kane, Sweden
Bruno Dumas, Belgium
Carla Maria Dal Sasso Freitas, Brazil
Célia Martinie, France
Chi Vi, UK
Christine Bauer, Austria
Daniel Buzzo, UK
Daniela Trevisan, Brazil
Davide Spano, Italy
Denis Lalanne, Switzerland
Dhaval Vyas, Australia
Dorian Gorgan, Romania
Effie Law, UK
Elisa Mekler, Switzerland
Fabio Paterno, Italy
Frank Steinicke, Germany
Frode Eika Sandnes, Norway
Gavin Sim, UK
Gerhard Weber, Germany
Giuseppe Desolda, Italy
Jan Gulliksen, Sweden
Jan Stage, Denmark
Jan Van den Bergh, Belgium
Janet Wesson, South Africa
Jenny Darzentas, Greece
Jo Lumsden, UK
Jolanta Mizera-Pietraszko, Poland
Jose Abdelnour Nocera, UK

José Creissac Campos, Portugal
Katrina Attwood, UK
Kaveh Bazargan, Iran
Kibum Kim, South Korea
Laurence Nigay, France
Luis Teixeira, Portugal
Lynne Coventry, UK
Marcin Sikorski, Poland
Margarita Anastassova, France
Marta Laursdottir, Iceland
Matistella Matera, Italy
Nervo Verdezoto, UK
Nikolaos Avouris, Greece
Özge Subasi, Austria
Patrick Langdon, UK
Paula Kotze, South Africa
Pedro Campos, Portugal
Peter Forbrig, Germany
Peter Johnson, UK
Philippe Palanque, France
Regina Bernhaupt, The Netherlands
Sayan Sarcar, Japan
Simone Barbosa, Brazil
Simone Stumpf, UK
Stefania Castellani, France
Tom Gross, Germany
Torkil Clemmensen, Denmark
Valentin Schwind, Germany
Virpi Roto, Finland
Yoshifumi Kitamura, Japan
Zdenek Mikovec, Czech Republic

Reviewers

Adalberto Simeone, Belgium
Aditya Nittala, Germany
Adriana Vivacqua, Brazil
Aekaterini Mavri, Cyprus
Agneta Eriksson, Finland
Aidan Slingsby, UK
Aku Visuri, Finland
Alaa Alkhafaji, UK
Alasdair King, UK
Alberto Boem, Japan
Alberto Raposo, Brazil
Albrecht Schmidt, Germany
Aleksander Bai, Norway
Alessio Malizia, UK
Alexander Wachtel, Germany
Alexandra Covaci, UK
Alexandra Mendes, Portugal
Alexandre Canny, France
Ali Rizvi, Canada
Ali Soyoof, Iran
Alisa Burova, Finland
Alistair Edwards, UK
Alla Vovk, UK
Amina Bouraoui, Tunisia
Ana Cristina Garcia, Brazil
Ana Paula Afonso, Portugal
Ana Serrano, Spain
Anders Lundström, Sweden
Anderson Maciel, Brazil
Andre Suslik Spritzer, Brazil
André Zenner, Germany
Andrea Marrella, Italy
Andreas Sonderegger, Switzerland
Andrew Jian-lan Cen, Canada
Andrew MacQuarrie, UK
Andrew McNeill, UK
Andrey Krekhov, Germany
Andrii Matviienko, Germany
Andy Dearden, UK
Angus Forbes, USA
Anind Dey, USA
Anja Exler, Germany
Anke Dittmar, Germany

Anna Bramwell-Dicks, UK
Anna Feit, Switzerland
Anna-Lena Mueller, Germany
Annette Lamb, USA
Anthony Giannoumis, Norway
Antigoni Parmaxi, Cyprus
Antonio Gonzalez-Torres, Costa Rica
Antonio Piccinno, Italy
Arash Mahnan, USA
Arindam Dey, Australia
Aristides Mairena, Canada
Arjun Srinivasan, USA
Arminda Lopes, Portugal
Asam Almohamed, Australia
Ashkan Pourkand, USA
Asim Evren Yantac, Turkey
Aurélien Tabard, France
Aykut Coşkun, Turkey
Barbara Barricelli, Italy
Bastian Dewitz, Germany
Beiyu Lin, USA
Ben Morrison, UK
Benedict Gaster, UK
Benedikt Loepp, Germany
Benjamin Gorman, UK
Benjamin Weyers, Germany
Bernd Ploderer, Australia
Bineeth Kuriakose, Norway
Bosetti Bosetti, France
Brady Redfearn, USA
Brendan Cassidy, UK
Brendan Spillane, Ireland
Brian Freiter, Canada
Brianna Tomlinson, USA
Bruno Dumas, Belgium
Burak Merdenyan, UK
Cagatay Goncu, Australia
Cagri Tanriover, USA
Carlos Silva, Portugal
Carmen Santoro, Italy
Cecile Boulard, France
Célia Martinie, France
Chaolun Xia, USA

Charlotte Magnusson, Sweden
Chee Siang Ang, UK
Chelsea Kelling, Finland
Chloe Eghtebas, Germany
Christian Sturm, Germany
Christina Schneegass, Germany
Christina Vasiliou, UK
Christophe Kolski, France
Christopher Johnson, UK
Christopher Lueg, Switzerland
Christopher Power, UK
Christos Mousas, USA
Cinzia Cappiello, Italy
Clarisse Sieckenius de Souza, Brazil
Claudio Jung, Brazil
Clauirton Siebra, Brazil
Cléber Corrêa, Brazil
Clodis Boscarioli, Brazil
Cornelia Murko, Austria
CRI Putjorn, Thailand
Cristina Gena, Italy
Cynara Justine, India
Daisuke Sato, Japan
Damien Mac Namara, Ireland
Dan Fitton, UK
Daniel Lopes, Portugal
Daniel Mallinson, USA
Daniel Orwa Ochieng, Kenya
Daniel Ziegler, Germany
Daniela Fogli, Italy
Danula Hettiachchi, Australia
Dario Bertero, Japan
David Navarre, France
David Zendle, UK
Davy Vanacken, Belgium
Debaleena Chattopadhyay, USA
Deepak Akkil, Finland
Dejin Zhao, USA
Demetrios Lambropoulos, USA
Denis Berdjag, France
Dennis Wolf, Germany
Deqing Sun, USA
Dhaval Vyas, Australia
Dimitra Anastasiou, Luxembourg
Diogo Cabral, Portugal
Dmitrijs Dmitrenko, UK

Donal Rice, Ireland
Dorian Gorgan, Romania
Dorothé Smit, Austria
Dragan Ahmetovic, Italy
Ebtisam Alabdulqader, UK
Ee Xion Tan, Malaysia
Elena Not, Italy
Elizabeth Buie, UK
Elizabeth Shaw, Australia
Emad Aghayi, USA
Emma Nicol, UK
Emmanuel Pietriga, France
Englye Lim, Malaysia
Eric Barboni, France
Éric Céret, France
Erica Halverson, USA
Eva Cerezo, Spain
Evangelos Karapanos, Cyprus
Fabien Ringeval, France
Fabio Morreale, New Zealand
Fausto Medola, Brazil
Federico Botella, Spain
Felipe Soares da Costa, Denmark
Filippo Sanfilippo, Norway
Florence Lehnert, Luxembourg
Florian Daniel, Italy
Florian Güldenpfennig, Austria
Florian Heller, Belgium
Florian Weidner, Germany
Francesca Pulina, Italy
Francesco Ferrise, Italy
Francisco Nunes, Portugal
François Bérard, France
Frank Nack, The Netherlands
Frederica Gonçalves, Portugal
Frode Eika Sandnes, Norway
Gabriel Turcu, Romania
Ganesh Bhutkar, India
George Raptis, Greece
Gerd Berget, Norway
Gerhard Weber, Germany
Gerrit Meixner, Germany
Gianfranco Modoni, Italy
Giulio Mori, Italy
Giuseppe Desolda, Italy
Giuseppe Santucci, Italy

Goh Wei, Malaysia
Guilherme Bertolaccini, Brazil
Guilherme Guerino, Brazil
Günter Wallner, Austria
Gustavo Tondello, Canada
Hatice Kose, Turkey
Heidi Hartikainen, Finland
Heike Winschiers-Theophilus, Namibia
Heiko Müller, Finland
Hsin-Jou Lin, USA
Hua Guo, USA
Hugo Paredes, Portugal
Huy Viet Le, Germany
Hyunyoung Kim, France
Ian Brooks, UK
Ilaria Renna, France
Ilya Makarov, Russia
Ilya Musabirov, Russia
Ilyena Hirskyj-Douglas, Finland
Ioanna Iacovides, UK
Ioannis Doumanis, UK
Isabel Manssour, Brazil
Isabel Siqueira da Silva, Brazil
Isabela Gasparini, Brazil
Isidoros Perikos, Greece
Iyubanit Rodríguez, Costa Rica
Jaakko Hakulinen, Finland
James Eagan, France
James Nicholson, UK
Jan Derboven, Belgium
Jan Plötner, Germany
Jana Jost, Germany
Janet Read, UK
Janki Dodiya, Germany
Jason Shuo Zhang, USA
Jayden Khakurel, Denmark
Jayesh Doolani, USA
Ji-hye Lee, Finland
Jingjie Zheng, Canada
Jo Herstad, Norway
João Guerreiro, USA
Joe Cutting, UK
Johanna Hall, UK
Johanna Renny Octavia, Belgium
Johannes Kunkel, Germany
John Mundoz, USA

John Rooksby, UK
Jolanta Mizera-Pietraszko, Poland
Jonas Oppenlaender, Finland
Jonggi Hong, USA
Jonna Häkkilä, Finland
Jörg Cassens, Germany
Jorge Cardoso, Portugal
Jorge Goncalves, Australia
José Coelho, Portugal
Joseph O'Hagan, UK
Judith Borghouts, UK
Judy Bowen, New Zealand
Juliana Jansen Ferreira, Brazil
Julie Doyle, Ireland
Julie Williamson, UK
Juliette Rambourg, USA
Jürgen Ziegler, Germany
Karen Renaud, UK
Karin Coninx, Belgium
Karina Arrambide, Canada
Kasper Rodil, Denmark
Katelynn Kapalo, USA
Katharina Werner, Austria
Kati Alha, Finland
Katrin Wolf, Germany
Katta Spiel, Austria
Kellie Vella, Australia
Kening Zhu, China
Kent Lyons, USA
Kevin Cheng, China
Kevin El Haddad, Belgium
Kiemute Oyibo, Canada
Kirsi Halttu, Finland
Kirsten Ellis, Australia
Kirsten Ribu, Norway
Konstanti Chrysanthi, Cyprus
Kris Luyten, Belgium
Kurtis Danyluk, Canada
Kyle Johnsen, USA
Lachlan Mackinnon, UK
Lara Piccolo, UK
Lars Lischke, The Netherlands
Lars Rune Christensen, Denmark
Leigh Clark, Ireland
Lene Nielsen, Denmark
Lilian Motti Ader, Ireland

Oscar Mayora, Italy
Panayiotis Koutsabasis, Greece
Panos Markopoulos, The Netherlands
Panote Siriaraya, Japan
Paola Risso, Italy
Paolo Buono, Italy
Parinya Punpongsanon, Japan
Pascal Knierim, Germany
Pascal Lessel, Germany
Patrick Langdon, UK
Paul Curzon, UK
PD Lamb, UK
Pedro Campos, Portugal
Peter Forbrig, Germany
Peter Ryan, Luxembourg
Philip Schaefer, Germany
Philipp Wacker, Germany
Philippe Palanque, France
Philippe Renevier Gonin, France
Pierre Dragicevic, France
Pierre-Henri Orefice, France
Pietro Murano, Norway
Piyush Madan, USA
Pradeep Yammiyavar, India
Praminda Caleb-Solly, UK
Priyanka Srivastava, India
Pui Voon Lim, Malaysia
Qiqi Jiang, Denmark
Radhika Garg, USA
Radu Jianu, UK
Rafael Henkin, UK
Rafał Michalski, Poland
Raian Ali, UK
Rajkumar Darbar, France
Raquel Hervas, Spain
Raquel Robinson, Canada
Rashmi Singla, Denmark
Raymundo Cornejo, Mexico
Reem Talhouk, UK
Renaud Blanch, France
Rina Wehbe, Canada
Roberto Montano-Murillo, UK
Rocio von Jungenfeld, UK
Romina Kühn, Germany
Romina Poguntke, Germany
Ronnie Taib, Australia

Rosa Lanzilotti, Italy
Rüdiger Heimgärtner, Germany
Rufat Rzayev, Germany
Rui José, Portugal
Rui Madeira, Portugal
Samir Aknine, France
Sana Maqsood, Canada
Sanjit Samaddar, UK
Santosh Vijaykumar, UK
Sarah Völkel, Germany
Sari Kujala, Finland
Sayan Sarcar, Japan
Scott Trent, Japan
Sean Butler, UK
Sebastian Günther, Germany
Selina Schepers, Belgium
Seokwoo Song, South Korea
Sergio Firmenich, Argentina
Shah Rukh Humayoun, USA
Shaimaa Lazem, Egypt
Sharon Lynn Chu, USA
Shichao Zhao, UK
Shiroq Al-Megren, USA
Silvia Gabrielli, Italy
Simone Kriglstein, Austria
Sirpa Riihiaho, Finland
Snigdha Petluru, India
Songchun Fan, USA
Sónia Rafael, Portugal
Sonja Schimmler, Germany
Sophie Lepreux, France
Srishti Gupta, USA
SRM Dilrukshi Gamage, Sri Lanka
SRM_Daniela Girardi, Italy
Stefan Carmien, UK
Stefano Valtolina, Italy
Stéphane Conversy, France
Stephanie Wilson, UK
Stephen Snow, UK
Stephen Uzor, UK
Steve Reeves, New Zealand
Steven Jeuris, Denmark
Steven Vos, The Netherlands
Subrata Tikadar, India
Sven Mayer, Germany
Taehyun Rhee, New Zealand

Takuji Narumi, Japan
Tanja Walsh, UK
Ted Selker, USA
Terje Gjøsæter, Norway
Tetsuya Watanabe, Japan
Thierry Dutoit, Belgium
Thilina Halloluwa, Australia
Thomas Kirks, Germany
Thomas Neumayr, Austria
Thomas Olsson, Finland
Thomas Prinz, Germany
Thorsten Strufe, Germany
Tifanie Bouchara, France
Tilman Dingler, Australia
Tim Claudius Stratmann, Germany
Timo Partala, Finland
Toan Nguyen, USA
Tomi Heimonen, USA
Tommaso Turchi, UK
Tommy Dang, USA
Troy Nachtigall, The Netherlands
Uran Oh, South Korea
Val Mitchell, UK
Vanessa Cesário, Portugal
Vanessa Wan Sze Cheng, Australia
Venkatesh Rajamanickam, India
Verena Fuchsberger, Austria
Verity McIntosh, UK
Victor Adriel de Jesus Oliveira, Austria

Victor Kaptelinin, Sweden
Vincenzo Deufemia, Italy
Vinoth Pandian Sermuga Pandian,
  Germany
Vishal Sharma, USA
Vit Rusnak, Czech Republic
Vita Santa Barletta, Italy
Vito Gentile, Italy
Vung Pham, USA
Walter Correia, Brazil
Weiqin Chen, Norway
William Delamare, Japan
Xiaoyi Zhang, USA
Xiying Wang, USA
Yann Laurillau, France
Yann Savoye, UK
Yannis Dimitriadis, Spain
Yiannis Georgiou, Cyprus
Yichen Lu, Finland
Ying Zhu, USA
Yong Ming Kow, SAR China
Young-Ho Kim, South Korea
Yue Jiang, USA
Yu-Tzu Lin, Denmark
Z Toups, USA
Zdeněk Míkovec, Czech Republic
Zhanna Sarsenbayeva, Australia
Zhihang Dong, USA
Zhisheng Yan, USA

Sponsors and Partners

Sponsors

Research Centre on **Interactive** Media
Smart Systems and **Emerging** Technologies

 Springer

Partners

International Federation for Information Processing

 Cyprus
University of
Technology

 TALLINN UNIVERSITY

 *In-Cooperation*

In-cooperation with ACM

SIGCHI

In-cooperation with SIGCHI

Contents – Part I

Assistive Technology for Mobility and Rehabilitation

Assistive Technology for Visually Impaired

Co-Design and Design Methods

Crowdsourcing and Collaborative Work

Cyber Security and E-voting Systems

Design Methods

Design Principles for Safety/Critical Systems

Accessibility Design Principles

A Serious Game for Raising Designer Awareness of Web Accessibility Guidelines

Fotios Spyridonis$^{(\boxtimes)}$ and Damon Daylamani-Zad

University of Greenwich, Park Row, London SE10 9LS, UK
{F. Spyridonis, D. D. Zad}@greenwich. ac. uk

Abstract. Accessibility of products and services is key for people living with a disability to ensure that they are easier to use. However, web accessibility guidelines have been shown to be cumbersome to understand, which impacts on designers' intention to use them. Several tools have been proposed in the literature, but they mostly focus on automatic accessibility testing, a process that is performed after a product has been developed. Little attention has been paid to using web accessibility guidelines during the design phase. In this paper, we present GATE, a serious game to help raise designer awareness of web accessibility guidelines, which is part of our work in progress on gamified technologies for this purpose. Its usability and perceived effectiveness were evaluated through an empirical study using a mixed methods approach. Our initial findings show that GATE is a promising solution that scored high in its playability and potential for use. This work has important potential contributions for the wider adoption of web accessibility guidelines.

Keywords: Human computer interaction · Accessibility · Web · Guidelines · Gamification · Game mechanics · Serious games · Usability

1 Introduction

There are currently around 80 million people in the European Union who have a disability and this figure is expected to increase to 120 million by 2020 [1]. It is therefore imperative to design accessible products for people living with a disability to ensure that barriers to use are minimized. However, a recent survey of web accessibility practitioners [2] revealed that while web accessibility is part of their daily job responsibilities, the majority reported that they implement accessibility part time. Further findings from the same survey and from recent research by Scott et al. [3] identified that lack of awareness and/or understanding of the Web Content Accessibility Guidelines (WCAG) and lack of relevant skills or knowledge are the main factors that they don't engage with accessibility design. This poses an important challenge and calls for an action to **raise designers' awareness** towards using WCAG.

Serious games, which are defined as digital games that don't have entertainment as their main focus, have been shown to be an effective platform for improving training, education or modifying objectives [4]. The use of established game mechanics is central in this effort, especially when carrying out work-related activities. Despite their popularity, in current serious games literature, web accessibility is scarcely addressed.

© IFIP International Federation for Information Processing 2019
Published by Springer Nature Switzerland AG 2019
D. Lamas et al. (Eds.): INTERACT 2019, LNCS 11746, pp. 3–12, 2019.
https://doi.org/10.1007/978-3-030-29381-9_1

The work presented in this paper is part of an ongoing project that aims to study and develop gamified technologies in order to engage with and raise awareness about the importance of web accessibility guidelines. Therefore, in this paper, we present GATE – a serious game developed to raise designers' awareness about WCAG – and we further report our findings from its initial evaluation.

2 Background and Related Work

2.1 Web Accessibility and Tools

The World Wide Web Consortium (W3C) was first to establish the WCAG standard, which involves 12 guidelines categorized under four principles: Perceivable, Operable, Understandable and Robust [5]. Together these form the guidelines suggested for ensuring accessibility on the web. When assessing web designs for compliance, W3C recommend that a design could be classified as "Level A", "Level AA" or "Level AAA," with Level A representing the minimum level of conformance. So far, WCAG has been the main point of reference for web accessibility and has been incorporated to a number of tools used to evaluate designs for their conformity to accessibility standards across various application areas [6, 7]. W3C also recommend a number of tools [8] that could be used in this effort. Evidence from the literature suggests that most work has focused on providing tools that incorporate and use WCAG to test for issues later in the project lifecycle. However, it has been suggested that "accessibility is solved at the design phase" [9]. Accordingly, GATE builds upon this through a serious game to raise designers' awareness about using the WCAG during design.

2.2 Serious Games for Raising Awareness

Serious games are increasingly applied in various areas, as well as becoming more complex. Recent research has focused on areas such as healthcare and rehabilitation [10], environment [11], military [12], education and training [13], and decision making [14, 15]. Serious games offer interactivity coupled with immersive experiences in order to engage people in tasks and activities. Research has demonstrated many examples of serious games used for increasing engagement [16]. The body of research also indicates that serious games have been successfully used for raising awareness, for example, in communal policing [17] and stress awareness [18]. In engineering, they have been used to raise awareness on agile methodologies [19] and software security [20]. Cultural awareness and historical heritage have also benefited from serious games [21]. Accordingly, serious games are a successful medium for raising awareness through engaging individuals with activities around the topic at hand and will therefore be utilized as the solution in this work.

3 Design and Development

The serious game was designed based on two dimensions of requirements: A. Game design elements identified based on the Gamification User Types HEXAD Framework [22], and B. Game scenarios that would enable implementation of the WCAG and the game design elements identified in (A) (see Table 1), which were devised based on the framework proposed in [23]. HEXAD proposes six user types (Socializers, Free Spirits, Achievers, Philanthropists, Players, Disruptors)[1] that can be used to screen a target audience and choose adequate game design elements. We designed GATE based on game design elements proposed by [24] for each user type above.

Table 1. Game scenarios mapping to WCAG guidelines and game elements based on [23]

WCAG guidelines		Game scenarios	
Perceivable	Text Alternative	Mystery Box	Ground Floor
	Time-based Media	Mystery Box	
	Adaptable	Keys and Doors	
	Distinguishable	Tactical Assassination	
Operable	Keyboard Accessible	Discovery & Coordinated Action	Floor 1
	Enough Time	Timed tower defense	
	Seizures	Loss aversion & Interactive Narrative	
	Navigable	Discovery	
Understandable	Readable	Puzzle	Floor 2
	Predictable	Room Escape	
	Input Assistance	Connect the dots	
Robust	Compatible	Connect the circuit	Floor 3

The game was implemented with Unity and C#. The current version is ported as a desktop PC game and as a web-based game that is playable in a browser. The use of this engine allows for future releases on suitable mobile platforms, such as tablets and smartphones. GATE uses a secure NoSQL database to store user data, user progress, and achievement and certification capabilities. The theme used was a contemporary setting with a futuristic touch to ensure that there is a greater abstraction between the real world scenario and the game scenario, so that enjoyment is increased in line with the findings from [25]. The location is an office building to match the player's perception with the reality of working as a designer. The building has multiple rooms spread across four floors, which are connected via an elevator. Each floor represents a 'Principle' of the WCAG and would encompass rooms that act as levels with specific challenges which are dedicated to a specific guideline (Fig. 1). The incorporation of levels and challenges supports the 'Achiever' user type. A companion assistive robot that helps/guides the player and a leader board mechanic have also been designed into the game, as the former

---

[1] HEXAD User Types are available at https://www.gamified.uk/user-types/.

allows for the implementation of Knowledge sharing mechanics for the 'Philanthropist' user type, while the latter helps to enable social competition and discovery in line with the 'Achiever', 'Socializer' and 'Player' user types. Both provide for a sense of belonging and ownership [26], and support a competitive experience.

Fig. 1. A hallway where doors would lead to rooms with various scenarios (Left). A Mystery Box scenario in progress in one of the rooms (Right)

To illustrate the gameplay, in the Mystery Box game scenario for the 'Text Alternative' guideline in Fig. 1, a player enters a dimly lit room and finds a box at its center. The player tries to open the box, but the item inside is unclear. The assistive robot will explain what it can scan, and the player is presented with an HTML code box and must write the item's description in the ALT tag of an image. If the player enters a correct description, the item will appear clearly and can be collected.

Finally, the player is free to enter and explore the various floors and rooms in any order they wish to in support of the 'Free spirit'. This also supports in transitioning 'Disruptors' into more engaged user types through incorporating an Anarchic gameplay. Upon overcoming challenges, the player would receive an achievement badge for the corresponding guideline, supporting the 'Player' user type, and will be provided with a briefing about a specific guideline for more in-depth information. This is in line with the 'Achiever' user type who are looking to learn new skills and improve themselves. Once the player overcomes a guideline challenge at Level A, the challenge at Level AA is unlocked. This mechanic supports Progression for 'Achievers' and Unlockable content for the 'Free Spirit'. Once all the levels for a 'Principle' are completed, the player is issued a certificate at the corresponding level (A, AA, or AAA) in support of the 'Achiever'. This game structure allows players to learn about the guidelines through different challenges and understand the importance of classification and success criteria.

4   User Evaluation

An empirical user study was carried out to address two main questions: 1. Is GATE a playable game? 2. What is its perceived effectiveness? The user evaluation was performed in two stages. The first stage used the well-established Heuristic Evaluation for

Playability (HEP) [27]. HEP consists of 43 heuristics relevant to Game Play, Game Story, Mechanics, and Usability. The perceived effectiveness was assessed by obtaining qualitative data through a demonstration of GATE and follow-up short semi-structured interviews in the second stage to gain more in-depth information.

4.1 Participants and Procedure

Stage 1. A purposive sampling approach was used whereby 20 designers (8 female; 12 males; Mean age = 33.7; SD = 7.24) were recruited to participate via online postings and through related professional networks. All of them played video games regularly and had some previous experience with WCAG. All participants were initially briefed about the purpose and functionality of GATE and they were asked to use the game freely for a few minutes. They were then told to work through the game focusing on how the game supports or violates each of the 43 heuristics, as well as to think-aloud during the process. Each heuristic was rated on a 1 (Strongly disagree) to 5 (Strongly agree) point Likert scale. Think-aloud comments were recorded and transcribed by the authors. Each user test lasted approximately 40 min.

Stage 2. GATE was further demonstrated to an additional participant group that consisted of two designers (DS), two developers (DV) and a product manager (M) (2 female; 3 males; Mean age = 40.8; SD = 7.32) from a London-based design company who were recruited through the authors' professional contacts. The study took place over one day in their offices. All had previous experience with WCAG. Each participant was then interviewed about its perceived effectiveness which was recorded and transcribed for analysis purposes. Each interview lasted approximately 35 min.

4.2 Evaluation Results

Stage 1: HEP Findings. In each HEP category, we present the top two supported and top two violated heuristics. These were further validated using the Wilson confidence interval (Fig. 2), which revealed that most responses have averaged above the chance line (value 3 would be the average for a 1–5 scale).

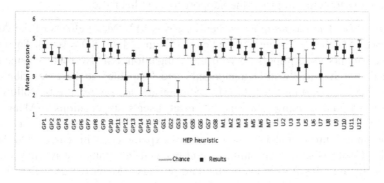

Fig. 2. Wilson confidence interval of HEP.

Game Play (GP). The heuristic GP7 "Player is taught skills early that you expect the players to use later, or right before the new skill is needed" was considered the most supported (Mean = 4.67, SD = 0.65). The participants commented that the companion assistive robot was always in time for teaching and informing them of any new skills that they needed, and they never felt like that they needed skills that they were not aware of. The heuristic GP1 "Player's fatigue is minimized by varying activities and pacing during game play" was the second most supported (Mean = 4.58, SD = 0.51) as participants felt that the free roaming nature of the game allowed them to pace the game as they were comfortable, which kept the game fresh and engaging. The two most violated heuristics were GP12 "Player's should perceive a sense of control and impact onto the game world" (Mean = 2.92, SD = 1.44) and GP14 "The game should give rewards that immerse the player more deeply in the game by increasing their capabilities (power-up) and expanding their ability to customize" (Mean = 2.58, SD = 1.00). Whilst GATE remembers achievements, all levels would be reset on re-entry as it was important that players should be able to attempt any level as many times as they would like. In terms of GP14, the low scoring participants identified that whilst the player is increasing their capabilities as a designer, their capabilities as a player are not increased by completing each level. On the other hand, the high scoring participants identified that there are levels that introduce new capabilities, and the player would have new available options in terms of rewards and certificates.

Game Story (GS). The most supported heuristic was GS1 "Player understands the story line as a single consistent vision" (Mean = 4.83, SD = 0.39). All participants agreed that the game story followed a clear vision and the design elements complemented the goal and the story of the game. The second most supported was GS4 "The Player feels as though the world is going on whether their character is there or not" (Mean = 4.58, SD = 0.79), where the participants appreciated the autonomy and the setting of the game as an environment. The most violated heuristic was considered GS3 "The Player spends time thinking about possible story outcomes" (Mean = 2.25, SD = 0.97), as participants did not feel that the outcome of the game was important to them and most mentioned that they had predicted a straightforward outcome. Similarly, GS7 "The game transports the player into a level of personal involvement emotionally" was the second most violated heuristic (Mean = 3.17, SD = 1.47), as participants felt that the game did not emotionally involve them. Better use of sound effects and background music could potentially improve the support for this heuristic.

Mechanics (M). The most supported heuristic was M2 "Make effects of the Artificial Intelligence (AI) clearly visible to the player" (Mean = 4.75, SD = 0.62). The majority of the participants were impressed with the companion assistive robot's behavior and mentioned that it was "well-characterized" and "capable" to best describe it. The second highest supporting heuristic M5 "Shorten the learning curve by following the trends set by the gaming industry to meet user's expectations" (Mean = 4.67, SD = 0.65) demonstrates that most participants found the game easy to use and the mechanics and controls matched their previous experiences with games. On the other hand, M6 "Controls should be intuitive, and mapped in a natural way; they should be customizable and default to industry standard settings" (Mean = 4.25, SD = 0.45) and M7 "Player should be given controls that are basic enough to learn quickly yet expandable for advanced options" (Mean = 3.67, SD = 1.07) were identified as the most violated heuristics. Participants commented that the controls could not be customized and there are not many options with regards to controls.

Usability (U). The most supported heuristics were U6 "Players should be given context sensitive help while playing so that they do not get stuck or have to rely on a manual" (Mean = 4.75, SD = 0.45) and U12 "Art should be recognizable to player and speak to its function" (Mean = 4.67, SD = 0.49). The players highlighted the role of the companion assistive robot in providing prompts and context sensitive help without being a nuisance. Many commented on the design and the art work used in the game as suitable and they recognized the pictures that were used in the corridors and hallways (such as the W3C logo and HTML code screens). On the other hand, U7 "Sounds from the game provide meaningful feedback or stir a particular emotion" (Mean = 3.08, SD = 1.08) was identified as the top violated heuristic. The comments showed that the sound effects and the background music could have been used more effectively in eliciting emotions and adding to the immersion of the game. Similarly, U4 "The Player should experience the menu as a part of the game" (Mean = 3.42, SD = 1.44) was also identified as an area of improvement, as participants felt that they wanted more in-game incorporated menus.

Stage 2: Interview Findings. Overall, the participants felt that GATE has potential for use in practice. Responses indicated that participants were positive towards its potential to draw attention to the importance of WCAG emphasizing on its usefulness in portraying all guidelines in an engaging, yet informative manner. When they were asked whether GATE presents an accurate representation of the guidelines through its gameplay, participants responses varied, but were generally in agreement: "…I can see that everything is included from the guidelines…in a way, it (the game) helps to see relations that I hadn't noticed before…for me the validity (correctness) of the them (scenarios for each guideline) is the impressive thing" (DS1). In our question how practical GATE could be, participants agreed that their workload could be better supported through GATE's impact on their understanding of accessibility guidelines: "…the detail here (in the game) is very interesting. I feel like even I am getting to know some of the guidelines better than I used to… just thinking about page linking (Navigable) I can see that I wasn't exactly explaining it to our intern the right way… I should get them to have a go at it (the game)" (DV2). However, it was mentioned that GATE may come across barriers that need to be overcome before it is accepted in practice: "GATE is great for entry level or especially as a refresher, but it is not yet something that one could use to understand or find a solution for a problem at hand. As an introduction or review, I can see a lot of potential here, maybe having the team go through it on a monthly basis to refresh their knowledge…" (M). Overall, results from the semi-structured interviews indicated that participants acknowledged the potential effectiveness of GATE in increasing awareness about WCAG and it is heartening to hear that they could use it in practice.

5   Concluding Discussion

In this paper we introduced GATE – a novel serious game that was developed to raise designers' awareness about the WCAG. An empirical study was reported which evaluated its playability and perceived effectiveness. The results indicated that it is a playable system that ranked high in terms of user satisfaction and its potential in practice. A number of contributions arose from this work. We demonstrated that lack of awareness of WCAG could be moderated with GATE by increasing designers' engagement with the process (GP1). However, research has shown that this is influenced by how satisfying a game is for a player [28]. Our user evaluation indicated that GATE's overall playability was high (Fig. 2), which points to an equally high level of engagement with the game. Interestingly, participants commented that they would appreciate a higher level of immersion (GS7), which seems to be important to designers. Dominguez et al. [29] found that emotional engagement is crucial for successful games. Additionally, our findings indicated that designers found engaging with WCAG through play as an attractive approach to learn about a new work process and increase their skills as a designer (GP14). This is in line with previous findings that employees enjoy work activities that include elements of play [30]. We found that turning accessibility design into a play activity could be enabled through certain game mechanics that are shown to be most appealing to designers, such as free roaming (GP1). Exploration and learning are therefore important elements of play to designers and should be investigated by further studies based on appropriate behavioral theories. Participants also identified that the ability to provide players with flexible controls and additional menus (U4) is important. Past research indicated that customization is related to the feeling of "ownership" [31], which is an element that designers identify with in serious games according to our findings.

Our findings present certain limitations. We acknowledge that the relatively small number of participants may have an impact on the generalization of our findings. However, given the limited efforts in this area, they can be useful as they could offer significant insights and could be used as a point of reference for future efforts. We also acknowledge that we only used a heuristics evaluation and interviews to ascertain GATE's usability. Employing additional methods could lead to more insights. Our findings finally present two main avenues for future work. First, a further study is needed to fully address the effectiveness of GATE through a well thought out design process underpinned by appropriate behavioral theory. Second, the recently published WCAG 2.1 will be incorporated into GATE. Overall, this work can contribute in ongoing efforts to adopt good accessibility practices when designing products.

References

1. Nadkarni, I.T.: European Accessibility Act: Parliament and Council negotiators strike a deal. http://www.europarl.europa.eu/news/en/press-room/20181108IPR18560/european-accessibility-act-parliament-and-council-negotiators-strike-a-deal
2. WebAIM: Survey of Web Accessibility Practitioners #2 Results. https://webaim.org/projects/practitionersurvey2/

3. Scott, M.J., Spyridonis, F., Ghinea, G.: Designing for designers: Towards the development of accessible ICT products and services using the VERITAS framework. Comput. Stand. Interfaces **42**, 113–124 (2015). https://doi.org/10.1016/j.csi.2015.05.004
4. Michael, D., David, R.: Serious Games: Games that Educate. Train and Inform. Thomson Course Technology, Boston (2006)
5. W3C: Web Content Accessibility Guidelines (WCAG) 2.0. https://www.w3.org/TR/WCAG20/
6. IBM Research: IBM aDesigner. https://www-03.ibm.com/able/dwnlds/aDesigner_accessible.pdf
7. University of Cambridge: Impairment simulator software. http://www.inclusivedesigntoolkit.com/simsoftware/simsoftware.html
8. Chisholm, W., Kasday, L.: Evaluation, Repair, and Transformation Tools for Web Content Accessibility (2005). https://www.w3.org/WAI/ut3/ER/existingtools.html
9. Lambert, S.: Designing For Accessibility And Inclusion. https://www.smashingmagazine.com/2018/04/designing-accessibility-inclusion/
10. Meijer, H.A., Graafland, M., Goslings, J.C., Schijven, M.P.: Systematic review on the effects of serious games and wearable technology used in rehabilitation of patients with traumatic bone and soft tissue injuries. Arch. Phys. Med. Rehabil. **99**, 1890–1899 (2018)
11. Aubert, A.H., Bauer, R., Lienert, J.: A review of water-related serious games to specify use in environmental multi-criteria decision analysis. Environ. Model Softw. **105**, 64–78 (2018)
12. DeFalco, J.A.: Detecting and addressing frustration in a serious game for military training. Int. J. Artif. Intell. Educ. **28**, 152–193 (2018)
13. Lamb, R.L., Annetta, L., Firestone, J., Etopio, E.: A meta-analysis with examination of moderators of student cognition, affect, and learning outcomes while using serious educational games, serious games, and simulations. Comput. Hum. Behav. **80**, 158–167 (2018)
14. Daylamani-Zad, D., Agius, H., Angelides, M.C.: Reflective agents for personalisation in collaborative games. Artif. Intell. Rev. 1–46 (2018). https://doi.org/10.1007/s10462-018-9665-8
15. Daylamani-Zad, D., Angelides, M.C., Agius, H.: Lu-Lu: a framework for collaborative decision making games. Decis. Support Syst. **85**, 49–61 (2016). https://doi.org/10.1016/j.dss.2016.02.011
16. Papaioannou, T.G., Hatzi, V., Koutsopoulos, I.: Optimal design of serious games for consumer engagement in the smart grid. IEEE Trans. Smart Grid. **9**, 1241–1249 (2018)
17. Sorace, S., et al.: Serious Games: An Attractive Approach to Improve Awareness. In: Leventakis, G., Haberfeld, M.R. (eds.) Community-Oriented Policing and Technological Innovations. SC, pp. 1–9. Springer, Cham (2018). https://doi.org/10.1007/978-3-319-89294-8_1
18. Holz, H., Brandelik, K., Beuttler, B., Brandelik, J., Ninaus, M.: How to train your syllable stress awareness. Int. J. Serious Games **5**, 37–59 (2018)
19. Stettina, C.J., Offerman, T., De Mooij, B., Sidhu, I.: Gaming for agility: using serious games to enable agile project & portfolio management capabilities in practice. In: 2018 IEEE International Conference on Engineering, Technology and Innovation (ICE/ITMC), pp. 1–9. IEEE (2018)
20. Yasin, A., Liu, L., Li, T., Fatima, R., Jianmin, W.: Improving software security awareness using a serious game. IET Softw. **13**(2), 159–169 (2018)
21. Idrobo, C.C.S., Vidal, C.M.I., Marceles, V.K., Burbano, C.L.: Characterization of the serious games applied to the historical heritage. In: Mata-Rivera, M.F., Zagal-Flores, R. (eds.) WITCOM 2018. CCIS, vol. 944, pp. 135–144. Springer, Cham (2018). https://doi.org/10.1007/978-3-030-03763-5_12

22. Tondello, G.F., Wehbe, R.R., Diamond, L., Busch, M., Marczewski, A., Nacke, L.E.: The gamification user types hexad scale. In: Proceedings of the 2016 Annual Symposium on Computer-Human Interaction in Play - CHI PLAY 2016, pp. 229–243. ACM Press, New York (2016)

23. Spyridonis, F., Daylamani-Zad, D., Paraskevopoulos, I.T.: The gamification of accessibility design: a proposed framework. In: 2017 9th International Conference on Virtual Worlds and Games for Serious Applications (VS-Games), pp. 233–236. IEEE (2017)

24. Marczewski, A.: Even ninja monkeys like to play : gamification, game thinking & motivational design. Gamified UK (2015)

25. Daylamani Zad, D., Angelides, M.C., Agius, H.: Collaboration through gaming. In: Angelides, M.C., Agius, H. (eds.) Handbook of Digital Games, pp. 235–273. IEEE/Wiley & Sons Inc., New Jersey (2014)

26. Pavlus, J.: The game of life (2010). http://www.nature.com/doifinder/10.1038/scientificamerican1210–43

27. Desurvire, H., Caplan, M., Toth, J.A.: Using heuristics to evaluate the playability of games. In: Extended abstracts of the 2004 Conference on Human factors and Computing Systems - CHI 2004, p. 1509 (2004)

28. Yang, H.E., Wu, C.C., Wang, K.C.: An empirical analysis of online game service satisfaction and loyalty. Expert Syst. Appl. **36**, 1816–1825 (2009). https://doi.org/10.1016/j.eswa.2007.12.005

29. Domínguez, A., Saenz-De-Navarrete, J., De-Marcos, L., Fernández-Sanz, L., Pagés, C., Martínez-Herráiz, J.J.: Gamifying learning experiences: Practical implications and outcomes. Comput. Educ. **63**, 380–392 (2013). https://doi.org/10.1016/j.compedu.2012.12.020

30. Gomes, N., et al.: Steptacular: An incentive mechanism for promoting wellness. In: 2012 Fourth International Conference Communication System Networks (COMSNETS 2012), pp. 1–6 (2012). https://doi.org/10.1109/comsnets.2012.6151377

31. Ondrejka, C.R.: Escaping the gilded cage: user created content and building the metaverse. New York Law Sch. Law Rev. **49**, 81–101 (2004)

Aestimo: A Tangible Kit to Evaluate Older Adults' User Experience

Iyubanit Rodríguez[1](✉)(iD), Maria Karyda[2], Andrés Lucero[2],
and Valeria Herskovic[3](iD)

[1] Universidad de Costa Rica, San José, Costa Rica
`iyubanit.rodriguezramirez@ucr.ac.cr`
[2] Aalto University, Helsinki, Finland
`maria.karyda@aalto.fi, lucero@acm.org`
[3] Pontificia Universidad Católica de Chile, Santiago, Chile
`vherskov@ing.puc.cl`

Abstract. Surveys and questionnaires are commonly used to capture people's experiences with technology. However, some older users experience issues when reading and filling out forms, and inexperienced computer users may not be comfortable with web-based versions. To improve the report of user experience, we designed and implemented *Aestimo*, a tangible interface based on a shortened version of the AttrakDiff questionnaire. The interface was evaluated during a study with 20 older adults (age avg. = 65.6). Although completing the *Aestimo* questionnaire took longer than a paper-and-pen version of AttrakDiff, 60% of participants preferred *Aestimo* over AttrakDiff. *Aestimo* was found to be innovative and inviting, and to stimulate the senses and the mind. Participants liked feeling guided by the interface, and also found their experience to be playful and fun. Overall, the evaluation of *Aestimo* was highly positive and suggests that some user groups may benefit from the availability of innovative evaluation experiences.

Keywords: User experience · Older adults · Tangible interface

1 Introduction

An important part of the design of products or systems is to measure user experience (UX) to understand users' perception about a product [1]. The dominant UX evaluation type are questionnaires [2]. Surveys or questionnaires are used to collect opinions, data, perceptions or feelings about the use of technology in a short period of time [3]. AttrakDiff is one of the questionnaires that have been used to evaluate UX. More specifically, the questionnaire is used to understand the usability and design of an interactive product, and measure hedonic and pragmatic qualities of a product [4].

At what age we humans become *older adults* cannot be universally defined due to cultural and historical differences. In some parts of the world, a person

© IFIP International Federation for Information Processing 2019
Published by Springer Nature Switzerland AG 2019
D. Lamas et al. (Eds.): INTERACT 2019, LNCS 11746, pp. 13–32, 2019.
https://doi.org/10.1007/978-3-030-29381-9_2

over 50 is considered an older adult [5]. United Nations considers people over 60 to be older adults [6], which coincides with the retirement age in Chile, where this study took place [7]. Partly, this is because the aging process is not uniform, due to differences in lifestyle, genetics and health [8]. As older adults, we may experience issues when asked to answer surveys or questionnaires. Questionnaires can often be long [9], and users with reduced vision may have trouble reading them [10], while users with hand-eye coordination issues may have difficulty writing with a pen [11]. It is claimed that some older adults tend to choose "I do not know" when answering a questionnaire [12], or to respond randomly [11]. Evaluations of technology in this type of situation have occasionally used shorter or adapted versions of standard questionnaires [13] or interviews [10].

Although web-based questionnaires solve some of the accessibility problems of paper-based questionnaires, some potential evaluation participants are inexperienced computer users or lack the necessary equipment. A lack of familiarity in technology use may produce anxiety [14]. Besides the aforementioned contextual differences in identifying when we become older adults, there are similar differences in the use of technology between the Western world and developing countries. In Chile, where this project was developed, some studies suggest that the use of technology by older adults is limited, finding that around 60% have no computer experience [15]. Therefore, a part of the population in the developing world is currently being neglected in their needs with the assumption that most people have easy access to current technology and that anybody can get by using a mobile device.

Multi-touch interaction may be uncomfortable for users with reduced coordination between motor and cognitive skills [16]. Some researchers have recommended the use of tangible user interfaces (TUI), e.g. tangible interfaces with push-buttons [17]. Physical interactions may remind users of devices we are all familiar with [18]. In the case of users who are insecure in their abilities to interact with technology, this may allow confidence to increase [19].

In this paper, we aim to explore the following research questions: (1) *Are the results obtained through a TUI similar to those from a paper-and-pen-based questionnaire?*, and (2) *What is the perception of older adults of a TUI for reporting UX?* To answer these questions, we designed a tangible interface kit called *Aestimo* (based on a prototype described in [20]), which allows users to input their user experience, emotion and overall opinion. Subsequently, we recruited 20 older adults to test our interface. During the evaluation we asked participants to evaluate a simple puzzle application on a tablet device, and then to answer a paper-and-pen questionnaire and a shortened version of the questionnaire on the *Aestimo* device.

This paper extends previous HCI research on the use of tangible technologies to enable data collection [21, 22]. However, this work is focused on improving the way UX is reported by older users. We describe in this paper the *Aestimo* device, a tangible interface that allows UX reporting, as well as our findings regarding how such an interface compares to a paper-based questionnaire, and our insights about the preferences and needs of older adults when recording their user experience. We found that the participants enjoyed that the interface was built with familiar materials and physical interaction styles, and that in the case of participants with little experience with technology, an interface such as this one should be designed to be intuitive and self-explanatory.

2   Related Work

2.1   Older Adults and Tangible Interfaces

Research on creating technological systems for older adults reports that TUIs may be more efficient and familiar than current digital technologies. Studies have focused on creating TUIs with diverse goals, e.g. to improve social communication [23–26], playing [27], entertainment [28], and cognitive training [29,30].

There are several techniques that may be used to design TUIs, combining digital interfaces with familiar physical objects. There are several examples of interfaces designed for a specific population of older adults, e.g. an interface in which people may compose digital messages in a way that resembles traditional ways of writing a letter [31], using individual tangible tokens on a digital board [28], or creating a multimedia book that combines pictures and sounds for reminiscing purposes [29]. During the evaluation of those systems it appeared that there were often unclear instructions, need for improvement in the feedback or even physiological characteristics (e.g. tremor) that were not taken into account when designing those systems. This work is based on the understanding that utilizing familiar elements in the design of the tangible interface is key when designing for older adults with little technological experience.

In terms of modalities we can see the aforementioned projects involve projection or a digital screen complementing a physical prototype. Blossom [25], a TUI for asynchronous voice messages, is an example of combining digital and physical modalities. The prototype includes a fake vase with flowers, which resemble messages waiting for a response. A frame which includes a picture of close family members complements the physical prototype.

Several works have described their prototypes as tangible when they are actually touch-screen, mobile, or computer-based [26]. Our work combines several modalities such as sound, haptic feedback and visual modalities, without any visible digital information or interaction. A similar prototype, TanCu [32], does not use screens, rather relying on haptic and visual engagement with the user. In terms of aesthetics, we believe it is the closest to *Aestimo*, since it avoids screens and focuses on other modalities.

2.2   Tangible Interfaces to Collect People's Opinion

Tangible interfaces have been used to provide support in the collection of data through physical interaction. The creation of such tangible interfaces has been used mostly in crowded public spaces. Among these, VoxBox [21] was designed to collect public opinion of an event in a playful way, finding that the anxiety of using a novel technology can be mitigated by familiar physical interactions. Another example of an interface to collect information from people is an electronic poster that allows community voting, which was found to be as intuitive as conventional posters, but with the advantages of online surveys [33]. To collect the opinion of communities, a tangible interface was designed with two buttons on the ground (yes/no) to allow voting. This type of interaction attracted the attention of the participants and was easy to use [34]. Sens-Us is an interface that allows collecting personal and sensitive information. The questions are answered by means of sliders, rotary dials, toggle, check buttons and yes/not push buttons, and it was found that people knew intuitively how to interact with the interface despite it being new to them [22]. Tangible interfaces have been used to improve the capacities of attraction and participation to provide information to people, since physical characteristics encourage people to approach these types of devices [35].

In the same way, tangible interfaces have been used to collect the perception of children through surveys in age-appropriate ways. SmallTalk is a tangible survey system designed to be used within a theater space to capture what children thought of a show they just watched [36]. Another example is a paper rating scale for children to provide their answers visually by means of non-adhesive stickers [37]. In general, although tangible interfaces have been created to collect and crowdsource the perception of people, they have not taken us older users into account, with our specific physical characteristics and limitations, and they have also not been used in this way in a more private space to collect user experience information.

3   *Aestimo*

Aestimo is based on a previous work (published as late breaking work) focusing on the design of *Aestimo*, which was at the time a non-functional prototype [20]. Instead, this paper presents (1) *Aestimo*'s implementation and (2) the evaluation of the functional prototype with 20 older adults.

Aestimo is a tangible interface kit to evaluate UX. The kit includes the evaluation of the user experience, emotional dimensions and the general opinion about the technology that is being evaluated. *Aestimo* uses familiar interactive styles and proposes a playful experience.

3.1   Design

The motivation to make *Aestimo* arose from the challenges observed in several evaluations while using questionnaires, in which e.g. some older adults wanted to hear the questions out loud. This section explains the design rationale behind *Aestimo*.

First, we selected AttrakDiff, a validated questionnaire that measures UX, which we have used in several prior evaluations. Based on our experience using

AttrakDiff with older adults, we decided to make a shorter version of the questionnaire to better fit their needs. The number of AttrakDiff questionnaire items was reduced from 28 to 16 questions. In this step the 4 dimensions of AttrakDiff were maintained, but instead of having 7 questions for each dimension, we reduced them to 4 (i.e., two positive and two negative adjectives). Each pair of adjectives was then turned into a question, e.g. *Conservative-Innovative* became "Is the application innovative?". In addition to reducing the number of questionnaire items, we also noticed in previous evaluations that most participants ended up using only three points on the scale instead of the seven available points. Therefore, we simplified the scale to three points to answer the questionnaire: *Yes*, *Neutral* and *No*.

Second, we looked into 27 electronic devices from the 1970s, e.g. Walkman personal stereos, washing machines, and typewriters, to get inspired about classic interaction styles that may seem familiar and playful to older adults. We found 45 types of interaction styles that require physical manipulation. The most commonly used interaction styles were buttons, sliders and knobs.

Third, continuing on the idea of using familiar, approachable elements, we decided to design AttrakDiff as a book and a handset. Each page of the book displays a question with large print. The handset works in conjunction with the book, as it reads the question that the book presents. Combining a book with a handset further served the purpose of providing users with double feedback: visual and auditory, to give support to the person in case that have any limitations in these two areas. A physical knob similar to that of a cooking appliance was selected as the main means to provide an answer to a given question on our three-point scale.

Fourth, we decided to incorporate two more dimensions to report user experience. The first one was an **emotional aspect**, in which the user can indicate how they felt while using the product or service to be evaluated. This decision was inspired by customer feedback that one can normally find in stores and airports [1], which show 4 faces: *very happy, happy, sad* or *very sad*. A slider (similar to that of an old radio) was included as a way for the users to select one of the four faces. The second aggregate dimension was **overall feedback** where the person can express in their own words how they felt while using the product or service. A vintage type tape recorder with two buttons was used for this. One button was used to start recording, the other to stop recording. The person can hear and feel the buttons when they are being pressed, which allows them to receive feedback while using the recorder.

Fifth, the interface can guide the user through instructions, which are presented in the form of text engraved on the surface, and are also heard by the handset. Finally, with respect to materials, *Aestimo* was made using laser-cut plywood (for the exterior, buttons, slider and knob) and paper (for the book). The materials were chosen with the purpose of being inviting and manageable.

Table 1 presents the explanation of each dimension.

---

[1] https://www.happy-or-not.com/en/.

Table 1. *Aestimo* dimensions

Dimension	Interaction	Description
User experience	Book	Displays questions
	Handset	Plays audio of the instructions and the currently open question in the book
	Knob	Allows answering each question, with three options: yes, no, neutral
Emotional	Handset	Play audio instructions
	Slider	Allows to select the emotional state (4 faces)
Overall opinion	Handset	Plays audio instructions
	Buttons	Record the user's opinion

3.2   How Is *Aestimo* Used?

To use *Aestimo*, the user first reads a set of instructions directly from the device, leading them to open a lid, where the user finds a handset and picks it up (see Fig. 1). The handset plays the instructions and questions about the user experience, which are synchronized with the questions in the book. After listening to each question, the user is invited to answer by choosing one of three options (yes, neutral, no) using the knob on the right front of the prototype. The system reminds people in case they have not responded to a question from the book that they cannot continue to the next phase until they answer all the questions from the book.

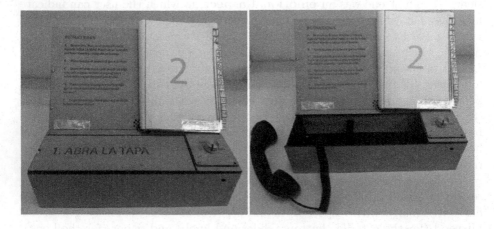

Fig. 1. *Aestimo*: tangible interface kit (33.9 cm, 26 cm, 23.8 cm).

After closing the last page of the book, a new part of the interface is revealed (see Fig. 2), in which users are asked to record an emotion and their overall opinion. The emotional dimension presents four faces with different moods and the user has to select the face that identifies the most with his/her feelings by means of a slider. The last part is the general opinion. The user is invited to record their thoughts on the prototype by pressing the *rec* button and then press the *stop* button to complete the recording. When a button is pressed, the corresponding sound of a mechanical tape recorder button is played.

Fig. 2. Left: book. Right: emotional aspect and the overall feedback.

3.3 Implementation

The interface was implemented using Arduino Mega 2560 R3 as a controller, a real-time clock (DS1307 I2C), classic headset, an 8-relay card with opto-coupled channels, a 12 V battery and a SparkFun MP3 Player Shield for sound and information storage. The interface also has an on/off switch (see Fig. 3). The implementation of each element of the interface is described next.

Book. The book presents 16 questions, a shortened version of the UX questionnaire AttrakDiff, which were selected using as a base the version used in [20]. The final version of the questionnaire is presented in Table 2 in Spanish and English.

The book uses magnets so that the system knows which page of the book is open: if a page is making contact on both sides, the page is closed; otherwise, if the contact of the magnets is released the page is open. The system can then provide the corresponding question orally through the handset. The system also recognizes if the question was already answered, indicating to the user to proceed to the next question.

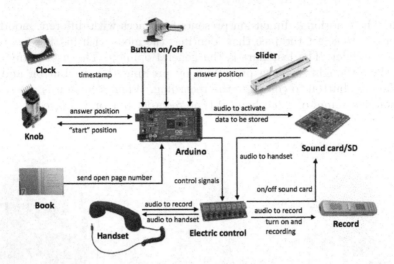

Fig. 3. Diagram of the components of *Aestimo*.

Table 2. *Aestimo*: book questions.

N	Spanish question	English question
1	¿Es la aplicación complicada de usar?	Is the application *cumbersome*?
2	¿La aplicación me motiva a usarla?	Does the application *motivate* me to use it?
3	¿Siento que la aplicación es desagradable?	Do I feel that the application is *disagreeable*?
4	¿La aplicación es atractiva?	Is the application *attractive*?
5	¿La aplicación es poco placentera?	Is the application *unpleasant*?
6	¿La aplicación no me cautiva?	Does the application not *captivate* me?
7	¿Usar esta aplicación representa un reto para mí?	Is using this application *challenging* for me?
8	¿La aplicación es convencional?	Is the application *conventional*?
9	¿La aplicación es innovadora?	Is the application *innovative*?
10	¿La aplicación es poco profesional?	Is the application *unprofessional*?
11	¿Siento que esta aplicación me acerca a la gente?	Do I feel that this application *brings me closer to people?*
12	¿Esta aplicación tiene una apariencia presentable?	Does this application have a *presentable* appearance?
13	¿La aplicación me aísla de la gente?	Does the application *isolate* me from people?
14	¿Es la aplicación manejable?	Is the application *manageable*?
15	¿La aplicación es simple de usar?	Is the application *simple* to use?
16	¿Fue confuso usar la aplicación?	Was the application *confusing*?

A knob is used to answer the questions. The knob was implemented using a Micro Metal Gearmotor HPCB 12 V with Extended Motor Shaft, and a Magnetic Encoder Pair Kit for Micro Metal Gearmotors, 12 CPR, 2.7–18 V (HPCB compatible). The space of the knob is divided into 4 positions (*yes*, *no*, *neutral* and *start*), which are demarcated by a range. The knob works by using a motor: when the person responds and turns the page, the motor positions the knob at *start* spot, so that the person answers the next question. The motor works in conjunction with the book's magnets.

Emotional Aspect. The emotional state displays four faces (representing four emotions: *very happy*, *happy*, *sad* or *very sad*), and asks the user to select one using the slider. The slider was implemented by means of a linear potentiometer, divided into five positions (*start* and the four emotions). After the user is asked to select a face, the system reads the slider's final position.

Overall Opinion. The recorder uses two push buttons and a recorder (Voice Recorder Pen 8 Gb Digital Usb). The recorder is turned on internally, when the instruction audio of that part of the evaluation starts. The recorder stores the information in its internal memory.

4   Method

4.1   Participants and Recruitment

We recruited 20 older adults (14F, 6M, 60–83 years, Avg. = 65.6, SD = 5.46). Participants were compensated with a 15 USD gift card for their time. The inclusion criteria was the following: 1) being 60 years of age or older, since the Ministry of Social Development in Chile considers people over 60 to be older adults [7]; 2) not having cognitive problems; and 3) speaking and understanding Spanish. Snowball sampling and signs near the entrance of campus were used to contact people to participate in the study. Out of 20 participants, eight had *none* and five had *low* digital skills, three had *basic* skills, and four had *above basic* digital skills, according to a digital skills questionnaire [38,39]. 13 people had never previously used a Tablet device. Table 3 provides the participants' information.

Ethical Considerations. The research protocol was approved by the university ethics committee (170711013). Each participant received oral and written information about the aim of the research, and written consent to the overall study was subsequently provided. Participants were informed that their involvement was voluntary, that anonymity would be guaranteed, and that they could withdraw from the study at any time.

Table 3. Description of study participants

P	Age	Gender	Occupation	Educational level	Digital skills	Lives with
P1	70	F	Retired	University	Above basic	Family
P2	65	M	Retired	School	Low	Family
P3	62	M	Manager	High School	Low	Family
P4	65	F	Retired	Technical	Basic	Alone
P5	60	F	Cleaning	School	Low	Family
P6	66	F	Housewife	School	None	Family
P7	63	M	Manager	Technical	Above basic	Family
P8	62	F	Cleaning	School	Low	Family
P9	64	F	Cleaning	School	None	Family
P10	69	F	Hairdresser	Technical	Low	Family
P11	60	M	Security Guard	High School	None	Family
P12	83	M	Housewife	None	None	Family
P13	60	F	Chemistry	University	Above basic	Family
P14	61	M	Chemistry	University	Above basic	Family
P15	71	F	Housewife	School	None	Family
P16	66	F	Cook	Technical	None	Family
P17	67	F	Merchant	High School	Basic	Alone
P18	62	F	Housewife	School	None	Alone
P19	72	F	Housewife	School	None	Family
P20	63	M	Manager	High School	Basic	Family

4.2   Study Procedure

This study was carried out at the researchers' university and lasted between 30 and 50 min per participant during August 2018.

First, a researcher provided a brief explanation about the purpose of the research and the participant signed the informed consent form, then the demographic data (age, profession and educational level) were collected. Afterwards, the participant completed a digital skills questionnaire [38, 39]. The participants then interacted with a simple puzzle application on a iPad Pro 9.7 [40]. This application was chosen because of its generic design (i.e., no elements specifically designed for children), being simple enough for users without digital skills, and because it allowed us to tailor its content by including photos that would be appealing to adults and not childish. The participants had to put together two different puzzles. The images of the puzzles were buildings or locations in the city they were living in, selected randomly from a set of 10 photographs.

After finishing the game, the participants answered the AttrakDiff [41] questionnaire and the Aestimo device questionnaire (half the participants started with one and the other half with the other). AttrakDiff was completed on paper, and in Spanish and it has four dimensions: *pragmatic quality (PQ)*, is focused on determining how easy the task was completed, *hedonic quality-identity (HQ-I)*, what is that message transmitted to others while the product is used, *hedonic quality-stimulation (HQ-S)*, if the user's abilities are developed when using the product, and *attraction (ATT)*, or the overall charm of the product. Answers are on a scale of −3 to 3 (0 represents neutrality) [4]. The first author then conducted a semi-structured interview to know the perception of the use of *Aestimo* compared to the traditional paper questionnaire. The interview focused on asking the opinion of the participants (positive and negative aspects) after using both types of questionnaires, then, the participants were asked which method they preferred, and finally, what they would change to the *Aestimo* interface. The interviews lasted 10 to 15 min per participant.

During the evaluation a researcher observed and took notes. *Aestimo* stored the duration of time each participant used the interface. In the case of the traditional questionnaire a researcher used a stopwatch to measure the time it took for the participant to fill it out. Figure 4 shows some participants during different stages of the study.

In this study, we used a translation of the complete AttrakDiff questionnaire in paper (Spanish) and a short version of AttrakDiff in *Aestimo* with 16 questions (Spanish). The reason to compare the two questionnaires was mainly to understand whether a shortened tangible version could capture user experience similarly to the full paper-based questionnaire.

Fig. 4. Participants during the study.

5   Analysis and Results

A thematic analysis was conducted by one researcher to analyse the interviews and notes made during the evaluation [42]. The first step was to transcribe the interviews. The transcripts of the interviews were made in Spanish, which is the first language of both the participants and the researcher. Then, all the interviews were read to become familiar with the data. As a second step, the initial themes emerged, then the list of topics was taken and classified. In this process, a description of the themes were used to select similar themes and place them in a new sub-list. At this point, we had 9 themes, but some themes were not supported to be candidates (1 was eliminated) and 2 themes were merged with existing themes, resulting in 6 final themes. Quotes from the participants are presented here translated from Spanish.

5.1 Are the Results Obtained Through a TUI Similar to Those from a Paper-and-Pen-Based Questionnaire?

We obtained data from *Aestimo* and AttrakDiff, which allows us to compare several aspects: dimensions, questions, preferences and execution time.

Dimensions. Regarding the dimensions, it can be seen that the short version of AttrakDiff used in *Aestimo* had very similar values in two dimensions: *hedonic quality-identity (HQ-I)* and *attraction (ATT)* with a difference of 0.09 and 0.06, respectively. *Pragmatic quality (PQ)* is very similar with 0.33 difference, and finally, *hedonic quality-stimulation (HQ-S)* presents a greater difference with 1.21, being in both cases the dimension with the lowest scores (see Fig. 5).

Questions. When comparing the score each *Aestimo* question score with the scores received in AttrakDiff, we found that three questions (6, 7 and 8) had scores with a difference greater than 2.4, which is the difference between the two results of those questions in Aestimo and the paper version. The values of AttrakDiff have a range between −3 and 3 (0 is neutral). Therefore, the difference between these two results (Aestimo and paper version) is greater than 2.4.

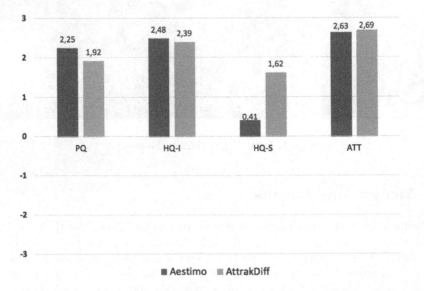

Fig. 5. Comparison of results according to dimensions: *Aestimo* and AttrakDiff.

The questions were formulated following the same form as the long version of AttrakDiff. However, some words did not have a direct translation in Spanish and were therefore used as a negation of another word. This resulted in a final question with strange wording for Spanish speakers. For example: question 6 was phrased with a negative (*Does the application* **not** *captivate me?*), which was confusing - some participants said that the application was captivating out loud, but answered yes to the question on the device.

Preferences. Out of the 20 participants, seven stated they preferred AttrakDiff over the paper questionnaire to report their user experience. The reasons they gave were that it was *"simpler and faster"* (P7, above basic) and that the AttrakDiff questionnaire is *"easier because you can choose between two alternatives"* (P11, none), and that *"these little dots are clearer, it's easier for me"* (P18, none). Contrarily, 12 participants preferred *Aestimo*, because the questions in it were easier to understand: *"it was difficult to understand the differences between both words. The questions are easier here."* (P10, low). Other participants liked that *Aestimo* would give them instructions: *"It's more practical, it tells me what to do. I think this little box is easier."* (P12, none). A participant with visual problems mentioned *"It's more fun, I liked it. Hearing things is easier than reading, since I have problems with my eyesight"* (P17, basic). One participant stated that they liked both methods equally.

Execution Time. We measured execution time, i.e. the time in which each participant filled the AttrakDiff and the time in interacting with *Aestimo*.

The average time users spent on AttrakDiff was 4 min and 31 s, while they spent 8 min and 37 s on *Aestimo*. Although *Aestimo* took a longer time to answer, none of the participants mentioned that this was a problem. During the experiment, three participants asked the researcher to read the paper questionnaire out loud, which reduced the average time (the average of those 3 participants was 3 min and 18 s).

5.2 What Is the Perception of Older Adults of a TUI for Reporting UX?

From the interviews and observation, we obtained 6 themes about the experience of the participants after using *Aestimo*.

Innovation and Nostalgia. An interesting aspect of the results is that the participants perceived *Aestimo* as novel, saying that they had never seen something like it, but also as something that seemed handmade and reminded them of previous times. They felt that using it was like going back to the time of their childhood: *"it kind of took me back to my times, because in those times we used things like this, made out of wood. It was what was at school or during my studies, these things were manual, we used our hands"* (P17, basic). They identified elements that they knew from the past, such as the telephone handset: *"There are things that I already know. This [the handset] was the first thing that connected me to others in my childhood"* (P13, above basic).

Guide. The fact that *Aestimo* has instructions and these can be read and heard, guides the participants during the use of the interface: *"It guided me, it was friendly. A girl was talking to me from the inside through the phone, she read me the questions, she read me everything I needed to do"* (P14, above basic). Also, the interface itself instructed them on how to use it: *"... it instructed me to use it, something I never used before. I liked the handset telling me things"* (P12, none).

Inviting. The participants felt motivated and invited to use technology: *"I like the way it works, the way it asks the question, it's like a phone and motivates me to work with modern technology"* (P8, low), and they do not feel intimidated or nervous: *"It's kind of nice, it doesn't make me feel dumb or distant, it invites me to get closer to technology, which I'm currently interested in, not to quit. It invites me to do it and I can do it, it doesn't make me feel dumb or ridiculous, because sometimes I quit because of that"* (P13, above basic). Likewise, one participant mentioned that she could use the interface despite her age: *"I never expected to use something like this at my age"* (P15, none).

Stimulates Senses and Mind. The participants mentioned that they felt their senses were activated and challenged by performing the activities: *"I feel that here I have hearing, I have touch, reading, seeing - I feel that several senses are involved here and that it activates them. That's what I liked: to hear, touch, see and at the same time develop my brain"* (P13, above basic). Participants felt their minds were engaged as well: *"It's great because it awakens the imagination, and you try to answer the question correctly, because you have to know how to answer, although the questions are simple... but I'm still clear headed and I can answer it"* (P10, low), *"You learn and you try to think about what you're doing. I liked the handset and the knob, because I have to use both hands, one for the handset and one for the knob and to turn the page"* (P15, none).

Playful and Easy to Use. Several participants mentioned that the interface was easy to use due to its characteristics *"It's a good size, the knob is easy to find, the font is a big size, so it's perfect... it's easy to use"* (P1, above basic). Three participants also stated that *Aestimo* could be used by people with less physical abilities, low educational levels or people with visual limitations. Although, as previously mentioned, three of the participants requested the paper questionnaire to be read out loud by the researcher, they used *Aestimo* without help.

The playful aspect was something that arose during the evaluation of *Aestimo*: *"Using the interface was entertaining"* (P2, low). After using the interface, some participants said they had expected it was going to be difficult, but rather it was fun. One of the aspects that they liked most was the surprise, when they saw the phone or when the book ended and other questions appeared: *"The phone impressed me... what is in there? I was going to put my hand inside and I didn't know what it was, and it was a phone, and it communicates you with someone else. I hadn't thought before that there would be someone else, asking for the answer"* (P20, basic).

Difficulties of Using Aestimo. The participants had some difficulties with the book. The problem was caused by having to stick the magnets of the new page to the previous page, since in some occasions the magnet did not make contact, and the user had to press with greater force the area of the magnets: *"I would change the manipulation of the magnets, to make it more precise, because the magnet did not get stuck correctly every time, but after awhile I got used to sticking it correctly."* (P16, low). Another problem was the position of the buttons on the recorder, since they are vertical and the label was difficult to see. Therefore, many participants asked what each of the buttons did. Some participants mentioned that the inability to change the volume on the telephone was a problem, since the proposed volume was too low for them. Finally, some participants did not read *Aestimo*'s instructions, and began by opening the book (instead of removing the telephone).

6 Discussion

What emerged from our study was the enthusiasm of the participants when faced with an interface that they did not perceive to be threatening or complex. One previous study found that some older adults do not easily use previous knowledge when faced with new technology [43]. However, the participants in our study were positive and felt invited to use the interface, similarly to previous studies in which familiar physical interactions mitigated participants' anxiety when using new technology [21]. Some of our participants did not read the provided instructions and therefore did not begin with the first activity, highlighting the importance of designing clear affordances into interfaces, especially tangible ones, to ensure that users will follow the flow of the designed actions. Simpler interfaces have been found to be more intuitive, e.g. for patients with dementia [44]. Thus, a design challenge to consider when designing such interfaces is configuring an interface that is able to control the activities itself and not load this task on the user. For example, in [35], users read the textual information before starting the interaction, since the interaction flow was activated automatically. This problem has been reported in previous studies in the implementation stage or during the evaluation [45].

In the interviews a dichotomy between innovation and nostalgia emerged. Some participants found that our interface was innovative as it was something new for them in terms of function. Aesthetically, it felt familiar: it was made out of wood and paper, and used physical interactions, with which participants felt invited to use it. Wood has been found to attract people to interact with it [35], which was also evident in our experiment.

Regarding the shortened version of AttrakDiff, it was evident that it is important to select the appropriate synonyms and wording so that the same message is expressed in the Spanish and English version, especially in the hedonic quality-stimulation (HQ-S) dimension. This dimension (HQ-S) is composed of questions 6,7, 8 and 9, out of which three of them (6, 7 and 8) were the questions that had different values between AttrakDiff and Aestimo. Therefore, we believe that this is the reason for the difference in values.

Regarding the results obtained from the comparison of the full version of AttrakDiff on paper and the short version of AttrakDiff in Aestimo, we are aware that, to actually compare paper vs. digital versions of AttrakDiff, the shortened version should be used in both cases. However, in this study we tried to understand if the short version of AttrakDiff could evaluate the user experience in a similar way to the complete questionnaire. The results obtained in this study encourage us to continue with the comparison of this short version of AttrakDiff in both paper and tangible formats. Additionally, the participants mentioned that the questions were simple and easy to understand, which agrees with [10] arguing that older adults respond better to questions rather than statements.

The development of *Aestimo* was based on the specific characteristics of some older adults in developing countries who have had little interaction with technology. *Aestimo* has the potential to be used by other user groups (e.g. people with a disability or people with low digital skills), who would benefit from this type of technology. However, we propose that *Aestimo* must be modified to better adapt to other groups of users. Additionally, we could study the use of *Aestimo* to collect information in public spaces, to make this a more playful user experience.

Aestimo is not designed for all older adults in the world. Our prototype was developed for a subgroup of this population: those older adults who feel rejection, have little knowledge about, and may even fear technology. Therefore, we believe that there should be a greater discussion of how to approach this issue in the HCI community, so as not to neglect this population.

Finally, our results indicate the importance of a playful element when users approach technology that is new to them. The use of different elements (sounds, haptic or text) made the participants enjoy using the interfaces e.g. [29]. These playful elements should be adjusted to the age of the people in ways that are not seen as childish or distant.

We would like to acknowledge the following limitations. The evaluation was conducted with a group of older adults with different digital skills. In addition, the online version of the AttrakDiff questionnaire was not used in this study. Finally, AttrakDiff was compared with *Aestimo* using an application and with a small number of participants, so these results cannot be further generalized.

7   Conclusions and Future Work

In this paper we presented the implementation and evaluation of *Aestimo*, a tangible system to report the user experience of a subgroup of older adults who have had with little experience with technology. The proposed interface had high user acceptance. Our findings indicate that our participants felt that such an interface can be encouraging to introduce technology and that physical interaction can activate the senses and the mind. In the same way, it is evident that an interface such as this one should provide instructions and use familiar elements to support feelings of security and reassurance.

The next steps in this research will be to improve the usability problems found in *Aestimo* e.g. the implementation of the book regarding the use of magnets for the recognition of every page. Likewise, it would be interesting to make a comparison of the *Aestimo* questionnaire, the paper version of AttrakDiff and the online version of AttrakDiff.

References

1. ISO DIS 9241–210. Ergonomics of human system interaction - part 210. Technical report, Inter. Organization for Standardization, Switzerland (2010)
2. Bargas-Avila, J.A., Hornbæk, K.: Old wine in new bottles or novel challenges: a critical analysis of empirical studies of user experience. In: Proceedings of the SIGCHI Conference on Human Factors in Computing Systems, CHI 2011, pp. 2689–2698. ACM, New York (2011)
3. Roto, V., Obrist, M., Väänänen, K.: User Experience Evaluation Methods in Academic and Industrial Contexts (2009)
4. Isleifsdottir, J., Larusdottir, M.: Measuring the user experience of a task oriented software. In: Proceedings of the International Workshop on Meaningful Measures: Valid Useful User Experience Measurement, pp. 97–101 (2008)
5. World Health Organization. Definition of an older or elderly person. Accessed 06 June 2016
6. García-Peñalvo, F.J., Conde, M.Á., Matellán-Olivera, V.: Mobile apps for older users – the development of a mobile apps repository for older people. In: Zaphiris, P., Ioannou, A. (eds.) LCT 2014. LNCS, vol. 8524, pp. 117–126. Springer, Cham (2014). https://doi.org/10.1007/978-3-319-07485-6_12
7. Ministerio Desarrollo Social. Casen sobre previsión social muestra importante aumento de la cobertura de la pensión básica solidaria de vejez en cuatro años [casen on social welfare shows significant increase in the coverage of the basic solidarity pension for old age in four years] (2017). Accessed 06 Jan 2019
8. Singh, S., Bajorek, B.: Defining 'elderly' in clinical practice guidelines for pharmacotherapy. Pharm. Pract. **12**(4), 489 (2014)
9. Gerling, K., Schild, J., Masuch, M.: Exergaming for elderly persons: analyzing player experience and performance. In: Mensch & Computer 2011, Chemnitz, Germany (2011)
10. Heerink, M., Krose, B., Evers, V., Wielinga, B.: Studying the acceptance of a robotic agent by elderly users. J. Assistive Robot. Mechatron. **7**, 33–43 (2006)
11. Harjumaa, M., Isomursu, M.: Field work with older users-challenges in design and evaluation of information systems. Electron. J. Inf. Syst. Eval. **15**, 50–62 (2012)

12. Park, D.C., Gutchess, A.H.: Cognitive Aging and Everyday Life. Psychology Press, New York (2000)
13. Gerling, K.M., Schulte, F.P., Masuch, M.: Designing and evaluating digital games for frail elderly persons. In: Proceedings of the 8th International Conference on Advances in Computer Entertainment Technology, ACE 2011, pp. 62:1–62:8. ACM, New York (2011)
14. dos Santos, T.D., de Santana, V.F.: Computer anxiety and interaction: a systematic review. In: Proceedings of the Internet of Accessible Things, W4A 2018, pp. 18:1–18:10. ACM, New York (2018)
15. OECD. Skills matter: Further results from the survey of adult skills. In series: OECD Skills Studies (2016). http://www.oecd.org/skills/piaac/Skills-Matter-Chile.pdf
16. Sciarretta, E., Ingrosso, A., Volpi, V., Opromolla, A., Grimaldi, R.: Elderly and tablets: considerations and suggestions about the design of proper applications. In: Zhou, J., Salvendy, G. (eds.) ITAP 2015. LNCS, vol. 9193, pp. 509–518. Springer, Cham (2015). https://doi.org/10.1007/978-3-319-20892-3_49
17. Price, B.A., Kelly, R., Mehta, V., McCormick, C., Ahmed, H., Pearce, O.: Feel my pain: design and evaluation of painpad, a tangible device for supporting inpatient self-logging of pain. In: Proceedings of the 2018 CHI Conference on Human Factors in Computing Systems, CHI 2018, pp. 169:1–169:13. ACM, New York (2018)
18. Nilsson, M., Johansson, S., Håkansson, M.: Nostalgia: an evocative tangible interface for elderly users. In: Extended Abstracts on Human Factors in Computing Systems, CHI EA 2003, pp. 964–965. ACM, New York (2003)
19. Häikiö, J., Wallin, A., Isomursu, M., Ailisto, H., Matinmikko, T., Huomo, T.: Touch-based user interface for elderly users. In: Proceedings of Conference on Human Computer Interaction with Mobile Devices and Services, MobileHCI 2007, pp. 289–296. ACM, New York (2007)
20. Rodríguez, I., Karyda, M., Lucero, A., Herskovic, V.: Exploring tangible ways to evaluate user experience for elders. In: Extended Abstracts of the 2018 CHI Conference on Human Factors in Computing Systems, CHI EA 2018, pp. LBW589:1-LBW589:6. ACM, New York (2018)
21. Gallacher, S., et al.: Getting quizzical about physical: observing experiences with a tangible questionnaire. In: Proceedings of the 2015 ACM International Joint Conference on Pervasive and Ubiquitous Computing, UbiComp 2015, pp. 263–273. ACM, New York (2015)
22. Golsteijn, C., Gallacher, S., Capra, L., Rogers, Y.: Sens-Us: designing innovative civic technology for the public good. In: Proceedings of the 2016 ACM Conference on Designing Interactive Systems, DIS 2016, pp. 39–49. ACM, New York (2016)
23. Ehrenstrasser, L., Spreicer, W.: kommTUi – a design process for a tangible communication technology with seniors. In: Holzinger, A., Ziefle, M., Hitz, M., Debevc, M. (eds.) SouthCHI 2013. LNCS, vol. 7946, pp. 625–632. Springer, Heidelberg (2013). https://doi.org/10.1007/978-3-642-39062-3_42
24. Foverskov, M., Binder, T.: Super dots: making social media tangible for senior citizens. In: Proceedings of the 2011 Conference on Designing Pleasurable Products and Interfaces, p. 65. ACM (2011)
25. Zhao, M., Chen, Z., Lu, K., Li, C., Qu, H., Ma, X.: Blossom: design of a tangible interface for improving intergenerational communication for the elderly. In: Proceedings of the International Symposium on Interactive Technology and Ageing Populations, ITAP 2016, pp. 87–98. ACM, New York (2016)
26. Bong, W.K., Chen, W., Bergland, A.: Tangible user interface for social interactions for the elderly: a review of literature. Adv. Hum. Comput. Interact. **2018**, 15 (2018)

27. Kern, D., Stringer, M., Fitzpatrick, G., Schmidt, A.: Curball-a prototype tangible game for inter-generational play. In: WETICE 2006 Proceedings of the 15th IEEE International Workshops on Enabling Technologies: Infrastructure for Collaborative Enterprises, pp. 412–418. IEEE (2006)
28. Al Mahmud, A., Mubin, O., Shahid, S., Martens, J.-B.: Designing and evaluating the tabletop game experience for senior citizens. In: Proceedings of the 5th Nordic Conference on Human-computer Interaction: Building Bridges, NordiCHI 2008, pp. 403–406. ACM, New York (2008)
29. Huldtgren, A., Mertl, F., Vormann, A., Geiger, C.: Reminiscence of people with dementia mediated by a tangible multimedia book. In: 2nd International Conference on Information and Communication Technologies for Ageing Well and e-Health (ICT4AWE 2016), ICT4AWE 2016; Conference date: 21–04-2016–22–04-2016, pp. 191–201, May 2016
30. Boletsis, C., McCallum, S.: Augmented reality cubes for cognitive gaming: preliminary usability and game experience testing. Int. J. Serious Games **3**(1), 3–18 (2016)
31. Davidoff, S., Bloomberg, C., Li, I.A.R., Mankoff, J., Fussell, S.R.: The book as user interface: lowering the entry cost to email for elders. In: CHI 2005 Extended Abstracts on Human Factors in Computing Systems, CHI EA 2005, pp. 1331–1334. ACM, New York (2005)
32. Wolfgang, S.: Tangible interfaces as a chance for higher technology acceptance by the elderly. In: Proceedings Conference on Computer Systems and Technologies, CompSysTech 2011, pp. 311–316. ACM, New York (2011)
33. Vlachokyriakos, V., et al.: Postervote: expanding the action repertoire for local political activism. In: Proceedings of the 2014 Conference on Designing Interactive Systems, DIS 2014, pp. 795–804. ACM, New York (2014)
34. Steinberger, F., Foth, M., Alt, F.: Vote with your feet: local community polling on urban screens. In: Proceedings of The International Symposium on Pervasive Displays, PerDis 2014, pp. 44:44–44:49. ACM, New York (2014)
35. Patle, N.: Linkingpark: design of a physical interface to enhance public engagement in an emerging smart city. Technical report, UCL Interaction Centre, University College London (2016)
36. Gallacher, S., Golsteijn, C., Rogers, Y., Capra, L., Eustace, S.: Smalltalk: using tangible interactions to gather feedback from children. In: Proceedings of the TEI 2016: Tenth International Conference on Tangible, Embedded, and Embodied Interaction, TEI 2016, pp. 253–261. ACM, New York (2016)
37. Sylla, C.M., Arif, A.S., Segura, E.M., Brooks, E.I.: Paper ladder: a rating scale to collect children's opinion in user studies. In: Proceedings of the 19th International Conference on Human-Computer Interaction with Mobile Devices and Services, MobileHCI 2017, pp. 96:1–96:8. ACM, New York (2017)
38. Ferrari, A.: Digital competence in practice: an analysis of frameworks. Technical report, Research Centre of the European Commission, Seville, Spain, September 2012
39. European Commission. Measuring digital skills across the EU: EU wide indicators of digital competence. Technical report (2010). http://ictlogy.net/bibliography/reports/projects.php?idp=2685
40. Minkov, S.: Educativos juego puzzles para niños pequeños niñas [educational game puzzles for little boys and girls] (2018)
41. AttrakDiff (2018). http://www.attrakdiff.de. Accessed 30 Mar 2018
42. Braun, V., Clarke, V.: Using thematic analysis in psychology. Qual. Res. Psychol. **3**(2), 77–101 (2006)

43. Lawry, S., Popovic, V., Blackler, A., Thompson, H.: Age, familiarity, and intuitive use: an empirical investigation. Appl. Ergon. **74**, 74–84 (2019)
44. Chen, L.-H., Liu, Y.-C.: Affordance and intuitive interface design for elder users with dementia. Procedia CIRP **60**, 470–475 (2017). Complex Systems Engineering and Development Proceedings of the 27th CIRP Design Conference Cranfield University, UK 10th – 12th May 2017
45. Golsteijn, C., et al.: Voxbox: a tangible machine that gathers opinions from the public at events. In: Proceedings of the Ninth International Conference on Tangible, Embedded, and Embodied Interaction, TEI 2015, pp. 201–208. ACM, New York (2015)

Towards Reliable Accessibility Assessments of Science Center Exhibits

Till Halbach$^{(\boxtimes)}$ and Ingvar Tjøstheim

Norwegian Computing Center, Oslo, Norway
{till.halbach,ingvar.tjostheim}@nr.no

Abstract. A methodology for assessing the degree of accessibility of museum and science center exhibits is proposed in this work. It consists of an exhibit-centric framework with a corresponding score for the accessibility indicators vision, hearing, mobility, motor, and cognition. The scores are achieved by combining the results of an observational study with a supplementary expert evaluation for high reliability. The methodology was successfully applied with pupils in an informal-learning context at Oslo Science Center. We believe it has relevance for and can be applied to other areas such as self-service machines and interactive technical artifacts in general due to its generic nature.

Keywords: Accessible interactives · A11Y · Universal design · UD · Digital inclusion · Museum · Exhibition · Installation · Visitor experience

1 Introduction

In how far are exhibits at museums and science centers universally designed? Are there the same opportunities for pleasing visitor experiences for all, regardless of ability or disability? If not, what kind of barriers do visitors with disabilities encounter? These are some of the questions addressed in this study, for which we cooperated with Oslo Science Center. These centers target a very broad audience, but in this study we have focused on how pupils experience and use interactive and electronic artifacts.

According to statistics from 108 Norwegian museums for 2017 and 2018, 73% of the museums have employed accessibility measures in terms of braille labeling, use of sign language, large print, and easy-to-read information [1]. We believe that these numbers are biased because they are based on institution self-reports, and they lack the proper documentation and description of methodology. Also, the list of criteria is very limited and does not cover important aspects like multimodality, video captions, color contrasts, etc. There is anyhow a potential for improvement, given that 15-20% of the Norwegian population have some form of disability [2].

The work is organized as follows: We present the assessment framework and corresponding measurement methods first. Then it is demonstrated how exhibits at Oslo Science Center can be assessed with school-children as visitors. Finally, we present our conclusions and outlook for future research.

© IFIP International Federation for Information Processing 2019
Published by Springer Nature Switzerland AG 2019
D. Lamas et al. (Eds.): INTERACT 2019, LNCS 11746, pp. 33–41, 2019.
https://doi.org/10.1007/978-3-030-29381-9_3

2   Related Work

One of the earliest publications regarding museums and accessibility dates back to 1977 and originates from The Smithsonian Institution [3]. The Smithsonian has later published extensive and detailed guidelines linked to their dedicated Accessibility Program [4]. Related to this are the recommendations for universal design of exhibitions in science museums, which is the work of a number of experts in the field with the lead of the Museum of Science in Boston [5]. Included in this document is also a checklist, which can be used to get a quick impression for how inclusive an exhibition is. An earlier research report from the Museum of Science studied not only the visitor experiences of persons with disabilities but also the relationship of universal design and informal learning contexts in general [6]. The author argues that some accessibility measures for one particular group may counteract the measures for other visitor groups with different needs, but most of the accessibility measures also benefit persons without disabilities.

In general, accessibility measures in museums are necessary but not sufficient for learning and interest [7]. A strategy to achieve both is the application of recommendations from Universal Design for Learning, or short UDL [8]. Basic elements here are the use of multiple modalities, specific measures for the creation of engagement and motivation, and giving visitors several options for interaction and ways of expressing themselves. Rappolt-Schlichtmann argues that the UDL recommendations not only can give visitors with disabilities access to exhibits but may also lead to increased motivation and improved learning for all. Many factors for learning in science museums are, however, not sufficiently understood [9], such as effect of the surroundings and context. According to the author, measures could be counteracting if used without reflection about their impact, and there are many potential pitfalls: For instance, confusion caused by too many selection options and choices, distraction due to many interaction possibilities, disruptions through simultaneous interaction mechanisms, and failing to grasp the main learning objective due to multiple content alternatives. The author concludes that there are no generic solutions, and that the key for good learning experiences is the combination of user-centric design and universal-design measures with a special focus on cognitive accessibility.

3   Assessment Framework

It is common to categorize disabilities into three main areas: *Sensor, motor,* and *cognition* [10]. However, it makes sense to distinguish between *hearing* and *vision* as the most important sensors. This is also done by the WHO. Next, *motor* is a broad term which does not adequately mirror the difference between using one's legs, in our study referred to as *mobility*, and the use of hands and arms to interact with something, which is the meaning used here. In addition, we suggest a category for voice control. This gives the six areas *vision* (V), *hearing* (H), *mobility* (M), *motor* (MT), *voice* (VC), as well as *cognition* (C), here called accessibility indicators. *Cognition* compounds a variety of processes, including orientation, language, reasoning, memory, concentration, coordination, learning and engagement.

The guidelines on universal design of self-service machines [11], by Norway's Agency for Public Management and eGovernment (Difi), are also relevant for interactive exhibits. The agency recommend the following four main areas for development and assessment: *Finding the machine, getting there, surroundings and area of use*, and *use of the machine*. While this is a useful approach, it lacks two important topics, which are addressed in the WCAG 2.1 standard [12]: *perceivable* and *understandable*. Combined with Difi's areas, this leads to the topics *getting to/from, perceive, control*, and *understand. Findability* is then part of *perceive, use* belongs to *control*, and *surroundings and area of use* relates to *getting to/from*. WCAG's *robust* principle is no longer an area of its own but included with the other four; see Fig. 1. The inner circle is associated with the visitor's movement to a particular exhibit or installation. Within interaction distance, the visitor's actions are dominated by a combination of perceiving, controlling, and understanding (outer circle). The disability indicators can now be mapped to exhibit areas: *Mobility* relates to *getting to/from, vision* and *hearing* to *perceive, motor* and *voice* to *control*, and *cognition* to *understand*.

To quantify each indicator, we propose a grading system with four levels/points. This number is a compromise considering that the scale should have as few levels as possible, be easy to understand, and allow for quantifying different degrees of (in-) accessibility. The levels are:

- 1 point: Absolute barrier(s). A true "showstopper", no work-around.
- 2 points: Significant barrier(s). Increased use of time, high risk for making mistakes, as well as significantly reduced user experience.
- 3 points: Minor barrier(s). Somewhat reduced user experience.
- 4 points: No barrier. Normal user experience.

In the following, it is discussed how the rating can be compiled.

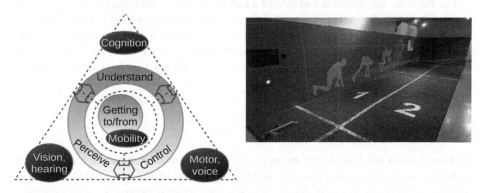

Fig. 1. Mapping of accessibility indicators to exhibit areas (left), and the exhibit "Running track" (right)

4 Methodology

In accessibility and usability research, it is the user or group of users who have the final verdict for how accessible or usable a given solution is [13]. Therefore, trials and studies involving a wide range of users with different backgrounds are mandatory for correct results [10]. Unfortunately, this is often difficult to achieve as recruiting users to form a representative population is not a straightforward process. Moreover, user trials may give inconclusive or contradictory results for different user groups [7], and conducting them can be quite time-exhaustive and expensive [14].

Evaluations carried out by experts are usually cheaper and more efficient in terms of the number of accessibility issues found per invested time [14]. Also, trained experts typically have the knowledge needed to bridge the gap between opposite user groups. On the other hand, experts might not get the same results as studies with actual users, and different experts do not necessarily agree in their conclusions [15]. A combination of user assessment with expert assessment can therefore be the right strategy to reduce the weaknesses with each method. The findings from the user trials should guide the experts in their own assessment, minimizing the potential for diverging results and disagreements. Moreover, the experts can interpret inconclusive user trial data, use their knowledge to fill potential gaps, and collect more data points where this is possible.

To determine the appropriate indicator level in the assessment framework, all data points in terms of observation notes, quotes, questionnaire answers, camera recordings and others are mapped to one of the accessibility indicators. In case of missing data points, experts can conduct empathetic walk-throughs and/or sessions with simulated impairments and a particular accessibility area in mind and note down any challenges and barriers. With the given definition of accessibility indicator levels, the resulting (final) dataset is then used to decide how many points an exhibit should be given in a particular area. It is stressed that each exhibit typically relates to multiple indicators.

For instance, the position and size of a button, as well as how easy it can be pushed, is associated with the indicator *motor*. Text on the button, and in how far it is lightened up, is mapped to *vision*. How well it can be understood what it controls is related to *cognition*. A button is usually not linked to *mobility, voice* or *hearing* in any way (if there is no auditory feedback upon a button push) and has hence no influence on the choice of levels in these areas.

5 Case Study

We have carried out a first step in verifying the assessment framework and proposed method through a case study that included the assessment of 15 exhibits at Oslo Science Center, undertaken in Autumn 2018. Oslo Science Center is primarily targeting school classes and family visits, meaning that most visitor experiences happen in small groups, and that there are no real restrictions to the visitor age. Pupils with the ability to read and general knowledge in math and science, however, may benefit the most from a visit.

We recruited 34 informants in total, 25 pupils and nine adults, distributed over two families and three school classes. The pupils were between nine and 12 years old, and almost two out of three were male. Some of them had visited the Science Center previously, a few even several times. Three had low vision, 23 had hearing disabilities (both cochlear implant and other hearing aids), and one had cerebral parese. We assume that many also had hidden impairments like dyslexia and learning difficulties. Among the adults, there were two parents, three teachers, one assistant, and three interpreters.

The pupils could choose their own route around the venue either alone or in small groups of up to six. They were typically followed by teachers and/or interpreters, as well as observing researchers. The observers were passive for most of the time but sometimes had to intervene the situation with explanations and demonstrations, and they also asked questions about the pupils' experience during and after a session, which lasted 45 to 60 min. Thus, when the collection of user data was finished, there was a multitude of data points in terms of observation notes, quotes, questionnaire answers, and camera recordings.

The objective of the subsequent expert assessment was, as already mentioned, to add data points for missing accessibility areas. No exhibit had voice control, so there were no *voice*-related challenges. Next, we had a lot of user data regarding *vision* and *hearing* but few data points related to *mobility* and *motor*. Our expert assessment focused therefore on both areas and was guided by technical report ISO TR 22411:2008, which – while not being an international standard – provided useful recommendations for the optimum height of control elements, minimum width for passages and other areas, maximum reach to screens and controls, minimum audio volume, and more. When it comes to *cognition*, it is stressed that it was outside the scope of this project to thoroughly collect data regarding whether or not the pupils had understood the given phenomena, and what they might have learned after their visit. We did, however, have a number of indications from the user trials regarding the pupils' comprehension and engagement. The expert evaluation thus concentrated on a limited set of cognitive aspects, such as language- and reading-related issues, dyslexia, as well as basic reasoning.

6 Example Assessment

We illustrate the use of the assessment framework and proposed method by means of a concrete example, the exhibit "Running track" at Oslo Science Center, depicted in Fig. 1 (right side). In the following, the various assets and aspects of an exhibit are coded with appropriate accessibility indicators to clarify their contribution to the given indicator level (V, H, M, MT, VC, C).

The exhibit's learning purpose is to teach its users about the relation of distance, velocity, and time. Two participants compete in running 10 m beside each other and as fast as they can on tartan tracks. Prior to this, a countdown must be started by pushing a button, counting both on a screen and on a loudspeaker (3-2-1-"shot"). The participants run straight ahead until they pass the finish line (and are eventually stopped by a mattress against the wall), upon which their time is taken, and a slow-motion video of the participants' performance is shown together with their result (on the finish screen). It is possible to run alone, too, but more fun doing so pair-wise. On the days of the trials, the starting screen was out of order (V), leaving only the auditive countdown for its users, and sometimes the finish line sensors would not capture the correct running time (C), confusing the users with irrelevant numbers.

The corresponding label associated with the exhibit is found on a nearby wall at a readability-friendly height (V) and uniquely identifies (C) the exhibit, it gives instructions (C) and tries to inspire the visitor by the use of illustrations and engaging questions (C), and it explains the exhibit's learning purpose (C). It contains text in both Norwegian and English - a plus for non-native speakers (C) - with short and easily comprehensible sentences (C). (Labels at other exhibits sometimes contain technical terms which are too difficult for the majority of pupils, let alone those with reading/learning difficulties.) The English text is solely set in italics, which should be avoided due to poor readability (V). Text and illustrations have sufficient contrast (V), but an x-height of 3 mm means that the font size is too small (V). We noticed that pupils with low vision had to get really close (10–20 cm) to the labels to be able to read them. (Labels at other exhibits sometimes have a glossy surface with many undesirable reflections (V).) There are no auditive labels or provision of other modalities for entirely blind people (V).

The exhibit is located in the center of the exhibition, well illuminated, and very easy to find/get an eye on (V). There is plenty of space around and no obstacles except for a small 3-cm edge around the tartan floor, which can be problematic for wheelchairs (M). The luminescent (V) countdown button is easy to reach, easy to target, and easy to push (MT). It is also possible to adjust the starting blocks, but this requires some finger strength (MT).

Both screens and the loudspeakers are placed in a readability- and hearing-friendly height but only mounted in one position on the left wall (V, H). The pupils with hearing impairments in our trials had to turn their heads away from the tracks and towards the wall in order to capture the signal. In addition, the audio is quite low (roughly 48 dB near the starting block farest away), challenging those with hearing aids in our trials (H). Both screens have sufficient brightness and contrast (V), but the font size is only average (V), meaning that some pupils with low vision had to stand quite close to it to be able to read, and sometimes this conflicted with those running. Had the starting screen worked, it would have shown some instructions ("get ready for countdown") which are not given by the loudspeaker (V). There is no result service for entirely blind users (V).

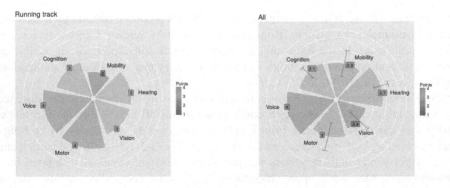

Fig. 2. Example assessment of the exhibit "Running track" (left), and mean and standard deviation of the accessibility indicators for all evaluated exhibits (right)

According to notes from the observers, the vast majority of pupils understood the exhibit's concept right away (C). A few did not notice the starting button, most likely because it is not prominent enough (V, C), and almost nobody understood where the finish line was (C); they all run until they hit the mattress. The result screen shows the time and average and maximum speed of both participants, but does not inform about which track the numbers relate to, and who has won (C). In our trials, this lead to situations where pupils argued about the "ownership" of numbers, and sometimes they were unable to say who had won, because they were not capable of comparing two given numbers. Also, the correct understanding of the unit "km/h" cannot be expected by pupils in the lower ages (C).

All in all, this was a very engaging exhibit and it meant a lot of fun to all who tried, as we could easily tell from the pupils' reactions and from how much time they spend here. Even wheelchair users could use it (if the change in floor level is reduced), and with some minor modifications (an auditory result service) even blind visitors. It was interesting to see that even though many with hearing impairments encountered problems with the countdown, they were able to cope with this by helping each other, by counting themselves and giving signs to each other for when to start. The learning purpose of this exhibit is likely a bit overrated; its inspiration factor is quite high, though.

Figure 2 (left) summarizes our assessment. There are no *voice*- or *motor*-related barriers in this exhibit, so both indicators yield a maximum point score (4 points). The problems encountered on the areas *vision*, *hearing*, and *cognition* are all rated as minor as specified in the definition of indicator levels above, so 3 points here. The edge on the floor is viewed as severe for those with *mobility* issues, and it is hence given only 2 points. There are no absolute barriers with this exhibit, so no indicators are on the minimum point score.

We have followed the same procedure for 15 exhibits in total and, based on this, calculated the average levels including the standard deviation (avg./std.dev.) for each indicator. The resulting numbers indicate where there is most potential for improvement with the exhibition, and where accessibility measures vary the most. As can be seen in Fig. 2 (right side), the fewest challenges lie in the areas *voice* (4.0/0.0) and *hearing* (3.7/0.6). No exhibit is voice-controlled yet, and with many, hearing is not required in order to use them. (However, some of the other exhibits show phenomena related to sound waves.) We have found minor hinders in the areas *mobility* (2.9/1.1), *motor* (3.0/1.2), and *cognition* (3.1/0.6). The high standard deviation for *mobility* and *motor* can be explained by the fact that there are exhibits which have inherent absolute barriers and only achieve 1 point. Obviously, *vision* (2.4/1.0) is the area with the least degree of accessibility. This is because most of the exhibits require vision to some extent, and virtually all have indisputable barriers for entirely blind visitors.

7   Limitations

Both framework and method have been in use in a single study only. In our trials, we have used a qualitative approach with relatively few informants (34) and few (15) exhibits. In particular, our observations would have benefit from informants with mobility and motor impairments, and also from pupils with different ages and severe cognitive impairments. However, we believe that we have minimized the problem of a non-representative population by the aforementioned expert assessment.

We are aware of the fact that all observers and expert opinions are to some extent subjective, and we have tried to counterbalance this effect by summarizing all observations and impressions across all researchers for each exhibit asset and exhibit. It would nevertheless have been an advantage to have multiple experts evaluate the exhibits in the last phase, and to have a higher number of exhibits for the statistical analysis. In this project, with the given project budget, though, this was not feasible. On the other hand, more experts would not necessarily have led to different results as most of the expert assessment is based on rather objective measures, such as the width of a passage, the height of buttons, a screen's font sizes, the volume settings of loudspeakers, and so on.

8   Conclusion and Outlook

In this work, a novel framework and methodology for assessing the degree of accessibility (and hence universal design) of museum and science center exhibits has been proposed. The framework is exhibit-centric and consists of six indicators and a score from one to four (where four is best). The indicators can be bar-plotted graphically for easy comprehension. The assessment method is characterized by a user study followed by a supplementary expert evaluation. The entire approach is rather generic and can thus be applied to other areas, too, such as self-service machines and interactive technical artifacts in general. Framework and method have been successfully tested by the assessment of 15 exhibits at Oslo Science Center.

It can be concluded that the approach is well suited to measure and quantify an exhibit's degree of accessibility and uncover its strengths and weaknesses in a reliable manner. The approach is demanding with regard to time consumption and costs, though. For future research, we suggest to compare the assessments from user trials and expert trials to determine if experts (and if so, how many) can reliably replace users.

An important observation from our trials is that both engagement and social aspects can counterbalance the downsides with barriers and hinders in informal learning. Engaged visitors usually do not give up so quickly when they meet barriers, and peer visitors can help working around hinders and also contribute to engagement. On a final note, a high number of exhibits in an exhibition is an accessibility measure in itself, as visitors who encounter barriers often will leave for other exhibits with more pleasing experiences. This argument should not, though, serve as a resting pillow for not addressing existing accessibility issues with exhibits, as everybody should be given the same opportunity to experience all phenomena in a science center, as called for by the UN's Convention on the Rights of Persons with Disabilities [16].

References

1. Kulturrådet. Statistikk for museum 2017 (2017)
2. Otnes, B., Ramm, J.: SSBs Levekårsundersøkelse. Statistisk sentralbyrå (2016)
3. Snider, HW.: Museums and Handicapped Students: Guidelines for Educators. Smithsonian Institution (1977)
4. Majewski, J.: Smithsonian Guidelines for Accessible Exhibition Design. Smithsonian (2011)
5. Reich, C.: Universal Design Guidelines for Public Programs in Science Museums. Boston Museum of Science & NISE Network (2008)
6. Reich, C.A.: Universal Design of Interactives for Museum Exhibitions. Museum of Science, Boston (2005)
7. Rappolt-Schlichtmann, G., Daley, S.G.: Providing access to engagement in learning: the potential of universal design for learning in museum design. Curator Mus. J. **56**(3), 307–321 (2013)
8. CAST. Universal design for learning guidelines. National Center for Universal Design for Learning (2011)
9. Allen, S.: Designs for learning: studying science museum exhibits that do more than entertain. Sci. Educ. **88**, S17–S33 (2004)
10. Fuglerud, K.S.: Inclusive Design of ICT: The Challenge of Diversity. University of Oslo, Faculty of Humanities (2014)
11. Agency for Public Management and eGovernment (Difi) Krav til automater|Universell utforming. In: uu.difi.no. https://uu.difi.no/krav-og-regelverk/automater/krav-til-automater. Accessed 2 Apr 2019
12. W3C. Web Content Accessibility Guidelines (WCAG) (2018)
13. Norman, D.: The Design of Everyday Things: Revised and Expanded. Basic books, New York (2013)
14. Røssvoll, T.H., Fuglerud, K.S.: Best practice for efficient development of inclusive ICT. In: Stephanidis, C., Antona, M. (eds.) UAHCI 2013. LNCS, vol. 8009, pp. 97–106. Springer, Heidelberg (2013). https://doi.org/10.1007/978-3-642-39188-0_11
15. Brajnik, G., Yesilada, Y., Harper, S.: Is accessibility conformance an elusive property? a study of validity and reliability of WCAG 2.0. ACM Trans. Access Comput. **4**(2), 8 (2012)
16. United Nations. Convention on the Rights of Persons with Disabilities (2006)

Understanding the Authoring and Playthrough of Nonvisual Smartphone Tutorials

André Rodrigues[1(✉)], André Santos[1], Kyle Montague[2], Hugo Nicolau[3], and Tiago Guerreiro[1]

[1] LASIGE, Faculdade de Ciências, Universidade de Lisboa, Lisbon, Portugal
afrodrigues@fc.ul.pt, abranco@lasige.di.fc.ul.pt, tjvg@di.fc.ul.pt
[2] Open Lab, Newcastle University, Newcastle upon Tyne, UK
kyle.montague@newcastle.ac.uk
[3] INESC-ID, Instituto Superior Técnico, Universidade de Lisboa, Lisbon, Portugal
hman@inesc-id.pt

Abstract. Mobile device users are required to constantly learn to use new apps, features, and adapt to updates. For blind people, adapting to a new interface requires additional time and effort. At the limit, and often so, devices and applications may become unusable without support from someone else. Using tutorials is a common approach to foster independent learning of new concepts and workflows. However, most tutorials available online are limited in scope, detail, or quickly become outdated. Also, they presume a degree of tech savviness that is not at the reach of the common mobile device user. Our research explores the democratization of assistance by enabling non-technical people to create tutorials in their mobile phones for others. We report on the interaction and information needs of blind people when following 'amateur' tutorials. Thus, providing insights into how to widen and improve the authoring and playthrough of these learning artifacts. We conducted a study where 12 blind users followed tutorials previously created by blind or sighted people. Our findings suggest that instructions authored by sighted and blind people are limited in different aspects, and that those limitations prevent effective learning of the task at hand. We identified the types of contents produced by authors and the information required by followers during playthrough, which often do not align. We provide insights on how to support both authoring and playthrough of nonvisual smartphone tutorials. There is an opportunity to design solutions that mediate authoring, combine contributions, adapt to user profile, react to context and are living artifacts capable of perpetual improvement.

We thank Fundação Raquel and Martin Sain in Lisbon (Portugal) and all participants. This work was partially supported by Fundação para a Ciência e Tecnologia (FCT) through scholarship SFRH/BD/103935/2014, funding of project mIDR (AAC 02/SAICT/- 2017), INESC-ID research unit UID/CEC/50021/2019, and LASIGE Research Unit, ref. UID/CEC/00408/2019.

D. Lamas et al. (Eds.): INTERACT 2019, LNCS 11746, pp. 42–62, 2019.
https://doi.org/10.1007/978-3-030-29381-9_4

Keywords: Tutorials · Blind · Smartphones · Accessibility · Assistance

1   Introduction

Mobile devices are pivotal tools for inclusion and independence. The inability to operate them proficiently, and quickly adapt to new usages, is likely to have deep social and professional repercussions. Blind people encounter challenges when first adopting these devices and with each new application and update [23]. The wide variety of interface templates and workflows mandates users to create different mental models and constantly adapt to them. Moreover, users are often confronted with accessibility issues that, without assistance, render the app, feature, or even device, inaccessible. In prior work [22,23], users reported to primarily rely on the assistance of others, when they felt helpless with their smartphones. However, depending on the issue, their support network might not be able to help effectively. Sighted users with no accessibility experience often could not cope with the interaction changes caused by the assistive technology [23]. In contrast, for issues relating to missing labels or hidden screens, sighted assistance is required. Nevertheless, there are situations whereby knowledgeable users, capable of assistance, might not always be available and co-located.

Another key strategy to overcome technology challenges is to browse the web for answers and guidance. Possible knowledge sources are online video tutorials (e.g. on YouTube), including channels dedicated to accessibility such as the Tech Accessibility Tutorial [28], where users can listen to tutorials on a variety of tasks. Alternatively, people can resort to dedicated fora and mailing lists, for example AppleVis [1] or Eyes-Free [6]. Despite the availability of tutorials, it is not always easy or possible for blind users to translate the content to their own devices or settings. Less tech savvy users often lack the initiative to search for content when it's not where they expect it. Equally, they do not necessarily ask the right questions, or possess the ability to understand the answers and know how to apply them to their specific context [22].

It is commonplace for applications and OS to have onboarding tutorials that guide users through their core features, thus supporting only initial learnability of the system. Developers typically create tutorials for what they believe to be the most relevant features, which can result in limited coverage of assistance. They also often overlook nonvisual accessibility, relying solely on visual metaphors to guide users (e.g. overlay to obscure content, animation depicting required gestures). Therefore, onboarding tutorials are not always accessible to blind people. Recognizing the existing challenges of mobile nonvisual interaction, there is an opportunity to leverage the benefits of in-context, and always available, help provided by tutorials. Our research explores the feasibility and the requirements for tools that enable the authoring and playthrough of effective nonvisual smartphone tutorials at scale. We believe that only then we will be able to support users in both initial and extended learnability as described in Grossman et al. [10].

To maximize the number of possible tutorial authors, it is essential to look beyond just app developers, and support other users to contribute with assistive content. We report on a study exploring the authoring and playthrough of nonvisual tutorials, where untrained individuals are at both ends of the technology. First, we conducted an authoring session with five blind, and five sighted participants where we asked them to create tutorials for four smartphone tasks. To evaluate the quality of the created tutorials, we conducted a playthrough session with 12 blind participants. Participants were asked to follow the tutorials, while interacting with the researcher whenever they needed additional assistance.

Our contributions include: (1) understanding of the instructions given by sighted and blind people when creating nonvisual tutorials; and (2) the interaction and information needs of blind people when following tutorials created by other users.

2 Related Work

In this section, we discuss previous work in four topics: nonvisual mobile accessibility and its open challenges; current support mechanisms; in-context assistance; and attempts to democratize assistance in other contexts.

2.1 Nonvisual Mobile Accessibility

Researchers have quickly become aware of the opportunities and challenges smartphones could bring to blind people. There has been a large body of work focusing on the interaction challenges of smartphones. At first, there was a focus on enabling access to surfaces with no physical buttons, and novel interaction techniques emerged. Kane et al. [14] developed and evaluated a set of multi-touch interaction techniques to provide nonvisual access to multiple applications. Nowadays, the main smartphone OS come packaged with a native screen reader (e.g., VoiceOver on iOS, Talkback on Android). Users perform directional swipes to navigate through content or rely on Explore by Touch by dragging one finger around the screen while elements are read aloud; to select, users can double tap anywhere on the screen. Since one of the first challenges is learning how to perform gestures on touchscreens, prior work has investigated how sonification can be used to support gesture learning [20].

Despite the efforts, gaining proficiency with such devices is still a challenge. In an eight-week study of the smartphone adoption process by blind people [23], Rodrigues et al. found that learning how to use the device is still an arduous task that most often requires help from peers. Others have looked at the open challenges touchscreen interactions create for blind people [12], which go beyond touch, gestures, and text-entry. In Rodrigues et al. [22], a series of workshops on smartphones, featuring users of varied expertise levels, confirmed difficulties beyond touchscreen interaction and the need to rely on others to surpass them.

Challenges often spawn from the overwhelming number of apps and features users need to adapt to. A possible solution is to simplify the interaction by replacing the entire system with a single application (e.g. Mobile Accessibility [5]) guaranteeing consistency, coherence of layouts, and app behaviors. However, it has the severe drawback of negating the benefits of all other apps available, and to disallow people with disabilities to have access to the same applications as others [25]. Another option is to adapt how content is rendered and navigated to maximize its accessibility [30]. Zhang et al. [30] proposes the use of interactions proxies to allow third-party developers to address apps accessibility issues. However, for a successful adaptation one must be aware of each application's issues and adapt them to the end users' specific needs without compromising any features. Thus, it relies on a limited population of third-party developers. Moreover, apps can be fully accessible and still pose a challenge for the untrained user [23].

2.2 Supporting Smartphone Learning

Aware of the differences and difficulties of learning how to use a smartphone, both VoiceOver and Talkback feature training tutorials for their users. VoiceOver provides a training canvas for gestures and relies on customer service to get users started with the device. On the other hand, Talkback has five interactive lessons to cover the basics of screen reader usage: Basic Navigation, Scrolling, Talkback Menus, Text Navigation and Text Editing. The tutorials available are limited in their scope, only addressing gestures and screen reader control. There is a lack of assistance in guiding the users through their holistic needs from basic navigation to complex task guidance (e.g. 'Add a contact', 'Forward a message').

Previous work found that blind people prefer the assistance of peers who are familiar with assistive technologies (e.g., screen readers), and have overcome similar issues [22]. Despite such perception, some screen information is likely to be accessible solely via visual feedback (e.g. describing layout or identifying a missing tag). To our knowledge, instruction-giving has not been explored in a nonvisual smartphone usage setting.

2.3 In-Context Assistance

Providing inline or in-context interactive assistance can facilitate users' learning process, as it has been shown in desktop applications [10,16]. Kelleher et al. [16] investigated an interaction technique for presenting in-context tutorials. The proposed technique, now commonly used in smartphone onboarding tutorials, features an overlay to obscure the non-relevant content and restrict user interaction. This approach has showed to be more efficient than traditional tutorials, reducing errors, time, and required assistance [16].

Interactive tutorials can be applied to a variety of contexts and population. Hagiya et al. [13] reported a text-entry tutorial for older adults that detects errors and provides instructions to correct them. Also, it detects when the user is taking too long to type the next letter/word and provides instructions simultaneously through voice, text and finger animations. In a study with 28 elderly participants, the tutoring system significantly increased typing speed (by 17%) and reduced errors (by 59%).

Tutorials can be designed to be engaging experiences to boost user performance. In Fernquist et al. [7], the system guides users through the interface providing assistance while sketching. Using a step navigation dialog, in each step, the user is shown how, where, and when to change settings, as well as when and where to draw. Yet, interactive tutorials should not restrict users of following the steps. In Lieberman et al. [18], the authors argue that at various points during the tutorial, users may require different levels of assistance (e.g. 'let me do it', 'show me how', and 'guide me through it'). At each step, users can delve into its particularities and freely navigate between steps.

As for interactive assistance, in-app onboarding has become more common with apps, guiding users on their first interactions. Unfortunately, they are limited in their scope, only supporting first usage, heavily relying on restricting users' interactions, and conveying instructions through visual metaphors. In EverTutor [29], researchers have investigated how to broaden the reach of interactive tutorials by allowing the creation of system-wide tutorials from user demonstration. When a tutorial is played, it uses overlays with visual metaphors, and an obscuring overlay to convey the next target and gesture in-context; additionally, it prevents users from performing incorrect steps.

To our knowledge, there are no tools with the ability to create nonvisual interactive tutorials on smartphones nor studies on how blind people cope with the instructions provided. Moreover, there are no insights into their efficacy nor how to design them.

2.4   Democratizing Assistance

The limitations in the success of the available tutorials on commodity smartphones put forward a stereotypical and limited view on the challenges smartphones impose to blind people. The variety of applications, and the complexity of their interactions and workflows, require for support to be flexible. One solution found by tech savvy users is to resort to online sources, for example, posing a question in a dedicated forum. There have been efforts to allow for this type of flexible on-demand support building on contributions from volunteers and/or crowd workers [2,22,24,26]. Bigham et al. [2] developed VizWiz, a mobile application that enabled users to ask visual questions by taking a photo and have crowd-workers answer in nearly real-time. In a follow-up study, researchers explored how blind users were taking advantage of the platform to ask for assistance with a variety of real-world tasks [3].

In the context of web accessibility, the Social Accessibility project [26] has shown how to take advantage of a network of domain knowledgeable sighted volunteers to provide document metadata (e.g. image labeling, document structure). After 20 months, the project had 350 volunteers that created about 19,000 metadata items for over 3000 web pages [24], revealing the potential of human powered approaches for assistance reliant on volunteers. In contrast with previous work, the Social Accessibility project can aggregate and reutilize the knowledge to assist others without the need of additional interventions by volunteers. Past work has explored how an in-context Q&A system relied on sighted volunteers to provide answers to support nonvisual access [22]. Insights from that work rallied for support tools that promote self-organized learning. Moreover, it unveiled some of the challenges present in relying on sighted people, with no accessibility knowledge, to support blind people in using their smartphones.

While there seems to be an opportunity to develop tools that enable and foster the provision of assistance by volunteers (i.e. the crowd), there is the need to better understand how those tools can be designed to be effective. In this paper, we examine how blind and sighted people provide instructions in this context and how they support, or fail in doing so, blind people in performing smartphone tasks.

3 Methodology

We sought to understand how people provide instructions to others, knowing that the end-user is a blind person. In line with capturing the broader set of possible authors, we conducted authoring sessions with two user groups: blind and sighted people. We recruited sighted smartphone users with no prior screen reader experience; and experienced blind smartphone users. We asked participants to create four tutorials for different tasks. Participants were made aware the intended audience were blind users. Sighted participants were given a set of tips (discussed in the following section) that were previously discussed with two accessibility instructors. Instructions given by the two groups allowed us to identify the information that we can gather to be leveraged by interactive tutorials. However, we did not know whether the instructions created were enough for people to be able to successfully follow them, and if not what was missing.

In a preliminary study [21], we had 11 blind participants following the tutorials created with a playthrough prototype. At every step, participants would hear the instruction followed by the screen reader announcing the target they needed to find and select in that step. However, only 30% of the tutorials were successfully completed; participants struggled to follow instructions and it became clear that having pre-recorded in-context instructions (plus step target) as the sole assistance would not suffice. However, we did not know what was missing for users to be successful.

To understand how to design effective tutorials, in a playthrough session, we again, exposed the content created to a new group of blind participants and allowed them to ask additional assistance to the researcher that acted in place of an ideal interactive tutorial similar to the question-asking protocol introduced by Kato [15]. The protocol was designed to have an expert coaching a user with the system. During the process users could ask questions that would help understands needs in context, identify information needs, difficulties and how users perceived the system. The approach has been previously identified for its potential in uncovering learnability issues [11]. We adopted the approach, and in addition, we observed and analyzed the interactions between participant, smartphone, tutorial and researcher. We were particularly interested in understanding the limitations of the instructions provided, what were the problems they caused and how one could complement them to enable users to complete the tutorials. Thus, we investigated how to deal with previously identified challenges by understanding the interaction and content needs of end-users.

3.1   Task Design

Participants created tutorials for six tasks (T) during the authoring session. Two were training tasks (TT) and were designed by the research team. In an effort to minimize the differences in difficulty between the tutorials, all tasks could be completed with six selections. Three of the tasks were doubts previously asked to members of the research team by blind people. T1 was added by the research team, as an OS task, that could also be completed with six selections. The tasks apps and description were as follow: TT1 *SimpleNote* - Delete an existing note; TT2 *SimpleNote* - Share existing note on WhatsApp; T1 *Settings* - Clean data from an app; T2 *Messages* - Forward an SMS; T3 *WhatsApp* - Create a group chat; T4 *RadioNet* - Add a station to favorites.

Tips for Accessible Tutorial Authoring. Sighted participants were informed the tutorials were to be used by blind people. However, some people are not aware of how screen readers work and go as far as not knowing smartphones can be accessible to blind people. In synchronous assistance, people have the ability to ask questions and explain their requirements. On the other hand, for assistance provided through technology (e.g. tutorials, Q&A [22, 26]) there is an opportunity to inform helpers of the user requirements. To this end, we had a session with two blind IT instructors where we devised a description of a mobile screen reader and set of tips to provide to sighted authors:

The tutorials you will be creating today will be used by blind people. Nowadays, smartphones come with screen readers, an accessibility software that allows blind people to interact with touchscreens. When active they change the way users interact with the device. To navigate, taps that used to select options now focus the tapped element and read it using text-to-speech technology. Alternatively, users can swipe left or right to change focus to the next or previous element. To select, instead of a tap, users need to double tap. When creating a tutorial please remember the following tips: (1) Do not reference visual elements (e.g. tap the green arrow); (2) If possible, indicate the textual description of the elements; (3) Indicate the functionality/purpose of the elements; (4) If possible, indicate the element location.

3.2   Authoring Tutorials Towards Democratization

Users created tutorials while performing the task, first they described a step and then they perform it. Upon finishing, users were asked to name and provide a description for the tutorial. Tutorials were segmented by each selection (e.g. 'Contacts', 'John') and associated with the respective audio snippet; this constitutes what we refer to as a step. To record the tutorials we developed an Android tool that allowed us to audio record authors and detect the steps performed to complete a certain task. The tool was designed to be unobtrusive to user interaction and usable with and without screen readers. We purposelessly asked participants to demonstrate the task while recording it, as authoring through demonstration can be an effective teaching approach [17,29].

3.3   Participants

For the authoring session, we recruited five sighted participants with no previous screen reader experience, ages ranging between 19 and 23 (M = 20.8, SD = 1.64) years old, three Android users and two iOS, experience between 3 and 4 years; and five blind participants, ages ranging between 25 and 51 (M = 38.8, SD = 9.49) years old, three iOS users and two Android, experience between 5 and 11 years, and two were IT instructors. Experienced users were chosen because of their knowledge and because people often rely on them to overcome challenges [22]. We considered users to be experienced if they had a smartphone for over four years and were able to perform the following list of tasks: place/receive calls, send/read emails/messages, install new applications, configure accessibility settings, browse the internet, use communication apps (e.g. Messenger, WhatsApp, Skype) and assistive applications (e.g. BeMyEyes). In the following sections we will refer to authoring participants as Authors.

For the playthrough session, we recruited 12 blind participants, ages ranging between 29 to 59 (M = 49.58, SD = 10.36), six Android users and six iOS, experience with smartphones between three months and four years. None of the participants took part in the first session. Participants had a wide range of expertise, with three participants meeting the task requirements to be experienced users, and two novice users that currently only place/receive calls and receive messages. Only one participant had previously done the 'forward task' in an Android device. There were three participants that had previously forwarded a message but on iOS devices. Additionally, one had previously created a group in WhatsApp. In the following sections we will refer to playthrough participants as Consumers.

3.4   Apparatus

We used a device running Android 7.1.2. and Talkback, the default screen reader. In the authoring session, participants were invited to use headphones to prevent recording the screen reader feedback. All applications were made available a priori on the device home screen. For the playthrough session, a laptop computer was used to control the audio instructions given to the participants during the tasks. We controlled for concurrent feedback only providing the next instruction when the screen reader was silent pausing/starting when needed.

3.5 Procedure

In both sessions, participants were informed the purpose of the study was to understand how interactive tutorials might facilitate smartphone use. Then participants completed a brief demographics and smartphone usage questionnaire.

Authoring Session. Authors were recruited in advance and given the list of tasks at least one day before meeting with the research team. They were asked to become acquainted with the applications and the tasks if they were not already. Participants were tasked with creating six tutorials. Sighted users were also presented with the introduction and set of tips aforementioned. Prior to creating a tutorial for each task, users were instructed to explore and perform it. For the first training tutorial (TT1), participants were guided through the creation process. Participants were informed that each step should start with an explanation of the step followed by its demonstration. Participants were then asked to create a tutorial for TT2. All participants successfully created a tutorial, thus completing the training phase. The order of the remaining four tasks was randomly chosen. Participants started every recording from the home screen. Although every task could be completed with six selections, participants were free to take alternative paths. The study concluded with a debriefing questionnaire to assess the user's opinions about the authoring process.

Pre-processing Content. For the playthrough session, we discarded four tutorials for having missteps (i.e. a incorrect step followed by a "back" action), one for having stereotypical references to difficulties felt by blind people, and three for poor audio quality. When recording tutorials, users had to demonstrate the task while giving instructions which resulted in audio files with long periods of silence. To address this issue, we removed the silences of all audio recordings. We intentionally did not control tutorial delivery, precision of vocabulary or required level of skill. In this study, our goal was to assess how to go from human generated tutorials with all their idiosyncrasies to accessible tutorials.

Playthrough Session. First, Consumers were informed they would be asked to complete a set of tasks. During the tasks they would be following instructions that had been previously recorded by other people, both sighted and blind. At any point during the task when participants wanted to control the playthrough of the instructions (e.g. stop, play, repeat) or when they required additional information or assistance, they could prompt the researcher. When a clear question was asked the researcher answered it (e.g. "Where is it?"). When participants asked for assistance but could not verbalize what they needed (e.g. "I cannot find it anywhere. What should I do?") the researcher would help them based on what he observed caused the issue (e.g. "You already went through the target but it is not 'create' it is 'new conversation'").

Instructions were given step by step or whenever the participant asked. To avoid audio conflicts, instructions only started when the screen reader had nothing else to announce. Participants were asked to complete the task by following the instructions and encouraged to think aloud whenever they stopped to require assistance. The only limitations imposed were: (1) the researcher could not physically assist in any way; (2) the researcher could not take the initiative to provide further instructions unless the participant was stuck in a step for more than three minutes. We audio recorded the entire session and observed user interactions with the smartphone. A second researcher annotated all requests and assistance provided by the intervening researcher.

For Consumers to get accustomed to the device and the study procedure, they completed TT1 created by the research team. Once they completed the task and felt comfortable navigating the device, we asked Consumers to complete the four tasks. Prior to starting each, they were informed what they would be attempting to do by following the instructions (e.g., 'Creating a group chat in WhatsApp'). Each participant followed tutorials created by both groups. Order of the tasks was counterbalanced, and every validated tutorial was followed at least once. We had a debriefing session whereby participants could discuss the experienced challenges and provide insights on possible features. Finally, we asked Consumers what information they believed to be essential to a instruction.

3.6   Data and Analysis

We conducted a thematic analysis leveraging the flexibility of the method in reflecting over the data collected [4]. We transcribed the instructions provided by Authors while creating the tutorials. For the authoring session we sought to understand the characteristics of each instruction. Therefore, two researchers inductively created two codebooks from ten tutorials, one from each participant and at least one per task. Codebooks were iterated, and merged. Another set of ten tutorials were coded independently and reached a Cohen's Kappa agreement of k = 0.82. The final codebook is shown on Table 1 aggregated by theme.

During the playthrough session, a researcher was observing interactions, behaviors, annotating requests, their motivation, and the additional assistance

Table 1. Code frequency in the tutorials' instructions.

Codes	Type					Screen	
	Visual	Text	Incorrect Text	Function	Type	Function Description	Layout Description
Blind (%)	0.0	77.8	0.0	9.4	7.7	8.5	2.6
Sighted (%)	8.6	74.3	19.2	21.0	8.6	2.9	1.9

Codes	Action			Location			Feedback	
	Selection	Navigation	Gesture Explanation	Absolute	Relative	Hierarchical Functional	Audio	State
Blind (%)	59.0	33.3	52.1	7.7	2.6	1.7	7.7	22.2
Sighted (%)	61.9	18.1	1.0	19.0	13.3	11.4	1.0	21.0

- *Now we do the up down gesture to go to the last element of the page. Now we are on **Next** we double tap. (BA)*
- *We click forward. (SA)*

- *Now its showing a list of radio stations, we are going to swipe from left to right with one finger until Radio Comercial. It will say radio logo, radio and name. (...) (BA)*
- *Multiple stations appear, we choose the one we want, Radio Comercial. (SA)*

Fig. 1. Two examples of two steps described by four different authors. Two blind authors (BA) and two sighted (SA).

provided. Thus, given the different focus of the second session, we created a second codebook from all the information collected that was iterated and refined by the two researchers. We aggregated the observations, requests and motivations in four major categories: Instructions' Content; Gesture & Navigation; Location & Layout; and Feedback.

3.7 Findings

In the authoring session, we collected 40 tutorials, 20 from each group, with a total of 128 individual instructions recorded by sighted Authors and 128 by blind Authors (summing a total of 256). Three tutorials created by blind people included extra steps during the recording (e.g. enabling Bluetooth). One blind participant, in one task, only demonstrated the steps without giving any instructions. The remaining tutorials were created successfully. In the playthrough session, the twelve participants explored all tasks successfully by following the tutorials and relying on the assistance of the researcher. In total, participants followed 240 steps and requested additional assistance in all tutorials. Specifically, in 83 (34.6%) of the steps, requesting information that was not present in the instruction given.

Below, we detail our findings organized into the four major themes that emerged from the playthrough session: Instructions' Content, Gesture & Navigation, Location & Layout and Tutorial Feedback (Table 2). The discussion on each topic is also supported by the analysis conducted on the tutorial instructions (Table 1). Frequencies are used to illustrate the findings, however they should not be taken as quantitative measures of the relevance of each problem. Finally, we report on the participant's feedback about the tutorial authoring process and on the value of the tips provided.

Table 2. Code Frequencies of the major categories of issues found during playthrough. A single step may possess multiple overlapping categories.

Category	Instructions Content	Gesture & Navigation	Location & Layout	Tutorial Feedback
In steps (%)	21.3	13.3	15.8	17.5

Instructions' Content. In 51 (21.3%) of the instructional steps provided, Consumers could not understand or identify the content being described in relation to the current screen.

Textual Descriptions Were Not Always Provided. In most steps (above 75%), the instructions had the target textual description. *"In the main menu click the app RadiosNet" [S1].* For some of the remaining instructions, Authors gave less detailed information focusing on the tutorial goal:

"We want a group conversation with one of the contacts, after you select a contact (...)." [S1] "(...)until we find the intended message" [B4].

At times, sighted Authors were unable to provide a target description leading to long and possibly confusing instructions. One example from T2 (WhatsApp): the sighed Authors did not know what to call the confirmation button, a green arrow, and gave a long confusing instruction:

"After you select the subject it will appear on the bottom of the screen and then click. Click not on the upper right corner but a little bit below, but still in the far-right side of the screen and click" [S1].

Blind Authors Were More Verbose. Sighted Authors provided shorter instructions only indicating what to do in each step Fig. 1. Blind Authors provided additional information about the current state of the tutorial and its overall goal (33% and 9% of instructions respectively) Fig. 1. Despite being more verbose, only 8% of blind people instructions referenced any kind of audio feedback. *"It will say in all of them the radio logo, radio followed by the name." [B1]* Moreover, none described any type of audio cue.

Target Description. Although most instructions had text descriptions, 19% of the ones provided by sighted people did not match the item label. Which is to be expected given the known issues with the variability of vocabulary used by people when interacting with systems [8]. Not surprisingly, on the debriefing questionnaire all sighted participants mention how hard it was to translate a visual icon into a textual description. Therefore, at times (21% of the instructions) they relied on describing the target function rather than its name. *"In the bottom right corner, look for the icon that starts a conversation." [S5].* For Blind Authors, target function (in 9% of the instructions) appears to be described to alert users about the outcome of their interactions. *"Now we get to Radio Channel and we are going to make it play" [B3].*

When following instructions, if the target was anything but verbatim (e.g. *"New Conversation"* vs. *"Create Conversation"*) Consumers assumed there would be another option that they had yet to find that corresponded exactly. This is particularly relevant in the first utterances of the word which are relied on to quickly skim through content.

Gesture & Navigation. In 32 (13.3%) of steps, Consumers required additional assistance due to issues with gestures and navigation. This includes issues that resulted from a combination of the navigational content of the instructions and the participants navigational behaviors.

Blind Authors Instructed More Often to Navigate. For sighted Authors mentioning navigation is only relevant when the target element is not visually available on the screen. However, for blind people that rely on swipe gestures to navigate, every target needs to be navigated to. Sighted Authors instructed users to navigate in 18% of their instructions, while blind Authors did it in 33% of the instructions. *"We are going to look for the message by swiping with one finger until we find the message that in this case says 'Hello'"* [B2].

Blind Authors Were More Aware of Gesture Subtleties. Only one instruction by a sighted Authors contained a brief explanation on how to perform a particular action. *"I am going to keep it pressed"* [S2]. On the other hand, 52% of blind authored instructions contained the additional information on how to perform a gesture. *"Now, we locate or we swipe from left to right or by exploring the screen until we find the message we want to forward. Then we double tap and hold on the second one"* [B1]. However, how to instruct the user raised some questions.

Conflicts with User Expertise and Interaction Preferences. Instructions that guide the user by saying 'go to the right corner and select X' or 'swipe until you find X' can be disruptive for users who are only familiar with one interaction method (i.e. Explore by Touch versus Swipe Navigation). In multiple instances, Consumers tried using an unfamiliar method with no success. Moreover, they were convinced that since the tutorial instructed them to do so, it was the only way to reach the target. Thus, participants of both methods had to request help to understand how to proceed. The same problem happens when sighted Authors instruct participants to perform gestures (e.g. to forward a message with a screen reader users have double tap with a long press on the second tap; without one is just a long press). Since neither sighted Author nor Consumer were aware of the dissonance between the interactions, the latter required further assistance.

Navigational Deadlocks. Although we observed that instructions that include how to reach a target can be problematic, the exact opposite can also be true. For novice users that still struggle understanding some navigational behaviors such as lists, information on how to reach a target can be fundamental. To reach the option "Applications" in the device "Settings" users have to either perform a scroll or navigate by swiping from left to right until they reach the end of the list displayed on the screen. However, if the user is relying on navigating from right to left, the list will not scroll down, it will just cycle through the elements on the screen repeatedly. Thus, the user will never find the intended target, leading to a navigational deadlock. Moreover, when multiple lists are present on the screen, the user can get "locked" navigating one until it reaches the end of its content, which in auto updated views can be never.

Location & Layout. In 38 (15.8%) of steps, Consumers required some assistance related with the location of the target element or further details about the overall layout of the screen.

Sighted Authors Gave More, and Often Useless, Location Instructions. Blind Authors gave location instructions (absolute, relative or hierarchical) 15 times while sighted Authors did it 46 times. Although 42% (absolute 19%, relative 13%, and hierarchical 11%) of instructions by sighted Authors came with location, many of them were inadequate and even misleading *"I am going to click in the OK that is on the bottom right corner of the pop-up" [S4].* In this example, while location was provided, the Consumer was unaware of the location and dimensions of the pop-up menu.

Target Location Was Complementary. Consumers wanted to be notified about the absolute locations of the target they needed to reach. Since some relied on 'Explore by Touch', absolute location could be crucial to find the target effectively. Others asked for location instructions when they got stuck in navigational deadlocks. A few that rely on mixed interaction methods wanted to optimize their navigation behaviors. To do so, they needed to know the target whereabouts to be able to start their navigation closer to the intended target, prior to linear scanning. Location seems to be complementary, and when given, one must be aware of its potential consequences. It all depends on the user expertise and interaction behaviors.

Describe the Screen Overall Layout. For multiple Consumers it was important to create a mental model of the screen before starting to navigate. However, less than 10% of the instructions contained additional information about other functionalities available in the screen. Sighted Authors made no attempts to describe layout, despite being able quickly grasp a screen structure. From the 128 instructions given by sighted Authors only two attempted to describe screen layout. In contrast, for a blind Author to describe a layout he/she must first explore all the interface. Even so, three of the 128 instructions, by blind Authors, contained layout descriptions.

Consumers asked how the content organized as they tried to figure out how the elements were disposed (*"Is it a grid?"*). In some cases where the screen was composed by two or three major structures (e.g. title bar and list) the answer was simple. However, there are complex layouts that can be time consuming to describe and at times even confusing (e.g. multiple list views, some horizontal others vertical, with other unstructured content). In these instances, the researcher providing additional assistance struggled to provide a clear and concise description of the layout.

Tutorial Feedback. In this section we aggregated instances where feedback should have been provided to facilitate user interaction at a key point during navigation or when feedback was provided inappropriately causing users to request assistance.

Confirm Target. Similarly, to has been previously reported in Vigo et al. [27] on the coping tactics employed by visually impaired people on the web, Consumers asked for reassurance and confirmation. Confirming what to do prior to engaging in a navigation and confirming once they reached a target. For a successful interactive tutorial, one may need to ensure users are given appropriate feedback to enable them to seamless detect they have reached the target and reassure them they are following the intended steps.

Consumers Did Not Understand Why They Could Not Find Their Target. When Consumers spent a significant amount of time exploring the screen and detected repetitions without finding the target element, they prompted the researcher for assistance. This could be because the element was not displayed on the screen; or Consumers were stuck in navigational deadlock; or because during exploration they missed the target element. Although the consequences are the same, the required actions to address them are distinct. Thus, it can be crucial to understand how to detect each scenario.

Consumers Were Unaware of Incorrect Steps. In 21 (8.8%) of the steps Consumers deviated from the intended path. In all, Consumers were unaware they did so. In two instances the step was a shortcut that jumped the tutorial two steps forward. In these instances, the researcher controlling the audio tutorial compensated and skipped the middle step. In the remaining steps, participants were notified they had deviated from the intended path after they asked the researcher for further instructions; it is noteworthy that all requested assistance to resume their previous state.

Authoring and Tips. Sighted Authors at times did not follow the provided tips; struggled to provide descriptions to visual elements; and at times, even to provide location. *"I will press again (hadn't mentioned or previously pressed that button) in the button on the right line below, in the bottom right corner." [S2]*.

4   Discussion

We explored the ways in which people create tutorials for mobile interactions, and the challenges faced by blind people when following those tutorials. Herein, we discuss the lessons learned, which should be of interest to researchers and practitioners working on nonvisual mobile accessibility.

4.1   Required Information and Feedback

Different people will require different instructions and control depending on a variety of factors. The only common requirement for all instructions and across participants was accurate target description. All other information can be beneficial or detrimental to the users. The types of information/feedback required were the following: target location; target function; screen state; layout description; target focus confirmation; alert on path deviation; gesture guidance; and task/feature clarifications.

In past work, Lieberman et al. [18] have explored three levels of control over each step. However, with an understanding of the information and interaction needs, we can go further and, not only provide different levels of guidance, but also adapt contents within each instruction. It is important to collect different types of information for all tutorial steps during the authoring process to be able to develop flexible playthrough tools. This may come with the cost of overburdening authors; thus, we must work towards solutions that support the authoring process.

4.2   Authoring Support

Blind and sighted people created instructions with different content. Blind people were more verbose and often provided guidance on how to navigate, which again can be beneficial or detrimental.

On the other hand, despite the tips, sighted participants still provided inaccurate instructions, suggesting we may need to find alternatives. Discarding sighted people from the pool of authors is not one we should willingly follow due to its impact in availability and coverability of tutorials. Particularly, when we consider that some of the information required during playthrough is easier to be provided by sighted people. Sighted people in previous work have been successfully leveraged to provide answers to visual questions [2]. Future solutions should be able to leverage the differences in content created, by both author groups, to provide accessible tutorials.

One possibility is to increase the authoring burden by increasing training. However, we believe a more scalable approach can be collecting additional data during the authoring process (e.g. layouts, steps, workflows, labels) to reduce the dependency on the accessibility knowledge of tutorial authors.

To collect all the different information required we can explore how to break down the authoring process in steps and prompt people (Authors) to provide different types of information in small tasks (e.g. Item location, Layout Structure), without any training or particular understanding of the underlying requirements; similar to what has been previously proposed and achieve by Gleason et al. [9] in enabling non-expert participation in the installation and maintenance of indoor localization infrastructure.

This approach would enable us to both guide contributors through the authoring process, and if need be, rely on different contributors for different types of information. Furthermore, we can explore how to make the most of contributions by maximizing the information collected and/or derived automatically. For instance, since we can ask contributors to demonstrate tasks, we use the opportunity to collect target descriptions, thus avoiding inaccurate descriptions. Moreover, by breaking down the authoring process we can combine contributions of multiple people to create a complete representation of the task and all its peculiarities. In addition to relying on authors as the sole contributors, in line with previous work [17], consumers interactions with content can also be leveraged to enhance the content provided (e.g. providing multiple demonstrations of the sequence of navigational steps taken).

Only by supporting the authoring process and leveraging multiple sources of information will we be able to design adaptable playthrough solutions.

4.3   Account for User Expertise, Behaviors and Preferences

The same instructions can be interpreted differently by users, and what prevents some from completing the task can be what enables others to do so. For example, for users who primarily rely on Explore by Touch, it is of the utmost importance to understand the interface underneath. If users understand they are interacting with a grid they will scan very differently than if they believe they are facing a list. We must also be aware that user requirements might change per step or even in the same step when certain navigation patterns occur (e.g. detecting users are stuck navigating an auto-updating list and their target is not on that list but in another element of the layout). We believe part of the solution can be to continuously model and monitor user interaction behaviours during playthrough. Previous research in user modelling [19] has already explored continuously updating models based on current behaviors, leveraging its information to provide optimal settings for each interface. We can imagine a similar approach to tutorial playthrough where, one can adapt based on: user profile; interaction behaviors (i.e. past and current); navigation pattern detection; content instructions and personalization.

4.4   Flexible Instructions and App Modeling

If we can collect different types of information and develop solutions that take into consideration user interaction behaviors and immediate needs, we will be able to provide flexible instructions. As recognized by Lieberman et al. [18], at different steps users may require different levels of guidance. By default, users should be able to access all types of instructions during playthrough by request or based on triggering interactions. Moreover, we may start to adapt instructions verbosity and gestures guidance. Expert users felt instructions were too long with unnecessary content. However, for less experienced users detailed instructions may be crucial since they are not as aware of the navigation nuances of different interface elements. One example is providing users with additional information on navigational locks or if the target element is or ever was on screen. When possible, instructions should be generated or adapted to current context and past actions. Moreover, interactive tutorials should detect the variety of available paths to complete a task, alerting users on deviations and providing mechanisms to recover. Building such systems will require a deeper understanding of app structure and navigation workflows, currently out of reach for third party assistive technologies. However, if we can model application structures and workflows we will be in a position to creater smarter assistive tools.

4.5   Enable Dialog, a Fallback Mechanism

The previous considerations stem from the unpredictability of the user individual requirements when trying to learn or accomplish a task. We discuss how we can broaden the adaptability of instructions and assistance by considering the variety of points of failure and doubts, and preemptively prepare for them. As our findings suggest, invariable instructions were not enough. With adapted solutions we might get closer to fully automatize assistance. However, we believe the only answer to byzantine problems is to rely on others once more. To do so, we can create solutions that take advantage of peers/crowdworkers/users beyond a single contribution and enable a dialog mediated by the technology. The outcomes of this channel will further fuel the accessibility and adaptability of the content, thus creating living artifacts capable of perpetual improvement.

4.6   Limitations

We conducted a study with five blind and five sighted authors that created tutorials for four tasks, that we exposed to 12 blind participants. Although this is a small number of participants and tasks per user group, it allowed us to identify a variety of novel information needs triggered by nonvisual tutorials. Nonetheless, further research with a larger user pool, with different expertise levels, and set of tasks (e.g. navigate a video, play a game) may uncover additional needs.

5   Conclusion

We inform future work on the design of solutions that rely on untrained individuals to provide asynchronous technical assistance. We believe both to be valuable contributions for the community in future efforts to design assistive technologies that empower and enable peer support.

We identified the different information required by users during playthrough when following instructions by others. We found that instructions by sighted people were more concise and often had misleading target information due to the challenges of converting visual references to accurate textual descriptions. Even though blind instructions were accurate it was clear, in both tutorial types, that users required additional assistance that was not contemplated in the instructions provided. When following a tutorial, the differences in users' expertise, interaction behaviors and preferences dictate the type of instruction adequate for each user. There is a need for novel solutions in interactive nonvisual tutorials both in authoring and playthrough.

Future research should seek to explore how to support users during authoring to create useful information, taking advantage of each author specific knowledge. Moreover, we can start leveraging the data collected during the authoring process to enrich or even create new instructions. On the other end of the spectrum, we need to compensate for the unavoidable flaws that come from: (1) the authoring process by non-specialists; (2) the limitations of rigid instructions by looking into novel playthrough mechanisms for nonvisual interactive tutorials.

References

1. AppleViz: iOS blind and low-vision support community (2018). https://www.applevis.com/. Accessed 3 Jan 2019
2. Bigham, J.P., et al.: Vizwiz: nearly real-time answers to visual questions. In: Proceedings of ACM Symposium on User Interface Software and Technology, UIST 2010, pp. 333–342 (2010). https://doi.org/10.1145/1866029.1866080. http://doi.acm.org/10.1145/1866029.1866080
3. Brady, E., Morris, M.R., Zhong, Y., White, S., Bigham, J.P.: Visual challenges in the everyday lives of blind people. In: Proceedings of the SIGCHI Conference on Human Factors in Computing Systems, CHI 2013, pp. 2117–2126. ACM, New York (2013). https://doi.org/10.1145/2470654.2481291. http://doi.acm.org/10.1145/2470654.2481291
4. Braun, V., Clarke, V.: Using thematic analysis in psychology. Qual. Res. Psychol. 3(2), 77–101 (2006). https://doi.org/10.1191/1478088706qp063oa. http://www.tandfonline.com/doi/abs/10.1191/1478088706qp063oa
5. CodeFactory: Mobile Accessibility (2011). http://codefactoryglobal.com/app-store/mobile-accessibility/. Accessed 17 May 2018
6. Eyes-Free: eyes free (2010). https://groups.google.com/forum/#!forum/eyes-free. Accessed 3 Jan 2019
7. Fernquist, J., Grossman, T., Fitzmaurice, G.: Sketch-sketch revolution: an engaging tutorial system for guided sketching and application learning. In: Proceedings of the 24th Annual ACM Symposium on User Interface Software and Technology, UIST 2011, pp. 373–382. ACM, New York (2011). https://doi.org/10.1145/2047196.2047245. http://doi.acm.org/10.1145/2047196.2047245
8. Furnas, G.W., Landauer, T.K., Gomez, L.M., Dumais, S.T.: The vocabulary problem in human-system communication. Commun. ACM 30(11), 964–971 (1987). https://doi.org/10.1145/32206.32212. http://doi.acm.org/10.1145/32206.32212
9. Gleason, C., et al.: Crowdsourcing the installation and maintenance of indoor localization infrastructure to support blind navigation. Proc. ACM Interact. Mob. Wearable Ubiquitous Technol. 2(1), 9:1–9:25 (2018). https://doi.org/10.1145/3191741. http://doi.acm.org/10.1145/3191741

10. Grossman, T., Fitzmaurice, G.: ToolClips: an investigation of contextual video assistance for functionality understanding. In: Proceedings of the SIGCHI Conference on Human Factors in Computing Systems, CHI 2010, pp. 1515–1524. ACM, New York (2010). https://doi.org/10.1145/1753326.1753552. http://doi.acm.org/10.1145/1753326.1753552

11. Grossman, T., Fitzmaurice, G., Attar, R.: A survey of software learnability: metrics, methodologies and guidelines. In: Proceedings of the SIGCHI Conference on Human Factors in Computing Systems, CHI 2009, pp. 649–658. ACM, New York (2009). https://doi.org/10.1145/1518701.1518803. http://doi.acm.org/10.1145/1518701.1518803

12. Grussenmeyer, W., Folmer, E.: Accessible touchscreen technology for people with visual impairments: a survey. ACM Trans. Access. Comput. 9(2), 6:1–6:31 (2017). https://doi.org/10.1145/3022701. http://doi.acm.org/10.1145/3022701

13. Hagiya, T., Yazaki, T., Horiuchi, T., Kato, T.: Typing tutor: automatic error detection and instruction in text entry for elderly people. In: Proceedings of the 17th International Conference on Human-Computer Interaction with Mobile Devices and Services Adjunct, MobileHCI 2015, pp. 696–703. ACM, New York (2015). https://doi.org/10.1145/2786567.2793690. http://doi.acm.org/10.1145/2786567.2793690

14. Kane, S.K., Bigham, J.P., Wobbrock, J.O.: Slide rule: making mobile touch screens accessible to blind people using multi-touch interaction techniques. In: Proceedings of the 10th International ACM SIGACCESS Conference on Computers and Accessibility, Assets 2008, pp. 73–80. ACM, New York (2008). https://doi.org/10.1145/1414471.1414487. http://doi.acm.org/10.1145/1414471.1414487

15. Kato, T.: What "question-asking protocols" can say about the user interface. Int. J. Man Mach. Stud. 25(6), 659–673 (1986). https://doi.org/10.1016/S0020-7373(86)80080-3. http://www.sciencedirect.com/science/article/pii/S0020737386800803

16. Kelleher, C., Pausch, R.: Stencils-based tutorials: design and evaluation. In: Proceedings of the SIGCHI Conference on Human Factors in Computing Systems, CHI 2005, pp. 541–550. ACM, New York (2005). https://doi.org/10.1145/1054972.1055047. http://doi.acm.org/10.1145/1054972.1055047

17. Lafreniere, B., Grossman, T., Fitzmaurice, G.: Community enhanced tutorials: improving tutorials with multiple demonstrations. In: Proceedings of the SIGCHI Conference on Human Factors in Computing Systems, CHI 2013, pp. 1779–1788. ACM, New York (2013). https://doi.org/10.1145/2470654.2466235. http://doi.acm.org/10.1145/2470654.2466235

18. Lieberman, H., Rosenzweig, E., Fry, C.: Steptorials: mixed-initiative learning of high-functionality applications. In: Proceedings of the 19th International Conference on Intelligent User Interfaces, IUI 2014, pp. 359–364. ACM, New York (2014). https://doi.org/10.1145/2557500.2557543. http://doi.acm.org/10.1145/2557500.2557543

19. Montague, K., Hanson, V.L., Cobley, A.: Designing for individuals: usable touchscreen interaction through shared user models. In: Proceedings of the 14th International ACM SIGACCESS Conference on Computers and Accessibility, ASSETS 2012, pp. 151–158. ACM, New York (2012). https://doi.org/10.1145/2384916.2384943. http://doi.acm.org/10.1145/2384916.2384943

20. Oh, U., Kane, S.K., Findlater, L.: Follow that sound: using sonification and corrective verbal feedback to teach touchscreen gestures. In: Proceedings of the 15th International ACM SIGACCESS Conference on Computers and Accessibility, ASSETS 2013, pp. 13:1–13:8 (2013). https://doi.org/10.1145/2513383.2513455. http://doi.acm.org/10.1145/2513383.2513455

21. Rodrigues, A., Camacho, L., Nicolau, H., Montague, K., Guerreiro, T.: AidMe: interactive non-visual smartphone tutorials. In: Proceedings of the 20th International Conference on Human-Computer Interaction with Mobile Devices and Services Adjunct, MobileHCI 2018, pp. 205–212. ACM, New York (2018). https://doi.org/10.1145/3236112.3236141. http://doi.acm.org/10.1145/3236112.3236141

22. Rodrigues, A., Montague, K., Nicolau, H., Guerreiro, J., Guerreiro, T.: In-context Q&A to support blind people using smartphones. In: Proceedings of the 19th International ACM SIGACCESS Conference on Computers and Accessibility, ASSETS 2017, pp. 32–36. ACM, New York (2017). https://doi.org/10.1145/3132525.3132555. http://doi.acm.org/10.1145/3132525.3132555

23. Rodrigues, A., Montague, K., Nicolau, H., Guerreiro, T.: Getting smartphones to talkback: understanding the smartphone adoption process of blind users. In: Proceedings of ACM SIGACCESS Conference on Computers and Accessibility, ASSETS 2015, pp. 23–32 (2015). https://doi.org/10.1145/2700648.2809842. http://doi.acm.org/10.1145/2700648.2809842

24. Sato, D., Takagi, H., Kobayashi, M., Kawanaka, S., Asakawa, C.: Exploratory analysis of collaborative web accessibility improvement. ACM Trans. Access. Comput. **3**(2), 5:1–5:30 (2010). https://doi.org/10.1145/1857920.1857922. http://doi.acm.org/10.1145/1857920.1857922

25. Shinohara, K., Wobbrock, J.O.: In the shadow of misperception: assistive technology use and social interactions. In: Proceedings of the SIGCHI Conference on Human Factors in Computing Systems, CHI 2011, pp. 705–714. ACM, New York (2011). https://doi.org/10.1145/1978942.1979044. http://doi.acm.org/10.1145/1978942.1979044

26. Takagi, H., Kawanaka, S., Kobayashi, M., Itoh, T., Asakawa, C.: Social accessibility: achieving accessibility through collaborative metadata authoring. In: Proceedings of ACM SIGACCESS Conference on Computers and Accessibility, Assets 2008, pp. 193–200 (2008). https://doi.org/10.1145/1414471.1414507. http://doi.acm.org/10.1145/1414471.1414507

27. Vigo, M., Harper, S.: Coping tactics employed by visually disabled users on the web. Int. J. Hum. Comput. Stud. **71**(11), 1013–1025 (2013). https://doi.org/10.1016/j.ijhcs.2013.08.002. http://www.sciencedirect.com/science/article/pii/S1071581913001006

28. Vyshnavi: Tech Accessibility Youtube Channel (2018). https://www.youtube.com/channel/UCOVwNKy4c_jDllBXUntbh5Q/about. Accessed 3 Jan 2019

29. Wang, C.Y., Chu, W.C., Chen, H.R., Hsu, C.Y., Chen, M.Y.: EverTutor: automatically creating interactive guided tutorials on smartphones by user demonstration. In: Proceedings of the SIGCHI Conference on Human Factors in Computing Systems, CHI 2014, pp. 4027–4036. ACM, New York (2014). https://doi.org/10.1145/2556288.2557407. http://doi.acm.org/10.1145/2556288.2557407

30. Zhang, D., Zhou, L., Uchidiuno, J.O., Kilic, I.Y.: Personalized assistive web for improving mobile web browsing and accessibility for visually impaired users. ACM Trans. Access. Comput. **10**(2), 6:1–6:22 (2017). https://doi.org/10.1145/3053733. http://doi.acm.org/10.1145/3053733

User Study: A Detailed View on the Effectiveness and Design of Tactile Charts

Christin Engel[✉] and Gerhard Weber[✉]

Faculty of Computer Science, Chair of Human-Computer-Interaction, TU Dresden,
01062 Dresden, Germany
{christin.engel,gerhard.weber}@tu-dresden.de

Abstract. Charts such as bar or pie charts are often used to represent data and their relation. Tactile charts are widely used to enable blind and visually impaired people to explore charts through the sense of touch. Effective tactile chart design differs from its visual counterpart due to sequential nature of touch. Accordingly, in a study with 48 blind and visually-impaired participants we investigated the preferences for chart types, design features and errors in reading data values. We developed bar, line and pie charts as well as scatterplots with different layouts and novel design properties. Participants answered questions concerning the readability, content and data, specific design aspects as well as a personal rating. Overall, participants answered 80% of nominal questions regarding minima, maxima, and comparisons, correctly. Blind participants achieved a corrected mean error rate of 4.5%, when reading single points or intersections, for example. More specifically, we directly compare chart types, and discuss the results for specific design considerations (e.g. distances between bars, width of bars, design and use of grid lines in scatterplots) by comparing different charts.

Keywords: User studies · Blind and visually impaired people ·
Tactile chart design

1 Introduction

Graphics are important to communicate and represent ideas, relations or spatial information. Information graphics such as bar or line charts are often used in our daily life to represent data and its meaning. Analysing data by using information visualisations is a common way to gain insights from the data. Information visualisations have been developed for the visual sense and make use of domain specific skills. Due to the preattentive perception, it is easy to quickly detect outliers or patterns in visualisations. The development of new information visualisation techniques is ongoing since Cleveland has presented his seminal work (e.g. [4]). The design and type of visualisation depends on the underlying data as well as the analysis tasks. Different visualisation types are suitable for specific analysis tasks such as details-on-demand, overview or filter [19]. Analysing data effectively is a main requirement in many professions and daily life. Blind and

© IFIP International Federation for Information Processing 2019
Published by Springer Nature Switzerland AG 2019
D. Lamas et al. (Eds.): INTERACT 2019, LNCS 11746, pp. 63–82, 2019.
https://doi.org/10.1007/978-3-030-29381-9_5

visually-impaired people cannot access information graphics and its underlying data. Therefore, accessibility guidelines such as BITV (Barrier-Free Information Technology Ordinance) state to provide a verbal description of non-textual content. The basic verbalisation of common chart types like bar charts, line charts or scatterplots is well defined. Existing guidelines (e.g. BANA guidelines [3]) recommend describing the elements and structure of a chart while providing the underlying data within a data table. This is not useful for complex charts or for understanding the content of the chart. Analysis of raw data in a table data is very difficult, whereby especially gaining an overview or detecting trends.

Tactile charts are suitable to provide access to charts for blind people. They comprise raised elements and can be perceived by the sense of touch two-handed. Colours in visual charts are replaced by line styles, symbols and textures to distinguish data sets from each other. Tactile charts allow blind and visually-impaired people to explore and analyse the represented data independently. In addition, tactile charts provide spatial information, which supports the understanding and memorability of the content.

Readability of tactile charts is influenced by their design. Most guidelines concerning tactile chart design recommend a design similar to the visual counterpart (e.g. [3,17,18]). Visual design differs from tactile design because the two senses have different perception properties. Given that tactile perception has a small resolution, tactile charts have to be adapted for the tactile sense [9,14]. In addition, there is not always a visual counterpart. Furthermore, existing guidelines are lacking of specific use cases of tactile charts. For example, BANA guidelines recommend avoiding grid lines in scatterplots because the purpose of this chart type is to show correlations. This may be true for some but not all use cases. Most guidelines are too general and do not provide precise design recommendations for effective tactile chart design. In addition, specifications of necessary distances or sizes of chart-specific elements are often only vaguely provided. For instance, the size of point symbols in scatterplots is determined by the required space between point symbols [3]. Other guidelines simply provide examples for transcriptions [17]. Prescher et al. [15] developed general guidelines for tactile graphics and provide clear examples and precise specifications. In the following, we investigate such general recommendations and their application to different chart types.

2   Research on Tactile Chart Design

There is initial research concerning tactile chart design. Panëels et al. [14] reviewed the field of haptic data visualisations for blind people, discussing haptic line, bar and pie charts regarding the representation, quantitative information, overview, exploration and automation. The authors show the wide range of multimodal approaches and force-feedback systems for the representation of haptic charts. They underline the need for effective visualisation methods. A few studies have highlighted the effectiveness of tactile charts. Watanabe et al. [21] compared the usability of a Braille table, a digital data table and a scatterplot with three blind students. Tactile scatterplot outperformed the other representation methods when identifying trends quickly. The authors repeated this study with ten blind participants aged from 19 to 27 years [20]. Second, Watanabe et al. used identical data sets to compare a tactile table, a tactile scatterplot and a digital table to ascertain which representation method is most effective. Their charts represent four relation types: linear, quadratic, inverse proportional and non-correlated (12 data sets overall). They show blind people are able to identify relations in a scatterplot more quickly than in a tactile table or a digital table. Tactile chart was understood in the shortest time. At the same time, error rates between the three conditions were comparable.

Especially the design of grid lines in tactile charts is commonly discussed. In a study with twelve female students (six blind), Aldrich et al. [1] compared three formats for the representation of tactile line charts. They used a line chart with standard x and y axes without grid lines (L/no-grid), one with duplicated axes (box/no-grid) and one with duplicated axes and grid lines (box/grid). The box/grid condition led to the most accurate answers. The L/no-grid format achieved the shortest response time. Lederman et al. [12] evaluated four grid formats with 20 adult participants: no-grid, grid-on-graph (extended tick marks into graph area), grid-overlay (separate sheet served as an overlay) and grid-underlay where a separate sheet was placed underneath the chart. The study shows no correlation between age of blindness and the graph-reading performance of participants. The grid-on-graph and grid-underlay condition performed best. Barth et al. [2] evaluated line charts with an incised grid/raised data curve condition (grids were embossed on the other side of the sheet) with 24 blind students. This incised grid condition significantly improves the reading time in comparison with the raised-grid and no-grid condition. Their aimed to find effects of different design characteristics on graph-reading performance (extreme and intersections points, line tracing, reading time).

Goncu et al. [11] investigated several formats of bar charts with twelve blind participants. They created three formats for three types of bar charts (simple, grouped, stacked). Grid and values at the top of each bar led to the lowest error rate in comparison with the no grid/no values and grid/no values conditions. In addition, grid and values were preferred by participants. Surprisingly, the tactile data table was preferred over the tactile chart (6 participants, 8 data points).

More general research focuses on the discriminability of embossed elements. Culbert et al. [5] identified a set of eleven textures that are discriminable. Nolan et al. [13] defined a high legible set of eleven point symbols and seven line symbols designed for tactile maps. Furthermore, Prescher et al. [16] present a consistency set of nine tactile patterns that are recognisable over different production media.

Overall, research in tactile chart design only focuses on a few chart types, whereby line charts and bar charts are the most popular. There is initial research concerning the effectiveness of tactile charts. While some studies focus on the comparison with other data representation methods, others describe the effectiveness based on the reading performance. Effectiveness among different chart types has not been considered. Further research is necessary to understand their limitations [10]. Research should focus in particular on designing tactile charts for data analysis. Furthermore, design parameters are not evaluated for different chart types. For example, the use of grid lines is commonly discussed for line charts but not for scatterplots. The results of the studies are only comparable to a limited extent due to different design parameters. Current research indicates certain chart elements influence the readability of the chart. Many design features for specific chart types remains unclear (e.g. distance between bars, textures in bar charts, point symbols in scatterplots). Most studies only compare single data sets or data sets with few values and do not use real data sets (apart from Goncu et al. [11]). Accordingly, current studies do not evaluate real-world scenarios where the user has to understand the data and its meaning in the context to the given chart. Data sets often include only a few data points and rarely multiple data sets. The data is optimised for tactile output. For example, overlapping symbols in scatterplots, charts without clear correlations and outliers, thin columns, very close data lines or different point symbols in scatterplots had not yet been investigated. Several analysis tasks need to be explored such as identifying clusters in scatterplots. Furthermore, it is not known if certain design features are intuitively understood and whether blind people can access tactile charts independently. If tactile charts need to be designed differently for different user groups is unclear.

In this context, it is important to evaluate tactile charts with blind participants having a different background. This is a major problem with prior studies, because they were carried out with a small group of participants who are mostly homogeneous regarding their experiences or age (e.g. female students largely of a similar age [1]). Overall, there is a need to investigate the effectiveness and design of tactile charts based on different criteria through user studies. It remains unclear whether tactile charts can be understood by blind people who are unfamiliar with them.

Accordingly, we investigated several studies about tactile chart design. First, we analysed the design of tactile charts collected from online libraries, publications and transcribing institutes [6]. In an online survey with 71 sighted, visually-impaired and blind creators and users of tactile charts [7] we included questions about the current production process of tactile charts, chart types known, exploration strategies as well as the design of tactile charts. Based on several pilot studies in which we evaluated the readability of specific design criteria, we developed a total of 21 tactile bar charts, line charts, scatterplots and pie charts, which we evaluated with 48 blind and visually-impaired people. In [8] we presented first results of this remote study. In this paper, we describe our study and results in detail for specific design parameters that have not been discussed in detail in prior research. In addition, we investigate whether characteristics of the user group influence the reading performance.

3 Remote User Study with Blind and Visually Impaired People

For a remote user study we mailed the tactile charts to participants. Accordingly, they were free to perform the study at any time and place. This design avoids traveling to far away or to unknown places. Participants could work in their personal setup and use their own assistive technologies. We reached a large number of diverse participants who completed the study based on our instructions.

3.1 Study Design

Within the remote study, participants should complete an online survey and simultaneously explore the tactile charts. We emailed invitation to blind and visually-impaired people in Germany and posted invitations in social network groups, forums and mailing lists. We also asked associations of blind people as well as schools for the blind for participation. In addition, we attached the invitation to the study as black print and as a Braille version. Interested people could contact us to receive the materials by mail. In addition, they obtained a detailed description about the study via e-mail. Each participant received the following materials:

- A brief description about the study in Braille
- A description how to mail the materials back to us (including an address label with our address on it)
- 21 individually-sorted tactile charts
- Personalised URL to the online survey with an access key

We put Braille labels on the envelope so that blind participants could identify the envelope independently. We requested the participants to send the materials back to us after performing the study to save paper resources and re-use them. It was advised to perform the study within at most a few days without longer breaks. We instructed the participants to carry out the study without any aids (e.g. ruler, other people).

Overall, our mailing consists of seven bar charts, six line charts and three pie charts as well as five scatterplots. The charts were randomised by chart type (the paper on the top was the first). Each chart was identifiable by a number within a box in the upper left corner and referenced within the online survey. Accordingly, participants could always check ordering of the charts. We defined six randomisation configurations to avoid learning effects while exploring. Only pie charts were not randomised; rather, they were always last in the pile. The structure and elements of pie charts strongly differ from other chart types. Minor learning effects were expected. In addition, pie charts are the least suitable for data analysis because they can only represent a small amount of data. All six permutations of line charts, bar charts and scatterplots were used. The order of charts within the pages for each chart type was fixed. The full completion of two out of four chart types (where pie charts are always in fourth position)

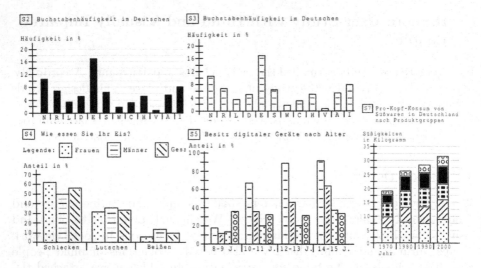

Fig. 1. Simple, grouped and stacked bar charts that we generated for evaluation (from left to right: S2, S3, S4, S5, S7)

were mandatory to receive a voucher amounting to 15 Euros for participation. Finally, the participants were asked to complete an additional survey to rate the study design and its content.

3.2 Stimuli

The charts represent real data sets to stimulate interest in the results. Charts were embossed on A4 format, mostly in landscape orientation (except from the stacked bar chart). While some charts include a legend on the same sheet, three charts come with a legend on a separate sheet. Each chart has a title at the top, a box with an ID as well as labelled axes. The sizes and design of chart elements and distances are based on existing guidelines [3,15,18], the results of our own analysis (e.g. [6]) and pilot studies. Repeating chart elements were designed consistently. Axes and tick marks are about 1 mm (one embossed line). The line styles and textures used are well evaluated by Prescher et al. [15,16] for general use. Moreover, we evaluated various design parameters that have not yet been considered. Therefore, we developed charts with different design characteristics to evaluate their effectiveness. In addition, we compared design alternatives directly where we developed two charts that only differ in one design parameter.

Bar Charts. We generated three simple bar charts (S1–S3), three grouped bar charts with multiple data sets (S4–S6) and the stacked bar chart S7 (see Fig. 1). The wider bars have a width of about 2 cm, the smaller are 1 cm wide [3]. While bars of S2 are filled, S3 makes use of a texture consisting of horizontal grid lines to mark scale units. S2 has thin grid lines in the background of the chart area.

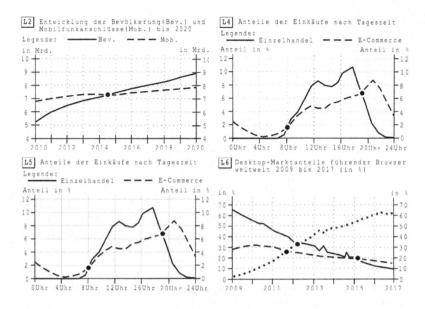

Fig. 2. Line charts used for evaluation (from left to right: L2, L4, L5, L6)

The charts represent the frequencies of usage of letters in German. Condition S4 is a grouped bar chart with three textures. The bar width is 2 cm in accordance with accepted guidelines. S5 represents the same textures whereby one texture was added. The bars of S5 are only half as wide as those in S4. In contrast to S5, S6 increased distances between all bars within each group. The stacked bar chart S7 was embossed in portrait format and utilizes five textures in every sub-segment. The chart contains segments in a suitable height as well as very small segments. The chart represents the per capita consumption of sweets in different years.

Line Charts. We created six line charts, each of which represents between one to three data lines (see Fig. 2). The vertical axis is duplicated in all charts. We used solid, dashed and dotted line styles. L2, L3, L4 and L6 have a thin, dotted grid. Two pairs were generated. With L2 (marked) and L3 (not marked), we compared the effectiveness of marking intersection points with point symbols. While L4 makes use of thin, dotted grid lines, L5 uses solid ones. Both charts represent one solid and one dashed data curve with two intersection points. S6 is the most complex line chart, containing three intersection points of three different lines.

Scatterplots. Four tactile scatterplots (P1, P2, P3, P5) with one to three data sets were developed (see Fig. 3). P2 and P3 differ in the use of grid lines. Because grid lines often cause confusion in scatterplots, we used an incised grid in condition P3. Therefore, the grid lines were embossed separately on the background

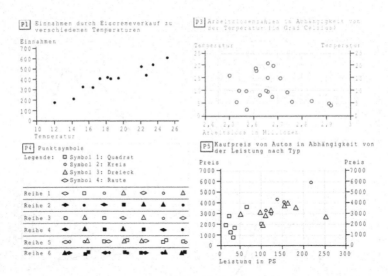

Fig. 3. We generate in fact four scatterplots and one condition to evaluate point symbols separately (from left to right: P1, P3, P4, P5)

of the sheet. Data points were embossed with a high outline and a filling with a much lower high. Points have a diameter of about 0.6 cm. Additionally, we evaluated the readability of four alternative point symbols (square, rhombus, triangle, circle). Therefore, we randomly arranged seven symbols in each of six rows. Each row contains all four symbols. Two design alternatives were used: first, the symbols have a high outline and were filled with much lower filling (row 1, 3, 5); and second, the symbols and outline were embossed with equal high (row 2, 4, 6). The first two rows compare the readability of single symbols in both design conditions. The third and fourth row added a thin grid line to the symbols to evaluate their influence on symbol readability. The final two rows represent two overlapping symbols at a time. P5 represents three data sets with the use of circles, squares and triangles. The symbols are not described, so participants should interpret their meaning by themselves. Especially in the centre of the chart, several symbols overlap each other. In order to ensure readability, we add an incised grid embossed on the background.

Pie Charts. As pie charts require many textures, we developed just three pie charts. K2 is divided into four slices and uses the same number of textures. Textures are separated by white spaces. K3 omits textures and is divided into seven outlined segments. Labels were placed within the slices. If required, labels were positioned outside the chart. On the outer side of the circle, we added markers in 5% steps (Fig. 4).

Fig. 4. Three pie charts - with and without textures - used in the study (from left to right: K1 to K3)

3.3 Procedure of the Online Survey

We carried out a pre-test to evaluate the accessibility and feasibility of the study with one blind participant. Therefore, the participant checked the printed Braille texts. Afterwards, the participant performed the online study while exploring the charts. The participant used own setup, in particular a laptop with a standard keyboard and a refreshable Braille display as well as JAWS. The study investigator could monitor on a display the progress. The pre-test lasted about 6 h, during which issues were discussed immediately. Several issues were identified and fixed later.

At the very beginning of the survey, participants were asked about their experiences with tactile charts. They were instructed to explore the materials independently. The exploration process starts with a training phase that can be skipped when participants are familiar with tactile charts. We provided a training chart with a detailed description containing the general structure and content of the chart. Participants should explore one chart after another and control the ID placed within the box in the upper left corner of each chart. Specifications for each chart type were introduced by a training chart (S1, L1, P1, K1). Participants received a description of the chart if they did not understand it independently. Accordingly, we ensure that every participant could understand the chart type in general.

For most of the charts, we used the following six question types:

1. $Q_{Readability}$: Judgement of the understanding of the chart (without instructions): Agreement with the statement "I could understand the content and the structure of the chart very well." on a five-point Likert scale from "Fully agree" to "Not agree". Those who did (rather) not agree with the statement received an additional description of the chart.
2. $Q_{Nominal}$: Questions concerning the retrieval of nominal values such as naming categories for minimum and maximum values or comparisons (1 to 4 per chart).
3. $Q_{Accuracy}$: Questions on metric values such as reading out values, comparing different data sets or single values, finding extremes or intersection points (1 to 4 per chart).

4. Q_{Design}: Statements concerning the readability and design of specific design parameters that should be rated on a five-point Likert scale.
5. Q_{Rate}: Rating of the chart on a scale from 1 to 6.
6. Q_{Text}: Free-text input field for additional comments.

The participants were allowed to finish the study already after two of four chart types. Finally, demographic data were recorded, in particular age, level of blindness, profession and Braille reading skills.

3.4   Participants

Overall, 48 participants (43 blind, 5 visually-impaired) completed our study. 50% of the participants were born with a visual impairment, 15% became blind at an age less than 10 years, while 4% are late-blinded (becoming blind at an age between 41 and 60). The participants are heterogeneous concerning different properties. The age of the participants ranged from 16 to 77 years with a median of 44. Overall, 27 females and 21 males completed the study. Only one participant had no experience with reading Braille. About 70% indicated having good Braille reading skills. The professions of participants are diverse, with teachers, students, pupils as well as three pensioners taking part. Besides professions in the information technology field (e.g. computer science, software developer), there were also participants from the social domains as well as Braille transcribers.

Overall, 74% have experience in exploring tactile charts. 47% of them stated having "very high" or "high" experience. Of the twelve participants who had no experience with tactile charts, eight knew the general structure of charts, while four participants did not know anything about charts. Above all, most participants had experience with exploring tactile bar charts (89%) and tactile line charts (94%). Furthermore, 71% had experience with tactile pie charts. Scatterplots (23%) and stacked bar charts (31%) were still unknown to most participants. By comparison, among participants without experience with exploring tactile charts, line charts were only known by 67%. Participants with tactile chart experience (35 of 48) mostly used charts to gain access to a visual chart (63%) and read out values (69%). More than half of them use tactile charts to gain an overview, while only 31% made use of tactile charts to analyse data. In addition, swellpaper and Braille printers are most familiar for participants (71%). 57% explore tactile graphics primarily made from thermoformed foils, while 29% primarily use a graphic embosser as used in our study.

3.5   Statistical Measurements

First, we identified unclear answers, in particular when ranges or multiple values were entered instead of single values or spelling mistakes. They were excluded from the calculations. For each chart, we computed frequencies for $Q_{Readability}$, the relative number of *Correct Answers* for $Q_{Nominal}$ as well as the *Mean Error* for every chart based on Q_{Metric}. We defined agreement as the sum of "Fully agree" and "Rather agree" for $Q_{Readability}$ and Q_{Design}. We computed the *Mean*

Error as the average of deviations from all answers to the correct value based on valid numerical values. For the analysis, we excluded incorrectly answered responses as *Mean Error*$_{corrected}$ as follows. For example, when the value of the highest value instead of the smallest value (mentioned in the question) was named, the question was misunderstood. We also excluded all answers outside the value range of the axis. In some cases, these answers could be identified by the corresponding $Q_{Nominal}$. For example, participants were asked to find two bars with the same height. Afterwards, participants should name the value of the two bars with the same height. If the first question was answered incorrectly, the required value for second question would be incorrect. Q_{Design} measures subjective data and addresses chart-specific design parameters. However, some questions are identical for different charts so that e.g. the readability of bars can be compared among charts with different design aspects. Finally, we calculated the median for ratings. In addition, we compared the results by dividing participants into groups concerning the degree of experience with exploring tactile charts (E_1: have experiences, E_2: no experiences) and the age of blindness (B_1: birth-blind, B_2: not birth-blind). We used the Mann-Whitney U test for pairwise significant tests and non-parametric Friedman test for multiple comparisons.

4   Results

Overall, 37 participants completed all chart types, among whom 11 participants performed two chart types completely. Participants needed a minimum of 2 h to complete the whole study. We estimate based on the measured times and comments that most participants needed 3 to 4 h. In this section, we first summarise results of all charts, before proceeding in detail and showing the results for specific conditions per chart type.

4.1   Overall Results

First, we analysed how well participants understood the chart contents individually ($Q_{Readability}$). Overall, about 59% fully agree with this statement. 23% of participants "Rather agree", while on average 1.5% "Fully disagree" with the statement. Concluding from this, most of the charts are well understandable without the need for additional instructions. K1 has the highest rate with agreement of 100% (sum of "Fully agree" and "Rather agree"), followed by L2 with 90%. Overall, less complex charts (e.g. training chart, first three charts of each chart type) have a higher agreement rate (>85%) than more complex charts (e.g. line charts with three data lines, stacked bar charts). A non-parametric Friedman test of differences in agreement among $E_{1/2}$ and $B_{1/2}$ was not significant (p = .9). Furthermore, we compared the mean rate of *Correct Answers* for $Q_{Nominal}$ among all charts. On average, 80% of nominal questions were answered correctly. The differences between groups $B_{1/2}$ and $E_{1/2}$ are not significant (p = .4). L2 (100%), K3 (95%) and S5 (95%) achieved the best correct rate, where only one nominal question was asked. The scatterplot P2 has the lowest rate with 49%. Here, participants had problems with counting data points within a specific range without having a grid.

Overall, there is a significant difference (p = .008) between the *Mean Error* (11.8%) and *Mean Error*$_{corrected}$ (4.5%). For example, stacked bars achieved the worst results with a *Mean Error* of 22.7% (see Table 1) while the corrected error is much smaller (5.4%). This can be explained by the fact that many participants indicated the value of the whole column if the value for a sub-segment was asked for. The difference between the *Mean Error* and *Mean Error*$_{corrected}$ is highest among birth-blind participants (about 11%). There was neither a significant difference in *Mean Error*$_{corrected}$ between group E$_1$ and E$_2$ nor between B$_1$ and B$_2$. S2 (1.7%) and K3 (2.1%) achieved best *Mean Error*$_{corrected}$. Eight out of fourteen charts have a corrected error rate below 5% which indicates a high level of correctness when reading out values. Scatterplots achieved the highest corrected error rate of 6%, followed by line charts with 5.8%. These findings could not be generalised for all chart types because we cannot quantify the level of difficulty for each question of every chart.

However, finally we compared the ratings that participants assigned to every chart. This may reflect individual preferences as well as difficulties created by a chart. Overall, the median of all ratings is 2 ("Good"). The pie chart K3 rated with the best mark of 1. L4, L6 and K2 are rated worst by a mark of 3 as median. All results depend on several parameters, such as the number of questions, level of difficulty and number of charts of this chart type. We present detailed results for specific charts in the following.

4.2   Bar Charts

Bar charts achieved a *Mean Error*$_{corrected}$ of 3.2%. We investigated the design of fillings and grid lines, distances between bars, sizes of bars and textures.

Design of Grid Lines (S2, S3). S3 makes use of a horizontal texturing to replace grid lines, while S2 has filled bars and conventional grid lines. S2 leads to more *Correct Answers* as well as a lower *Mean Error* rate (see Table 1). Because grid lines within the bars are unfamiliar to most participants, fewer participants recognised them in S3 than in S2, which may be the reason for the higher error rate. Recognising bars is more suitable in condition S2 (100%) than in condition S3 (89%). Moreover, participants rate reading out values and comparing data

Table 1. Direct comparison of *Correct Answers* (in %), *Mean Error* rate (in %), corrected *Mean Error* rate (in %) and ratings of all charts.

Chart ID	S2	S3	S4	S5	S7	P2	P3	P5	L2	L4	L5	L6	K2	K3
Correct Answers	74	77	71	95	74	49	76	94	100	81	81	82	77	95
Mean Error	2.4	3.2	3.1	4.2	22.7	13.5	12.6	60.8	17.7	4.4	5.7	7.3	4.8	3.1
Mean Error$_{corrected}$	1.7	3.0	2.2	3.9	5.4	7.0	6.3	4.8	7.7	4.4	5.7	5.2	4.8	2.1
Rating (Median)	2	2	2	2	2.5	2	2	2	2	3	2	3	3	1

among bars as much higher in S2. Overall, only 15% of the participants prefer the design in condition S3. We conclude that condition S2 is more effective than condition S3, although thin grid lines in bar charts are suitable to read out values. Other supporting users elements should be explained in advance. One participant recommended combining both types of grid lines.

Comparison of Bar Width (S4, S5). In this comparison, we investigated the influence of the column width on the readability of textures. Participants could recognise bars and textures better in S4 than in S5 (see Table 2). The corrected *Mean Error* is lower in S4 (no significance). Width of bars influences the readability of the chart. Textures and bars in condition S4 are better readable.

Table 2. Comparison of Agreement (sum of "Fully agree" and "Rather Agree") for design statements of condition S4 and S5 (N = 32).

Statement	S4	S5
I could recognize all bars immediately	93.5	77.3
I could distinguish all textures easily	95.7	77.8
I could reference all textures in legend	95.7	75.5
Help lines inside the bars were helpful to read out values	73.91	77.8

Distance Between Bars (S5, S6). We investigated the influence of distances between bars on the readability of bars. Adding distances between bars in groups increases the comparability of values between bars as well as the readability of single bars for most participants (see Table 3). By contrast, about one-quarter of participants prefer omitting distances.

Table 3. Comparison of Agreement (sum of "Fully agree" and "Rather Agree") and Disagreement (sum of "Fully disagree" and "Rather Disagree") of condition S5 and S6 in % (N = 31).

Statement	Agree	Disagree
Single bars are better distinguishable in *S6* than in *S5*	71.0	24.5
The comparison among bars is better in *S5*	27.0	60.0
No difference in readability between S5 and S6	34.0	52.3
I prefer condition *S5*	22.7	68.2

Stacked Bar Charts (S7). Most participants were unfamiliar with stacked bars (69%). More than 41% fully or rather agree that it was difficult to distinguish all textures within the bars. Textures in stacked bar charts reduce the readability (61%). By contrast, only 22% prefer omitting textures (simply using the order of segments in a bar for orientation). Help lines are suitable to read out values in stacked bar charts (83%). When participants were asked to read the value of the upper section of a bar, 41% indicated the total value of the bar. The meaning of stacked bar charts can be misunderstood. Participants reported high mental effort when analysing data in stacked bar charts.

4.3   Line Charts

We investigated the design of intersection points and grid lines in line charts as well as the readability of a complex line chart with three data curves.

Design of Intersection Points (L2, L3). Participants rated both designs roughly equally. In L2, 80% could recognise the intersection point very easily. 14% cannot find any difference in the readability of intersection points. By contrast, 56% prefer the marked intersection point in L2, whereas 28% also prefer condition L3. Therefore, marking single intersection points may influence chart readability less. There is little evidence that marking intersection points increases the readability of crossing data lines.

Design of Grid Lines (L4, L5). Participants rate solid grid lines in L5 better than dotted grid lines in L4 (see Table 1). Solid grid lines are significant better recognised ($p = .03$) than dotted grid lines (see Table 4). The design of the grid lines also influences the perceptibility and traceability of the data lines. Overall, 86% of the participants prefer solid grid lines in line charts, especially when dashed and solid data lines were used.

Table 4. Comparison of Agreement (sum of "Fully agree" and "Rather Agree") for design statements of condition L4 and L5 in % ($N = 42$).

Statement	L4	L5
I could recognize all lines easily	69.1	78.5
It was easy to distinguish lines	76.7	79.5
I could follow lines easily	72.1	85.7
I could recognize help lines very easy	69.8	90.5
Help lines were very helpful to read out values	80.9	92.6
I could recognize all intersection points very well	74.8	83.3

Complex Line Charts (L6). L6 represents three data lines (solid, dotted, dashed) as well as three intersection points. It is very difficult to read this chart because solid and dashed line are very close to each other. Furthermore, a thin, dotted grid was added. Lines in this chart can be recognised very well with a rate of 56%. Line tracing is easiest for the solid line (83% of agreement), while the dashed (57%) and dotted lines (60%) are rated as roughly equal. In addition, 31% agree that it was difficult to distinguish between dotted and dashed lines. For 82%, it was easy to distinguish data curves and grid lines. Grid lines are used by 88% to read out values. Only 63% recognise intersection points very well.

4.4 Scatterplots

We compared the usage of grid lines in scatterplots as well as point symbols and the readability of complex scatterplots.

Usage of Grid Lines (P2, P3). In the first condition P2 (without grid lines), participants gave 20% fewer *Correct Answers* than in the second condition (with grid lines). Especially counting data points in a certain area is challenging without grid lines (about 30% fewer *Correct Answers*). It was easy to recognise single data points for 90% of participants. Help lines in P3 do not influence the readability of data points (97.3%), while they could be recognised very well by 93.1%. In condition P2, it was difficult for 37% to read out precise values, while in condition P3 only 27% agree with it. From these findings, it can be concluded that grid lines clearly influence the readability of scatterplots. Incised grid lines are suitable to support reading out values, whereby they can be recognised very well and do not influence the readability of data points provided that they have a suitable size.

Point Symbols (P4). P4 compares four point symbols (square, circle, rhombus, triangle), whereby the task was to name the correct symbols within each row. In the last two rows, participants should name one of the two symbols that overlap each other. Overall, the first four rows have similar recognition rates. In addition, 48% preferred the outlined symbols over filled points. In the first row, participants named 90% of symbols correctly, which is the highest value over all rows. Overlapping symbols in rows five and six leads to a lower correct rate of answers (71%). Here, overlapping reduced the correct recognition of tactile symbols by about 20%. The overall correct answers per symbol type are similar. In general, 75% of participants could distinguish all symbols very well. However, 32% state that the identification of symbols in rows five and six was very difficult. For 46% of participants, it was difficult to distinguish between the rhombus and square. In additional comments, several participants reported challenges in separating square and circle symbols. One participant proposed combining both design alternatives in one chart when multiple data sets are shown.

Complex Scatterplots (P5). Overall, this chart has the lowest *Mean Error*$_{corrected}$ and *Correct Answers* for of all scatterplots (see Table 1). The high uncorrected *Mean Error* can be explained by a large outlier, which probably results from a typo by one user. P5 has a mean corrected error rate of

4.8%. Only one quantitative question was taken into account. 36% could recognise overlapping symbols easily, while 82% could identify the number of overlapping symbols correctly. 75% of participants agreed that triangles and circles could be easily distinguished. Almost one-third had problems recognising the distribution of the data points. Nearly all participants used incised help lines and rated them as very useful. Additionally, grid lines did not interrupt the recognition of symbols (72.7%).

4.5   Fillings in Pie Charts (K2, K3)

With the pie charts, we compared the design of segments as well as the use of tick marks. K3 is the best-rated chart overall (median 1), while K2 is one of the worst-rated charts (median 3). K3 leads to many more *Correct Answers* and fewer errors. 78% could distinguish all textures in K2 well. Accordingly, only 24% agree that textures in slices increase estimating their sizes. There is also a strong difference relating the readability of slices, whereby 89% could recognise all slices in K3, compared with 59% in K2. Additionally, 17% prefer textures in pie charts over outlined slices. Despite the fact that K3 makes use of different label types, 84% of participants could assign labels to slices very well. Furthermore, tick marks on the outer circle of the chart are useful (87%). Overall, textures in pie charts strongly influence the readability of the chart and thus they should be omitted in pie charts. In addition, they are not suitable to represent more than five single values, in contrast to outlined slices.

4.6   Limitations

The results reflect the effectiveness of tactile grouped and stacked bar charts, line charts, scatterplots as well as pie charts. Due to the remote study design, we do not know the reasons for any incorrect answers. The results may be biased by misunderstandings of the question, typing errors or handling problems of the online questionnaire. Accordingly, we conducted a manual error analysis for *Mean Error* calculation and identified answers with correct value. Especially typing errors (e.g. comma errors) lead to strong outliers, which strongly influenced the final results. Answers outside the value range of axes were excluded. On the other hand, we cannot guarantee that the participants did carry out the study on their own, even if they were instructed to do so. Nominal questions can be measured well with this study design because they provide evidence of the understanding and readability of the chart without instruction. Reasons for incorrect answers can at least be provided by text comments. Moreover, we could not measure the time that it took the participants to answer questions. Therefore, efficiency cannot be measured with this study. Nevertheless, despite 26% of participants having never explored a tactile chart before, even complex charts could be read and understood by most participants.

In order to ensure the feasibility of the study, we provided many explanations and – if needed – chart descriptions. This replaces the study leader's additional explanation in laboratory studies. In order to obtain information about user experiences, we invited the participants to rate the study design in a separated short questionnaire.

5   Evaluation of the Study Design

We identified thirteen aspects that are important in remote studies with blind people. All participants (28) rate the whole study design, the chart descriptions as well the communication as "very good" or "good". While the personal benefit from the study is rated at 77%, 92% rate the fun factor with mark 1 or 2. Information about the study, materials, accessibility and comprehension of the questions were rated very high with more than 95%. By contrast, the duration to perform the study achieved the worst rating with 65%. Overall, we receive very positive feedback. Some participants reported that they had learned much while performing the study, while others commented on the preparation of materials, which gave them a safety feeling. One participant state that he/she learned within the study how tactile charts could provide a benefit. Another person expressed the wish to produce such kinds of charts oneself. Especially those participants who had no prior experience with tactile charts rate the tutorial at the beginning of the study as very helpful. Twenty-one out of 28 participants read it completely. Sixteen participants learned the structure or rather the exploration of charts with the help of the training phase (including tutorial and charts). Many participants also commented on the long duration of the study and the high level of effort that performance required. Several participants recommended not to use computer Braille in tactile charts. One participant stated it would be better to omit the number sign instead of using computer Braille when a space is required. In addition, numbering questions is very helpful.

6   Discussion and Outlook

We have analysed quantitative and subjective data from 48 blind and visually-impaired participants about specific design properties as well as the readability of tactile charts. We ascertained that there are individual user preferences that the design should fit. In the following, we will summarise the major findings:

- Solid grid lines are suitable in bar charts. Grid lines within bars can be used but should be explained in advanced.
- Distances between bars of a group can increase the comparability of values between bars and the recognition of single bars.
- Wider bars with texture are preferred over thinner ones with texture. Even thin bars (about 1 cm) with textures are readable.
- It is advised to use as few textures as possible in stacked bar charts. Stacked bar charts should only be used if the value of the sum of a bar is very interesting; otherwise, the use of grouped bars is recommended.

- Marking intersection points with a circle in line charts does not strongly influence the readability of the chart.
- The usage of solid help lines instead of dotted grid lines is recommended in line charts.
- Solid line style for curves are best readable in line charts, even if solid help lines were used.
- Duplicated vertical axes increase reading out values in line charts and scatterplots.
- Help lines in scatterplots are recommended for reading out values and counting points.
- Incised help lines are suitable in scatterplots with data points of an appropriate size (about 1 cm).
- Three to four different symbols in scatterplots are readable. Circles and triangle are very well distinguishable. Rectangles and rhombus shapes and more specifically circles and squares should significantly differ.
- Omitting textures in pie charts increases the readability.
- Adding tick marks to pie charts increases the reading accuracy.

We have shown that the design of tactile charts (e.g. grid lines, design of elements) influences the readability, depending on the whole design, the chart type and the represented data. Blind people are able to read trends, outliers, clusters and specific values out of charts. Even complex charts with three data lines or multiple symbols are readable for most participants, including novices in tactile chart reading. We found no significant difference in performance (mean error, correct answers) of birth-blind and not-birth-blind participants. Surprisingly, we could not demonstrate a significant difference between experienced and inexperienced participants. To conclude, tactile charts are usable for commonly-known chart types, whereby blind people are able to analyse data effectively. While other authors have identified the effectiveness of tactile charts by comparing them with other data-representing methods (e.g. a tactile or digital table), we will compare the calculated effectiveness of the charts with another user group. Accordingly, we are currently conducting a comparative study in which sighted participants receive the same charts (black printed, not embossed) and questions as blind participants. The aim of this study is to compare the effectiveness among blind and sighted people when analysing charts. Additionally, the results of this study have highlighted many more design alternatives we will take into account when re-designing charts for further user studies. Furthermore, we will implement well-chosen guidelines for tactile charts based on these results.

Besides improving the production process to increase the availability of tactile charts, there is a need for more user studies in tactile chart design. Especially the design of more chart types with useful data and tactile variables – such as line width, symbols, line styles, and help elements – should be explored in detail. The results can be used to design tactile charts effectively for different use cases that support blind people by fulfilling many tasks that are needed in several professions.

References

1. Aldrich, F.K., Parkin, A.J.: Tangible line graphs: an experimental investigation of three formats using capsule paper. Hum. Factors **29**(3), 301–309 (1987). https://doi.org/10.1177/001872088702900304

2. Barth, J.L.: Incised grids: enhancing the readability of tangible graphs for the blind. Hum. Factors **26**(1), 61–70 (1984)

3. Braille Authority of North America, Canadian Braille Authority: Guidelines and Standards for Tactile Graphics (2011)

4. Cleveland, W.S.: Visualizing Data. Hobart Press, Summit (1993)

5. Culbert, S.S., Stellwagen, W.T.: Tactual discrimination of textures. Percept. Mot. Skills **16**(1957), 545–552 (1963). http://www.ncbi.nlm.nih.gov/pubmed/14024190

6. Engel, C., Weber, G.: Analysis of tactile chart design. In: Proceedings of the 10th International Conference on PErvasive Technologies Related to Assistive Environments, PETRA 2017, pp. 197–200. ACM, New York (2017). https://doi.org/10.1145/3056540.3064955. http://doi.acm.org/10.1145/3056540.3064955

7. Engel, C., Weber, G.: Improve the accessibility of tactile charts. In: Bernhaupt, R., Dalvi, G., Joshi, A., Balkrishan, D.K., O'Neill, J., Winckler, M. (eds.) INTERACT 2017. LNCS, vol. 10513, pp. 187–195. Springer, Cham (2017). https://doi.org/10.1007/978-3-319-67744-6_12

8. Engel, C., Weber, G.: A user study to evaluate tactile charts with blind and visually impaired people. In: Miesenberger, K., Kouroupetroglou, G. (eds.) ICCHP 2018. LNCS, vol. 10897, pp. 177–184. Springer, Cham (2018). https://doi.org/10.1007/978-3-319-94274-2_24

9. Goncu, C., Marriott, K.: Tactile chart generation tool. In: Proceedings of the 10th International ACM SIGACCESS Conference on Computers and Accessibility - Assets 2008, p. 255 (2008). https://doi.org/10.1145/1414471.1414525

10. Goncu, C., Marriott, K., Aldrich, F.: Tactile diagrams: worth ten thousand words? In: Goel, A.K., Jamnik, M., Narayanan, N.H. (eds.) Diagrams 2010. LNCS (LNAI), vol. 6170, pp. 257–263. Springer, Heidelberg (2010). https://doi.org/10.1007/978-3-642-14600-8_25

11. Goncu, C., Marriott, K., Hurst, J.: Usability of accessible bar charts. In: Goel, A.K., Jamnik, M., Narayanan, N.H. (eds.) Diagrams 2010. LNCS (LNAI), vol. 6170, pp. 167–181. Springer, Heidelberg (2010). https://doi.org/10.1007/978-3-642-14600-8_17

12. Lederman, S.J., Campbell, J.I.: Tangible graphs for the blind. Hum. Factors J. Hum. Factors Ergon. Soc. **24**(1), 85–100 (1982)

13. Nolan, C.Y., Morris, J.E.: Improvement of tactual symbols for blind children. Final Report, p. 88 (1971). http://eric.ed.gov/?id=ED070228

14. Paneels, S., Roberts, J.C.: Review of designs for haptic data visualization. IEEE Trans. Haptics **3**(2), 119–137 (2010). https://doi.org/10.1109/TOH.2009.44

15. Prescher, D.: Guidelines for image descriptions and tactile graphics (2016). http://nbn-resolving.de/urn:nbn:de:bsz:14-qucosa-196167

16. Prescher, D., Bornschein, J., Weber, G.: Consistency of a tactile pattern set. ACM Trans. Access. Comput. **10**(2), 7:1–7:29 (2017). https://doi.org/10.1145/3053723

17. Round Table on Information Access for People with Print Disabilities Inc.: Guidelines on Conveying Visual Information (2005). http://printdisability.org/guidelines/guidelines-on-conveying-visual-information-2005/

18. Schuffelen, M.: On editing graphics for the blind (2002). http://piaf-tactile.com/docs/Tactile_Graphics_Manual.pdf

19. Shneiderman, B.: The eyes have it: a task by data type taxonomy for information visualizations. In: Proceedings 1996 IEEE Symposium on Visual Languages, pp. 336–343, September 1996. https://doi.org/10.1109/VL.1996.545307
20. Watanabe, T., Mizukami, H.: Effectiveness of tactile scatter plots: comparison of non-visual data representations. In: Miesenberger, K., Kouroupetroglou, G. (eds.) ICCHP 2018. LNCS, vol. 10896, pp. 628–635. Springer, Cham (2018). https://doi.org/10.1007/978-3-319-94277-3_97
21. Watanabe, T., Yamaguchi, T., Nakagawa, M.: Development of software for automatic creation of embossed graphs. In: Miesenberger, K., Karshmer, A., Penaz, P., Zagler, W. (eds.) ICCHP 2012, Part I. LNCS, vol. 7382, pp. 174–181. Springer, Heidelberg (2012). https://doi.org/10.1007/978-3-642-31522-0_25

Assistive Technology for Cognition and NeuroDevelopment Disorders

A User-Centred Methodology for the Development of Computer-Based Assistive Technologies for Individuals with Autism

Raquel Hervás[1]([⊠]), Virginia Francisco[1], Gonzalo Méndez[2],
and Susana Bautista[3]

[1] Facultad de Informática, Universidad Complutense de Madrid, Madrid, Spain
{raquelhb,virginia}@fdi.ucm.es
[2] Instituto de Tecnología del Conocimiento (UCM), Madrid, Spain
gmendez@fdi.ucm.es
[3] Escuela Politécnica, Universidad Francisco de Vitoria, Pozuelo de Alarcón, Spain
susana.bautista@ufv.es

Abstract. The design and development of computer assistive technologies must be tied to the needs and goals of end users and must take into account their capabilities and preferences. In this paper, we present MeDeC@, a Methodology for the Development of Computer Assistive Technologies for people with Autism Spectrum Disorders (ASD), which relies heavily in our experience working with end users with ASD. The aim of this methodology is not to design for a broad group of users, but to design highly customizable tools so that they can be easily adapted to specific situations and small user groups. We also present two applications developed using MeDeC@ in order to test its suitability: Emo Traductor, a web application for emotion recognition for people with Asperger Syndrome, and ReadIt, a web browser plug-in to help people with ASD with written language understanding difficulties to navigate the Internet. The results of our evaluation with end users show that the use of MeDeC@ helps developers to successfully design computer assistive technologies taking into account the special requirements and scenarios that arise when developing this kind of assistive applications.

Keywords: Computer assistive technologies · Interactive systems ·
Autism Spectrum Disorder · Asperger Syndrome ·
User-Centered Design

1 Introduction

The design and development of interactive technologies must be tied to the goals and requirements of end users. This is even more important when the system is aimed to users with cognitive impairments, and more specifically with Autism

© IFIP International Federation for Information Processing 2019
Published by Springer Nature Switzerland AG 2019
D. Lamas et al. (Eds.): INTERACT 2019, LNCS 11746, pp. 85–106, 2019.
https://doi.org/10.1007/978-3-030-29381-9_6

Spectrum Disorder (ASD), who present very specific goals and restrictions and find unexpected difficulties when using interactive systems. For example, whereas many applications are configured with general profiles that try to cover all the possibilities for a specific group of users, in fact capabilities and individual preferences are not the same for two different people even if they share the same impairment.

Although user-centered methodologies are the most appropriate for this kind of developments, developers usually find it difficult to work with users with ASD. The problem is not only that these users may face extra difficulties to express their needs or desires, but also that they may not be available to be involved during such complex and usually long processes. In the case of users with low functioning cognitive impairments, or even children, the burden of this involvement may be too big [11]. When talking about high functioning cognitive impairments, end users may be reluctant to be involved in research over and over again. In our experience, young adults with Asperger Syndrome, for example, state that they feel like "guinea pigs", and there are studies, such as [13], which describe similar motivations of these users to avoid taking part in research.

Therefore, it is important to employ user-centered methodologies that rely less on the availability of these users and can take advantage of other stakeholders, such as experts, caregivers or tutors. Therefore, these experts must be directly involved in the design process, not only because they can enhance the communication with end users, but because they provide a wider context of the needs and problems faced by a collective of people with impairments that can be important in the development process [2,18,19,25]. Some authors have pointed out the difficulties of working with experts (e.g. [2]), but these difficulties must be faced when either end users are not available or not willing to take part in the study, or when, to some extent, the success of the project depends on the involvement of experts.

Taking this context into account, we present MeDeC@, a Methodology for the Development of Computer Assistive Technologies that adapts classic User-Centered Design approaches to the special requirements of applications for people with ASD. MeDeC@ comprises four main tasks (requirements elicitation, design, implementation and evaluation) that are subdivided in several subtasks. This methodology has been applied to the creation of two applications: *Emo-Traductor*, a web application for emotion recognition in texts aimed at people with Asperger Syndrome, and *ReadIt*, a web browser plug-in to foster digital inclusion of people with ASD. MeDeC@ has been evaluated on two aspects: the appropriateness of the applications for end users' scenarios and their impact on daily activities and the satisfaction of end users and experts with both the process and the results. Results suggest that MeDeC@ can make the development of computer assistive technologies more tied to the requirements and scenarios that arise when developing applications in such a complex and sensitive scope.

The rest of the paper is organized as follows. In Sect. 2 we present a description of previous approaches to formalize the development of computer assistive technologies. Section 3 provides an overview of MeDeC@ and its driving principles. A detailed description of the methodology is then provided in Sect. 4. After that, Sect. 5 describes two case studies of applications developed using MeDeC@. Finally, Sect. 6 includes the discussion of the main contributions of this work, and Sect. 7 depicts some conclusions and future worklines.

2   Related Work

The development of computer assistive technologies has been tackled in very different ways, but currently User-Centered Design (UCD) and Participatory Design (PD) approaches seem to be widely spread [5]. In general terms, UCD focuses on the needs of the user in an iterative process, and its aim is to optimize the final product taking into account the needs, wants, and limitations of end users. Designers not only analyze and predict how users are likely to use the product, but also test the validity of their assumptions through evaluations with end users. On the other hand, in PD users have a more active participation than in UCD, as they become a key group of stakeholders. The idea behind PD is that end users become co-designers by empowering them to propose and generate design alternatives.

A number of assistive systems for people with impairments have been developed using UCD approaches. A three-phase UCD methodology to rapidly develop connected health systems is described in [15]. In the first phase, the authors propose the construction of a document detailing the context of use of the system through the use of storyboarding, paper prototypes, and mock-ups along with user interviews to gather user feedback. In the second phase, they emphasize the use of expert usability inspections, such as heuristic evaluations and cognitive walkthroughs, with small multidisciplinary groups to review the developed prototypes. In the third phase, they propose to use classical testing with end users, using various metrics to measure the user experience and improve the final prototypes. However, the report on the application of this methodology to the development of only one connected health system makes it hard to evaluate its robustness or the adequacy to develop other kinds of systems.

The use of UCD *Personas* [6] to design Augmentative and Alternative Communication (AAC) devices for individuals with speech impairments due to amyotrophic lateral sclerosis is studied in [26]. The authors report on the used method to validate the representativeness and utility of the designed *Personas*. Overall, although the authors present favourable results, they also report on the difficulty to create enough *Personas* for all the different user profiles or to represent users with changing symptoms.

USERfit [1,24] is a UCD methodology for assistive technology design that provides a framework to ensure that human issues are adequately considered during the design process. This methodology covers the design of the product and the understanding of the context in which a product will be used, and aspects of the support environment (e.g. intended documentation and training). Design activities involve matching requirements to the technological alternatives, and then developing a functional specification for the product to satisfy requirements. Subsequent steps involve design, test and redesign until the design is complete.

Once a fully working product is available, USERfit assists in the selection of methods for evaluation as well as establishing evaluation criteria. The USERfit methodology is too broad, as it is aimed at a wide spectrum of assistive technologies based on the Design for All paradigm, and that it does not address in detail the role of experts in the design process, as it sets its main focus on the end users. In addition, USERfit is a summarizing methodology that advices on tools and techniques that can be used in the different steps of the methodology, but it does not describe in detail how to take users and experts into account.

From the point of view of PD approaches, the authors of [23] present the PD process followed to develop interactive technologies for people with ASD to support collaboration and social conversation skills. During the process, ASD children regularly participated in design and evaluation activities to inform the development of the prototypes. The response of ASD children and teachers involved in the pilot test was very positive: children enjoyed the initiative and the teachers found the process useful. According to the authors, one of the main reasons for the good feedback obtained in the pilot test is the significant participation of teachers and children throughout the development of the prototypes. They believe that this involvement has shaped the content, the usability and the suitability of the technologies used.

Cooperative Inquiry (CI) is a PD method where developers, designers and end users come together to explore issues of concern and interest. In CI, everyone must decide which questions should be addressed and what ideas may be of help, eliminating the split between designers, developers and end users. CI is applied to the design of a sports video game with children with learning challenges in [8]. The authors concluded that CI was effective but they recognize that there were limitations, as only ten children participated.

Although PD has been used frequently, some difficulties have been encountered when using it. Sometimes end users are unable or unwilling to collaborate [3,16] and sometimes there are difficulties that hinder their full integration into the process [11]. As explained in [22], children with ASD are characterized by deficiencies in social interaction (difficulties understanding non-verbal behavior or social cues, difficulties to establish and maintain an adequate peer relationship. . .), in communication (inability to initiate and maintain conversations, tendency to interpret idiomatic expressions literally. . .) and by a rigidity of thought and behaviour (need of structured data and routines, inability to generalize information. . .). Nevertheless, it is important to note that ASD is very heterogeneous, so the difficulties encountered when working with this impairment can be very different depending on the specific users.

Different solutions have been tried to overcome these last limitations. In [12], the CI method is extended to develop IDEAS [4], where drawing templates are used to help children in prototyping and a visual timeline is used in the sessions to clearly define beginning and end. The authors of [20] suggest ways to integrate users with impairments in the PD process. The authors of [10] present a tool to support children with ASD in design critique, an activity in which users and designers discuss the qualities of a design, allowing participants to express their criticisms and contribute to the design in a creative way. This tool was used with seven children to criticize a prototype of the ECHOES system. The tool not only helped children with ASD to annotate the prototype but also facilitated the interaction with the facilitator.

3   Overview of MeDeC@

Over the last few years, we have implemented a number of computer assistive applications for people with ASD, such as a predictive editor for pictogram messages, a text-to-pictogram translator, an application for emotion recognition and an assistant for web navigation. The results and lessons learned in those experiences have been used to formalize MeDeC@ (Methodology for the Development of Computer Assistive Technologies), a UCD methodology that covers all the tasks necessary to create this kind of applications from requirements elicitation to evaluation. We decided to adopt a UCD approach instead of a PD one as we did not have access to end users during all the stages of the development process. The schools and associations we worked with considered that our presence, the interruption of the users' routines or their participation in the design process would affect them quite negatively. As stated previously, PD approaches can only be successful if some access to end users is granted, but when users are not reachable, it is necessary to draw on UCD approaches that rely less on end users and take advantage of other stakeholders, such as experts, caregivers or tutors.

MeDeC@ is built around three basic principles: (1) Personalization, (2) Interaction with Users and Experts, and (3) Service-Oriented Implementation.

3.1   *Principle #1.* Personalization-Based Approach

Solutions for people with ASD must be highly configurable, since each person has specific capabilities and needs that do not always coincide with those of others, even within the same impairment. MeDeC@ proposes, following the approach advocated by Harper [14], a design-for-one approach instead of a design-for-all one. Therefore, MeDeC@ is driven by the importance of personalization not only of general functionalities and controls, but of their usage depending on the specific user needs. We propose the customization of the developed applications to the specific needs of associations and educational centers where they will be deployed. At the same time, applications must present mechanisms for their configuration according to the specific requirements of each user or situation in which they will be used.

3.2   *Principle #2.* Interaction with Users and Experts

Although the main end user of assistive technologies is the person with impairments, our experience has shown us that end users are not always available, or they may not be able or willing to collaborate in the design process. In those cases, experts become a valuable resource for obtaining the required information, and will become a collateral user as well. Therefore, MeDeC@ aims to integrate not only end users in the design and implementation processes, but also their tutors, caregivers and/or relatives as experts in their needs and capabilities. Consequently, experts, together with end users, will be consulted and integrated in the tasks related to requirements elicitation, system design, implementation and evaluation. Both actors will provide differentiated and complementary information in each stage: end users are of course authorities in living with their condition, whereas experts do have a wider context of the problems and difficulties faced by a collective, even when these problems may not be perceived by the end users themselves.

3.3 *Principle #3*. Service-Oriented Implementation

MeDeC@ proposes to implement computer assistive applications following a Service-Oriented Architecture (SOA). This kind of software architectures organize the implementation in units of functionality called services that can be accessed remotely and work in an individual fashion. In this way, each service solves a small problem, and the main application uses service composition to perform its complete functionality. We consider that SOA is specially appropriate for the implementation of assistive technologies aimed at people with ASD for two fundamental reasons. First, this approach allows these users to have tools that are adaptable to their personal needs, since the application will help them to decide what services they need and how they should be configured. Second, the designers or programmers of new computer assistive applications will be able to integrate the already created services in their implementations, thus saving an enormous cost in research and development of these accessible technologies.

4   Detailed Description of Tasks in MeDeC@

This section provides insights on the tasks and subtasks proposed by the methodology in a reproducible manner so that other researchers can apply it.

4.1   Requirements Elicitation

As a previous step to the design and implementation of an application, developers must obtain and comprehend some basic information about end users and their intended use of the application. This task must be based on the importance of personalization (Principle #1), so the subsequent design phase can be oriented not only to a collective of users but to individual users inside this group. MeDeC@ proposes to collaborate in this task with end users and also with professionals, tutors and/or relatives who work with end users on a daily basis, as we consider them as experts with respect to end users goals, needs and capabilities (Principle #2). End users will therefore provide information about their goals and how the application can help to achieve them, and experts will present a wider context taking into account problems and needs that end users may not be aware of. This collaborative analysis process is essential to achieve the goal of developing tools that are useful for end users, and it is also one of the most challenging ones due to the diverse fields in which the different actors perform. Therefore, it is of utmost importance that developers identify clearly the environment and needs of end users and why a certain assistive tool can be useful for them, whereas experts and end users must understand the affordances and limitations of available technologies. The main output of this task is a document with formalized answers to the following aspects:

- **User goals with respect to the application**: The initial step of this task is to obtain information about users' goals and expectations with respect to the use of the application, that is, what they are going to use the tool for and why it will be useful for them. It is also important to take into account how the use of the application will affect their daily activities.
- **Description of scenarios, environment and activities in which the tool will be used**: The scenarios of use typically describe how and when the tool will be used, as well as the people or other actors that will interact with the users during their usage of the application. These scenarios must include information related to the physical and digital environment and the specific activities that will be performed in each scenario.
- **Technological capabilities and limitations of end users**: An important aspect to be considered from the point of view of end users is to understand their technological capabilities and limitations. For example, whereas some users might be able to use the mouse or the keyboard, other users may need alternative input options such as speech recognition interfaces.

4.2 Design

Once the main purpose of the application has been agreed by experts, end users and developers, this information must be transformed into a detailed specification of both the general behaviour of the tool and its interface and interactions. Although related, these two issues are not the same and must be treated separately. On the one hand, the behaviour of the tool comprises the tasks that can be performed in it and their relative importance to the general operation. On the other hand, the same tasks can usually be accomplished by using different types of controls and interactions (mouse or keyboard, contextual menu or keyboard shortcuts, etc.). These decisions must always take into account Principle #1 (Personalization). As the developers are not the ones that can decide which options are better in each case, they will rely on prototypes and mock-ups to discuss different alternatives with end users and experts, and find the best designs for each aspect of the final tool. This interaction between developers, end users and experts is based on Principle #2. The application design can therefore be subdivided into three subtasks:

- **Design of the behavior of the application**: The high-level description of the application goals and scenarios of use must be used to decide its general behavior. General aspects like platforms and devices where the application will be used must be defined at this point, always having the scenarios, environment and activities already defined as a starting point. For example, if the application will help users with autism to communicate out of school or at home, a mobile app will surely be the best option. At this point, designers must also decide the main functionalities that will be available.

- **Design of the interaction with the application**: The expected behavior and functionalities of the application must be translated into controls and widgets from the point of view of both interactions and interfaces. Questions like how data will be presented, how the users will interact with these data or how they will activate the controls must be answered at this point. Designers will study different answers to these questions, capturing them in a series of mock-ups and prototypes, always taking into account that they can not make the right decisions without the help of end user and experts.
- **Evaluation of the different alternatives with the help of experts and end users**: For both the behavior and interactions of the application, designers must study different alternatives (in the form of mock-ups or prototypes) so they can discuss them with experts and end users. In this subtask, different solutions must be discussed from the point of view of end users capabilities, limitations and expectations. The output of this subtask must be an agreement about how to face the implementation of the working prototypes that will be tested afterwards.

The main output of the design task is a document with sufficient information to start the implementation of different prototypes.

4.3   Implementation

Following Principle #3, we propose the implementation of computer assistive applications following a Service-Oriented Architecture (SOA). Therefore, the design outputs must be translated into development decisions not only from the point of view of the final tool, but also of the small pieces of functionality that will be implemented as services and then used to compose the application. The implementation phase receives the design outputs produced in the previous task as its main input, and it is composed of two subtasks:

- **Implementation of services**: An important part of the implementation task consists in deciding the services that will encapsulate the functionalities that conform the application. For example, in a text simplification application we could find services for the lexical simplification of a word, the syntactical simplification of a sentence, or the summarization of a text. Then, all these pieces could be integrated as different functionalities in the final tool.
- **Implementation of application prototypes**: Different application prototypes will be implemented using the services that have been defined in the previous subtask as basic pieces. When composing the intended application, developers must bear in mind the desired personalization of this kind of applications (Principle #1). Following this kind of architecture, it would be easy

to configure the application differently for each user just by selecting which services must be activated in each case, for example.

The main outputs of this task are one or more working prototypes that can be evaluated with users, and an API of fully functional services that are used to compose the developed prototypes.

4.4   Evaluation

In an assistive application, two main aspects must be evaluated: the appropriateness of the application from the point of view of end users goals and scenarios, and the satisfaction of end users and experts with both the process and results. To study these aspects, we propose a user-centered evaluation where experts and end users can explore the application prototypes (Principle #2), so they can try out possible options and find bugs, technical errors or usability flaws. When possible, these evaluation sessions should be organized around the following phases:

- **Prototype presentation**: The prototypes must be presented and explained to end users before they can use them. Depending on their cognitive level or specific impairments, the tools can be presented just before the evaluation, or they can be introduced previously by professionals or tutors in separate sessions prior to the evaluation.
- **Task-oriented testing**: We propose the first part of the evaluation sessions to be task-oriented. This means that the evaluators will prepare a set of predefined tasks that must be completed by end users with the application. This task-oriented testing allows to cover the most important functionalities and scenarios so they can be evaluated in the first place. This approach allows the research team to control the difficulty of the tasks to be carried out, starting with easy tasks and then continuing with a more complex use of the tool during the evaluation session.
- **Free testing**: At some point of the evaluation, preferably after the task-oriented testing, users must be allowed to explore the tool freely. This kind of testing not only allows the research team to study how end users interact with the application when they are not told what to do, but also serves to discover unexpected ways to use it or assumptions about the users that had not been considered before. This step is specially useful when it was possible to involve end users in previous stages of the design process.
- **Acquisition of users opinions and findings**: During the whole evaluation session, developers will rely on different techniques to collect user opinions and findings. Not only questionnaires and interviews are useful, but also techniques like user observation can be very helpful to extract the desired information. All these data will later be analyzed and changes and improvements will be proposed for the next prototypes of the application.

Materials for end users must be adapted to their limitations and needs. To carry out this adaptation, the help of experts is essential as the vocabulary, punctuation scales, possible answers or devices to be used must be adapted to the target group. The output of this task is a set of proposed modifications to any of the sub-products of the other tasks (requirements and design documents and/or prototypes).

5   MeDeC@ in Practice: Case Studies

This section explains in detail how MeDeC@ has been applied to the creation of two computer assistive applications: EmoTraductor, a web application for emotion recognition in written texts aimed at people with Asperger Syndrome, and ReadIt, a web browser plug-in to promote the digital inclusion of people with written language understanding difficulties.

5.1   EmoTraductor: A Web Application for Emotional Text Analysis

EmoTraductor [7] is a web application that automatically detects the presence of each of the five basic emotions (joy, sadness, disgust, fear and anger) in a given text. Not only does the application show the main emotions transmitted in a text using emoticons and colors, but it also highlights the words in the text that are considered emotional and therefore lead to the presented emotions. EmoTraductor was designed and implemented following the MeDeC@ methodology. In this case study, end users did not participate in the preliminary stages of requirements elicitation and design, but only in the evaluation stage. As expressed by the experts involved in the development of EmoTraductor, these users were quite reluctant to participate in experiments over and over again, so they only agreed to be involved in the tool evaluation. Therefore, only experts with a global understanding of the needs of this collective were involved throughout the whole process.

Requirements Elicitation. EmoTraductor was designed and implemented with the help of experts from *Asociación Asperger Madrid*[1], a local association aimed to help people with Asperger Syndrome (AS). We met with a group of experts from the association, from psychologists to social workers, who introduced us to the capabilities and daily life of people with this syndrome. Experts let us know that one of the main difficulties that people with AS face is the detection of the emotions of others, as well as the difficulty to express their own. However, people with AS find themselves in many situations where the correct identification of emotions is fundamental for their social integration. For example, when they publish or comment on a blog, they may express in a way that does not comply with social conventions: if what they read has annoyed them, they will post a comment with a disproportionate tone of anger. This comment could then start a chain of unpleasant responses transmitting different emotions that could be difficult for them to handle. They can also find difficulties in more

---

[1] http://www.aspergermadrid.org.

common situations, such as answering an email: they may misinterpret the tone of an email from their boss or teacher and answer in an inappropriate way.

In all these cases, it would be very useful for them to have an "emotional translator" capable of suggesting them the emotions that are transmitted by the text they are reading or writing. With a tool like this, they could check if the emotion they perceive in a text they are reading is correct or if the emotion transmitted by a text they have written matches the emotion they wanted to convey. Although language is very subjective, and a machine is far from being able to perfectly interpret the emotions of a text, any aid in this path can be very helpful for this collective. Experts also indicated that the application should not only express the overall emotion of a text, but also give clues about which elements of the text influence this global emotion. These clues are vital if the user finds that the emotion conveyed by a text is not the desired one, as they will help him to identify what must be changed in order to transmit the desired emotion correctly. Although end users were not directly present in these meetings, experts provided us with real examples of problems experienced by people with AS that could be avoided using a tool with the described functionalities.

From the point of view of the scenarios of use and activities, most members of the association are young adults in their twenties who spend lots of time in social networks and the Internet. They mostly find problems with emotions transmitted in WhatsApp and Telegram groups, entries in Facebook or blogs where they read, write and comment, or communications through email. Conversely, people with AS are usually very capable from the point of view of technology.

Design. Once the main purpose of the application was agreed by experts and developers, we had to transform it into a detailed specification. From the point of view of the general behavior of the application, we decided to implement the translator as a web application. Thus, the application could be used on any device with Internet access. Regarding the emotions detected by our application, we decided to use the five basic emotions: joy, sadness, fear, anger and disgust.

The design of the application was discussed with experts in two different sessions. First, we analyzed with them different options for representing emotions, which was probably the most important decision from the point of view of the design. Three different possibilities were considered: to use emoticons to represent each of the emotions, to use a scale representing the polarity (positive or negative) of the emotion or to use different colors for the words in the text according to the emotion they represent. The experts discarded the polarity scale and the colors in the text from the start, as they thought they could confuse end users, and they suggested that the best choice was to associate each emotion with an emoticon that could be accompanied by a color and a textual label such as *anger* or *joy*.

Then, in order to design the rest of the interface and the interactions with the web application, we employed a parallel design process: each developer designed a mock-up of the application independently. The aim was to explore a series of ideas without developers influencing each other, so there would be more variety

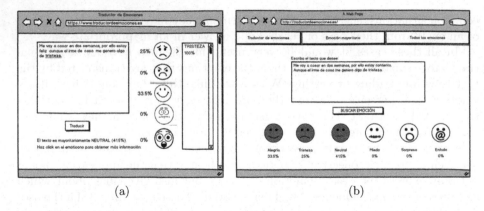

Fig. 1. Two of the mock-ups created during the parallel design process

of functionalities as well as different designs for the same functionality. Once the individual prototypes were ready, they were studied and compared by the developers, and a final mock-up of the application was built to be analyzed by experts. This mock-up had, in some cases, different options for the same data to be represented or the same functionality to be used (as shown in Fig. 1), so these options could easily be discussed with the experts. Different alternatives for the main decision points of the design were discussed in a new meeting with the group of experts. The main issues that were discussed were the following: how to represent the emotions and its values, where to position the results, and what was the appropriate granularity for this representation.

When asked if the intensity of the emotions could be represented with percentages next to the emoticons, the experts considered that percentages could mislead potential users of the application. They recommended a more visual way with a bar divided by emotions, associating each emotion with a color, and a division of this bar proportionally among the emotions according to the results obtained from the emotional analysis of the text. Taking into account the textual labels accompanying the emoticons, the specific use of the word "neutral" to express the absence of emotions was considered ambiguous. In this case, the experts recommended the use of a message like "this text has no emotions". As emoticons, they recommended the use of the ones provided by ARASAAC[2], since end users were already familiar with them. When discussing the best position for the obtained results (to the right of the text or below the text box), the experts considered that both solutions could work, but they preferred the one with the results below the text. When asked if this should be an option that could be configured, they thought that personalizing this aspect would not add any benefit to the application and could mislead the user. From the point of view of the granularity of the results to be shown, the experts were asked if it

---

[2] ARASAAC is an extensive database of pictograms for an ample vocabulary in Spanish. More information in: http://www.arasaac.org/.

would be better to show all the emotions that were present in the text or only the predominant emotion, for which they preferred the former.

In general, the experts considered that the functionalities included in the prototype were adequate for the application to be useful for the daily activities of the end users. They also indicated that personalization is very important in this type of applications. For example, they pointed out that it would be very useful to allow the change of the colors associated with the emotions, since people with AS are more likely to have synesthesia[3] than other population groups. The experts also indicated that it would be very useful to be able to change the emoticons associated with each emotion, as this could help some users to better interpret the results.

Implementation. EmoTraductor was implemented following a service-oriented architecture. The main interface had to be created following the decisions and mock-ups obtained in the design phase, and the functionality had to be decomposed in smaller pieces that could be implemented as web services. The idea was to design these web services so that they could also be used as pieces in future developments and other applications.

A complete API of the emotional web services[4] was implemented considering three levels of text granularity: word, sentence and multi-sentence text. Although there are more auxiliary services, the most important ones are the following:

– *Web service to obtain the emotions expressed by a word.* Given a word, this service returns information about the degree of intensity of each emotion in the word, expressed with a value between 1 (lack of emotion) and 5 (full of emotion). This information is extracted from a series of pre-existent emotional dictionaries that associate the basic emotions and a very extensive vocabulary in Spanish. For example, given the word *"enfermedad" (illness)*, the service returns the following values for each emotion: <sadness:4.13; fear:3.96; joy:1.0; anger:2.93; disgust:2.43>.
– *Web service to obtain the emotions expressed by a sentence.* This service is based on the previous web service, and returns the emotional values of the sentence along with the list of words that have led to those results. For example, for the sentence *"Estoy alegre y feliz" (I'm glad and happy)*, the service returns the following values for each emotion: <sadness:1.1; fear:1.21; joy:4.73; anger:1.05; disgust:1.02>, and the following list of emotional words: <*alegre (glad), feliz (happy)*>.
– *Web service to obtain the emotions expressed by a multi-sentence text.* In order to obtain the emotions of a text, this service splits the whole text into sentences and obtains the emotional degrees of each sentence using the previous web service. Enunciative, interrogative and admiration sentences are given different weights when calculating the final emotional values.

---

[3] Condition by which a mixture of the senses is experienced. For example, colors are seen when sounds are heard or emotions are felt.

[4] The emotional web services API is publicly available in http://sesat.fdi.ucm.es/apiEmoTraductor/.

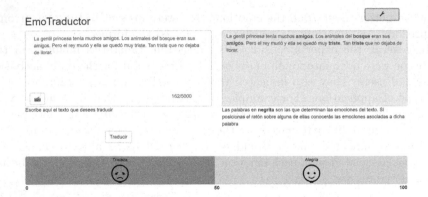

Fig. 2. Final version of the EmoTraductor interface.

A complete functional application[5] was implemented using these web services in a responsive web application, always following the design decisions from the previous phase. The interface of the application can be seen in Fig. 2. More technical and detailed information about the implementation of the web services API and the application can be found in [7].

Evaluation. Thanks to *Asociación Asperger Madrid*, it was possible to evaluate the EmoTraductor with end users and experts. The main goal of this evaluation was to figure out the suitability of the application for different users, and the satisfaction of both end users and experts with the process and the results obtained with the application. The evaluation of EmoTraductor was performed with a total of 9 users with AS and 2 experts from the association.

First, the application was briefly presented to the evaluators. Then, during a task-oriented testing phase, the evaluators were provided with different texts to test in the application (texts lacking emotion, texts expressing a single emotion and texts with several emotions). For each text, evaluators had to indicate in a questionnaire which was the information presented by the application: the emotions in the text, the predominant emotion and the emotional words. The aim of this phase was to verify if users could interact with the application and comprehend the information presented in it. The evaluators were not asked which was the emotion they thought the text conveyed, but which was the emotion the application assigned to the text and words. The aim was to check if the application was intuitive and offered the information in an understandable way, and if the users could understand the results.

Next, the evaluators were asked to explore the application freely in the free testing phase. In this way, they could use their own texts and test if the results would help them to interpret the emotions. At the end of this phase, the evaluators completed a form to assess the usability of the application. All the questionnaires were designed in collaboration with experts. Most of the questions

---

[5] EmoTraductor is publicly available in http://sesat.fdi.ucm.es/traductor/.

were answered with a 5 point Likert scale, the granularity recommended by the experts, and we made sure that potentially emotion-based subjective responses were not used. In addition to the questionnaires, the developers of the application were observing the evaluators, taking notes of their suggestions and comments during the whole session.

All these data were later analyzed and several conclusions were obtained. The application was positively valued by both experts and end users, including the colors and emoticons used by default and the available personalization options. The emotional bar that shows the emotions related to the text and their degrees was considered intuitive. However, the emotional results obtained for some texts were not accurate in those cases where there were words with ambiguous meanings or negations. Slang language was also problematic for the application. From the point of view of the process, the experts specially valued the effort made during the design and implementation process for taking into account the information about end users, their necessities and requirements.

5.2 ReadIt: A Browser Plug-In to Enhance Web Navigation

ReadIt [17] is a web browser plug-in that supports and enhances web navigation for people with written language understanding difficulties. Considering the characteristics of these users, who may have problems when reading or interpreting a text, this application has been developed in order to facilitate web navigation. Through the use of web services, ReadIt provides a simple set of tools to help these users understand the texts they encounter in web pages. ReadIt was designed and implemented following the MeDeC@ methodology. In this case, end users participated mainly in the evaluation stage because the experts who work with them considered that our presence, the interruption of their routines or their participation in the design process would affect them in a rather negative way. Discussions about requirements elicitation and design were held only with the experts, who gave us a global view of the problems that this collective usually faces.

Requirements Elicitation. ReadIt was designed and implemented with the help of experts from *Estudio 3 Afanias School*[6], a school aimed to attend the special needs of children with learning difficulties that cannot study in a regular school, including children with ASD and other cognitive impairments. We met with teachers and psychologists who helped us to obtain and comprehend some basic information about the end users and their use of Internet technologies, as they usually encounter problems reading, writing or understanding text from web pages. Although there are certain guidelines to make the web more accessible, like choosing simple vocabulary and sentence structures to make the text easier to read, these guidelines are not fulfilled in most web pages. Despite the fact that the end users did not actively participate in the conversations, part of our

---

[6] https://afanias.org/que-hacemos/educacion/colegio-estudio-3/.

meetings consisted in observing them working on the computer, so we could grasp some of the difficulties they usually face.

Estudio 3 Afanias students are teenagers under 21 who are educated in both regular studies and adult life according to their intellectual capabilities. The experts selected a specific class of students from 16 to 21 years old who could benefit the most from a tool for enhancing and facilitating web navigation, as they spend many hours consulting the web pages of their favorites singers or actors, or use the Internet as part of their studies. Considering the characteristics of this specific class, who were mostly capable of reading and writing but usually found problems when interpreting a text, the goal of ReadIt was set to providing a set of tools to help them understand the texts they encounter in the web.

From the point of view of the scenarios of use, these users could benefit from tools that allowed them to obtain additional textual information for a word, to generate a summary of a text, or access YouTube videos and Wikipedia articles corresponding to the words they do not understand. It was important to take into account that these students, who were in general capable of using a computer and a web browser, could have problems for certain interactions such us selecting text or using the keyboard. Therefore, the experts emphasized the importance of being able to customize the tool for each of them.

Design. The information obtained from the first task was transformed into a detailed specification of both the general behavior and interactions. As the application was intended as an assistant to browse the web, we decided to implement it as an extension for Google Chrome, since it is currently one of the most popular web browsers. The tool was designed as a series of functionalities that can be activated at any time, such as looking up synonyms or definitions of a word or creating a summary of the content of a web page.

In order to discuss different design options with the experts, we created two mock-ups with alternative solutions to activate the available functionalities, selecting the text that is considered difficult, and the general layout:

– *Mock-up 1: Right button click.* After activating the extension in the browser, there was no special interface to be shown. When the user selects a difficult word or a short part of the text, the list of functionalities can be activated by using the right mouse button. The response is shown in a modal window.
– *Mock-up 2: Toolbar.* After activating the extension, a new toolbar appears, displaying the different functionalities offered by the application. The users can then select the text as in mock-up 1 and then click on the toolbar button that corresponds to the desired function, or they can write the text in a search field instead. The response is also shown in a modal window.

Experts preferred mock-up 2 without any doubt, as they pointed out that a user with ASD would be confused if after activating the plug-in there was no visual feedback in the browser window. In addition, although *Estudio 3 Afanias* students who are going to use ReadIt are able to work with the keyboard and mouse, the right click interaction is usually difficult for them. Experts considered as a good idea to make it possible to introduce the difficult text by selecting or writing it, so users can decide depending on their capabilities or the situation. They also remarked that it was very important to be able to configure the available functionalities for each user, so they are not confused by the options they are not going to use. In addition, they recommended the use of simple vocabulary for the texts in the plug-in. For example, these users do not understand what a synonym is, but will understand an option called "similar words".

Implementation. Taking into account the conclusions obtained in the design phase, a completely functional instance of the plug-in was implemented[7]. Figure 3 shows the ReadIt toolbar with all the functionalities activated and the additional option of writing text in a search space. The toolbar is visible in all websites during the navigation, and the options can be configured easily.

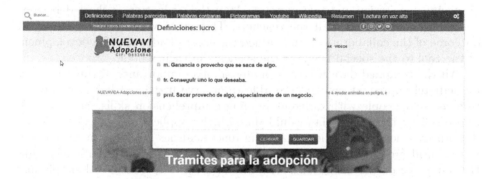

Fig. 3. ReadIt plug-in interface with the search of definitions for *"lucro"* (*profit*).

This implementation follows a service-oriented architecture, with eight web services encapsulating the implementation of each functionality available in the plug-in: (1) obtaining the definitions of a word using the Royal Academy of the Spanish Language (RAE) dictionary[8]; (2) getting the synonyms and (3) antonyms of a word; (4) obtaining a pictogram translation of a text; (5) accessing the Youtube video for a word or text; (6) accessing the Wikipedia article for a word or text; (7) generating an automatic summary of the selected text; and (8) listening to a conversion of the written text into spoken words. More technical and detailed information about the implementation of the plug-in can be found in [17].

Evaluation. A user-centered evaluation where experts and end users could explore the application prototype was carried out in *Estudio 3 Afanias School*.

---

[7] ReadIt is publicly available in the Chrome Web Store.
[8] http://www.rae.es/.

We tested the implemented plug-in with 10 students and 2 teachers in their computer classroom. First, a presentation was made to students to show them the application and its functionalities. Then, during the task-oriented testing, we proposed a series of guided activities to use all the options and functionalities in the plug-in. As the class was about to go on a trip to Tarragona, we oriented the activities to different ways of looking for information about what they were going to see, and how to use the plug-in to better understand the web pages they were navigating. Next, users could use the plug-in freely during one hour, always with the help of developers and teachers. Finally, we asked both students and teachers to complete a questionnaire with different questions about the application and their experience. In the case of the students, we had to adapt a typical questionnaire so that people with ASD could understand and complete it. The solution was to use a semaphore scale, where they could choose the red color if they did not agree with a statement, yellow if they were not sure, and green if they did. In addition to this final questionnaires, the developers were observing the session and taking notes. After the evaluation, a short debriefing session was performed with the teachers. They were very satisfied about the outcome of the collaboration, and valued the effort of adapting the development of the tool to the special needs of the students in their school.

All the compiled data was later analyzed. The importance of this work was immediately apparent, as we were able to observe first-hand how the application assisted people with different reading comprehension skills. Students felt impressed by the things they could do with the application, and eager to use it both at school and at home. All the functionalities available in the plug-in were considered very helpful by both students and teachers, specially some like the summary or the definitions. The interface was also considered simple and practical, although teachers highlighted that some vocabulary in the menus and options could be simplified. An interesting finding was that ReadIt not only made it easier for users to understand the texts in a web page, but also promoted and encouraged them to improve their learning and independence. For example, a student found an unknown word (*"sarcophagus"*) and was very happy when she discovered the meaning by herself using the tool. The same happened to another student who did not understand the word *"bovine"*.

6   Discussion

The methodology presented in this work relies heavily in our experience. Throughout these years of experience we have learned that organizations that work with people with ASD are very willing to collaborate, but it is usually difficult to have an appropriate access to end users. Therefore, one of the main contributions of our methodology is to recommend the inclusion of experts (as other authors have previously done, such as [9,27,28]), along with end users, in all the stages of the development process. This makes it necessary to adapt phases like requirements elicitation or evaluation to the presence of two different actors that provide different and complementary information for the task at hand.

However, we acknowledge that the MeDeC@ methodology relies mainly in the involvement of experts throughout the design process, which may imply several drawbacks according to other authors. For example, the authors of [2, 21] have analyzed some of these drawbacks in the development of two assistive hand-held applications. One of the drawbacks has to do with the experts' interests, perspectives and expectations, as they may differ from the researchers' ones or even the users' ones. This has been the case in our experience, although in the two presented case studies we have managed to take their needs into account in the resulting product, as they did not clash with our own. Another drawback that the same authors point out is the possible interference between the roles of domain experts. Again, we have experienced this problem as our domain experts acted both as representatives of and liaisons with the end users. Therefore, we have had to take their needs into account so that we made sure that they would eventually grant us access to the end users to carry out the necessary evaluations of our applications. In addition, in their roles of teachers and caregivers, these experts have been considered as side users of our applications. Finally, the authors of [2, 21] also point out how beneficial it can be to work with existing support organizations. Although it is true that they have provided us with valuable information related to the users' needs, we cannot deny that they have also imposed some limitations that have affected our working plans. First, these organizations have been quite reluctant to let us work with the end users, which is reflected in the MeDeC@ methodology in the prominent role that experts have over end users. Subsequently, this is one of the reasons why we have favoured User-Centered Design over Participatory Design, as a purely PD approach has not been possible without a bigger involvement of the end users. In addition, different organizations had conflicting expectations about the functionality of the final applications, which has made us design different solutions for each of them, as a design-for-all strategy would not have lead us to a satisfactory solution.

Another contribution of our methodology is not to design for a wide collective of users with a specific impairment, but to adapt UCD to specific situations and smaller groups. The applied MeDeC@ approach has the potential to assist developers to rethink the development of computer assistive applications by listening to, and focusing on, the needs and aims of potential users of those applications. The involvement of end users or experts throughout the development process can lead to a more effective design and the development of more accessible applications that obtain a high degree of satisfaction for the end users.

Finally, although more tied to the implementation than to the design, the idea of using a Service-Oriented Architecture with small pieces of reusable code has demonstrated to be highly flexible for the configuration and personalization of computerized assistive tools. The availability of services that solve small accessibility problems simplifies the design process, because once the operations are given, the choices that remain are mostly about interface and interaction. That makes it easier and faster to develop new tools that solve similar problems but must be personalized for a different group of users. Harper [14] expresses a similar idea: the separation between user interface and functionality allows universal access to applications, since the interface can be adapted to the user without modifying the code that implements the functionality. Therefore, we consider that the exploration of this kind of implementation architectures can greatly enhance the development of computerized assistive technologies, with a lower cost and effort and shorter development times.

7   Conclusions and Future Work

This paper has presented a Methodology for the Development of Computer Assistive Technologies (MeDeC@) that adapts the classic UCD approaches to the design and implementation of applications for people with ASD. The MeDeC@ methodology, along with the two applications developed using it, are some of the results obtained in the IDiLyCo (*Digital Inclusion, Language and Communication*) research project. The main objective of the two applications has been to assist users with their difficulties in the use of language. Interestingly enough, the main limitations of both applications come from the Natural Language Processing (NLP) research field. In the case of EmoTraductor, advances in the detection of negation or in emotional analysis are likely to improve the obtained results. In the case of ReadIt, advances in summarization and machine translation are also likely to improve the quality of the texts presented to the users. Even so, the results of both evaluations show that the users are satisfied with their use and that the experts are willing to keep collaborating using MeDeC@.

The use of a service-oriented architecture in MeDeC@ results in services that solve small problems that facilitate their reuse in other applications. We are currently integrating some of the emotional services created for the EmoTraductor emotional translator into the ReadIt plug-in to emotionally mark words, sentences or texts. This integration would have a higher cost with other kind of software architectures. In addition, the architectural approach using web services will allow us to incorporate NLP improvements to the applications without bothering the users, which is likely to help improve their quality of life.

In the near future, our work is planned to evolve in two different directions. In the case of MeDeC@, we are using the methodology to develop other applications, such as a tool that helps people with ASD to understand complex words by comparing them with easier ones or an editor of pictogram boards. In addition, we are getting in touch with more organizations in order to test the suitability of MeDeC@ with a wider range of cognitive impairments. Regarding the applications, our aim is to create a repository of web services that can be composed to build configurable applications in a fast and simple way, helping developers and users to satisfy their needs as effortlessly as possible. We are also preparing an observational longitudinal study in collaboration with schools in order to better understand the benefits that the developed applications may imply for the end users.

Acknowledgements. The work presented in this paper has been partially funded by the projects IDiLyCo: Digital Inclusion, Language and Communication, Grant.

No. TIN2015-66655-R (MINECO/FEDER) and InVITAR-IA: Infraestructuras para la Visibilización, Integración y Transferencia de Aplicaciones y Resultados de Inteligencia Artificial, UCM Grant. No. FEI-EU-17-23. The authors want to thank Lorena Jiménez, Paloma Gutiérrez, Elena Kaloyanova and Gema Eugercios for their work in the implementation of the presented case studies.

References

1. Abascal, J., Nicolle, C.: The application of *USERfit* methodology to teach usability guidelines. In: Vanderdonckt, J., Farenc, C. (eds.) Tools for Working with Guidelines, pp. 209–216. Springer, London (2001). https://doi.org/10.1007/978-1-4471-0279-3_20
2. Allen, M., Leung, R., McGrenere, J., Purves, B.: Involving domain experts in assistive technology research. Univ. Access Inf. Soc. **7**(3), 145–154 (2008)
3. Allsop, M.: Involving children in the design of healthcare technology. Ph.D. thesis, University of Leeds (2010)
4. Benton, L., Johnson, H., Ashwin, E., Brosnan, M.J., Grawemeyer, B.: Developing IDEAS: supporting children with autism within a participatory design team. In: CHI 2012: The 2012 ACM Annual Conference on Human Factors in Computing Systems (2012)
5. Börjesson, P., Barendregt, W., Eriksson, E., Torgersson, O.: Designing technology for and with developmentally diverse children: a systematic literature review. In: Proceedings of the 14th International Conference on Interaction Design and Children, pp. 79–88. ACM, New York (2015)
6. Cooper, A., Reimann, R., Cronin, D., Noessel, C.: About Face: The Essentials of Interaction Design, 4th edn. Wiley Publishing, Hoboken (2014)
7. Eugercios, G., Gutiérrez, P., Kaloyanova, E.: Análisis emocional para la inclusión digital (2018). https://eprints.ucm.es/48834/
8. Foss, E., Guha, M.L., Papadatos, P., Clegg, T., Yip, J., Walsh, G.: Cooperative inquiry extended: creating technology with middle school students with learning differences. J. Spec. Educ. Technol. **28**(3), 33–46 (2013)
9. Frank Lopresti, E., Mihailidis, A., Kirsch, N.: Assistive technology for cognitive rehabilitation: state of the art. Neuropsychol. Rehabil. **14**(1–2), 5–39 (2004)
10. Frauenberger, C., Good, J., Alcorn, A., Pain, H.: Supporting the design contributions of children with autism spectrum conditions. In: Proceedings of the 11th International Conference on Interaction Design and Children, pp. 134–143. ACM (2012)
11. Frauenberger, C., Good, J., Keay-Bright, W.: Designing technology for children with special needs: bridging perspectives through participatory design. CoDesign **7**(1), 1–28 (2011)
12. Guha, M.L., Druin, A., Fails, J.A.: Designing with and for children with special needs: an inclusionary model. In: Proceedings of the 7th International Conference on Interaction Design and Children, IDC 2008, pp. 61–64. ACM, New York (2008)
13. Haas, K., Costley, D., Falkmer, M., Richdale, A., Sofronoff, K., Falkmer, T.: Factors influencing the research participation of adults with autism spectrum disorders. J. Autism Dev. Disord. **46**(5), 1793–1805 (2016)
14. Harper, S.: Is there design-for-all? Univ. Access Inf. Soc. **6**(1), 111–113 (2007)
15. Harte, R., et al.: A human-centered design methodology to enhance the usability, human factors, and user experience of connected health systems: a three-phase methodology. JMIR Hum. Factors **4**(1), e8 (2017)

16. Holone, H., Herstad, J.: Three tensions in participatory design for inclusion. In: Proceedings of the SIGCHI Conference on Human Factors in Computing Systems, CHI 2013, pp. 2903–2906. ACM, New York (2013)
17. Jiménez-Corta, L.: Herramienta de apoyo a la navegación web para personas con discapacidad (2018). https://eprints.ucm.es/48863/
18. Keay-Bright, W.: The reactive colours project: demonstrating participatory and collaborative design methods for the creation of software for autistic children. Des. Princ. Pract. 1(2), 7–15 (2007)
19. Kientz, J.A., Hayes, G.R., Westeyn, T.L., Starner, T., Abowd, G.D.: Pervasive computing and autism: assisting caregivers of children with special needs. IEEE Pervasive Comput. 6(1), 28–35 (2007)
20. Lazar, J., Feng, J.H., Hochheiser, H.: Research Methods in Human-Computer Interaction. Morgan Kaufmann, Cambridge (2017)
21. Leung, R., Lumsden, J.: Designing mobile technologies for individuals with disabilities. In: Lumsden, J. (ed.) Handbook of Research on User Interface Design and Evaluation for Mobile Technology, pp. 609–623. IGI Global, Hershey (2008)
22. Murray, D., Lesser, M., Lawson, W.: Attention, monotropism and the diagnostic criteria for autism. Autism 9(2), 139–156 (2005). https://doi.org/10.1177/1362361305051398
23. Parsons, S., Millen, L., Garib-Penna, S., Cobb, S.: Participatory design in the development of innovative technologies for children and young people on the autism spectrum: the cospatial project. J. Assist. Technol. 5(1), 29–34 (2011)
24. Poulson, D., Richardson, S.: USERfit - a framework for user centred design in assistive technology. Technol. Disabil. 9(3), 163–171 (1998)
25. van Rijn, H., Stappers, P.J.: Expressions of ownership: motivating users in a co-design process. In: Proceedings of the Tenth Anniversary Conference on Participatory Design 2008, pp. 178–181. Indiana University (2008)
26. Subrahmaniyan, N., Higginbotham, D.J., Bisantz, A.M.: Using personas to support augmentative alternative communication device design: a validation and evaluation study. Int. J. Hum.-Comput. Inter. 34(1), 84–97 (2018)
27. Sullivan, J., Fischer, G.: Mobile architectures and prototypes to assist persons with cognitive disabilities using public transportation. In: 26th International Conference on Technology and Rehabilitation (2003)
28. Tee, K., et al.: A visual recipe book for persons with language impairments. In: Proceedings of the SIGCHI Conference on Human Factors in Computing Systems, pp. 501–510. ACM (2005)

Classifying Sensitive Issues for Patients with Neurodevelopmental Disorders

Torben Wallbaum[1](✉), Tim Claudius Stratmann[1], and Susanne Boll[2]

[1] OFFIS - Institute for Information Technology, Oldenburg, Germany
{torben.wallbaum,tim.stratmann}@offis.de
[2] University of Oldenburg, Oldenburg, Germany
susanne.boll@uni-oldenburg.de

Abstract. ADHD has an estimated worldwide prevalence of 2–3% and is one of the most frequent neurodevelopmental disorders. Many problems in an ADHD-patient's life arise from the lack of self-management abilities and social interaction with others. While medication is considered the most successful treatment for disorders such as ADHD, patients often seek support in therapeutic sessions with trained therapists. These aim to strengthen self-awareness of symptoms, emotional self-regulation, and self-management. However, sharing personal insights can be a burden for patients while therapists would benefit from understanding important issues a patient is facing. Our work aims to support therapy for patients and therapists by providing classification of digital diary entries for therapy sessions while protecting patients privacy. Additionally, we provide insights into important issues and topics including their affective interpretation for patients suffering from ADHD.

Keywords: ADHD · Social communities · Classification · Text analysis

1 Introduction and Prior Work

One of the most commonly diagnosed psychiatric disorders for children as well as adolescents is ADHD (Attention-deficit-hyperactivity disorder). The prevalence of ADHD in adults is around 2–3% [20], often starts in childhood and persists in up to 50% into adulthood. In recent years an increase in diagnosis, as well as medication, can be found in multiple sources (e.g., [5,19]). Core symptoms of the disorder are inattention, hyperactivity, and impulsivity, however patients suffering from various combinations of these and further symptoms. A common instrument in ADHD diagnosis and therapy are self-reporting scales (such as ADHD Rating Scale-IV [12]), which are assessing behavioral patterns that are considered ADHD risk factors. The use of such self-reporting questionnaires is often criticized, due to the lack of a missing specific situational context. Patients need to imagine and predict their own behavior for situations described within

© IFIP International Federation for Information Processing 2019
Published by Springer Nature Switzerland AG 2019
D. Lamas et al. (Eds.): INTERACT 2019, LNCS 11746, pp. 107–114, 2019.
https://doi.org/10.1007/978-3-030-29381-9_7

these assessments. Because of a missing self-awareness of their own reaction, patients may have difficulties in evaluating oneself objectively or may differ in their ability for introspection. Previous works have suggested that additional behavioral data could allow for more objective measures.

In previous works Sonne et al. have suggested a framework to support therapy with technological on-body systems [17]. Based on this, concepts and systems have been presented which support self-management of psychological disorders for young adults unobtrusively in everyday life. Sensing modules are used to detect symptoms that are relevant by using unobtrusive sensors that continuously collect data about a person's movements [13,18], heart-rate variability [7,15], eye-movements [10], contextual parameters e.g., body temperature [4] and in-situ experience sampling [11]. Current moods and self-evaluations are queried through a mobile device in appropriate moments.

One other successful measure is the use of retrospective or emotional diaries, that provide patients a save space to collect and reflect experiences from their day-to-day life. This method is used often by therapists when applying techniques from cognitive behavioral therapy (CBT) [3]. Essentially, cognitive behavioral therapy aims to change behavior by identifying negative and distorted thinking patterns. These diaries provide a tool for monitoring feelings of anxiety, fear, hurt, anger, shame, guilt, or sadness as well as when and where these feelings were experienced. This successful form of therapy emphasizes the link between thoughts, feelings, and behavior. However, some patients might feel uncomfortable to later share their experiences with therapists during sessions due to privacy reasons and therefore miss the chance to get helpful feedback or learn helpful strategies specific to their own personal circumstances. At the same time therapists could benefit from these inputs to better understands common issues and links between subjects, involved people, and emotional interpretations. By gaining knowledge from these experiences, therapists can improve the quality of their therapy over time.

To address these shortcomings of traditional diaries, we propose a support system that aims to classify digital diary entries using text-analysis and detect the overarching topic of a diary entry. In addition, our approach performs a sentiment analysis of each diary entry to understand how a patient emotionally rates specific topics personally e.g. social interactions are perceived negatively. The privacy conserving overarching topics based on a patients personal experiences might be shared with therapists, to provide a basis for future therapy sessions and indicate changes in topics important to patients for long-term self-reflection. Patients can decide if or when to share diary entries with therapists. If only privacy conserving keywords and sentiments are shared, therapists can use them as a conversation starter during which more details might be revealed by the patient. The reuse of diary entries in therapy session might additionally encourage patients to keep engaged in regularly documenting important things, emotional states and reflections of their day-to-day experiences.

With this work, we aim for two main goals: (1) Discover and understand important issues and topics including their affective interpretation for patients suffering from ADHD or similar neurodevelopmental disorders. (2) Support therapy for patients and therapists by providing in-situ classification of digital diary entries collected to provide important topics for therapy sessions. To understand important topics and gather create a dataset for training a classification model, we collected posts from an active online community. Following we describe our approach.

2   Crowdsourcing Topics for Classification

2.1   Data Mining and Analysis

We collected our initial dataset from the ADHD Subreddit[1], which is an active community, of at that time about 221,382 users, to share and discuss topics related to ADHD. We collected the 1000 *TOP* posts of *ALL* times (upvoted by users of the community). After cleaning up and removing duplicates, the dataset resulted in 998 posts from 823 different authors. We choose the ADHD Subreddit community because of two main attributes: First, similar to diary entries, posts vary in length and grade of detail and second, users often share important subjects with the community in a way they would collect them in a diary, such as:

> [..]I feel nervous or numb mostly and can't think clearly most of the time. I don't particularly feel like a pleasant human being and I have quite a disheveled past. Luckily nothing too horrible but just many many SO many fuck ups and experiences and broken relationships that feel like a weight on my back. [..]

We first aimed to retrieve overarching topics from the dataset itself. Based on initial topics from a literature review e.g. problems at work or with loved ones, we used techniques from NLP to understand the data corpus. We analyzed the existing overall text corpus with regard to word frequencies, clustering as well as term correlations. After cleaning the dataset and removing stop words (english and custom ADHD-related ones), we used stemming and removed white spaces. Based on the corpus we created a tf-idf weighted document-term-matrix [14] with 10% sparse terms removed as basis for further analysis. While we analyzed the corpus with different clustering algorithms (hierarchical clustering, K-means), we could not find any particular interesting correlations. However, we will continue our analysis in the near future, in cooperation with experts from the medical domain to further search for extending topics of interest.

2.2   Classification of Posts

We included three experts (therapists, medical professionals) to help us identify general important topics and issues that often or regularly occur during therapy sessions with patients and are known from professional literature. Together with

---

[1] (https://www.reddit.com/r/ADHD/; last retrieved: 06-28-2018).

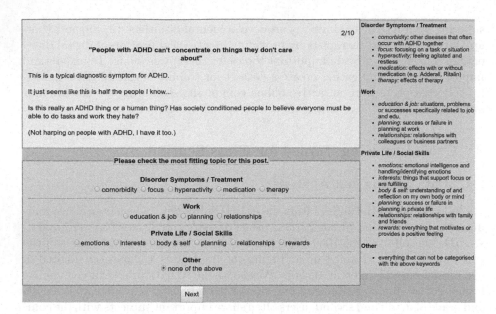

Fig. 1. Snapshot of the crowdsourcing website, to categorize social media postings into one of fifteen overarching topics.

the experts, we identified 14 topics (listed in Fig. 2a for the following three overarching areas: *ADHD-related, Work, Private Life/Social Skills*. The topics for relationships and planning occur in two areas, for private and professional life accordingly.

In a next step, we built a website to crowdsource the mappings of overarching topics for each entry of our dataset to retrieve labels for a later model training (shown in Fig. 1). The website was accessible for crowd-workers hired through a crowdsourcing service (We hired 100 crowd-workers through https://www.prolific.ac/ with an incentive of about $8/hour) Workers were presented one post at a time, which they had to read and choose an appropriate overarching topic for. Each categorization tasks consisted of 10 posts and took about 15–30 min per worker. We asked workers to categorize by 1 in 14 categorize or select *other* if none of the available options seemed appropriate. Figure 2a shows the frequencies of topics identified as a result of the crowdsourcing task for our dataset.

3   Analysis and Model

3.1   Sentiment-Analysis of Topics

To understand affective interpretation of topics, we used sentiment analysis for our dataset. Each post (categorized into one of the overarching topics by the crowd-workers) was analyzed using the VADER Sentiment Analysis[2]. VADER is a lexicon and rule-based sentiment tool, specifically trained to classify sentiments expressed in social media [6]. It was already successfully used for similar data in related research [1,16]. The resulting overall distribution of sentiments (53.9% positive, 13.1% neutral, 33.0% negative) is shown in Fig. 2b. The median associated sentiment for each separate topic is represented in Fig. 3. For six topics the median classification is neutral, nine correspond to positive, none of the topics is mostly associated with negative feelings. Similar to a bias towards a positive sentiment of the posts from Reddit, we expect a positive bias in later diary entries as these are a way to get help by outsiders (either other users or a therapist using the diaries).

Topic	Count
comorbidity	15
education	98
emotions	104
focus	147
hyperactivity	49
inbodyment	85
interests	40
medication	82
planning_private	74
planning_work	43
relationship_private	79
relationship_work	10
rewards	22
therapy	40
other	110
Total	998

(a) Distribution of topics.

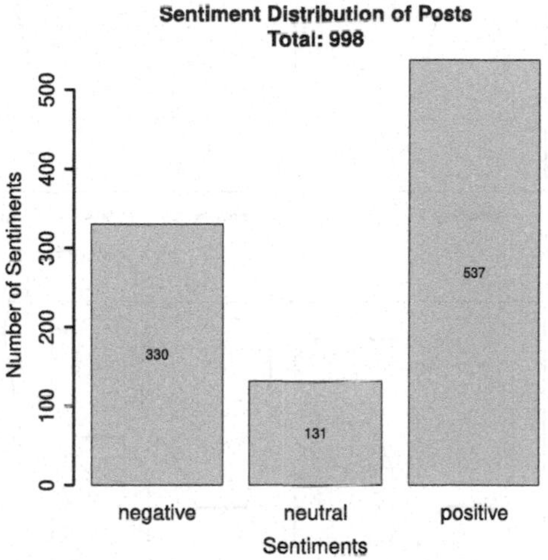

(b) Distribution of sentiments.

Fig. 2. Distribution of topics classified from our sourced reddit postings and distribution of sentiments (positive, neutral, negative) over all analyzed posts.

3.2 Model-Training for Classification

For training the model to classify in-situ diary entries from patients into overarching topics we used a supervised learning approach. As a basis, we used our existing dataset including 9,647 words and the fifteen topic labels created by the crowd-workers. Following we used the FastText [9] library to train our classification model as it proofed to be well suited in related research [2,8]. We trained our model for 500 epochs with a learning rate of 0.5. For testing the trained model we used 20% of our dataset per topic for testing (to prevent underrepresented topics). As we are currently implementing the mobile application for

---

[2] (https://github.com/cjhutto/vaderSentiment; last retrieved 01-07-2018).

in-situ diaries, we have not yet evaluated the overall performance of the model
with regard to classification accuracy. However, our first tests showed a precision
of 0.215 as well as a recall of 0.215 (performs better than pure chance = 0.06).
While the classification accuracy can be further improved e.g. by using n-grams
to set words into context, we see first promising results in our current results.

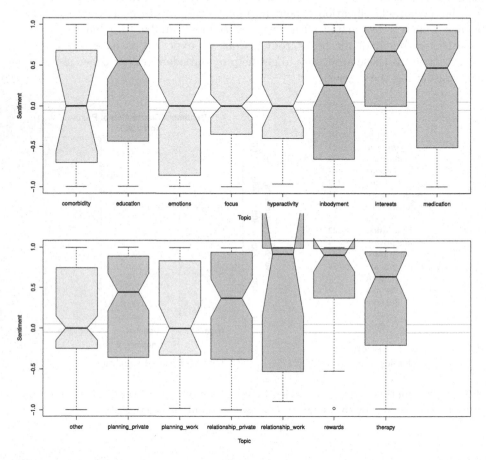

Fig. 3. Overarching topics and their associated sentiment (entries colored in green
represent a positive sentiment, while yellow related to neutral). (Color figure online)

4   Next Steps and Research Agenda

Our next step is to experiment further with learning approaches for diary entry
classification. Furthermore, we are currently completing the development of the
first digital diary prototype for Android, while also planning a field test with
patients. In this field evaluation, we want to test our Application (see digital

diary for patients Fig. 4a and overview screen including classified entries with sentiment rating for therapists Fig. 4b) against a baseline *analog* diary during therapy sessions. We aim to better understand (1) how patients and therapists can be supported during therapy sessions, (2) how good our approach performs in comparison with existing techniques and (3) how we can improve our classification model to be further generalized for real-life applications with patients suffering from other neurodevelopmental disorders.

(a) Diary-application for patients.   (b) Application for therapists.

Fig. 4. Using a smartphone application, the patients are enabled to keep a diary. Each entry can be hidden from the therapist, if the patient is choosing to do so. Therapists can see diary entries for each patient individually. Each entry is presented including (a) keywords, (b) a color coded sentiment (red = negative, green = positive, grey = neutral) as well as the entries text, if not hidden by the patient. (Color figure online)

References

1. Althoff, T., Clark, K., Leskovec, J.: Large-scale analysis of counseling conversations: an application of natural language processing to mental health. Trans. Assoc. Comput. Linguist. **4**, 463–476 (2016). https://doi.org/10.1162/tacl_a_00111
2. Badjatiya, P., Gupta, S., Gupta, M., Varma, V.: Deep learning for hate speech detection in tweets. In: Proceedings of the 26th International Conference on World Wide Web Companion, WWW 2017 Companion, pp. 759–760. International World Wide Web Conferences Steering Committee, Republic and Canton of Geneva, Switzerland (2017). https://doi.org/10.1145/3041021.3054223
3. Beck, J.S.: Cognitive Behavior Therapy: Basics and Beyond. Guilford Press, New York (2011)
4. Bijlenga, D., et al.: Associations between sleep characteristics, seasonal depressive symptoms, lifestyle, and ADHD symptoms in adults. J. Attention Disord. **17**(3), 261–275 (2013)

5. Brault, M.C., Lacourse, É.: Prevalence of prescribed attention-deficit hyperactivity disorder medications and diagnosis among Canadian preschoolers and school-age children: 1994–2007. Can. J. Psychiatry **57**(2), 93–101 (2012)
6. Gilbert, C.H.E.: Vader: a parsimonious rule-based model for sentiment analysis of social media text. In: Eighth International Conference on Weblogs and Social Media (ICWSM-14) (2014). http://comp.social.gatech.edu/papers/icwsm14.vader. hutto.pdf. Accessed 20 Apr 2016
7. Griffiths, K.R., et al.: Sustained attention and heart rate variability in children and adolescents with ADHD. Biol. Psychol. **124**, 11–20 (2017)
8. Jha, A., Mamidi, R.: When does a compliment become sexist? Analysis and classification of ambivalent sexism using Twitter data. In: Proceedings of the Second Workshop on NLP and Computational Social Science, pp. 7–16. Association for Computational Linguistics, Vancouver, August 2017. https://doi.org/10.18653/v1/W17-2902. https://www.aclweb.org/anthology/W17-2902
9. Joulin, A., Grave, E., Bojanowski, P., Mikolov, T.: Bag of tricks for efficient text classification. arXiv preprint arXiv:1607.01759 (2016)
10. Matsuo, Y., et al.: Gap effect abnormalities during a visually guided pro-saccade task in children with attention deficit hyperactivity disorder. PloS One **10**(5), e0125573 (2015)
11. Murphy, P., Schachar, R.: Use of self-ratings in the assessment of symptoms of attention deficit hyperactivity disorder in adults. Am. J. Psychiatry **157**(7), 1156–1159 (2000)
12. Pappas, D.: ADHD rating scale-IV: checklists, norms, and clinical interpretation. J. Psychoeducational Assess. **24**(2), 172–178 (2006)
13. Pina, L., Rowan, K., Roseway, A., Johns, P., Hayes, G.R., Czerwinski, M.: In situ cues for ADHD parenting strategies using mobile technology. In: Proceedings of the 8th International Conference on Pervasive Computing Technologies for Healthcare, pp. 17–24. ICST (Institute for Computer Sciences, Social-Informatics and Telecommunications Engineering) (2014)
14. Ramos, J., et al.: Using TF-IDF to determine word relevance in document queries. In: Proceedings of the First Instructional Conference on Machine Learning, vol. 242, pp. 133–142 (2003)
15. Rukmani, M.R., Seshadri, S.P., Thennarasu, K., Raju, T.R., Sathyaprabha, T.N.: Heart rate variability in children with attention-deficit/hyperactivity disorder: a pilot study. Ann. Neurosci. **23**(2), 81–88 (2016)
16. Song, K., Feng, S., Gao, W., Wang, D., Yu, G., Wong, K.F.: Personalized sentiment classification based on latent individuality of microblog users. In: Twenty-Fourth International Joint Conference on Artificial Intelligence (2015)
17. Sonne, T., Marshall, P., Obel, C., Thomsen, P.H., Grønbæk, K.: An assistive technology design framework for ADHD. In: Proceedings of the 28th Australian Conference on Computer-Human Interaction, pp. 60–70. ACM (2016)
18. Sonne, T., Obel, C., Grønbæk, K.: Designing real time assistive technologies: a study of children with ADHD. In: Proceedings of the Annual Meeting of the Australian Special Interest Group for Computer Human Interaction, pp. 34–38. ACM (2015)
19. Toh, S.: Datapoints: trends in ADHD and stimulant use among children, 1993–2003. Psychiatric Serv. **57**(8), 1091 (2006)
20. de Zwaan, M., et al.: The estimated prevalence and correlates of adult ADHD in a German community sample. Eur. Arch. Psychiatry Clin. Neurosci. **262**(1), 79–86 (2012)

Effects of Menu Organization and Visibility on Web Navigation for People with Dyslexia

Helen Petrie[(⊠)] and Ili Farhana Md Mahtar

Department of Computer Science, University of York, York YO10 5GH, UK
{helen.petrie, ifmm500}@york.ac.uk

Abstract. People with dyslexia have reported difficulties with navigating websites, yet very little research has investigated the nature of these difficulties. This study investigated the effects of two aspects of web navigation, menu organization and visibility on the eye gaze behaviour, performance and preferences of dyslexic and non-dyslexic participants. Participants undertook four tasks on a website with either unified or fragmented main menu organization and either static or dynamic submenus. Dyslexic participants had significantly longer menu scanpaths (i.e. looked at more menu items), due to looking at more different menu items and revisiting more items in comparison to non-dyslexic participants. They also had more fixations and longer dwell times on submenus than non-dyslexic participants. They were also slower to select their first menu item and complete tasks. However, the perceptions of the different menu presentations did not differ between the two participant groups, although all participants preferred the unified menu presentation to the fragmented. Directions for further research to deepen the understanding and implications of these results are discussed.

Keywords: People with dyslexia · Web navigation · Menu organization · Menu visibility · Eye gaze patterns

1 Introduction

People with dyslexia have difficulties in processing language, which manifests itself in difficulties with reading, writing and spelling [53]. However, people with dyslexia often have difficulties beyond language, and may also have difficulties with numbers, spatial orientation, hand-eye coordination, and short-term memory. Whether these additional difficulties are part of dyslexia, or relate to other conditions which co-occur frequently with dyslexia, is a subject of fierce debate [8, 32]. However, from a practical point of view, people with dyslexia do often have these additional difficulties and 5%–10% of the population have dyslexia to a greater or less extent [51], depending on their native language [12]. For example, in the United Kingdom, it is estimated that 10% of the population have some aspects of dyslexia, with 4% of the population being severely affected [5, 31].

D. Lamas et al. (Eds.): INTERACT 2019, LNCS 11746, pp. 115–133, 2019.
https://doi.org/10.1007/978-3-030-29381-9_8

A growing body of research in HCI has explored the difficulties that people with dyslexia have with technology and how to use technology to support them in overcoming their difficulties. Most of the research has explored how to make text easier to read, both in terms of the presentation of standard typefaces [33, 35, 38–40, 42–44, 48, 49, 52] but also by developing new typefaces especially for dyslexic readers [7, 34, 37, 55]. Research has also investigated how to support writing and particularly spell-checking [13, 14], reading and producing mathematics [10] web search [21–23, 28], computer coding [25, 36] and the use of multimedia [3].

One area in which people with dyslexia have been shown to have difficulties is in the navigation of digital material. Freire, Petrie and Power [11] found that navigation problems were the second most common problem on websites for participants with dyslexia, accounting for 12.4% of all their problems. However, little research has been undertaken about the detailed nature of these problems and how web navigation might be improved for people with dyslexia, apart from some exploratory work by Al-Wabil and colleagues [1, 2]. On the other hand, there has been a considerable amount of research on how best to present web navigation for users in general [30]. Therefore, this study investigated the effects of two aspects of web navigation, the organization and visibility of menus with a sample of dyslexia participants and compared their performance, eye gaze patterns and opinions on a range of measures with a similar sample of non-dyslexic participants. We hope this will provide some initial useful results and stimulate further research on this topic.

2   Related Work

Most of the research in HCI for people with dyslexia has investigated how best to present text on screens for this user group. A number of different aspects of text have been investigated, including typeface [39], font size [33, 39, 40], character and line spacing [44, 48, 49, 52], line length [43, 48] and text and background colour [35, 38, 42]. A comprehensive review of this literature is beyond the scope of this paper, however current recommendations from this body of research are to use 18 point sans serif text with relatively short line lengths and wider vertical line and character spacing. Although there is much discussion about the possible effects of text and background colour on reading for people with dyslexia, there are no strong recommendations on this aspect of text presentation, as research results are mixed [28, 35, 42]. In all, these recommendations do largely agree with recommendations which have existed for some years from user organizations which have probably been based on more anecdotal evidence [5].

Another area related to the optimal presentation of text for people with dyslexia has been the development of a number of typefaces which it is argued are easier for people with dyslexia to read, for example Dyslexie [7], OpenDyslexic [34], ReadRegular[TM] [37], and Sylexiad [55]. However, the current scientific evidence is that these typefaces do not improve reading speed or accuracy (most studies have used the sans serif typeface Arial as a comparison) and participants do not prefer them compared with standard typefaces [17, 18, 24, 35, 39, 41, 56]. Most of this research has been conducted with children, although Rello and Baeza-Yates [39, 41] worked with participants with a wide range of ages (11–50 years).

Research has also investigated other areas of the use of digital technologies by people with dyslexia. For example, a number of researchers have investigated how dyslexic and non-dyslexic people conduct searches on the web. MacFarlane and colleagues [21–23] found that search behaviour of dyslexic and non-dyslexic web users is very different, with dyslexic users finding fewer relevant search returns in a given time and having very different eye gaze patterns. Morris et al. [28] also found that dyslexic web users have difficulty identifying relevant search returns, perhaps because they are seeking pages which are not cluttered or dense in information. These differences in judgements of relevance were further supported by an online study.

Al-Wabil, Zaphiris and Wilson [1, 2] appear to be the only researchers who have investigated difficulties specifically in web navigation for people with dyslexia. In their first study [1] they interviewed 10 people with dyslexia about their experiences with web navigation. A number of interesting themes emerged, particularly that the interviewees did not find common navigational support tools such as breadcrumb trails and site maps very useful and that they preferred to navigate with the Back and Forward buttons on a website, as they could more clearly see the effects of their actions. On the use of menus for navigation, all interviewees stressed the importance of having menus consistent throughout a site, but opinions on dynamic menus differed. Some interviewees found them hard to interact with, while several interviewees found having dynamic menus reduced the visual clutter on a page which was helpful. In a second study, Al-Wabil et al. [2] investigated the eye gaze patterns of dyslexic and non-dyslexic web users in navigating three websites. Unfortunately, only two dyslexic web users participated and one of the control group of four non-dyslexic web users may have been an undiagnosed dyslexic (but was kept in the non-dyslexic group). However, the results suggested that the number of fixations, fixation duration and eye gaze patterns were different in relation to navigation between dyslexic and non-dyslexic web users.

While little research has investigated the performance or opinions of dyslexic web users with navigation and specifically menus on websites, there has been a substantial body of research on both aspects of web navigation for users in general, a recent review [30] covers 13 studies, without going into more unconventional and innovative menu types such as floating pie [46], radial [29, 47], flower [4] and leaf [45] menus. Some studies have found that there is no difference in performance between menus placed on the left or right of a webpage [9, 16], although left is now much more common, at least in English language websites. Similarly, some research has found [27] that static or dynamic menus do not affect performance or the perception of being lost. However, other research [19] has found that static menus are faster and easier (as measured by eye fixations) than dynamic ones, although this may interact with task complexity. Clearly a great deal more research could be conducted on this topic, although it may have little effect on web design fashions.

In this study we decided to investigate the effects of two aspects of web navigation for participants with dyslexia which had been investigated or mentioned in previous research, the organization and visibility of menus. The performance, eye gaze patterns and preferences were compared with a similar sample of non-dyslexic participants in order to investigate whether dyslexic web users would benefit from particular web menu presentations.

3 Method

3.1 Design

Participants navigated through a website about tourism in Canada and answered four questions, the answers to which were in different parts of the website. They were not allowed to use a search engine to find the answers. The order of tasks was counterbalanced.

The experiment had a $2 \times 2 \times 2$ between-participants design with Participant Group (Dyslexic vs Non-Dyslexic), Menu Organisation (Unified vs Fragmented, see Sect. 3.2) and Menu Visibility (Visible vs Dynamic, see Sect. 3.2) as the between participants variables. The choice of these two variables in menu organization was motivated by the fact that they have been investigated with non-dyslexic web users [e.g. 19, 27], although no clear results have emerged as to which configuration is more appropriate. Thus our results contribute to the body of knowledge about non-dyslexic web users as well as dyslexic ones. In addition, dyslexic participants in [1] were asked to comment on static versus dynamic menus, although there was no consensus about whether they were helpful or difficult.

There were three groups of dependent variables: (1) eye gaze behaviour, (2) performance and (3) participants' opinions.

The eye gaze measures were divided into two further groups, menu scanpath measures and Areas of Interest (AoI) measures.

Menu scanpath measures. The menu scanpath is the sequence of fixations of the eyes as participants look at the menus on the webpages.

The measures taken were:

- total length of the scanpath (i.e. total number of fixations)
- number of different items in the scanpath (i.e. number of different places where the participant looked)
- number of revisits (i.e. number of places to which the participant returned). Thus, total length = number of different items + number of revisits.

In addition, the following eye gaze measures were taken for three Areas of Interest (AoIs): main menus, sub-menus and target menu item (the item the participant should follow to complete the task):

- First fixation duration in the AoI (measured in milliseconds, msec)
- Number of fixations in the AoI
- Mean fixation duration in the AoI (msec)
- Total dwell time in the AoI (msec)

The first fixation duration is thought to reflect the attention-getting property of an AoI, the number of fixations and number of revisits are thought to be good indicators of the importance of an AoI or its noticeability, while mean fixation duration and total dwell time are thought to reflect engagement of a participant with the AoI [6].

The performance measures were:

- Time from opening the page to first mouse click (whether it is the correct or wrong target) (measured in msec)
- Task completion time (measured in msec)
- Number of correct answers to comprehension questions

The participants' opinion measures were ratings on 7-point Likert items of the website in terms of 'ease of use', 'ease of remembering' and 'ease of learning'. A lower rating indicated a more positive opinion.

Ethics approval for this study was granted by Physical Science Ethics Committee of the University of York.

3.2 Participants

On recruitment, participants were asked to complete a validated screening tool for dyslexia [54] (see Sect. 3.3). A total of 64 participants took part, 32 were classified as non-dyslexic and 32 as dyslexic. All participants were native English speakers with normal vision or vision correctable with spectacles.

The non-dyslexic group comprised 13 females and 19 males with ages ranging from 18 to 42 years ($M = 22.25$, $SD = 4.59$). Nineteen were undergraduate students, five were Masters students, five were PhD students (one was working part time) and three were employed. All of them had more than six years web experience (mean: 5.78, SD = 1.07, on a 7-point Likert item).

The dyslexic group were matched as closely as possible to the dyslexic group, they comprised 18 females and 14 males with ages ranging from 18 to 44 years ($M = 20.61$, $SD = 4.70$). Twenty-five were undergraduate students, six were Masters students and one was employed. All of them had more than six years web experience (mean: 5.32, SD = 0.98).

Participants were given a £10 Amazon gift voucher to thank them for participating in the experiment.

3.3 Materials and Equipment

The equipment set-up for the experiment is illustrated in Fig. 1. Participants used a wireless keyboard, a wireless mouse and a monitor to read and navigate the website and answer questions, while the researcher used a laptop. The laptop was connected to the eye tracker camera (SMI Red250 Mobile[1]), below the participant's monitor (via USB cable) and their monitor (via VGA cable). A Bluetooth USB dongle for the participant's wireless mouse and keyboard were also attached to the laptop. Viewing distance between the participant and the monitor screen was approximately 60 cm (see Sect. 3.4).

---

[1] https://www.smivision.com/.

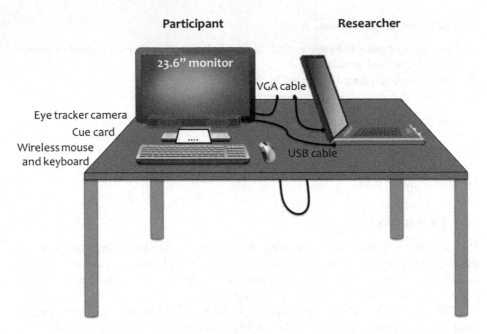

Fig. 1. Equipment set up

An online version of the Adult Self-Report of Dyslexia (ARQ, [54]) was used to establish whether participants were dyslexic or not, in addition to their self-report. The questionnaire asks information about reading habits, literacy and any dyslexia symptoms. Participants were categorised as non-dyslexic if their score was between 0 to 10, and dyslexic if their score was above 10.

An initial questionnaire collected information about participants' use of the web and demographic information.

Two web sites (a practice web site and an experimental web site) and five navigational tasks (one practice and four experimental tasks) were developed. Each task involved answering one multiple choice question with three answer options.

The experimental web site was about tourism in Canada, developed using content adapted from the Lonely Planet Canada web site[2] and [20]. Four versions of the experimental web site were developed, one each for the combinations of the Menu Organization and Menu Visibility variables. Menus were either Unified (located only on top of the page, see Figs. 2 and 3) or Fragmented (split between the top and left side of the webpage, see Figs. 4 and 5). Sub-menus were either Visible (visible to the participant at all times, see Figs. 2 and 4) or Dynamic (appearing only when the participant hovered over with the mouse, see Figs. 3 and 5).

---

[2] https://www.lonelyplanet.com/canada.

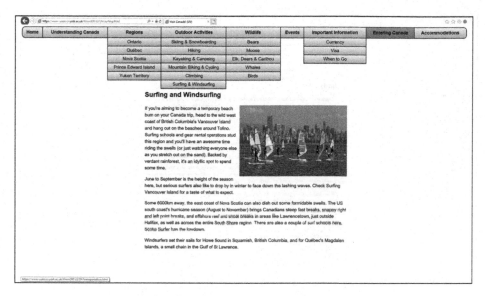

Fig. 2. Experimental website page with unified and visible menus

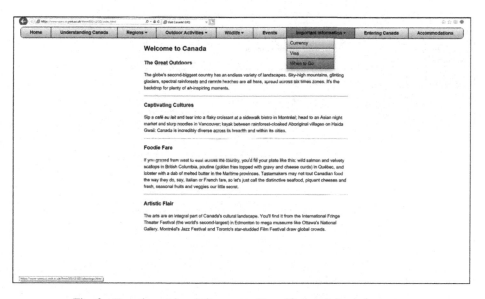

Fig. 3. Experimental website page with unified and dynamic menus

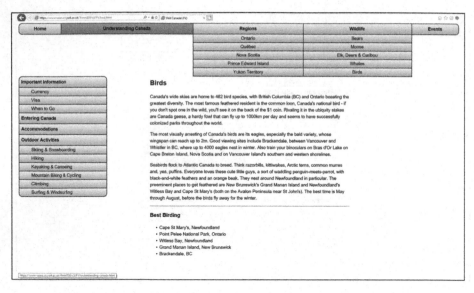

Fig. 4. Experimental website page with fragmented and visible menus

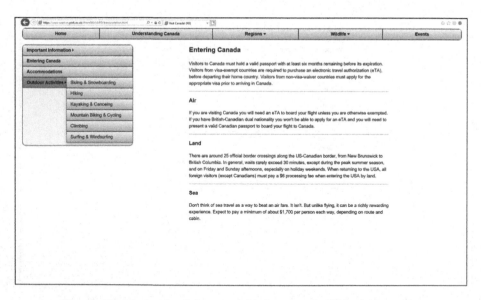

Fig. 5. Experimental website page with fragmented and dynamic menus

The text on the web pages was presented left-justified, 80–90 characters per line (not including spaces), font size 14 point, 1.5 line spacing, black on a white background. A limited number of images were included so as not to distract the participants too much from the text and menus. Menus had a linear gradient colour from light grey (#c1c1c1, RGB (193, 193, 193)) to very light grey (#f5f5f5, RGB (245, 245, 245)).

When hovered over with a mouse, the menu item temporarily changed its background colour, a linear gradient colour from pure orange (#f8ac00, RGB (248, 172, 0) to soft orange (#fac754, RGB (250, 199, 84)). All menus, text passages and images fit into one screen on the monitor, so no scrolling was required to find information (that would have made the eye gaze analysis much more complicated).

A practice website was created with a very similar design to the experimental website, although the material was on a different topic, the biology of insects.

Questions were developed for participants to search for answers in the website. Multiple choice questions were used to make the task less onerous for the participants and easier for the researchers to score. A typical question was "How many official border crossings are there along the US-Canadian border?". A pool of 9 questions was generated and their difficulty assessed. Five participants (students and staff in the Deparmtnet of Computer Science) searched the website and answered the questions. After each question they rated how difficult it was to find the answer (on a 9 point Likert item, 1 = very difficult to 9 = not at all difficult) and indicated whether they had known the answer before viewing the website. Four questions from the pool were chosen, based on accuracy (all five participants were able to find the answer), difficulty (two questions were relatively easy, mean rating of 5.8, two questions were more difficult, mean ratings 7.0 and 7.6), and the fact that none of the participants knew the answer beforehand.

Small cue cards (9 cm × 12 cm) with the questions were created and placed below the participant's monitor as they tried to answer each question, so if the participant forgot the question, they could glance down and remind themselves of it.

A final questionnaire measured participants' opinion of the ease of use, ease of remembering and ease of learning of the menu structures on 7-point Likert items. It was decided not to use a standardized usability questionnaire such as the SUS as we wanted to specifically measure participants' opinions of the menus, not the whole website. All the standardized questionnaires considered were found to be too broad in their scope for the current study.

3.4   Procedure

Participants were asked to complete the ARQ before they came for their experimental session, in order to assign them to the appropriate participant group. The experiment session took place in a quiet room so participants could concentrate on the task (particularly important for the dyslexic participants). Participants were given a brief explanation about the purpose of the study and the tasks they were going to undertake. They were given a chance to ask any questions, before completing an informed consent form and the initial questionnaire.

Participants were asked to sit comfortably and adjust the height of the chair and the gap between their body and the desk. The monitor was then adjusted so the viewing distance from the participant to the screen was as close to 60 cm as possible. Participants were asked to minimise head and body movement during the experiment to optimise the accuracy of the eye tracking equipment.

The eye tracking equipment was then used to calibrate and validate the participant's eye gaze. After a successful calibration, the participant was given a task on the practice website to familiarise them with the experimental procedure. They then moved to the experimental website and completed the four experimental tasks. The calibration and validation of their eye gaze was repeated at the beginning of each task. Questions were provided on screen, but also on a small cue card placed under the monitor (see Fig. 1), so if the participant forgot what they were looking for, they could glance at the card. The order of tasks was counter-balanced between participants. After all four tasks were completed, participants completed the final questionnaire, were encouraged to ask questions about the study and offered the Amazon gift voucher.

3.5   Data Preparation

Data were summed across the four tasks from each participant. Areas of Interest (AoIs) were created for the main menu, sub-menus and the relevant target menu item for each task and each version of the website. Data for first fixation duration in the AoI, number of fixations in the AoI, mean fixation duration for the AoI, total dwell time in the AoI, first time of mouse click, task completion time were all extracted from the eye tracking program.

For the menu scanpath analysis, each item in the main menu and sub-menus was allocated a code and the sequence of items visited was manually extracted from the eye tracking recording. Then the total length of the scanpath, the number of different items in the scanpath and the number of revisits to items were calculated. For example, if the sequence of items visited was ABCDEDEDC, the total length would be 9, the number of different items would be 5 and the number of revisits would be 4.

All dependent variables were visually analysed using histograms to check for normality of distribution. Outliers for all variables in eye gaze behaviour measures and some variables in performance measures (time of first mouse click, task completion time) were adjusted using the *winsorization* technique [15]. In this technique, outliers were adjusted if the values below or above than *Mean* $\pm$ *2SD*.

The majority of the data were normally distributed and the variances were homogeneous, so parametric statistics were used.

4   Results and Discussion

4.1   Eye Gaze Behaviour: Menu Scanpaths

$2 \times 2 \times 2$ ANOVAs were conducted with participant group (non-dyslexic and dyslexic), menu organisation (unified and fragmented) and menu visibility (visible and dynamic) as the between participants independent variables. The dependent variables were total length of scanpath, number of different Items in the scanpath and number of revisits.

On the ANOVA for total length (measured in number of items in the scanpath), there was a significant main effect for participant group with a large effect size, $F(1, 49) = 9.02$, $p = .004, \eta_p^2 = .15$. Dyslexic participants had significantly longer paths than non-dyslexic participants (mean Dyslexic: 25.79, SD: 17.11; mean non-dyslexic: 19.34, SD: 13.37).

There was also a significant main effect for menu organization with a medium effect size, F $(1, 49) = 3.88$, p $= .05$, $\eta_p^2 = .07$. Scanpaths were significantly longer in the fragmented menu condition compared to the unified menu condition (mean fragmented: 24.05, SD: 16.20; mean unified: 20.87, SD: 14.88). No other effects were significant.

On the ANOVA for the number of different items in the scanpath, there was a significant main effect for participant group with a medium effect size, F $(1, 49) = 5.46$, p $= .024$, $\eta_p^2 = .10$. Dyslexic participants viewed more menu items than non-dyslexic participants (mean Dyslexic: 12.18, SD: 6.81; mean non-dyslexic: 10.47, SD: 6.35). No other effects were significant.

On the ANOVA for number of revisits, there was a significant main effect for participant group with a large effect size, F $(1, 49) = 9.06$, p $= .004$, $\eta_p^2 = .16$. Dyslexic participants made significantly more revisits to menu items than non-dyslexic participants (mean dyslexic: 13.37, SD: 10.95; mean non-dyslexic: 8.80, SD: 7.81). There was also a significant main effect for menu organization with a medium effect size, F $(1, 49) = 3.82$, p $= .05$, $\eta_p^2 = .07$. There were significantly more revisits in the fragmented menu condition compared to the unified menu condition (mean fragmented: 12.05, SD: 10.25; mean unified: 9.98, SD: 9.09). No other effects were significant.

These results show strong differences in menu scanpaths between the dyslexic and the non-dyslexic participants. Dyslexic participants had significantly longer scanpaths, so they looked at more items in the menus before making a selection than non-dyslexic participants. This was due both to the fact that they looked at significantly more different menu items and they revisited significantly more menu items than the non-dyslexic participants. So, they look around at more menu items and go back to items more before selecting a menu item to move to. Further research is needed to understand whether this is a robust effect and if so, why this is the case. Bylinskii et al. [6] argue that the number of revisits to an item reflects its noticeability, however as this is a differential effect between dyslexic and non-dyslexic participants it could be that the dyslexic participants found the menu items more difficult to read or that they have a greater need to be sure of where they are going before they make a selection, as they are more worried about navigating through web pages. This behaviour certainly slows down their use of the web.

There was also an effect of menu organization on scanpaths for both dyslexic and non-dyslexic participants. Fragmented menu presentation resulted in significantly longer scanpaths and this was due to a significantly higher number of revisits rather than a greater number of different items visited (as there was no significant different in the number of different items visited). So, fragmenting the menu may create uncertainty in all web users, and they need to revisit items before making a selection. Only one of the previous studies found [25] investigated the pattern of scanpaths in relation to different menu organisation. Although it conducted interesting analyses, that study only investigated scanpaths in terms large areas of the web page, one of which was the menu. Thus, the researchers were not able to investigate how the menu organization affected the way in which participants interacted with components of the menu at a fine-grained level of individual menu items. Our results suggest that investigating the effects of menu structure in more detail could yield useful results.

4.2   Eye Gaze Behaviour: Areas of Interest

$2 \times 2 \times 2$ ANOVAs were conducted with participant group (non-dyslexic and dyslexic), menu organisation (unified and fragmented) and menu visibility (visible and dynamic) as the between participants independent variables. The dependent variables were first fixation duration, number of fixations, mean fixation duration, and dwell time, all for each type of AoI (main menu, submenus, target menu Item).

The ANOVA on first fixation duration (measured in msec) showed no significant effects for any of the AoIs.

The ANOVA on number of fixations for main menus showed no significant main effects but a significant interaction between menu organization and menu visibility, F $(1, 56) = 6.17$, $p = .02$, $\eta_p^2 = .10$. Figure 6 shows that in unified menus there were more fixations with visible submenus, but with fragmented menus there were more fixations with dynamic submenus.

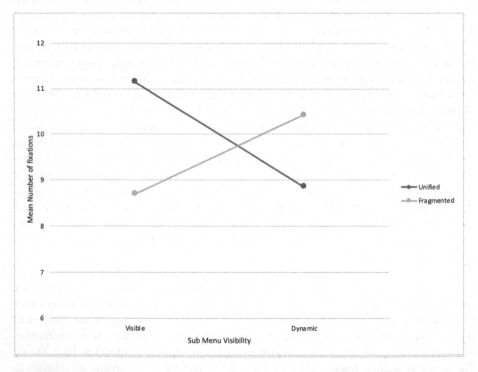

Fig. 6. Interaction for number of fixations between menu organization and visibility for main menu AOI

The ANOVA on number of fixations on submenus showed a significant main effect for participant group, F $(1, 56) = 5.69$, $p = .02$, $\eta_p^2 = .09$. Non-dyslexic participants had a significantly lower number of fixations on the submenus (mean: 9.94, SD: 3.86) than dyslexic participants (mean: 12.31, SD: 4.12).

The ANOVA on number of fixations on target menu items showed no significant effects.

The ANOVA on mean fixation duration (measured in msec) showed no significant effects for either main menus, submenus or target menu item.

The ANOVA on dwell time (measured in msec) showed no significant effects for main menus. However, the ANOVA for dwell time on submenus showed a significant main effect for participant group with a moderate effect size, $F (1, 56) = 4.19$, $p = .02$, $\eta_p^2 = .07$. Non-dyslexic participants had a significantly shorter dwell times on the submenus (mean: 2.58, SD: 1.13) than dyslexic participants (mean: 3.18, SD: 1.20).

The ANOVA on dwell time on target menu item showed no significant effects.

There were fewer interesting differences in the eye gaze measures related to AOIs than the overall scanpath measures. The first fixation duration, which it has been argued measures the attention getting property of an item [6], showed no significant effects. This is perhaps not surprising, as the experimental website was deliberately kept rather bland with mainly text, so there were not particularly attention-grabbing elements, particularly in the menus.

There were significant differences in the number of fixations on menu items, with dyslexic participants having significantly more fixations on submenus than non-dyslexic participants. However, the meaning of this result is not clear: in terms of interest in visual elements, more fixations are thought to indicate greater interest, but in terms of reading the text in menu items, more fixations are thought to indicate greater difficulty in reading. So, it may be that it was taking the dyslexic participants longer to read the text of the menu items.

There was also a significant interaction between menu organization and visibility on number of fixations (see Fig. 6), with unified menus with visible submenus having more fixations than with dynamic submenus, whereas for fragmented menus the number of fixations was reversed between visible and dynamic submenus. The first result makes obvious sense: if the main menu is all in one place and the submenus are visible, there will be more items to immediately look at, so more fixations will occur. However, the second result is more difficult to understand, why should dynamic menus create more fixations if the main menu is fragmented? Further research is needed to investigate whether this effect is replicable.

Mean fixation duration also showed no significant effects. However, overall dwell time on submenus showed a significant effect with dyslexic participants spending longer time on submenus than non-dyslexic participants. This result fits with the other results from the scanpath analysis and the number of fixations, that dyslexic participants are spending more time looking at the menus, particularly the submenus.

The two previous studies which investigated number of fixations in menu exploration [19, 25] did not conduct as fine-grained an analysis as presented here, so it is hard to make comparisons. Leuthhold et al. [19] only investigated the number of fixations before the first mouse click and found dynamic menus produced significantly more fixations than simple menus. This is similar to our finding that there was a significant interaction for number of fixations between menu organization and visibility, but it does not help explain the interaction. As mentioned in the previous section, McCarthy et al. [25] did not conduct an analysis below the whole menu structure, so their investigation of number of fixations is not comparable with ours. Further research is needed, both comparing dyslexic and non-dyslexic participants and the effects of menu organization and visibility on all participants, to establish whether these effects are robust.

4.3   Performance Variables

$2 \times 2 \times 2$ ANOVAs were conducted with participant group (non-dyslexic and dyslexic), menu organisation (unified and fragmented) and menu visibility (visible and dynamic) as the between participants independent variables. The dependent variables were time to first mouse click and task completion time as dependent variables. There was a ceiling effect in the number of correct answers to the comprehension questions, with most participants answering all questions correctly, so no analysis was undertaken on that dependent variable. However, this did mean that both dyslexic and non-dyslexic participants answered the questions very largely correctly.

On the ANOVA for time to first mouse click (measured in msec), there was a significant main effect for participant group with a large effect size, $F(1, 56) = 7.64$, $p < .01$, $\eta_p^2 = .12$. Non-dyslexic participants clicked sooner dyslexic participants (mean non-dyslexic: 5.56 s, SD: 2.07; mean dyslexic: 7.41, SD: 3.18). No other effects were significant.

On the ANOVA for task completion time (measured in msec), there was a significant main effect for participant group with a large effect size, $F(1, 56) = 5.34$, $p = .02$, $\eta_p^2 = .09$. Non-dyslexic participants completed the tasks faster than dyslexic participants (mean non-dyslexic: 26.78 s, SD: 10.69; mean dyslexic: 32.97, SD: 10.88). No other effects were significant.

Not surprisingly, given the differences in the scanpath behaviour between dyslexic and non-dyslexic participants, there were also differences in performance between the two participant groups. Dyslexic participants were significantly slower in making their first mouse click and in completing tasks.

4.4   Participant Opinions

Participants separately rated three aspects of the menu structures: their ease of use (EoU), ease of remembering (where items were, EoR) and ease of learning (EoL), each on a 7-point Likert item (with low ratings indicating most positive values). However, there were significant correlations between the three sets of ratings (EoU-EoR $r = .49$, EoU-EoL $r = .56$, EoR-EoL $r = .63$, all $p < .01$), suggesting they were measuring one underlying construct. Therefore, a mean rating (MenuRating) was calculated from the three ratings, which also creates a more robust measure.

A $2 \times 2 \times 2$ ANOVA was conducted with participant group (non-dyslexic and dyslexic), menu organisation (unified and fragmented) and menu visibility (visible and dynamic) as the independent variables and MenuRating as the dependent variable. There was a significant main effect for menu organization with a large effect size, $F(1, 55) = 14.95$, $p = .00$, $\eta_p^2 = .21$. The unified menu organization was rated significantly more positively than the fragmented menu organization (mean unified: 1.90, SD: 0.82; mean fragmented: 2.82, SD: 1.01). No other effects were significant.

Interestingly the differences between dyslexic and non-dyslexic participants eye gaze behaviour and consequent performance did not lead to different opinions of the website. There were no differences between the groups in their ratings of the overall ease of use/remembering/learning the website. However, there was a significant difference in participants' ratings of menu organization, with the unified menu presentation rated significantly better than the fragmented presentation. There were no significant differences between ratings of the visible or dynamic submenus.

5 Discussion and Conclusions

This study investigated the effects of two aspects of web navigation, the organization and visibility of menu items on the eye gaze patterns, performance and preferences of dyslexic and non-dyslexic web users. A number of interesting results have emerged.

On the eye gaze measures, the scanpaths followed by participants showed significant differences between dyslexic and non-dyslexic participants and between fragmented and unified menu organization. Dyslexic participant had significantly longer scanpaths, which was due to both a significantly larger number of different menu items visited and a significantly larger number of revisits to menu items. Thus, the scanning behaviour of dyslexic and non-dyslexic participants was different. There were also significantly longer scanpaths for all participants in the fragmented menu conditions, which was due to a significantly greater number of revisits to items. Thus, fragmented menus slowed participants down as they revisited items before making a decision of where to go to next in the website.

On the analysis of eye gaze on specific areas of interest (AoIs), only the number of fixations and the overall dwell time (which are related as measures) showed significant effects. For all participants there was a significant interaction between number of fixations between menu organization and visibility, although the result was rather difficult to interpret and further research is needed. In addition, dyslexic participants made significantly more fixations and have significantly longer dwell times on submenus. Combined with the results that dyslexic participants had longer scanpaths than non-dyslexic participants, this shows that dyslexic participants are spending more time (and potentially effort) exploring the menus.

The differences between dyslexic and non-dyslexic participants in terms of eye gaze behaviour also showed themselves in the performance measures. Dyslexic participants were significantly slower in making their first mouse click on a webpage than non-dyslexic participants, not surprising given their scanpaths were significantly longer. In addition, dyslexic participants were significantly slower in completing the tasks, which may have been due to slower reading times of the texts as well as slower times to investigate the menus. There were no effects of the menu organization or visibility on the performance measures.

Finally, there were significant effects in participants' opinions of the menu organization, but no differences between dyslexic and non-dyslexic participants in their opinions. Overall, all participants were significantly more positive about the unified menus than the fragmented menus; there were no significant differences in opinions of visible or static menus.

The study has a number of limitations which need to be considered. The main limitation is that the participants, both dyslexic and non-dyslexic, were almost all university students. While this makes them comparable groups, it probably means that the dyslexic participants have learnt good coping strategies to deal with their problems, to have reached higher education. It would be interesting to collect a further sample of participants with more severe dyslexia and compare their data with the current samples and with a matched non-dyslexic sample. A further limitation is that only one website was used, so some of the results could be due to the particularities of this website and its menus. It is important to replicate these results with a range of websites. Using a number of websites would also allow for a within participants design, so that the participants could experience the different menu presentations and compare them. This was not possible in the current study, as once participants had undertaken the tasks with one menu presentation, they would know where menu items and information were and be to answer the questions very quickly.

Nonetheless, we believe these results are an interesting and useful first set of detailed results of the eye gaze behaviour, performance and preferences of dyslexic and non-dyslexic web users in relation to several aspects of menu organization on websites. The eye gaze data is time consuming to analyse and it seems that analysing the scanpaths yielded the most useful data with little extra information being added by analysing the number of fixations and fixations durations, although these are standard eye gaze measures in the research literature. Interesting future research could use a retrospective verbal protocol, showing the participant their scanpath after they have completed a task, and asking them to explain why they looked where they did. This would throw light on why the dyslexic participants looked at more menu items and revisited more items before making a selection. In turn, this could lead to guidelines for better menu organization for both dyslexic and non-dyslexic web users.

Acknowledgements. We would like to thank all the dyslexic and non-dyslexic participants in the study for their time and effort. We would also like to thank our colleagues in the Department of Computer Science for their help in establishing the difficulty of the questions for the study.

References

1. Al-Wabil, A., Zaphiris, P., Wilson, S.: Web navigation for individuals with dyslexia: an exploratory study. In: Stephanidis, C. (ed.) UAHCI 2007. LNCS, vol. 4554, pp. 593–602. Springer, Heidelberg (2007). https://doi.org/10.1007/978-3-540-73279-2_66
2. Al-Wabil, A., Zaphiris, P., Wilson, S.: Examining visual attention of dyslexics on web navigation structures with eye tracking. In: Proceedings of the International Conference on Innovations in Information Technology (IIT 2008), pp. 717–721. IEEE (2008)
3. Andresen, A., Anmarkrud, Ø., Bråten, I.: Investigating multiple source use among students with and without dyslexia. Reading and Writing, (2009, in press)
4. Bailly, G., Lecolinet, E., Nigay, L.: Flower menus: a new type of marking menu with large menu breadth, within groups and efficient expert mode memorization. In: Proceedings of the Working Conference on Advanced Visual Interfaces (AVI 2008), pp. 15–22 (2008)
5. British Dyslexia Association: Background. https://www.bdadyslexia.org.uk/about. Accessed 2 Feb 2019

6. Bylinskii, Z., Borkin, M.A., Kim, N.W., Pfister, H., Oliva, A.: Eye fixation metrics for large scale evaluation and comparison of information visualizations. In: Burch, M., Chuang, L., Fisher, B., Schmidt, A., Weiskopf, D. (eds.) ETVIS 2015. MV, pp. 235–255. Springer, Cham (2017). https://doi.org/10.1007/978-3-319-47024-5_14
7. Dyslexie font. https://www.dyslexiefont.com/. Accessed 15 Jan 2019
8. Elliott, J.G., Grigorenko, E.L.: The Dyslexia Debate. Cambridge University Press, Cambridge (2014)
9. Faulkner, X., Hayton, C.: When left might not be right. J. Usability Stud. 6(4), 245–256 (2011)
10. Freda, C., Pagliara, S.M., Ferraro, F., Zanfardino, F., Pepino, A.: Dyslexia: study of compensatory software which aids the mathematical learning process of dyslexic students at secondary school and university. In: Miesenberger, K., Klaus, J., Zagler, W., Karshmer, A. (eds.) ICCHP 2008. LNCS, vol. 5105, pp. 742–746. Springer, Heidelberg (2008). https://doi.org/10.1007/978-3-540-70540-6_108
11. Freire, A.P., Petric, H., Power, C.: Empirical results from an evaluation of the accessibility of websites by dyslexic users. In: Proceedings of the Workshop on Accessible Design in the Digital World, Lisboa, Portugal. CEUR-WS.Org (2011)
12. Goulandris, N.E.: Dyslexia in Different Languages: Cross-linguistic Comparisons. Whurr Publishers, London (2003)
13. Gregor, P., Dickinson, A., Macaffer, A., Andreasen, P.: SecWord - a personal word processing environment for dyslexic computer users. Br. J. Edu. Technol. 34(3), 341–355 (2003)
14. Gregor, P., Newell, A.F.: An empirical investigation of ways in which some of the problems encountered by some dyslexics may be alleviated using computer techniques. In: Proceedings of the Fourth International ACM Conference on Assistive Technologies. ACM Press, New York (2000)
15. Hellerstein, J.M.: Quantitative Data Cleaning for Large Databases (2008). http://db.cs.berkeley.edu/jmh/papers/cleaning-unece.pdf. Accessed 28 Jan 2019
16. Kalbach, J., Bosenick, T.: Web page layout: a comparison between left and right justified site navigation menus. J. Digital Inf. 4(1) (2003)
17. Kuster, S.M., van Weerdenburg, M., Gompel, M., Bosman, A.M.: Dyslexie font does not benefit reading in children with or without dyslexia. Ann. Dyslexia 69(1), 25–42 (2018)
18. Leeuw, R.: Special font for dyslexia? Phd thesis, University of Twente (2010)
19. Leuthold, S., Schmutz, P., Bargas-Avila, J.A., Tuch, A.N., Opwis, K.: Vertical versus dynamic menus on the world wide web: Eye tracking study measuring the influence of menu design and task complexity on user performance and subjective preference. Comput. Hum. Behav. 27(1), 459–472 (2011)
20. Miller, K., et al.: Lonely Planet Canada. Lonely Planet (2017)
21. MacFarlane, A., Al-Wabil, A., Marshall, C., Albrair, A., Jones, S., Zaphiris, P.: The effect of dyslexia on information retrieval: a pilot study. J. Documentation 66(3), 307–326 (2010)
22. MacFarlane, A., Albrair, A., Marshall, C.R., Buchanan, G.: Phonological working memory impact on information searching: an investigation of dyslexia. In: Proceedings of the 4th Information Interaction in Context Symposium, pp. 27–34. ACM Press, New York (2012)
23. MacFarlane, A., Buchanan, G., Al-Wabil, A., Andrienko, G., Andrienko, N.: Visual analysis of dyslexia on search. In: Proceedings of Conference on Human Information Interaction and Retrieval (CHIIR 2017), pp 285 – 288. ACM Press, New York (2017)
24. Marinus, E., Mostard, M., Segers, E., Schubert, T.M., Madelaine, A., Wheldall, K.: A special font for people with dyslexia: does it work and if so, why? Dyslexia 22(3), 233–244 (2016)

25. McChesney, I., Bond, R.: Gaze behaviour in computer programmers with dyslexia – considerations regarding code style, layout and crowding. In: Proceedings of EMIP 2018. ACM Press, New York (2018)
26. Meindertsma, J.: The power of typefaces: Dyslexie. TXT **2016**(8–9), 56–59 (2016)
27. Melguizo, M.C.P., Vidgay, U., van Oostendorp, H.: Seeking information online: the influence of menu type, navigation path complexity and spatial ability on information gathering tasks. Behav. Inf. Technol. **31**(1), 59–70 (2012)
28. Morris, M.R., Fourney, A., Ali, A., Vonessen, L.: Understanding the needs of searchers with dyslexia. In: Proceedings of the 2018 CHI Conference on Human Factors in Computing Systems (CHI 2018). ACM Press, New York (2018)
29. Murano, P., Khan, I.N.: Pie menus or linear menus which is better? J. Emerg. Trends Comput. Inf. Sci. **6**(9), 476–481 (2015)
30. Murano, P., Sander, M.: User interface menu design performance and user preferences: a review and ways forward. Int. J. Adv. Comput. Sci. Appl. **7**(4), 355–361 (2016)
31. National Health Service: Overview – dyslexia. https://www.nhs.uk/conditions/dyslexia/. Accessed 2 Feb 2019
32. Nicolson, R.: Dyslexia: beyond the myth. Psychol. **18**(11), 658–659 (2005)
33. O'Brien, B.A., Mansfield, J.S., Legge, G.E.: The effect of print size on reading speed in dyslexia. J. Res. Reading **28**(3), 332–349 (2005)
34. Open Dyslexic. https://www.opendyslexic.org/. Accessed 29 Jan 2019
35. Pijpker, C.: Reading performance of dyslexics with a special font and a colored background. Phd thesis, University of Twente (2013)
36. Powell, N., Moore, D., Gray, J., Finlay, J., Reaney, J.: Dyslexia and learning computer programming. In: Proceedings of the 9th annual SIGSCE/SIGCUE ITiCSE Conference on Innovation and Technology in Computer Science Education (ITICSE 2004). ACM Press, New York (2004)
37. Read Regular. http://www.readregular.com/english/intro.html. Accessed 29 Jan 2019
38. Rello, L., Baeza-Yates, R.: Optimal colour to improve readability for people with dyslexia. Text Customization for Readability Online Symposium (2012). https://www.w3.org/WAI/RD/2012/text-customization/
39. Rello, L., Baeza-Yates, R.: Good fonts for dyslexia. In: Proceedings of the 15th International ACM SIGACCESS Conference on Computers and Accessibility. ACM Press, New York (2013)
40. Rello, L., Baeza-Yates, R.: How to present more readable text for people with dyslexia. Univ. Access Inf. Soc. **16**(1), 29–49 (2015)
41. Rello, L., Baeza-Yates, R.: The effect of font type on screen readability by people with dyslexia. ACM Trans. Accessible Comput. (TACCESS) **8**(4), 15 (2016)
42. Rello, L., Bigham, J.P.: Good background colours for readers: a study of people with and without dyslexia. In: Proceedings of the 19th International ACM SIGACCESS Conference on Computers and Accessbility. ACM Press, New York (2017)
43. Rello, L., Kanvinde, G., Baeza-Yates, R.: Layout guidelines for web text and a web service to improve accessibility for dyslexics. In: Proceedings of the International Cross-disciplinary Conference on Web Accessibility (W4A 2012). ACM Press, New York (2012)
44. Rello, L., Pielot, M., Marcos, M.-C., Carlini, R.: Size matters (spacing not): 18 points for a dyslexic-friendly Wikipedia. In: Proceedings of the 10th International Cross-Disciplinary Conference on Web Accessibility (W4A 2013). ACM Press, New York (2013)
45. Roudaut, A., Bailly, G., Lecolinet, E., Nigay, L.: Leaf menus: linear menus with stroke shortcuts for small handheld devices. In: Gross, T., Gulliksen, J., Kotzé, P., Oestreicher, L., Palanque, P., Prates, R.O., Winckler, M. (eds.) INTERACT 2009. LNCS, vol. 5726, pp. 616–619. Springer, Heidelberg (2009). https://doi.org/10.1007/978-3-642-03655-2_69

46. Rubio, J.M., Janecek, P.: Floating pie menus: enhancing the functionality of contextual tools. In: Adjunct Proceedings of the 15th Annual ACM Symposium on User Interface Software and Technology (UIST 2002). ACM Press, New York (2002)
47. Samp, K., Decker, S.: Supporting menu design with radial layouts. In: Proceedings of the International Conference on Advanced Visual Interfaces. ACM Press, New York (2010)
48. Schneps, M.H., Thomson, J.M., Chen, C., Sonnert, G., Pomplun, M.: E-readers are more effective than paper for some with dyslexia. PloS One 8(9), e75634 (2013)
49. Schoonewelle, A.: Typographical support for dyslexics: the effect of textual alternations on dyslexics' test scores. PhD thesis, Vrije Universiteit, Amsterdam (2013)
50. Schulz, T.: Internal validity in experiments for typefaces for people with dyslexia. In: Miesenberger, K., Bühler, C., Penaz, P. (eds.) ICCHP 2016. LNCS, vol. 9759, pp. 335–338. Springer, Cham (2016). https://doi.org/10.1007/978-3-319-41267-2_47
51. Siegel, L.S.: Perspectives on dyslexia. Paediatr. Child Health 11(9), 581–587 (2006)
52. Sjoblom, A.M., Eaton, E., Stagg, S.D.: The effects of letter spacing and coloured overlays on reading speed and accuracy in adult dyslexia. Br. J. Educ. Psychol. 86(4), 630–639 (2016)
53. Snowling, M.J.: Dyslexia, 2nd edn. Blackwell Publishers, Malden (2000)
54. Snowling, M.J., Dawes, P., Nash, H., Hulme, C.: Validity of a protocol for adult self-report of dyslexia and related difficulties. Dyslexia 18(1), 1–15 (2012)
55. Sylexiad. http://www.robsfonts.com/fonts/sylexiad. Accessed 29 Jan 2019
56. Wery, J.J., Diliberto, J.A.: The effect of a specialized dyslexia font, OpenDyslexic, on reading rate and accuracy. Ann. dyslexia 67(2), 114–127 (2017)

ELE - A Conversational Social Robot for Persons with Neuro-Developmental Disorders

Davide Fisicaro[✉], Franca Garzotto, Mirko Gelsomini, and Francesco Pozzi

Politecnico di Milano, P.zza Leonardo da Vinci, Milan, Italy
{davide.fisicaro,franca.garzotto,mirko.gelsomini,
francesco.pozzi}@polimi.it

Abstract. Several studies explore the use of social robots in interventions for persons with cognitive disability. This paper describes ELE, a plush social robot with an elephant appearance that has been designed as a conversational companion for persons with Neuro-Developmental Disorders (NDD). ELE speaks through the live voice of a remote caregiver, enriching the communication through body movements. It is integrated with a tool for automatic gathering and analysis of interaction data that support therapists in monitoring the users during the experience with the robotic companion. The paper describes the design and technology of ELE and presents an empirical study that involved eleven persons with NDD using the robot at a local therapeutic center. We compared user engagement in two story-telling experiences, one with ELE and one with a face-to-face human speaker. According to our results, the participants were more engaged with ELE than with the human storyteller, which indicates, although tentatively, the engagement potential of conversational social robots for persons with NDD.

Keywords: NDD (Neurodevelopmental Disorder) · Disability · Social robot · Conversational companion · Engagement · Storytelling

1 Introduction

Social robots are characterized by the capability of communicating and interacting with users in a social and engaging manner [17, 18]. Several studies explore the use of social robots in interventions for persons with Neuro-Developmental Disorders (NDD). NDD is a general term for a group of conditions with onset in the developmental period [1] that are associated primarily with the functioning of the brain and the neurological system and are characterized by impairments in the personal, social, academic, and occupational spheres. Examples of NDD include Attention-Deficit Hyperactivity Disorder (ADHD), Autism Spectrum Disorder (ASD) and Down Syndrome.

Electronic supplementary material The online version of this chapter (https://doi.org/10.1007/978-3-030-29381-9_9) contains supplementary material, which is available to authorized users.

© IFIP International Federation for Information Processing 2019
Published by Springer Nature Switzerland AG 2019
D. Lamas et al. (Eds.): INTERACT 2019, LNCS 11746, pp. 134–152, 2019.
https://doi.org/10.1007/978-3-030-29381-9_9

Social robots are thought [2, 7, 38–40] to elicit specific, desirable behaviors among persons with NDD, and to have the potential of promoting specific social skills. It is easier for persons with NDD to interact with robots than with humans because the former creates situations in which they can practice and learn in a safer and more pleasant manner [6, 9, 16]. Robots enable forms of embodied interactions that are appealing for these persons. They can offer human-like social cues (e.g., speaking, smiling) while maintaining object-like simplicity (e.g., limited facial expressions) and more generally provide sensory stimuli that are more predictable, less complex and less confusing [5, 7, 16].

The paper describes the design, implementation, and evaluation of ELE, a plush social robot that is intended to be used as a conversational companion during regular therapies for persons with NDD. ELE speaks through the digitally modified live voice of a remote caregiver and enriches verbal communication through body movements. The robot is integrated with a tool for automatic gathering and analysis of interaction data to support therapists' monitoring of the users during the experiences with ELE. We performed an empirical study at a local therapeutic center that aimed at evaluating the potential of ELE as a conversational companion for persons with NDD. The study involved eleven persons attending the center and their therapists. We compared participants' engagement in a story-telling experience with ELE against a similar one performed with a co-located human speaker. The results, although preliminary, show that participants were more engaged with ELE than with the face-to-face human storyteller, and indicate that conversational robots have a potential to increase engagement and motivation in interventions for subjects with NDD.

2 Related Work

In the last years, many researchers have investigated the application of social robots for persons with NDD, mainly considering children with autism (e.g., [3, 15, 16, 18–24, 30, 38–40]). Differently from other devices such as computers, tablets, and smartphones, social robots can engage children in the real world physically and emotionally, and offer unique opportunities of guided, personalized, and controlled social interaction and learning tasks [25]. Many social robots used in NDD interventions are remotely controlled by caregivers [16, 22, 26]. Autonomous behavior is implemented only in few cases, to support a specific learning task such as imitation, attention, communication, question-answering ability [27–29].

Several researchers explore the physical and dynamic characteristics of robots in relationship to subjects with NDD. Different shapes have been studies, e.g., "abstract", cartoon-like, or simplified or realistic human-like [3]; research suggests that individuals with NDD tend to prefer for something that is clearly "artificial" with respect to agents that have human-inspired characteristics [6, 31]. Some authors suggest that the shape of the robot should evoke a familiar element, such as a toy that the subject likes, or a cartoon character. For example, Teo [28] - a robot designed specifically for children with autism - resembles the popular cartoon characters of Minions. Puffy [7, 40] - an egg-shaped, inflatable, soft, and mobile robot – is inspired to Baymax, the inflatable healthcare robot of the popular movie Big Hero 6. The research reported in [32] and [33] shows that subjects with NDD may respond faster when cued by a robotic movement than human movement, and some social robots used in NDD therapy can move body parts [15, 22, 34, 35] or the entire body [7, 28, 40].

Several social robots exploit emotional features that seem to benefit children with NDD. Puffy [7] supports multisensory stimuli and multimodal interaction, can interpret child's intentions and emotion from her gestures and facial expressions, and can communicate emotions using sound and speech-based utterances, movements in space, and lights and projections embedded in its body. Keepon [22, 26] is a creature-like robot that is capable of expressing its attention (directing its gaze) and emotions (pleasure and excitement). An empirical study with autistic children showed that this robot triggered a sense of curiosity and security; the subjects spontaneously engaged in dyadic interaction with it, and then shared with the adult caregiver's the pleasure and the surprise they found in Keepon. KISMET [36] is an emotional robot which exploits eyebrows, ears, and mouth movements to expresses emotions depending on the way a human interacts with the robot. Teo [2, 41] supports the user's manifestation of emotions through the personalization of the robot body. Teo is equipped with a set of a detachable pieces like eyes, eyelids, or mouths that can be attached to its body and enables children to create "face" expressions. Its sensorized body can distinguish among caresses, hugs, and two levels of violent punches or slaps; the robot reacts to the different type of manipulations and expresses corresponding emotional states – happiness, angriness, or fear - using light, sound, vibrations, and movements.

3   The Design of ELE

ELE is a social robot that speaks through the live voice of a remote caregiver and enriching the communication using non-verbal signals, i.e., the movements of its body (i.e. trunk, eyes, ears). The goal of ELE is to play as a conversational companion, engaging users in dialogues or story-telling or story-listening tasks.

ELE is intended to address several needs: to mitigate a person's stress during therapies; to create moments of fun and trigger engagement; to enable the verbal communication between a person with NDD and a remote caregiver (e.g., therapist or educator) in situations when the former is unable to leave his/her home or to receive specific on-site intervention; to improve communication skills; to help therapists monitor the person's behavior remotely and automatically gather data that can be helpful for therapeutic and assessment purposes.

ELE is inspired by Huggable [10], a robotic teddy bear developed at MIT and used as a conversational mediator between hospitalized children and their caregivers. With Huggable, the remote operator can listen to the user via microphones; he/she can talk to the child by typing on a mobile device the text for the robot to speak, or by interacting directly with the robot through the embedded speaker (voice deformation features make the operator's voice not recognizable).

ELE has similar capabilities but provides some original features.

(1) It is integrated with a powerful application for therapists that enables caregivers to control the body behavior of the robot (not only eyes), i.e., movements of ears, eyes and trunk (and associated sounds). These therapist-controlled body expressions during a session of dialogue convey a personality-rich character to ELE. In addition, they are means to offer contextualized non-verbal backchanneling during the conversation. The term *backchannel* is used in linguistic to denote phatic expressions, primarily serving a social or meta-conversational purpose (e.g., to assess or acknowledge what is being said, to express attention or interest). The importance of verbal and non-verbal backchanneling in human-robot interaction has been demonstrated by a study using the robot Tega [12]. This study shows that humans are more engaged when interacting with a robot that is able to move (e.g., nodding) according with the semantic behind the conversation rather than a robot moving randomly.

(2) The application integrated with ELE also supports the transmission of both the audio and the *video* stream to and from the robot and enables to monitor the behavior of the person using ELE remotely. Therapists can monitor the user during the conversation, viewing the video recording and visualizing the evolution of the NDD person's emotions that are detected automatically from the streamed video. The same information can be visualized and inspected after a session, which is helpful for therapists to reflect on the person's behavior, inspect his or her progression, and tune future interventions.

(3) The design process of ELE has taken into account the replicability of the robot at *affordable* cost, which is an important issue for the adoption of a technology in real-life settings. Rather than building a new toy fully from scratch and at a high cost, as it happens for Huggable, we created ELE by reusing a cheap commercial plush toy provided with body movement capability and equipped it with off-the-shelf devices for input/output, control and connectivity devices. The result is a smart toy that can be developed, and replicated, at an affordable cost.

The first step in our design process was to identify a commercial plush toy that addressed the above requirements. Our choice was based on some needs pinpointed by NDD therapists we collaborate with:

- small size, because ELE is intended to be used also with children [3, 15];
- low cost;
- a shape different from the ones of typical pet toys (e.g., a dog, a cat, a teddy bear) to make the robot a unique entity;
- movement capabilities;
- colors that have positive psychological qualities [14] and are not problematic for persons with visual impairments.

We analyzed the rich catalogue offered by a worldwide known toy manufacturer - Giochi Preziosi - and finally selected a stuffed elephant (Fig. 1) sized 14 × 7 × 5.5 in. Embedded in this commercial toy there are motors to move ears, trunk, and eyes. Movements of eyes and ears exploit a single DC (Direct Current) motor that rotates forward and backward. Another DC motor is used for moving the trunk up and down.

The skin colors are pale blue (most of the body), and, in some specific body parts, pale grey, pink and white. Blue is the color of the sky and sea; it is often associated with depth and stability and symbolizes trust, loyalty, wisdom, confidence, intelligence, and truth. Pink is thought to have a calming effect on people. Pale grey is considered to be a non-deflective neutral color that provokes neither a positive nor negative reaction [14].

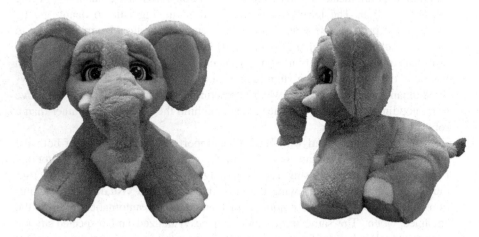

Fig. 1. Front and left view of ELE.

We equipped the commercial toy with input/output devices and an embedded board. Input devices consists in a microphone and a camera, while the output device is a non-amplified speaker. The speaker and the microphone are positioned inside ELEs body, and the camera is positioned over ELE's head and hidden by a hat. These components as well as the native motors are controlled by an embedded board that also manages the communication with the dashboard application for the remote therapist.

4   Dashboard for Therapists

Therapists can control ELE remotely through an application called *dashboard* available on PC, tablet, or smartphone. The dashboard is accessible via a web page hosted on ELE's *internal* web server, automatically loaded when the system is turned on. The visual interface has been co-designed with the therapists participating in the project and its usability was evaluated during an empirical test with external therapists from a different therapeutic center.

A control panel (Fig. 2-right side) enables therapists to control ELE movements and define the audio settings. Predefined combination of sounds and movements, defined with therapists, are provided to facilitate control and provide backchanneling during the conversation. An example is the "Trumpeting": while ELE reproduces a bellow, it moves its trunk up-down-up and ears move back and forth one time. Audio/video stream can be activated by the operator at any time.

Fig. 2. Dashboard as seen by the remote operator during a session. On the left side, video stream and emotion graph. On the right side, ELE's control (voice modification and motors).

The progression of emotions extracted from the video are visualized as graphs on a separate visualization panel, which also offers a "filter" function to select a subset of the available emotions to display (Fig. 3).

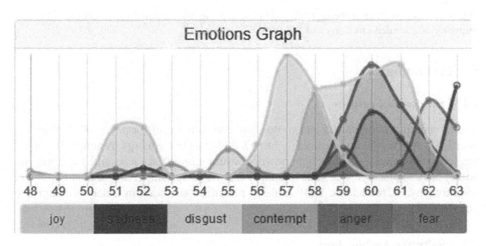

Fig. 3. Focus on the emotions graph.

At the end of the session, therapists can save all emotional information as well as with the audio/video streams, and the movements of ELE performed during the interaction. All data are locally stored in the therapist's device and are accessible at any time (Fig. 4).

Fig. 4. Review section of the dashboard. On the left side, the recorded video. On the right side, summary of recorded emotions and log of ELE's action.

5 Technology

5.1 Hardware Features

All input/output components and motors are connected to a Raspberry Pi 3 Model B board (RaspberryPi Foundation - https://www.raspberrypi.org) running Raspbian Stretch Lite operating system. The power consumption is very low, and a commercial power bank is placed inside ELE to supply the whole system, giving almost five hours of autonomy. A retractable USB cable is placed on the back in order to charge the power bank.

5.2 Software Architecture

The web application implementing the dashboard for therapists exploits a web server that is hosted inside ELE itself and is automatically loaded when the system is turned on. Network connection between ELE and the application is handled by a proxy.

The software module that manages the connection, as well as the modules used to manage the commands received from the operator activating ELE's motors and the other input/output devices, are coded in Python. Sensible data (as well as all the other data) from ELE to the therapist's device are transferred over HTTPS protocol and all data are encrypted. A full-duplex audio/video streaming is opened between the operator and the NDD person using ELE; a specific component is devoted to modifying the therapist's voice.

The real-time emotion analysis component –coded in JavaScript - exploits the ELE user's person's facial expression retrieved from the camera streaming is performed on the therapist's browser. Facial expression analysis relies on *Affdex*, a commercially available recognition software [11]. The software collects information about facial position and facial key points to provide a value between 0 and 100 every 100 ms. This value represents the probability that the subject is feeling a particular emotion; emotions set includes joy, sadness, disgust, contempt, anger and fear. Every second, an average of ten values for each emotion is calculated and the generated sequences are displayed in real-time via the emotion graph in the control panel. This information is logged, saved and synchronized with the video recording of the session and the movements ELE did.

6 Empirical Study

6.1 Goal

We performed an exploratory empirical study at a local care center to investigate the potential of ELE as a conversational companion for persons with NDD. We focused on a specific aspect, namely, the robot capability of promoting *engagement* among this target group. To this end, we compared the engagement potential of ELE against the one of a therapist speaking face-to-face.

Engagement is a broad concept and there is limited agreement on the definition and operationalization of the construct. We embraced the definition from Chapman ([4], p. 3), who defines engagement as *"...something that draws us in, that attracts and holds our attention."*. Engagement is widely acknowledged learning *facilitator* [12] and, for subjects with NDD, it has an even stronger role. The impairments associated to NDD create a persistent state of insecurity and uncertainty, a tendency to withdrawal and self-inhibition, and a difficulty to stay focused on something for a prolonged time, which hinders the willingness and capability to be involved in a task and to act upon the associated objects. Among subjects with NDD, reaching and maintaining a state of engagement is a *precondition* for any learning process to take place [37].

6.2 Engagement Metrics

Prior work with persons with cognitive impairments [42] suggests that *gaze* is a good quantitative indicator of engagement. For the purpose of our study, we assumed that the person with NDD – hereinafter referred to as *"participant"* - is *engaged* when *he/she looks at* the face of the *"speaking agent"*, i.e., the on-site therapist (in experimental situation S1) or ELE (in experimental situation S2).

Engagement metrics were defined using the terms and expressions reported below.

- *Area of interest:* the *face* of the speaking agent (ELE or the face-to-face therapist);
- *Total Session Time (T_{tot}):* total duration of an experimental session;
- *Focus Interval:* an interval of time during a session in which the participant *maintains* her gaze on a point within the area of interest;
- *Total Focus Time (T_f):* the sum of all Focus Intervals during a session, i.e., the total time during which the participant looks at the area of interest during a session.
- *Total Focus Change (C):* the number of times the participant *moves* her gaze from *outside* to *inside* the area of interest.

Areas of interest are calculated starting from simplified geometric models of ELE's and the therapist's face. ELE's face is modeled as a circumference while the human speaker's one as an ellipsis where the two principal axis are the head width and height.

We used a commercial eye tracker (https://steelseries.com) to gather gaze measures. The data retrieved from the eye tracker are sequences of tuples containing information on where the subject is looking at (x and y coordinates referred to a reference system whose origin is on the setting) at a specific time instant. These data are aggregated in order to measure Focus Intervals: a tuple belongs to a Focus Interval when its coordinates are inside the area of interest.

T_f and C are calculated from the set of Focus Intervals for each participant and each session, and are then normalized with respect to the session duration to obtain the following two measures:

- *Performance on Focus Change:* $P_{fc} = \frac{C}{T_{tot}}$
- *Performance on Focus Time:* $P_f = \frac{T_f}{T_{tot}}$

The *Performance on Focus Time* can be interpreted as the *probability* that at a given time instant the subject is looking at the area of interest.

We can assume that an *increase* of *Performance on Focus Time* indicates an *increase of engagement*. Still, this single measure should be considered together with *Performance of Focus Change*: for instance, if a subject has the same P_f in two sessions but P_{fc} increases in the second session, the latter session should be considered *less* engaging because the duration of the single intervals of focus on the area of interest decreases. For this reason, we assume that a *decrease* in *Performance on Focus Change* indicates an *increase of engagement*.

This information is used to create a scoring function $E(P_f, P_{fc})$ called *session performance* that give us the possibility to compare two sessions for a single participant. This value also represents the engagement.

Assuming that $E = f(P_f) \circ g(P_{fc})$, where f and g are two unknown functions and $\circ$ an unknown operator between the two functions, we must define f, g and $\circ$ in order to perform the scoring. Since we want to maintain proportionality, we consider the operator "$\circ$" as a multiplication: at this point $E = f(P_f)g(P_{fc})$.

Some considerations on the nature of functions f and g should be made: both of them must be defined, at least, in the interval $[0, 1]$, because data are positive and can be null. Furthermore f must be an increasing monotone function because its argument, P_f, is directly proportional to E, while g must be a decreasing monotone function because its argument, P_{fc}, is inversely proportional to E. Having in mind the above constraints, the choice fell on a negative exponential function for g, while f is linear. The scoring function E is defined as follows:

$$E(P_f, P_{fc}) = P_f * e^{-P_{fc}}$$

This definition must be completed to take into account some particular cases:

- when $P_f = 0$ (the participant never looked in the area of interest), $E = 0$;
- when $P_{fc} = 0$ there are two possibilities:
  - the participant never looked inside the area of interest, then $E = 0$;
  - the participant always looked inside the area of interest without exiting from it, then $E = P_f e^0 = P_f$. Since $P_f = 1$ when the participant always looks in the area of interest, then $E = 1$;
  - when $P_f = 1$ (the maximum value), then $P_{fc} = 0$ and $E = 1$ (see previous point);
  - when P_{fc} grows, tending to infinite, the number of interactions is very high but the permanence inside the area of interest for each interaction is almost 0, then E should be equal to 0. In fact, $\lim_{P_{fc} \to \infty} P_f * e^{-P_{fc}} = 0$ due to the negative exponential;
  - for any other value of P_{fc} (which is always positive, without considering the already discussed case in which $P_{fc} = 0$), $e^{-P_{fc}} < 1$ and $0 < P_f < 1$ by definition, so $0 < E < 1$.

In summary, the completed definition of the scoring function is the following:

$$E(P_f, P_{fc}) = P_f * e^{-P_{fc}}, \text{ with } 0 \leq E \leq 1.$$

6.3   Participants

Finding a homogeneous group of participants and controlling bias introduced by individual differences is acknowledged as very difficult in any study involving persons with NDD. We involved 11 participants recruited among the persons attending the center where the study took place. Their age range was 25–43 ($\mu = 31.09$, $\sigma = 5.1$). The group was heterogeneous with respect to their diagnosis but homogenous with respect to intellectual functioning level (medium), as described in Table 1.

Table 1. Subject's age, gender (G) and diagnosis

Subject	Age (years)	G	Diagnosis
1	35	F	Mental retardation of medium degree with severe limitations of personal autonomy, polyvoltine syndrome, obesity
2	28	F	Mental retardation of medium-severe entity associated with behavioral disorders symptomatic of cerebral malformation
3	30	M	Mental retardation in genetic syndrome with minor malformative aspects
4	25	M	Autism spectrum disorder
5	27	F	Mental retardation of medium degree, global hypoututism, growth hormone deficiency, diabetes mellitus
6	28	M	Spastic dysplasia with a medium to severe cognitive delay as outcomes of neonatal distress
7	36	F	Severe mental insufficiency and deficit psychosis
8	31	M	Cornelia de Lange syndrome with serious mental retardation
9	29	M	Mental retardation of medium degree with behavioral disorders
10	30	F	Borderline personality disorder with behavioral abnormalities in mental retardation with very limited relational skills
11	43	F	Average oligophrenia on a cerebropathic basis

6.4   Method

The study respected the ethical rules and procedures required by our university and the study was approved by our Ethical Committee and the one at the care center where we performed the study took. The head of the therapeutic team at the center identified a set of potential participants, explained them the study, and asked them if they wanted to participate. The same procedure was carried out among therapists and families. An informed consent (also including data treatment rules) was signed by parents/guardians. All digital data were anonymized and were stored in a certified secure server, while paper documentation was kept in a dedicated lock-room.

The study had a two-conditions within-subjects design. Each participant attended *two sessions*, and experienced a different experimental condition in each session: S_1 = *"Talking with a face-to-face human speaker"* and S_2 = *"Talking with ELE"*. The order of conditions was *randomized* among participants.

Instruments, stimulus, set-up, and test protocol (time of exposition to the stimulus, physical distance between the participant and the speaking agent, room setting, session scheduling) were defined carefully to control as much as possible for the many potentially confounding variables. The most challenging requirement was to standardize the stimulus in the two experimental conditions (human speaker and ELE), minimizing the differences in content and voice features.

Since storytelling is a frequent activity in interventions among persons with NDD [8], we created two short tales that had the same number of words, similar plot and environment, same number of characters, resolution pattern and duration. According to therapists, they could be regarded as "equivalently engaging". They were randomly assigned to each experimental condition. The *same therapist* (unknown to all participants) told the story through ELE and face-to-face. To exclude differences due to individual voice characteristics, ELE spoke using the *pre-recorded reading of the story;* the therapist's voice was digitally modified to hide its human nature and simulate the voice of a fantasy character. The therapist was trained to tell the other story trying to use the same voice tone and speech rhythm as much as possible.

The experimental sessions took places in a dedicated room. The setting included two tables, some chairs, very neutral furniture (bookshelf, baskets) and a frame, and remained the same for all sessions. The frame had the purpose of hiding the technological instruments (an eye tracker to collect the fixation point and a camera to record the session). The frame represents a simple natural landscape, which was designed with the help of a therapist and was used in all sessions. (see Fig. 5). The frame was placed on the table, with the participant sitting in front of it, while the speaker was placed behind the subject (Figs. 6 and 7). The chair was located between 50 and 80 cm from the frame (otherwise his/her gaze would not be detected by the eye tracker). a psychologist and a member of the design team participated as observers, taking notes during sessions.

Each session followed the same protocol:

1. Before entering the study room, the participant is informed on what is going to happen ("You will enter, sit on the chair placed in front of the table where a nice frame is placed, and listen to a story") and the two observers are introduced to him/her.
2. The participant enters the room and is guided to the chair. The two observers move behind the participant, out of the camera vision angle.
3. The participant listens to the story; when it ends, he/she is invited to cheer the speaker and is accompanied out of the room.

Fig. 5. Frame used in the study.

Fig. 6. Session with human speaker (S1).

Fig. 7. Session with ELE as a speaker (S2)

6.5   Main Results

The analysis of the data collected during the study does not consider participant #11 (aged 43) who attended one session only. In the rest of this section, we will use the expression "*sessions i*" (i = 1, 2) to indicate sessions with experimental condition S_i.

The results concerning *Performance on Focus Time (P_f)* and *Performance on Focus Change (P_{fc})* in the two types of sessions –are summarized in Tables 2 and 3.

Table 2. Data gathered during Sessions 1 - with human speaker

Subject	P_f [%]	P_{fc} (ms^{-1}) [%]
1	6.73	0.05
2	50	0.5
3	0	0
4	0.1	0.01
5	6	0.01
6	16	0.70
7	70	0.03
8	0	0
9	37	0.02
10	0	0

Table 3. Data gathered during Sessions 2 - with ELE

Subject	P_f [%]	P_{fc} (ms^{-1}) [%]
1	66	0.1
2	31	0.3
3	6	0.1
4	95	0.01
5	49	0.05
6	10	0.05
7	97	0.02
8	49	0.05
9	83	0.08
10	98	0.02

Participants' Scores in the two experimental conditions, and respective variations, are shown in Table 4 and visualized in Figs. 8 and 9.

Table 4. Scores and score differences in the two experimental conditions

Subject	Scoring (E) [%]		$\Delta E = E_2 - E_1$ [%]
	Session 1 (E_1)	Session 2 (E_2)	
1	6	66	60
2	50	31	−19
3	0	5.8	5.8
4	0.1	95	94.9
5	6	48	42
6	17	10	−7
7	70	97	27
8	0	49	49
9	37	83	46
10	0	98	98

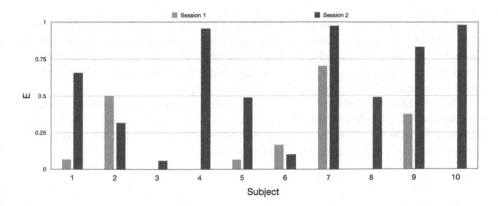

Fig. 8. Absolute scores for each participant in each experimental condition

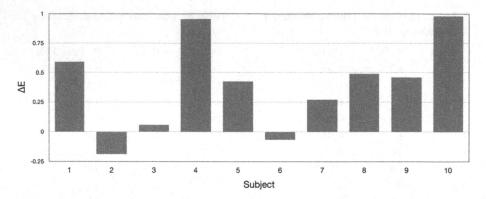

Fig. 9. Variations of the scores for each participant in each experimental condition

6.6   Discussion

The main finding is that for 8 participants out of 10 *(80%)* we measured a higher engagement score in the session with ELE than in the ones with the face-to-face therapist. This result may encourage the future adoption of ELE as conversational companions in interventions for persons with NDD at the therapeutic center where the study was performed. Still, our study is exploratory and has a number of limitations.

We involved the participants in one session for each type of stimulus (ELE and face to face human speaker). A longer exposure to both experimental conditions would increase the validity of our results. We may wonder if the positive results for ELE could be ascribed to the "novelty effect" of the robot. The answer is "probably not". For all subjects involved in our study (like for many people with NDD), the "unknown" is often a source of distress and discomfort and these persons tend to manifest rigidity towards any new situation. Novelty therefore should not be considered a facilitator of engagement.

The number of participants (11) was relatively small, although this sample size is similar to many studies on robots for persons with NDD [2, 16, 23, 30]. The main critical issue is the variability between the participants: even if their cognitive level is comparable to neuro-typical children aged 8–10, they have relevant differences in of age, impairments, severity of the disorders, capability of processing and reacting to sensory stimuli.

Participant variability is a typical problem in empirical research among persons with disability and are one of the main reasons why statistical methods can hardly be applied in this field. Particularly, the descriptive analysis of our data indicates that the distance from the Gaussian Curve was too high to allow an inferential analysis, and we opted to present individual data and results by participants.

The individual variability also makes difficult to generalize the results of our study: persons with NDD different from our participants, or the same persons experiencing ELE and the human speaker in different ambient conditions, may not manifest similar engagement/disengagement trends as in our study.

7   Conclusion

We have presented the design, technology, and evaluation of ELE, a novel plush social robot with an elephant appearance that has been designed as a conversational companion for persons with NDD. ELE speaks through the live voice of a remote caregiver and is integrated with a tool for automatic gathering and analysis of interaction data.

Even if ELE is inspired to an existing smart toy that offers conversational proxy facility (MIT Huggable [43]), our research has some peculiar features that makes it an interesting contribution to research on social robots for persons with NDD.

In ELE, the physical design per se is not original as we reused a commercial toy. Still, "smartifying" an existing toy rather than building a new one from scratch (like Huggable) has an advantage in terms of development cost and therefore in terms of the potential for adoption.

The dashboard for caregivers integrated with ELE offers more features than Huggable's telecontrol application, and enables monitoring, analyzing and visualizing various kinds of user's data including emotion flows.

An additional contribution of our research is the empirical exploration of the engagement potential of conversational social robots. The operationalization of engagement and its metrics are novel. To our knowledge, conversational social robots were never studied among persons with cognitive impairments. Huggable for example was designed for and tested with neurotypical hospitalized children and was evaluated in terms of effects on user relaxation and communication. Engagement of smart toys for persons with NDD was explored in one previous work only [44] that used non-conversational e-toys and weaker metrics for engagement evaluation. Our initial empirical study suggests that ELE might be a more engaging conversational companion for persons with NDD than human speakers. This outcome needs to be validated in future research. Engagement is a necessary precondition for any learning process to take place among our target group. If our results are confirmed, ELE could be used as a complement to traditional interventions for this target group, e.g., to promote verbal communication skills. In addition, since reaching a state of engagement is known to help releasing tension, ELE could be used to alleviate a person's stress during any therapy. An additional benefit of ELE that will deserve future research is related to the use of the robot for remote therapy, where a distant caregiver provides verbal interventions remotely. In this respect, ELE can be a useful tool for persons with NDD who cannot leave home.

A further direction for future research concerns the data collected by ELE. Initial feedbacks by therapists pinpoint the utility of the visualization and analysis tools for monitoring the emotional expression and communication attitude of the persons with NDD who use ELE. Still, little is known about the way therapists could use this information to improve their interventions. Finally, the audio and video streams collected by ELE represent a wealth of information on the behavior of persons with NDD: they could be analyzed with appropriate art AI tools and exploited for NDD diagnosis.

Acknowledgements. The authors are grateful to Gianmarco Giummarra, Salvatore Ferrigno and Mattia Melli for their contribution to the development of ELE and to the execution of the empirical study. We warmly thank all persons at the therapeutic center Fraternità e Amicizia (Milan) who participated in our research.

References

1. American Psychiatric Association: Diagnostic and Statistical Manual of Mental Disorders (DSM-5®). American Psychiatric Pub., Arlington (2013)
2. Bonarini, A., Garzotto, F., Gelsomini, M., Romero, M., Clasadonte, F., Yilmaz, A.N.C.: A huggable, mobile robot for developmental disorder interventions in a multi-modal interaction space. In: 2016 25th IEEE International Symposium on Robot and Human Interactive Communication (RO-MAN), pp. 823–830. IEEE (2016)
3. Cabibihan, J.J., Javed, H., Ang, M., Aljunied, S.M.: Why robots? A survey on the roles and benefits of social robots in the therapy of children with autism. Int. J. Social Robot. 5(4), 593–618 (2013)
4. Chapman, P.M.: Models of engagement: intrinsically motivated interaction with multimedia learning software. Ph.D. thesis, University of Waterloo (1997)
5. Dautenhahn, K., Werry, I.: Issues of robot-human interaction dynamics in the rehabilitation of children with autism. Proc. Anim. Animats 6, 519–528 (2000)
6. Dautenhahn, K., Werry, I.: Towards interactive robots in autism therapy: background, motivation and challenges. Pragmat. Cogn. 12(1), 1–35 (2004)
7. Garzotto, F., Gelsomini, M., Kinoe, Y.: Puffy: a mobile inflatable interactive companion for children with neurodevelopmental disorder. In: Bernhaupt, R., Dalvi, G., Joshi, A., Balkrishan, D.K., O'Neill, J., Winckler, M. (eds.) INTERACT 2017. LNCS, vol. 10514, pp. 467–492. Springer, Cham (2017). https://doi.org/10.1007/978-3-319-67684-5_29
8. Garzotto, F., Paolini, P., Sabiescu, A.: Interactive storytelling for children. In: Proceedings of the 9th International Conference on Interaction Design and Children, IDC 2010, pp. 356–359. ACM, New York (2010)
9. Huijnen, C.A., Lexis, M.A., Jansens, R., de Witte, L.P.: Mapping robots to therapy and educational objectives for children with autism spectrum disorder. J. Autism Dev. Disord. 46(6), 2100–2114 (2016)
10. Jeong, S., et al.: Designing a socially assistive robot for pediatric care. In: Proceedings of the 14th International Conference on Interaction Design and Children, pp. 387–390. ACM (2015)
11. McDuff, D., Mahmoud, A., Mavadati, M., Amr, M., Turcot, J., Kaliouby, R.e.: AFFDEX SDK: a cross-platform real-time multi-face expression recognition toolkit. In: Proceedings of the 2016 CHI Conference Extended Abstracts on Human Factors in Computing Systems, CHI EA 2016, pp. 3723–3726. ACM, New York (2016)
12. O'Brien, H.L., Toms, E.G.: What is user engagement? A conceptual framework for defining user engagement with technology. J. Am. Soc. Inform. Sci. Technol. 59(6), 938–955 (2008)
13. Park, H.W., Gelsomini, M., Lee, J.J., Breazeal, C.: Telling stories to robots: the effect of backchanneling on a child's storytelling. In: Proceedings of the 2017 ACM/IEEE International Conference on Human-Robot Interaction, pp. 100–108. ACM (2017)
14. Pauli, D., Egerton, J., Carpenter, B.: The sunfield colour impact project. PMl. Dl. inl 12(2), 12–16 (1999)
15. Robins, B., Dautenhahn, K., Te Boekhorst, R., Billard, A.: Robotic assistants in therapy and education of children with autism: can a small humanoid robot help encourage social interaction skills? Univ. Access Inf. Soc. 4(2), 105–120 (2005)
16. Scassellati, B., Admoni, H., Matarić, M.: Robots for use in autism research. Annu. Rev. Biomed. Eng. 14, 275–294 (2012)
17. Feil-Seifer, D., Matarić, M.J.: Socially assistive robotics. IEEE Robot. Autom. Mag. 18(1), 24–31 (2011)

18. Stiehl, W.D., Lieberman, J., Breazeal, C., Basel, L., Lalla, L., Wolf, M.: Design of a therapeutic robotic companion for relational, affective touch. In: IEEE International Workshop on Robot and Human Interactive Communication, ROMAN 2005, pp. 408–415. IEEE, August 2005

19. Chella, A., Barone, R.E., Pilato, G., Sorbello, R.: An emotional storyteller robot. In: AAAI Spring Symposium: Emotion, Personality, and Social Behavior, pp. 17–22, April 2008

20. Den Brok, W.L.J.E., Sterkenburg, P.S.: Self-controlled technologies to support skill attainment in persons with an autism spectrum disorder and/or an intellectual disability: a systematic literature review. Disabil. Rehabil. Assistive Technol. 10(1), 1–10 (2015)

21. Diehl, J.J., Schmitt, L.M., Villano, M., Crowell, C.R.: The clinical use of robots for individuals with autism spectrum disorders: a critical review. Res. Autism Spectr. Disord. 6(1), 249–262 (2012)

22. Kozima, H., Michalowski, M.P., Nakagawa, C.: Keepon. Int. J. Social Robot. 1(1), 3–18 (2009)

23. Michaud, F., Duquette, A., Nadeau, I.: Characteristics of mobile robotic toys for children with pervasive developmental disorders. In: 2003 IEEE International Conference on Systems, Man and Cybernetics, vol. 3, pp. 2938–2943. IEEE, October 2003

24. Ricks, D.J., Colton, M.B.: Trends and considerations in robot-assisted autism therapy. In: 2010 IEEE International Conference on Robotics and Automation (ICRA), pp. 4354–4359. IEEE, May 2010

25. Short, E., et al.: How to train your DragonBot: socially assistive robots for teaching children about nutrition through play. In: 2014 RO-MAN: The 23rd IEEE International Symposium on Robot and Human Interactive Communication, pp. 924–929. IEEE, August 2014

26. Kozima, H., Nakagawa, C., Yasuda, Y.: Children–robot interaction: a pilot study in autism therapy. Prog. Brain Res. 164, 385–400 (2007)

27. Robins, B., et al.: Scenarios of robot-assisted play for children with cognitive and physical disabilities. Interact. Stud. 13(2), 189–234 (2012)

28. Bonarini, A., Clasadonte, F., Garzotto, F., Gelsomini, M.: Blending robots and full-body interaction with large screens for children with intellectual disability. In: Proceedings of the 14th International Conference on Interaction Design and Children, pp. 351–354. ACM, June 2015

29. Kory Westlund, J., et al.: Tega: a social robot. In: The Eleventh ACM/IEEE International Conference on Human Robot Interaction, p. 561. IEEE Press, March 2016

30. Dautenhahn, K., Werry, I., Salter, T., Boekhorst, R.T.: Towards adaptive autonomous robots in autism therapy: varieties of interactions. In: Proceedings of the 2003 IEEE International Symposium on Computational Intelligence in Robotics and Automation, vol. 2, pp. 577–582. IEEE, July 2003

31. Robins, B., Dautenhahn, K., Dubowski, J.: Does appearance matter in the interaction of children with autism with a humanoid robot? Interact. Stud. 7(3), 509–542 (2006)

32. Bird, G., Leighton, J., Press, C., Heyes, C.: Intact automatic imitation of human and robot actions in autism spectrum disorders. Proc. Roy. Soc. Lond. B Biol. Sci. 274(1628), 3027–3031 (2007)

33. Pierno, A.C., Mari, M., Lusher, D., Castiello, U.: Robotic movement elicits visuomotor priming in children with autism. Neuropsychologia 46(2), 448–454 (2008)

34. Shamsuddin, S., et al.: Initial response of autistic children in human-robot interaction therapy with humanoid robot NAO. In: 2012 IEEE 8th International Colloquium on Signal Processing and its Applications (CSPA), pp. 188–193. IEEE, March 2012

35. Shibata, T., Mitsui, T., Wada, K., Tanie, K.: Subjective evaluation of seal robot: parotabulation and analysis of questionnaire results. J. Robot. Mechatron. 14(1), 13–19 (2002)

36. Breazeal, C.: A motivational system for regulating human-robot interaction. In: AAAI/IAAI, pp. 54–61, July 1998
37. Ferrara, C., Hill, S.D.: The responsiveness of autistic children to the predictability of social and nonsocial toys. J. Autism Dev. Disord. **10**(1), 51–57 (1980)
38. Colombo, S., Garzotto, F., Gelsomini, M., Melli, M., Clasadonte, F.: Dolphin Sam: a smart pet for children with intellectual disability. In: Proceedings of the International Working Conference on Advanced Visual Interfaces, pp. 352–353. ACM, June 2016
39. Tam, V., Gelsomini, M., Garzotto, F.: Polipo: a tangible toy for children with neurodevelopmental disorders. In: Proceedings of the Eleventh International Conference on Tangible, Embedded, and Embodied Interaction, pp. 11–20. ACM, March 2017
40. Bonarini, A., Clasadonte, F., Garzotto, F., Gelsomini, M., Romero, M.: Playful interaction with Teo, a mobile robot for children with neurodevelopmental disorders. In: Proceedings of the 7th International Conference on Software Development and Technologies for Enhancing Accessibility and Fighting Info-exclusion, pp. 223–231. ACM, December 2016
41. Hu, F. (ed.): Virtual Reality Enhanced Robotic Systems for Disability Rehabilitation. IGI Global, Hershey (2016)
42. Armstrong, T., Olatunji, B.O.: Eye tracking of attention in the affective disorders: a meta-analytic review and synthesis. Clin. Psychol. Rev. **32**(8), 704–723 (2012)
43. Stiehl, W.D., et al.: The huggable: a therapeutic robotic companion for relational, affective touch. In: ACM SIGGRAPH 2006 Emerging Technologies, p. 15. ACM, July 2006
44. Beccaluva, E.A., et al.: Exploring engagement with robots among persons with neurodevelopmental disorders. In: 2017 26th IEEE International Symposium on Robot and Human Interactive Communication (RO-MAN), pp. 903–909. IEEE, August 2017

S²C²: Toward an App to Support Social Story™ Comprehension Checking in Children with ASD

Aurora Constantin[1](iD), Nicholas Georgiou[1], Cristina Adriana Alexandru[1](✉),
and Jessica Korte[2]

[1] The University of Edinburgh, Edinburgh, UK
{aurora.constantin,cristina.alexandru}@ed.ac.uk,
nicholas.g1993@hotmail.com
[2] The University of Queensland, Brisbane, QLD, Australia
j.korte@uq.edu.au

Abstract. Children with Autism Spectrum Disorders (ASD) have difficulties with social communication and interaction. Social Stories™ are a well-known intervention to help them overcome these difficulties. During these interventions, practitioners must check children's understanding of various concepts that are taught. However, this activity - comprehension checking - is often skipped as practitioners find it difficult and time consuming. Our project explores how a technology-based tool (the S²C² app) can be designed and developed to support Social Story™ comprehension checking in children with ASD (aged 7–12) by involving typically developing children (TD) and experts in ASD and HCI. An initial pilot evaluation with sixteen TD children and five experts in ASD and HCI suggested that the S²C² app provides appropriate engaging activities for children and facilitates Social Story™ comprehension checking. However, caution must be taken in extending the results and more studies involving children with ASD are planned to be conducted in the future.

Keywords: Autism · ASD · Educational technology · App design · Reading comprehension

1 Introduction

Autism Spectrum Disorder (ASD) is a group of disorders characterised by impairments in three core domains: social interaction, social communication and social imagination [25]. Social interaction deficit social interaction, includes lack of understanding others' intentions, emotions, and mental states. For example, individuals with ASC have difficulties in analysing common social situations, are unable to react to them, or react with delay or in an unusual way. Communication deficits include delay in the development of language skills and sometimes total lack of spoken language. Social imagination is defined as the ability to detach from normal routines and look at them from a different perspective.

D. Lamas et al. (Eds.): INTERACT 2019, LNCS 11746, pp. 153–160, 2019.
https://doi.org/10.1007/978-3-030-29381-9_10

Various educational interventions have been designed which help reduce the core difficulties in individuals with ASD [12,16,23]. A particular example of an educational intervention which is widely used by practitioners and parents is Social Stories[TM], defined as short stories written following ten specific criteria, which describe social situations, social skills or concepts [18]. Social Stories[TM] address the social interaction and communication difficulties encountered by children with ASD. They are implemented to improve social understanding and celebrate the achievements of children with ASD.

One problem with Social Stories[TM] is that, even if the child reads the story, there is no guarantee that he/she has understood the concept [18]. Therefore it is important to test the child's understanding through a comprehension check method. However, anecdotal evidence from Constantin revealed that, in spite of being aware of this, practitioners do not check Social Story[TM] comprehension in children with ASD because they find it difficult and time consuming, partly due to the lack of standard tools [6].

Recently, with the spread of mobile devices, there is an increased interest in exploring the potential of technology to support children with ASD by addressing their challenges, such as joint attention [2], social and communication skills [17] and behavioural problems [20]. Empirical data shows promise for the effectiveness of educational technology for children with autism [13,15]. Moreover, most of these children have an attraction for technology [7]. This justifies researchers' efforts in designing new applications to aid children with ASD.

In this project we explore how technology can be designed and developed to best support Social Story[TM] comprehension checking in children with ASD. In particular, we propose the S^2C^2 tablet app for children with ASD, which practitioners can use with them within the school environment to check their Social Story[TM] comprehension.

The project is in its preliminary stages and we decided not to include children with autism before getting evidence that our solution may work for them. Therefore, in the initial stages that we report here, the design was informed by research literature (related to methods for checking Social Story[TM] comprehension in children with ASD, designing technology for children in general and for children with autism), and empirical studies with typically developing (TD) children and experts in the fields of ASD and Human Computer Interaction (HCI).

The results of the pilot evaluation were very promising, and suggest, based on the feedback received from TD children and experts in ASD and HCI, that the new technology could be used to aid in Social Story[TM] comprehension checking in children with ASD. However, caution must be taken in extending the results until design and evaluation studies involving children with ASD are conducted - which is what we are planning for the near future.

2   Designing the App

To design the app, we first reviewed the literature on methods used or recommended for checking Social Story[TM] comprehension in children with ASD. We

identified the following: (1) asking "5W+H" questions[1] after the story [1,8];
(2) partial sentences[2] [18], and (3) using computer-based games [3,5]. Additionally, we reviewed the literature on design guidelines for technology for children
(e.g. [4,10]) and for children with autism (e.g. [9]).

Although including children with ASD in a software design process is possible
through a number of methods and techniques, it is also very time and resource
consuming. Moreover, TD children (bringing their age-related expertise) and
HCI experts can contribute to the design of a technology-based tool with good
usability for children, and experts in ASD can provide initial feedback about
what is appropriate for children with ASD for checking Social Story™ comprehension. TD children were also successfully included in the past as proxies
because of the difficulties to carry out studies with children with ASD [14,19]. We
therefore decided, for the first iteration of the design of the app, to involve TD
children and experts in ASD and HCI. Our next step in this project, presented
as future work, is to involve children with ASD in further design studies.

We ran a design workshop with TD children between the ages of 7 and 12.
As research reveals that rewards embedded into educational technology can be
motivational and enhance learning performance [11,21], this workshop was also
an opportunity to investigate what kinds of rewards children between the ages
of 7 and 11 enjoy. An iterative process of developing a prototype was carried
out and formative evaluation was conducted with four experts in ASD and HCI.
The main aims of the formative evaluation were to improve the usability of
the S²C² app, its suitability for checking Social Story™ comprehension and its
appropriateness for children with ASD.

The final prototype included one example story (about sharing) and three
methods to check its comprehension which the child could select based on their
preferences (Fig. 1).

Once children read a story, they can check (with or without support from
practitioners) their comprehension using their favourite method. In the question and answer method, three choice answers are provided. If they choose the
incorrect answer, they are encouraged to try again. If they choose to try again,
they are re-directed to the page with the question they got wrong, but this time
the incorrect answer(s) they chose earlier is (are) not available. Similarly, for
the partial sentences and for the game, if children choose an incorrect solution,
they are encouraged to try again. Then, if they opt for trying again they are re-
directed to the screen with the proposed solutions, but the incorrect solution(s)
they had chosen is (are) not available. In this way, we avoided the alternative of
providing children with negative feedback when they give wrong answers, which
can lead to frustration and disappointment. However, our approach may have
the disadvantage of leading to the correct answer if all the incorrect ones are
eliminated, and this makes it unclear whether the child understood or not the
concepts taught in the story. To compensate this, a log file was implemented to
record the number of attempts taken to get the correct answer. Future develop-

---

[1] "5W+H" = Who, What, Why, Where, When and How.
[2] Partial sentences are incomplete sentences in which the reader must fill in the gaps.

Fig. 1. Screenshots: [*left*] a question for checking comprehension and a correct answer; [*middle*] a partial sentence for checking comprehension; [*right*] a game for checking comprehension

ment will provide this information in the practitioner interface (which was not our focus at this stage).

3   Evaluation

An evaluation study was conducted with sixteen TD children aged 7–12 and five experts in ASD and HCI. The main aim of the study was to understand to what extent the new technology supports children with ASD in checking Social Story™ comprehension. Additionally, the study aimed to evaluate whether the S^2C^2 app is easy to use by the target population and to collect suggestions for further improvements of the app to make it appropriate for children with ASD.

The children were asked to independently read the story about sharing and then to complete the three comprehension check methods on an Android tablet. At the end, they were asked a series of questions related to their experience in using the app and preference with regards to the checking method. Each session lasted 30–40 min.

The experts used the Think Aloud protocol [22] while exploring the app individually. Then, they were asked a series of questions including their experience with the app, their perception about the suitability of the activities for checking Social Story™ comprehension, and appropriateness of the app for children with ASD. It is worth mentioning that all experts had some knowledge of Social Stories™ and two of them had experience in working with Social Stories™ with children with ASD. Each evaluation session with an expert lasted about 45 min.

All the sessions (both with children and experts) were video recorded (with the participants' written consent) and the videos were transcribed.

4   Results and Preliminary Findings

To make sense of the data, we employed open coding and axial coding as described by Saldaña [24]. The results showed that both children and experts received the app positively.

4.1   General Experience

All the children answered that they enjoyed using the app and were enthusiastic during its exploration. Child C7 stated:

"I really like the comprehension check methods as they are really easy to understand".

Out of the sixteen children, five inquired whether the app was available for download on the app stores, and stated that if it was they would want to download it.

All the children said they enjoyed the storyline of the game where they were collecting fruit for their virtual friend (e.g. an elephant), while also helping others on the way.

All the experts commented that they liked the app:

"Overall I like the application, it is well built and I think it has great potential." (E3)

4.2   Ease of Use

None of the children had any issues with navigating through the app or understanding what the steps to accomplish their goals were.

All the experts found the app easy to use. Expert E5 commented:

"I have young children. They are typically developing, but I believe they would be able to use this application very easily".

4.3   Appropriateness for Children with ASD

All the experts considered that the app is appropriate for the target users due to the language it uses and its simplicity:

"Using this application, there is nothing which would cause any issues to the target user, as there are no distracting features and the overall language used is simple enough". (E1)

4.4   Suitability for Checking Social Story™ Comprehension

All the experts who evaluated the app considered that the three methods were very good in extracting the important information from the story and considered that the app fulfilled its purpose for checking comprehension. Expert E3 explained:

"The questions and answers and partial sentences extract the important information from the Social Story^{TM} and I believe it would be a good way for testing Social Story^{TM} comprehension".

Also, expert E4 made the following comment:

"I really like how the questions asked in the application go from a general concept to more specific situations in regard to the story read [...]".

4.5   Rewards

All the children and experts appreciated the use of rewards within the app. Child C13 stated:

"It was really fun answering the questions and collecting the stars as rewards".

Another child, C5, also commented:

"I really liked how the fruit I collected in the game were then used to feed my character at the end".

Similarly, expert E4 added:

"I also like how the game comprehension check method ends with the user sharing their fruit with the character they chose, as this tests the concept of the Social Story^{TM} I read which was about sharing".

Child C16 suggested:

"I would like it if there was a big reward when all the comprehension check methods were completed".

5   Conclusions and Future Work

This research explored how technology could aid in checking Social Story^{TM} comprehension in children with ASD by involving TD children and experts in ASD and HCI in the design and evaluation of an app, S^2C^2. Preliminary results showed that both children and experts had a positive experience with the S^2C^2 app and perceived it as easy to use. Experts considered that it has potential to support children with ASD in checking Social Story^{TM} comprehension. Our research brings the following contributions to the INTERACT community, particularly to researchers with interest in educational technology for ASD: (1) a design solution for facilitating Social Story^{TM} comprehension checking in children with ASD informed by research literature and empirical data; (2) a tablet app implementation for this solution; (3) empirical evidence from the evaluation with TD children and experts in ASD and HCI that the app may aid in checking Social Story^{TM} comprehension for children with ASD.

The next step is to implement the suggestions collected from TD children and experts (i.e. animations, sound effects and customisation of the game characters). Then, we will recruit children with ASD from schools for children with special needs from across Edinburgh, and by contacting the Lothian Autistic Society[3], for a second round of evaluation.

---

[3] http://lothianautistic.org/.

Alongside further improvements to the child interface to the S²C²app that these steps would result in, we would like to further extend this work by adding a practitioner interface for the school environment. Such an interface would allow practitioners to create Social Stories™ and set up comprehension check methods for them which are adapted to each child's abilities and preferences, but also to the content of the story. For example, practitioners could use editors to prepare their own questions and answers using different fonts and colours, or to create comprehension check games using a child's favourite characters and environments. Moreover, we could add more types of rewards that practitioners could choose from depending on the child. We would like to evaluate these ideas with practitioners from schools for children with special needs from across Edinburgh.

In the long term, this work could also be extended to include other target groups (e.g. children with learning disabilities or hearing impairments) and other educational interventions.

Acknowledgments. We thank all the children and experts who participated to our studies for their contribution and effort.

References

1. Akin, L., MacKinney, D.: Autism, literacy, and libraries. Child. Libr. J. Assoc. Libr. Serv. Child. **2**, 35–43 (2004)
2. Bernardini, S., Porayska-Pomsta, K., Smith, T.J.: ECHOES: an intelligent serious game for fostering social communication in children with autism. Inf. Sci. **264**, 41–60 (2014)
3. Charlton, B., Williams, R.L., McLaughlin, T.: Educational games: a technique to accelerate the acquisition of reading skills of children with learning disabilities. Int. J. Spec. Educ. **20**(2), 66–72 (2005)
4. Chiasson, S., Gutwin, C.: Design principles for children's technology. Interfaces **7**, 28 (2005)
5. Chuang, T.Y., Chen, W.F.: Effect of computer-based video games on children: an experimental study. In: 2007 First IEEE International Workshop on Digital Game and Intelligent Toy Enhanced Learning (DIGITEL 2007), pp. 114–118. IEEE (2007)
6. Constantin, A.: Supporting practitioners in social story interventions: the ISISS authoring tool (2015)
7. Constantin, A., Johnson, H., Smith, E., Lengyel, D., Brosnan, M.: Designing computer-based rewards with and for children with autism spectrum disorder and/or intellectual disability. Comput. Hum. Behav. **75**, 404–414 (2017)
8. Crozier, S., Sileo, N.M.: Encouraging positive behavior with social stories: an intervention for children with autism spectrum disorders. Teach. Except. Child. **37**(6), 26–31 (2005)
9. Davis, M., Dautenhahn, K., Powell, S., Nehaniv, C.: Guidelines for researchers and practitioners designing software and software trials for children with autism. J. Assist. Technol. **4**(1), 38–48 (2010)
10. Druin, A., et al.: The Design of Children's Technology. Morgan Kaufmann Publishers, San Francisco (1999)

11. Eisenberger, R., Cameron, J.: Detrimental effects of reward: reality or myth? Am. Psychol. **51**(11), 1153 (1996)
12. Fails, J.A., Guha, M.L., Druin, A.: Methods and techniques for involving children in the design of new technology for children. Found. Trends Hum.-Comput. Interact. **6**(2), 85–166 (2013). https://doi.org/10.1561/1100000018
13. Fletcher-Watson, S., Pain, H., Hammond, S., Humphry, A., McConachie, H.: Designing for young children with autism spectrum disorder: a case study of an iPad app. Int. J. Child-Comput. Interact. **7**, 1–14 (2016)
14. Frauenberger, C., Good, J., Alcorn, A.: Challenges, opportunities and future perspectives in including children with disabilities in the design of interactive technology. In: Proceedings of the 11th International Conference on Interaction Design and Children, pp. 367–370. ACM (2012)
15. Frauenberger, C., Good, J., Keay-Bright, W.: Designing technology for children with special needs: bridging perspectives through participatory design. CoDesign **7**(1), 1–28 (2011). https://doi.org/10.1080/15710882.2011.587013
16. Frauenberger, C., Good, J., Keay-Bright, W., Pain, H.: Interpreting input from children: a designerly approach. In: Proceedings of the SIGCHI Conference on Human Factors in Computing Systems, pp. 2377–2386. ACM (2012)
17. Garzotto, F., Gelsomini, M., Clasadonte, F., Montesano, D., Occhiuto, D.: Wearable immersive storytelling for disabled children. In: Proceedings of the International Working Conference on Advanced Visual Interfaces, pp. 196–203. ACM (2016)
18. Gray, C.: The New Social Story Book. Future Horizons, Arlington (2010)
19. Hirano, S.H., Yeganyan, M.T., Marcu, G., Nguyen, D.H., Boyd, L.A., Hayes, G.R.: vSked: evaluation of a system to support classroom activities for children with autism. In: Proceedings of the SIGCHI Conference on Human Factors in Computing Systems, pp. 1633–1642. ACM (2010)
20. Kim, S., Clarke, E.: Case study: an iPad-based intervention on turn-taking behaviors in preschoolers with autism. Behav. Dev. Bull. **20**(2), 253 (2015)
21. Lai, E.R.: Motivation: a literature review research report (2011). Accessed 30 May 2013
22. Lewis, C.: Using the 'thinking-aloud' method in cognitive interface design. Research Report RC9265, IBM TJ Watson Research Center (1982)
23. McConnell, S.R.: Interventions to facilitate social interaction for young children with autism: review of available research and recommendations for educational intervention and future research. J. Autism Dev. Disord. **32**(5), 351–372 (2002)
24. Saldaña, J.: The Coding Manual for Qualitative Researchers. Sage, Thousand Oaks (2015)
25. Wing, L., Gould, J., Gillberg, C.: Autism spectrum disorders in the DSM-V: better or worse than the DSM-IV? Res. Dev. Disabil. **32**(2), 768–773 (2011)

Assistive Technology for Mobility and Rehabilitation

(How) Can an App Support Physiotherapy for Frozen Shoulder Patients?

Thomas Stütz[✉] [ID]

Department of Multimedia Technology, Salzburg University of Applied Sciences,
Puch, Salzburg, Austria
thomas.stuetz@fh-salzburg.ac.at
https://www.fh-salzburg.ac.at/

Abstract. People affected by the frozen shoulder syndrome show limited shoulder mobility which is often accompanied by pain. The frozen shoulder syndrome often lasts from months to years, and mostly affects people in the age group of 40 to 70 years. The frozen shoulder syndrome severely reduces the quality of life and the ability to work. A common treatment method is physiotherapy. Patients are referred to a physiotherapist, who selects specific exercises adapted for the specific patient. Physiotherapy requires patient compliance, time, and effort. Correct exercise performance and compliance are the main issues in physiotherapy. A smartphone app could support patients by providing detailed exercise instructions and motivation through exercise logging, as is common for fitness and sport. In this work, such an app for frozen shoulder syndrome, the ShoulderApp, is evaluated in two user studies. The main contribution is that the user studies were conducted in an ambulatory assessment setting, which allows to draw conclusions about real-world usage, usability and user acceptance. The app was regularly used and study participants were satisfied. Additionally, we researched the usability and usage of interactive 3D and multi-modal exercise instructions, motivational aspects, exercise correctness and the interplay of physiotherapy and app usage. Measurements of shoulder mobility are the key assessment tool for the state and progress of the frozen shoulder syndrome. A smartphone sensor-based measurement tool, which only required a simple band in addition to the smartphone, was developed and evaluated. Interventions with the ShoulderApp were evaluated in a three-week short-term intervention and an 18-week midterm evaluation with 5 patients each. For the evaluation of the results, we used standardized questionnaires, SUS, TAM-2, and USE. In addition, semi-structured interviews and automatic logging of user-interactions in the app were included as the outcome measurements. Overall, the results for both the short-term and mid-term user studies showed that the ShoulderApp could support physiotherapy for frozen shoulder patients. The positive results of the studies show the potential of a generalization of the ShoulderApp concept to the large group of musculoskeletal disorders such as lower back pain and knee injuries.

Keywords: eHealth · mHealth · Co-creation ·
Multimodal information representation · Evaluation · User study · Patients

ⓒ IFIP International Federation for Information Processing 2019
Published by Springer Nature Switzerland AG 2019
D. Lamas et al. (Eds.): INTERACT 2019, LNCS 11746, pp. 163–183, 2019.
https://doi.org/10.1007/978-3-030-29381-9_11

1 Introduction

Patients with frozen shoulder syndrome show a decreased mobility of the upper extremities often accompanied by severe pain. Frozen shoulder syndrome may occur in one or both shoulders. The incidence of the frozen shoulder syndrome is reported to be 2–5% in the general population [25] and patients in the age group between 40 and 70 are affected more frequently [8]. The frozen shoulder syndrome is diagnosed by a physician, often patients are then referred to shoulder specialists for diagnosis. A common treatment option is physiotherapy, including mobilization and strength exercises [15]. In most cases, mobilization and strength exercises are conducted at home and not under the constant supervision of a physiotherapist. However, even with treatment the frozen shoulder syndrome is long lasting and patients may require years to fully recover and in some cases limitations in the range of motion persist.

Physiotherapy is often prescribed for a limited number of sessions (around 10) as health insurance does not cover more sessions (at least in Austria). Patients with frozen shoulder syndrome are thus likely to pinball between physicians (prescribing physiotherapy) and physiotherapists (conducting physiotherapy) in the course of their disease, which leads to gaps in treatment and information.

Home-based physiotherapy has two main issues: correct exercise performance and compliance [12, 13]. In [36] non-compliance rates as high as 70% are reported and in [19] it is reported that the majority of patients are not performing the home-exercises correctly two weeks after their initial instruction. In previous work, a smartphone app that supports patients during therapy in order to reduce the problems of exercise compliance and correctness has been proposed and evaluated in a short-term intervention. The app used a 3D avatar to show the correct exercise conduct and also provided text and audio descriptions of the exercises. Compared to traditional methods for home-instructions, which are either paper-based (text and illustrations) or videos [29], 3D animations allow better communication of complex 3D movements. Even for interactive video-based physiotherapy, the 2D representation complicates the understanding of 3D body movements [1], because of the missing depth information. Exercises that are performed by a 3D avatar allow the user to freely adjust the view point. Thus depth and therefore exact body movements can be perceived and the animated exercise allow vicarious learning. Additionally, the app for frozen shoulder patients offers more functionality such as an exercise diary and progress assessment, which support the patient exercising compliance.

Home-exercising requires a significant behavior change. According to Fogg's behavior model (FBM) [22], successful behavior change depends on three main factors, motivation, ability and triggers. While frozen shoulder patients have an intrinsic motivation to perform home-based exercises to improve their condition, a study context is expected to raise motivation and provide extrinsic motivation by regular supervision and follow-up meetings. A main contribution of an app is towards the factor ability in FBM. The app increases the ability to perform the home-based exercises correctly as it provides the patients with precise instructions on how to perform the exercises. Additionally, the permanent availability of a smartphone and the included diary and progress monitor provide constant triggers.

A user study in a short-term intervention (3 weeks) showed great potential of the app as support system for home-based physiotherapy. However, the frozen shoulder syndrome is a long-term disease and thus a short-term success is only a precondition for an evaluation over a longer period. In this work, the results of a short-term and a mid-term intervention (18 weeks) are presented and thoroughly analysed in order to answer whether an app can support physiotherapy and whether an app is general feasible in the context of home-based physiotherapy. The main focus is on the analysis of the interviews of the patients and the physiotherapists with respect to usability, 3D interaction and multimodal exercise instructions, motivation, mobility measurements in the app, and the interplay of physiotherapy and app usage.

The implemented study design did not require a formal approval by the ethics committee as the regular treatment remained unchanged and the app did not classify as a medical device (see Sect. 3.5).

2   Related Work

There has been a tremendous interest in industry of assistance technology of fitness and well-being of the general (healthy) population, e.g., by major companies, such as Google (Google Fit) and Apple (Apple Health). Apart from general health and fitness, several specific medical and rehabilitation issues have been addressed in the HCI and the medical community. Among these issues were stroke rehabilitation [6], Parkinson's disease [34], cerebral palsy [16], autism [28] and, most importantly for the focus of this work, musculoskeletal disorders (MSDs) [12,13] including disorders of the knee [5] and the shoulder [21,27].

A smartphone app could tackle important obstacles for physiotherapy at home in the context of musculoskeletal disorders: comprehensible and easily accessible exercise instructions, compliance and progress monitoring as established by Chandra et al. [12,13].

Previous work can be classified in terms of the used technology and hardware, which ranges from the application of professional tracking hardware to everyday smartphones.

Professional tracking systems capable of precisely tracking patient motion have been used by Tang et al. for physiotherapy at home [39,40]. The application of virtual reality systems to support physiotherapy was proposed by Gourlay et al. [23] and by Yim et al. [43]. Augmented reality head sets for physiotherapy were investigated by Dezentje et al. [17] and in follow-up work by Cidota et al. [14]. Liu et al. employed a humanoid robot in an interactive training system of motor learning [28].

Also the application of the Kinect body tracking system for physiotherapy was proposed by Nixon et al. [31], Anderson et al. [4], by Zhao et al. [44], by Smeddinck et al. [37] and by Fikar et al. [21].

The Nintendo Wii system was investigated by Deutsch et al. [16] and off-the-shelf Nintendo Wii Fit exer-games were evaluated with respect to the retention of motor skills of patients with Parkinson's disease by do Santos Mendes et al. [34].

Doyle et al. proposed an IMU-sensor based system for exercises [18]. A wearable device for knee rehabilitation was proposed by Ananthanarayan et al. [3] and by

Ayoade et al. [5]. Huang et al. proposed a cap with an IMU (Sense-Cap) to monitor balance exercises [24]. Schönauer et al. proposed an IMU-based system to provide motion guidance [35].

Buttussi et al. proposed a mobile system for fitness training [10, 11]. Op den Akker gave an overview of user-tailored activity coaching systems [2]. Smartphone apps were investigated for physiotherapy by Postolache et al. [33]. A reminder app for stroke patients was proposed by Micalle et al. [30]. Vorrink et al. developed and evaluated a mobile phone app to encourage activity in COPD patients [42].

The strength of our contribution is that actual patients used the system in their everyday setting over an extended period of time. This strength is especially noteworthy with respect to most related contributions of the HCI community which mostly focus on laboratory studies. Laboratory studies are not able to capture the complexities which arise out of actual systems in real life application settings.

3   Methods

In this work the results of a three-week short-term intervention and an 18-week midterm evaluation of home-based physiotherapy supported with an smartphone app, the ShoulderApp, are presented. The app was developed with the support of a shoulder surgeon and four physiotherapists from the department of physiotherapy.

3.1   ShoulderApp

The ShoulderApp starts with the main screen (see Fig. 1a), which shows five buttons for the five different screens of the app.

Training Mode. The most frequent task of a user affected by the frozen shoulder syndrome, exercising, is supported by a training mode. Pressing the first button starts the training mode ("Trainingsmodus"), in which an animation with audio description shows the exercises selected for the user (see Fig. 1b). A basic exercise is repeated several times, usually 10–20 times, in a set. After each set the patient confirms the set, by pressing the ok button (see Fig. 1b in the bottom right of the screen). 2–3 sets are commonly selected by physiotherapists. After the last set, the app returns to the main screen.

Sensor-Based Mobiltiy Measurement. The second button starts the mobility measurement ("Beweglichkeitstest"). Shoulder mobility is measured along four different movement axes (see Fig. 2). These measurements are the key metrics to track the progress and monitor the course of the frozen shoulder syndrome.

The patient could choose between two methods of assessing the mobility by pressing the corresponding button (see Fig. 3a). In the manual input mode, the patient uses a slider to adjust the avatar's arm position (see Fig. 2). In the sensor-based mobility measurement, the smartphones IMU (inertia measurement unit) is used. The smartphone is placed in a common smartphone band, which is commonly used for exercising, e.g. running (see Fig. 4). This approach needs minimal additional hardware, only a very cheap band is additionally necessary. The patient puts the band with the smartphone on the upper-arm (for the lateral and frontal arm lift) and on the forearm (for the lateral rotation and the back scratch). The patient presses the large start button (see Fig. 3b), moves the arm into the starting position and waits for an audible beep (3 s after pressing the start button). The patient should move the arm to the maximal extent without pain. The maximum extent of movement, i.e. the maximum angle, is recorded and the next measurement along a different axis is started.

Calendar Overview. The third button starts a calendar overview of the performed trainings and the mobility measurements (see Fig. 5a). Left and right arrow allow to change the month. The home button returns to the main screen.

Exercise Configuration. The fourth button starts the planning view, in which the patient or the physiotherapist can choose exercises and the number of sets appropriate for the patient (see Fig. 5b). Left and right arrow allow to change the exercise. The numer of sets can be by the minus and plus buttons. The home button returns to the main screen.

(a) Main screen

(b) Screenshot of the first exercise, appeared after tap on training button on main screen

Fig. 1. Features of the ShoulderApp

3.2 Study Design

The studies were designed as an ambulatory assessment where the participants were briefed before the intervention [20]. The main motivation for this design choice was to get as closely as possible to real at-home usage as possible within the study. The studies were conducted using a within-subject design [26]. While the percentage of people affected by the frozen shoulder syndrome in a life time is relatively high (around 10% are reported),

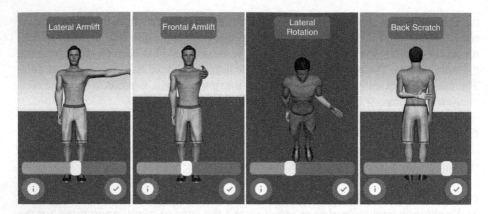

Fig. 2. Mobility assessment feature of the ShoulderApp: The four different axes of shoulder mobility assessment

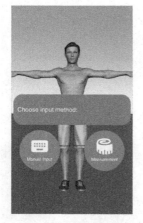 

(a) Mobility assessment feature of the ShoulderApp: Option selection for mobility assessment

(b) Sensor-based mobility assessment: Start button

Fig. 3. Mobility measurement

the percentage of people affected by frozen shoulder syndrome at any given moment is comparably low (2–5% are reported). Participants were acquired by a physician among his/her patients diagnosed with frozen shoulder. Inclusion criteria were a diagnosis of frozen shoulder and the willingness to voluntarily participate in the study. Exclusion criteria were other chronic diseases, which would rule out the idiopathic nature of the shoulder stiffness. Different patients were used for the short-term intervention and the mid-term intervention. As one of the main issues in the treatment of frozen shoulder is the long duration of the disease, fewer patients and longer study durations were chosen.

(a) Band with smartphone strapped on the upper arm

(b) Band with smartphone strapped on the forearm

Fig. 4. Sensor-based mobility measurement with smartphone in band

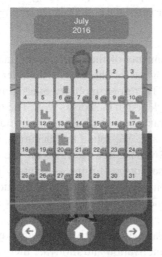

(a) Progress view with logged exercise activities and mobility assessments

(b) Planning view to select exercises and number of sets

Fig. 5. Calendar overview and planning mode

The plan was to start with a user study based on 3 week short-term intervention and in the case of success, extend the duration to gain more insights in the long-term usage. After the success of the first short-term user study, the length of the second mid-term intervention user study was extended to 18 weeks.

The main focus of the user studies was the long-term usage and the assessment of the general feasibility of an app in the context of home-based physiotherapy.

Usage, Usability, and 3D Interaction and Multi-modality. It was unclear whether the patients and the physiotherapists would accept an app to support the treatment of the frozen shoulder syndrome. The question was in particular whether an app can support the home-based therapy over an extended period. Also, it was not clear whether patients would accept the interaction with animated 3D content and which modality is suited to communicate physiotherapy exercises.

Correct Exercise Performance and Concordance of Physiotherapy and App. A main question was whether the exercises are performed correctly, which can only be assessed by a professional physiotherapist. Also, the concordance and inter-relations between standard physiotherapy sessions and app usage was considered an interesting topic in the study design. In the first study, the patients continued their individual physiotherapy with their own therapists (who were not part of the study team). In the second study, the participants were provided with physiotherapy sessions from the study team. They discontinued the therapy with their own therapists. All participating physiotherapists were under supervision of a leading physiotherapist, who provided guidelines for the physiotherapy sessions. This design decision assured the concordance of physiotherapy and app intervention.

Mobility Measurement. As mobility measurements of the joint are the main clinical parameters in the assessment of the state/progress of the frozen shoulder treatment, these measurements are of great importance. Therefore, mobility measurements were part of the physiotherapy sessions and were included in the app as well. The focus of the study of the app measurements was not accuracy, but whether patients would actually perform such measurements with a band at home. We found that accuracy was not an issue if high-quality smartphones were used. Given the trend towards mobile augmented and virtual reality, the accuracy of the IMU sensors will improve anyway in the near future. Therefore, accuracy is not interesting in this context, but the question whether patients accept this method with the smartphone in a band at all is crucial.

Motivation. A further interest in the studies was patient motivation: which elements of the intervention and the app increase patient motivation and motivate them to conduct the exercises accurately and regularly at home.

Further Improvements and Pain Logging. We wanted to know which ideas for improvements, especially to increase motivation for regular exercising, were derived by the patients during their experience with the provided app. Specifically, we were interested whether patients would like to integrate the possibility to log pain. Nightly pain often causes severe sleep deprivation for frozen shoulder patients. Regular nightly pain over an extended period would in fact be an argument for surgical intervention.

3.3 Study Flow

The first step was the design, conduct and evaluation of a short-term intervention.

Short-Term Intervention. In the first meeting patients were instructed by the physiotherapist and the app was made available for the following three weeks. In the second meeting, the outcome measures were evaluated (usability questionnaires and individual semi-structured interviews (for details see Sect. 3.4).

Mid-Term Intervention. After the successull short-term intervention, the study duration was significantly extended to 18 weeks. The study was again designed as an ambulatory assessment where the participants were briefed before, in-between and after the intervention [20]. Additionally, weekly physiotherapy session were provided. The outcome measures were evaluated in the second and the third (final) session (see Sect. 3.4).

In the first meeting with the patients, patients were informed about the study and its goals. The ShoulderApp was made available. The exercises and the app usage were explained by a physiotherapist and a computer scientist.

A patient information sheet, including study goals and details, the voluntary participation, the data collected by the app and a privacy statement was signed. Patients were instructed to use the app daily to log the training, and to conduct at least one mobility assessment per week. In order to rule out interference with their regular physiotherapist, physiotherapy was provided by the department of physiotherapy at most twice per week. The physiotherapy sessions were provided under the supervision of the leading physiotherapist. However, the app and the exercises in the app were deliberately not part of these physiotherapy sessions in order to get insight into the stand-alone app usage over a longer period. Furthermore, the study period over Christmas lead to around three weeks without seeing a physiotherapist and to app usage and home-exercising in a usually rather unstructured period for the patients (public holidays and Christmas vacations).

In the second meeting (in-between) and third meeting (final) with the patients, standardized questionnaires were evaluated and a personal semi-structured interview with each patient was conducted.

In the second meeting, patients were instructed to use the app only if they wanted and to continue therapy with their regular physiotherapist.

3.4 Outcome Measures

The outcome measures included standardized questionnaires, automatic logging of user-interactions in the app, and semi-structured interviews. The interviews were recorded (audio) and a qualitative content analysis (see [32]) was performed.

Usage, Usability, and 3D Interaction and Media. For the evaluation of the participants' satisfaction we conducted the System Usability Scale (SUS) by [9]. Additionally, selected parts (intention to use, perceived usefulness, perceived ease of use) of the revised Technology Acceptance Model (TAM-2) [38,41], and the USE (Usability, Satisfaction, and Ease of use) questionnaire which was used in previous work [42], were evaluated. For the interpretation of SUS scores we referred to [7].

The app tracks usage details in log files. The log files from the participants' smartphones were collected and analysed in order to gain insight into the actual usage in everyday life.

Participants were asked about their interactions with the app (e.g., did you change the view port?, did your read the instructions?) and their app usage contexts, e.g. alone at home.

Mobility Measurement. Mobility measurements are recorded in the log files of each user. As the short-term intervention revealed usability issues of the mobility measurement with smartphone sensors, this part of the app was revised and optimized (more explanation and an in-detail walk-through for the user of the necessary steps). Additionally, the USE: Ease of Learning questionnaire was rephrased such that questions 3 and 4 were specific to the sensor-based measurement routine.

Motivation. Our semi-structured interviews contained questions on the motivating effects of individual app aspects.

Correct Exercise Performance and Concordance of Physiotherapy and App. The physiotherapists assessed the correctness of the exercise performance in both interventions.

In the mid-term intervention we asked whether the app could replace actual physiotherapy sessions. The physiotherapists assessed the correctness of patients' exercise performance (of the exercises shown in the app). The leading physiotherapist was interviewed twice in the mid-term intervention.

Improvements and Pain Logging. To gather app improvement possibilities we asked each participant open questions about what they liked and what they disliked about the intervention and the app. We asked for suggestions for improvements in the overall conduct of the study and whether the initial personal instructions about how to use the app were necessary.

Specifically we asked whether patients would like to add a pain logging module.

3.5 Ethics Committee

We have informed the ethics committee of the county of Salzburg of the studies, however, the implemented study design did not require a formal approval by the ethics committee. A formal approval of a study from the ethics committee is needed if (a) regular treatment is changed (b) a medical device is tested. In the presented studies, the physician and physiotherapists and physicians assured, that only patients were selected for which the app was completely in line with their regular treatment. Based on the recommendation of the ethics committee we have carefully reviewed EU directive on medical devices (MEDDEV 2.1/6) to determine wether the evaluated app is a medical device. According to the definitions in the guidance document, the app is "stand-alone software". However, the software (app) does not perform an action on data different from storage, archival, communication or simple search (see Figure 1 of the Guidance Document MEDDEV 2.1/6 July 2016). The ShoulderApp stores the 3D instructions for home-based exercises (which would commonly just be explained by the physiotherapists) and provides exercise and mobility logging (which would commonly be done individually by the patients using their preferred tools, such as a paper or online calendar). Therefore, to the best of our assessment, the app is not covered by the medical device directive and not considered a medical device and standalone medical software. Therefore, a formal ethics committee approval process was determined to be not applicable.

3.6   Patient Recruitment

The patients were selected from the patient pool of the physician. Patients meeting the inclusion criteria were selected from the patient database of the head shoulder surgeons practice and contacted by the office of the head shoulder surgeon. Special care was taken that the regular treatment plan of the included patients was in line with the implemented treatment with app support in the studies. The patients were informed of the outline of the study, the timeline and their eligibility for free and voluntary participation.

4   Results

A short-term intervention was conducted in July 2016 for a duration of three weeks. Five patients (4f, 1m) with the frozen shoulder syndrome participated voluntarily. One physiotherapist was part of the study execution.

A mid-term intervention with 5 patients (3f, 2m) was conducted from December 21 2016 to April 24 2017. For this study, the instructions for the mobility measurement with sensors were improved in the app. On December 21 the user study started with a personal meeting of the patients and the leading physiotherapist (FH) and the computer scientist (TS) who was responsible for the app development. Patients were provided with physiotherapy sessions up to two times a week, which were conducted by 6 physiotherapists in training under the supervision of the leading physiotherapist. After the second in-between session (Feb 20), patients continued their regular treatment with their own therapists and were free to use the app and its exercises. A third and final session on April 24 was held to gather information on the app usage "in the wild" without accompanying measures by the study team. Four patients showed up to the third and final session (one patient did not show up).

4.1   Usage, Usability, 3D Interaction and Multi-modality

In the short-time intervention, patients reported that they used the app almost daily to get instructions and to track exercising. Their statements were confirmed by the usage log files. The results of standardized questionnaires (SUS, TAM-2, USE) are given in Table 1. Overall, these results indicate a usable and well-accepted system that is easily learnt.

Also in the in-between evaluation of the mid-term intervention, patients reported that they used the app almost daily to get instructions and track exercising. Their statements were confirmed by the usage log files, but mobility measurements were only conducted a few times except for one patient. The results of standardized questionnaires (SUS, TAM-2, USE) are given in Table 2. Overall, these results indicate again a usable and well accepted system that is easily learnt.

Even when the patients were free to continue to use the app after the in-between meeting, only one patient stopped using the app, as her condition had very much

Table 1. Short-term intervention: questionnaire results

Questionnaire	Mean	Standard deviation
TAM-2 Intention to use	4.2	1.5
TAM-2 Perceived Usefulness	3.9	0.8
TAM-2 Perceived Ease of Use	4.4	0.5
USE Ease of Learning	4.2	0.8
USE Satisfaction	4.7	0.8
SUS	88	6

Table 2. Mid-term intervention, in-between evaluation: questionnaire results

Questionnaire	Mean	Standard deviation
TAM-2 Intention to Use	4.1	0.9
TAM-2 Perceived Usefulness	3.8	1.1
TAM-2 Perceived Ease of Use	4.7	0,49
USE Ease of Learning	3,4	0.6
USE Satisfaction	4.0	0,9
SUS	89	9

improved. Three patients reported that they had continued to use the app almost daily, which was again confirmed by the log files. These three patients are considered for the standardized questionnaires. The results are given in Table 3 and indicate again a usable and well-accepted system that is easily learnt.

Patients reported that they usually performed the exercises at home and mostly alone, either in the morning or the evening. One patient added that he performed the exercise alone in his hotel room on a business trip in the evening.

Table 3. Mid-term intervention, final evaluation: questionnaire results

Questionnaire	Mean	Standard deviation
TAM-2 Intention to Use	4.0	0,8
TAM-2 Perceived Usefulness	4,3	1.1
TAM-2 Perceived Ease of Use	4.7	1.1
USE Ease of Learning	3.3	1.6
USE Satisfaction	4.0	0.8
SUS	88	2

3D Interaction and Media. All patients of the short-time intervention changed the view port in order to view the exercises from different angles and to have better control of their own conduct of the exercise. Only two patients reported that they did not read the instructions at all, three patients and one partner used the text instructions. In the mid-term evaluation, two patients reported that they changed the view port of the animation. One of these two patients reported that "I have rotated the animation in order to see exactly how to correctly perform the exercise". The other said, "that he prefers a 3D animation compared to video or illustrations, because one can zoom-in on the interesting parts". The other three patients watched the 3D animations from the default view port. All patients reported that the avatar was sufficient and that they did not require further options, e.g., a female avatar.

In the short-term intervention, three patients said the audio was helpful. Two patients and the partner of a patient did not find the audio instructions helpful. Three patients reported that the audio description helped a lot at the beginning, while two patients did not find the audio description of the animation helpful. In the mid-term intervention, three patients did not read the exercise description (3D animation and audio was sufficient), but two read the description several times at the beginning. In the mid-term evaluation, one patient said that he really liked the visualization/animation of the exercises, which made it easy to understand how to perform the exercises.

4.2 Motivation

In the short-term intervention, one patient said that she liked that the app motivated her to regularly and properly conduct the exercises. One patient reported that she especially liked a certain exercise (stretching in the door). One patient reported that she liked the simplicity of the program and that the app would even be usable for someone with no smartphone usage experience. The introduction to the app and the exercises in the first meeting were positively mentioned as well. All patients reported that they found the support of physiotherapy with an app useful. One patient asked to use the app after the study, because she found the app motivating.

In the mid-term intervention's in-between interview, one patient remarked that she liked the intervention because it is nice that you are taken seriously. Another patient liked that the app helps remembering the exercises and gives an overview of the conducted trainings. Another patient liked the detailed explanation and the strict schedule imposed by the app. That patient remarked: "I know that I can make the entries without doing the exercises, but I liked the feeling of control/empowerment when I could check off a training". In the mid-term intervention's final evaluation, one patient noted, that "I liked to see the improvements in the mobility measurements over time. This motivated me to keep on exercising." All four patients found the study/mid-term intervention useful. One patient added that "also the intervention itself, the study context, motivated me".

Asked about an outlook and improvements for the app, one patient noted that she would be motivated by the physiotherapist looking into her app data.

4.3 Mobility Measurement

In the short-time intervention, one patient reported that they conducted the manual mobility measurement (without sensors) together and that the joint usage of the app was enjoyable. Another patient said that the instructions for the mobility measurement were insufficient. One patient reported that a different choice of bands would be recommended, which allow the usage on the upper arm und forearm without adjustment. One patient said that the current manual mobility measurement required a second person. Three patients used the measurement with the sensors. One did not know how to conduct the measurements and one smartphone did not support the sensor measurement. Furthermore one patient slightly misunderstood the measurement process, which made it more cumbersome, as she thought she had to press the accept measurement button at the maximum angle of movement (which does no not lead to repeatable results). Two patients reported that the sensor-based mobility measurement would benefit from better instructions in the first meeting and in the app. One patient recommended that at least one measurement should be done by the patient in the first meeting. In the mid-term intervention's in-between evaluation, we investigated whether the improvements of the sensor-based measurements were successful. However, a closer look at the results for the sensor-based mobility measurement (see Table 5 and compare to the results of the short-term study in Table 4) shows that the improvements of this module were not successful. The patients did not find the sensor-based mobility measurement easy to learn (Table 6).

Table 4. Short-term intervention: detail results of USE, no reference to sensor-based measurement

Questionnaire	Mean	Standard deviation
USE Ease of Learning (q1,q2)	4,3	4,3
USE Ease of Learning (q3,q4)	4.0	4.2

Table 5. Intermediate session: detail results of USE, non-sensor measurement related and sensor measurement related questions.

Questionnaire	Mean	Standard deviation
USE Ease of Learning (q1,q2)	4,8	4,6
USE Ease of Learning (q3,q4)	2.0	2.0

Table 6. Final session: detail results of USE, non-sensor measurement related and sensor measurement related questions.

Questionnaire	Mean	Standard deviation
USE Ease of Learning (q1,q2)	5.0	4.0
USE Ease of Learning (q3,q4)	2.0	2.0

Four patients did not use the sensor-based measurements regularly, only one patient did. This patient did the mobility measurements with the help of her partner (as one patient of the short-term intervention did). This patient reported that "[the partner] put it on me [the smartphone] and pressed the button for me." Two patients said that the sensor-based mobility measurement on the back was too complicated. Another patient explained that she did not do the measurements, as the physiotherapist did the measurement in the session and she preferred it that way. Also, more time to learn the sensor-based assessment did not help to improve the acceptance of the sensor-based measurement module.

In the final interview of the mid-term intervention, three patients stated that they would prefer it if the physiotherapist conducted the mobility measurements.

4.4 Correct Exercise Performance and Concordance of Physiotherapy and App Usage

In the short-term intervention patients we were able to perform the exercises almost flawlessly after three weeks of initial instruction. Only minor differences to the optimal exercise conduct were present, e.g. one patient did not bend the legs in a lying-down exercise, which did not affect the shoulder movement strongly.

In the mid-term intervention, all but one patient performed the exercises almost flawlessly. In four patients only minor differences to the optimal exercise conduct were present, but one patient made significant errors in the exercises. In the mid-term intervention we asked whether app instruction could replace the provided physiotherapy sessions. All patients answered that they did not believe that the app could have replaced the provided physiotherapy sessions. The exact results were on average 1 on a five-item Likert scale (1: strongly disagree to 5: strongly agree) for the statement: "I could have skipped the physiotherapy sessions because of the app." The leading physiotherapist noted that "all patients liked the intervention". He pointed out that the pain situation is a major factor and that especially one patient had severe pain over the Christmas weeks. At this time the patient was unhappy with the intervention, but when the pain was reduced and the patient had a much more positive outlook on the intervention. The physiotherapist's main concern was the appropriate choice of exercises and how to adapt the exercises to the current state of patients. He noted that two patients were already too fit for the selected exercises. In the final interview of the mid-term intervention, all patients answered that they did not believe that the app could have replaced their regular physiotherapy sessions. The exact results were on average 1.5 on a five-item Likert scale (1: strongly disagree to 5: strongly agree) for the statement: "I could have skipped the physiotherapy sessions because of the app." At the end of the final session, the physiotherapist stated that all patients were satisfied with the intervention and the exercises, but that it is a longer process to adjust the exercises, especially in the painful stages. The physiotherapist concluded that at the start of the intervention, more supervision for the exercises would be recommended. The physiotherapist added that the app was a useful support tool, especially after finishing the personal sessions with a physiotherapist.

4.5   Further Improvements and Pain Logging

In both interventions we asked for possible improvements of the app and the overall intervention. One patient noted that changes in the training regime (e.g., 2 times daily) are not well-reflected by the current app design (training can only be confirmed once per day). Another patient noted that checking off the exercises is only possible on the same day, but: "when I have forgotten to enter the performance of the exercises, I could not add them later". Another patient remarked that the "timing [of the exercises] is not clear, is it exactly the same timing as I should perform the exercise, can I do it faster?". This patient continued that "feedback on exercise correctness is missing ... I did perform the exercises too rigorously so pain followed in the night". The feedback on correct exercise performance was mentioned by a second patient as well: "Feedback on exercise correctness would be nice in the app". One patient stated that "the app could be used when explained by a physiotherapist or someone like a medical assistant, but not without explanation." Another patient noted that "I am interested in the other different exercises [included the planning mode of the app]". Another patient missed feedback in physiotherapy sessions on exercise performance (of the exercises presented in the app). Two patients stated that reminders in the app would be appreciated. One patient added that intelligent reminders coupled with geo-location would be a nice feature, such that one is reminded when arriving at home. The same patient also thought that gamification would be nice, with achievements and weekly goals.

One patient noted that a simple check-off of the entire exercises (all exercises and all sets) would be sufficient after a few times.

In both interventions, we asked specifically whether patients would like a module in the app to report pain. In the short-term intervention, three patients and one partner did not wish to document pain. Two patients wished to document pain, but did not have a proposal how they would like to do it. In the mid-term intervention, three patients found the idea to integrate a tool to log pain in the app interesting, two patients were strongly opposed. These patients argued that they did not want to be reminded of their pain at all, but tried hard to ignore it.

5   Discussion

A weakness of the study is the limited number of patients. However, the results are very similar for both the short-term and the mid-term intervention and thus the number of patients (overall 10) is believed to be sufficient to draw preliminary conclusions.

In both the short-term and the mid-term intervention, the scores in the standardized questionnaires were high, e.g. the SUS score was consistently in the range of 88 to 89, which indicates a very usable system [7]. The app was used almost daily in the 3-weeks and in the first 9 weeks (of the 18 weeks) by all patients and even when app usage became optional, the majority of patients continued to use the app almost daily. Therefore, the conclusion is that the app can successfully support physiotherapy for frozen shoulder patients in a mid-term time frame. 3D interaction and mulitmodal exercise instructions were appreciated.

During the mid-term intervention, patients noticed significantly more possible improvements for the app, e.g., with respect to different training regimes (twice daily) and the ability to check-off exercises in the following days.

The mobility measurements are of significant interest for physicians and shoulder surgeons, but are not well-accepted in its current implementation in the app by the patients. Most patients felt more comfortable if a physiotherapist conducted these measurements. Overall, one conclusion of the studies is that the consideration of the physiotherapists as users of the system needs to be more intensively researched, e.g. band with separate IMUs such as smart watches.

Most patients would also appreciate a joint usage with the physiotherapist, especially for the mobility measurements. Also, some patients would like to share their app usage data with the physiotherapist and believe that this sharing would increase their motivation.

An interesting question was whether patients would think that an app alone would suffice. Patients in the mid-term study firmly stated that the usage of the app without support from physiotherapy sessions would not be sufficient.

Overall, we believe that patients benefit from an app that supports home-based physiotherapy. However, in the further design the role of the physiotherapist as user of the system has to be carefully revisited in order to design a satisfying and usable system for all user groups. Also, the interaction with the physician in the long-term usage of the system needs to be clarified. If conservative treatment (physiotherapy and pain medication) fails, the physician has to decide if an operation is necessary. A well-documented course of the disease can greatly support the physician in the decision, i.e., the reliable and continuous mobility measurements and records of pain over the last years would be helpful.

6   Conclusion

Patients with frozen shoulder syndrome used an app to support their home-based physiotherapy in a short-term and a mid-term intervention. Both interventions showed that an app can sustainably support physiotherapy for the frozen shoulder syndrome as shown by the feasibility over a short-term and a mid-term period. Furthermore, the studies show that the ShoulderApp-based intervention was well accepted by the frozen-shoulder users over a short-term and a mid-term period. Patients would appreciate automatic feedback on their progress, but the usability of the automatic mobility measurement process has to be improved. The evaluation of novel hardware, such as smart-watches, is a promising new direction for that end. Most musculoskeletal disorders have similar characteristics and are treated with home-based physiotherapy as well. Therefore, we believe our results can be generalized for a large group of musculoskeletal disorders, which e.g. includes lower back pain and knee injuries. The analysis of the presented studies also showed the complexities which arise in the design of systems with multiple user-groups, in this case patients, physiotherapists and physicians. The role of the physiotherapists and physicians as co-users of the system has to be subject of further research. This work provides insights into their requirements, motivations, and needs. The inclusion of novel results from persuasive technology and habit formation is a promising line of research as well.

Overall, long-term and larger studies, such as RCTs (Randomized Controlled Trials) to research improvements on medical relevant outcomes, are warranted.

Acknowledgments. Thomas Stütz was responsible for writing the paper; he was the project leader and responsible for the conduct of the studies. He implemented prototypes of the app. Gerlinde Emsenhuber implemented the final version of the app. Nicholas Matis (shoulder surgeon) provided the medical background for the app, the studies, and was responsible for patient acquisition. He also provided the initial idea for an app for Frozen Shoulder patients. Daniela Huber and Felix Hofmann (physiotherapists) lead the team of physiotherapists. Daniela Huber co-designed the studies. Michael Domhardt performed the analysis of the log files of the first study (not part of this paper) and reviewed the study design of the mid-term study.

References

1. Aggarwal, D., Ploderer, B., Vetere, F., Bradford, M., Hoang, T.: Doctor, Can You See My Squats? In: Proceedings of the 2016 ACM Conference on Designing Interactive Systems - DIS 2016, pp. 1197–1208. ACM Press, New York (2016). https://doi.org/10.1145/2901790.2901871
2. op den Akker, H., Jones, V.M., Hermens, H.J.: Tailoring real-time physical activity coaching systems: a literature survey and model. User Model. User-Adap. Inter. **24**(5), 351–392 (2014). https://doi.org/10.1007/s11257-014-9146-y
3. Ananthanarayan, S., Sheh, M., Chien, A., Profita, H., Siek, K.: Pt Viz. In: Proceedings of the conference on human factors in computing systems - CHI 2013, p. 1247 (2013). https://doi.org/10.1145/2470654.2466161
4. Anderson, F., Grossman, T., Matejka, J., Fitzmaurice, G.: YouMove. In: Proceedings of Symposium on User Interface Software and Technology - UIST 2013, pp. 311–320. ACM Press, New York (2013). https://doi.org/10.1145/2501988.2502045
5. Ayoade, M., Baillie, L.: A novel knee rehabilitation system for the home. In: Proceedings of the Conference on Human Factors in Computing Systems - CHI 2014, pp. 2521–2530. ACM Press, New York (2014). https://doi.org/10.1145/2556288.2557353
6. Balaam, M., et al.: Rehabilitation centred design. In: Proceedings of the Conference on Human Factors in Computing Systems, Extended Abstracts - CHI EA 2010, p. 4583. ACM Press, New York (2010). https://doi.org/10.1145/1753846.1754197
7. Bangor, A., Kortum, P.T., Miller, J.T.: An empirical evaluation of the system usability scale. Int. J. Hum.-Comput. Inter. **24**(6), 574–594 (2008). https://doi.org/10.1080/10447310802205776
8. Bridgman, J.F.: Periarthritis of the shoulder and diabetes mellitus. Ann. Rheum. Dis. **31**(1), 69–71 (1972)
9. Brooke, J.: Sus - a quick and dirty usability scale. In: Jordan, P.W., Thomas, B., Weerdmeester, B.A., McClelland, I. (eds.) Usability evaluation in industry, pp. 189–193. Taylor and Francis, London (1996)
10. Buttussi, F., Chittaro, L.: MOPET: a context-aware and user-adaptive wearable system for fitness training. Artif. Intell. Med. **42**(2), 153–163 (2008). https://doi.org/10.1016/j.artmed.2007.11.004

11. Buttussi, F., Chittaro, L., Nadalutti, D.: Bringing mobile guides and fitness activities together. In: Proceedings of the Conference on Human-Computer Interaction with Mobile Devices and Services - MobileHCI 2006, p. 29. ACM Press, New York (2006). https://doi.org/10.1145/1152215.1152222

12. Chandra, H., Oakley, I., Silva, H.: Designing to support prescribed home exercises. In: Proceedings of the Nordic Conference on Human-Computer Interaction Making Sense Through Design - NordiCHI 2012, p. 607. ACM Press, New York (2012). https://doi.org/10.1145/2399016.2399108

13. Chandra, H., Oakley, I., Silva, H.: User needs in the performance of prescribed home exercise therapy. In: Proceedings of the Conference on Human Factors in Computing Systems, Extended Abstracts - CHI EA 2012, p. 2369. ACM Press, New York (2012). https://doi.org/10.1145/2212776.2223804

14. Cidota, M.A., Lukosch, S.G., Dezentje, P., Bank, P.J., Lukosch, H.K., Clifford, R.M.: Serious gaming in augmented reality using HMDs for assessment of upper extremity motor dysfunctions. i-com 15(2), 155–169 (2016). https://doi.org/10.1515/icom-2016-0020

15. Dennis, L., Brealey, S., Rangan, A., Rookmoneea, M., Watson, J.: Managing idiopathic frozen shoulder: a survey of health professionals' current practice and research priorities. Shoulder Elbow 2(4), 294–300 (2010). https://doi.org/10.1111/j.1758-5740.2010.00073.x

16. Deutsch, J.E., Borbely, M., Filler, J., Huhn, K., Guarrera-Bowlby, P.: Use of a low-cost, commercially available gaming console (wii) for rehabilitation of an adolescent with cerebral palsy. Phys. Ther. 88(10), 1196–1207 (2008). https://doi.org/10.2522/ptj.20080062

17. Dezentje, P., Cidota, M.A., Clifford, R.M., Lukosch, S.G., Bank, P.J., Lukosch, H.K.: designing for engagement in augmented reality games to assess upper extremity motor dysfunctions. In: International Symposium on Mixed and Augmented Reality - Media, Art, Social Science, Humanities and Design - ISMAR MASH'D, pp. 57–58. IEEE, September 2015. https://doi.org/10.1109/ISMAR-MASHD.2015.24

18. Doyle, J., Bailey, C., Dromey, B., Scanaill, C.N.: BASE - an interactive technology solution to deliver balance and strength exercises to older adults. In: Proceedings of the 4th International ICST Conference on Pervasive Computing Technologies for Healthcare. IEEE (2010). https://doi.org/10.4108/ICST.PERVASIVEHEALTH2010.8881

19. Faber, M., Andersen, M.H., Sevel, C., Thorborg, K., Bandholm, T., Rathleff, M.: The majority are not performing home-exercises correctly two weeks after their initial instruction - an assessor-blinded study. PeerJ 3, e1102 (2015). https://doi.org/10.7717/peerj.1102

20. Fahrenberg, J., Myrtek, M. (eds.): Progress in Ambulatory Assessment - Computer-Assisted Psychological and Psychophysiological Methods in Monitoring and Field Studies. Hogrefe, Seattle (2001)

21. Fikar, P., Schönauer, C., Kaufmann, H.: The Sorcerer's Apprentice: A serious game aiding rehabilitation in the context of Subacromial Impingement Syndrome. In: Proceedings of the ICTs for Improving Patients Rehabilitation Research Techniques, pp. 327–330. IEEE (2013). https://doi.org/10.4108/icst.pervasivehealth.2013.252224

22. Fogg, B.: A behavior model for persuasive design. In: Proceedings of the 4th International Conference on Persuasive Technology, Persuasive 2009, pp. 40:1–40:7. ACM, New York (2009). https://doi.org/10.1145/1541948.1541999

23. Gourlay, D., Lun, K.C., Lee, Y., Tay, J.: Virtual reality for relearning daily living skills. Int. J. Med. Inform. 60(3), 255–261 (2000). https://doi.org/10.1016/s1386-5056(00)00100-3

24. Huang, K., et al.: A technology probe of wearable in-home computer-assisted physical therapy. In: Proceedings of the Conference on Human Factors in Computing Systems - CHI 2014, pp. 2541–2550. ACM Press, New York (2014). https://doi.org/10.1145/2556288.2557416

25. Kelley, M.J., et al.: Shoulder pain and mobility deficits: adhesive capsulitis. J. Orthop. Sports Phys. Ther. **43**(5), A1–A31 (2013). https://doi.org/10.2519/jospt.2013.0302
26. Keren, G.: Between- or Within-Subjects Design - A Methodological Dilemma, chap. 8, pp. 257–272. Psychology Press, New York (1993)
27. Liu, S.F., Lee, Y.L.: A simple and reliable health monitoring system for shoulder health: proposal. J. Med. Internet Res. **16**(2), e11 (2014). https://doi.org/10.2196/resprot.2584
28. Liu, X., et al.: An interactive training system of motor learning by imitation and speech instructions for children with autism. In: Liu, H., Jo, K., Manic, M. (eds.) 9th International Conference on Human System Interactions (HSI), pp. 56–61. Institute of Electrical and Electronics Engineers (IEEE), Los Alamitos (2016). https://doi.org/10.1109/hsi.2016.7529609
29. May, M.A.: The psychology of learning from demonstration films. J. Educ. Psychol. **37**(1), 1–12 (1946). https://doi.org/10.1037/h0058528
30. Micallef, N., Baillie, L., Uzor, S.: Time to exercise! In: Proceedings of the Conference on Human-computer Interaction with Mobile Devices and Services - MobileHCI 2016, pp. 112–123. ACM Press, New York (2016). https://doi.org/10.1145/2935334.2935338
31. Nixon, M.E., Howard, A.M., Chen, Y.P.: Quantitative evaluation of the Microsoft Kinect for use in an upper extremity virtual rehabilitation environment. In: 2013 International Conference on Virtual Rehabilitation (ICVR), pp. 222–228. IEEE, August 2013. https://doi.org/10.1109/ICVR.2013.6662131
32. Patton, M.Q.: Qualitative Research & Evaluation Methods - Integrating Theory and Practice, 4th edn. Sage, Thousand Oaks (2015)
33. Postolache, G., Girao, P.S., Postolache, O.: Applying smartphone apps to drive greater patient engagement in personalized physiotherapy. In: 2014 IEEE International Symposium on Medical Measurements and Applications (MeMeA), pp. 1–6. IEEE, June 2014. https://doi.org/10.1109/MeMeA.2014.6860094
34. dos Santos Mendes, F.A., et al.: Motor learning, retention and transfer after virtual-reality-based training in parkinson's disease - effect of motor and cognitive demands of games: a longitudinal, controlled clinical study. Physiotherapy **98**(3), 217–223 (2012). https://doi.org/10.1016/j.physio.2012.06.001
35. Schönauer, C., Fukushi, K., Olwal, A., Kaufmann, H., Raskar, R.: Multimodal motion guidance. In: Proceedings of the International Conference on Multimodal Interaction - ICMI 2012, p. 133. ACM Press, New York (2012). https://doi.org/10.1145/2388676.2388706
36. Sluijs, E.M., Kok, G.J., van der Zee, J.: Correlates of exercise compliance in physical therapy. Phys. Ther. **73**(11), 771–782 (1993)
37. Smeddinck, J.D., Herrlich, M., Malaka, R.: Exergames for Physiotherapy and Rehabilitation. In: Proceedings of the Conference on Human Factors in Computing Systems - CHI 2015, pp. 4143–4146. ACM Press, New York (2015). https://doi.org/10.1145/2702123.2702598
38. Szajna, B.: Empirical evaluation of the revised technology acceptance model. Manag. Sci. **42**(1), 85–92 (1996). https://doi.org/10.1287/mnsc.42.1.85
39. Tang, R., Alizadeh, H., Tang, A., Bateman, S., Jorge, J.A.: Physio@Home: exploring visual guidance and feedback techniques for physiotherapy exercises. In: Proceedings of the Conference on Human Factors in Computing Systems, Extended Abstracts - CHI EA 2014, pp. 1651–1656 (2014). https://doi.org/10.1145/2559206.2581197
40. Tang, R., Bateman, S., Yang, X.D., Jorge, J., Tang, A.: Physio @ Home : Exploring Visual Guidance and Feedback Techniques for Physiotherapy Exercises. In: Proceedings of the Conference on Human Factors in Computing Systems - CHI 2015, pp. 4123–4132. ACM Press, New York (2015). https://doi.org/10.1145/2702123.2702401

41. Venkatesh, V., Davis, F.D.: A theoretical extension of the technology acceptance model: four longitudinal field studies. Manag. Sci. **46**(2), 186–204 (2000). https://doi.org/10.1287/mnsc.46.2.186.11926

42. Vorrink, S.N., Kort, H.S., Troosters, T., Lammers, J.W.J.: A mobile phone app to stimulate daily physical activity in patients with chronic obstructive pulmonary disease: development, feasibility, and pilot studies. JMIR mHealth uHealth **4**(1), e11 (2016). https://doi.org/10.2196/mhealth.4741

43. Yim, J., Graham, T.C.N.: Using games to increase exercise motivation. In: Kapralos, B., Katchabaw, M., Rajnovich, J. (eds.) Proceedings of the 2007 Conference on Future Play, pp. 166–173. ACM, New York (2007). https://doi.org/10.1145/1328202.1328232

44. Zhao, W., Feng, H., Lun, R., Espy, D.D., Reinthal, M.A.: A kinect-based rehabilitation exercise monitoring and guidance system. In: 5th International Conference on Software Engineering and Service Science, pp. 762–765. IEEE, Los Alamitos, June 2014. https://doi.org/10.1109/icsess.2014.6933678

A Digitally-Augmented Ground Space with Timed Visual Cues for Facilitating Forearm Crutches' Mobility

Beatriz Peres[1], Pedro F. Campos[1,2(✉)], and Aida Azadegan[3]

[1] Madeira-ITI, Funchal, Portugal
{beatriz.peres, pedro.campos}@m-iti.org
[2] ITI/Larsys and University of Madeira, Funchal, Portugal
[3] Intelligent Systems Research Laboratory, University of Reading, Reading, UK
aida.azadegan@gmail.com

Abstract. Persuasive technologies for physical rehabilitation have been proposed in a number of different health interventions such as post-stroke gait rehabilitation. We propose a new persuasive system, called *Augmented Crutches*, aimed at helping people to walk with crutches. People with injuries, or with any sort of mobility problem typically use assistive devices such as crutches, walkers or canes in order to be able to walk more independently. However, walking with crutches is a learning skill that needs continuous repetition and constant attention to detail in order to walk correctly with them and without suffering negative consequences, such as falls or injuries. In close collaboration with therapists, we identify the main issues that patients face when walking with crutches. These vary from person to person, but the most common and hardest challenges are the position and coordination of the crutches. *Augmented Crutches* studies human behavior aspects in these situations and augments the ground space around the user with digital visual cues where timing is the most important factor, without the need for a constant therapist providing manual help. This is performed through a mini-projector connected to a smartphone, worn by the user in a portable, lightweight manner. Our system helps people to learn how to walk using crutches with increased self-confidence and motivation. Additionally, our work identifies timing, controllability and awareness as the key design dimensions for the successful creation of persuasive, interactive experiences for learning how to walk with crutches.

Keywords: Persuasive technologies · Behavior change · Rehabilitation · Augmented experiences · User experience · Interaction design

1 Introduction

The number of people with the need for learning to walk with assistive devices is increasingly rising [1]. Mobility is an important prerequisite for equal participation in social life and satisfaction of basic human needs. Mobility impairments can restrict the participation in social life of those affected such that people lack fair opportunities for fulfilling their needs [20]. Loss of physical mobility makes maximal participation in

© IFIP International Federation for Information Processing 2019
Published by Springer Nature Switzerland AG 2019
D. Lamas et al. (Eds.): INTERACT 2019, LNCS 11746, pp. 184–201, 2019.
https://doi.org/10.1007/978-3-030-29381-9_12

desired activities more difficult and in the worst case fully prevents participation [21] Among those with mobility impairment, the number of people with the need for learning to walk using assistive technology is increasingly rising [3].

Restoration of walking is a primary goal for people with stroke and their therapists. In many cases although the patient can resume walking, he/she has to face restrictions. Few people with stroke are able to mobilize outside the house as they wish, and approximately 20% are unable to get out of the house unaided at all [23]. Another example of physical impairment is Cerebral palsy (CP) which is the most common childhood motor disability and often results in debilitating walking abnormalities, such as flexed-knee and stiff-knee gait.

Current medical and surgical treatments are only partially effective and may cause significant muscle weakness. However, emerging walking technologies can substantially improve gait patterns and promote muscle strength in patients [24]. People with Multiple sclerosis (MS) also experience gait impairments being one of the most common symptoms of the disease [23] and they require training in using walking aids like canes, crutches. These aids are also commonly recommended for balance problems, pain, weakness, joint instability, and to recover locomotion. Many assistive devices can mitigate gait disturbance. However, the most common assistive devices are crutches [1, 19].

The two most common models of crutches are: axillary crutches and forearm crutches, or Lofstrand. Forearm crutches are the dominant type used in Europe, whether one considers them for short- or long-term usage. Crutches help an individual to maintain the balance and can help in the elimination of weight bearing - partially or completely - on the injured leg. Crutch gait patterns include two-points, three-point, four-point, swing-to, and swing-through patterns. Changes from the position of the crutch, and the amount of weight bearing in the injured leg occur according to the crutch gait that depends on the amount of weight that the individual can put on the injured leg [1].

However, the use of this mobility aid can be associated to some negative consequences related to its incorrect use. Walking with crutches requires an understanding of a technique. It is a learning process that needs continuous repetition and constant attention to detail in order to walk correctly with them, not suffering negative consequences, such as falls or other injuries.

Walking with crutches crutches is, in general, a theme about which people have a lot of doubts. Feedback from an instructor can often be useful for walking correctly. Physiotherapists often give instantaneous feedback by gradually correcting the patient's position. However, there is a lack of opportunity for receiving permanent intervention from the physiotherapist leaving patients to rely on themselves for moving using crutches. Moreover, self-confidence can quickly be replaced with anxiety, especially if an accident or injury occurs [19]. In this context, we present Augmented Crutches, a novel system aimed at helping people to walk with crutches. Working in close collaboration with therapists, we identify the main issues that patients face when walking with crutches. These vary from person to person, but the most common and hardest challenges are the position and coordination of the crutches.

In this context, our main research question (RQ) was: *Can a ground-projection mobile system be effective in correctly training people to learn how to walk with crutches?*

A secondary research question (RQ2) was whether such system could increase motivation and self-confidence, since it is a long, repetitive process that requires a lot of motivation and effort.

Augmented Crutches studies human behavior aspects in these situations and augments the space around the user with digital indications where timing is the most important factor, without the need for a constant therapist providing manual help. This is performed through a mini-projector connected to a smartphone, worn by the user in a portable, lightweight manner. This paper presents the interactive design aspects of the system and identifies *timing*, *controllability* and *awareness* as the key design dimensions for the successful creation of interactive experiences for motivating patients and for learning how to walk with crutches.

2 Background and Related Work

Technologies focusing on augmentation have the capability of creating an interactive, motivating environment for patients with mobility impairment in which practice, learning and feedback can be manipulated to create individualized treatments to retrain movement [26].

Many of the technologies focusing on augmentation of the user experience are persuasive by nature. Persuasive technologies for physical rehabilitation have been proposed in a number of different health interventions such as post-stroke gait rehabilitation [13, 18]. For example, Luo et al. [28] developed a training environment that integrates augmented reality (AR) with assistive devices for post-stroke rehabilitation and training.

Cueing is defined as using external temporal or spatial stimuli to facilitate the initiation and continuation of movement (gait) [30], providing the necessary trigger to switch from one movement to other sequences of movements. This could explain why people with Parkinson, in the absence of external cues, show slowed movements and low execution times. These can significantly improve with the use of external cues.

An effective mobility-training program involves the use of external cues. Movement speed (gait speed), and movement length (stride length) have been shown to improve when visual cues or auditory cues are present, improving gait and contributing to a more active and independent life.

There is also indicative evidence in support of the use of verbal instructions (also another kind of cues), to take big steps in walking training for stride length improvement in people with mild to moderate Parkinson's disease who are without cognitive impairment [31].

Auditory signals are a form of rhythmic cues which reportedly also improve gait. Cueing techniques such as musical beats [32, 33], metronomes [32], rhythmic sound [34] or verbal instructions [35] have been implemented to improve gait. Auditory cues have been demonstrated to increase speed gait [33].

Suteerawattanannon et al. [35] studied the effect of auditory cues and visual cues and conclude that using metronomes significantly improve gait. Gait speed significantly improve with auditory cues.

Visual cues have been also found to help gait. These cues are since placement of visual floor markers [36], adaptive glasses [37]. Recently, laser guided walking visual cue such as projection of visual cues [29], projection of lines [3], and laser-guided walking canes [40] have been used.

In traditional motor rehabilitation visual cues have normally used of a series of stripes placed on the floor in traverse line for patients walk all over. Floor markers were reported to being effective in improving gait [10].

Some studies found that placing visual cues can effectively in regulation of stride length, improving gait [9, 11] and also that patients retained a positive carryover effect over after the cues being remove [9, 11]

Both visual and auditory cues have highly effective in improving gait walking in persons with Parkinson. However, they have some limitations when used outdoors, such as external noise (auditory cues) and bright areas (visual cues). In this context, researchers started to study the effects of other type of cues: rhythmic somatosensory (vibration). The results from these studies also show they can improve gait and stride length [41].

Some studies were performed to conclude that simultaneous uses of cues do not improve significantly gait more that each one alone [35].

Suteerawattanannon et al. [35] show that both visual or auditory cues significantly improve gait performance but each one has a different impact. Gait speed was significantly increases with auditory cues and stride length was effectively influenced by the use of visual cues.

In order to design digitally-augmented crutches, we used textual cues as well as visual cues. Through the application of textual cues within the design of the crutches, users experience memory retrieval which improves their walking performance [2]. Visual cues play an important role in helping patients, as they are self explanatory and facilitate users when remembering their interactions through the use of visual working memory (VWM). In this section, we review current approaches in terms of persuasive systems for rehabilitation processes (Sect. 2.1) and we provide background information on the domain problem: learning to walk with crutches (Sect. 2.2).

2.1 Persuasive Systems for Rehabilitation

Persuasive technologies for physical rehabilitation have been proposed in a number of different health interventions such as post-stroke gait rehabilitation. There are a large number of digital systems for physical rehabilitation [13, 18]. We review the ones that correlate best with our own system, especially in terms of persuasion.

Task guidance is one approach: computers can help users perform better when they use crutches, by showing them how they are performing by visually projecting what the user is doing and receiving guidance about what to do better and which aspects should be improved. For instance, Tsuda et al. [2] created a robot that provides textual cues based on information such as body acceleration. The textual cues are about the walking stride: whether it is short, long or correct. This improves the walking performance because it acts like a memory recall about the task (walking correctly) [2]. In our system, we also decided to include textual cues for the user to know how to walk with crutches and persuade the user towards changing his behavior. Visual cues are also popular, as they are a signal of something or a reminder of something, aiming at being self-explanatory and pre-attentive. Visual elements were used to e.g. improve the walking skills of Parkinson disease patients [3, 4]. LightGuide [5] explored the use of video projections. A projection was made into the user, using his own body as a projection screen. Visual cues were then projected into the user's hand in order to guide him through the movement. Projecting the information directly in the body, helped the user to keep concentrated and not distracted by the external factors [5].

Rehawalk [6] is a rehabilitation system that projects the visual cues (footprints) on a treadmill during the gait training of the patient. Similarly, Slekhavat et al. [7] developed a projection-based approach AR feedback system that shows visual cues and feedback in order to provide an effective understanding of the relationship between body perception and movement kinematics in rehabilitation exercises. The visual cues depend on the type of exercise. If it is a stepping exercise the footprint icons are presented on the surface of the treadmill, if it is an obstacles' exercise the visual obstacles are presented on the treadmill.

These projection-based approaches for gait disorders' training are based on walking on a surface (usually a treadmill). In contrast to this, our approach is suited for gait training with crutches and projects visual cues (footprints and crutches icons) directly on the floor. With this we want to explore how the user reacts to the visual cues and if it helps the user to know how to walk with crutches, becoming more focused in his task. Another advantage of projecting the visual cues on the floor is portability: as long as it is visible (i.e. not hit by direct sunlight), the system can be used anywhere.

Persuasive systems and Behavior Change Support Systems (BCSS) show great potential for improving the efficacy and efficiency of the rehabilitation process. For instance, Van Delden [8] propose movement-based games for gait rehabilitation with personalization based on gait characteristics. In a similar approach to ours, based on digital augmentation of the environment, they used an eight by one-meter pressure sensitive interactive LED floor and developed interactive games to steer different dimensions of people's gait, increase motivation, provide an enjoying experience, and create an additional platform for gait rehabilitation by physical therapists [8].

Kim and Mugisha [9] present a paradigm called "visual feedback distortion" in which they manipulate the visual representation of step length and study whether that distortion influences gait spatial pattern. They concluded that perturbation of visual information about subjects' movement can cause unintentional motor functions. A related approach with ours is presented by Merrett et al. [10], who describe the research and development of an instrumented forearm crutch that was developed to wirelessly and autonomously monitor a patient's weight bearing over the full period of their recovery, including its potential use in a home environment. Initial results highlighted the capability of the instrumented crutch to support physiotherapists and patients in monitoring usage, thus making use of the reflective mind [11] as an approach to consciously motivate the user.

Other persuasive systems worth noting include physical computer games for motivating physical play among the elderly [13], and modular interactive tiles for short-term training of community-dwelling elderly [14, 15].

A virtual environment like the existing ones is not adequate for the specific problem of learning to walking with crutches, since the patient will need to learn how to adapt to the virtual environment itself. Also, solutions like these are obviously not portable, and therefore the patient is limited to using it only in certain cases. Early examples of persuasive technologies argued for Ambient Intelligence for Persuasion (AmI) [12]. Surrounding the user with persuasive technology (in everyday life) opens up the possibility for implementing persuasive interventions just at the right time and in the right place. This is extremely effective for learning crutch walking. Based on this context, our approach provides persuasive and motivational feedback in two different ways: (i) through persuasive sentences as well as information about gait training, and (ii) through carefully-timed visual cues, including the remaining time the patient has to complete each phase of the gait training.

2.2   Walking with Crutches

There are different types of crutches for different situations. Our work focused on forearm crutches, illustrated in Fig. 1, since forearm crutches are the dominant type used in Europe, whether it is for short- or long-term usage. These crutches are indicated for people undergoing rehabilitation of an injury to the lower limb, and are commonly prescribed to enable functional mobility for people with walking problems [2].

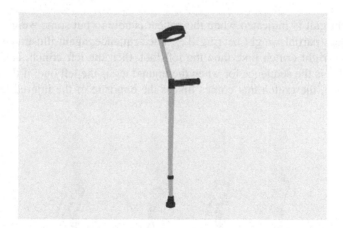

Fig. 1. Forearm crutches.

Additionally, there are several different methods for walking with crutches. These depend the on the weight bearing that the patient can put on the injured side. In collaboration with therapists we learned that the more common types of crutch gait used are: (i) three-point gait; (ii) four-point gait; and (iii) single crutch gait. There has to be specific training for each of these three gaits, although the ones that are more challenging are the three- and four-point gaits.

Three-point gait is used when there is inability to discharge the weight in one of the lower limbs [2]. The sequence, is illustrated by Fig. 2: both crutches and the affected leg move forward together, then the other leg moves forward by the patient (voluntarily). This type of gait is employed when the patient has no strength in the injured leg.

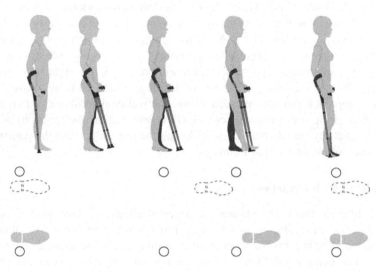

Fig. 2. Three-point gait.

Four-point gait is indicated when the patient is able to put some weight bearing in the injured leg (partial weight bearing) [2]. The sequence, again illustrated (Fig. 3) is the following: right crutch first, then the left foot, then the left crutch, and finally the right foot. This is the sequence for when the injured leg is the left one; if the injured leg is the right one, the crutch that comes first is the opposite of the injured leg.

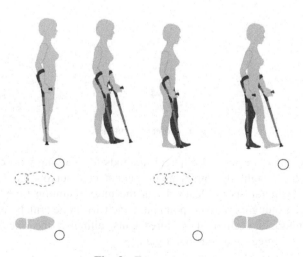

Fig. 3. Four-point gait.

Finally, single crutch gait (Fig. 4). When the weight bearing in the injured leg is 100%. The crutches should be on the arm opposite to the injured leg. For instance, considering the injured leg is the left one, the sequence is the following: the right arm and the crutch move together, with the weaker leg, then the stronger leg moves by itself.

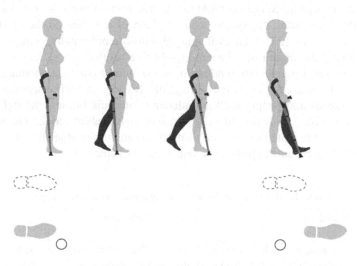

Fig. 4. Single crutch gait.

Many studies of crutch walking have been made by researchers. For example, studies about the amount of weight bearing during crutch walking and studies to improve the user's walking with crutches [1, 17, 18]. However, we could not find any study or device related to crutch gait, i.e. the coordination between the foot step and the crutch, which exhibits changes throughout the rehabilitation process.

We discarded audio cues because of the nature of the learning process itself. Visual cues can help in a more effective way. This is inline current literature that refers e.g. its effectiveness in issues like Parkinson's disease gait training [29].

3 Method

The main challenge that we addressed was the learning of correct positioning and coordination of the crutches. Position and coordination as main challenges were identified through three different sources which we will clarify in the next version of the manuscript: (i) known literature, e.g. [1–3]; This literature includes illustrated manuals of nursing practice as well, which document the problem in a very clear manner[1]; (ii) extensive interviews which were made to experienced physical therapists,

---

[1] See e.g. *Illustrated Manual of Nursing Practice*, Springhouse Ed., 3rd ed, ISBN-10 1582550824.

who all independently agreed as to the reasons that actually make it difficult for people to learn how to walk with crutches (again, position and coordination); and finally (iii) the first author's own personal experience as a chronic user of crutches. This is also inferred from simple consultation to different specialized websites that provide advice on how to safely and efficiently walk with crutches, as position and coordination are evident as most common problem, and credible websites such as the American Academy of Orthopedic Surgeons (AAOS). In this section, we describe our method, which involved designing the system with the help of experienced therapists, developing in an agile way [27], then evaluating it with a representative sample of target users, and finally discussing the clustered qualitative results.

An ideal system for ambulation rehabilitation should be compact, modular, flexible, versatile, easy to use, easy to switch on and off, friendly to both categories of users (physical therapists and people with ambulation-related disabilities) through the adequate interfaces [16, 22]. It should be a portable, high-usability tool, able to provide training, assistance (adapted to the user's limitations and to the objective of the training program), challenges, constraints, drive and support (Table 1).

Table 1. Relationship between design goals and visual cues.

Design goals	Visual cues	Rationale
Good visibility	Designed as bright white visual cues imposed over a black background	The system should be used in a variety of ground spaces. Therefore, having clean, bright visual cues is paramount to achieve this goal
Well-timed animations	Designed and thoroughly tested with experienced therapists so that they would match the real life training process	Timing is important when helping users to walk with crutches
Improved motivation	Persuasive textual cues	Learning to walk with crutches is typically performed under stressful conditions as the patients need extrinsic motivation in order to succeed. Cues should be designed in order to improve motivation

Other design goals include a precise and real-time diagnosis, evaluation and assessment and to become a biofeedback tool that is persuasive, comprehensible and comprehensive in real-time [16, 39].

Current VR solutions require the use of special equipment that is simply too costly (e.g. VR CAVEs) or too cumbersome to use with crutches (e.g. HMDs). All these alternative techniques were found to be confusing, including from the first author's own personal experience as well as from the user research we performed. We are striving for portability and effectiveness. Interviews with therapists (corroborated by other sources of research such as user observations), clearly point out that people need to train their crutch-walking alone, ideally *anytime, anywhere*. The goal is not to replace the physical therapist, but rather have a cost-effective, portable solution that addresses the real needs of people who unfortunately need to learn how to walk with crutches. The visual cues were designed having in mind the crutch-walk learning process. They were validated by the therapists and then we proceeded to evaluate them in the context of the ground-projection system.

Having some of these goals in mind, Augmented Crutches was designed and developed as a projection-based system for assisting the user who is learning how to walk with crutches. All current projection-based approaches for gait training disorders are based on walking on a surface (usually a treadmill). In contrast, our solution projects visual cues (footprints and icons) directly into the floor, augmenting the physical space surrounding the crutches. It presents the user with digital feedback, precisely-timed cues and motivating elements like textual quotes. Figure 5 illustrates the system in use.

Augmented Crutches is worn as a belt that contains a front pocket where a Philips PicoPix mini-projector is connected to an Android phone running the system. This setup allows for portability and avoids the complicated task of VR treadmills, which would require additional training and would confuse learners or even people with significant crutch-walking experience.

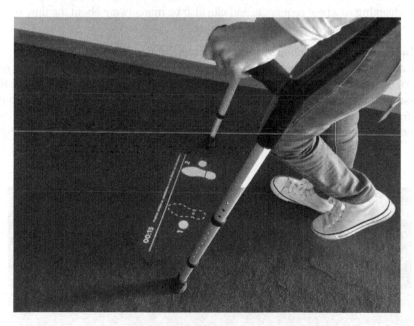

Fig. 5. Augmented Crutches.

To provide guidance when walking with crutches, the visual cues need to convey a sense of where to start and *what goes first, the foot or the crutch?* Users are motivated by the combination of what is projected on the floor (the visual cues) with the timed challenge of moving along a path, thus correctly performing a training session.

The design considerations that were addressed included personalization, timing, visual cues and feedback.

Personalization. As described in Sect. 2.2, there are different types of gait training with crutches. Through close collaboration with physical therapists, we designed Augmented Crutches as a solution to address the main three different gait training types: three-point gait, four-point gait and single crutch gait. Personalization provides a gait training adapted to the condition of the patient through a questionnaire that is available in the mobile application. The questionnaire's results perform a triage and sets the system accordingly. Through the user's answers about his physical condition, the system generates the adequate gait training. The questions include: "Which one is the injured side?", "What is the amount of weight that can be put in the injured leg?", age, height, and others.

Visual Cues. The visual cues provide information about the position of the foot and the crutch, as well as the sequence of movements. With this visual guide, the user improves the performance on the correct gait training.

Timing. In our design there is a system-imposed timing, as users follow the visual cues (footprints and the crutches' icons) which are displayed at specified speeds. The user can observe how much time there is to conclude a sequence of the gait training before changing to a new sequence, and can also be more aware about the time that was spent performing any given training sequence.

Feedback. Feedback components provide information about the gait training. This feedback can appear after finishing a sequence of visual cues transmitting to the user a sense of continuation (ex: motivational messages to continue the effort). This feedback can also help the user about the progress of the gait training sessions, again without the need for a human intervention.

Figure 6 illustrates a particular gait training sequence (in this case, for three-point gait).

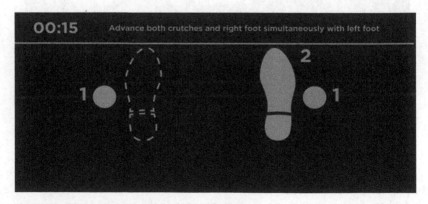

Fig. 6. Augmented crutches showing a sequence of gait training.

3.1 Participants and Procedure

The focus of our evaluation was on understanding the user's behavior regarding the visual cues during the gait training process. We recruited 21 participants (7 who walked with crutches and 14 who never walked with crutches). We made sure that the participants were not visually-impaired, and only participants with normal visual performance were included in the study. Ages ranged from 18 to 56 years old. It is important to point out that the evaluation was documented with informed consent and all image rights belong to the authors.

The following table characterizes the participants in detail (Table 2).

Table 2. Participants' chacteristics.

Subject	Gender	Age	Experience on walking with crutches
U1	F	21	Yes
U2	M	55	Yes
U3	F	56	Yes
U4	M	23	No
U5	F	30	No
U6	F	23	Yes
U7	F	27	Yes
U8	F	44	Yes
U9	F	22	Yes
U10	F	23	No
U11	F	23	No
U12	F	54	No
U13	F	27	No
U14	F	19	No
U15	F	24	No
U16	F	30	No
U17	F	24	No
U18	M	26	No
U19	F	19	No
U20	M	25	No
U21	M	22	No

3.2 Procedure

Each participant was asked to answer the system's built-in questionnaire. The participants that already used crutches were asked to remember the moment that they started using crutches. For the remaining participants, we asked them to imagine that they have an injury and that they have to use crutches without having been taught on how to do it. The questionnaire was deemed very easy to understand by all participants.

The second task, performed by all participants, was to experiment with the system and follow the visual cues (essentially the footprint and the crutch icon as exemplified in Fig. 5). The first sequence of visual cues was shown for 15 s before changing to the next one. Participants could understand and follow the visual cues.

Users were interviewed after each session, and filled-in a small questionnaire. An observer (first author) took notes. The main criteria for the questionnaire's design was: (i) the understanding of the visual cues, (ii) why was this understanding effective or not, and (iii) what was the participant's opinion regarding the timing of visual cues in our system. Focusing the questions on the "why" helped us assess exactly what had been learned by the users, in terms of crutch walking. All data was triangulated between the different sources, so that the researchers' observations were found consistent with the participants' answers in the questionnaires.

With the data collected and clustered, we analyzed the three main issues that arise when designing behavior change support systems for gait training sessions, described in the following section.

4   Results and Discussion

4.1   Qualitative Results

Most users involved in this qualitative study were quite interested in the walking process and noted the importance that our system brings in terms of awareness, e.g. *"This is useful for understanding the crutch walking process"* (U7). There were some general, broad issues that were pointed out. For instance, some users mentioned difficulty using the crutches for the first time, especially during the beginning of the training process: *"I was not sure if the length of my step was correct, besides that I had to memorize the instructions because once I moved the foot, the positioning of the image changed"* (U5, U8).

In terms of feedback, we observed that during the display of visual cues (footprint and crutches icons) which build the gait training, all users were able to understand the visual cues and the position of them, but they often expressed some frustration with the time. As one participant expressed: *"It is too fast, it requires some speed to perform the position of the visual cues"* (U9). Users also noted some lack of explanation regarding the type of crutch that the users have to use in order to perform the training. As one user explained, *"I didn't understand clearly through the image what was the type of crutch that is required"*. The problem here is if the user doesn't employ a forearm crutch (Fig. 1), then the gait training supplied by the system will be not adequate.

Users reported high levels of motivation, however this is somewhat expected due to the novelty effect of the system. We were not focused on measuring motivation, but rather making sure that users were engaged and felt motivated. The system showed motivational messages, such as the one illustrated in Fig. 7. With this feedback, we decided to improve our approach by providing more time in each sequence of the visual cues, and also to explain in the beginning which is the type of crutch that the user needs to have.

Fig. 7. Augmented crutches' motivating visual cue (an example).

With the data collected and clustered, we analyzed the three main issues that arise when designing behavior change support systems for gait training sessions. We discuss the main takeaways in terms of (i) timing, (ii) controllability, and (iii) awareness.

4.2   Timing

Timing was clearly the most important design dimension for this type of system. Independently of the persuasive icons, textual or visual cues can only be effective if they are displayed at the proper timing.

The stipulated time aimed at helping people improve their locomotion (walking properly with crutches) and not their speed. The *"timer also aims to encourage the person to learn to walk better with crutches"* (U9[2]). Other users are also inline with this motivating capability provided by the well-timed cues. For instance, U8 referred that *"Regarding the timer, in my case I would set it faster, so I did not have to wait for the rest of the time to continue. But time will depend from person to person to people who make faster slow others"* (U8). Also, the motivating aspect comes from making the process less monotonous, e.g. *"Without the timer, it would be monotonous"* (U9).

Another user suggested to *"make the timing intervals defined by each user, according to the training experience"* (U6), i.e. the more experienced the user is, the lower the timing intervals.

4.3   Controllability

Controllability implies being self-confident that the process is going well. The user should feel assured that the training is effective. In this perspective, qualitative data seems clear: *"Positioning, and coordination of the solution was easy to use"* (U1, U2, U3, U4, U6, U7, U9), the *"numbers helped"* (U4, U6, U7, U9). Even *"without stepping, the projection helps you see the sequence and what goes first (...) and I had no doubts thanks to the [visual cues] that were being displayed"* (U8). *"Without this I do not know if I could feel confident enough on how to walk with crutches"* (U8).

In this aspect, the qualitative data seems to suggest a negative point involved in this solution: the fact that the projection moves along with the user was sometimes referred as *"being a little confusing at the beginning"* (U5, U8).

---

[2] Throughout this section, U*i* refers to the user (i.e. the participant's ID in our evaluation).

4.4 Awareness

Being aware of their progress was also highlighted by the users in this experiment. The notion of progress is particularly important in behavior change support systems, as it motivates the user towards achieving a desired goal, even when the progress is slow.

In our case, the system was regarded almost as a game. In fact, some suggestions were given to "*gamify the system*", e.g. "*Maybe instead of showing different timings, [the system] could present different challenges: stairs, ramps*" (U4).

All these design considerations, empirically tested, are extremely useful for facilitating the design of persuasive systems, especially when those systems need to motivate people on how to proceed correctly with their training processes.

4.5 Limitations of the Study

As with all qualitative studies approaching novel systems for assistive technologies, this study has its own strengths and weaknesses.

In terms of limitations of the study, we highlight the following:

- The majority of participants had never walked with crutches before. This was not considered to be a major concern, since the target of the system is on helping users to learn how to walk with crutches, as specified in our RQ. However, it would be important to further assess the effect of ground space visual cues on users that have extensive crutch experience and/or major motor impairments.
- The study had a limited time duration. This means nothing can be claimed regarding the study's efficacy on the long term. To address this weakness, we are preparing a longitudinal study involving a representative sample of users.
- No study or assessment was performed regarding other types of gait training.

5 Conclusions and Future Work

Crutch walking is very different from gait rehabilitation in the sense there are no degrees of freedom. For instance, balance is limited, and the amount of applied strength is fine-tuned throughout the rehabilitation process itself. The main advantages of Augmented Crutches are portability and a reduced need for human intervention during gait training processes. However, Augmented Crutches also brings an important element of persuasiveness to a physical rehabilitation process that can be painful and can even lead to significant losses of self-confidence and self-awareness. Van Delden reports patients complaining about over stimulation of reflective light due to the led floor they used [8]. Our approach does not suffer from this effect. Subtle solutions are needed for achieving usable behavior change support systems.

By digitally augmenting the physical space around the user, our system helps people to learn how to walk using crutches with increased levels of self-confidence and motivation. Additionally, our work identifies timing, controllability and awareness as the key design dimensions for the successful creation of persuasive experiences for learning how to walk with crutches.

Future work, as suggested by some of the participants in the study, could include the development of an audio-enhanced version for the blind (suggested by U2), but should be essentially dedicated to improving the persuasive elements of the system. It should also focus on improvements to the technical design of the system in order to allow more detailed real-time adaptation to the users' gait speed and consideration regarding predictable achievement of the users' desired proficiency when using crutches.

Acknowledgements. We thank the therapists for helping us design an effective solution. This project was partially funded by projects FCT UID/EEA/50009/2019, M1420-01-0145-FEDER-000002, and M1420-01-0247-FEDER-000019.

References

1. Li, S., Armstrong, C., Cipriani, D.: A three-point gait crutch walking: variability in ground reaction force during weight bearing. Arch. Phys. Med. Rehabil. **82**(1), 86–92 (2001)
2. Tsuda, N., Tarao, S., Nomura, Y., Kato, N.: Attending and observing robot for crutch users. In: Companion of the 2018 ACM/IEEE International Conference on Human-Robot Interaction (HRI 2018), pp. 259–260. ACM, New York (2018)
3. Vitório, R., Lirani-Silva, N., Pierucinni-Faria, F., Moraes, R., Gobbi, L., Almeida, Q.: Visual cues and gait improvement in Parkinson's disease: which piece of information is really important? Neuroscience **277**, 273–280 (2014)
4. Sidaway, B., Anderson, J., Danielson, G., Martin, L., Smith, G.: Effects of long-term gait training using visual cues in an individual with Parkinson disease. Phys. Ther. **86**(2), 186–194 (2006)
5. Rajinder, S., Hrvoje, B., Andrew, W.: LightGuide: projected visualizations for hand movement guidance. In: Proceedings of the SIGCHI Conference on Human Factors in Computing Systems (CHI 2012), pp. 179–188. ACM, New York (2012)
6. Rehawalk homepage. https://samcon.nl/Rehabilitation/Gait-rehab/Zebris-Rehawalk. Accessed 03 May 2019
7. Sekhavat, Y., Namani, S.: Projection-based AR: effective visual feedback in gait rehabilitation. IEEE Trans. Hum. Mach. Syst. **48**, 1–11 (2018)
8. Delden, R.V., et al.: Personalization of gait rehabilitation games on a pressure sensitive interactive LED floor. In: Orji, R., Reisinger, M., Busch, M., Dijkstra, A., Stibe, A., Tscheligi, M. (eds.) Proceedings of the Personalization in Persuasive Technology Workshop, Persuasive Technology 2016, Salzburg, Austria, 05 April 2016 (2016). http://ceur-ws.org
9. Kim, S., Mugisha, D.: Effect of explicit visual feedback distortion on human gait. J. Neuroeng. Rehabil. **11**, 74 (2014)
10. Merrett, G., Ettabib, M., Peters, C., Hallett, G., White, N.: Augmenting forearm crutches with wireless sensors for lower limb rehabilitation. Measur. Sci. Technol. 21(12) (2010)
11. Kahneman, D.: Thinking, Fast and Slow. Farrar, Straus and Giroux, New York (2011)
12. Reitberger, W., Tscheligi, M., de Ruyter, B., Markopoulos, P.: Surrounded by ambient persuasion. In: CHI 2008 Extended Abstracts on Human Factors in Computing Systems (CHI EA 2008), pp. 3989–3992. ACM, New York (2008)
13. Jessen, J., Lund, H., Jessen, C.: Physical computer games for motivating physical play among elderly. Gerontechnology **13**(2), 220 (2014)
14. Lund, H., Jessen, J.: Effects of short-term training of community-dwelling elderly with modular interactive tiles. Games Health J. **3**(5), 1–7 (2014)

15. Lund, H.: Modular interactive tiles for rehabilitation: evidence and effect. In: Proceedings of ACS 2010, pp. 520–525 (2010)
16. Tabac, M., Hermens, H., Burkow, T., Ciobanu, L., Berteanu, M.: Acceptance and usability of an ambulant activity coach for patients with COPD. In: Proceedings of the IADIS International Conference e-health, Prague, 24–26 July, pp. 61–68. IADIS Press (2013)
17. Youdas, J., Kotajarvi, B.J., Padgett, D.J., Kaufman, K.: Partial weight-bearing gait using conventional assistive devices. Arch. Phys. Med. Rehabil. **86**(3), 394–398 (2005)
18. Goh, J., Toh, S., Bose, K.: Biomechanical study on axillary crutches during single-leg swing-through gait. Prosthet. Orthot. Int. **10**, 89–95 (1986)
19. Carpentier, C., Font-Llagunes, J., Kövecses, J.: Dynamics and energetics of impacts in crutch walking. J. Appl. Biomech. **26**(4), 473–483 (2010)
20. Sammer, G., et al.: Identification of mobility-impaired persons and analysis of their travel behavior and needs. Transp. Res. Rec. **2320**, 46–54 (2013)
21. Cowan, R.E., Fregly, B.J., Boninger, M.L., Chan, L., Rodgers, M., Reinkensmeyer, D.J.: Recent trends in assistive technology for mobility. J. Neuroeng. Rehabil. **9**(20), 9–20 (2012)
22. Campos, P., Nunes, N.J.: Principles and practice of work style modeling: sketching design tools. In: Clemmensen, T., Campos, P., Orngreen, R., Pejtersen, A.M., Wong, W. (eds.) HWID 2006. IIFIP, vol. 221, pp. 203–219. Springer, Boston, MA (2006). https://doi.org/10.1007/978-0-387-36792-7_12
23. Tyson, S.F., Rogerson, L.: Assistive walking devices in non-ambulant patients undergoing rehabilitation after stroke: the effects on functional mobility, walking impairments and patients' opinion. Arch. Phys. Med. Rehabil. **90**, 475–479 (2009)
24. Rose, J., Cahill-Rowley, K., Butler, E.: Artificial walking technologies to improve gait in cerebral palsy: multichannel neuromuscular stimulation. Artif. Organs **41**(11), E233–E239 (2017)
25. Andreopoulou, G., Mercer, T., van der Linden, M.: Walking measures to evaluate assistive technology for foot drop in multiple sclerosis: a systematic review of psychometric properties. Gait Posture **61**, 55–66 (2018)
26. Merians, A.S., et al.: Virtual reality-augmented rehabilitation for patients following stroke. Phys. Ther. **82**, 898–915 (2002)
27. Constantine, L., Campos, P.: CanonSketch and TaskSketch: innovative modeling tools for usage-centered design. In: OOPSLA 2005, 16–20 October, San Diego, USA (2005)
28. Luo, X., Kline, T., Fischer, H., Stubblefield, K., Kenyon, R., Kamper, D.: Integration of augmented reality and assistive devices for post-stroke hand opening rehabilitation. In: International Conference of the IEEE Engineering in Medicine and Biology Society, Shanghai, China (2005)
29. Schlick, C., Ernst, A., Bötzel, K., Plate, A., Pelykh, O., Ilmberger, J.: Visual cues combined with treadmill training to improve gait performance in Parkinson's disease: a pilot randomized controlled trial. Clin. Rehabil. **30**, 463–471 (2015)
30. Azulay, J.P., Mesure, S., Blin, O.: Influence of visual cues on gait in Parkinson's disease: contribution to attention or sensory dependence? J. Neurol. Sci. **248**, 192–195 (2006)
31. Fok, P., Farrell, M., McMeeken, J., Kuo, Y.L.: The effects of verbal instructions on gait in people with Parkinson's disease: a systematic review of randomized and non-randomized trials. Clin. Rehabil. **25**(5), 396–407 (2011). https://doi.org/10.1177/0269215510387648
32. Hayashi, A., Nagaoka, M., Yoshikuni, M.: Music therapy in Parkinson's disease: improvement of Parkinsonian gait and depression with rhythmic auditory stimulation. Parkinsonism Relat. Disord. **12** (2006). https://doi.org/10.1016/j.parkreldis.2006.05.026
33. Thaut, M., McIntosh, G., Rice, R., Miller, R., Rathbun, J., Brault, J.: Rhythmic auditory stimulation in gait training for Parkinson's disease patients. Mov. Disord. **11**(2), 193–200 (1996)

34. Ledger, S., Galvin, R., Lynch, D., Stokes, E.K.: A randomised controlled trial evaluating the effect of an individual auditory cueing device on freezing and gait speed in people with Parkinson's disease. BMC Neurol. **8**, 46 (2008). https://doi.org/10.1186/1471-2377-8-46

35. Suteerawattananon, M., Morris, G.S., Etnyre, B.R., Jankovic, J., Protas, E.J.: Effects of visual and auditory cues on gait in individuals with Parkinson's disease. J. Neurol. Sci. **219** (1), 63–69 (2004)

36. Luessi, F., Mueller, L.K., Breimhorst, M., Vogt, T.: Influence of visual cues on gait in Parkinson's disease during treadmill walking at multiple velocities. J. Neurol. Sci. **314**(1–2), 78–82 (2012). https://doi.org/10.1016/j.jns.2011.10.027

37. Ferrarin, M., Brambilla, M., Garavello, L., Di Candia, A., Pedotti, A., Rabuffetti, M.: Microprocessor-controlled optical stimulating device to improve the gait of patients with Parkinson's disease. Med. Biol. Eng. Comput. **42**(3), 328–332 (2004)

38. Mendes, D., et al.: Collaborative 3D visualization on large screen displays. In: Powerwall-International Workshop on Interactive, Ultra-High-Resolution Displays, ACM CHI 2013 Extended Abstracts, 27 April–2 May 2013, Paris, France (2013)

39. Maximilien, M., Campos, P.: Facts, trends and challenges in modern software development. Int. J. Agile Extreme Softw. Dev. **1**, 1 (2012)

40. McCandless, P.J., Evans, B.J., Janssen, J., Selfe, J., Churchill, A., Richards, J.: Effect of three cueing devices for people with Parkinson's disease with gait initiation difficulties. Gait Posture **44**, 7–11 (2005). https://doi.org/10.1016/j.gaitpost.2015.11.006

41. van Wegen, E., et al.: The effect of rhythmic somatosensory cueing on gait in patients with Parkinson's disease. J. Neurol. Sci. **248**(1), 210–214 (2006)

42. Glisoi, S., Ansai, J., Silva, T., Ferreira, F., Soares, A., Cabral, K.: Auxiliary devices for walking: guidance, demands and falls prevention in elderly. Geriatr. Gerontol. Aging **6**(3), 261–272 (2012)

43. Dean, E., Ross, J.: Relationships among cane fitting, function, and falls. Phys. Ther. **73**(8), 494–500 (1993)

44. Bateni, H., Maki, B.: Assistive devices for balance and mobility: benefits, demands, and adverse consequences. Arch. Phys. Med. Rehabil. **86**(1), 134–145 (2005)

Analyzing Accessibility Barriers Using Cost-Benefit Analysis to Design Reliable Navigation Services for Wheelchair Users

Benjamin Tannert[1][(✉)], Reuben Kirkham[2], and Johannes Schöning[1]

[1] University of Bremen, Bibliothekstr. 5, 28359 Bremen, Germany
{btannert, schoening}@uni-bremen.de
[2] Monash University, 900 Dandenong Rd, Caulfield East, VIC 3145, Australia
reuben.kirkham@monash.edu

Abstract. This paper explores 'A to B' routing tools designed to chart accessible routes for wheelchair users. We develop and present a novel measurement framework based upon cost-benefit analysis in order to evaluate the real-world utility of routing systems for wheelchair users. Using this framework, we compare proposed routes generated by accessibility tools with the pedestrian routes generated by Google Maps by means of conducting expert assessments of the situation on the ground. Relative to tools aimed at pedestrians, we find that these tools are not significantly more likely to produce an accessible route, and more often than not, they present longer routes that arise from imaginary barriers that do not exist in the real world. This analysis indicates how future routing tools for wheelchair users should be designed to ensure that they genuinely ameliorate the effects of accessibility barriers in the built environment.

Keywords: Accessibility · Disability · Wheelchair users ·
Pedestrian navigation · Routing

1 Introduction and Motivation

Getting from 'A to B' is an important task in day-to-day life. It is a fundamental part of being integrated into wider society. For most people, this is something that can usually be taken for granted: the existing pedestrian paths are all accessible to them, and modern tools (e.g. Google Maps) operate seamlessly to plot an accurate route for them to travel to their desired destination. However, the same cannot be said for people with mobility impairments and other disabilities (e.g. people with visual impairments) that impact their movement within the built environment [8]. One group who are particularly disadvantaged in this regard are wheelchair users, who require a smoothly surfaced set of paths in order to safely drive a wheelchair. This is a substantial group of people with disabilities with a specific and well-defined set of accessibility needs,

Electronic supplementary material The online version of this chapter (https://doi.org/10.1007/978-3-030-29381-9_13) contains supplementary material, which is available to authorized users.

D. Lamas et al. (Eds.): INTERACT 2019, LNCS 11746, pp. 202–223, 2019.
https://doi.org/10.1007/978-3-030-29381-9_13

with there being 65 million people worldwide that are reliant on a wheelchair in their day-to-day lives [28]. This is more common in westernized countries: e.g. the Federal Statistical Office in Germany indicates that 1.5 million people use a wheelchair in Germany on a day-to-day basis [37], with a similar picture in the UK (1.2 million people [49]) and the USA (3.3 million people [48]).

In response, there has been a range of research aimed at documenting the built environment, so accessibility barriers can be identified (and thus be avoided or addressed). One aspect of this work focuses upon the accessibility of sidewalks, including the detection of surface quality for wheelchair users. These measurements have been made using both technical means such as depth cameras or acceleration sensors (e.g. [11, 13, 16, 17, 24]), or direct inspections, be they via crowdsourcing [45], or more formal inspections by experts (e.g. [46, 51]). These approaches either suffer from limited accuracy (i.e. the automated or crowdsourced approaches) or a paucity of coverage (in respect of the formal inspections by experts) [19].

Accordingly, there is an inevitable limitation in respect of a routing system for wheelchair users: it will always be operating on the basis of imperfect and incomplete information (and thereby make misdirection's, see Fig. 1 for an example). An effective routing tool will be optimised to manage the risk that arises from this uncertainty. There have been nascent efforts to build routing systems for wheelchair users, including OpenRouteService [50], Routino [52], and Google has recently offered a separate prototype to serve wheelchair users [33]. There are also predecessors to these systems that were developed as academic prototypes (e.g. [4, 21, 26, 41]). Yet one limitation of these existing works is that they have not been subject to a real-world evaluation approach.

This paper makes two primary contributions. First, drawing upon both the literature concerning the experiences and needs of wheelchair users and separately the tool of cost-benefit analysis from economics, we develop a real-world evaluation approach for 'A to B' routing systems for wheelchair users. Second, we apply this framework to compare Google Maps – a *pedestrian* routing tool (and the most widely used mapping tool [30]) – with two different Wheelchair Routing systems in a real-world scenario. As with [42], our emphasis is upon the metrics and appropriate means for evaluation. We find that Google Maps is more effective than the existing Wheelchair Routing systems in identifying accessible routes for wheelchair users. By analysing how Google Maps is more effective, we are able to propose algorithmic and practical improvements to future 'A to B' systems for wheelchair users, as well as proposing new directions for research in respect of the documentation of accessibility barriers.

2 'A to B': The Task of Wheelchair Routing

We frame the problem of wheelchair accessibility in respect of the 'A to B' problem, setting out the specific types of wheelchairs and wheelchair users, the effect of less than ideal driving conditions, and how this might in practice be mitigated. It must be emphasised that this is distinct to the *at* A or *at* B problem, which considers the accessibility of a location when someone *arrives* at it (e.g. does it have elevators to travel between floors?) and which is evaluated by a different set of tools (examples of which include Wheelmap [23] or Euan's Guide [47]). The aim is to broadly frame and capture the problem in question, so that we can fully justify our proposed approach towards the identification and measurement of barriers.

Fig. 1. A real example of a misdirection made by a wheelchair routing tool. On the left side of the street there is a narrow pavement with a horizontal slope (purple – diagonal strips). In addition, there is a street sign (yellow – horizontal strips) and a bin (red - squares) which hamper the use of this sidewalk. On the right side the narrow pavement has not only a horizontal slope but is also blocked by a bike (orange - full) and a car (pink – vertical strips). Even without the temporary barriers this sidewalk would not be usable for electric wheelchair drivers because of their narrow width. For manual wheelchair users it would only be possible with increased power and by travelling on the road itself (which itself presents substantial safety issues). (Color figure online)

2.1   Living with and Navigating Around Barriers in the Built Environment

In day-to-day life, an important task is getting from 'A to B', where A is one geographical location and B is another geographical location. This can be done using a broad range of transportation, including public transport or a private car, but in practice, there will be a portion of most trips that involve navigation of pedestrian routes of some kind (e.g. there are no roads leading to a location, a limited number of car parks and so forth). For a wheelchair user, those pedestrian routes may contain one or more obstacles: if they do, then they are either impassable, inconvenient or uncomfortable depending upon the person. The problem therefore is a matter of determining which route to take and how someone can know this in advance of traversing it, much as someone would use Google Maps. The distinction is that mapping software needs to take into account the barriers in determining which route to take and there is less of a possibility to 'ask for directions' (because most people are not wheelchair users and are therefore not familiar relevant with the barriers in the built environment). An example of a scenario involving a range of obstacles encountered after the failure of a routing system is provided in Fig. 1.

There are substantial practical effects upon the day-to-day lives of manual wheelchair users. The most notable recent work that directly considers 'A to B' routing systems is [12], which provides an extensive account of the way that Google Maps and other means are adapted by those with mobility impairments in order to assist with navigation (e.g. by performing 'reccies' to check routes in advance, or using Google Streetview to check a location): that work also proposed approaches for redesigning such systems. What is clear is that the uncertainty imposed upon people with mobility impairments – in respect of the accessibility of routes that are not already known to the person in question – has a substantial impact on their day-to-day lives, not only for the reasons given in [12], but also the wider socio-economic difficulties that often impact upon disabled people (e.g. a disproportionate number are on social security [22] and have low incomes, limiting the availability of alternatives such as taxis or more advanced mobility equipment).

2.2   Wheelchairs and Wheelchair Users

There are a multiplicity of underlying reasons why someone might be a wheelchair user. The common ground is that they are unable (or less able) to ambulate using their legs due to one or more impairments. The most usual case is manual wheelchairs driven using the arms of the wheelchair user: this group make up around 85% of all wheelchair users [35]. Manual wheelchairs generally comprise two large rear wheels (with grips known as 'pushrims') for propulsion, supported by two smaller caster wheels at the front of the chair [5]. Typically, these wheelchairs are highly customised to the specific anatomical requirements of the individual user [39].

In some cases, there are additional features, for instance a one-armed propulsion mechanism for someone who has had a stroke (and only has full use of one side of their body), or the use of a battery pack for someone who has limited strength and less ability to climb gradients. In others, a manual wheelchair is propelled by a caregiver or assistant, for those who may be unable to operate the chair themselves (e.g. due to a comorbid cognitive impairment): in this case there can be considerable physical demands placed on this operator [1, 2]. For persons who lack physical strength, coordination or control in respect of their upper arms, or those who simply lack physical stamina due to a health condition, an electric wheelchair or scooter would be used: as with manual wheelchairs, there can be a considerable degree of customisation involved in the design of these systems: they are bespoke to the user [18, 20, 39]. In general, an electric wheelchair or scooter is a four wheeled vehicle which is powered electrically by one or more motors, and normally controlled by some kind of joystick or steering wheel.

2.3   The Direct Effect of an Individual Barrier in the Built Environment

Despite this breadth in wheelchair users and wheelchairs, there is a point of considerable commonality. This starts with the *ideal* driving conditions for *any* kind of wheelchair which are the same in general, which in turn means that an accessibility barrier can be well-defined with reference to be a *deviation* from this ideal. To be specific, these ideal driving conditions are a sufficiently flat, smooth surface (albeit with sufficient grip), with sufficient space to maneuver their chair. Anything outside of that has consequences for wheelchair users: the precise effects are different depending on the individual and their abilities. They range from simple inconvenience, onto discomfort, gradual injury from repetitive interaction with the environment (or a more immediate injury were a feature to cause an accident), to impassability. To provide a concrete understanding, we now describe the main types of barriers and the different effects that they can have.

- **Surface gradient.** If a slope is too steep, physical fitness limits driving, it also involves undue effort and exertion for those who are able to navigate this [6]. In respect of gradients perpendicular to the direction of travel (i.e. with a notable camber), these can be uncomfortable, especially for (two-handed) manual wheelchair users, as they have to propel the wheelchair in an unbalanced manner [14].
- **Surface deformation.** These typically take the form of an abrupt discontinuity in the surface, which raises the risk of a person driving an electric wheelchair getting stuck, or a manual wheelchair user falling out of the wheelchair. It is not just the risk in tripping that is detrimental, but also the additional concentration required in an effort to avoid these hazards (not all of which are readily visible).
- **Rough surface.** As well as being a potential trip hazard and increasing the work required by a manual wheelchair user, it also increases harmful whole-body vibration, with a long term negative effect upon health [9, 44].
- **Lack of a dropped curb (or curb cut).** These are impassable for existing electric wheelchairs but can be passed (uncomfortably) by 'hopping' in a manual wheelchair (presuming a suitably fit rider).
- **Stairs.** For obvious reasons, these are generally impassable to a wheelchair user.
- **Narrow pavement or passageway.** Wheelchairs are wider than most pedestrians and need a certain width in order to travel a given path. Accordingly, if a pavement is not wide enough (or is obstructed by a transient barrier such as a parked car or wheelie-bin), then a wheelchair driver may have to use the road (with the obvious risks) or the route is entirely inaccessible.

These features exclude barriers that go beyond wheelchair users: for example, whether there are sufficient tactile markings for visually impaired people [31], or if there is sufficient crowd management for people with relevant impairments (e.g. age related frailty or anxiety). By focussing upon a relatively fixed set of concrete barriers, our approach avoids subjectivity and enables a focus on the mechanical accessibility issues that apply specifically for wheelchair users.

3   Developing a Measurement Framework

3.1   The Task of a (Wheelchair) Routing System

It is necessary to briefly set out the task of a pedestrian routing system and provide some terminology. A routing systems task is to plot a route between geographical location A and geographical location B. This route will be a sequence of paths. An *optimal* route will be the one which allows the person to *most efficiently* traverse 'A to B'. Typically, 'most efficiently' means the *shortest distance*, however it can be important to take into account the *complexity* of the route (because navigation can itself take additional time and effort, especially when a route is unfamiliar or more complex [10, 15]). In some cases, other factors might be optimised, for example the flatness of the route. We will say a route is *effective* if it is traversable by the person traversing it, i.e. it is *not impassable*. For someone who is not a wheelchair user, that means that the route *exists* and is *not obstructed*, for example by construction work. For someone who is a wheelchair user, this means that the route is not obstructed *for them*: in addition to that, it means that there are no *accessibility barriers for them* (i.e. those features as identified in Sect. 2.3 or a subset of them, depending on the person) impeding their route. The task of a wheelchair routing system is therefore to provide an *optimal* route from 'A to B' that (i) *exists*, (ii) is *not obstructed* and (iii) has *no accessibility barriers* for the wheelchair user in question.

3.2   What Errors Can Be Made by a Wheelchair Routing System?

Following on from the task of a routing system, it is important to be more specific as to what an error actually is and how it might arise. With *respect to a given wheelchair user* there are two primary types of errors that can be made by such a tool: A *Type 1 error*, where a longer route is proposed that presumably arises from a 'virtual' or 'imaginary' accessibility barrier which does not physically exist (i.e. a suboptimal route), and a *Type 2 error*, where a route is declared to be wheelchair accessible, but in fact has substantial obstacles within it. These errors have different consequences. In respect of a Type 1 error, the wheelchair user unnecessarily spends more time going to their destination than they otherwise would. In some cases, this may also mean additional time navigating, because longer routes on average are more likely to be complicated with an increased number of turns, in turn requiring further in-situ references to the route in question [43]. In respect of a Type 2 error, the result is the person has to do a 'go around', i.e. amend their journey in real time. A 'go around' has two implications, both of which substantially reduce efficiency: the first is that time is wasted travelling a route that is inaccessible; the second is that time has to be taken in order to identify or investigate an alternative route. Figure 2 depicts each type of error in turn.

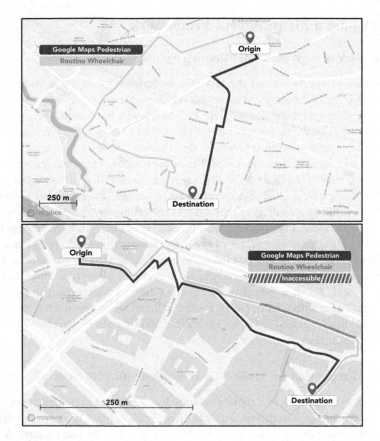

Fig. 2. Examples of the types of errors that can be made by an 'A to B' wheelchair routing system. A Type I error (top), is where a longer route is proposed that presumably arises from a virtual or imaginary barrier. A Type II error (bottom) is where the routing algorithm sends a user down an inaccessible route, when there is an alternative accessible one.

3.3   Cost-Benefit Analysis

Cost-benefit analysis is a widely-used comparative approach used to make decisions between options based on economic analysis. More specifically, it is defined as *"the systematic and analytical process of comparing benefits and costs in evaluating the desirability of a project or programme"* [32]. In our case, this is whether a wheelchair user should use a given routing algorithm. Cost-benefit analysis is an *objective* balancing exercise: it involves determining the costs and benefits of a given option. However, there are a variety of ways as to which this might be done: for example, there are different ways of measuring cost and benefit, including in respect of the units of analysis employed (e.g. time, financial cost). This means a bespoke approach must be designed for each individual scenario. This is what we do next.

3.4   Making the Subjective Objective: Classifying Individual Routes for Populations

One difficulty in developing any framework is the diverse nature of wheelchair users and their particular impairments in respect of accessing the built environment: this is captured in Sect. 2.2. Moreover, how this can impact upon a given individual is innately subjective. However, this does not mean we cannot adopt an objective approach towards evaluating wheelchair routing systems. This is because we are considering *populations* of individuals, not individuals per se, because the systems are supposed to be designed for wheelchair users at large. The remedy is to consider extrema, because it offers a strong indication in respect of the intermediate space which many wheelchair users fit within. For our purposes, this means the following broad categories of wheelchair users, with **C1** and **C3** capturing the extrema:

- **C1 (Electric/All users)**: A route which is fully accessible for an electric wheelchair or scooter user, which means it does not contain one or more errors identified in Sect. 2.3. *Note: a route that is accessible for an electric wheelchair user will almost always be accessible for most manual wheelchair users.*
- **C2: (Manual, Not Electric)** A route that has one or more errors noted in **C1**, but is not inaccessible to a manual wheelchair user (i.e. there was no need for a 'go around' by them).
- **C3 (Not Accessible for *all* Wheelchair Users)**: A route which is impassable even to a highly skilled and able manual wheelchair user without any impairments asides in respect of using their legs to ambulate.

These categories can be readily considered pairwise to produce Type I and Type II errors, *(i)* Scenario 1 by comparing C1 vs C2 and C3 combined (hereon **electric**_wheelchair user accessibility), and separately *(ii)* Scenario 2 by comparing C1 and C2 vs C3 (hereon **manual** wheelchair user accessibility). This provides two different scenarios where a cost-benefit analysis can be performed on a set of routing algorithms.

3.5   Drawing This Together: How to Perform a Cost-Benefit Analysis

For our purposes, cost-benefit analysis takes two routing algorithms at a time, RA1 and RA2 and then compares them. To do so, one needs to prepare a *sample*[1] of 'A's and 'B's: i.e. two different geographic locations and then use RA1 and RA2 in turn to compute routes. These routes can then be evaluated in turn, by computing *(i)* the length and complexity of the routes in question and *(ii)* the proportion of routes in which there is an accessibility barrier encountered, with reference to Scenario 1 and Scenario 2. A simple cost-benefit analysis would then involve computing – for each element of the sample – the additional distance and complexity between RA1 and RA2 by quantifying it as a numerical time, before deducting time for additional go-arounds.

---

[1] For an individual user, what would matter is the sample of routes (rather than focussing on one route) in any event. This is because an effective tool would be used regularly for navigation, as opposed on a 'one off' basis.

For example, one could take distance at 6 km/h (the standard speed for moving in a wheelchair – thus 6000 m = 1 h), complexity at 5 s per turn (to take account of additional consultations of a smartphone) and a time penalty of 5 min for encountering an accessibility barrier. Now suppose RA1 was 24 km (so 4 h) over a sample of routes and RA2 was 30 km (so 5 h), but RA1 involved 30 more turns than RA2 and encountered 16 extra barriers, then RA1 would perform marginally worse than RA2, because the 30 extra turns (150 s or 2 and half extra minutes) and the 16 additional detours (80 min) add up to more time taken in total.

4 Methodology: Applying Our Framework in an Investigation of Wheelchair Routing Algorithms

As mentioned before, our method is a Cost-Benefit Analysis, following the framework set out in the foregoing section. Any analysis is based upon data. This work is no exception. We therefore collected a dataset for this investigation to which cost-benefit analysis could then be applied. There are three facets to this exercise: *(i)* the design of an expert assessment of routes to obtain a ground truth; *(ii)* the determination of how routes were to be generated using existing navigation tools and then *(iii)* how these routes were to be sampled (given the burdens of performing an expert investigation).

4.1 Making an Expert Assessment of a Route

Our goal was to produce an expert accessibility assessment of the routes generated by the mapping algorithms in order to act as an effective ground truth. Two manual wheelchair users with expertise in accessibility assessments independently traversed each of the routes in question to ensure that all the potential issues were captured. This 'double annotation' is in line with best practice when collecting accurate datasets [29]. The assessments took place in daytime to ensure sufficient visibility so that no features were occluded from the assessment. Whilst travelling the route, a detailed record was taken of all potential barriers (see the discussion in Sect. 2.3 above) within the built environment for wheelchair users of all abilities. If the route was impassable in a manual wheelchair, this was recorded and then a 'go around' was performed to travel as much of the proposed route as possible. To help ensure the necessary objectivity, there was a detailed checklist that had to be completed for each trip. Any discrepancies were resolved between the two annotators. The resulting exercise involved the collection of an extensive amount of data, with 160 km of routes being directly assessed by our two experts.

4.2   Navigation Tools

There are two existing systems for routing Wheelchair users from 'A to B', OpenRouteService ('ORS') [50] and Routino [52], which *(i)* presently operate in German cities and *(ii)* which also have an publicly available API that enables automated access to them. For each of these platforms, we generated 2715 routes. We adopt the approach towards generating origin-destination pairs as per Tannert et al. [38] This approach involves determining all possible routes 'A' and 'B' within a city, where in 'A' is a publicly available bathroom, and 'B' is a point of interest. Bathrooms are used because their locations are critical for wheelchair users in two respects: *(i)* the nature of many mobility impairments means an increased need to visit the bathroom (e.g. Spina Bifida is well known for having such an incidence [40]) and *(ii)* public **accessible** toilets are a rarity when compared to the facilities available for non-wheelchair users. Bremen was chosen because it is heavily populated, as well as having a variety of terrain (e.g. a medieval city centre) as to present a diverse range of challenges for a routing algorithm.

4.3   Sampling Approach

Our sampling approach has two goals. The first was to allow for an effective test of whether Type I or Type II errors (as defined in Sect. 3.2) impeded routes, so we could gain an insight into how (or more accurately why) a system offered the routes that it did. The second was to ensure that the overall sample was reasonably representative of how a wheelchair user might use the system, thereby enabling cost-benefit analysis. The challenge was to have a process that efficiently used expert assessments, given the degree of effort involved in collecting (and annotating) the data, whilst also meeting these goals. The way we achieved this was to have three different groups of routes, of which 15 examples were sampled (making 45 pairs for each comparison, totalling around 160 km of routes evaluated) These groups of routes were determined on the basis of the degree of overlap or alignment between RA1 and RA2 (where RA2 was always Google Maps): examples of each can be found in Fig. 3:

1. **MAX (overlap)** the case where the route was closest to the one generated by Google Maps for fully ambulant pedestrians (i.e. starting from 100% overlap and descending until we have 15 routes). This is designed to help identify Type II errors, because it is highly probable that routes for wheelchair users that are equal to the routes of pedestrians could create a virtual barrier of Type 2.

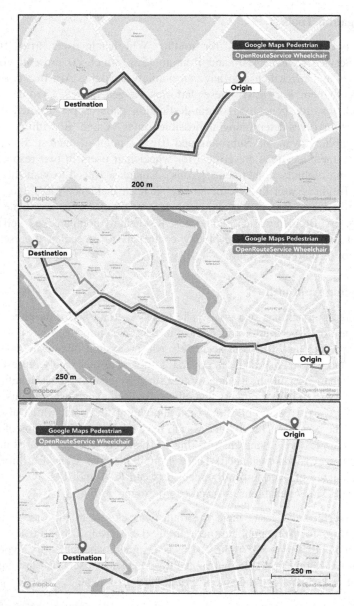

Fig. 3. These images provide examples of the generated routes in respect of each case. At the top is Case 1 (near 100% overlap/MAX), the middle is Case 2 (near 50% overlap/MID) and the bottom is Case 3 (near 0% overlap/MIN).

2. **MID (overlap)** those in the middle (with $\sim 50\%$ overlap). This was added to provide a more balanced sample for cost-benefit analysis, given that cases 1 and 3 were extrema.

3. **MIN (overlap)** those routes with the least overlap (i.e. starting from 0% overlap and ascending until we had 15 routes). This is designed to help identify Type I errors, because if the routes for wheelchair users and pedestrians are almost different it is very possible that there could occur virtual barriers of Type 1.

To compute the degree of overlap between routes we used a fine grid to represent each path (with 10 m by 10 m cells) in order to identify which elements were overlapping and thus estimate the % overlap (which is different from the difference in distance) [34].

5   Results

5.1   The Routes Chosen by the Algorithms

We begin by summarizing the general (non-accessibility related) features of the routes we sampled. As one might expect (Fig. 4), the routes for the minimum overlap (whose average length is over 1.5 km) with Google Pedestrian are significantly longer that those with a maximum overlap (all of which are under 500 m), albeit there is substantial variance in lengths. Another key feature (Fig. 4) is that the routes generated by the wheelchair routing systems are on average both longer (in distance) and more complex (they have substantially more turns, indeed on average there are more than twice as many in each route). This is also to be expected: the algorithms of ORS[2]. and Routino[3] both focus on *(i)* avoiding steps and *(ii)* providing paved routes whereby the ORS route has to be 100% paved and for the Routino route 90% must be paved.

5.2   Are the Routes Generated by a Wheelchair Routing System More Likely to Be Accessible?

The confusion matrices in Fig. 5 provide a comparison between Google and both of the mapping tools for each of the settings in question. The difference between the two approaches is mostly marginal, asides Routino's relative failure in respect of electric wheelchair users, and ORS being better (by providing three more accessible routes compared to Google) for manual wheelchair users. In total 39 of the 45 ORS routes were accessible for manual wheelchair users and 29 for electric wheelchair users. Out of the 45 Routino routes, 34 were accessible for manual wheelchair users and only 21 for electric wheelchair users. For electric wheelchair users, both tools less often provide a more accessible route, meaning that the tools were (insofar as our sample was concerned) less accurate than using Google Maps, especially in respect of Routino. This appears to be for the reason that *(i)* the routes in question are longer and involve

---

[2] https://github.com/GIScience/openrouteservice-docs.

[3] https://github.com/twinslash/routino/blob/master/xml/routino-profiles.xml.

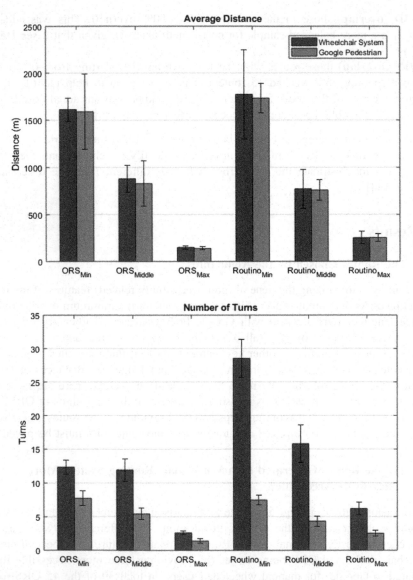

Fig. 4. A summary for the routes generated by each system, in respect of each sample, with its paired pedestrian route in Google Maps. Each graph presents the mean values, with the error bars being one standard error. A proportion of the variance is explained by the fact that Google had up-to-date information on construction sites that necessitated substantial details, but neither wheelchair routing system was aware of them.

more turns and *(ii)* there is more likely to be a missing dropped curb within a given route (this only needs to happen once for the route to fail): see Table 1 which shows the increased number of average number of curbs and missing curbs (especially in respect of the longer routes with less overlap: i.e. Routino$_{min}$ and ORS$_{min}$).

ORS Manual Wheelchair

Google:In   Google:Acc

	Google:In	Google:Acc
ORS:In	5	1
ORS:Acc	4	35

Routino Manual Wheelchair

Google:In   Google:Acc

	Google:In	Google:Acc
Routino:In	5	2
Routino:Acc	3	31

ORS Electric Wheelchair

Google:In   Google:Acc

	Google:In	Google:Acc
ORS:In	9	5
ORS:Acc	4	25

Routino Electric Wheelchair

Google:In   Google:Acc

	Google:In	Google:Acc
Routino:In	16	8
Routino:Acc	0	21

Fig. 5. Confusion Matrices comparing Google Maps Pedestrian Routing with the specialist Wheelchair Routing systems. The general picture is that under each condition, there is little or any practical difference between using a Wheelchair Routing system and simply using a general Pedestrian Routing system in terms of the accessibility (:Acc) or inaccessibility (:In) of the routes in question. The majority of the results are within the leading diagonal, i.e. neither system proposed a route that encountered an accessibility barrier.

5.3   Our Cost-Benefit Analysis

In Table 2 we compute the *additional time cost (denoted [Z] in the table)* per additional accessible route identified. We make assumptions that generally favour the 'A to B' systems, including that it would take 5 min (on average) to perform a 'go around' in respect of a given accessibility barrier and that it would take only five seconds extra per turn to navigate the route in question. We also provide the *success probability (denoted by [X] in Table 2 for Google, and [Y] for the respective routing system)*: namely the proportion of routes that were completely passable for each type of wheelchair user.

Table 1. This table provides a summary of the number of missing dropped curbs in respect of each routing algorithm. It can be seen that Google Maps is generally more successful in avoiding them.

Routes	Total number of *missing* dropped curbs		Total number of dropped curbs		Total number of curbs	
	Wheelchair routing system	Google	Wheelchair routing system	Google	Wheelchair routing system	Google
Routino_Max	11	11	40	40	51	51
Routino_Middle	7	**4**	109	116	116	120
Routino_Min	16	**4**	280	240	296	244
ORS_Max	5	5	23	23	28	28
ORS_Middle	**4**	8	127	158	131	166
ORS_Min	15	**6**	251	216	266	222
Routino_Mean	11.33	**6.33**	143	132	154.3	138.3
ORS_Mean	8	**6.33**	133.7	132.3	141.7	138.7
Overall_Mean	9.67	**6.33**	138.3	132.2	148	138.5

Table 2. This table details the underlying cost-benefit analysis of each Wheelchair Routing Algorithm compared to Google Maps. As the Increased Accessibility Probability for Electric Wheelchairs is negative to begin with (and the routing tools produce routes that are already on average longer), the table is only complete for Manual Wheelchair Users. The same modelling assumptions are used as in our example in Sect. 3.5.

Scenario	Google success probability [X]	'A to B' success probability [Y]	Average additional distance	Average additional turns	Increased accessibility probability	Time lost/extra accessible route (at 6 kph)	Time lost from turns/extra accessible route (assume 5 s/turn)	Total time cost per extra accessible route [Z]
ORS_Electric	**30/45**	29/45	182 m	4.11	–1/45	N/A	N/A	N/A
ORS_Manual	36/45	**39/45**	182 m	4.11	3/45	27 m 45 s	5 m 8 s	32 m 53 s
Routino_Electric	**29/45**	21/45	118 m	12.07	–8/45	N/A	N/A	N/A
Routino_Manual	33/45	**34/45**	118 m	12.07	1/45	53 m 6 s	44 m 15 s	1 h 37 m 21 s

The best-case scenario is the Manual Wheelchair user with no other mobility impairments, as we have already found that the systems showed no improvement *at all* for Electric Wheelchair users (making the result of any cost benefit analysis be that Google Maps is more effective). For manual wheelchairs the ORS would need to be over *six* times more effective simply just to break-even (it takes over 30 min extra travelling time to avoid one accessibility barrier, so dividing by 5 min – our assumed time to perform a 'go around' gives us the figure in question), let alone to actually have a substantive impact on the wheelchair users chances of getting from 'A to B' in a timeous fashion. The picture is worse with Routino, which would need to be *over 19* times more effective. We find that neither routing tool is effective compared to Google Maps under a cost-benefit analysis, even if profoundly more favorable assumptions were applied.

5.4   Virtual Barriers

As explained in our introduction, our concern was that these systems may be sending their users around the houses (i.e. on longer routes) to deal with imaginary accessibility barriers (i.e. making Type 1 errors). Table 3 makes it clear that this is so. As can be seen from Fig. 6 the most aggressive interventions appear to be made on the occasions where only the wheelchair routing system produces an accessible route (especially with respect to Routino): similarly, the increased distance of using a wheelchair routing system is markedly reduced on occasions where only Google Maps is accessible. This suggests where longer routes are being used, there is a real accessibility barricr in play, for Google Maps, we observed this was where a construction site was missed by the Wheelchair routing tool (in total, we identified four such occasions).

6   Discussion

6.1   Google (Normally) Knows Best

The result of our cost-benefit analysis is surprising: it was better to use Google Maps than a specialist routing tool to travel as a wheelchair user, even for manual wheelchair users. As Google Maps was able to identify transient barriers, such as construction sites (whereas the wheelchair mapping tools directed our user straight through them), it has an evident informational advantage over the alternative tools. This informational advantage partly explains why Google Maps is more effective.

Accordingly, rather than striking out alone for wheelchair users, it might be more appropriate to focus upon improving Google Maps and similar platforms, or at the least, integrate these additional sources of information into the analysis offered by a wheelchair routing tool. This is particularly so given that Google Maps is more developed: it provides a range of features both in the moment (where someone discovers a barrier) and offline (e.g. Street View for inspections), meaning that the foregoing analysis is an underestimate of the increased burden imposed by wheelchair-routing tools. Whilst Google Maps may have a disadvantage in that it is not Open Source (unlike the two tools we used), the reason for its advantage is the level of

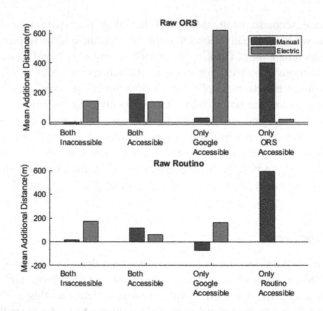

Fig. 6. These two charts illustrate the additional travelling distance involved in using the tools in question, grouped by the same categories used in the confusion matrices.

Table 3. This table enumerates the Types of Errors made in line with our Taxonomy in Sect. 3.2. of this document.

	Type I Error	Type II Error
ORS	4	7
Routino	6	12

resource which arises from it not be purely focused upon Wheelchair users: there is no reason to expect that this advantage would not apply to similarly resourced Open Source tools.

6.2   Real Versus Synthetic Evaluations

There are a number of existing works that analyze the efficacy of a given routing algorithm on the basis of a synthetic evaluation. This includes two works which were the basis for the ORS system itself [26, 27]. Our investigation shows that in the real world, these synthetic analyses are not even sufficient to ensure that the routes offered are accessible, let alone the most effective ones. There are two specific flaws with these tools *(i)* they do not pick accessible routes often enough (which would have been identified if this was tested with a direct inspection) and *(ii)* they are not being optimized using metrics that are orientated from the perspective of the end user (i.e. they do not involve an effective cost-benefit analysis).

These are synthetic problems of different flavours, but ultimately the lesson is that some form of physical inspection process (i.e. obtaining ground truth) is required when evaluating any 'A to B' tool, as well as taking into account the real data that is likely to be available when navigating, rather than some idealized expectation of it. There is a further implication, namely that these tools cannot be used as proxies for the general accessibility of a city as proposed in [38], because (unlike what someone would reasonably expect) they simply do not sufficiently reflect the real world.

6.3 Reporting Routing Options

There is always a risk that accessibility data will be inaccurate: even for expert assessments, accessibility information is as only as good as the time of the assessment. In practice, simply due to resource constraints, most data is not even gathered by experts, making it inherently unreliable at the point of collection. The real concern is one of high-level strategy: Google Maps (and similar systems) may offer more direct (and more up to date) information about additional barriers (e.g. construction sites) and routes, but there is a need to merge that with reliable accessibility information.

How should these two information sources be combined? We suggest that a starting point should be the lived experiences of wheelchair users using 'A to B' tools, as sharply captured in [12]. These experiences are multifarious in nature, being a combination of the impairment that the person in question has, as well as their wider life circumstances and the particular city that they are based. Ultimately, this must be an exercise in exposing choices and the risk associated with them, so wheelchair users can decide in advance whether its worth (for example) the risk of being 'X minutes late' or having to go Y metres further, rather than having to do 'reccies' in advance or laboriously exploring routes using Google StreetView [12]. Given that Wheelchair users sometimes use existing networks, the information arising from this could also be provided, including perhaps the sharing of location and acceleration data to the mutual benefit of other wheelchair users.

Making meaningful choices would involve a system exposing what it knows about the accessibility of given segments, before presenting it as a range of choices. Taking into account that Google Maps is likely to suggest a shorter route, the choices would in effect amount to proposed 'detours', together with the information known about that detour (e.g. how much longer, what accessibility barrier it might be avoiding and the probabilities involved). Overall, this would be an exercise in exposing trade-offs that recognizes the imperfection inherent in any accessibility tool. Other advanced algorithms have been successful in a range of complex route-planning contexts (e.g. for ships at sea [3], pedestrians travelling at night [7] or personalized routing [36]), so adapting such approaches may be a partial remedy for wheelchair mapping as well.

6.4 Cost-Benefit Analysis and the Bigger Picture

In so far as we know, this paper is the first attempt at using cost-benefit analysis in analyzing individual assistive technologies. It is therefore important to recap the benefits of this approach. In this case, the further analysis allowed for a consideration that took into account a more holistic set of factors and considered the true utility of a system to someone with a disability. Whilst any cost-benefit analysis (like any model) has its limitations (it only captures what is modelled), the success in this example may mean that it could be appropriate for it to be considered more widely in respect of assistive technologies and thereby capture the wider benefits to individual lives. We consider this approach to be complementary to qualitative methods used to understand individual experiences and an efficient alternative where these studies might not be easily available (e.g. due to the well-known difficulty of easily accessing a pool of participants due to delays in ethical approval [25], or where a longer term consideration is required in advance of deployment), or at preliminary stages in design (thereby ensuring a better design to be tested and explored in a qualitative study or deployment).

6.5   Limitations

Our investigation was constrained to wheelchair users, meaning that its findings may not generalize to people with other impairments that limit their opportunity to access the built environment. This paper focusses on one city with a diverse landscape: future work may compare the effects identified within this paper with other cities. In particular, given that our city may have had limited accessibility, a more accessible city may well produce different results and be more (or less) effective a place for using 'A to B' tools (on the other hand, it is possible that the trade-off could in fact be worse). Similarly, where a city has been more (or less) thoroughly documented in respect of accessibility, this would also potentially impact on performance. For the comparison of the routes we chose Google Maps because it is the most widely used tool: future work may benefit with a comparison between other mapping tools (e.g. Apple Maps).

7   Conclusion and Future Work

We have explored the viability of 'A to B' mapping tools for wheelchair users, by developing a novel framework based on cost-benefit analysis in order to explore their real-world efficacy. In respect of existing tools aimed at wheelchair users the overall result is unfortunate: these tools are of little or no practical benefit when compared to Google Maps, with Routino also presenting routes that were less accessible overall. In arriving at this conclusion, we have also determined that the approaches used to evaluate 'A to B' tools are potentially misleading, and an economic approach based upon cost-benefit analysis from the perspective of wheelchair users would be more appropriate instead. Our analysis also suggests more appropriate means of presenting the data generated by these systems that reflects their real-world performance and the uncertainty inherent in that. It is hoped that this work would be the basis for 'A to B' mapping tools which are of genuine and long-lasting utility to Wheelchair users going forwards.

Acknowledgements. The project was supported through the Volkswagen foundation through a Lichtenbergprofessorship and the University of Bremen. Reuben Kirkham was supported by an EPSRC Doctoral Prize Fellowship.

References

1. Abraham, B., Davidson, R.I.: A best space for assisted wheelchair users. Br. J. Occup. Ther. **80**(3), 163–172 (2017)
2. Abraham, B.B., et al.: A novel four-caster manual vehicle manoeuvring investigation: Higher loading-weights require larger turning spaces. Proc. Inst. Mech. Eng. Part H J. Eng. Med. **229**(5), 403–416 (2015)
3. Andersson, P., Ivehammar, P.: Cost benefit analysis of dynamic route planning at sea. Transp. Res. Procedia **14**, 193–202 (2016). https://doi.org/10.1016/j.trpro.2016.05.055
4. Beale, L., et al.: Mapping for wheelchair users: route navigation in urban spaces. Cartographic J. **43**(1), 68–81 (2006)
5. Boninger, M.L., et al.: Manual wheelchair pushrim biomechanics and axle position. Arch. Phys. Med. Rehabil. **81**(5), 608–613 (2000)
6. Choi, Y.O., et al.: Effects of ramp slope on physiological characteristic and performance time of healthy adults propelling and pushing wheelchairs. J. Phys. Ther. Sci. **27**(1), 7–9 (2015)
7. Fang, Z., et al.: An artificial bee colony-based multi-objective route planning algorithm for use in pedestrian navigation at night. Int. J. Geogr. Inf. Sci. **31**(10), 2020–2044 (2017). https://doi.org/10.1080/13658816.2017.1346795
8. Froehlich, J.E., et al.: Grand challenges in accessible maps. Interactions **26**, 78–81 (2019)
9. Garcia-Mendez, Y., et al.: Health risks of vibration exposure to wheelchair users in the community. J. Spinal Cord Med. **36**(4), 365–375 (2013)
10. Gartner, G., et al.: Human-centred mobile pedestrian navigation systems. Mitteilungen der Österreichischen Geographischen Gesellschaft **153**, 237–250 (2011)
11. Hara, K., et al.: Combining crowdsourcing and Google street view to identify street-level accessibility problems. In: Proceedings of the SIGCHI Conference on Human Factors in Computing Systems, pp. 631–640. ACM (2013)
12. Hara, K., et al.: The design of assistive location-based technologies for people with ambulatory disabilities: a formative study. In: Proceedings of the 2016 CHI Conference on Human Factors in Computing Systems, pp. 1757–1768 ACM (2016)
13. Holloway, C., Tyler, N.: A micro-level approach to measuring the accessibility of footways for wheelchair users using the capability model. Transp. Plann. Technol. **36**(7), 636–649 (2013)
14. Ishida, T., et al.: Evaluation of sidewalk unevenness based on wheelchair traveling resistance. Transp. Res. Rec. J. Transp. Res. Board **1956**, 68–75 (2006)
15. Ishikawa, T., et al.: Wayfinding with a GPS-based mobile navigation system: a comparison with maps and direct experience. J. Environ. Psychol. **28**(1), 74–82 (2008)
16. Iwasawa, Y., et al.: Combining human action sensing of wheelchair users and machine learning for autonomous accessibility data collection. IEICE Trans. Inf. Syst. **99**(4), 1153–1161 (2016)
17. Iwasawa, Y., Yairi, I.E.: Life-logging of wheelchair driving on web maps for visualizing potential accidents and incidents. In: Anthony, P., Ishizuka, M., Lukose, D. (eds.) PRICAI 2012. LNCS (LNAI), vol. 7458, pp. 157–169. Springer, Heidelberg (2012). https://doi.org/10.1007/978-3-642-32695-0_16
18. Kirkham, R., et al.: Build me a ubicomp: bespoke ubiquitous accessibility in live television production environments. Pervasive Ubiquitous Comput. **19**(5–6), 853–880 (2015)
19. Kirkham, R., et al.: WheelieMap: an exploratory system for qualitative reports of inaccessibility in the built environment. In: Proceedings of the 19th International Conference on Human-Computer Interaction with Mobile Devices and Services, p. 38. ACM (2017)

20. Maltais, C., et al.: Assessment of geometric and mechanical parameters in wheelchair seating: a variability study. IEEE Trans. Rehabil. Eng. **7**(1), 91–98 (1999)
21. Matthews, H., et al.: Modelling access with GIS in urban systems (MAGUS): capturing the experiences of wheelchair users. Area **35**(1), 34–45 (2003)
22. Meyer, B.D., Mok, W.K.: Disability, earnings, income and consumption. J. Public Econ. **171**, 51–69 (2018)
23. Mobasheri, A., et al.: Wheelmap: the wheelchair accessibility crowdsourcing platform. Open Geospatial Data Softw. Stand. **2**(1), 27 (2017)
24. Mourcou, Q., et al.: Wegoto: a Smartphone-based approach to assess and improve accessibility for wheelchair users. In: IEEE EMBS 2013, pp. 1194–1197 IEEE (2013)
25. Munteanu, C., et al.: Situational ethics: re-thinking approaches to formal ethics requirements for human-computer interaction. In: CHI 2015, pp. 105–114 (2015). https://doi.org/10.1145/2702123.2702481
26. Neis, P.: Measuring the reliability of wheelchair user route planning based on volunteered geographic information. Trans. GIS **19**(2), 188–201 (2015)
27. Neis, P., Zielstra, D.: Generation of a tailored routing network for disabled people based on collaboratively collected geodata. Appl. Geogr. **47**, 70–77 (2014)
28. Newdisability.: Wheelchair Statistics: How Many Wheelchair Users Are There? http://www.newdisability.com/wheelchairstatistics.htm
29. Nowak, S., Rüger, S.: How reliable are annotations via crowdsourcing: a study about inter-annotator agreement for multi-label image annotation. In: Proceedings of the International Conference on Multimedia Information Retrieval, pp. 557–566. ACM (2010)
30. Panko, R.: The Popularity of Google Maps: Trends in Navigation Apps in 2018. https://themanifest.com/app-development/popularity-google-maps-trends-navigation-apps-2018
31. Parkin, J., Smithies, N.: Accounting for the needs of blind and visually impaired people in public realm design. J. Urban Des. **17**(1), 135–149 (2012)
32. Quah, E., Haldane, J.: Cost-Benefit Analysis. Routledge, Abingdon (2007)
33. Blair-Goldensohn, S.: A better world for wheels on Google Maps (2017). https://www.blog.google/products/maps/better-world-wheels-google-maps/
34. Shirabe, T.: A method for finding a least-cost wide path in raster space. Int. J. Geogr. Inf. Sci. **30**(8), 1469–1485 (2016)
35. Smith, E.M., et al.: Prevalence of wheelchair and scooter use among community-dwelling Canadians. Phys. Therap. **96**(8), 1135–1142 (2016)
36. Socharoentum, M., Karimi, H.A.: Multi-modal transportation with multi-criteria walking (MMT-MCW): personalized route recommender. Comput. Environ. Urban Syst. **55**, 44–54 (2016). https://doi.org/10.1016/j.compenvurbsys.2015.10.005
37. StatistischesBundesamt. https://www.destatis.de/DE/Publikationen/Thematisch/Gesundheit/BehinderteMenschen/SozialSchwerbehinderteKB5227101159004
38. Tannert, B., Schöning, J.: Disabled, but at what cost?: an examination of wheelchair routing algorithms. In: Proceedings of the 20th International Conference on Human-Computer Interaction with Mobile Devices and Services, p. 46 ACM (2018)
39. Trefler, E., Taylor, S.: Prescription and positioning: evaluating the physically disabled individual for wheelchair seating. Prosthet. Orthot. Int. **15**(3), 217–224 (1991)
40. Verhoef, M., et al.: High prevalence of incontinence among young adults with spina bifida: description, prediction and problem perception. Spinal Cord **43**(6), 331 (2005)
41. Völkel, T., Weber, G.: RouteCheckr: personalized multicriteria routing for mobility impaired pedestrians. In: ASSETS 2008, pp. 185–192. ACM, New York (2008). https://doi.org/10.1145/1414471.1414506
42. Ward, J.A., et al.: Performance metrics for activity recognition. ACM Trans. Intell. Syst. Technol. **2**(1), 6:1–6:23 (2011). https://doi.org/10.1145/1889681.1889687

43. Winter, S.: Modeling costs of turns in route planning. GeoInformatica **6**(4), 345–361 (2002)
44. Wolf, E., et al.: Vibration exposure of individuals using wheelchairs over sidewalk surfaces. Disabil. Rehabil. **27**(23), 1443–1449 (2005)
45. AXS Map. https://www.axsmap.com/
46. DisabledGo. http://www.disabledgo.com/
47. Euan's Guide - Disabled Access Reviews. https://www.euansguide.com/
48. KDS   Smartwheelchair.   https://kdsmartchair.com/blogs/news/18706123-wheelchair-facts-numbers-and-figures-infographic
49. NHS Wheelchair Services Statistics. https://www.england.nhs.uk/wheelchair-services/
50. OpenRouteService. (https://www.openrouteservice.org)
51. PhotoRoute. http://www.photoroute.com/
52. Routino. (https://www.routino.org)

Bridging the Gap: Creating a Clinician-Facing Dashboard for PTSD

Elaine Schertz[1]([⊠]), Hue Watson[1]([⊠]), Ashok Krishna[1]([⊠]), Andrew Sherrill[2]([⊠]), Hayley Evans[1]([⊠]), and Rosa I. Arriaga[1]([⊠]) [iD]

[1] Georgia Institute of Technology, Atlanta, GA, USA
elaine.schertz@gmail.com, {hwatson,hayley.evans}@gatech.edu,
ashok.r.krishna@gmail.com, arriaga@cc.gatech.edu
[2] Emory University, Atlanta, GA, USA
andrew.m.sherrill@emory.edu

Abstract. Post-traumatic stress disorder (PTSD) is a serious mental health condition. Prolonged Exposure (PE) therapy has been shown to have the greatest therapeutic efficacy in treating PTSD. However, clinicians face significant challenges in delivering PE therapy successfully. We conducted a two-part study with 17 clinicians where we (1) gathered requirements for a PE therapy dashboard and (2) had clinicians assess the relevance and usability of our dashboard prototypes. The first part of our study showed that clinicians wanted (1)improved workflow for their PE sessions (2)improved methods of monitoring their patients' self-report data and (3)a way to assess their patients' progress outside of sessions. The second part showed that our dashboard prototypes were highly usable. Our study provides preliminary steps in designing user-centered tools that assist clinicians in the delivery of PE therapy by improving data access and workflow efficiency.

Keywords: PTSD · Post traumatic stress disorder · PE Therapy · Prolonged exposure therapy · Clinician dashboard

1 Introduction

Post-traumatic stress disorder (PTSD) is a mental health disorder that can develop after a person experiences a traumatic incident [2]. PTSD is characterized by four symptom clusters: (1) trauma re-experiencing, (2) avoidance of trauma related situations, thoughts, and feelings (3) negative alterations in thought and mood and (4) hyperarousal [2]. Furthermore, PTSD has serious comorbidities including suicidal ideation [19], substance abuse [21], and domestic violence [23]. The lifetime prevalence of PTSD in the United States is around 9% [2].

In this research, we focus on the treatment of PTSD using Prolonged Exposure (PE) therapy, a manualized therapeutic approach which has been shown to have one of the greatest therapeutic efficacies [4,12]. PE therapy has its theoretical underpinnings in Emotional Processing Theory of PTSD; a theory that

© IFIP International Federation for Information Processing 2019
Published by Springer Nature Switzerland AG 2019
D. Lamas et al. (Eds.): INTERACT 2019, LNCS 11746, pp. 224–233, 2019.
https://doi.org/10.1007/978-3-030-29381-9_14

emphasizes processing the traumatic memory in the reduction of PTSD symptoms [10]. The two main determinants of successful PE Therapy are repeated *in vivo* (real world) exposure to situations that the patient is avoiding due to trauma-related anxiety, and repeated, prolonged imaginal exposure where the patient revisits the trauma memory by visualizing and recounting the traumatic event aloud [10]. The fundamental takeaway of the in vivo and imaginal exposure components is for the patient to learn that the traumatic memory and the trauma itself are two distinct entities [10]. Successful PE therapy results in patients being able to reclaim control over their lives by reducing the excessive fear and anxiety [10].

PE therapy can be administered via traditional weekly sessions or daily in intensive outpatient programs. During sessions, clinicians discuss the patient's progress, review previous homework assignments, conduct imaginal exposure sessions, guide the patient through emotional and cognitive processing, and assign new homework. The therapist must keep track of the patients's self-report measures via instruments such as the PTSD Checklist (PCL) and Subjective Units of Discomfort scale (SUDs). The PCL is used to assess a patient's PTSD symptoms [15] while the SUDs scale measures how distressed the patient is feeling in the current moment. This scale ranges from 0, a state of no distress, to 100, a state of the most distressed the patient has ever experienced [10].

Our work explores opportunities for the development of technology to support clinicians in the delivery of PE therapy. While technology currently exists to support patients during their treatment [5,6,13,16,18], there is a lack of clinician-focused technology. We address this gap by first examining the challenges that PE clinicians face when delivering therapy through semi-structured interviews. Then we propose and evaluate two clinician-facing design solutions to improve clinicians' abilities to document and monitor patient progress and more effectively target treatment.

2   Related Work

Prior work on the treatment of PTSD using PE includes a variety of interfaces. Numerous mobile applications have been developed to diagnose and treat symptoms of PTSD [17]. One of the most popular mobile applications, PE Coach, was developed with the goal of facilitating PE therapy for the patient [13,16]. Functionality of this application includes the ability to record imaginal exposure sessions, enter SUDs, and schedule appointment reminders. Kuhn *et al.* found that clinicians generally have favorable perceptions of PE Coach [13], however, PE Coach does not currently have a clinician interface. Recent work in the computing field has explored the user requirements for the design of future technology which incorporates the perspectives of various stakeholders including both clinicians and patients [9].

Virtual reality (VR) based applications have also been used to improve PE therapy by enabling scenarios that are realistic yet safe for the patient [5,6,18]. VR has been used to simulate combat environments for veterans [18]. Furthermore, there is hope that the use of VR could increase the utilization of PE therapy [5]. As in the case of mobile applications, VR applications for PTSD have been primarily developed as a tool for patients [6].

Currently technology for PE therapy is geared toward the patient, however, there is also ample opportunity to help clinicians. For example, these professionals have specific challenges based on their level of experience administering PE therapy [24]. Novice clinicians are often overwhelmed by the manualized nature of PE therapy; they often focus on the implementation of in vivo and imaginal therapy and forego key clinical skills such as listening. Successful PE therapy depends on patients fully engaging with their traumatic memories, and novice clinicians often fear that patients may over engage. Thus, even though PE therapy has high efficacy, its delivery can be improved.

PE is known to be one of the most effective and highly used therapies for PTSD. We presented examples that highlight the range of low-tech (app) and high-tech (VR) options geared toward improving PE practice for patients. We have also shown that clinicians have pressing needs that have gone unmet. In our work we opt to target a practical solution to aid clinicians. Specifically, we see the opportunity for development of a clinician-facing dashboard that could, in combination with PE Coach, improve the ability of clinicians to target treatment and monitor patient progress.

3   Methods and Results

The university's ethics review board authorized the study protocol and all participants signed informed consent forms before participating. We conducted a two-part study where we gathered (1) requirements for a clinician-facing PE Therapy system and (2) feedback about two PE Therapy systems that we designed.

3.1   Interviews

In the first part of our study, 12 clinicians (10 females, 2 males, age range 30 to 58 years) that practice PE therapy participated in semi-structured interviews that lasted about 45-min. The goals were: (1) to understand the challenges clinicians face when delivering PE therapy, (2) to better comprehend how clinicians assess patient progress and (3) to determine what data clinicians are missing from their existing processes. Audio from the interviews were both recorded and transcribed. Two of the researchers used thematic analysis [7] to analyze these interviews. The researchers met to analyze, iterate, and develop 28 themes from 120 transcript excerpts. From these discussions, three main themes emerged.

The first theme highlighted the need for improved workflow during the therapeutic sessions. The current process for collecting and reviewing patient data is inefficient; clinicians want a system that enables them to quickly digest relevant information. PE clinicians have to balance time spent collecting and analyzing data and engaging in therapeutic tasks. The compromise is typically to either not collect some (or all) data or to briefly review subjectively reported data by asking the patient questions. This theme is exemplified in the following quotes:

"[Any data] needs to be easily accessible, not time intensive, and immediate because if those are not readily available, or I got to figure it out, then I'm not going to do it." -Clinician 07

"One thing that is a challenge for me as a clinician is that there are so many things to be, you know, um, be aware and assess in a short amount of time [. . .] you want to focus on the therapeutic tasks." -Clinician 05

Another theme was that self-reports are an important part of monitoring patient progress, but clinicians struggle to effectively monitor all of the self-report scores. This is due to the large amount of self report homework and data that needed to be processed and analyzed by the clinicians before therapy sessions. Past research has emphasized the utility of visualizing such time-oriented patient variables [1,14]. Research on therapeutic processes within PE suggest several indicators, including decreases in SUDs between exposures and completion of homework tasks [8,20], that are predictive of treatment outcome. Clinicians expressed this sentiment and stated:

"I put a lot of faith in [self-reports]. I definitely use them to drive treatment, to know when to terminate, when to change." -Clinician 04

"Your desk starts to explode with paperwork and of course the writing the notes, and inputting their scores each week and trying to mention their SUDS." -Clinician 04

The third major theme was that clinicians would like a better way to asses their patients' symptoms and behaviors outside of therapy and expressed a desire for more frequent assessments of symptoms in the patient's home, and information about the patient's daily life. Clinicians stated:

"More frequent assessment of symptoms or anything like that in their home environments." - Clinician 08

"Information about what they're actually doing in their real life. So if there's a way to observe them and see if they're doing... engaging in safety behaviors [. . .] just a little bit more information not based on their self-report." -Clinician 02

Based on these themes, we developed prototypes for two different design alternatives. To address the third theme, we designed a "social sensing system" that would enable clinicians to gather collateral information from people that the patient trusts, or "trusted others." Trusted others are people close to the patient, such as a spouse or sibling, who can provide another prospective on the patient's treatment progress. Other research has incorporated the perspectives of trusted others with success. Foong *et al.* explored the value of volunteer knowledge in the care of dementia patients and found that these individuals provided effective, reliable information [11]. The second design addresses the first and second themes. It is a clinician-facing information dashboard aimed at automating the collection and visualization of patient self-report and homework data.

3.2 Design Solutions

The social sensing prototype has three main sections: (1) a social sensing overview section that would enable a clinician to view a trusted other's assessment of a patient's progress (Fig. 1A), (2) an in vivo section that displays a trusted other's assessment of a patient's in vivo session (Fig. 1B), and (3) a messaging section that would enable a clinician to message a trusted other with pre-formulated questions pertaining to a patient's state and progress (Fig. 1C).

A. Social Sensing Overview   B. In Vivo   C. Messaging

Fig. 1. Clinician facing feedback from trusted others

The information dashboard prototype focuses on the digitization of the PE manual's paper forms to allow for automated visualization of self-report data throughout the therapy. Variables were selected for the dashboard based on interviews with clinicians, the therapy manual, and research into the predictive power of various self-report measures [8,10,20]. The dashboard design consists of three screens. The first provides a patient overview which graphically displays the patient's PCL score, in vivo hierarchy progress, in-session imaginal exposure SUDS and the clinician's notes (Fig. 2A). The second screen provides a session agenda, homework review graphics, homework assignment capabilities and in-session notes (Fig. 2B). The third screen provides an overview of the imaginal exposure sessions. It allows for real-time graphing of SUDS and physiological measures, such as heart rate, one-click capture of patient engagement signs, such as crying or clenching fists, and clinician note entry (Fig. 2C).

A. Patient Overview   B. In Session   C. Imaginal Exposure

Fig. 2. PE therapy information dashboard

3.3   Feedback Sessions

In the second part of the study, we conducted feedback sessions with five clinicians (4 females, 1 male, age range 31 to 39 years). They had been practicing
PE therapy for an average of 4.4 years ($\pm$2.4 years).

Feedback sessions for the social sensing interface had six components (1) a
device usage survey, (2) think-aloud tasks for each of the three sub-components:
the general social sensing feature (*see* Fig. 1A), the in vivo feature (*see* Fig. 1B)
and the messaging feature (*see* Fig. 1C), (3) a task interview for each of the three
sub-components, (4) a post-task interview, and lastly (5) a System Usability
Scale (SUS) questionnaire for the social sensing interface as a whole ([3]).

The purpose of the device usage survey was to gain insight into the clinicians'
technology usage habits. These habits were uniform, as they all used laptops/PCs
for their clinical work, though some expressed a desire to use a tablet when
interacting with a patient. Think-aloud tasks were performed to both assess
whether the clinicians could complete specific tasks using the interface and to
gather feedback on features as they were using them. Task-specific questions
allowed for further explication of the system features. The post-task interview
and the SUS were performed to obtain the clinician's assessment of the system
as a whole.

As part of the feedback process, clinicians were asked to rank the three social
sensing sections in order of importance, all five agreed unanimously on the order:
(1) the in vivo section (most important), (2) the general social sensing section,
and (3) the messaging section (least important). This consistency in ranking
indicates the specific use cases for which clinicians want collateral data. Overall,
clinicians had positive feedback regarding the fact the social sensing system as
whole could provide them with important, missing data. Clinicians stated:

*"I had an outpatient before; it would've been useful to have feedback from his
wife about how he was, she was a huge part of his treatment." -User 01*

*"I always want to hear more about what other people think is going on. I
get a skewed picture talking to one person." -User 05*

The results of the System Usability Scale were positive as well, with an average
score of 89.5 which corresponds to an "excellent" usability rating [22].

Clinicians voiced concerns that the social sensing system as a whole might
lead to privacy and confidentiality issues that would need to be discussed with
the patient prior to inclusion of the trusted other. Clinicians also noted that the
social sensing section could better emphasize the problematic behavior notice
and visualization of what the emoticons meant. Regarding the in vivo section,
clinicians mentioned that it did not clearly indicate that the SUDs assessment
was that of the trusted other and not that of the patient, but found this section
the most important in assessing the patient. However, they liked that the messaging section had a pre-populated question form that allowed them to quickly
send desired queries.

In order to evaluate the information dashboard, clinicians were first asked to complete a background survey about their experience with PE therapy and rate their current satisfaction with the process of delivering PE therapy on a seven-point Likert scale. Clinicians then completed the following four think-aloud tasks on the information dashboard: (1) prepare for an upcoming appointment with patient John Doe, (2) review John Doe's homework, (3) conduct an imaginal exposure session with John Doe and (4) assign John Doe his next set of home-work. After each task, clinicians were asked to rate their satisfaction with the process using the dashboard, and were asked follow-up questions about their experience using the system. After completing all tasks, clinicians were asked to provide three words to describe the system and were interviewed about their overall impressions of the system as a whole. The goal of the information dashboard feedback session was to understand whether a clinician-facing dashboard centered on visualizing self-report data would be useful to clinicians.

Overall the information dashboard received positive feedback with clinicians describing it as comprehensive (n = 2), intuitive (n = 2) and helpful (n = 2). Clinicians thought the system would improve accountability, both for the patient and the clinician, saying:

"This seems much more organized and much easier to notice any discrepancies." -User 04

"I like that it's more holistic, and it could be more accurate." -User 02

Clinicians often described the system as a tool their patient's could use directly or collaboratively with the clinician. One clinician stressed the importance of allowing the patient to remain in control of the treatment saying:

"Usually now, you bring your form, and you tell me how those things went, and it's in the patient's ballpark in terms of how they want to talk about it [. . .] they take ownership of their work." -User 05

Clinicians were skeptical of two features: (1) clinician notes and (2) the ability to mark suspected SUDs as over or under reported by the patient. Since all clinicians in this study already took notes in a separate system, they did not see the need to record or transfer notes to another system. Clinicians thought that the ability to mark SUDs as over or under reported made their judgment seem too official. Instead, one clinician purposed a companion metric, such as a perceived unit of distress, that would allow the clinician to rate their perception of the patient's distress without placing official judgment on the reported SUDs.

The in vivo hierarchy and homework review sections of the dashboard had the most usability issues, and several design changes were identified to improve these features. Clinicians were most excited about the imaginal exposure feature, with many saying that it would increase the likelihood of them visualizing the session and that it would save them time by allowing them to graph SUDs and engagement signs in real-time.

The results of the Likert questions were positive with all dimensions showing improvement using the dashboard compared to the current process (3). The biggest improvement was in the process of tracking a patient's mental health status, which was one of the main goals of the system (Fig. 3).

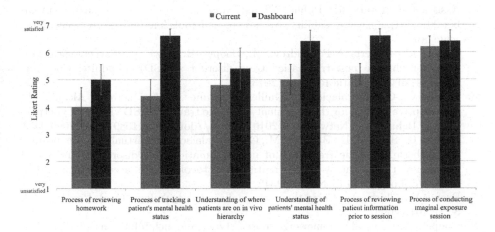

Fig. 3. Mean clinician satisfaction with current process versus mean dashboard-assisted process (bars represent standard error)

4   Conclusion

To our knowledge, no clinician-facing dashboards have been developed for PE or other PTSD psychotherapies. Our research bridges a gap in PTSD therapy, the design of an interface to streamline the clinician's workflow during PE therapy. In the first part of our study we found that clinicians wanted (1)improved workflow for their PE sessions (2)improved methods of monitoring their patients' self-report data and (3)a way to assess their patients' behavior in the "real world." We prototyped and evaluated two systems to meet these needs. On the positive side, both of the systems were well received and clinicians believe that we are on the right track. Thus, a next step is to combine the best features of both interfaces to develop a single system that allows clinicians to access self-report and social sensing data seamlessly. On the negative side, clinicians noted that there were practical privacy matters that needed to be addressed. These will require meeting with patients (and their trusted others) to understand under what conditions social sensing would be acceptable to them. It is also important to identify features that will encourage patients to maintain ownership of their treatment, such as the ability for patients to indicate specific homework or self-report data that they would like to discuss in sessions. Our study provides preliminary steps in designing user-centered tools that assist clinicians in the delivery of PE therapy by improving data access and workflow efficiency.

References

1. Aigner, W., Miksch, S., Schumann, H., Tominski, C.: Visualization of Time-Oriented Data, January 2011. https://doi.org/10.1007/978-0-85729-079-3
2. American Psychiatric Association: Diagnostic and statistical manual of mental disorders 5th Edn. American Psychiatric Association (2013)
3. Assistant Secretary for Public Affairs: System usability scale (sus), September 2013. https://www.usability.gov/how-to-and-tools/methods/system-usability-scale.html
4. Bisson, J.I., Roberts, N.P., Andrew, M., Cooper, R., Lewis, C.: Psychologicaltherapies for chronic post-traumatic stress disorder (PTSD) in adults. Cochrane Database of Systematic Reviews (2013)
5. Botella, C., García-Palacios, A., Guillen, V., Baños, R.M., Quero, S., Alcaniz, M.: An Adaptive display for the treatment of diverse trauma PTSD victims. Cyberpsychology Behav. Soc. Networking (2010). https://doi.org/10.1089/cyber.2009.0353
6. Botella, C., Serrano, B., Baños, R.M., Garcia-Palacios, A.: Virtual reality exposure-based therapy for the treatment of post-traumatic stress disorder: A review of its efficacy, the adequacy of the treatment protocol, and its acceptability (2015). https://doi.org/10.2147/NDT.S89542
7. Braun, V., Clarke, V.: Using thematic analysis in psychology. Qual. Res. Psychol. **3**, 77–101 (2006)
8. Cooper, A.A., et al.: Homework "dose," type, and helpfulness as predictors of clinical outcomes in prolonged exposure for PTSD. Behav. Ther. **48**(2), 182–194 (2017)
9. Evans, H., Lakshmi, U., Ismail, A., Watson, H., Kumar, N., Arriaga, R.: Engaging a plurality of caring perspectives in treating veterans with PTSD. In: CSCW 2019 (2019)
10. Foa, E.B., Hembree, E.A., Rothbaum, B.O.: Prolonged Exposure Therapy for PTSD: Emotional Processing of Traumatic Experiences: Therapist Guide. Oxford University Press, Oxford (2007)
11. Foong, P.S., Zhao, S., Tan, F., Williams, J.J.: Harvesting caregiving knowledge. In: Proceedings of the 2018 CHI Conference on Human Factors in Computing Systems - CHI 2018, pp. 1–12. ACM Press, New York (2018). https://doi.org/10.1145/3173574.3173653, http://dl.acm.org/citation.cfm?doid=3173574.3173653
12. Harvey, A.G., Bryant, R.A., Tarrier, N.: Cognitive behaviour therapy for posttraumatic stress disorder. Clin. Psychol. Rev. **23**, 501–522 (2003)
13. Kuhn, E., et al.: Clinician characteristics and perceptions related to use of the pe (prolonged exposure) coach mobile app. Prof. Psychol. Res. Pract. **46**, 437–443 (2015)
14. Lanatà, A., Valenza, G., Nardelli, M., Gentili, C., Scilingo, E.: Complexity index from a personalized wearable monitoring system for assessing remission in mental health. IEEE J. Biomed. Health Inform. **19**(1), 132–1339 (2014). https://doi.org/10.1109/JBHI.2014.2360711
15. McDonald, S.D., Calhoun, P.S.: The diagnostic accuracy of the PTSD checklist: a critical review. Clin. Psychol. Rev. **30**, 976–987 (2010)
16. Reger, G.M., et al.: The "PE coach" smartphone application: an innovative approach to improving implementation, fidelity, and homework adherence during prolonged exposure. Psychol. Serv. (2013). https://doi.org/10.1037/a0032774
17. Rodriguez-Paras, C., et al.: Posttraumatic stress disorder and mobile health: app investigation and scoping literature review. JMIR mHealth and uHealth 5(10) (2017). https://doi.org/10.2196/mhealth.7318

18. Rothbaum, B.O., et al.: Virtual realityexposure therapy for ptsd vietnam veterans: a case study. J. Trauma. Stress **12**(2), 263–271 (1999). https://doi.org/10.1023/A:1024772308758

19. Schnurr, P.P., Green, B.L.: Trauma and Health: Physical Health Consequences of Exposure to Extreme Stress. Washington American Psychological Association, Washington, D.C (2004)

20. Sripada, R.K., Rauch, S.A.: Between-session and within-session habituation in prolonged exposure therapy for posttraumatic stress disorder: a hierarchical linear modeling approach. J. Anxiety Disord. **30**, 81–87 (2015)

21. U.S. Department of Veterans Affairs: Substance abuse in veterans - PTSD: National center for PTSD (2014)

22. User Experience Magazine: Determining what individual sus scores mean: Adding an adjective rating scalejus (2009)

23. Washington University in St. Louis: Growing problem for veterans: Domestic violence (2008)

24. Zoellner, L.A., et al.: Teaching trauma-focused exposure therapy for PTSD: critical clinical lessons for novice exposure therapists. Psychol. Trauma Theory Res. Pract. Policy **3**, 300–308 (2011)

Using Artificial Intelligence for Augmentative Alternative Communication for Children with Disabilities

Rodica Neamtu[1](✉) , André Camara[2] , Carlos Pereira[3] ,
and Rafael Ferreira[2]

[1] Worcester Polytechnic Institute, Worcester, MA 01609, USA
rneamtu@wpi.edu
[2] Departamento de Computação,
Universidade Federal Rural de Pernambuco, Recife, Brazil
{andre.camara,rafael.mello}@ufrpe.br
[3] Livox, Orlando, USA
carlos@livox.com.br

Abstract. According to the World Health Organization, an estimated one billion people live with a disability. Millions of them are non-verbal, and also experience motor-skill challenges. The limitations on activity and restrictions on participation due to such disabilities often lead to discrimination and social exclusion. A UNICEF study analyzing data from 15 countries found that almost 50% of children with disabilities are out of school, and 85% of them did not receive any formal education. Affording enhanced and accelerated communication for disabled people, who continue to form the world's largest minority to experience social discrimination, is central to making the world a more inclusive place. Our LIVOX application incorporates artificial intelligence algorithms to reduce the so-called "reciprocity gap" that acts as a communication barrier between disabled people and their interlocutors, thus enabling people with disabilities, especially children, to participate in daily social and educational activities. Integrating them into the existing social structures is central to making the world a more inclusive place.

Keywords: Augmentative alternative communication ·
Children interfaces · Artificial intelligence ·
Interaction with large and small displays

Electronic supplementary material The online version of this chapter (https://doi.org/10.1007/978-3-030-29381-9_15) contains supplementary material, which is available to authorized users.

1 Introduction

1.1 Motivation and Background

The foundation of human interaction involves some form of communication, whether through voice, symbols, numbers, pictures or signs. Whether they happen face-to-face or online, interactions can be challenging for people with disabilities. Disabilities and disorders such as cerebral palsy, aphasia and autism can lead to social isolation mostly to the difficulty of communicating. People with disabilities find it hard and tiresome to express their thoughts, while their interlocutors often lose patience waiting for delayed responses. The communication challenges create severe problems for the intellectual development of young children, further preventing and delaying their integration into the society. A recent UNICEF study [13] analyzing data from 15 countries shows that almost 50% of children with disabilities do not go to school, and 85% never received a formal education. Even for those few who actually attend school, there is evidence suggesting that traditional teaching methods are often not suitable for children with disabilities, especially those who are both non-verbal and have motor-skill challenges. Thus, overcoming the first barrier and bringing children with disabilities into a formal educational setup is crucial, and it has to be complemented by educational methods and strategies that can facilitate communication and reduce the so-called "reciprocity gap" often due to delays in responses.

Adaptive applications such as Augmentative and Alternative Communication (AAC) [5] have emerged as crucial players in enabling effective communication for people with disabilities [2]. Based on the manner in which they facilitate communication, there are two main categories AAC devices: (1) devices that synthesize speech through message composition [9], in which the user constructs sentences by selecting subsets of suggested words and then synthesizing them [18]; and (2) devices that offer alternative ways of communication through pictograms [5], in which the user expresses thoughts, desires and requests by selecting specific images. Although both are invaluable because they empower people with disabilities to communicate, the first group tends to be costly prohibitive [11], while also having reduced mobility due to size and shape.

We focus here on the devices in the latter category, namely the systems that provide pictogram-based communication. In these solutions the main idea is to

Fig. 1. Scenarios showing the sequence of steps expressing the desire to eat an apple (interactions/selections (touches on the screen) indicated by light yellow background). (Color figure online)

somehow mimic the traditional communication boards, and expand them into the mobile computing context. Thus, there is always a trade-off between the versatility of communication, limited by the number of available pictograms, and the space available on the screen to display the images in a manner consistent with specific motor and cognitive skills of individuals. To circumvent this limitation, pictograms are usually organized in categories, and they can be accessed by interactively navigating through hierarchies of items or through "pages" shown on the screen. Nevertheless, this raises another challenge: the "deeper" or further down an item is placed on the hierarchy, the more physical effort is required from the user, due to the increased number of interactions (i.e. multiple pages to explore) necessary to reach the final item. We show in Fig. 1 the scenario where the disabled person wants to eat an apple as a snack. To express this desire, there are several steps to follow, each one corresponding to choosing an item on the screen and then moving to a "follow-up" screen. The selections are marked with a light background contrasting with the overall choices that are displayed on blue backgrounds. In Fig. 1 first selecting "I want to...", is followed by the next selection "Eat...", then "Fruit...", and finally "Apple". The three dots at the end of a selection signal that there are subsequent selections to be made, while the lack of ending dots means that there are no more available options.

Although trivial for a person with good motor skills, this sequence of choices can be quite slow and difficult for people with motor-skill challenges, thus it is crucial to present them with the most appropriate choices using the least number of steps or screens to navigate. One of distinguishing features of our LIVOX addresses precisely this challenge that often acts as a barrier in communication. Using machine learning algorithms to enhance communication, LIVOX reduces the number of necessary interactions to reach a desired item.

Figure 2 gives an on appreciation of the capabilities of LIVOX to apply personalised online learning algorithms to infer the most probable items for a child who cannot speak and also has motor skill challenges, based on a given time and location. For example, subfigure A indicates that based on the fact that LIVOX detects the location of the disabled person as "home", and the time as "8am", the customized choices are "I want to" (for expressing desires, such as "I want to eat") and 'I am' (for expressing needs, such as "I am hungry") and shows them as items available at the start of the conversation, on the first "page". Similarly, the remaining subfigures customized screens based on location and time recommenders, and will be later discussed in Sect. 3.

1.2   Limitations of the State of the Art

Crucial challenges of Alternative and Augmentative Communication (AAC) continue to be related to the length of time to communicate, improving overall conversational reciprocity, and reducing the physical effort for people with motor challenges [12]. Many existing pictogram-based systems [1,7] use static pages that people with disabilities browse to find the appropriate images to express their thoughts and needs. A rich experience necessarily involves the use of large collections of images, thus leading to increased response time and effort to find

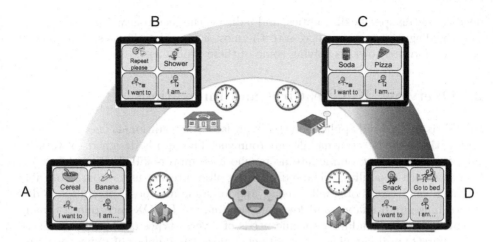

Fig. 2. Example of LIVOX context-aware pictogram recommenders suggesting itemsets based on location and time. The customized screen as per user choice here displays four pictograms for each "page", two recommendations and two standard items (blue boxes). (Color figure online)

the appropriate items [15]. Sc@ut [16] and IMLIS [17] use more than 2,200 pictograms for interaction, available on different platforms like tablets and Nintendo DS, increasing the time needed to browse them. Similarly, Proloquo2go [19] and Tobii Dynavox [8] are AAC commercial systems that aim to reduce the communication gap, where the interlocutor waits for an answer and eventually loses interest due to the slow pace of the conversation. To mitigate this, others [10] use reduced functionality to allow users to call emergency services by tapping pictograms instead of using calls/text messages.

Although these applications are popular, they do not focus on customizing the pictogram selection, and thus suffer from increased gaps in communication. To our knowledge, our current application is the first to use Machine Learning without an active internet connection to make pictogram recommendations based on spatial and temporal context in mobile devices, thus reducing the effort needed to find the most appropriate images.

More recently, there are new efforts to explore the integration of various devices of the domestic environment through IoT protocols, allowing users to interact with the surrounding smart objects [14].

Several works studying the impact of using AAC on adults' behavior [3, 4, 6] revealed that: (1) an increased number of people with aphasia, brainstem impairment, dementia, amyotrophic lateral sclerosis (ALS) and traumatic brain injury (TBI) use AAC; (2) the use of AAC is more effective under the supervision of professional staff; (3) the utilization time is usually low (25% of the time) especially due to the lack of support.

In summary, there is a need for AAC apps that can address many challenges simultaneously: portability, mobility, ease of use and customization to various needs based on specific disabilities, and reducing the reciprocity conversation gap by providing fast and easy access to the most appropriate images. Our LIVOX is a step forward towards solving some of these problems.

2   Overview, Key Features and Innovations

LIVOX is an Android application that translates the traditional concept of "communication boards" to a mobile environment. The app is designed to work on tablets, mostly to accommodate users who have motor-skill challenges in addition to speech disabilities. These disabilities often prevent users from being able to touch small areas of small screens, and for some also pose difficulties in distinguishing small shapes and low contrast images. LIVOX incorporates many distinct features to address specific needs of diverse types of disabilities. These allow parents and caregivers to easily customize the number of items shown on the screen, to use high contrast images, to adjust for repetitive touch behavior, and many others. Most of these features were inspired by observation and empirical evaluation in clinics during the development of the app.

The app is highly flexible and customizable, allowing for multiple users to co-exist, each with their own specific interface settings and collections of pictograms. The minimalist look of the user interface allows caregivers to easily learn how to setup and use the communication board in a short amount of time. Additional information can be added and accessed through a web interface, where the parent or caregiver can see all his devices and their respective users. This makes LIVOX a viable solution both for personal use by one person, and for sharing the same app over multiple users in educational and social settings such as schools, hospitals, clinics, recreation centers, etc. We first list here in short some of the many features of LIVOX, which although some might seem trivial, the combination of several features into the same app is not trivial, and it majorly contributes to better communication. Then we focus on our unique approach to using artificial intelligence to facilitate communication and increase engagement in social and educational activities.

Number/Size of Items on the Screen. By increasing or decreasing the number of columns and rows our app increases or decreases the number and size of the items in the user's screen. This is especially important for people with visual impairments, making images easier to be viewed. For people with motor disabilities, the size of the items is directly connected to the physical effort required to choose them. Larger items are more easily accessed while smaller ones pose greater challenges. Similarly, the font sizes are adjusted accordingly.

Black/White and High Contrast Images. These customizations are especially important for people with cognitive impairments and vision disabilities.

Show Full-Sized Image After Click. This feature is particularly relevant if the user needs to get visual confirmation that an item was selected, and it is achieved by displaying the item image in full size upon the item being touched.

This can assist with the comprehension that an action was completed, and it is particularly helpful for children with cognition-related disabilities.

Click Interval. Some disabilities lead to repetitive movements, causing multiple involuntary touches, which can flood and slow down the system. Livox uses a customizable "click interval" that can be adjusted to wait a for a specified number of seconds before allowing a next valid click on the tablet screen.

Screen as Actuator. Some physical disabilities prevent users from touching the screen. In such cases, including those with severe coordination challenges, LIVOX allows automatic scanning of items. As each individual item is sequentially highlighted, the user just needs to wait for the desired item to be highlighted and then touch anywhere on the screen (no need to click on the highlighted item). This way the entire screen acts as a switch.

Navigation Adjustments. Livox enables customized navigation through hidden/virtual navigation buttons and the use swiping.

Return to Initial Screen. This feature can be enabled to return to the home (initial) screen after a specified time interval. This contributes to the reduction of the physical effort who would otherwise have to touch the "back" button repeatedly to return to the home screen. For users with cognitive disabilities, this feature helps with cognitive adaptation. To put it metaphorically, after selecting the desired items, Livox returns to the home screen, like closing a book to restart the selection process.

Keep Items' Relative Position on the Screen. For people on the autistic spectrum it is important to keep the relative position of items on the screen, even when the item is not being currently displayed. When enabled, this feature leaves a blank space in the place of hidden items on the screen instead of replacing them with new items.

Automated Imprecise Touch Adjustment (IntelliTouch). Users with poor motor coordination find it difficult to touch specific screen areas, even for large sized-pictograms. This algorithm checks how many fingers are touching the screen, if the hand was dragged on the tablet screen, how long the touch lasted and other factors to correct the imperfect touch performed by a disabled person.

Using Artificial Intelligence to Make Context-Base recommendations. Our first step towards introducing Machine Learning was successful in leveraging fast, **contextual communication** in mobile devices. LIVOX analyzes past usage data (i.e. item used, time of usage, GPS data, X and Y coordinates on screen, touch time), to predict what a person with a disability may want to say in a specific context as shown before in Fig. 2).

Natural Language Processing. In order to allow disabled users to answer questions faster, our existing work incorporates Natural Language Conversation for disabled users, enabling them to engage in conversation using LIVOX speech recognition. This feature continuously listens to the environment looking for trigger words such as the name of the disabled person, and activates communication

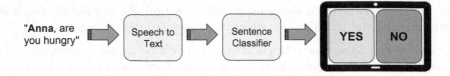

Fig. 3. LIVOX Natural Language sentence classifier. The activation word (here Anna, the name of the user) triggers the trained sentence classifier. Once the sentence is classified as a Yes/No type of question, the Yes/No screen is presented as a choice.

based on sentences. We showcase in Fig. 3 the use of the NLP sentence classifier, triggered by the activation word.

3 Usability and Real Life Case Scenarios

We showcase here four scenarios of using LIVOX to enable a person with disabilities to communicate in four specific contexts: (1) in the morning, at home with a caregiver; (2) at school with a teacher; (3) in a restaurant; and finally (4) at home again, in the evening. For simplicity and natural flow, we use here a fictional character named Anna as the person who is non-verbal and has severe motor-skill limitations. Her specific disability is expressed by her inability to speak as well as severe difficulties in moving her hand to the desired item in the screen. To assist with both challenges, her LIVOX account has been configured to display four items at a time. The four pictograms are the "combined" recommendation of the various recommenders as well as the customized settings.

We note that the recommendations are hierarchical, consisting of subsequent "levels" of groups of four images. For example, in order to select "Cereal", Anna would have to first select "I want to...", then "Eat...", followed by "Breakfast..." and finally "Cereal". The further in the hierarchy a suggested item is, the higher are the gains in terms of time and physical effort to communicate.

The pictogram recommender is trained on the device, with the problem being posed as a multiclass classification problem, considering previously clicked items as classes for a given location. The model updates itself at regular time intervals by performing automated machine learning steps, including data preprocessing (stay point detection from GPS coordinates, time feature transformation, etc.), model training and, finally, storing the trained model on the local Android file system in order to use it for upcoming predictions. Random Forest is the default classification algorithm, chosen because it is computationally less intensive than other algorithms such as neural networks and that it can handle noisy data.

1. Communicating Basic Needs and Desires. Figure 4 (1) displays four pictograms presented as choices to Anna in the morning. These images have been selected by the LIVOX context aware recommender system as the most appropriate for this context. The recommendations are always presented with a different background color. For example, the first image gives Anna the opportunity to express the natural desire to eat breakfast, and this image shows as a

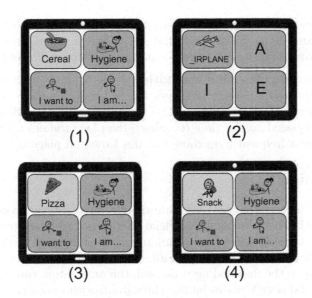

Fig. 4. Case scenarios for LIVOX usage during the day. Recommendations can be enabled or disabled, according to the needs and context for a given time and activity: (1) in the morning, at home with a caregiver, LIVOX recommender suggests the preferred breakfast food for Anna; (2) at school with a teacher, the LIVOX recommendations are disabled, in order to have more space to work on a literacy class; (3) in a restaurant, LIVOX recommender is active, and recommends Anna's preferred food at that place; and finally (4) at home again, in the evening.

top choice given the time of day (8am), the place (home) and the consideration of previous choices by Anna (she usually eats cereal at this time every day when she is home). We note here that LIVOX learns from the usage habits by keeping track of the frequency with which specific images are chosen, thus insuring that items that are favored show up ahead of other that are seldom used.

2. Teaching/Learning Literacy. One of the first steps in teaching literacy is assisting students in recognizing vowels and consonants. Such activities include verbal pronunciation, writing of the letter, giving and soliciting examples of words that begin with that letter, etc. We show in Fig. 4 subfigure (2) a scenario where Anna has to decide what is the initial vowel in the picture displaying an airplane. As an introductory step to this activity, LIVOX shows the letter in its written form handwriting and typed, it pronounces it out loud to generate awareness of the sound, and it gives Anna the option to see other images and listen to short songs featuring the letter in diverse contexts. To have more screen space, the teacher opts here to disable LIVOX recommendations during class.

3. Interacting in Diverse Social Contexts. We showcase here the case of a social interaction involving Anna being at a restaurant. As shown in Fig. 4 subfigure (3) she can now use the home screen to select her favorite food in that specific restaurant We want to emphasize that the suggestions presented to

Anna at this moment are based on the existing context (time: late afternoon, place: restaurant, item: pizza) and they are different than she would get as recommendations if she was at home or another restaurant, for example.

4. Communicating Routine Activities. Now Anna is back home, in the evening, and the recommender is suggesting to her a "Snack", as she usually asks for a snack before going to bed. This recommendation shown in Fig. 4 subfigure (4) is based on the time (evening), the place (home) as well as usage pattern (the most frequent item chosen at this time and place is the snack).

4   Conclusion

LIVOX is the first pictogram-based alternative augmentative communication mobile application to incorporate artificial intelligence to adapt to the needs of people with motor skill and verbal communication challenges. First, our system combines a wide range of algorithms to afford flexibility in creating custom items to be presented to the disabled user. Second, the application can adapt itself to diverse motor and cognitive disabilities through algorithms such as IntelliTouch, and Livox Natural Conversation.

References

1. Baldassarri, S., Rubio, J.M., Azpiroz, M.G., Cerezo, E.: Araboard: a multiplatform alternative and augmentative communication tool. Procedia Comput. Sci. **27**, 197–206 (2014)
2. Beukelman, D., Mirenda, P.: Augmentative and alternative communication (2005)
3. Beukelman, D.R., Ball, L.J., Fager, S.: An AAC personnel framework: adults with acquired complex communication needs. Augment. Altern. Commun. **24**(3), 255–267 (2008)
4. Beukelman, D.R., Fager, S., Ball, L., Dietz, A.: AAC for adults with acquired neurological conditions: a review. Augment. Altern. Commun. **23**(3), 230–242 (2007)
5. Beukelman, D.R., Mirenda, P.: Augmentative and Alternative Communication: Supporting Children and Adults with Complex Communication Needs. Paul H. Brookes Publishing, Baltimore (2013)
6. Bilyeu, D.V., Beukelman, D.R.: Duration of AAC technology use by persons with ALS. J. Med. Speech Lang. Pathol. **15**(4), 371–381 (1998)
7. Desai, T., Chow, K., Mumford, L., Hotze, F., Chau, T.: Implementing an iPad-based alternative communication device for a student with cerebral palsy and autism in the classroom via an access technology delivery protocol. Comput. Educ. **79**, 148–158 (2014)
8. Dynavox, T.: myTobiiDynavox (2019). https://www.tobiidynavox.com/. Accessed 28 Mar 2019
9. Higginbotham, D.J.: Humanizing vox artificialis: the role of speech synthesis in augmentative and alternative communication. In: Computer Synthesized Speech Technologies: Tools for Aiding Impairment, pp. 50–70. IGI Global (2010)
10. Hosono, N., Inoue, H., Nakanishi, M., Tomita, Y.: Urgent mobile tool for hearing impaired, language dysfunction and foreigners at emergency situation. In: Proceedings of the 16th International Conference on Human-computer Interaction with Mobile Devices & Services, pp. 413–416. ACM (2014)

11. Kagohara, D.M., et al.: Behavioral intervention promotes successful use of an iPod-based communication device by an adolescent with autism. Clin. Case Stud. **9**(5), 328–338 (2010)
12. Light, J., et al.: Challenges and opportunities in augmentative and alternative communication: research and technology development to enhance communication and participation for individuals with complex communication needs. Augment. Altern. Commun. **35**, 1–12 (2019)
13. Mizunoya, S., Mitra, S., Yamasaki, I.: Towards inclusive education: the impact of disability on school attendance in developing countries. UNICEF (2016)
14. Modoni, G.E., Veniero, M., Trombetta, A., Sacco, M., Clemente, S.: Semantic based events signaling for AAL systems. J. Ambient Intell. Hum. Comput. **9**(5), 1311–1325 (2018)
15. Pino, A., Kouroupetroglou, G.: Ithaca: an open source framework for building component-based augmentative and alternative communication applications. ACM Trans. Access. Comput. (TACCESS) **2**(4), 14 (2010)
16. Rodríguez-Fórtiz, M., Fernández-López, A., Rodríguez, M.: Mobile communication and learning applications for autistic people. In: Autism Spectrum Disorders-From Genes to Environment. IntechOpen (2011)
17. Schelhowe, H., Zare, S.: Intelligent mobile interaction: a learning system for mentally disabled people (IMLIS). In: Stephanidis, C. (ed.) UAHCI 2009, Part I. LNCS, vol. 5614, pp. 412–421. Springer, Heidelberg (2009). https://doi.org/10.1007/978-3-642-02707-9_47
18. Schlosser, R.: Roles of speech output in augmentative and alternative communication: narrative review. Augment. Altern. Commun. **19**(1), 5–27 (2003)
19. Ware, A.: Proloquo2go (2019). https://www.assistiveware.com/products/proloquo2go. Accessed 28 Mar 2019

Assistive Technology for Visually Impaired

Comparing User Performance
on Parallel-Tone, Parallel-Speech, Serial-Tone
and Serial-Speech Auditory Graphs

Prabodh Sakhardande[1(✉)], Anirudha Joshi[1], Charudatta Jadhav[2],
and Manjiri Joshi[1]

[1] Industrial Design Center, IIT Bombay, Mumbai, India
{prabodhs, anirudha, manjirij}@iitb.ac.in
[2] Tata Consultancy Services Limited, Mumbai, Maharashtra, India
charudatta.jadhav@tcs.com

Abstract. Visualization techniques such as bar graphs and pie charts let sighted users quickly understand and explore numerical data. These techniques remain by and large inaccessible for visually impaired users. Even when these are made accessible, they remain slow and cumbersome, and not as useful as they might be to sighted users. Previous research has studied two methods of improving perception and speed of navigating auditory graphs - using non-speech audio (such as tones) instead of speech to communicate data and using two audio streams in parallel instead of in series. However, these studies were done in the early 2000s and speech synthesis techniques have improved considerably in recent times, as has the familiarity of visually impaired users with smartphones and speech systems. We systematically compare user performance on four modes that can be used for the generation of auditory graphs: parallel-tone, parallel-speech, serial-tone, and serial-speech. We conducted two within-subjects studies - one with 20 sighted users and the other with 20 visually impaired users. Each user group performed point estimation and point comparison tasks with each technique on two sizes of bar graphs. We assessed task time, errors and user preference. We found that while tone was faster than speech, speech was more accurate than tone. The parallel modality was faster than serial modality and visually impaired users were faster than their sighted counterparts. Further, users showed a strong personal preference towards the serial-speech technique. To the best of our knowledge, this is the first empirical study that systematically compares these four techniques.

Keywords: Auditory graphs · Auditory feedback · Sonification · Human computer interaction

1 Introduction

Graphs or charts are a visual representation of some type of relational data. They are widely used across domains and disciplines. Different types of graphs like a bar graph, line graph, pie chart, histogram, etc. are chosen by the designers of the graph depending upon the nature of the information they want to convey. Due to the inherently visual

D. Lamas et al. (Eds.): INTERACT 2019, LNCS 11746, pp. 247–266, 2019.
https://doi.org/10.1007/978-3-030-29381-9_16

nature of graphs, it is difficult for visually impaired users to access or even understand their benefits.

Graphs provide several benefits and affordances to a sighted user. They provide multiple layers of information that allows the user to explore and discover the information in the sequence and to the level of detail that they desire [22]. Graphs allow users to quickly discover trends in the data such as "Has the value of a stock been generally increasing in the last 5 years?", look for specific information like "What was the highest or lowest value for the stock in the last 5 years?" or discover the relationship between two points in the graph such as "Which of the two countries have similar landmass size?". An inquisitive mind can gain multiple insights from the same graph. Graphs on web pages can be made accessible through attributes like "alt" [16]. While such mechanisms allow the author to describe the contents of the graph, it does not allow the user to explore or discover beyond what has already been "canned" by the author.

Research on making graphs accessible is not new. Two main techniques that have been explored are making graphs tangible and making graphs auditory. In this paper, we focus on auditory graphs, specifically focussing on the modalities of tones and speech, along with serial and parallel.

As we will discuss in the related work section, previous research on sonification has compared the use of synthesized speech with non-speech audio (such as tones) and found that non-speech audio decreases workload and task time [8]. However, this study was done in the early 2000s. With the recent advances in technology, speech synthesis has reached a level of maturity. Through multiple devices like smart speakers, speech input and output is now much more ubiquitous. Moreover, visually impaired users have gained a lot of experience with speech-based screen readers. Hence a comparison between speech and tone is worth investigating again.

Audio is perceived sequentially, so a potential downside of using audio is that it can slow the user down. Thus, at least some advantage of data becoming more accessible is lost because of slow speeds. Some research has explored the effect of using two audio streams in parallel instead of in series in order to speed up the process [2]. It found that parallel audio leads to faster task completion time than audio in series.

To the best of our knowledge, no study has been conducted that compares the performance of auditory graphs in both dimensions simultaneously: speech vs. tone and parallel vs. serial. In this paper, we systematically compare the effect of the four modes (parallel-tone, parallel-speech, serial-tone, and serial-speech) on user perception. We investigate the performance of both sighted and visually impaired users. We present the results of two within-subjects studies - one with 20 sighted users and the other with 20 visually impaired users.

2   Related Work

In order to make graphics like charts, graphs and images accessible to users of screen-readers, W3C [30] recommends adding a short description to identify contents of the image and a longer description that can contain detailed information such as the scales, values or trends in the data. While making the graph accessible, this method does not allow the user to explore the data creatively on his/her own and may not fulfill the needs of some users. Also, presenting all the information in speech form increases the task load when graphs are long [48].

The visual medium communicates a lot of information in parallel [35], allowing sighted users to use visual graphs in diverse ways. In contrast, by and large, audio communicates information serially. One of the challenges in designing auditory graphs is retaining this rich diversity in a serial medium. In literature, auditory graphs have been used for presenting data with several goals. SoundVis [2] uses audio to communicate detailed information of a graph. TeDUB [21, 31] describes an automatic/semi-automatic way of making diagrams accessible. Audio has also been used to quickly provide an overall gestalt effect of a graph [1, 2, 36, 37].

In this paper, we focus on enabling users to estimate (e.g. the highest point) and compare values (e.g. two similar points) of bars in a bar graph. While a sighted user may explore a bar graph for other purposes, we argue that comparison and estimation are the most common use cases of a bar graph.

Tactile [20], auditory [28, 32, 36] and combined [33, 47] modalities have been used to make graphs accessible by visually impaired users. Tactile graphs have been explored to allow exploration of line graphs [47], bar graphs [47], georeferenced data [38], etc. alongside auditory feedback. Tactile graphs themselves are limited by the amount of data that can be presented at the same time [34].

In this paper, we focus on the use of audio to make graphs accessible. In literature, several terms have been used for graphs that use audio for communication including "auditory data representation" [29], "auditory graphs" [5, 9, 13], "sonification" [2, 3, 7, 10, 11], etc. In this paper, we use the term "auditory graphs" as against "visual graphs" to include any graph that communicates numerical information through audio.

While speech is considered a natural form of communication, tones are non-speech sounds like musical instruments, earcons, everyday sounds, synthesized sounds and so on. Different parameters of sound like pitch [1, 2, 4, 13], loudness [13, 17], duration [10], frequency [10], timbre [3, 39], panning [2–4] have been used to map data to auditory graphs.

Mansur et al. [1] compared the performance of tactile graphs and auditory graphs for conveying characteristics of the curve such as the slope, monotonicity, convergence, symmetry and whether the line graph was exponential. The study was done with sighted and visually impaired users. Results showed that the auditory graph was faster to use while the tactile graph was significantly more accurate than the auditory graph. The authors also concluded that the accuracy of auditory graphs could improve with some practice. In this study, music i.e. continuous tone and not discrete tones convey graph information. Ramloll et al. [8] investigated the use of speech and non-speech audio and speech-only interface for accessing numerical data (between 0-100) in 26 rows and 10 columns. They found that making data available in non-speech audio form resulted in lower subjective workload and higher task successes and significantly lower mean task completion time.

Different strategies of encoding data in sound to leverage the relationships between the sound parameters have been explored [12, 19, 27, 28]. For example, frequency and pitch have a logarithmic relationship, for logarithmic data set or for multivariate data set the dimension that varies exponentially is mapped onto frequency. Peres et al. [3] conducted an experiment to investigate whether using redundant design i.e., using two parameters of sound to represent the information redundantly is useful. They found that the benefit depends upon the properties chosen for the mappings. Using pitch and loudness ("integral parameters") to map the data to auditory graphs was found to be beneficial whereas using pitch and timing ("separable parameters") together were not found to be useful.

While some studies have suggested that panning in parallel mode may not be sufficient to make data streams differentiable [40, 41], others reported that panning does help certain types of tasks when presenting multiple data series in parallel [4]. Audio is perceived sequentially, so a potential downside of the use of audio is that it can tend to slow the user down as audio needs to be perceived sequentially. Thus, at least some advantage of data becoming more accessible is lost because of slow speeds. Previous research has explored the effect of using two audio streams in parallel instead of in series to represent two or more data series [2, 4]. It was found that parallel audio leads to faster task completion time than audio in series in sonified graphs with two data series, for finding intersection of the two lines. Audiograph [22] compared two ways of playing tones: note-sequence where all tones between the note for origin and that for the current value were played and note-pair, where only the notes for origin and the note for the value were played. Note-sequence had the advantage of conveying the value in pitch and in the time, while Note-pair had the advantage of being brief. Note-sequence emerged as the more accurate method. Many studies investigated the effect of providing context information in auditory graphs, the visual graph equivalent of gridlines along X and Y axes [11, 17, 35].

Nees et al. [17] investigated the effect of varying the loudness of the context audio relative to the data audio on the performance and found that keeping the loudness lower or higher than that of the data audio was beneficial to the performance of point esti-mation tasks. Magnitude estimation tasks have been used to study preferred mappings of data to the sound parameters and whether they were the same for sighted and visually impaired users [10]. Three parameters of sound were varied: pitch, tempo, or spectral brightness. Users were presented with a sound stimuli and asked to estimate its value. The study aimed to understand whether users associated higher pitch or spectral brightness and faster tempo with higher or lower values for entities like dollar, size, temperature, pressure and velocity and whether this was same for sighted and visually impaired users.

Different kinds of data has been represented using auditory graphs. Stockman et al. [36] investigated the use of sonification to allow users to get an overview of data in the spreadsheets. They explored auto-sonification that gives an overview of the data automatically and also manual sonification where a visually impaired user could select ranges of data to sonify in order to quickly understand trends in the selected range and identify characteristics such as outliers [36]. Flower et al. used binned data to generate auditory histograms with a musical pitch to present statistical information like shape of the distribution [49]. AUDIOGRAPH developed by Rigas et al. [22] used auditory tones to convey information like shape, size of the shape, location of the object in space, etc. to enable users to manipulate objects in space.

While the human ear can detect small pitch changes very well, studies show that there is no linear relationship between pitch perception and the actual frequency of the auditory signal and that it is user dependent [8, 50, 51]. In our study design, like

Ramloll et al. [8], we did not include value estimation tasks. Brown et al. [3] recommend using instruments with wide pitch like the Piano and Trumpet and MIDI tones 35–100 as they are easily perceived and differentiable. In our design, we used pitch variation to show differences in values in a graph. In the next section, we describe in more detail how data in bar graphs were mapped to MIDI tones with piano timbre. While sonification gives a quick overview of the data [6, 13] and reduces cognitive load for tabular and graph datasets [8], it cannot provide an absolute perception of value at a point. Speech-based auditory graphs, on the other hand, can provide exact value at a point.

3 Design of the Auditory Graphs

In this experiment, we used a simple bar graph with a single data series, such as the one shown in Fig. 1 below. A sighted user may explore such a bar graph in different ways, depending on what task s/he is trying to do. S/he may be interested in a point estimation task (such as which city gets the lowest rainfall). Or s/he may be trying to do a point comparison task (such as which city gets similar rainfall to my city). Our goal was to provide similar flexibility of exploration to a blind user. Here we describe how the information contained in a bar graph was conveyed to the user through each of the four auditory graph techniques.

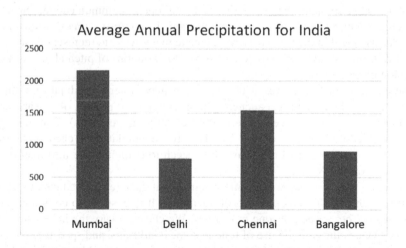

Fig. 1. Graph showing annual average rainfall in different cities in India in mm.

3.1 Serial-Parallel

By default, audio information is communicated to the user sequentially, i.e., one after the other. For example, the user would hear "Mumbai 2168, Delhi 790, Chennai 1541, Bangalore 905". We call this "serial" modality. Unfortunately, serial communication would take at least as much time as it might take to play the audio files, and more time if the user needs repetition. It is possible to speed up the audio playback, and several users (especially visually impaired users who use screen readers) are used to perceiving spoken audio at very high speeds.

Yet, another way to reduce the time is to playback multiple elements of the audio simultaneously. In the example above, we could play back the words "Rainfall in mm, (Mumbai = 2168), (Delhi = 790), (Chennai = 1541), (Bangalore = 905)". Wherein the brackets imply that the words in the brackets (e.g. "Mumbai" and "2168") are played simultaneously. We call this "parallel" modality.

In our study, we compared serial modalities with parallel modalities. While it may seem natural to assume that parallel modalities will be faster than serial modalities, this may in fact not be so effective. Firstly, the amount of time taken to communicate the actual information about the elements may be not much in comparison with the other time taken. A bar graph may have other information that needs to be communicated (e.g. the title). The user may need time to perceive and process the information and to navigate the graph. Secondly, the user may find it harder to perceive the information presented in the parallel modalities in comparison with the serial modalities, leading to errors or repetitions. The goal of our study is to explore if parallel modalities actually result in time-saving, whether they induce more errors, and whether the users prefer them to serial modalities.

3.2   Speech-Tone

Our interest is to compare the effect of speech and tone in communication. "Speech" is considered a natural modality of communication. In contrast, "tones" need interpretation. As discussed in the related work, there are many ways to represent data in tones. However, for this study, we restricted ourselves to variations of pitch alone, as a single dimension of variation.

The elements of the X-axis of the bar graph may either be ordinal (e.g. ranks of athletes), related by a natural sequence or progression (e.g. months of a year), or may be unrelated by any natural sequence or progression (e.g. countries). Considering that in a general case, elements of the X-axis may be unrelated to each other in any predictable way, we decided to always use speech to communicate information about the elements on the X-axis.

In contrast, the Y-axis always contains numerical data, (e.g. time taken by athletes, rainfall in each month, or population of countries). It is possible to communicate this data through either speech or tone modalities. We chose to vary the information about the Y-axis values through the use of tone in some conditions, and speech in the others. Thus, in tone modalities, the user would hear, "Rainfall in mm, Mumbai beep 1, Delhi beep 2, Chennai beep 3, Bangalore beep 4", where beeps 1–4 represent tones representing 2168, 790, 1541 and 905 respectively. In speech modalities, the user would hear "Rainfall in mm, Mumbai 2168, Delhi 790, Chennai 1541, Bangalore 905".

3.3   Auditory Graphs

We used combinations of the parallel-serial and speech-tone modalities described above resulting in four modes of our study, namely parallel-tone, serial-tone, parallel-speech, and serial-speech. We selected eight datasets to create auditory bar graphs of real-world data sourced from The World Bank [24]. We selected the topics of rural population, surface area (sq km), incidence of tuberculosis (per 100,000 people), total population (thousands), population growth (%), forest area (%), CO2 emissions (kt), and GDP growth (%) of various countries. We chose these topics because we expected that participants would not be too familiar with such data, and would need the graphs to find answers to the questions asked in the tasks. We wanted the data to be realistic so that our study will have good external validity. Four datasets (rural population, surface area, tuberculosis, and total population) contained six data points on the x-axis (the "short" graphs). The other four datasets contained 15 data points on the x-axis (the "long" graphs). The number 15 was chosen to safely be beyond the short term memory limit [23]. In order to counter the variation in the time required to speak out the names of different countries (e.g. "United Kingdom" and "India"), all the short graph datasets had the same set of countries. Similarly, all the long graph datasets had the same set of countries. Thus, we created a total of (8 datasets × 4 four modes = 32) auditory graphs.

We made some specific design decisions for each modality. In the speech modalities, the numeric readout of values was limited to 3 digits (most significant bits). For example, if the value was 25.263, we rounded it off to 25.3. If it was 2.5263, we rounded it off to 2.53, and if it 25,263, we rounded it off to 25,300. As our study was done in India, we used "Animaker Voice" [26] with the Indian English female voice "Raveena" at the default speed to generate the speech.

In the tone modalities, the method of converting numerical data to auditory tones was derived from Brown et al. [2], where data values were mapped to MIDI notes. The data was mapped to MIDI notes linearly. The lowest pitch was chosen as a MIDI value of 20 and the highest was MIDI 100. We used "Sonic Pi" [25] with the "Piano Synthesizer" option as the musical instrument for generating tones as they were reported to be perceived more easily [8, 18].

In the parallel modalities, the sounds were "left aligned", i.e. both sounds started playing at the same time, although they may end at different times depending on their lengths. In both the serial and parallel modalities, the two audio streams representing the X and Y-axes were spatially separated. The audio representing the X-axis was always played to the right ear and the audio representing the Y-axis was always played to the left ear.

Once the audio clips for all modalities were generated, the audio was combined and spatially modified, mapping X-axis to the right ear and Y-axis to the left ear in Audacity [42]. All source clips were brought to the same volume gain. The means and standard deviations in seconds of the total duration of audio recordings for graphs in each mode if all information in that graph was heard without repetition or delay are shown in Table 1. An attempt was made towards making all tone audios of the same length. In most cases, the duration of tone playback (for X-Axis) was shorter than the duration of speech playback (for Y-Axis). Thus as the graphs of a set (short or long) had the same Y-Axis (countries), in Table 1 the tonal modalities show a small standard deviation.

Table 1. The means and standard deviations of the duration of audio recordings in the four modes for the two graph lengths.

	Short Graphs (s), N = 4		Long Graphs (s), N = 4	
	Mean	SD	Mean	SD
Parallel tone	3.70	0.00	9.35	0.00
Serial tone	6.43	0.10	16.45	0.12
Parallel speech	8.85	2.35	16.95	6.41
Serial speech	12.42	2.61	25.71	6.90

We created a prototype running on a laptop computer for the studies. We used Processing [46] to create the keyboard based user interface and link keystrokes to respective audio playback.

The users navigated the graphs using the up (↑), right (→) and left (←) arrow keys and the enter key (↵) of a keyboard. While we acknowledge that navigation is a crucial aspect of an auditory graph, in order to systematically study the effect of the modes on perception, we kept the navigation complexities at a minimum. When the user presses the enter key (↵), the audio corresponding to the first bar of the graph is played. When the user presses the right arrow key (→), the audio corresponding to the next bar is played after the audio corresponding to the first bar is over. When the user pressed the left arrow key (←), the audio corresponding to the previous bar is played. When the user presses the up arrow key (↑), the audio corresponding to the current bar is repeated. Audios do not interrupt or overlap each other. If the user tries to go beyond the first or the last values on the X-axis, a tone is played back indicating that the user has reached the end.

Here we illustrate each mode using data from Fig. 1. Irrespective of the mode, the user first hears a "title", such as "Rainfall in four major cities in India in millimeters". When the user is ready, s/he presses the enter key (↵). Then in the parallel-tone mode, the user hears "Mumbai" and "beep 1" simultaneously. On pressing the right arrow key (→), s/he hears "Delhi" and "beep 2" again simultaneously, and so forth. In serial-tone mode, the user hears "Mumbai", followed by "beep 1", and after (→) "Delhi", followed by "beep 2", and so forth. In parallel-speech mode, the user hears "Mumbai" and "two thousand one hundred and sixty" simultaneously, and after (→) "Delhi" and "seven hundred and ninety" simultaneously, and so forth. In serial speech mode, the user hears "Mumbai", followed by "two thousand one hundred and sixty", and after (→) "Delhi", followed by "seven hundred and ninety", and so forth. In all of these cases, the values on the X-axis ("Mumbai", "Delhi" etc.) are heard in the right ear and the corresponding values on the Y-axis (in speech or tone) would be heard in the left ear.

4   Method

We conducted two within-subject studies to compare speed, errors, and preference of users. One study was conducted with sighted users and the other with visually impaired users. The study compared across parallel-serial and speech-tone modalities, resulting in four modes of auditory graphs - parallel-tone, serial-tone, parallel-speech, and serial speech. In each mode, we studied auditory graphs of two lengths, a 6-point graph (short) and a 15-point graph (long). On each graph, users performed three tasks - estimating the highest point (task 1), the two most similar points (task 2), and the lowest three points (task 3). The wording of the tasks was modified to suit the contents of the graph. For example, for the graph of the rural population, the task 1 was "Which country has the highest rural population?" None of the tasks required the participants to guess exact values, but only to compare values.

Thus we had 4 modes, with 2 graph lengths per mode, and 3 tasks per graph, resulting in 24 tasks per user. The order of the modes was counterbalanced across participants through a balanced Latin square. The order of graphs was kept the same across modes - the participants first used the short graph, and then the long graph. The order of the three tasks for each graph was kept the same for all graphs. Thus the complete design of the experiment across the independent variables was speech-tone (2) x parallel-serial (2) x graph length (2) x tasks (3) x user type (2 - between subjects).

All participants went through a training protocol before performing the tasks. The training protocol was the same for sighted and visually impaired participants. The experimenter first familiarised the participant with bar graphs. He presented two versions of a bar graph, namely a printed version and a transparent tactile overlay. This graph contained information about rainfall for a city by month from April to September. The experimenter asked the participant to explore this graph on his/her own and perform a talk aloud. If the participant was not familiar with graphs (which was the case for some visually impaired participants), the experimenter explained concepts of the X-axis, Y-axis points, and plotting. After this, the experimenter explained and demonstrated the four modes of auditory graphs used in the experiment. The order of modes for the training was parallel-tone, serial-tone, parallel-speech, and serial-speech. The same rainfall data was used as examples. The experimenter asked the participant one question for each mode. The participant was allowed to listen to these examples multiple times if required.

After the training, the participant performed the tasks. When the participant was ready, s/he heard the title of a graph. Then the experimenter verbally gave the participant the first task for that graph. The participant was instructed that after s/he finds the answer, s/he should immediately say it aloud. For the tasks requiring multiple answers, the participant had to be ready with all the answers before answering. Before starting with the task, the participant had the option to listen to the graph title and the task as many times as required. When s/he was ready to do the task, s/he pressed the enter key (↵) and started navigating the graph. The task time started when the participant pressed the enter key (↵). A soft limit of 5 min was initially kept for every question after which the task was to be abandoned, but this was not required as no one exceeded this limit. As soon as the participant started answering, the experimenter pressed a key on another keyboard, which stopped the navigation and logged the time. After the participant had told the answer(s), s/he was told if his/her answer was correct and if not, the error rank (see below). This was done to keep the participant engaged with the study.

After completing the three tasks of the short graph of the first assigned mode, the participant moved on to do the tasks of the long graph of the same mode. After completing the six tasks of the two graphs of the first mode, the participant was assigned the next mode. After completing the 24 tasks for the 8 graphs of the 4 modes, the participant was asked to fill out the system usability score (SUS) [14] to record his/her feedback for each mode. If s/he had a problem recalling a particular mode, s/he could hear to the training graph of that mode again.

The dependent variables of the study were task time, the error rank of the given answer, and the SUS score. The task time was the time from when a participant started an exploration of the graph to when s/he started giving the answer. The error rank of a task was calculated by ranking all possible answers of that task in ascending order of correctness starting with zero. Thus the error rank of an answer was 0 if the answer given by the user was correct, 1 if it was the second best answer and so forth.

4.1 Participants

We conducted two studies. The first study was done with 20 sighted participants and the second study was done with 20 visually impaired participants. Anonymous demographic information regarding self-reported hearing ability, age, level of education, musical training and prior familiarity with graphs was recorded.

Sighted participants were university students (mean age = 24.7 years, SD = 4.65). The selection criteria were that they had to be currently enrolled and between the ages of 18 to 36. None of them were familiar with the research or with the people involved in the studies. They were recruited through word of mouth and through online groups. As these users walked to the experiment center, they were not compensated for travel. Instead, they were given a token of appreciation in the form of a gift voucher worth INR 150 (about USD 2).

Visually impaired users were recruited from across the city (mean age = 29.71 years, SD = 11.33). They were initially recruited through word of mouth and then through a snowballing process. Selection criteria was any visually impaired individual with more than 8–10 years of formal education. They were compensated for their travel to and from the experiment venue.

4.2 Experiment Apparatus

The experiment was conducted in a quiet room with minimal human movement around the seating. A Hewlett Packard laptop running Windows 10 was used for conducting the experiment. Philips DJ series headphones were used for all participants and the default volume was kept at 38. The experimenter asked the participant if s/he were comfortable with the volume and changed it if necessary. Users were given an external USB keyboard with mechanical button keys for navigating the graph. The arrangement was such that the participant could not see the screen from where s/he was seated. Only one participant participated in the experiment at a time.

5   Results

We performed two within subjects repeated measures ANOVAs with time and error as dependent variables and parallel-serial (2), speech-tone (2), graph length (2), tasks (3), and user type (2, between subject) as independent variables. We found the following differences significant for time: Tone is faster than speech ($F(1,38) = 8.093$, $p = 0.007$), parallel is faster than serial ($F(1,38) = 4.928$, $p = 0.032$), short graphs are faster than long graphs ($F(1,38) = 234.031$, $p < 0.0005$), task 1 (highest point) is faster than task 2 (two similar points) and task 3 (three lowest points) ($F(2,37) = 18.74$, $p < 0.0005$), and visually impaired participants are faster than sighted participants ($F(1,38) = 8.246$, $p = 0.007$). The significant results for errors are: speech is more accurate than tone ($F(1,38) = 15.242$, $p < 0.0005$), short graphs are more accurate than long graphs ($F(1,38) = 19.069$, $p < 0.0005$) and task 1 is more accurate than task 2 and task 3 ($F(2,37) = 15.154$, $p < 0.0005$). We elaborate on these results below.

5.1   Tone vs. Speech

Tone (mean time = 43.53 s, SD = 1.81, 95% CI = 39.87 to 47.20) was found to be significantly faster than speech (mean time = 49.81 s, SD = 1.61, 95% CI = 46.55 to 53.08) ($F(1,38) = 8.093$, $p = 0.007$, $\eta_p^2 = 0.176$). At the same time, speech (mean error rank = 0.59, SD = 0.12, 95% CI = 0.35 to 0.83) was significantly more accurate than tone (mean error rank = 1.63, SD = 0.24, 95% CI = 1.13 to 2.12) ($F(1,38) = 15.242$, $p < 0.0005$, $\eta_p^2 = 0.286$) (Fig. 2). Thus, though tone improved user speed in comparison with speech to an extent, it did so at the cost of accuracy. The implication to design is that if it is important that the users interpret the data accurately, speech works better though task time may increase.

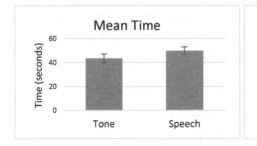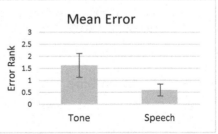

Fig. 2. Graphs showing mean time (seconds) and error rank for tone and speech modes.

5.2   Serial vs. Parallel

Parallel modality (mean time = 45.20 s, SD = 1.46, 95% CI = 42.24 to 48.15) was found to be significantly faster than serial modality (mean time = 48.15 s, SD = 1.48, 95% CI = 45.15 to 51.15) (F(1,38) = 4.928, p = 0.032, η_p^2 = 0.115). However, error was higher in the case of parallel modality (mean error rank = 1.26, SD = 0.23, 95% CI = 0.78 to 1.73) than serial modality (mean error rank = 0.96, SD = 0.12, 95% CI = 0.71 to 1.20) (Fig. 3), though the difference was not significant. Thus, the parallel modes performed significantly faster than the serial modes without affecting user accuracy by much.

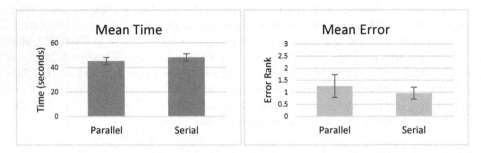

Fig. 3. Graphs showing mean time (seconds) and error rank for serial and parallel modes.

5.3   Graph Length

In case of short graphs, there were only 6 data points and users could rely solely on short term memory in order to answer after traversing the graph once. This is not the case with long graphs as there were 15 points and participants were required to go back and forth to find the correct answer. As expected, participants took significantly more time to navigate longer graphs (mean time = 58.71 s, SD = 1.86, 95% CI = 54.96 to 62.47) than they did shorter graphs (mean time = 34.63 s, SD = 1.12, 95% CI = 32.38 to 36.89) (F(1,38) = 234.031, p < 0.0005, η_p^2 = 0.86). Likewise, participants made significantly more errors with longer graphs (mean error rank = 1.62, SD = 0.25, 95% CI = 1.12 to 2.13) than shorter graphs (mean error rank = 0.59, SD = 0.07, 95% CI = 0.45 to 0.73) (F(1,38) = 19.069, p < 0.0005, η_p^2 = 0.334) (Fig. 4).

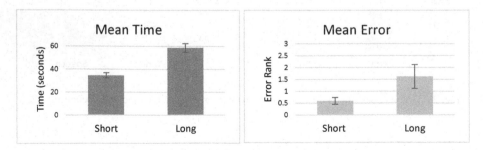

Fig. 4. Graphs showing mean time (seconds) and error rank for different graph lengths (short and long).

5.4   Task

All tasks were point estimation and point comparison tasks with varying levels of difficulty. The first task (highest point) required one answer, the second task (two most similar) required the participant to retain and compare multiple values to give two answers, and the third task (lowest three) required three answers. As expected, there were significant differences in the ANOVA because of the tasks in time (F(2,37) = 18.74, p < 0.0005, η_p^2 = 0.33) and errors (F(2,37) = 15.154, p < 0.0005, η_p^2 = 0.285). Performing pairwise comparisons after applying Bonferroni adjustment for multiple comparisons, we found that task 1 (mean time = 39.76 s, SD = 1.34, 95% CI = 37.05 to 42.47) was significantly faster than task 2 (mean time = 50.97 s, SD = 2.00, 95% CI = 46.93 to 55.01) and task 3 (mean time = 49.29 s, SD = 1.82, 95% CI = 45.62 to 52.97) (p < 0.0005). Task 1 was also more accurate (mean error rank = 0.18, SD = 0.05, 95% CI = 0.07 to 0.28) than task 2 (mean error rank = 1.86, SD = 0.34, 95% CI = 1.18 to 2.54) and task 3 (mean error rank = 1.29, SD = 0.20, 95% CI = 0.89 to 1.69) (p < 0.0005) (Fig. 5). The differences between tasks 2 and 3 on task time and errors was not significant.

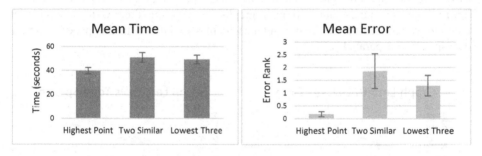

Fig. 5. Graphs showing mean time (seconds) and error rank for the three tasks.

5.5   User Type

The experiment was conducted with two groups of participants, sighted and visually impaired. Figure 6 shows the mean time and error values for both these user types. Visually impaired participants were significantly faster (mean time = 42.90 s, SD = 1.86, 95% CI = 39.15 to 46.66) than their sighted counterparts (mean time = 50.44 s, SD = 1.86, 95% CI = 46.69 to 54.20)(F(1,38) = 8.246, p = 0.007, η_p^2 = 0.178). While sighted users (mean error rank = 1.01, SD = 0.20, 95% CI = 0.61 to 1.41) were more accurate in their answers than visually impaired users (mean error rank = 1.21, SD = 0.20, 95% CI = 0.81 to 1.61), this difference is not significant.

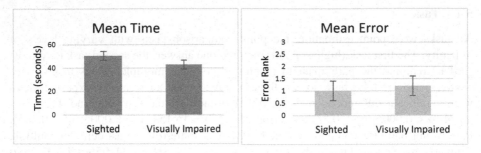

Fig. 6. Graphs showing mean time (seconds) and error rank for sighted and visually impaired participants.

5.6   Significant Interactions

In case of speed, we found four significant interactions, namely graph-length * user-type ($F(1,38) = 11.323$, $p = 0.002$, $\eta_p^2 = 0.23$), graph-length * tone-speech ($F(1,38) = 5.02$, $p = 0.031$, $\eta_p^2 = 0.117$), tone-speech * task ($F(2, 37) = 6.303$, $p = 0.003$, $\eta_p^2 = 0.142$) and tone-speech * graph-length * task ($F(2, 37) = 7.129$, $p = 0.001$, $\eta_p^2 = 0.158$). Figure 7 represents these interactions in graphs. We note that there were no significant interactions between the two independent variables of interest in this paper - namely tone-speech and parallel-serial.

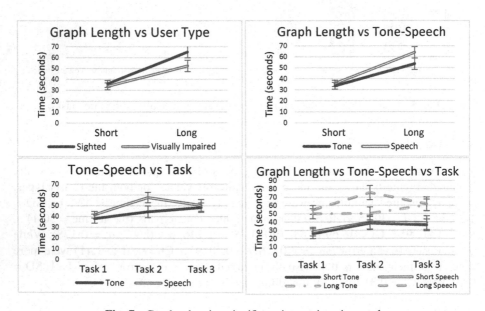

Fig. 7. Graphs showing significant interactions in speed.

In case of errors, we found two significant interactions, namely tone-speech * task $(F(2, 37) = 3.873, p = 0.025, \eta_p^2 = 0.092)$ and graph-length * task $(F(2, 37) = 3.892, p = 0.025, \eta_p^2 = 0.093)$. Figure 8 represents these interactions in graphs. There were no significant interactions between the two independent variables of interest - namely tone-speech and parallel-serial.

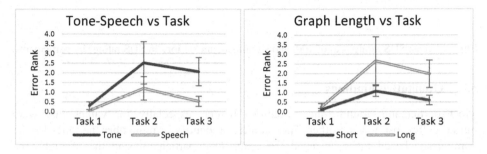

Fig. 8. Graphs showing significant interactions in error.

5.7 User Preference

User preference was calculated through a system usability score (SUS) [14] for each of the four modes, viz. parallel-tone, serial-tone, parallel-speech and serial speech (Fig. 9). In the case of sighted participants, two participants reported they were not confident enough on giving a rating as they had not paid enough attention to the technique while performing the tasks. These participants were dropped from the SUS evaluation and thus N = 18 for sighted users. All 20 visually impaired users gave SUS ratings confidently.

We performed a within subjects repeated measures ANOVA with SUS scores as dependent variables and parallel-serial (2), speech-tone (2) and user type (2, between subject) as independent variables. We found that users preferred speech (mean SUS = 83.63, SD = 1.97, 95% CI = 79.63 to 87.63) over tone (mean SUS = 61.25, SD = 2.80, 95% CI = 55.56 to 66.93) $(F(1,36) = 46.283, p < 0.0005, \eta_p^2 = 0.562)$. Users also preferred serial modes (mean SUS = 77.51, SD = 2.05, 95% CI = 73.35 to 81.66) over parallel modes (mean SUS = 67.37, SD = 2.03, 95% CI = 63.25 to 71.48) $(F(1,36) = 26.157, p < 0.0005, \eta_p^2 = 0.421)$. Visually impaired users gave significantly higher SUS ratings (mean SUS = 76.31, SD = 2.45, 95% CI = 71.34 to 81.29) compared to sighted users (mean SUS = 68.56, SD = 2.59, 95% CI = 63.32 to 73.80) $(F(1,36) = 4.732, p = 0.036, \eta_p^2 = 0.116)$. This was probably because visually impaired users are a lot more familiar with audio-interfaces in general than sighted users.

We found only one significant interaction, namely parallel-serial * user-type $(F(1,36) = 5.775, p = 0.022, \eta_p^2 = 0.138)$. Figure 9 represents these interactions in a graph. We note that there were no significant interactions between the two independent variables of interest in this paper - namely tone-speech and parallel-serial.

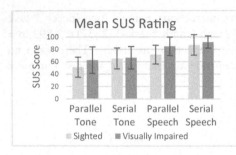
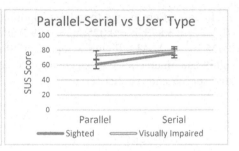

Fig. 9. Mean SUS rating (out of 100) and significant interactions in SUS ratings by participants.

5.8 Qualitative Findings

Most participants found tone modalities harder, especially for values that were numerically close to each other. They could not identify or remember the tones for the comparison based tasks or recall the scale. One participant said that though tone modalities took less time to play out, it took longer to analyze the data as comprehension still took more time. Participants stated that tone modalities were easy for comparing adjacent points, but difficult for longer graphs.

Likewise, users found it harder to concentrate in parallel modalities as they had to pay attention to both ears. Users noted that this might be hard when they are listening casually, while multitasking, or in places with noise. Interestingly, users found parallel speech more distracting than parallel tone. In spite of this, the response for parallel-speech was generally positive as participants found that it was fast and conveyed all the information necessary. Users found parallel tone acceptable only for adjacent values. For longer graphs, this was much harder.

Participants made several design suggestions. For example, using different instruments in the tonal modalities to indicate data values. A participant also suggested using different voices to indicate the magnitude of a data point as well as changing the pitch of voices. Previous research has explored using multiple instruments to denote multiple data series [3]. It would be worth exploring a technique where different instruments are used to denote the magnitude of the data.

We noticed that users rarely used the up arrow to repeat a bar, preferring instead to go back and forth with left and right arrow keys, leading to more repetitions. When asked why, they mentioned it helped get a better relational reference.

6   Discussion

Tone modalities were faster than speech modalities. Through this study, we found that while the tone modalities have substantially less recorded time than speech modalities, this results in only a small amount of saving in the actual task time. Further, this saving comes at a cost of significantly higher error rates and lower user preference. Tones are a poor substitute for speech to communicate numeric data, but they provide a way to reach the required data quickly. While prior work has found that tone modalities may provide context and help in augmenting the information in graphs [15], our users felt that tones do not convey the complete information and demand higher attention. User preference was higher for speech modalities than tonal modalities.

Parallel modalities showed more promise, though they too have a price. As expected, the parallel modalities were faster than the serial modalities in recorded time. Our studies show that task times have some gains in parallel modalities compared to serial modalities, and although accuracy is degraded, the difference is not significant. These results are consistent with earlier studies [2] which showed the effectiveness of using parallel audio streams. While users did not prefer parallel modalities over serial modalities because of increased attention demands, participants were nonetheless positive about parallel modalities, as they conveyed all the information in a short time.

We acknowledge some limitations in our studies. Our participants were familiar with speech technologies, including conversational agents such as Google Assistant [43] and Siri [45], and in case of visually impaired users with screen readers such as TalkBack [44]. None of the participants had prior familiarity with tones which depict numerical values. Our studies did not give the users an opportunity to practice the tone and parallel modalities. The advantages of using these modalities may become more evident after practice.

Our studies have identified opportunities for future work. Firstly, we focussed on bar graphs only. Several other types of graphs could be explored. The tasks performed in our studies were point estimation and point comparison tasks. Choosing a different task could lead to different results. We did not explicitly evaluate the effect of practice of the first task on subsequent tasks. This is something that could be systematically controlled for, and explored. It would be interesting to evaluate interfaces which switch between modalities, either automatically or manually. There was a significant increase in task time and errors from short graphs to long graphs. It will be interesting to explore techniques required for very long graphs containing hundreds of points. Future studies could study more interactive graph navigation techniques, data sorting and filtering techniques, and/or voice input based interactions.

7 Conclusion

In this paper we presented a systematic evaluation of tone and speech and parallel and serial modalities for auditory bar graphs in four modes - parallel tone, serial tone, parallel speech, and serial speech. We found that although tone was consistently faster than speech, it was less accurate. Parallel modalities were significantly faster than serial modalities without affecting accuracy significantly. We also found that users preferred serial modalities over parallel modalities and speech modalities over tone modalities. Serial speech mode was the most preferred. To the best of our knowledge, this is the first paper that presents a systematic comparison of these modes. We hope this work will be beneficial to creators of auditory graphs and pave the way towards new methods of effective auditory graph generation.

Acknowledgements. This research was supported by Tata Consultancy Services. We would like to thank all the participants who took part in this study for their valuable feedback. We would also like to thank the anonymous reviewers of this paper for their reviews which helped shape the final version of this paper.

References

1. Mansur, D.L.: Graphs in sound: a numerical data analysis method for the blind (No. UCRL-53548). Lawrence Livermore National Lab., CA (USA) (1984)
2. Brown, L., Brewster, S., Ramloll, R., Yu, W., Riedel, B.: Browsing modes for exploring sonified line graphs. In: Proceedings of BCS-HCI (2002)
3. Brown, L.M., Brewster, S.A.: Drawing by Ear: Interpreting Sonified Line Graphs. Georgia Institute of Technology, Atlanta (2003)
4. Brown, L.M., Brewster, S.A., Ramloll, S.A., Burton, R., Riedel, B.: Design guidelines for audio presentation of graphs and tables. In: International Conference on Auditory Display (2003)
5. Flowers, J.H.: Thirteen Years of Reflection on Auditory Graphing: Promises, Pitfalls, and Potential New Directions. Georgia Institute of Technology, Atlanta (2005)
6. Kildal, J., Brewster, S.A.: Providing a size-independent overview of non-visual tables. In 12th International Conference on Auditory Display (ICAD2006), pp. 8–15, June 2006
7. Peres, S.C., Lane, D.M.: Sonification of Statistical Graphs. Georgia Institute of Technology, Atlanta (2003)
8. Ramloll, R., Brewster, S., Yu, W., Riedel, B.: Using non-speech sounds to improve access to 2D tabular numerical information for visually impaired users. In: Blandford, A., Vanderdonckt, J., Gray, P. (eds.) People and Computers XV—Interaction without Frontiers, pp. 515–529. Springer, London (2001). https://doi.org/10.1007/978-1-4471-0353-0_32
9. Walker, B.N., Mauney, L.M.: Universal design of auditory graphs: a comparison of sonification mappings for visually impaired and sighted listeners. ACM Trans. Accessible Comput. (TACCESS) 2(3), 12 (2010)
10. Walker, B.N., Lane, D.M.: Psychophysical Scaling of Sonification Mappings: A Comparison of Visually Impaired and Sighted Listeners. Georgia Institute of Technology, Atlanta (2001)
11. Bonebright, T.L., Nees, M.A., Connerley, T.T., McCain, G.R.: Testing the Effectiveness of Sonified Graphs for Education: A Programmatic Research Project. Georgia Institute of Technology, Atlanta (2001)
12. Nees, M.A., Walker, B.N.: Encoding and representation of information in auditory graphs: descriptive reports of listener strategies for understanding data. In: International Community for Auditory Display (2008)
13. Peres, S.C., Lane, D.M.: Auditory Graphs: The Effects of Redundant Dimensions and Divided Attention. Georgia Institute of Technology, Atlanta (2005)
14. Brooke, J.: SUS-a quick and dirty usability scale. Usability Eval. Ind. 189(194), 4–7 (1996)
15. Smith, D.R., Walker, B.N.: Effects of training and auditory context on performance of a point estimation sonification task. In: Proceedings of the Human Factors and Ergonomics Society Annual Meeting, vol. 48, no. 16, pp. 1828–1831. SAGE Publications, Los Angeles, September 2004
16. Resources on Alternative Text for Images. https://www.w3.org/WAI/alt/. Accessed 20 Jan 2019

17. Nees, M.A., Walker, B.N.: Relative intensity of auditory context for auditory graph design. Georgia Institute of Technology, Atlanta (2006)
18. Brewster, S.A., Wright, P.C., Edwards, A.D.: Experimentally derived guidelines for the creation of earcons. In: Adjunct Proceedings of HCI, vol. 95, pp. 155–159, August 1995
19. Nees, M.A., Walker, B.N.: Listener, task, and auditory graph: toward a conceptual model of auditory graph comprehension. In: Proceedings of ICAD 2007 (2007)
20. Wall, S.A., Brewster, S.: Sensory substitution using tactile pin arrays: human factors, technology and applications. Sig. Process. **86**(12), 3674–3695 (2006)
21. Horstmann, M., et al.: Automated interpretation and accessible presentation of technical diagrams for blind people. New Rev. Hypermedia Multimedia **10**(2), 141–163 (2004)
22. Jankun-Kelly, T.J., Ma, K.L., Gertz, M.: A model and framework for visualization exploration. IEEE Trans. Vis. Comput. Graph. **13**(2), 357–369 (2007)
23. Cowan, N.: The magical number 4 in short-term memory: a reconsideration of mental storage capacity. Behav. Brain Sci. **24**(1), 87–114 (2001)
24. The World Bank. https://data.worldbank.org/. Accessed 01 May 2019
25. Sonic Pi - The Live Coding Music Synth for Everyone. https://sonic-pi.net/. Accessed 01 May 2019
26. Animaker Voice, Create free human-like voice overs for your videos, https://www.animaker.com/voice. Accessed 01 May 2019
27. Pollack, I., Ficks, L.: Information of elementary multidimensional auditory displays. J. Acoust. Soc. Am. **26**(2), 155–158 (1954)
28. Bly, S.: Presenting information in sound. In: Proceedings of the 1982 Conference on Human Factors in Computing Systems, pp. 371–375. ACM, March 1982
29. Yeung, E.S.: Pattern recognition by audio representation of multivariate analytical data. Anal. Chem. **52**(7), 1120–1123 (1980)
30. Web Accessibility Tutorials. https://www.w3.org/WAI/tutorials/images/complex/. Accessed 01 May 2019
31. The TeDUB-Project (Technical Drawings Understanding for the Blind). https://www.alasdairking.me.uk/tedub/index.htm. Accessed 01 May 2019
32. Brown, A., Pettifer, S., Stevens, R.: Evaluation of a non-visual molecule browser. In: ACM SIGACCESS Accessibility and Computing, no. 77–78, pp. 40–47. ACM, October 2004
33. Kennel, A.R.: Audiograf: a diagram-reader for the blind. In: Proceedings of the Second Annual ACM Conference on Assistive Technologies, pp. 51–56. ACM, April 1996
34. Challis, Ben P., Edwards, Alistair D.N.: Design principles for tactile interaction. In: Brewster, S., Murray-Smith, R. (eds.) Haptic HCI 2000. LNCS, vol. 2058, pp. 17–24. Springer, Heidelberg (2001). https://doi.org/10.1007/3-540-44589-7_2
35. Carpenter, P.A., Shah, P.: A model of the perceptual and conceptual processes in graph comprehension. J. Exp. Psychol. Appl. **4**(2), 75 (1998)
36. Stockman, T., Nickerson, L.V., Hind, G.: Auditory Graphs: A Summary of Current Experience and Towards a Research Agenda. Georgia Institute of Technology, Atlanta (2005)
37. Gardner, J.A., Lundquist, R., Sahyun, S.: TRIANGLE: a tri-modal access program for reading, writing and doing math. In: Proceedings of the CSUN International Conference on Technology and Persons with Disabilities, Los Angles. Converging Technologies for Improving Human Performance (pre-publication on-line version), vol. 123, September 1998
38. Zhao, H., Plaisant, C., Shneiderman, B., Lazar, J.: Data sonification for users with visual impairment: a case study with georeferenced data. ACM Trans. Comput. Hum. Interact. (TOCHI) **15**(1), 4 (2008)

39. Flowers, J.H., Whitwer, L.E., Grafel, D.C., Kotan, C.A.: Sonification of Daily Weather Records: Issues of Perception, Attention and Memory in Design Choices, p. 432. Faculty Publications, Department of Psychology (2001)
40. Deutsch, D.: Grouping mechanisms in music. In: The Psychology of Music, pp. 299–348. Academic Press (1999)
41. Bregman, A.S.: Auditory scene analysis: The perceptual organization of sound. MIT Press, Cambridge (1990)
42. Audacity - Free, open source, cross-platform audio software. https://www.audacityteam.org/. Accessed 01 May 2019
43. Google Assistant. https://assistant.google.com. Accessed 01 May 2019
44. Talkback - Google Accessibility. https://www.google.com/accessibility/. Accessed 01 May 2019
45. Apple Siri. https://www.apple.com/siri/. Accessed 01 May 2019
46. Processing Programming Language. https://processing.org/. Accessed 01 May 2019
47. McGookin, D., Robertson, E., Brewster, S.: Clutching at straws: using tangible interaction to provide non-visual access to graphs. In: Proceedings of the SIGCHI Conference on Human Factors in Computing Systems, pp. 1715–1724. ACM, April 2010
48. Gomez, C.C., Shebilske, W., Regian, J.W.: The effects of training on cognitive capacity demands for synthetic speech. In: Proceedings of the Human Factors and Ergonomics Society Annual Meeting, vol. 38, no. 18, pp. 1229–1233. SAGE Publications, Los Angeles, October 1994
49. Flowers, J.H., Hauer, T.A.: "Sound" alternatives to visual graphics for exploratory data analysis. Behav. Res. Methods Instrum. Comput. 25(2), 242–249 (1993)
50. De Cheveigne, A.: Pitch perception models. In: Plack, C.J., Fay, R.R., Oxenham, A.J., Popper, A.N. (eds.) Pitch, pp. 169–233. Springer, New York (2005). https://doi.org/10.1007/0-387-28958-5_6
51. Newman, E.B., Stevens, S.S., Davis, H.: Factors in the production of aural harmonics and combination tones. J. Acoust. Soc. Am. 9(2), 107–118 (1937)

Factors that Impact the Acceptability of On-Body Interaction by Users with Visual Impairments

David Costa[✉] and Carlos Duarte

LASIGE, Faculdade de Ciências, Universidade de Lisboa, Lisbon, Portugal
dcosta@lasige.di.fc.ul.pt, caduarte@di.fc.ul.pt

Abstract. On-body interaction is a growing alternative way of controlling everyday interactive devices. Despite on-body gestures being natural
for humans, there is still a lack of research on how this type of interaction
can improve accessibility for people with visual disabilities. The first step
must be to acknowledge if users from this population group are willing to
use on-body interaction for mobile interaction scenarios and under what
conditions. In this article we present a qualitative study with 18 interviewees to understand what factors impact the willingness of visually
impaired users to control their mobile devices through on-body interaction in different environments and settings. We observed a set of factors
and conditions that affect positively or negatively their willingness to
use on-body interaction. The factors range from the location and type
of audience to safety, privacy, and embarrassment or even the characteristics of the gestures themselves.

Keywords: On-body interaction · Social acceptance · Accessibility ·
Visually impaired people

1 Introduction

Visually impaired users of smartphones have to be able to interact with their
devices without visual cues. Current mobile operating systems already offer assistive options that make this task possible (Talkback for Android and VoiceOver
for iOS). However, existing assistive options still require the user to interact
with the device's screen even though it cannot be seen. For blind users, this usually requires both hands (one to hold the device, another to touch the screen),
which limits their use of these devices in some mobile contexts. For example, a
blind person using a cane or assisted by a guide dog will have at least one hand
occupied. In these situations they will usually delay their interaction with the
device until they reach a place where they feel safe and are confident enough to
use both hands [7]. One alternative is speech based interaction. However, this
also raises issues in mobile contexts. For instance, the user might shy away from
providing private information via speech when not confident of being alone [7].

© IFIP International Federation for Information Processing 2019
Published by Springer Nature Switzerland AG 2019
D. Lamas et al. (Eds.): INTERACT 2019, LNCS 11746, pp. 267–287, 2019.
https://doi.org/10.1007/978-3-030-29381-9_17

Another alternative for interacting with smartphones is non-screen based gestural interaction, or body based interaction. By interacting via gestures that resort only to our body parts, without requiring a foreign interaction surface, the device's screen is no longer needed, and the blind user does not even need to pick or touch the device. Also, if the gestures are inconspicuous enough they can be private to the user. To be used in a mobile context, this solution requires a wearable gesture recognizer that is capable of recognizing gestures made by hands or arms, sensitive enough to recognize inconspicuous gestures. Solutions have emerged in recent years that make this a technologically viable alternative now. Wilhelm et al. [21] present a ring with a transmitter on it. Whenever the fingers move there is a change in the electromagnetic field around the ring thus enabling finger gestures recognition. Zhang et al. [23] enable gesture recognition via a ring with an oscillator built-in which emits an active signal while a sensor band with four pairs of electrodes, placed on the user's wrist, is used to capture and measure the signal. Rossi et al. [17] use 4 sEMG sensors placed on the user's forearm to recognize hand and finger gestures.

However, being a novel interaction paradigm for these users, we still need to understand how it can support people with visual impairments [12] and what variables are important for the adoption of such a solution from the users' perspective. Without this knowledge, we risk designing solutions that, even if technologically sound, will not be adopted by the target users.

Our main objective is to create an interaction model that characterizes how visually impaired users might use body based interaction to interact with mobile devices, and then explore this model to increase the accessibility of these devices. To create this model there are different dimensions that must be taken into account (e.g., technology requirements and limitations, actions that can be performed with this type of interaction, user characteristics). In this document we want to address the social dimension, i.e., the human behavior and interactions in society. More specifically, we want to answer two research questions:

- RQ1: Are users with visual impairments willing to use on-body interaction to control their smartphones?
- RQ2: What are the main factors that affect, positively or negatively, the acceptability of on-body interaction by people with visual impairments?

To understand people's behaviors and attitudes towards on-body interaction we conducted a qualitative study with visually impaired users. The next section presents work related with body based sensing technology, its use on ameliorating the accessibility and social studies regarding body interaction. The methodology followed in this study is described after. This is followed by a results section presenting the topics identified in the study and a discussion section where the main findings are described. Finally, the main conclusions and future work are stated in the last section.

2   Related Work

2.1   Body Based Interaction and Technology

Starting in the past decade, the idea of using our body as a platform for interaction is present in a rising number of research projects. Harrison et al. paved the way with several well known works such as Scratch Input [4], Skinput [6] or Armura [5]. More recent research in on-body interaction is found on SkinTrack [23], the virtual trackpad [10], iSKin [20], ThumbSlide [1] and many others.

A plethora of different kinds of sensors are presented in these works (piezo-electric films [6], modified stethoscope [4], infrared camera [5], capacitive sensors [20,23], electromyography [10] and photo-reflective sensors [1]), which are able to recognize multiple points of touch in several parts of our body (fingers [20], hand [6,20,23], forearm [6,23] and legs [4]) and mid-air gestures also made by different parts of the body (fingers [1], hand [5,10], arms [5].

Additionally, the increasing miniaturization and low-power consumption of sensing technology makes interaction with mobile devices possible. Games [1,23], hierarchical navigation [6], picking up calls [20], music players [20] and text input [20] were the main focus of some projects when using smartphones [4,6,20] and smartwatches [1,23].

2.2   Body Based Interaction and Accessibility

Other works have looked at how on-body interaction can improve the accessibility of interactive systems. They have focused on leveraging proprioception, gesture recognition and micro-interactions. Virtual Shelves [9], an interaction technique that leverages proprioception capabilities to support eyes-free interaction by assigning spatial regions centered around the user's body to applications shortcuts, compared the performance of this technique between sighted users and visually impaired users. Although sighted users had significantly better performance, people with visual disabilities were still able to launch shortcuts correctly 88.3% of the time. Costa and Duarte [3] developed a gesture recognizer with the goal of removing unnecessary calibration procedures and at the same time being robust for a mobile environment. Oh et al. [13] also studied the potential of using on-body input for micro-interactions in mobile devices for people with visual impairments. Findings suggest that gestures should be location independent (e.g., swiping the hand or the leg results in the same action) mainly because it is easier to learn and remember the gestures than recalling where a gesture should be performed on your body.

2.3   Social Acceptability

It is already known that VI people are concerned with looking "normal" and avoiding strange-looking assistive technologies [18] which can cause embarrassment [2]. Body based interaction techniques, which are a possible technology addressing those concerns, were already subject of several social acceptability studies. The willingness to perform these gestures will largely be dictated by how appropriate those actions look and feel when performed in public. Profita et al. [14] and Rico et al. [15,16] findings show that there is a significant relation between audience and location with the willingness to perform certain gestures. Findings also show that users are more fond of subtle movements, movements that are similar to what already exists in current technology, and movements similar to the ones used in our everyday lives and enjoyable movements. On the other hand, participants stated that uncommon, large or noticeable movements would look weird in public settings.

Williamson et al. [22] developed an application based on in-air gestural inter-action. Despite being considered subtle by the authors, it was observed that some gestures were considered unacceptable in certain settings by the study partici-pants. Consequently, the participants developed new ways of performing the same gesture. To address this issue, such systems much be flexible and develop correc-tion mechanisms in the recognition process. Additionally, the authors found that the willingness to perform gestures in a public setting depends on the characteris-tics of the audience, such as if they are a sustained spectator (e.g. other passenger on a bus) or a transitory spectator (e.g. a person walking by).

Focused on our target population, Oh et al. [12,13] investigated preferences for and design of accessible on-body interaction. The authors' findings show that location specific gestures rose concerns regarding social acceptability in public settings. The least preferred areas were the face/neck and the forearm, while locations on the hands were considered to be more discrete and natural. The findings also suggest that participants may prioritize social acceptability over ease of use and physical comfort when assessing the feasibility of input at different locations of the body.

3   Methodology

We sought to collect rich opinions of potential end users of an on-body interaction based solution for mobile interaction. We conducted a qualitative study focused on interviews, as they provide richer data than questionnaires or online surveys. With an interview we can work directly with the person which gives us the opportunity to probe or ask follow up questions and enrich our findings.

To understand in what conditions people with visual impairments are willing to perform body based gestures we chose a set of different factors that may affect their decisions. Here we present the main factors we saw fit to discuss and why:

The **environment** where the person is located is a factor that could decide whether the person feels it is opportune or not to perform on-body gestures (e.g., home might provide a safer place for gestural interaction than a bus).

Living in a society means to get along with other individuals. The **degree of relationship** between two or more individuals restrains or encourages certain actions thus we see it as a factor when considering performing on-body gestures.

Humans can assume different **stances**, i.e., walk, run or sit. Those are associated with different actions and can affect the predisposition to perform gestures (e.g., seated stance can enable inconspicuous gestures while walking not).

In spite of the possibility of several negative factors deterring a person from doing certain actions (e.g., security, embarrassment, discomfort), there are occasions when the **emergency** of the situation can overcome these factors.

While we discussed these factors in the interviews, we also explored possible gestures. The gestures explored first on the interview ranged from mid-air gestures to on-body touches. We provided a wide variety of examples during the conversations so that interviewees could have a better understanding of the possibilities. These examples did not take into account technological limitations associated with gesture recognizers. We opted to exemplify gestures with different characteristics in terms of amplitude, body parts involved, meaning, etc., with the aim to generate discussion around the **subtleness of gestures**.

Still on this topic, we asked participants to rate the subtleness of specific gestures with different characteristics such as finger, hand and forearm amplitude and conveyed meaning. The gestures from that list were categorized based on a two-level taxonomy (movement and style) similar to the one presented in [8]. Gestures can be static, i.e., do not change over time; Or they can be dynamic, i.e., may involve multiple strokes and the whole movement conveys the gesture's meaning. More specifically, we seek to understand if the gesture's movement characteristics affects its subtleness.

In what concerns its style, gestures can be defined as: Semaphoric (any gesturing system that employs a stylized dictionary of static or dynamic hand or arm gestures), Pantomimic (gestures that simulate performing an action), Iconic (gestures that are used to clarify a verbal description of a physical shape or form through the use of gestures that depict those characteristics), Manipulative (gestures with a close relation between the gesture movement and an object with the intent to control said object) and Deictic (gestures that involve pointing to an entity to be established as the target subject of an action). With this set of gestures we hope to know if and what characteristics can affect the perception of subtleness by people with visual impairments.

We also wished to explore the social aspects of using speech commands as an alternative interaction approach to standard accessible mobile interaction options. Similar to on-body gestures, speech commands also raise concerns regarding social acceptance. Thus, we want to compare the main differences and similarities between the two modalities.

In order to answer our research questions we followed a qualitative approach supported on semi-structured interviews. We chose this type of study based on all the aspects pointed out previously. Conducting an interview with baseline topics where we are able to generate a discussion will be more advantageous to collect meaningful conclusions supported by the reasoning of the participants. Additionally, it can generate new, unexpected, topics for discussion.

3.1   Interviews' Procedure

The interviewer took notes and the interviews were audio recorded for posterior analysis. The interviewer firstly asked for authorization to record the interview and then proceeded to gather demographic information and cellphone usage habits from the participants. The interviewer then explained the goal of the study and how the session will proceed.

During the interviews we presented participants with different situations and asked them if they would perform gestures to interact with their smartphone in those situations and then discussed the motivations for their answers.

Table 1. Gestures exemplified to the participants and their classification

Gesture	Type
"Ok" sign - thumbs up	Static - Semaphoric
"V" sign - index and middle finger spread	Static - Semaphoric
"No" sign - wave hand repeatedly with index finger up	Dynamic - Semaphoric
"Swipe right" sign - move hand from left to right	Dynamic - Semaphoric
"Double click" sign - stroke twice with index finger	Dynamic - Semaphoric
"Grab cup of tea" - simulate grabbing a cup of tea by holding thumb on index	Static - Pantomimic
"Pinch" gesture - move thumb and index closer or farther of each other	Static - Iconic
"Scissors" - move index and middle finger up and down on opposite directions	Dynamic - Iconic
"Rotate an object" - thumb and index up while rotating the wrist	Dynamic - Manipulation
"Point forward" - index pointing with arm stretched	Static - Deictic

As we seek to understand what factors impact the willingness to perform body based gestures to interact with their smartphones we selected a set of domains as basis for the situations to be discussed in the interviews: (1) Gesture subtlety [subtle, not so subtle and unsubtle]; (2) Environment context [home, street with passersby, street with people standing by and workplace]; (3) People around [alone, family, stranger and colleague]; (4) Posture [seated, standing up and walking]; (5) Emergency of the action [emergency, no emergency].

We also wanted to understand what the participants consider to be a subtle gesture. Therefore, we described orally the gesture being discussed. If they could not understand and reproduce the gesture we assisted them in performing it until they correctly understand it. In this part of the interview we discussed a total of 10 gestures (see Table 1). Finally, we asked how they feel regarding speech commands in some of the situations described before.

3.2 Data Analysis

The interviews were transcribed manually from audio to text for further analysis. We then carried out an inductive category analysis [19]. Two coders were, individually, in charge of reviewing notes and discover common factors that affect the acceptability of body based interaction for controlling smartphones in different conditions. The coding task was processed in the online tool QCAMAP [11]. In the next stage, coders shared their interpretations of the interviews and proceeded to obtain a single list of codes. The two coders then reanalyzed the interviews. The results of this analysis will be described in the following section.

3.3 Participants

We recruited 18 visually impaired participants from an institution supporting visually impaired people. However, one participant was excluded from the analysis for not being able to conclude the interview. Each session with a single participant lasted around one hour. Due to problems with the audio recording we could not analyze the recording of 10 participants. For those participants only the interviewer notes were considered in the analysis.

The participants ranged from 25 to 64 years of age ($M = 46.88, SD = 13.27$), 8 were female (9 male) and all had some kind of visual impairment (5 participants reported to have some residual sight, the remaining were blind). On average, participants lost their vision since their teen years ($M = 15.92, SD = 14.84$).

Table 2. Main themes generated after the interview analysis.

Themes	Sub-themes
Acceptability	Gestures
	Task
	Gesture subtlety
	Place
	Who is present
	Stance
	Hand occupancy
	Gesture familiarity
	Emergency situations
Advantages	
Reaction to others	
Participants perception of subtle gestures	
Ethics and other concerns	Privacy
	Security
	Politeness
Technology and devices	

Of the 17 participants, eleven use smartphones (4 iOS) and use VoiceOver or Talkback as their main assistive technology.

4   Results

Expectedly, the analysis of the transcripts and interviewer's notes revealed themes aligned to the dimensions that grounded the interviews. However, new themes emerged from the analysis and new factors were found regarding the acceptability of on-body interaction. We now discuss the themes presented in Table 2.

4.1   Gesture Acceptability

When discussing on-body interaction some of the participants initially showed no concerns about performing gestures. P10 said *"I do not have any issues with touching my body or in my arm"* and *"We, blind people, already raise attention with our canes, it would not be because of doing gestures. What about the deaf and mute people? Don't they already perform gestures to communicate?"* P15 stated *"I am imagining myself on the subway if necessary doing a movement to reject a call, I think the gesture would be similar to other gestures that others do in other devices."* However, some concerns were raised about the **type of gestures** they would be doing. The same participant, P15, now said *"I am imagining being on a restaurant [...] it would depend on the gesture's characteristics."* P18 supported this by expressing *"The gestures must be well thought."*

Frequent gestural interaction, and its consequences, was a legitimate concern. P1 exemplifies this with *"if it is a frequent interaction maybe I would not do it, it would be tiring."*

Some participants expressed their concerns about gestures that already have a **meaning** (e.g., waving hand for "Hello", thumbs up for "OK"). P13 stated *"I think it would be a little weird, others would think that I am waving at them."* P18 added *"It depends on the gestures, right? If I do this [performs a waving gesture] others would think I am talking to them."*

Participants also showed strong concerns about gestures having **offensive meanings**. P11 said *"You should not point at others, it is rude."* P14 exemplified it with *"if we do this [performs offensive gesture] others might get offended, right?"* And P17 summarized it with *"as long as the gestures are not offensive to anyone, it would not affect me."* Still on this topic, when shown a specific gesture – V sign – P18 raised a **cultural** concern when performing gestures: *"This sign could be offensive in the UK."*

According to participants, **comfort** also plays a role on the willingness to perform gestures to interact with their smartphones. On this subject, P15 said *"It would depend [..] if it would be more comfortable to hold the cellphone on my hand or keep it on the pocket.".* When the interviewer asked participants to replicate a specific gesture (scissors), this factor was evident together with concerns for **injuries** or **limitations**. P11 said *" The right hand does not want* to cooperate [...] this one is bad for the tendinitis." P17 added "[...] it is fine, but there are people with motor impairments, it could be harder for them."

Gesturing being something that is **natural** for humans also contributes to the acceptability of this interaction. P10 said that it is more natural than using speech input, "[...] more natural than talking with and listening to a machine."

One major acceptability factor for this interaction is **what it allows users to do**. This could offset some concerns and drive its adoption as can be seen in the comments of P4 ("If it brings advantages to me I cannot feel embarrassed"), P10 ("Everything that eases the interaction with my cellphone is not an inconvenient to me. Don't people talk already with gestures normally?") and P16 ("[...] if it could ease my life, why would I care about what others think?").

4.2 Perceived Advantages

During the interviews the participants stated some perceived advantages from using on-body interaction to control their smartphones. Participants mentioned several times the ability to **interact without having to take the phone out of the pocket**. This was more important when discussing specific tasks.

When discussing walking outside P13 said "it suits me better as I do not have to take out the phone, stop and accept the call. I could walk [...] without having to hold the phone in one hand [...] having a cane this would be beneficial."

Some participants mentioned advantages when cooking. P15 stated "[...] or I am cooking, it is very interesting to me!" and P17 said "[...] it would be advantageous, I could be gutting the fish at the same time for instance."

When discussing desk work, P16 mentioned "If I have the phone on the table and I am working I would not have to move to grab the phone, it would help."

However, the same participant raised the concern of performing gestures that could interrupt a conversation: "as long as it does not interrupt my conversation with another person by doing the gesture [...]".

Other participant saw advantages concerning **privacy** issues. P16 exemplified it with "If I am seated, I can do the gestures under the table" and "if I do it like this [demonstrates gesture], no one else would notice."

Others stated that it would be a great advantage regarding **security** concerns if they could keep the cellphone in their pocket. For example, P4 stated "[...] this way I would not run the risk of being robbed."

Participants also stated that using on-body interaction to control their cellphones is a technology that not only helps them but also can **help everyone**. Examples of this came from P10 ("it is an easier way [to interact with his phone], I think it would be better for everyone.") and P15 ("[...] I became aware that this is not only good for persons with visual disabilities, but for everyone else too!")

4.3 Gesture Subtlety

Gesture subtlety is a major factor in the acceptability of this interaction technique as could be seen in the comments of most participants when faced with different levels of gesture subtleness.

If gestures were **subtle** and the interviewee was assured that no one else would notice it, the overall reaction is very positive. For example, P1 said *"I would do it in any circumstance as they are subtle gestures."* In the same line, P13 stated *"I would feel comfortable doing gestures, no one would notice so."*

Being on public environments (e.g., street), makes this factor even more important as could be seen in several comments. For instance, P2 mentioned *"For me the benefit of using subtle gestures would be even better in this situation."*

When discussing not so subtle gestures that could be noticed by others the reaction was less positive. For example, if asked to do these gestures on the street, P11 commented *"Right, I do not know if I would feel very comfortable."*

However, not all participants expressed the same level of concern. P4 stated *"Even being less subtle, people also scratch their shoulders and no one notices it [...] there are always ways to avoid people noticing me doing gestures."*

When presented with gestures that surely would be noticed by others, the reaction grew more negative. Even P4 stated *"it is more complicated to do it. [...] it is a little embarrassing"* and *"I would prefer to pick up the phone than using gestures."* **Embarrassment** was a concern expressed by most participants. P8 saw no point in doing such gestures to interact with his cellphone specially in front of family or strangers, *"I would feel embarrassed [...] I do not feel necessary to do such gestures with big movements to control the phone."* P10 outrightly stated that *"At home alone I would do it, but on the street I would not."*

Some participants expressed additional concerns about the dangerous aspects of performing such **extreme movements** being blind. P10 exemplified this by stating *"[...] we can not see if we will hit someone."* P14 also discussed this when saying *"Most of the times we have to have perception of our surroundings, If I am in my house I would be able to do it. However, for instance if we are talking about raising our arm in front of us, I could be sitting on a table and a bottle of water could be on the table, we have to be aware of what we are doing. I could be surrounded by people and hit someone."*

Near the end of the interviews we discussed what makes a gesture subtle in their opinion. This is important since we had discussed the effect of the subtlety of gestures. To this end we defined a set of ten gestures (Table 1) and we asked what they thought about them.

In general all gestures were well understood when described aurally by the interviewer. However, three gestures had to be explained physically. The "ok" and "Pinch" signs where not understood by 4 participants while the "Victory" sign was not understood by 3 participants.

All except one gesture were generally perceived as subtle (Fig. 1). With this result we could not find any difference between static and dynamic gestures.

Further analyzing, we observed that the two **iconic** gestures exemplified to the interviewees were the most perceived as subtle (15 out of 17 participants). One of the reasons stated for the iconic gestures being subtle is that those gestures are known and used in our daily lives. Referring to the *scissors* gesture, P16 said *"these are gestures that we have used for a long time."* The *point forward* gesture

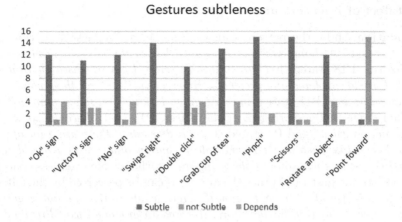

Fig. 1. Gesture subtlety perceived by the interviewees.

was seen as not subtle by the majority of participants (15 out of 17). P11 even reported it as being offensive, *"You should not point, it is rude."*

Gesture subtleness is not only categorized by the characteristics of the gesture but also by external factors such as the person's **stance**. While seated, gestures could be performed in a more inconspicuous way as they can be hidden. P16 said *"If I am seated I would do it under the table, or I would do it like this [demonstrates the gesture]."* Differences between walking and standing were referred regarding the subtlety of the gesture. For instance, P13 stated *"as I said before, it depends if we are walking, if we are stationary"*, referring that while walking it would be noticed.

Other factor is how the person performs the gesture. **Where the gesture is done**, i.e., on air or close to body as well as **how fast** it can be performed were the two main reasons pointed out by the interviewees. Gestures closer to the body and without abrupt movements are perceived as subtle. P8 said *"It depends on the gestures' speed and if you do it on air or on your leg."* P18 stated *"It depends on how you do the gesture, if I do it like this [performs gesture closer to the body] [...] This way it is ok [subtle]."*

4.4 Effect of Gesture's Complexity

Not only the subtlety but also the **complexity** of the gestures affects the willingness to interact with gestures. P2 said *"These more complex gestures, I would perform them only inside."* P13 stated *"If the gestures are simple yes [I would do it]."* P18 said *"one will pick a simple gesture to pick up calls"*, *"I think in any situation I would opt for simpler gestures."*

P13 stated that the issue is not the embarrassment of doing it in front of other people but the **quickness** when compared with the traditional way of interacting, *"I would not have any problems but probably I would not do it because I would have more work than getting the phone out of my pocket."*

4.5   Effect of Location and People Present

The **location** where the person is also affects the willingness to perform gestures. P10 said *"At home alone I could do it but in the street it would be more complicated."* P18 stated that *"in situations where I am in closed environments [home], I would not have any problems. However in the street they would not be so practical to do."* P11 states that *"At home I would feel much more willing."*

When discussing gesturing in public places, P11 said *"I would do it, if the place is not crowded"* and P9 stated that *"It depends if there are a lot of people and confusion like rush hour, I would do it, but in other cases I would refrain from using gestures with others observing me."* Others were even less concerned about performing gestures in these locations, as can be perceived by the following comments. P5 stated *"I do not know if others would notice me doing gestures, but I would do it anyway. Furthermore, if it was an urgency I would really do it."* P1 said *"People are too busy to notice"* regarding passers-by or people standing by. P8 said that *"Shy people would feel embarrassed but not me."*

While in public places, the presence of **family** is something that can affect positively the willingness to perform gestures. P6 said *"Perhaps I would feel more comfortable if I were with my family"* and P11 stated *"yes, if I was accompanied with my family it would be easier."*

In the presence of **strangers** the subtleness of the gestures plays an important role in the willingness to perform them. When gestures are subtle P13 says *"I would feel comfortable, the gestures are so imperceivable."* If the gestures are not subtle, P7 instead states that *"I would avoid doing gestures around strangers."* P9 shares this opinion when expressing *"I would feel constrained to do it in front of others."* Nevertheless, it is important to mention that this attitude is not shared by every participant. P15 is uncomfortable with performing gestures in front of strangers, independently of the subtleness, as expressed by *"In the case of being with a stranger I would think twice."*

We also discussed in the interviews other degrees of acquaintances between family and strangers. For instance, **work colleagues** may affect the willingness to perform gestures. P3 stated that only if he trusts the colleague he would perform gestures: *"Only if I trust him because I do not want him to tell my boss I am doing gestures."* P4 said that he would do it in front of colleagues but not in front of his boss adding *"if it is a colleague, I would explain it to him [why he is doing gestures]."* P9 stated that he would only do gestures in the presence of a work colleague if he understood his situation: *"Taking into account that the other person knows I need help for being blind."*

4.6   Effect of Stance and Free Hands

We also discussed the impact that stance might have on the willingness to perform gestures. In particular we considered seating, standing and walking. There were not many comments on this subject. A few participants would prefer to avoid performing gestures while **walking**, like P11 who said *"[...] If I was stationary I would in fact do it, without any problem."* P15 related the stance with the subtlety of gestures when stating *"Maybe if I was seated it would be more discreet wouldn't it?"*

Given that blind people when walking outside usually have at least one of their **hands occupied** with a cane or a guide dog's leash, we also discussed what effect this could have. P10 and P18 said respectively, *"No [issues with doing gestures while walking on the street], if I was only using one hand"* and *"[...] it could be solved by just changing the hand holding the cane, that would not be a problem."* P2 also said *"[...] using my non-dominant hand or I could use my index finger while holding the cane."*

While gestures made with one hand only, or more inconspicuous ones that could be done only with fingers, raised no concerns if one hand is free, more ample gestures originated a different reaction. P1 summed it up when stating *"Normally I have both hands occupied. I would stop to interact."*

4.7 Effect of Other People Noticing

In many situations participants commented how they would react when **noticed by others** doing gestures to interact with their smartphones. P14 said he would just ignore offensive comments by others, *"[...] people could sometimes say this guy must have nervous twitches and I would say yes yes."* P15 stated that he would quickly forget that others are observing him (*"Probably others will look but I will stop noticing that, I do not care"*) although he also stated that *"I have the tendency to explain everything to others, to make them aware of our reality."*

The **willingness to explain** what is going on can be seen in the comments of several other participants. P4, P8, P10, P16 and P17 mentioned this explicitly in their interviews. For example, P4 said *"If anyone asked me what I was doing, I would explain it to him."* P10 contextualized with the action being done when commenting *"[...] I am accepting a call [using] a new easier way to do it."*

4.8 Effect of Gesture Familiarity

For those participants who owned a smartphone and were familiar with Talk-back and VoiceOver gestures, we discussed what they think about using similar gestures to what they already use but done in-air or on the body.

Almost all participants agreed that using **gestures they already knew** would affect positively their willingness to use on-body interaction. P4 said *"If we were using the same set of gestures we use on the touchscreen, I would feel more comfortable to do it in any situation."* P9 stated *"I would prefer the ones I already know, it would be easier and I would be more comfortable."* P13 said *"I would prefer Talkback's gestures for being simpler."*

Other participants were indifferent to it (P5) or emphasized not the gestures but how they are performed. P8 said *"If all of [the gestures] would be performed close to the body it would be the same [as Talkback]. On air they would not."*

4.9   Effect of Task Urgency

During the interviews we discussed, especially with who was less prone to perform gestures in public settings, about their willingness to perform non subtle gestures (eventually with large amplitude of movements) when they urgently needed to use the smartphone (e.g., to call an ambulance, or to answer an important call).

The opinions covered the whole spectrum. Most said they would do it in an **emergency context**. For example, P2 stated *"Yes I would do it even if someone would call me crazy!"* while P6 said *"If I were afflicted I would do it."* Some showed to be less keen to do it. P4 and P5 said if it was the only option then they would do it. Finally others were not willing to do these gestures even in extreme situations. P9 said *"[...] I think I would prefer to use the traditional way"* while P14 stated *"I would try to avoid doing it."*

4.10   Effect of Ethics and Security

When discussing the use of gestures for interacting with a smartphone when at the work place, we initially identified a common concern that is not related with gestures. Many participants refrain from **using their smartphone in the workplace**, as can be seen in the words of P5: *"On the workplace I always keep my phone away [...] I would only use it if it is an emergency."* From the interviews we concluded that for those that do not use their phone at work, not even the gestures being subtle would make them use it. For those that use it, then on-body interaction would not change it. For example, P14 said *"[...] Yes I think I would do it, as long as it has no consequences."*

The **ethical concerns** extended to outside the workplace, as can be seen in this statement from P17: *"Of course we can not obstruct the sidewalk [while doing the gesture] [...] and [I would] move to one of the sides to do it."*

Another factor that was frequently raised during the interviews was **security**, and how on-body interaction has the potential to make them feel safer. Various participants expressed their fears of having their smartphones stolen from them. P10 said that *"I do not like to pick up my cellphone, I am scared that someone near me takes it."* P14 stated *"Because we can be on the street and someone takes my phone of my hand."*

4.11   Speech Recognition

At the end of the interview we discussed what did the participants think about using speech to control their smartphones. Participants were asked to comment on this subject based on all the topics that had been discussed previously.

The major concern raised by participants regarding the use of speech was **privacy**. P1 said *"Only at home and with people I really trust."* P2 stated *"I would prefer to write over talking [...] I would even try to learn the touchscreen gestures rather than using voice."* When discussing the public location with a stranger setting, P14 said *"[I would not use voice] because I do not know that person and I would not trust her."*

Other interviewees are used to and currently use voice commands. These had a different opinion. P4 said *"I use it on the bus, for example, to search contacts."* P7 stated that *"When I had Internet [on my phone] I usually used it [...] I would use voice commands in any situation even in public."* Other participants (P10) accepted using voice commands due to its familiarity and popularity. P11 said he would prefer voice over gestures.

Besides privacy, other participants showed **ethical** concerns regarding the use of voice in crowded spaces. P8 said *"At home or on a place alone I would use voice [...] In public transportation or places with a lot of people I would avoid it, so I don't bother them."*

Similar to what happened with on-body interaction, **security** issues were also mentioned. P10 said *"I would avoid it maybe ... and the cellphone would have to be in my hand?"* P13 stated that *"for instance, my cellphone can be ringing and other person hears it and says accept and I did not want to answer it"* referring to other people issuing commands on his behalf.

Another aspect that was not specific to on-body interaction is **embarrassment**. For a subset of the participants, speech is potentially more embarrassing than on-body gestures. P9 said *"If I were to use it, it would never be on the street. I think it is worse than using the gestures we discussed."* P10 stated that *"I would do it but I think gestures would be better."* Also, P13 stated that for certain situations gestures are also better than speech: *"I would prefer gestures over speech but the street is where it is really advantageous."*

5   Discussion

This study explored the acceptability of on-body interaction by visually impaired users as a potential interaction technique to increase smartphone's accessibility.

Our findings supplement previous studies that investigated gestures and touches on our body as a means of interaction for people with this impairment [12]. Past studies limited gesture creation to finger gestures and body touch in three different body locations (hand, forearm and face). While in our study we did not explore gesture creation, participants were given examples of gestures and touches that showed the freedom of on-body interaction which is not restricted only to fingers and hands. We believe that in this way participants could be more creative when confronted with the situations described during the interview (e.g., P15 suggested to use the tongue or foot taps for subtle gestures).

While our end goal is to understand what are the design implications for an on-body based interaction model for users with visual impairments, in this document we provide more insight on the social acceptability aspect and what are the factors that impact the willingness of the users to interact with gestures.

The themes that emerged in this study were in accordance with the literature. Rico and Brewster [15] studied the social acceptability based on a survey where a set of 18 gestures were described to participants. They concluded that demographics or previous experience with technology usage are not the only factors that impact social acceptability. There are a lot more factors than embarrassment or politeness. In [16], the same authors state that it can range from appearance, social status, to culture. In their studies, the authors concluded that audience and location are factors that affect the willingness to perform body based gestures. Authors also reported gesture subtleness; similarity to existing technology; similarity to everyday actions/uncommon movements, enjoyable/uncomfortable movements and interference with communication are important factors as well. Our study focused on the acceptability by visually impaired people, unlike Rico and Brewster's study which did not consider this target group. Nevertheless, it is interesting to register that our findings were similar.

Regarding the **location** where the individual is at, it was evident that home was the most acceptable location to perform gestures and public places were the least accepted locations. This is, of course, a result of public locations being coupled with an **audience** that can perceive the gestures being made [16]. However, we learned that being at **home** brings an added confidence to perform gestures even when around strangers. By being in a "safe place" our participants are more confident of their knowledge of their surroundings and feel more at ease to explain what they are doing.

Besides the audience factor that is associated with public locations and that potentially can cause **embarrassment** as explained by some of our interviewees, we uncovered other reasons attached to the willingness to perform gestures in certain locations. Among this, the **security** of the blind person was often mentioned. Our participants felt that a solution that removes the need to take the phone out of a pocket or bag to be able to interact with it would address their fears of having the phone stolen from them while holding it in a public place. Another acceptability factor that was discussed is the **ethics** of using a smartphone in a public setting. Several participants revealed that in their workplace they refuse to interact with their smartphone. Even if using inconspicuous gestures to interact with the smartphone, our participants maintained their unwillingness to use the devices in the workplace if that was their initial position.

As aforementioned, audience plays a major role in social acceptance of on-body interaction. When alone, most participants accepted doing gestures, some even in the street or at their workplace. The **type of audience** can affect positively the users to perform gestures in public locations. Family presence comforts and increases user's confidence to interact with gestures. Work colleagues offered a mixed experience. Participants reported that the confidence in using on-body interaction is based on trusting that their colleagues will not get them in trouble.

The main causes that affect the acceptance in front of others have to do with **embarrassment** and **privacy** issues. Gesture **subtleness** is a major contributing factor to the embarrassment or lack of privacy of the interaction, thus it is a major factor impacting the willingness to perform gestures. While subtle gestures were welcome and even seen as a great feature and advantage of on-body interaction, attention grabbing gestures were not welcome at all. The perceived disadvantages of these gestures weighed more heavily on the participant's willingness to use them than positive factors like the location and type of audience. Some participants were not willing to do these gestures in their home or when alone in public places. This was more evident in public places when they could not be sure that there weren't any observers around (e.g., train station). In this situation almost no one wanted to perform these gestures although the presence of family still affected positively some of our participants.

The more ample the gestures are, the more embarrassment they cause. However, this was not the single concern raised. Participants also mentioned **safety** reasons (e.g., hitting someone while doing the gestures) for not wanting to perform those gestures. However, in **emergency** situations, such as needing to call an ambulance, the subtleness factor loses importance to some of our participants.

Hand occupancy was also discussed by Oh and Findlater [12]. Our results are in agreement with theirs. During our discussions the interviewees declared that when holding a cane or a guide dog's leash they would prefer to do gestures with the non-dominant hand or, if with the dominant hand, they need to be allowed to do gestures or touches while holding the cane (e.g., index finger tapping the cane while holding it).

We also investigated if **stance** would affect the willingness to perform on-body interaction. However, participants shown almost no concerns when talking about different stances (seating, standing and walking), except for the walking stance. The majority of participants did not point any differences in being seated or standing regarding, for instance, the ability to disguise the interaction. Only one participant mentioned this situation. This perception applied irrespectively of the location where the interaction was taking place. The walking stance impact was mentioned only in those situations where the cane is needed, i.e., on the street. At places that are well known, e.g., home or at work, participants feel that they will have no problems performing the gestures while walking.

The **tasks** users have at hand were also identified as a factor impacting the acceptability. As Rico and Brewster [16] state, there are gestures that may interfere and disrupt a conversation with another person. Gestures that already convey a communication meaning should be avoided. When navigating from one point to another in the presence of obstacles or other factors that might be dangerous for the person, this type interaction was not welcomed by some participants. However, in this setting any interaction with the smartphone is avoided, which means that is not a concern exclusive to on-body interaction. Interestingly enough, there are tasks where both hands are occupied and participants were enthusiastic with the idea of using gestures (e.g., cooking).

Gesture **familiarity** also contributes for on-body interaction acceptance. Replicating on-screen gestures or other gestures already popular via current technology (e.g., Wii remote control) might help to ease the acceptance for this novel type of interaction [12,16]. The use of these well-established gestures might also contribute to reduce the embarrassment of doing such gestures.

Gestures' characteristics and **meanings** also affect their social acceptance when the user might be observed. We already discussed the importance of avoiding gestures with a meaning. For example, waving hands could mean a communication starter. Doing these gestures "alone" while on a public place would lead to misunderstandings. Gestures may not only convey offensive meanings but they are also **culturally dependent**.

All the factors above contribute to answer RQ2. Besides these, we received multiple statements suggesting that if this technology is well implemented and in fact brings accessibility advantages for the user, they will use it despite other factors (embarrassment) that would normally deter them from accepting this interaction. This contributes to answering RQ1.

One additional aspect we investigated is how on-body interaction compares with **speech interaction**. Regarding speech recognition the results suggest that it is a better accepted technology due to its familiarity and popularity among all population. However, it also shares acceptability concerns with on-body interaction. Embarrassment, privacy and security are some of them. When comparing speech with on-body interaction, gestures were mostly preferred probably because if subtle they can overcome privacy and embarrassment.

6   Conclusions

On-body interaction is an interaction technique with the potential to increase the accessibility of mobile devices for visually impaired people. For this potential to be realized, we must first understand if this population is willing to use on-body gestures and in what conditions. To contribute to this understanding we conducted a qualitative study with 18 interviewees with visual impairments to acknowledge what are the main factors that can impact the willingness to use on-body interaction. In this paper, we present a set of factors and conditions that affect positively or negatively their willingness to use on-body interaction.

To answer RQ1, we can state that people with visual impairments are indeed willing to use on-body interaction to control their mobile devices. This statement is even more reinforced if this new interaction technique proves to be faster, more robust and easier to use than standard mobile interaction techniques. Furthermore, the participants saw immediate advantages over their current assistive technologies regarding the practicality and safety aspects of not having to hold their phone on one hand.

In what concerns RQ2, findings also showed that regarding location, home is their most acceptable location to do gestures and public places are the least preferred for this kind of interaction. However, the advantages of on-body interaction are more valuable in public places, with on-body interaction being seen as more practical in this situation than standard interaction. Audience also plays a role in the acceptance: when alone, this population feels more willing to perform gestures even in public places. When in less desirable places to interact, family helps to diminish the embarrassment. The stance is not as important for adoption and only walking was perceived as a stance that can affect negatively the usage of on-body interaction. However, the task the user is performing is a factor that brings up one of the advantages of on-body interaction (i.e., not being required to hold the phone). The characteristics of the gesture is an important factor when deciding to use on-body interaction. The gesture's subtleness is prioritized over location and audience by people with visual impairments. Additionally, using well established gestures (e.g., similar to what is used in Talkback and VoiceOver) can improve the acceptability of on-body interaction.

Although with this study we reached interesting findings that helped us in answering RQ2, we can not at this stage conclude which ones are the most important factors or which ones are only relevant when combined with others. For that to happen we have to address one of the study's limitations: the interviewees did not get to try the technology. When using such technology, the opinions might diverge from current conclusions, which was already shown to happen especially when experiencing non-hypothetical situations [16]. To address this limitation, we have developed an accessibility service for Android smartphones based on gestures made with the hand or fingers (thus making them fairly inconspicuous). The development of this prototype was inspired by the findings reported here. In our future work we plan to use this prototype in a longitudinal study with visually impaired people in order to get feedback from real life situations and compare their user experiences with the findings from this study.

Acknowledgements. This work was supported by LASIGE Research Unit, ref. UID/CEC/00408/2019. I thank the Fundação Raquel e Martin Sain for providing their trainees for our study.

References

1. Aoyama, S., Shizuki, B., Tanaka, J.: Thumbslide: an interaction technique for smartwatches using a thumb slide movement. In: Proceedings of the 2016 CHI Conference Extended Abstracts on Human Factors in Computing Systems, CHI EA 2016, pp. 2403–2409. ACM, New York (2016). https://doi.org/10.1145/2851581. 2892435, http://doi.acm.org/10.1145/2851581.2892435
2. Cimarolli, V.R., Boerner, K., Brennan-Ing, M., Reinhardt, J.P., Horowitz, A.: Challenges faced by older adults with vision loss: a qualitative study with implications for rehabilitation. Clin. Rehabil. **26**(8), 748–757 (2012). https://doi.org/10.1177/ 0269215511429162. pMID: 22169832
3. Costa, D., Duarte, C.: From one to many users and contexts: a classifier for hand and arm gestures. In: Proceedings of the 20th International Conference on Intelligent User Interfaces, IUI 2015, pp. 115–120. ACM, New York (2015). https://doi. org/10.1145/2678025.2701388, http://doi.acm.org/10.1145/2678025.2701388
4. Harrison, C., Hudson, S.E.: Scratch input: creating large, inexpensive, unpowered and mobile finger input surfaces. In: Proceedings of the 21st Annual ACM Symposium on User Interface Software and Technology, UIST 2008, pp. 205–208. ACM, New York (2008). https://doi.org/10.1145/1449715.1449747, http://doi.acm.org/ 10.1145/1449715.1449747
5. Harrison, C., Ramamurthy, S., Hudson, S.E.: On-body interaction: armed and dangerous. In: Proceedings of the Sixth International Conference on Tangible, Embedded and Embodied Interaction, TEI 2012, pp. 69–76. ACM, New York (2012). https://doi.org/10.1145/2148131.2148148, http://doi.acm.org/10. 1145/2148131.2148148

6. Harrison, C., Tan, D., Morris, D.: Skinput: appropriating the body as an input surface. In: Proceedings of the SIGCHI Conference on Human Factors in Computing Systems, CHI 2010, pp. 453–462. ACM, New York (2010). https://doi.org/10.1145/1753326.1753394, http://doi.acm.org/10.1145/1753326.1753394

7. Kane, S.K., Jayant, C., Wobbrock, J.O., Ladner, R.E.: Freedom to roam: a study of mobile device adoption and accessibility for people with visual and motor disabilities. In: Proceedings of the 11th International ACM SIGACCESS Conference on Computers and Accessibility, Assets 2009, pp. 115–122. ACM, New York (2009). https://doi.org/10.1145/1639642.1639663, http://doi.acm.org/10.1145/1639642.1639663

8. Karam, M., Schraefel, M.C.: A taxonomy of gestures in human computer interactions. Project report, University of Southampton (2005)

9. Li, F.C.Y., Dearman, D., Truong, K.N.: Leveraging proprioception to make mobile phones more accessible to users with visual impairments. In: Proceedings of the 12th International ACM SIGACCESS Conference on Computers and Accessibility, ASSETS 2010, pp. 187–194. ACM, New York (2010). https://doi.org/10.1145/1878803.1878837, http://doi.acm.org/10.1145/1878803.1878837

10. Liu, X., Zhang, M., Richardson, A., Lucas, T., Spiegel, J.V.D.: The virtual trackpad: an electromyography-based, wireless, real-time, low-power, embedded hand gesture recognition system using an event-driven artificial neural network. IEEE Trans. Circuits Syst. II Express Briefs **PP**(99), 1 (2016). https://doi.org/10.1109/TCSII.2016.2635674

11. Mayring, P.: Qualitative content analysis: theoretical foundation, basic procedures and software solution (2014)

12. Oh, U., Findlater, L.: Design of and subjective response to on-body input for people with visual impairments. In: Proceedings of the 16th International ACM SIGACCESS Conference on Computers & Accessibility, ASSETS 2014, pp. 115–122. ACM, New York (2014). https://doi.org/10.1145/2661334.2661376, http://doi.acm.org/10.1145/2661334.2661376

13. Oh, U., Stearns, L., Pradhan, A., Froehlich, J.E., Findlater, L.: Investigating microinteractions for people with visual impairments and the potential role of on-body interaction, October 2017. https://doi.org/10.1145/3132525.3132536

14. Profita, H.P., et al.: Don't mind me touching my wrist: a case study of interacting with on-body technology in public. In: Proceedings of the 2013 International Symposium on Wearable Computers, ISWC 2013, pp. 89–96. ACM, New York (2013). https://doi.org/10.1145/2493988.2494331, http://doi.acm.org/10.1145/2493988.2494331

15. Rico, J., Brewster, S.: Gestures all around us: user differences in social acceptability perceptions of gesture based interfaces. In: Proceedings of the 11th International Conference on Human-Computer Interaction with Mobile Devices and Services, MobileHCI 2009, pp. 64:1–64:2. ACM, New York (2009). https://doi.org/10.1145/1613858.1613936, http://doi.acm.org/10.1145/1613858.1613936

16. Rico, J., Brewster, S.: Usable gestures for mobile interfaces: evaluating social acceptability. In: Proceedings of the SIGCHI Conference on Human Factors in Computing Systems, CHI 2010, pp. 887–896. ACM, New York (2010). https://doi.org/10.1145/1753326.1753458, http://doi.acm.org/10.1145/1753326.1753458

17. Rossi, M., Benatti, S., Farella, E., Benini, L.: Hybrid EMG classifier based on HMM and SVM for hand gesture recognition in prosthetics. In: IEEE International Conference on Industrial Technology (ICIT), pp. 1700–1705, March 2015. https://doi.org/10.1109/ICIT.2015.7125342

18. Sandnes, F.E.: What do low-vision users really want from smart glasses? Faces, text and perhaps no glasses at all. In: Miesenberger, K., Bühler, C., Penaz, P. (eds.) ICCHP 2016. LNCS, vol. 9758, pp. 187–194. Springer, Cham (2016). https://doi.org/10.1007/978-3-319-41264-1_25

19. Thomas, D.R.: A general inductive approach for analyzing qualitative evaluation data. Am. J. Eval. **27**(2), 237–246 (2006). https://doi.org/10.1177/1098214005283748

20. Weigel, M., Lu, T., Bailly, G., Oulasvirta, A., Majidi, C., Steimle, J.: iSkin: flexible, stretchable and visually customizable on-body touch sensors for mobile computing. In: Proceedings of the 33rd Annual ACM Conference on Human Factors in Computing Systems, CHI 2015, pp. 2991–3000. ACM, New York (2015). https://doi.org/10.1145/2702123.2702391, http://doi.acm.org/10.1145/2702123.2702391

21. Wilhelm, M., Krakowczyk, D., Trollmann, F., Albayrak, S.: eRing: multiple finger gesture recognition with one ring using an electric field. In: Proceedings of the 2nd International Workshop on Sensor-based Activity Recognition and Interaction, WOAR 2015, pp. 7:1–7:6. ACM, New York (2015). https://doi.org/10.1145/2790044.2790047, http://doi.acm.org/10.1145/2790044.2790047

22. Wiliamson, J.R., Crossan, A., Brewster, S.: Multimodal mobile interactions: usability studies in real world settings. In: Proceedings of the 13th International Conference on Multimodal Interfaces, ICMI 2011, pp. 361–368. ACM, New York (2011). https://doi.org/10.1145/2070481.2070551, http://doi.acm.org/10.1145/2070481.2070551

23. Zhang, Y., Zhou, J., Laput, G., Harrison, C.: SkinTrack: using the body as an electrical waveguide for continuous finger tracking on the skin. In: Proceedings of the 2016 CHI Conference on Human Factors in Computing Systems, CHI 2016, pp. 1491–1503. ACM, New York (2016). https://doi.org/10.1145/2858036.2858082, http://doi.acm.org/10.1145/2858036.2858082

Faster and Less Error-Prone: Supplementing an Accessible Keyboard with Speech Input

Bhakti Bhikne[1(✉)], Anirudha Joshi[1], Manjiri Joshi[1],
Charudatta Jadhav[2], and Prabodh Sakhardande[1]

[1] Industrial Design Centre, IIT Bombay, Mumbai, India
mailbhaktibhikne@gmail.com,
{anirudha,manjirij}@iitb.ac.in,
prabodh.sakhardande@gmail.com
[2] Tata Consultancy Services Limited, Mumbai, Maharashtra, India
charudatta.jadhav@tcs.com

Abstract. Swarachakra is an Abugida text input keyboard available in 12 Indian languages. We enhanced an accessible version of Swarachakra Marathi with speech input. However, speech input could be error-prone, and especially so for languages where speech recognition technologies are new. Such errors could either slow the user down due to the need for editing, or go unnoticed, leading to high uncorrected error rates. We therefore conducted a within-subject empirical study to compare the user performance of keyboard-only input method with keyboard+speech input method with 11 novice visually impaired users. We found that keyboard+speech input was almost 11 times faster, reaching 182 characters per minute, and had a lower uncorrected error rate than the keyboard-only input, and in spite of having higher corrected error rates. Though we used a wide variety of phrases in our study, we observed that all phrases were faster on average with the keyboard+speech input method. To the best of our knowledge, ours is the first empirical study to evaluate the performance of speech enabled text input in Marathi for visually impaired people. This is the highest reported speed by visually impaired users in any Indian language.

Keywords: Speech-based text entry · Accessibility · Longitudinal study · Visually impaired users

1 Introduction

In this paper, we investigate the question, "With the advancement of speech recognition technologies, can speech augment text input by visually impaired users in Indian languages?"

Despite technological advancements, text input for the visually impaired people remains a hurdle. Although there has been a widespread adoption of smartphones and screen-readers such as Talkback [11] and VoiceOver [12] by visually impaired users, typing on mobile phones remains slow and laborious for them [1–3, 7]. This is even more so for Indian languages. In recent years, research for text input in Indian languages by sighted users has gathered steam [5–8, 10, 13–15]. On the other hand,

© IFIP International Federation for Information Processing 2019
Published by Springer Nature Switzerland AG 2019
D. Lamas et al. (Eds.): INTERACT 2019, LNCS 11746, pp. 288–304, 2019.
https://doi.org/10.1007/978-3-030-29381-9_18

research in text input in Indian languages by visually impaired people is notably under-developed.

Text entry in Indian languages has always been a challenge for users, including low speeds and high error rates, mainly due to the complex structure of the Devanagari script. Studies with sighted users were reported to have text input speeds between 35 to 45 characters per minute (CPM) on four keyboards [6]. The only study for text input by visually impaired users for an Indian language reported 15 CPM using the Swarachakra keyboard and 13 CPM using the Google Indic keyboard [7]. In our recent study, we found that enhancing the keyboard with speech input could enable sighted users achieve mean speeds of 118 CPM in Hindi [8]. In this paper, we investigate if we could we achieve similar improvements in performance for visually impaired users. We found that enhancing a keyboard with speech increases the text input speed of visually impaired users by about 11 times compared to keyboard-only input, reaching a mean of 182 CPM (Fig. 1). This is the highest reported speed by visually impaired users in any Indian language.

In the next section, we discuss the background related to our work. Next, we introduce the keyboards and the method we used for our study. We next present our results, and finally present our conclusions.

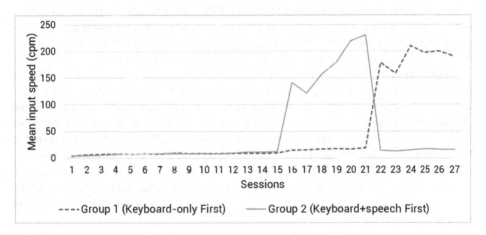

Fig. 1. The improvement in text entry rates due to speech as seen by the large peaks when speech is used as an input method between sessions 16 to 21 for group 1 and between sessions 22 to 27 for group 2.

2   Background

Our work deals with Marathi, a language spoken in India by about 72 million native speakers and 84 million total speakers [19]. Marathi uses the Devanagari script, which is an Abugida script used by several other languages including Hindi, Konkani, Kashmiri, and Sanskrit [20]. Users have found Devanagari, and other Abugidas scripts challenging to input on digital devices, something that has been extensively discussed in literature [5–7]. We summarise below the key challenges for the purpose of completeness.

Typically, there are four types of glyphs in the Devanagari script, which can combine together to form words. Firstly, a consonant in Devanagari may stand alone as an independent glyph, with an inherent vowel. Likewise, a vowel can stand independently. Thirdly, a consonant (C) may be "modified" by a vowel modifier (V), leading to a C+V glyph. In such a glyph, the vowel modifier may appear before, after, above or below the consonant, which often causes confusions in the mind of the users about the sequence they should use to input the vowel modifier. Fourthly, two or more consonants can combine to form a conjunct, which in turn may have a vowel modifier. Conjuncts are particularly difficult for users, as, at times, the visual representation of a conjunct glyph can be significantly different than the constituent consonants. Devanagari also uses a large number of characters (34 commonly used consonants, 14 commonly used independent vowels, 14 corresponding vowel modifiers, a *halant* to join consonants into conjuncts, and 3 commonly used diacritic marks, leading to about 66 unique, commonly used Unicode characters), which adds to the complexity of the text input task.

Researchers have explored the effect of adding speech recognition technologies to keyboards. Traditionally, researchers have reported text entry speeds ranging from 19 to 53 words per minute (WPM) (or 95 to 256 CPM) for English [2, 16, 17, 21]. After adding speech, Ruan et al. reported 161 WPM (about 805 CPM) for English, 108 WPM (about 540 CPM) for Mandarin Chinese as compared to 53 WPM (about 265 CPM) and 38 WPM (about 195 CPM) without speech, respectively [16, 17].

While speech may improve the speed, it may also cause more errors, and hence analysis of errors is important. Ruan et al. reported a mixed result. In their case, uncorrected error rates with speech were higher - 0.35% and 1.69% for English and Chinese respectively in contrast to 0.19% and 1.40% without speech. On the other hand, the corrected error rates with speech were lower at 2.58% and 5.8% compared to 3.49% and 19.14% without speech [16, 17]. Moreover, speech does not necessarily increase speed in all kinds of input tasks. For example, Rudnicky et al. [23] conducted a longitudinal study in which participants carried out 40 spreadsheet tasks alternating between keyboard and speech input. They observed that tasks took longer to finish through voice input.

As mentioned above, the much slower text entry rates have been reported for Indian languages, and speech seems to help particularly in these languages. After a between-subject longitudinal study with novice users lasting several weeks and providing about 300 min of controlled typing practice, we reported peak speeds between 35 to 45 CPM on four Marathi keyboards, namely Swarachakra Marathi, CDAC InScript Devanagari, Swiftkey Marathi and Sparsh Marathi [8]. In our more recent study, we reported substantial gains by adding speech input to the Swarachakra Hindi keyboard [8]. We found that novice users could achieve mean speeds of up to 118 CPM with speech, compared to 47 CPM without speech. We found that speech increased both the uncorrected error rate (0.75% to 1.63%) and the corrected error rate (7.5% to 21.6%). The increase in the corrected error rate (unlike [16, 17]) implies that in the speech condition, users found and needed to correct many errors, which could be attributed to the relative immaturity of speech recognition technology for Indian languages.

While the smooth-screened smartphones are generally considered to be more "advanced" than the feature phones with hardware buttons, these were considered to be a "giant leap backwards" by the visually impaired users – especially for tasks such as text input. Fortunately, advances in accessibility research has led to somewhat more accessible text input methods. For example, Perkinput used Input Finger Detection (IFD) for non-visual touch screen input [3], which could then enable the visually impaired to input text with one hand. In their studies, users could achieve average text input speeds of 6 WPM (30 CPM) for Perkinput and 4 WPM (20 CPM) for VoiceOver. Their uncorrected error rates were also observed to be low for Perkinput at 3.52% and 6.43% for VoiceOver. Consequently, the corrected error rates were higher for Perkinput with an error rate of 12.23% and 8.32% for VoiceOver. Gaines modelled Tap123 after a standard QWERTY keyboard that does not require users to tap specific keys and achieved entry speeds of 19 WPM (95 CPM) and uncorrected error rates of 2.08% [2].

Much research has also been done using gestural interactions in accessible text entry. Kane et al. in their study described Slide Rule which is a gesture based technique that was compared with button based Pocket PC Screen Reader [4]. Although Slide Rule was significantly faster than the button-based system, more errors were found while using the gesture based system. On the contrary, NavTap used a navigational method and evaluated text entry speeds in real-life settings. The text entry speeds increased from 0.2–2.7 WPM in the first session to 1.6–8.46 WPM in the 13th session over a period of 16 weeks [9].

The advancement of text input research in Indian languages for visually impaired is limited. To the best of our knowledge, the only work in this area was conducted by Bharath et al., who conducted an empirical study that provided benchmark speeds for visually impaired users in Indic scripts [7]. They conducted a within subject study with two accessible keyboards – Google Indic and Swarachakra. The overall mean speeds were 14.2 CPM for Swarachakra and 12.8 CPM for Google Indic. The mean accuracy for Swarachakra was higher at 96% in contrast to 94% for Google Indic.

Only limited amount of prior work has been done for visually impaired people that analysed speech input in English. Azenkot et al. carried out a survey with 169 blind and sighted users and later conducted a study with 8 blind users [1]. Their study evaluated the use of speech input on iPod vs on an on-screen keyboard. They found that although speech was 5 times faster than the keyboard, users spent an average of 80.3% of their time editing the errors. Bonner et al. describe No-Look Notes as an eyes-free text entry system that uses multi-touch input and audio output [22]. They evaluated No-Look Notes against Apple's accessibility component VoiceOver and found that No-Look Notes performed better than VoiceOver in terms of speed, accuracy and user preference. They found the overall speed for No-Look Notes to be 1.32 WPM (about 7 CPM) in contrast with 0.66 WPM (about 3 CPM) for VoiceOver.

To the best of our knowledge, there is no work reported that systematically evaluates the effect of applying speech recognition technologies to a given keyboard on the performance of visually impaired users. Further, we believe that we are the first to explore and evaluate speech as a method of text input in Indian languages for visually impaired people.

3   Keyboard Description

We conducted our study with the Swarachakra keyboard [5–7, 10] as it had emerged as the better performing keyboard in earlier studies for Marathi and Hindi. Swarachakra is a logically organised keyboard. The layout of the consonants in Swarachakra mimics the structure of the Devanagari script [6]. In the version for sighted users, when the user touches a consonant, Swarachakra displays a pie menu pop-up around the finger, which includes the 11 most frequently used vowel modifiers. The independent vowels are in a separate pie menu of its own. Swarachakra also supports previews of conjuncts, which is helpful for the sighted users.

Anu Bharath et al. adapted the design of Swarachakra to make it accessible [7]. In their variation, the interaction technique of the pie menu was changed. The user first explores the keyboard by touch to locate the desired consonant. As the user moves the finger, the screen reader reads out the consonant below the finger. Once the user reaches the desired consonant, she puts down a second finger, below which the vowel modifier pie menu is displayed (Fig. 2). The user can further explore the pie menu with the second finger until the desired vowel modifier is found. The keyboard has special gestures for backspace and for entering space.

Fig. 2. Accessible version of Swarachakra from [7]. The user first explores by touch to locate the desired consonant while following the feedback from the screen reader. Once the desired consonant is located, she puts the second finger down under which a pie menu with 11 frequently used vowel modifiers is shown. The user further explores the pie menu by touch to select the desired vowel modifier.

Based on the user feedback from the study done by Bharath et al., and some pilot studies that we conducted, we modified the layout of the accessible version of Swarachakra slightly (Fig. 3). In the original design, the independent vowel pie menu was in the bottom row, and was difficult to locate. We moved it to the top row because independent vowels are reasonably frequent, and it is common for users to start exploring the keyboard from the top. In the original design, the less frequent vowel modifiers and diacritics such as rukar, anusvar, chandrabindu and visarga were absent.

Fig. 3. The modified layout of accessible Swarachakra layout that we used in our study. The interaction technique was identical to the one shown in Fig. 2.

We added an additional pie menu of these characters in the top row alongside the independent vowel key. We moved other infrequent keys such as trakar, rafar and nukta to the rightmost column in their order of frequency. We added the navigation keys and the punctuation keys to the penultimate row and the Shift, Space and the Enter key to the last row of the layout.

In addition, we integrated Marathi speech recognition ability through the Liv.ai API[1]. When the user wishes to invoke speech recognition, she explores the keyboard till she reaches the microphone button in the third-last row on the right. When she reaches the button, she puts down a second finger anywhere on the keyboard. This invokes the speech recognition engine. When the speech engine is ready, it plays a beep sound, after which the user can speak into the phone. The user indicates that she has finished speaking by lifting the second finger. The keyboard plays another beep which indicates the end of listening and then relays the user's speech to the Liv.ai server. The server interprets the speech and sends back the recognised text, which the keyboard enters in the text box and also reads out through the screen reader. The user may then edit the text if she finds any recognition errors.

---

[1] https://liv.ai/.

4 Method

The study protocol was a within-subject design that compared the performance of users in the keyboard-only condition with their performance in the keyboard+speech input condition. The protocol was partly derived from [5–8]. Each user did five tasks: a training task, a first-time usability task, a keyboard familiarization task, and two main tasks. The keyboard familiarization task and the two main tasks were longitudinal tasks – i.e. they were performed in multiple sessions spread across several days.

On the first day of the study, moderators trained the user to type and edit the texts in Marathi using the Accessible Swarachakra keyboard. The users were also familiarized with special gestures for backspace and for entering space. The users were trained on 10 words. All the tasks were conducted on a mobile application that displayed the words/phrases to be transcribed, and logged all user input, input time and input errors. The application also gave audio feedback with regards to the accuracy of the phrase typed after the user submitted the phrase. The users were trained to read (with the screen reader) the phrase to be typed, the transcribed phrase, and the feedback.

After the training task, the user conducted a first-time usability task (FTU) by typing 20 words of various levels of difficulty. In the FTU, the user was allowed two attempts per word. In the first attempt no help was provided. If the user failed in the first attempt, a second attempt was allowed. Minimal help was provided in the second attempt if the users failed to type the word again. The user was considered to be trained successfully if she could type a significant proportion of words in the FTU without help.

After completion of the training and FTU on the first day, the users commenced the keyboard familiarization task. This task comprised of 15 sessions in each of which the user transcribed 8 phrases without any help from the moderator. If the user struggled to type a specific word during the session, the moderator provided additional practice for that word at the end of the session. We limited the number of such sessions that user could do in a single day to three, with an interval of at least 15 min between sessions. The training, the FTU task and the keyboard familiarisation task constituted the practice phase of the study.

At the conclusion of the practice phase, the users were assigned an input method for the first main task (keyboard-only or keyboard+speech input). Each main task comprised of 6 sessions in each of which the user transcribed 8 phrases. After completing the first main task, the users completed the second main task using the second input method. The sequence of input methods was counterbalanced across users. While performing the main tasks, we restricted the users to a maximum of two sessions in a day with at least 15 min between sessions.

Just before the users performed the main task involving the keyboard+speech input method, we gave a demonstration to the users about how they could use the speech input option. To locate the microphone button, the users were trained to use the right edge using their second digit and then to use the index finger to activate the speech service. To use the speech service, the users were asked to speak after they hear a beep and to lift both fingers after they finish speaking. The system reads back the recognized sentence after a beep. In case of an error, the participant could edit it using either the speech input or the keyboard.

To ensure that the users performed the tasks accurately and attain a good speed, we incentivized the users like Dalvi et al. [6]. The users won a "speed prize" every time they typed a phrase at a speed higher than their previous best speed on a phrase. Besides the speed prizes, the users could also win an "accuracy prize" at the end of each session if they typed all the 8 phrases in that session with 100% accuracy. We describe how we calculated accuracy in the results section below.

4.1   Users and Study Context

We conducted the study with visually disabled children in a residential Marathi-medium school for the visually disabled girls in the city of Nashik, Maharashtra, India. Permissions were obtained from the school authorities and hostel authorities for the participation of the children in the study. The school in turn informed the parents of the children and sent them a copy of the project information. We recruited fourteen volunteers from classes seven to nine (all girls). All users were native Marathi speakers and were learning Marathi as their first language in the school. None of the users had used a smartphone or a computer previously. They could read and write the Braille Marathi script and used it for their academic work.

Fourteen users volunteered for the study. Out of these, 11 users completed all the sessions in time. Three users could not complete the study or had to take long breaks lasting several days between sessions. While we let them complete the study to the extent possible, to avoid bias, for the purpose of the analysis, we dropped these users from the results of this paper.

The sessions were carried out in an "office quiet" environment in a school classroom. At any given time, no more than 4 users performed the tasks in the room and they were supervised by at least 2 moderators. Prizes mentioned above were provided after consulting the school, and these included small items of stationery or cosmetics such as set of markers, drawing books, hair clips, hair ties, hair pins, pencil-box etc. At the end of the study, all users were given participation certificates and a "participation prize".

The study was conducted on Motorola G6 Android phones. We used a 4G cellular network to connect to the internet for speech recognition during the study.

4.2   Phrase Set

We selected ten words for the training session and twenty words for the first-time usability test. Like [6–8], these words were selected such that the users had enough opportunity to learn and explore typing in Marathi. For the keyboard familiarisation task, we selected 120 conversational phrases that were representative of everyday Marathi language used among native speakers. Phrases included conversational phrases, proverbs, lines from popular songs and poems, and phrases from school textbooks. Table 1 shows some examples of the selected phrases. For the main tasks, we selected another set of 48 similar phrases. The same sets of 48 phrases were used for both main tasks.

Table 1. Examples of selected phrases.

चहा गरम आहे	तो सकाळी लवकर उठला
तू कशी आहेस	सागरा प्राण तळमळला
दीपक पाणी आण	झाली सकाळ सरली रात
विजय पाट उचल	थेंबे थेंबे तळे साचे
किती वेळ लागेल	जजकडे वतकडे लख लख लख
आज खूप उकडत आहे	शरदने कॅमेऱ्याने फोटो काढले
अजयने चेंडू आणला	उषःकाल होताहोता काळरात्र झाली

5 Results

The main purpose of the study was to compare the user performance in the two conditions (keyboard-only and keyboard+speech input). During each of the two main tasks of the study, each user typed (8 sessions × 6 phrases =) 48 phrases that are relevant to our analysis. We first present the analysis of errors followed by typing speed of these phrases and then discuss the efficacy of text entry with and without speech.

Transcribing text with the help of a screen reader has several limitations for a visually impaired user, which leads to a peculiar set of errors in Indian languages that the user cannot avoid. These are similar to the problems faced by visually impaired users of English, where the user may occasionally miss an unwanted space (e.g. it is difficult to differentiate between "output" and "output" with a screen reader). In Indian languages, it is particularly difficult to distinguishing between a long and a short vowel (e.g. the difference between the "u" sound of word "put" and the "oo" sound of the word "cool"). In our screen reader, we tried to enhance the difference by adjusting the tone of voice, but this too was not enough.

Hence, during the study, we used a "lenient" model for error calculation for vowel modifiers. Thus, while giving error feedback to the users and while calculating their eligibility for prizes, we tolerated errors such as substitution of a similar sounding vowel modifier, or an additional space. However, for the purpose of error analysis in this section of the paper, we report all the errors strictly. We computed uncorrected error rate (UER) and corrected error rate (CER) as described by William Soukoreff et al. [18]. Figure 4 below shows the CER and UER for the keyboard-only and keyboard+speech input conditions for all the sessions of the main tasks.

The mean UER for the keyboard-only condition was higher at 7.07% (N = 11, SD = 4.76%, 95% CI 3.91% to 10.24%) than the UER for the keyboard+speech input condition, which was 4.61% (N = 11, SD = 2.16%, 95% CI 3.18% to 6.04%). A paired t test revealed that the differences are not significant (N = 11, $p = 0.06$). Nevertheless, the direction of the difference is surprising, and contrary to results found

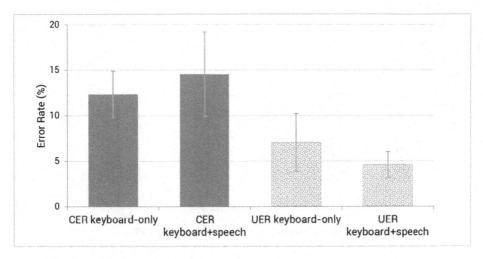

Fig. 4. Mean corrected error rate (CER) and uncorrected error rate (UER) for keyboard-only and keyboard+speech input modes. The error bars show 95% confidence intervals.

in studies with sighted users in English, Chinese and Hindi ([8, 16, 17] respectively), where UER was found to be higher for speech. This suggests that visually impaired users in our study did not notice some errors that were more evident to sighted users, and hence left them uncorrected.

The mean CER for the keyboard-only condition was lower at 12.33% (N = 11, SD = 3.85%, 95% CI 9.78% to 14.89%) than keyboard+speech input condition, which was 14.53% (N = 11, SD = 6.98%, 95% CI 9.90% to 19.17%). A paired t test reveals that the differences are not significant (N = 11, p = 0.44). The direction of this result is consistent with the results found in [8], a study with sighted users in Hindi, though inconsistent with [16, 17], a study with sighted users in English and Chinese. This is probably due to the speech recognition accuracy of Indian languages.

Figures 5 and 6 show session-wise corrected and uncorrected error rates for keyboard-only method and keyboard+speech method. In both the input methods, the UER had little variation across sessions, while CER tended to fall as is visible from the trendlines in the graphs. We can attribute this to a practice effect in both conditions, and speculate that CER could reduce further with more practice.

We compared the accuracy of the typed phrases in both the input methods. We found that out of 48 phrases, only three phrases (6%) had an accuracy of 100% in the keyboard+speech input method for all 11 users. The lengths of such phrases were between 12–25 characters and the average time required was 6.3533 s. These phrases are किती वेळ लागेल, दुष्काळात तेरावा महिना and तो सकाळी लवकर उठला. Two of these phrases are conversational phrases and one is a proverb. The average accuracy for these phrases using the Keyboard-only method was 94.48% and time was 70.23%.

To calculate speed, we used a similar method as reported by Bhikne et al. in their study [8]. For the keyboard-only method, the phrase task time was considered from the time the user typed the first character till the time of the user made the last alteration to

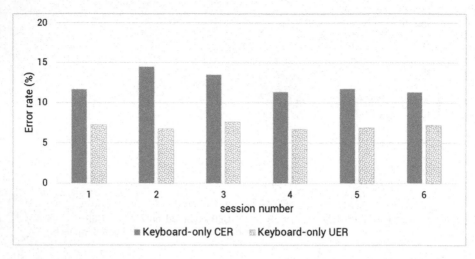

Fig. 5. Session-wise mean corrected and uncorrected error rates for keyboard-only input mode.

the transcribed phrase. If n was the number of Unicode characters in the typed phrase, the speed was calculated by dividing n–1 by the phrase task time in minutes. For the keyboard+speech input method, the phrase task time was considered from the time the user pressed the mic button till the time the user made the last modification to the typed phrase. In contrast to the keyboard-only method, the speed for the keyboard+speech input method was calculated by dividing n by the phrase task time, where n is the number of Unicode characters typed by the user.

Most often, users submitted well-formed phrases with an occasional uncorrected error. On rare occasions though, users accidentally pressed the submit button of the

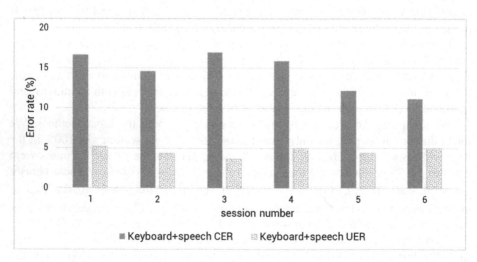

Fig. 6. Session-wise mean corrected and uncorrected error rates for keyboard+speech input mode.

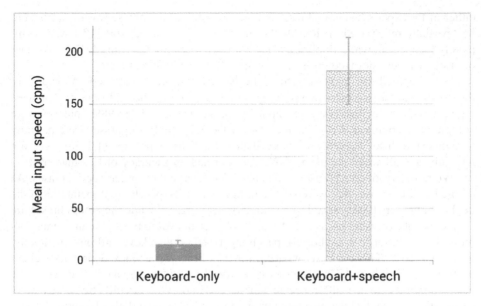

Fig. 7. Mean input speed (CPM) for keyboard-only and keyboard+speech input modes. The error bars show 95% confidence intervals.

logging tool before they meant to, perhaps while they were exploring the keyboard by touch. In such cases, this led to a unusually high uncorrected error rate for that phrase, and often, an unusually high input speed. We attribute this higher speed to the study situation rather than to the input method. To reduce this bias, we dropped phrases that had an uncorrected error rate of more than 20% for the purpose of analysis of speed. Out of the total of (2 tasks × 6 sessions × 8 phrases per session × 11 users =) 1,056 phrases that were typed during the main tasks, 66 phrases (6.25%) had an uncorrected error rate of more than 20%, and were dropped in this way. We note here that this number is much higher than the study reported with sighted users [8] who had reported only 0.75% such phrases.

Figure 7 shows the results of the analysis of speed differences. The keyboard-only condition had a mean speed of 16.04 CPM (N = 11, SD = 5.22, 95% CI 12.58 to 19.50). The keyboard+speech input condition had a mean speed of 182.13 CPM (N = 11, SD = 48.05, 95% CI 150.25 to 214.02). As can be guessed, a paired t test revealed that the differences are significant (N = 11, $p < 0.0005$).

To investigate the effect of speech recognition engine on the performance of the user, we had selected a phrase set consisting of a variety of phrases including popular poems, songs, proverbs and conversational phrases. Similar to Bhikne et al. [8], we created a "ground truth" of the phrase recognition accuracy in our lab. Two expert users who were native Marathi speakers spoke out the phrases in an "office-quiet" environment. A phrase was determined to be "completely recognised" (CR) and requiring no edits if the transcribed phrase matched with the given phrase for both experts. If either of the experts had any phrases that needed editing, the phrase was determined to be "partially recognised" (PR). Of the 48 phrases, 29 phrases (60.41%) were completely recognised, while 19 phrases (39.58%) were partially recognised. There were no phrases that were not recognised by the speech recognition engine.

We compared the "ground-truth" with the performance of the users. As expected, the results varied somewhat from the ground truth. Out of the 528 phrases that were typed using the keyboard+speech input by the 11 users, 275 (51.98%) phrases were completely recognised (CR). Another 248 of the 528 (46.88%) phrases were partially recognised with an accuracy of more than 65%. Only 6 phrases (1.13%) were not recognised at all when the users spoke them, or had an accuracy of less than 65%.

We also performed a phrase-wise analysis to observe the "underwater" phrases. As defined in [8], phrases that were slower in the keyboard+speech input method than the keyboard-only method are said to be "underwater phrases" while the other phrases are said to be "above water phrases". Of the 48 phrases that were typed, on an average, all phrases were faster with keyboard+speech input method than keyboard-only method by more than 10%. This contrasts with the findings from [8], a study done with sighted users in Hindi, where 12.7% phrases were found to be "underwater". This could be partly attributed to the difference in language (Hindi vs. Marathi), but much more substantially to the fact that visually impaired users had a much lower base rate for text input in keyboard-only method than sighted users.

To explore if there is any correlation between the mean speeds of the users in the keyboard-only method and keyboard+speech method, we calculated Pearson's Correlation Moment. There was a low negative correlation between the speeds of the users in the two input methods but the correlation is not significant ($r = -0.347$, $p = 0.295$). Figure 8 illustrates the scatter plot for the two distributions. It is possible that users who type faster with the keyboard-only method perform somewhat slower with the keyboard+speech input method than users who are not so fast. The other possibility is that

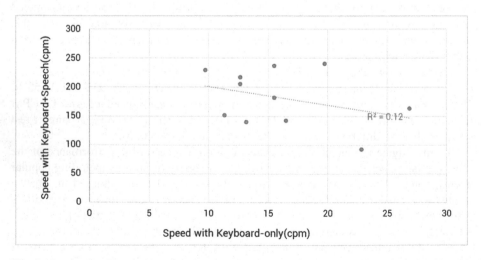

Fig. 8. Pearson's Correlation moment between the mean speeds of each user ($n = 11$, $r = -0.347$, $p = 0.295$).

the skills required to type quickly with the two methods are independent of each other. Please note that our study is quite small (N = 11), and it needs to be repeated with a larger sample for strengthening either of these results (Fig. 8).

5.1 Other Findings

There were some other interesting findings during our study. The layout of the Swarachakra keyboard is based on the sequence and the structure of the Devanagari script. The sequence (and the structure) is taught to sighted children from childhood. Novice users use this sequence/structure to locate keys on the keyboard. This has been one of the strengths of the design of the Swarachakra keyboard. However, during our study we learnt that Devanagari Braille is taught in a different sequence and thus the visually impaired children are not familiar with the original sequence/structure of Devanagari. To an extent, this hampered the learning of the keyboard. While this issue is relatively less important in this paper, which aims to compare the performance of visually impaired users with speech enabled keyboards, it could have a broader implication on the design of keyboards.

We tried to analyse the speech recognition errors, and found some interesting patterns. As could be expected, some words were misrecognised as similar sounding more frequent words or spelling alternatives (e.g. पँट as पॅन्ट, मुलं as मुले). We found that words with lower frequencies such as झरझर and कुऱ्हाडीचा were misrecognized as जर्जर (which is completely different, though similar sounding word) and कुर्हाडीचा (which is a wrong spelling). More popular words including words such as दुसऱ्या, कॅमेऱ्याने and सरड्याची, though arguably equally complex to type, were recognized accurately.

When a phrase contained clusters of repeated words for a poetic effect (e.g. झुक झुक झुक झुक and लख लख लख) such clusters were often recognized as a single words, i.e. without the spaces (e.g. झुकझुकझुकझुक and लखलखलख respectively). This could be a result of the users speaking the phrases without pauses or in a rhythm.

6 Conclusion

We conducted an empirical study with 11 visually impaired children to compare performances of keyboard-only method with keyboard+speech input method. We observed that in spite of speech recognition errors, the keyboard+speech input method was almost 11 times faster than keyboard-only method.

Ours is the first empirical study that evaluates the two input modalities of text entry in Indian languages. We also document the highest ever text entry speeds reported for Indian languages by visually impaired users, and, in fact, by any group of users. It is interesting to note that the speeds achieved by the visually impaired users in our study with keyboard+speech input was 182 CPM, which was substantially above the speed reported by Bhikne et al. [8] of 118 CPM by sighted users. The languages used in the two studies were different (Marathi and Hindi). Consequently, phrase sets were different. Also, the user groups were different. Hence the results of the two studies are not strictly comparable. Nevertheless, the two languages are related enough, and the phrase sets, the methods and users in the two studies are similar enough to interest us in a future study to compare such effects more systematically.

Of the 48 phrases that were typed in our study, none were "underwater". That means, on an average, all phrases were faster with keyboard+speech input method than the keyboard-only method by more than 10%. This contrasts with the findings from [8], a study done with sighted users in Hindi, where 12.7% phrases were found to be "underwater". This is possibly because the baseline speeds of typing (i.e. in the keyboard-only mode) is higher for sighted users than the visually impaired users. In other words, speech input helps the visually impaired users a lot more than it helps the sighted users. Of course, as noted above, the studies are not strictly comparable, as the languages of the two studies are different. Future work could explore this finding more systematically.

We were surprised to find that the uncorrected error rate (UER) for the keyboard-only condition was higher than for keyboard+speech input condition, though the difference is not significant. This is contrary to reported studies with sighted users in English, Chinese and Hindi [8, 16, 17], where UERs were found to be higher for speech. UER for sighted users in keyboard-only condition was reported at only 0.75% for Hindi, 1.40% for Mandarin and 0.19% for English, compared to 7.07% in our study with visually impaired users in Marathi.

One possible explanation for this could be that at the baseline (i.e. without speech) visually impaired users leave behind a larger number of uncorrected errors in the text because they are not able to detect such errors with the help of screen readers. As mentioned above, short and long vowel errors in Indian languages are particularly hard to differentiate with screen readers. When automatic speech recognition engines recognize text, such systems use dictionaries, which do not have not have too many errors of those kinds. On the other hand, speech recognition systems create errors of their own (which could be of a different nature than the ones that creep in because of screen readers), and a sighted person may miss correcting those errors, as his mind is already conditioned by the "correct speech" he believes he has said, and then such errors get left behind uncorrected in the transcribed text, leading to higher UER in the speech condition for sighted users. A visually impaired user may somehow have been alert to such errors, again perhaps because of the screen reader interface. Future research could analyse the different types of errors made by users and the role of error perception in different media (visual vs. audio).

Consistent with [8] (and in turn, inconsistent with [16, 17]), we found that corrected error rates for the keyboard+speech condition were higher than the keyboard-only condition (though our differences are not significant). This implies that our users (and those in [8]) found and corrected many errors in speech recognition, implying that the speech recognition technologies for Indian languages have yet to mature.

In both the input methods, the UER had little variation across sessions, while CER tended to fall with sessions. This is understandable as our study was done with novice users. With practice, the need for error correction seems to be going down in both keyboard-only and keyboard+speech input conditions. Correspondingly, speeds seem to be still on the rise. Future work needs to investigate effects of even longer term practice, by perhaps working with expert users.

We acknowledge that with N = 11, our study was quite small. Given that text input in Indian languages by visually impaired users on mobile phones is new, it was necessary for us to train up novice users and, this implied a longitudinal study. Given the constraints of resources and logistics, and availability of visually impaired users, this was the best that we could do in this study. Yet, we believe that we have contributed a lot to the knowledge in this space, and we hope that our study will light the way forward for future research in this area.

Acknowledgements. This project was funded by Tata Consultancy Services. We are thankful to all our participants and administration from National Association for Blind in Nashik, India for their invaluable feedback and support.

References

1. Azenkot, S., Lee, N.B.: Exploring the use of speech input by blind people on mobile devices. In: Proceedings of the 15th International ACM SIGACCESS Conference on Computers and Accessibility (ASSETS 2013), 8 p. ACM, New York. Article 11 (2013). http://dx.doi.org/10.1145/2513383.2513440
2. Gaines, D.: Exploring an ambiguous technique for eyes-free mobile text entry. In: Proceedings of the 20th International ACM SIGACCESS Conference on Computers and Accessibility (ASSETS 2018), pp. 471–473. ACM, New York (2018). https://doi.org/10.1145/3234695.3240991
3. Azenkot, S., Wobbrock, J.O., Prasain, S., Ladner, R.E.: Input finger detection for nonvisual touch screen text entry in Perkinput. In: Proceedings of Graphics Interface 2012 (GI 2012), pp. 121–129. Canadian Information Processing Society, Toronto (2012)
4. Kane, S.K., Bigham, J.P., Wobbrock, J.O.: Slide rule: making mobile touch screens accessible to blind people using multi-touch interaction techniques. In: Proceedings of the 10th International ACM SIGACCESS Conference on Computers and Accessibility (Assets 2008), pp. 73 80. ACM, New York (2008). https://doi.org/10.1145/1414471.1414487
5. Dalvi, G., et al.: A protocol to evaluate virtual keyboards for Indian languages. In: Proceedings of the 7th International Conference on HCI, IndiaHCI 2015 (IndiaHCI 2015), pp. 27–38. ACM, New York (2015). https://doi.org/10.1145/2835966.2835970
6. Dalvi, G., et al.: Does prediction really help in Marathi text input? Empirical analysis of a longitudinal study. In: Proceedings of the 18th International Conference on Human-Computer Interaction with Mobile Devices and Services (MobileHCI 2016), pp. 35–46. ACM, New York (2016). https://doi.org/10.1145/2935334.2935366
7. Anu Bharath, P., Jadhav, C., Ahire, S., Joshi, M., Ahirwar, R., Joshi, A.: Performance of accessible gesture-based indic keyboard. In: Bernhaupt, R., Dalvi, G., Joshi, A., Balkrishan, D.K., O'Neill, J., Winckler, M. (eds.) INTERACT 2017. LNCS, vol. 10513, pp. 205–220. Springer, Cham (2017). https://doi.org/10.1007/978-3-319-67744-6_14
8. Bhikne, B., Joshi, A., Joshi, M., Ahire, S., Maravi, N.: How much faster can you type by speaking in Hindi? Comparing keyboard-only and keyboard+speech text entry. In: Proceedings of the 9th Indian Conference on Human Computer Interaction (IndiaHCI 2018), pp. 20–28. ACM, New York (2018). https://doi.org/10.1145/3297121.3297123
9. Guerreiro, T., Nicolau, H., Jorge, J., Gonsalves, D.: NavTap: a long term study with excluded blind users. In: Proceedings of the 11th international ACM SIGACCESS Conference on Computers and Accessibility (Assets 2009), pp. 99–106. ACM, New York (2009). https://doi.org/10.1145/1639642.1639661

10. Joshi, A., Dalvi, G., Joshi, M., Rashinkar, P., Sarangdhar, A.: Design and evaluation of Devanagari virtual keyboards for touch screen mobile phones. In: Proceedings of the 13th International Conference on Human Computer Interaction with Mobile Devices and Services (MobileHCI 2011), pp. 323–332. ACM, New York (2011). https://doi.org/10.1145/2037373. 2037422

11. Google TalkBack. Wikipedia. https://en.wikipedia.org/w/index.php?title=Google_TalkBack &oldid=849832493. Accessed 27 Jan 2019

12. VoiceOver.   Wikipedia.   https://en.wikipedia.org/w/index.php?title=VoiceOver&oldid= 870848560. Accessed 27 Jan 2019

13. Sharma, M.K., Samanta, D.: Word prediction system for text entry in Hindi **13**(2), 29 (2014). https://doi.org/10.1145/2617590. Article 8

14. Jung, Y., Joshi, D., Narayanan-Saroja, V., Desai, D.P.: Solving the great Indian text input puzzle: touch screen-based mobile text input design. In: Proceedings of the 13th International Conference on Human Computer Interaction with Mobile Devices and Services (MobileHCI 2011), pp. 313–322. ACM, New York (2011). https://doi.org/10.1145/ 2037373.2037421

15. Hinkle, L., Brouillette, A., Jayakar, S., Gathings, L., Lezcano, M., Kalita, J.: Design and evaluation of soft keyboards for Brahmic scripts. **12**(2), 37 (2013). http://dx.doi.org/10.1145/ 2461316.2461318. Article 6

16. Ruan, S., Wobbrock, J.O., Liou, K., Ng, A.Y., Landay, J.A.: Speech is 3x faster than typing for English and Mandarin text entry on mobile devices. CoRR abs/1608.07323 (2016)

17. Ruan, S., Wobbrock, J.O., Liou, K., Ng, A., Landay, J.: Comparing speech and keyboard text entry for short messages in two languages on touchscreen phones. In: Proceedings of the ACM on Interactive, Mobile, Wearable and Ubiquitous Technologies, vol. 1, no. 4, pp. 1–23 (2018). https://doi.org/10.1145/3161187

18. William Soukoreff, R., Scott MacKenzie, I.: Recent developments in text-entry error rate measurement. In: CHI 2004 Extended Abstracts on Human Factors in Computing Systems (CHI EA 2004), pp. 1425–1428. ACM, New York (2004). https://doi.org/10.1145/985921. 986081

19. List of languages by number of native speakers in India - Wikipedia. https://en.wikipedia. org/wiki/List_of_languages_by_number_of_native_speakers_in_India. Accessed 28 Jan 2019

20. Devanagari - Wikipedia. https://en.wikipedia.org/wiki/Devanagari. Accessed 28 Jan 2019

21. MacKenzie, S.I., Soukoreff, W.R.: Text entry for mobile computing: models and methods, theory and practice. Hum. Comput. Interact. **17**(2–3), 147–198 (2002)

22. Bonner, M.N., Brudvik, J.T., Abowd, G.D., Edwards, W.K.: No-look notes: accessible eyes-free multi-touch text entry. In: Floréen, P., Krüger, A., Spasojevic, M. (eds.) Pervasive 2010. LNCS, vol. 6030, pp. 409–426. Springer, Heidelberg (2010). https://doi.org/10.1007/978-3-642-12654-3_24

23. Rudnicky, A.I., Sakamoto, M., Polifroni, J.H.: Evaluating spoken language interaction. In: Proceedings of the Workshop on Speech and Natural Language (HLT 1989), pp. 150–159. Association for Computational Linguistics, Stroudsburg (1989). https://doi.org/10.3115/ 1075434.1075459

Investigating Feedback for Two-Handed Exploration of Digital Maps Without Vision

Sandra Bardot[1], Marcos Serrano[1], Simon Perrault[2],
Shengdong Zhao[3], and Christophe Jouffrais[1,4,5(✉)]

[1] IRIT, University of Toulouse, Toulouse, France
{sandra.bardot,marcos.serrano,
christophe.jouffrais}@irit.fr
[2] Singapore University of Technology and Design (SUTD),
Singapore, Singapore
[3] NUS-HCI Lab, National University of Singapore, Singapore, Singapore
[4] IRIT, CNRS, Toulouse, France
[5] IPAL, CNRS, Singapore, Singapore

Abstract. Digital Interactive Maps on touch surfaces are a convenient alternative to physical raised-line maps for users with visual impairments. To compensate for the absence of passive tactile information, they provide vibrotactile and auditory feedback. However, this feedback is ambiguous when using multiple fingers since users may not identify which finger triggered it. To address this issue, we explored the use of bilateral feedback, i.e. collocated with each hand, for two-handed map exploration. We first introduced a design space of feedback for two-handed interaction combining two dimensions: spatial location (unilateral vs. bilateral feedback) and similarity (same vs. different feedback). We implemented four techniques resulting from our design space, using one or two smartwatches worn on the wrist (unilateral vs. bilateral feedback respectively). A first study with fifteen blindfolded participants showed that bilateral feedback outperformed unilateral feedback and that feedback similarity has little influence on exploration performance. Then we did a second study with twelve users with visual impairments, which confirmed the advantage of two-handed vs. one-handed exploration, and of bilateral vs. unilateral feedback. The results also bring to light the impact of feedback on exploration strategies.

Keywords: Users with visual impairment · Accessibility · Wearable devices · Smartwatches · Multimodal feedback · Map exploration

1 Introduction

In special education centers for people with visual impairments, raised-line maps are particularly important. An advantage of these maps is that they can be explored with both hands, allowing efficient two-handed exploration strategies [4]. However, making

Electronic supplementary material The online version of this chapter (https://doi.org/10.1007/978-3-030-29381-9_19) contains supplementary material, which is available to authorized users.

raised-line maps is a tedious process, which requires tactile document specialists to adapt and simplify visual maps. Moreover, maps have to be printed out on a special paper that generates raised lines when heated. As a result, raised-line maps cannot be changed or updated easily when the content is out-of-date.

Digital Interactive Maps (DIMs) are a good alternative to raised line maps [13]. They can be generated on demand and are easily modifiable. DIMs can be displayed on a touch sensitive surface (e.g. a tablet) and explored with the fingers. DIMs are not combined with any physical objects, i.e. they are entirely digital. During exploration, they provide auditory and/or vibrotactile feedback according to touch positions on the map [13]. Previous work has proposed to explore DIMs on multitouch surfaces using one [39] or several fingers (usually one finger of each hand) [5, 19]. However, single-finger exploration raises perceptual and cognitive issues [29]. Two-handed interaction allows for preserving exploration strategies [19] but raises the challenge of providing the appropriate feedback for each hand without ambiguity. As bimanual interactions support cognitive processes related to spatial perceptions, it is then necessary to design and evaluate them to explore DIMs in ubiquitous context (e.g. with the use of an Xperia Touch). To the best of our knowledge, no previous work has: (1) explored the design of appropriate feedback for two-handed exploration of digital maps (2) compared the impact of feedback on the performance and strategies used during one- vs. two-handed map exploration.

In this work, we investigated these two research questions. First, we studied the design of unilateral vs. bilateral feedback for two-handed exploration of digital maps without vision. To this end, we proposed a design space for two-handed exploration feedback (see Fig. 1), which combines two axes: location of the feedback (unilateral vs. bilateral), and feedback similarity (same vs. different feedback). To compare the usability of the different techniques, we conducted a first study with 15 blindfolded subjects. Results revealed that bilateral feedback outperforms unilateral feedback, and that the feedback similarity has little influence on exploration performance.

Then, we explored the impact of unilateral vs. bilateral feedback on performance and exploration strategies in a study with 12 people with visual impairments. In that study, the one-handed technique with unilateral feedback is similar to existing map exploration techniques on a tablet with accessibility feature activated. The results show that the two-handed technique with bilateral feedback is between 30% and 43% faster than the other techniques, and is preferred. We also identified, for each study and task, the two-handed exploration strategies used by the participants, revealing the impact of the feedback on such strategies.

To summarize, we explored the design and the evaluation of two-handed exploration techniques with different feedback on digital maps, and compared it with one-handed exploration. Our contributions are: (1) the exploration of all techniques resulting from the combination of our two axes (spatial location of the feedback and feedback similarity); (2) the results of an evaluation of this design space with 15 blindfolded people; (3) the results of an evaluation with 12 users with visual impairments comparing one-handed exploration vs. two-handed exploration techniques (with unilateral and bilateral feedback) for map exploration.

2   Related Work

2.1   Exploring DIMs on Touch Sensitive Surfaces

Digital interactive maps (DIMs) can be explored by directly moving the finger over the display surface. Important elements of the map (buildings, streets, regions, etc.) are rendered by auditory and/or vibratory feedback. For instance, TouchOverMap was designed for a smartphone [33] and provided a basic overview of a map layout. Other prototypes were designed on tablets and provided access to maritime, choropleth or city maps [8, 25, 37]. Some projects have also been developed on large tabletops [26]. One persistent issue with DIMs based on multitouch is that feedback can be ambiguous: when multiple fingers are moving on the surface, the user does not know which finger triggers the feedback. To release ambiguity, the user must raise up all the fingers and touch back, one finger after the other, to locate the rendered elements. Another possibility is to use only one finger to explore the map [31]. For instance, Bardot et al. [3] designed a one-handed technique to explore DIMs using a smartwatch. Vocal and vibratory feedback was provided by the smartwatch according to the finger location on the DIM. In this technique, the feedback was collocated with the moving hand.

Although users can use gestures with several fingers (two, three or four fingers) to access menus, two-handed exploration is not possible with VoiceOver or TalkBack. Hence map applications depending on them (e.g. Plans, Google Maps, Ariadne GPS, etc.) do not rely on two-handed exploration. For instance, it is not possible to use one finger as a reference point (anchor) while the other is moving around, which can provide the relative location of different elements in the map.

2.2   Multimodal Feedback

Giudice et al. [16] designed multimodal (audio and tactile) feedback that was triggered when graphics were explored by touch on a tablet. They showed that vibro-audio interface is a good multimodal solution for providing access to dynamic graphical information. They also showed that it supports the development of mental representations of the explored graphics. Goncu et al. [17] designed a more complex device that allowed the user to use the index finger of both hands, and that provided vibrations with small vibrators attached to the fingers and controlled by the tablet. The results showed that blind participants were able to understand different graphics including tables, line graphs and floorplans. Although multimodal feedback distributed on both hands may intuitively seems more efficient that single multimodal feedback, it has never been evaluated systematically.

2.3   Parallel Feedback

The "cocktail party effect" is a known research problem [1, 22]. It is the ability for a person to focus on a single speaker among several parallel conversation or background noise. Results showed that the ability of a listener depend on different factors (such as the type, the number or the location). How many information can be gather from several conversations while focus on one is unclear. Guerreiro et al. [18] proposed a study using several concurrent speech channels. They aimed to understand how people with VI can glean relevant information over two, three or four channels. The results showed that users where able to easily get the relevant information over two or three concurrent channels.

2.4 Haptic Exploration Strategies

Single hand exploration of an unknown digital map relies on a few strategies [38, 43]. The perimeter strategy consists in exploring an area for the identification of shape, size and contour characteristics. The gridline strategy involves searching for elements of a configuration with a systematic exploration of the display. The cyclic strategy consists in moving from one element to another in the same order, and then returning to the starting point. The reference point strategy is a back and forth movement between two elements. Previous studies [38] showed that grid and perimeter strategies are specially used for the first step of the exploration called "discovery phase", whereas cyclic and reference point strategies better serve the memorization of the map configuration.

In a recent study [19], Guerreiro et al. investigated strategies used during one-handed and two-handed target finding on a touchscreen. Complex behaviors involving both hands have been observed and six two-handed strategies have been identified: path scan consists in a structured scanning path; focused consists in searching a small sub-section; to-the-point corresponds to a path starting close to the target, which is already known by the user; freeform represents an unstructured strategy, while freeform symmetry describes the same strategy with two-hands; finally, trailing finger is a variant of freeform with an offset between hands. Although authors did not specifically compare one-handed vs. two-handed performance, they pointed out that they found no difference in exploration time. These strategies are consistent with previous work on how people with VI explore unknown spaces by foot [15, 23] or using tactile input [28].

In our study, we designed different types of bilateral feedback for digital map exploration. We then assessed the effects of unilateral vs. bilateral feedback on exploration strategies used with different one- vs. two-handed interaction techniques.

3 Bilateral Feedback for Two-Handed Exploration

While unilateral feedback can be easily produced using a multitouch surface, bilateral feedback requires locating both hands and providing unambiguous cues. The use of two wearable devices such as smartwatches can comply with this requirement since they have sound and vibration capabilities. A smartwatch or a vibrating bracelet can be worn on each hand, providing bilateral feedback that is collocated with each hand. To render the elements of a map (i.e. region, cities and borders), we used TTS to render the name of cities or regions, and vibratory feedback to locate map elements, such as borders between regions.

Interaction for one-handed exploration of digital maps (e.g. on tablets and smart-phones) is based on audio and vibratory feedback [25, 39]. Audio feedback is often used to render text and descriptions (e.g. name of regions) while vibratory feedback is preferred to render elements that must be located accurately (e.g. points or lines). We leveraged this approach for two-handed exploration. The challenge was to provide feedback corresponding to both hands actions, while still being cognitively manage-able. We know that using different feedback for each hand, for instance using different voices (e.g. male or female) and different vibration patterns (e.g. single or dual), can help to identify which hands triggers it [32]. Then we proposed a design space based on the combination of two design factors: spatial location of the feedback (unilateral or bilateral) and similarity of the feedback (same or different).

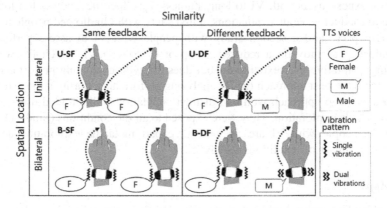

Fig. 1. The design space combines two feedback dimensions: spatial location and similarity.

The combination of these two design factors resulted in four feedback techniques (see Fig. 1): (1) unilateral with the same feedback (SF) for both hands (U-SF); (2) unilateral with different feedback (DF) for each hand (U-DF); (3) bilateral with the same feedback for both hands (B-SF); and (4) bilateral with different feedbacks for each hand (B-DF). It is interesting to note that the condition U-SF is similar to exploring a DIM on a touch screen with two fingers. We also designed a Control condition including one hand only, which is similar to exploring a DIM with only one finger on a tablet with the accessibility feature activated.

For the conditions with different feedback (U-DF and B-DF), we used a female voice and one vibration for the left hand, and a male voice and two vibrations for the right hand. For the unilateral conditions (U-SF and U-DF), if the user moves both hands at the same time, the feedback corresponds to the latest detected movement.

4 Materials and Methods

In the current paper, we present two studies on two-handed exploration of maps without vision. In this section, we detail the rationale for such an approach, as well as the experimental task and apparatus, which was the same for both studies.

4.1 Rationale

Including people with visual impairments (VI) in controlled studies is not a simple task due to limited availability [35]. Three different approaches might be adopted to evaluate interaction techniques for people with VI: (1) Gathering sighted people and people with VI in the same study, which is appropriate when the study is not too long because we cannot expose users with VI to long studies; (2) When the study is too long, it is possible to conduct separate evaluations: a first study with blindfolded people to reduce the design space, and a second study with people with VI to assess performance; (3) Conducting a study on a reduced group of users with VI, which fits well with evaluating qualitative user experience, but does not with evaluating performance.

We chose the best approach (2) for analyzing performance during a long study. We adopted a two-step approach with two distinct populations: blindfolded users are non-experts of tactile exploration. They were exposed to all the conditions (Study 1). On the other hand, people with VI are, in general, expert in tactile exploration and were exposed to a subset of conditions (Study 2).

4.2 Maps

We asked participants to explore digital maps similar to country maps, i.e. composed of regions. To create the digital maps, we used the Voronoi algorithm [14], configured to randomly generate 30 regions of different areas fitting an A3 format (29.7 × 42 cm). We included constraints in our Voronoi algorithm to define the targets regions: each map has the same complexity but with different target positions and size. The maps were different for each participant and each task.

4.3 Task and Instructions

Each session included two tasks corresponding to the discovery and memorization phases observed during haptic map exploration [38]. The first task was to explore a digital map and find 4 regions as fast as possible. To simplify the task, the names of the 4 regions were the same for all trials but their location was pseudo randomly changed. After 2 min, if the participant did not find the 4 regions, we considered the trial as a failure. Before switching to the second task, we indicated the eventual missing regions to the participant.

The second task was to compare the distance between 3 regions among the 4 regions found in task 1. For each trial, the three target regions were pseudo randomly chosen (the regions were chosen in order to remove comparisons that were too easy; and the trials order was random). After 2 min, if the participant did not answer the question, we considered the trial as a failure.

During the training session, we explained the techniques and the tasks. Participants started with a training map for each technique. Participants notified the experimenter when they found a specific region, and when they identified the two regions with the shortest distance.

4.4   Design and Procedure

The experiment followed a within-participant design with Interaction Technique as main factor. A block included three trials with the same technique. We counterbalanced the blocks order across participants using a Latin Square. We informed participants that they could take a break between blocks. Before using each technique, participants completed a familiarization session during which the technique was explained, and they completed a few trials of each task until they felt comfortable with the technique (around 5 min).

4.5   Apparatus

For finger tracking, we used TopCodes tags [24] attached to the index fingers of each hand (Fig. 2). We tracked them with a Logitech C270 webcam (1280 × 720 px, 50 Hz) located above the exploration surface. We used two SimValley AW-414 Android smartwatches (91 g, 45 × 44 × 14 mm), connected to the computer running the study with TCP sockets over a local Wi-Fi.

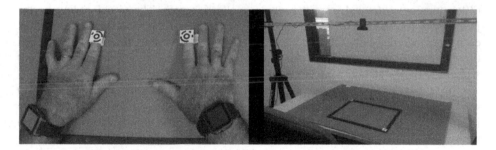

Fig. 2. Tags on index fingers (left) and setup (right).

4.6   Collected Data

We logged all tracking data, completion times and success rates for the two tasks. At the end of each block, participants had to fill a NASA-TLX questionnaire [21] about the technique they just used. At the end of the study, users had to classify the techniques by preference order and subjective effectiveness.

4.7   Identification of Exploration Strategies

We coded the exploration strategies according to Simonnet and Vieilledent [38] and Guerreiro et al. [19] (see Related Work section). We first unified equivalent strategies (i.e. gridline and path scan; back-and-forth and to-the-point). As a result, we had a set of eight strategies corresponding to the discovery (path scan, perimeter, freeform, freeform symmetry) and memorization (focused, back-and-forth, cyclic and point-of-reference) phases. During data analysis, we also included an additional discovery strategy named asymmetry (i.e. a different strategy with each hand).

The "Path scan" strategy corresponds to hand movements that clearly show a systematic and well organized exploration of the drawing. The "Perimeter" strategy is another discovery strategy that consists in corresponds to displacements along the physical limits of the interactive surface. The "Freeform" strategy represents an unstructured strategy, which does not explicitly show any form of organization. The "Freeform symmetry" is another unstructured strategy, but with the two-hands moving in similar directions (in mirror or in parallel). The "Focused" strategy consists in searching a small sub-section of the drawing in order to relocate a previously detected element of the drawing. The "Back-and-forth" strategy corresponds to back and forth movements between two elements of the drawing that have been previously located. The "Cyclic" strategy is a movement between three or more elements of the drawing, which are relocated one after the other before coming back to the starting element (e.g. A – B – C – A). Finally, the "Point-of-reference" strategy consists in star-like movements between three or more targets (e.g. A – B – A – C – A). The memorization strategies can help to locate the elements relative to each other.

In order to detect the discovery strategies in each trial, we relied on three independent judges inspecting the exploration paths. We generated one image showing the complete exploration path, and a set of images corresponding to successive periods (30 s duration) extracted from the whole exploration path. The visual coding by the judges was divided in two steps: first, they coded 5% of the trials set, and then they compared their respective coding in order to agree on the coding. Finally, they encoded the entire set of trials, and they collectively decided (i.e. reach a consensus if needed) which discovery strategy was the most observed in each trial.

Since three memorization strategies (back-and-forth, cyclic and point-of-reference) were difficult to identify visually, we developed three algorithms to perform the identification process. We validated the three algorithms with unit tests and with thorough visual exploration of many subparts of the exploration traces. In the following sections of the paper, when the memorization strategies were observed in every trials, we report the average number of occurrences per trial. When the memorization strategies were observed in some trials only, we report the percentage of trials in which these strategies were observed.

4.8   Analysis

Recently, the null-hypothesis significance testing (NHST) has come under criticism within the statistics [2, 9] and HCI communities [11, 12]. We thus report our results using estimation techniques with confidence intervals (0.95), instead of p-value statistics, consistent with APA recommendations [40].

5   Study 1: Exploration of the Design Space

The goal of this first study was to compare the impact of the design factors during map exploration.

5.1   Participants

We recruited 15 sighted participants (3 females) aged between 19 and 29 (M = 23, SD = 3). Participants were blindfolded for the study. They were recruited at the university: 12 of them were undergraduate students, 2 were PhD students, and one was research assistant. Fourteen participants were right-handed and one left-handed. Six participants owned a smartwatch. None of them had hearing problems.

5.2   Interaction Techniques

We compared the four two-handed techniques from our design space (U-SF, U-DF, B-SF and B-DF) and the control technique. As mentioned earlier, the control technique is similar to exploring a DIM with one finger on a tablet with the accessibility feature activated; and U-SF condition is similar to exploring a DIM with two fingers.

5.3   Results

In total, we collected 5 techniques × 2 tasks × 3 repetitions × 15 participants = 450 trials.

Task 1: Completion Time and Success Rate. On average, participants took 64.4 s (CI [55.8, 72.4]) using one hand only (Control), 68.9 s (CI [61.4, 76.5]) using two hands with unilateral feedback (average completion time for U-SF and U-DF because they are similar), and 45.5 s (CI [40.2, 51.6]) using two hands with bilateral feedback (average completion time for B-SF and B-DF because they are similar). Hence, results show a difference between techniques concerning completion time (Fig. 3). The Control and unilateral techniques were slower than bilateral techniques. Results did not show any difference regarding the feedback similarity factor (i.e. between U-SF and U-DF, or between B-SF and B-DF). Among all the trials, only nine trials were considered as failure. For each condition, it represents: 2 for Control (4.44%), 6 for U-SF (13.3%) and 1 for U-DF (2.22%).

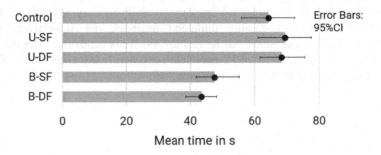

Fig. 3. Mean time in s to complete Task 1.

Task 2: Completion Time and Success Rate. Concerning the comparison of map elements location (task 2), we observed that, very often, participants remembered the position of the regions to be compared from task 1, and hence answered directly without re-exploring the map (62.5% of the trials). For the remaining trials with map exploration, we observed no difference in completion time between techniques: on average it took participants 24.8 s to complete the task. Regarding success rates, only 2 U-SF trials were incorrect (4.44%).

Strategies Used. During task 1, across the different conditions, the most used strategies were "Path scan" (71% of the trials) and "Freeform" (15.5%). The prevalence of the "Path scan" strategy was true for all the techniques (Control: 73.3%; U-SF: 61.1%; U-DF: 66.6%; B-SF: 76.7% and B-DF: 77.2%).

During task 2, when users re-explored the map, the most used discovery strategies were "Freeform" (75.7% of the trials) and "Path scan" (13.7%). Participants also used memorization strategies: "Back-and-forth" movements with the same hand between two regions were observed in 28.8% of the trials for Control, 20% for U-SF, 26.6% for U-DF, 22.2% for U-SF, 31.1% for B-SF, and 28.8% for B-DF. "Cyclic" strategy over three regions was observed in 4% of the trials for Control, and not observed with the other techniques. The participants did not used the "Point-of-reference" strategy.

Simultaneous Hand Movements. To further investigate two-handed exploration, we identified simultaneous movements for the different techniques. Simultaneous movements correspond to exploratory movements with both hands at the same time. On average, participants used simultaneous movements in 15.7% of the trials using U-SF, in 17.4% using U-DF, in 72.1% using B-SF, in 75.8% using B-DF. This clearly illustrates how the feedback impacts behavior. With bilateral feedback, participants did use their two hand at the same time without any difficulty to manage parallel audio and vibratory feedback.

Subjective Report. *User Preference.* Overall, participants preferred using the bilateral technique with different feedback (B-DF). Among the 15 participants, 10 chose this technique as their favorite, 3 chose the bilateral with same feedback (B-SF), and 2 the unilateral with different feedback (U-DF).

User Feedback. All the participants appreciated moving both hands at the same time, and most of them added positive comments about the bilateral feedback. P3 appreciated not "wasting time on determining which hand I'm using". P5 found that "feedback is stronger" with bilateral feedback. Regarding the B-DF technique, users enjoyed "listening to different voices because it allows me to easily identify which hand triggered the feedback" (P11). Concerning unilateral feedback, P8 subjectively reported exploring slowly, and explained that he had to "move his hands one after the other in order not to miss any regions". P12 felt "less confident using U-SF and U-DF techniques because the exploration was less intuitive".

5.4   Discussion

In this first experiment, we found out that bilateral feedback techniques allow participants to perform task 1 faster than the other techniques (control and both unilateral techniques). This result confirms that bilateral feedback makes it easier for participants to locate elements on the digital map. The type of feedback (same or different) did not affect performance, as we found no differences between B-SF and B-DF in terms of accuracy or completion time. However, a large majority of participants (10/15) preferred having a different feedback (B-DF) compared to the same feedback (B-SF). In addition, most users were able to build an accurate mental representation of the map during exploration (task 1), and active comparison of elements location during task 2 was not necessary in a majority of trials.

6   Study 2: Impact of Feedback on Performance and Exploration Strategies

We ran a second experiment with 12 users with VI, who have an expertise in two-handed exploration of raised-line diagrams compared to the participants of the previous study. Since feedback similarity did not raise differences in the first study, we focused on the location of the feedback (unilateral vs. bilateral) for two-handed exploration.

6.1   Interaction Techniques

In order to shorten the experiment time in this study, we focused on three conditions only: Control, U-SF and B-DF. We made that choice according to the results of the first study. Indeed, there was no difference between U-SF and U-DF on one side, and B-SF and B-DF on the other side (see Fig. 3). Secondly, as mentioned earlier, the Control and U-SF conditions are similar to exploring a digital map on a tablet, with one or two fingers respectively. We selected the Control condition because there is no feedback ambiguity, and because people with visual impairment already use a similar technique on regular phones and tablets. Hence, as stated in its name, it represents a good control condition. B-DF was selected because it is the best and preferred technique identified in the first study.

6.2   Participants

We recruited 12 people with VI (5 females) aged between 21 and 73 years old (M = 52, SD = 15). The level of visual impairment varied: 9 of them were totally blind, and 3 had residual light perceptions. All participants use VoiceOver daily, and three of them use a map application (i.e. Ariadne GPS) on their smartphone. Seven participants had already used a smartwatch before, and two participants own a smartwatch. None of them had hearing problems. All of them were used to exploring raised-line diagrams (Table 1).

Table 1. Description of the visually impaired participants

Subject	Gender	Age	Vision	Device owned	Map application	Raised-line Expertise (1–5)
1	M	58	Light	Smartphone Smartwatch	None	2
2	M	50	Blind	Smartphone Smartwatch	Plans Ariadne GPS	3
3	F	21	Blind	Smartphone	None	4
4	M	58	Light	Smartphone Tablet	None	2
5	F	62	Blind	Smartphone	None	4
6	F	47	Blind	Smartphone Tablet	Ariadne GPS BlindSquare	3
7	M	27	Blind	Smartphone	Ariadne GPS	3
8	M	68	Blind	Smartphone	None	4
9	F	45	Blind	Smartphone	None	2
10	F	73	Light	Smartphone	None	4
11	M	61	Blind	Smartphone	None	3
12	M	55	Blind	Smartphone	None	2

6.3 Maps

To design the maps, we used the Voronoi algorithm to randomly generate 30 regions on each map. We generated 216 maps in order to use a different map in each trial (for each participant, condition, and task). In addition, in order to verify whether bilateral feedback improves performance on the comparison task too, we systematically changed the map between task 1 and task 2, which means that participants had to locate four new regions in task 2 before comparing them. Then, both discovery and memorization strategies should appear in task 2.

6.4 Results

In total, we collected 3 techniques × 2 tasks × 3 repetitions × 12 participants = 216 trials.

Task 1: Completion Time and Success Rate. Results show a clear difference between techniques concerning completion time to find the four regions (task 1). Participants completed the task faster with bilateral feedback (50 s, CI [42.9, 58.8]) than with Control (76 s (CI [66.7, 88.3]) or unilateral (93 s, CI [80.7, 107.2]), as illustrated in Fig. 4. This difference is quite important, since B-DF is 31.2% faster than Control and 42.9% than U-SF. Eleven trials that lasted longer than 2 min were considered as failure: 7 Control (19.4%) and 4 U-SF (11.1%).

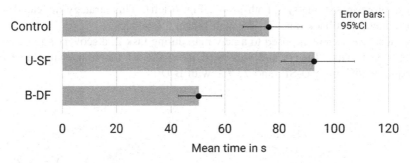

Fig. 4. Mean time in s to complete Task 1.

Task 2: Completion Time and Success Rate. On average, participants completed the comparison task, i.e. finding the four regions and answering the question, in 92.8 s (CI [69.7, 118.5]) with B-DF, in 110 s (CI [92.8, 141.3]) with Control and in 137 s (CI [113.1, 171]) with U-SF. The ratio analysis confirmed the difference between B-DF and U-SF: the ratio and the corresponding CIs was above 1 (meaning that the B-DF is faster than U-SF) (Fig. 5).

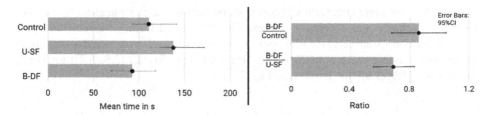

Fig. 5. Mean completion time in seconds (left), and ratio (right) for Task 2.

The time needed to find the four regions for the first time was, on average, 83 s with B-DF, 94 s with Control and 122 s with U-SF. These times are higher than those observed in task 1 because participants mixed up discovery and memorization strategies from the beginning of task 2.

The percentage of correct answers was 77% (CI [54.5, 99.5]) with the Control condition, 50% (CI [27.5, 72.50]) with U-SF, and 77% (CI [57.25, 96.75]) with B-DF. Because the task had to be completed within 4 min, 2 trials were considered as failure, corresponding to 1 Control (0.9%) and 1 U-SF (0.9%).

Strategies Used. During task 1, when exploring with the control technique, the most used strategy was the "Path scan" (83.3% of the trials), and then "Perimeter" (8.3%). When exploring with two hands and unilateral feedback (U-SF), the most used strategy was the "Path scan" (66.6% of the trials) then "Freeform" (16.6%; see Fig. 6 right). When exploring with two hands and bilateral feedback (B-DF), the most used strategy was the "Path scan" (74.9%) and then "Freeform" (11.1%). We also identified when hands explore in symmetry ("Path scan"; Fig. 6 left). This strategy appeared 41.6% with unilateral feedback, and 72.2% with bilateral feedback.

Because users were exposed to a new map during task 2, discovery strategies were also observed. The "Path scan" was used in 88.9% of the trials with the Control technique, 91.6% with U-SF, and 77.7% with B-DF.

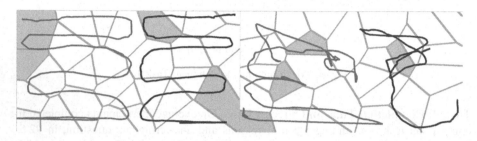

Fig. 6. Example of strategies used (the underlying digital map is virtual. It is displayed for illustration purpose only). Left: "Path scan" strategy (P4 with B-DF, task 1, simultaneous hand movements). Right: "Freeform" (P2 with U-SF, task 2, sequential hand movements). Brown and blue line correspond to left and right hands movements respectively. (Color figure online)

In task 2, we more specifically focused on the memorization strategies ("Back-and-forth", "Cyclic", and "Point-of-reference"). "Back-and-forth" movements were observed in every trials, and the number of occurrences in each trial varied according to the technique being used: 5.3 (CI [4.1, 6.3]) for Control, 3.6 (CI [2.8, 5.4]) for U-SF, and 2.4 (CI [1.9, 3.8]) for B-DF (see Fig. 7).

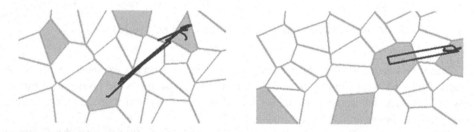

Fig. 7. Example of "Back-and-forth" strategies used (the underlying digital map is virtual. It is displayed for illustration purpose only). Left: P2 with U-SF, task 2. Right: P7 with B-DF, task 2. The blue line corresponds to right hand movements. (Color figure online)

Contrary to "Back-and-forth" strategy, "Cyclic" and "Point-of-reference" strategies were observed in some trials only. The "Cyclic" strategy with the same hand (i.e. going from region A, to B, to C, and back to A) over 3 regions was observed in 33.3% of the Control trials, 38.8% of the U-SF trials, and 22.2% of the B-DF trials. "Cyclic" strategy over 4 regions was observed in 30.5% of the Control trials, and only 5.5% of the U-SF and B-DF trials (see Fig. 8).

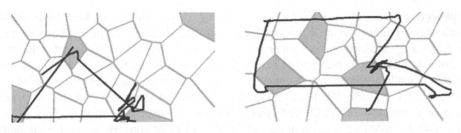

Fig. 8. Example of "Cyclic" strategies used (the underlying digital map is virtual. It is displayed for illustration purpose only). Left: P12 with U-SF, task 2. Right: P9 with B-DF, task 2. The blue line corresponds to right hand movements. (Color figure online)

The "Point-of-reference" strategy with the same hand (going from A to B, back to A, and then to C) was observed in 58.3% of the Control trials, 41.6% of the U-SF trials, and 33.3% of the B-DF trials (see Fig. 9).

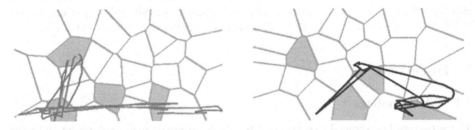

Fig. 9. Example of "Point-of-reference" strategies used (the underlying digital map is virtual. It is displayed for illustration purpose only). Left: P5 with U-SF, task 2. Right: P5 with B-DF, task 2. Brown and blue lines correspond to left and right hands movements respectively. (Color figure online)

Finally, we observed the number of occurrences of memorization strategies realized with two hands (i.e. placing one hand on one target region, as an anchor, and using the other hand to re-locate other target regions): 2.5 (CI [2.27, 3.06]) occurrences per trial for U-SF, and 2.8 (CI [2.27, 3.37) occurrences for B-DF. These results show that participants combined the use of both hands during two-handed exploration to compare the relative location of two regions.

In the Annex of the paper, we have added many figures corresponding to the different strategies used during exploration.

Simultaneous Hand Movements. With unilateral feedback (U-SF), 37% of the exploration time was based on simultaneous hands movements. This percentage increased to 70% with bilateral feedback (B-DF), which highlights the impact of feedback on the use of the two hands. Even though both hands were involved with U-SF, users mainly did sequential movements. On the contrary, they effortlessly do simultaneous hand movements with B-DF.

Subjective Report. *User Preference.* 9 out of 12 participants ranked the bilateral technique as their favorite, 2 preferred the control condition (none of these two people use any map application on his/her smartphone or tablet), and 1 preferred unilateral feedback. Participants preferring bilateral feedback mentioned that using both hands in parallel, and hence hearing two concurrent voices, "does not raise any cognitive issue" (P1, P3, P4, P7, P8, P9, P10, P11 and P12). Two of them reported that they are regularly "confronted to different audio stimuli at the same time in their daily lives" (P3, P4) (i.e. listening to street noises while talking to a person). However, two of them reported that bilateral feedback requires "more concentration and cognitive load" (P2, P5), but that using it for such a short task was not disturbing. All participants reported feeling the vibration. Eleven out of twelve participants reported that wearing two smartwatches for the bilateral technique was convenient as "it is easy to understand where the feedback comes from" (P1, P10). One participant said that "wearing two smartwatches is useless" (P6 - same participant that scored unilateral technique first).

NASA-TLX. We did not observe any major difference on the different dimensions of the NASA TLX questionnaire (mental demand, physical demand, temporal demand, effort and frustration) between the three techniques. Participants evaluated the performance of B-DF and U-SF (M = 75 and M = 74 respectively) better than control (M = 63).

7 Discussion

7.1 Main Findings

These two studies showed that bilateral feedback improves map exploration and more specifically the localization and comparison of specific elements on the map. We can consider [4] that there is a difference of raised-line exploration expertise between users with VI (study 2) and blindfolded users (study 1). Because the results show the same trends in these two studies, it seems that expertise does not have any effect on the usability of the bilateral techniques. A more surprising result is that exploring the map with two hands but triggering unilateral feedback was not faster than one-handed exploration. This is an important result showing than an efficient two-handed exploration technique for digital maps must provide bilateral feedback.

7.2 The Effect of Bilateral Feedback on Exploration Strategies

We observed different exploration strategies depending on the technique being used. With the two-handed technique and bilateral feedback, users explored the map with their two hands, and each hand mainly explored one half of the map only. In task 2 (comparison of map elements), users also took advantage of using two hands: quite often, one hand was used as an anchor while the other hand was moving around. Consequently, they did less back and forth movements between elements. With these bimanual strategies, based on adapted bilateral feedback, users were more efficient when exploring a map and when comparing the location of different regions. When the bilateral feedback was not provided (U-SF), users were less efficient and preferred using one hand only.

7.3   Recommendation for Touch Devices

It is important to note that two of our experimental conditions (Control and U-SF) may correspond to a situation where users with VI explore maps on a tablet with TTS activated (e.g. VoiceOver or TalkBack). In such a situation, they are free to explore the map with one or two fingers (corresponding to Control and U-SF respectively), but with ambiguous feedbacks. When it is not possible to use bilateral unambiguous feedback, our results show that it is more efficient to use one finger only.

Our results also show that bilateral feedback may improve tactile exploration, provided that both hands are identified during exploration. In order to implement bilateral feedback on touchscreens, it is mandatory to identify and track each finger unambiguously (or at least right and left hands if only one finger is used on each hand). Recent studies show that finger identification can be based on finger orientation [41], or on external hardware such as a wearable device, or a camera [20].

7.4   Other Applications for Bilateral Feedback

A recent study [4] has shown that people with VI intuitively use two hands to explore different types of raised line graphics, such as common drawings, mathematical graphs or neighborhood maps. Bilateral feedback could be of interest to render these different graphics accessible on touch surfaces. For instance, a two-handed exploration of digital graphs could allow the user to explore the horizontal or vertical axes with one hand, and the graph itself with the other [34]. It could also be used on tagged drawings or photos (e.g. on Facebook) to explore tags with both hands, which is similar to our experimental task. Previous work [4] showed that the average of simultaneous exploration time for people with VI on raised-line diagrams is 74.6%. In the current study, we observed that simultaneous exploration using bilateral technique was 70%. These two results are comparable and show that people with VI can perform similar two-handed exploration on raised-line diagrams and digital maps.

8   Conclusion and Future Work

In this paper, we designed and evaluated four feedback techniques for two-handed exploration of digital interactive maps by users with visual impairments. These techniques resulted from a design space combining feedback location and similarity. The results, which were comparable for both blindfolded and users with visual impairments, show the advantages of two-handed vs. one-handed exploration, providing that bilateral feedback is available and unambiguous. Although we observed these results on graphics that represent maps, we are convinced that they can apply to other interactive accessible graphics (figurative drawings, graphs, etc.). Future work will focus on how to design affordable hand and finger tracking techniques that could provide multimodal bilateral feedback. Moreover, future work will investigate bimanual interactions on complex digital maps (i.e. with different data sets).

Acknowledgments. We thank all the users who participated to the studies. We also thank the special education Center IJA, and the "Cherchons pour Voir" lab, both in Toulouse, FR. This work was part of the AccessiMap project (research grant AccessiMap ANR-14-CE17-0018).

References

1. Arons, B.: A review of the cocktail party effect. J. Am. Voice I/O Soc. **12**(7), 35–50 (1992)
2. Baker, M.: Statisticians issue warning over misuse of P values. Nature **531**(7593), 151 (2015). https://doi.org/10.1038/nature.2016.19503
3. Bardot, S., Serrano, M., Jouffrais, C.: From tactile to virtual: using a smartwatch to improve spatial map exploration for visually impaired users. In: Proceedings of the 18th International Conference on Human-Computer Interaction with Mobile Devices and Services (MobileHCI 2016), pp. 100–111. ACM, New York (2016). https://doi.org/10.1145/2935334.2935342
4. Bardot, S., Serrano, M., Oriola, B., Jouffrais, C.: Identifying how visually impaired people explore raised-line diagrams to improve the design of touch interfaces. In: Proceedings of the 2017 CHI Conference on Human Factors in Computing Systems (CHI 2017), pp. 550–555. ACM, New York (2017). https://doi.org/10.1145/3025453.3025582
5. Brock, A., Lebaz, S., Oriola, B., Picard, D., Jouffrais, C., Truillet, P.: Kin'touch: understanding how visually impaired people explore tactile maps. In: CHI 2012 Extended Abstracts on Human Factors in Computing Systems (CHI EA 2012), pp. 2471–2476. ACM, New York (2012). https://doi.org/10.1145/2212776.2223821
6. Brock, A.M., Truillet, P., Oriola, B., Picard, D., Jouffrais, C.: Interactivity improves usability of geographic maps for visually impaired people. Hum. Comput. Interact. **30**(2), 156–194 (2015). https://doi.org/10.1080/07370024.2014.924412
7. Chakraborty, T., Khan, T.A., Alim Al Islam, A.B.M.: FLight: a low-cost reading and writing system for economically less-privileged visually-impaired people exploiting ink-based Braille system. In: Proceedings of the 2017 CHI Conference on Human Factors in Computing Systems (CHI 2017), pp. 531–540. ACM, New York (2017). https://doi.org/10.1145/3025453.3025646
8. Carroll, D., Chakraborty, S., Lazar, J.: Designing accessible visualizations: the case of designing a weather map for blind users. In: Stephanidis, C., Antona, M. (eds.) UAHCI 2013, Part I. LNCS, vol. 8009, pp. 436–445. Springer, Heidelberg (2013). https://doi.org/10.1007/978-3-642-39188-0_47
9. Cumming, G.: The new statistics: why and how. Psychol. Sci. **25**(1), 7–29 (2014). https://doi.org/10.1177/0956797613504966
10. Delogu, F., Palmiero, M., Federici, S., Plaisant, C., Zhao, H., Belardinelli, O.: Non-visual exploration of geographic maps: does sonification help? Disabil. Rehabil. Assist. Technol. **5**(3), 164–174 (2010). https://doi.org/10.3109/17483100903100277
11. Dragicevic, P.: Fair statistical communication in HCI. In: Robertson, J., Kaptein, M. (eds.) Modern Statistical Methods for HCI. HIS, pp. 291–330. Springer, Cham (2016). https://doi.org/10.1007/978-3-319-26633-6_13
12. Dragicevic, P., Chevalier, F., Huot, S.: Running an HCI experiment in multiple parallel universes. In: Extended Abstracts on Human Factors in Computing Systems, pp. 607–618. ACM, New York (2014). http://dx.doi.org/10.1145/2559206.2578881
13. Ducasse, J., Brock, A.M., Jouffrais, C.: Accessible interactive maps for visually impaired users. In: Pissaloux, E., Velázquez, R. (eds.) Mobility of Visually Impaired People, pp. 537–584. Springer, Cham (2018). https://doi.org/10.1007/978-3-319-54446-5_17

14. Fortune, S.: A sweepline algorithm for Voronoi diagrams. Algorithmica **2**(1–4), 153–174 (1987)
15. Gaunet, F., Martinez, J.L., Thinus-Blanc, C.: Early-blind subjects' spatial representation of manipulatory space: exploratory strategies and reaction to change. Perception **26**(3), 345–366 (1997)
16. Giudice, N.A., Palani, H.P., Brenner, E., Kramer, K.M.: Learning non-visual graphical information using a touch-based vibro-audio interface. In: Proceedings of the 14th International ACM SIGACCESS Conference on Computers and Accessibility - ASSETS 2012, pp. 103–110. ACM Press, New York (2012). https://doi.org/10.1145/2384916. 2384935
17. Goncu, C., Marriott, K.: GraVVITAS: generic multi-touch presentation of accessible graphics. In: Campos, P., Graham, N., Jorge, J., Nunes, N., Palanque, P., Winckler, M. (eds.) INTERACT 2011. LNCS, vol. 6946, pp. 30–48. Springer, Heidelberg (2011). https://doi. org/10.1007/978-3-642-23774-4_5
18. Guerreiro, J., Gonçalves, D.: Text-to-speeches: evaluating the perception of concurrent speech by blind people. In: Proceedings of the 16th International ACM SIGACCESS Conference on Computers & Accessibility (ASSETS 2014), pp. 169–176. ACM, New York (2014). https://doi.org/10.1145/2661334.2661367
19. Guerreiro, T., Montague, K., Guerreiro, J., Nunes, R., Nicolau, H., Gonçalves, D.J.V.: Blind people interacting with large touch surfaces: strategies for one-handed and two-handed exploration. In: Proceedings of the 2015 International Conference on Interactive Tabletops & Surfaces (ITS 2015), pp. 25–34. ACM, New York (2015). https://doi.org/10.1145/2817721. 2817743
20. Gupta, A., Balakrishnan, R.: DualKey: miniature screen text entry via finger identification. In: Proceedings of the 2016 CHI Conference on Human Factors in Computing Systems - CHI 2016, pp. 59–70 (2016). https://doi.org/10.1145/2858036.2858052
21. Hart, S.G., Staveland, L.E.: Development of NASA-TLX (Task Load Index): results of empirical and theoretical research. In: Hancock, P.A., Meshkati, N. (eds.) Human Mental Workload, pp. 139–183. Elsevier (1988). http://doi.org/10.1016/S0166–4115(08)62386–9
22. Hawley, M.L., Litovsky, R.Y., Culling, J.F.: The benefit of binaural hearing in a cocktail party: effect of location and type of interferer. J. Acoust. Soc. Am. **115**(2), 833–843 (2004)
23. Hill, E.W., Rieser, J.J., Hill, M.M., Hill, M.: How persons with visual impairments explore novel spaces: strategies of good and poor performers. J. Vis. Impair. Blind. **87**, 295–301 (1993)
24. Horn, M.T.: TopCode: Tangible Object Placement Codes. http://hci.cs.tufts.edu/topcodes/
25. Kaklanis, N., Votis, K., Tzovaras, D.: Open touch/sound maps: a system to convey street data through haptic and auditory feedback. Comput. Geosci. **57**, 59–67 (2013)
26. Kane, S.K., et al.: Access overlays: improving non-visual access to large touch screens for blind users. In: Proceedings of the 24th Annual ACM Symposium on User Interface Software and Technology (UIST 2011), pp. 273–282. ACM, New York (2011). https://doi. org/10.1145/2047196.2047232
27. Kane, S.K., Wobbrock, J.O., Ladner, R.E.: Usable gestures for blind people: understanding preference and performance. In: Proceedings of the SIGCHI Conference on Human Factors in Computing Systems (CHI 2011), pp. 413–422. ACM, New York (2011). https://doi.org/ 10.1145/1978942.1979001
28. Lahav, O., Mioduser, D.: Haptic-feedback support for cognitive mapping of unknown spaces by people who are blind. Int. J. Hum. Comput. Stud. **66**(1), 23–35 (2008)
29. Loomis, J.M., Klatzky, R.L., Lederman, S.J.: Similarity of tactual and visual picture recognition with limited field of view. Perception **20**(2), 167–177 (1991). https://doi.org/10. 1068/p200167

30. McGookin, D., Brewster, S., Jiang, W.: Investigating touchscreen accessibility for people with visual impairments. In: Proceedings of the 5th Nordic Conference on Human-Computer Interaction: Building Bridges (NordiCHI 2008), pp. 298–307. ACM, New York (2008). http://dx.doi.org/10.1145/1463160.1463193

31. Morash, V.S., Connell Pensky, A.E., Tseng, S.T.W., Miele, J.A.: Effects of using multiple hands and fingers on haptic performance in individuals who are blind. Perception **43**(6), 569–588 (2014)

32. Moray, N.: Attention in dichotic listening: Affective cues and the influence of instructions. Q. J. Exp. Psychol. **11**, 56–60 (1959)

33. Poppinga, B., Magnusson, C., Pielot, M., Rassmus-Gröhn, K.: TouchOver map: audio-tactile exploration of interactive maps. In: Proceedings of the 13th International Conference on Human Computer Interaction with Mobile Devices and Services (MobileHCI 2011), pp. 545–550. ACM, New York (2011). https://doi.org/10.1145/2037373.2037458

34. Ramloll, R., Brewster, S.: A generic approach for augmenting tactile diagrams with spatial non-speech sounds. In: CHI 2002 Extended Abstracts on Human Factors in Computing Systems - CHI 2002, p. 770. ACM Press, New York (2002). http://doi.org/10.1145/506443. 506589

35. Sears, A., Hanson, V.: Representing users in accessibility research. In: Proceedings of the SIGCHI Conference on Human Factors in Computing Systems (CHI 2011), pp. 2235–2238. ACM, New York (2011). https://doi.org/10.1145/1978942.1979268

36. Shilkrot, R., Huber, J., Ee, W.M., Maes, P., Nanayakkara, S.C.: FingerReader: a wearable device to explore printed text on the go. In: Proceedings of the 33rd Annual ACM Conference on Human Factors in Computing Systems (CHI 2015), pp. 2363–2372. ACM, New York (2015). https://doi.org/10.1145/2702123.2702421

37. Simonnet, M., Ryall, E.: Blind sailors' spatial representation using an on-board force feedback arm: two case studies. Adv. Hum. Comput. Interact. **2013**, 1 (2013). https://doi.org/10.1155/2013/163718. Article 10

38. Simonnet, M., Vieilledent, S.: Accuracy and coordination of spatial frames of reference during the exploration of virtual maps: interest for orientation and mobility of blind people?". Adv. Hum. Comput. Interact. **2012**, 14 (2012)

39. Su, J., Rosenzweig, A., Goel, A., de Lara, E., Truong, K.N.: Timbremap: enabling the visually-impaired to use maps on touch-enabled devices. In: Proceedings of the 12th International Conference on Human Computer Interaction with Mobile Devices and Services (MobileHCI 2010), pp. 17–26. ACM, New York (2010). https://doi.org/10.1145/1851600. 1851606

40. VandenBos, G.R. (ed.): Publication Manual of the American Psychological Association, 6th edn. American Psychological Association, Washington, DC (2009). http://www.apastyle. org/manual/

41. Wang, F., Cao, X., Ren, X., Irani, P.: Detecting and leveraging finger orientation for interaction with direct-touch surfaces. In: Proceedings of the 22nd Annual ACM Symposium on User Interface Software and Technology (UIST 2009), pp. 23–32. ACM, New York (2009). https://doi.org/10.1145/1622176.1622182

42. Wall, S., Brewster, S.: Providing external memory aids in haptic visualisations for blind computer users. Int. J. Disabil. Hum. Dev. **4**(4), 331–338 (2011). https://doi.org/10.1515/ IJDHD.2005.4.4.331. Accessed 19 Sep 2018

43. Wijntjes, M.W.A., van Lienen, T., Verstijnen, I.M., Kappers, A.M.L.: Look what I have felt: unidentified haptic line drawings are identified after sketching. Acta Psychol. (Amst) **128**(2), 255–263 (2008)

Perception of Tactile Symbols by Visually Impaired Older Adults

Vojtech Gintner, Miroslav Macik$^{(\boxtimes)}$, and Zdenek Mikovec

Faculty of Electrical Engineering, Czech Technical University in Prague,
Prague, Czech Republic
macikmir@fel.cvut.cz

Abstract. We present a design of an indoor orientation terminal for visually impaired older adults. Interaction is based on buttons, tactile symbols, and audio feedback. The terminal consists of five parts dedicated to a particular function. The tactile symbols mimic real-world objects. We performed three design iterations and conduct evaluations with a total of 17 participants, their mean age was 84.2 years. The results show that usage of real-world objects and low level of symbol abstraction leads to an unambiguous pairing of user expectations and real functions. Introduction of complicated and abstract artifacts like contour objects or complex tactile map was very hard to understand and recognize. Our final design was well accepted by all participants and allowed the participants to orient themselves in the indoor environment.

Keywords: Tactile perception · Visually impaired · Older adults

1 Introduction

Visually impaired people challenged with severe impairment or even blindness (according to WHO classification [12]) appear mostly among older adults. According to Bourne et al. [3], 86.3% of blind people are older than 50 years and 52.8% older than 70 years.

Unfortunately, the research attention on visually impaired older adults is limited. We have analyzed 39 papers focusing on visually impaired people presented on last three CHI conferences (2016–2018). When excluding studies focused primarily on children and young adults, the mean age of study participant was 37.3 years (weighted mean, sample size as weight). This clearly reveals a bias in favor of the younger part of the population that forms a minority of the visually impaired population.

As visual impairment limits mainly a person's mobility and reduces travel-related activities [6], solutions helping visually impaired people with spatial orientation and navigation are of high importance. A tactile user interface is one of the efficient ways of interaction for visually impaired people as their passive tactile acuity is superior [5].

© IFIP International Federation for Information Processing 2019
Published by Springer Nature Switzerland AG 2019
D. Lamas et al. (Eds.): INTERACT 2019, LNCS 11746, pp. 325–334, 2019.
https://doi.org/10.1007/978-3-030-29381-9_20

In our research, we focus on the design of tactile symbols used for buttons of an interactive indoor orientation system helping visually impaired older adults with orientation and navigation inside a large complex building. The previous research [10] shows, that visually impaired older adults experience serious problems with understanding the meaning of abstract tactile symbols. Our research shows a way how to design tactile symbols whose meaning is understandable by visually impaired older adults.

2   Related Work

There exist extensive research in the field of tactile symbols used especially in the framework of tactile maps like [1,15]. Besides 2D symbols researches experiment also with 3D (volumetric) tactile symbols [7,8]. Moreover, the tactile perception of visually impaired people is superior [5].

There are also other approaches to solve the orientation and navigation by means of a combination of active and passive elements. PERCEPT [4] uses RFID tags with a special glove to read them. Another similar solution [16] is based on RFID tag grid on the floor and speaker placed on the white cane. Other solutions typically use a smartphone or another dedicated electronic device which should be carried by the user in combination with Bluetooth beacons like [9].

Unfortunately, all currently widely used orientation and navigation systems require the user to carry a special artifact or electronic device. We want to avoid that as our user group can often include people with mobility issues [13] or mental illness (approximately 20% of adults aged 60 and over suffer from a mental disorder) [11].

Analysis of related work shows that there is a lot of research dedicated to tactile symbols and alternative solutions. However, there is a lack of research focusing on tactile symbols for visually impaired older adults being a majority in the user group of visually impaired.

3   Design of Tactile Symbols

As the tactile symbols were designed in the context of an orientation system, we had to define the user requirements related to orientation and navigation at first. We cooperated with special housing for visually impaired older adults and gathered all requirements and recruited experiment participants there. Following the methodology of participatory design [14], we conducted a workshop with four employees of the special housing (two nurses and two social workers), 21 semi-structured interviews with residents, and numerous observations. From the requirements we can state four primary purposes of the system: spatial orientation, navigation to a known place, general information (about time, date, schedule and lunch menu) and emergency call for help. The proposed orientation system consists of three types of components (orientation terminals, guiding lines, and mini-info buttons). In this paper, we focus on the design of the tactile symbols of the orientation terminal.

The orientation terminal is a small box placed on the wall on the most strategic places in the building, like entry halls or next to elevators; it outputs all the information as natural language voice instructions. It serves as the central hub of interaction for the other parts of the system that relate to the information provided by an orientation terminal. It serves the following functions:

- Orientation – where I am, what's around me, where this direction leads.
- Navigation – how do I get back to safety (to my room).
- Information – what time is it, what's the date today, what's for lunch or dinner, what's the weather, what's today's schedule.
- Emergency – call for help.

Specifics of the target user audience create significant challenges for designing interactive devices. We decided to use buttons that will invoke the voice recordings (or TTS). The choice of buttons was made with three factors in mind. It is one of the simplest types of interaction, and it can be easily used by visually impaired as well as sighted individuals and everyone ever used a button at some point in their life (elevator, radio or television, etc.).

The previous research [10] showed that simplified or abstract tactile pictograms did not work for visually impaired older adults. The symbol representing a clock (circle with little and big hand), for instance, was recognized by one participant only. On the other hand, simple abstract symbols, like a triangle, were recognized by almost everybody, but without any notion what function it can represent. We started looking for a different tactile representation of corresponding terminal functions, that will be both easy to recognize and assign a corresponding function of an orientation terminal.

3.1   Design A - Mimic the Real World

We organized a design studio [2] with four employees of the special housing (two nurses and two social workers) and came out with an idea to focus on the objects from daily-life of clients they are used to from past period. We also decided to mimic the real world as much as possible during the design of the symbols. We created a lo-fi prototype of an orientation terminal with four squared panels corresponding to four functions of the terminal (see Fig. 1). On each panel, there was an object representing a function and a square button. We have picked the following four objects as symbols:

- Wristwatch – represents time-related information. The button provides information about current time and date, daily schedule and weather.
- A spoon – represents eating. The button provides information about lunch time and lunch menu.
- A key – represents going in/out of the room, walking. The button provides spatial information about the nearby surroundings and directions as well as navigation instructions back to a known place (their room).
- A whistle – represents loud noise, draw attention to yourself. The button provides a way to call for help.

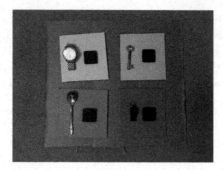

Fig. 1. Design A – lo-fi prototype introducing four panels with real-world symbols and buttons representing four functions of an orientation terminal.

Participants. We recruited six visually impaired older adults from the special housing (5 women, 1 man), mean age 87.7 ($MED = 86$, $MIN = 81$, $MAX = 98$, $SD = 5.8$), see Table 1. The recruitment and execution of all experiments were under the supervision of the special housing authorities.

Table 1. Table of participants for evaluation of design A, P5 is also P3 from evaluation of design C

Participant	Sex	Age	Impairment	Impairment duration
P1	F	90	Severe	5+
P2	M	86	Blind	70
P3	F	86	Severe	70
P4	F	85	Blind	8
P5 ($P3_C$)	F	81	Blind (light perception)	10
P6	F	98	Blind (light perception)	5+

Procedure. The low-fi prototype was introduced to the participants, and then they were asked to perform exploration. We encourage them to comment aloud their exploration. Then we asked them to inspect the explored objects and identify them. After that, participants were given a task to determine what information would be provided by the orientation terminal if they would press the button next to the corresponding object.

Results. All participant correctly identified all four objects. All of them also assigned wristwatch to information about time or schedule. All participants assigned the key to a movement; three assigned it to "getting back to room", three assigned it to "leaving a room" or "leaving a building". All participants assigned a spoon to food and drink, four of six assigned spoon to a lunch menu, two assigned the information to the time of the lunch. All participants assigned the whistle to a call for help action.

Conclusion. The real-life objects were identified without any error. Moreover, the assignment to a terminal function was except the navigation function unambiguous. This can be explained by overloading this option with more slightly different functions (what is nearby and way back to a room). Our suggestions were to split these functions into more objects on the orientation terminal.

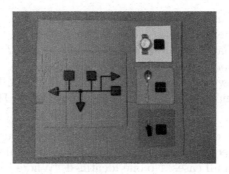

Fig. 2. Design B – lo-fi prototype introducing a tactile map replacing the panel with a key symbol.

Table 2. Table of participants for evaluation of design B, P4 is P5 from evaluation of design C

Participant	Age	Sex	Impairment	Impairment duration
P1	81	F	Blind (light perception)	13
P2	94	F	Severe	5
P3	81	F	Severe	23
P4 ($P5_C$)	70	M	Severe	10
P5	79	F	Blind (light perception)	1
P6	90	F	Severe	30
P7	86	F	Blind (light perception)	5

3.2 Design B - Adding a Tactile Map

According to results from the *Design A*, we focused on splitting "what is nearby" and "way back to room" functions. We have replaced the panel with a key symbol by a tactile map, which consisted of four symbols: square representing a room, triangle/arrow representing a continuation of a corridor, a line representing corridor, and a small dot representing the current position (see Fig. 2).

Participants. We recruited 7 visually impaired older adults (6 female) from the special housing, mean age 83 ($MED = 81, MIN = 70, MAX = 94, SD = 7, 9$).

Procedure. Participants were standing in a hall next to the elevator on the second floor in front of the lo-fi prototype of the terminal. They were asked to explore the terminal and describe aloud the parts of it. We used the Wizard of Oz technique to play corresponding voice information from a nearby tablet after pressing the buttons. After exploration, participants answered the following six questions one by one.

1. Can it tell you what time is it? How? Which button?
2. Can it tell you where you are? How? Which button?
3. Can it tell you what is for lunch? How? Which button?
4. Can it tell you what is around? How? Which button?
5. Can it tell you how to get to a room XY? How? Which button?
6. Can it tell you which direction the nearest staircase is? How? Which button?

Results. *P2* and *P7* did not recognize whistle, they thought it is a keychain. All participants correctly recognized all other objects. Questions 1 and 3 were answered correctly in all cases. No one identified "Where I am" button. *P1* and *P6* missed the tactile map part of the terminal. *P1*, *P2*, and *P6* did not realize it is a map. *P3* and *P7* though it is a side projection instead of a floor plan. *P5* did not explore the whole range of the tactile map, only near surroundings. *P4* answered that the hierarchy and connections are too confusing.

Conclusion. The real-world objects worked again almost perfectly, however, the tactile map did not work at all. It seems that the tactile map is too complicated and too abstract for our target group.

3.3 Design C - Replacing a Map with Tactile Cursor

Evaluation of the *Design B* showed that tactile map integrating more functions at once become too complicated and not understandable. We decided to introduce back the key symbol, but we reduced the functionality to "navigating back to the room" only. For the remaining functions "What is around me" and "Current position" we have introduced new artifact called tactile cursor. It consists of three triangle/arrow buttons and square button. The arrow buttons describe what is on the left/right-hand side and behind the participant. The square button describes the current location.

The whistle was changed for a metal one as these were more common during the time participants could encounter them during their life. The design of an orientation terminal now consisted of five color panels with corresponding symbols and buttons on it (see Fig. 3). All distances between objects on the panels were defined to ensure discovery of all object on a particular panel. The distances (button-to-symbol, or button-to-button) are set to a width of one finger.

Fig. 3. Design C – lo-fi prototype introducing a tactile cursor providing information about the surrounding and current location. The panel with key symbol served to navigate the user back to the room. Other three panel's function did not change.

To manifest clearly the borders between panels, the distance between objects and the edge of a panel and the distance between edges of two neighboring panels is set to the width of two fingers. All panels also have different colors to support recognition for people with residual sight.

Participants. We recruited 6 visually impaired older adults (4 female) from the special housing, mean age 79.5 ($MED = 86$, $MIN = 52$, $MAX = 93$, $SD = 15.8$).

Table 3. Table of participants for evaluation of design C, P3 is P5 from evaluation of design A, P5 is P4 from design B

Participant	Age	Sex	Impairment	Impairment duration
P1	90	F	Severe	20
P2	93	F	Blind	15
P3 ($P5_A$)	82	F	Blind (light perception)	10
P4	90	F	Moderate	2
P5 ($P4_B$)	70	M	Severe	10
P6	52	M	Blind	27

Procedure. Participants were standing in a hall next to the elevator on the second floor in front of the lo-fi prototype of the terminal. They were asked to explore the terminal a describe aloud the parts of the prototype. We used the Wizard of Oz technique to play corresponding voice information from a nearby tablet after pressing the buttons. Participants were asked to predict what function or information could the buttons serve. After the exploration, participants answered the following eight questions one by one.

1. Can it tell you what time is it? How? Which button?
2. Can it tell you where you are? How? Which button?
3. Can it tell you what's for lunch? How? Which button?

4. Can it tell you what's around? How? Which button?
5. Can it call you help? How? Which button?
6. Can it tell you how to get back to your room? How? Which button?
7. Can it tell you how to get to a room XY? How? Which button?
8. Can it tell you which direction is the nearest staircase? How? Which button?

Results. All objects on the panels were correctly identified. This also includes tactile cursor and its buttons. This panel was often described as a signpost or pointer. Exchanging the whistle for a metal one improved identification. All predictions of functions were correct except for *P5* who could not assign a key to any reasonable function. All participants correctly answered each of the eight questions. Every participant had a suggestion on modifications of the instructions and information given. Some requested enhanced information and more details; others suggested shortening the information.

Conclusion. Tactile cursor was correctly connected with the meaning of directions and movement by all participants. Real-world objects again proved to work as intended. Even the key object (back to my room) was experiencing correct predictions of purpose caused by narrowing down possible functions by the neighboring tactile cursor. Diversion in requests on information granularity and detail suggest further possible improvements by using different possible activations (single push, double push, long push) or usage of the contextual model and serving of personalized information (Table 3).

4   Discussion

The level of abstraction is the key to our design. As we observed, the more abstract is the interface, the less correct mental connections are made between the interface and expected functionality. The usage of real-world objects worked in its full capability exactly as intended as real-world objects are the lowest level of abstraction we could employ. It is also important how close and related are the objects to the intended functionality and interaction context. We observed that even minor details, like the material of the object, can play a key role. For example, the metal whistle worked better than the plastic one. As the metal whistle represented exactly the object visually impaired older adults had a chance to encounter in an earlier life period.

Overloading of a single symbol with too many functions and meanings leads to ambiguous expectations and thus less reliable functionality. It turned out that fine-tuning of minor details of the symbols can improve the functionality of the design. The next step is a series of experiments exploring which aspects are important. For example, if the wristwatch should have a leather or metal watchband. Should it produce a typical tick-tock sound or be tactfully readable. An interesting idea could be the usage of the main function of the symbols. The wristwatch could really show time and date, as well as the whistle, could be blown on to draw attention.

We also observed that various people with various mental capabilities and preferences require different information and even different level of detail and granularity of the information given. The terminal should then provide a way of identification of the user and user's needs and contextual adaptation of the provided information.

5   Conclusion and Future Work

We have conducted several iterations of participatory design and qualitative evaluation leading to a functioning interaction with orientation terminal. Usage of real-world objects and low level of symbol abstraction leads to an unambiguous pairing of user expectations and real functions with our user group of visually impaired older adults recruited from special housing.

According to our observation, future steps should be focused on improvements in audio feedback and especially contextual level of detail based on individual user's capabilities and cognitive load as users directly asked for this. In terms of both extremes, some users asked for more detail while others for less detailed audio feedback.

Acknowledgments. This research has been supported by the TACR research program TE01020415 and the project RCI (reg. no. CZ.02.1.01/0.0/0.0/16_019/0000765) supported by EU.

References

1. Amick, N.S., Corcoran, J.M., Hering, S., Nousanen, D.: Tactile graphics kit. Guidebook (2002)
2. Blevis, E., Lim, Y.-k., Stolterman, E., Wolf, T.V., Sato, K.: Supporting design studio culture in HCI. In: CHI'07 Extended Abstracts on Human Factors in Computing Systems, pp. 2821–2824. ACM (2007)
3. Bourne, R.R.A., et al.: Magnitude, temporal trends, and projections of the global prevalence of blindness and distance and near vision impairment: a systematic review and meta-analysis. Lancet Global Health **5**(9), e888–e897 (2017)
4. Ganz, A., Schafer, J., Gandhi, S., Puleo, E., Wilson, C., Robertson, M.: PERCEPT indoor navigation system for the blind and visually impaired: architecture and experimentation. Int. J. Telemed. Appl. **2012**, 19 (2012)
5. Goldreich, D., Kanics, I.M.: Tactile acuity is enhanced in blindness. J. Neurosci. **23**(8), 3439–3445 (2003)
6. Golledge, R.G.: Geography and the disabled: a survey with special reference to vision impaired and blind populations. Trans. Inst. Br. Geograph. **23**(8), 63–85 (1993)
7. Gual, J., Puyuelo, M., Lloveras, J.: The effect of volumetric (3D) tactile symbols within inclusive tactile maps. Appl. Ergon. **48**, 1–10 (2015)
8. Gual-Ortí, J., Puyuelo-Cazorla, M., Lloveras-Macia, J.: Improving tactile map usability through 3D printing techniques: an experiment with new tactile symbols. Cartogr. J. **52**(1), 51–57 (2015)

9. Zikitapp Ltd.: Right Hear - App for Visually Impaired & Blind People (2019). https://www.right-hear.com/
10. Macik, M., Gintner, V., Palivcova, D., Maly, I.: Tactile symbols for visually impaired older adults. In: 2018 9th IEEE International Conference on Cognitive Infocommunications CogInfoCom. IEEE (2018)
11. World Health Organization. Mental health of older adults, 12 December 2017. https://www.who.int/news-room/fact-sheets/detail/mental-health-of-older-adults
12. World Health Organization. International Classification of Diseases 11 - Vision impairment including blindness (2018). https://icd.who.int/browse11/l-m/en#/ http://id.who.int/icd/entity/1103667651
13. World Health Organization. Musculoskeletal conditions, 15 February 2018. https://www.who.int/news-room/fact-sheets/detail/musculoskeletal-conditions
14. Spinuzzi, C.: The methodology of participatory design. Tech. Commun. **52**(2), 163–174 (2005)
15. Wang, Z., Li, B., Hedgpeth, T., Haven, T.: Instant tactile-audio map: enabling access to digital maps for people with visual impairment. In: Proceedings of the 11th International ACM SIGACCESS Conference on Computers and Accessibility, pp. 43–50. ACM (2009)
16. Willis, S., Helal, S.: RFID information grid for blind navigation and wayfinding. In: ISWC 2005, pp. 34–37 (2005)

Co-Design and Design Methods

Able to Create, Able to (Self-)Improve: How an Inclusive Game Framework Fostered Self-Improvement Through Creation and Play in Alcohol and Drugs Rehabilitation

Franco Eusébio Garcia[✉][iD], Roberta Pereira Brandão,
Gabriel Cheban do Prado Mendes, and Vânia Paula de Almeida Neris[iD]

Departamento de Computação, Universidade Federal de São Carlos (UFSCar),
São Carlos, SP, Brazil
{franco.garcia,vania}@dc.ufscar.br

Abstract. We are working towards establishing a framework to enable more people to create and play digital games. Our focus is on skills, communication, and collaboration, since these qualities can enable more people to co-create inclusive games. In this paper, we describe how the framework assisted adults involved in an alcohol and drugs rehabilitation program to co-create their own games. Ten adults in a healthcare service co-created games using the framework as a part of their rehabilitation, in ten meetings spanning four months. Two healthcare professionals evaluated the activities. Five additional collaborators (three with a Computer Science and two with a Nursing background) provided accessibility features and artistic improvements to the projects. During the meetings, we observed that game creation and playing helped the participants. They started in an uncertain frame of mind, with low-self esteem, and were scared to use computers and games, since they doubted they could succeed. However, they ended up more confident on their abilities and proud of their creations, as they were able to share their games and knowledge with their peers, and teach people how to play. The models and systems of the framework allowed the people to achieve better results. The game co-creation empowered the participants, and, hence, their abilities became opportunities for further collaborations. Co-creation consisted of a journey in which self-improvement superseded the created games.

Keywords: End-user development · Game development ·
Game accessibility · Universal design · Meta-design ·
Human-centered computing

This study was financed in part by the Coordenação de Aperfeiçoamento de Pessoal de Nível Superior – Brasil (CAPES) – Finance Code 001 and FAPESP (# 2015/24523-8).

1   Introduction

In the same way that traditional literacy defined reading and writing skills as being essential for gathering knowledge and communicating, digital games are now encouraging educators to seek modern types of literacy [8,14,18,36,48]. In light of this, we should, ideally, allow everyone to create and play them. However, there are still a limited number of audiences for game creation strategies. For instance, a systematic review of Game Based Learning found that only 6 out of 494 studies (1.21%) took account of a public who were, at least, 23 years old, while 351 studies (71.05%) targeted children, youngsters, and teenagers [8]. The review also comments that inclusion tended to focus on *"game making as a strategy for addressing the underrepresentation of girls and women in computing"* [8].

Our analysis of academic studies that describes the end-user development of digital games obtained similar results. In particular, young Anglophone students (normally children and teenagers attending elementary and high schools in the United Stated of America; for instance, in [1,5–7,9,17,18,21,22,24,26,29,32,34–36,41,45,47,48,54,57]) seem to be most often the intended audience for the design and evaluation of game creation strategies. Modder (people who modify their favourite games) communities were the second most common audience (for instance, in [42,43,55]). Although older (the average age of the participants was 31 years old in [42]), modders grew up playing digital games. The term "average users" [11,38] describes users belonging to a group with a normal distribution of skills, but excluding, for instance, users with disabilities, a low level of literacy, or who are older. Thus, to the best of our knowledge, the usual audiences (average users) for game creation and modding are young people within a normal distribution of user abilities and interaction needs.

When investigating the potential barriers to game creation and playing (for instance, age, socioeconomic status, literacy, language, and (dis)abilities), audiences of potential creators can be found that have not yet been included. Game accessibility provides resources that can help developers to enable more people to play [3,10,13,15,20,59]. Although these studies are currently aimed at professional developers, another route for inclusion can be explored, by fostering inclusive co-creation as a means of enabling people with heterogeneous interaction needs to make their own games, by encouraging creation and use alike. This could benefit key areas such as education and healthcare. For instance, healthcare professionals can exploit these games as rehabilitation tools that can allow their patients to address their mental, physical, and behavioral condition [2,27,28,44]. Thus, by selecting suitable strategies, domain experts (such as healthcare professionals and educators) could explore game creation as well as playing the games themselves to assist their activities.

In an attempt to be more broadly inclusive, our framework has been defined to promote the inclusive co-creation of digital games. Our lemma is "games *by* everyone, *for* everyone". However, this lemma and our goals do not assume that everyone will be able to create and play every game. Rather, it means that we should always strive for inclusion: even if a system cannot become universal, it can always become more inclusive. The framework aims at extending modding to "accessibility modding", and, thus, allow people to add content as well as accessibility features to promote inclusion.

In this paper, we describe how our framework has helped participants who are currently digitally (and socially) marginalized to create and play digital games, by including their peers and becoming changed in the process. Some adults in an alcohol and drugs rehabilitation program in a public healthcare service (Psychosocial Care Center – Alcohol and Drugs; in Portuguese, Centro de Atenção Psicossocial – Álcool e Drogas (CAPS/AD)) used our framework as a support activity for their rehabilitation so that they could create and play their own games[1]. In the process, creation became a "sandbox", in which participants designed games for self-expression and to share their experiences and knowledge with others. Ultimately, the framework enabled them to create and play for a greater end, by providing participants with opportunities for self-expression, learning, and growth.

2   A Framework Towards Inclusive Game Co-creation

To achieve broader inclusion, there is a need to focus game creation on abilities, knowledge and skills, and provide opportunities for collaboration based on what people are able to do. In this way, people with heterogeneous interaction needs can start contributing, co-creating, and playing games. In particular, it should be noted that the interaction needs of the creators may be different from those of the players. Thus, inclusion should encompass creation (game making) *and* play (the resulting games).

We have defined a framework to enable people with heterogeneous abilities to work with communities, and co-create accessibility features for inclusive play. This involved overcoming barriers, by providing better communication, collaboration, and inclusion in a combined collective effort to cater for individual needs. These requirements were met based on three key pillars: (i) a flexible software architecture that allows use-time modification of human-computer interaction; (ii) a collaborative working model that can turn inclusion into a community problem (that is, it can be addressed by the collaboration of the community); (iii) tools to create the workflow. As proof of concept, these tools are, currently, accessible to a subset of interaction needs (traditional audiences, hearing disabilities, and a low rate of literacy) and a single genre (storytelling).

The architecture enables developers to implement games for adaptation, based on "semantics of use" rather than physical-level activities (what a player can do, instead of how she/he will do it). These adaptable systems were called tailorable games. Like tailors, we create and adjust the input and output (IO) interaction that can suit a player's ability to command and follow the game based

---

[1] As end-users (including people with disabilities and/or situations of vulnerability) took an active part in our study, we complied with research ethics protocols throughout the entire process. Certificado de Apresentação de Apreciação Ética from Plataforma Brasil: CAAE: 89477018.5.0000.5504.

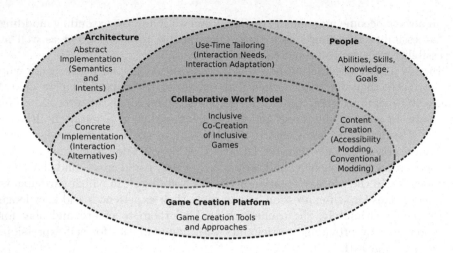

Fig. 1. The pillars of the framework supporting people.

on her/his interaction needs. Our use-time tailoring architecture allows an arbitrary re-definition of human-computer interaction at the time of use. It explores game entities and components (from Entity-Component Systems [16,33,40]), events and event handlers (from Event-Driven Architectures [16,33,40]), and data-driven architectures [16,33] so that interaction alternatives can be introduced to (or removed from) a game at run-time [12,13]. As a result, interaction becomes similar to plug-and-play add-ons for game accessibility. This approach lets developers address different interaction needs iteratively, one audience a time, to allow the creation and play.

With this architecture, a "one core fits most" version as well as multiple accessible game versions can co-exist in the same digital system. Developers can create interfaces to suit the needs of the widest range of people, as well as custom interfaces for specific interaction needs. The users can choose and combine alternatives to define their best way of interacting with the system. For instance, text, audio, video, and/or graphics can convey a given entity; controllers, assistive technologies, and/or automation can handle it. With this architecture, players can choose which features they want for their game and define the customized ways of playing, based on their own needs. Thus, access can be given to new audiences; a better experience of use, usability and interaction choices can be provided for those already included.

The collaborative working model makes use of the architecture for both game creation and modding, by providing a dynamic and iterative process to scaffold community-powered inclusion. We applied the communist slogan "*from each according to their abilities, to each according to their needs*" [30] to game creation: the architecture allowed people to add new content to a game, co-creating inclusion as a community. The community can improve inclusion (through accessibility modding), as well as content (through conventional modding).

In this way, the end-users can provide broader accessibility even if the original developers failed to do so. The members of the community can provide their own abilities, knowledge, and skills to create and improve the content of the game *and* provide accessibility features so that it can be played by new audiences. Thus, collaborative practices (such as modding, co-design [37,58] and co-creativity [23,51,52,60]) can be employed towards co-creation of inclusion and game content. As a result, the people who are included can further co-create and enable new people to play, by forming "cycles of inclusion" based on their abilities. Rather than being excluded, the people become "yet to be included". Once they have been included, they are potentially able to enable new audiences to co-create and play.

As the end-users are not, necessarily, programmers, tools are needed for inclusive end-user creation of tailorable games. As a proof of concept, we implemented Lepi for storytelling-based games. Lepi currently caters for traditional audiences, people with hearing disabilities (by providing graphics and text content for all kinds of media, and sign language support such as videos) and people with low literacy (by providing audio descriptions, large icons, and audio voice recordings).

Figure 1 outlines strategies explored in the framework to support people. The collaborative working model is the inner part of the figure, as it merges people, the architecture and the game creation platform into a system that can assist end-user game creation. The other parts cooperate in the co-creation of tailorable games. Interaction needs result from the architecture and people (for instance, disabilities) to provide interaction alternatives. The intersection between the architecture and the game creation platform abstract this task into slots for accessible content (for instance, audio-description, closed-captions, translations, alternative input devices, graphical, aural or haptic effects). Slots represent placeholders for interaction alternatives to convey an item of information. The intersection between people and the game creation platform represents how people create and implement the alternatives. Once someone creates an alternative, she/he can add the artifact into its slot (from drawings, voice recordings, text, sign language videos, or other media). In this way, the resulting game can combine features to produce accessible versions for different audiences of players.

3   Fostering Self-Improvement Through Game Creation and Play with Adults in Alcohol and Drugs Rehabilitation Programs

Ten meetings were held in the CAPS/AD, spanning a period of four months. These were concerned with end-user game creation and playing activities and how to evaluate and refine the framework. The service was designed to assist the rehabilitation of adults suffering from alcohol and drug addiction. Our meetings became an additional activity provided by the service with the aim of helping its users. They followed a similar pattern: (i) They started with a brief description of the planned activities. (ii) They completed a cycle of the collaborative working model, consisting of: (1) **Conception:** idealization of the project; (2) **Conversion:** first prototype of the game; (3) **Evaluation:** evaluation and guidance from the Supervisor; (4) **Creation:** development of the game; (5) **Enrichment:** improvement of the game's features and usability, inclusion of accessibility alternatives; (6) **Distribution:** assembling of playable games; (7) **Use:** play sessions with other participants; (8) **Conclusion:** end of the project. The working model set out "transient roles", which were defined on the basis of what the participants were carrying out at a given time. They could be Supervisors, Creators, Collaborators, and Players. In particular, the Collaborators could act as Enablers (for instance, by providing accessibility features to enable others to create and play), and/or Enhancers (for instance, by improving the quality of existing features and thus refine the game). (iii) They finished by discussing the activities and results with the healthcare professionals to obtain feedback and inform them about the next meeting.

In the first meeting, we set out our project to the users of the CAPS/AD, and invited them to participate. The recruitment and meetings were held at the healthcare service center as a biweekly activity, and each lasted two hours. We explained our goals (refining and evaluating the framework, and employing game creation as a support therapy) to users of the service and provided a schedule of planned activities per meeting. Interested users of the service took part of their own free will, without any incentives or rewards. Attendance was optional (both at the activity and for the service itself).

From the second meeting onwards, the participants only interacted with games and our game creation platform. As most participants had never used a computer before, the second and third meeting involved playing games to teach them how to use the mouse and keyboard: a game designed to teach basic mouse skills [56], and a therapeutic game designed for elderly people with depression [39], and a visual novel in Portuguese (Carcará, by Supernova Games) at the third meeting. The visual novels emphasized the storyline rather than the other technical features (such as mechanics), and the storytelling was closer to traditional media (for instance, books, movies, and soap operas). This allowed the participants to create content from the third meeting, with an incremental introduction of more complex strategies and game mechanics (by exploring "gentle slopes" [4, 46] even within non-programming activities – for instance, from linear stories to non-linear, branching stories).

From the fourth meeting onwards, the participants stopped making use of the existing games and started to create their own. They used Lepi, our game creation platform, and exploited the working model to create, share, and play their games. Each meeting introduced new features and added complexity to the development process. This continued until the last two meetings, during which our participants showed their games to other users of the service, who had never taken part in our activities.

3.1   Participants and Their Goals

Our team consisted of the authors of this paper and three additional support-ers (a MSc in Computer Science, and a undergraduate student and a PhD in Nursing). The supporters and two authors (undergraduate students in Computer Science) acted as Collaborators in the working model. Two CAPS/AD health-care professionals assisted and monitored the meetings; they were involved in the research as Supervisors. In the case of the professionals, the meetings provided an additional strategy for carrying out their responsibility of aiding the CAPS/AD's users. Finally, ten CAPS/AD users agreed to participate in our study (hereafter called participants). They were recovering from alcohol and drug abuse, receiv-ing non-compulsory support (for instance, guidance to stop use and avoid lapses) at the service center. The participants were not hospitalized and were not surro-gates. In the working model, they acted as Creators, Collaborators, and Players, depending on the different phases of the working model and activities that were carried out.

The participants were adults (29 or older) from a lower socioeconomic back-ground, with no programming experience, low literacy skills (ranging from not being able to read and write, to a primary level of literacy skills in Portuguese), and different computer skills (from never having used a computer before to being able to use office productivity suites). Emotionally-wise, they displayed a subset of features that are characteristic of young drug addicts described by Rodrigues et al. [49], such as: emotional vulnerability and insecurity, anxiety, low self-esteem and performance levels, internal and external pressures (their own, from colleagues, and from society), and a lack of self-confidence and hope. Unlike the young drug addicts however, they were not, for instance, aggressive, impulsive, and hyperactive. Owing to their cognitive and emotional condition, it was important to avoid situations that might lead to failure during their creative activities. Otherwise, the participants might assume they were unable to carry out activities, blame themselves (rather than the tools), and give up.

Figures 2 and 3 illustrate some participants and created games. Table 1 out-lines the motivations, needs, goals, and wishes of the participants and how the framework helped, goals, and wishes of the participants and how the framework helped to achieve them. It provides a summary of the following subsections. The features and strategies in the table summarize how each pillar of the framework helped the participants to create and play games.

3.2   Becoming Able to Create: Exploiting the Framework to Suit the Interaction Needs of the Participants

Overall, the participants wanted to have opportunities and succeed (Goal 1.1 in Table 1), and also to feel they were members of society, as they felt excluded from it ("*I hear in the streets: 'you can't do that, because you are an addict, you are this, you are that'; no, we are not like that, we can do it*"; "*I want to be able to do it*"; "*I can do it, I will be able to*"). Goal 1.1 became the ultimate goal of the study, which the framework had to support. The systems (Lepi and

(a) Participants meeting each other at a room in the service.

(b) Two participants meeting at a town square.

(c) Game to promote the health-care service. A person invites his friend to seek aid in the service.

(d) Scene resulting from seeking aid in the service, following Figure 2c.

Fig. 2. Examples of three games created by our participants using Lepi.

(a) P_2 creating his game.

(b) P_2 proud of his game.

(c) Participants creating their games.

(d) P_3 playing a game on which her image was not her.

(e) Supervisor helping a Creator.

(f) The Creator from Figure 3e decided to dictate his story.

Fig. 3. Participants creating and playing games over multiple meetings.

Table 1. Summary of how the framework supported the goals of the participants.

Goal	Participants needs/wishes	Pillar(s)	Framework features/strategies
1.1	Be able to succeed	A, M, L	Increase creation complexity over time (M, L); avoid creation errors (L)
1.2	Learn how to use computers	L	Prefer easier interactions (L)
1.3	Create the game	A, M, L	Provide alternatives for creation (A, M, L); promote external aid with Collaborators (M)
1.4	Help friends to play the game	A, M, L	Provide alternatives for use (A, L); promote creation of accessible content (M) and external aid (Collaborator) (M)
1.5	Understand what the game is presenting	A, M, L	Provide interaction alternatives (text, speech, sign) for play (A, L); promote creation of alternatives (M); explore aid for creation and play (M)
1.6	Be part (inside of) the game	M, L	Co-create image of participants (M); include images into game (L)
1.7	Be with friends in-game, in a common physic space	M, L	Co-create assets (M); inclusion of assets in game (L)
1.8	Show what was being learned in the service	M, L	Define game choices with different outcomes and scores (L); play and discuss games with domain experts (M)
1.9	Promote the healthcare service, removing negative stigmas	L	Co-create as marketing, game play as publicity (L)
1.10	Help players to develop character and values – especially kids	M, L	Co-create to teach (L); provide scores to provide feedback (L); play and discuss to learn (M)
1.11	Express ideas (share ideas in a different media)	M, L	Co-create for self-expression (L); supervision for evaluation (M)
1.12	Feel important, at least for a day	M, L	Co-create to self-express, demonstrate skills and knowledge, and demonstrate progress (L); validation from community use (M)
1.13	Learn with a game created by others	M, L	Play to experience creation from others, receive feedback from domain experts, and foster community discussion (M); scores to measure performance (L)
1.14	Understand what would happen after bad choices	M, L	Perceive outcomes from choices (L); receive advice, guidance, and support from main experts (M)
1.15	Share opinions, discuss similar experiences	M, L	Play to foster discussion (L); discuss with community and receive guidance from domain expert (healthcare professional) (M)
1.16	Share the game with friends (with different interaction needs)	A, M, L	Define interaction alternatives (M); include alternatives in project and export project as games with different accessibility features (A, L)
1.17	Share experiences and perceptions	M, L	Co-create to teach and self-express (L); share game to communicate with others (M)

Pillars: Architecture (A), Collaborative Work Model (M), Lepi (L)

architecture) had to suit the interaction needs of the audience for creation and play. The Creators, Supervisors, and Collaborators had to work together to co-create games (work model).

The process to achieve the Goal 1.1 was incremental, and set out by enabling creation. The participants needed basic computer skills for this (Goal 1.2). Among the participants, there were people who had never used computers or played digital games before. Some were scared, and afraid they would be unable to interact with the computer ("*I never thought I would be able to use the computer; I had seen others using it, but never thought I would"*); others did not have access to computers (*"you know, it is a very good experience, because children in school have computers, and I was never able to have one"*), nor could afford to do computing courses (*"I never thought I would do a computing course in my life"*). The participants made their first contact and were provided with basic training by playing games to practice basic mouse and keyboard skills at the second and the third meetings.

At the fourth meeting, there began the creation activities based on the framework (Goal 1.3). The architecture made it possible to implement multiple IO schemes and interactions to suit the needs of our participants. Lepi provided abstract commands for creation (for instance, for adding media and characters, and editing the dialogues), that allowed us to implement physical-level interactions (for instance, by adding media and characters with the mouse or keyboard; editing dialogues with a keyboard or voice recording). We were able to define custom bindings for any available feature in the platform, and for any input device we wanted to use. Likewise, Lepi supported interchangeable graphical (image and video), textual, and aural output to convey information.

As our intended audience had fine motor skills, the participants used the mouse and keyboard to provide input (Fig. 3d). The strategies to map abstract commands into the input devices varied in accordance with the interaction needs of the participants. For instance, although some participants could not read nor write, they were able to listen, speak, and draw. To overcome the writing barrier, we decided to provide editing alternatives in Lepi or exploit the working model for collaboration – in a similar way to the scaffolding practices which have been previously employed in technologically-enhanced learning environments [25,50,53]. This resulted in independent and assisted approaches for game creation. In the independent approach, a Creator carried out activities on her/his own. In the assisted approach, a Collaborator (acting as Enabler) helped the Creator to carry out her/his activities. The Collaborator acted as a form of human-powered assistive technology, by extending the Creator's abilities with her/his own to overcome interaction barriers (Fig. 3f). The Collaborator also acted as an interaction interpreter and/or mediator. For input, she/he translated commands from the Creator to the system. For output, she/he transformed content information from the System to the Creator.

By adopting content creation approaches, the participants could make a contribution that was based on their own abilities and skills. The strategies that involved producing a first prototype in The Conversion phase: (i) typing stories and exploring the visual programming language offered by Lepi. This was the strategy of choice for participants who had previous experience with computers and could write well. (ii) Creating low-fidelity prototypes with paper and pencil containing drawings, sketches, graph-based schemes, or comic books. These were strategies adopted by participants who preferred to communicate visually. The participants who could write annotated their illustrations. Those who could not write dictated the content to Collaborators. (iii) Creating low-fidelity prototypes via speaking, with voice recordings or transcription. The participants who did not like to draw or preferred speaking, followed this strategy. The collaborators transcribed the text for the participants who could not write.

After Conversion, the healthcare professionals (Supervisors) performed the Evaluation phase to analyze the projects. They advised the Creators on how best to proceed to achieve a successful rehabilitation. For instance, they asked questions to prompt reflections, requested descriptions of past experiences, provided alternative scenarios for thinking, and asked the Creators to explain the reasoning and rationale behind their story branches and their impact on the Player's score. Game-wise, the Creators responded to the content-related requests during the Creation phase. In the case of the most independent participants, the Conversion and Creation phases were similar; they used Lepi to create high-fidelity game prototypes. With regard to the assisted participants, the strategies employed for implementing a high-fidelity prototype varied according to their preferences. The Creators used the visual constructs of Lepi for characters, environments, scenes and story flows (transitions and branches), and decisions (choices and consequences). The Creators defined their stories by typing them, recording a voice-over narration, or asked a Collaborator to type it for them. To each according to their abilities.

After iterations of Creation and Evaluation phases, the participants played games with each other in the Distribution and Use phases. They could also play games created by the Collaborators (for instance, Collaborators with a nursing background created several games involving drug and alcohol usage in daily activities.), which showcased more Lepi features. Following this process during several meetings, some participants who had initially, adopted the assisted approach, started using Lepi on their own (in some cases, Collaborators transcribed narrations or dictated characters, to allow the Creators to type their stories). The participants who were initially given assistance the whole time, started becoming more independent (their games became longer, more complex, and relied on more features and resources provided by Lepi). Overall, the participants stated that they enjoyed the creative activities (*"creating is very good. It is the experience of my own life"*; *"it is, a new experience, a good experience"*); it was something that they looked forward to doing at the service (*"I don't mind missing the lunch, I want to create my game"*; *"I count the time when I can go to the workshop"*).

3.3   Making Creation Easier, Enhancing Play: An Accessible Platform for Creators, Accessible Games for Players

We tweaked Lepi every meeting with new features, improvements in accessibility and usability to cater interaction needs of the participants. The changes to improving accessibility and usability included the following: alternative color schemes (from darker to lighter); increased contrast; larger font sizes; typefaces with better readability; short and objective text instructions (whenever possible); large graphical icons; voice instructions. For input, we avoided difficult interactions (such as holding to drag), and offered large areas for selection. As people with drug addiction may have difficulty in concentrating [49], we also tried to provide automated input features whenever applicable (for instance, for audio scene playback) to avoid errors and minimize user input (by reducing the chance of mistakes). We tried to keep activities flowing continuously, by avoiding idle intervals, dispersion, and errors, to help concentration. The Supervisors and Collaborators were always present and the Creators could request assistance whenever needed.

The resulting games had to be accessible as well, because the Players' abilities could be different from those of the Creators. This was addressed with the architecture: it was possible to change IO interactions of the resulting games during the Distribution phase to suit the Players' needs in the Use phase. Default assets provided images, textual description, speech narrative, and sign language videos as output alternatives. With regard to content that was Creator-made, the participants had to define and include their own alternatives. With the aid of the working model, Creators and Collaborators could provide alternatives based on their abilities and skills. In the Enrichment phase of the working model, a Supervisor requests the Collaborators to refine the game assets and usability, or provide accessibility features and alternatives for use.

At the CAPS/AD, the Creators told their stories using text, speech, and drawings. In Lepi, the stories were often created as text; this meant that the participants who were unable to read, could not play unassisted (*"Can you read this for me?"*; *"What is she saying?"*). This was a concern for the participants in Goal 1.4 and Goal 1.5: the main requirement was to make independent play possible for the participants who could not read with the voice content. Between the meetings, the Collaborators acted as Enablers to record text into voice. After the content had been added to a project, the Players who were able to hear it, could play it. Although these were external contributions, Creators greatly appreciated being included, because it meant they improved their projects. Furthermore, it enhanced the playing experience, and also allowed their friends to play. Some participants noted that they could record their voices and include the recording in their future games to postpone the experience and enable their friends to play. As one of our Collaborators knew basic Língua Brasileira de Sinais (LIBRAS), some games offered sign language videos to enable people with hearing disabilities to play them. Although the participants did not need them, they thought that the videos were important.

Furthermore, in practice, following an assisted approach, a Collaborator can act as an Enabler during the Use phase to translate any content to those who cannot perceive it[2]. In particular, the roles in the working model are transient, and participants can make a contribution on the basis of their skills and abilities, as well as the context of use. Thus, whenever the activity occurs in a shared environment (such as this service or a classroom), a Creator can become a Collaborator and provide assistance. For example, a Supervisor requested that one Creator should read his story to help his friend who could not read (Fig. 3b). This Creator, thus, became a Collaborator (Enabler) at that point, since he

---

[2] In the case of motor disabilities, a Collaborator could also help a Player to play (for instance, with automation features or assistive technologies).

was able to assist his friend. He provided a skill (reading) that was necessary to overcome the accessibility barrier, by exploiting another ability that he possessed (speaking) and one that his friend had (listening). At other meetings, the participants who were acting as the Players employed this strategy during the Use phases whenever an audio transcription of the story had not yet been added to the project.

3.4   Being Part of the Game: Creators Within the Creation

In the first meeting, one participant (hereafter called P_1) wanted his *"game character to be inside the game"*; it *"should look like me and walk like me!"* (Goal 1.6). In response to the request, a Collaborator started designing a game model representing P_1, which became available at the fifth meeting. On one occasion, a friend (P_2) saw the model. He promptly (and happily) identified P_1 (*"Look, it is P_1!"*), and requested a character to represent himself as well. When he had both models, P_2 realized that he and his friends could become his stories' characters. He further requested the CAPS/AD as an environment (a place) (Goal 1.7), to share stories about users and the activities that were carried out in the service. P_2 also discovered that he could give a *"voice to my characters to help my friends to play my game"*.

Being in a "magic circle" can serve as a metaphor for game playing [19]. P_2 became a Creator of his own "magic circles". Other participants joined him, and requested their models as well (Fig. 2a). A healthcare professional and a participant co-created a game to promote the service (Goal 1.9): they described how it worked (by trying to demystify the public opinion about it), and explained that users were well received and benefited from it (Fig. 2c and d).

3.5   Self-Improvement Through Games: Self-expression Leading to Self-Knowledge

In the first meeting, we encouraged participants to create games based on their experiences with alcohol and drug abuse using fictitious characters. During the meetings, healthcare professionals suggested that the participants could explore any other themes that they wanted as well. In both cases, there were participants who decided to portray themselves in the stories, instead of fictitious characters, for self-expression (*"I will do this story for myself, because I want to live this moment, show that I can do it. I am able, because no one is born knowing"*). This became more apparent once they could include their own images and the environment of the service into their games. One healthcare professional stated that most of the participants' stories were (directly or indirectly) related to their own lives, regardless of the subject.

The participants who portrayed themselves in alcohol and drug related stories admitted their own addiction and abuse in their creations; they were honest about the facts (for instance, how they happened, what they had done, when something happened, and whom they were with). Moreover, the stories acted as a support for therapeutic practices. The Professionals could analyze them and help participants, by suggesting different ways of addressing situations (for example, other ways to act) from the decisions made in the stories. During the Evaluation phases, the healthcare professionals started broadening the scope of their advice, by suggesting that the Creators should consider alternative scenarios and ways of coping with a given situation. By analyzing their past experiences and reflecting on them, the participants could find other ways of acting in their original scenario, each of which could lead to different outcomes. This helped the participants "to think more about life". These kinds of reflections and lessons learned shaped their game stories. They started in a linear way, on the basis of their memories and then progressed to branching, based on the lessons learned.

The Supervisors defined attributes (health, social relationships, and work attributes) as part of the creative practices to reinforce this learning. In the case of the Players, the scores provided the means of tracking their progress during the play. The Creators made modifications based on their own judgement: good choices increased the number of attributes, while bad choices reduced them. With the aid of multiple choices, the Creators could compare prompts and outcomes to see how far they could affect their own lives. From the standpoint of the Creators, they provided another way of showing and applying what they were learning in the service, as well as sharing this knowledge with others ("*if you add what you are experiencing in the game, you can go much further than you think*"). This helped to materialize abstract ideas into concrete, quantifiable outcomes based on decisions and their results, with could foster reflection during the creation and play (Goal 1.8). The participants applied the knowledge provided by the professionals in practice, even if they were unaware of it.

The games were a self-expression of what the participants experienced (or imagined) and analyzed, expressed digitally as game features (Goal 1.11). Their prompts for decisions had consequences that they could foresee and judge according to the parameters. From the standpoint of Computer Science, the sole objective of the framework was creation and playing. However, when used for serious activities, the games became means rather than ends. More significant results can emerge from enabling participants to make something and collaborate. Like play [2, 31, 44], creation can have a therapeutic value in themselves, as, according to one participant, "*creation occupies the mind with fun. I avoid thinking bad things*". The participants could share values and teach others (Goal 1.10). Their games could help others ("*people will learn a lot from my game, they can start thinking that they can re-start their lives if they believe in it*"), and could also help themselves ("*creation helps to find paths, and weigh up the consequences of each*"; "*creating games is great for participation and learning*"). The Creators could "*recount experiences, learn good things, always move forward, and interact with friends*". Players could learn that "*in any path, there is always a better exit*".

3.6   Sharing Knowledge: Learning and Experiencing from Playing

In the working model, the Supervisor decides who can play a game, as well as defines available interaction features for the Players. The architecture combines these features to generate playable games that are compatible with a Player's abilities and skills. In the first meeting, P_1 mentioned that game creating and playing could be good for his own therapeutic treatment and also for that of others. In the third, P_1 realized that his game could heighten awareness of the effects of drugs and alcohol abuse: he could advise players to avoid abusive substances on the basis of his experience. He, thus, wished to share his game in schools, because, then, *"kids can play my game and learn from my mistakes"*. In future meetings, other participants reinforced this opinion (for instance, *"people can do what I did, see what I did, what I created (...) then the person can say 'I can change, it only depends on me, we can find a way to tackle everything'"*).

Initially, the participants were uncertain if they could create games; some of them had not even played digital games (or used a computer) before. During the meetings, they became more confident, skilled, and proud. In their games, the Creators expressed how they could overcome their doubts, insecurities, and fears. They could track how their games evolved and hence measure their progress: each new scene and added feature showed this evolving pattern. As well as what they achieved in their game, the participants also progressed therapeutically, owing to their service support (*"when I started, I wanted to learn many things, but I see that I have learned a lot already"*). The Players could also learn from the experiences of others (Goal 1.13). Games were a safe environment: the negative outcomes from bad choices provided feedback for learning (Goal 1.14). In the end, once the projects were completed, participants shared their games (Goal 1.16). They started teaching their peers how to play their own games, and took pride in it (Goal 1.12): *"knowing that someone will play my game is very good"*; *"it is great fun to show people my game; you keep thinking 'how is it possible to create a game and see your friends playing it?'"*.

Interactions between Creators and Players during the Use phase (such as playtesting) were helpful for the participants in three different ways. First, the Creators adopted a new attitude when showing their games to their Player peers (for instance, a participant who was initially scared to use the mouse taught a friend to use it when interacting with her game). Second, the Creators felt proud at seeing their games in use (*"seeing my friends playing, for me, is an honour, because I can share the game with them here to see that they care about me"*). Third, the games can serve as tools to assist Supervisors in their professional practices. For instance, a Supervisor requested that a Creator explained his rationale for assigning scores to his peers during the game. On the basis of his explanation, the Creator, Players and the Supervisor discussed the game (Goal 1.15) and shared similar experiences Goal 1.17. The Supervisor advised a large number of participants at the same time; the Creator reflected on his choices and showed what he had learned; and the Players received and provided assistance: learned from the Creator's game and from the Supervisor, and helped the Creator by describing similar real world situations that had happened to them.

3.7   The Way Games Can Transform Participants: Anecdotes

Previous sections can be illustrated by sharing the reactions of one participant (P_2) in a meeting, whose experiences motivated another (P_3) to further partic-ipate (Fig. 3a, b). In the Use phase, a Supervisor asked P_2 to explain his game to the public (Goal 1.11, Goal 1.15, Goal 1.17). As there were participants who could not read, she requested P_2 to read his story aloud (Goal 1.5). At first, P_2 was nervous and insecure about the value of his creation (*"I don't know..."*, *"I am not sure..."*). However, as he proceeded to read his story and answer questions, he became more confident. His attitude improved and he started to smile and laugh; at a certain point, his eyes started glowing. As a result of peer acceptance (Goal 1.12), he was proud and pleased with his creation, because it was successful (Goal 1.1; Fig. 3b). When the Collaborators showed the enhanced version of his game, P_2 became enthusiastic about the changes, as they improved its quality and allowed his friends to play the game without his help (Goal 1.3, Goal 1.5). The enhanced version enabled P_3 to play. She shared her experiences (Goal 1.17), providing her own insights and personal response to his story. P_2 and the Supervisor appreciated her insights (Goal 1.8, Goal 1.13). Her comments showed admiration and appreciation for P_2, who asked if he could present his game to the community in an upcoming soirée at the CAPS/AD. In the case of the Supervisor, it offered new information regarding P_3, which she could make use of to help the participant further.

After this experience, P_3 became motivated to create her own games in the following meetings (she had not participated in creation activities before). P_3 had never been to school, nor used computers; he was one of the participants who had been scared of using computers and touching a mouse. P_3 saw P_1's and P_2's models, and requested her own (Goal 1.6). As the meetings progressed, she started using a keyboard (Goal 1.2) to create her own game (Goal 1.3): she narrated her story to a Collaborator, who transcribed it, and, later, dictated the characters to P_3. Sometimes, she narrated her stories with her own voice (Goal 1.11). P_3 included herself, her friends, and the CAPS/AD's environment in her stories (Goal 1.7; Fig. 2a and b). As a Creator, she advised her friends how to make better decisions in her stories (Goal 1.10, Goal 1.17), in the same way that her Supervisor had advised herself (Goal 1.15). She wanted her children to be proud and motivated by her games (*"I want my kids to [play my game and] think, 'wait a second; my mother is making games, I can also do it'. It is very beautiful"*). As a Player, she always chose the best options when prompted to make decisions; she also played her own games several times (Goal 1.13, Goal 1.8). P_3 spoke about her games to her daughter, who could not believe her: *"my daughter thought I was lying when I told her I created a game"*. At a later meeting, when the healthcare professionals invited other users to play the games (Goal 1.16), P_3 started teaching others (including her boyfriend) to play her game (Goal 1.4). From being scared of using computers, she reached the point of teaching other people how to use them.

Finally, with her own character, P_3's model became an asset for creation (Fig. 3d). In P_3's stories, her model was always herself (*"I wanted to put myself in the game to show that I could do it, I can be there, I can be anywhere, I can think about what I should do, what I should not do"*). In stories from others, her model was someone else (with different names). Although it was her own image, it was not her. Whenever she saw her image, she asked: *"is this me?"* She was an actress. She felt important for a day (Goal 1.12). She (and other participants) had succeeded (Goal 1.1). Even though she had *"never imagined I would be able to do it"*, she found that she was able to do it, could further improve (*"you can create lots of things there to show people"*), and had opportunities for social inclusion (*"I had never had as many opportunities as this in my life"*). This feeling was shared by the other participants, *"I could never imagine something like that could come out of my head"*), as well as by a healthcare professional who stated the following: creation together with therapeutic activities *"enabled patients to have contact with technology, develop their cognitive skills and creativity, encourage game creation, [self-]identify with the activity, and provide opportunities to think about real or imaginary situations. This allowed them to learn behaviors to deal with daily situations of conflict [in real life], acquire self-esteem during [the act of] creation, and teach patients that they are responsible for their choices and [their] consequences"*.

4   Design Recommendations from Lessons Learned

The following design recommendations summarize the strategies described in Sect. 2 as being necessary to achieve Table 1's goals:

1. **Design for semantics of use.** If semantics of use are designed, we do not assume any abilities are required for use, and, thus, people are not excluded by design.
2. **Implement for modification.** We can re-shape human-computer interaction at-use time to enable people to perceive, understand and command digital games according to their needs and abilities.
3. **Provide different ways to create and play.** Digital inclusion does not have to imply "one-size fits all solutions"; rather, a game may have the same rules, but can be played differently (for instance, there are multiple accessible versions in one game).
4. **Compose interaction.** We can provide interaction alternatives and (re-)combine them to define custom user interfaces that can enable interaction. We can group alternatives into profiles aimed at particular interaction needs (for instance, for visual or hearing or motor disabilities) – or allow people to define their own.
5. **Focus on abilities and skills.** People can always make a contribution on the basis of their own strengths (abilities, skills, knowledge, interests, experience). Therefore, one important goal for co-creation is to identify and provide opportunities for people to make contributions.
6. **Foster community inclusion.** Accessibility to inclusion can be an iterative process, based on abilities.

7. **Consider inclusion as a dynamic process.** Once people are included and able to create, they can enable more people to use the system and/or create. In particular, people with disabilities can become contributors once they have been included.

8. **Foster community collaboration.** People can teach, learn and benefit from each other's strengths, and understand how they can achieve more as a community, than individually. This workflow benefits both the sharer and receiver: they may feel empowered, important and valued, as well as creating bonds with each other. In serious contexts, domain experts can further benefit from communal collaboration and discussions and, thus, provide advice, guidance, and feedback to their participants.

5   Concluding Remarks

Although there are a number of approaches that can enable people to create their own digital games, their intended audience is, currently, narrow; enabling people to play and create are important stages in achieving digital and social inclusion. In this paper, we have examined our experiences in establishing a framework that can enable more people to create and play digital games. Co-creation was supported by a framework for game accessibility moving towards accessibility modding. By combining an architecture, a collaborative working model, and a game creation platform that could suit the interaction needs of the participants, the framework enabled participants to co-create games. The architecture allowed us to build creation tools and games able to modify IO interactions arbitrarily, at use-time. With the aid of the model, we were able to guide end-users to create games collaboratively, with the prospect of learning from (non-computing) domain experts in the process. The game creation platform helped the participants to create and share their own games.

In this study, it was found that the framework promoted inclusive game creation for an initial audience. We have explored inclusive game co-creation in an attempt to support therapeutic practices (that involve assisted self-improvement) by adults with low levels of literacy in a drug and alcohol abuse rehabilitation program. The outcomes from several workshops were analyzed to demonstrate how the framework supported the participants' self-improvement. It was found that game co-creation promoted self-expression and self-improvement. The participants took part in creative projects to teach and share what they knew, received guidance and support from healthcare professionals, and played games so that they could gain experience and learn from others.

Instead of an end in itself, game creation became a journey, in which the participants acquired and shared knowledge and skills, while crafting a game in the process. They learned and showed that they were capable of improving themselves, by creating, sharing and teaching. If they had any doubts, the Supervisors were there to support them. The game was the artifact, their way of expression, and their gift to others. It started from acceptance, believing in oneself and that one would be able to do it. Next, in working towards this end, iterating to improving the creation, and continuously observing the progress made towards its completion. Thus, what the Creators achieved was self-improvement, more self-confidence and hope, and the recognition that they are able to do whatever they put an effort into, even if it seemed impossible at first.

Establishing a framework is a step towards enabling more people to create and play digital games. We are currently working with new audiences (for instance, people with visual and motor disabilities as creators and players with text-to-speech and voice input for simple commands) and mechanics, as well as setting out new goals (for instance, digital co-creation as therapy).

References

1. Ahmadi, N., Jazayeri, M.: Analyzing the learning process in online educational game design: a case study. In: Proceedings of the Australian Software Engineering Conference, ASWEC, pp. 84–93 (2014). https://doi.org/10.1109/ASWEC.2014.34
2. Atilla, T.: Video games in psychotherapy. Rev. Gen. Psychol. **14**(2), 141–146 (2010). https://doi.org/10.1037/a0019439
3. Barlet, M.C., Spohn, S.D.: Includification: a practical guide to game accessibility (2012)
4. Basawapatna, A.R., Repenning, A., Koh, K.H., Savignano, M.: The consume - create spectrum: balancing convenience and computational thinking in stem learning. In: Proceedings of the 45th ACM Technical Symposium on Computer Science Education, SIGCSE 2014, pp. 659–664. ACM, New York (2014). https://doi.org/10.1145/2538862.2538950
5. Berland, M., Martin, T., Benton, T., Petrick, C.: Programming on the move: design lessons from IPRO. In: Conference on Human Factors in Computing Systems - Proceedings, pp. 2149–2154 (2011). https://doi.org/10.1145/1979742.1979932
6. Carbonaro, M., et al.: Interactive story authoring: a viable form of creative expression for the classroom. Comput. Educ. **51**(2), 687–707 (2008). https://doi.org/10.1016/j.compedu.2007.07.007
7. Denner, J., Werner, L., Ortiz, E.: Computer games created by middle school girls: can they be used to measure understanding of computer science concepts? Comput. Educ. **58**(1), 240–249 (2012). https://doi.org/10.1016/j.compedu.2011.08.006
8. Earp, J.: Game making for learning: a systematic review of the research literature. In: Proceedings of 8th International Conference of Education, Research and Innovation, ICERI2015, pp. 6426–6435. IATED Academy, Seville (2015)
9. El-Nasr, M.S., Smith, B.K.: Learning through game modding. Comput. Entertain. **4**, 1 (2006). https://doi.org/10.1145/1111293.1111301
10. Ellis, B., et al.: Game accessibility guidelines: a straightforward reference for inclusive game design (2013). http://www.gameaccessibilityguidelines.com/
11. Fischer, G.: User modeling in human-computer interaction. User Model. User-Adap. Inter. **11**(1–2), 65–86 (2001). https://doi.org/10.1023/A:1011145532042
12. Garcia, F.E.: Um Motor para Jogos Digitais Universais. Universidade Federal de São Carlos, São Carlos, Dissertação (2014)
13. Garcia, F.E., de Almeida Neris, V.P.: A data-driven entity-component approach to develop universally accessible games. In: Stephanidis, C., Antona, M. (eds.) UAHCI 2014. LNCS, vol. 8514, pp. 537–548. Springer, Cham (2014). https://doi.org/10.1007/978-3-319-07440-5_49

14. Gee, E.R., Tran, K.M.: Video game making and modding. In: Guzzetti, B., Lesley, M. (eds.) Handbook of Research on the Societal Impact of Digital Media, pp. 238–267. Information Science Reference, Hershey (2015)
15. Grammenos, D., Savidis, A., Stephanidis, C.: Unified design of universally accessible games. In: Stephanidis, C. (ed.) UAHCI 2007. LNCS, vol. 4556, pp. 607–616. Springer, Heidelberg (2007). https://doi.org/10.1007/978-3-540-73283-9_67
16. Gregory, J.: Game Engine Architecture, Second Edition, 2nd edn. A K Peters/CRC Press, Boca Raton (2014)
17. Hayes, E.: Game content creation and IT proficiency: an exploratory study. Comput. Educ. **51**(1), 97–108 (2008). https://doi.org/10.1016/j.compedu.2007.04.002
18. Hayes, E., Gee, J.: No selling the genie lamp: a game literacy practice in the sims. E-Learning **7**(1), 67–78 (2010). https://doi.org/10.2304/elea.2010.7.1.67
19. Huizinga, J.: Homo Ludens: A Study of the Play-Element in Culture. Angelico Press, Kettering (2016)
20. International Game Developers Association: Accessibility in Games: Motivations and Approaches. Technical report, International Game Developers Association, June 2004
21. Ioannidou, A., Repenning, A., Webb, D.C.: AgentCubes: incremental 3D end-user development. J. Vis. Lang. Comput. **20**(4), 236–251 (2009). https://doi.org/10.1016/j.jvlc.2009.04.001
22. Jazayeri, M., Ahmadi, N.: End-user programming of web-native interactive applications. In: Proceedings of the 12th International Conference on Computer Systems and Technologies, CompSysTech 2011, pp. 11–16. ACM, New York (2011). https://doi.org/10.1145/2023607.2023610
23. Kantosalo, A., Toivonen, H.: Modes for creative human-computer collaboration: alternating and task-divided co-creativity. In: Proceedings of the Seventh International Conference on Computational Creativity, pp. 77–84 (2016)
24. Kauhanen, M., Biddle, R.: Cognitive dimensions of a game scripting tool. In: Proceedings of the 2007 Conference on Future Play, Future Play 2007, pp. 97–104. ACM, New York (2007). https://doi.org/10.1145/1328202.1328220
25. Ke, F.: Designing and integrating purposeful learning in game play: a systematic review. Educ. Technol. Res. Dev. **64**(2), 219–244 (2016). https://doi.org/10.1007/s11423-015-9418-1
26. Keser, H., Ozcinar, Z., Kanbul, S., Webb, D.C.: Troubleshooting assessment: an authentic problem solving activity for it education. Procedia Soc. Behav. Sci. **9**, 903–907 (2010). https://doi.org/10.1016/j.sbspro.2010.12.256
27. Kharrazi, H., Faiola, A., Defazio, J.: Healthcare game design: behavioral modeling of serious gaming design for children with chronic diseases. In: Jacko, J.A. (ed.) HCI 2009. LNCS, vol. 5613, pp. 335–344. Springer, Heidelberg (2009). https://doi.org/10.1007/978-3-642-02583-9_37
28. Kharrazi, H., Lu, A.S., Gharghabi, F., Coleman, W.: A scoping review of health game research: past, present, and future. Games Health J. **1**(2), 153–164 (2012). https://doi.org/10.1089/g4h.2012.0011
29. Lin, H.Z.S., Chiou, G.F.: Modding commercial game for physics learning: a preliminary study. In: 2010 Third IEEE International Conference on Digital Game and Intelligent Toy Enhanced Learning (DIGITEL), pp. 225–227, April 2010. https://doi.org/10.1109/DIGITEL.2010.41
30. Liu, P., Ding, X., Gu, N.: "Helping Others Makes Me Happy": social interaction and integration of people with disabilities. In: Proceedings of the 19th ACM Conference on Computer-Supported Cooperative Work & Social Computing, CSCW 2016, pp. 1596–1608. ACM, New York (2016). https://doi.org/10.1145/2818048.2819998

31. Mader, S., Natkin, S., Levieux, G.: How to analyse therapeutic games: the player/game/therapy model. In: Herrlich, M., Malaka, R., Masuch, M. (eds.) ICEC 2012. LNCS, vol. 7522, pp. 193–206. Springer, Heidelberg (2012). https://doi.org/10.1007/978-3-642-33542-6_17

32. McArthur, V., Teather, R.J.: Serious mods: a case for modding in serious games pedagogy. In: 2015 IEEE Games Entertainment Media Conference (GEM), pp. 1–4, October 2015. https://doi.org/10.1109/GEM.2015.7377224

33. McShaffry, M.L., Graham, D.: Game Coding Complete, Fourth Edition. Course Technology PTR, 4 edn., March 2012

34. Morais, D., Gomes, T., Peres, F.: Desenvolvimento De Jogos Educacionais pelo Usuário Final: Uma Abordagem Além do Design Participativo. In: Proceedings of the 11th Brazilian Symposium on Human Factors in Computing Systems, IHC 2012, pp. 161–164. Brazilian Computer Society, Porto Alegre (2012)

35. Mota, M.P., Faria, L.S., de Souza, C.S.: Documentation comes to life in computational thinking acquisition with agentsheets. In: Proceedings of the 11th Brazilian Symposium on Human Factors in Computing Systems, IHC 2012, pp. 151–160. Brazilian Computer Society, Porto Alegre (2012)

36. Moumoutzis, N., Christoulakis, M., Pitsiladis, A., Sifakis, G., Maragkoudakis, G., Christodoulakis, S.: The ALICE experience: a learning framework to promote gaming literacy for educators and its refinement. In: 2014 International Conference on Interactive Mobile Communication Technologies and Learning (IMCL), pp. 257–261, November 2014. https://doi.org/10.1109/IMCTL.2014.7011143

37. Mouws, K., Bleumers, L.: Co-creating games with children: a case study. Int. J. Gaming Comput.-Mediated Simul. 7(3), 22–43 (2015). https://doi.org/10.4018/IJGCMS.2015070102

38. Ncris, V.P.d.A.: Estudo e Proposta de um Framework para o Design de Interfaces de Usuário Ajustáveis. Tese (Doutorado), Universidade de Campinas, Campinas (2010)

39. Nishikawa, D., et al.: Se cuidar, cuidar de algo, se divertir e aprender fazem bem! Demonstração de um jogo para apoiar o tratamento da depressão. In: Anais Do XV Simpósio Brasileiro Sobre Fatores Humanos Em Sistemas Computacionais, São Paulo (2016)

40. Nystrom, R.: Game Programming Patterns, 1st edn. Genever Benning, Carrollton (2014)

41. Petre, M., Blackwell, A.F.: Children as unwitting end-user programmers. In: IEEE Symposium on Visual Languages and Human-Centric Computing (VL/HCC 2007), pp. 239–242, September 2007. https://doi.org/10.1109/VLHCC.2007.52

42. Poor, N.: Computer game modders' motivations and sense of community: a mixed-methods approach. New Media Soc. 16(8), 1249–1267 (2014). https://doi.org/10.1177/1461444813504266

43. Postigo, H.: Video game appropriation through modifications: attitudes concerning intellectual property among modders and fans. Convergence 14(1), 59–74 (2008). https://doi.org/10.1177/1354856507084419

44. Preschl, B., Wagner, B., Forstmeier, S., Maercker, A.: E-health interventions for depression, anxiety disorders, dementia and other disorders in older adults: a review. J. CyberTherapy Rehabil. 3(4), 371–385 (2011)

45. Rea, D.J., Igarashi, T., Young, J.E.: PaintBoard: prototyping interactive character behaviors by digitally painting storyboards. In: Proceedings of the Second International Conference on Human-Agent Interaction, HAI 2014, pp. 315–322. ACM, New York (2014). https://doi.org/10.1145/2658861.2658886

46. Repenning, A., Basawapatna, A., Klymkowsky, M.: Making educational games that work in the classroom: a new approach for integrating STEM simulations. In: IEEE Consumer Electronics Society's International Games Innovations Conference, IGIC, pp. 228–235 (2013). https://doi.org/10.1109/IGIC.2013.6659151
47. Repenning, A.: Conversational programming: exploring interactive program analysis. In: Proceedings of the 2013 ACM International Symposium on New Ideas, New Paradigms, and Reflections on Programming & Software, pp. 63–74. Onward! 2013. ACM, New York (2013). https://doi.org/10.1145/2509578.2509591
48. Robertson, J.: Making games in the classroom: benefits and gender concerns. Comput. Educ. **59**(2), 385–398 (2012). https://doi.org/10.1016/j.compedu.2011.12.020
49. Rodrigues, K., Garcia, F.E., Bocanegra, L., Gonçalves, V., Carvalho, V., Neris, V.P.d.A.: Personas-driven design for mental health therapeutic applications. SBC J. Interact. Syst. **6**(1), 18–34 (2015)
50. Romero, M., Ouellet, H.: Scaffolding digital game design activities grouping older adults, younger adults and teens. In: Zhou, J., Salvendy, G. (eds.) ITAP 2016. LNCS, vol. 9754, pp. 74–81. Springer, Cham (2016). https://doi.org/10.1007/978-3-319-39943-0_8
51. Sawyer, R.K., DeZutter, S.: Distributed creativity: how collective creations emerge from collaboration. Psychol. Aesthetics Creativity Arts **3**(2), 81 (2009)
52. Schmoelz, A.: Enabling co-creativity through digital storytelling in education. Thinking Skills Creativity **28**, 1–13 (2018). https://doi.org/10.1016/j.tsc.2018.02.002
53. Sharma, P., Hannafin, M.J.: Scaffolding in technology-enhanced learning environments. Interact. Learn. Environ. **15**(1), 27–46 (2007). https://doi.org/10.1080/10494820600996972
54. Smith, D.C., Cypher, A., Tesler, L.: Novice programming comes of age. In: Lieberman, H. (ed.) Your Wish Is My Command, Interactive Technologies, pp. 7–19. Morgan Kaufmann, San Francisco (2001)
55. Sotamaa, O.: When the game is not enough: motivations and practices among computer game modding culture. Games Cult. **5**(3), 239–255 (2010). https://doi.org/10.1177/1555412009359765
56. de Souza, P.M., Silva, M.A.P., Proença, F.R.: Mouseando - Jogo Educacional Computacional que Auxilia no Aprendizado e no Uso Correto do Mouse. In: de Oliveira Borges, V., Proença, F.R., de Castro Borges, A., Ferreira, E.A., Godinho, R.F. (eds.) Aplicações de Tecnologias de Informação e Comunicação No Processo de Ensino Aprendizagem, vol. 1, pp. 108–124, Limeira (2018)
57. Uzunboylu, H., Baytak, A., Land, S.M.: A case study of educational game design by kids and for kids. Procedia Soc. Behav. Sci. **2**(2), 5242–5246 (2010). https://doi.org/10.1016/j.sbspro.2010.03.853
58. Walsh, G., Donahue, C., Pease, Z.: Inclusive co-design within a three-dimensional game environment. In: Proceedings of the 15th International Conference on Interaction Design and Children, IDC 2016, pp. 1–10. ACM, New York (2016). https://doi.org/10.1145/2930674.2930721
59. Yuan, B., Folmer, E., Harris, F.: Game accessibility: a survey. Univ. Access Inf. Soc. **10**(1), 81–100 (2011). https://doi.org/10.1007/s10209-010-0189-5
60. Zeilig, H., West, J., van der Byl Williams, M.: Co-creativity: possibilities for using the arts with people with a dementia. Qual. Ageing Older Adults **19**(2), 135–145 (2018). https://doi.org/10.1108/QAOA-02-2018-0008

Cinévoqué: Design of a Passively Responsive Framework for Seamless Evolution of Experiences in Immersive Live-Action Movies

Jayesh S. Pillai[1]([⊠]), Amarnath Murugan[2], and Amal Dev[3]

[1] IDC School of Design, IIT Bombay, Mumbai, India
jay@iitb.ac.in
[2] Next Tech Lab, SRM Institute of Science and Technology, Chennai, India
[3] Design Discipline, IIITDM Jabalpur, Khamaria, India

Abstract. In this paper, we present a passively responsive framework for immersive movies, called Cinévoqué. The framework seamlessly alters the narrative and visual elements within an immersive live-action movie, based on real-time passive data, such as gaze direction and system time, obtained during the experience. The paper primarily focuses on the design and storytelling aspects of Cinévoqué, such as possible narrative structures and the design challenges involved in creating responsive experiences. We further examine the potential of this framework through two prototypes of varying complexity and responsive features, and the insights from them are used to suggest approaches that can lead to effective seamless narrative experiences.

Keywords: Virtual reality · VR storytelling · Responsive narrative · Presence

1 Introduction

Traditional non-immersive movies guide the viewers through the story by displaying events within a fixed rectangular frame determined by the filmmaker, thereby making them focus on the intended points-of-interest (POIs). In contrast, within an *immersive movie*, experienced in Virtual Reality, the viewers (users) are completely surrounded by the environment of the narrative. Due to its nature of pushing the user beyond being merely an observer, it gives them complete freedom to change the point-of-view (POV) throughout the experience. Immersive movies being relatively new and less explored than frame-bound movies, the storytelling and filmmaking techniques are still evolving [1, 2]. Studies on the grammar of VR cinema point towards the potential of new storytelling opportunities [3]. The idea of a responsive narrative that we explore here stems from the very basic properties of an immersive movie experience.

Electronic supplementary material The online version of this chapter (https://doi.org/10.1007/ 978-3-030-29381-9_22) contains supplementary material, which is available to authorized users.

D. Lamas et al. (Eds.): INTERACT 2019, LNCS 11746, pp. 359–367, 2019.
https://doi.org/10.1007/978-3-030-29381-9_22

In this study, we present a novel framework based on the concept of seamlessly evolving narratives in live-action immersive movies, that we call Cinévoqué. The term Cinévoqué is derived from Cinema Évoqué (evoked cinema) to represent a form of responsive narrative that evolves based on the user's passive interactions, such as changes in POIs throughout the experience. Although our study explores storytelling as well as technical challenges in creating a Cinévoqué experience, in this paper, we focus mainly on the storytelling aspects, i.e. narrative structures and approaches. In a spectrum of immersive experiences arranged in the order of their interactivity, ranging from a 360° immersive movie to a high-end VR experience (Fig. 1), we believe that a Cinévoqué experience falls between an immersive movie and an interactive immersive movie experience which allows the user to make conscious choices about the progression of the story.

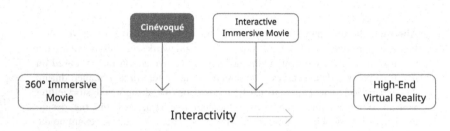

Fig. 1. Interactivity spectrum

2   Background

Within an immersive movie, the users' ability to choose their own POV makes it difficult to ensure that they look at the important events in the experience and are following the story consistently. VR filmmakers and researchers have tried to address this problem through visual & auditory cues [3, 4] and through specific editing techniques. For instance, the intended POIs across consecutive scenes are aligned to be in the same viewing direction so that the users are more likely to not miss them [5]. Though these approaches may be effective in directing the attention of the majority of users, it may still not guarantee that all of the users would follow the intended POIs consistently. Another drawback of these techniques is that they become less effective when there are large number of POIs within a scene [6].

Some techniques try to force the user to look in a specific direction by limiting the information in the other locations within the immersive space, or by displaying UI elements within the scene that point to the intended direction. However, sometimes these techniques were observed to cause discomfort to the users [7, 8]. Cinévoqué takes a different approach by using real-time data such as the user's gaze direction, to seamlessly adapt the experience to the user. It dynamically modifies the narrative and other elements within the environment based on the POIs the user has focused on.

2.1   Responsive Narratives

The Cinévoqué experience is conceptualized as a narrative that dynamically responds to passive interactions from the user, unbeknownst to them, as opposed to actively interactive movies that allow the users to make conscious choices about the progression of the narrative [9]. Thus to the user, a Cinévoqué experience would seem to be the same as watching a normal VR movie.

The concept of seamlessly switching storylines based on passively collected data has been explored in traditional movies through the use of eye tracking to measure the user's interest to alter the narrative [10], or by using data from sensors that measure bio-signals of the viewers [11, 12]. Creating a responsive narrative within traditional movies require specialized hardware on top of the system running the experience. In contrast, all immersive VR experiences implicitly generate the core data used by Cinévoqué, which makes it relatively more accessible to end users.

Researchers have previously proposed the application of a passively responsive narrative approach to live-action VR movies [3] and some have explored the idea in parallel to a limited extent [13]. Cinévoqué explores a similar direction while investigating the fundamental design and development challenges that exist in such a system.

3   Cinévoqué

Similar to interactive movies, the narrative structure of a Cinévoqué experience would also have a branched construct, that allows for multiple possible storylines. The storylines within Cinévoqué are structured as directed graphs i.e. the overall story is divided into smaller segments which point to one or more segments. This structure is broadly composed of *Levels* and *Nodes* which contain certain condition-based entities called *Hotspots* that influence the evolution of the storylines.

3.1   Narrative Structure - Levels and Nodes

A node is a segment/snippet of the larger possible experience and a level is a collection of multiple nodes which are alternate possibilities at the same point of the story. The story always begins from a *start level* and concludes on a *terminal level*. If the start level contains multiple nodes, one node is chosen based on data collected prior to the beginning of the experience or at random.

Figure 2 shows the structure of a simple Cinévoqué experience, here L1 is the start level, followed by the terminal level L2. Each node is denoted by the nomenclature *L (level number)N(node number)*. The lines diverging from a node lead to the possible nodes that it can transition to. Each node has a predetermined default *transition time* and *transition duration* associated with it. When the node reaches the default transition time it transitions to a node in the succeeding level over the given transition time. The transition to a particular node would primarily be influenced by the user's interest in certain events or objects within the immersive environment. These events/objects are associated with Hotspots.

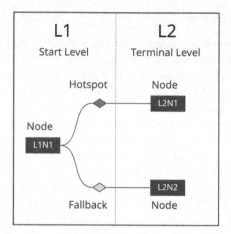

Fig. 2. Levels and nodes in a basic narrative structure

3.2   Hotspots

A hotspot is a region (predefined or dynamically marked) within the immersive environment of a node that has a set of conditions, that when met (triggered), helps the system make changes to the user's experience dynamically. A hotspot could exist throughout a node or for a specific duration depending on the event/object it's associated with. Each hotspot can lead to one or more target nodes, of which one would be played after the current node if that particular hotspot is triggered. The target node of the hotspot could exist in any level, so the storyline could skip levels or go back if required. If multiple target nodes are given, one final target is chosen based on the conditions set by the storyteller or at random (if the narrative requires it). A hotspot could also be used to alter the dynamic elements within its own node or in the nodes that follow. A node may contain one or more hotspots that influence the experience. In Fig. 2, the experience would start from the node L1N1 and would conclude at L2N1 if the hotspot leading to it is triggered. If none of the hotspots in a node are triggered, the experience would transition to a predetermined node called *fallback node*. In Fig. 2, the node L2N2 is the fallback. Cinévoqué consists of multiple types of hotspots that operate primarily based on the user's POV and gaze. In an experience where gaze-time is used to derive the user's interest, the hotspots could be broadly classified as *timer-based* and *immediate*. If other factors are used to derive user's interest (such as heart rate, skin conductance, Brain-Computer Interface, etc.), the classification of the hotspots would vary accordingly.

A *timer-based hotspot* measures the number of seconds it has been gazed at. If a node were to contain multiple timer-based hotspots, then the next node would usually be the target node of the hotspot which was gazed at the most. The hotspots can also be assigned different priorities within a node if a certain storyline is to be given more importance. Hotspots with a specific gaze-time threshold could have the ability to override the conditions met by other hotspots with equal or lower priorities. In this case, the transition to the next node always starts at the predetermined transition start time.

An *immediate hotspot*, as the name implies, would immediately decide the next node, thereby overriding all the other hotspots. In this case, the transition to the next node can start either immediately or after a certain amount of time specified by the storyteller.

4 Prototypes

The framework which was developed in the game engine Unity3D was utilized to create two prototypes in order to test our concept and investigate storytelling possibilities. These prototypes were deployed in both mobile VR and HTC Vive to be experienced by the users.

4.1 Schrödinger's Vada-Pav

Schrödinger's Vada-Pav is the first prototype that was built using Cinévoqué. In this experience, the user is introduced into the first person view of a character (Schrödinger) working in an office, and a waiter walks in and takes an order (a vada-pav) from him. After some time, the waiter returns with the vada-pav and knocks on the office door, noticing that the character is busy. From this point, there are two possible outcomes to this narrative. If the user gazes at the waiter within a certain amount of seconds after the knock, he would walk in and place the vada-pav near the character. If the user were to concentrate on something else, the waiter would leave without delivering the vada-pav.

Fig. 3. (a) Equirectangular frame with an active hotspot (grey region), the region of user's POV (within green outline) and corresponding user's view (right) in *Schrödinger's Vada-Pav*. (b) Hotspot detected (yellow region) within the POV and corresponding user's view (right) (Color figure online)

This experience is composed of two levels L1 & L2 (Fig. 2), where L1 has one node (L1N1) which shows the waiter taking the order and returning with the vada-pav. An immediate hotspot (Fig. 3) that corresponds to the waiter's position within the immersive environment is activated after the knock. If the user were to gaze on it (Fig. 3b), the node would transition to L2N2, which shows him walking in and placing the vada-pav near the character. In case the user doesn't gaze at the hotspot (as seen in Fig. 3a), the experience would transition to L2N1, which shows the waiter leaving with the order. This prototype also has a virtual body on a chair, that rotates to correspond to the user's physical body (as seen in Fig. 3a and b). This approach could provide a relatively better sense of embodiment while reducing the discomfort caused by placing a fixed virtual body [7].

4.2   Shapeshifter

Shapeshifter is a relatively complex Cinévoqué prototype. The narrative has three levels, seven nodes and four hotspots in total. The story immerses the user into the first-person perspective of a character stuck in an office along with two coworkers during an invasion by a shape-shifting alien race. The experience starts at L1N1 (Fig. 4) with the user's character and the coworkers watching the news. As the coworkers react to the news, two timer-based hotspots corresponding to each of them are activated. If the user gazes at Coworker-1 the most, the narrative transitions to L2N1 and if they focus on Coworker-2 more, node L2N2 would follow. L2N2 was assigned also as the fallback node, in case none of these two hotspots were gazed at.

Node L2N1 shows both coworkers arguing about leaving the building to seek help. For a small time frame, part of Coworker-2's hand changes colour subtly. During this phase, an immediate hotspot corresponding to Coworker-2 is activated. If the user gazes on this hotspot, the narrative would transition to L3N1 and reveal Coworker-2 as an alien. If the user doesn't gaze at the hotspot, the movie would conclude at N3L2 with Coworker-1 being exposed as an alien.

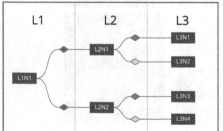

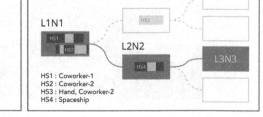

Fig. 4. Narrative structure of *Shapeshifter*   **Fig. 5.** Example   narrative   sequence   in *Shapeshifter*

In node L2N2, a similar argument takes place. At the same time, a spaceship whizzes past the window near the user, thereby activating an immediate hotspot associated with it. If the user gazes at the hotspot, the narrative would transition to L3N3 and conclude the movie by showing an alien entering the room. If the user focuses elsewhere, it concludes at L3N4 by revealing the user's character as the alien.

Shapeshifter also explored the possibility of varying the genre of the experience across storylines. The tone of Nodes L3N3 and L3N4 is light and if they were to be seen by the user, the interactions between the characters would point towards a sci-fi comedy genre. On the other hand, if the user's experience concludes at L3N1 or L3N2 the genre of the movie would be more of a sci-fi thriller.

The progression of a possible narrative sequence in *Shapeshifter* is shown in Fig. 5. In this case, the rectangular nodes denote the progression of time as we move from left to right. The small rectangles within the nodes show the timeframe within which a hotspot is active. The yellow highlights in the hotspot timeframe indicate the duration for which the user has gazed at the hotspot. In this example sequence, the user has gazed at both hotspots in L1N1, but since the second hotspot was gazed at the most, the narrative transitions to L2N2. At L2N2, as the user has gazed at the immediate hotspot, the narrative concludes at L3N3.

5 Discussion

Shooting live-action immersive narratives that dynamically alter itself imposes new challenges on top of the existing issues that plague production for cinematic VR [14]. In general, care must be taken to ensure that all the objects within the environment aren't altered between successive scenes captured in the same location. Since the user has more visual information that can be observed in an immersive environment, they are more likely to notice any inconsistencies in spatial continuity between consecutive scenes. In a Cinévoqué experience, when multiple nodes across consecutive levels are required to depict the same environment, each node in the succeeding level must start out with an environment that looks exactly the same as that of the preceding node. Achieving such a consistency over all the possibilities becomes increasingly difficult based on the number of succeeding nodes, especially if one of these nodes require changes in existing objects/camera position or if it introduces/removes objects in the surroundings. *Schrödinger's Vada-Pav* and *Shapeshifter* brought these issues to light and provided crucial insights on the ways to address them. These prototypes were also helpful in developing the different storytelling approaches that can be implemented in Cinévoqué and the constraints imposed by each of them.

5.1 Insights from Prototypes

When capturing a narrative for a Cinévoqué experience, the nodes with the same predecessor must be captured in the order of least to most disruptive to the immersive environment i.e. if a particular node requires more changes in the position/orientation of multiple objects or if it adds/removes objects in the environment, it must be captured after its alternative nodes. To further ensure that the environment remains consistent between multiple nodes, some parts of the environment could be replaced with static images or looped videos during post-production similar to approaches in traditional films. It is also advisable to keep the number of objects that are subject to change and in close proximity to the user's POV as low as possible.

In immersive experiences, ambisonic (spatial) audio also helps in directing the user's attention to the necessary event/object [4]. If the nodes were to contain non-ambisonic audio, the audio cues could be spatialized by converting them to an ambisonic format. The transitions between nodes could also be made more seamless by having a global ambient sound that spans across multiple nodes, as the difference in audio would be less noticeable during the transition.

Apart from the storyline, Cinévoqué could also alter other components within the experience, using the data provided by the user before the experience or real-time data. One of the primary uses of this idea is to dynamically recenter the orientation of a new scene or the title and credits. This ensures that the user looks at the intended information within the immersive environment. Another application of this concept is the addition of a virtual body on a chair that rotates with respect to the user's orientation, as shown in *Schrödinger's Vada-Pav* (Fig. 3a and b).

5.2   Storytelling Approaches

Some of the fundamental approaches of storytelling derived from our prototypes, that could define a narrative structure and the story universe, are as follows:

1. *One story - multiple order*: the narrative structure contains a single node in each level, but the order in which the levels are traversed is determined by the framework. Here different interpretations would be derived by the users based on the order in which the nodes are presented to them.
2. *Unique story - same story-universe*: a user would experience one unique storyline (which is complete in itself) that exists within the same story-universe as other experiences; Each story may or may not be connected to storylines of other users.
3. *Partial story - same story-universe*: based on the POIs gazed at, a user would experience only a part of a larger story within the same story-universe. Each user's experience would be closely connected to experiences of other users, and post-experience discussions among the users will lead to a better closure of the story.
4. *Same premise - parallel story-universes*: although starting with a similar premise each user experiences a unique story, that may exist across parallel universes.

6   Conclusion

Depending on the story content, the branched narrative structures may be diverging, converging or even have circular storylines. One may also create genre-defying narrative structures with the possibilities of each narrative sequence leading to a unique genre of experience. Ultimately it is the storyteller's creativity that will contribute to an effective narrative structure, but these insights could help them create a perfectly seamless experience. For the users, we believe that through the features of Cinévoqué we could maintain coherent storylines more effectively than regular immersive movies, thus giving them further freedom to explore the narrative environment as the story evolves and adapts to them.

References

1. Brillhart, J.: The Language of VR: Concepts and Ideas. https://medium.com/the-language-of-vr. Accessed 05 Apr 2019
2. Alger, M.: Visual Design Methods for Virtual Reality. http://mikealger.com/professional. Accessed 07 Apr 2019
3. Pillai, J.S., Ismail, A., Charles, H.P.: Grammar of VR storytelling: visual cues. In: Proceedings of the Virtual Reality International Conference-Laval Virtual 2017, p. 7. ACM (2017)
4. Bender, S.: Headset attentional synchrony: tracking the gaze of viewers watching narrative virtual reality. Media Pract. Educ. 1–20 (2018)
5. Brillhart, J.: In the Blink of a Mind - Attention. The Language of VR. https://medium.com/the-language-of-vr/in-the-blink-of-a-mind-attention-1fdff60fa045. Accessed 05 Apr 2019
6. Brillhart, J.: In the Blink of a Mind - Engagement. The Language of VR. https://medium.com/the-language-of-vr/in-the-blink-of-a-mind-engagement-part-1-eda16ee3c0d8. Accessed 05 Apr 2019
7. Nielsen, L.T., et al.: Missing the point: an exploration of how to guide users' attention during cinematic virtual reality. In: Proceedings of the 22nd ACM Conference on Virtual Reality Software and Technology, pp. 229–232. ACM (2016)
8. Fearghail, Colm O., Ozcinar, C., Knorr, S., Smolic, A.: Director's cut - analysis of aspects of interactive storytelling for VR films. In: Rouse, R., Koenitz, H., Haahr, M. (eds.) ICIDS 2018. LNCS, vol. 11318, pp. 308–322. Springer, Cham (2018). https://doi.org/10.1007/978-3-030-04028-4_34
9. Rouse, R., Dionisio, M.: Looking Forward, Looking Back: Interactive Digital Storytelling and Hybrid Art Approaches, pp 93–108 (2018)
10. Vesterby, T., Voss, J.C., Hansen, J.P., Glenstrup, A.J., Hansen, D.W., Rudolph, M.: Gaze-guided viewing of interactive movies. Dig. Creativity 16(04), 193–204 (2005)
11. Kirke, A., et al.: Unconsciously interactive Films in a cinema environment—a demonstrative case study. Dig. Creativity 29(2–3), 165–181 (2018)
12. Tikka, P., Vuori, R., Kaipainen, M.: Narrative logic of enactive cinema: Obsession. Dig. Creativity 17(4), 205–212 (2006)
13. Rico Garcia, O.D., Tag, B., Ohta, N., Sugiura, K.: Seamless multithread films in virtual reality. In: Proceedings of the Eleventh International Conference on Tangible, Embedded, and Embodied Interaction, pp. 641–646. ACM (2017)
14. The Cinematic VR Field Guide, Jaunt Studios. https://www.jauntvr.com/cdn/uploads/jaunt-vr-field-guide.pdf. Accessed 07 Apr 2019

P(L)AY ATTENTION! Co-designing for and with Children with Attention Deficit Hyperactivity Disorder (ADHD)

Gyöngyi Fekete and Andrés Lucero[✉] (iD)

Aalto University, Helsinki, Finland
gyongyi.fekete.mail@gmail.com, lucero@acm.org

Abstract. In recent years, children's mental health problems, including Attention Deficit Hyperactivity Disorder (ADHD), have been a growing phenomenon. However, there are limited examples of designing for and with children with ADHD. This work views conditions such as ADHD through the lens of neurodiversity as different cognitive styles, focusing on "*cool*abilities" and enhanced competences instead of *dis*abilities. This paper explores how to engage children with ADHD in co-design activities. Taking the Diversity for Design (D4D) framework as a starting point, an adaptation of the framework for ADHD was first driven by theoretical considerations and three expert interviews, followed by an empirical study consisting of three co-design workshops with four male participants (aged 7–10). Based on observations and audio recordings from the co-design workshops, a qualitative analysis was carried out. Our results show that when their needs, preferences, and individual desires are taken into account, children with ADHD can be meaningfully engaged in co-design activities. By offering an adapted version of the D4D framework tailored for ADHD, designers can structure the environment and provide scaffolds so that children with ADHD can become active participants in co-design workshops. This research informs the design community on how to engage and involve children with ADHD into the design process.

Keywords: Co-design · Children · ADHD · Diversity for Design · D4D

1 Introduction and Related Work

Children's mental health, as well as social and emotional well-being are a growing concern in today's society. The number of individuals requiring diagnosis and treatment is expected to rise in the near future. Besides anxiety and depression, numerous young people are affected by Attention Deficit Hyperactivity Disorder (ADHD), approximately 7–10% of the global population [10]. ADHD in children is often treated with psychostimulants, which has been proven to reduce playfulness [24]. Play improves self-control and attention, while reducing the symptoms of hyperactivity, therefore research suggests that it could be applied as prevention in some cases of ADHD [27].

© IFIP International Federation for Information Processing 2019
Published by Springer Nature Switzerland AG 2019
D. Lamas et al. (Eds.): INTERACT 2019, LNCS 11746, pp. 368–386, 2019.
https://doi.org/10.1007/978-3-030-29381-9_23

Prior studies have noted the importance of looking at different cognitive styles from a critical perspective, through the lens of neurodiversity [2]. Accordingly, this study focuses on "*cool*abilities" [13] and enhanced competences instead of *dis*abilities. While many studies have focused on involving children with Autism Spectrum Disorder (ASD) in the design process, there are limited examples of designing for and with children with Attention Deficit Hyperactivity Disorder (ADHD) [5].

The advantages technology can bring in the context of neurodiversity are broadly recognized by the Child-Computer Interaction (CCI) community [5]. A growing number of projects focus on involving children with special needs into the design process through participatory design activities, with different levels of involvement [11,14]. Previous studies have explored the possibilities to include children, also with special needs and conditions, into the design process. One of the most influential scholars in designing with children is Allison Druin, who identified four levels of involvement regarding the role of children in designing technology [8]. To involve children with special needs in designing technology, Guha and colleagues created a three-layer-model [14]. Still, these researchers mainly focus on how to conquer difficulties in involving children into the design process. More recently, attention has focused on the shift of viewing disability from another perspective, and adapting the neurodiversity mindset. Dalton [7] proposes the development of new design methods for participatory design in the context of neurodiversity. In their systematic literature review, Börjesson and colleagues [5] present three examples of involving children with ADD/ADHD in the technology design process [1,12,29]; all addressing matters that individuals with ADHD have difficulties with, and varying in the level of user involvement. While children with Autism Spectrum Disorder have been frequently involved in the design process, little attention has been paid to children with ADHD [5].

Participatory design can be defined as the practice of *collective creativity* between participants. The designer acts as facilitator, and supports participants in idea generation and other activities by supplying different tools for expression [25]. Co-design (or collaborative design) [26] is rooted in participatory design (PD). It usually describes an activity where target users are engaged in contributing and creating their ideas in different design situations. As a result, novel solutions can be created together, not only with adults, but with children as well, based on the knowledge-sharing and experiences of the participants [28]. Personas can be used in the design process, for instance in envisioning fictional use-cases [6]. Co-created personas have been tested with participants with diverse needs, and have been found to be an empowering and effective way to generally engage people in participation [23].

This paper explores how to engage children with ADHD in co-design activities. Building on previous research regarding the Diversity for Design Framework (D4D) framework [3], this study attempts to apply and further develop a framework of methods in theory and practice in the context of ADHD through an empirical case study. Co-design workshops were organized to develop tools and methods for engaging children in meaningful participation in co-design.

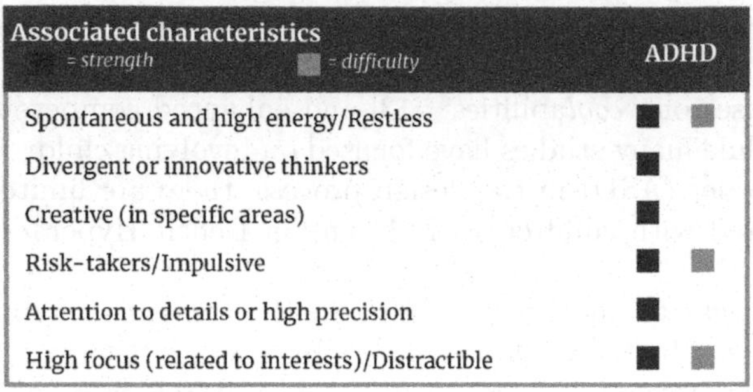

Associated characteristics	ADHD
■ = strength ■ = difficulty	
Spontaneous and high energy/Restless	■ ■
Divergent or innovative thinkers	■
Creative (in specific areas)	■
Risk-takers/Impulsive	■ ■
Attention to details or high precision	■
High focus (related to interests)/Distractible	■ ■

Fig. 1. Characteristic strengths and difficulties related to ADHD [3].

The outcomes of the workshops were used to provide the basis for adapting and extending the D4D framework to ADHD. The updated framework can be used to design digital services (apps) or toys that take the needs of children with ADHD into account and support their development. Such apps or toys could further be used for therapeutic purposes.

2   Background

2.1   ADHD and Creativity

A large amount of research is focused on disabilities and the negative effects of being diagnosed with ADHD. However, from a designer's point of view, the perspective needs to be shifted into looking at strengths when involving people with ADHD in design activities. Neurodiversity attempts to change how conditions are perceived by suggesting that they establish alternative cognitive processing styles appearing along a broad spectrum. The term Neurodiversity indicates several neurological conditions, such as Autism Spectrum Disorder, ADHD, dyslexia, anxiety, and intellectual disabilities, among others [2]. Grundwag [13] proposed the term "coolability" instead of "disability" regarding enhanced abilities and competences. An overview of characteristic strengths and difficulties related to ADHD can be found on Fig. 1.

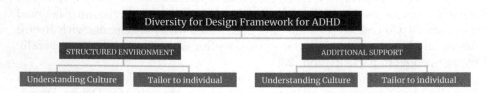

Fig. 2. The Diversity for Design (D4D) framework by Benton et al. [3]

Many children with ADHD have difficulties to sit still for extended periods of time, following rules, and consequently are sometimes unable to perform well in a traditional school system. Certain characteristics that modern society believes to be disabilities (such as impulsivity and distractibility) in fact provide a high degree of adaptability; this was extremely useful for our hunter-gatherer ancestors, and eventually led to forming a unique DNA cluster, the so-called Edison gene. Thom Hartmann describes this gene in his book The Edison gene: ADHD and the gift of the hunter child [16]. He portrays Thomas Edison - the inventor of the phonograph and many other things - as an easily distractible person. Edison had many projects proceeding at the same time, and would work on one until new inspiration struck or until he got bored. This means that a distractible person can be flexible, which is a key in innovation [17]. People with ADHD can move on quickly from negativity if the setting or activity changes. They are also very adaptive, and tend to get forgetful and disorganized in everyday situations. Consequently, they must learn how to solve particular problems creatively, becoming damage control experts (as Mahamane reported in his TEDx talk, in 2015). If they can control their attention by concentrating on what is interesting to them, they can be productive in their careers, for example in creative or other fields [9], such as the well-known chef Jamie Oliver.

2.2 The Diversity for Design Framework (D4D)

The Diversity for Design (D4D) framework was established by Benton et al. [3] with the objective of discussing challenges and strategies for facilitating participatory design activities with neurodiverse children. In the context of neurodiversity, the whole construction of the activities and the design environment becomes even more relevant due to their influence on how creativity is manifested. Therefore, in the D4D framework, the focus is both on the structured environment and on activities supporting strengths, while difficulties are balanced out 'structuring the environment and providing support' (Fig. 2). The general characteristics of neurodiverse conditions should be considered, in addition to the abilities and talents of individuals participating in the workshops: 'understanding culture and tailoring to the individual'. Even though the two case studies presented in Benton's article were based on Autism Spectrum Disorder (ASD) and dyslexia, it discussed characteristics of ADHD, and the framework was proposed to be applied to and further expanded to ADHD. The D4D is intentionally named a framework instead of a strict method - it is intended to be applied as a flexible set of tools that enables neurodiverse populations in meaningful participation.

Two additional approaches were taken into consideration in the case study, namely Universal Design for Learning (UDL) approach and growth mindset [21]. These theories are both looking at strengths and difficulties from the lens of neurodiversity, and therefore their perspective is in line with the D4D Framework. The three principles of UDL are established on giving multiple ways of engagement, representation, action and expression to provide an optimal learning experience that builds on flexibility and choices. Children with ADHD are reported to have lower self-esteem than average [15]. Looking at everyday setbacks as challenges that can create opportunities for building skills that help overcome difficulties; adopting and training a growth mindset can empower children with attention issues, and develop their resilience [21].

3   Methods and Data Collection

The D4D Framework is adapted to ADHD in two steps. First, a theory- and expert-informed version is established based on insights from literature, and two expert interviews (Fig. 3). One of the interviewees is the chief pediatrician at ADHD Ambulance at Bethesda Hospital in Budapest, with 20 years of experience. The other interviewee is a clinical child psychologist, general neuropsychologist, and relaxation therapist with more than 10 years of experience. Based on the two expert interviews, further elements were added in the adapted D4D framework, so as to refine strategies to support participation in follow-up workshops.

Second, a practice-informed version is developed by testing the framework during three co-design workshops (Fig. 9). Three experts (i.e., two psychologists and a social worker) helped plan and provided feedback on the first workshop program draft. Next, three facilitators with diverse background (i.e., design, psychology, and social care) conducted the co-design sessions. The latter had experience in mentoring children with ADHD, and had ADHD himself. Before the workshops, the facilitators discussed the background of the study, and the workshops were rehearsed in advance.

After the workshops, the final step was to qualitatively analyze the observations and audio recordings. To further develop the practice-informed D4D, the three facilitators reflected on the design practice and the observed behaviors of the children, and comparatively analyzed features of the theory-informed version based on what was anticipated regarding engagement during the three workshops.

4   Adapting the D4D Framework to ADHD

While the theoretical foundations have been laid to include neurodiverse population in the D4D Framework, there has been a lack of practical guidelines for involving children with ADHD in co-design activities. Therefore, we explored how the D4D framework could be adapted to children with ADHD. The first step was to search the literature and look for characteristics of ADHD; these helped in identifying the basis of the theoretically-inspired methods of the framework. Since some typical characteristics overlap for different neurological conditions [20], some of the features can be transferred from Benton's two case studies. On Fig. 3, these features are annotated with the letters "A" from the ASD, and "D" from the Dyslexia case studies [3]. Furthermore, insights from expert-interviews are marked with the letter "E", while features confirmed from the UDL approach are annotated with the letter "U". Features were added as boxes in the four categories, on how to tailor activities to the individual, and how to structure the environment to encourage participation.

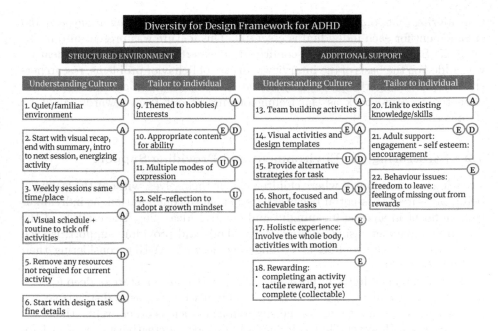

Fig. 3. The theory- and expert-informed version of the Diversity for Design (D4D) framework adapted for ADHD. Features on how to tailor activities to the individual and how to structure the environment to encourage participation were added as boxes, and labeled: "A" for ASD, "D" for Dyslexia, "E" for expert-interviews, and "U" for the UDL approach.

4.1 Tailor to Individual

The D4D framework highlights the need for tailoring design activities to individuals, considering their skills and competences [3]. To execute this, a questionnaire should be sent out to parents before the first of three co-design workshops. Questions should be aimed at understanding children's *hobbies and interests*, as they might be engaged more, and could possibly reach a deeper focus regarding these particular topics. The findings from the survey should then be used in motivating children in different activities, for example through embedding them in a story that is relevant for a particular child. Furthermore, strengths and potential difficulties should be assessed through the questionnaire to provide *appropriate content for ability*, to help reduce the risk of failure for the children. This feature was confirmed by the two experts as well. In addition, the feature *multiple modes of expression* from the Dyslexia study is in accordance with the findings from the UDL approach. Participants are encouraged to select from different methods that fit their personal interest, to express themselves. Various tools are available for them as long as they are completing the session goals [21].

When providing support for each individual, Benton proposes in the ASD study that children's *existing knowledge* could be integrated into the composition of the design activities [3], which might be possible after the first workshop.

Considering that some children also have low self-esteem [15], *adult support*, and engagement for each individual is essential. This feature was present also in the Dyslexia Study [3], while it was confirmed by experts too. An additional feature was added on the basis of the interviews: in case of behavior problems, researchers should offer the participant the *freedom to leave*. In most cases, children are expected to come back as the feeling of missing out from rewards might be stronger.

4.2   Structuring the Environment and Providing Support

Creating an environment where children can be themselves, without the feeling of being pressured, is essential because it can enhance collaboration, as individuals feel confident in sharing meaningful and creative ideas [25]. The crafting of the design environment, using appropriate methods and providing support, is even more critical in the context of (young) people with ADHD, considering their easy distractibility.

Focusing on children's interest, helping them to reach a state of deep focus is important to augment their creativity. Children who are easily distractible will pay attention to other things in the environment, such as other events, thoughts, or experiences. However, that is in fact a key aspect of creativity as well. It happens for example when mixing ideas together from different areas, that are not related to each other at first glance [17]. Furthermore, materials and tasks are also intended to invite and encourage participants in idea generation and exploration [19]. Hence, *removing any resources not required for the current activity* is suggested, similarly to the Dyslexia case study. Based on the findings of the ASD case study, at the beginning of each session, the structure and agenda are explained with a *visual schedule*, and the session is finished with a *visual summary and introduction to the next session* [3]. Building on children's strong visual skills, *visual design templates* are adopted, where, for instance, text is supported with pictograms. This feature was also supported by the expert interviews.

Adult support is also important: when children get distracted, the facilitator might intervene and provide inspiration. Similar to the Dyslexia Study [3], *short and well-structured tasks* were needed, because the attention-span of children with ADHD is shorter than average. Usually no longer than 10–15 min for each task, as it was suggested in the interviews. In addition, energizing activities that involve the *whole body in motion* are advised, to provide a holistic experience.

Rewarding is essential for children with ADHD. Research shows that the constant need for rewards has a biological background in their brain, causing deficits in their motivational system [15]. In one of the expert interviews, it was suggested to spark the interest of the children with a *tangible reward that is not yet complete* that they can take home, such as an individual personal workshop diary. The diary would be a place where rewards (such as stickers) could be collected when tasks are completed.

Building on the UDL approach presented earlier, the methods for the workshops were further improved and clarified. At the end of each session, guiding questions aid self-reflection: in realizing the participant's own strengths and challenges, reflecting on their own strategies for each activity to adopt the basics of growth mindset [21], and increasing the motivation for participation. In addition, it was suggested by one of the experts to support texts visually with small icons or pictograms for each question, as some children are stronger in visual skills than reading plain text. The first version of the theory- and expert- informed D4D Framework inspired the next research phase, namely the co-design workshops.

5   Co-design Workshops

To investigate how children with ADHD can be engaged in co-design activities, a series of three workshops was conducted in Budapest, Hungary during three consecutive weeks in May 2018. Rather than producing refined artifacts, the main purpose of these workshops was to create an environment where children with ADHD could try different methods and tools in a co-design context.

5.1   Participants

Four children (all male, aged 7–10) were recruited from a local Montessori primary school. The Montessori educational approach [22] supports children in self-initiated discovery, and learning through interaction with the constructed environment, rather than following direct instructions. All participants had received a diagnosis of ADHD, except for one who was under assessment for ADHD and dyslexia as a co-morbidity. Written consent was obtained both from the school's principal and the children's parents, who were otherwise not involved in the co-design sessions. Although we see potential benefits in involving other stakeholders in co-design (e.g., parents and other school staff), we decided it was important to build trust and engage with children first, and make sure they would not act differently in the presence of their parents (e.g., acting shy or overplaying themselves).

5.2   Setting

Before the first workshop session, an online survey assessed children's *hobbies, interests*, which were integrated in the form of rewards and reflective diaries. Based on the answers from parents, four workshop diaries were created with different themes (i.e., Minecraft, cars, bicycles, soccer) for each participant (see Fig. 5, left).

In preparing the workshops, it was important to find a *quiet/familiar environment*. The sessions took place in the afternoon in a classroom at the children's school. To separate the workshops from the school setting, the environment was divided into "zones". Similar to the dialogue-labs method [19], each task was set up at a different location, to inspire children and encourage participants to move around the area.

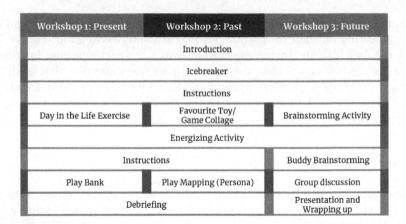

Workshop 1: Present	Workshop 2: Past	Workshop 3: Future
Introduction		
Icebreaker		
Instructions		
Day in the Life Exercise	Favourite Toy/ Game Collage	Brainstorming Activity
Energizing Activity		
Instructions		Buddy Brainstorming
Play Bank	Play Mapping (Persona)	Group discussion
Debriefing		Presentation and Wrapping up

Fig. 4. The main structure of the three co-design workshops. Workshop sessions consisted of different activities and had a particular theme for each day (i.e., *Present*, *Past* and *Future*).

5.3 Procedure

The general structure of the three workshops followed the path of expression [25]. Each workshop session started with a concise visual *introduction* where participants were told about the structure of the session, followed by an *ice-breaker*. Two design-related activities per session (i.e., session 1: a *day in the life*, *play bank*; session 2: *collage*, *persona*; session 3: *brainstorming*, *buddy brainstorming*) formed the basis of the sessions, divided by an *energizing activity* (i.e., session 1: Switch places, if you have...; session 2: Secret Conductor; session 3: chair battle). The activities were all *short and focused*, each within a time frame of maximum 10 min (+ explanation). The duration of each workshop was one hour. After each activity, participants ticked off boxes on a *visual schedule*, which engaged children in volunteering, even before accomplishing the current task. The workshops were closed by a *debriefing* (outro), which provided a visual recap, and a summary of the session, and gave a brief introduction to the next session. An overview of the structure of the three sessions is presented on Fig. 4.

The theme of the first session immersed participants in current experiences, by focusing on the *present*. The *day in the life* exercise (ibid.) helped children reflect upon their day, with the aim to prepare them for the generative session. In addition, this activity supported them in separating the levels of knowledge, from stories to a description of their needs and values. The second design-related task (i.e., *play bank*) aimed to collect as many play activities as possible in form of a competitive exercise, while facilitators documented the two teams' ideas.

The second session intended to activate feelings and memories from the *past*. Consequently, generative methods facilitated the investigation of past experiences (ibid.) and participants were instructed to make a *collage* of their favorite

Fig. 5. Workshop diary with children's customized drawings (left) and persona (right).

toys or games. Next, for the second design-related activity, children created a *persona* [6]. The aim of this task was to investigate participant's wants, hopes, and dreams for the future regarding play experiences. One of the participant's body was drawn around as a silhouette, after asking him to lie down on a piece of wrapping paper (Fig. 5, right). Next to the themes "school" or "home", participants shared their associations on small sticky notes. To adapt the activity for children with ADHD, and make it a bit more engaging and rewarding, we used colorful cake topper flags, which participants had to pierce through the paper.

Finally, the last workshop invited children to dream about *future* possibilities. The intention was to facilitate a co-design activity to generate and express fresh ideas related to children's ideal experiences, and thus shape the future of play [18] for children with ADHD. Children were invited to design their own game. The first step was to individually *brainstorm* and create a story. Characters were chosen from cartoon animals, and the participants had to fill in two sets of storyboards given to them using a set of other characters. The next step was intended to facilitate team work - in a form of a *buddy brainstorming* session, as well as a *group discussion* to evaluate ideas. Finally, for the presentation and wrapping up, parents were extended an optional invitation so they could see what had happened during the workshops.

Fig. 6. Running on tables (left), and engaging others in playing "Chair Battle" (right).

The workshops were audio recorded, and pictures were taken with the permission from the parents. Analyzing the participants' behavior during the co-designs sessions was beyond the scope of this study, thus there was no need to capture everything on video.

6   Findings

6.1   Workshop 1: Present

During the first workshop, children were invited to participate in a *day in the life* exercise, and were observed by the three facilitators. All of them appeared to be proactive, when something sparked their interest. After a small warm-up, children became engaged with the tools available. In spite of having strengths and weaknesses assessed by parents in the questionnaire beforehand, *appropriate content for ability* needed to be adjusted. Self-reflective questions were too abstract and beyond children's ability to analyze their own performance.

Most of the *energizing games* were a great success, participants became engaged. Still, many rules were overwhelming for three children. Surprisingly, at the end of the first workshop one of the participants proactively suggested his own game-idea (musical chairs or "Chair Battle") (Fig. 6, right), and engaged others in play.

Fig. 7. A collage from the second workshop. Despite challenges in completing this task due to the large amount of materials available to children, this collage combines images, pre-defined words, drawings, and a handwritten word "ijesztő" or scary.

6.2   Workshop 2: Past

During the second workshop, children had to make a *collage* (Fig. 10, left), and a *persona*, and were observed by the two female facilitators. Most of them could express their ideas most easily through their own drawing, in addition to describing orally what they were making. Making a *collage* was rather challenging, as participants seemed overwhelmed by the amount of materials presented to them [19], especially by the number of words.

One participant picked out words, and also images first, but at one point he decided to draw his favorite game instead, as sort of a comic strip. Another participant fully engaged with the task (Fig. 7), as he was able to pick out more than one word, and pictures. Moreover, he proposed his own word (i..e, "ijesztő" or scary), as well as drew something on the paper. It was confirmed that *removing materials* for the current activity was important, otherwise children sparked interest towards everything. In addition, when introducing any new activity or tool, it was important to *communicate short, clear goals*, which might be at the expense of understanding the exact task sometimes.

If a participant struggled with an activity, an *adult* provided additional *support* (e.g., in reading), to help the child accomplish a task. A lot depends on the overall mood or having a good or bad day for individuals with ADHD, and taking their medication or not. Participants' engagement and co-operative attitude varied during the workshops. For instance, based on one of the participant's engagement

Fig. 8. Storyboard of "Feri the cat and the Zombie attack" from the third workshop.

towards the energizing activity, the facilitators offered him the *freedom to leave* the workshop. Although it may seem like things got out of control, after a few minutes of energizing activities, running on tables and jumping (Fig. 6, left), the workshop could still continue.

6.3   Workshop 3: Future

The last workshop invited children to *brainstorm* and design their own game story, while three facilitators were present making observations. When introducing characters or pictures, gluing could only be implemented with the help of the facilitators. On the other hand, stickers were always a great success as they were easy to install on the templates. The youngest participant interpreted the task slightly differently than others; his storyboard did not follow the template provided, but he was keen on explaining the story in detail. Another participant drew several different games in each frame, but also included the same controller for each of them. At the same time, the last participant created a full story for a lion, who at the end got scared. This detail was added later, when also discussing stories with other participants, whose story was drawn as a complete comic of "Feri the cat and the Zombie attack" (Fig. 8). An overall impression was that children created anything beyond ordinary during the construction of the game story.

Interestingly, the second phase of the ideation *(i.e., buddy brainstorming)* was partly successful. One group was observed to be working together just fine, even though in previous sessions they did not get along well. The other group, however, could not finish presenting their stores to each other, as one of the participants left the room after the energizing activity. This was probably a result of personal differences between the children.

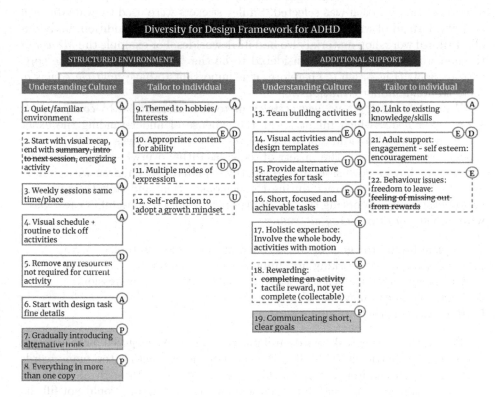

Fig. 9. The practice-informed version of the Diversity for Design (D4D) framework adapted for ADHD. Findings added after the methods were tested in practice with children with ADHD were added as gray boxes labeled "P". Revised aspects of the framework are illustrated with dashed lines.

7   Discussion

7.1   Revised D4D Framework for ADHD

Based on our empirical findings, we have revised the D4D framework for ADHD. On Fig. 9, boxes filled with gray and annotated with the letter "P" indicate findings added after the methods were tested in practice with children with ADHD; these were reflected upon to further develop the framework. Some other aspects also needed to be revised, illustrated with dashed lines.

At the end of the first workshop, a participant proposed their own game, which left children energized. This was a better closing of the session, instead of having to concentrate on an *intro to the next session*. This might be important for children with ASD, but during the other workshops, we experimented with having an energizing activity at the end of the session instead, with successful results.

For the second workshop, regarding *self-reflection to adopt a growth mindset*, a more visual approach was selected. Smiley stickers were used to evaluate each activity, instead of writing answers to reflective questions. In addition, individually tailored workshop material also had its downsides. For example the *Minecraft* themed workshop diary was considered to be the "coolest" but only one copy was available (Fig. 5, left). Therefore, it is important to have *multiple copies of tools* to avoid similar situations.

When introducing any new activity or tool, it is essential to *communicate short, clear goals*, which might be at the expense of understanding the exact task sometimes. Providing *multiple modes of expression* was useful in some cases, however in others, the variety of tools was rather overwhelming. Too many options can have a downside: due to lengthy explanations, children with limited attention span can lose track during the demonstration, and shift their interest to something else. Adopting the following strategy might be useful in these cases while *gradually introducing alternative tools*:

1. Explain briefly the goal of the activity, and provide one tool.
2. Participants start working and immersing into the topic.
3. Gradually introduce other options, and alternatives for expression.
4. Participants can now select their preferences.
5. Remove tools that are unnecessary.

During the collage task, words and images would have required more abstract thinking than participants' ability. It is advised not to include too many words and images, as children might quickly give up browsing through all of them. The blank A3-size paper can be overwhelming, as participants could not fill the whole page, therefore it is better to use pre-structured templates.

Even though rewarding is essential in the context of ADHD, it was not necessary to provide *small rewards after each activity*. In accordance with parents' observations, positive reinforcement, feedback and recognition were more important than snacks. Still, a *tangible reward that is not yet complete*, such as a sticker split into three parts, was successful. On the other hand, the feeling of missing out from rewards did not affect children's decision on whether they want to stay in the workshop or not.

Group work among individuals with ADHD was partly successful in its aims. The original intention was to facilitate co-design activities among the children. However, only one team succeeded in presenting their concepts to each other (Fig. 10, right). While organizing co-design activities even with neurotypically developing children, Vaajakallio, Mattelmäki & Lee observed similar challenges regarding creative collaboration, such as different group dynamics among the

Fig. 10. Participants creating a collage during the second workshop (left), and presenting concepts to each other (right).

children, in addition to different abilities and skills, which is even more critical among neurodiverse children [28]. Hence, a greater flexibility from methods and facilitators is required than with adults or children, and *team building activities* should be reconsidered according to the needs of the group.

7.2   Limitations of This Study

One limitation regarding the methodology applied in the empirical case study is that the workshops included only four male participants, therefore the results cannot be generalized to all children with ADHD. It was not easy to find participants with the eligible criteria. In the school where recruitment took place, girls could not be found with ADHD. Thus, the outcomes might be one-sided due to gender preferences. This might be less of a problem because according to one of the experts, in childhood, the statistical rate in diagnosed cases is 4:1 in male vs. female (whereas in adulthood, it is 1:1). The small sample was chosen firstly because of the difficulty in recruiting helpers in facilitation, and the inexperience of the researchers with children with ADHD. For the purpose of this research, it was more important to gather qualitative data about testing design methods and involving children in the design process, rather than producing refined design artifacts. Nevertheless, increasing the number of participants would have improved the reliability of the study.

A further limitation is that no more than two in-depth interviews with experts from mental health care were conducted. This was a result of the limited time schedule and the difficulty to find relevant interviewees. Despite its limitations, the research reached its goal in informing the design community about engaging and involving children with ADHD into the design process.

7.3   Further Research

To develop a full picture of co-designing with children with ADHD, additional studies will need to focus on the dynamics of group work. In reality, collaboration between individuals with ADHD was partly successful. The findings suggest that inclusion might be a promising direction. Co-design sessions could involve several mixed teams with neurotypically developing children. Each of these teams could integrate children with ADHD who can be the catalyst of creativity in innovation.

The mapped experiences could be used not only when designing treatment games specifically, but in other games targeted at children with ADHD that they would be able to 'play for the sake of play' [4]. The main goal is that play does not seem like homework for children, an extra obligatory task to carry out. By taking into account their experiences, it would be possible to leverage the potential of youngsters being *digital natives*, by taking advantage of their previous knowledge in games and other digital services.

One of the main findings from the expert interviews in this study was related to the important role of parents in therapy and development of their children. It was commented that *"parents are absenting themselves from play in the life of their child [...] nowadays."* In the future, the next phase of research could gain valuable insights about involving parents and families in addition to teachers and commercial experts in co-design workshops.

8   Conclusions

This paper explored how to engage children with ADHD in co-design activities. The Diversity for Design (D4D) framework was adapted by first looking into theory, conducting expert interviews, and finally putting everything into practice during co-design workshops. Our results show that, when their needs, preferences, and individual desires are taken into account, children with ADHD can be meaningfully engaged in co-design activities. By offering an adapted version of the D4D framework tailored for ADHD, designers can structure the environment and provide scaffolds so that children with ADHD can become active participants in co-design workshops. The updated framework can be used to design digital services (apps) or toys that take the needs of children with ADHD into account and support their development. Such apps or toys could further be used for therapeutic purposes.

Consequently, together these results provide important insights about how to involve and engage children with ADHD in design activities. Reflecting on the theory-, expert- and practice-informed D4D in the context of ADHD, it is worth noting that involving and engaging children in design activities was successful. However, it was partly successful in building on collaboration between participants, which is a core element of co-design. Further research is needed on how to involve and engage participants in group work activities, where they are capable of building upon each other's ideas. Firstly, among individuals with ADHD, and next in mixed teams to study how engagement and productivity would change.

This empirical case study aimed to reflect on the opportunities and challenges of involving children with ADHD in co-design, and thus is an important tool for the design community that contributes to collective knowledge of ADHD through its findings. Additionally, it represents one the first investigations into involving children with ADHD in human-centered innovation. The study was carried out by exploring, testing and further refining the framework of already existing design methods. The article presented an adapted version of the Diversity for Design (D4D) framework for ADHD, including modified features and proposed additions. The theory- and expert-informed version was tested during three workshops, and by reflecting on the design practice, a practice-informed D4D was established. The second main contribution of this study was a research-informed, initial model of the design process when designing for children with ADHD.

References

1. Al-Wabil, A., Meldah, E., Al-Suwaidan, A., AlZahrani, A.: Designing educational games for children with specific learning difficulties: insights from involving children and practitioners. In: 2010 Fifth International Multi-conference on Computing in the Global Information Technology, pp. 195–198. IEEE (2010)
2. Armstrong, T.: Neurodiversity: Discovering the Extraordinary Gifts of Autism, ADHD, Dyslexia, and Other Brain Differences. Da Capo Press, Reading (2010)
3. Benton, L., Vasalou, A., Khaled, R., Johnson, H., Gooch, D.: Diversity for design: a framework for involving neurodiverse children in the technology design process. In: Proceedings of the SIGCHI Conference on Human Factors in Computing Systems, pp. 3747–3756 (2014)
4. Besio, S., Bulgarelli, D., Stancheva-Popkostadinova, V.: Play Development in Children with Disabilties. Walter de Gruyter GmbH & Co. KG, Berlin (2016)
5. Börjesson, P., Barendregt, W., Eriksson, E., Torgersson, O.: Designing technology for and with developmentally diverse children: a systematic literature review. In: Proceedings of the 14th International Conference on Interaction Design and Children, pp. 79–88 (2015)
6. Cooper, A., Reimann, R.: Persona. In: Erlhoff, M., Marshall, T., Bruce, l. (eds.) Design Dictionary: Perspectives on Design Terminology. Birlshauser, Boston (2008)
7. Dalton, N.S.: Neurodiversity & HCI. In: CHI 2013 Extended Abstracts on Human Factors in Computing Systems, pp. 2295–2304 (2013)
8. Druin, A.: The role of children in the design of new technology. Behav. Inf. Technol. **21**(1), 1–25 (2002)
9. Eisenberg, D., Campbell, B.: The evolution of ADHD. San Francisco Medicine, pp. 21–22 (2011)
10. Mental Health Foundation: Fundamental Facts About Mental Health 2016. Mental Health Foundation, London (2016)
11. Frauenberger, C., Good, J., Keay-Bright, W.: Designing technology for chidren with special needs: bridging perspectives through participatory design. CoDesign **7**(1), 1–28 (2011)

12. Garcia, J.J., de Bruyckere, H., Keyson, D.V., Romero, N.: Designing personal informatics for self-reflection and self-awareness: the case of children with attention deficit hyperactivity disorder. In: Augusto, J.C., Wichert, R., Collier, R., Keyson, D., Salah, A.A., Tan, A.-H. (eds.) AmI 2013. LNCS, vol. 8309, pp. 109–123. Springer, Cham (2013). https://doi.org/10.1007/978-3-319-03647-2_8

13. Grundwag, C., Nordfors, D., Yirmiya, N.: "Coolabilities" - enhanced abilities in disabling conditions (2017)

14. Guha, M.L., Druin, A., Fails, J.A.: Designing with and for children with special needs: an inclusionary model. In: IDC Proceedings-Workshop on Special Needs, pp. 61–64. ACM Press (2008)

15. Hallowell, E.M., Ratey, J.J.: Driven to Distraction (Revised): Recognizing and Coping with Attention Deficit Disorder. Anchor, New York (2011)

16. Hartmann, T.: The Edison Gene: ADHD and the Gift of the Hunter Child. Inner Traditions/Bear & Co., Rochester (2005)

17. Honos-Webb, L.: The Gift of ADHD: How to Transform Your Child's Problems into Strengths. New Harbinger Publications, Oakland (2010)

18. Lucero, A., Karapanos, E., Arrasvuori, J., Korhonen, H.: Playful or gameful? Creating delightful user experiences. Interactions 21(3), 34–39 (2014)

19. Lucero, A., Vaajakallio, K., Dalsgaard, P.: The dialogue-labs method: process, space and materials as structuring elements to spark dialogue in co-design events. CoDesign 8(1), 1–23 (2012)

20. Mesibov, G.B., Shea, V., Schopler, E.: The TEACCH Approach to Autism Spectrum Disorders, 1st edn. Springer, New York (2005). https://doi.org/10.1007/978-0-306-48647-0

21. Meyer, A., Rose, D.H., Gordon, D.: Universal Design for Learning: Theory and Practice. CAST Professional Publishing, Wakefield (2014)

22. Montessori, M.: The Montessori Method. Transaction Publishers, London (2013)

23. Neate, T., Bourazeri, K., Roper, A., Stumpf, S., Wilson, S.: Co-created personas: engaging and empowering users with diverse needs within the design process 2(018)

24. Panksepp, J.: Can PLAY diminish ADHD and facilitate the construction of the social brain? J. Can. Acad. Child Adolesc. Psychiatry (Journal de l'Academie canadienne de psychiatrie de l'enfant et de l'adolescent) 16(2), 57 (2007)

25. Sanders, E.B.N., Stappers, P.J.: Convivial Toolbox: Generative Research for the Front End of Design. BIS, Amsterdam (2012)

26. Sanders, E.B.-N., Stappers, P.J.: Co-creation and the new landscapes of design. CoDesign 4(1), 5–18 (2008)

27. Six, S., Panksepp, J.: ADHD and play. Scholarpedia 7(10), 30371 (2012)

28. Vaajakallio, K., Mattelmäki, T., Lee, J.J.: Co-design lessons with children. Interactions 17(4), 26–29 (2010)

29. Weisberg, O., et al.: TangiPlan: designing an assistive technology to enhance executive functioning among children with ADHD. In: Proceedings of the 2014 Conference on Interaction Design and Children, pp. 293–296. ACM (2014)

Technology, Theatre and Co-design: Impact and Design Considerations

Christina Vasiliou[1(✉)] and Tom Schofield[2]

[1] Northumbria University, Newcastle upon Tyne, UK
christina.vasiliou@northumbria.ac.uk
[2] Newcastle University, Newcastle upon Tyne, UK

Abstract. The paper documents the co-design methodology followed by Northern Stage theatrical company for the design of a theatrical production, rich in digital elements. Drawing on our data from fieldwork, interviews and questionnaires, we initially report on the co-design activities, then using thematic analysis, we review the impact of technology in the co-design activities, the dynamics of using digital technologies in a performance and the limitations for small-medium theatrical companies. Our work extends research and practice on co-design and participatory design in creative industries and their experimentation with technology. More specifically, we contribute by casting light on the nature of activities and the level of digital maturity and readiness. The paper concludes with considerations of co-design and HCI work in attracting a new generation of performers and audiences for the digital era.

Keywords: Participatory design · Co-design · Theatre · Digital maturity · Technology adoption

1 Introduction

Co-design and participatory design activities are tightly interwoven with youth theatre, as young people often get involved not only in performing but also in writing, devising and contributing to the design of a theatrical piece. Incorporating technology is often an integral part of youth theatre as it allows experimentation and exploration of new ideas. However, the co-design activities in the theatrical context may differ from the academic perspective. One of the issues with designing and producing a performance is the difficulty of capturing and documenting the multiple interconnections between people and procedures.

In this work, we report on an ethnographic field study on a youth program to develop a digital theatre production. The aim is two-fold. We aim to capture the structure of the co-design approach for the development of a digitally-augmented professional performance with young adults as co-designers and digital performers. We further aim to bring to the forefront ideas from a different field and reflect on the potential uses of technology in a professional theatre, tackling the digital agenda of cultural organizations [8].

© IFIP International Federation for Information Processing 2019
Published by Springer Nature Switzerland AG 2019
D. Lamas et al. (Eds.): INTERACT 2019, LNCS 11746, pp. 387–396, 2019.
https://doi.org/10.1007/978-3-030-29381-9_24

2 Related Work

2.1 Co-design Activities

In the last few years, there has been an evolution in design research from user-centred approaches to co-designing, highlighting the need for a collective creativity [19]. As Sanders and Stappers [19] indicated, co-design reflects a collective effort that spans throughout the whole design process, where both designers and "people not trained in design" work together. The multidisciplinarity of the area, blending work from design, psychology, computer science, led to the generation of different paradigms and approaches for practice [11]. Researchers have used co-design practices extensively in domains where democratising a process is crucial, and there is a need to give the power to the end-users and communities with interest to design products or services that they will use [15].

Involving users as partners instead of subjects of study may improve the end product [1], build ownership reducing the risk for the product to fail [12] and encourage sustainable engagement [16]. Co-design and participation empowers users and creates a secure space for design experts and non-experts to equally contribute to the final product [2]. For instance, Penuel, Roschelle and Shechtman [17] brought together teachers, researchers, and developers to collaboratively design an educational assessment tool. Co-design activities are also often explored in cultural venues, such as museum settings allowing visitors or museum volunteers to contribute towards creating digitally augmented and interactive exhibitions [5, 6] encouraging audiences to engage with art, culture and heritage.

Furthermore, when working with young participants as in our case study, researchers adapted the co-design approaches to meet the needs of the specific population [13]. For example, Weiss et al. [22] situated the design workshops in the context of investigation (shopping area), that increased the creativity of young participants, allowing them to make context related reflections. Instead of bringing the participants to the context, "Living Labs" explored the use of construction kits, bringing the makers' environment to the participants [18]. Children and young people used the tools in the construction kit to build prototypes of their ideas, making their thoughts and views tangible, highlighting the need for hand-on activities and scaffolding to structure the co-design activities.

2.2 Theatre Practice and Technology

In an attempt to reinstate audience engagement in theatrical performances, researchers have also explored the use of co-design approaches during production and marketing activities. For instance, Dima [7] involved participants in pre-production activities of a theatrical play to build a storytelling application, namely Mobile Stories, to engage audiences before a performance. Schofield et al. [20] provided a set of workshops for a year-long participatory design process, with the goal to create and present a theatrical performance mixing technology, monologues and visuals. The design process incorporated introductory, technical, and design workshops to allow the young adults to learn the basics of directing and performing with technology.

However, existing literature on co-designing in theatrical productions is limited to either experimental groups for one-off theatrical performances [20] or co-design of pre-performance promotional material for sustainable engagement [7]. To the best of our knowledge, results have not been reported on co-design activities in a technology-augmented professional production with the involvement of young members of the audience. This paper not only documents the process used to engage young adults in a professional theatrical production through co-design and digital augmentation, but further provides a case study of technology use, adoption and limitations of technology in a professional theatre, focusing on a sustainable future for theatre and audiences.

3   Methodology

3.1   Context

The Production is part of a Northern Stage project for engaging young adults of the region in theatre and empowering them into understanding the use technology in theatre as well as developing their own professional portfolios. The Production aimed to explore co-design activities with young adults in professional theatre and to create a digitally-infused performance to attract young audiences. The role of Researchers was to observe the collaboration, and get immersed in the Production culture.

The recruitment process for the theatrical production resulted in a total of 34 participants (19 female, one transgender, 14 male) aged 16 to 21 (M = 17.2). Participants had the opportunity to enrol in more than one session throughout the co-production activities. That resulted in 16 young adults for Session 1, 10 for Session 2, 18 for Session 3, and 16 for Session 4. During all four sessions, there was a mixture of both new participants and participants from previous weeks. Regarding participants' background and abilities related to theatre, the young adults were a blend of students from secondary schools or sixth-form institutes of the region, or attending universities and colleges with an interest or direction to fine or performing arts. There was also a blend of people who were new to the idea of theatrical productions, and a blend of people who had previous experience with performing. The Creative Professionals team working on the Production - collaborating with the Young Company - included five professional artists as experts in directing, sound editing, movement, filming.

3.2   Data Collection and Analysis

The data from the project were collected through field ethnography at Northern Stage theatre company to gain an in-depth understanding of the co-design activities focusing on understanding the "what", "how", and "why" [10]. The fieldwork included observation of the co-design activities that took place over a period of a month (4 weeks). At the end of the process, the Researchers conducted interviews with Creative Professionals and attended briefing meetings, central to the production. We also conducted an open-ended questionnaire with the young participants focusing on their experience of the co-design process and their role as digital performers to the Production. The interviews and questionnaires were administered on a voluntary basis, collecting a total of three one-hour interviews with Creative Professionals and eight questionnaire responses from Young Company. The interviews were audio-recorded, transcribed and then the researchers coded the whole data corpus using a thematic analysis [3].

4   Findings

4.1   Co-design Activities for Digitally Augmented Theatre

In what follows we present the co-design activities the company followed to design a theatrical production, involving young adults. The co-design process, Fig. 1, aimed to cultivate a new method for involving young adults in professional theatrical making as a step towards their future development as professional artists. The activities spanned over 4 weeks with each week addressing a different section of the script.

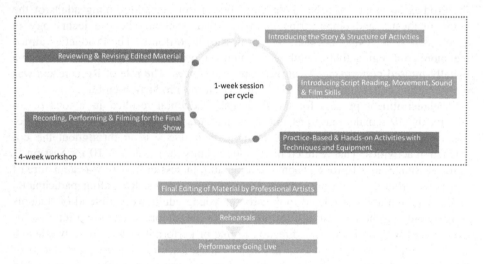

Fig. 1. Procedure for co-design activities for a digitally infused theatrical production (Color figure online)

Each week began by introducing Creative Professionals as collaborators, constructing a sense of community among the Young Company, and presenting the structure of the daily activities and the story of the play. This introduction served as a warm-up for the Young Company to feel comfortable within the context of work and their peers. As highlighted in interviews and field notes, during this first session, the Creative Professionals also clarified the terms of this co-design Production, communicating expectations clearly to the young adults, a vital step for good collaboration between different parties in long-term projects [14]. More particularly, as one of the creative professionals mentioned, *"managing the expectation of young people to understand that they were part of this project, but they wouldn't be central to the live event in the same way that they would be as live performers"* [CP2].

The next session as seen in Fig. 1, was the introduction to technical skills necessary for them to actively contribute to the Production. In this session, the Creative Professionals, internal or external to the company, would lead the sessions and introduce different skills, such as movement on stage, filming, sound composition, as well as script reading and acting on stage. The session also presented the script that the Young Company was going to be working on throughout the week, serving as a stepping stone to build fundamental understanding about the play and technical language.

The following sessions included practice-based activities to work towards designing and capturing the material for the Production. The Young Company were initially practising different techniques for movement, script reading, creating sound, as well as setting up equipment for filming through hands-on activities. The Creative Professionals covered areas such as filming, sound composition, how to move and perform, and rotated individuals through different roles each time to allow them to understand all the various aspects in each field and how they work altogether.

The activities were designed to strengthen the technical skills of the Young Company as artists and creatives, as well as boost their confidence and trust in their abilities [4]. As one of the external Creative Professionals indicated during the interview, *"these activities followed learning-by-doing approach, such as learning how to handle the camera or frame the shot as first steps towards filmmaking. "[CP3]* This method is often used in technical training emphasising that learning through practice can be more beneficial that recalling only from memory [9]. In this context, the activities took place over an intensive week. However, the Creative Professionals considered this period as short for building deep skills for the Young Company and thus incorporated the practice-based activities early in the process. By fusing the hands-on activities early in the co-design process, they intended to allow the young adults to familiarise themselves with the techniques and equipment, and then build the production material, an approach drawing on fundamental ideas of constructionism [4].

Following the practice-based learning, the next session focused on capturing the Production material. The Young Company took a general direction from the director of the Production and were encouraged to explore and interpret that on their own. At this point, the Creative Professional limited their role as observers and tutors of the Young Company and avoided giving exact directions. For instance, in the case of filming, the Young Company would set the scene based on the director's needs, position the camera, light and other equipment and film the scene. The role of the filming professional was to support, allowing them to apply their new skills.

As a concluding session each week, the group had the opportunity to review the outcome of their work throughout the week, with Creative Professionals encouraging the Young Company to make suggestions for revisions. However, the editing of the raw material, such as sound and film, was only performed by the Creative Professionals as it was a time-consuming and demanding activity, outside the time-limits and scope of this case.

4.2   Thematic Analysis

Participation as Digital Performers Expanded the Sense of "Being on Stage". The performance itself had a single female performer, and the stage was set so that the digitally recorded material of the young adults would be projected as a backdrop on stage, as seen in Fig. 2. The protagonist narrates the story and draws the audience into her world, with the digital chorus witness her tale and contribute to its progress. The projections remained in use throughout and aimed to transport the audience "out of the theatre" into a sequence of remembered incidents of the story, pre-recorded with the young participants. The young participants felt they were a significant part of the performance:

> "I wasn't digitally on-stage a lot since I only did a week but it did feel weird seeing myself there because it's something new and different. I was quite excited to think that I was technically on-stage and part of such a spectacular performance and people would see me. I think it's a brilliant way to extend the metaphorical 'self-life' of theatre."

Fig. 2. Digital projection of young company recordings in "A Song for Ella Grey"

The technology was felt as an integral and necessary aspect of the play, working towards extending their role. Their role in the performance took the form of a digital Greek "chorus" where the protagonist would be able to talk to and discuss her thoughts with, and thus becoming an integral part of the performance. What was strongly expressed through their post-show questionnaire responses was the ability to feel on-stage without physically being there and the inclusiveness that the technology allowed in such a new format. As individuals voiced:

> "It was really cool to see the work that we had spoken about actually in front of you. The digital format worked really well in the show."

> "I thought it would be everything I had expected. Despite not knowing how the shape of the show would eventually come together, I was happy with the final outcome."

Technology-Infused Theatre Could Modernize Theatre and Attract Young Audiences. All of the young adults participating in the co-design activities went to see the performance, with individuals attending more than once. The young participants expressed that the technology in the show also provided a new dimension in the performance, one that the young audience could relate to. As one of the indicated, the show is *"very relatable to teenagers I think, and the use of modern technology kind of made everybody seem connected, since our culture is so heavily influenced by it today."*

What was also expressed was the close connection between what was happening on stage with what was happening pre-production, without always focusing on one's self in the show. As the young participants indicated:

> *"It was completely surreal, as an audience member I detached myself from the filming/sound, hearing and seeing my voice and face as a part of the piece rather than identifying myself and taking away from the story. It was also incredibly heart-warming as, despite being able to detach, I could really feel the joy within the scene, the same joy I felt filming it."*

> *"It was a different experience because we were still in the show, we were just live on stage. At the start I was really focused on myself and my peers, but as the play progressed I started to become less selfish and actually focus on the actress and the play as a whole."*

Technology and Resource Limitations Within the Theatre. The company explored a number of ideas before finalizing the plan for this performance, taking into consideration resources, technical knowledge and expertise limitations and possibilities within the timeline of the performance. As indicated by one of the Creative Professionals,

> *"there was a while were the show was going to be a show that was going to happen entirely on mobile phones, and you turned up at the box office at [...] and you download the app on your phone and went out, walked through the city and experience the whole thing on little videos. There was a while where there was going to be a bit that would happen in the theatre and a bit that happens with you walking around, looking at things on your phone. You keep having ideas, and testing this form against the story, and also testing the form against the parameters of what is possible within the time, within the resources, within all of that" [CP1].*

5   Discussion

The ultimate goal of the analysis is two-fold: to initially document the co-design practices for a professional and digitally-infused performance, and then provide a means to explore on the framing of technology within the context of theatre and co-design activities. In this section, we reflect on our findings regarding the co-design activities and the nature of participation, as well as the considerations for technology use.

One of the most prominent worries of the professionals was to manage young adults' expectations of what the activities would include and what their role would be in the show. The literature suggests that in practical or long-term projects between young learners and supervisors or facilitators of learning, communicating expectations can improve the quality of collaboration between the different parties [14]. This is particularly true in vocational education and training where the supervising style and learning style are not always a match. However, the use of technology allowed the participants to feel as an integral part of the live performance, extending their role as performers and creators, as well as their legacy as professional creatives.

Further, a number of aspects should be taken into account in a co-design process:

- To what extent do we incorporate technology in the performance? Is the company ready and digitally mature? The use of technology in this performance was limited to projection of pre-recorded video, audio and live streaming of mobile video. However as indicated in the interviews, the resources, technical knowledge and expertise should match the script and storyline of a performance, a tricky balance.
- To what extent do we allow users/audience to influence the final performance? Stages displayed in lighter blue in Fig. 1, indicate sessions where young participants have a passive or no role, with minimal impact on the final performance. While overall the process increased the democratisation of the design of a play, the finality of the play remained in the hands of the creative professionals [20].
- To what extent the co-design activities are beneficial for the participants? The co-design activities developed a sense of belonging in a community, through the hands-on activities or the development of technical skills. Thus the co-production activities, as guided by the basic understanding of what participatory design is all about, also provided a set of technical skills that would benefit the participants in this context preparing them for the digital marketplace [21].
- To what extent is the process sustainable and transferable to future productions? Involving young adults for a young adult performance allowed the use of tools and technologies that would enthuse them and their peers, increasing the engagement of young people with "modern" theatre, an easily replicable process.

Limitations of this work are bound by the limitations of qualitative and ethnographic studies. Ethnographic research is often providing "thick descriptions" that cannot generalize beyond the context of the study, but can be transferable to other settings identifying opportunities for further research. Our aim as future work in this area is to further expand design prototyping in technology-infused theatre and theatre making and explore the influence of the context in co-design activities, working towards creating a sustainability framework for co-designing theatre for the digital era.

6   Conclusion

This case study was an initial step to document the co-design activities in a theatrical context and develop insights into how professionals and amateur youth work together in designing a digitally-infused theatre production. This work provides an opportunity to rethink how to frame co-design approaches in different settings as well as form an exemplary case for technology use in theatre.

Acknowledgement. We thank Northern Stage (Theatrical Productions) Limited for their invitation and warm welcome to experience the production as well as their contributions to this research. We also thank the Young Company participants and Creative professionals for their time and effort. This research was supported by KTP010714, a Knowledge Transfer Partnership supported by Innovate UK and UK Research and Innovation.

References

1. Beyer, H., Holtzblatt, K.: Contextual Design: Defining Customer-Centered Systems. Elsevier, Amsterdam (1997)
2. Borar, P., Karnam, D., Agrawal, H., Chandrasekharan, S.: Augmenting the textbook for enaction: designing media for participatory learning in classrooms. In: Bernhaupt, R., Dalvi, G., Joshi, A., Balkrishan, D.K., O'Neill, J., Winckler, M. (eds.) INTERACT 2017. LNCS, vol. 10516, pp. 336–339. Springer, Cham (2017). https://doi.org/10.1007/978-3-319-68059-0_24
3. Braun, V., Clarke, V.: Using thematic analysis in psychology. Qual. Res. Psychol. 3(2), 77–101 (2006)
4. Brown, B.L.: Applying constructivism in vocational and career education. Information Series No. 378 (1998)
5. Ciolfi, L., et al.: Articulating co-design in museums: reflections on two participatory processes. In: Proceedings of the 19th ACM Conference on Computer-Supported Cooperative Work & Social Computing, pp. 13–25. ACM (2016)
6. Damala, A., Hornecker, E., van der Vaart, M., van Dijk, D., Ruthven, I.: The loupe: tangible augmented reality for learning to look at Ancient Greek art. Mediterr. Archaeol. Archaeometry 16(5), 73–85 (2016)
7. Dima, M.: Engaging theatre audiences before the play: the design of playful interactive storytelling experiences. In: Proceedings of the 2013 Inputs-Outputs Conference: An Interdisciplinary Conference on Engagement in HCI and Performance, p. 5. ACM (2013)
8. European Commission: European Agenda for Culture (2018). https://ec.europa.eu/culture/sites/culture/files/staff_working_document_-_a_new_european_agenda_for_culture_2018.pdf
9. Gallagher, S.A.: Problem-based learning: where did it come from, what does it do, and where is it going? J. Educ. Gifted 20(4), 332–362 (1997)
10. Hammersley, M., Atkinson, P.: Ethnography: Principles in Practice. Routledge, London (2007)
11. Kensing, F., Blomberg, J.: Participatory design: issues and concerns. Comput. Supp. Coop. Work (CSCW) 7(3–4), 167–185 (1998)
12. Kujala, S.: User involvement: a review of the benefits and challenges. Behav. Inf. Technol. 22(1), 1–16 (2003)
13. Leong, T.W., Robertson, T.: Voicing values: laying foundations for ageing people to participate in design. In: Proceedings of the 14th Participatory Design Conference: Full Papers, vol. 1, pp. 31–40. ACM (2016)
14. Myers, K.K., Sadaghiani, K.: Millennials in the workplace: a communication perspective on millennials' organizational relationships and performance. J. Bus. Psychol. 25(2), 225–238 (2010)
15. Parmaxi, A., Vasiliou, C.: Communities of interest for enhancing social creativity: the case of Womenpower platform. In: Proceedings of INTED2015 Conference, pp. 2838–2847 (2015)
16. Parmaxi, A., Vasiliou, C., Ioannou, A., Kouta, C.: Empowerment of women through an innovative e-mentoring community platform: implications and lessons learned. J. Commun. Inform. 13(3) (2017)

17. Penuel, W.R., Roschelle, J., Shechtman, N.: Designing formative assessment software with teachers: an analysis of the co-design process. Res. Pract. Technol. Enhanced Learn. **2**(01), 51–74 (2007)
18. Reichel, M., Schelhowe, H.: Living labs: driving innovation through civic involvement. In: Proceedings of the 7th International Conference on Interaction Design and Children, pp. 141–144. ACM (2008)
19. Sanders, E.B.N., Stappers, P.J.: Co-creation and the new landscapes of design. Co-design **4**(1), 5–18 (2008)
20. Schofield, T., Vines, J., Higham, T., Carter, E., Atken, M., Golding, A.: Trigger shift: participatory design of an augmented theatrical performance with young people. In: Proceedings of the 9th ACM Conference on Creativity & Cognition, pp. 203–212. ACM (2013)
21. Vyas, O., Bahadur, K.R.: A digital employability marketplace. In: Bernhaupt, R., Dalvi, G., Joshi, A., Balkrishan, D.K., O'Neill, J., Winckler, M. (eds.) INTERACT 2017. LNCS, vol. 10516, pp. 321–325. Springer, Cham (2017). https://doi.org/10.1007/978-3-319-68059-0_21
22. Weiss, A., Wurhofer, D., Bernhaupt, R., Beck, E., Tscheligi, M.: This is a flying shopping trolley: a case study of participatory design with children in a shopping context. In: Proceedings of the Tenth Anniversary Conference on Participatory Design 2008, pp. 254–257. Indiana University (2008)

Visual Fixations Duration as an Indicator of Skill Level in eSports

Boris B. Velichkovsky[1]([✉]), Nikita Khromov[2], Alexander Korotin[2], Evgeny Burnaev[2], and Andrey Somov[2]

[1] Moscow State University, Mokhovaya 11/5, 125009 Moscow, Russia
velitchk@mail.ru
[2] Skolkovo Institute of Science and Technology,
Bolshoy Boulevard 30, bld. 1, 121205 Moscow, Russia
{nikita.khromov, a.korotin, e.burnaev,
a.somov}@skoltech.ru

Abstract. Using highly interactive systems like computer games requires a lot of visual activity and eye movements. Eye movements are best characterized by visual fixation – periods of time when the eyes stay relatively still over an object. We analyzed the distributions of fixation duration of professional athletes, amateur and newbie players. We show that the analysis of fixation durations can be used to deduce the skill level in computer game players. Highly skilled gaming performance is characterized by more variability in fixation durations and by bimodal fixation duration distributions suggesting the presence of two fixation types in high skill gamers. These fixation types were identified as ambient (automatic spatial processing) and focal (conscious visual processing). The analysis of computer gamers' skill level via the analysis of fixation durations may be used in developing adaptive interfaces and in interface design.

Keywords: eSports · eSports athletes · Amateurs · Skill level · Eye movements · Eye-tracking · Fixation duration · Ambient · Focal

1 Introduction

eSports involves highly dynamic interactions with complex computer-mediated environments. It is a complex activity the success of which depends on many factors – technological, cognitive, personal, and even social. From the Human-Computer Interaction (HCI) perspective, eSports is an interesting activity as it provides for the study of human-user interaction under the conditions of stress and the need for high performance [8, 10]. For instance, it is vital for the study of the visual aspects of the interaction as contemporary user interfaces are still mainly visually oriented. This suggests the importance of studying the patterns of eye activity in eSports as the eye movements are the most important prerequisite for the gathering of visual information [11].

Human vision is an active vision system [3]. It depends on the eye movements to allow for a detailed exploration of objects in the environment. That is why the analysis of the eye movements can reveal a lot about the organization of visual information processing. Today, the analysis of eye movements is made much easier by the availability of

D. Lamas et al. (Eds.): INTERACT 2019, LNCS 11746, pp. 397–405, 2019.
https://doi.org/10.1007/978-3-030-29381-9_25

affordable non-invasive video-based eye-trackers. For instance, eye movements are often studied in users interacting with computers [1, 9].

Eye movements are complex and have many subtypes. Important events within the eye activity are fixations – time intervals during which the eyes stand relatively still (although there is always some jitter) with the gaze pointed at an external object under detailed inspection [13]. Visual perception is said to be accomplished during fixations while there is no visual processing during the ballistic eye movements between fixations (saccades, "saccadic suppression"). Fixations are characterized by (1) their location within the visual field and (2) by their duration. It is the fixation duration that we focus on in this paper. Fixation durations differ a lot during eye movements. Typical durations may be as short as 50 ms and as long as over 2000 ms. The distributions of fixation durations are skewed to the left with typical median durations 0f 200–250 ms, mean durations of 300–350 ms, and a long right tail of long and very long fixations. Fixation durations are used for a distinction between subtypes of fixations with "short" fixations considered ambient (spatial processing) and "long" (over 300–500 ms) fixations considered focal (conscious perception) [5, 12]. Fixation durations are sensitive to many factors like the skill level of the user and the cognitive load experienced by the user.

In this paper, we study the differences in fixation durations between eSports athletes of different proficiency levels (amateurs with less experience, experienced amateurs, and professional players) during the gameplay. We computed individual distributions of fixation durations and compared various parameters of these distributions. The rationale was to discover how differences in the parameters of individual fixation durations distributions may reflect differences in the eSports athletes' proficiency level under realistic conditions of an emotion-provoking competition (Counter-Strike: Global Offensive, CS:GO).This study is novel to HCI in that it, for the first time, uses the analysis of individual fixation duration distributions to measure skill level to drive possible human-computer interface changes in a high-performance HCI scenario.

2   Method

2.1   Subjects

In this experiment players with different CS:GO experience were invited. Some players have had only limited CS:GO experience (amateurs with less than 700 h playing the game). This was the low skill group (N = 10). Other amateur players have had more experience with the game (over 700 h) and were in the high skill group (N = 7). There also were some professional eSports athletes (N = 4) with over 10.000 h of playing the game which means they play more than 4 h per day (they are designated as the pro group below) The athletes are from the professional Monolith team, Russia. This team is affiliated with the Skoltech Cyberacademy. Amateur players are Skoltech MS/PhD students as well as research and administrative staff from Skoltech.

2.2 Equipment

An in-house IoT platform for the eSports data collection and analysis was used. The platform block diagram is shown in Fig. 1. It includes three units: a sensing unit, a gaming PC, and a CounterStrike (CS:GO) server. It allows for data collection from heterogeneous sensors and a game service deployed on the CS:GO server.

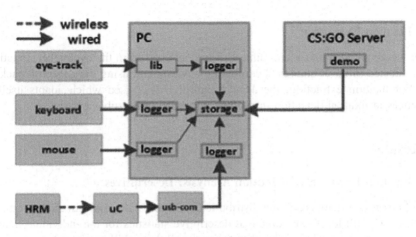

Fig. 1. Block diagram for the platform for eSports data collection

In terms of sensing, the proposed platform contains the following sensors: Tobii EyeX eye-tracker, Garmin Heart Rate Monitor (HRM) belt, key/mouse logger, in-game data logger (CSGO HLTV demo). We used the Tobii eye-tracking library for eye-position measurements and developed a custom script for capturing the data-stream from the Tobii library and recording these data to a local.csv text file. We measured the gaze position at 30 Hz. PC unit is an advanced (storage and processing capability) gaming PC to which all external physiological sensors, i.e. eye-tracker and HRM, are connected. Apart from the physiological data we performed logging of mouse and keyboard on the PC, as well as collection of game statistics

2.3 Game Scenario

There are two roles for the Retake modification of CS:GO discipline: a terrorist team and counter-terrorist team. The terrorist team (2 players) is characterized by the defensive role. They have a bomb planted on the territory and have to defend it. The counter-terrorist team (3 players) has to deactivate the bomb or to kill the enemy team. The system shows the bomb location on the map at the beginning of each round. Players are also asked to buy exactly the same set of weapons for each round. Each round lasts for 40 s while there are 12 rounds in total. This scenario must be played without any breaks between the rounds.

2.4 Procedure

Prior to participate in the experiment, all participants were informed about the project, its goals, and the experiment. We obtained a written consent from each participant in the experiment. Afterwards, we ensured by a questionnaire that all the participants are in a good form and do not take any drugs in order to avoid the interference with the experimental results

2.5 Fixation Extraction

Raw eyegaze data (x- and y-coordinates) were obtained from the eyetracker. Fixations were extracted in the R statistical computing environment using the *gazepath* package [11]. For fixation extraction, the *Mould* algorithm was used which adapts itself to differences in fixation detection thresholds on a subject-by-subject basis.

3 Results

3.1 Fixation Duration Distribution Analysis: Descriptives

To find possible differences in the distributions of fixation durations in eSports athletes with different skill level, we computed descriptive statistics for the individual fixation duration distributions. The averaged statistics for all three skill levels and the results of testing for significant differences (ANOVA) are presented in Table 1.

Table 1. Descriptive statistics for the individual fixation duration distributions averaged over skill levels

Skill level	Mean	Median	SD	Minimum	Maximum
Low	250	213	122	117	800
High	278	223	197	72	1188
Pro	282	218	223	55	1229
F(2,18)	0.53	0.04	9.72	3.53	4.54
p	n.s.	n.s.	<0.001	0.051	<0.05

This analysis shows that mean and median durations are not different between skill levels. Differences are observed for the measures of the variability of duration. In the low skill group, minimum durations are higher and maximum durations are lower than in the more skilled groups. The professional group is characterized by very low minimal durations (technically, 50 ms is a typical cut-off for the identification of a fixation) and very large maximum durations. The standard deviations of the durations show a systematic increase with skill level. Thus, higher skill levels are characterized by more "wide" duration distributions with more variability.

Additional analysis using post-hoc multiple comparison test (Sheffe's test) showed that the differences in the standard deviations are differences between the low skill group and both the high skill and the pro group, that the differences in the minimums are mainly differences between the low skill group and the pro group, and that the differences in the maximums are again driven by the differences between the low skill group and both the high skill group and the pro group. This suggests that the pro and the high skill group are relatively similar while the low skill group is distinctively different from them. Overall, these results suggest that higher skill level leads to wider fixation duration distributions.

3.2   Vincentile Analysis

A more formal analysis of a frequency distribution form may be given by a Vincentile analysis [2]. The Vincentile analysis consists in separating distributions in five equal bins ("the vincentiles", each comprising 20% of the distribution), computing averages over the bins, and statistically analyzing differences in these averages. For example, if there are significant differences in the first vincentile, than the left tail of the distribution with a smaller first vincentile is shifted to the left.

We computed mean fixation durations over five bins (Fig. 2). The previous analysis suggests that the line connecting bin means for the pro group should start lower than the line connecting the means for the bin means for the low skill group and cross it. The line for the high skill group should be in between these two lines. This is exactly what is seen in the Fig. 2. We submitted the binned data to a two-way 3×5 rm-ANOVA and obtained a highly significant Bin $\times$ Skill Level interaction, $F(8,72) = 10.3$, $p < 0.001$. Generally, these results formally support the idea that progressing skill level makes the fixation duration distribution more wide.

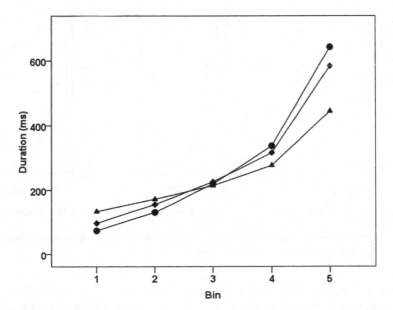

Fig. 2. Mean fixation durations (ms) for the five bins for different skill levels (low – triangles, high – diamonds, pro – circles)

3.3   Kernel Density Estimation Analysis

We further also applied a kernel density estimation procedure to the fixation duration distribution in the three skill groups. Kernel density estimation is a statistical procedure to compute a probability distribution of a random variable (like fixation duration) from a finite number of observations. Kernel density estimation is often used to reveal whether the "true" distribution of a variable is unimodal or bimodal. That is, it is used to assess whether the distribution of random variable values is homogenous or there are two (or more) clusters of values.

To analyze the specific form of fixation duration distributions at different skill levels we applied kernel density estimation to raw frequencies data. We were specifically interested in obtaining bimodal density plot for higher skilled groups as these may indicate the presence of two type of fixations – ambient (lower mean durations around 100 ms) and focal (higher mean durations around 300–350 ms). These two types of fixations have often been reported in eye-movements research. They seem to reflect either unconscious spatial processing (ambient) or conscious identification of visual objects and events (focal). To this end, the standard *density()* function from the R statistical computing environment was used with the Gaussian kernel and the band-width estimated with the 'js' method (see Fig. 3).

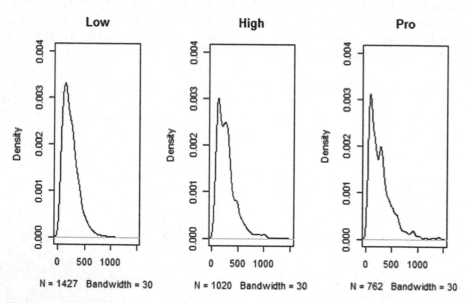

Fig. 3. Probability densities of fixation durations (in ms) in the low, high, and pro player groups estimated with the Gaussian kernel at bandwidth 30.

Overlaying the densities (not shown) reveals that they coincide to a large extent which explains why the above analysis of the means and medians didn't reveal significant differences. However, the form of distributions is clearly different suggesting the existence of two clusters of fixation durations in the higher skill groups. This is in line with the distinction between short ambient fixations and long focal fixation. This is also supported by the finding that the modes in the higher skill distributions are about 100 ms and 300 ms as is typically reported for ambient and focal fixations [12]. Overlaying the density of the low skill group over the pro group also indicates that there are more "very long" (over 500 ms) fixations in the pro group. Actually, these are virtually not present in the low skill group, contrary to the pro group.

4 Discussion

The results presented above suggest a clear difference in the distribution of fixation durations between low skilled amateurs, advanced amateurs, and professional eSports athletes while engaged in a realistic gaming experience. The low skill group shows a typical left shifted unimodal distribution of fixation durations. Fixation durations are mostly within the typical 200–400 ms range. With progressing skill level, there is a clear tendency for the variability in fixation durations to become larger. That is, there are more short fixations and more long fixations in the high skilled amateurs and, even more pronounced, in the professional gamers. A specific characteristics of the both advanced groups is the presence of very long fixations over 500 ms which are virtually absent in the low skill group.

A more detailed analysis of the distributions (kernel density estimation) revealed that the source of increased variability of fixation durations in the higher skilled groups may be the presence of different types of fixations in the latter. That is, in the low skill group the fixation duration distributions is highly uniform and unimodal. This suggests the presence of only one fixation cluster in this skill group. In the high skilled amateurs and, especially, in the professional players the distributions are bimodal with the two modes around 100 and 300 ms. Thus, there may be two clusters of fixations typically associated with short (100 ms) and long (300 ms) fixations in the two higher skilled groups. This is a qualitative difference in the distribution of fixation duration which may depend on the skill level of cyberathletes which deserves further exploration.

There is a well-founded distinction of visual fixations into ambient fixations and focal fixations [3, 5]. Ambient fixations are associated with spatial analysis of visual scenes, specifically, with the localization of objects. Ambient visual fixations are driven largely by automatic processes, are associated with the dorsal "Where" visual processing system in the human brain [6], and don't permit for conscious identification of objects. On the contrary, focal fixations reflect conscious perception of objects and are associated with the conscious ventral visual processing system in the brain (the "What" system). Studies have shown the importance of this distinction for predicting visual memory success and traffic accidents, for example [12]. Objectively, ambient fixations are short (clustering in the range 50–150 ms) and focal fixations are long (clustering around 250–350 ms). This allows identifying the two fixation clusters obtained in the both high skill groups as ambient and focal.

The ability to assess eSports athletes skill level based on the analysis of fixation duration distributions (and, generally, to assess the skill level in performing any complex computer-mediated visual interactions) may be of some importance for HCI. It may serve as input to developing personalized interfaces which adapt to the skill level of a user. Such interfaces may be adaptive to changes in the user's skill level which inevitably will occur over time. It is also important for supporting visual-motor interactions with computers as individually-tailored identification of ambient and, important, focal fixations will inform the interface what interface events were consciously processed by the user. Such analyses may also be of importance in interface design in order to assess the effectiveness of visual scanning of different interface layouts.

Game interface design solutions may be based on the analysis of the fixation durations. First, if an important screen element is mostly covered with short (ambient) fixation, it may be made visually more salient (size/color/animation) to grab players' focal attention. Second, a clear conjecture in interface design is that display elements which are focally fixated are subjectively the most important ones and so must be design with more care. Third, the ratio of ambient of focal fixations may reveal the cognitive load players experience when navigating and acting in the virtual world. It is to note that we choosed a highly specific shooter game (CS:GO) as a case study. So, our results may not generalize directly to other kinds of video games. However, in any game which employs sophisticated visualizations, there will be room for a detailed analysis of players' eye movements in order to improve the interface.

5   Conclusions

eSports athletes with different skill levels (low, high, and professional) play computer game under realistic conditions. Eye movements were recorded and the distributions of fixation durations were analyzed. It was found that increasing skill leads to more variable fixations durations (more shorter and more longer fixations). It was also found that high skill was characterized by bimodal fixations durations distributions suggesting the presence of two fixation types. These fixation types were identified as ambient and focal fixations. The results were interpreted as indicating a complex interplay of automatic ambient visual processing and conscious focal visual processing in high skilled gamers. The objective identification of skill level of users performing complex visual-motor interactions with computers may be used in developing adaptive user interfaces and in interface design.

Acknowledgements. The reported study was funded by RFBR according to the research project No. 18-29-22077\18. Authors would like to thank Skoltech Cyberacademy, CS:GO Monolith team and their coach Rustam "TsaGa" Tsagolov for fruitful discussions while preparing the paper. The authors thank Alexey "ub1que" Polivanov for supporting the experiments by providing a slot at the CS:GO Online Retake server.к.

References

1. Al-Samarraie, H., Sarsam, S.M., Guesgen, H.: Predicting user preferences of environment design: a perceptual mechanism of user interface customization. Behav. Inf. Technol. **35**(8), 644–653 (2016). https://doi.org/10.1080/0144929X.2016.1186735

2. Balota, D.A., Yap, M.J., Cortese, M.J., Watson, J.M.: Beyond mean response latency: response time distributional analyses of semantic priming. J. Mem. Lang. **59**, 495–523 (2008)
3. Berman, R., Colby, C.: Attention and active vision. Vis. Res. **49**(10), 1233–1248 (2009)
4. Eisenberg, M.L., Zacks, J.M.: Ambient and focal visual processing of naturalistic activity. J. Vis. **16**(2), 5 (2016). https://doi.org/10.1167/16.2.5
5. Fitts, P.M., Posner, M.I.: Human Performance. Brooks/Cole, Belmont (1967)
6. Follet, B., Le Meur, O., Baccino, T.: New insights into ambient and focal visual fixations using an automatic classification algorithm. Iperception. **2**(6), 592–610 (2011). https://doi.org/10.1068/i0414
7. Goodale, M.A., Milner, A.D.: Separate visual pathways for perception and action. Trends Neurosci. **15**(1), 20–25 (1992)
8. Graham, T.C.N., et al.: Usability and computer games: working group report. In: Doherty, G., Blandford, A. (eds.) DSV-IS 2006. LNCS, vol. 4323, pp. 265–268. Springer, Heidelberg (2007). https://doi.org/10.1007/978-3-540-69554-7_22
9. Jacob, R.J.K.: The use of eye movements in human-computer interaction techniques: what you look at is what you get. ACM Trans. Inf. Syst. **9**(3), 152–169 (1991)
10. Roccetti, M., Marfia, G., Semeraro, A.: Playing into the wild: a gesture-based interface for gaming in public spaces. J. Vis. Commun. Image Representation **23**(3), 426–440 (2012)
11. Starke, S.D., Baber, C.: The effect of four user interface concepts on visual scan pattern similarity and information foraging in a complex decision making task. Appl. Ergon. **70**, 6–17 (2018)
12. Van Renswoude, D.R., Raijmakers, M.R.F., Koornneef, A., Johnson, S.P., Hunnius, S., Visser, I.: Gazepath: an eye-tracking analysis tool that accounts for individual differences and data quality. Behav. Res. Methods **50**(2), 834–852 (2018)
13. Velichkovsky, B.M., Dornhoefer, S.M., Kopf, M., Helmert, J., Joos, M.: Change detection and occlusion modes in road-traffic scenarios. Transp. Res. Part F Traffic Psychol. Behav. **5**(2), 99–109 (2002)
14. Velichkovsky, B.M., Dornhoefer, S.M., Pannasch, S., Unema, P.: Visual fixations and level of attentional processing. In: Proceedings of the Eye Tracking Research & Application Symposium, ETRA 2000, Palm Beach Gardens, Florida, USA, 6–8 November 2000. https://doi.org/10.1145/355017.355029

Crowdsourcing and Collaborative Work

#TheDay: Triggering User Generated Videos in Participatory Media Productions

Sandy Claes[1(✉)], Maarten Wijnants[2], Chaja Libot[1],
and Rik Bauwens[1]

[1] VRT Innovation, Brussels, Belgium
{Sandy.claes,chaja.libot,rik.bauwens}@vrt.be
[2] Hasselt University – tUL, Expertise Centre for Digital Media,
Diepenbeek, Belgium
maarten.wijnants@uhasselt.be

Abstract. Traditional media such as television are increasingly adopting interaction logic as a way to engage viewers. In this paper, we report on the design of a smartphone application that facilitates the participatory production process of #TheDay, a two-minute item in an infotainment TV show, which is broadcasted twice a week on national television. #TheDay leverages a co-creation approach as it allows viewers to submit and discuss self-produced video content, this way empowering them to share their take on topics imposed by TV producers. We report on #TheDay's eight-month deployment. Through a mixed methods approach, we learn how the TV producers succeeded in triggering viewer interaction, also on a long-term. From our findings, we distill three considerations for the design of interactive applications that support professional producers in deploying participatory forms of media production with sustained user commitment.

Keywords: Co-creation · Participatory TV · User-Generated Content (UGC) · User-Generated Video (UGV) · Social media · Evaluation · Engagement

1 Introduction and Background

Given the increasing popularity of social media, television broadcasters started to embrace social media logic in multiple ways in an attempt to stay relevant [3]. In particular, the logic of programmability includes the transformation of one-way traffic, which is typical for television consumption, to two-way communication between users and producers—a process that affected both the technological and social mediation of content [3]. Merging such User-Generated Content (UGC) with professionally produced video has already been found to form one particular way to enhance audience engagement [8]. Yet we know little about how interaction design facilitates media producers to engage viewers in the co-creation process of media productions [6]. Furthermore, participatory media productions are often studied in the context of specific niches like interactive documentaries (e.g., [11]), interactive film (e.g., [1]) or online music experiences [5], yet in general they are still exceptions in the media landscape [9].

D. Lamas et al. (Eds.): INTERACT 2019, LNCS 11746, pp. 409–417, 2019.
https://doi.org/10.1007/978-3-030-29381-9_26

Our research is based on #TheDay, a two-minute item in an infotainment TV show that is broadcasted twice a week during prime time on national television in Flanders, Belgium. #TheDay invites viewers of the show to share specific audiovisual contributions that relate to the trending topics of that day via a smartphone application. The targeted "assignments" in relation to the interaction design of the application facilitate responses in the form of both text (i.e., users can chat with TV producers) and User-Generated Video (UGV). We hypothesize that exactly this focus on conversational interactions contributes to the engagement of users in submitting (audiovisual) content.

#TheDay has been included in the broadcast schedule for about a full year. To address our research question, we evaluate the objective data that has been captured in this time frame and complement this data with qualitative insights yielded by conducting semi-structured interviews with both contributing users of the application and professional producers of #TheDay. In particular, we study the (reasons for) engagement of contributing users, especially those who participated multiple times in generating audiovisual content for the television show and offset these user engagement incentives against the viewpoint of professional producers.

Our primary research contribution, then, is a formulation of three pragmatic considerations for designing interactive (smartphone) applications that support media professionals to trigger user generated audiovisual materials.

2   Design

#TheDay is part of the TV show "Iedereen Beroemd" (translated as "Everybody Famous") of public broadcaster VRT (in Flanders, Belgium), which is aired every day of the workweek during prime time (i.e., immediately after the evening news bulletin, around 7.30 PM). The show aims to present the viewpoint of *'John Doe'* on current events, in a lightweight fashion. #TheDay occurs each Tuesday and Thursday and includes a call-to-action for viewers to install a dedicated #TheDay smartphone application in order to send footage of "their day" to the producers of the show.

The assignment-based approach of #TheDay affords viewers the opportunity to co-create stories with the TV producers, while at the same time granting the latter stakeholder group tighter control over the storyline and facilitating the "tying together" of the incoming footage in a meaningful way. The design of the #TheDay smartphone front-end is driven by three requirements elicited from the producers. First, as the show targets a broad audience with divergent demographics and backgrounds, the application should be easy to use. Secondly, the application should grant viewers full creative freedom when creating video footage. The producers aim to receive footage with a 'DIY aesthetic' in order to highlight the sincerity and authenticity of the viewers' contributions in the final edit (i.e., the montage that is aired on TV). Producers also envision this aesthetic to connect to existing social media practices such as adding graphic elements (e.g., emojis). Therefore, they requested not to work with rigid templates or overlay instructions, in contrast to comparable UGC systems (e.g., [7]). Instead, as third requirement, viewers should be able to contact the producers for guidance.

Professional producers expressed the wish that the editorial interface should enable them to immediately consult the incoming UGV footage and to directly communicate with contributing users. Secondly, the system should allow the production team members to label the footage before sending it to post-production to enable a quick and efficient workflow.

2.1   User Flow

When opening the smartphone application for the first time, viewers are presented with a login screen where they can create a user profile for the online platform of VRT or log in with an existing one. Because of the General Data Protection Regulation (GDPR) in Europe that went in effect on May 25, 2018, the application can only be accessed by registered users, which already forms a threshold for viewers to open and inspect the application [4]. However, the use of connected user profiles allows the producers to check whether the contributing user is over 18 years old and has given his or her consent to appear on television. Then, the first screen presents an overview of open assignments (see Fig. 1.1) and a camera button (below) that immediately allows users to select and upload video footage from their smartphone media gallery. When uploaded, users receive a thank you response via a Conversational User Interface (CUI), as shown in Fig. 1.3. Videos can also be uploaded from within this screen, to grant users the option to weave their footage into a conversation with the producers. If not immediately uploading video footage, users are able to access their chat conversations and other settings via an overlay menu or via a chat bubble button in the top right of the screen (see Fig. 1.2).

The design rationale of the application mainly focused on establishing conversations, which were a requirement for both the professional producers' and users' end of the application. Therefore, second (and multiple)-time users enter the application via a conversational user interface (see Fig. 1.3), after they clicked a push notification with the assignment(s) of that day. CUIs allow users to interact with producers in their natural language (text). CUIs can support interactions with another human or with a chatbot (simple software program). This design was introduced to lower the barrier for users to engage with the application in order to chat with the producers. This approach builds upon the sense of belonging to the media production team that is already triggered by user generated visual materials [11], which is further augmented via the conversational design. It is also a way for the producers to give feedback to users, on their submitted audiovisual content as well as on their filming techniques.

The editorial interface then enables producers to request users to contextualize their footage or to ask for additional footage via the CUI. Chat messages that announce the assignment(s) or thank the users after submitting footage are sent automatically (by a chatbot). Personal chat messages issued by producers are signed with their real name, and every user that submits a video receives such a personal message to indicate whether their footage has been included in the TV item or not. The professional producers also receive an overview of all uploaded videos in this editorial tool. Each incoming video is examined

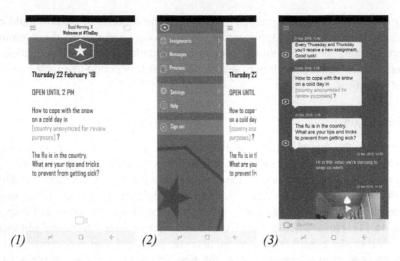

Fig. 1. User flow of the #TheDay smartphone application: (1) Open assignments, (2) Overlay menu, (3) Chat messages with the TV production team.

and labeled by a professional producer and, if deemed usable, is sent to the broadcaster's ingest system for integration in their post-production environment, where the final edit is produced. Then, when the submission period ends (i.e., approximately 1.5 h before broadcast, at 6 PM), each contributing user receives a message with a link to the final edit as it will be broadcasted later that day.

3   Study

The evaluation focused on how the #TheDay application, and the CUI specifically, facilitates user engagement. The item was first aired March 6, 2018, after which it ran twice a week until June 30, 2018. After a two-month summer break, #TheDay launched again on September 4, 2018 with an average of 701.212 viewers [2] that day and ran until December 27, 2018. During these two television seasons, we logged all interactions of both viewers and producers with the application via Google Analytics. We managed a mixed methods approach, combining quantitative data with qualitative insights from semi-structured interviews with frequently contributing users (N = 7) and professional producers (N = 3).

In total, 4501 users[1] installed the application in the analyzed period of approximately eight months, of which 2025 were female. Most users were relatively young, i.e. 18,4% of the female users were between 18 and 24 years old versus 10,4% of men. The gender distribution is more evenly spread in the age category of 35–44 years old (13% female versus 12% male), while men even take the upper hand in older age groups

---

[1] We use the term *user* to refer to someone who has installed and opened the #TheDay smartphone app without necessarily contributing UGV. People who uploaded at least one video via the app are referred to as *contributing users*.

(i.e., >44 y.o., 9% female versus 13% male). Finally, there exists a clear inversely proportional relationship between application installation and age (i.e., lower installation rate in older age ranges), which is a strong indicator that the application and the #TheDay concept appeals mostly to younger people. Users sent 3979 messages in total, of which 944 text messages (in contrast to 3035 video messages). Most users thus submitted their video contributions without any additional text.

3.1 Study Participants

On December 28, 2018, a call for participation was administered via the smartphone application, asking users to complete a concise digital survey. The survey covered topics like users' assessment of the witnessed degree of freedom, the guidance provided by producers, their completed assignment count and their motivation for contributing. 14 Users completed the survey; from this pool of users, 10 were contacted for a follow-up interview. Our main participant selection criterion here was "to have at least a minimal level of #TheDay experience", i.e. contributing UGV more than twice and having more than 2 months of experience with the application. 7 Participants voluntarily accepted the invitation. The semi-structured interviews occurred via telephone and lasted approximately 10 min. In addition, we organized semi-structured interviews with three professional #TheDay producers who are responsible for identifying interesting topics, formulating assignments, contacting and coaching contributing users and giving directions to the post-production team. These interviews lasted approximately 30 min each. For both the user and producer interviews, resulting data were transcribed per interview and then divided into quotes. Via a grounded theory approach, two researchers independently coded and categorized these quotes [9], and then reached consensus on their individual codes. The participant profiles for both our user and producer stakeholder groups are summarized in Table 1.

Table 1. Overview of study participants who are representative of long-term engaged users and professional producers, respectively.

User ID	Age	Gender	Self-reported number of participations	Date of app installation	Member of 'frequent user pool' (see Sect. 4.3)
U1	41	F	4–5	Nov 2018	No
U2	32	M	6–7	May 2018	No
U3	21	M	Every week	May 2018	Yes
U4	24	M	3	May 2018	No
U5	40	F	20–25	June 2018	No
U6	25	M	Every (two) week(s)	May 2018	Yes
U7	26	F	Every time	May 2018	Yes
Producer ID	Gender	Role as professional producer			
P1	M	Chief editor #TheDay			
P2	F	Editor #TheDay			
P3	M	Chief editor of hosting infotainment TV show			

4 Results and Discussion

4.1 Viewer and Producer Motivation

In #TheDay's first season, the application was mostly opened when a new assignment was released, i.e. on Tuesdays and Thursdays, which was also the moment for sending text and video messages. In the second season, this pattern was more spread over several days, which overlapped with the producers' strategic decision to deploy the assignments earlier than the broadcast date. This decision was informed by feedback from users who sent this spontaneously via the CUI. Such immediate and direct feedback from their audience was a novel experience for the participating producers. In specific, those users mentioned the time constraint to be a factor for disengagement. Therefore, in the beginning of the second season, producers adapted their approach to send out (most) assignments a day earlier (i.e., on the evening before broadcast).

U4 expressed to open the application in order to read the assignments as they triggered him to reflect on current topics and stay up-to-date, as he does not have the time or interest to explore the news. In that sense, the creative challenges posed by #TheDay succeeded in engaging him to explore relevant topics. Furthermore, U2 initially participated in #TheDay as he believed it could be a platform for his activist agenda. Although he did not submit footage concerning such an agenda, he appreciated learning about how to deploy media. U6 is a journalist by profession and stated how creating #TheDay footage connects to his daily work in a different, more relaxed way. In this context, U6 mentioned how he enjoys giving his footage 'out of his hands' and to discover what the professional producers did with it. The openness of the assignments was also found to foster creativity (i.e., being able to fulfill an assignment without imposed constraints, mentioned by U1, U4, U6), which most participants mentioned to be crucial in their motivation to continue sending in content.

From the production side, P2 recalled one particular experiment in which UGV contributed by different fans of a specific professional cyclist was mixed with professional footage from the sports department of the broadcaster. The final edit thus combined objective and subjective coverage of the involved cyclist, which P2 felt resulted in a story that was exciting and emotional. This experiment hints that UGV can be a valuable means to complement professional coverage in order to tell a compelling story. Furthermore, the conversational approach with individual users encouraged producers to reflect on their pre-composed storyline, which might support them in the editing process and even in identifying new stories and assignments [5], a process that might not occur when communicating to a group of users.

Design Guideline #1: Initial engagement was triggered by intrinsic motivation factors such as curiosity and learning, which should be supported by the interaction design of the application. The conversational interface seemed to lower barriers to discuss the production process of the television item, which also supported the producers in learning how to trigger user generated content.

4.2   Social Aspects

Four user participants referred to the social aspect of completing assignments together with others as key for their motivation and long-term engagement. U7, who has participated in every assignment thus far, used to shoot footage during her lunch break together with two colleagues. When one of these colleagues left their company, all three continued participation yet added a competitive element, in the sense that the former colleague now competes with U7 (and the remaining colleague) for the 'best' footage (i.e., the footage that makes it to the final edit). U1 similarly mentioned she is currently planning to execute assignments together with her colleagues. U1 also reported how she sees her participation as a collaborative effort, generating footage together with other people, including her children. U6 claimed to initiate the participation yet always collaborates with fellow students to make footage. U6 also mentioned how the participatory assignments "seem to bring people together" by giving the example of receiving several text messages from people who he had not spoken to for more than 5 years after appearing on #TheDay. U1 mainly repeated participation on request of her children. They enjoy the process of pondering what to film, the actual filming and the reward of seeing their contribution being included in the TV show. U5 similarly reported she engages with the assignments in order to share an activity with her children.

Design Guideline #2: Integrate collaboration or even competition amongst users when designing an application for triggering user generated videos. We learned how the social aspect of working together on an assignment caused contributing users to be engaged to repeatedly co-create. Often, they referred to this collaborative aspect in a competitive way, e.g. against colleagues, family and friends, or other unknown users.

4.3   Personal and Automated Conversations

The personal contact between users and professional producers that was facilitated via the CUI was found to contribute positively to the collaborative aspect of #TheDay. P2 felt she has built relationships with several contributing users who she learned to know over time, through their conversations and submitted video footage. This led to a 'pool of frequent users', i.e. 20 participants (see also Table 1), who the producers trust to deliver promising UGV. When needed, the producers contact these viewers with targeted (yet voluntary) requests to produce additional footage. U6 and U7 reported that receiving such requests are exciting and enticed a sense of belonging, yet they also felt annoyed if they could not oblige due to time or other constraints.

U1, U2, U4 and U5 reported not to have engaged in such chat conversations with the producers. However, they expressed to have personal contact with the producers, which might indicate the automatic contact supports this sense of belonging. In general, the chatbot was well-received by all of our participating users as it provided them initial confirmation and they were aware these messages were automatically generated (as the messages of producers were signed by name). Two producers, however, mentioned how this is feasible for the small frequent user pool, yet they envision this to be too time consuming when scaling up. Although P1 and P2 were initially weary of integrating a chatbot to discuss the user generated videos with users (i.e. in the design phase), through their actual experience with the automated messages, they saw opportunities to support their work.

Design Guideline #3: When designing for participatory media productions, the interaction design should establish personal conversations. Indeed, we learned how messages from the producers were key for building a lasting relationship with the users and sparked a sense of belonging. In fact, even without 'real' conversations, the ability to have contact supported the feeling of belonging to the production team.

5 Conclusions and Future Work

We have presented the design and evaluation of a smartphone application that supports the co-creation process of #TheDay, a UGV-driven TV format that is aired twice a week as part of a daily infotainment show and that has been included in the broadcast schedule for almost one year now. Via #TheDay's dedicated smartphone application, producers elicit specific contributions from the audience, based on the trending topics of that day. Using #TheDay as a lens and by wielding a mixed methods approach, we have formulated three design considerations to facilitate long-term viewer as well as professional producer commitment in participatory media contexts. These design considerations can be summarized as follows: (i) foster intrinsic motivation factors, (ii) invest in social collaboration and even competition, and (iii) promote a conversational approach, either through personal or automated contact, as it contributes positively to user engagement.

As part of future work, we will explore the role of gamification strategies, which have already been studied quite extensively in other domains (e.g., education [2], healthcare [6]), as a stimulating means to increase audience involvement and to contribute to the establishment of co-creation communities. Secondly, based on existing #TheDay conversational data, we will more deeply study how chatbots can alleviate the work of producers by suggesting or even automatically giving constructive feedback to users on the generation of videos and content. Finally, we will investigate opportunities to involve the UGV community in the post-production editing process.

Acknowledgments. This project has received funding from the European Union's Horizon 2020 research and innovation programme under grant agreement No 761802. Maarten Wijnants is funded through a VLAIO Innovation Mandate (project number HBC.2016.0625), co-sponsored by Androme.

References

1. Bartindale, T., Schofield, G., Crivellaro, C., Wright, P.: TryFilm: situated support for interactive media productions. In: Proceedings of the 19th ACM Conference on Computer-Supported Cooperative Work & Social Computing (CSCW 2016), pp. 1412–1422 (2016). https://doi.org/10.1145/2818048.2819929
2. Centre for Information on Media (CIM) in Belgium. Daily report of number of viewers. https://www.cim.be/nl/televisie/openbare-resultaten
3. van Dijck, J., Poell, T.: Understanding social media logic. Media Commun. 1(1), 2–14 (2013). https://doi.org/10.17645/mac.v1i1.70
4. Geerts, D., Leenheer, R., De Grooff, D., Negenman, J., Heijstraten, S.: In front of and behind the second screen: viewer and producer perspectives on a companion app. In: Proceedings of the 2014 ACM International Conference on Interactive Experiences for TV and Online Video - TVX 2014, pp. 95–102 (2014). https://doi.org/10.1145/2602299.2602312
5. Green, D.P., et al.: Beyond participatory production: digitally supporting grassroots documentary. In: Proceedings of the 33rd Annual ACM Conference on Human Factors in Computing Systems (CHI 2015), pp. 3157–3166 (2015). https://doi.org/10.1145/2702123.2702203
6. Kroon, A.: More than a Hashtag: Producers' and Users' Co-creation of a Loving "We" in a Second Screen TV Sports Production (2017). https://journals.sagepub.com/doi/abs/10.1177/1527476417699708. Accessed 31 Jan 2019
7. Schofield, G., Bartindale, T., Wright, P.: Bootlegger: turning fans into film crew. In: Proceedings of the 33rd Annual ACM Conference on Human Factors in Computing Systems (CHI 2015), pp. 767–776 (2015). https://doi.org/10.1145/2702123.2702229
8. Stollfuß, S.: Between television, web and social media: on social TV, About:Kate and participatory production in German Public Television. Particip. J. Audience Recept. Stud. 15 (1), 36–59 (2018)
9. te Walvaart, M., Van den Bulck, H., Dhoest, A.: Engaging the audience in a digitised television production process. J. Pract. 12(7), 901–917 (2018). https://doi.org/10.1080/17512786.2017.1343093

A Literature Review of the Practice of Educating Children About Technology Making

Leena Ventä-Olkkonen, Heidi Hartikainen, Behnaz Norouzi,
Netta Iivari, and Marianne Kinnula(✉)

INTERACT Research Unit, University of Oulu, Pentti Kaiteran katu 1,
90014 Oulu, Finland
{leena.venta-olkkonen, heidi.hartikainen,
behnaz.norouzi, netta.iivari, marianne.kinnula}@oulu.fi

Abstract. Inspired by the Maker Movement and attempts of integrating Making into formal education of children, we have examined how practice-oriented the research on Making and education is in Child-Computer Interaction field. Our results show that despite the growing interest practice-orientation is still weak. Making efforts rarely aim for longitudinal durable patterns and practices even though practice-driven research has started to gain prominence in the whole Human-Computer Interaction field. General ideas of what Making integrated with education can be and should be seem to be well shared among practitioners, however. We demonstrate what aspects should be considered when doing practice-oriented Making research and point out gaps in our current understanding of the practice. We also provide guidelines for how to study Making in order to develop sustainable practices.

Keywords: Making · Maker Movement · Fab Lab · Makerspace · School · Education · Curriculum · Child · Youth · Teen · Teacher · Practice

1 Introduction

Maker Movement has spread quickly over different continents, partly influenced by creation of the Fab Lab concept in MIT by Gershenfeld and colleagues in 2002 [58]. Making, i.e., crafting and tinkering with different materials, is actually an integral element in being human. However, when integrated with utilizing the possibilities of digital fabrication, it has been seen as revolutionary; as providing opportunities for 'ordinary people' to create something that only engineers with access to expensive machinery previously had [18]. The idea of combining digital fabrication and Making with formal education has also raised interest within researcher and practitioner communities alike. Maker Movement and Making skills are argued to have an important role in countering the digital divide by supporting development of skills in relation to digital technology [11, 15, 32, 34]. Even calls for seeing Making related skills as allowing children to grow to be "future digital innovators" [32] or protagonists as regards technology [26, 37] have been presented. In line with Maker Movement, the

© IFIP International Federation for Information Processing 2019
Published by Springer Nature Switzerland AG 2019
D. Lamas et al. (Eds.): INTERACT 2019, LNCS 11746, pp. 418–441, 2019.
https://doi.org/10.1007/978-3-030-29381-9_27

central vision here is that children learn to see technology as something they can create and shape by themselves, not merely use [e.g. 5, 7, 15, 17, 22, 25, 27, 31].

A great research and practical challenge is how to implement such vision in the education of children. Researchers and practitioners alike have explored what Making in educational context could be. For example, in 2008 FabLab@School project in Stanford University was started and Fab Labs started to appear in K-12 schools around the world [5]. In 2011, the FabLearn conference series started as a "Digital Fabrication in Education Workshop" at Stanford University and has since been arranged yearly. In 2016, already six different FabLearn conferences/events were arranged in as many countries spreading over the globe. A related trend is that countries are placing increasing emphasis on STEM (Science, Technology, Engineering, and Mathematics) education and experimenting with integration of programming into the K-12 curricula [e.g. 2, 59]. There are also plenty of Child-Computer Interaction (CCI) studies on educating and engaging children in Making activities in the school context [e.g. 5, 6, 11, 12, 30, 38, 73, 78]. The existing studies, however, mostly describe one-time and relatively short-term projects with schoolchildren, while integration of Making into basic education of children necessitates much longer and thorough engagement. So far, this has been addressed in a very limited number of studies [11, 12, 34].

We argue that there is a need for practice-oriented studies on this topic. To show this, in this study we conduct a critical review of the existing CCI literature on Making within education of children, utilizing practice approach [e.g. 40, 48, 60, 67, 81], to see how practice oriented such research currently is and what critical research gaps there can be identified. Existing Human Computer Interaction (HCI) studies have been criticized as focusing on people's short-term encounters with novel technology and as neglecting more in-depth and long-term practice studies on how such novel technology becomes embedded into and intermingled with the everyday practices of people [e.g. 48, 81, 82]. In a similar vein, we point out that the existing CCI research has focused on shorter-term encounters and neglected more in-depth and long-term studies on how Making becomes embedded into and intermingled with the everyday lives of people (i.e. how it becomes a part of teachers' and pupils' practices). Thus, our definition of 'practice' relates to Making being studied in terms of its potential to become a practice (i.e. an integrated part of everyday activity). Based on the practice approach, we offer proposals on how researchers and practitioners working with children, Making, and education should conduct their studies and cultivate the emergence of practices around Making. We acknowledge that there are various views on what Making as a practice entails and on whose values and interests have been embedded within it [84]. In this paper we seek for an understanding of how Making as a practice has been approached in CCI research on children's education.

Next, we present our analytic lens together with the methodology for the literature review. Then, we outline the literature review findings, and finally summarize the results and discuss their implications for Making research, practice, and education.

2   Theoretical Lens: Practice Approach

Interest in practice approach originates from social sciences while practice lens has gained prominence also in technology-related disciplines such as HCI [48]. Kuutti and Bannon [48] contrast Interaction paradigm and Practice paradigm in contemporary HCI. Within Interaction paradigm, the interest is on people interacting with novel technology and on how they perceive it and what they do with it, the focus being on ahistorical events quite detached from situational aspects. Practice approach, instead, emphasizes exploring in-depth how technology is integrated into the fabric of everyday life, and focuses on how things come to matter in their context from historical, social, cultural, spatial, and temporal perspectives. Practice approach studies trajectories instead of isolated events and thus requires longitudinal studies. It acknowledges material aspects, bodily and mental activities, emotions and motivational factors, which are all studied as interconnected and inseparable elements [40, 48, 60, 67, 81].

Aspects from different practice theories have been combined into a "toolkit approach" by Nicolini [60] for studying practices. The approach guides to *zooming in* on a local practice and studying it from different perspectives, but also to *zooming out* to see the bigger picture: to studying the history behind the practice, its effects on and connections with other practices and discourses circulating around. Nicolini's toolkit represents a widely cited and respected treatment of practices and it comprehensively captures aspects of several separate, famous practice theories. Hence, it enables studying practices in quite a complexity, which is needed as practices indeed are complex.

Zooming in lens studies different aspects that relate to the local practice in a specific place and time. The focus is on actual local performances, related material and bodily aspects, aims of the practice, creativity, and durability. The zoom in lens heavily takes its inspiration from ethnomethodologically influenced approaches [60]. Regarding practices as *performances*, practices are basically real time doings and sayings in specific times and places and they actually exist only when enacted and re-enacted. Thus, analysis of practices should start from observing the local accomplishments. Moreover, practice always involves an active contribution of tools. Thus, the second step is to zoom in by focusing on the active role of *material aspects* involved in practicing such as bodily choreography and tools, artifacts, and mediation work. One should acknowledge the contribution of both material and symbolic tools. It is important to study the active role of all material artifacts and how they establish relationships between practices. The *aim* of the practice is also important to study to understand what the practitioner considers should be done and what is the reason for the practice. The tension between *creativity* and normativity needs to be studied as well to understand what the norms and rules of the practice are. Finally, *durability* of the practice from the perspective of legitimacy and learning is to be examined to see how the practice can become part of a larger configuration as a resource for another practice.

Zooming out lens emphasizes that practices never happen in isolation. They cannot be carried out separately from other practices: "In order to understand what happens here and now, we also need to understand what happens somewhere else" [60]. After analyzing the accomplishment of local practices, one proceeds to identifying and trailing the *connections* between practices, *historical* trajectories regarding the emergence and evolution of practices, *discourses* circulating around practices, and links between practices. It is important to consider how local practices are *affected* by other practices and discourses, and vice versa.

Our Approach. Studying local practices usually entails long-term involvement with the practice itself through ethnographic approach. However, in this paper we use Nicolini's practice toolkit as an analytic framework to focus our attention to how the central aspects of the practices are reported in the current CCI literature on Making and education of children in the central CCI forums. This is a fresh and needed perspective in Making research in CCI – critically examining our own practice in order to be able to develop it. Utilization of a predefined categorization as an analytic framework - rather that analyzing the literature in a purely data-driven manner – helps to focus our attention to the key points in the reported practices, to spot possible research gaps, as well as to ensure that no important issues are left out. The Nicolini's toolkit of studying practices guides us to study the literature through focusing on the following nine aspects: zooming in by looking into whether and how (1) local performances, (2) aims, (3) material aspects, (4) durability, and (5) creativity have been examined in the papers, and zooming out by looking into whether and how (6) emergence and evolution of Making practice, i.e., historical trajectories, (7) effects of the practice, (8) connections between practices, and (9) discourses circulating around have been studied.

3   Methodology for the Literature Review

For this review, we have chosen to examine specifically how practice-oriented the research on Making and education is in the CCI field. We relied on a systematic review process of the following high quality, leading HCI and CCI conferences and journals that publish research on children: Nordic Conference on Human-Computer Interaction (NordiCHI), Human Factors in Computing Systems (CHI), Interaction Design and Children (IDC), Participatory Design Conference (PDC), Designing Interactive Systems (DIS), and International Journal of Child-Computer Interaction (IJCCI). We acknowledge that children's education and Making related papers have been published also elsewhere (e.g. in educational forums) but we decided first to focus only on the state of the art in the HCI and CCI field, to map out current knowledge and to point out research gaps and paths for future work. We also excluded some less authoritative, relatively new HCI forums that publish shorter papers on the topic (e.g. FabLearn). We maintain that in shorter papers thorough treatment of practices is unlikely. Hence, we did not carry out a systematic review of those publication forums.

The search for the conference papers was carried out using the Scopus database. The journal articles were searched using their own systems. Publication dates were limited to 2010 or later to gain as rich picture as possible of the current research. Used keywords included *Making*, *digital fabrication*, *children*, and *education* and different variations of those. A search carried out in the Scopus database is as follows: (TITLE-ABS-KEY ("child" OR "youth" OR "teen" OR "teenager" or "children") AND ("education" OR "school") AND ("Making" OR "maker" OR "fabrication" OR "3D"))). A paper trail was established to keep track of what was done to avoid repeating the same search tasks during the process. The collected material was organized into an online database accessible to all authors. A total of 73 papers were found fitting our initial criteria. It was further decided to exclude papers not presenting empirical accounts of working with children and papers shorter than 4 pages. This inclusion/exclusion criteria were based on our own insight and judgment of the relevance of the examined studies [cf. 8, 21]. This left us with a final dataset of 45 papers. Each paper was coded into a table featuring the nine aspects of Nicolini's practice lens as columns. The coding was done by authors 1 and 2 of this paper collaboratively. The coding process was iterative, and all the materials were gone through several times to identify content in the paper representing these categories. After coding, the results were discussed between all authors and summarized in tables seen in this paper, with accompanying text. As the dataset was relatively small, quantitative analysis was not meaningful. Instead, we prepared a narrative synthesis using the collected papers to provide understanding of the current knowledge in the area and highlighting the significance of new knowledge [16].

4 Zooming in and Out

4.1 Zooming in: Making Activity as a Local Performance

All of the reviewed papers featured an explanation of the making activity. The local performances were most often workshop style activities organized for children. These workshops had a predefined structure consisting of: (1) some kind of warm-up and review of the topic and the used techniques, (2) ideation and design phase, (3) Making and testing phase, and (4) Presentation and reflection phases. The warm-up phase included often an introduction and motivation to the selected topic such as energy forms [11] or archaeological findings [55]. This was followed by going through the different techniques of Making. The ideation and design phases consisted of e.g. sketching and storyboarding [30] and the actual Making phase included constructing, programming, and implementing [e.g. 78]. Often the process included also some sort of a final reflection stage, where outcomes were presented and evaluated. Emphasis of different phases varied, some highlighting and spending more time on learning the Making skills, others stressing ideation and design or Making. Workshops consisted typically of 1–10 short sessions. One-time workshops were reported in 16/45 papers [e.g. 38, 42], and longer-term efforts in 18/45 publications such as bi-weekly sessions throughout a school year [61] or routines lasting for several months or even years with same group of children [e.g. 11, 85]. Drop-in Making was also mentioned in the literature [e.g. 4, 53]. In the drop-in makerspaces children were free to enter and start Making, self-motivated, without a necessity to attend a specific workshop structure.

4.2 Zooming in: Material Aspects

Space. All of the reviewed papers described the location where the Making practice took place. About two thirds (31/45) of locations were informal learning contexts such as after-school clubs and centers [53, 57], summer programs [69], learning and computer clubs [86], youth centers, libraries [4, 51], and museums [53]. Sometimes Making activities were conducted in more unusual settings, e.g. in youth prison [74] or a refugee camp [86]. In addition, Making in virtual space (Minecraft) was discussed [70]. Although these activities were carried out in informal learning contexts, some of them took place inside school premises and utilizing school facilities, but were not part of the curriculum [e.g. 51, 86]. About one third (13/45) were organized in school as part of formal teaching and curriculum. In school, the Making practice took place as part of science teaching [12, 55], as an elective course [30, 79, 80] or as project weeks throughout the semester [11]. Multi-space approach was also visible in the literature. For example, Tittarelli and Iocono present a workshop program taking place in three different contexts in order to "make practices that normally take place in an archaeology lab, a fab lab and a primary school, available as resources for design" [55: p. 3]. In [30] workshops were organized both in school premises and in the university fab lab.

Materials. Making is an activity largely dependent on materials, and they were well described in majority of (42/45) the reviewed papers. At least five types of materials were listed in the literature: (1) *Electronic components (21/45)*: micro-controllers, battery packs, rotating motors, vibrating motors, LEDs, paper electronics, paper circuits, programmable projections, sewable circuits, copper tape, conductive thread and fabric, coin cell batteries, sensors and actuators, Arduino board; (2) *Crafting materials (18/45)*: cardboard, wood, paper, paint, scissors, tape, glue, pipe cleaners, fabric, colored pencils, recycled materials, Play-Doh, graphite, aluminum, beads, sequins, acrylic; (3) *Devices (15/45)*: computers, 3D printer, laser cutter, 3D scanner, headphones, and speakers. (4) *Toolkits (14/45)*: Arduino, Lilypad Arduino, Makey Makey, Circuit Scribe, PicoBoard, Lego WeDo and littleBits, TALKOO kit, fundakit, Dolly 2.0, Spark!, ID toolbox, Lego RCX, Crickets; (5) *Software (10/45)*: Scratch, Meshmixer, Thingiverse platform, Tinkercad, graphics design software; The usage and rationale for choosing different materials was usually described well.

4.3 Zooming in: Aim of the Making Activities

The literature described at least two different types of aims for the Making practice: firstly, educating children on micro level and empowering them as makers, and secondly, higher level integration of making type working into curriculum.

Educating Children. Educating children was the most often (23/45) described aim of the Making activity in the literature. Making was used for teaching different skills and empowering children as technology makers. Learning was mentioned in different levels: (1) *Empowerment*: advocating children's genuine participation and aiming at offering children design and technology skills and competencies [30], exploring ways to increase motivation and engagement in maker activities among girls and groups underrepresented in science and engineering [23]; (2) *Learning of skills*: how elements of design thinking and digital fabrication could provide pupils with new learning possibilities [73] and creating a collaborative culture of "learning and doing" [74]; (3) *Self-expression*: supporting and providing means for self-expressing through Making [e.g. 3, 38, 44, 62]; engaging children in creating multiple representations of their personal experiences [62]; allowing a group of children and teachers to create, share, and tell stories together [3]; motivating productive and expressive hands-on Making for at-risk children [49]; (4) *Related knowledge*: specific learning goals such as awareness of environmental issues, ability to design creative solutions for environmental challenges [86] or teaching facts about materials [86], history [55], anatomy and physiology [61].

Integrating Making into Curriculum. Higher level goal for Making practices was for example integrating Making into the science curriculum (6/45) [e.g. 11, 15]. Researchers considered how Making could have a role in the modern classroom to support scientific modeling [12] and specifically how 3D printing could be integrated into educational settings [6]. Making was also proposed to enrich arts curriculum e.g. in [22].

4.4 Zooming in: Durability of the Making Practice

Some papers explicitly stated aiming for integration of Making into the official school curricula in long term [e.g. 15, 19], hoping for durable and stable Making practice to emerge and stay as part of teaching. The papers aiming for creating a maker identity [e.g. 23] and for teaching needed skills [e.g. 20] had a similar goal, although not explicitly mentioned. Most of the papers, however, did not aim specifically for durable, continuing action patterns. Several aspects may enhance the durability of the practices of Making. Nicolini [60] names at least four of those:

Communities of Practice Enhancing Durability. People with similar skills and concerns make practices durable and stable [60]. The role of involved people is thus very important when practices are in the stage of establishment [60], whether the Making activity happens in school or in an informal learning context. Different communities can be seen as forming when introducing Making into education context. They usually consist of (1) children participating in the Making activities, (2) teachers, (3) research team members, and (4) domain experts. School administrators, classroom helpers, facilitators of the activities, parents, and other adult stakeholders collaborating with children can also be identified. Next, we open up the most prominent roles and their interaction.

Children were, naturally, an inseparable part of the reviewed literature. Importance of group work and collaboration among children was highlighted in many studies. Different ways to arrange the collaboration were tried out, for instance group members allocating different roles to each other by themselves [73], engaging in idea sharing, discussion and negotiation [12, 20, 49, 57, 70, 76, 78, 79], overcoming problems by observing each other [57, 85], more experienced children assisting less experienced ones (peer mentoring) [70], nomination of some children by their peers as 'experts' [86], grouping children based on knowing each other [41], or on different range of interests and skills [57] or letting children to choose their partners freely and interacting with others openly [51]. Building of community through uninterrupted natural group collaboration among children was also tried out, children playing both the roles of a teacher and a learner [74]. Within same-age-groups, teen teams were found to help each other more compared to teams consisting of younger children [65].

Teachers' presence was specified in many of the studies, mostly as providing pupils with instructions, guidance, and assistance [1, 5, 12, 15, 20, 30, 39, 72–74, 77, 79, 80, 85, 86]. This was particularly important when starting the activities; initially children can have a tendency of requesting help constantly from their teacher but when progressing in the activity they may come to the realization that through trying out, failing, and trying out again they can find their own way of working [73]. Sometimes teachers led the discussions of pupils [15] or the digital fabrication process [73]. Other times they joined the team of children and played the role of a learner [74], or had informal interaction with pupils while accomplishing some specific Making activities [39]. Other responsibilities of teachers mentioned included ensuring the baseline of the science knowledge of the pupils [11], providing consent for children' participation [65], assessing participants' skills [52], observing the children' activities [52], lecturing on the topic [12], dividing children into groups [30], or simply accompanying children in a workshop [20]. The ability of the teacher to support the complex process of digital fabrication was a considerable challenge that should be addressed [36] as well as challenges regarding hardware/software provision and teaching some complex topics to children [77]. Teachers were also specified to be closely linked with other stakeholders and they collaborated in developing the activities by providing feedback on the design concept/tool [1, 3, 5, 15, 30, 38, 52, 66, 72, 79, 80].

Research team members were reported to act as designers, developers, or revisers of the Making practices [62, 84]; instructors, tutors, or helpers in Making [15, 30, 39, 47, 49, 75, 86]; lecturers providing children with introduction to the concept [14, 52]; leaders of children' activities [15, 65]; motivators, who encourage children in the conversations [49], or supervisors of the work of junior researchers [30]. By observing children's activities and inquiring pupils' choices and actions, researchers strived to attain a deeper understanding of the creative processes of the children [73]. Sometimes research team members also assisted teachers [1] or helped pupils in Making [1, 52]. Formal and informal interaction between researchers and children was highlighted [39], formal interaction taking place when researchers acted as instructors teaching the group, informal interaction showing up through doing Making activities with children.

Different domain experts' presence was emphasized in many studies regarding their collaboration with other stakeholders and specifically with researchers. Their presence was instrumental in grounding the Making activities in real-life issues and problems, helping researchers to understand the domain-specific issues, and helping children to make their ideas come true by providing practical help and instructing and tutoring them during Making activities. Those mentioned included, e.g., game developers and content area experts [66]; an artist [63]; archaeologists [52]; a psychologist [52]; MA students participating as experience designers [52]; a fashion designer, magician, dance educator, and sport teacher [44]; teaching artists [84]; a design researcher [73]; a design team [1]; a lead designer involved in prototyping the developed sketches and helping with the manufacturing materials [1]; and experts in electrical engineering and computer science [15]. Many domain experts were mentioned in relation to planning and designing the practical work with children, such as a design researcher creating design concept template for pupils [73]; teaching artists helping in developing and revising a framework for Making [84]; design students and design researchers focusing on a digital design toolkit for children [5]; and, educational scientists providing input to the process [5]. Some domain experts such as scientists, publishers, and policy makers were mentioned as helping by giving feedback on the design concepts [5].

Parents were considered as active actors in only few studies. Involvement of parents by asking them to "post-report on the interactions of children in the days following the workshop" was suggested [13] and makerspace design was proposed to be such that it is felicitous for family engagement and children's interaction with their parents, therefore encouraging to conveying their thoughts and feelings regarding their abilities and achievements [84]. In one study, parents acted as outside audience, who contributed in structuring the feedback from other actors [56]. Many studies mentioned parents as the consent providers for their children's participation [1, 4, 11–13, 15, 39, 52, 65].

Helpers, facilitators, instructors, tutors, and *moderators* were also identified from the studies. Classroom helpers might be present in the sessions to provide help if pupils asked for it [6, 12, 14, 15, 63, 65]. Facilitators [23, 24, 43, 53, 56, 62, 68, 75] engaged in various tasks such as (1) engaging children in activities and encouraging them to express their thoughts [62], (2) adopting different facilitation approaches such as "problem-focused" or "playful" [53] and "probing into the process by asking questions" [69: p. 3], suggesting ideas to children and discussing with them about their ideas in an open way, leading the personalization of the idea by children with some flavors of creativity [75], (4) guiding children in STEM topics additional to the project [56] and (5) encouraging children by positioning them as 'experts' [56]. Instructors were mentioned as collaborating with a teacher in designing and facilitating sessions as well as data collection [41, 80], assisting children during activities [20], or explaining the model to the children [12]. Moderators were responsible for supporting children with autism [70]. Tutors provided verbal and technical assistance [78, 85].

Learning Enhancing Durability. To achieve durable practices, the practitioners need to learn the norms of the practice. To understand development of practice, the way of how learning happens, how novices are taken as part of the practice, and who teaches whom can be examined. Concerning Making, there are some central issues the reviewed literature focused on. Regarding the norms of the Making practice, it is important to learn the *practical Making skills* including use of different techniques, coding, 3D modelling and printing, but also knowledge of the design process etc. As described earlier, learning in different levels was often in the focus of the reviewed literature. Teaching the needed skills was often highlighted, including for example: circuitry, coding [63], basic skills in language and numeracy, and technology [74], 3D printing [6]; laser cutting, using Makey Makey and Touch Board [30]. On higher level, also *gaining digital literacy* and *developing maker identity* were underscored in order to maintain the Making practice in the long run [e.g. 11]. Common was to empower groups of children who are underrepresented in science and engineering, for example girls [23], refugees [86], children in the risk of exclusion [49, 56], or children with autistic diagnosis [70]. Regarding how learning happened, teachers or instructors usually guided children in the Making practice. However, children also tutored each other as described in the previous section [74]. Newcomers could be integrated into more experienced maker groups during maker activities [57]. Learning seemed to be more self-guided and self-motivated in drop-in style makerspaces, where mentors and facilitators were there to "offer assistance when the kids encounter hurdles in the Making process" [4: p. 596].

Tools and Instruments Enhancing the Practice Durability. Tools and instruments also maintain the durability of practices – they carry the scripts of the practices, which the designers and developers have embodied in them [60]. To be able to build durable practices, tools have to be available and functioning. Making practice is very much tool dependent. Thus, to build lasting Maker culture to schools, the first thing is to start building infrastructure. Most (32/45) of the activities in the literature were organized outside of official makerspaces (school class, computer labs, club rooms). The material provided by these spaces varied and the provided tools (devices, materials etc.) seemed to be limited, which does not enhance the durability of the practices. However, Smith et al. [73] describe Making and design activities within schools' fab lab environment. Such environment has natural enhancing effect to the establishment of Making activities as the availability of Making equipment makes it more likely for them to be used as part of teaching. Design of the space for Making needs also to be considered. In order to Making practice emerge, youth makerspaces should be designed as "interactive, technologically enriched spaces and programs to support youth exploration and creativity" [51: p. 310]. In general, the material space and facilities (other than the used materials) where the Making practice took place were rarely described in detail in the literature, with a few exceptions: resource availability [53], layout and the furniture of the workshop space [38, 49, 51], and the building process of Making environment [74].

Other Practices Enhancing Making Practice Durability. Finally, the durability of the practice may be achieved by a practice becoming part of a larger configuration as a resource for another practice [60]. When Making practice becomes a natural part of everyday routines attached to other practices, it becomes persistent and durable. This indeed was the goal of the studies, which clearly stated that their goal was to integrate teaching into the curriculum [14]. When Making becomes natural part of for example STEM curriculum, it becomes a routine of everyday schoolwork. Making can also become durable as part of other recurrent practices such as e.g. after school clubs. In the studies, Making had been integrated into teen center activities [56] and after-school centers that "aim to promote the social inclusion of youth living in economically-disadvantaged communities" [57: p. 91]. Proximity, safety, and inclusivity of the centers and "freedom of choice" can help in acquiring otherwise hard to obtain knowledge and skills and even seeing new career possibilities [57: p. 91]. Authors [57] beautifully describe the centers as "interruptive institutions where the cycle of exclusion can be broken, and youth development addressed, over the long-term" [57: p. 91].

4.5 Zooming in: Creativity in the Making Practice

Practices are re-produced every time they are performed, but at the same time, they are bound. Two practices are never identical, but still hold something in common [60]. Creativity as such was mentioned in many of the reviewed papers. To really study creativity of a practice, however, one should be able to study it for a longer period of time, to be able to see how it changes. This sort of longitudinal tracking of Making practice is currently absent in the literature. In some cases (18/45), work with the same group of children continued on regular basis for months or years [e.g. 11]. In these cases, the authors reported how working changes within the practice while the children gained knowhow, from instruction guided to more creative and open assignment mode [11]. For example, Chu et al. [11] report that after learning Making skills within classroom constraints (lockstepped instructions, fixed goals, minimal choices, etc.) for 1.5 years, the students could produce significant technology-based science dioramas in a Maker activity that was more in line with the spirit or essence of Making. Thus, after learning basic skills, the Making practice became more open and creative.

A summary of findings generated with the zooming in lens is presented in Table 1.

Table 1. Summary of zooming out lens inspired analysis of the literature.

Zoom in Lens	Described in the reviewed literature
Local accomplishment	Making practice described in pre-designed workshop style structure lasting 1–10 sessions consisting of following stages with varying emphasis: (1) warm-up and review of the topic and the used techniques, (2) ideation and design, (3) Making and testing, and (4) presentation and reflection
Material aspects: space	(31/45) of maker activities conducted in unofficial learning contexts such as after-school clubs and libraries. (13/45) in school context as part of school elective or science classes, as project weeks during school
Material aspects: tools & materials	Materials and tools reported in detail; materials include crafting materials (18/45), electronic components (21/45), toolkits (14/45), software (10/45), and devices (15/45)
Aim	Aiming to educate children (23/45) through learning Making skills and knowledge, providing means for self-expression, learning general learning skills. Integration making into curricula mentioned as a goal in (6/45)
Creativity	No longitudinal tracking of local practices which would enable analysis of how much practice varies within time. Creativity increases when children have learned the basic skills needed in Making
Durability: community	Community around Making consisting of following groups: (1) Children participating in the Making activities, collaborating in teams, (2) Teachers providing with instructions, guidance and assistance, (3) Research team members as developers of the Making process and instructors in the Making activities, and (4) Domain experts grounding the activities in real-life issues
Durability: learning	Learning highlighted as an important goal (23/45). Learning discussed in different levels. To gain durable practices, explicit Making knowledge and skills and development of maker identity brought out. Learning more self-guided and self-motivated in drop-in style makerspaces with help of mentors and facilitators, whereas in Making workshops activities more guided and structured

(continued)

Table 1. (*continued*)

Zoom in Lens	Described in the reviewed literature
Durability: tools & instruments	Most of the maker activities not organized in official "makerspaces" (32/45). Spaces not usually described in detail. Other spaces (e.g. classrooms, computer labs, club rooms) usually used in workshop style Making practices, which are time and place dependent, offer fewer equipment for Making, and do not support that well the durability of practices. Minority (12/45) of the activities organized in "official" makerspaces which support better the durability of the practice by providing available facilities as well as mentors and are used in both workshop style as well as in drop-in Making practices
Durability: other practices	Recurrent Maker activities integrated as part of after-school programs or school work

4.6 Zooming Out: The Emergence and Evolution of the Practices

While zoom in lens concentrates on local practices, zoom out lens expands the scope in both time and place. One should look back in time and try to find out how the practice emerged and how it has changed since through historical investigation. Historical analysis helps to understand the power relations determining the current situation [60].

The background of Making was typically reviewed in the literature review part of the articles. That is, the Making practice is grounded in the existing research as is typical scientific practice. However, notes about local history, stakeholders involved and their contribution, possible power struggles and varying motivations in general, and the steps taken before being able to conduct the current Making activity were scarcer. As an exception, one paper focused on different aspects of building of the Making environment: "The CLL (Constructionist Learning Laboratory) project was built upon a desire to build an alternative learning environment unencumbered to the greatest extent possible by the policies, practices and heuristics of traditional schooling. This goal was not entirely realized due to issues involving personnel, regulations, lack of trust and hostility imposed by the prison bureaucracy where the CLL was located" [74: p. 487].

The historical trajectory of the local practices can still be seen implicitly through continuing elements. The literature demonstrated at least four types of historical continuity in the local practices. For example, work with a *group of same children* lasting for several months or years either in school [e.g. 11] or as an after-school activity [e.g. 76] was reported in 18 articles. Another example of continuity is when the *same workshop structure* was run for several times with different participating child groups and possibly in different settings (in 6/45 articles) [e.g. 69, 85]. The third type of continuity is when the longitudinal work of researchers around the *same topic of Making* continued for years (11/45). This kind of historical trajectory was visible in [e.g. 44]: "For more than a decade, we have designed, conducted and evaluated constructionist learning environments for digital fabrication with physical computing material focusing on children... In total, we conducted approximately 40 workshops with programmable construction kits (including Lego RCX, Crickets, Arduino and

Arduino LilyPad)" [44: pp. 3–4]. Continuity is also visible in the level of *community* where the Making practice is taking place (13/45). Making efforts can be conducted within the same school or youth center where the maker culture is thus taking root. For example, [79] described a programming focused course offered for the students of the same school four times a year as an elective. Iivari et al. [30] reported also of long-term collaboration with researchers and local schools and Meintjes et al. [57] described longitudinal work with the same after school center.

4.7 Zooming Out: Effects of the Practice

Zooming out requires also studying the effects of the practices on other practices and how the local practice acts at a distance. Interesting is how the practice contributes to a wider picture and how the phenomena take place in distant times and places [60]. Most studies neglected this aspect, while Chu et al. [11] connected to this discussion the following way: "Why is it important to begin thinking about Making literacy? We expect the Maker Movement to evolve beyond being a 'movement' or a subculture. Making is poised to become a generalized rather than a specialized practice, essentially a literacy, just like textual and visual literacy today. Children learn to read till around third grade, after which they read to learn. The same may perhaps be expected for Making in the future: children may learn how to make and then use Making as a tool for learning" [11: p. 321]. Hence, some studies touched upon the broader issue of Making practice affecting other practices: e.g., children's learning and teachers' teaching practices. Another noteworthy observation is that in this literature review we have observed similar type of practices performed in different places. Hence, Making practice seems quite bound; it is distributed through Making related courses, the Fab Lab institute, and the Fab Academy, spreading the practice around the world. The community of interested researchers also help in distributing the practices to new venues. Thus, it is not surprising that there were a lot of similarities within the Making practices.

4.8 Zooming Out: Connections Between Practices

When zooming out, one should empirically track the associations between practices, asking how the practice is causally or materially connected with other practices [60]. The reviewed literature presented many related practices that the practice of Making is related to and taking influences of. The literature connected the practice of Making for example with *design* practices e.g. Design thinking, [5]; Design-based learning [5]; *learning* practices such as Collaborative learning [39, 63]; Constructive learning/constructionism [12, 39, 63, 74, 85]; Active Learning [39]; Digital literacy [5]; *education* practices such as STEM & computer science education [11, 39, 63]; *computer science* practices such as Electronics [13, 15, 39, 44, 54]; Programming [15, 43, 44, 54, 63, 72, 79]; Robotics [63]; Computational thinking [43]; Physical computing [43]; and *art and play* practices such as Storytelling [13]; Theatre [13]; Constructive play [38]; Open-ended Play [38]; Interactive music [38]; and gaming [72]. However, the studies did not discuss much how the Making practice is connected with the other practices of the participating children, teachers and schools.

4.9   Zooming Out: Discourses

The spirit of empowering children as technology makers seems to be the common ethos for all, with varying flavors; that was the central academic discourse and motivating factor for the studies. None of the studies, however, examined discourses produced and reproduced in situ, in the actual Making projects, in formal education (Table 2).

Table 2. Summary of zooming out lens inspired analysis of the literature.

Zoom out Lens	Described in the reviewed literature
Emergence and evolution of the practice	Historical trajectory of local Making practice rarely described in detail. Traces of historical trajectory and continuity of the local practices seen in different levels: (1) Work with same group of participating children continues on regular basis for months or years (18/45), (2) Same type of workshop structure/maker activity run for several times with different children and in different settings (6/45), (3) Researchers' longitudinal work around same topic of Making (11/45),(4) Longitudinal work with the same community (e.g. school) (13/45)
Effects of the practice	Not considered in the current literature with a few exceptions
Connections between practices	Making practice linked with several other practices, most often with education (e.g. collaborative and constructive learning) and computer science related practices (e.g. programming, electronics and robotics). In addition, also design related practices are linked with Making (e.g. design thinking and participatory design). However, limited focus on how Making practice connects with other practices of the participants in their everyday life
Discourses	Not considered in the current literature

5   Concluding Discussion

Inspired by the recent Maker Movement and the attempts of integrating Making into formal education of children, we conducted a review of the existing CCI literature on Making in education, utilizing the Nicolini's practice toolkit approach [60] for examining how practice-oriented such research currently is. This approach helped us make sense on the current situation in Making practice and envision how it could be better studied as well as integrated into the fabric of everyday life in the education of children. Next, we discuss what we can learn from this examination.

5.1   How to Study and Nurture Durable Making Practices?

We can summarize that the existing CCI literature on Making and education of children is not very practice-oriented. Moreover, many of the studies do not consider supporting or nurturing of durable practices for the practitioners, i.e. for children and teachers. If Making enthusiasts, both researchers and practitioners, think that all children need to learn Making skills to become digital innovators of the future [31], if the goal truly is to develop a maker mindset or identity in children [11, 15], to transform their education with Making [11, 12, 15], or to empower children to adopt a protagonist role as regards technology [26, 35], then we need to seriously consider how we can nurture durable making practices that become weaved into the fabric of everyday life. In Table 3 we give suggestions with this on mind: how the practice lens can be applied to guide and evaluate our research and practice around Making on Micro (local practice in specific time and place), Meso (related to local practice but extension in time and space), and Macro (not related to local practice) levels.

Table 3. Guidance for practice oriented CCI research on Making practices

Level	Perspective	Questions to ask
Micro-level	Local performances	What is actually being done? What children do, what teachers do? Is the working recurrent? How longitudinal is it? Does the working progress from lock-step instructions to more creative and free learning processes?
	Individual learning	What are children (or teachers) learning and how (e.g. practical Making skills, digital literacy)? Do children's and teachers' skills, competencies, and maker identity develop? Do they feel empowered?
	Aim	What is the goal of the local Making activity (e.g. specific skills, learning to learn, related knowledge)? Whose goals are acknowledged?
	Material aspects	What materials and tools are available? What is the layout of the space? How open is the space? How materials, tools and space inspire, shape or limit the performances? How accessible are they? Are they available in the longer timespan?
Meso-level	Communities	Who are involved? What kind of roles and responsibilities are involved? How new members are taken along? Is there peer learning and teaching (helping new members to join the community)?
	Other practices	Is Making part of some other activity (as part of another practice)? Does school curriculum include and/or enable Making activities?
	History of the local practice	How did we get where we are? Who are/were the stakeholders' involved? What are their interests? Who has the power?
Macro-level	Connections between practices	To which activities (such as design, learning, IT related) the current practice is connected to and how? How other practices are shaping Making practice?
	Effects of the practice	How practice travels to other places? How the same practice is expressed in another setting? How the practice in question is inspiring, shaping or delimiting other practices?
	Discourses	What are the ongoing related societal discourses (e.g. related to education, skills of 21st century, constructive learning) circulating around? What are the ongoing discourses in families (e.g. technology is good/bad)? How these discourses affect the local practice and vice versa?

Next, we discuss our findings and guidelines on these three different levels.

Local Performances. From the perspective of Nicolini's [60] toolkit approach, we can say the aspect of local performances was quite well addressed in the literature. The studies quite well described what was happening in the Making practice. We wish to point out, however, that there was a lack of observational or ethnographic studies describing in richness and detail what was happening, what the participants were saying and doing in minute detail. We think this type of inquiries are needed to understand and better support Making practice in education.

Individual Learning. Learning was also acknowledged by the existing literature quite well. Mostly children's learning was addressed, but occasionally also teachers'. The current research described learning goals quite well, but it was quite vague in examining whether those were actually met. Moreover, from the perspective of durability, longer-term studies are needed.

Aims. The reviewed studies quite well addressed the aims of the practice but almost exclusively from adults' perspective, with empowerment of children, teaching children valuable skills, as their aim. Children's own aims for the practice were not discussed. The work mostly seemed not to be initiated by children or based on their own issues and interests; hence, it is not such a surprise that their aims were not the most central in these studies. We call for more child driven projects as well as for studies on the aims from children's perspective in any type of a project (in line with [32, 45]).

Material Aspects. Another relatively strong aspect in the studies was the acknowledgement of material issues in Making. The studies comprehensively listed the tools and technologies they utilized, even if more mundane arts and crafts materials were less well described. Usually the space where the activity took place was mentioned, but it was often not very well described: its effects on the Making practice was not contemplated upon much. The same goes for the tools and equipment in many studies: they were listed but their role in and intrigue influence on children's activities were not well addressed, even if some studies discussed their influence on creativity of children (see also [36, 46]). The participants' detailed bodily choreographies in the space while interacting with each other and the tools and equipment in question were also neglected in the reviewed studies. This type of analysis often relies on observational or ethnographic studies with video data in situ. We invite researchers to collect such data. For durability of a practice, the material aspects are very important: the tools and equipment, if available in the longer run, capture and transmit aspects of the practice. Only few studies concentrated particularly on this aspect in the sense of building of suitable environments for Making practice. More this type of work is needed in the future.

Communities. Important is to point out that various kinds of practitioners can be identified as producers and bearers of the practice in the studies. Interestingly, these divergent groups of people were placed into various kinds of roles in the practice, too. Most widely discussed groups were teachers and children, who both were also assigned different kinds of roles. Mostly, however, the studies merely mentioned these groups and roles, without going into detail as regards the responsibilities, contributions and challenges associated with them. We think that practice studies focusing on the perspective of each of these stakeholder groups and their roles is warranted in the future. The groups and roles definitely have differing skills, competencies, interests, expectations, needs, and desires that should all be examined and acknowledged in the practice. Moreover, although many studies showed the variety of actors and communities that are to be involved in this practice, any group of people interacting does not automatically form a community, not to mention a community of practice [50, 86], which requires the group to have a joint enterprise, a shared practice supporting the enterprise, mutual relationships, a shared identity and new members learning by observing the expert member and learning by doing. The existing literature does not address these types of issues yet very well, but future studies on the emergence of communities of practice around Making in education are very much welcomed.

Other Practices. For durability of a practice, it is important to connect the practice with other practices, which was indeed emphasized by the studies highlighting the need to integrate Making with education and school practices.

History of Local Practice. As regards zooming out, i.e., acknowledging the broader context, the studies were quite limited. The studies described the history of the Maker Movement and related research, but the local history, i.e., local happenings and trajectory behind the study, and various stakeholders with vested interests and power relations were not described. Such analyses are warmly welcomed.

Connections Between Practices. We were surprised to see how similar the Making practice was in the studies – carried out by different people with differing backgrounds, in different schools with their particular cultures and practices, in different countries with their specific educational systems and practices. Naturally, some differences in the studies were easily observable (e.g. regarding equipment used), but as Making practice in education involves such a variety of participants (most notably children, teachers, researchers) as bearers and producers of the practice that is embedded within such a variety of rich and evolving contexts, interesting differences should also be observable. They should also be brought up – also to reveal the variety in the values and agendas embedded in the Making practices [84]. Then again, as Maker culture is a world-wide movement; it is not that surprising that Making projects with children are somewhat similar around the world – many assumptions and principles are shared. In addition, in studies in other contexts it has been shown that children's technology use practices in public spaces bear interesting similarities to their use practices with different technology at home [82]; hence, practices may travel between contexts or heavily shape other practices. Studies have overall shown that our knowledge, background, and experiences shape our current action [29, 47]. This requires attention also in Making research: it would be interesting to study what kind of baggage the participants bring into Making, how their experiences and knowledge shape what they do, how their practices elsewhere influence their current activities, and how the experiences with Making practice influence and enrich practices elsewhere: at school, at home, during leisure time.

Effects of the Practice. As regards the effects of the practice on other practices, it has already been pointed out that learning and the need for (cultural) change were highlighted in the studies, while longer term studies would be needed to really observe the effects, As regards participatory design, this type of attempts have been published, examining longer term influences of participatory design projects [9, 10]. Along these lines, studies inquiring the effects of these Making endeavors are also needed in the future. Effects on the participants are naturally interesting, but the practice lens guides to study effects on school practices or even educational systems. So far, the studies in their discussion sections mostly argue for such effects and give recommendations on how to achieve those, while it is yet a question mark how well they work in practice.

Discourses. As the last point, we wish to highlight that there was a lack of studies examining in situ discourses produced and reproduced during Making practice in education. Research has shown that discourses circulating around – in situ or broader ones in society – heavily influence what people say and do [e.g. 19, 28, 71]. Definitely interesting discourses on Making could be identifiable in situ by listening to how the participants talk about it, but also by carrying out broader analyses addressing talk about Making in education in society – shaping the opinions of the public as well as that of the policy makers. These studies remain yet to be carried out.

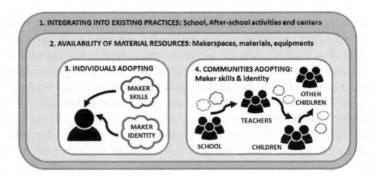

Fig. 1. Nurturing durable making practice in education.

Way Forward. The way forward in nurturing durable Making practice is demonstrated in Fig. 1. In order to develop practices that last and become durable, Making practice should be integrated with other recurrent daily practices such as schoolwork or after-school clubs. Although integrating into school curriculum would reach children in a wide spectrum, informal contexts, such as after school clubs, may be even more efficient in teaching children to become makers, as the activity is voluntary and does not have the burden of learning goals. In this endeavor, availability of material resources is critical: easy access to makerspaces with needed material and equipment as well as guidance are necessary. The participants should first learn the basic Making skills, which in the longer run should contribute to the adoption of a maker identity and ideology. In school context, it is also critical that teachers learn the Making skills and how to integrate Making naturally into everyday schoolwork. Only after that, the practice can become a durable part of education of children. To truly ensure durable practices, communities of practice should emerge, within which individuals learn from each other and novices are encultured and educated to become full members.

5.2   Conclusion

Previous literature reviews on Making and children have focused on Making as a social action and the histories of participants and interactions between them [34], potential of Making in empowering children to become digital innovators of the future [33], or potential on Making in the educational contexts [88; 64], while our interest has been in the potential of the practice of Making to become integrated as part of everyday activity in educational contexts. Our results show that even though Making in the context of children's education has raised much interest within both researcher and practitioner communities, it is still an undeveloped practice and much is needed to truly understand what it means to integrate Making with education of children. Many gaps exist in our current understanding of the practice but it can also be seen that some general ideas on what Making integrated with education can be and should be is surprisingly shared among the practitioners. As there is a vivid interest within practitioner communities all around the world, researchers have good possibilities to both study this emerging practice and to affect how it develops. By adopting the practice lens, it is possible to understand the Making practice in-depth as well as to help it to fit into the everyday life of schools.

We wish to point out, however, that there are also alternative ways to do practice research and we do not see the Nicolini's [60] toolkit approach as the only way forward (see also [81]). The toolkit's strength is that it very comprehensively captures aspects that are relevant in practice studies and it hence provided a very useful lens for this examination of how well practice approach has been utilized in the existing literature. However, at the same time the toolkit combines such a variety of theories and traditions that its coherence can be questioned. For a detailed practice study in practice, it might be wiser to select one of the theories Nicolini utilizes. Each of them has its own strengths and weaknesses; hence, the selection needs to be done case by case, considering the specific needs and interests of the study.

As to the limitations of this study, due to the existing research not being very practice-oriented, the number of the papers analyzed in this review is relatively small and therefore the actual practice in real life surely is more varied than pictured here. We also acknowledge that Nicolini's toolbox is meant for serving as a methodological lens for ethnographic studies. Here, we have applied it to reviewing literature which tell the interpretations and analysis of the authors of the papers, instead of the original local practices. Moreover, one could criticize the validity of the whole lens, which combines several practice theories with distinct assumptions and ontologies into one framework. Despite these weaknesses, we think that the benefits of using the analysis framework are greater than the drawbacks. By utilizing the toolbox, we are able to identify issues, which we wouldn't be able to spot without.

References

1. Angello, G., Chu, S.L., Okundaye, O., Zarei, N., Quek, F.: Making as the new colored pencil: translating elementary curricula into maker activities. In: Proceedings of the IDC, pp. 68–78. ACM, New York (2016)

2. Balanskat, A., Engelhardt, K.: Computing our future: computer programming and coding-priorities. School Curricula and Initiatives Across Europe. European SchoolNet (2014)
3. Baranauskas, M.C.C., Posada, J.E.G.: Tangible and shared storytelling: searching for the social dimension of constructionism. In: Proceedings of the IDC, pp. 193–203. ACM, New York (2017)
4. Bar-El, D., Zuckerman, O., Shlomi, Y.: Social competence and STEM: teen mentors in a makerspace. In: Proceedings of the IDC, pp. 595–600. ACM, New York (2016)
5. Bekker, T., Bakker, S., Douma, I., van der Poel, J., Scheltenaar, K.: Teaching children digital literacy through design-based learning with digital toolkits in schools. Int. J. Child-Comput. Interact. 5(C), 29–38 (2015)
6. Berman, A., Deuermeyer, E., Nam, B., Chu, S.L., Quek, F.: Exploring the 3D printing process for young children in curriculum-aligned making in the classroom. In: Proceedings of the IDC, pp. 681–686. ACM, New York (2018)
7. Blikstein, P.: Digital fabrication and 'making' in education: the democratization of invention. In: Walter-Herrmann, J., Büching, C. (eds.) FabLabs: Of Machines, Makers and Inventors, pp. 1–21. Transcript Verlag, Bielefeld (2013)
8. Boell, S.K., Cecez-Kecmanovic, D.: On being 'systematic' in literature reviews in IS. J. Inform. Technol. 30(2), 1–13 (2014)
9. Bossen, C., Dindler, C., Iversen, O.: Impediments to user gains: experiences from a critical participatory design project. In: Proceedings of the PDC, pp. 31–40. ACM, New York (2012)
10. Bossen, C., Dindler, C., Iversen, O.S.: User gains and PD aims: assessment from a participatory design project. In: Proceedings of the PDC, pp. 141–150. ACM, New York (2010)
11. Chu, S.L., et al.: Becoming makers: examining "making" literacy in the elementary school science classroom. In: Proceedings of the IDC, pp. 316–321. ACM, New York (2017)
12. Chu, S.L., Deuermeyer, E., Quek, F.: Supporting scientific modeling through curriculum-based making in elementary school science classes. Int. J. Child-Comput. Interact. 16, 1–8 (2018)
13. Chu, S.L., Quek, F., Bhangaonkar, S., Ging, A.B., Sridharamurthy, K.: Making the maker: a means-to-an-ends approach to nurturing the maker mindset in elementary-aged children. Int. J. Child-Comput. Interact. 5, 11–19 (2015)
14. Chu, S.L., Saenz, M., Quek, F.: Connectors in maker kits: investigating children's motor abilities in making. In: Proceedings of the IDC, pp. 452–462. ACM, New York (2016)
15. Chu, S.L., Schlegel, R., Quek, F., Christy, A., Chen, K.: "I Make, Therefore I Am": the effects of curriculum-aligned making on children's self-identity. In: Proceedings of the CHI, pp. 109–120. ACM, New York (2017)
16. Cronin, P., Ryan, F., Coughlan, M.: Undertaking a literature review: a step-by-step approach. Br. J. Nurs. 17(1), 38–43 (2008)
17. Dougherty, D.: The maker movement. Innovations 7(3), 11–14 (2012)
18. Gershenfeld, N.: How to make almost anything: the digital fabrication revolution. Foreign Affairs 91(6), 43–57 (2012)
19. Halkola, E., Iivari, N., Kuure, L.: Infrastructuring as social action. In: Proceedings of the ICIS, pp. 1–19 (2015)
20. Hamidi, F., et al.: Using robotics and 3D printing to introduce youth to computer science and electromechanical engineering. In: Proceedings of the CHI, pp. 942–950. ACM, New York (2017)
21. Hart, C.: Doing a Literature Review: Releasing the Social Science Research Imagination. SAGE Publications Ltd., London (1999)
22. Hatch, M.: The Maker Movement Manifesto. McGraw-Hill Education, New York (2014)

23. Holbert, N.: Bots for tots: building inclusive makerspaces by leveraging "ways of knowing". In: Proceedings of the IDC, pp. 77–88. ACM, New York (2016)

24. Holbert, N.: Leveraging cultural values and "ways of knowing" to increase diversity in maker activities. Int. J. Child-Comput. Interact. **9–10**, 33–39 (2016)

25. Honey, M., Kanter, D.E. (eds.): Design, Make, Play: Rowing the Next Generation of STEM Innovators. Routledge, New York (2013)

26. Iivari, N., Kinnula, M.: Empowering children through design and making: towards protagonist role adoption. In: Proceedings of the PDC. ACM, New York (2018)

27. Iivari, N., Kinnula, M.: Inclusive or inflexible - a critical analysis of the school context in supporting children's genuine participation. In: Proceedings of the NordiCHI, pp. 1–10. ACM, New York (2016)

28. Iivari, N., Kinnula, M., Kuure, L.: With best intentions - a Foucauldian examination on children's genuine participation in ICT design. J. Inf. Tech. Peop. **28**(2), 246–280 (2015)

29. Iivari, N., Kinnula, M., Kuure, L., Molin-Juustila, T.: Video diary as a means for data gathering with children - encountering identities in the making. Int. J. Hum. Comput. Stud. **5**(5), 507–521 (2014)

30. Iivari, N., Kinnula, M., Molin-Juustila, T.: You have to start somewhere - Initial meanings making in a design and making project. In: Proceedings of the IDC, pp. 80–92. ACM, New York (2018)

31. Iivari, N., Kinnula, M., Molin-Juustila, T., Kuure, L.: Multiple voices in the maker movement – a nexus analytic review of children and making research. In: Proceedings of the ECIS, pp. 1919–1933 (2017)

32. Iivari, N., Molin-Juustila, T., Kinnula, M.: The future digital innovators: empowering the young generation with digital fabrication and making. In: Proceedings of the ICIS, p. 18 (2016)

33. Iivari, K., Molin-Juustila, K.: Multiple voices in the maker movement – a nexus analytic literature review on children, education and making. In: Proceedings of the ECIS, pp. 1919–1933 (2017)

34. Iversen, O.S., Smith, R.C., Dindler, C.: From computational thinking to computational empowerment: a 21st century PD agenda. In: Proceedings of the PDC, pp. 1–11. ACM, New York (2018)

35. Iversen, O.S., Smith, R.C., Blikstein, P., Katterfeldt, E., Read, J.C.: Digital fabrication in education: expanding the research towards design and reflective practices. Int. J. Child-Comput. Interact. **5**, 1–2 (2015)

36. Iversen, O.S., Smith, R.C., Dindler, C.: Child as protagonist: expanding the role of children in participatory design. In: Proceedings of the IDC, pp. 27–37. ACM, New York (2017)

37. Jakobsen, K.B., Stougaard, J., Petersen, M.G., Winge, J., Grønbæk, J.E., Rasmussen, M.K.: Expressivity in open-ended constructive play: building and playing musical lego instruments. In: Proceedings of the IDC, pp. 45–57. ACM, New York (2017)

38. Johnson, R., Shum, V., Rogers, Y., Marquardt, N.: Make or shake: an empirical study of the value of making in learning about computing technology. In: Proceedings of the IDC, pp. 440–451. ACM, New York (2016)

39. Jurmu, M., Ventä-Olkkonen, L., Lanamäki, A., Iivari, N., Kukka, H., Kuutti, K.: Emergent practice as a methodological lens for public displays in-the-Wild. In: Proceedings of the PerDis, pp. 124–131. ACM, New York (2016)

40. Kafai, Y., Vasudevan, V.: Hi-lo tech games: crafting, coding and collaboration of augmented board games by high school youth. In: Proceedings of the IDC, pp. 130–139. ACM, New York (2016)

41. Katterfeldt, E.-S., Cuartielles, D., Spikol, D., Ehrenberg, N.: Talkoo: a new paradigm for physical computing at school. In: Proceedings of the IDC, pp. 512–517. ACM, New York (2016)

42. Katterfeldt, E.-S., Cukurova, M., Spikol, D., Cuartielles, D.: Physical computing with plug-and-play toolkits: key recommendations for collaborative learning implementations. Int. J. Child-Comput. Interact. **17**, 72–82 (2018)

43. Katterfeldt, E., Dittert, N., Schelhowe, H.: Designing digital fabrication learning environments for bildung: implications from ten years of physical computing workshops. Int. J. Child-Comput. Interact. **5**, 3–10 (2015)

44. Kinnula, M., et al.: Cooperation, combat, or competence building – what do we mean when we are 'empowering children' in and through digital technology design? In: Proceedings of the ICIS, p. 21. AIS (2017)

45. Kinnula, M., Molin-Juustila, T., Sanchez Milara, I., Cortes, M., Riekki, J.: What if It Switched on the Sun? Exploring creativity in a brainstorming session with children through a Vygotskyan perspective. Comput. Support. Coop. Work **26**(4), 423–452 (2017)

46. Kuure, L., Halkola, E., Iivari, N., Kinnula, M., Molin-Juustila, T.: Children imitate! Appreciating recycling in participatory design with children. In: Proceedings of the PDC, pp. 131–140. ACM, New York (2010)

47. Kuutti, K., Bannon, L.J.: The turn to practice in HCI: towards a research agenda. In: Proceedings of the CHI, pp. 3543–3552. ACM, New York (2014)

48. Kuznetsov, S., Trutoiu, L.C., Kute, C., Howley, I., Siewiorek, D., Paulos, E.: Breaking boundaries: strategies for mentoring through textile computing workshops. In: Proceedings of the CHI, pp. 2957–2966. ACM, New York (2011)

49. Lave, J., Wenger, E.: Situated Learning: Legitimate Peripheral Participation. Cambridge University Press, Cambridge (1991)

50. Lee, V.R., Lewis, W., Searle, K.A., Recker, M., Hansen, J., Phillips, A.L.: Supporting interactive youth maker programs in public and school libraries: design hypotheses and first implementations. In: Proceedings of the IDC, pp. 310–315. ACM, New York (2017)

51. Linke, R., Kothe, T., Alt, F.: TaBooGa: a hybrid learning app to support children's reading motivation. In: Proceedings of the IDC, pp. 278–285. ACM, New York (2017)

52. Litts, B.K.: Resources, facilitation, and partner-ships: three design considerations for youth makerspaces. In: Proceedings of the IDC, pp. 347–350. ACM, New York (2015)

53. Lochrie, M., et al.: Co-designing a physical to digital experience for an onboarding and blended learning platform. In: Proceedings of the IDC, pp. 660–665. ACM, New York (2016)

54. Marti, P., Tittarelli, M., Iacono, I.: Itinerarium: co-designing a tangible journey through history. In: Proceedings of the NordiCHI, pp. 1–6. ACM, New York (2016)

55. McBeath, J.K., Durán, R.P., Harlow, D.B.: Not my gumdrop buttons! Youth tool use in designing an electronic Shrek-themed bean bag toss. In: Proceedings of the IDC, pp. 61–72. ACM, New York (2017)

56. Meintjes, R., Schelhowe, H.: Inclusive interactives: the transformative potential of making and using craft-tech social objects together in an after-school centre. In: Proceedings of the IDC, pp. 89–100. ACM, New York (2016)

57. Mikhak, B., Lyon, C., Gorton, T., Gershenfeld, N., McEnnis, C., Taylor, J.: Fab Lab: an alternate model of ICT for development. In: Proceedings of the International Conference on Open Collaborative Design for Sustainable Innovation, pp. 1–7 (2002)

58. National Research Council: Successful K-12 STEM education: Identifying effective approaches in science, technology, engineering, and mathematics. National Academies Press (2011)

59. Nicolini, D.: Practice Theory, Work, and Organization: An Introduction. Oxford University Press, Great Britain (2012)
60. Norooz, L., Froehlich, J.: Exploring early designs for teaching anatomy and physiology to children using wearable e-textiles. In: Proceedings of the IDC, pp. 577–580. ACM, New York (2013)
61. Panjwani, A.: Constructing meaning: designing powerful story-making explorations for children to express with tangible computational media. In: Proceedings of the IDC, pp. 358–364. ACM, New York (2017)
62. Papavlasopoulou, S., Giannakos, M.N., Jaccheri, L.: Creative programming experiences for teenagers: attitudes, performance and gender differences. In: Proceedings of the IDC, pp. 565–570. ACM, New York (2016)
63. Papavlasopoulou, S., Giannakos, M.N., Jaccheri, L.: Empirical studies on the Maker Movement, a promising approach to learning: a literature review. Entertain. Comput. **18**, 57–78 (2017)
64. Papavlasopoulou, S., Sharma, K., Giannakos, M., Jaccheri, L.: Using eye-tracking to unveil differences between kids and teens in coding activities. In: Proceedings of the IDC, pp. 171–181. ACM, New York (2017)
65. Radu, I., Doherty, E., DiQuollo, K., McCarthy, B., Tiu, M.: Cyberchase shape quest: pushing geometry education boundaries with augmented reality. In: Proceedings of the IDC, pp. 430–444. ACM, New York (2015)
66. Reckwitz, A.: Toward a theory of social practices - a development in culturalist theorizing. Eur. J. Soc. Theory **5**(2), 243–263 (2002)
67. Richard, G.T., Kafai, Y.B.: Making physical and digital games with e-textiles: a workshop for youth making responsive wearable games and controllers. In: Proceedings of the IDC, pp. 309–402. ACM, New York (2015)
68. Richard, G.T., Giri, S., McKinley, Z., Ashley, R.W.: Blended making: multi-interface designs and E-crafting with elementary and middle school youth. In: Proceedings of the IDC, pp. 675–680. ACM, New York (2018)
69. Ringland, K.E., Boyd, L., Faucett, H., Cullen, A.L.L., Hayes, G.R.: Making in minecraft: a means of self-expression for youth with autism. In: Proceedings of the IDC, pp. 340–345. ACM, New York (2017)
70. Scollon, R.: Nexus Analysis: Discourse and the Emerging Internet. Routledge, London (2004)
71. Simões Gomes, T.S., Pontual Falcano, T., Cabral de Azeve-do Restelli Tedescoa, P.: Exploring an approach based on digital games for teaching programming concepts to young children. Int. J. Child-Comput. Interact. **16**, 77–87 (2018)
72. Smith, R.C., Iversen, O.S., Hjorth, M.: Design thinking for digital fabrication in education. Int. J. Child-Comput. Interact. **5**, 20–28 (2015)
73. Stager, G.S.: Papert's prison fab lab: implications for the maker movement and education design. In: Proceedings of the IDC, pp 487–490. ACM, New York (2013)
74. Tan, V., Peppler, K.: Creative design process in making electronic textiles. In: Proceedings of the IDC, pp. 327–330. ACM, New York (2015)
75. Tarkan, S., et al.: Toque: designing a cooking-based programming language for and with children. In: Proceedings of the CHI, pp. 2417–2426. ACM, New York (2010)
76. Tinapple, D., Sadauskas, J., Olson, L.: Digital culture creative classrooms (DC3): teaching 21st century proficiencies in high schools by engaging students in creative digital projects. In: Proceedings of the IDC, pp. 380–383. ACM, New York (2013)
77. Trappe, C.: Creative access to technology: building sounding artifacts with children. In: Proceedings of the IDC, pp. 188–191. ACM, New York (2012)

78. Tsan, J., Lynch, C.F., Boyer, K.A.: "Alright, what do we need?" A study of young coders' collaborative dialogue. Int. J. Child-Comput. Interact **17**, 61–71 (2018)

79. Vasudevan, V., Kafai, Y., Yang, L.: Make, wear, play: remix designs of wearable controllers for scratch games by middle school youth. In: Proceedings of the IDC, pp. 339–342. ACM, New York (2015)

80. Ventä-Olkkonen, L.: The characteristics and development of urban computing practices: utilizing practice toolkit approach to study public display network. Ph.D. dissertation Thesis, University of Oulu, Finland (2017)

81. Ventä-Olkkonen, L., Iivari, N., Kuutti, K.: Zooming in and out – studying children's and their families' smart device practices with public and private screens. In: Proceedings of the ECCE, pp. 129–136. ACM, New York (2017)

82. Vossoughi, S., Bevan, B.: Making and tinkering: a review of the literature. National Research Council Committee on Out of School Time STEM (2014)

83. Wardrip, P.S., Brahms, L.: Learning practices of making: developing a framework for design. In: Proceedings of the IDC, pp. 375–378. ACM, New York (2015)

84. Weibert, A., Marshall, A., Aal, K., Schubert, K., Rode, J.A.: Sewing interest in e-textiles: analyzing making from a gendered perspective. In: Proceedings of the DIS, pp. 15–24. ACM, New York (2014)

85. Weibert, A., et al.: Creating environmental awareness with upcycling making activities: a study of children in Germany and palestine. In: Proceedings of the IDC, pp. 286–291. ACM, New York (2017)

86. Wenger, E.: Communities of Practice: Learning, Meaning, and Identity. Cambridge University Press, New York (1998)

87. Vossoughi, S., Hooper, P.K., Escudé, M.: Making through the lens of culture and power: toward transformative visions for educational equity. Harvard Educ. Rev. **86**(2), 206–232 (2016)

Effect of Cognitive Abilities
on Crowdsourcing Task Performance

Danula Hettiachchi[1](✉)(iD), Niels van Berkel[1](iD), Simo Hosio[2](iD),
Vassilis Kostakos[1](iD), and Jorge Goncalves[1](iD)

[1] School of Computing and Information Systems,
The University of Melbourne, Melbourne, Australia
{danula.hettiachchi,niels.van,
vassilis.kostakos,jorge.goncalves}@unimelb.edu.au
[2] Center for Ubiquitous Computing, University of Oulu, Oulu, Finland
simo.hosio@oulu.fi

Abstract. Matching crowd workers to suitable tasks is highly desirable
as it can enhance task performance, reduce the cost for requesters, and
increase worker satisfaction. In this paper, we propose a method that
considers workers' cognitive ability to predict their suitability for a wide
range of crowdsourcing tasks. We measure cognitive ability via fast-paced
online cognitive tests with a combined average duration of 6.2 min. We
then demonstrate that our proposed method can effectively assign or
recommend workers to five different popular crowd tasks: Classification,
Counting, Proofreading, Sentiment Analysis, and Transcription. Using
our approach we demonstrate a significant improvement in the expected
overall task accuracy. While previous methods require access to worker
history or demographics, our work offers a quick and accurate way to
determine which workers are more suitable for which tasks.

Keywords: Crowdsourcing · Cognitive ability · Task performance

1 Introduction

Although crowdsourcing is actively used for a wide variety of both academic
and industry tasks, ensuring that the crowd produces data of appropriate quality remains an important challenge. As a result, a wide range of quality assurance
mechanisms have been proposed, from straightforward approaches, such as the
use of golden standard questions [13] to more complex approaches like monitoring
worker activity on crowdsourcing markets [54]. Researchers have also explored
ways to predict which workers are likely to perform a task well and facilitate
appropriate task assignment [22,60]. For instance, this can be achieved through
the analysis of historical records on completed tasks over a certain period [40,46].
However, this method is only applicable when such records exist and can be
matched to individual workers, which is often not the case. Furthermore, mechanisms that do not rely on the historical performance of workers are better suited

© IFIP International Federation for Information Processing 2019
Published by Springer Nature Switzerland AG 2019
D. Lamas et al. (Eds.): INTERACT 2019, LNCS 11746, pp. 442–464, 2019.
https://doi.org/10.1007/978-3-030-29381-9_28

in certain scenarios, such as one-time crowdsourcing tasks/campaigns or when considering new workers of a platform. In these cases, there is no past performance data to predict how well workers would perform on similar or relevant tasks [22].

More robust approaches entail predicting worker performance using different worker attributes, such as age [34], location [34,56], technical skills [43], and personality [33,41]. In this paper, we investigate a promising but understudied worker attribute to predict performance in a crowdsourcing setting – cognitive ability. Cognitive ability tests are one of the many methods used by organisations during the recruitment process to identify potential employees with the highest job compatibility. Furthermore, Psychology research has extensively shown that a person's cognitive ability is a good indicator of work performance [55]. In particular, the literature presents three core executive functions of the brain (Inhibition Control, Working Memory, and Cognitive Flexibility) as the basis to describe cognitive ability, which can be measured using appropriate tests [9]. In a crowdsourcing setting, a recent study by Goncalves et al. [22] reported promising results regarding the successful prediction of crowd worker performance based on their cognitive skills. However, the completion of the cognitive ability tests (visual and verbal) and crowdsourcing tasks was conducted in a lab study with a limited sample of 24 participants instead of workers from a crowdsourcing platform. Further, the researchers used the Educational Testing Service (ETS) cognitive kit [16], a collection of comprehensive yet complex and time-consuming cognitive tests that are not practical for an online setting. Goncalves et al. [22] report that the experiment lasted between 90 to 120 min per participant, which would be considered overly long in most online crowdsourcing scenarios.

In this paper we aim to establish a link between the metrics of simple and established online cognitive tests and worker task performance. This link could be used in routing tasks to enhance the efficiency and outcomes of crowd work. As a result, task requesters and crowdsourcing platforms would be able to distinguish the optimum set of workers for a particular crowd task. We conducted an online study on Amazon Mechanical Turk (MTurk)[1] with 102 workers. We asked workers to complete a set of simple and quick (i.e., workers spent on average 6.2 min to complete five tests) online cognitive tests (Stroop [42], Flanker [17], N-back [49], Task switching [47], Pointing [50]) that capture the three core executive functions of the brain. This was followed by the completion of typical tasks available in crowdsourcing platforms (Classification, Counting, Proofreading, Sentiment Analysis, Transcription). Our results show a strong relationship between the cognitive ability of crowd workers and their performance in crowdsourcing tasks. We also identify relationships between specific cognitive tests and crowd tasks based on executive functions. Finally, we assign workers to tasks based on their cognitive test scores and demonstrate that our method can significantly improve crowd task accuracy when compared to a baseline generic task assignment.

---

[1] https://www.mturk.com.

2   Related Work

2.1   Human Cognitive Ability and Executive Functions

Human cognitive ability has been extensively studied in Psychology and is often described using executive functions [9]. Executive functions are known to be vital for mental and physical well-being, as well as success in school [3] and at work [2]. The general consensus is that there are three core executive functions: inhibition control, working memory, and cognitive flexibility. These functions form the basis of higher order functions such as reasoning, problem-solving, and planning [9]. *Inhibition control* is the conscious or unconscious restriction of a process or behaviour, especially of impulses or desires. *Working memory* is the ability to hold information in memory and mentally work with it. *Cognitive flexibility* (also known as Switching) is the ability to adapt behaviours in response to changes in the environment and is often associated with creativity [9].

A wide variety of psychological tests such as Stroop [42], Task Switching [47], and N-Back [49] have been developed to assess executive functions. A collection of such tasks is known as a cognitive kit (*e.g.,* Cambridge Neuropsychological Test Automated Battery (CANTAB) [51], Test My Brain [21], The Addenbrooke's Cognitive Examination [45]) and is extensively used in medical and psychological research [9]. Cognitive ability measured from such tests is known to be a good indicator of performance at work, among other predictors such as personality, emotional intelligence, and job experience [55]. This is also well supported by the Person-Job fit theorem which is broadly defined as the compatibility between individuals and jobs [37]. The two aspects of the theory are the suitability of a person for the requirements of a job, and the match between the expectations of a person and the attributes of the job [37]. In theory, any organisation would benefit from optimising their employee selection processes to achieve Person-Job fit, as the literature identifies several positive outcomes such as job performance, satisfaction, and motivation [14].

In a study involving software developers, Chilton *et al.* [4] reported that a misfit between cognitive style and that of the job environment could diminish performance while increasing strain. Similar links between cognitive style and work performance have been established in a number of studies [29,57]. Although cognitive style or the way individuals think, perceive, and remember information slightly differ from cognitive ability, it correlates with cognitive ability [19]. We also note that several studies have shown that there is no significant relationship between cognitive style and performance at work [38,53].

In this study we aim to investigate the impact of worker cognitive ability on their task performance in crowdsourcing platforms by measuring cognitive ability using online cognitive tests that capture the three widely established executive functions of the brain.

2.2   Measuring Cognitive Ability Online

Previous work has shown that accurately measuring cognitive ability through online tests is feasible. For instance, Germine *et al.* [21] explored the validity of using the web for timed, performance-based, and/or stimulus-controlled experiments which are critical for measuring cognitive aptitude online. They reported that web samples do not differ significantly from traditionally recruited or lab-tested samples. Furthermore, participants of their study were anonymous, uncompensated, and unsupervised.

In another example, Crump et al. [6] examined the viability of conducting behavioural experiments on crowdsourcing platforms. In a study conducted on MTurk, workers completed tests that are used in cognitive science and cognitive psychology (e.g., Stroop, Flanker, Attentional Blink) with the results being comparable to those collected in laboratory settings. These experiments lasted up to 30 min and have characteristics such as multi-trial designs, stimulus presentation, complex instructions, rapid response recording, and requirement of sustained attention of participants. Given these findings and the fact that we based our online cognitive tests on the extensive literature in Psychology on this topic, we anticipate that our online cognitive tests will effectively gauge the cognitive aptitude of crowd workers by testing the three executive functions of the brain.

2.3   Cognitive Ability of Crowdworkers

Eickhoff [15] examined the effect of cognitive biases in crowdsourced relevance labelling tasks and reported that biases could significantly deteriorate the quality of output. A cognitive bias is a systematic error in thinking that affects judgements and decisions. For instance, the framing effect is one such cognitive bias where people respond to a particular option in different ways based on how it is presented. Though cognitive biases differ from cognitive aptitudes, they are closely related and the literature suggests that people with higher cognitive abilities are better at avoiding cognitive biases when making decisions [59].

Alagarai et al. [1] investigated different cognitive elements of crowd task design and its effect on performance. They showed that higher task accuracy could be obtained by reducing the demand for visual search and working memory within the task. Previous work by Goncalves et al. [22] predicted the accuracy of participants when performing crowd tasks based on cognitive skills measured. However, this experiment was conducted in a laboratory setting, with a small sample, and using the ETS cognitive kit [16], which consists of laborious and time-consuming tests. We aim to investigate this further using straightforward and quick online cognitive tests with a larger sample and explore its applicability for task assignment in crowdsourcing.

2.4   Task Assignment Based on Worker Attributes

Previous work has shown that both demographic and behavioural attributes of workers impact their work quality [33,34,41]. In practice, apart from more common attributes such as approval rate, the number of tasks completed, and location, crowd platforms allow requesters to narrow down the worker selection at a premium price. For example, MTurk allows requesters to select a subset of workers based on worker gender, age, daily internet usage, job, among others.

While there is a strong relationship between crowd worker accuracy and their location in relevance labelling [24,34] and content analysis [56], studies have confirmed that gender has no significant effect on task accuracy in crowd-sourcing [34]. Beyond demographics, personality of the worker is known to affect accuracy. In a study on labelling relevance, Kazai et al. [33] segmented crowd workers into five categories based on personality dimensions and reported a significant correlation between personality type and the mean accuracy of the worker. In a subsequent study, Kazai et al. [34] also reported that certain personality traits relate to higher task accuracy. Lykourentzou et al. [41] examined the effect of personality on the performance of collaborative crowd work on creative tasks and reported that balanced teams containing multiple personalities produce better work in terms of the quality of outcome.

Rzeszotarski and Kittur [54] showed that it is feasible to build predictive models of task performance based on behavioural traces of the user. They introduced a method that analyses the sequence of actions (e.g., mouse movements, scrolling, key-strokes) performed by the user to complete a task, which can be used to measure task accuracy and content quality. Han et al. [28] explored annotating the semantic structure of the web using crowdsourcing and reported that most of the behavioural factors of the worker are correlated with the annotation quality. In addition, behaviours of trained professional workers have been successfully used as golden standard to identify those with poor performance [35]. However, behaviour based task performance prediction methods can only be used as post-processing techniques to exclude subpar contributions, which differ from task routing methods. Another approach is to extract the interests of users from social media activity and serve tasks accordingly [11]. We note practical and ethical difficulties in linking worker profiles with social media data.

3   Method

In this study we measured the cognitive ability of crowd workers using five cognitive tests. We then recorded worker performance in five crowdsourcing tasks, and examined if we can utilise cognitive aptitude as an indicator of crowd task performance. We used established cognitive tests to measure the three executive functions of the brain. Table 1 describes the primary executive function measured by each test.

3.1   Cognitive Tests

A description of each cognitive test is provided below.

Stroop *Test* [42]. The classic Stroop test presents two types of trials (incongruent and congruent). As shown in Fig. 1, incongruent trials present names of colours (such as "green") displayed in a different colour ("red") whereas congruent trials present names in matching colour. We also included a third trial type (unrelated)

Table 1. Cognitive tests and associated executive functions [9]

Cognitive test	Executive function
Stroop	Inhibition control
Flanker	Inhibition control
Task switching	Cognitive flexibility
N-Back	Working memory
Pointing	Working memory

where non-colour words (such as "monkey") appear in either red, green, or blue colour. Participants were asked to press the key corresponding with the first letter of the colour of the word. When asked to focus on the colour of the ink and ignore the meaning of the word (*i.e.*, suppress our prepotent response to words), people are found to be slower and less accurate. This is known as the Stroop effect. Our test contained a total of 18 trials, with a total of 6 trails per type.

*Eriksen **Flanker** Test* [17]. In each trial crowd workers were presented with a sequence of five arrow symbols (*e.g.,* >>>>>, <<><<) and were asked to pick the centre symbol and press the corresponding arrow key. This task contained 8 congruent (all arrows pointing in the same direction) and 8 incongruent (centre symbol pointing to the opposite direction from the rest) trials. The task effect is similar to the Stroop test.

***Task Switching** Test* [47]. This test presented a letter and a number in each trial. Depending on whether the pair appears on the upper or lower half of the display, participants were asked to indicate whether the letter is a vowel or consonant, or whether the number is even or odd. The test contained 8 repeating and 8 switching trials.

***N-Back** Test* [49]. In the N-Back test, crowd workers were presented with a sequence of stimuli. For each stimulus, participants were asked to decide if the current stimulus is the same as the one presented N trials ago, where N can be 1, 2, or 3. We used the 3-back version of this test with each worker completing 16 trials.

*Self-ordered **Pointing** Test* [50]. In this task, crowd workers were shown 3 to 12 randomly distributed identical squares and were asked to click one box at a time, in any order and without repetition, making sure to click all boxes.

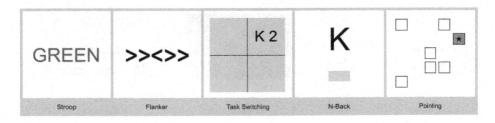

Fig. 1. Screenshots from cognitive tests (Color figure online)

Workers received visual feedback after each choice. We tested workers' ability to remember which items they have clicked. The test contained 5 rounds with the total number of squares increasing in each round.

For each test, we specified instructions and included an example prior to the test to ensure workers fully understood the test. Except for the Pointing test, we also configured each trial within the tests to expire after 3.5 s. This allowed us to avoid crowd workers pausing the study in the middle of a test and get them to promptly complete each trial. For the Stroop, Flanker, Task Switching, and N-Back tests we recorded accuracy, response time, and trial type (if applicable) for each trial. Based on the trial type, for the Stroop, Flanker, Task Switching tests, test effect was calculated (*e.g.,* Stroop effect in terms of accuracy is the difference in accuracy between congruent and incongruent trials).

3.2   Crowdsourcing Tasks

We used crowdsourcing tasks that are representative of typical tasks available in popular crowdsourcing platforms. Crowd task taxonomy [20] and task availability [10] reported in the literature were also considered. The sentiment analysis and proofreading tasks were adopted from previous work by Goncalves *et al.* [22], and the counting task from Rogstadius *et al.* [52] and Goncalves *et al.* [23,25]. The transcription and item classification tasks were created specifically for this study. Screenshots from the crowdsourcing tasks are shown in Fig. 2 and a description of each task is given below. All tasks had varying complexity as shown in Fig. 3 and were presented to participants in random order.

Sentiment Analysis. Crowd workers were asked to identify the sentiment of a sentence (*i.e.,* point of view, opinion). A sentence's sentiment was classified as either 'negative', 'neutral', or 'positive'. The task contained a total of 16 unique sentences. Half of the sentences were straightforward (*e.g.,* "The weather is great today"), while the other half were more challenging due to sentiment ambiguity, context, or sarcasm (*e.g.,* "I'm so pleased road construction woke me up with a bang").

Counting. In this task, workers were presented with an image of a petri dish and asked to count malaria-infected blood cells. Workers were provided with specific instructions on how to differentiate an infected blood cell from an ordinary blood cell. The task contained 8 images that were generated algorithmically containing

Fig. 2. Screenshots from crowdsourcing tasks

varying numbers of infected and ordinary blood cells. Accuracy for each image was determined by $max(0, 1 - \frac{|response-ground\_truth|}{ground\_truth})$.

Item Classification. In this task, crowd workers were presented with 16 paintings (primarily from The Metropolitan Museum of Art[2] and the remaining from Flickr[3], all images licensed for public use) and were asked to identify and mark the items appearing in each painting from a given list of four items. Images represent different painting styles from different countries and contain one or more of the listed items. Certain items could be easily spotted, whereas others were more challenging (*e.g.*, the classification image shown in Fig. 2 contains both objects 'Ship' and 'Sword', where the latter is more challenging to locate).

Proofreading. In this task, crowd workers were asked to proofread 12 sentences. Two sentences contained no errors. The remaining sentences contained a single error such as a misspelled word, a grammatical error, or an incorrect word. Workers were asked to type the correct word which should replace the identified erroneous word.

Transcription. Crowdworkers were required to type out a piece of text from a given image. We included 12 images extracted from The George Washington Papers at the Library of Congress [58] in the task. As shown in Fig. 3, manuscripts had varying complexity based on the writing style, date, and content. We calculated Levenshtein distance (*LD*) [7] between the response string and the ground truth and measured accuracy using $max(0, 1 - \frac{2 \times LD}{length(ground\_truth)})$.

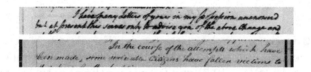

Fig. 3. Transcription tasks of high (top) and low (bottom) complexity.

The cognitive tests were implemented using *jsPsych*, a JavaScript library for online behavioural experiments [39]. Our experiment was integrated with MTurk using *psiTurk* [26], which let us host the experiment on our own server without the need of redirecting users and asking them to submit a completion code.

All tests were encapsulated to a single *Human Intelligent Task* (HIT) and posted to MTurk. When participants accepted the HIT, they were required to electronically sign an informed consent form to start the study. Workers first completed the five cognitive tests, followed by the five crowdsourcing tasks. Both the order of the tests and tasks was randomised. In the last step of the study, participants were requested to provide demographic information (age, gender, and education level). From a pilot study, we estimated that workers would spend around 40 min to complete the study. Based on the prevailing federal minimum

---

2 https://www.metmuseum.org/art/collection.
3 https://www.flickr.com.

wage of the United States of $7.25, we payed $5.00 (USD) for each worker who completed all the tests and tasks. The amount we payed for a worker is comfortably above the average pay one would receive for regular tasks in MTurk [10].

We considered the executive functions associated with each crowdsourcing task during task selection in order to be able to relate them to the different cognitive tests. For example, our counting and classification tasks require sustained attention (Inhibition Control), and demands Working Memory skills while going through the different elements [9]. For the Proofreading task, it is critical to relate to and apply different grammar rules and language patterns (Working Memory and Cognitive Flexibility) [5]. Initially, three of the paper's authors individually identified executive functions linked to each crowdsourcing task based on the literature and their own judgement. The authors then discussed the results, which led to the mapping shown in Table 2.

Table 2. Crowdsourcing tasks and related executive functions

Task	Executive functions
Classification	Inhibition control & Working memory
Counting	Inhibition control & Working memory
Proofreading	Working memory & Cognitive flexibility
Sentiment analysis	Cognitive flexibility & Inhibition control
Transcription	Cognitive flexibility & Working memory

4   Results

A total of 102 workers completed the study (Female 48, Male 54). On average, workers spent 43.6 min to complete the study, with 37.0 min spent on the crowdsourcing tasks ($SD = 10.7$) and 6.2 min on the cognitive tests ($SD = 2.1$). Based on a Pearson Correlation test, we found a significant correlation between the worker scores for the cognitive tests and the mean accuracy for the crowdsourcing tasks ($r = 0.47, p < 0.01$), as shown in Fig. 4.

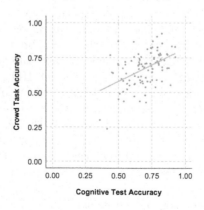

Fig. 4. Accuracy of crowdsourcing tasks vs accuracy of cognitive tests.

4.1   Cognitive Tests

Figure 5 shows worker performance across the five cognitive tests. Workers found the Stroop test to be relatively easier than the rest. In contrast, the mean accuracy of the N-back task is consistently low. Workers are slightly faster in responding to the two tests that measure inhibition control, Stroop and Flanker.

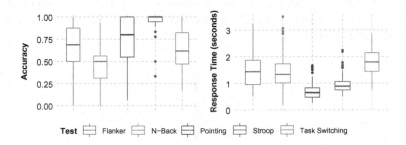

Fig. 5. Accuracy and response time for cognitive tests.

Figure 6 summarises the observed Stroop, Flanker, and Task Switching effects in terms of response time and error rate. As indicated by ANOVA results, for both Stroop and Flanker tests, workers were less error prone ($F(1, 202) = 26.88, p < 0.01, F(1, 202) = 8.80, p < 0.01$) and faster ($F(1, 202) = 16.16, p < 0.01, F(1, 202) = 5.22, p < 0.05$) when presented with congruent tasks. In the Task Switching test workers were generally faster ($F(1, 202) = 6.78, p < 0.01$) when the same type of task was repeated as opposed to switching from one type to another. This confirms that the effect of the tests was in the expected direction [17, 42, 47].

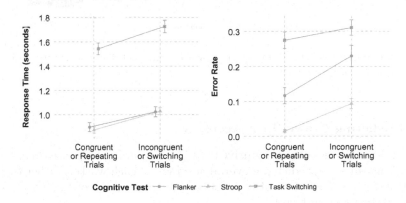

Fig. 6. Stroop, Flanker, and Task Switching effects.

4.2   Crowdsourcing Tasks

Figure 7 shows that workers were generally faster and more accurate in the Sentiment Analysis task as compared to other tasks. Worker accuracy was lowest for the Proofreading task. Figure 8 visualises the accuracy of workers for each sub task of the crowdsourcing tasks (*e.g.,* an individual sentence in the sentiment task). This demonstrates that there is a varying level of complexity within each of our crowdsourcing tasks, an aspect we aimed for in the initial study design. Finally, we do not observe a significant impact of gender, age, or education level on crowd task performance.

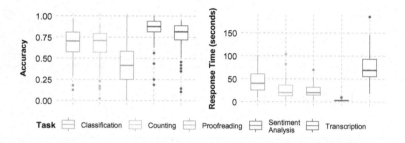

Fig. 7. Accuracy and response time for crowd tasks.

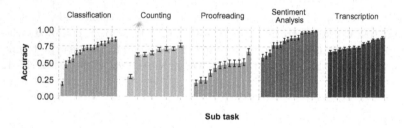

Fig. 8. Accuracy of sub tasks for each crowdsourcing task (Sub tasks are ordered in ascending order of mean accuracy).

4.3   Predicting Crowd Task Accuracy

We used the outcomes of the cognitive tests (*e.g.,* accuracy, response time, Stroop effect) as features to predict the overall accuracy of each worker. Other features include mean response time of instructions and demographic information (age, gender, and education level).

We used Generalised Linear Models, Random Forest, and Beta Regression to predict the overall task accuracy. Mean Absolute Error (MAE), Root Mean Square Error (RMSE), and R-Squared values for the models with 5-fold cross validation with 10 repeats are shown in Table 3. Inter-correlations were checked prior to constructing the models and the variance inflation factors values of our predictors were below the often-used threshold of 5 to detect multicollinearity [27]. As Beta Regression is optimised for datasets where the output value is in the range (0,1), we had to slightly modify the accuracy values (y) using the equation, $(y * (n - 1) + 0.5)/n$ where n is the number of observations.

Table 3. Results of predictive models (5-fold cross validation with 10 repeats)

Method	MAE	RMSE	R^2
Generalised Linear Model	0.085	0.105	0.320
Random Forest	0.085	0.105	0.303
Beta Regression	0.083	0.105	0.290

Table 4. Significant features and related executive functions

Crowd task	Hypothesis	Significant features	Imp. score	Related executive functions
Classification	In. Control	Pointing (Accuracy)	4.95	In. Control
	W. Memory	Flanker (Response Time)	3.07	W. Memory
		Stroop (Accuracy)	2.45	
Counting	In. Control	Flanker (Effect Accuracy)	5.57	In. Control
	W. Memory	Pointing (Response Time)	3.72	W. Memory
		Stroop (Accuracy)	3.37	
Proofreading	W. Memory	Task Switching (Accuracy)	7.93	W. Memory
	Cog. Flexibility	Pointing (Accuracy)	5.60	Cog. Flexibility
		Instructions (Response Time)	4.08	
Sen. Analysis	Cog. Flexibility	Stroop (Response Time)	9.68	In. Control
	In. Control	Instructions (Response Time)	6.90	
		Flanker (Effect Accuracy)	5.74	
Transcription	Cog. Flexibility	Task Switching (Accuracy)	3.03	Cog. Flexibility
	W. Memory	Task Switching (Effect Accuracy)	2.98	

We also predicted the accuracy for individual crowdsourcing tasks using the same procedure. Based on the results (MAE, RMSE, and R-Squared values), we selected Random Forest for further investigation and prediction as it produces slightly better results over the other two models in this analysis. Table 4 presents the features that were shown to be the most important based on feature importance scores of Random Forest models and the respective executive functions that those features relate to, as well as the executive functions we hypothesised each crowdsourcing task covers (Table 2).

In addition, we applied Principal Component Analysis (PCA) separately for both the cognitive test and crowdsourcing task results. PCA can be used to show the distance and relatedness among a population. We visualise this analysis in Figs. 9 and 10. These figures, known as variable correlation plots, visualise the relationship between all variables. In Fig. 9, we observe that the N-back and Pointing tests are grouped together, implying they are highly correlated. Both tests measure Working Memory. Similarly, Stroop and Flanker tests, which both measure Inhibition Control, are positively correlated as shown in Fig. 9. More importantly, Fig. 9 confirms that our cognitive test results are in agreement with the literature regarding the measured executive functions (as presented in Table 1). The yellow circle indicates a 100% representation of a variable in the given space. The length of the arrows (close to the edge of the circle) indicates that all variables are well represented in both plots.

We make two important observations in Fig. 10. First, workers are spread throughout the space, which shows the diversity in terms of worker expertise. For example, worker marked as 'W1' in Fig. 10 did not perform well on Proofreading and Transcription tasks, but performs above average on Sentiment Analysis and Counting tasks. Our aim is to capture these differences via cognitive tests to facilitate effective task assignment. Second, we identify strong positive correla-

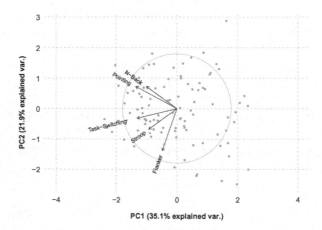

Fig. 9. Principal Component Analysis (PCA) of cognitive tests. (Color figure online)

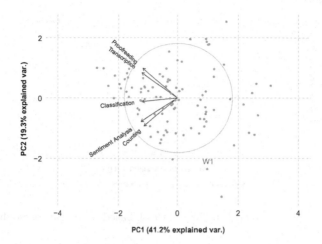

Fig. 10. Principal Component Analysis (PCA) of crowdsourcing tasks. (Color figure online)

tions among Proofreading and Transcription task pair, and Sentiment Analysis and Counting task pair. This suggests a similarity between tasks in terms of underlying executive functions. According to our findings (Table 4), Cognitive Flexibility is important for both Proofreading and Transcription tasks while Inhibition Control is significant for Sentiment Analysis and Counting tasks.

4.4 Task Assignment Based on Cognitive Skills

Next we developed a strategy to exemplify how cognitive tests can be used for task assignment. To evaluate our strategy, we first select workers for tasks solely based on cognitive test scores, and then compare their task performance as recorded in the study. Here, we transform our prediction from a regression problem to a binary classification problem and focus on predicting if a particular worker should be assigned to a particular crowdsourcing task or not.

For any specific task, we can select a subset of workers from a worker pool in order to maximise the predicted accuracy. For each task, we trained a Random Forest model with 5-fold cross validation using measures from cognitive tests and demographic information as features. Using the models, we predicted the expected accuracy for each worker for each task. Then for each task, based on predicted worker accuracy, we categorised workers into two classes ('Selected' or 'Not Selected'). We used a variable 'Worker Qualification Limit' (L) to determine which portion of workers to consider for assignment. For instance when $L = 40$ for the Classification task, the top 40% of workers in terms of their predicted accuracy in this task are labelled as 'Selected' and the remaining 60% are labelled as 'Not Selected'.

The observed accuracy for workers based on prediction outputs for all five tasks with different L values is shown in Fig. 11. For instance, for the Sentiment

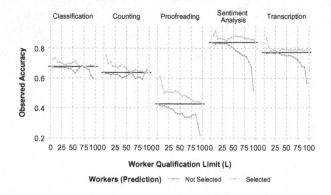

Fig. 11. Accuracy of workers for each task based on output of prediction.

Analysis task, if we select the top 51 workers out of 102 ($L = 50$) in terms of our predictive model, we observe that those 51 selected workers actually achieve a mean accuracy of 0.88 whereas the 51 unselected workers achieve a mean accuracy of 0.80. The overall mean accuracy for the Sentiment Analysis task for all 102 workers is 0.84 (shown in black horizontal line in Fig. 11). Also, we note that for any L value, our assignment method selects a subset of workers whose mean accuracy for the task is better than the mean accuracy of the remaining workers or the mean accuracy of the entire worker pool.

Next we investigated to what extent our method leads to worker discrimination. In other words, does it always favour a handful of skillful workers? We calculate the total number of tasks each worker would be assigned to once we select workers for all five tasks based on our approach. Figure 12 summarises the outcome distribution. If task assignment is carried out based on our model with L as 50, we observer that 11 (10.8%) workers are selected for all five tasks, and 18 (17.6%) workers are not assigned any task. A higher L value (e.g., $L = 75$) assigns more workers to all five tasks. For lower values (e.g., $L = 25$), which represent a more "exclusive" model, we observe that no worker is assigned to all 5 tasks. In other words, at low L values, task routing is so exclusive that there is no single worker in our sample that would meet the expectations for all 5 tasks.

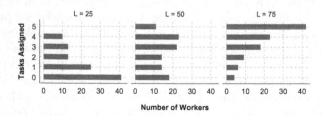

Fig. 12. Number of workers against the total number of tasks assigned to each worker.

5   Discussion

5.1   Using Cognitive Tests to Predict Performance

Apart from cognitive skills, previous work has explored the relationship between crowd task performance and a number of worker attributes, such as age [34], location [34,56], skills [43], and personality [33,41]. However, we note a common pitfall in these studies: evaluation is based on a single type of task. For example, Kazai et al. [33,34] only used relevance labelling tasks; Shaw et al. [56] used content analysis questions; Mavridis et al. [43] used a set of multiple choice questions on the topic of 'Computer Science'; and Lykourentzou et al. [41] explored collaborative advertisement creation. To ensure the applicability of our findings to generic crowd work, our study included five different crowdsourcing tasks.

Previous work by Goncalves et al. [22] demonstrated that it is possible to predict the accuracy of crowd workers based on their cognitive skills. While their study used 8 different crowdsourcing tasks to validate their findings, we note three major deficiencies. First, aptitude tests (visual and verbal) as well as the crowdsourcing tasks were conducted in a lab study, using a limited sample of 24 participants that are not representative of the crowd worker population. In contrast, we deployed our entire study on MTurk where 102 actual crowd workers completed the study. Second, compared to the ETS cognitive kit [16] used by Goncalves et al. [22], the tests we used to assess the cognitive ability of participants contained fewer trials which were mostly fast-paced. According to the specifications of ETS kit, it takes 44 min in total to complete the first part of each cognitive test employed in [22]. In contrast, workers spent on average 6.2 min to complete all five of our tests which indicates a significant reduction in required time. Third, unlike ETS tests which are not practical for an online setting (e.g., one task requires paper folding), our online tests can be readily utilised by crowd platforms or task requesters with low effort. Thus, we eliminate any uncertainty associated with the previous study and establish that it is viable to use online cognitive tests to predict crowd task performance.

Furthermore, our prediction model can also be used along with other task routing frameworks. For example, Zheng et al. [60] proposed a task assignment system that uses expectation maximisation to populate an *estimated distribution matrix* containing estimated task accuracies. They select optimum tasks to be assigned to a worker based on this matrix. One could easily apply our model based on cognitive skills to predict task accuracy and then generate the estimated distribution matrix.

5.2   Conducting Cognitive Tests Online

We observed Stroop, Flanker, and Task Switching effects that replicate the results of classic Psychology experiments [17,42,47]. More importantly, our findings are in line with previous work by Crump et al. [6], that demonstrated that these effects could be effectively observed in online experiments. However, the effects we observed indicate a smaller effect size when compared to previous work. One reason for this could be the fact that we used a lower number of trials. For instance, we used 18 trials per worker with 102 workers for Stroop task, whereas the previous work by Crump *et al.* [6] is based on a total of 40 workers, each completing 96 trials.

Furthermore, our study identifies a strong relationship between each crowd task and several cognitive tests, validating our assumption that corresponding executive functions have an extensive impact on the crowd task (see Table 4). Based on this finding, a task requester could either select cognitive tests based on our results or pick executive functions that best explain the nature of the work and choose matching tests. Alternatively, the requester could implement multiple tests covering all executive functions and then figure out which tests to be used by piloting with a small set of workers. From a crowdsourcing platform perspective, it is more viable to implement a collection of cognitive tests similar to the tests applied in our study, so that the outcomes of such tests can be used to route or recommend a wide variety of tasks to workers.

5.3   Task Assignment

Assigning tasks based on historical performance of workers in crowdsourcing platforms may be impractical for many reasons including anonymity, fluctuations in worker availability [31], or the lack of ground truth data to assess the historical accuracy of workers. On the other hand, using post-processing techniques to reject work could have consequences like workers avoiding the requester in future [44]. Here, we attempt to address these issues by using cognitive tests as predictors of crowd task performance. Our approach for assigning or recommending users, whereby we select a subset of workers who would possibly perform better at each task, can also be seen as a top-N recommendation task [8]. As shown in Fig. 12 (for $L = 50$), we observe that tasks are well-distributed amongst workers – despite selecting the best workers for each task. Only 18 workers out of 102 end up not assigned to any task, while 11 workers are selected for all five tasks. This indicates that our proposed model is able to capture different expertise of workers and assign tasks accordingly. Fair task distribution is extremely important when we consider the task assignment problem from the perspective of the crowd workers. In contrast to widely used methods such as approval rate [32], our method does not aim to reward a superior set of workers who are capable in all tasks. Instead, our method focuses on finding the best suited task or tasks for each worker. This will allow workers to complete tasks that are more compatible with their skill set, which has been shown to improve worker satisfaction and reduce the likelihood of task abandonment [30,36].

Due to budget constraints, crowd task requesters often have to either limit the number of answers expected for each question or reduce the payment for each answer. Both of these actions can reduce output quality [10]. We show that it is possible to obtain higher accuracy by selecting a subset of workers based on cognitive skills (Fig. 11), therefore reducing the total number of answers and task cost. In a situation where the requester opts to use cognitive tests as a qualification test, an additional cost would incur for running the cognitive tests.

However, typically the number of questions in each task is large enough [10,31] to recover this initial investment.

5.4   Limitations

We acknowledge several limitations in our study. First, as we wanted to ensure that the cognitive tests took as little time as possible to complete, the total number of trials for each test was kept to a minimum. While measures of cognitive tests would become more accurate and distinct when increasing the number of trials, the limited number of trials was sufficient for our predictions. Second, human cognitive ability is known to demonstrate subtle variations during the day [12], this is an aspect that we do not account for in our study. Third, similar to any supervised learning method, in the initial stages, our model needs to be trained using data captured from a set of workers performing cognitive tests followed by a set of crowdsourcing tasks similar to those presented in this study.

6   Conclusion and Future Work

In this paper we demonstrate the possibility of using brief online cognitive tests to predict the performance of crowd workers across a range of tasks. We present a study conducted on Amazon Mechanical Turk with 102 workers, where each worker completed a set of cognitive tests followed by a series of crowdsourcing tasks. Through our analysis we highlight the relationships between particular cognitive tests that measure one or more specific executive functions and crowdsourcing task performance.

We show that our proposed method can effectively assign or recommend workers to 5 distinct crowd tasks from a pool of 102 workers with significant improvements to task accuracy while also utilising the majority of the worker pool. Our results also suggest that suitability of a worker for a specific crowdsourcing task could be predicted using the outcome of two or three cognitive tests. Given that each of our cognitive tests could be completed within less than 2 min and can be seamlessly integrated with online crowdsourcing platforms, our findings could be readily adopted by researchers, general task requesters, and crowdsourcing platforms.

Further research on the longitudinal impact of the process of measuring cognitive ability would allow us to decide on the optimum frequency with which these tests should be repeated. Cognitive tests should not be repeated too often as it could lead to workers being familiarised with tests. It is known that training obtained in cognitive tests could contribute towards an improvement in metrics of those particular tests but has no impact on other tests or general performance of other tasks [48]. As there are a number of different tests that measure the same executive function [9], one alternative would be to randomly select tests from a pool of tests instead of using identical dedicated tests. In addition, a future study that dynamically routes tasks based on worker cognitive ability and compares the results with other routing methods can further establish the effectiveness of the proposed method in practice.

In our evaluation, we consider assigning workers to tasks one after the other, which will result in repeatedly selecting some workers for multiple tasks. In future work, we intend to explore how we could assign or recommend tasks to workers based on cognitive skills when we have multiple tasks at hand. For this we could either adopt task routing frameworks presented in the literature [18,40,60] or propose a novel approach considering additional parameters such as the number of unique questions in each task, the number of answers required for each question, and payment.

References

1. Alagarai Sampath, H., Rajeshuni, R., Indurkhya, B.: Cognitively inspired task design to improve user performance on crowdsourcing platforms. In: Proceedings of the SIGCHI Conference on Human Factors in Computing Systems, CHI 2014, pp. 3665–3674. ACM, New York (2014). https://doi.org/10.1145/2556288.2557155
2. Bailey, C.E.: Cognitive accuracy and intelligent executive function in the brain and in business. Ann. N. Y. Acad. Sci. **1118**, 122–141 (2007). https://doi.org/10.1196/annals.1412.011
3. Borella, E., Carretti, B., Pelegrina, S.: The specific role of inhibition in reading comprehension in good and poor comprehenders. J. Learn. Disabil. **43**(6), 541–552 (2010). https://doi.org/10.1177/0022219410371676
4. Chilton, M.A., Hardgrave, B.C., Armstrong, D.J.: Person-job cognitive style fit for software developers: the effect on strain and performance. J. Manag. Inf. Syst. **22**(2), 193–226 (2005). https://doi.org/10.1080/07421222.2005.11045849
5. Clair-Thompson, H.L.S., Gathercole, S.E.: Executive functions and achievements in school: shifting, updating, inhibition, and working memory. Q. J. Exp. Psychol. **59**(4), 745–759 (2006). https://doi.org/10.1080/17470210500162854
6. Crump, M.J.C., McDonnell, J.V., Gureckis, T.M.: Evaluating Amazon's mechanical Turk as a tool for experimental behavioral research. PLoS ONE **8**(3), 1–18 (2013). https://doi.org/10.1371/journal.pone.0057410
7. Damerau, F.J.: A technique for computer detection and correction of spelling errors. Commun. ACM **7**(3), 171–176 (1964)
8. Deshpande, M., Karypis, G.: Item-based Top-N recommendation algorithms. ACM Trans. Inf. Syst. **22**(1), 143–177 (2004). https://doi.org/10.1145/963770.963776
9. Diamond, A.: Executive functions. Annu. Rev. Psychol. **64**(1), 135–168 (2013). https://doi.org/10.1146/annurev-psych-113011-143750
10. Difallah, D.E., Catasta, M., Demartini, G., Ipeirotis, P.G., Cudré-Mauroux, P.: The dynamics of micro-task crowdsourcing: the case of Amazon MTurk. In: Proceedings of the 24th International Conference on World Wide Web, WWW 2015, pp. 238–247. IW3C2, Switzerland (2015). https://doi.org/10.1145/2736277.2741685
11. Difallah, D.E., Demartini, G., Cudré-Mauroux, P.: Pick-a-crowd: tell me what you like, and I'll tell you what to do. In: Proceedings of the 22nd International Conference on World Wide Web, WWW 2013, pp. 367–374. ACM, New York (2013). https://doi.org/10.1145/2488388.2488421

12. Dingler, T., Schmidt, A., Machulla, T.: Building cognition-aware systems: a mobile toolkit for extracting time-of-day fluctuations of cognitive performance. Proc. ACM Interact. Mob. Wearable Ubiquitous Technol. **1**(3) (2017). https://doi.org/10.1145/3132025

13. Downs, J.S., Holbrook, M.B., Sheng, S., Cranor, L.F.: Are your participants gaming the system?: Screening mechanical Turk workers. In: Proceedings of the SIGCHI Conference on Human Factors in Computing Systems, CHI 2010, pp. 2399–2402. ACM, New York (2010). https://doi.org/10.1145/1753326.1753688

14. Edwards, J.R.: Person-Job Fit: A Conceptual Integration, Literature Review, and Methodological Critique. Wiley, New York (1991)

15. Eickhoff, C.: Cognitive biases in crowdsourcing. In: Proceedings of the Eleventh ACM International Conference on Web Search and Data Mining, WSDM 2018, pp. 162–170. ACM, New York (2018). https://doi.org/10.1145/3159652.3159654

16. Ekstrom, R.B., Dermen, D., Harman, H.H.: Manual for Kit of Factor-referenced Cognitive Tests, vol. 102. Educational Testing Service, Princeton (1976)

17. Eriksen, B.A., Eriksen, C.W.: Effects of noise letters upon the identification of a target letter in a nonsearch task. Percept. Psychophys. **16**(1), 143–149 (1974)

18. Fan, J., Li, G., Ooi, B.C., Tan, K.l., Feng, J.: iCrowd: an adaptive crowdsourcing framework. In: Proceedings of the 2015 ACM SIGMOD International Conference on Management of Data, SIGMOD 2015, pp. 1015–1030. ACM, New York (2015). https://doi.org/10.1145/2723372.2750550

19. Federico, P.A., Landis, D.B.: Cognitive styles, abilities, and aptitudes: are they dependent or independent? Contemp. Educ. Psychol. **9**(2), 146–161 (1984). https://doi.org/10.1016/0361-476X(84)90016-X

20. Gadiraju, U., Kawase, R., Dietze, S.: A taxonomy of microtasks on the web. In: Proceedings of the 25th ACM Conference on Hypertext and Social Media, HT 2014, pp. 218–223. ACM, New York (2014)

21. Germine, L., Nakayama, K., Duchaine, B.C., Chabris, C.F., Chatterjee, G., Wilmer, J.B.: Is the web as good as the lab? Comparable performance from web and lab in cognitive/perceptual experiments. Psychon. Bull. Rev. **19**(5), 847–857 (2012). https://doi.org/10.3758/s13423-012-0296-9

22. Goncalves, J., Feldman, M., Hu, S., Kostakos, V., Bernstein, A.: Task routing and assignment in crowdsourcing based on cognitive abilities. In: Proceedings of the 26th International Conference on World Wide Web, WWW 2017, pp. 1023–1031. IW3C2, Switzerland (2017). https://doi.org/10.1145/3041021.3055128

23. Goncalves, J., et al.: Crowdsourcing on the spot: altruistic use of public displays, feasibility, performance, and behaviours. In: Proceedings of the 2013 ACM International Joint Conference on Pervasive and Ubiquitous Computing, UbiComp 2013, pp. 753–762 (2013). https://doi.org/10.1145/2493432.2493481

24. Goncalves, J., Hosio, S., van Berkel, N., Ahmed, F., Kostakos, V.: CrowdPickUp: crowdsourcing task pickup in the wild. Proc. ACM Interact. Mob. Wearable Ubiquitous Technol. **1**(3), 51:1–51:22 (2017). https://doi.org/10.1145/3130916

25. Goncalves, J., Hosio, S., Rogstadius, J., Karapanos, E., Kostakos, V.: Motivating participation and improving quality of contribution in ubiquitous crowdsourcing. Comput. Netw. **90**(C), 34–48 (2015). https://doi.org/10.1016/j.comnet.2015.07.002

26. Gureckis, T.M., et al.: psiTurk: an open-source framework for conducting replicable behavioral experiments online. Behav. Res. Methods **48**(3), 829–842 (2016). https://doi.org/10.3758/s13428-015-0642-8

27. Hair, J., Black, W., Babin, B., Anderson, R.: Multivariate Data Analysis. Prentice-Hall, Upper Saddle River (2010)

28. Han, S., Dai, P., Paritosh, P., Huynh, D.: Crowdsourcing human annotation on web page structure: infrastructure design and behavior-based quality control. ACM Trans. Intell. Syst. Technol. **7**(4), 56:1–56:25 (2016)

29. Hoffman, B.J., Woehr, D.J.: A quantitative review of the relationship between person-organization fit and behavioral outcomes. J. Vocat. Behav. **68**(3), 389–399 (2006). https://doi.org/10.1016/j.jvb.2005.08.003

30. Hosio, S., Goncalves, J., Lehdonvirta, V., Ferreira, D., Kostakos, V.: Situated crowdsourcing using a market model. In: Proceedings of the 27th Annual ACM Symposium on User Interface Software and Technology, UIST 2014, pp. 55–64. ACM, New York (2014). https://doi.org/10.1145/2642918.2647362

31. Jain, A., Sarma, A.D., Parameswaran, A., Widom, J.: Understanding workers, developing effective tasks, and enhancing marketplace dynamics: a study of a large crowdsourcing marketplace. Proc. VLDB Endow. **10**(7), 829–840 (2017). https://doi.org/10.14778/3067421.3067431

32. Kazai, G.: In search of quality in crowdsourcing for search engine evaluation. In: Clough, P., et al. (eds.) ECIR 2011. LNCS, vol. 6611, pp. 165–176. Springer, Heidelberg (2011). https://doi.org/10.1007/978-3-642-20161-5_17

33. Kazai, G., Kamps, J., Milic-Frayling, N.: Worker types and personality traits in crowdsourcing relevance labels. In: Proceedings of the 20th ACM International Conference on Information and Knowledge Management, CIKM 2011, pp. 1941–1944. ACM, New York (2011). https://doi.org/10.1145/2063576.2063860

34. Kazai, G., Kamps, J., Milic-Frayling, N.: The face of quality in crowdsourcing relevance labels: demographics, personality and labeling accuracy. In: Proceedings of the 21st ACM International Conference on Information and Knowledge Management, CIKM 2012, pp. 2583–2586. ACM, New York (2012). https://doi.org/10.1145/2396761.2398697

35. Kazai, G., Zitouni, I.: Quality management in crowdsourcing using gold judges behavior. In: Proceedings of the Ninth ACM International Conference on Web Search and Data Mining, WSDM 2016, pp. 267–276. ACM, New York (2016). https://doi.org/10.1145/2835776.2835835

36. Kittur, A., et al.: The future of crowd work. In: Proceedings of the 2013 Conference on Computer Supported Cooperative Work, CSCW 2013, pp. 1301–1318. ACM, New York (2013). https://doi.org/10.1145/2441776.2441923

37. Kristof, A.L.: Person-organization fit: an integrative review of its conceptualizations, measurement, and implications. Pers. Psychol. **49**(1), 1–49 (1996)

38. Kristof-Brown, A.L., Zimmerman, R.D., Johnson, E.C.: Consequences of individuals' fit at work: a meta-analysis of person-job, person-organization, person-group, and person-supervisor fit. Pers. Psychol. **58**(2), 281–342 (2005)

39. de Leeuw, J.R.: jsPsych: a javascript library for creating behavioral experiments in a web browser. Behav. Res. Methods **47**(1), 1–12 (2015)

40. Liu, X., Lu, M., Ooi, B.C., Shen, Y., Wu, S., Zhang, M.: CDAS: a crowdsourcing data analytics system. Proc. VLDB Endow. **5**(10), 1040–1051 (2012)

41. Lykourentzou, I., Antoniou, A., Naudet, Y., Dow, S.P.: Personality matters: balancing for personality types leads to better outcomes for crowd teams. In: Proceedings of the 19th ACM Conference on Computer-Supported Cooperative Work & Social Computing, CSCW 2016, pp. 260–273. ACM, New York (2016)

42. MacLeod, C.M.: Half a century of research on the stroop effect: an integrative review. Psychol. Bull. **109**(2), 163 (1991)
43. Mavridis, P., Gross-Amblard, D., Miklós, Z.: Using hierarchical skills for optimized task assignment in knowledge-intensive crowdsourcing. In: Proceedings of the 25th International Conference on World Wide Web, WWW 2016, Switzerland, pp. 843–853. IW3C2 (2016). https://doi.org/10.1145/2872427.2883070
44. McInnis, B., Cosley, D., Nam, C., Leshed, G.: Taking a hit: designing around rejection, mistrust, risk, and workers' experiences in Amazon mechanical Turk. In: Proceedings of the 2016 CHI Conference on Human Factors in Computing Systems, CHI 2016, pp. 2271–2282. ACM, New York (2016)
45. Mioshi, E., Dawson, K., Mitchell, J., Arnold, R., Hodges, J.R.: The Addenbrooke's cognitive examination revised (ACE-R): a brief cognitive test battery for dementia screening. Int. J. Geriatr. Psychiatry **21**(11), 1078–1085 (2006)
46. Mo, K., Zhong, E., Yang, Q.: Cross-task crowdsourcing. In: Proceedings of the 19th ACM SIGKDD International Conference on Knowledge Discovery and Data Mining, KDD 2013, pp. 677–685. ACM, New York (2013)
47. Monsell, S.: Task switching. Trends Cogn. Sci. **7**(3), 134–140 (2003)
48. Owen, A.M., et al.: Putting brain training to the test. Nature **465**, 775 (2010). https://doi.org/10.0.4.14/nature09042
49. Owen, A.M., McMillan, K.M., Laird, A.R., Bullmore, E.: N-back working memory paradigm: a meta-analysis of normative functional neuroimaging studies. Hum. Brain Mapp. **25**(1), 46–59 (2005). https://doi.org/10.1002/hbm.20131
50. Petrides, M., Alivisatos, B., Evans, A.C., Meyer, E.: Dissociation of human mid-dorsolateral from posterior dorsolateral frontal cortex in memory processing. Proc. Natl. Acad. Sci. **90**(3), 873–877 (1993)
51. Robbins, T.W., James, M., Owen, A.M., Sahakian, B.J., McInnes, L., Rabbitt, P.: Cambridge Neuropsychological Test Automated Battery (CANTAB): a factor analytic study of a large sample of normal elderly volunteers. Dement. Geriatr. Cogn. Disord. **5**(5), 266–281 (1994). https://doi.org/10.1159/000106735
52. Rogstadius, J., Kostakos, V., Kittur, A., Smus, B., Laredo, J., Vukovic, M.: An assessment of intrinsic and extrinsic motivation on task performance in crowdsourcing markets. In: Proceedings of the Fifth International AAAI Conference on Web and Social Media, ICWSM, California, USA, vol. 11, pp. 17–21. AAAI (2011)
53. Ruble, T.L., Cosier, R.A.: Effects of cognitive styles and decision setting on performance. Organ. Behav. Hum. Decis. Process. **46**(2), 283–295 (1990). https://doi.org/10.1016/0749-5978(90)90033-6
54. Rzeszotarski, J.M., Kittur, A.: Instrumenting the crowd: using implicit behavioral measures to predict task performance. In: Proceedings of the 24th Annual ACM Symposium on User Interface Software and Technology, UIST 2011, pp. 13–22. ACM, New York (2011). https://doi.org/10.1145/2047196.2047199
55. Schmidt, F.L., Hunter, J.: General mental ability in the world of work: occupational attainment and job performance. J. Pers. Soc. Psychol. **86**(1), 162 (2004)
56. Shaw, A.D., Horton, J.J., Chen, D.L.: Designing incentives for inexpert human raters. In: Proceedings of the ACM 2011 Conference on Computer Supported Cooperative Work, CSCW 2011, pp. 275–284. ACM, New York (2011)
57. Verquer, M.L., Beehr, T.A., Wagner, S.H.: A meta-analysis of relations between person-organization fit and work attitudes. J. Vocat. Behav. **63**(3), 473–489 (2003). https://doi.org/10.1016/S0001-8791(02)00036-2
58. Washington, G.: George Washington papers, series 5, financial papers: Copybook of invoices and letters, 1754-1766 (1766). https://www.loc.gov/item/mgw500003

59. West, R.F., Toplak, M.E., Stanovich, K.E.: Heuristics and biases as measures of critical thinking: associations with cognitive ability and thinking dispositions. J. Educ. Psychol. **100**(4), 930 (2008)
60. Zheng, Y., Wang, J., Li, G., Cheng, R., Feng, J.: QASCA: a quality-aware task assignment system for crowdsourcing applications. In: Proceedings of the 2015 ACM SIGMOD International Conference on Management of Data, SIGMOD 2015, pp. 1031–1046. ACM, New York (2015)

Insights on Older Adults' Attitudes and Behavior Through the Participatory Design of an Online Storytelling Platform

Diogenis Alexandrakis[1]([⊠]), Konstantinos Chorianopoulos[1],
and Nikolaos Tselios[2]

[1] Department of Informatics, Ionian University, Corfu, Greece
{c15alex,choko}@ionio.gr
[2] Educational Sciences and Early Childhood Education Department,
University of Patras, Patras, Greece
nitse@ece.upatras.gr

Abstract. While digital technology adoption by older adults rises constantly, the design of new technologies often overlooks the culture of the end users, which, in turn, has an impact on the acceptance and use by many of them. Based on the fact that technology adoption by this age group in Greece remains low, compared to the vast majority of the EU countries, our goal in this paper is to gain further insights into the user requirements of older adults as web 2.0 storytellers in order for designers to better address their needs. For this purpose, we implemented participatory design with five older adults in Greece over a twelve-week period, combined with an evolutionary prototyping approach, as we noticed during our sessions that our participants had a difficulty in envisioning and proposing novel technologies. In order to analyze and interpret the feedback that we collected during the design sessions, the digital storytelling sessions and the in-depth interviews, we made use of the Activity Theory, as well as age-related and self-presentation frameworks. Through probing our participants' usage and design preferences of the storytelling platform, we came up with a set of attributes and motives that seem to expound their online choices. Issues of loneliness and social inclusion, generativity and computer mediated communication, among others, have emerged. Additionally, differences and similarities with findings from other studies have been indicated.

Keywords: Older adults · Participatory design · Digital storytelling

1 Introduction

The global population of older adults has doubled since 1980 and, as it seems, in 2050 the number of people aged 60 years or more will be twice as large as it is now. By then, it is estimated that Japan (42.4%), Spain (41.9%), Portugal

© IFIP International Federation for Information Processing 2019
Published by Springer Nature Switzerland AG 2019
D. Lamas et al. (Eds.): INTERACT 2019, LNCS 11746, pp. 465–474, 2019.
https://doi.org/10.1007/978-3-030-29381-9_29

(41.7%) and Greece (41.6%) will be the countries with the largest percentage of older citizens [35].

Older adults are one of the fastest growing groups of ICT users [1]. The elderly population is not homogeneous, but comprises of individuals with different characteristics, experiences, mental and physical states [25]. Contrary to the preserved stereotype that ageing and new technology adoption do not get along, researchers argue that older adults are just a different kind of users compared to the younger ones, with different capabilities, handicaps, usage patterns and expectations from technology [2,23,25].

Stories and narratives are significant cultural means through which knowledge can be shared. The benefits of creating written or digital artifacts have an important effect on the individual's well-being and the community. Through life stories people construct their identities, reflect their culture, and often help themselves maintain their mental health [27]. According to Ricoeur [32], our narratives are interwoven with a social dimension and contribute to our efforts for understanding who we are. Also, Jerome Bruner [4], based on Jean-Paul Sartre's arguments, emphasized that one's life stories should be placed and interrelated within a community of other people's narratives. Likewise, it seems that older adults can benefit from sharing digital stories in a variety of different ways, such as social engagement, motivation, and connectedness with younger generations [21].

Nowadays, research on digital technologies for storytelling, communication, and content sharing has been a significant field in HCI and CSCW (e.g., [3,8,36, 37]). However, ICT is not culturally neutral [33] and, notably, Greek older adults are almost the least connected to the Internet age group in the European Union [12]. Hence, it is a matter of importance for designers to focus on their distinct attributes and involve them further in the design process [15,23]. In order to gain better insights into the needs and attitudes of Greek older adults as storytellers, in this article we describe a participatory design [19] combined with an evolutionary prototyping approach [30] for the creation of a web 2.0 storytelling platform.

2   Methodology

The research presented in this paper lasted twelve weeks and included five participants. It consisted of three phases: (1) exploratory sessions in order to examine participants' needs and record their attitudes and preferences on digitally written narrations, (2) design and iterative refinements of the storytelling platform, and (3) implementation of the platform. In each phase, semi-structured in-depth interviews were conducted with the participants and, mainly during the second phase, short storytelling and design workshops were implemented. Our goal was to trigger further discussions and gain deeper insights into older adults' feedback, concerning issues of usefulness, design and usability.

Participants were recruited by word-of-mouth. Initially, the design group included six older adults, three men and three women, but one woman withdrew before the second phase. All of them were healthy, had retired from work, lived in their houses with their spouses and their age ranged from 59 to 73 years old.

In this article, they are referred to by a distinct abbreviation, which reflects the gender and the age of each participant (F59, F65, M66, M67, M73).

By exploring the platform specifications, our purpose is to broaden our knowledge regarding the experiences, attitudes, and preferences of the ageing population in Greece as digital storytellers, in order for designers to better address their needs as active technology users and citizens. Because of the restrictions that derived from the participants' shortage of spare time and the fact that they were geographically remote, the project sessions were conducted mostly individually with each older adult and included several iterations. The sessions of the project took place in their houses in order for them to feel more comfortable. Most of the participants never met each other. As we have previously mentioned, a participatory design methodology has been applied. During the initial exploratory sessions of our project we observed that they often struggled when trying to imagine possible technologies that do not exist. In order to overcome this difficulty, we decided to implement an evolutionary prototyping approach [30], as a grounded starting point during the participatory design sessions, in order to trigger and provoke further discussions.

For the analysis of the qualitative data, we implemented the Activity Theory (AT) framework. Since the late '80s, AT has been broadly used in HCI [6] and CSCW [9,14] for analyzing the context and development of digital artifacts that support human activities. As AT focuses on the relationship between individuals, the community they participate in, and the tools they use, it has been also proposed as a valuable framework for understanding design and social initiatives within specific cultural contexts [34]. Thus, in our study, AT is a practical lens that could help us code and analyze older adults' online storytelling activities. The main elements of an activity are: the object, the tool, the community, the rules, the division of labor and the outcome [20], as well as the motives, which have been included in the object of the activity [10,34].

3   Results

3.1   Subject: The Participants

The younger participant was F59. She had two adult children and was fluent with technology. She had a university degree, she was highly socialized and she had recently lost a relative that she admired. M73 and F65 were married to each other and had two adult children. Also, they both had a university degree, they were usually very busy and had low skills in ICT usage. M66 had graduated from Secondary Education, was extrovert, he did not have any children and could handle ICT at a medium level. M67 had rounded Primary Education, he was rather introvert, was at the novice level of ICT expertise and had two adult children, one of which was living in the same house with him and his wife.

3.2   Object: Digitally Written Narrations

Ten stories were posted on the collective map of the prototype. The shortest story contained 75 words and the longest 936 words (mean = 296.90, sd = 246.68). The main themes that emerged were (i) grief or remembrance of a deceased person (two stories: F59, F65), (ii) memories from childhood (four stories: F59, M66, M67, M73), (iii) having fun with friends during adulthood (two stories: F59, M66) and (iv) a personal achievement (two stories: M73, M66). The two most frequent feelings during the storytelling process were nostalgia and a tendency to provide guidance to the next generation. According to the responses of the participants, their motivation to post online narrations is due to their need for writing down their memories (M66, M67, M73) or in order for the descendants to know some historical facts about their family (F65, M67). As memory deficits come with age, some participants regarded that the digital platform can provide them a means for personal memory storage, which can be easily accessed and, in contrast to other tangible media, it cannot be lost or forgotten somewhere in the house (F59, M67). Furthermore, as this platform is on the web, a medium which is extensively used by younger generations, it was also regarded as a valuable tool for promoting their memories to young users (F59, M67). All participants also mentioned that people who try to confront their feelings of loneliness could benefit from the use of the platform, either to communicate directly with specific users through it or to share their own memories, express themselves, and be part of an anonymous ad hoc storytelling community.

3.3   Tool: The Web 2.0 Platform

Based on features and guidelines for older adults' software, which derived from other studies (e.g. [2, 23, 31]), as well as the feedback during the interviews and the workshops (Fig. 1A), we constructed a basic digital prototype of the story-telling platform (Figs. 1B and 2A). Its main functions were (a) a collective map containing all story pointers (Fig. 2A), (b) the page with the full narrative of each story, which could also include the viewers' public comments (Fig. 1B), (c) the input/edit form that each user could type a new narration or make changes to an existing one, and (d) the private discussions area, where each user could have private chats with others.

In the iterations which followed, the participants decided to focus mainly on the initial page and sketched the main areas and functions that they would like to include (Fig. 2B). The most basic suggestions included: (1) The initial page should also include a timeline with the stories, as well as an informative list of the stories that were recently posted. (2) An awareness tool in order for each user to know who else is online. (3) The implementation of cheerful colors (F59, F65) in the interface and removal of bouncing elements (M66). (4) The platform should be properly adjusted to different screen sizes and devices (mainly for tablets and desktop or laptop computers). (5) The storytellers of each narration should have the option to make their stories private or public to other viewers. (6) The storyteller of each narration should have the option to allow or deny receiving public comments or private messages from other users. (7) All platform users should be anonymous. The participants would like to use the application both indoors, e.g. in their living room, and outdoors, e.g. on the beach during the

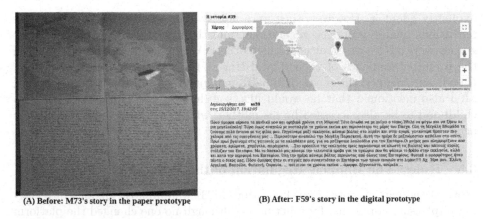

(A) Before: M73's story in the paper prototype   (B) After: F59's story in the digital prototype

Fig. 1. A paper storytelling prototype made during workshops (A) and its implementation in the digital platform (B).

summer (F59) or in the boat while fishing (M73). A screenshot of the initial page of the final prototype can be seen in Fig. 2C.

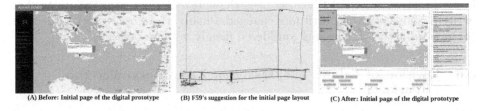

(A) Before: Initial page of the digital prototype   (B) F59's suggestion for the initial page layout   (C) After: Initial page of the digital prototype

Fig. 2. The evolution of the initial page in the course of the participatory design sessions.

3.4 Community: The Narrators and the Audience

According to the participants' responses, the community of the storytelling activity comprises of two major groups: the users of the platform and the desirable audience. As no one of the users ever communicated digitally with the others, although they could, the community of the platform reflects mostly the notion of the imagined audience [24] in our study. In general, as the majority of the storytellers (F59, F65, M66, M73) preferred being part of small intimate storytelling communities, they suggested that the platform should have a small number of users, ranging from five (F65, M73) to fifteen (F59). Also, one of the main arguments for keeping a small audience was that they were anxious of receiving offensive messages on their stories (F65, M66, M73). Apart from the potential negative incoming messages, they were also unease about posting their narrations on a platform with unfamiliar users, although they did not explicitly admit it. However, they were mostly in favor of people reading their narrations, mainly younger generations, and they regarded that most of their stories were life lessons that could help others. When our discussions focused on the preferred audience of their digital stories, they all mentioned their closest friends and, mainly, those who had been mentioned in their narrations. Notably, M66 also mentioned that he would like, somehow, a particular story from his childhood to be also accessed by his mother, who had passed away many years ago.

3.5　Rules: The Implicit Regulation of the Web 2.0 Platform

Most of the participants (F59, F65, M66, M73) were almost anxious of receiving unpleasant comments by other users, although no one changed the platform settings to avoid interactions with others. The fact that they did not write any public comment or private message themselves to others' stories was not just a matter of reciprocity. After deeper discussions and examinations of their beliefs, we discovered that the phrase 'write a comment' that we used in the corresponding field of the prototype was responsible, at some extent, for their negative attitudes on communicating with other narrators. According to their point of view, the Greek translation of the word 'comment' meant mostly 'criticism', which had a negative meaning. When we used the phrase 'leave a message', instead of 'write a comment', their attitudes changed. Finally, the most essential rule that emerged from our discussions considered mainly netiquette issues.

3.6　Division of Labor: The Task that Each Storyteller Has to Perform

The prototype was initially designed in order for users to post their narrations independently from other users' operations, if they wished to act individually. However, some of the interviewees thought about having their stories co-written or edited by their friends, as platform users, who might have something to add to the digital narration. Eventually, after further discussions, they concluded that they preferred to write and edit their stories by themselves and if any viewer wished to make changes to a specific story, he/she should write a message to the narrator and ask for it.

3.7　Outcome: The Results of the Storytelling Process

At the end of the digital storytelling workshops, besides the final collection of their personal memories, participants had also three significant outcomes from the process. First, having their stories online created a liberating feeling of security to many narrators (F59, F65, M66, M73), that their selected memories will not be forgotten or perished. Second, the features of the storytelling platform, such as the common map, the narrations, the list with the most recent posts, and the ability to send messages to other users provided them with a sense of community, despite the fact that they never communicated with each other as we have previously mentioned. Third, they discovered how much they enjoyed writing down their most valuable memories, which was something that the majority had never tried in the past. Notably, M66 continued the digital storytelling process on his own after the end of the project.

4   Discussion

4.1   General Observations

Our participants experienced a clear difficulty in envisioning and proposing possible technologies that could meet their needs [23], regardless of their level of proficiency in using ICT. However, the implementation of the evolutionary prototyping approach [30] acted as a catalyst during the participatory design sessions and helped our participants overcome their initial struggle.

Similar to other studies [22,29], older adults regarded memory recording as a useful tool to resist oblivion, as well as to communicate their memories to young users [22]. The feeling of security that some narrators had after they had posted their stories online was associated not only with the perceived endurance of the web as a file storage medium, according to their point of view, but also with their previous experiences with other media, especially paper, which can be put in places that will be later forgotten. The desirable audience, as well as the themes of their recorded narrations, was not limited to their friends, relatives or strangers, but also included beloved persons who had passed away [18]. Notably, the two stories that were about deceased persons were written by the female users, while the stories concerning personal achievements were posted by male users.

Unlike the use of social media by other older adults [2], our participants did not make any public comments or send private messages to other authors. Although similar behavior has been observed in other studies (e.g. [17,29]), in our case the main reason for not commenting seems to be related to their deep concern upon issues regarding offensive online actions. Additionally, our storytellers preferred not having their personal stories edited by others [29]. Also, they enjoyed having their stories posted on a common storytelling area and they wanted to have awareness upon the online presence of other users, which also varies among different cultures [26]. All these findings draw a profile of an average user with a mixture of preferences regarding online behavior.

4.2   Online Performance vs Online Exhibition

Based on Ervin Goffman's [13] notion upon presentation of the self, Bernie Hogan [16] distinguished users' activities in online social media into two categories: performances and exhibitions. The former includes real time interactions such as online chats, whereas the latter mainly considers the online presentation of artifacts, such as status updates in social networking sites, picture uploads, or even previous synchronous performances that have become asynchronous artifacts.

All presentation activities require two parts: the actor/presenter and the audience that monitors the actor. Under this scope, it seems that our participants used the platform only as an exhibition tool as they just posted their personal memories. Although they read others' memories, they never sent any private or public message. This also seems to be in contrast to other older adults' online behavior [2]. The participants' views, that presenting one's personal memories to an anonymous audience could also help the narrator confront social isolation and feelings of loneliness, reminds us of a similar study on facebook users, according to which feelings of loneliness were reduced when they posted status updates, whether they had feedback from their audience or not [7].

4.3 Generativity vs Socioemotional Selectivity Theory

According to the interviewees, all of the stories posted on the platform had also an implicit function as life lessons or advice to others, especially for younger generations and family. Due to generativity, a term used in Erik Erikson's theory of human development, individuals often have a need to act creatively and productively in a way that others can benefit from it, targeting mainly to the next generation [11]. However, the majority preferred the platform to include only five to fifteen users, which seems to contradict, in practice, the aforementioned issue of generativity. This online behavior resembles older adults' attitudes in the real world: On the one hand studies upon generativity (e.g. [28]) have revealed that there is often a decline after midlife and, on the other hand, according to socioemotional selectivity theory [5], contrary to younger adults, older adults usually prefer a small range of social partners, focusing mainly on selected, emotionally meaningful, social relationships.

5 Conclusion

During the last decade, a variety of digital technologies focused on older adults have been designed and implemented. However, despite the fact that ICT should not be considered as culturally neutral [33], there still seems to be an implicit notion of 'one size fits all' [34]. In this article we made an attempt to highlight Greek older adults' distinct insights on ICT usage as storytellers and digital content producers through a participatory design approach. We were based on a variety of studies, theories and frameworks for analyzing, comparing and interpreting their attitudes, motives and online behavior, which are partly differentiated from the outcomes found in other studies. Among others, issues regarding loneliness, generativity, computer mediated communication and preservation of personal memories have been discussed. It is evident that due to the small sample size of our study, we cannot generalize our findings. Nevertheless, they could be used as a prompt for future work in order for designers to engage further with this group of users as digital narrators. Besides, promoting the benefits for older adults derived from using storytelling technologies is advantageous not only for themselves but also for the broader community.

References

1. Anderson, M., Perrin, A.: Tech Adoption Climbs Among Older Adults. Pew Research Center (2017)
2. Brewer, R., Piper, A.M.: Tell it like it really is: a case of online content creation and sharing among older adult bloggers. In: Proceedings of the 2016 CHI Conference on Human Factors in Computing Systems, pp. 5529–5542. ACM (2016)
3. Brewer, R.N., Jones, J.: Pinteresce: exploring reminiscence as an incentive to digital reciprocity for older adults. In: Proceedings of the 18th ACM Conference Companion on Computer Supported Cooperative Work & Social Computing, pp. 243–246. ACM (2015)
4. Bruner, J.: Life as narrative. Soc. Res. **54**, 11–32 (1987)
5. Carstensen, L.L., Isaacowitz, D.M., Charles, S.T.: Taking time seriously: a theory of socioemotional selectivity. Am. Psychol. **54**(3), 165 (1999)
6. Clemmensen, T., Kaptelinin, V., Nardi, B.: Making HCI theory work: an analysis of the use of activity theory in HCI research. Behav. Inf. Technol. **35**(8), 608–627 (2016)
7. Deters, F.G., Mehl, M.R.: Does posting facebook status updates increase or decrease loneliness? an online social networking experiment. Soc. Psychol. Pers. Sci. **4**(5), 579–586 (2013)
8. Dimond, J.P., Dye, M., LaRose, D., Bruckman, A.S.: Hollaback!: the role of storytelling online in a social movement organization. In: Proceedings of the 2013 Conference on Computer Supported Cooperative Work, pp. 477–490. ACM (2013)
9. Engeström, Y.: Expansive visibilization of work: an activity-theoretical perspective. Comput. Support. Coop. Work (CSCW) **8**(1–2), 63–93 (1999)
10. Engestrom, Y.: Activity theory as a framework for analyzing and redesigning work. Ergonomics **43**(7), 960–974 (2000)
11. Erikson, E.H.: Childhood and Society. Norton, New York (1950)
12. Eurostat: A look at the lives of the elderly in the EU today (2017)
13. Goffmann, E.: The Presentation of Self in Everyday Life. Doubleday, New York (1959)
14. Halverson, C.A.: Activity theory and distributed cognition: or what does cscw need to do with theories? Comput. Support. Coop. Work (CSCW) **11**(1–2), 243–267 (2002)
15. Harley, D., Fitzpatrick, G.: Youtube and intergenerational communication: the case of geriatric1927. Univ. Access Inf. Soc. **8**(1), 5–20 (2009)
16. Hogan, B.: The presentation of self in the age of social media: distinguishing performances and exhibitions online. Bull. Sci. Technol. Soc. **30**(6), 377–386 (2010)
17. Hope, A., Schwaba, T., Piper, A.M.: Understanding digital and material social communications for older adults. In: Proceedings of the SIGCHI Conference on Human Factors in Computing Systems, pp. 3903–3912. ACM (2014)
18. Huberman, J.: Dearly departed: communicating with the dead in the digital age. Soc. Anal. **61**(3), 91–107 (2017)
19. Kensing, F., Blomberg, J.: Participatory design: issues and concerns. Comput. Support. Coop. Work (CSCW) **7**(3–4), 167–185 (1998)
20. Kuutti, K.: Activity theory as a potential framework for human-computer interaction research. In: Nardi, B.A. (ed.) Context and Consciousness: Activity Theory and Human-computer Interaction, pp. 17–44. MIT Press, U.S.A. (1996)
21. Lili, L., Rincon, A.R., Cruz, A.M., Daum, C., Neubauer, N.: Digital storytelling in interventions with older adults-what does the literature say? Innov. Aging **2**(Suppl 1), 317 (2018)

22. Lindley, S.E.: Before i forget: from personal memory to family history. Hum. Comput. Interact. **27**(1–2), 13–36 (2012)

23. Lindsay, S., Jackson, D., Schofield, G., Olivier, P.: Engaging older people using participatory design. In: Proceedings of the SIGCHI Conference on Human Factors in Computing Systems, pp. 1199–1208. ACM (2012)

24. Litt, E.: Knock, knock. who's there? the imagined audience. J. Broadcast. Electron. Media **56**(3), 330–345 (2012)

25. Loos, E.: Senior citizens: digital immigrants in their own country? Observatorio (OBS*) **6**(1), 1–23 (2012)

26. Lowry, P.B., Cao, J., Everard, A.: Privacy concerns versus desire for interpersonal awareness in driving the use of self-disclosure technologies: the case of instant messaging in two cultures. J. Manage. Inf. Syst. **27**(4), 163–200 (2011)

27. McAdams, D.P.: The psychology of life stories. Rev. Gen. Psychol. **5**(2), 100–122 (2001)

28. McAdams, D.P., de St Aubin, E., Logan, R.L.: Generativity among young, midlife, and older adults. Psychol. Aging **8**(2), 221 (1993)

29. Morganti, L., Riva, G., Bonfiglio, S., Gaggioli, A.: Building collective memories on the web: the nostalgia bits project. Int. J. Web Based Communities **9**(1), 83–104 (2013)

30. Muller, M.J.: Participatory design: the third space in HCI. Hum. Comput. Interact. Dev. Process **4235**(2003), 165–185 (2003)

31. Peesapati, S.T., Schwanda, V., Schultz, J., Cosley, D.: Triggering memories with online maps. In: Proceedings of the 73rd ASIS&T Annual Meeting on Navigating Streams in an Information Ecosystem, vol. 47, p. 69. American Society for Information Science (2010)

32. Ricoeur, P.: Life in quest of narrative. In: Wood, D. (ed.) On Paul Ricoeur, pp. 34–47. Routledge, London (2002)

33. Tedre, M., Sutinen, E., Kähkönen, E., Kommers, P.: Ethnocomputing: ICT in cultural and social context. Commun. ACM **49**(1), 126–130 (2006)

34. Tjahja, C., Yee, J., Aftab, M.: Objects of design: activity theory as an analytical framework for design and social innovation. In: Conference Proceedings of the Design Management Academy, vol. 3, pp. 931–947. Design Management Academy (2017)

35. United Nations: World Population Ageing: Highlights. United Nations, New York (2017)

36. Wallbaum, T., Matviienko, A., Ananthanarayan, S., Olsson, T., Heuten, W., Boll, S.C.: Supporting communication between grandparents and grandchildren through tangible storytelling systems. In: Proceedings of the 2018 CHI Conference on Human Factors in Computing Systems, p. 550. ACM (2018)

37. Waycott, J., et al.: Older adults as digital content producers. In: Proceedings of the SIGCHI Conference on Human Factors in Computing Systems, pp. 39–48. ACM (2013)

Participatory Evaluation of Human-Data Interaction Design Guidelines

Eliane Zambon Victorelli[1]([✉]), Julio Cesar dos Reis[1],
Antonio Alberto Souza Santos[2], and Denis José Schiozer[2]

[1] Institute of Computing, University of Campinas (UNICAMP),
Campinas, Brazil
{eliane.victorelli,jreis}@ic.unicamp.br
[2] Center for Petroleum Studies, University of Campinas (UNICAMP),
Campinas, Brazil
{alberto,denis}@cepetro.unicamp.br

Abstract. The design of visual analytics tools for facilitating human-data interaction (HDI) plays a key role to help people identifying useful knowledge from large masses of data. Designing data visualization based on guidelines is relevant. However, it is necessary to further promote the engagement of people in evaluation activities in the design process. Stakeholders need to comprehend the guidelines to help with the evaluation results and design decisions. In this paper, we propose participatory evaluation practices based on HDI design guidelines. The practices aim to create the conditions to participants from any profile collaborate with the design guidelines evaluation. The practices were used on a design problem involving interactions with coordinated visualization. The context of application was a visual analytic tool supporting decisions related to the production strategy in oil reservoirs with the participation of key stakeholders. The results indicate that participants were able to understand the design guidelines and took advantage from them in the design decisions.

Keywords: Human-data interaction · Design guidelines ·
Design evaluation · Participatory design · Visual analytics ·
Oil reservoirs

1 Introduction

Nowadays, the success of organizations depends on the analysis of large amounts of data [4] and solid decision making based on them. Through the evaluation of different possibilities and scenarios one can lay the foundations for a consistent decision making. Analyzing information taking into account facts and data can increase the chances of success in decisions.

Data analysis process requires human judgment to make the best possible evaluation of incomplete, inconsistent and potentially deceptive information in

© IFIP International Federation for Information Processing 2019
Published by Springer Nature Switzerland AG 2019
D. Lamas et al. (Eds.): INTERACT 2019, LNCS 11746, pp. 475–494, 2019.
https://doi.org/10.1007/978-3-030-29381-9_30

face of rapidly changing situations. Visual analytic (VA), the science of analytically reasoning facilitated by interactive visual interfaces, aims to extract and identify useful information and knowledge from large volumes of data [31]. Unfortunately, there is a natural correlation between the complexity of the data and the complexity of the tools to study them [8]. This complexity requires that the VA tools design addresses the challenges of facilitating interaction to support understanding, manipulation and analysis of large number of information.

Recently, the Human-data interaction (HDI) area has investigated how people interact with data in a manner analogous to the research conducted by the Human-computer Interaction (HCI) area on the relationship between people and computers [12,15]. HDI is referenced as the "human manipulation, analysis and meaning creation from bulky, unstructured and complex datasets" [11]. We consider HDI aspects related to VA tools. We adopt an approach to the HDI that highlights the importance of taking into account the various stakeholders during all the development cycle.

Designing VA tools based on guidelines is an important approach to help materializing the knowledge and experience acquired by various experts in the field [11,26]. However, this approach does not favour the engagement of people in the process of shared construction of software design. Similarly, participatory approaches [16,21] allow obtaining diverse knowledge to improve products through people's vision who potentially are affected by their construction. Nevertheless, the participation of people with diverse profiles does not favor the use of technical inputs *e.g.*, design guidelines. We claim that the option for the use of design approach based on guidelines should not necessarily exclude the possibility of taking advantage of the participation of people with different profiles.

In this study, we propose evaluation techniques for supporting the design decisions of VA tools based on HDI guidelines to be taken in a participatory way. The challenges brought by our approach involve research and exploration of methods to select and clarify the guidelines relevant to a given decision, as well as the definition of appropriate practices to ensure the adequate participation of key stakeholders in the project decision on the use of guidelines. The contribution of this investigation consists in new practices to create the necessary conditions to help participants of all profiles collaborate with the design process.

Our methodology started with a research on participatory practices that can be used in the evaluation phase and with a study of alternatives to adapt the practices to the context of the HDI design guidelines. Then, we investigated and selected design guidelines related to the design problem and looked for examples and systems to facilitate the guidelines understanding by the involved stakeholders. We created tasks for the participants to carry out and we elaborated questions to guide the decision making.

This investigation was conducted and applied in a case study related to a data intensive environment. The evaluation of the proposed practices was carried out in the context of the UNISIM laboratory of the Center for Petroleum Studies (CEPETRO) at University of Campinas, which develops methodologies and tools to assist in the decision analysis process [30]. In this context, one of the research lines emphasizes the study concerned with the selection of production strategy in oil fields based on a 12-steps methodology. In this research, the practices were conducted in workshops involving design decisions about SEPIA, a VA tool developed by the UNISIM laboratory. This tool supports VA tasks commonly performed by domain engineers and researchers. In particular, we addressed how to design coordinated visualizations [2]. Obtained results based on the conducted workshops indicate that the participatory practices for the evaluation of the visualization guidelines was relevant for the design decisions in SEPIA.

The remainder of this article is organized as follows: Sect. 2 presents the background with the fundamental concepts and related work. Section 3 reports on the proposed practices. Section 4 describes the conducted case study. Whereas Sect. 5 discusses the findings and lessons learned, Sect. 6 presents our final considerations and directions for future research.

2 Background and Related Work

The proposal for design practices presented by Churchill [9] attempted to demystify the "genius designer" whose instincts and intuition lead to great design decisions. Her work states that is needed to take a proactive and critical stance to design, develop, or evaluate products that incorporate the capture, storage and data analysis. In this sense, we address the design of VA tools based on guidelines in a participatory design approach.

Participatory Design. The field of Participatory Design spans a rich diversity of theories, practices, analyses and actions, with the goal of working directly with users and other stakeholders in the design of social systems that are part of human work [16]. This approach considers that everyone involved in a design situation is capable of contributing for it [21].

The area is rich in terms of practices and extent of theoretical development. There is a large number of practices that vary in relation to the phase of development life cycle and address who participates with whom in what, and appropriate group size and the type of project that has been used [16, 21].

In our proposal, workshops with a participatory approach is used for taking advantage of people's participation in activities in all the design cycle. We use some practices described in the literature and propose new participatory practices with the goal of conducting guidelines evaluation.

Design Guidelines. From their experience in various projects, design specialists can compile recommendations and provide designers with the ability to determine the consequences of their design decisions. The use of these recommendations allows less experienced designers to enjoy knowledge of the most experienced. Design rules in the form of standards and guidelines provide direction for design. They are recommendations a designer can follow to enhance the interactive properties of the system [10]. Design guidelines vary in their level of abstraction, generality and authority.

We use the term guideline in a broad sense to talk about design recommendations made by experts that can be used in the design of other systems in a comprehensive way, without distinguishing the level of generality, abstraction or authority. One example of guideline is the information density guideline that suggests "to provide only necessary and immediately usable data; do not overload your views with irrelevant data" [29]. We use HDI guidelines, in the phase of evaluation, as an approach to bring specialists' knowledge to help the identification of points for redesign that favour HDI.

Coordinated Visualizations Guidelines. A multiple view system uses two or more distinct view to support the investigation of a single conceptual entity [2]. The advantages of using multiple visualization coordination are improved user performance; discovery of unforeseen relationships; and unification of view [24]. The design of this kind of system involves decisions, ranging from determining layout to constructing sophisticated coordination mechanisms and interactions between the various dimensions of space. Some guidelines were provided to support decisions involved in this context [2]. In this context, there are two set of guidelines. The first supports the decision of using or not coordinated visualizations, *e.g.*, the rule of complementarity: *"Use multiple views when different views bring out correlations or disparities"* [2]. Other set of guidelines helps deciding how to design coordinated visualizations, *e.g.*, the rule of self-evidence *"Use perceptual cues to make relationships among multiple views more apparent to the user"* [2]. In this study, we explore both set of coordinated visualizations design guidelines associated with other more generic interaction guidelines.

Evaluation Techniques. Evaluation tests are used to assess the usability, functionality and acceptability of an interactive system. Some approaches are based on experts' evaluation whereas others involve users. Evaluation seeks to assess the quality of an interface design, both during the development process and when the software is almost ready. An evaluation method must be chosen carefully and must be suitable for the system under analysis [10].

Among several methods, we highlight the Heuristic Evaluation [23], which consists in conducting the inspection of the interface based on a list of heuristics. Heuristic evaluation refers to a method for finding usability problems in user interface design. A review of Nielsen's Heuristic evaluation method based on participatory approaches was proposed by including users (work-domain experts) as inspectors by Muller *et al.* [22]. He extended the original Nielsen's heuristic set with several process-oriented heuristics. The evaluation method guided an iterative designs process.

This technique is similar to one of the practices proposed in our work, but it is focused in a specific Nielsen's heuristics set extension. Our initial set of guidelines includes the Nielsen heuristic set and further covers a larger set of heuristics in the context of HDI and specific issues, *e.g.*, coordinated visualizations guidelines. This type of assessment is generally adopted for the design phase. However, it is not appropriate to our participatory approach, because it is important to have input from stakeholders at all stages of the project. We propose adaptations to the heuristic evaluation method for engaging stakeholders while aggregating the knowledge and experience provided by the experts through the use of guidelines.

The online community was the target of a study that applied a combination of participatory design and development methods with heuristic evaluation [27]. A specific set of heuristics was developed, extending the Nielsen's heuristics and adding a specific set of sociability heuristic. The set of heuristics was then turned into a questionnaire that was iteratively tested with online communities. Refining the set of sociability heuristics was one of the goals of the study.

The studies conducted by Muller *et al.* [22] and Preece *et al.* [27] conceived practices of evaluation by guidelines combined with participatory methods. However, these studies did not involve VA neither emphasize HDI. These facts highlight the innovation of our proposed practices which combines stakeholders participation and HDI guidelines for a VA tool in a complex domain.

Leman *et al.* [17] studied typical data visualizations that results from linear pipelines that start by characterizing data and end by displaying the data. The proposal goal was to provide natural means to adjust the displays to support good HDI. This method supports a dynamic process for defining visualizations in which users learn from visualizations and the visualizations adjust to the expert's judgment. This proposal differs from ours mainly because it is a method for the execution time and not a process for design VA in the HDI context.

3 Participatory Practices for HDI Guidelines Evaluation

Our proposal supports design decisions based on guidelines to be taken in a participatory way. Subsect. 3.1 presents an overview of a design process for HDI [32], in which our evaluation techniques are developed. The following sections detail the defined evaluation tasks for supporting the design decisions. These activities involve selection of HDI design guidelines (*cf.* Subsect. 3.2); preparation of workshops (*cf.* Subsect. 3.3); procedure to assist participants in the understanding of HDI design guidelines (*cf.* Subsect. 3.4); and a technique for conducting participatory evaluation with HDI guidelines (*cf.* Subsect. 3.5).

3.1 Overview of the Process for HDI Designing

We summarize the entire design process for HDI that combines guidelines with participatory practices [32]. It includes several activities that are orchestrated by the flow illustrated in Fig. 1. It starts with problem clarification activities. Initially, it is necessary to know the stakeholders, understand the concepts and values of each one involved in the design problem (*cf.* item A of Fig. 1). All stakeholders and their interest have to be identified [19]. We explore supporting artifacts that help thinking beyond traditional participants [3]. It is possible to discover people who are not directly involved with the tasks of the selected design scope, but they are affected by the results produced by these tasks. From the obtained stakeholders, it is important to know the problems and issues as well as the ideas and solutions related to each stakeholder [3]. They can have different perspectives about the subject. In this context, the well known elicitation techniques of requirements engineering are used to understand the subject.

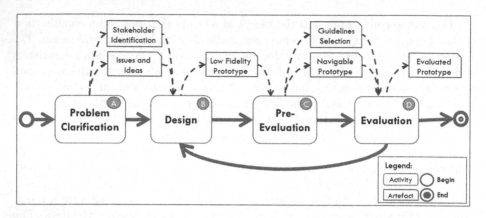

Fig. 1. Process for HDI design by combining guidelines with participatory design approaches (adapted from [32])

Design activities should focus on meeting the needs of stakeholders by providing solutions to the problems and issues reported by them. Participants of all hierarchical levels should give their contributions during the participatory design workshops (*cf.* item B of Fig. 1). We use Storyboarding and BrainDraw [21] as the main techniques to support design activities.

In our proposal, during design activities the group creates a low fidelity prototype without design guidelines orientation. The participants should propose alternatives freely in the design phase without worrying about guidelines. In this sense, they do not stop thinking in creative ways to solve the problem for fear of not attending a guideline. The guidelines are introduced afterwards.

Before beginning the evaluation activities, there is a pre-evaluation phase (*cf.* item C of Fig. 1). It includes the selection of guidelines (*cf.* item E of Fig. 2) and the preparation of the workshops for evaluation (*cf.* item F of Fig. 2), detailed in Subsects. 3.2 and 3.3, respectively. In this phase, a non-functional navigable prototype must be constructed so that participants can interact with it and better understand how their suggestions given in previous activities would be mapped to the software.

We need to verify to which extent users think the prototype might help them accomplishing their tasks; and how the prototype can be improved. All the activities of evaluation phase help making decisions about the prototype refinement (*cf.* item D of Fig. 1). To know the impression that a prototype cause we use techniques such as the Participatory Thinking-aloud Evaluation [18] and User Evaluation. In the first, a participant is invited to interact with the navigable prototype to complete an use case, conducting a pre-defined task. In our proposal, all participants in a workshop speak aloud while one participant interacts with the prototype. When the design of the prototype is mature, an user evaluation based in the Query Technique [10] is conducted asking the participants about the results directly. It is applied by interview or questionnaire.

The navigable prototype and the selected guidelines support the evaluation activities. We recommend the use of guidelines in more advanced phases of the design. They are introduced to the participants only in the evaluation phase. This phase includes the understanding of guidelines for all participants (*cf.* item G of Fig. 2) and the participatory evaluation with the guidelines (*cf.* item H of Fig. 2), detailed in Subsects. 3.4 and 3.5, respectively.

After the evaluation activities, the team has the opportunity to decide if they are going to make a redesign activity to adjust the prototype to the issues identified. The decision to be taken, as a result of the activities of evaluation, is whether the guidelines will be adopted in the prototype solution. The activities may also result in suggestions of how to use them. If the group decision is to change the prototype, it may be necessary to return to the design activities. This cycle can be repeated more than once until participants feel that the prototype design is appropriate for their needs.

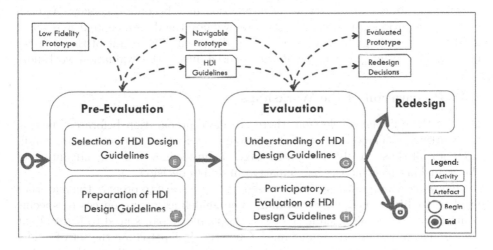

Fig. 2. Pre-evaluation and evaluation activities for evaluation of HDI design guidelines

3.2   Selection of HDI Design Guidelines

At the beginning of the evaluation process, before the evaluation workshops, it is necessary to conduct tasks with the objective of defining which guidelines are relevant for supporting decisions in a specific context (item E of Fig. 2). The designer should select guidelines considering specific problems being addressed in the design, characteristics of the solutions being analyzed, and design phase.

The selection activity should be based on a large set of guidelines related to the subject. Given the complexity of the problem of facilitating the HDI for VA application, we aggregate guidelines of the VA, HCI and HDI area. We draw upon a previously compiled set of guidelines and heuristics [26]. It brings together the guidelines found in influential contributions in the VA and HCI areas. We add HDI guidelines found in the literature [5–7, 13–15, 20, 28].

We need to include in the set the guidelines those for the application domain or standards used by the target organization if they exist. For example, if the design problem involves a particular type of interaction or visualization, the designer should look for specific guidelines in that context.

At this stage, you group the guidelines by subject to facilitate the selection of the recommendations that matter to one specific scope. One group of guidelines could aggregate, *e.g.,* guidelines related to decision about using a specific type of resource; and other group join all guidelines about how to use this resource.

This large set is a facilitator for the next task of deciding which guidelines will be useful in the workshops. However, it is unfeasible to work with so many guidelines at the same time. Then, you need to analyze which design decisions need to be made due to the design situation at that time and the subjects involved. You should select the specific guidelines more closely related to the prototype issues and interactions that are discussed in a given design phase.

With the progress of the design and refinement of prototype, new features may be introduced or new types of interaction may become necessary. At each cycle of the process, it is important to re-evaluate the design context and select guidelines regarding the new issues being discussed. The result of this activity consists in a set of guidelines that will be used during the evaluation workshop.

3.3   Preparation of the Workshops

Besides the guidelines selection, there are more preparation before conducting the workshops. The objective of this activity (*cf.* F of Fig. 2) is to create conditions for all those involved to understand the guidelines and take advantage of them, making possible the participation in design decisions.

Knowing what guidelines will be used, it is necessary to prepare the materials used to facilitate their understanding. The guidelines are resources to specific contexts of design; we assume that workshop's participants need to learn about the content of the involved guidelines. Once the designer chose the set of guidelines, it is necessary to find ways to unravel, explain and facilitate their understanding to allow participants comprehending them and to decide on their use. The designer must prepare a form to support the understanding of the guidelines by the following steps.

1. Evaluate the best ways of organizing and explaining the guidelines selected. It should be clear what decisions the participants have to make and what they need to be concerned about in each evaluation workshop. In this regard, the participants' background should be considered. If participants are not familiar with the use of design guidelines, you need to prepare explanations that relate the concepts involved to things they know.
2. For each guideline, choose simple examples to explain the involved concepts to the participants without the specific background. It is convenient to use examples from different contexts that involve interactions similar to those being analyzed in order to avoid biases. During the analysis of literature on the guidelines, it is possible to find illustrated examples that can be used.

3. To complement the explanation, look for websites or VA tools that allow the practical exercise of interaction. Use references from the literature and consult other designers and users to find websites or VA tools that have prototype-like interactions. The focus of the choice should be HDI. Then, choose the visualizations and scenarios for analysis that involve interactions and data types similar to the design context. For example, if the design problem involves interacting the location of some elements, look for systems exploring interactions with maps.

4. At this stage, you can navigate and explore the interaction alternatives and information presented in the visualizations from the chosen tools. List points that users should observe focusing on the interactions being studied, *e.g.*, if the study is about coordinated visualizations, it is important to highlight interactions in a visualization that impact other visualizations.

5. Select different alternatives available for the same type of interaction, *e.g.*, if the application involves maps, choose websites that react in different way to similar interactions, as zoom operations. Some websites may automatically update the contents of coordinated visualizations while others do not.

6. Find alternatives related to the moment when actions are triggered due to user interaction, *e.g.*, if the user changes the position in a slider altering the value of some visualization parameter, in some websites other visualizations are regenerated and updated while the user moves the mouse and others do this only when the mouse is released.

7. Prepare some tasks for the participants to do using the websites or VA tools to exercise the content of the guidelines. For example, if a website regarding real estate is used for the exploration, it may be interesting that participants choose a property to rent in a particular region of the city.

The result is an activity guide to support the participants in the understanding of guidelines. For each guideline, list all the relevant points for participants to explore and tasks to be executed. A form should be defined and should clearly state the decisions that must be made and ask questions that drive the decisions.

3.4 Participants' Understanding of HDI Design Guidelines

During the workshops, initial activities aim to ensure that all participants understand the guidelines and they are prepared to participate in the evaluation. The materials generated in the preparation step (*cf.* F of Fig. 2) is used as a support in the understanding phase (*cf.* G of Fig. 2). In this step, users should be guided through the following steps:

1. Guide the participants in the understanding of the guidelines so they can make sense of them. Introduce each guideline or group of guideline to participants with explanation and examples of applications.

2. The participants must explore by themselves the interactions in websites or VA tools in different context from the design under evaluation. The exploration should be conducted in small groups of 2 or 3 people. They should answer the questions set out in the form.

3. We understand that HDI guidelines analysis should be done in a practical way. The participants should perform tasks involving the interaction to understand the aspects related to their accomplishment. The exploration of selected websites helps the understanding of the interaction aspects, since the participants have the opportunity to exercise the interaction.

4. After the exploitation of the websites, all the participants are gathered to discuss their understanding of the guidelines. At the end of this activity, participants must understand well the guidelines and their application in the explored websites or VA tools.

3.5   Participatory Evaluation of HDI Design Guidelines

The last activity is held in a participatory workshop (*cf.* H of Fig. 2). The guidelines are evaluated by participants led by a designer. The participants should map the guidelines for the prototype interactions and make the relevant design decisions. This is conducted through the following steps:

1. You should clarify which design questions need to be answered in the workshop. It may be convenient to discuss the related guidelines in a grouped way. Each evaluation workshop should focus on a well-defined decision and discuss a set of related guidelines that can support that decision making.

2. Participants explore the navigable prototype. It may be convenient to explore the prototype in a thinking-aloud activity (*cf.* Subsect. 3.1).

3. Highlight and clarify the relationship between the guideline and the prototype. Show participants possible alternatives for mapping the guidelines in the prototype under analysis.

4. Make sure that the participants are aware that the suggestions of design mappings are a starting point for the discussions, and there are alternatives that need to be sought and discussed. They are used to help participants collaborate with the design process.

5. In the light of the previous steps, participants should discuss the application of the guidelines to the interactions covered by the prototype. Participants should discuss the impacts as well the advantages and disadvantages of the adoption of the guideline. The outcome of the discussion is the decision of the participants on the adoption of the guidelines. The activity generates a subset of the discussed guidelines potentially useful and the associated ideas for redesign.

4   Case Study

One of the challenges being addressed by UNISIM consists in the investigation of technologies for optimal production strategy selection in oil fields [30]. This process involves a lot of efforts in analysis of voluminous data. SEPIA is a VA software tool developed to facilitate this process. The results of this study consist of requirements for the tool and in future will be incorporated the production version of SEPIA.

One step for optimization of the production strategy requires, among other activities, the performance of many simulations, with some variations among them. After some simulations, it is necessary to make comparisons to verify the impact in results of the changes from one simulation to another. SEPIA supports several types of VA activities, but does not have specific functionalities to support this scenario. We addressed how to allow the enhancement of SEPIA with HDI design for comparisons among different oil production strategies.

The project was conducted in 2 cycles. The first cycle of the process resulted in the prototype for the comparison interface screens to be supported by SEPIA. In the second cycle, we dealt with design aspects related to the specific type of interaction with coordinated visualizations.

In this study, we emphasized evaluation activities based on design guidelines conducted in the second cycle. The application of the process for the second cycle required 2 workshops lasting approximately 3 h each. Thus, the whole process was conducted in approximately 6 h of meeting with 6 participants on average. In addition, 12 h of effort were required for the designers prepare the presentations and practices for each workshop.

The activities of this study involved 2 Computer Science researchers and 4 participants from UNISIM playing different roles with different reasons for engagement. One of the Computer Science researcher (one of the authors) played the role of designer throughout the process. We present the results for the evaluation activities carried out in the second cycle.

4.1   Results of the Design Activities

In the first cycle, the process began with stakeholders identification followed by issues and requirements elicitation. The stakeholders identified involved developers, designers, development project manager, researcher and users of the VA tool. The UNISIM team involves engineers and researchers who are very important stakeholders. Some of them are real users of SEPIA tool and others develop their own visualizations due to specific demands of their research.

In the elicitation phase, there were many meetings and presentations about the complex domain of strategies for petroleum exploration. To deepen the understanding of the domain, we conducted individual interviews with the purpose of clarifying the problem and eliciting the requirements. The results of the interviews revealed that one of the important issues was the comparison between the results of several attempts to optimize results. This subject was chosen as the central requirement to be addressed in the prototype (cf. Subsect. 4.2).

The issues, problems, ideas and solutions identified during the problem clarification activities were the source for the initial design activities conducted with storyboard and braindraw techniques. After getting consensus for the first version of the storyboard, it was possible to identify the goal of each interface involved in the process. We conducted one separated braindraw for each state identified in the storyboard.

We selected the guidelines that were most related to the prototype scope and they supported a participatory evaluation. One example of a VA guideline included was about information density: "Provide only immediately usable data; do not overload visualizations with irrelevant data" [29]. A preliminary participatory thinking-aloud evaluation of the prototype was undertaken.

4.2   Prototype

The time, volume of data and number of files involved in these attempts pose difficulties the execution of comparisons among obtained results from simulations. Participants suggested alternatives for the design of the comparison functionality so that users could quickly focus on the points being compared without being distracted by the other data or visualizations not involved. The decision made by the group adhered to the previously mentioned guideline, (*cf.* Subsect. 4.1), and the new prototype reduced the density of information by providing only immediately usable data and not overloading views with irrelevant data.

In the first cycle, the results of the braindraw workshops, the low fidelity prototypes, were transformed into a navigable prototype. This was very useful during evaluation activities and helped to raise issues, questions and suggestions. Figure 3 presents two screens of the SEPIA prototype defining the design for the visualization functionality of results comparison.

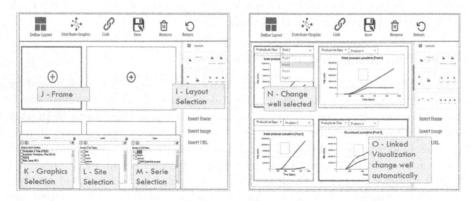

Fig. 3. Screens of SEPIA prototype for oil production simulation results comparisons

According to the new design, after the user chooses the comparison feature and selects the parameters for comparison, the system shows the comparison dashboard. To format this dashboard, the system allows the user to opt for a layout previously constructed (*cf.* item I of Fig. 3) or choose manually the position and format of the frames (*cf.* item J of Fig. 3). The user must define the visualizations to be shown in each frame defining types of graphics, *e.g.*, production time curve or bar chart (*cf.* item K of Fig. 3); the sites, *e.g.*, a specific producer well or reservoir (*cf.* item L of Fig. 3); and the data series, *e.g.*, production of oil or water (*cf.* item M of Fig. 3).

To facilitate the task of constructing views, the system must allow the user to copy the definitions of visualization from one frame to another and modify it later. The user can ask the system to link, two or more frames indicating which parameter, *e.g.*, site, should be linked. When the user changes one information, *e.g.*, the site in one of the linked frames (*cf.* item N of Fig. 3), the system must automatically change a related information in other linked frames as well (*cf.* O of Fig. 3). In this sense, when the user requests to change an information in a given frame, the system should verify if it is needed to change the information in other different frames, maintaining consistency between them and facilitating user data analysis. Therefore, linked frames in SEPIA must be treated as coordinated views. In the second cycle, we dealt with design challenges related to various aspects of coordination between visualizations.

4.3   Results of the Selection of HDI Design Guidelines

Before the evaluation phase, we selected the useful guidelines explored in each specific workshop. The guidelines were chosen based on the large set of guidelines we had assembled and on the issues being addressed in each workshop.

The design decision taken to the prototype required to deepen the understanding of the guidelines for coordinated visualizations. These recommendations were incorporated into the set of guidelines. One guideline included to deal with coordinated visualizations was: "Use perceptual cues to make relationships among multiple views more apparent to the user" [2].

In this study, it was necessary to decide if coordinated visualizations would be used (decision I). If the decision was positive to this question, it was required to decide how they would be used (decision II). In this context, two separate groups of guidelines were organized.

First, we decided whether using coordinated visualizations. In this context, we selected guidelines that helped identifying which features of the prototype required the use of coordinated visualizations. We used guidelines regarding: (1) the diversity of information; (2) correlations and disparities revealed by visualizations; (3) the partitioning of information into manageable parts; and (4) the parsimony in the use of complex resources [1, 2, 20].

The second decision was about how to support coordinated visualizations. The selected guidelines addressed very specific aspects of coordinated visualizations such as: (1) the identification of the visualizations to be used in a coordinated way; (2) the presentation of coordinated visualizations; (3) the actions in each visualization that affect other visualizations; (4) the techniques of interaction; and (5) how to make the coordination clear to the user [2, 25].

4.4   Results of the Preparation for the Workshops

Preparation activities were necessary to arrange the materials used during the explanation of guidelines and the workshops. We organized the materials for two workshops, one for each decision (I and II). For each workshop, we organized the materials related to the specific decision, which included: (1) the explanation of the specific set of guidelines; (2) the definition of examples; (3) ways of participants exploring similar interactions; and (4) forms with questions to guide the activities and design decisions.

We prepared a presentation to show the guidelines. We looked for simple examples to explain the concepts involved in the guidelines. We avoided to use examples of the oil production area. First, we search for examples of similar interactions adopted in tools used by all the participants in their daily activities, *e.g.*, file manager applications and spreadsheets. Afterwards, we used more complex and complete examples.

We looked for websites to allow a practical exploration of similar interactions. When it was impossible to find websites pointed out in the literature, we looked for websites that dealt with subjects similar to those mentioned in the literature examples, *e.g.,* restaurant selection based on quality and location using a map or a site about the stock price index.

We prepared a list of questions included in the form to guide the workshops and design decisions, as follows.

1. Exploration of Websites
   - Does the guidelines apply to the context of the website?
   - How the interactions handled by the guidelines are supported?
   - What are the positive and negative points? Justify.
2. Mapping to the prototype:
   - Do the guidelines apply to the prototype interactions? In what contexts?
   - How could it be supported? It could be supported in the same way as the exploration examples, with some adaptation, or with another approach?
   - What are the design alternatives for the prototype?
   - What are the positive and negative points? Justify.
3. Open questions
   - Are there other similar design situations that could be addressed?
   - What other questions should we ask ourselves about the guidelines?

4.5   Results of the Participant's Understanding the Guidelines

We held two workshops in separated days, one for each decision. The first part of each workshop considered activities to ensure understanding and enable the participation of all. The activities of understanding took on average 2 h in each workshop. All those who participated in the decision-making activities also participated in the understanding activity. In this stage, 3 groups of 2 participants were organized to carry out the exploration, which was directed by the activity guide form.

Participants used the QuintoAndar[1] website for the explorations with the aim of familiarizing with the interaction techniques used in coordinated visualization. We requested participants to search apartments with 3 bedrooms in a specific neighborhood and then compare with the offers of another neighborhood. As another exercise, participants were invited to compare the interaction techniques in the website regarding crimes in Seatle[2].

---

[1] www.quintoandar.com.br.

[2] http://www.seattle.gov/police/information-and-data/crime-dashboard.

We suggested the participants to use the Yahoo's Finance[3] website to explore ways of making relationships between visualizations more evident. We asked participants about the coordination between the closing price and the negotiated volume. In addition, we proposed explorations to be carried out with the website Kekanto[4]. The goal was to enable participants to compare different ways of coordination between textual information and maps, besides the time to trigger consistency maintenance actions.

Participants with a user profile reported great knowledge gain with the proposed activities. Knowledge among the various participants was equated and everyone was able to participate in the next activity in which decision-making was actually easily carried out.

4.6 Results of the Participatory Evaluation of Guidelines

In each workshop, the selected guidelines were explained to the participants and they explored the different websites. Afterwards, the participants were able to decide whether the orientation made by the guidelines could benefit the prototype. After the activities, we consolidated the answers to the questionnaires.

In the first workshop conducted, the set of guidelines evaluated was regarding the benefits, costs, advantages and disadvantages involved in the use of coordinated views. The guideline that oriented all evaluation and can summarize the work is: "Participants should balance the benefits of having multiple coordinated visualizations and the complexity that comes with their introduction" [2]. Regarding decision I, the group indicated that it was convenient to maintain the coordinated visualizations in the solution of the comparison feature.

The second workshop reviewed the set of guidelines on how to support interactions between coordinated views. The most discussed guideline in this workshop was: "Make the interfaces for multiple views consistent, and make the states of multiple views consistent attention" [2].

The discussion of this guideline began by dealing with the comparison dashboard in a general way. However, the participants were unable to evolve due to the large number of possible situations that require consistency between visualizations. Then, the strategy adopted was to choose more specific scenarios for discussion. Once all the scenarios have been discussed, a detailed analysis identified the possible points of generalization.

We discussed a specific scenario about analyzing the production curve of oil and water, the curve for the net present value for a given period and specific wells. It also included a bar chart with the accumulated amount of the production for all the wells. The participants subdivided the decision II into 5 more specific design decisions. The following are the issues and decisions taken for the specific scenario discussed.

---

[3] https://www.financas.yahoo.com/quote.

[4] https://kekanto.com.br/sp/campinas/restaurantes/.

1. **Issue:** How should coupling be done between views? What are the mapping functions? **Decision:** Coupling must be done when the user includes or change a simulation model; and when the user changes the production time.
2. **Issue:** What are the perception tips used to make relationships self evident? **Decision:** The same color is used for the same simulation model in different visualizations. There should be a bar to indicate that the time of the production curve has changed.
3. **Issue:** What information should be kept consistent across multiple views? What attributes need to be kept consistent and what consistency rules should be used? **Decision:** The value of the total time used to calculate the accumulated production value should be kept consistent with the position in the time bar.
4. **Issue:** What situations require the consistency rule to be triggered? **Decision:** When the user changes the considered time.
5. **Issue:** At what specific time should consistency updates be triggered? **Decision:** When the user releases the mouse from button in the time bar.

4.7   Participants' Assessment of the Activities

The participants were invited to evaluate the activities via a questionnaire and open questions. We used a Likert scale to understand participants' assessment of the activities in which they were engaged. We considered the following grades: 1 to poor; 2 for bad; 3 for indifferent; 4 for good and 5 for very good. Table 1 presents the obtained results. Evaluations were considered positive when the notes are equal to or greater than 4.

Five participants answered the questionnaire. All of them participated in the design and evaluation activities. The process overall evaluation, time involved, practices, achieving the goal and quality of results were considered positive for 100.0% of the participants and presented average grade 4.0. The items with the best grade were about the understanding of guidelines and support to think about problems and solutions, followed by the help given by the examples in this understanding. The worst aspect considered by the participants was the value of their own participation in the workshop, which was considered positive by only 60% of them.

5   Discussion

We proposed a methodology for evaluating guidelines through participatory practices focusing on HDI design for decisions supported by VA. We faced the challenges of identifying suitable methods for selecting and clarifying the relevant guidelines; and the appropriate definition of practices to the activities that ensure effective participation of key stakeholders.

Our achieved results indicated that the methodology application produces good effects. The participatory practices allowed to observe how the shared

Table 1. Participants' assessment of the evaluation activities.

Question	Aver. Grade	% Positive
What is your overall evaluation of the workshops you attended?	4.0	100.0
How was the use of the time involved in the workshops?	4.0	100.0
Were the practices used adequate for the objectives?	4.0	100.0
Did you understand the explanation of the guidelines?	4.6	100.0
Did the examples help you understand the guidelines?	4.4	100.0
Did the explorations of the websites helped to propose alternatives to apply the guidelines?	4.0	80.0
Were guidelines helpful to think about possible problems and solutions?	4.6	100.0
Did you consider your participation in the workshop fruitful?	3.6	60.0
Was the goal of deciding the design of interactions with coordinated views reached?	4.0	100.0
What is the quality of the results obtained with the workshops?	4.0	100.0

understanding about the problem domain can be obtained and different viewpoints conciliated.

Our findings suggest that it is necessary to create conditions for all involved to understand the guidelines and to take advantage of them for the guidelines evaluation practices to be truly participatory. To facilitate the understanding of the concepts it is relevant to use simple examples and exploration from different scenarios. Afterwards, when the participants are clear about the guidelines, it is important to help them map to the context of the evaluation.

The use of examples from other contexts familiar to the users avoids the bias that using examples from the domain itself can bring. We merged very simple examples that illustrated the concepts with more sophisticated examples to give new ideas of application. The examples were well evaluated and appeared to be useful to all participants.

We introduced guided explorations of websites that support interactions similar to the ones under analysis. The participants (users and domain experts) considered it very relevant, mainly for the understanding of the details related to the interactions. It helped all participants to know several alternative types of interaction and stimulated the generation of new ideas on how to apply them in SEPIA in a way that is useful for their daily work. However, the exploration practice did not have a uniform assessment. The developers did not consider the practice very helpful for themselves and reported that they already knew the possibilities of interaction in coordinated visualizations. Our understanding is that exploration is very interesting for people who are unaware of the possibility of interaction and unproductive for those who dominates the subject.

We found that it was not easy to analyze the use of guidelines based on generic scenarios. The use of specific scenarios facilitates discussion and understanding. Even for general purpose tool such as a dashboard, we noticed that the discussion flowed better when it came to simple, concrete scenarios based on a day-to-day project task. In this sense, everyone can follow the discussion, think of possibilities and contribute with suggestions.

During the preparation and conduction of the workshops we found limitations for the construction of the navigable prototype to support a better understanding of multiple coordinated visualizations. In general, prototyping tools do not have sufficient resources to allow exploring the effects of user interaction in multiple areas with multiple possible paths with different results in each area.

As future steps, we consider to identify scopes in the domain of oil production strategy that can be easily explained to design specialists and conduct guidelines evaluation with classical approach. This would make it possible to compare the results obtained by guidelines evaluation involving several design specialists and those obtained in a participatory approach.

6   Conclusion

The adequate use of design guidelines requires the definition of participatory practices to improve design decisions. This article presented the feasibility of including diversified profiles in participatory evaluation practices based on HDI design guidelines. Our methodology defined practices to create the necessary conditions for the understanding of the guidelines using examples and explorations of similar interactions. We applied the evaluation activities in a VA tool created to support optimal production strategy selection in oil fields by involving complex decisions and make good usage of participants knowledge. Our results lead to believe that the participatory evaluation of complex guidelines is favored by the use of examples and the exploration of interaction in other contexts, followed by the mapping to the domain under evaluation. We plan to evaluate the guidelines for coordinated visualizations in other scenarios of the optimization domain of petroleum production strategy.

Acknowledgments. We thank Petrobras; Energi Simulation inside of the R&D of ANP; Center for Petroleum Studies (CEPETRO-UNICAMP); Energy Department (DE-FEM-UNICAMP); and from the Research Group of Simulations and Management of Petroleum Reservoirs (UNISIM-UNICAMP) at CEPETRO.

References

1. Amar, R., Stasko, J.: A knowledge task-based framework for design and evaluation of information visualizations. In: IEEE Symposium on Information Visualization, pp. 143–149 (2004). https://doi.org/10.1109/INFVIS.2004.10

2. Baldonado, M.Q.W., Kuchinsky, A.: Guidelines for using multiple views in information visualization. In: AVI 2000 Proceedings of the Working Conference on Advanced Visual Interfaces, pp. 110–119 (2000)
3. Baranauskas, M.C.C., Martins, M.C., Valente, J.A.: Codesign de Redes Digitais: tecnologia e educação a serviço da inclusão social. Penso Editora (2013)
4. Behrisch, M., et al.: Commercial visual analytics systems-advances in the big data analytics field. IEEE Trans. Vis. Comput. Graph., 1–20 (2018). https://doi.org/10.1109/TVCG.2018.2859973
5. Cabitza, F., Zotti, F.D., Locoro, A.: Probing interactivity in open data for general practice. An evidence-based approach. In: VVH@ AVI, pp. 35–42 (2016)
6. Cafaro, F.: Using embodied allegories to design gesture suites for human-data interaction. In: Proceedings of the 2012 ACM Conference on Ubiquitous Computing, pp. 560–563. ACM (2012). https://doi.org/10.1145/2370216.2370309. http://dl.acm.org/citation.cfm?id=2370216.2370309
7. Cavoukian, A., Chibba, M.: Cognitive cities, big data and citizen participation: the essentials of privacy and security. Stud. Syst. Decis. Control 63, 61–82 (2016). https://doi.org/10.1007/978-3-319-33798-2
8. Ceneda, D., et al.: Characterizing guidance in visual analytics. IEEE Trans. Vis. Comput. Graph. 23(1), 111–120 (2017). https://doi.org/10.1109/TVCG.2016.2598468
9. Churchill, E.F.: Designing data practices. Interactions 23(5), 20–21 (2016). https://doi.org/10.1145/2983401
10. Dix, A., Finlay, J., Abowd, G.D., Beale, R.: Human-Computer Interaction, 3rd edn. Pearson/Prentice-Hall, Upper Saddle River (2004)
11. Elmqvist, N.: Embodied human-data interaction. In: ACM CHI 2011 Workshop Embodied Interaction: Theory and Practice in HCI, pp. 104–107 (2011)
12. Holzinger, A.: Extravaganza tutorial on hot ideas for interactive knowledge discovery and data mining in biomedical informatics. In: Ślęzak, D., Tan, A.-H., Peters, J.F., Schwabe, L. (eds.) BIH 2014. LNCS (LNAI), vol. 8609, pp. 502–515. Springer, Cham (2014). https://doi.org/10.1007/978-3-319-09891-3_46
13. Hornung, H., Pereira, R., Baranauskas, M.C.C., Liu, K.: Challenges for human-data interaction – a semiotic perspective. In: Kurosu, M. (ed.) HCI 2015, Part I. LNCS, vol. 9169, pp. 37–48. Springer, Cham (2015). https://doi.org/10.1007/978-3-319-20901-2_4
14. Hutton, L., Henderson, T.: Beyond the EULA: improving consent for data mining. In: Cerquitelli, T., Quercia, D., Pasquale, F. (eds.) Transparent Data Mining for Big and Small Data. SBD, vol. 11, pp. 147–167. Springer, Cham (2017). https://doi.org/10.1007/978-3-319-54024-5_7. http://www.arxiv.org/abs/1701.07999
15. Knight, S., Anderson, T.D.: Action-oriented, accountable, and inter(active) learning analytics for learners. CEUR Work. Proc. 1596, 47–51 (2016)
16. Kuhn, S., Muller, M.: Participatory design. Commun. ACM 36(4), 25–28 (1993). https://doi.org/10.1145/153571.255960
17. Leman, S.C., House, L., Maiti, D., Endert, A., North, C.: Visual to Parametric Interaction (V2PI). PLoS ONE 8(3), 1–12 (2013). https://doi.org/10.1371/journal.pone.0050474
18. Lewis, C.: Using the 'thinking-aloud' method in cognitive interface design. Research Report RC9265, IBM TJ Watson Research Center (1982)
19. Liu, K.: Semiotics in Information Systems Engineering. Cambridge University Press, Cambridge (2008). http://medcontent.metapress.com/index/A65RM03P4874243N.pdf

20. Locoro, A., Cabitza, F., Actis-Grosso, R., Batini, C.: Static and interactive infographics in daily tasks: a value-in-use and quality of interaction userstudy. Comput. Hum. Behav. **71**, 240–257 (2017). https://doi.org/10.1016/j.chb.2017.01.032

21. Muller, M.J., Haslwanter, J.H., Dayton, T.: Participatory practices in the software lifecycle. In: Handbook of Human-Computer Interaction, 2nd edn., vol. 11, pp. 256–296. Elsevier Science B.V. (1997). https://doi.org/10.1016/0141-9382(90)90110-f

22. Muller, M.J., Matheson, L., Page, C., Gallup, R.: Participatory heuristic evaluation. Interactions **5**(5), 13–18 (1998). https://doi.org/10.1145/285213.285219

23. Nielsen, J.: Usability inspection methods. In: Conference Companion on Human Factors in Computing Systems, pp. 413–414. ACM (1994)

24. North, C., Shneiderman, B.: A Taxonomy of Multiple Window Coordination. Technical report, National Science Foundation Engineering Research Center Program, University of Maryland, Harvard University and Industry (1997)

25. North, C., Shneiderman, B.: Snap-together visualization: a user interface for coordinating visualizations via relational schemata. In: The Craft of Information Visualization, pp. 341–348 (2007). https://doi.org/10.1016/b978-155860915-0/50043-3

26. de Oliveira, M.R.: Adaptção da Avaliação Heurística para Uso em Visualização de Informação. Master thesis, Universidade Estadual de Campinas (2017). https://www.repositorio.unicamp.br/jspui/handle/REPOSIP/322040%0A

27. Preece, J., Abras, C., Krichmar, D.M.: Designing and evaluating online communities: research speaks to emerging practice. Int. J. Web Communities **1**(1), 2 (2004). https://doi.org/10.1504/IJWBC.2004.004795. http://www.inderscience.com/link.php?id=4795

28. Roberts, J., Lyons, L., Cafaro, F., Eydt, R.: Interpreting data from within: supporting human data interaction in museum exhibits through perspective taking. In: Proceedings of the 2014 Conference on Interaction Design and Children (IDC 2014), pp. 7–16 (2014). https://doi.org/10.1145/2593968.2593974. http://dl.acm.org/citation.cfm?id=2593974

29. Scapin, D.L., Bastien, J.M.: Ergonomic criteria for evaluating the ergonomic quality of interactive systems. Behav. Inf. Technol. **16**(4–5), 220–231 (1997). https://doi.org/10.1080/014492997119806

30. Schiozer, D.J., Santos, A.A.S., Santos, S., von Hohendorff Filho, F.: Model-based decision analysis applied to petroleum field development and management. Oil Gas Sci. Technol. Rev. IFP (2019). https://doi.org/10.2516/ogst/2019019

31. Thomas, J., Cook, K.: Illuminating the path: the research and development agenda for visual analytics. IEEE Computer Society (2005). https://doi.org/10.3389/fmicb.2011.00006, http://vis.pnnl.gov/pdf/RD_Agenda_VisualAnalytics.pdf

32. Victorelli, E., dos Reis, J.C., Santos, A.A.S., Schiozer, D.J.: Design process for human-data interaction: combining guidelines with semio-participatory techniques. In: Proceedings of the 21st International Conference on Enterprise Information Systems, ICEIS, vol. 2, pp. 410–421. INSTICC, SciTePress (2019). https://doi.org/10.5220/0007744504100421

Cyber Security and E-voting Systems

Comparative Evaluation of Node-Link and Sankey Diagrams for the Cyber Security Domain

Rotem Blinder[1], Ofer Biller[2], Adir Even[1], Oded Sofer[2], Noam Tractinsky[1], Joel Lanir[3(✉)], and Peter Bak[4]

[1] Ben-Gurion University of the Negev, Beer Sheva, Israel
[2] IBM Security, Beer Sheva, Israel
[3] University of Haifa, Haifa, Israel
ylanir@is.haifa.ac.il
[4] IBM Research Haifa Lab, Haifa, Israel

Abstract. Visualization tools are critical components of cyber security systems allowing analyzers to better understand, detect and prevent security breaches. Security administrators need to understand which users accessed the database and what operations were performed in order to detect irregularities. The current work compares the Sankey diagram with the more commonly used node-link diagram as an alternative visualization technique for cyber security tasks in a controlled experiment. The results indicate, that the Sankey tool showed a consistent advantage in task completion time and was more effective (measured by the percent of correct answers) in synoptic tasks, while the Node-link diagram was more effective in basic, elementary tasks. Further results revealed that performance had only a small effect on user satisfaction and preferences. Our results suggest that the Sankey tool may be a viable option for cyber security visualization tools and strengthens the need to provide personalized visualization tools based on user preferences.

Keywords: Cyber security · Visualization · Sankey diagram

1 Introduction

The growing threats to cyber security have motivated the search for solutions that detect, prevent, and minimize the damage associated with security breaches and cyber-attacks on data resources and information systems. Visualizing cyber security-related data suggest using the perceptual capabilities of humans in order to complement machine analysis and enable better analytical support in understanding this complex data. Studies show that effective visualization tools can help security analysts identify hostile activity and analyze its characteristics, thereby significantly increasing the safety level of data [5, 26, 31].

The design of effective cyber security visualization tools depends on the type of data collected, the tasks users need to perform using the visualization, and

© IFIP International Federation for Information Processing 2019
Published by Springer Nature Switzerland AG 2019
D. Lamas et al. (Eds.): INTERACT 2019, LNCS 11746, pp. 497–518, 2019.
https://doi.org/10.1007/978-3-030-29381-9_31

the design decisions of the visualization solutions that aim to meet these requirements. One of the most common tasks in cyber security is trying to understand database access [16,23]. Modern database servers log users' activity to allow automatic or manual detection of violations either in real-time or on log history. Administrators need to understand which users accessed what table, and what type of operations were performed. However, this may not be a simple task as users are usually described by their IP-address, user name, operation system and other attributes, and database access is described by different database systems and views that reference multiple tables. System administrators are left with the difficult task of looking for irregularities and possible security violations within this data.

One of the most common visualizations used in cyber security, and especially when analyzing database access, is the node-link diagram [30]. Node-link diagrams, usually layed out using a force-directed algorithm (as was done in our study), enable the projection of the complex interlinking structure of the users and databases access graph onto a two-dimensional screen by applying the right layout algorithms [15]. While the node-link diagram is widely used in cyber security it does have some disadvantages. The readability of node-link diagrams has been investigated and found to be often limited and too complex, especially when the number of nodes and links increase [15].

The Sankey diagram is a type of flow chart in which the width of the stream reflects the quantity of the flow [28]. Similar to a node-link diagram, Sankey diagrams show a directional relationship between different entities. However, the largest difference is that Sankey diagrams are constrained in their layout, grouping the nodes into layers displayed from left to right. In some versions of Sankey diagrams, the nodes can be grouped into semantic groups that depict the layers of the chart. The layout constraints, in form of clustering, has been proven to provide an advantage to graph readability for a number of tasks [18].

We posit that for database access analysis, Sankey diagrams can be a better choice than node-link diagrams. In order to assess the possible use of the Sankey diagram for cyber security visualizations, we compared its use with the more traditional node-link diagram by conducting an empirical quantitative user study on a large number of participants. We used real-world security data, asking participants to complete a set of tasks following a formal task taxonomy. We complemented the quantitative analysis with interviews with domain experts. Results indicate that the Sankey diagram was more effective (measured in completion accuracy) in general, synoptic tasks, while the node-link diagram was more effective in more basic, elementary tasks. In terms of user efficiency (measured by task completion time) results show that the Sankey diagram was overall more efficient than the node-link diagram. Finally, results suggest that performance had only a small effect on user preferences. We discuss the implications of these results and provide guidelines for the design of cyber security visualization tools.

2   Related Work

Cyber security visualization is a well-established research field. Previous efforts created many tools and techniques to support and improve cyber security tasks. Moreover, multiple surveys provide comprehensive reviews and more details on existing visualization techniques and systems for the cyber security domain [13, 14, 30, 34]. However, while many tools and techniques exist, very few works have performed usability studies with users, and evaluations if they exist, are usually done per system in an ad-hoc and unsystematic way [30, 31]. There is a clear lack of empirical evaluations that aim to add theoretical knowledge to the field [30].

The node-link diagram is often used in the cyber security domain for the visualization of packet traces, intrusion alerts and database access [30]. The visual language of node-link diagrams can help to observe global patterns of connectivity [36], spot the presence of unexpected connections, and study trivial correlations between topology and the properties of nodes and edges through visual features. The topic of network and graph visualization is well-studied and has become a commodity in cyber security applications [4, 14]. A general overview of node-link diagrams is beyond the scope of this paper. We refer readers to some of the available surveys in this field for in-depth information [15, 20, 25].

The Sankey diagram is a counterpart to this visualization. It depicts a flow from one set of values to another. The elements being connected are called nodes and the connections are called links. Node height and link width usually denote the volume of the flow. Sankeys are best used to show a many-to-many mapping between two domains or multiple paths through a set of stages. The interactive Sankey diagram allows selection, rearrangement, and filtering to select a specific category, and to see the associated inflows and outflows [27, 28]. The Sankey technique is widely used in other domains, such as energy or water management, health-related applications and event sequence data analysis [29, 35, 37]. Although it is rarely used in the cyber security domain, some commercial systems, such as the IBM Security Guardium system, have started using it for various tasks. We propose that Sankey diagrams can be useful in depicting the *flow of information* from users to database tables and vice versa when monitoring and detecting anomalies in database access.

Evaluating visualization techniques for applicability is a major challenge and an important research direction in general [6, 8]. Practices and guidelines for conducting valid and repeatable empirical evaluation have been proposed in [7, 9, 24]. Specifically, for graphs and networks, Huang [22] provides a comprehensive overview of measuring the effectiveness of graphs under different conditions of cognitive load. Usability studies involving Sankey and Node-link diagrams were performed in [19]. Their work focused on users' ability to create such diagrams programmatically using the *Prefuse* framework in an efficient way. Specifically, the Sankey diagram has been proved efficient in contrast to other visualization frameworks in [21]. In addition, the Sankey diagram was used as the main tool in the *Outflow* system for investigating event sequence data [35]. A user evaluation showed that users were able to learn how to use the diagram easily with little training and perform a range of tasks both accurately and rapidly.

Despite efforts to evaluate and compare many information visualization techniques, we did not find a systematic evaluation of performance between node-link and Sankey diagrams. The current study focuses on this issue, given the practical importance of such a comparison for the development of visualizations for cyber security systems.

3   Method

We postulate that performance and subjective evaluations depend on the type of visualization tool used and that these effects could be mitigated by the type of tasks in which the users engage. We thus conducted a controlled laboratory experiment to test the effects of the two visualizations (Sankey and node-link) on user effectiveness, efficiency, satisfaction, and preference. To complement the controlled experiment, we also conducted interviews with security analysts, asking their opinion on the two visualization methods in relation to the task of understanding user access to a database.

3.1   Data Preparation

We extracted real log files from a large data security platform of database access information in a large organization containing user information, details of the database accessed, and a timestamp. To create the visualizations, we processed, cleaned, and summarized these information sources in the following form:

Who performed the activity? This includes the database *user*, and the *IP address* of the source, among many other related attributes (which were not included in this research).

What activity was performed? This indicates the type of activity; (*verb*) such as selection, modification, or others. There was a very limited variance in the data on activity types, the most frequent activity being "selection" and then "execution" for the period in which we investigated the data.

On what was this activity performed? Contains the database system, the *database* and the table or view that was accessed.

When was it performed? This shows the time of the activity, which was only used for filtering purposes. We filtered the data, limiting the time span to one specific hour of database access information.

How many of these activities were performed by the user? This was computed by counting the access requests within the selected timeframe. This was aggregated over the time span.

These numbers and settings reflect a real-world scenario, and were used in the empirical evaluation.

3.2   Visual Design

We encoded the above information using two different techniques: node-link diagrams and Sankey diagrams. Care was taken to ensure that the same information is represented using only different channels and marks.

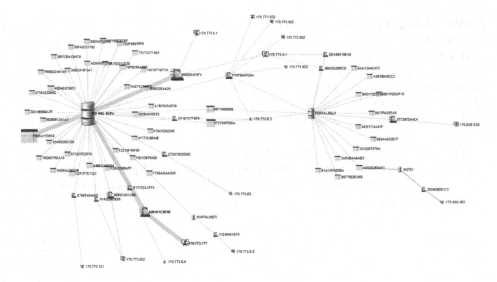

Fig. 1. Node-link diagram shows four selected layers of information: IP address, user, database, and database-table

Node-Link Diagram. Figure 1 represents a one hour time span for activity overview using the node-link diagram. To construct the node-link diagram, objects of the information layers are encoded as symbols (IP as a computer with "IP" on its screen, database as a disk-symbol, user as a person with a database symbol, and tables as grid-icons). Lines show the connection between the objects. Line thickness and symbol size encode the number of database transactions conducted. The type of activity, which we refer to as "verb", is depicted as a separate node type with its own icon. For interaction, we supported selection and tooltips. When an object was selected, all corresponding connections are highlighted, and unselected objects fade out. When an object is hovered over, a tooltip including the name and number of transactions is presented.

The resulting visual encoding reflect the data and lead to a comprehensive network of activities in the system. The view simultaneously shows the topology of activities (who accesses what database), and specific details of each user's access patterns. As there are alternative encodings possible, we verified these with security domain experts, who confirmed that this reflects the common state of node-link diagrams in security systems. Study participants were able to investigate the activities of database users by selecting an icon and consecutively highlighting all corresponding connections. For demonstration purposes, Fig. 1 shows activities on an MS SQL server with two major users (connected with thick lines to the server) and one high frequency table access (also connected to the server).

Sankey Diagram. Figure 2 shows the Sankey diagram created on the database access information. The Sankey diagram uses a horizontal positioning for the four information layers; IP, users, database, and tables in a left-to-right order (the same layers as in the node-link diagram). Objects corresponding to one of these information layers are placed in a vertical position. Information layers are given a label on the horizontal position. Objects are represented as rectangular nodes, and connections between nodes as splines. The height of the node and the width of the lines encode the number of transactions. Color distinguishes nodes from each other within a layer. The activity type (verb), was added as one of the information layers, connecting the database objects with the users. For interaction, selection and tooltips were used exactly the same way as in the node-link diagram.

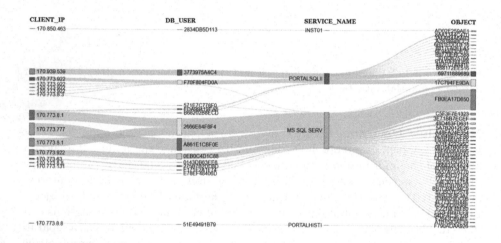

Fig. 2. Sankey diagram shows four selected layers of information: IP address, user, database, and database-table

The resulting image in Fig. 2 shows the *flows* of data from the IP addresses and the users to the databases and tables. Study participants could point out databases or tables that are used more frequently than others, and select corresponding users with either high or low transaction counts.

Compared to the node-link diagram, the Sankey diagram has a much more constrained layout, due to the horizontal fixed positions of the information layers. As a result, in the Sankey diagram, users have to search horizontally for an information layer, and then vertically for a particular object. In contrast, in the node-link diagram, objects can appear at any position in the display and can only be recognized by the icons.

In node-link diagrams, users of the real-world systems could usually reposition items and select different information layers. For the Sankey diagram, users of real-world systems could usually change the horizontal position of the information layers. However, to avoid confounding, the software in the experiment allowed participants to only select and hover over objects in both chart types.

3.3 Participants

We had 135 third-year undergraduate engineering students participate in the experiment. All participants were enrolled in a database class and received course credit for their participation.

3.4 Procedure and Design

Participants were assigned randomly to one of two groups: treatment and control. In the treatment group, 77 participants used the two visualization tools mentioned above to address 14 tasks. The control group was used to validate the benefits of the two visualization tools compared to the use of a standard spreadsheet. Thus, in the control group, 58 participants used an Excel worksheet with the raw data to perform the same tasks.

At the start of the experiment, the participants were given a written description of the experimental purpose and signed a consent form. The experimenter then introduced and demonstrated the two visualization tools. Next, participants performed the tasks using two sets of structurally equivalent tasks in two consecutive blocks. In each block, the participants interacted with one of the two visualization tools (Sankey diagram or Node-Link diagram). The order in which the visualization tools were used was counterbalanced.

Each block began with four training tasks, to acquaint the participants with the visualization tool and the tasks. Next, they were presented with 14 experimental tasks. Participants were asked to work as quickly and accurately as possible. They answered each task by selecting from a predefined list of alternative answers. After choosing an answer, the participant pressed the "Next" button to move to the next task. Completion time and the selected answer for each task were recorded. At the end of the second session, participants responded to items asking about their satisfaction with each tool (using a 1 to 5 Likert scale) and indicated which of the tools they preferred. Each experimental block (i.e., working with one visualization tool) lasted between 30 and 40 min.

The control group received the same data sets and the same training and experimental tasks as the two visualization groups. The control group performed the tasks using the raw data set in an Excel worksheet, without the aid of a visualization tool.

All sessions were conducted in a quiet lab equipped with an Intel Core i5-4570 3.2 GHz computers and 24" monitors with a resolution of 1920 × 1080 pixels.

3.5 Experimental Tasks

We classified the experimental tasks according to the model proposed by
Andrienko et al. [3], distinguishing between *elementary* and *synoptic* tasks. Elementary tasks are defined as simple, basic tasks that usually require a single
or only few basic operations (such as identify, locate or compare) to complete.

Table 1. List of experimental tasks. The same tasks were used for both visualization
tools, with different attribute values for each tool.

	Task	Task type	Other attributes
1	What was the number of transactions of database "Grades" at 15:00?	Elementary	Ov, L
2	Which ClientIPs did the User "Yotam" use at 15:00?	Elementary	Ov, L
3	Which User had the highest number of transactions at 15:00?	Elementary	Ov, IL
4	When was the lowest number of transactions of database "Students"?	Elementary	Ov, IL
5	Did ClientIP "773.922.841" use more Verbs than ClientIP "773.922.858" at 15:00? How many more?	Elementary	Ov, C
6	For DB "Grades" and "Students", which performed more diverse activities of different Users at 15:00?	Elementary	Ou, C
7	Mark 2 Verbs on which number of transactions of DBUser "Aviv" was higher than DBUser "Nimrod" at 15:00	Elementary	Ov, RS
8	Find the time (hour) which DBUser "Nimrod" used less than 3 Client IPs	Elementary	Ou, RS
9	What was Database "Lecturers" trend between 15:00–16:00?	Synoptic	Ou, PI
10	For 16:00. Which user used the database (DB Name), Verb, and Client IP that no other User used?	Synoptic	OU, PI
11	What is the most common Verb on database "Grades" at 15:00?	Synoptic	Ov, BC
12	Which User used the most diverse DBNames at 15:00?	Synoptic	Ou, BC
13	For Users "Shlomi" and "Yotam", which one has the largest growth rate of transactions between 13:00 and 14:00?	Synoptic	Ou, RS
14	Which Verb increased the most from 16:00–17:00?	Synoptic	Ou, RS

Synoptic tasks are more general, more complex and usually require multiple operations. Each task question had a different number of response options varying from 3 to 10 options. We created two structurally equivalent task sets, each for use with a different visualization tool. The 14 tasks included 8 elementary tasks and 6 synoptic tasks. Our data analysis concentrated on this low level classification. Table 1 presents the tasks and provides additional information about other task attributes according the classification of Andrienko et al. [3].

3.6   Datasets

The source of data for the experiments was a cyber security system installed at a large company, with data gathered during a working day in 2016. The description given to participants in the experiment was that the data belonged to students in a "Databases" course, who check their personal data in the university information system. The students access the system's databases and carry out various activities. Each access includes the student's username ('User') and receives a 'ClientIP'. Other data included the name of the action performed by the user ('Verb'), for example- Select, Execute, Update, Truncate, Create, If, and Delete. The data also showed the database 'DBName' used by the students, for example- Grades, Students, Lecturers, Courses, Faculties, and Departments. The attribute values were replaced to match the cover story. For example, the 'ServiceName' "MS SQL SERVER" was changed to "Grades", the 'DBUser' "F70F804FD0A" was replaced by "John". To reduce carry over due to task familiarity between the two experimental blocks, we used different values for the attributes in each block. For example, the 'User' named "John" in the first block was presented with another name in the second block.

3.7   Expert Interviews

To complement the results of the controlled experiment, we conducted semi-structured interviews with seven database administrators working in a big software company. We used a list of set questions that were elaborated on according to each interview. We asked their opinion on the suitability of the two visualization methods in relation to database access security tasks. Each expert was asked to work with both the Sankey and the node-link diagram on several tasks using a real-world dataset. The dataset shown to the experts was not the same as used in the quantitative experiment, but rather was one that was not constrained by the needs of a formal user study (e.g. larger, and more representative of a real system). Tasks included identification and pattern definition for Users, Databases and Verbs separately, and in a pair-wise combination. Experts were asked to verbalize their thoughts (Thinkaloud) when completing the tasks, and were interviewed at the end of the session regarding their opinions.

4   Results

All participants completed the assignments successfully. The distribution of correct answers ranged from 17 to 28 (best possible result) with an average of 24.8 and a median of 25. The minimal completion time of all tasks combined was 794 s and the maximal time was 2,332 s, with a mean of 1,383 s and a median of 1,353 s.

4.1   Data Cleaning

The criterion for discarding outlier data was set in terms of task completion times. Outliers were defined as answers whose task completion times were 10 times smaller or greater than the sample's median completion time on that specific task. We found 7 such cases, distributed over 4 individuals. We set those times to missing values. In addition, examination of individual tasks identified 1 specific task in which performance measures differed greatly between the 2 visualization tools. The task (Task 12, see Table 1), was the only task in our battery that was classified as a combination of behavior comparison and outlier detection according to the low-level task taxonomy of [3]. It took much longer to complete using the Sankey tool (mean = 108.9, median = 103.8, SD = 55. vs. mean = 59.4, median = 50.3, SD = 28.8 in node-link) and answers were considerably less accurate (M = .57, SD = .50 in Sankey vs. M = .88, SD = 32, in node-link). Both differences were highly significant (paired-sample $t(75)$ = 6.88, $p < .001$ for completion time and $t(76) = 5.03$, $p < .001$ for correctness). Due to the clear advantage of node-link in performing this task, we considered it separately from the other 13 tasks.

4.2   Main Analysis

Table 2 summarizes the experimental groups and the associated demographics. We analyzed the data using R Studio 1.1.383.

We first examined the potential effects of the demographic variables. Age was very weakly correlated with the three dependent variables ($r < .1$ for all variables). Separate t-tests for differences between males and females on all three dependent variables were insignificant ($p > .47$ in all tests). Therefore, we did not consider those control variables in further analyses.

Table 2. Experimental groups and demographic data

Group	Sample size (M/F)	Age Mean/SD
Sankey first	38 (11/27)	24.7/1.2
Node Link first	39 (11/28)	24.9/1.2
Control (Excel)	58 (33/25)	25.8/1.1
Overall	135 (55/80)	24.8/1.7

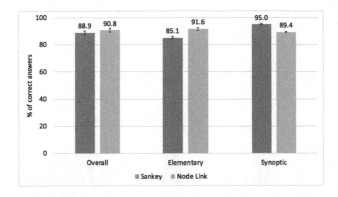

Fig. 3. Average effectiveness scores (percent correct answers with standard-error) of all tasks, elementary tasks only (8 tasks) and synoptic tasks only (5 tasks).

Effectiveness and Efficiency Compared to the Excel Baseline. We performed a one-way ANOVA with three levels (Sankey, Node-Link, Excel) for effectiveness and efficiency results. Both analyses were significant (F(2,209) = 15.31, $p < .001$ for effectiveness, F(2,209) = 296, $p < .001$ for efficiency). Post-hoc analyses (Tukey HSD) revealed that, on average and over all tasks, the Excel group performed substantially lower on both measures. This finding established the superiority of the visualization tools over the default format. Therefore, in the subsequent analyses we focused on comparing the two visualization tools.

Effectiveness and Efficiency Without Task 12. Figures 3 and 4 present the overall effectiveness and efficiency results, as well as results broken down by task type (elementary vs. synoptic) in each visualization tool. We analyzed the data using separate two-way (visualization tool and task type) within-subjects analyses of variance with effectiveness and efficiency as dependent variables. The analysis of the overall effectiveness score (percent of correct answers) found no difference between the groups (F(1,76) = .115, p = .12). There was a main effect for Task Type. Synoptic tasks had more correct answers than elementary tasks (F(1,76) = 8.53, p = .005). However, this result was qualified by a significant Tool x Task Type interaction (F(1,76) = 28.10, $p < .001$). The interaction stemmed from a higher percentage of correct answers to the elementary tasks in node-link (paired-sample t(76) = 4.27, $p < .001$) and a higher percentage of correct answers to the synoptic tasks in Sankey (t(76) = 3.31, p = .001).

A two-way within-subjects analyses of variance with efficiency (task completion time) as the dependent variable found the main effects to be visualization tool and task type (F(1,76) = .12.82, p = .001 and F(1,76) = 15.43, $p < .001$, respectively). There was no interaction effect (F(1,76) = 1.92, p = .17). Participants answered more quickly with Sankey than in node-link on both task types. In addition, synoptic tasks were answered more quickly than elementary tasks.

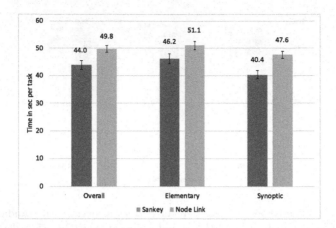

Fig. 4. Average efficiency (time in seconds with standard-error) of all tasks, elementary tasks only (8 tasks) and synoptic tasks only (5 tasks).

Subjective Evaluation and Preference. There was no difference in participant satisfaction from each tool (M = 3.73, SD = .91 for Sankey, M = 3.90, SD = .95 for node-link; paired sample t(76) = .94, p = .35). However, when asked which of the two tools they preferred, 50 participants (65%) preferred the node-link tool compared to 27 who preferred the Sankey tool. Regardless, there were only low correlations between the participants' achievements in the experiment and their tool of choice.

Figure 5 describes the relationships between performance measures, user satisfaction, and user preference. The data plotted are from the 77 individuals who participated in the experiment. Circles filled with orange denote participants who preferred the node-link tool; circles filled with blue denote those who preferred the Sankey tool. The circles' outline (stroke) denote differences in satisfaction, whereas the size of the circles represents the magnitude of the difference. Larger circles represent larger differences in satisfaction score. For example, Participant #5, just to the right and above the center, preferred the node-link tool, despite reporting considerably more satisfaction with the Sankey tool. Participant #16, just to the left and below the center, showed the same preference and satisfaction pattern.

The x-axis in Fig. 5 presents effectiveness differences between the two visualization tools (Sankey correct − Node-Link correct). Positive values (right half) denote participants whose effectiveness using Sankey was better than their effectiveness using Node-link. The y-axis denotes differences in efficiency, expressed as Node-Link completion time − Sankey completion times. Positive numbers (upper half) denote that using Sankey was more efficient (took less time). The values on this axis are the differences in seconds divided by 100, for simplicity of presentation. The two participants (#5 and #16) discussed earlier (with more satisfaction for the Sankey, but preference for the node-link diagram) show very different performance patterns: #5 is more effective and more efficient with the Sankey, the other #16 with the node-link diagram.

The resulting matrix can be interpreted as follows. Quadrant II denotes participants who performed better on both aspects (effectiveness and efficiency) using *Sankey*. Quadrant IV denotes participants who performed better on both aspects using *node-link*. Quadrants I and III include users with performance trade-offs. In Quadrant I participants were more effective using node-link but more efficient using Sankey, whereas Quadrant III includes participants with the opposite type of tradeoff. For example, Participant #31 at the top of Quadrant I performed more effectively using node-link but was faster using Sankey. Participant #53 on the right-hand side of Quadrant III was more effective using Sankey but faster using node-link.

To test which factors affected the participants' evaluations, we conducted separate regression analyses for the two satisfaction items. In each model, the predictors were effectiveness (number of correct answers) and efficiency (average task completion time) of the two visualization tools. The results (Table 3) were very similar in terms of the explained variance (about 10% for each tool) and the fact that the only significant predictor was the effectiveness score of that tool.

Table 3. A regression model to predict user satisfaction with the visualization tool

Predictors	DV = Node-Link Satisfaction			DV = Sankey Satisfaction		
	Beta	t	sig	Beta	T	sig
Sankey correct answers	−.204	−1.723	.089	.323	2.772	.007
Sankey time per task	−.042	−.353	.725	.049	.421	.675
Node Link correct answers	.300	2.550	.013	−.184	−1.588	.117
Node Link time per task	.086	.731	.467	.120	1.042	.301

A logistic regression with effectiveness, efficiency, and satisfaction scores on both tools as predictors correctly classified 83% of the participants' preferences (Table 4). The model's Cox & Snell's R2 was .384. The only significant predictors in the model were the two satisfaction items (Table 5).

4.3   Expert Interviews

The expert opinions elicited through the interviews showed a slight overall preference for the Sankey diagram. However, preference of tool was mostly dependent on the user task. When entities (Users, Databases and Verbs) had to be

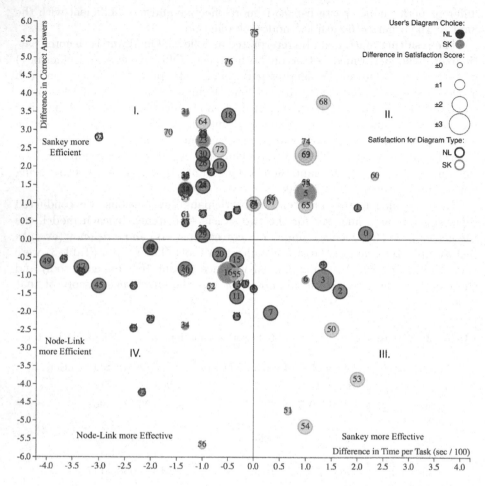

Fig. 5. Participant preference of a diagram (node-link or Sankey) is indicated by the colored circles on the scatter-plot. Differences in effectiveness (number of correct answers) are mapped to the x-axis, efficiency (average completion time in seconds/100) is mapped on the y-axis, and differences in satisfaction scores are plotted for each participant (labeled by the numbers) as the size of the circles.

Table 4. Classification table for the logistic regression analysis

		Predicted choice %		
		NL	SK	Correct
Observed Choice	NL	44	6	88.0
	SK	7	20	74.1
Overall				83.1

Table 5. Logistic regression model of predictors of preferred visualization

	B	S.E	Wald	df	Sig	Exp(B)
Sankey correct	.311	.349	.794	1	.373	1.365
Node-Link correct	−.278	.291	.913	1	.339	.757
Sankey time per task	.023	.024	.898	1	.343	1.023
Node-Link time per task	−.031	.032	.923	1	.337	.970
Sankey satisfaction	1.135	.473	5.757	1	.016	3.110
Node-Link satisfaction	−.996	.387	6.615	1	.010	.369
Constant	−1.079	4.480	.058	1	.810	.340

investigated on their own, experts stated that this was harder to perform with the Node-Link diagram, mostly due to the spread-out layout which sometimes caused entities "to be all over the place". As one expert said: "It is hard finding the users, they are all placed in different positions". For these type of tasks, the constrained layout of the Sankey diagram seemed to be an advantage. However, For finding groups of Users connected to Databases, experts thought that the node-link diagram has a clear advantage since they were grouped in the layout closer together. Experts found it very intuitive that "close proximity indicates stronger connections". In the Sankey diagram this is more difficult as connecting lines need to be visually highlighted one user at the time. For comparison tasks between entities of the same type, both visualizations "require additional manual work" and there was no clear preference for either of the techniques. Finally, for tasks involving Databases and Verbs only, some of the experts expressed preference for the node-link diagram, where color coding helped the association between the entities, even though they stated that much effort needs to be put into this task using both types of visualizations.

5   Discussion

We conducted a systematic experimental comparison of two visualization solutions for the cyber security domain, specifically, for the analysis of database-related activities. The visualizations represent various design trade-offs that facilitate or hamper users' decision making in different types of tasks. Consequently, our research model postulated that the type of tasks in which the users engage could moderate the effects of the visualization tools on user performance. Thus, the participants in the main part of the experiment completed 14 well-defined tasks that were classified into 2 main types, based on [3] high-level classification of tasks to elementary and synoptic. In the first analysis, we compared the performance of participants who were aided by the visualization tools to the performance of participants who viewed the data using a spreadsheet. Finally, we complemented the controlled experiment with interviews with seven domain experts.

Using the data from 135 participants in a between-groups design, the results first demonstrate that visualization tools are superior to the spreadsheet presentation of the database access data, in terms of both effectiveness and efficiency, confirming the benefit of visualizations as an analysis tool over the use of a spreadsheet. Subsequent analyses concentrated on the results of the within-subjects part of the experiment, in which 77 of the participants used 2 visualization tools. We compared the tools in terms of their effectiveness, efficiency, and user satisfaction and preference. During the analyses we found exceptional user performance data on a task that combined synoptic behavior comparison and outlier detection. We will discuss this task separately following a discussion of the results of the other 13 tasks and the implications of those results.

5.1   Effectiveness of the Visualization Tools Is Contingent on Task

The analyses of the effectiveness data demonstrate the importance of considering the moderating effect of task type when evaluating the performance of visualization tools. This was also emphasized by the experts in their interviews. Without considering task type, the study's results would suggest that the two visualization tools provide the same degree of support for the cyber security context studied in this project. However, our analysis indicates that the node-link diagram helped users complete the elementary tasks more correctly relative to the Sankey diagram. At the same time, synoptic tasks were answered more correctly using the Sankey diagram.

A possible explanation for the moderating effect of task type is that the node-link diagram provides a semantic organization of the layout, bringing related objects closer together and pushing unrelated objects farther away. As a result, finding related objects, as required in elementary tasks, may benefit from this type of layout. In addition, the line-widths in the Sankey correspond to node sizes in a more explicit manner, thus it supports tasks requiring comparison better than node-link diagrams, where nodes and lines have different scales, and thus may be more suitable for synoptic tasks.

5.2   Efficiency of Visualization Tools

The results analysis revealed that, on average, using the Sankey diagram resulted in shorter task completion times. This was the case for both the elementary and the synoptic tasks, and thus suggests an inherent advantage to the Sankey diagram in terms of speed. On the one hand, this advantage represents speed-accuracy tradeoff for elementary tasks. Users performed faster with Sankey but more accurately with node-link. On the other hand, it represents a clear advantage for using Sankey when users engage in synoptic tasks; performance is both more accurate and faster.

From a practical perspective, these findings call for the incorporation of Sankey diagrams in support of database administrators who are interested in understanding database-access activities. Our conjecture about the reasons behind these findings is that the Sankey diagram provides constraints and super-imposes a kind of organization to the layout by the horizontal positioning of the information layers. In contrast, location and orientation of nodes and links may change substantially in the node-link diagram. Thus, the greater structure of the Sankey diagram improves familiarity and consistency, which can lead to faster performance when conducting any of the task types.

These findings are especially important given the ubiquity of node-link dia-grams in cyber security systems. Our research suggests the possibility that at least certain types of cyber security tasks can be better handled by other types of visualizations. In our study, the Sankey visualization provided more effective support for users engaged in synoptic tasks and a higher overall efficiency. Con-sidering different user goals (e.g., exploration rather than detection) or different task classifications (e.g., [2]) suggests that additional visualization tools could also be beneficial for cyber security experts.

5.3   Subjective Evaluation of the Visualization Tools

User evaluation of the visualization tools revealed several interesting findings. First, although users expressed their satisfaction only after using both tools, their satisfaction was only correlated with the effectiveness of the tool for which a satisfaction score was given. In other words, performance on the other tool did not play a role in the satisfaction score, nor did the completion times of the evaluated tool. Second, the predictors used in our regression model explained only a small portion of the variance of the satisfaction score (about 10%). This finding may point to the existence of other factors affecting satisfaction, e.g., learnability and ease of use [1] or aesthetics [33]. Third, although the majority of users (about two-thirds) preferred the node-link tool, there was no differ-ence in user satisfaction between the two tools. The logistic regression findings suggest that the only predictors for preference were user satisfaction with both tools. Performance measures had no effect on preference. Thus, user preference may result from a complex combination of factors, of which performance may not be the most important. Figure 5 provides a detailed view of user prefer-ences, given satisfaction scores and performance measures in both systems. It can be argued that this figure portrays a story of diversity. Diversity in terms of effectiveness and efficiency, in terms of whether these performance aspects are traded-off against each other, and in terms of user satisfaction and preferences. The observed diversity in this study provides support for recent calls for the personalization of visualization tools [10].

In more general terms, the idea that performance depends on how support tools are commensurate with task demands is not new. Early research on decision support systems identified the importance of such a contingency view [11]. Later research provided evidence for the need to match the support tools to the task at hand [12,17]. As [17] suggests, "task-technology fit, when decomposed into its more detailed components, could be the basis for a strong diagnostic tool to evaluate whether information systems and services in a given organization are meeting their needs".

In this context, it is worth mentioning that user performance with the node-link diagram dominated their performance using the Sankey diagram for one specific task, Task 12. The task, "Which User used the most diverse DBNames at 15:00?" is classified as a synoptic task that involves behavior comparison and outlier detection. Our retrospective analysis of this task suggests that while using Sankey, users had a hard time completing this task because they needed to consult two diagram axes that were on the opposite sides of the screen. The axis representing the user was on the left of the screen, whereas the axis representing the database was on the right of the screen. Using node-link, on the other hand, highlighting of a specific node causes unrelated values to fade out, leaving a relatively clear view of the relevant values of the associated entities. The immediate implication of this finding is that tasks of this type are better performed using node-link. However, it is also possible to conceive an adaptation of the Sankey diagram to the context of the task, such that remote axes can be brought closer by the user. While such a solution is more complex and requires greater expertise by the users, it is nonetheless feasible. In fact, it is likely desirable in a personalized system or if the Sankey diagram is chosen as the only visualization tool for the cyber security system.

6 Limitations

Experimental work usually requires the researchers to consider multiple design tradeoffs. In the following, we list the limitations of our study in light of the design decisions we made and their potential threats to the validity of the findings.

Our study used students as participants, which may reduce the external validity of the findings. The reason for using students was mainly due to the difficulty of arranging a large sample of professionals for the controlled user study. To mitigate this effect, we framed the experimental scenario as one that the participants were familiar with (i.e., the university environment). They were also familiar with database essentials and aware of data security issues given the university scenario. We note that the tasks themselves were not trivial and the participants treated them seriously, taking on average close to 50 s to complete a task. Finally, from the perspective of isolating the net effects of the visualization tools and the experimental tasks on user performance and preferences, using participants who are not already involved in data security operations alleviates the confounding effects of previous experience (e.g., in using the familiar node-link diagram in cyber security systems or being previously engaged in similar or identical tasks).

Another limitation is the fact that tasks were classified and analyzed in our research only according to the highest level of classification in [3]. Tasks were also identified in terms of lower-level classifications; however, due to limitations on sample size and length of experimental session, we decided not to expand the number of tasks and thus did not include lower-level classifications as independent factors in the experimental designs. Moreover, other task classifications exist, which can also be used in the domain of this research. As an initial investigation, we used relatively short tasks based on a formal task taxonomy, rather than open-ended domain-based tasks. However, the tasks that we used in the study are sub-tasks that are used when investigating security breaches. Future studies will investigate domain-based tasks as well as examine these issues in the field, in real-world settings. Finally, the questions were multiple choice type questions with varied amount of answers. This may give rise to chance findings (on average, slightly below 0.25 chance to get the answer by guessing). However, we note that this is common in such experiments and the chance is divided equally between conditions.

It is possible that giving the participants feedback on their tasks would have made their subjective assessments of the visualization tools more reflective of their performance. However, such explicit feedback is rarely available in the real world, and thus we opted not to include it. Given the discrepancy between performance and subjective measures, it would be useful to study how much of this discrepancy can be attributed to lack of feedback on performance and how much is due to other aspects influencing users' subjective evaluations.

We have used a force-directed layout for our node-link representation. However, there are other possible layout options to represent node-link diagrams. Using the force-directed layout was motivated by the popularity of this technique by the literature and commonly available tools. Unfortunately, the comparison of different layout algorithms is beyond the scope of the current effort, but should be considered in future research. Finally, the question of scalability of visualization techniques would have posed a significant complexity to our empirical setting, and would have prolonged the experiment for the participants. Therefore, we fixed the amount of data to a level typical for small- and medium-size enterprises. The effect of scalability on user performance in the visualization of security systems is a crucial research question, and is left to be investigated in future research.

7   Design Recommendations

The objective of this study was to compare two visualization systems in the cyber security context of database-activity monitoring in terms of their performance and users' subjective evaluations. The experiment's data included some clear and statistically significant results that can be used to devise design guidelines. Although appropriate scientific caution should be applied regarding the generalization of these guidelines beyond the study's cyber security context, we believe these guidelines can apply to other contexts that use tasks with a similar structure to those we used. We recommend the following design guidelines, taking into consideration the limitations described above:

- For elementary tasks, the node-link diagram produces more effective (i.e., correct) responses than the Sankey diagram.
- For synoptic tasks, the Sankey diagram produces more effective and more efficient responses than the node-link diagram. Thus, our results unequivocally support the use of Sankey for synoptic tasks.

– If efficiency (speed of completing tasks) is an important criterion, then the Sankey diagram is preferred over the node-link diagram. This result was statistically significant across both task types. Still, designers should consider the effectiveness-efficiency tradeoff when it comes to elementary tasks.

– For the special case of tasks that require synoptic behavior comparison of outliers, node-link was clearly the superior tool.

– Users preferred the node-link diagram over the Sankey diagram by a ratio of 2:1. However, user preference and satisfaction did not closely match performance, indicating that factors other than preference may be influencing satisfaction.

– Given users' diversity in performance and preference, and given that task type moderates the effects of visualization type on performance, we recommend that designers consider supporting users with more than one visualization method. Furthermore, designers should consider giving users the means to switch between methods as a function of the task and of their preference, either by user control, or by utilizing user-adapted techniques [10,32].

References

1. Albo, Y., Lanir, J., Bak, P., Rafaeli, S.: Off the radar: comparative evaluation of radial visualization solutions for composite indicators. IEEE Trans. Visual Comput. Graphics **22**(1), 569–578 (2016)
2. Amar, R., Eagan, J., Stasko, J.: Low-level components of analytic activity in information visualization. In: IEEE Symposium on Information Visualization, INFOVIS 2005, pp. 111–117. IEEE (2005)
3. Andrienko, N., Andrienko, G., Gatalsky, P.: Exploratory spatio-temporal visualization: an analytical review. J. Vis. Lang. Comput. **14**(6), 503–541 (2003)
4. Ball, R., Fink, G.A., North, C.: Home-centric visualization of network traffic for security administration. In: Proceedings of the 2004 ACM Workshop on Visualization and Data Mining for Computer Security, pp. 55–64. ACM (2004)
5. Best, D.M., Endert, A., Kidwell, D.: 7 key challenges for visualization in cyber network defense. In: Proceedings of the Eleventh Workshop on Visualization for Cyber Security, pp. 33–40. ACM (2014)
6. Best, D.M., Endert, A., Kidwell, D.: 7 key challenges for visualization in cyber network defense. In: Proceedings of the Eleventh Workshop on Visualization for Cyber Security, VizSec 2014, pp. 33–40. ACM, New York (2014). https://doi.org/10.1145/2671491.2671497
7. Boyandin, I., Bertini, E., Lalanne, D.: A qualitative study on the exploration of temporal changes in flow maps with animation and small-multiples. In: Computer Graphics Forum, vol. 31, pp. 1005–1014. Wiley Online Library (2012)
8. Carpendale, S.: Evaluating information visualizations. In: Kerren, A., Stasko, J.T., Fekete, J.-D., North, C. (eds.) Information Visualization. LNCS, vol. 4950, pp. 19–45. Springer, Heidelberg (2008). https://doi.org/10.1007/978-3-540-70956-5_2
9. Chen, C., Yu, Y.: Empirical studies of information visualization: a meta-analysis. Int. J. Hum. Comput. Stud. **53**(5), 851–866 (2000)
10. Conati, C., Carenini, G., Toker, D., Lallé, S.: Towards user-adaptive information visualization. In: AAAI, pp. 4100–4106 (2015)

11. Dickson, G.W., Senn, J.A., Chervany, N.L.: Research in management information systems: the Minnesota experiments. Manage. Sci. **23**(9), 913–934 (1977)
12. Elam, J.J., Mead, M.: Can software influence creativity? Inf. Syst. Res. **1**(1), 1–22 (1990)
13. Ferebee, D., Dasgupta, D.: Security visualization survey. In: Proceedings of the 12th Colloquium for Information Systems Security Education University of Texas, p. 124. Citeseer (2008)
14. Fink, G.A., North, C.L., Endert, A., Rose, S.: Visualizing cyber security: usable workspaces. In: 6th International Workshop on Visualization for Cyber Security, VizSec 2009, pp. 45–56. IEEE (2009)
15. Ghoniem, M., Fekete, J.D., Castagliola, P.: A comparison of the readability of graphs using node-link and matrix-based representations. In: IEEE Symposium on Information Visualization, pp. 17–24 (2004). https://doi.org/10.1109/INFVIS.2004.1
16. Girardin, L., Brodbeck, D.: A visual approach for monitoring logs. LISA **98**, 299–308 (1998)
17. Goodhue, D.L., Thompson, R.L.: Task-technology fit and individual performance. MIS Q. **2**, 213–236 (1995)
18. Hascoët, M., Dragicevic, P.: Interactive graph matching and visual comparison of graphs and clustered graphs. In: Proceedings of the International Working Conference on Advanced Visual Interfaces, pp. 522–529. ACM (2012)
19. Heer, J., Card, S.K., Landay, J.A.: Prefuse: a toolkit for interactive information visualization. In: Proceedings of the SIGCHI Conference on Human Factors in Computing Systems, pp. 421–430. ACM (2005)
20. Herman, I., Melançon, G., Marshall, M.S.: Graph visualization and navigation in information visualization: a survey. IEEE Trans. Visual Comput. Graphics **6**(1), 24–43 (2000)
21. Hoekstra, R., Groth, P.: PROV-O-Viz - understanding the role of activities in provenance. In: Ludäscher, B., Plale, B. (eds.) IPAW 2014. LNCS, vol. 8628, pp. 215–220. Springer, Cham (2015). https://doi.org/10.1007/978-3-319-16462-5_18
22. Huanga, W.: Measuring effectiveness of graph visualizations: a cognitive load perspective. Inf. Vis. **8**, 139–152 (2009)
23. Kamra, A., Terzi, E., Bertino, E.: Detecting anomalous access patterns in relational databases. VLDB J. Int. J. Very Large Data Bases **17**(5), 1063–1077 (2008)
24. Lam, H., Bertini, E., Isenberg, P., Plaisant, C., Carpendale, M.S.T.: Empirical studies in information visualization: seven scenarios. IEEE Trans. Visual Comput. Graphics **18**, 1520–1536 (2012)
25. Liu, S., Cui, W., Wu, Y., Liu, M.: A survey on information visualization: recent advances and challenges. Visual Comput. **30**(12), 1373–1393 (2014)
26. Ma, K.L.: Cyber security through visualization. In: Proceedings of the 2006 Asia-Pacific Symposium on Information Visualisation-Volume 60, pp. 3–7. Australian Computer Society, Inc. (2006)
27. Perer, A., Wang, F.: Frequence: interactive mining and visualization of temporal frequent event sequences. In: Proceedings of the 19th International Conference on Intelligent User Interfaces, pp. 153–162. ACM (2014)
28. Riehmann, P., Hanfler, M., Froehlich, B.: Interactive Sankey diagrams. In: IEEE Symposium on Information Visualization, INFOVIS 2005, pp. 233–240. IEEE (2005)
29. Schmidt, M.: The Sankey diagram in energy and material flow management. J. Ind. Ecol. **12**(1), 82–94 (2008)

30. Shiravi, H., Shiravi, A., Ghorbani, A.A.: A survey of visualization systems for network security. IEEE Trans. Visual Comput. Graphics **18**(8), 1313–1329 (2012)
31. Staheli, D., et al.: Visualization evaluation for cyber security: trends and future directions. In: Proceedings of the Eleventh Workshop on Visualization for Cyber Security, pp. 49–56. ACM (2014)
32. Toker, D., Conati, C., Steichen, B., Carenini, G.: Individual user characteristics and information visualization: connecting the dots through eye tracking. In: Proceedings of the SIGCHI Conference on Human Factors in Computing Systems, pp. 295–304. ACM (2013)
33. Tractinsky, N.: Visual aesthetics. In: The Encyclopedia of Human-Computer Interaction, 2nd edn. (2013)
34. Wagner, M., et al.: A survey of visualization systems for Malware analysis. In: EG Conference on Visualization (EuroVis)-STARs, pp. 105–125 (2015)
35. Wongsuphasawat, K., Gotz, D.: Exploring flow, factors, and outcomes of temporal event sequences with the outflow visualization. IEEE Trans. Visual Comput. Graphics **18**(12), 2659–2668 (2012)
36. Yin, X., Yurcik, W., Treaster, M., Li, Y., Lakkaraju, K.: VisFlowConnect: NetFlow visualizations of link relationships for security situational awareness. In: Proceedings of the 2004 ACM Workshop on Visualization and Data Mining for Computer Security, pp. 26–34. ACM (2004)
37. Zhao, J., Liu, Z., Dontcheva, M., Hertzmann, A., Wilson, A.: MatrixWave: visual comparison of event sequence data. In: Proceedings of the 33rd Annual ACM Conference on Human Factors in Computing Systems, pp. 259–268. ACM (2015)

Comparing "Challenge-Based" and "Code-Based" Internet Voting Verification Implementations

Oksana Kulyk[1,4]($\boxtimes$), Jan Henzel[2], Karen Renaud[3], and Melanie Volkamer[4]

[1] IT University of Copenhagen, Copenhagen, Denmark
okku@itu.dk
[2] Technische Universität Darmstadt, Darmstadt, Germany
[3] Abertay University, Dundee, Scotland
k.renaud@abertay.ac.uk
[4] Karlsruhe University of Technology, Karlsruhe, Germany
melanie.volkamer@kit.edu

Abstract. Internet-enabled voting introduces an element of invisibility and unfamiliarity into the voting process, which makes it very different from traditional voting. Voters might be concerned about their vote being recorded correctly and included in the final tally. To mitigate mistrust, many Internet-enabled voting systems build verifiability into their systems. This allows voters to verify that their votes have been *cast as intended, stored as cast* and *tallied as stored* at the conclusion of the voting period. Verification implementations have not been universally successful, mostly due to voter difficulties using them. Here, we evaluate two *cast as intended* verification approaches in a lab study: (1) "Challenge-Based" and (2) "Code-Based". We assessed cast-as-intended vote verification efficacy, and identified usability issues related to verifying and/or vote casting. We also explored acceptance issues post-verification, to see whether our participants were willing to engage with Internet voting in a real election. Our study revealed the superiority of the code-based approach, in terms of ability to verify effectively. In terms of real-life Internet voting acceptance, convenience encourages acceptance, while security concerns and complexity might lead to rejection.

Keywords: User study · Usable security · Verifiability · Electronic voting

1 Introduction

Internet voting has been the topic of public discussion in many countries. Estonia and Switzerland, for example, conduct legally-binding elections using Internet voting as a voting channel. Internet voting does deliver advantages, such as providing support to voters who are abroad or housebound. On the other hand,

D. Lamas et al. (Eds.): INTERACT 2019, LNCS 11746, pp. 519–538, 2019.
https://doi.org/10.1007/978-3-030-29381-9_32

new security risks are also undeniably introduced into the process due to the deployment of technology where previously only paper has been used [22]. Unless effective security measures are implemented, hackers can indeed manipulate the election on a large scale, possibly changing the outcomes of elections [9,14]. End-to-end verifiability [13] is a way to alleviate concerns related to the threat of illicit manipulations. End-to-end verifiable systems allow voters to verify that their votes have been *cast as intended*, *stored as cast* and *tallied as stored* to lead to a credible and trustworthy election outcome. A voting system that is end-to-end verifiable provides reassurance that the election outcome does indeed reflect the will of the voters.

"*Cast-as-intended*" verification allows the voter to verify that his/her vote has not been manipulated during vote casting. However, verification only detects manipulations if voters are: able to *complete* the verification task effectively. Moreover, the effort that is expended affording verification is only warranted if voters are *willing* to cast their vote using Internet voting technology in elections. It is important to note that cast-as-intended verification *has* to be performed by the voters themselves, to preserve vote secrecy. This makes the usability and understandability of the verification process crucial.

We report on a study that compared the usability of two alternative cast-as-intended verification approaches: *challenge-based* and *code-based*, primarily in terms of efficacy. Both are significant players in the field of Internet voting.

We commence by presenting the background to our study (Sect. 2), including a discussion of the security of the two tested approaches, and a brief review of other verification studies. Section 3 details our research questions and hypotheses. Section 4 then details our methodology and research questions. Section 5 reports on the outcome of the study and provides the answers to our research questions. Section 6 discusses the results and suggests future directions for research. Section 7 concludes.

2   Background

Challenge-Based Approach: This approach requires the voter to choose a voting option on the voting website, and encrypt their option. They are now faced with two options: (1) cast the encrypted vote, or (2) confirm that the system has encrypted the vote correctly by using a verifier to reveal the contents of the encrypted vote. A verified vote cannot be cast: it has to be discarded so that the verifier's output cannot be used to facilitate vote selling. The challenge-based approach is most commonly used by the so-called Benaloh challenge [6,7].

Depending on the implementation, the verifier software can run either on a vote-casting device, on an external device owned by the voter, or via a 3rd party website. Another difference is that the verified vote can either automatically be re-encrypted by the voting system, or discarded, requiring the voter to start again from scratch. The latter is the preferred course of action because it preserves vote secrecy — re-randomisation essentially casts the same vote, and vote secrecy is thereby compromised. If the voter commences making their choice from scratch, vote secrecy is preserved.

A number of Benaloh implementations have been proposed [4,18,27]. Of these, the so-called mobile approach [27], which uses an installed Smartphone *verifier app* (Fig. 1), seems the most promising, in terms of both security and usability [25]. The variant of the challenge-based approach that we tested in this study used a Smartphone verifier app, and required voters to discard verified votes.

The individual steps of the verification process are (see Fig. 1): (1) The voter marks her chosen voting option, which is then encrypted by the voting client. (2) The cryptographic hash of the encrypted vote is displayed as a QR-code. (3) The voter scans the QR-code using the Smartphone verifier app and (4) chooses either the "cast" or the "verify" option. (5) If the voter chooses the "verify" option, the voting client displays a QR-code with the chosen voting option and the randomness used for encrypting the vote. (6) The voter scans the QR-code. (7) The verifier app encrypts the voting option with the displayed randomness code. The resulting encrypted vote is compared to the check code scanned in previous step. If they are identical, the voting client has encrypted the vote correctly. If the encryption does not match the code, verification has failed. (8) If encrypted code matches the QR code, the verifier app displays the voting option from the verification data to the voter. (9) The voter compares the voting option output by the verifier app with her intention. If the options match, the vote has been verified. Otherwise, the vote has been manipulated. (10) Once verification is complete, the voter returns to step (1), where she goes through the entire process again.

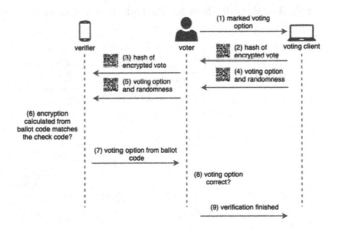

Fig. 1. Verification using the challenge-based approach.

Code-Based Approach: Each voter is issued with an individualised *code sheet*, which is distributed to voters before the election, via snail mail. The sheet provides a check code for each individual voting option (the sheets differ from voter when it comes to all the shown codes). When the voter casts a vote, his/her individual check code for that option is displayed by the voting client. To verify, the voter confirms that the displayed output code matches his/her sheet's check code which is next to his/her voting option. Diverse variants of this approach exist, including one used in the actual Swiss elections [34]. Some code sheets contain both confirmation *and* finalisation codes, which, again, are unique to each voter. The voter inputs the confirmation code after he/she has checked the validity of the displayed check code. The finalisation code is displayed to reassure the voter that the voting system has (1) indeed cast the vote as intended, and (2) that the vote has been verified and confirmed by the voter. An example of the code sheet is provided in Fig. 2.

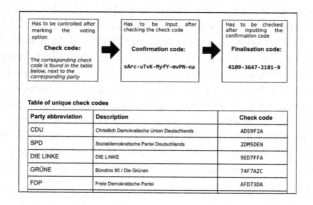

Fig. 2. The code sheet for the code-based approach.

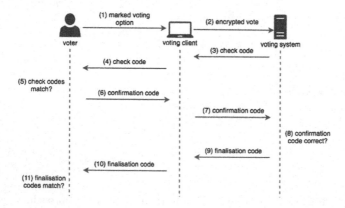

Fig. 3. Verification using the code-based approach.

The code-based verification process is depicted in Fig. 3. The individual verification steps are as follows: (1) The voter marks her chosen voting option via the voting client. (2) The voting client encrypts the chosen option and sends it to the voting system. (3) Upon receiving the cast vote, the voting system searches for the person's individualised return code corresponding to the cast voting option[1] and sends the return code back to the voting client. (4) The voting client displays the return code. (5) The voter checks whether the output return code matches the return code provided on her individualised code sheet. If the codes match, the voter knows that the voting system has received the intended vote. (Otherwise, the vote has been manipulated.) (6) If the voter is happy that the codes match, she inputs the so-called *confirmation code*, which is also found on her code sheet. (7) The voting client sends the input confirmation code to the voting system. (8) The voting system checks whether the provided confirmation code is correct. If the code is correct, the voter has verified that the cast vote reflects her intention. Otherwise, the voter has failed to confirm the correctness of the vote, either due to receiving an invalid return code or due to failing to perform the verification at all. In that case, the vote will not be stored by the voting system. (9) If the confirmation code is correct, the *finalisation code* is sent to the voting client. (10) The voting client displays the finalisation code. (11) The voter compares the displayed finalisation code to the finalisation code on her code sheet. If the codes match, the voter knows that her vote has been permanently stored in the voting system. A failure to receive the correct finalisation code would be evidence of hacker activity.

2.1 Security of the Approaches

In this section, we provide details of the security assumptions required by the two approaches.

Challenge-Based Approach: As shown in Fig. 1, the challenge-based approach involves the following entities: the voter, the voting client, the verifier and the voting server. The verifiability assured by the challenge-based approach relies on the assumption that the voting client does not know, in advance, whether the encrypted vote will be cast or verified. It is therefore crucial to encourage voters to perform the verification, and to do so repeatedly. Otherwise, if each voter either only verifies once, or not at all, an adversary controlling the voting client could change votes after a single verification, knowing that their actions are unlikely to be detected. Another assumption is that either the voting client or the verifier is trustworthy. If they collaborate, manipulations will not be detected. That is why independent verifies are usually considered.

Code-Based Approach: As shown in Fig. 3, the code-based approach involves the following entities: the voter, the voting client, the registrar, the code generator and the voting server.

The verifiability assured by the code-based approach relies on the assumption that the voting client can display the correct check code corresponding to the voter's chosen voting option only if the vote has indeed been cast as intended.

---

[1] Note that this search is performed via cryptographic anonymisation techniques, so that vote secrecy remains intact.

Note that we do not elaborate on the other security properties of the corresponding voting systems (e.g. vote privacy), or on other aspects of verifiability (e.g. whether the stored votes have been tallied correctly), see [4, 12] for more information.

2.2 Previous Studies on Human Factors in Verifiable E-Voting Systems

A number of studies have investigated human factors of verifiable e-voting systems. The research has focused on several aspects, including usability of verifiable voting systems, verification-related mental models and empirical studies of voter behaviour in verifiable real-world elections.

Several studies focused on usability at the polls. A number evaluated usability of the investigated systems in terms of satisfaction, e.g. [23, 24, 30, 37]. While the results of some studies revealed high satisfaction scores, they did not measure verification effectiveness in terms of the extent to which the participants were actually able to verify their votes. The evaluation of effectiveness was included in other studies, such as Pret-a-Voter and Scantegrity II [1, 2], BingoVote [5], StarVote [3] and EasyVote [8]. While some of these studies report high rates of success in terms of verifications [3, 8], the results of other studies [1, 2, 5] reveal several issues. These include misconceptions related to the verification process, leading to study participants being unable to complete the verification successfully. Other papers focus on evaluating the usability of verifiable Internet voting systems. In particular, different variants of the Helios voting system, which implements challenge-based verification approach, have been evaluated [1, 18, 25, 36], all revealing verification process issues. Of these, those that specifically measured verification success reported between 43% [1] and 81.25% [25] success rates. The usability of the code-based approach was investigated by [11], revealing usability issues, such as participants being confused about the different kinds of codes used for voting and verification. Marky et al. [26] investigated the usability of a variant of a code-based approach, the so-called 'code voting', by comparing different code modalities. The study reported that all of the participants were able to cast their vote successfully using all the modalities, and that the modality of using a QR code for entering the voting codes received the highest SUS score. However, no evaluation of verification has been done. The usability, in terms of satisfaction (without considering effectiveness), and acceptance of code-based verification (and variants) was evaluated in [20], which found that the participants were more willing to use a system with the highest security assurance in a real-world election, even if they also found it less usable due to complexity of entering and comparing different kinds of codes. Distler et al. [10] investigated the user experience related to the Selene voting system, which uses a verification approach based on tracking codes. While they did not evaluate the effectiveness of the verification, their results have shown that the participants felt less secure after verifying than before, and that displaying the security mechanisms, such as mentioning of encryption during vote casting, makes the participants feel more secure, but at the same time perceive the voting app to be less understandable.

Other studies focused on the voters' verification-related mental models [28,29,32]. These studies revealed a number of factors that would potentially prevent voters from verifying, such as a lack of knowledge of verification procedures, perceived verification effort or misconceptions about verification itself.

Finally, empirical studies using data from real-world elections have evaluated the extent to which the voters actually verify their votes. As such, only 31.4% of surveyed voters verified their votes using the challenge-based approach in the Helios voting system in the IACR (International Association of Cryptographic Research) elections [19]. In the Estonian Internet voting system, where the verification process is similar to that used in the challenge-based approach[2], only 4% of voters verified their votes [17]. The surveys of the code-based approach report successful verifications between 70% [31] and 90% [35] (self-reported by the survey participants who participated in an election which used a voting system with code-based verification).

While many of the aforementioned studies revealed usability shortcomings and mental models preventing voters from verification in different voting systems, most of them did not attempt to compare different verification approaches directly. As such, only very few empirical comparisons between various cast-as-intended verifiability implementations in terms of effectiveness have been carried out [2,25], none considering a code-based verification approach. It is furthermore difficult to compare the approaches using the data from the real-world elections, due to the differences in elections scenarios (i.e. elections conducted in different countries and in different settings) and in the methods the data was collected (i.e. log audits vs. self-reporting). When it comes to a comparison between code-based and challenge-based approaches, it therefore remains an open question, which one of them is more suitable to ensure the effectiveness of the verification.

3 Research Questions

We want to compare verification *effectiveness* of the two approaches. We also want to reveal usability issues leading to difficulties for participants during both vote casting and verification, in order to identify the need for further improvements.

Note, that we do not compare other metrics related to the voting itself, such as efficiency of the verification or satisfaction with the process. As such, comparing efficiency is particularly challenging: verification is conducted repeatedly in the challenge-based approach, as described in Sect. 2, while the voters using the code-based approach only have to verify once. Furthermore, because participants were confronted with manipulations, this could bias their perceptions of trustworthiness, rendering satisfaction measures unreliable.

RQ1: Our first research question is: *Are there any differences between the challenge- and code-based approaches, in terms of verification effectiveness?*

---

[2] The main difference is that the verified vote in the Estonian voting system does not have to be discarded and can be cast post-verification. We refer to [15,17] for more details.

As mentioned in Sect. 2.2, various previous studies investigating the effectiveness of the two approaches report the rate of successful verifications to be between 70% and 90% for the code-based approach, and between 43% and 81.25% for the challenge-based approach. While, as mentioned previously, the results of these studies are not strictly comparable due to different study settings, they do give us an indication that the code-based approach might make it easier for voters to verify. We therefore propose to conduct a one-tailed comparison of the approaches and to test the following hypotheses:

H_0: Participants detect the manipulation of their vote equally using the code-based and challenge-based approaches.

H_1: Significantly more participants are able to detect the manipulation of their vote using the code-based approach compared to challenge-based approach.

To uncover usability problems that might explain efficacy issues, we also explore:

- Can participants complete verification? (If not, what prevents this?)
- Can participants verify their cast vote effectively i.e. do they detect anomalies that the verification process is designed to reveal? (If not, what prevents this?)

RQ2: Our second question is: *What factors encourage or discourage acceptance of Internet voting in real world elections?*

The next section will explain how we went about answering these questions in our study.

4   Methodology

The main goal of our investigation was to compare the verification effectiveness afforded by the two approaches. To do this, a between-subjects user study was carried out, with participants randomly assigned to one of the two verification approach groups. All participants were instructed to use a mock Internet voting system and requested to verify their votes. We recorded participants' feedback throughout the experiment to help us to identify verification process issues and to garner insights into potential interface and process improvements.

The purpose of the cast-as-intended verification step is to give the voter the opportunity to detect vote manipulations. If anomalies are detected as quickly as possible, during the election, the authorities can be informed and are able to take immediate remediation steps. Hence we engineered our system to deliberately change cast votes. This helped us to test verification efficacy. Participants who detected the manipulation were told to cast and verify a second vote in a so-called *second run*, and this second vote was not manipulated. Participants who did not detect the manipulation completed the experiment as normal, and were not required to cast another vote.

4.1   Ethics

The study adhered to the guidelines of the ethics commission at the first author's institution, where the research was carried out. All participants completed a consent form at the outset. The consent form informed them that their interactions with the website would be recorded via screen recording software, that the data collected from the study would be stored and processed anonymously for research purposes, and that the participants could drop out at any time without negative consequences. They were paid proportionally, according to the amount of time they spent doing the experiment.

4.2   Implementation

For the purpose of the study, a mock variant of each of the two approaches was implemented: one of which implemented the challenge-based approach, and the other the code-based approach. The German parliament elections were used as the election scenario. Correspondingly, the list of candidates included the political parties that were also present on the ballot during the 2017 parliament election. The mock website ballot interface provided in Fig. 4[3]. The participants of the study accessed the mock website via a lab laptop provided to them during the study. The website was accessed via the URL "https://bundestagswahlen. de". This actually directed the browser to the local host[4].

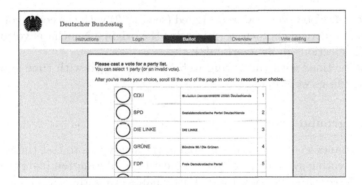

Fig. 4. The voting interface.

Challenge-Based: The mock voting system was based on the mobile approach introduced in [27] and evaluated by [25]. For the purposes of this study, a verifier

---

[3] All the screenshots provided in the paper are translated from German. The study itself was conducted in German.

[4] This was achieved by modifying the local hosts on the laptop. In order to communicate website credibility, a SSL certificate was issued by creating a new certificate chain starting with a new certificate authority. The SSL certificate was imported into the browser, so that the participants of the study could see the reassuring green lock in the browser address bar.

app was developed and installed on a lab Smartphone (see Fig. 5). The app collects timestamps of participants' interactions to support analysis.

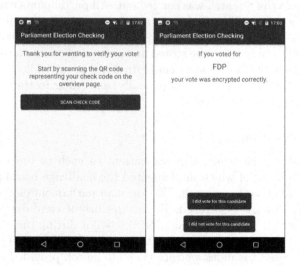

Fig. 5. The verifier app for challenge-based voting.

Code-Based: Code sheets were designed (see Fig. 2) with the codes consisting of seven alphanumerical characters (mirroring the original Neuchâtel voting system used in the elections in Switzerland[5]).

All interactions with the voting website were logged with time stamps, and screen recordings were made.

4.3 Background Story

The participants were told that the goal of the study was to test the usability of an Internet voting system. They received election information materials, as well as instructions related to their tasks. Participants evaluating the challenge-based approach used a lab Smartphone with the installed verifier app. Participants in the code-based group received a code sheet (similar to the one used in Switzerland).

Participants were given instructions in the form of a role card. For the code-based approach, the voter was instructed to cast a vote for the SPD[6] party and subsequently to verify their vote. For the challenge-based approach, the voter was instructed to verify a vote for SPD, and then to cast a vote for the Green party[7].

---

[5] Note, that even though the population in Switzerland is much smaller than Germany's, the code length allows for the generation of 36^7 unique codes, which makes the system suitable for the population of ca. 62 million. The code sheet resembled the original voting system's code sheets.

[6] German Social-Democratic Party.

[7] Note, re-casting is mandated by the challenge-based approach.

Pre-defined parties were used to preserve vote secrecy because their interactions with the system were observed and recorded during the experiment.

4.4 Manipulation

The first cast vote was surreptitiously manipulated by the system to check that the voters are able to verify effectively. It was changed from SPD to FDP[8]. FDP was chosen due to its similarity to SPD and the proximity of these parties on the ballot, which made the manipulation harder to detect. The challenge-based approach makes this manipulation detectable because the verifier app correctly reflects the manipulated vote (FDP), instead of the intended vote (SPD) (see Fig. 5 on the right). Using the code-based approach, the voting system outputs a check code assigned to FDP on the code sheet (in our study, "AFD73DA" instead of "2DM5DEN", see Fig. 6).

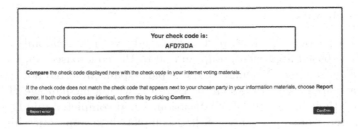

Fig. 6. The voting software's output during code-based verification.

4.5 Procedure

The study consisted of the following phases:

(1) Manipulation phase: Participants were welcomed and signed the consent form. The participants were given a role card outlining their tasks, as well as the voting information materials. After familiarising themselves with the role card, they proceeded to carry out their tasks. For the challenge-based approach group, this meant verifying a vote for SPD and casting a vote for the Green party; and, for the code-based approach group, casting and verifying a vote for SPD.

(2) Run-up phase: If a participant detected a manipulation, she was made aware that the manipulation had been introduced deliberately. The experimenter then installed an uncompromised voting system, and told the participant this. The participant was instructed to verify and cast their vote again. This time, no manipulation occurred, and participants could verify and cast their votes without hindrance.

---

[8] German Free Democratic Party.

(3) Conclusion phase: Having used the system and not noticed the manipulation, or after the run-up phase, participants completed questionnaires. They were encouraged to express their opinions of the systems (i.e. whether they experienced any issues verifying), and demographic data was collected. We also asked them the question *"Would you use this Internet voting system in a real parliament election? Please explain your answer."* We asked this to detect factors that would encourage or discourage acceptance of Internet voting in the future. Participants were debriefed.

5   Results

Participants were recruited via a snowball principle. They were told that the study would take approximately 15 to 30 min, based on pre-test experience, and offered remuneration of €10.

5.1   Participants

A total of 61 participants took part in the study, with 31 randomly assigned to the challenge-based approach group and 30 to the code-based approach group. Of these, 35 were male, 25 female and one participant preferred not specify their gender. Participant ages ranged from 19 to 67, with a median age of 33. When asked about their highest level of education, 7 had completed middle school, 10 had graduated from high school, 8 had completed an apprenticeship, 9 had a degree from the university of applied sciences, 25 had a university degree, and 2 had a doctorate.

5.2   RQ1: Verification Effectiveness

All the participants in the code-based approach group were able successfully to verify their vote and detect the manipulation during the manipulation phase. Furthermore, all were able successfully to complete the verification during the run-up stage. In the challenge-based group, seven of the participants were unable to perform verification during the manipulation stage.

A one-tailed Fisher's exact test compared the number of successful verifications during the manipulation phase and revealed a significant difference between the groups ($p < 0.01$). H_1 is thereby supported.

Usability Issues

We observed the participants' behaviours as they used the system. If a participant commented on some issue while completing the tasks, this was recorded. We also examined the screen recordings to see whether the participants made errors while engaging with the vote casting or verification interface. For example, they could have clicked on the wrong button or entered the wrong code. We also analysed the participants' responses to the final questionnaire.

Usability Issues with Challenge-Based Approach. A number of participants were unable to verify. Furthermore, several participants experienced problems casting their votes during the run-up phase. We describe the issues these participants experienced, as well as issues mentioned by successful participants.

One important issue was the **confusion about the verification process.** Some comments: *"too cumbersome, difficult to understand"* or mentioning that they had to *"develop an understanding of the system and what has to be scanned"*. They were also confused due to presence of two QR codes that had to be scanned in the correct order when using the verifier app. They expressed the need for clearer instructions: *"Make it clearer, which QR code should be scanned"*. Further improvement suggestions focused on overall better and more understandable instructions for verification: *"Purpose of the verification, and maybe a flowchart: What is assured during each step?"*.

Indeed, such confusion also affected participants' ability to verify their vote. Of 31 participants, seven were unable to verify. One did not attempt to verify, admitting that the process seemed too complicated despite the instructions. The other six only scanned the check code (Step (3) in Fig. 1), then not knowing how to proceed. Half thought that they had verified successfully, while the other half admitted that they had problems verifying.

Some participants experienced **confusion about vote re-casting**, as the challenge-based approach requires the voter to discard verified votes: *"Evidently, I only verified, but did not cast my vote. Have not understood the system yet"*. *'At the end I forgot, that the vote will be deleted after verification, and almost did not cast a vote"*.

Improvement suggestions: *"Maybe the hint that the vote has to be cast again after verifying needs to be more visible and salient on every page"*.

As evidenced from the screen recordings and observations, three of the participants in the challenge-based group also failed to recast their vote, and another three only succeeded in casting their vote after several attempts. In all cases, the participants proceeded to verification by clicking on the "Verify" button when they tried to cast their vote. Because the challenge-based approach does not allow the casting of a verified vote, the ballot was discarded and the participants were redirected to a page requiring them to cast their vote again. Some were able to figure out how to cast their vote, but others gave up.

In addition to mentioning the issues related to the non-intuitive process of verifying and vote casting, a number of participants lamented the **complexity of the voting system.** They asked for more information: *"Additional information for people with less technical experience"*. Other proposed improvements to clarity of the website interface included: *"Clearer instructions (another formulations, reordering of buttons, another choice of colors"*. *"Reflect status with colors and symbols, e.g. red for a failed verification"*.

Usability Issues with Code-Based Approach. All participants detected the manipulation, completed the verification and cast their votes during the run-up phase. Nonetheless, a number of issues emerged during the study, highlighting the potential for improvement.

The **complexity and length of the codes** was raised as an issue by several participants: *"Usability can be better; especially regarding complex codes"*. When asked to propose improvements, several participants focused on making it easier to enter and compare codes. As such, use of additional hardware, such as tokens similar to TAN-generators for online banking, or RFID-cards, have been suggested: *"A transponder, such as in [anonymised] or online banking..."*. Indeed, the issue of code complexity emerged from the screen recordings. While all participants were able to verify and cast their votes, two did so only after several attempts.

A number of participants expressed their **need for more information** and desire to know more about the technical details of the system: *"As an IT-specialist I would love to know more about the storage of data and encryption"*. This was also mentioned as an important predicor of system acceptance: *"The need/comprehensibility of the check code should be explained better (for acceptance). Same for the code of 'encryption"*.

A number of participants suggested **improving the instructions** and information materials. Several suggested aligning different instructions more effectively: *"Build in step-by-step screenshots in the information materials"*. *"Use symbols for simpler matching between verification steps on paper and on computer screen"*.

Several participants required **more reassurance** from the system, or extra options to confirm vote verification: *"As the last step, not just a finalisation text, but a button"*. *"I would like to confirm the finalisation code"*. *"The confirmation page can be more formal and leave a code with which one could confirm that the voting was successful"*.

A few responses included suggestions for maintaining the **security of the verification process**: *"It is good when the system provides the option to report a manipulation or highlights the possiblity – with this, the user will be more careful and attentive"*. *"If the codes of different parties are too similar, the comparison by the voter is prone to making errors"*.

Finally, a number of **user interface design improvements** were suggested. In particular: (*"Bigger buttons and images, support for the visually impaired"*); (*"For inputting the confirmation code, focus should move to the next form field"*).

Provision of a demo system was proposed, so that potential voters can familiarise themselves with the voting and verification processes before the election: *"Set up a test election with fake parties"*.

Some participants were **sceptical about the integrity of the verification.** Even a positive verification did not alleviate mistrust: *"Still not clear, how the verification can ensure that at the end the vote that is being transferred and processed and has not been manipulated"*.

5.3   RQ2: Acceptance of Internet Voting

We focused our analysis on the code-based approach, as it was better than the challenge-based one in affording effective verification, as demonstrated by the aforementioned analysis. The responses to all responses were analysed via independent and agreed-upon open coding by at least two authors.

Reasons for Acceptance. Overall, of 30 participants who used the code-based approach, 21 said that they would be willing to use the system in real-world elections. The following reasons were cited:

Convenience: This was a common theme: participants were positive about the proposed system: *"It saves me the way to the polling station, and if I want to apply for postal vote, the post traffic".*

Reassurance: The presence of verification procedure positively influenced the perceived security of the system among some of the participants: *"seems secure due to multiple verification steps."*

Reasons for Non-acceptance. 9 of the 30 participants were unwilling to use the system in a real-world election, citing the following reasons:

Security concerns: A general mistrust towards Internet voting were present among several participants: *"Does not matter how secure the Internet voting system can be, there are always ways to manipulate it".*

Complexity of the system and lack of transparency: This was commonly mentioned as one of the reasons for not using the proposed voting system: *"Too many random strings. Encryption? What is it? How does it work?".*

6   Discussion

Evaluation Results: Our study shows that the code-based approach outperforms the challenge-based approach with respect to effectiveness. Indeed, while all of our participants were able to verify their vote using the code-based approach, only 77.4% (24 out of 31) were able to do so with the challenge-based approach. Furthermore, of the seven participants who could not verify, three were convinced that they had indeed verified successfully. Such shortcomings would leave manipulations undetected.

For these reasons, we conclude that the code-based approach is superior to the challenge-based approach with respect to verification efficacy. However, as described in Sect. 2, these approaches rely on different security assumptions, such as the need to rely on the trustworthiness of various voting system components in the code-based approach, or the need to rely on the trustworthiness of the verifier (i.e. a smartphone with an installed verifier app) for the challenge-based approach. Therefore, the person deciding on which approach to be used in a particular election scenario has to take these assumptions into consideration.

Our study revealed a number of issues with the investigated approaches. The participants who used the challenge-based approach were particularly confused about the relationship between verification and vote casting, not appreciating that a verified vote cannot be cast. This confusion led to several participants failing to cast their votes. Although the interfaces provided instructions explaining that the vote had to be discarded after verification, these were evidently not understandable or noticeable enough. This issue was also revealed by other studies into the usability of the challenge-based approach, the most recent being the study reported by [25].

The process of discarding a verified vote, only to cast another *unverified vote*, is counter-intuitive and conflicts with pre-existing paper-based voting mental models. Moreover, asking voters to verify more than once will probably confuse them even more. There does not seem to be an easy way to improve this situation, from a usability perspective, because the problems are caused by the protocol of the underlying system.

Another issue related to the challenge-based approach was reported by [25]. This is the lack of feedback, which led some voters to abort verification prematurely, all the while thinking that they had indeed verified successfully. In particular, participants in our study stopped after scanning the first QR code (the check code). The instructions, both on the website and in the verifier app, asked them to scan a second QR code (the ballot code). These were seemingly overlooked.

For the code-based approach, the most prominent issue mentioned by the participants was the length and complexity of the codes that they had either to input or compare. This issue was also reported by [25]. While their study did not investigate the code-based approach, it included the evaluation of a variant of the challenge-based approach where the check code had to be written down and then compared manually, instead of using the verifier app. Similar to our study, the participants in [25] commented on the complexity of the code and expressed their concerns that the voters might make errors either writing down or comparing the codes. While the complexity of the codes is inherent in the system, to satisfy security requirements, the difficulties that the participants experienced suggest that other modalities for representing the codes should be investigated, such as, for example, passphrases or visual hashes.

The results of our study show that even though all of the participants were able to cast and verify their votes using the code-based approach; one third were still unwilling to use the system in a real-world election. They cite such reasons as security concerns, complexity of the system and lack of transparency. This suggests that while it is crucial to ensure that the Internet voting systems can be used effectively by the voters, this is not enough – a point that was also argued in previous research [21]. Yet, other studies show that voters would be ready to accept Internet voting systems that involve complex steps in both vote casting and verification, if the security of the system, which generates the complexity, is communicated to them [20]. This suggests that ways to inform the voters about the underlying mechanisms of the system, and the extent to which these ensure the security of the election, would be helpful in encouraging greater acceptance of Internet voting.

Finally, we should make the point that verification is explicitly provided in order to allay voter concerns about the integrity of a system that replaces paper-based voting. That being so, it is entirely possible that as people become accustomed to using Internet voting systems they will trust them more, and see even less need to verify. This would be a very interesting topic for a future study.

Limitations and Future Work: Many of the participants of our study were relatively young and highly educated. Because these demographics generally tend to be early adopters of new technologies, several studies on the demographics of Internet voting in different countries show that young and highly educated voters do tend to be over-represented among the voters who chose to cast their vote online [16,33,34]. Furthermore, people from these demographics generally have more advanced computer skills, as compared to the rest of the population. The usability issues they experiences are very likely affect other demographic groups, perhaps even more severely. It is worth noting that Internet voting is almost never the only available voting channel in practice, so that voters who do not feel confident using the Internet voting system still can cast their ballots in the traditional way. However, in order to study the effect of verification procedures amongst more general population, further studies might be needed.

The focus of our study was on the effectiveness of the verification process. As such, we did not measure the user experience and the satisfaction with the investigated systems. The reason for this was the design of our study, which included the manipulations of the vote. While these manipulations were necessary in order to measure the effectiveness with which they carried out the verification task, they also biased the user experience, as the voting system was intentionally designed to behave anomalously. The investigation of user experience in the cast-as-intended approaches, and the role it plays on the acceptance of the Internet voting systems, remains a topic for future research.

The participants were explicitly requested to verify their vote. However, empirical studies have shown that voters are often not motivated enough to verify [17]. This becomes a particular problem when verification is optional and not incentivised. Moreover, while the verification step is mandatory in the code-based approach, it is entirely possible for a participant simply to click through the verification of the check code without comparing it to their code sheets. Further studies are necessary in order better to model the voter's behaviour with respect to cast-as-intended verification in real-world elections.

Finally, our study only considered the attack scenario where an adversary manipulates a cast vote. We did not consider cases where the adversary might also attempt to manipulate the interface of the voting website (see [21] for examples). Such an attempt might be detected by attentive voters but voters could misunderstand verification instructions or overlook important information – as we observed during our study. Investigating the extent of such manipulations, and developing countermeasures, is an important direction for future investigations.

7 Conclusion

We carried out a study to compare the implementations of two verification approaches, one being challenge-based and the other code-based. We wanted to see whether people could verify their cast votes successfully, which entailed spotting a deliberately-introduced vote manipulation. We observed them carrying out the tasks, and recorded any errors they made, as well as their reservations, difficulties they experienced during the process, and suggestions for improvement. We found that participants in the code-based group could verify more successfully, and that this group also detected our introduced manipulation more reliably than those in the challenge-based group. In other words verification effectiveness in the code-based group was superior to that of the challenge-based group. We also revealed a worrying unwillingness to engage with Internet voting, even amongst our young and educated participants. If they do not accept voting it is even less likely that older demographics will do so.

Our analysis revealed that the idea of verification, being a fairly alien concept, is problematic. More needs to be done to familiarise voters with the differences between paper and Internet voting, to prepare them for the requirements of the new digital voting era.

Acknowledgements. This work was partially conducted within the Center of Information Security and Trust at the IT University of Copenhagen (ITU CIST) and also supported by the German Federal Ministry of Education and Research within the Competence Center for Applied Security Technology (KASTEL).

References

1. Acemyan, C.Z., Kortum, P., Byrne, M.D., Wallach, D.S.: Usability of voter verifiable, end-to-end voting systems: baseline data for Helios, Prêt à Voter, and Scantegrity II. USENIX J. Election Technol. Syst. **2**(3), 26–56 (2014)
2. Acemyan, C.Z., Kortum, P., Byrne, M.D., Wallach, D.S.: From error to error: why voters could not cast a ballot and verify their vote with Helios, Prêt à Voter, and Scantegrity II. USENIX J. Election Technol. Syst. (JETS) **3**(2), 1–19 (2015)
3. Acemyan, C.Z., Kortum, P., Byrne, M.D., Wallach, D.S.: Summative usability assessments of STAR-vote: a cryptographically secure e2e voting system that has been empirically proven to be easy to use. Hum. Factors (2018). https://doi.org/10.1177/0018720818812586
4. Adida, B.: Helios: web-based open-audit voting. In: USENIX Security Symposium, vol. 17, pp. 335–348. USENIX Association, Berkeley (2008)
5. Bär, M., Henrich, C., Müller-Quade, J., Röhrich, S., Stüber, C.: Real world experiences with bingo voting and a comparison of usability. In: IAVoSS Workshop on Trustworthy Elections (WOTE 2008) (2008)
6. Benaloh, J.: Simple verifiable elections. In: Electronic Voting Technology Workshop EVT 2006 (2006)
7. Benaloh, J.: Ballot casting assurance via voter-initiated poll station auditing. In: Electronic Voting Technology Workshop EVT 2007 (2007)

8. Budurushi, J., Renaud, K., Volkamer, M., Woide, M.: An investigation into the usability of electronic voting systems for complex elections. Ann. Telecommun. **71**(7–8), 309–322 (2016)

9. Chang-Fong, N., Essex, A.: The cloudier side of cryptographic end-to-end verifiable voting: a security analysis of Helios. In: Proceedings of the 32nd Annual Conference on Computer Security Applications, pp. 324–335. ACM (2016)

10. Distler, V., Zollinger, M.L., Lallemand, C., Roenne, P., Ryan, P., Koenig, V.: Security-visible, yet unseen? How displaying security mechanisms impacts user experience and perceived security. In: Proceedings of ACM CHI Conference on Human Factors in Computing Systems (CHI 2019) (2019)

11. Fuglerud, K.S., Røssvoll, T.H.: An evaluation of web-based voting usability and accessibility. Univ. Access Inf. Soc. **11**(4), 359–373 (2012)

12. Galindo, D., Guasch, S., Puiggalí, J.: 2015 Neuchâtel's cast-as-intended verification mechanism. In: Haenni, R., Koenig, R.E., Wikström, D. (eds.) VOTELID 2015. LNCS, vol. 9269, pp. 3–18. Springer, Cham (2015). https://doi.org/10.1007/978-3-319-22270-7_1

13. Gharadaghy, R., Volkamer, M.: Verifiability in electronic voting-explanations for non security experts. In: Electronic Voting, pp. 151–162 (2010)

14. Halderman, J.A., Teague, V.: The New South Wales iVote system: security failures and verification flaws in a live online election. In: Haenni, R., Koenig, R.E., Wikström, D. (eds.) VOTELID 2015. LNCS, vol. 9269, pp. 35–53. Springer, Cham (2015). https://doi.org/10.1007/978-3-319-22270-7_3

15. Heiberg, S., Martens, T., Vinkel, P., Willemson, J.: Improving the veriability of the Estonian Internet Voting scheme. In: International Joint Conference on Electronic Voting, pp. 92–107. Springer (2016)

16. Heiberg, S., Parsovs, A., Willemson, J.: Log analysis of estonian internet voting 2013–2014. In: Haenni, R., Koenig, R.E., Wikström, D. (eds.) VOTELID 2015. LNCS, vol. 9269, pp. 19–34. Springer, Cham (2015). https://doi.org/10.1007/978-3-319-22270-7_2

17. Heiberg, S., Willemson, J.: Verifiable internet voting in Estonia. In: 6th International Conference on Electronic Voting, Verifying the Vote (EVOTE), pp. 1–8. IEEE, October 2014

18. Karayumak, F., Olembo, M.M., Kauer, M., Volkamer, M.: Usability analysis of Helios-An open source verifiable remote electronic voting system. In: Proceedings of the 2011 Conference on Electronic Voting Technology/Workshop on Trustworthy Elections, EVT/WOTE 2011. USENIX Association, Berkeley (2011)

19. Kiayias, A., Zacharias, T., Zhang, B.: Ceremonies for end-to-end verifiable elections. In: Fehr, S. (ed.) PKC 2017. LNCS, vol. 10175, pp. 305–334. Springer, Heidelberg (2017). https://doi.org/10.1007/978-3-662-54388-7_11

20. Kulyk, O., Neumann, S., Budurushi, J., Volkamer, M.: Nothing comes for free: how much usability can you sacrifice for security? IEEE Secur. Priv. **15**(3), 24–29 (2017)

21. Kulyk, O., Volkamer, M.: Usability is not enough: lessons learned from 'human factors in security' research for verifiability. In: E-Vote-ID 2018, p. 66 (2018)

22. Langone, A.: An 11-Year-Old Hacked Into a U.S. Voting System, 14 August 2018. http://time.com/5366171/11-year-old-hacked-into-us-voting-system-10-minutes/

23. Mac Namara, D., Gibson, P., Oakley, K.: A preliminary study on a dualvote and prêt à voter hybrid system. In: CeDEM 2012 Conference for E-Democracy and Open Government 3–4 May 2012 Danube-University Krems, Austria, p. 77. Edition-Donau-Univ. Krems (2012)

24. Mac Namara, D., Scully, T., Gibson, P.: DualVote addressing usability and verifiability issues in electronic voting systems (2011). http://citeseerx.ist.psu.edu/viewdoc/summary?doi=10.1.1.399.7284

25. Marky, K., Kulyk, O., Renaud, K., Volkamer, M.: What Did I Really Vote For? In: Proceedings of the 2018 CHI Conference on Human Factors in Computing Systems, p. 176. ACM (2018)

26. Marky, K., Schmitz, M., Lange, F., Mühlhäuser, M.: Usability of code voting modalities. In: CHI Conference on Human Factors in Computing Systems, Glasgow, Scotland UK. ACM (2019). Late Breaking Work

27. Neumann, S., Olembo, M.M., Renaud, K., Volkamer, M.: Helios verification: to alleviate, or to nominate: is that the question, or shall we have both? In: Kő, A., Francesconi, E. (eds.) EGOVIS 2014. LNCS, vol. 8650, pp. 246–260. Springer, Cham (2014). https://doi.org/10.1007/978-3-319-10178-1_20

28. Olembo, M.M., Renaud, K., Bartsch, S., Volkamer, M.: Voter, what message will motivate you to verify your vote. In: Workshop on Usable Security, USEC (2014)

29. Olembo, M.M., Bartsch, S., Volkamer, M.: Mental models of verifiability in voting. In: Heather, J., Schneider, S., Teague, V. (eds.) Vote-ID 2013. LNCS, vol. 7985, pp. 142–155. Springer, Heidelberg (2013). https://doi.org/10.1007/978-3-642-39185-9_9

30. Oostveen, A.M., Van den Besselaar, P.: Users' experiences with e-voting: a comparative case study. J. Electron. Gov. $2(4)$, 357–377 (2009)

31. Puiggalí, J., Cucurull, J., Guasch, S., Krimmer, R.: Verifiability experiences in government online voting systems. In: Krimmer, R., Volkamer, M., Braun Binder, N., Kersting, N., Pereira, O., Schürmann, C. (eds.) E-Vote-ID 2017. LNCS, vol. 10615, pp. 248–263. Springer, Cham (2017). https://doi.org/10.1007/978-3-319-68687-5_15

32. Schneider, S., Llewellyn, M., Culnane, C., Heather, J., Srinivasan, S., Xia, Z.: Focus group views on Prêt à Voter 1.0. In: 2011 International Workshop on Requirements Engineering for Electronic Voting Systems (REVOTE), pp. 56–65. IEEE (2011)

33. Serdült, U., Germann, M., Harris, M., Mendez, F., Portenier, A.: Who are the internet voters? Innov. Public Sect. 27, 27–41 (2015)

34. Serdult, U., Germann, M., Mendez, F., Portenier, A., Wellig, C.: Fifteen years of internet voting in Switzerland [History, Governance and Use]. In: 2nd International Conference on eDemocracy & eGovernment, ICEDEG 2015, pp. 126–132. IEEE, April 2015

35. Stenerud, I.S.G., Bull, C.: When reality comes knocking. Norwegian experiences with verifiable electronic voting. Electron. Voting 205, 21–33 (2012)

36. Weber, J.L., Hengartner, U.: Usability study of the open audit voting system Helios (2009). http://www.jannaweber.com/wpcontent/uploads/2009/09/858Helios.pdf. Accessed 22 Dec 2017

37. Winckler, M., et al.: Assessing the usability of open verifiable e-voting systems: a trial with the system Prêt à Voter. In: Proceedings of ICE-GOV, pp. 281–296 (2009)

Mouse Behavior as an Index of Phishing Awareness

Kun Yu[1,2(✉)], Ronnie Taib[2], Marcus A. Butavicius[3],
Kathryn Parsons[3], and Fang Chen[1]

[1] University of Technology Sydney, Ultimo, NSW 2007, Australia
{Kun.yu,Fang.chen}@uts.edu.au
[2] Data61, CSIRO, Eveleigh, NSW 2015, Australia
Ronnie.taib@csiro.au
[3] Defence Science and Technology Group, Edinburgh, SA 5111, Australia
{Marcus.Butavicius,
Kathryn.Parsons}@dst.defence.gov.au

Abstract. Phishing attacks are one of the most common security challenges faced by individuals and organizations today. Although many techniques exist to filter out phishing emails, they are not always effective leaving humans as the most vulnerable links in the information security chain. This paper presents a study investigating how human behavior, especially mouse movements, may reflect cybersecurity awareness, in particular to phishing emails. Using an email sorting task, we examined three key mouse movement features: hover, slow movement, and response time. The results suggest that slow mouse movements indicate high awareness of phishing emails and could be used to determine the likelihood of users falling victim to phishing attacks. However, contrary to intuition, response time and mouse hovering behaviors do not correlate with phishing awareness.

Keywords: Cybersecurity · Phishing · Mouse movements ·
Email classification

1 Introduction

Phishing refers to the fraudulent attempt to obtain sensitive information or access to the recipient's computer or system from people in electronic communications [1, 2] and is the most popular cyberattack method [3]. Although most organizations deploy technical defenses such as email filtering against cyber threats, employees still receive many phishing emails, due to more sophisticated and sometimes personalized content being crafted by attackers (e.g., spear phishing). In practice, humans remain the most vulnerable link in the information security chain, and in many cases it is the human behavior that makes a cyberattack possible and successful [4].

Extensive research has been conducted to investigate how and why people click on the suspicious URL or attachment in an email, and it is suggested that knowledge of phishing threats, usage of situational cues (such as the URLs in the email) and perceptions of severe negative consequences are possible indicators of phishing awareness [5–7].

© IFIP International Federation for Information Processing 2019
Published by Springer Nature Switzerland AG 2019
D. Lamas et al. (Eds.): INTERACT 2019, LNCS 11746, pp. 539–548, 2019.
https://doi.org/10.1007/978-3-030-29381-9_33

However, most of these studies are focused on theory verification or validation with very few addressing empirical techniques to predict whether a suspicious URL is likely to be clicked by a given person via their behavioral data, or at what stage a person should be warned of a potential phishing threat.

Besides theoretical investigations, various intervention methods have been devised to educate people to avoid being phished, and typical anti-phishing skills include examination of the sender information, the addressing of the email, the hyperlinks involved in the email and typographic errors in the text [5, 8]. Focusing on these characteristics of emails, anti-phishing training can improve the general phishing awareness [9]. However, a common challenge faced by the anti-phishing education schemes is that they do not customize education to different users – an approach which has been shown to be effective when the training is tailored to individual differences such as learning style preferences [10].

Many emails are still processed on personal computers today, with the mouse as most widely used interface to browse the contents of the emails, check the sender information, click on URLs or open attachments. Existing research has revealed that tracking user's mouse movements is effective for website usability evaluation [11, 12], that a mouse position gives an indication of the user's gaze during their online tasks [13–15], and corresponds to user's attention [16]. Huang et al. suggested that mouse hovering gestures are related to user observation and thinking when browsing online search results [17]. This finding motivated us to consider whether typical features related to mouse movements, e.g. mouse hover or slow mouse movements can be used as indicators of a user's likelihood to click a phishing link. For example, slow mouse movements may suggest that the subject is reading slowly which may indicate a less impulsive decision making style that has been empirically demonstrated to be linked to phishing email resistance [18]. However, to our knowledge no similar examination has been conducted to date.

Compared with existing phishing awareness examination methods, there are several advantages of a mouse behavior-based method: as mouse movements occur naturally, the examination can be done in real time in a non-intrusive way without interfering with the user's online interactions. Furthermore, a user can be warned, or links can be de-activated, whenever relevant mouse behaviors are detected that reflect high susceptibility to clicking on suspicious content. Finally, the personalized nature of mouse movements makes it possible to design personalized phishing interventions. Hence, we propose three research hypotheses on the relationship between mouse features and user response to phishing emails:

1. Response time can indicate a user's decision when processing phishing emails;
2. Mouse hovers can be used to gauge the level of phishing threat awareness;
3. Slow mouse movements can be used to identify whether a phishing threat can be identified.

2 Method

Based on a user study involving 30 email sorting tasks, we collected behavioral data, as well as post hoc subjective feedback.

2.1 Participants

Thirty-three volunteers, including thirteen females, from a multi-national research organization participated in the experiment. Thirty participants finished all the tasks although two participants used an iPad and therefore had no mouse input. As a result, we collected mouse data from twenty-eight subjects (10 females) with an age range of 30–39 years old. Participants had reasonable self-reported proficiency in English (on average 7.6 out of a 10-point scale) and good computer skills (on average 7.7 out of a 10-point scale). Most participants (27 out of 28) finished the experiment within twenty minutes. Ethics approval was obtained for this study, and all the subjects confirmed their consent before the experiment and were aware that they could opt out at any time. They were unpaid but received a small snack as acknowledgement of their time.

2.2 Email Interface

We adapted the real-life examples of phishing emails from the UC Berkeley Information Security and Policy Phishing Examples Archive [19], and adapted the URLs and logos embedded in the email to suit the local population. We converted the emails to images of fixed size and calibrated the location of the URLs to enable the hover effect of the mouse (Fig. 1). Specifically, each email had a hyperlink-enabled element which could be either text, URL or a button. When the mouse hovered on this element for a short time (browser tooltips typically trigger after 500 ms) without click, a popup message appeared, which revealed the real URL in a similar way that most modern email clients do. However, due to security reasons, none of the links were active during the experiment. In total thirty emails were crafted, including twenty phishing emails and ten legitimate ones, the latter being compiled from real emails received by the experiment designers in the past.

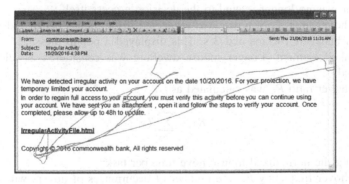

Fig. 1. A crafted phishing email with the retrieved traces of mouse movements from a user shown in blue. (Color figure online)

2.3   Experiment Procedure

The emails were presented to the participants in a randomized order, and the participants were asked to finish the tasks as soon as possible, although there was no time
limit for the tasks. For each email, the participant was asked to classify it into one of
three categories: high priority, low priority, or suspicious. We assume that participants
would only put emails with legitimate or innocuous content and links into the first two
categories. Upon completion of the email tasks, the participants answered three distinct
open-ended questions (one per text in curly brackets): "Of the emails you categorized
as {HIGH PRIORITY | LOW PRIORITY | SUSPICIOUS}, what aspects of the emails
influenced your decision?". They could answer 'not applicable' if they had never
selected that category during the tasks.

2.4   Data Collection

We used a crowdsourcing tool to present the email interfaces, organize the questionnaires, and capture mouse movements. In particular, we collected timestamped mouse
movements and click traces throughout the experiment. Using this information, we
were able to replay the mouse behaviors, as shown in Fig. 1.

We grouped data for the High Priority and Low Priority categories as we were only
interested in whether an email was considered suspicious or not. This resulted in a
binary decision for each email (*Suspicious/Non-suspicious*), from each participant. We
used a similar reclassification (i.e., *Suspicious/Non-suspicious*) for the qualitative
answers to the final questionnaire.

In this paper, we focus on the participants' responses to phishing emails only, hence
the data collected from the non-phishing emails is out of scope and not discussed
below. We derived the following variables for each email sorting task:

- Email category: the subjective decisions on whether a given email was phishing
  (*Suspicious*) or not (*Non-suspicious*);
- Response time T_r: the time elapsed before the participant selected a category for the
  email. We intentionally removed mouse movements within 200 ms prior to the
  mouse click on the email category (*Low Priority, High Priority* or *Suspicious*) as we
  considered that the decision has already been made by that time, and hence the user
  behavior was no longer related to the decision process itself.;
- Mouse hover time T_h: a hover was registered if the mouse cursor did not change
  location between 100 ms and 3 s. This displayed a popup message when over a
  hyperlinked element. Longer mouse dwelling was considered as idle state and
  discarded;
- Mouse hover ratio R_h was calculated as

$$R_h = \sum_{task} T_h / T_r \tag{1}$$

indicating the normalized mouse hove time per task;
- Mouse hover frequency F_h: the number of occurrences of hovers within an email
  sorting task;

- Slow mouse movements T_s: if the mouse movement speed fell in the bottom quartile (25%) of the overall speed within an email task, it was considered to be slow, and the corresponding time for slow movement was recorded;
- Slow mouse movement ratio R_s was calculated as

$$R_s = \sum_{task} T_s/T_r \qquad (2)$$

- Slow mouse movement frequency F_s: the number of occurrences of slow mouse movements within an email sorting task.

3 Results

We analyzed the mouse motion features with respect to human decisions, and further refined these findings with an attempt to categorize subjects that are more vulnerable to phishing threats. We used Welch's t-test to examine the differences for all the reported analytics due to the unequal variances involved in the data.

3.1 Response Time

The response time T_r was compared between the correct and incorrect classification of a phishing email, as shown in Fig. 2. There was no significant difference ($t(199) = .73$, $p > .05$), suggesting that the response time does not account for the differences between phishing email identification, which suggests our first hypothesis to be invalid.

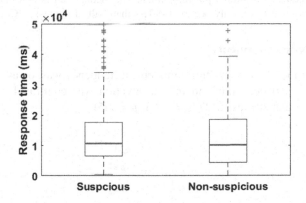

Fig. 2. Response time (T_r) of different decisions on a phishing email. The horizontal red line indicates the median value of each case. (Color figure online)

3.2   Mouse Hover

As mouse hovering is considered to indicate when a user is observing and thinking about the email content [17, 19], a high hover frequency should suggest that the subject has examined several elements in the email, hence the email sorting decision should be more thorough. The other variable R_h reflects the total time intentionally spent on examining the elements in an email, and it was expected to exhibit a similar pattern to F_h. However, the Welch's t-test suggested no significant difference for F_h ($t(362) = .44, p > .05$) or R_h ($t(304) = .55, p > .05$) between the correct and incorrect decisions to classify a phishing email. Figure 3 illustrates the hover frequency for correct and incorrect email classifications respectively. It can be seen that in either case, hover does not occur regularly – actually, for more than half of the emails the participants didn't hover their mouse at all, hence insufficient hover data is collected and could not be used for subjective phishing awareness examination. These findings invalidate our second hypothesis for the feasibility of using mouse hovers as indicators of phishing awareness.

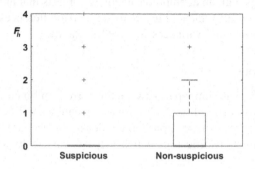

Fig. 3. Hover frequency (F_h) on a phishing email. The median values (red line) for both cases are zero, indicating that hover only occurred in less than half of the tasks. (Color figure online)

3.3   Slow Mouse Movements

As illustrated in Fig. 4(a), slow mouse movement frequency was, on average, lower for the *Suspicious* email decisions and this observation was confirmed by a significant difference in a Welch's t-test ($t(274) = -2.3, p < .05$).

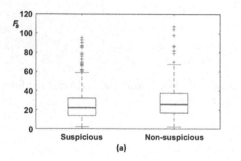
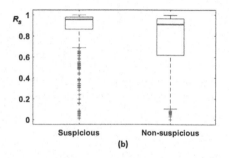

Fig. 4. (a) Slow mouse movement frequency and (b) slow mouse movement ratio of user decisions on a phishing email. The horizontal red line indicates the median value. (Color figure online)

For the slow movement ratio R_s, a significant difference was also identified via a Welch's t-test ($t(236) = 4.16$, $p < .01$), as shown in Fig. 4(b). This suggests that to reach the correct decision to identify a phishing email, the participants overall spent more time performing slow mouse movements.

Combining the examination above on slow mouse movements, correct *Suspicious* email identification by the users relates to high ratio of slow mouse movement time but low occurrences of slow mouse movements. This suggests that, on average, if the mouse is moving slowly and takes a long time, there is a high chance that the phishing email is correctly classified, however frequent slow mouse movements do not account for a correct classification decision.

4 Discussion

In this paper, we explored whether mouse behavior data can be used to characterize susceptibility to phishing threats. The results confirmed slow mouse movements can reflect awareness. However, contrary to intuition, neither response time to sort an email, nor mouse hovers were able to indicate phishing awareness.

Response time has been shown to reflect several aspects of the mental process, including thinking, interpreting, processing and decision generating [20, 21]. It is notable that although different decisions are made when sorting phishing emails, the decision time didn't differ significantly, suggesting that any difference in cognitive processing time may be orders of magnitude smaller than the physical response of moving the mouse and selecting an outcome in this experiment.

As reported by prior research that user's mouse position gives an indication of the user's gaze during their online tasks and corresponds to the user's attention, the mouse hover can be interpreted as a visual fixation at the mouse location. In the email sorting task, only one hyperlink is embedded in each email, limiting the hover gestures the participants needed to examine the hyperlink. Examining all the realistic phishing emails from Berkeley Information Security and Policy Phishing Examples Archive [19], we found that similarly to our tasks, most of them only involve a single hyperlink-enabled element per email. Therefore, the hover gestures can be very limited when a phishing email is encountered, making them unsuitable for phishing awareness detection. However, in practice the hyperlink itself remains crucial to identify phishing emails, which is recognized by some participants: 11 out of the 28 of them reported that the URL in the email influenced their decision to categorize an email as *Suspicious*.

Compared with mouse hovers, slow mouse movements exhibited a much higher rate of occurrences. Two features we derived – mouse movement frequency and ratio – are both good indicators of phishing awareness. We attribute this result to the amount of data available and to the mental processes involved. The slow mouse movements refer to how the participant slows down from time to time as the eyes may slow down as well to follow the mouse cursor, suggesting that the participant is focusing their attention on a specific part of the email message. This research established that such cognitive processing mechanism is related to the ability to discriminate suspicious emails. Specifically, we found that if many slow movements, or in other words, frequent fluctuation in mouse movement speed exist in one task, chances are that the phishing email will be misclassified. In comparison, long slow mouse movements with few fluctuations in mouse movement speed often result in correct identification of a phishing threat.

Our findings regarding two qualitatively different processing styles for emails aligns with the Dual Process Theory of human reasoning [22]. Accordingly, we have two qualitatively different systems for making decisions, i.e., System 1 focusing on implicit, automatic reasoning and System 2 which is deliberate and analytic. The former is characterized by intuitive, heuristic decision making that is highly efficient and automatic but also relatively error prone. The latter is more controlled, systematic and effortful.

Given that previous research has suggested that System 2 thinking is linked to better phishing email detection, the long slow mouse movements with few fluctuations in mouse movement speed evident in correct phishing classification in our study may in fact indicate functioning of System 2. In other words, the users' mouse activity (i.e., long, slow mouse movements) may be reflective of their decision-making quality (i.e., focus on details and deliberation with a high level of attentional control) when determining the legitimacy of an email. Future research into phishing email resistance should examine, empirically, the link between mouse movements, performance on the Cognitive Reflection Test [23] and accuracy in email categorization.

The features we derived, including the slow mouse movement frequency and ratio can both be calculated in real time before the user decision, and thus it would be possible to provide decision support to users based on their own mouse behavior pattern before they are about to click a link in a (phishing) email. The difference observed in slow mouse movement frequency and ratio before a decision can serve many other purposes, including the evaluation of anti-phishing education effectiveness, behavior recommendation for people who may fall victim to phishing attacks, or real-time inspection of phishing emails via crowdsourcing, or even general web browsing safety. For example, such decision support could dynamically block links or prompt the user to exert caution, when the user is deemed vulnerable to clicking on suspicious content, leading to better protection from drive-by download attacks or other malign web links.

There are several limitations to the current study. First, the sample was drawn from participants with a research background, which may not be representative of the wider population. Secondly, we posed the experiment as an email sorting task but didn't specify it was a phishing email detection study, to avoid the priming effect that previous research has shown will artificially improve performance [18]. In the post-experiment questionnaires we discovered one participant focused specifically on the discrimination between high priority and low priority emails (although their data indicated that appropriate phishing email selections were made).

As mouse remains a natural choice for email processing, we only analyzed mouse movement data in this paper. However, other user interaction data, e.g., mobile device use, or physiological data (eye tracking, galvanic skin response, or blood volume pulse) could be used to examine phishing awareness. However, these may lead to a more complicated experimental setup, hence may not be suitable for data collection via crowdsourcing platforms. It is also possible to combine mouse movement analysis with email text/content processing, as compound features to quantify phishing awareness, which will form part of our future work.

5 Conclusion

In this paper, we present a study using mouse movement features to identify subjective phishing awareness. Our experiment results show that slow mouse movements, rather than mouse hover and subjective response time, are good indicators of phishing threat detection. We also discuss the feasibility of using different mouse movement features to identify subjective phishing awareness, which is essential for the development of techniques that can protect vulnerable email users in real time. Our study adds to the general understanding of how humans use the mouse before processing potentially harmful email content, which could provide crucial novel, non-intrusive methods to assist people in phishing prevention and new ways of anti-phishing education through customized phishing detection.

References

1. Drake, C.E., Oliver, J.J., Koontz, E.J.: Anatomy of a phishing email. In: CEAS (2004)
2. Butavicius, M., Parsons, K., Pattinson, M., McCormac, A.: Breaching the human firewall: social engineering in phishing and spear-phishing emails. arXiv preprint arXiv:1606.00887 (2016)
3. Coopers, P.: Turnaround and transformation in cybersecurity: key findings from the global state of information security survey (2016)
4. Dhamija, R., Tygar, J.D., Hearst, M.: Why phishing works. In: Proceedings of the SIGCHI Conference on Human Factors in Computing Systems, pp. 581–590. ACM (2006)
5. Downs, J.S., Holbrook, M., Cranor, L.F.: Behavioral response to phishing risk. In: Proceedings of the Anti-Phishing Working Groups 2nd Annual eCrime Researchers Summit, pp. 37–44. ACM (2007)
6. Parsons, K., McCormac, A., Butavicius, M., Pattinson, M., Jerram, C.: Determining employee awareness using the human aspects of information security questionnaire (HAIS-Q). Comput. Secur. **42**, 165–176 (2014)
7. Conway, D., Taib, R., Harris, M., Yu, K., Berkovsky, S., Chen, F.: A qualitative investigation of bank employee experiences of information security and phishing. In: Thirteenth Symposium on Usable Privacy and Security, pp. 115–129 (2017)
8. Kumaraguru, P., et al.: School of phish: a real-world evaluation of anti-phishing training. In: Proceedings of the 5th Symposium on Usable Privacy and Security, p. 3. ACM (2009)
9. Sheng, S., Holbrook, M., Kumaraguru, P., Cranor, L.F., Downs, J.: Who falls for phish? A demographic analysis of phishing susceptibility and effectiveness of interventions. In: Proceedings of the SIGCHI Conference on Human Factors in Computing Systems, pp. 373–382. ACM (2010)
10. Pattinson, M., et al.: Adapting cyber security training to your employees. In: Proceedings of the 12th International Symposium on Human Aspects of Information Security & Assurance, Dundee, Scotland (2018)
11. Arroyo, E., Selker, T., Wei, W.: Usability tool for analysis of web designs using mouse tracks. In: CHI 2006 Extended Abstracts on Human Factors in Computing Systems, pp. 484–489. ACM (2006)
12. Atterer, R., Wnuk, M., Schmidt, A.: Knowing the user's every move: user activity tracking for website usability evaluation and implicit interaction. In: Proceedings of the 15th International Conference on World Wide Web, pp. 203–212. ACM (2006)

13. Navalpakkam, V., Jentzsch, L., Sayres, R., Ravi, S., Ahmed, A., Smola, A.: Measurement and modeling of eye-mouse behavior in the presence of nonlinear page layouts. In: Proceedings of the 22nd International Conference on World Wide Web, pp. 953–964. ACM (2013)

14. Hauger, D., Paramythis, A., Weibelzahl, S.: Using browser interaction data to determine page reading behavior. In: Konstan, J.A., Conejo, R., Marzo, J.L., Oliver, N. (eds.) UMAP 2011. LNCS, vol. 6787, pp. 147–158. Springer, Heidelberg (2011). https://doi.org/10.1007/978-3-642-22362-4_13

15. Huang, J., White, R., Buscher, G.: User see, user point: gaze and cursor alignment in web search. In: Proceedings of the SIGCHI Conference on Human Factors in Computing Systems, pp. 1341–1350. ACM (2012)

16. Smucker, M.D., Guo, X.S., Toulis, A.: Mouse movement during relevance judging: implications for determining user attention. In: Proceedings of the 37th International ACM SIGIR Conference on Research & Development in Information Retrieval, pp. 979–982. ACM (2014)

17. Huang, J., White, R.W., Dumais, S.: No clicks, no problem: using cursor movements to understand and improve search. In: Proceedings of the SIGCHI Conference on Human Factors in Computing Systems, pp. 1225–1234. ACM (2011)

18. Parsons, K., McCormac, A., Pattinson, M., Butavicius, M., Jerram, C.: Phishing for the truth: a scenario-based experiment of users' behavioural response to emails. In: Janczewski, L.J., Wolfe, H.B., Shenoi, S. (eds.) SEC 2013. IFIPAICT, vol. 405, pp. 366–378. Springer, Heidelberg (2013). https://doi.org/10.1007/978-3-642-39218-4_27

19. The Phish Tank | Information Security and Policy. https://security.berkeley.edu/resources/phishing/phish-tank. Accessed 20 Mar 2019

20. Anderson, E.W., Potter, K.C., Matzen, L.E., Shepherd, J.F., Preston, G.A., Silva, C.T.: A user study of visualization effectiveness using EEG and cognitive load. Comput. Graph. Forum 30(3), 791–800 (2011)

21. Sweller, J.: Cognitive load theory, learning difficulty, and instructional design. Learn. Instr. 4(4), 295–312 (1994)

22. Evans, J.S.B.: Questions and challenges for the new psychology of reasoning. Think. Reason. 18(1), 5–31 (2012)

23. Toplak, M.E., West, R.F., Stanovich, K.E.: The Cognitive Reflection Test as a predictor of performance on heuristics-and-biases tasks. Mem. Cogn. 39(7), 1275 (2011)

Perceptions of Risk, Benefits and Likelihood of Undertaking Password Management Behaviours: Four Components

Burak Merdenyan[✉] and Helen Petrie

University of York, York YO10 5DD, UK
bm815@york.ac.uk

Abstract. Passwords remain the most common form of authentication in the digital world. People have increasing numbers of passwords, and research suggests that many people undertake risky password management behaviours such as re-using passwords, writing them down and sharing them with friends and colleagues. It is not clear whether people persist in these behaviours because they do not understand the risks involved or the benefits of the behavior outweigh the risk. An online survey was undertaken with 120 MTurk workers in which they rated the risks, benefits and likelihood of undertaking 15 password management behaviours. They also completed the Marlow-Crowne Social Desirability Scale to investigate whether their responses, particularly of the likelihood ratings, were affected by social desirability. An interesting pattern of responses was found with some groups of behaviours more affected by perceptions of the benefits and others equally affected by the perceptions of the risks and the benefits. These results have implications for how information about risky password behaviours in presented to users and general education about password security.

Keywords: Passwords · Password management behaviour · Password risks · Password benefits · Usable security

1 Introduction

In spite of numerous technological innovations (e.g. graphical authentication, biometric authentication), passwords remain the most common form of authentication in the digital world [3, 24]. Numerous studies have investigated the extent to which people create strong passwords and their behaviours in relation to password management (*see* Related Work, below). Such studies have repeatedly shown that people make weak passwords and act in risky ways, for example re-using passwords, writing them down, and sharing them with friends and colleagues. However little research has investigated *why* people persist in these risky behaviours in the face of much information that they could lead to information and identity theft. Is it the case that people are not aware of these risks or do not understand them, or is it that people do understand the risks but believe that the benefits of the behaviours outweigh the risks?

This study undertook an exploratory study to assess people's perceptions of the risks of a range of password management behaviours, their perceptions of the benefits

D. Lamas et al. (Eds.): INTERACT 2019, LNCS 11746, pp. 549–563, 2019.
https://doi.org/10.1007/978-3-030-29381-9_34

of these behaviours, and their perceptions of the likelihood of undertaking the behaviours. The study will help us understand the relationship between these perceptions and address the question of what matters most to people in password management behaviour – risk or benefit? A greater understanding of these issues may influence future information disseminated about risky password management behaviours.

2 Related Work

Users' risky password management behaviours have been investigated in a number of studies. The most commonly researched risky password management strategies are reusing passwords, writing them down, and sharing them with others. Some users try to avoid the risks of having many passwords by using password management systems, although the use of these has been little researched. There are also behaviours which may risk a password being revealed to others such as logging in to accounts from shared computers or from a friend or colleague's device. We will briefly review the research on all these topics.

2.1 Password Reuse

Brown et al. [5] evaluated the generation and usage of passwords with 218 students in the United States. Participants were given a questionnaire and they were asked to describe the type of information or code they use for a set of services requiring passwords. 94% of the participants reported reusing at least one password for more than one system.

Gaw and Felten [10] conducted two studies about password management behavior. The first was a laboratory study in which participants were asked to log in to a wide range of sites to get an accurate estimate of the number of passwords they had and the amount of re-use of passwords. 49 American undergraduate students participated and it was found that the majority had three or fewer passwords and passwords were reused at least twice. The second study was a survey about password behaviours with 58 undergraduate students from the same pool of participants as in the first study. The survey explored why participants re-used passwords. By far the most common explanation was that it made passwords easier to remember, reported by 60% of respondents. Other explanations given were having too many accounts (14% of respondents), and the websites being of the same category (12% of respondents).

Notoatmodjo and Thomborson [19] conducted a survey with 26 university students in New Zealand. The survey found that these students could appropriately categorize their online accounts in relation to their importance: online banking accounts were categorized as *high importance* accounts, whereas newspaper accounts were categorized as *low importance* accounts. The more online accounts students had, the more they were likely to re-use passwords, although they reported that they avoided reusing passwords for high importance accounts. 35% of students reported that they re-used passwords because they were easier to remember, 19% reported that they re-used passwords for accounts of similar value and 18.5% reported that they re-used passwords for accounts of a similar type.

People also make small variations to passwords when re-using them across accounts, in an attempt to make them different but memorable and more secure. Researchers appear not to have given much attention to this strategy. Ur et al. [31] conducted a laboratory study in which participants created three passwords in different password policy conditions while performing a think aloud protocol. Three participants out of 49 (6%) used exactly the same password across all conditions, and 10 (20%) used the same password in two of the three conditions. A further 10 participants re-used a password with some variation, often a very minor one. Many participants were under the mistaken impression that such small variations make passwords more secure.

2.2 Writing Down Passwords

Writing down passwords is recommended for cognitive off-loading by some researchers [4], however, other researchers regard it as a 'bad habit' [5]. A password recorded, whether on paper or electronically, could be found by others and used maliciously. In the survey by Boothroyd and Chiasson [4], nearly half (15/31) of the Canadian university participants believed that the security of a password is highly related to where it is stored. A survey, albeit conducted some time ago (1999), with 997 computer users at the US Department of Defense found that 42% of respondents kept their password written down in their wallet [32].

Previous recommendations on this strategy have also highlighted security concerns: Boothroyd and Chiasson [4] found that over 70% of users had been previously advised that they should not write down their passwords. Nevertheless, 61% of these users reported that they would be less likely to re-use passwords if they were allowed to write them down.

2.3 Sharing Passwords

Apart from writing passwords down, users also share their passwords with others. A survey on password sharing strategies conducted with 122 respondents from a range of countries found that over 30% of the respondents shared their email password, and 25% shared their Facebook password with close friends or partners [10]. Sharing passwords is also used to establish trust and intimacy between people [1]. Interviews with 45 married and 11 cohabiting couples in Australia revealed that password sharing is seen as an easy way of managing bank accounts and a demonstration of trust between intimate couples [26].

2.4 Other Password Management Activities

Software systems known as password managers are also used by password holders as a strategy to manage their various passwords. Password managers are another form of cognitive off-loading, as users only need to remember one password and can create many strong passwords without having to remember them or write them down [7]. Users only have to manage a master password, to access and use their other passwords in their password manager. However, the consequences of forgetting the master password might be catastrophic [2].

Another risky password behaviour is logging in to password protected accounts from shared computers or from another person's device. We could find no research on how frequently people do this or their reasons for doing it.

Existing password research shows that users adopt one or more of the strategies mentioned above, to help them manage their passwords. However, existing password research also shows that such risky password activities were not caused by the users' lack of security knowledge [8, 22]. Users tend to have stronger passwords for the accounts which they consider to be of high importance, and tend not to reuse passwords as much as they do for less-important accounts [9, 10]. These findings suggest that users have at least an implicit security-benefit trade-off in their mind, in relation to their password management behavior.

Tam, Glassman, and Vandenwauver [29] highlighted the security-benefit tradeoff in people's password management behaviour. In an online survey, respondents were asked to list their motivations (i.e. positive and negative thoughts) about five password management behaviours: choosing a password for the first time, changing a password, letting someone else use their password, taping their password next to the computer, and sharing a password with family, friends or co-workers. Content analysis of responses from a diverse sample of 133 people from the USA suggested that bad password management is about convenience: even though respondents were aware of the risks they were taking, they continue to engage in the risky behaviours for the sake of convenience.

However, the behaviours investigated in the Tam et al. [29] study did not cover the full range of password management behaviours. A more extensive set of password management behaviours need to be investigated to better understand how people perceive the risk, benefits and likelihood of undertaking these behaviours, the security-benefit trade-off. The study presented here aimed to do that.

3   Method

This study was conducted via an online survey distributed via Amazon's Mechanical Turk (MTurk) crowdsourcing service.

15 potentially risky password management behaviours were identified (*see* Table 1), based on common sense knowledge and an analysis of previous research on passwords. Although previous research has shown that people adjust their password behavior in relation to the type of account being protected, our preliminary work found that assessment of risk was not affected by type of password, so the statements did not include an account domain (e.g. password for online banking, social networking account etc.).

To assess whether the range of behaviours represented good coverage of the password management space, the set of statements with a brief explanation of the rationale and purpose of the survey was sent to a number of senior researchers working in the area of usable security. Very useful comments were received from three researchers and some adjustments were made to the final set of behaviours as a result.

In the survey, the same set of 15 password statements was presented three times: to assess respondents' perception of the risk of the behaviour, the benefit of the behaviour, and their likelihood of undertaking the behaviour. Respondents rated each statement on a scale from 1 (Not risky at all/no benefits at all/not likely at all) to 7 (Extremely risky/beneficial/likely), respectively. Order of presentation of the statements was counterbalanced between respondents.

To check whether respondents were likely to be susceptible to social desirability in their ratings, they also completed the short version of the Marlowe-Crowne Social Desirability Scale (MCSDS) [27] which consists of 10 items, such as "I like to gossip at times". Respondents make a forced choice of "yes" or "no" on these items, for five items, "yes" is the socially desirable answer and for the other five, "no" is the socially desirable answer. When scored appropriately this creates an overall susceptibility to social desirability score from 10 (highly susceptible) to 0 (not at all susceptible). This scale was presented to respondents as a short personality questionnaire.

The survey concluded with a short set of demographic questions.

Respondents

Respondents were recruited via MTurk. To ensure good quality and homogenous data, the inclusion criteria for respondents to have a 'Human Intelligence Task (HIT) approval rate' of higher than 90%, 'Number of HITs approved' to be greater than 100, and location as United States.

Table 1. Password Management Behaviour Statements (and short names)

Password management behaviour	Short name
Storing passwords on paper at home	Store/Paper
Storing passwords in your wallet/purse	Store/Wallet
Storing passwords in a password manager (PM) on a local computer	Store/PM/Local
Storing passwords in a PM on the cloud	Store/PM/Cloud
Storing passwords in a file on the cloud	Store/File/Cloud
Storing passwords in a draft email in an email client	Store/Email
Reusing the same password across accounts	Reuse
Using variations of the same password across accounts	Variations
Not changing passwords at regular time intervals	NotChange
Sharing passwords with work/study colleagues	Share/Colleagues
Sharing passwords with a close friend	Share/Friend
Sharing passwords with life partner/close family member	Share/Partner
Logging in to password protected account from a shared computer in a library	Log/Shared
Logging in to password protected account from a close friend's digital device	Log/Friend
Logging in to password protected account from life partner's/close family member's digital device	Log/Partner

Table 2. Demographics of the respondents

Age	Range: 22–74 years Mean: 43 years Standard deviation: 12.2
Education	No Schooling: 1 (.8%) High School: 39 (32.5%) Undergrad: 64 (53.3%) Graduate: 14 (11.7%) Doctorate: 2 (1.7%)
Employment	Student: 3 (2.5%) Employed: 95 (79.2%) Retired/Not Working: 22 (18.3%)

120 respondents provided adequate data for analysis. Table 2 summarises the demographic information of the respondents. All 120 respondents are from the United States. Their mean age was 43 years, with an age range from 22 to 74 years. The sample was close to balanced for gender, with 46.7% men and 53.3% women.

Procedure

The online survey was distributed via MTurk. Potential respondents who accepted the HIT were provided a brief introduction about the study and the survey link. In the introduction, potential respondents were briefed about the topic of the survey, and the approximate time required for the HIT (15 min, established via a pilot study). Potential respondents who accepted the HIT were informed that all information they provided would be confidential and that they would not be asked for any of their passwords, or any information that might compromise the security of their passwords. All respondents who completed the survey appropriately received 0.50 USD.

4   Results

Distributions of the ratings on the 7-point Likert items were not normally distributed, and in addition as there is controversy about whether parametric statistics should be used on Likert item data [18], non-parametric statistics were used in the data analysis.

Table 3 shows the median ratings and ranges for each of the password management behaviours, organized from the most likely to the least likely to be undertaken. It is noteworthy that the median Likelihood ratings only range from 1 (not at all likely) to 4 (the midpoint of the 7-point Likert item), whereas the median Risk ratings range from 7 (extremely risky) to 4 (the midpoint). The Benefits median ratings cover a broader of the 7-point item, from 1 (not at all beneficial) to 5 (above the midpoint).

Table 3. Median (and range) for the 15 password management behaviours for ratings of Likelihood, Benefit and Risk

Password management behaviour	Likelihood	Benefit	Risk
NotChange	4.0 (6)	2.0 (6)	5.0 (6)
Variations	4.0 (6)	4.0 (6)	5.0 (6)
Reuse	4.0 (6)	4.0 (6)	6.0 (5)
Share/Partner	4.0 (6)	3.0 (6)	4.0 (6)
Store/Paper	3.0 (6)	4.0 (6)	4.0 (6)
Store/PM/Local	3.0 (6)	5.0 (6)	4.0 (6)
Log/Partner	3.0 (6)	3.0 (6)	4.0 (6)
Store/PM/Cloud	2.0 (6)	5.0 (6)	4.0 (6)
Store/File/Cloud	2.0 (6)	4.0 (6)	5.0 (6)
Log/Friend	2.0 (6)	2.0 (6)	5.0 (6)
Log/Shared	1.0 (6)	2.0 (6)	6.0 (5)
Store/Email	1.0 (6)	2.0 (6)	6.0 (6)
Share/friend	1.0 (6)	2.0 (4)	5.0 (5)
Store/Wallet	1.0 (6)	2.0 (6)	6.0 (6)
Share/Colleague	1.0 (6)	1.0 (5)	7.0 (4)

To investigate the relationship between respondents' perceptions of the risk, benefits and likelihood of undertaking the behaviours, the correlations between these three perceptions are needed. However, if we conducted a correlation analysis on the 15 individual statements, this would result in 45 correlations, and a severe problem with Type 1 errors (a 225% change of finding a significant difference when there is no significant difference). Therefore, analyses were first conducted to investigate how respondents grouped their ratings of the statements. This had the additional interest of investigating whether respondents grouped the statements in terms of our *a priori* classification into Storing, Sharing, Logging in and Change behaviours.

Principal Components Analysis (PCA)[1] was conducted on the ratings for Likelihood, Benefits and Risk separately. Initially a PCA without rotation and with any number of components was conducted. In each case, a four-component solution was optimal, accounting for between 61% and 68% of the variance in the data. Not surprisingly, the grouping of statements on the four components was slightly different for the Likelihood, Benefits and Risk ratings. As we are interested in predicting participants' perception of their Likelihood of undertaking password management behaviours, we concentrated on the groupings in the Likelihood ratings. Therefore, a second PCA was conducted on the Likelihood ratings with oblimin rotation and a fixed four component solution. Table 4 shows the component loadings and the four components which emerged (a loading of more than 0.500 was taken as the minimum loading for a statement to load on to a particular component). Only two statements did not load on to one of the four components, Log/Shared and Share/Colleague. There was a clear and

---

[1] PCA does not require normality of distribution of data, so was appropriate for this data [15].

meaningful component structure, although the components were not exactly the same as our a priori classification. Component 1 is about logging on to different systems with one's password and sharing passwords behaviours (henceforth Log/Share), Component 2 is about digital storing of passwords (in password managers in a file, in the cloud or locally, henceforth Store/Digital), Component 3 is about password change behaviour (e.g. reusing the same password across accounts, using variations of passwords for different accounts and not changing passwords regularly, henceforth PW/Change) and Component 4 is about storing passwords in generally more "low tech" ways (e.g. in a wallet or purse, on paper at home or in an email, henceforth Store/LoTech).

Table 4. Components from the PCA for Likelihood ratings (component loading which determined components are marked in grey).

Component	Component Loading			
	Comp 1	Comp 2	Comp 3	Comp 4
Log/Partner	.811	-.122	.198	-.102
Log/Friend	.772	.007	.020	.116
Share/friend	.698	.150	-.141	.251
Share/Partner	.570	.153	.217	-.207
Store/PM/Cloud	.012	.830	.060	-.113
Store/File/Cloud	.010	.801	-.115	.226
Store/PM/Local	.009	.765	.092	-.650
NotChange	.078	-.027	.836	.010
Reuse	.042	.064	.809	.199
Variations	.163	.061	.778	.106
Store/Wallet	.193	-.008	-.116	.771
Store/Email	-.148	.101	.114	.671
Store/Paper	-.053	-.050	.237	.507
Log/Shared*	.266	-.171	.175	.500
Share/Colleague*	.376	.083	-.311	.475

* No loading over .500, so not included on any factor.

Mean scores were calculated for each of the components for the three different sets of ratings: Likelihood, Benefits and Risks. Spearman correlations were calculated between the three ratings for each of the components, these are summarized in Table 5. This shows that for each component there is a significant positive correlation between Likelihood and Benefit ratings. This makes sense, people are more likely to undertake behaviours which they see as having a benefit. However, for three of the four components (PW/Change was the exception and this was very close to a significant correlation with p = 0.06) there was a significant negative correlation between Likelihood and Risk ratings. Again, this makes sense, people do not undertake behaviours which they see as risky. And finally, for all four components there was a significant negative correlation between Benefit and Risk ratings. This is interesting, as people might well see things as beneficial but risky (which would create a positive correlation), but this was not the case with these participants.

However, how do Benefit and Risk balance in people's choices in undertaking password management behaviours? To more fully understand how Likelihood relates to Benefit and Risk, we need to control for the inter-relationships between Benefit and Risk (be they negative or positive) in predicting Likelihood. In other words, can we predict Likelihood from Benefit when we control for the effect of Risk and can we predict Likelihood from Risk when we control for Benefit. To explore this question further, we performed Spearman partial correlations between the ratings on each component (a linear regression analysis would have been even more appropriate, but the data do not meet the parametric requirements for that analysis).

Table 6 summarizes the partial correlation analysis. By comparing the percentage of the variance explained in the entries for the four components in Tables 5 and 6 we can see how Benefit and Risk balance in predicting Likelihood. For example, for the Log/Share component, 23.5% of the variance in Likelihood is accounted for by Risk (without considering the effect of Benefit) (Table 5). However, when the effect of Benefit is controlled for, this percentage decreases to 6.1% (Table 6). Thus removing the effect of Benefit almost removes the effect of Risk. On the other hand, 36.2% of the variance in Likelihood is accounted for by Benefit (without controlling for Risk). When Risk is controlled for, this variance decreases to 21.7%. The effect Risk modulates the effect of Benefit, but the effect of Benefit is still important. Thus for Log/Share, perception of Benefit is much more important than perception of Risk, and perception of Risk does not cancel out the effect of Benefit.

For the Store/Digital component, the effects of Risk and Benefit are much more balanced. The percentage of variance in Likelihood accounted for by Risk goes down from 25.8% to 13.2% when the effect of Benefit is controlled for. Similarly, the percentage of variance in Likelihood accounted for by Benefit goes down from 25.3% to 12.7% when Risk is controlled for. So in each case, the effect of Risk and Benefit approximately half the percentage of the variance in Likelihood accounted for, and do not remove the effect of the other.

The PW/Change component presents a very different picture. Risk only accounts for 2.9% of the variance in Likelihood, and this reduces to 0% when the effect of Benefit is controlled for. Whereas, Benefit accounts for 23.0% of the variance in Likelihood and this only reduces to 20.7% when the effect of Risk is controlled for. Thus Benefit is the key factor in PW/Change and Risk has very little influence in predicting Likelihood.

Table 5. Spearman correlations between the four component scores for Likelihood, Benefit and Risk ratings.

	Relationship	Correlation	% variance
Log/Share	Likelihood - Benefit	.602**	36.2
	Likelihood – Risk	−.485**	23.5
	Benefit – Risk	−.527**	27.8
Store/Digital	Likelihood - Benefit	.503**	25.3
	Likelihood - Risk	−.508**	25.8
	Benefit - Risk	−.454**	20.6
PW/Change	Likelihood - Benefit	.480**	23.0
	Likelihood - Risk	−.171	2.9
	Benefit - Risk	−.338**	11.4
Store/LoTech	Likelihood - Benefit	.477**	22.8
	Likelihood - Risk	−.451**	20.3
	Benefit - Risk	−.375**	14.1

** $p < 0.01$

Table 6. Spearman partial correlations between the four component scores for Risk, Benefit, and Likelihood ratings

Component	Relationship	Correlation	% Variance
Log/Share	Likelihood – Risk Controlling for Benefit	−.247**	6.1
	Likelihood – Benefit Controlling for Risk	.466**	21.7
Store/Digital	Likelihood - Risk Controlling for Benefit	−.363**	13.2
	Likelihood – Benefit Controlling for Risk	.356**	12.7
PW/Change	Likelihood – Risk Controlling for Benefit	−.011	0.0
	Likelihood - Benefit Controlling for Risk	.455**	20.7
Store/LoTech	Likelihood - Risk Controlling for Benefit	−.334**	11.2
	Likelihood – Benefit Controlling for Risk	.372**	13.8

** $p < 0.01$

Finally, the Store/LoTech component presents a very similar pattern to the Store/Digital component. The percentage of variance in Likelihood accounted for by Risk goes down from 20.3% to 11.2% when the effect of Benefit is controlled for. Similarly, the percentage of variance in Likelihood accounted for by Benefit goes down from 22.8% to

13.8% when Risk is controlled for. So in each case, the effect of Risk and Benefit approximately half the percentage of the variance in Likelihood accounted for, but do not remove the effect of the other.

All the Likelihood ratings are of course of people's statement of what they say they would do, not their actual behaviours. It is well-known what people say they do and what they actually do are different things, and that people may be answering in the way they think they should answer, the *social desirability bias* [23]. We are constantly being told that we should not reuse passwords and change them regularly, so people may say they do not reuse their passwords and do change them regularly, as it is the right thing to say, not what they actually do. In the case of perception of Risk and Benefit we are actually interested in people's perceptions, which should be less influenced by social desirability bias. However, to investigate whether the ratings in this study might have been affected by social desirability bias, the effect of social desirability was investigated for all three sets of ratings. Respondents were divided into low, medium and high susceptibility to social desirability bias on the basis of their Marlowe-Crowne Social Desirability Scale (MCSDS) based on the distribution of scores (low = MCSDS score 0-3; medium = MCSDS score 4–6; high = MCSDS score 7 – 10). Kruskal-Wallis H tests were conducted comparing the ratings on each component for the three groups of respondents. The results are summarized in Table 7. As predicted, there were no significant differences in ratings between the three MCSDS groups on Risk or Benefits that would have indicated that respondents were answering in the socially desirable way. The significant effect on Risk in relation to PW/Change showed that participants with medium MCSDS scores answered with higher ratings of Risk, than those with the low and high MCSDS scores, so this does not reflect a socially desirable effect. However, on the Likelihood component, there was a significant effect of social desirability, with respondents with high MCSDS scores answering with lower ratings of Likelihood of undertaking PW/Change behaviours (mean for high MCSDS respondents: 3.19; mean for medium MCSDS respondents: 4.18; mean for low MCSDS respondents: 4.39). Those who are more susceptible to social desirability gave significantly lower ratings for their Likelihood of undertaking PW/Change behaviour, such as reusing a password or using slight variations of a password or not changing a password. Thus, they are responding in the socially desirable way.

Table 7. Kruskal-Wallis H tests on respondents' MCSDS scores for Risk, Benefit, and Likelihood ratings on the four components of password management behaviour

Rating/Component	Log/Share	Store/Digital	PW/Change	Store/LoTech
Risk	H = 4.187	H = .365	H = 6.679	H = 5.446
	n.s.	n.s.	p = .035	n.s.
Benefit	H = 4.898	H = 2.733	H = 2.923	H = 3.425
	n.s.	n.s.	n.s.	n.s.
Likelihood	H = 2.404	H = 1.974	H = 7.424	H = 3.258
	n.s.	n.s.	p = .024	n.s.

5 Discussion and Conclusions

This study investigated why people undertake risky password management activities in spite of much available information advising them not to do so. In an online survey respondents were asked to rate their perception of the risk of a range of password management behaviours, the benefits of the behaviours, and the likelihood of undertaking the behaviours. To check whether respondents were susceptible to social desirability in these self-reported ratings, a short scale to measure susceptibility to social desirability, respondents also completed the Marlowe-Crowne Social Desirability Scale (MCSDS) [27].

The PCA conducted on the ratings of the likelihood of undertaking password management behaviours found four meaning components: Log/Share, Store/Digital, Password/Change and Store/LoTech. These were somewhat different from our *a priori* grouping of the behaviours. Partial correlation analysis showed different patterns of the importance of the ratings of Benefit and Risk in predicting people's ratings of the Likelihood of undertaking these four types of password management behaviours. For two of the components, Log/Share (logging on to shared computers and sharing passwords with friends or partners) and PW/Change (not changing passwords regularly, re-using passwords across accounts identically or with variations), the effect of Benefit is much more important than the effect of Risk, and perception of Risk did not cancel out the effect of Benefit. In the case of Log/Share respondents' ratings suggest that while they do perceive the risk, the benefits of the behaviours outweigh them. In the case of PW/Change, respondents do not perceive risk, and the likelihood of their undertaking the behavior is predicted only from their perception of the benefits. Thus, when people think of reusing/not changing/using passwords with slight variations, they consider only the benefits they gain, and neglect the risks. Finally, for the Store/Digital and Store/LoTech components, the effects of Risk and Benefit are almost equally balanced. Perception of Risk reduces the perception of Likelihood of undertaking the behavior by approximately half, and perception of Benefit does the same.

Thus, from this self-report data we begin to see that people's perceptions of risks and benefits of different password management behaviours are fall into several different patterns which might help share future information campaigns and education of account users. When to emphasise benefits and when to emphasise risks could be important. For example, in relation to password change behaviours, an emphasis on the idea that the benefits are not worth the risks might be more effective, as participants clearly thought the opposite.

A weakness of self-report data is that they are based on what people say they *would* do, and not what they *actually* do. To mitigate as much as possible for this effect, respondents to the survey also completed a short social desirability scale, the MCSDS. There was no effect of susceptibility to social desirability on Risk and Benefit ratings, but on Likelihood ratings for PW/Change component, so respondents might not be admitting to their poor password change/reuse habits, by answering in a socially desirable way. Further research is needed to validate people's actual behaviour in relation to their perceptions of risks, benefits, and likelihood of undertaking different password behaviours. Unfortunately, undertaking ecologically valid research on passwords is very difficult. Several studies have leveraged naturally occurring real world events to study password behaviour. For example, Renaud and Ramsay [21] used the fact that a church commissioned a new website which stored private information and therefore required password protection to study the usability of a new handwriting-driven authentication system. Shay et al. [25] used a major change the password policy of their university to investigate password management behaviour. One can imagine using such events to study the relationship between perceptions of risk and benefit in relation to a particular password management behaviour. An ideal situation would be one in which a large group of people were invited to change their password, but it was not obligatory. One could then ask the entire group to rate risk and benefits of password change and cross-tabulate this information with those who did or did not respond to the invitation and change their password. Another possibility would be to send out messages about the dangers of not changing one's password regularly and investigate whether this prompted password change. Unfortunately, such opportunities are very difficult to arrange. An alternative is to set up a study in which participants are asked to do a task which requires storing private information and therefore needs password protection, and use that to study aspects of password management behaviour. A "cover" task is much easier to imagine, but some aspects of password management would be much less accessible to the researchers – would participants need to change their password (perhaps a security breach could be included in the scenario, but the ethics of the study are now getting somewhat dubious), but whether participants re-used passwords, wrote them down or shared them with others would not be available to the researchers.

The study has a number of other limitations which need to be considered. First, the respondents were recruited from Mechanical Turk. MTurk is a crowdsourcing service where requesters post jobs to collect data from the pool of workers online for small payments [6]. Researchers have been using the MTurk system, to run their studies online for some time [16] and MTurk is often used to collect data for behavioural research [17]. MTurk have also been used on numerous occasions for password research [14, 30]. Studies comparing laboratory behaviour and MTurk behaviour have found no significant differences in results between the two sources of data [12, 28]. Nonetheless, there are lingering doubts about the validity of data from MTurk [11], for example whether MTurk workers are investing sufficient attention in the task, are not who they say they are (there have been recent rumours of large numbers of people from Venezuela using private VPN connections to the USA to pose as American MTurkers to earn money) or are to experienced at participating in research. We attempted to mitigate against the possibilities by requiring respondent to have high MTurk approval ratings and numbers of HITS approved. Nonetheless, repeating this study with a non MTurk sample would be very useful.

Another limitation also related to the MTurk sample is that all respondents say they are from the United States. Even if this is true, this may mean they are a multicultural sample, which we did not attempt to control for. Previous research has found cultural differences in password management behaviours [20], conducting the same study with different populations may reveal different results.

A further limitation is about the effect of account domains on password management behaviour. There are many different types of password (banking, email, social networking, etc.), and these may affect different management behaviours (reusing, storing, sharing, etc.) differently. We did start with the idea of asking all the statements about a range of different account domains, but the need to ask respondents to rate each statement three times (for risk, benefit and likelihood of undertaking) made this unreasonable as a HIT. A different strategy would have been to ask different respondents to rate risk, benefit and likelihood of undertaking the behaviours, but that would have lost the relationship between these ratings for individual respondents, which is very important. Further work needs to be undertaken on specific account domains to investigate whether the relationships between the three variables is different in different domains.

This study has explored the relationship between perceptions of the risks and benefits of different password management behaviours and people's self-reports of the likelihood that they will undertake these behaviours. Interesting patterns of responses were found which could be helpful in formulating information and education about password management.

Acknowledgements. We would like to thank the usable security experts who commented on our initial pool of statements and all the respondents to the survey for their time and effort.

References

1. Bonneau, J., Preibusch, S.: The password thicket: technical and market failures in human authentication on the web. Inf. Secur. **8**, 230–237 (2010)
2. Bonneau, J., Herley, C., Van Oorschot, P.C., Stajano, F.: The quest to replace passwords: a framework for comparative evaluation of web authentication schemes. In: Proceedings of the IEEE Symposium on Security and Privacy, pp. 553–567 (2012)
3. Bonneau, J., Herley, C., van Oorschot, P.C., Stajano, F.: Passwords and the evolution of imperfect authentication. Commun. ACM **58**, 78–87 (2015)
4. Boothroyd, V., Chiasson, S.: Writing down your password: does it help? In: Proceedings of 11th Annual Conference on Privacy, Security and Trust, PST 2013, pp. 267–274 (2013)
5. Brown, A.S., Bracken, E., Zoccoli, S., Douglas, K.: Generating and remembering passwords. Appl. Cogn. Psychol. **18**, 641–651 (2004)
6. Buhrmester, M., Kwang, T., Gosling, S.D.: Amazon's mechanical Turk: a new source of inexpensive, yet high-quality, data? Perspect. Psychol. Sci. **6**(1), 3–5 (2011)
7. Chiasson, S., Oorschot, P. van, Biddle, R.: A usability study and critique of two password managers. In: 15th USENIX Security Symposium, pp. 1–16 (2006)
8. Dhamija, R., Perrig, A.: Déjà Vu: A user study using images for authentication. In: Proceedings of the 9th Conference on USENIX Security Symposium, p. 4 (2000)
9. Florencio, D., Herley, C.: A large-scale study of web password habits. In: Proceedings of the 16th International Conference on the World Wide Web (WWW 2007), pp. 657–666 (2007)
10. Gaw, S., Felten, E.W.: Password management strategies for online accounts. In: Proceedings of the Second Symposium on Usable Privacy and Security (SOUPS 2006), pp. 44–66 (2006)
11. Hauser, D.J., Paolacci, G., Chandler, J.: Common concerns with MTurk as participant tool: evidence and solutions. In: Handbook of Research Methods in Consumer Psychology, pp. 1–43 (2018)
12. Horton, J.J., Rand, D.G., Zeckhauser, R.J.: The online laboratory: conducting experiments in a real labor market. Exp. Econ. **14**, 399–425 (2011)

13. Kaye, J. "Jofish": Self-reported password sharing strategies. In: Proceedings of the SIGCHI Conference on Human Factors in Computing Systems, pp. 2619–2622 (2011)
14. Kelley, P.G., et al.: Guess again (and again and again): measuring password strength by simulating password-cracking algorithms. In: Proceedings of the IEEE Symposium on Security and Privacy, pp. 523–537 (2012)
15. Kim, D., Kim, S.K.: Comparing patterns of component loadings: Principal Component Analysis (PCA) versus Independent Component Analysis (ICA) in analyzing multivariate non-normal data. Behav. Res. Methods 44(4), 1239–1243 (2012)
16. Kittur, A., Chi, E.H., Suh, B.: Crowdsourcing user studies with mechanical Turk. In: Proceedings of the SIGCHI Conference on Human Factors in Computing Systems, pp. 453–456. ACM (2008)
17. Mason, W., Suri, S.: Conducting behavioral research on Amazon's mechanical Turk. Behav. Res. Methods 44(1), 1–23 (2012)
18. Murray, J.: Likert data: what to use, parametric or non-parametric? Int. J. Bus. Soc. Sci. 4 (11), 258–264 (2013)
19. Notoatmodjo, G., Thomborson, C.: Passwords and perceptions. Conf. Res. Pract. Inf. Technol. Ser. 98, 71–78 (2009)
20. Petrie, H., Merdenyan, B.: Cultural and gender differences in password behaviors. In: Proceedings of the 9th Nordic Conference on Human-Computer Interaction, p. 9. ACM (2016)
21. Renaud, K., Ramsay, J.: Now what was that password again? A more flexible way of identifying and authenticating our seniors. Behav. Inf. Technol. 26, 309–322 (2007)
22. Riley, S.: Password security: what users know and what they actually do. Usability News 8 (1), 2833–2836 (2006)
23. Rosenthal, R., Rosnow, R.L.: Essentials of Behavioral Research: Methods and Data Analysis, vol. 2. McGraw-Hill, New York (1991)
24. Seitz, T., Hartmann, M., Pfab, J., Souque, S.: Do differences in password policies prevent password reuse? In: Proceedings of the 2017 CHI Conference Extended Abstracts on Human Factors in Computing Systems, pp. 2056–2063. ACM (2017)
25. Shay, R., et al.: Encountering stronger password requirements: user attitudes and behaviors. In: Proceedings of the Sixth Symposium on Usable Privacy and Security, pp. 1–20 (2010)
26. Singh, S., Cabraal, A., Demosthenous, C., Asthrink, G., Furlong, M.: Password sharing: implications for security design on social practice. In: Proceedings of the SIGCHI Conference on Human Factors in Computing Systems, pp. 895–904 (2007)
27. Strahan, R., Gerbasi, K.C.: Short, homogeneous versions of the Marlow-Crowne social desirability scale. J. Clin. Psychol. 28(2), 191–193 (1972)
28. Suri, S., Watts, D.J.: Cooperation and contagion in web-based, networked public goods experiments. PLoS ONE 6(3), e16836 (2011)
29. Tam, L., Glassman, M., Vandenwauver, M.: The psychology of password management: a tradeoff between security and convenience. Behav. Inf. Technol. 29(3), 233–244 (2010)
30. Ur, B., et al.: How does your password measure up? The effect of strength meters on password creation. In: Security 2012 Proceedings of the 21st USENIX Conference on Security Symposium, pp. 65–80 (2012)
31. Ur, B., et al.: "I Added '!' at the End to Make It Secure": observing password creation in the lab. In: Proceedings of the Eleventh Symposium on Usable Privacy and Security - SOUPS 2015, pp. 123–140 (2015)
32. William, J., Zviran, M., Haga, W.J.: Password security: an empirical study. J. Manag. Inf. Syst. 15, 161–185 (1999)

Social Engineering and Organisational Dependencies in Phishing Attacks

Ronnie Taib[1]([⊠]) [iD], Kun Yu[2] [iD], Shlomo Berkovsky[3] [iD],
Mark Wiggins[3] [iD], and Piers Bayl-Smith[3] [iD]

[1] Data61 – CSIRO, Eveleigh, Sydney, Australia
ronnie.taib@csiro.au
[2] University of Technology Sydney, Ultimo, Australia
kun.yu@uts.edu.au
[3] Macquarie University, Sydney, Australia
{shlomo.berkovsky,mark.wiggins,
piers.bayl-smith}@mq.edu.au

Abstract. Phishing emails are a widespread cybersecurity attack method. Their breadth and depth have been on the rise as they target individuals and organisations with increased sophistication. In particular, social engineering in phishing focuses on human vulnerabilities by exploiting established psychological and behavioural cues to increase the credibility of phishing emails. This work presents the results of a 56,000-participant phishing attack simulation carried out within a multi-national financial organisation. The overarching hypothesis was that strong cultural and contextual factors impact employee vulnerability. Thus, five phishing emails were crafted, based on three of Cialdini's persuasion principles used in isolation and in combination. Our results showed that Social proof was the most effective attack vector, followed by Authority and Scarcity. Furthermore, we examined these results in the light of a set of demographic and organisational features. Finally, both click-through rates and reporting rates were examined, to provide rich insights to developers of cybersecurity educational solutions.

Keywords: Cybersecurity · Phishing · Social engineering · Simulation · Behavioural study

1 Introduction

In 2017, the average global annualised cost of cybercrime was $11.7M per organisation, representing a 22.7% increase over the previous year [28]. Phishing and social engineering were identified as the second highest type of attack after malwares. Phishing is a scalable act of deception whereby impersonation is used to obtain information from a target individual [15]. In practical terms, this involves sending malicious emails with the intent to deceive recipients and lure them into disclosing personal information or revealing their credentials. To increase credibility, phishing emails often mimic the design and content of genuine emails sent by reputable companies, government agencies, or personal contacts of the recipient.

© IFIP International Federation for Information Processing 2019
Published by Springer Nature Switzerland AG 2019
D. Lamas et al. (Eds.): INTERACT 2019, LNCS 11746, pp. 564–584, 2019.
https://doi.org/10.1007/978-3-030-29381-9_35

The breadth and depth of phishing attacks has expanded continuously in both individual and organisational settings. For the individual, the most destructive consequences will be identity theft or financial loss through electronic banking services. However, a successful attack on a company or an organisation can let the attacker access precious enterprise data and potentially cause significant financial, reputational, and security damage [28]. Hence, governments and financial institutions are seen as lucrative targets for phishing.

To mitigate potential losses, employees are continuously being trained to identify and report phishing attacks. But, in this 'armament race', phishing attacks have also been evolving, deploying more complex technical and psychological approaches. While early phishing methods primarily capitalised on mass-mailing of dubious content, recent methods involve the tailoring of emails to the recipients (spear-phishing or whaling), spoofing (links and email address manipulation), and even large scale methods, such as website forgery [18]. The attack vectors have also broadened significantly, with SMS and phone phishing being quite common.

To craft a phishing attack, one of the method most widely utilised to manipulate people into responding involves social engineering [14]. Social engineering exploits established psychological and behavioural principles to increase the credibility of emails and lessen the motivation to engage in the careful evaluation of incoming information, thereby increasing the likelihood of a successful attack. Among the methods widely-encountered in phishing emails are established persuasive principles such as authority or scarcity, which are exploited for the purposes of deception rather than persuasion [17].

As phishing poses a threat to organisations and individual users, much effort has been devoted to developing tools that protect the recipients of phishing emails and help them mitigate phishing attacks. Most of these are automated tools that scan and filter incoming emails for suspicious content (keywords, grammatical mistakes), or technical issues (inconsistent links, spoofed metadata, illegitimate senders) typical for phishing attacks. While such filters achieve substantially high levels of accuracy, they also have limitations, leaving users vulnerable to targeted or not yet detected types of attacks. Therefore, there is a need to empower humans to detect malicious emails, helping them to mitigate the risks associated with phishing.

Appropriate responses to phishing emails can be achieved through education. It has been demonstrated that less technically knowledgeable users are more vulnerable to phishing attacks [22]. We posit that customised content and regime can improve current education delivery methods. To achieve such customisation at a large scale, it is crucial to first identify solid predictors of vulnerability. Past research has touched upon basic demographic factors such as age and gender, but with mixed results, potentially due to small size and methodological limitations [21].

In this paper, we present and analyse the results of a large-scale phishing attack simulation carried out by a multi-national financial organisation, as a follow-up of a qualitative study [7]. The simulation involved virtually all the employees of the organisation (more than 56,000 staff) and five variants of a phishing attack, each deploying a different social engineering strategy or a combination of strategies. The simulated phishing attack was initiated by the organisation in a drill-style exercise, and emails were sent directly to the employees' corporate email addresses. We captured the employee responses to the phishing emails: *reporting* the attack, *clicking* on the link in the phishing email, or *ignoring* the email.

We report the observed responses of the employees and analyse them with respect to multiple demographic features, organisational categories, and the deployed social engineering strategies. To the best of our knowledge, this is among the first works to look beyond demographic factors into the more specific employment and organisational factors at such a large-scale, diverse role- and age-wise, and multi-national corporate environment. The outcomes surface important insights that should be considered by developers of future, tailored phishing education programs.

In summary, the contributions of our work are three-fold. First, we highlight demographic segments and categories of employees that are vulnerable to phishing attacks. Second, we compare the deceptive power of several social engineering strategies deployed for phishing purposes. Third, we discuss how organisations can operationalise these findings to develop tailored education campaigns and help employees mitigate phishing attacks.

2   Related Work

Phishing is an activity covering a range of media, approaches, attack vectors, and objectives. Hence, it has been difficult to establish a common definition for phishing, although Lastdrager, based on the lexical and semantic analysis of the literature, coined the following: "*phishing is a scalable act of deception whereby impersonation is used to obtain information from a target*" [15]. In this paper, we focus on phishing emails in a context where the information obtained from the target is for a malicious intent, such as to gain financial benefit or compromise an organisation's data or reputation.

Phishing emails typically contain a link to a fraudulent website or include malicious attachments. They often utilise a range of techniques to reach their target and entice them to disclose information. Protective methods can broadly be categorised into technological (filtering emails based on spoofed sender address or known harmful content), organisational (policies and procedures for recruitment, technology use) and human (training and educating users) [12, 18]. While all three categories must be addressed holistically to protect an organisation [12], this paper centres on human factors and social engineering attack vectors.

Social engineering refers to deception methods leveraging psychological mechanisms that reduce suspicion and increase trust in the malicious content. Several studies have attempted to define a taxonomy of social engineering attacks. At the highest level, they can be deconstructed into type (e.g., using social attributes to persuade the targets to divulge information), channel (e.g., email) and operator (e.g., sent by a purported human), and applied through a specific attack vector such as phishing [14].

Seamlessly persuading a target to disclose information is the main pillar of phishing attacks. Hence, the six basic principles of influence, originally proposed by Cialdini [6] in the field of marketing and human persuasion, can also be applied for phishing as "misused weapons" [1, 17].

The six core principles of persuasion are:

- Reciprocation: people tend to feel indebted to someone who did them a favour, e.g., they will positively regard a notification of account expiry and may enter their credentials to correct it;
- Commitment and consistency: people tend to honour their commitments, e.g., reviewing the bill of hotel they previously booked;
- Social proof: people tend to trust a source if others are believed to also trust that source;
- Liking: people tend to trust more a person they know or some content that looks familiar to them;
- Authority: people tend to comply with authority, be it in the form of a person's position, or an organisation's logo.
- Scarcity: people tend to hesitate less and act sooner if they believe that there is a limit in amount or time to obtain something of interest.

Authority is identified as one of the most effective principles in a number of studies [1, 3, 5, 11, 19], while the other principles may be more influential, depending on other characteristics. For example, while scarcity has been demonstrated to influence younger people, reciprocation is likely to influence older people [19]. Furthermore, the use of these principles by attackers is evolving over time, with an increasing use of scarcity, whereas reciprocation and social proof have been declining in usage [27].

Other efforts were made to combine Cialdini's principles with psychological profiling, e.g., the Big Five model [2], or with Gragg's psychological triggers and Stajano et al.'s principles of scams, leading to the principles of persuasion in social engineering [11]. The latter work lists and analytically compares the principles outlined by Cialdini, Gragg, and Stajano et al., showing that the three sets overlap for the authority and social proof principles, where distraction (scarcity) and authority were the most effective principles [10]. Combining the results from these studies, we selected social proof, scarcity and authority as the principles to deploy in the present study.

Considering the 'scalable' part of the phishing definition, we note that most of the existing studies are limited to a few hundred participants, often university students [4, 5, 8, 9, 19, 20, 23, 25]. A few studies included larger samples, such as Jagatic et al. with 1,731 participants in total (although only about 600 participated in the phishing component of their study) [13]. Mohebzada et al. engaged more than 10,000 students, staff and alumni [16]; however, again in a university environment. Sheng et al. collected 1,001 user responses, but noted that the use of crowdsourcing might have impacted the diversity of their sample population.

The only study using a large corporate-type of population has been reported by Williams et al. [26]. They used the results of nine phishing simulations administered to 62,000 public service employees, although they did not have access to the demographic characteristics of their participants. They focused on urgency and authority in isolation and showed that their application increased the effectiveness of spear phishing attacks. Our study extends [26] by also focusing on Social proof, as we posit that, in organisations, with a strong employee-identification culture, users may be at greater risk of Social proof, rather than of other types of attacks. Moreover, we examine the correlations between persuasion principles, demographic characteristics, and organisational parameters of the employees to test the links between multiple factors affecting vulnerability to phishing attacks.

Overall, while there has been some consideration of demographics in previous research, the results are inconclusive. In the context of gender, some studies report females as more vulnerable than males [8, 13, 19, 22], while others report the opposite [16]. In the context of age, younger participants appear most at risk [8, 13, 22], at least when exposed to scarcity-based material [19]. However, contradictory results are also reported, whereby young participants are less likely to fall victim [16]. To the best of our knowledge, only one study examined the links to corporate variables, namely tenure [4]. As expected, tenure positively correlated with age, but potentially, was a stronger predictor of phishing vulnerability. Correlations were negative, such that on average, more years of service were associated with a decrease in vulnerability.

Two main methodologies were used in previous research. Role-play studies typically present images of phishing emails to users and seek respondents' intended actions, e.g., clicking the link or deleting the email [9, 22, 23]. By contrast, drill-style studies send actual phish emails to participants and monitor their responses [4, 9, 13, 19, 25]. In some cases, participants were fully aware of the study taking place, e.g., because they installed specific monitoring software on their machine [19], while, in other cases, they were completely unaware of being used as participants [16], which caused post-study discussions [13]. To the best of our knowledge, the ecological validity of the role-play methods has not been fully investigated in prior works. Hence, drill-style studies with minimal warning seem to offer the highest levels of validity. Such warnings can materialise as a general email sent to an organisation, yet keeping in mind that a significant proportion of recipients may simply ignore the email [16].

3   Objectives

Building on existing research, this paper is part of a holistic approach to cybersecurity, aimed at empowering end-users to detect and respond to phishing attacks. We posit that the one-size-fits-all education approach, commonly used in large organisations misses its objective because it does not address the various needs and attitudes of employees. Hence, the overarching motivation of our work is to design tailored educational material crafted with various user profiles in mind.

However, the first step in designing such tailored education approaches lays in understanding the dependencies between demographic characteristics as well as organisational roles of the employees, and their vulnerability to various types of phishing attacks. To this end, in this work we set out to validate several hypotheses:

- Different age groups fall victim to different types of persuasion, and therefore, should receive educational content focusing on these specific types;
- Vulnerability decreases with tenure as employees become more familiar with the processes and structure of the organisation, and therefore, they are less likely to be vulnerable to an attack;
- Employees with managerial responsibility are more likely to exert caution than non-managers. Hence, the motivational messages for these groups would vary, e.g. focusing on the company image for manager, or on the consequences of non-compliance for non-managers.

Validating these dependencies would allow us to quantify individual or group-based vulnerability of employees to phishing attacks. In turn, not only this allows to tune the sensitivity of cybersecurity technologies, e.g., of the phishing filter deployed in email clients, but also the educational campaigns and cybersecurity trainings can be tailored to the specific risks faced by the target group of employees.

4 Experiment Setting

We first present the experimental setting, simulated phishing attack, data collection methods, and the evaluation metrics that were used in this study.

4.1 Participants

In this work, we carried out a controlled, organisation-wide phishing simulation. The organisation at hand is a multi-national financial institution operating in more than 30 countries. The present study included response data from 20 countries (Australia, Cambodia China, Fiji, Hong-Kong, India, Indonesia, Japan, Lao, New-Zealand, Papua New Guinea, Philippines, Samoa, Singapore, Solomon Islands, Taiwan, UK, USA, Vanuatu, Viet Nam), with data from 10 countries excluded due to low numbers. The organisation regularly conducts internal simulations and education campaigns with the intention of raising employee awareness of information security breaches, cybersecurity attacks, and phishing emails. As the attack simulation reported in this paper was, in part, conducted for research purposes, the experimental design and data collection methods were reviewed and approved by an accredited national Human Research Ethics Committee independent of the research team.

The reported phishing simulation was sent to more than 56,000 recipients from all departments and business units of the organisation in October 2017 and results collected over the following two weeks. Descriptive statistics of the demographic segments and employment categories are provided in Table 1. As the social engineering strategy was chosen randomly for each participant, the distribution of strategy type is uniform. In the context of gender, there were approximately equal numbers of female and male participants. The data were binned into three similar-sized age groups. For tenure, we used industry standards of 5 and 10 years to group the employees. As can be expected in most organisations, the distribution of managers versus non-managers is not balanced. Only 15% of the participants were managers (that is, had employees reporting to them), while 85% were non-managers.

Table 1. Distribution of the participants (total N = 56,365).

Feature	Distribution	Count	% population
Social engineering strategy	Social proof	11,268	20.0%
	Scarcity	11,267	20.0%
	Authority	11,285	20.0%
	Social proof + scarcity	11,281	20.0%
	Social proof + authority	11,264	20.0%

(*continued*)

Table 1. (*continued*)

Feature	Distribution	Count	% population
Gender	Female	28,430	50.4%
	Male	27,935	49.6%
Age	18–31	19,502	34.6%
	32–40	19,354	34.3%
	41+	17,509	31.1%
Tenure	0–5 years	32,032	56.8%
	5–10 years	11,714	20.8%
	10+ years	12,619	22.4%
Manager	Managers	8,376	14.9%
	Non-managers	47,989	85.1%

4.2   Methods

We deployed five variants of phishing email, all conforming with three of Cialdini's core principles of persuasion – *social proof*, *scarcity*, and *authority* – or their combinations. As explained earlier, these principles were selected based on the combination of prior works. Moreover, it can be noted that the other three principles – reciprocity, consistency, and liking – were considered less appropriate in the context of our simulation because (i) the one-off nature of phishing emails naturally could not leverage existing relationships and social ties between the sender and the recipient; and (ii) the risk of compromising the reputation of real employees or managers precluded us from using real names or roles within the organisation. As Cialdini's principles of persuasion are used in phishing attacks to deceive email recipients rather than to persuade them, we will refer to these hereafter as *social engineering strategies*.

In addition to the three core principles, we also considered two combinations of principles: *social proof + authority*, and *social proof + scarcity*. The authority+scarcity combination was considered but not studied, due to its low compatibility and less realistic outcome, when co-located in the same email. Consequently, we produced five variants of phishing emails. To verify their alignment with Cialdini's principles and with the organisation's corporate communication style, the crafted phishing emails were reviewed and iteratively revised by five human-computer interaction researchers and the security team of the organisation. The input of the latter ensured that the simulated phishing emails were broadly consistent with real phishing emails that had been previously detected at the organisation. Finally, minor typographic errors, grammatical mistakes, and language inconsistencies were intentionally introduced and uniformly distributed amongst the emails.

All of the emails were sent from an external email address with a domain name that closely resembles the organisation's, but has a minor typographic error. All the emails included a URL linking to the same domain. Although the domain name modification was minor, it was expected to be readily recognised by the employees of the organisation, frequently visiting web and intranet sites hosted by the original domain of the organisation. The emails were white-listed by the mail servers of the organisation and, as such, all reached their recipients.

Key excerpts from the five phishing emails are copied verbatim in the blocks below. For illustration purposes, we highlight those parts of the email that are associated with the deployed social engineering strategies. Linda Gardner, who is signed on the emails, is a fictitious name and not an employee of the host organisation.

Social proof

Check out this offer: Dinner carnival is coming! – based on recent survey, **more than 80% of our staff like** *to dine out with friends and family, so we have been negotiating with high-end local restaurants to bring you a meal discounted at 95% between now and the end of next week. I hope you'll take-up this unique chance to enjoy the delicious food and lovely dining environment.*

So far **over 100 staffs have enjoyed this discount.** *Please check [LINK] to find out which of your local restaurants are available for this nice offer and register accordingly.*
Linda Gardner

Scarcity

Check out this offer: Dinner carnival is coming! – we have been negotiating with high-end local restaurants to bring you a meal discounted at 95% between now and the end of next week. So I hope you'll take-up this unique opportunity to enjoy the delicious food and lovely dining environment.

However, opportunities are limited - only the **first 200 registrations** *will be able to secure the offer. So, hurry up and register at [LINK]*

The **registration may end anytime in the next couple of hours** *before COB today, so be quick!*
Linda Gardner

Authority

The Life Balance Team has announced an annual Dinner carnival. Based on the findings of **Prof. Clark** *and the Life Balance team, we want to be the perfect work-life balance place. We have been negotiating with high-end local restaurants to bring you a meal discounted at 95%. So, we suggest you take-up this unique chance to enjoy the delicious food and lovely dining environment.*

We strongly recommend *you check [LINK] to find out which of your local restaurants are available for this offer and register accordingly.* **This is an organisational priority for us,** *so we expect you to take part.*
Linda Gardner
Chief Officer

Social proof + scarcity

Dinner carnival is coming! – based on recent survey, **more than 80% of our staff** *like to dine out with friends and family, so we have been negotiating with high-end local restaurants to bring you a meal discounted at 95% between now and the end of next week. So, I hope you'll take-up this unique opportunity to enjoy the delicious food and lovely dining environment.*

*However, **opportunities are limited** - only the first **200 registrations** will be able to secure the offer. So, hurry up and register at [LINK]*
Linda Gardner

Social proof + authority
*The Life Balance Team has announced an annual Dinner carnival. Based on the findings of **Prof. Clark** and the Life Balance team, we want to be the perfect work-life balance place. Based on a recent survey, **more than 80% of our staff** like to dine out with friends and family, so we have been negotiating with high-end local restaurants to bring you a meal discounted at 95%. So, we suggest you take-up this unique chance to enjoy the delicious food and lovely dining environment.*

*So far **over 100 staffs have enjoyed this discount**. **We strongly recommend** you check link to find out which of your local restaurants are available for this offer and register accordingly. **This is an organisational priority for us**, so we expect you to take part.*
Linda Gardner
Chief Officer

4.3   Metrics

Upon receiving the emails, each participant could respond in three ways. The first would be to click on the link, virtually falling victim to the phishing attack. This is the undesired outcome of the simulation. In this case, the participant would be re-directed to an internal educational page articulating that the email was sent as part of a phishing attack simulation conducted by the organisation. Of course, clicking on a link may not result in users necessarily disclosing their credentials, but they are still vulnerable to drive-by download malware on some websites and other types of attacks which could compromise the organisation's security. Therefore, consistent with other research studies we considered clicking on a link as a risky behavioural response.

The second response, which is the desired outcome of the simulation, would be to report the email as a phishing attack. In this case, the participant would be automatically notified by email that they successfully recognised the attack and passed the phishing simulation. The host organisation considers reporting to be far superior to ignoring attacks because it can lead to swift protection of the whole organisation thanks to a snowball effect. From a psychological standpoint, it also reflects a totally different attitude: a healthy appreciation of the risk and locus of control, rather than perceiving the threat severity of phishing attacks as low.

The third response is essentially not to respond – neither report nor click – or to ignore the phishing email. It may reflect an undesirable condition where reporting is not performed because a user is 'unsure', which highlights flaws in the promotion of 'there is no dumb question when it comes to cyber'. This aspect could not be ascertained through our study data, and furthermore, the lack of reporting may not inform us as to the efficiency of social engineering attacks, so we treat it as an undesired outcome.

It should be noted that the responses of clicking and reporting are, in principle, not mutually exclusive. In fact, a small portion of participants reported phishing attacks after viewing the educational content. However, in the following analysis we discard this minor overlap.

Following this logic, we define two metrics allowing us to quantify the performance of a group of participants in response to a phishing attack. The metrics that quantify the success of the attack on a group and the success of a group in mitigating the attack are *Click Rate* (*CR*) and *Report Rate* (*RR*), respectively. More formally, let us denote by G_c and G_r the two subgroups in the entire population of phishing attack recipients G, who clicked on or reported the attack, respectively. *CR* and *RR* are computed as

$$CR = \frac{|G_c|}{|G|} \quad RR = \frac{|G_r|}{|G|}$$

where $|\cdot|$ denotes the number of employees within a group. Essentially, these metrics quantify the portion of group members, who clicked on or reported the attack.

5   Results

In this section, we present the results of the phishing attack simulation. Consistent with the aims of the study, we analyse the differences observed with respect to a number of demographic and organisational categories, and refine these findings by considering the effectiveness of various social engineering strategies. Therefore, as appropriate when analysing significant associations between categorical variables, Chi Square statistical tests were used for all comparisons and are noted in the diagrams below as * for $p < .05$ and ** for $p < .01$. No marking indicates that the difference was not statistically significant, $p > .05$. When more than two groups are compared, we initially report the combined Chi Square, before presenting further analysis where each group is tested against the rest of the sample (i.e., all other groups combined).

5.1   Overall Click Through and Reporting Rates

The overall headcount of the organisation at the time of the study was 57,089 employees. After filtering errors and missing values, we obtained reliable data related to the simulated phishing attack from 56,365 participants, which accounts to 98.7% of total employees and will be considered as the overall number of participants in the analyses reported below.

In total, 6,922 participants (*CR* = 12.28% of the employees), clicked on the phishing link and virtually fell victim to the attack. On the other hand, 12,219 participants (*RR* = 21.68% of the employees) reported the received email as a phishing attack, thus, successfully having passed the simulation, as shown in Fig. 1. The remaining 68.87% of employees did not respond actively to the simulation. Overall, we observe that the number of reports was 76% higher than the number of clicks, generally indicating a positive preparedness of the organisation to mitigate phishing attacks.

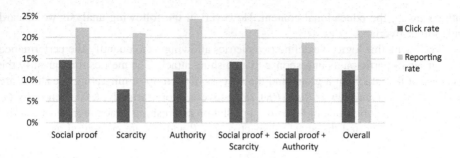

Fig. 1. Overall click-through and reporting rates.

Comparing the effectiveness of the three core social engineering strategies – Social proof, Scarcity, and Authority – we observe that the click-through rates differ substantially across these strategies, with Scarcity being perceived least credible ($CR =$ 7.8%), followed by Authority ($CR = 12.0\%$) and Social proof ($CR = 14.6\%$). Hence, the latter is 87.2% and 21.7% higher than the CRs of Scarcity and Authority, respectively. Despite the different click-through rates, the obtained reporting rates RR of the three core strategies are comparable, all placed within the 21.0–24.4% range.

We posit that this might be explained by the higher popularity of phishing emails leveraging Authority and Scarcity [26]. Therefore, the email recipients are familiar with this types of attack and are more likely to recognise them, as reflected by the lower CR of these strategies. In essence, a combination of the CR and RR results shows that *Social proof is the most effective social engineering strategy*, followed by Authority, and then by Scarcity.

Combining Social proof with the other social engineering strategies, does not provide an additive effect over and above a single strategy. The addition of either Scarcity or Authority to the Social proof strategy slightly compromises the credibility of the phishing emails, such that their respective CRs drop by 13.0% and 2.3% in comparison to the CR of Social proof deployed in isolation. Similarly, the RR decreases slightly when combining social engineering strategies (1.7% and 15.6%) in comparison to the RR of Social proof in isolation. In summary, we observe that the *addition of recognisable strategies decreases the effectiveness* of the phishing emails.

5.2 Gender

In contrast to previous studies [7, 13, 19, 22], the analysis of gender differences (Fig. 2) shows that there were no significant differences between female and male participants' click-through rates. Our population sample is much larger and more diverse in terms of age, occupation and country of origin than in prior research, so our result may have higher ecological validity within the general population. In terms of reporting phishing emails (Fig. 3), males were significantly more likely to report phishing emails than females, except for the Social proof + Scarcity attack strategy.

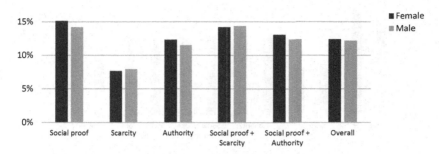

Fig. 2. Click-through rates per gender.

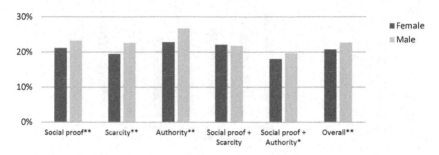

Fig. 3. Reporting rates per gender.

5.3 Age

Considering the differences observed with respect to the participants' age (Fig. 4), significant differences were evident between groups overall for all strategies except Scarcity and Authority.

Further analysis of each group versus the rest of the population provides more insights: the 41+ group is significantly more likely to fall victim to Social proof attacks than the other employees ($p < .01$). For Social proof + Scarcity, all age groups are significantly different from the rest of the employees ($p < .05$). Both the 18–31 and 41+ groups are significantly less likely to click than the rest of the population under the Social proof + Authority attack, but this is mostly due to an abnormally high click-through rate for the middle group.

In the context of reporting phishing emails (Fig. 5), we observe significant differences ($p < .01$) between the different age groups for Social proof, Scarcity, and overall. Further analyses show that the 18-31 group is significantly more likely to report Social proof ($p < .01$) or Scarcity ($p < .05$) attacks, while the group of 41+ employees are significantly less likely to report phishing using the same strategies (all $p < .01$, except Scarcity for 18–31: $p < .05$).

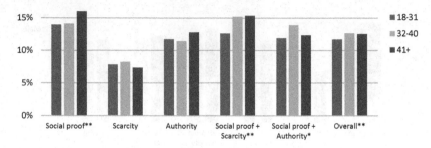

Fig. 4. Click-through rates per age.

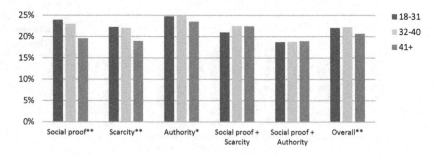

Fig. 5. Reporting rates per age.

These results indicate that *older participants are more vulnerable to phishing* than others. We posit that this observation might be attributed to lower a familiarity of the older employees with IT practices within the organisation and changes in modern technologies in general. This outcome is consistent with previous research examining phishing vulnerability of older adults [14].

5.4 Tenure

We now turn to the differences observed with respect to the number of years of service (tenure). While previous demographics-based analyses are applicable to the society at large, the following ones may be more relevant to large-scale organisations with established hierarchical structures.

Employees were grouped into three categories, including tenure of up to 5 years, 5 to 10 years, and more than 10 years (Fig. 6). We observed significant differences overall ($p < .01$) for all attack strategies. Further analyses also reveal significant differences between each group and the rest of the population for all types of attacks, apart from the 5–10 years of tenure employees and the rest for Scarcity or Social proof + Authority. In other words, the up to 5 years of tenure group is significantly more likely to click through than the rest of the population.

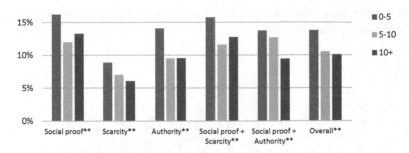

Fig. 6. Click-through rates per tenure (3 groups).

This is an interesting finding when contrasted with the age-focussed results discussed previously. Age in isolation may not be a reliable indicator of vulnerability, since organisational interventions are likely to override their effects. For example, regular training and awareness campaigns potentially decrease the vulnerability of staff during their first few years at the company, regardless of their age when joining. We tested this hypothesis further by grouping tenure into 9 comparable-size bins as shown in Fig. 7. This analysis allows us to isolate the group of new employees in their first year with the organisation. These employees are significantly more likely to click on phishing emails (overall and for each strategy: p < .01) than other staff.

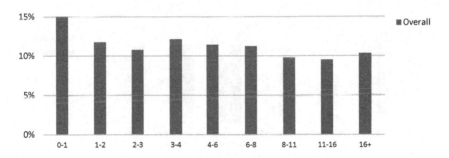

Fig. 7. Click-through rates per tenure (9 groups).

In the context of reporting rates (Fig. 8), the trend holds for newer employees whereby they were less likely to report the phishing email than the rest of the staff. However, while employees with longer tenure exhibited a fairly consistent behaviour for click-through rates, this time, the group with 5 to 10 years of tenure exhibited significantly more reporting than the rest of the population for all types of attacks (p < .01) except for Scarcity, where all groups were equally likely to report.

In summary, we conclude that *new employees (and, specifically, those in their first year of employment) are more vulnerable to phishing* than employees who have been with the organisation for a longer period of time. We posit that this can be explained by the lower familiarity of the former with the organisation's emails and communication styles. This may hamper their ability to distinguish between genuine emails and phishing attacks, hence, increasing their vulnerability. This is consistent with the results obtained in prior literature [16].

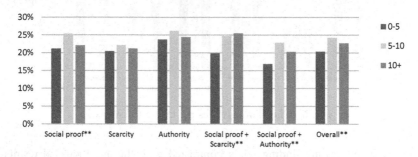

Fig. 8. Reporting rates per tenure (3 groups).

5.5 Managerial Status

Another important organisational feature is the manager/non-manager status, communicating whether other employees report to the phishing email recipient (Fig. 9). We observed that managers were significantly less likely to click on phishing emails overall and for all types of strategies ($p < .01$, except Authority $p < .05$) with the exception of Social proof and Social proof + Authority ($p > .05$).

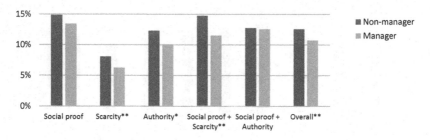

Fig. 9. Click-through rates per managerial status.

For reporting rates (Fig. 10), managers were significantly more likely to report phishing emails overall, and also for all types of attacks ($p < .01$, except for Scarcity and Social proof + Authority: $p < .05$).

We conclude that *non-managers are more vulnerable to phishing attacks* than managers. This outcome may be explained by the higher familiarity of managers with the organisation, which allows them to better recognise and mitigate phishing attacks.

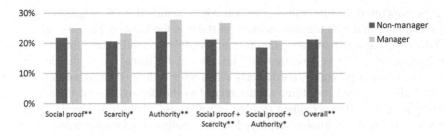

Fig. 10. Reporting rates per managerial status.

6 Discussion

We conducted a study of phishing attacks and vulnerability within a financial organisation. This study is uniquely large and diverse, with staff spanning across 20 countries and several cultures. It focuses on a number of demographic and organisational features, as well as on the social engineering strategies deployed. The main insights are:

- Females and males did not differ in their click-through rates of phishing emails, which contrasts previous research carried out with smaller or less diverse population samples. However, male employees demonstrated a higher rate of reporting phishing emails than females.
- Employees aged over 41 were generally more vulnerable to phishing attacks than other employees. They were particularly vulnerable to attacks deploying the Social proof strategy, as identified from the highest click-through rate and lowest reporting rate. Furthermore, employees younger than 32 years old were less vulnerable to all phishing attacks involving Social proof, while the employees aged between 32 and 40 were more likely to be the victimised by phishing attacks with combined strategies involving Social proof.
- Employees who have been with the organisation for fewer than five years (and, particularly, less than a year) were more vulnerable than others to phishing attacks, and also exhibited the lowest reporting rate, which was evident across all the social engineering strategies. Overall, employees who have worked in the organisation for a long period (more than 10 years) were less likely to fall victim to phishing attacks of any kind, although they may not report suspicious emails as frequently as those employees who have worked for a moderate time (5–10 years).
- Non-managers were more vulnerable to phishing attacks than managers. This finding was also observed across the board and did not depend on the social engineering strategy deployed.
- Generally, phishing attacks utilising the social proof strategy were more effective and dangerous than attacks using other strategies. This was clearly and evidently observable for all the analysed groups and organisational roles of participants.

While the first two findings related to the demographic factors reaffirm or nuance some previously reported works, the latter three, which are relevant to large organisations, are novel and original. The two findings related to tenure and manager status can be supported by the same common logic: familiarity of employees with the organisation – be it with the communication styles or the leadership team – allows them to better distinguish between genuine and fraudulent emails, and, thereby mitigate phishing attacks. We believe that this insight can be taken up by the designers of corporate training programs, particularly when on-boarding or targeting new staff.

We also observed insightful results related to the deployment of the social engineering strategies. It was evident that the effectiveness of phishing emails depends on the social engineering strategy deployed, with socially-driven manipulations being the most effective method, noticeably dominating both scarcity- and authority-driven attacks. We attribute these differences to prior familiarity of the participants and phishing email recipients in general with the deployed strategies. For example, authority-driven phishing attacks that pretend to be sent by the police, government agencies, or large companies like Apple or Microsoft, are relatively common. Likewise, numerous attacks use fraudulent scarcity-driven manipulations like "special prices for the day" or "lucky winner of a draw". We believe that, due to their sheer popularity, participants are naturally trained to recognise and mitigate such attacks better than the more uncommon social manipulations. In contrast, mentioning in the email that other employees of the organisation accepted an offer seems to be an effective means to deceive the recipients. A potential explanation might be that employees with a strong identification with the organisation look to decrease uncertainty by conforming to what others in their group are doing (i.e., self-categorisation theory [24]), and may be particularly susceptible to social manipulations. In other terms, companies with high organisational identification of employees may be more vulnerable to social proof than other types of deception.

The diversity observed in the vulnerability of various demographic segments and organisational roles calls for tailoring of future phishing education programs. For example, junior employees need to receive more encompassing phishing education than employees at the management levels. It is also evident that different social engineering strategies need to be emphasised for younger and older employees. Our findings undermine the validity of the current, one-size-fits-all phishing education campaigns and highlight the emergent need for group tailored (or even personalised) solutions, which can cater to the specific needs and weaknesses of every employee.

Several potential limitations of our work should be raised. The first refers to the reasonably low *a priori* effectiveness of the simulated phishing attack. The study did not tailor the phishing emails to group or individual characteristics of the recipients using demographic or organisational data available, which would have amounted to spear-phishing attacks. This was done in order not to compromise any departments within the organisation and to maintain the ecological validity of the study, because detailed personal information is typically not available at large scale to outside attackers. Hence, the level of attack effectiveness of our emails was deliberately limited.

The second limitation to be mentioned refers to the somewhat limited response rate of the simulation. As mentioned earlier, less than 35% of participants actively responded to the emails, i.e., clicked on the phishing link or reported the attack. This limitation is alleviated, however, by the large sample size of more than 56,000 participants. Therefore, we were able to obtain solid empirical evidence and analyse differences between participants with respect to social engineering strategies, as well as demographic and organisational factors.

The third potential limitation refers to the scope of the study, which involved a single phishing attack and was carried out in a single organisation operating in the financial sector. Again, we alleviate this limitation by the large sample size of the phishing attack simulation, which ensures representativeness with respect to a variety of countries, age groups, and other demographic and organisational factors. Furthermore, we should note the broad range of positions filled by the participants, including business/data analysts, financial advisers, administration staff, call centre staff, insurance specialists, and many more. Therefore, we believe that our findings are generalisable and will be also valid in other large organisations and economy sectors.

7 Conclusion

Phishing attacks have evolved over the last two decades into powerful and dangerous cybersecurity weapons. They are exploited in a multitude of cyber-attack scenarios, targeting organisations, companies, and individuals, and can be encountered in a range of domains and applications. While numerous technical solutions to phishing attacks have been developed, we argue that human users are one of the weakest links in the cybersecurity chain. Consequently, we believe in the emergent need to educate users and upgrade them into an active defence against cyber-attacks.

Large organisations rely on phishing simulations as an awareness tool and complement for a typical annual training. However, such a single point of measurement is fairly artificial and "ticking compliance boxes" does little to change users' attitudes and behaviours towards cybersecurity. While resisting the appeal of persuasive content may be difficult, a reliance on corporate protection can be reduced by emphasising locus of control, and conversely decreasing over-confidence in other users by managing threat appraisal. Our work departs from traditional, generic, cybersecurity educational content by identifying combinations of demographic and organisational factors that are most likely to lead to improvements in performance.

Indeed, everyone is different, and the same attack may be easily mitigated by some while victimising others. This brings forward the question of individual differences in phishing vulnerability, which we set out to investigate in this work. Our overarching hypothesis is that strong culture and context factors impact employee vulnerability. To this end, we conducted a large-scale phishing attack simulation focussing on demographic and organisational differences affecting the vulnerability to phishing, also considering the social engineering strategies deployed by phishing emails. The study was carried out within a real work environment of a multi-national financial organisation and involved more than 56,000 participants.

Our results surfaced several valuable insights related to the vulnerability of different participants to phishing attacks. While previous works linked differences in phishing vulnerability to demographic factors, to the best of our knowledge, this is among the first works to identify differences with respect to organisational features in a large corporate environment. This work also examined the deceptive potential of established persuasive strategies applied for phishing attack purposes. Finally, our work considered both click-through rates and reporting rates, which paves the way for the development of the next generation of phishing awareness tools and cybersecurity educational solutions.

One immediately realisable finding that stems from our work concerns the need to tailor or personalise future cybersecurity education programs. The differences observed between the participants clearly show the strengths and weaknesses of various segments of employees. Hence, it is beneficial to focus education on the specific weaknesses of each and every employee or group of employees, to better cater to their vulnerabilities. This task is not easy to accomplish, but it has the tremendous potential to improve the efficacy of educational programs and the individual strategies for mitigating phishing attacks.

This naturally leads to future research directions, one of which targets the evaluation of such tailored phishing education programs. We expect their efficacy to be superior to the efficacy of the non-tailored, one-size-fits-all education programs that are currently deployed by many organisations. This, however, can only be validated in a follow-up user study, comparing the observed changes in the responses to phishing attacks. We will embark on this research after developing the new education program.

Another promising direction refers to the use of alternative statistical models and approaches to data analysis, such as the generalised linear model frameworks and machine learning methods, to better predict the most relevant educational material for each employee or group of employees, based on their demographics, organisational and situational characteristics. Some of these characteristics are likely to evolve over time. Therefore, the learning mechanisms should be able to dynamically process this data. Such information is available in most organisations deploying phishing simulations, since they run the studies regularly, providing measures of vulnerability and capability to report over time.

Finally, we plan to incorporate psychological factors into the predictive model. Although high predictive accuracy can be achieved using behavioural features, we posit that another source of valuable information is the recipient's psychological model. For example, psychological factors, such as locus of control, impulsivity, and perceived threat severity have the potential to influence the decision-making processes and behaviour of the email recipients. In the future, we will construct psychological models of the employees and incorporate them into predictive models.

References

1. Akbar, N.: Analysing persuasion principles in phishing emails. University of Twente (2014)
2. Alkış, T.: (12) The impact of individual differences on influence strategies. ResearchGate. https://www.researchgate.net/publication/282720170_The_impact_of_individual_ differences_on_influence_strategies. Accessed 16 Feb 2018
3. Atkins, B., Huang, W.: A Study of social engineering in online frauds. Open J. Soc. Sci. **01** (03), 23–32 (2013). https://doi.org/10.4236/jss.2013.13004
4. Bullee, J.-W., Montoya, L., Junger, M., Hartel, P.: Spear phishing in organisations explained. Inf. Comput. Secur. **25**(5), 593–613 (2017). https://doi.org/10.1108/ICS-03-2017-0009

5. Butavicius, M., Parsons, K., Pattinson, M., McCormac, A.: Breaching the human firewall: social engineering in phishing and spear-phishing emails. In: Australasian Conference on Information Systems (2015). http://arxiv.org/abs/1606.00887
6. Cialdini, R.B.: Influence: Science And Practice. Allyn And Bacon, Boston (2001)
7. Conway, D., Taib, R., Harris, M., Yu, K., Berkovsky, S., Chen, F.: A qualitative investigation of bank employee experiences of information security and phishing. In: Thirteenth Symposium on Usable Privacy and Security (SOUPS 2017), pp. 115–129 (2017)
8. Coronges, K., Dodge, R., Mukina, C., Radwick, Z., Shevchik, J., Rovira, E.: The influences of social networks on phishing vulnerability. In: 2012 45th Hawaii International Conference on System Sciences, pp. 2366–2373 (2012). https://doi.org/10.1109/HICSS.2012.657
9. Downs, J.S., Holbrook, M., Cranor, L.F.: Behavioral response to phishing risk. In: Proceedings of the Anti-phishing Working Groups 2nd Annual eCrime Researchers Summit (eCrime 2007), pp. 37–44 (2007). https://doi.org/10.1145/1299015.1299019
10. Ferreira, A., Lenzini, G.: An analysis of social engineering principles in effective phishing. In: 2015 Workshop on Socio-Technical Aspects in Security and Trust, pp. 9–16 (2015). https://doi.org/10.1109/STAST.2015.10
11. Ferreira, A., Coventry, L., Lenzini, G.: Principles of persuasion in social engineering and their use in phishing. In: Tryfonas, T., Askoxylakis, I. (eds.) HAS 2015. LNCS, vol. 9190, pp. 36–47. Springer, Cham (2015). https://doi.org/10.1007/978-3-319-20376-8_4
12. Frauenstein, E.D., von Solms, R.: Phishing: how an organization can protect itself. In: Information Security South Africa Conference 2009 (ISSA 2009) (2009). https://www.researchgate.net/publication/220803149_Phishing_How_an_Organization_can_Protect_Itself. Accessed 16 Feb 2018
13. Jagatic, T.N., Johnson, N.A., Jakobsson, M., Menczer, F.: Social phishing. Commun. ACM 50(10), 94–100 (2007). https://doi.org/10.1145/1290958.1290968
14. Krombholz, K., Hobel, H., Huber, M., Weippl, E.: Advanced social engineering attacks. J. Inf. Secur. Appl. 22(C), 113–122 (2015). https://doi.org/10.1016/j.jisa.2014.09.005
15. Lastdrager, E.E.: Achieving a consensual definition of phishing based on a systematic review of the literature. Crime Sci. 3(1), 9 (2014). https://doi.org/10.1186/s40163-014-0009-y
16. Mohebzada, J.G., Zarka, A.E., Bhojani, A.H., Darwish, A.: Phishing in a university community: two large scale phishing experiments. In: 2012 International Conference on Innovations in Information Technology (IIT), pp. 249–254 (2012). https://doi.org/10.1109/INNOVATIONS.2012.6207742
17. Muscanell, N.L., Guadagno, R.E., Murphy, S.: Weapons of influence misused: s social influence analysis of why people fall prey to internet scams. Soc. Pers. Psychol. Compass 8 (7), 388–396 (2014). https://doi.org/10.1111/spc3.12115
18. Ohaya, C.: Managing phishing threats in an organization. In: Proceedings of the 3rd Annual Conference on Information Security Curriculum Development (InfoSecCD 2006), pp. 159–161 (2006). https://doi.org/10.1145/1231047.1231083
19. Oliveira, D., et al.: Dissecting spear phishing emails for older vs young adults: on the interplay of weapons of influence and life domains in predicting susceptibility to phishing. In: Proceedings of the 2017 CHI Conference on Human Factors in Computing Systems (CHI 2017), pp. 6412–6424 (2017). https://doi.org/10.1145/3025453.3025831
20. Parsons, K., McCormac, A., Pattinson, M., Butavicius, M., Jerram, C.: The design of phishing studies: challenges for researchers. Comput. Secur. 52, 194–206 (2015). https://doi.org/10.1016/j.cose.2015.02.008
21. Sarno, D.M., Lewis, J.E., Bohil, C.J., Shoss, M.K., Neider, M.K.: Who are phishers luring?: a demographic analysis of those susceptible to fake emails. In: Proceedings of the Human Factors and Ergonomics Society Annual Meeting, vol. 61, no. 1, pp. 1735–1739 (2017). https://doi.org/10.1177/1541931213601915

22. Sheng, S., Holbrook, M., Kumaraguru, P., Cranor, L.F., Downs, J.: Who falls for phish?: a demographic analysis of phishing susceptibility and effectiveness of interventions. In: Proceedings of the SIGCHI Conference on Human Factors in Computing Systems (CHI 2010), pp. 373–382 (2010). https://doi.org/10.1145/1753326.1753383

23. Tsow, A., Jakobsson, M.: Deceit and deception: a large user study of phishing. Indiana University, School of Informatics, Computing and Engineering, Bloomington (2007). https://www.cs.indiana.edu/cgi-bin/techreports/TRNNN.cgi?trnum=TR649. Accessed 16 Feb 2018

24. Turner, J.C., Hogg, M.A., Oakes, P.J., Reicher, S.D., Wetherell, M.S.: Rediscovering the Social Group: A Self-Categorization Theory. Blackwell, Oxford (1987)

25. Vishwanath, A., Harrison, B., Ng, Y.J.: Suspicion, cognition, and automaticity model of phishing susceptibility. Commun. Res. 0093650215627483 (2016). https://doi.org/10.1177/0093650215627483

26. Williams, E.J., Hinds, J., Joinson, A.N.: Exploring susceptibility to phishing in the workplace. Int. J. Hum.-Comput. Stud. **120**, 1–13 (2018). https://doi.org/10.1016/j.ijhcs.2018.06.004

27. Zielinska, O.A., Welk, A.K., Mayhorn, C.B., Murphy-Hill, E.: A temporal analysis of persuasion principles in phishing emails. In: Proceedings of the Human Factors and Ergonomics Society Annual Meeting, vol. 60, no. 1, pp. 765–769 (2016). https://doi.org/10.1177/1541931213601175

28. Cost of Cyber Crime Study. Accenture. https://www.accenture.com/t20170926T072837Z__w__/us-en/_acnmedia/PDF-61/Accenture-2017-CostCyberCrimeStudy.pdf

Vote-for-It: Investigating Mobile Device-Based Interaction Techniques for Collocated Anonymous Voting and Rating

Romina Kühn[1](✉), Mandy Korzetz[1](✉), Franz-Wilhelm Schumann[1],
Lukas Büschel[1], and Thomas Schlegel[2](✉)

[1] Institute of Software and Multimedia Technology, TU Dresden, Dresden, Germany
{romina.kuehn,mandy.korzetz,franz-wilhelm.schumann,
lukas.bueschel}@tu-dresden.de
[2] Institute for Ubiquitous Mobility Systems, Karlsruhe University of Applied Science,
Karlsruhe, Germany
thomas.schlegel@hs-karlsruhe.de

Abstract. During discussions in collocated work it is necessary to vote for results or to rate them to reach an agreement and continue working. To ensure impartiality and to avoid social embarrassment, the assessment should then be performed anonymously in so far as other groups members should not see directly how a person votes or rates. With a growing number of digital devices in collaboration, this requirement also concerns such kinds of equipment. Our approach of ensuring anonymity of individual votes and ratings submitted on personal mobile phones is to avoid shoulder surfing activities. For this purpose, we designed four device-based interactions that aim at being easy to use and eyes-free to perform to stay in touch with the environment and potential shoulder surfers. We conducted a user study to investigate these interaction techniques and observed seven groups with four participants each while testing the interactions. Participants evaluated usability and User Experience (UX) aspects as well as unobtrusiveness of the four device-based interactions. Furthermore, participants gave valuable user feedback and stated that our proposed interactions help to avoid shoulder surfing.

Keywords: Collocated interaction · Device-based interaction ·
Voting · Rating · Mixed-focus collaboration · Shoulder surfer

1 Introduction

Collocated collaborative group work often comes along with discussions about current progress, results or further proceeding [15,31]. Especially in case of discussing proposed partial solutions, it becomes crucial to vote on these solutions to continue working. While some votes can benefit from a joint direct discussion, others should happen anonymously to ensure impartiality or to protect a

© IFIP International Federation for Information Processing 2019
Published by Springer Nature Switzerland AG 2019
D. Lamas et al. (Eds.): INTERACT 2019, LNCS 11746, pp. 585–605, 2019.
https://doi.org/10.1007/978-3-030-29381-9_36

Fig. 1. Collocated collaborative work scenario with shoulder surfer (yellow). Group members apply our anonymous voting and rating interactions with their mobile devices. They either hide their mobile device (blue) from the shoulder surfer, observe the shoulder surfer while interacting (orange), or use a back-of-device interaction (red). (Color figure online)

voting person from social embarrassment [20]. Impartiality can be important to guarantee objective voting and rating results that are uninfluenced by opinion leaders within a group. For example, this can be the case if several employees of a company present their work and need to decide which approach they want to continue with. However, even though people attempt to vote anonymously, some people still try to catch a glimpse of the input or valuations of others. This phenomenon is known as both shoulder surfing [26] and visual hacking [9] and mainly occurs in the context of offices or public places [6]. We use both terms interchangeably although shoulder surfing is often equated only with looking over a victim's shoulder, not from different perspectives. Furthermore, we use these terms to describe the activity of obtaining information from or about others that actually should be kept private. We further refer to this activity as *shoulder surfing*. Independently from specific devices and used analog or digital tools, this issue must be addressed accordingly. Figure 1 illustrates this problem in a collocated collaborative scenario with mobile phones. People are sitting or standing around a table, collaborating and using their mobile phones to assess results. The person standing behind one of the sitting persons on the right side tries to get a look on the screen of the mobile device. Although, the others are not in focus of the shoulder surfer, they evade this problem by hiding their devices and/or keep an eye on their surrounding.

There are already many approaches that investigate shoulder surfing. The plethora of approaches address this problem on an individual level (one shoulder surfer and one "victim") although consequences of shoulder surfing can also be very big on a group level such as in companies [9]. In this work, we address the shoulder surfer problem in collocated group work by designing device-based interactions for mobile devices especially smartphones. Our approach is not limited to a specific application but applicable for groups in teaching or company domains. Furthermore, it addresses the mixed-focus collaboration activities

[15] and is reusable for comparing activities in general. Mobile devices enrich collocated group work in many respects and apply increasingly in spontaneous (ad-hoc) collaboration [10]. Smartphones have the advantage that they are small enough to keep the users' sight unhindered while working digitally, in contrast to laptops. Addressing digitization strategies in companies and the public sector [27], they also avoid media breaks by enabling users to directly perform actions digitally, in contrast to conventional paper-based methods. Additionally, each mobile device belongs to one user and is therefore mostly personal. Consequently, inhibitions in using such devices should be low. To use them as voting tool, such devices should not only include protocols, services, or tools for privacy and security but also interaction techniques for anonymous valuations that avoid or at least impede shoulder surfing. We focus on ways to apply smartphones to collocated group work efficiently by providing interaction techniques that are easy to perform and support the users' tasks. Thereby, we enable users to act self-determined in terms of keeping input and information anonymous. The contributions of this paper are the following:

- *Generalizable design goals* for device-based interactions in collocated groups
- Implemented and evaluated *mobile device-based interaction techniques for anonymous voting and rating* using mobile phones as direct valuation tool
- Recommendations derived from a *user study* that applied the proposed interactions in collocated collaboration and investigated usability and UX

To address the mentioned issues and contributions, we structured the paper as follows: First, we give an overview on related work that describes approaches on shoulder surfing and several interactions for voting. Based on this, we derive design goals concerning ad-hoc collaboration, device-based and eyes-free interaction that lead to interactions for anonymous voting and rating. The main part comprises the user study we performed by means of an interactive prototype. Our goals were to understand whether the interactions are easy to use, eyes-free to perform, and suitable for anonymous voting and rating in a collocated setting. This work concludes with findings, recommendations, and future work.

2   Related Work

Device-based interaction techniques have been investigated as additional way to interact efficiently in certain situations where input and output of data should be fast, unobtrusive or as easy as possible (e.g., [1,12,17,25]). Ashbrook and Starner [1] propose *mobile microinteractions* where interactions should take less than four seconds. Using mobile phones as physical input device that directly involve touching or moving the device has been analyzed, e.g., by Rico and Brewster [25] and Leigh et al. [17]. Lucero et al. [21] propose design principles (SSI principles) to embed multiple mobile devices for shared multi-user usage. Korzetz et al. [12] provide *mobile spaces*, a model for designing lightweight mobile-based interaction techniques to support individual as well as collaborative usage scenarios. Both approaches emphasize tangibility and spatiality as core concepts for interacting effortless especially during collaborative work. Our approach aims at supporting mixed-focus collaborative scenarios where people frequently move between individual tasks and shared work with other group members [7]. Such scenarios require the possibility to vote and rate individual results to continue joint working. Several different approaches have influenced our anonymous voting and rating interactions. We identified three main areas of related work. At first, we comprise the usage of mobile devices in collocated collaborative scenarios in general. Then, we present approaches that enable voting and rating with mobile devices. Third, we describe existing work on avoiding shoulder surfing.

2.1 Mobile Devices in Collocated Collaborative Scenarios

Collaborative scenarios can take various forms depending on the environmental conditions, the current task and the structure of the group. MobiSurf [29] outlines a collaborative scenario where various integrated personal mobile devices and one shared interactive surface in a home setting support collocated decision-making. The system Ubi-Jector [18] provides a shared information screen as whiteboard utilizing the personal tablets of the group members. Both systems use besides personal devices additional devices to display content. HuddleLamp [24] focuses on ad-hoc multi-device collaboration and uses only mobile devices. However, a lamp with an integrated camera is needed to detect and track the mobile devices.

The need for additional equipment, e.g., displays or tracking devices, is one of the reasons why mobile devices are still less well integrated into collaborative scenarios, although they are an indispensable part of our everyday life. Additionally, it is crucial to join a group spontaneously and start interacting with others in a fast and easy way for participating in mobile collocated interactions [3,21]. Lucero et al. propose device-based interactions, which only use mobile devices to support ad-hoc collaboration [19,22]. They focus on sharing content amongst group members. Our approach addresses mobile devices without external technology to overcome these issues and adds further collaborative activities.

2.2 Voting and Rating in Collaborative Scenarios

Related work mostly addresses direct voting and rating as part of discussions in collocated collaborative scenarios. McCrindle's et al. approach "t-vote" [23] enables digital collocated decision-making for children in a museum's context by using tangibles on a tabletop. The authors designed the application to rate content directly to foster joint discussions. MobiComics [20] is an application that allows for creating and editing comic panels collaboratively and distributing them among two public displays by performing tangible and spatial interactions according to the SSI principles. The application includes interactions for public voting to encourage discussions: By holding the mobile phone in the air with a thumb up or down image, a user can cast a vote. MobiLenin [28] allows for taking a vote on music videos shown on a public display by selecting an item in the voting menu of a mobile device. Kühn et al. [13] present interactions for mobile devices that support direct voting and rating for ad-hoc collaboration without additional technical equipment. Each mobile device represents one result of a specific task. By moving and arranging the physical devices, they digitize voting results in real time. The interactions aim at supporting seamless discussions to find a common rating or voting result.

Since opinion leaders can influence direct valuations it is sometimes necessary to avoid direct voting. To enable unbiased results, groups often use paper-based methods to hide their decision. Collaborators then write their decision on pieces of paper and put them into a box. After group members submitted their piece of paper, they count the results by hand. Then, in case of further digital processing, the results have to be digitized. There are also web-based tools that allow for setting up digital polls easily, e.g., Straw Poll [30]. They focus on providing textual response options for voting. However, although rating can be performed by entering values textually further processing options are missing, e.g., calculating an average value. Approaches for integrating personal mobile devices in collaboration should offer support for anonymous voting and rating to get an overall rating out of each single valuation. We address this issue by providing easy and eyes-free input, so that collaborators can pay attention to the surroundings and other group members while voting and rating. We propose device-based interactions following the SSI principles and *mobile spaces* without other equipment.

2.3 Shoulder Surfer Problem

Anonymous voting and rating in collocated settings requires techniques to avoid shoulder surfing to hide input from other collaborators. Approaches that address the shoulder surfer problem often focus on entering passwords or PINs (e.g., [2,32,33]) and only consider one-to-one scenarios (one shoulder surfer and one "victim"). They often adjust the displayed content on the mobile devices by using handwritten fonts [5] or password grids where users have to locate their password [11]. Instead of adjusting the user interface presentation, De Luca et al. [2] hide the interaction by acting on the device's backside. Our proposed interactions pick up that idea, as users also can act on the backside. Moreover, users can perform the interactions largely eyes-free, so that they are able to have a look at their surroundings to prevent shoulder surfing.

3 Design Goals for Collocated Collaborative Interactions

To design suitable interaction techniques that cover requirements for anonymous voting and rating by preventing shoulder surfing in collocated collaboration, we describe the following design goals to address this issues: (1) provide *unobtrusive and eyes-free* input to facilitate observing the surrounding to prevent shoulder surfing and that collaborators can feel comfortable while entering their vote, (2) provide device-based interaction techniques to enable an *intuitive and seamless* integration of mobile devices in collaboration, and (3) allow a group of collocated people to vote and rate ad-hoc only with their personal devices without further equipment to enable spontaneous collaboration activities. It is our purpose to adopt the easiness but at the same time to overcome the disadvantages of paper-based methods for rating and voting within collaborative sessions. The design goals focus on providing collocated anonymous voting and rating interactions but also address collocated collaboration interactions in general.

3.1   Unobtrusive and Eyes-Free Interactions

As shoulder surfing is a common issue while voting collocated, we aim at providing anonymous voting and rating interactions that users can perform as easy and unobtrusive as possible. From the users' perspective, interactions have to be simple and intuitive with little effort. The unobtrusiveness of interactions is twofold. The performance of an interaction technique should be unobtrusive to impede the identification of a particular interaction for shoulder surfers from different perspectives. Otherwise, the interaction input, especially the voting and rating result, should be as unobtrusive as possible in order to prevent the recognition.

Furthermore, to ensure prevention of shoulder surfing activities interactions should be *eyes-free* to perform. As a result of such an eyes-free interaction, users can keep an eye on the surrounding instead of looking permanently on the device screen to feel more safe and comfortable while making assessments. The objective is to demand less attention for input activities to facilitate additional observing of the surrounding. This, in turn, allows the user to judge when she can vote or rate. Users can act accordingly: entering valuations while being unobserved or hiding input activities with, e.g., hands, table or the backside of the device. With such simple interactions, we aim at providing a lightweight, fast, and easy privacy protection as proposed by Eiband et al. [4].

3.2   Intuitive Device-Based Interaction Techniques

To enable the usage of anonymous voting and rating interactions and to integrate mobile technology in a seamless and unobtrusive way, we use device-based interaction techniques. Mobile phones are physical devices that facilitate users to apply familiar interaction concepts. Our interaction techniques follow metaphors of conventional anonymous voting and rating methods (e.g., paper-based methods), so that they are easy to learn and to remember and, hence, *intuitive* to perform. Thus, users are still able to communicate face-to-face with group members and to keep an eye on the surrounding because there is low effort in using such interactions. This aspect addresses anonymous voting and rating interactions as a part of collaboration as well as collaboration interactions in general.

3.3   Supporting Ad-Hoc Collaboration

Collaborative groups, e.g., a group of students, often collaborate spontaneously. Therefore, special equipment, such as tabletops, large displays, or tracking systems, for collocated collaboration is not necessarily available. In contrast, users just use their mobile devices without the need for further technical equipment.

One benefit of using only mobile devices is that users can collaborate location-independently and spontaneously. If users own a mobile device, they can easily join or leave a group to participate in general collaboration activities as proposed in [15]. We thereby support groups of different sizes, because each person works with an own device. Furthermore, when the user is working digitally, there is no effort afterwards to digitize the results to continue working and users do not have to change permanently between media types (paper vs. digital content). Although, this is a general design goal for collocated collaboration interactions it also addresses the specific requirement of anonymous voting and rating interactions as one collaboration activity by enabling ad-hoc performance.

4   Anonymous Voting and Rating Interactions

We build on prior work that presents anonymous voting and rating interactions [14]. We revised and implemented the proposed conceptual interactions in order to evaluate them within a user study. They address the mixed-focus collaboration activity *comparing results* by setting in after group members discussed several interim results to reach an agreement anonymously [15]. We differentiate between rating and voting micro-activities. While voting only allows for accepting or rejecting a proposed solution, rating enables grading and therefore a higher level of granularity. The interactions are designed to be easy and eyes-free to perform and avoid shoulder surfing by enabling users either to observe their surrounding while entering content or easily shielding input from other eyes. Furthermore, they follow the before-mentioned design goals and base on everyday metaphors.

The interactions address the above-mentioned *mobile spaces* model (MSM) [12]. Collocated anonymous voting and rating as part of mixed-focus collaboration innately include individual as well as collaborative usage. Using their built-in sensors (MSM "technological"), mobile phones can identify their spatial arrangement (MSM "spatial"). Furthermore, due to their size and form, users can manipulate the devices physically (MSM "tangible"). Additionally, we offer multimodal feedback in terms of vibrations and enable users to choose between the several voting and rating interactions (MSM "representational").

4.1   Anonymous Rating Interactions

For rating solutions, we propose two interactions that can be performed alternatively (Fig. 2). The first interaction "Multiple Finger Tap to Rate" (1a, further referred to as *Fingerprint*) uses the fingerprint sensor to rate a result. By tapping the fingerprint sensor multiple times, the counter increases. For example, five taps represent the best rate. Since this interaction occurs on the backside of the device, it hides the input innately and shields it from other eyes. In case there is no fingerprint sensor or to provide an alternative interaction technique, the display acts as input area for ratings (1b, "Multi-Finger Tap to Rate" or *Touch*). The number of fingers tapping the display simultaneously corresponds to the value input. In Fig. 2, three fingers are tapping the display and the rating

	Interaction Technique	Interaction Name	Short Name	Used Device Sensors
RATING	(1a) 	"Multiple Finger Tap to Rate"	*Fingerprint*	Fingerprint sensor
	(1b) 	"Multi-Finger Tap to Rate"	*Touch*	Multi-touch display
VOTING	(2a) 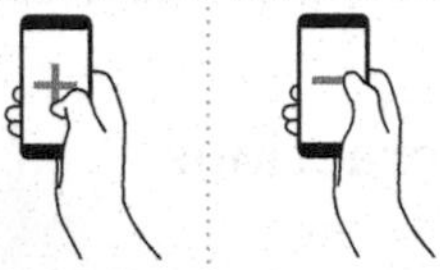	"Draw Plus to Accept" "Draw Minus to Reject"	*Draw*	Touch display
	(2b) 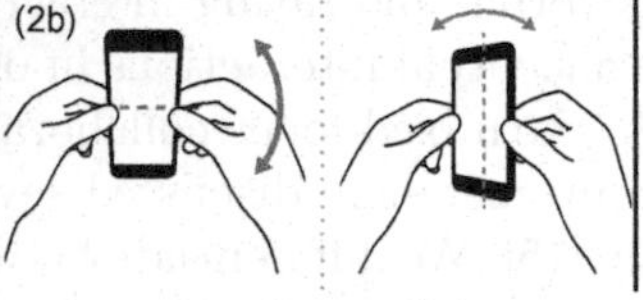	"Tilt Forwards to Accept" "Tilt Sidewards to Reject"	*Tilt*	Motion sensors (accelerometer, gyroscope)

Fig. 2. Interactions for anonymous rating and voting using standard mobile phones

"three" is given. To hide the input from shoulder surfers, users can shield the display, e.g., with their hand or an object, while entering the rating.

4.2 Anonymous Voting Interactions

To vote on results, group members can use the interactions "Draw Plus to Accept" or "Draw Minus to Reject" (2a, *Draw*) as well as "Tilt Forwards to Accept" or "Tilt Sidewards to Reject" (2b, *Tilt*). To accept a result users either draw a plus on their mobile phone display or tilt their device along the x-axis. If users draw a minus on the display or tilt their device along the y-axis, they reject a result. Users can perform these interactions alternatively depending on their preferences or hardware restrictions. To avoid shoulder surfers, users can either turn the device or shield it with another object while interacting.

5   User Study

We conducted a user study to examine the proposed interactions. In the following, we describe the participants, the interactive prototype, our procedure as well as the study design to answer the following questions:

1. How do the interaction techniques perform in terms of usability and UX?
2. How unobtrusive and eyes-free executable are the proposed interaction techniques to address the shoulder surfer issue properly?

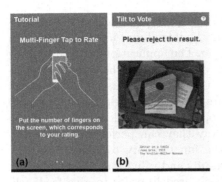

Fig. 3. Interactive prototype and study setting. (a) Tutorial describing each interaction textually and visually. (b) Participants try the interactions with given votes or ratings on several images. (c) Participants sat around a table in our lab, the study leader sat in the background. Each session was video recorded from this perspective.

5.1 Participants

We recruited 28 unpaid participants (11 female) from age 18 to 51 (M = 31.6, SD = 6.7) via e-mail or personally. All participants were familiar with the usage of smartphones, although two participants did not own such a device. We divided the participants into 7 groups with 4 people each. Within groups, participants knew each other beforehand as colleagues to establish a more realistic co-working scenario and to avoid inhibitions while interacting with each other.

5.2 Interactive Prototype

We implemented all interactions for Android devices with a minimum requirement of Android version 7.0. In addition, to conduct each interaction properly, all devices used for the user study had to provide an accelerometer, a gyroscope sensor, and a fingerprint sensor. We provided two Google Pixel phones and two ZTE Axon 7 devices for the participants to guarantee the availability of the necessary sensors and to control the setting. The devices are quite similar and communicate via Wi-Fi Direct. As shown in Fig. 2, both *Touch* and *Draw* use the touch screen to perform the interactions. For *Touch*, the device recognizes the number of touch points during a given time. Performing *Draw*, the touch screen recognizes one or two strokes. For *Fingerprint* the fingerprint sensor identifies a configured fingerprint in short time intervals. Each recognition represents an added rating point. *Tilt* uses both motion sensors - accelerometer and gyroscope. The accelerometer activates the tilt gesture whereas the gyroscope sensor measures how the mobile phone moves along the x- or y-axis.

We provided two Android applications to embed the interaction techniques in a plausible scenario. Both mobile applications use the same technical features. The first one involved a tutorial to become familiar with the anonymous voting and rating interactions (Fig. 3a) and the device. Furthermore, the tutorial application included a feedback form to assess first impressions on the interactions. The second application aimed at using the introduced interactions within a realistic but stipulated collaborative scenario. The application enabled to draw simple images, which became the valuation objects later. The second application also contained all interactions from the tutorial as well as further feedback forms. We added instruction text to facilitate the user to work through the app and the several tasks autonomously. Both applications included a help function in case users forgot an interaction or the way they can perform the gestures. Additionally, the second application had the functionality to connect to each other using Wi-Fi Direct to share working results and valuations. As soon as the users performed an interaction, the device vibrated in order to give feedback. Both applications logged the usage of the interactions, input errors, valuation results, and the completed feedback forms.

5.3   Procedure

After the participants arrived in our lab, we explained the global procedure of the user study. That included further proceeding and our focus on voting and rating anonymously. Then, the participants chose one of the provided mobile phones (Google Pixel or ZTE Axon 7) on their own. We used a square table where the participants could sit as shown in Fig. 3c. We also allowed the participants to move around within the room and to talk to each other. We emphasized that they should impede the others from noticing how they rate or vote. Furthermore, we encouraged the participants to stay curious during the study and try to see how the others vote and rate. We assume that in collaborative real-world scenarios all group members would act as shoulder surfer intrinsically motivated while they collaborate normally. In contrast, by assigning one person to the shoulder surfer role, we think that this person would have focused on observing and shoulder surfing instead of performing the collaboration task. That is why we decided to not appoint one explicit shoulder surfer within the group of participants. To address the order bias, we permuted the order of interactions. Furthermore, we recorded each session for retrospective analysis. In addition, the study leader was present during each session and observed the participants.

The participants started with the tutorial application simultaneously to become familiar with the interactions by perusing an introduction (Fig. 3a) and trying each interaction three times. The tutorial tasks included rating or voting on images of paintings of known artists (Fig. 3b). We predefined how participants ought to rate or vote in order to see whether they knew what to do or not. The participants received a positive feedback in form of a green check mark if the mobile phone recognized the right input value. After performing each interaction the participants got a questionnaire concerning the understandability of the tutorial and first impressions on the interactions including a short version of the User Experience Questionnaire (UEQ-S). At the end of the tutorial phase, the participants could try again all interactions independently.

Before starting the second application, the study leader reminded the participants to keep the input value anonymous and established a connection between the four mobile devices. The second application started with the task to draw a bird using a drawing functionality. The participants prepared content on their own to create a kind of an emotional link to vote and rate more realistic. After finishing drawing, every participant could see the other images on the device to vote and rate using a *stipulated* interaction technique. Then, each device showed the overall rating and voting results. Afterwards, every participant completed a questionnaire concerning the unobtrusiveness of the interactions. In a last run, we asked the participants to draw another image of an animal and to rate and vote on these images using *self-chosen* interactions. Finally, the participants completed the standardized User Experience Questionnaire (UEQ) and a questionnaire regarding demographic data. The study leader concluded by asking several semi-structured questions concerning the interactions and their usage in collaborative settings. Each group took about 70 to 80 min for the conduct.

5.4 Design

In order to answer the above-mentioned questions, we realized a within-subject design with the several interaction techniques as independent variable. We had two conditions for the interaction techniques: voting interactions (*Tilt* and *Draw*) and rating interactions (*Fingerprint* and *Touch*). We collected quantitative data by means of the standardized User Experience Questionnaire (UEQ) [8,16] at first after introducing and later after using the interactions several times at the end of the study. The UEQ contains three main scales: attractiveness, pragmatic quality (measuring perspicuity, efficiency, and dependability) and hedonic quality (measuring stimulation and novelty). Pragmatic quality describes goal-directed quality aspects, hedonic quality not goal-directed quality aspects. These three dimensions help us to evaluate usability and UX aspects. All data coming from the UEQs was assessed on 7-point Likert scales. Additionally, we provided questionnaires to investigate the unobtrusiveness and eyes-free performance of the interactions assessed on 5-point Likert scales. Finally, we collected qualitative data from observations during working with the interactive prototype, the prototype protocols as well as during semi-structured interviews.

6   Results

We received valuable insights concerning the usability and UX of our interactions as well as on the behavior of groups while rating and voting anonymously. For analyzing our data, we used logging protocols from both applications. These protocols included all voting and rating values, performed interactions and resulting errors as well as completed questionnaires. With 28 participants and 4 different interaction techniques, we received 112 responses to each questionnaire. We assessed and interpreted the following aspects also mentioned in Sect. 5:

- Usability aspects: attractiveness and pragmatic quality (perspicuity, efficiency, dependability)

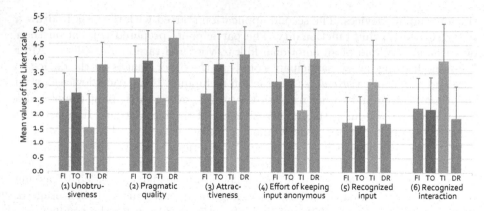

Fig. 4. Mean values (M) and standard deviation (SD) derived from the 5-point Likert scale (5 = best) concerning the unobtrusiveness of the interaction techniques, their pragmatic quality, their attractiveness, the effort of keeping the input anonymous, the perception of recognizing input, and the perception of recognizing each interaction for *Fingerprint* (FI), *Touch* (TO), *Tilt* (TI), and *Draw* (DR).

– UX aspects: hedonic quality (stimulation, novelty)
– Unobtrusive and eyes-free interaction: ease of recognizing voting and rating input as well as the respective interaction, effort of keeping input anonymous.

6.1   Usable Interactions for Anonymous Voting and Rating

From the protocols, we analyzed the errors that occurred while performing the interactions for the first time. Applying ANOVA showed that for the rating interactions the effect on the number of errors was not statistically significant ($F_{1,27} = 3.847$, $p > .05$). We could not analyze the voting interactions because the devices only could recognize the correct performance of *Tilt* and, therefore, did not document errors for analyzing. However, from the observation we noticed stronger responses to the voting interactions in case of errors.

After performing the tutorial, we asked the participants to assess each interaction regarding pragmatic quality on a 5-point Likert scale (5 = best). Furthermore, they assessed how unobtrusive the interactions were and how much they liked each interaction (attractiveness). Regarding these three criteria, participants assessed *Touch* as rating interaction better than *Fingerprint* and the voting interaction *Draw* better than *Tilt*. Figure 4 summarizes the mean values (M) as well as the standard deviation (SD) of the interactions. Overall, *Draw* has the lowest standard deviation, which we interpreted as strong consensus especially on pragmatic quality (SD = 0.6) and unobtrusiveness (SD = 0.8).

We compared the evaluation of the questionnaire with the results of the standardized UEQ-S. The UEQ-S as well as the long UEQ queried an assessment of contrasting pairs on a 7-point Likert scale ranging from −3 (worst) to 3 (best). Figure 5 (left) shows the mean values (M) from the UEQ-S completed

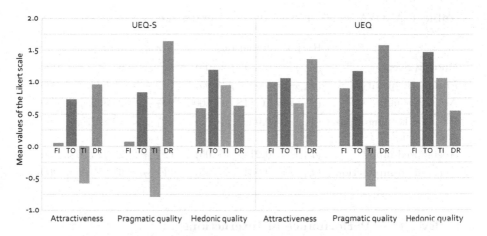

Fig. 5. Mean values from UEQ-S (left) and UEQ (right) concerning attractiveness, pragmatic quality and hedonic quality for *Fingerprint* (FI), *Touch* (TO), *Tilt* (TI), and *Draw* (DR). Values between −0.8 and 0.8 show a neutral evaluation (>0.8 = positive).

after the tutorial. Concluding, the UEQ-S confirms the evaluation of the first questionnaire. Participants assessed *Draw* best concerning pragmatic quality and attractiveness. *Touch* was rated better than *Fingerprint*. Although participants assessed *Tilt* worse than *Draw*, this interaction has the highest mean value regarding novelty of interaction (M = 1.5) as part of hedonic quality on the before-mentioned 7-point Likert scale. In contrast, *Draw* only got a neutral rating (M = 0.4) regarding novelty.

We compared both rating and voting interactions respectively by performing a t-test. With an alpha level of $\alpha = 0.05$, the voting interactions showed significant differences ($p < .05$) concerning attractiveness, perspicuity, efficiency, dependability, and novelty. Only stimulation showed no significant difference ($p = .18$). Comparing the rating interactions, the t-test showed significant differences in attractiveness, efficiency, and stimulation. We could not prove significant differences regarding perspicuity ($p = .06$), dependability ($p = .39$), and novelty ($p = .11$). We can derive that the voting interactions *Tilt* and *Draw* differ significantly concerning attractiveness and pragmatic quality, whereas the rating interactions *Fingerprint* and *Touch* only show significant differences in attractiveness. Finally, to substantiate our findings, we used ANOVA to investigate the significance of our results. The rating interactions (*Touch* and *Fingerprint*) only showed statistical significance concerning attractiveness ($F_{1,27} = 3.007$, $p < .005$). Analyzing our voting interactions, the effect of the respective interaction was statistically significant ($p < .0001$) concerning unobtrusiveness, pragmatic quality, and attractiveness. Table 1 shows the results in detail.

Table 1. ANOVA results showing the effect of the interactions on each aspect.

	Rating interactions	Voting interactions
Unobtrusiveness	$(F_{1,27} = 0.861, p > .05)$	$(F_{1,27} = 67.747, p < .0001)$
Pragmatic quality	$(F_{1,27} = 3.007, p > .05)$	$(F_{1,27} = 46.023, p < .0001)$
Attractiveness	$(F_{1,27} = 10.818, p < .005)$	$(F_{1,27} = 25.369, p < .0001)$
Effort of keeping input anonymous	$(F_{1,27} = 0.096, p > .05)$	$(F_{1,27} = 19.277, p < .0005)$
Recognized input	$(F_{1,27} = 0.213, p > .05)$	$(F_{1,27} = 22.216, p < .0001)$
Recognized interaction	$(F_{1,27} = 0.031, p > .05)$	$(F_{1,27} = 39.676, p < .0001)$

6.2   Eyes-Free Performance of Interactions

Participants ought to state why they looked at the mobile phone while performing the interactions. Half of the responses (56 of 112) comprised that participants did not look at the screen of the mobile device at all or only out of habit. This was especially the case for both *Fingerprint* (20 of 112) and *Draw* (15 of 112). The other half of responses showed that participants had to look at the screen since they either felt insecure (31 of 112) or unspecified unable to interact (25 of 112). Several participants mentioned that they marked these options to express that they needed the screens content to remember the input value that we predefined in the tutorial. Additionally, some mentioned that they wanted to see what happens next or "...to get a visual feedback" (P4). From these results, we derive that participants do not necessarily need the look at the mobile device during using our anonymous voting and rating interactions. Their look at the screen depended on the given task of the study. Consequently, we can state that the interaction techniques are eyes-free to perform.

6.3   Ensuring Anonymous Input Values by Unobtrusive Interactions

We asked the participants what they did to keep their input anonymous. About half of the responses (57 of 112) showed that participants hid their device under or behind an object, e.g., the table, or used their body to hide the device, e.g., shielded the device's screen with their hand or forearm (see Fig. 3). From our observations during the sessions and the recordings, we can confirm this and even reinforce that most of the participants changed their position when it came to rate and vote. However, about one third renounced keeping the interactions secret. For the *Tilt* interaction, some stated that it would not have helped at all to hide the interaction because it is very noticeable. Participants found the *Draw* interaction unobtrusive enough to omit hiding. The remaining participants either both observed the surrounding and interacted while they felt unobserved, distracted the others by moving, or varied the input rate. Using a 5-point Likert scale, the participants evaluated (4) the *effort* to keep the input anonymous

(5 = least effort), (5) the ease of *recognizing the input* value of others (5 = very easy) and (6) the ease of recognizing the *performed interactions* of other group members (see Fig. 4). Participants assessed *Draw* better regarding the effort to keep an input anonymous in contrast to *Tilt*. Furthermore, the *Draw* interaction itself makes it hard to recognize input value as well as interaction. Although *Tilt* received a worse rating, the standard deviation is high, which means that the participants' answers differed most regarding this interaction. *Touch* performs slightly better than *Fingerprint* regarding all three questions. Again, we performed an ANOVA to analyze the significance of the results (see Table 1). For the rating interactions the effect on the effort of keeping input anonymous, the recognized input as well as the recognized interaction was not statistically significant ($p > .05$). In contrast, the effect of the respective voting interaction on these three aspects was statistically significant.

6.4   Using Interactions in Collocated Settings

The last task aimed at using the interactions in a collaborative scenario whereas participants applied self-chosen interactions out of the presented interactions to rate or vote. Two participants used *Tilt* for voting and 26 participants used *Draw*. Comparing the rating interactions, 12 participants applied *Fingerprint*, whereas 16 participants used *Touch*. At the end of the user study, participants gave an overall assessment of all interactions regardless of rating or voting interaction. They confirmed that *Draw* is best concerning pragmatic quality (21 of 28) and unobtrusiveness (16 of 28). Participants also stated that *Draw* was fun (12 of 28). *Touch* also received positive feedback concerning fun factor (10 of 28).

With a concluding UEQ we asked the participants to assess usability and UX of their chosen interactions. Figure 5 (right) summarizes the mean values of the three aspects attractiveness, pragmatic quality, and hedonic quality. Although, the order of interactions at the end of the study is almost identical to the order after the tutorial, the mean values are better at the end. Only *Draw* slightly deteriorates concerning valuation. However, the results of the UEQ confirm the first impressions regarding popularity and functionality of the interactions. Furthermore, we derive a positive learning effect through repeating the interactions.

6.5   Qualitative User Feedback and Further Observations

After each session, participants had the opportunity to give additional verbal feedback on the interactions and to express further observations they made. We received user feedback and improvement suggestions concerning the technical implementation, several types of device feedback, and the tutorial.

Overall, the most discussed interactions were *Fingerprint* and *Tilt*. Whereas some participants enjoyed the voting interaction *Tilt* very much (P10 and P24: "Performing the tilt interaction was fun."), others described problems they had while interacting: "I only could reject results. Accepting did not work well." (P9). Concerning obtrusiveness one participant (P25) mentioned, "Tilt was [a] very effusive [gesture] and would benefit from being a little smaller." P18 suggested

"...it should also be possible to perform this gesture with one hand." Concerning *Fingerprint*, the participants stated that all in all this interaction was quite good to rate anonymously although "...it is unfamiliar to handle" (P16). P24 said, "I liked this interaction most because it is the most unobtrusive for me." The main point of criticism was that the fingerprint recognition "...took surprisingly long" (P2). We assume that the recognition time led to depreciation. As a result, we will revise the proposed interaction to reduce the recognition time.

Participants further commented on the given feedback possibilities of the interface. We provided vibrations in terms of haptic feedback but participants criticized it as noticeable. Nevertheless, participants highlighted the importance of feedback. They mentioned problems in understanding how they rated and thus wanted additional (visual) feedback (P5 and P9). Two participants (P3 and P27) also addressed the problem of correcting given input, which we did not enable directly during our tests but what would be crucial in real-world settings.

From the video recordings and the observations of the study leader during the study conduct, we received further insights on avoiding shoulder surfing, discovering new interactions, and acting in collaborative settings while assessing results. We observed that in the beginning of a session the group members sat closely at the table. They discovered the interactions as well as the tasks they had to perform during this time. When they started voting or rating, they mainly sat back in their chair and increased the space between each other. At the same time, they pulled their device closer towards their body and started looking around to observe the others. In this position, the participants primarily voted and rated. We also observed some other reactions. About one third of participants hid their device under the table while bending over. Occasionally, participants shielded their device with their hand (see Fig. 3) or with their legs crossed. These findings can be utilized for further improvement of the proposed interactions.

As described in Sect. 5, we decided to provide the participants a tutorial to become acquainted with the interactions. After reading the tutorial, participants tried the interactions the first time. We often observed that they had different kinds of difficulties during their first performances. For example, some participants did not touch the screen long enough performing *Touch*, some had problems with fingerprint recognition, or did not know instantly how fast to perform *Tilt*. Higher error rates coming from the specific logging protocol confirmed that observation. Since some participants mentioned missing information in the tutorial, e.g., execution speed, we recommend to investigate useful description methods for device-based interactions in depth. We further noticed that the group members normally talked to each other during the session. However, when the rating and voting started, the participants became much quieter in order to concentrate but easily resumed after performing the respective interaction. This shows that the participants could continue fluently and that the interactions did not obstructed them while collaborating.

7 Findings and Recommendations

From the results, we derived suggestions for improving the tested interactions as well as some further ideas and impressions for voting and rating activities using mobile devices in mixed-focus collaboration.

7.1 Device-Based Interaction Techniques and Their UX

The focus of the user study was on investigating the proposed interactions for anonymous voting (*Tilt* and *Draw*) and rating (*Fingerprint* and *Touch*) regarding their usability and user experience. The results from standardized UEQs and further questionnaires showed that overall interactions are useful and mostly suitable for anonymous voting and rating. However, there are some minor issues concerning each interaction. We implemented *Fingerprint* with two interaction steps to perform: first, tapping the fingerprint sensor and, second, confirming the input at the end of the rating. From our observations and user feedback, we assume that providing only one interaction step would lead to a better evaluation. However, participants described this interaction as very unobtrusive especially if the observation occurs from behind as illustrated in Fig. 1. An additional user study examining the application of the revised *Fingerprint* interaction in different local arrangements would be beneficial.

The *Touch* interaction received positive feedback, which possibly correlates with the fact that this interaction also resembles common smartphone interaction. We assume that this is also the case for *Draw*, which participants rated positively. However, the reason why the number of usage at the end of the performed study is that high remains vague: either they really liked *Draw* the most or they assessed *Tilt* as not suitable. Although, participants evaluated *Tilt* not as good as the other interactions the standard deviation had the highest value and shows that valuations differed most. *Tilt* was the only spatial interaction in terms of movement and most innovative according to the participants. This opens up possibilities for further investigations, e.g., on how such interactions can be better introduced or implemented to meet the users' preferences.

In general, we will revise the interactions in order to make them more precise in recognition and faster to perform. These are the main issues for designers and developers to address when implementing interaction techniques that are easy-free and unobtrusive to perform. Additionally, we need to reconsider device feedback modalities in terms of visual feedback versus non-visual feedback in context of shoulder surfing activities. This is due to the need of more intuitive correction options while voting and rating. Since we found that participants evaluated the interactions better at the end of the user study than at the beginning, we suggest addressing the learning phase of new interactions better even though they also need to be innately intuitive. We used a common type of mobile tutorial that showed a non-animated image of a certain interaction with additional text. Especially, interactions with a higher degree of novelty or more distinct movements could benefit from tutorials that, e.g., use short video sequences instead of images or more precise movement descriptions. While creating such interactions, designers should also consider the way of introducing the interaction techniques.

Performing new interactions was sometimes exhausting especially when they did not meet the expectations. In contrast, the participants stated that the performed drawing task was fun and that they could relax a little bit while drawing and talking. Therefore, we recommend providing tasks that are entertaining or easy to perform to prevent overworking.

7.2 Limitations and Future Work

Since the number of possible arrangements increases with a growing number of devices and participants, the user study limited the number of used devices to four. Of course, also larger groups can perform the interactions and the results can be fully exploited when more devices are used. Nevertheless, some limitations require further investigation. Although, we motivated the participants to stay curious and try to catch a glimpse on other devices, we did not appoint one or more explicit shoulder surfers within the group to receive a more realistic scenario. As a result, participants varied in performing shoulder surfer activities. It remains an open issue how one or more explicit shoulder surfers would change the participants' responses. In addition, other local arrangements, e.g., rows of seats instead of a table, should be further taken into account. This could extend the application area to other scenarios, e.g., polls in classrooms. Furthermore, the specifications of the mobile devices can influence the usage of the interaction techniques, e.g., the position of the fingerprint sensor, the device size, or the mobile platform. However, we provide a set of easy and useful interactions for anonymous voting and rating for further investigation.

Additional, further investigations should include a comparison with standard interactions for mobile devices, e.g., visual star rating. We did not include such interactions in our investigation yet because they do not follow our design goal to be performed eyes-free but need screen input. With our results in mind, we currently plan a usability study that examines this question. The results of our study provide the basis for further investigations using the revised interactions.

8 Conclusion

In this paper, we investigated interactions for anonymous voting and rating in collocated collaborative settings. The interactions' main aim is to avoid shoulder surfer activities by providing unobtrusive input and eyes-free performance. We introduced three design goals for mobile device-based interactions in collocated groups and described four derived interaction techniques and their implementation. The developed prototype was used in order to evaluate usability and UX aspects within a user study. We provided two Android applications that include all interactions and asked participants to use them for anonymous voting and rating. We collected data from observations, logging protocols, standardized UEQs, and semi-structured interviews.

Overall, participants assessed the interactions as suitable for anonymous voting and rating in terms of unobtrusive performance and eyes-free interaction to prevent shoulder surfing activities. From the questionnaires and interviews, we received some useful insights on revising the proposed interactions, especially *Fingerprint* and *Tilt*, and performing further user studies in collocated collaborative settings. According to the user feedback, we plan to apply our interactions to real-world scenarios with changing group sizes and local arrangements to extend the area of application and to investigate issues in different group settings.

Acknowledgements. The European Social Fund (ESF) and the German Federal State of Saxony have funded this work within the project CyPhyMan (100268299).

References

1. Ashbrook, D., Starner, T.: MAGIC: a motion gesture design tool. In: Mynatt, E., Schoner, D., Fitzpatrick, G. (eds.) Proceedings of the SIGCHI Conference on Human Factors in Computing Systems (CHI 2010), pp. 2159–2168 (2010)
2. De Luca, A., et al.: Now you see me, now you don't – protecting smartphone authentication from shoulder surfers. In: Proceedings of the SIGCHI Conference on Human Factors in Computing Systems (CHI 2014), pp. 2937–2946 (2014)
3. Dong, T., Churchill, E.F., Nichols, J.: Understanding the challenges of designing and developing multi-device experiences. In: Proceedings of the 2016 ACM Conference on Designing Interactive Systems (DIS 2016), pp. 62–72 (2016)
4. Eiband, M., Khamis, M., von Zezschwitz, E., Hussmann, H., Alt, F.: Understanding shoulder surfing in the wild: stories from users and observers. In: Proceedings of the 2017 CHI Conference on Human Factors in Computing Systems - CHI 2017, pp. 4254–4265 (2017)
5. Eiband, M., von Zezschwitz, E., Buschek, D., Hußmann, H.: My scrawl hides it all: protecting text messages against shoulder surfing with handwritten fonts. In: Proceedings of the 2016 CHI Conference Extended Abstracts on Human Factors in Computing Systems - CHI EA 2016, pp. 2041–2048. ACM Press (2016)
6. Goucher, W.: Look behind you: the dangers of shoulder surfing. Comput. Fraud Secur. **2011**(11), 17–20 (2011)
7. Gutwin, C., Greenberg, S.: Design for individuals, design for groups: tradeoffs between power and workspace awareness. In: Proceedings of the 1998 ACM conference on Computer Supported Cooperative Work (CSCW 1998), pp. 207–216 (1998)
8. Hinderks, A., Schrepp, M., Thomaschewski, J.: User experience questionnaire (2019). www.ueq-online.org
9. Ponemon Institute: Global visual hacking experimental study: analysis. Technical Report, Ponemon Institute, August 2016
10. Kim, S., Ko, D., Lee, W.: Utilizing smartphones as a multi-device single display groupware to design collaborative games. In: Proceedings of the 2017 ACM Conference on Designing Interactive Systems (DIS 2017), pp. 1341–1352. ACM (2017)
11. Kim, S.H., Kim, J.W., Kim, S.Y., Cho, H.G.: A new shoulder-surfing resistant password for mobile environments. In: Proceedings of the 5th International Conference on Ubiquitous Information Management and Communication - ICUIMC 2011. ACM Press (2011)

12. Korzetz, M., Kühn, R., Schlegel, T.: Turn it, pour it, twist it: a model for designing mobile device-based interactions. In: Proceedings of the 5th International Conference on Human-Computer Interaction and User Experience in Indonesia, CHIuXiD 2019, p. 4. ACM (2019)
13. Kühn, R., Korzetz, M., Büschel, L., Korger, C., Manja, P., Schlegel, T.: Natural voting interactions for collaborative work with mobile devices. In: Proceedings of the 2016 CHI Conference on Human Factors in Computing Systems, CHI EA 2016, pp. 2570–2575. ACM, New York, NY, USA (2016)
14. Kühn, R., Korzetz, M., Büschel, L., Schumann, F.W., Schlegel, T.: Device-based interactions for anonymous voting and rating with mobile devices in collaborative scenarios. In: Proceedings of the 15th International Conference on Mobile and Ubiquitous Multimedia - MUM 2016, pp. 315–317 (2016)
15. Kühn, R., Schlegel, T.: Mixed-focus collaboration activities for designing mobile interactions. In: Proceedings of the 20th International Conference on Human-Computer Interaction with Mobile Devices and Services (MobileHCI 2018), pp. 71–77 (2018)
16. Laugwitz, B., Held, T., Schrepp, M.: Construction and evaluation of a user experience questionnaire. In: Holzinger, A. (ed.) USAB 2008. LNCS, vol. 5298, pp. 63–76. Springer, Heidelberg (2008). https://doi.org/10.1007/978-3-540-89350-9_6
17. Leigh, S.w., Schoessler, P., Heibeck, F., Maes, P., Ishii, H.: THAW: tangible interaction with see-through augmentation for smartphones on computer screens. In: Proceedings of the 9th International Conference on Tangible, Embedded, and Embodied Interaction - TEI 2015, pp. 89–96 (2015)
18. Lim, H., Ahn, H., Kang, J., Suh, B., Lee, J.: Ubi-jector: an information-sharing workspace in casual places using mobile devices. In: Proceedings of the 16th International Conference on Human-Computer Interaction with Mobile Devices & Services (MobileHCI 2014), pp. 379–388 (2014)
19. Lucero, A., Holopainen, J., Jokela, T.: Pass-them-around: collaborative use of mobile phones for photo sharing. In: Proceedings of the 2011 Conference on Human Factors in Computing Systems - CHI 2011, pp. 1787–1796 (2011)
20. Lucero, A., Holopainen, J., Jokela, T.: Mobicomics: collaborative use of mobile phones and large displays for public expression. In: Proceedings of the 14th International Conference on Human-computer Interaction with Mobile Devices and Services, MobileHCI 2012, pp. 383–392. ACM (2012)
21. Lucero, A., Keränen, J., Jokela, T.: Social and spatial interactions: shared co-located mobile phone use. In: Proceedings of the 28th of the International Conference Extended Abstracts on Human Factors in Computing Systems, CHI EA 2010, pp. 3223–3228. ACM Press (2010)
22. Lucero, A., Porcheron, M., Fischer, J.E.: Collaborative use of mobile devices to curate sources of inspiration. In: Proceedings of the 18th International Conference on Human-Computer Interaction with Mobile Devices and Services Adjunct, MobileHCI 2016, pp. 611–616 (2016)
23. McCrindle, C., Hornecker, E., Lingnau, A., Rick, J.: The design of t-vote: a tangible tabletop application supporting children's decision making. In: Proceedings of the 10th International Conference on Interaction Design and Children, pp. 181–184 (2011)
24. Rädle, R., Jetter, H.C., Marquardt, N., Reiterer, H., Rogers, Y.: HuddleLamp: spatially-aware mobile displays for ad-hoc around-the-table collaboration. In: Proc. of the Ninth ACM International Conference on Interactive Tabletops and Surfaces - ITS 2014, pp. 45–54. ACM Press (2014)

25. Rico, J., Brewster, S.: Usable gestures for mobile interfaces: evaluating social acceptability. In: Proceedings of the 28th International Conference on Human Factors in Computing Systems - CHI 2010, pp. 887–896 (2010)
26. Roth, V., Richter, K.: How to fend off shoulder surfing. J. Bank. Finance **30**(6), 1727–1751 (2006)
27. Rott, B., Marouane, C.: Digitalization in schools – organization, collaboration and communication. In: Linnhoff-Popien, C., Schneider, R., Zaddach, M. (eds.) Digital Marketplaces Unleashed, pp. 113–124. Springer, Heidelberg (2018). https://doi.org/10.1007/978-3-662-49275-8_14
28. Scheible, J., Ojala, T.: MobiLenin - combining a multi-track music video, personal mobile phones and a public display into multi-user interactive entertainment. In: MULTIMEDIA 2005: Proceedings of the 13th Annual ACM International Conference on Multimedia, pp. 199–208 (2005)
29. Seifert, J., et al.: MobiSurf: improving co-located collaboration through integrating mobile devices and interactive surfaces. In: Proceedings of the 2012 ACM International Conference on Interactive Tabletops and Surfaces - ITS 2012, pp. 51–60. ACM Press (2012)
30. Straw poll - the place to create instant, real-time polls for free (2019). https://www.strawpoll.me/
31. Turnbull, D.: Rating, voting & ranking: designing for collaboration & consensus. In: CHI 2007 Extended Abstracts on Human Factors in Computing Systems, pp. 2705–2710. ACM, New York, NY, USA (2007)
32. Winkler, C., et al.: Glass unlock: enhancing security of smartphone unlocking through leveraging a private near-eye display. In: Proceedings of the 33rd ACM Conference on Human Factors in Computing Systems - CHI 2015, pp. 1407–1410. ACM (2015)
33. von Zezschwitz, E., De Luca, A., Brunkow, B., Hussmann, H.: SwiPIN - fast and secure PIN-entry on smartphones. In: Proceedings of the 2016 CHI Conference on Human Factors in Computing Systems, pp. 1403–1406 (2015)

Design Methods

Design Requirements of Tools Supporting Reflection on Design Impact

Qiong Peng(✉) and Jean-Bernard Martens

Eindhoven University of Technology, Eindhoven, The Netherlands
q.peng@tue.nl

Abstract. Designing for experience requires designers to pay attention to reflection on design impact. However, industrial design students are observed to have difficulty in demonstrating the impact of their design concepts due to insufficient thinking and reflection on design impact. There is a lack in the literature on both reflections on design impact and the tool support. The existing tools for general reflection purpose seem not to work well for this specific purpose. In response to the calls for designing for reflection, this paper presents two exploratory studies and the design requirements of tools for reflection on design impact. The purpose aims to facilitate design students for their reflection on design impact through developing appropriate tools. The design requirements could be generally used as guidelines or reference for future work of developing tools for reflection on design impact.

Keywords: Designing for reflection · Design impact · Tools · Design requirements

1 Introduction

Creative design is a process of co-evaluation of design problem and solution [1], involving a journey of self-exploration for designers [2]. It is defined as a reflective conversation with materials [3], reflection thus plays a vital role in such kind of process as a powerful tool of connecting thought [4] and promoting understanding of design space and problems [5]. Meanwhile, design is a situated and constructive making of meaning [6], it as an intervention influences people' thinking and action. The current designing for experience particularly fills designers with the responsibility to be aware of the impact of their design (concepts) on people and the world. Hence, designers actually design the impact, no the product [7, 8], and reflection on the design impact (or the impact of the design concept) allows industrial designers to think about the impact related aspects such as value, emotion, experience, feeling, and influence etc., instead of merely focusing on attributes of a product. However, industrial design students are prone to work around the product. Without thinking and reflection these impact aspects, design students are observed to have difficulty in demonstrating the design impact of their products when in communication with others.

D. Lamas et al. (Eds.): INTERACT 2019, LNCS 11746, pp. 609–622, 2019.
https://doi.org/10.1007/978-3-030-29381-9_37

There has been a substantial amount of literature of reflection on design. Different aspects such as reflection techniques and methods [9, 10], tools, reflection-in-action [11], etc., have been discussed in previous work, but relatively little work focuses on reflection on design impact. Reflection is viewed hard [12] and critical reflection is never effortless. It is still challenging for students [13]. Appropriate methods, techniques or tools for reflection practice are potentially helpful. Within HCI, the growing interest in designing for reflection [5, 14–16] allows designers to design technology-supported tools to facilitate their own design reflection practice as well as the reflective practice that is conducted by both the public and other professional practitioners for different purposes. There have been many tools, especially technology-based one, for design reflection, and most of them are more focused on encouraging reflection by enhancing awareness of the situation, providing and documenting materials and structuring the reflection process [17]. Since fewer prior studies about reflection on design impact and tool support can be found as reference, we proposed a study based on three main research questions to explore insights into reflection on design impact.

Q1: What do the industrial design students usually reflect upon in their design practice? (to identify the lack of reflection on design impact)

Q2: How do the design students perform reflection on design impact? (to identify the needs for alternative tools as support)

Q3: What could the tools for reflection on design impact be? (to identify the design requirements for developing tools for reflection on design impact)

In this paper, we present two separate exploratory studies related to answering these questions. Key findings indicated the needs for alternative tools in support of reflection on design impact. And the insights extracted from the studies helped us to outline the design requirements for tools supporting for this specific purpose. We aim to fill in the gap in the empirical studies in the area of design reflection by focusing on discussing designing tools for reflection on design impact. It is in accordance with designing for experience, and also in response of the calls for designing for reflection. The proposed design requirements could be used as guidelines or reference when designing specific tools for reflection on design impact.

The paper is started with a literature review on both the theoretic and empirical work around reflection in context of creative design, and then two studies are explained and the results are reported. It concludes with the discussion of the design requirements of tools supporting reflection on design impact.

2 Related Work

The growing interest in designing for reflection in HCI [5, 14–16, 18, 19] triggers both research and design for supporting reflection in the fields such as education, medical care and design, etc. The concept of reflection is primarily defined as a cognitive process of inquiry [20, 21] and a mechanism of learning from experience [21]. As it is often criticized as a fuzzy concept [22–27], people practice reflection with the same term but with different definitions in different domains [15] for different purposes. In design pedagogy, reflection is viewed the activities that designers do with to understand the design space, generate alternative solutions and test them by repeatedly reframing the problem [11]. Reflection is regarded crucial to creative design with a large body of studies [28–31] which are primarily informed by Schon's articulation of reflective practice and his distinction of three types of reflection: reflection-in-action, reflection-on-action [3, 11]. The benefits of design reflection are richly interpreted in literature such as making unconscious aspects of experience "available for conscious choices" [28], improving effectiveness and efficiency of design process [10], promoting design communication [32], facilitating design management [33] and supporting learning from design [10] etc. These benefits in turns confirm the increasing interest in designing for design reflection.

The focus of design nowadays has shifted from designing artefacts towards designing for experience [34], which allows designers to take the impact of design on people into account. It refers to the aspects such as user experience, emotions, values, etc. Friedman has early emphasized reflection on the value commitments embedded in a design through value-sensitive design [35]. Designing for experience, deeply based on user-centered design methodology, requires designers not to take their design concepts for granted without thinking about the impact on people. Reflection on the design impact is a deliberate process that can elicit thinking and analyzing the influence of the design on the targeted users and stakeholders, and even to the world. Hence, reflection on the design impact as well as the support for such kind of reflection should been given equal weight to when thinking about designing for reflection. Unfortunately, not many prior studies could be found.

When it comes to designing for reflection within design context, the principles and strategies of reflective design [28] are potentially helpful. Both the reflective informatics with three dimensions including breakdown, inquiry and transformation [16], and the five hierarchical levels of reflection [15] provide suggestions for designing for reflection. Slowness [36] which is in accordance with Reymens' suggestions of creating time [37] to encourage reflection could be intentionally designed to make space for reflection. However, as situated in design context, designing for design reflection is relatively more complex. This can be interpreted from two perspective. Design reflection broadly refers to the design process including both the design situation and the design activities [37], the design outputs like design concepts in the form of sketches, prototypes, etc., and other design materials generated during a design project, such as the reports, diaries, notes of communication, and audio or video records, ect. Whilst, there are different levels of design reflection which occurs at different phases as either reflection-in-action or reflection-on-action in the dynamic design process. Prior work has explored designing for design reflection by utilizing visualization. Examples are the Maps for reflection [38], Interactive Sketching [39] which increases the talk-back of design representation; Freed [40] which enables designers to create visual-spatial views of design work to support design reflection, the ReflectionSpace [41] and the ReflecT-able [42], etc. An approach of using two-dimensional positioning of objects is also presented as a means of reflection [43]. The support for revisiting and sharing by improved documentation or video is another design direction, examples are WorkSpace Nagivator [44], Designers' Outpost [45], Mindtap [46] and NOOT [47]. Besides, video is employed to support critical reflection in combination with story-making [29]. However, these tools are predominately designed either to encourage reflection by enhancing awareness of the situation, or to support reflection by improved documenting materials and structuring the reflection process. They are generally suitable when reflecting on the design process, design activities, design strategies, etc. Less focus was especially on reflection on design impact and the tool support. Hence, in designing for experience, we argue sufficient attention to the reflection on design impact (especially impact on people). And we particularly focus on designing (tools) for such kind of reflection. The lack of tool support calls for developing appropriate alternatives. We try to extent the exiting work by combining the fruitful results from literature review with our exploratory investigation.

3 Methodology

To meet the gap and facilitate design students for their reflection on design impact, we conducted two separate studies. We first made a set of interview sessions with 25 design students in our industrial design department to get a holistic understanding of their practice of design reflection. Each of the semi-structured interview session lasted for one hour and audio recorded, then later transcribed and analyzed. Participants included undergraduate students, master students and PhD students. They were first asked to interpret their own understanding of design reflection. This helped to ground the following questions focusing on the reflection on the design impact and the problems that they encountered. Participants were encouraged to provide explanation in more details. We also asked the participants to share their opinions on the tools that could better facilitate reflection on design impact in order to identify the needs for alternative better tools and collect insights and suggestions for tool design.

The results in the first study indicated that the design students' notions on design impact were not clear enough, and thus these vague notions influenced their practice of reflection on design impact. Meanwhile, it also implied a demand for alternative tools as the current tools didn't facilitate the specific reflection on design impact. Hence, in the second study, a co-design workshop with a task that to propose suggestions for developing tools in support of reflection on design impact was conducted with 12 design students. The reasons of co-workshop lay in the benefits of involving the design students in the design process, in which they contributed their personal experience and knowledge to generation of new ideas. Furthermore, they were more engaged and empathetic through designing for themselves. Reflection on design impact was explained to the participants when giving the task at the beginning of the work-shop. The researchers worked together with the participants to co-develop the design ideas. The workshops were structured designed, and the participants worked in groups following the procedure: getting the design task — task analysis — brainstorming (for divergence) — discussion the design ideas. The purpose of the workshop was to collect ideas about tool design, and a final design concept was not required. Instead, partici-pants were encouraged to contribute ideas with more detailed information such as features, attributes, functionalities, interaction, etc. The whole process of each work-shop lasted for 2 h and then closed with an informal interview as supplement to collect information that was not delivered during the design procedures.

4 Results

4.1 Results of Study 1

The interview sessions with 25 participants including 10 undergraduate students (42.9%), 10 master students (42.9%) and 5 PhD students (14.2%). The PhD students shared their opinions from the perspectives of being design practitioners rather than being design researchers. All of the participants reported that they had the experience in reflection upon the design practice either in the formal style like writing a report and making a presentation, or in the way that the believed as performing reflection such as sketching, discussion with team members, and self-thinking.

The answers to the questions (samples shown in Table 1) in the interviews were transcribed verbatim and individual quotes were extracted and labelled. 2 researchers were involved in the quote coding process separately to guarantee the consistency of the coding process. 5 categories with 219 quotes in total were finally identified.

Category 1 included 52 quotes related to the definition of reflection. 73% of them defined reflection in design practice with relatively clear purposes, for instance, "Reflection is the deep-thinking of the design activities and process", "Reflection means reviewing the design process and output to get new insights", and "Reflection for me is the process in which I carefully think of the related aspects of my design work and then I can gain knowledge and experience." While the other 27% quotes contained vague definitions which simply equated to the terms like thinking, discussion and meditation, etc. These quotes indicated that all the participants gave their definitions of reflection as a process or an activity that occurs in the design practice, and the difference lies in the purpose of doing it, since no quotes mentioned a clear distinction between reflection-in-action and reflection-on-action.

Table 1. Sample of questions that were asked in the interviews.

No.	Questions
1	How do you define design reflection? (your definition)
2	What do you usually reflect upon? (the content in your reflection)
3	Did you make reflection particularly on the design impact or on the impact of your design (concept)? Why/why not?
4	What are the problems that you encountered when you reflect on design impact?
5	Any methods or tools to support? Did they work well? Why/why not?
6	If any tool could help, what the tool could be? (suggestions for the tools)

Category 2: What to reflect upon (35 quotes): Each participant explained what they usually reflect upon. It covered nearly all the related aspects such as the design activities, design procedure, methods, tools, design strategies, design decision, design outcomes, etc. 28.5% quotes mentioned the terms like "influence", "affect", "impact" that were related to reflection on design impact.

Category 3: about reflection on design impact (65 quotes). 25 quotes were answers to experience in reflection on design impact, in which 20% quotes showed negative answers with the interpretations such as "I never think about the impact of the design. I usually make reflection when I have a problem and then think about how to solve it." "I must acknowledge that I might never or little think about the impact of my design. It seems that I actually neglected it." While, the remaining 80% quotes explained different consideration of reflection on design impact. For instance, "Yes, I think about the impact because I must envision the interaction between the user and my product." "User experience is important to think about. I think my reflection on design impact is related to the aspects of user experience." The other 40 quotes delivered problems that the students encountered when they reflect on the design impact. For instance, "I don't know how to reflect on design impact because I am not sure what the design impact means." "Design impact is too abstract to explain and reflect on. Guidelines or methods are necessary." "I don't know how to make reflection, and how to reflect on the design impact. I always perform reflection in my own way and I don't know whether it is right or not."

Category 4: Tools for support (30 quotes). 40% quotes showed no specific tools for reflection on design impact. The other 60% quotes mentioned the tools that were generally used for reflection (shown in Fig. 1). Both the traditional tools such as pen and

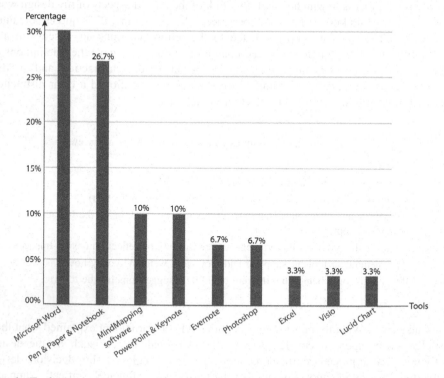

Fig. 1. Tools that were mentioned in the quotes by the students. Microsoft Word for 30%, the traditional tools like pen and paper, notebook for 26.7%, Mind mapping software for 10%, PowerPoint and Keynote for 10%, Evernote for 6.7%, Photoshop for 6.7%, Excel for 3.3%, Visio for 3.3%, Lucid Chart 3.3%.

notebooks, and the digital tools were applied. The diagram tools and mind map software were also introduced by the participants as tools for reflection for design impact.

Category 5: needs for alternative tools (37 quotes). Participants placed emphases on the needs for appropriate tool to support reflection on design impact. For instance, "Because I mostly make reflection in my own way which is time-consuming, I believe that it could be improved by some good tools." "I actually don't know how to reflect on the design impact, so methods or tools are necessary." "I believe that tools are in need. Design impact is too abstract to think about and I even don't know how to start the reflection." In addition, nearly half of the quotes in this category showed complaint or dissatisfaction with the existing tools, as the quotes explained "I didn't use any specific tools for reflection on design impact as these tools seem not appropriate." "Tools like Mindmap can be used for reflection on impact, as it helps to connect the aspects. The other tools might not facilitate."

4.2   Results of Study 2

In these workshops, 12 participants including the 50% undergraduate students and 50% master students participated in the co-design workshop. A task was given to the participants by introducing the items and requirements (shown in Table 2) to ensure our research purpose. More than 15 ideas based on the given design task were proposed and discussed (Fig. 2).

Table 2. Items of the task introduction.

Items	Requirement
Design for whom	Design students
Using context	Designing tools for reflection on design impact
To solve what problems	Need to identify the design problems when reflecting on design impact
What the design solutions (tools) could be?	Related technology to support Functionalities, interaction design…
How it works?	Identify how your design ideas support reflection on a design impact and how people use it
About design Impact	Identify the impact of your ideas on users

These ideas which were proposed for different specific problems were categorized into three main types. Some ideas were generated with emphasis on clear guidelines and procedures as the participants explained "only given specific support, the reflection on design impact could be easy to do." Some ones were about tools which provide the introduction and examples of design impact as explained that "If we don't know what design impact it is, we neither pay attention to it nor make good reflection on it." The ideas focusing on the support of visualizing and analyzing the design impact were also proposed.

Fig. 2. Photos of the workshop.

In the interview, participants added more information about explanation of the problem as well as their expectations on the solutions. The data was collected and transcribed verbatim into quotes, and then analyzed by sorting into 2 categories: C1: definition of the problems (27 quotes, shown in Table 3); C2: What the tool could be (59 quotes, shown in Table 4).

Table 3. Sub-categories of category 1 and example.

Sub-category	Quote No.	Example
[1] Lacking practical methods or guidelines	8	"Any specific procedures to support reflection on the design concept?"
[2] Lacking clear interpretation of design impact	6	"What is design impact? If I don't know what it is, how can I reflect on it?"
[3] No feedback on the results of reflection	4	"If the impact means values to the users, how can I get to know whether they get it or not after my reflection?"
[3] Design impact is abstract to reflect upon	9	"Design impact seems abstract. I don't know how to effectively think about them."

Table 4. Sub-categories of category 1 and example.

Sub-category	Quote No.	Example
[1] supporting interpretation of design impact	13	"The tool should provide tips or reminders to help designers to understand design impact."
[2] supporting visualization and analysis of the aspects related to describe design impact	21	"If there are some elements or factors to explain design impact, the tool should visualize them and support the analysis."
[3] supporting a structured way to review and connect design elements	25	"Maybe a framework or structure to connect the design concept, its impact and users, context together could help."

5 Discussion

5.1 Understanding Reflection on Design Impact

Designing for reflection should firmly be based on deep understanding of reflection itself, including the definition, content, purpose, method, tools and results, etc. The less known details of student designers' reflection practices not only paints reflection as an unstructured and inefficient process, but also results in limited support by tools for facilitation. Some insights are worth discussing as follows.

Lack Sufficient Attention to Reflection on Design Impact

The design students in our studies had relatively vague definition of design reflection because most of them interpreted their definition of design reflection with many different terms such as meditation, mindfulness, awareness, stillness, and deep-thinking, review, as well as discussion, self-assessment, etc. Students tended to associate the purposes or goals to reflection, and they mostly performed reflection triggered by a specific design need. Many aspects such as the design process, activities, methods, outputs, knowledge, as well as design problems, solutions etc. thus become the content to reflect on. Meanwhile, students seemed to be not clear about the notion of design impact. They articulated design impact based on their own understanding such as influence, benefits, values, and meanings, etc. Consequently, when reflecting on the design concepts, the reflection particularly focusing on design impact was relatively weak or easily neglected, as some participants in the first study clearly expressed that they never reflect on the design impact. The others who believed that they actually made reflection on design impact, but without more explanation of what the design impact is and how they did it. Design impact is primarily related to value [7] that a (product) design brings to people and the world. Based on user-centered design methodology and designing for experience, the meaning of design impact could be extended from value to the user-related aspects including emotion, experience, feeling, and the change in action, etc. [48, 49]. Without understanding of design impact, it is impossible for designer (students) to practice reflection on it.

Guidelines for Design Reflection on Design Impact are Beneficial

The student designers complained that they had difficulties in reflection primarily due to the lack of specific methods or guidelines. The unstructured process and chaotic procedure greatly affect effectiveness and efficiency of their reflection performance. Blaiklock highlights the benefits of structure in design that reaching a high level of academic literacy, critical reflection and knowledge construction [50]. Daudeline proposes structured approach to reflection as "coached" reflection which involves providing formal tools to help thinking through an experience in order to identify what they learned from [51]. Reymen's recommendation that to perform design reflection on action at the beginning or end of a design session guided in a structured procedure with three main activities consisting preparation, image forming, and conclusion [37] could be used as the methodology for reflection performance. The preparation refers to the materials that are the basis for reflection on action, as Schon stresses that design is a reflective conversation with the materials.

A Demand for Tools Support Reflection on Design Impact

The insights collected from our studies indicated the needs for appropriate tools in support of reflection on design impact. Design students predominately made reflection in their own ways with various tools including the traditional tools such as notebook, pen, post-it, and some digital tools such as Microsoft Word, PowerPoint, Evernote, Photoshop, etc. As to reflection on design impact, these tools potentially support, but seems not match well. This is one of important the reasons that participants in our studies called for alternative tools as support. Reflection is a cognitive activity which takes time and effort. Appropriate tools for support can enhance the efficiency, engagement of reflection performance, and improve the experience during the reflection process and the outputs.

5.2   Design Requirement of Tools Supporting Reflection on Design Impact

Tools for reflection are not absolutely essential, but appropriate tools can assist the reflection performance. What the tools for reflection on design impact would be? Based on the literature review and the results of our two studies, especially the insights from the workshops, we anchored the attention to the design requirements for such kind of tools rather than focusing on single tool design. Developing an appropriate tool is always challenging. These design requirements can be used as reference when thinking about designing tools for reflection on design impact. When it comes to design for reflection, design directions like design for pauses, design for detachments, design for serendipity are worthwhile pursuing. Dalsgaard et al. discuss some features like comparison and expansion for further development of their reflection maps [38]. Based on all of these prior research work, we summarize the design requirements of tools for reflection on design impact encompassing the following 3 aspects:

Firstly, with a unique style to differentiate from other tools.

Tools should be designed with clear features for supporting reflection design impact. Providing interpretation of design impact to the users is necessary, so that designers (students) can distinguish with the other tools that are for general reflection purposes. Explicit definition on functionality could work as scaffolding to avoid a random use of tools by the design students. Many existing tools that students utilize are not particularly developed for reflection, whilst some tools for reflection generally support design reflection like supporting documentation and visualization. It makes the tool users perplexed when deciding which tool is more appropriate for a specific purpose. The tool design thus is need-specific.

Secondly, narratives or storytelling could be used to provide a framework that involves in all the related elements to support discussion and reflection on design impact. Narratives or storytelling is regarded powerful for reflection and reflective practice [52–54]. Design impact is abstract and not easy to be interpreted. Reflection on design impact is challenging. Narratives or storytelling makes it accessible to thinking about impact by organizing the underlying aspects such as people, context and people's emotions, values into a structure. Hence, tools for reflection on design impact could be architecture with a narrative or storytelling framework. They can support designers to have discussion, envision and analysis on these aspects based on the narrative or storytelling framework. The narrative or storytelling itself is the material that designers (students) could have a conservation with.

Finally, designing tools for reflection on design impact should allow collaborative support either in the way of co-reflection or by involving in external feedback. The impact of a design is actually perceived by users or stakeholder, and designers design and reflect on the impact primarily based on their own judgement or imagination. Design reflection is different from design rationale or design critiques. It is large conceptualized as individual mental activity [55], but also has strong social dimensions [24]. Without external feedback, the reflection on design impact is performed in a blank box. The co-reflection, or collaborative reflection is a collaborative critical thinking process [56] which combines individual cognition and interaction between individuals. The sharing understanding through collaborative reflection can promote designers to critically re-think about the impact that their design would bring to people and even to the world. Technologies own unique advantages in supporting collaboration and feedback communication. Taking advantage of technology support is an important consideration when designing tools for reflection on design impact.

5.3   Limitations and Future Work

The huge body of research on reflection as well as design for reflection provides both opportunities and challenges for design research. In our research, we placed the background of designing for experience in which the design impact is highlighted, and the background of designing for reflection in which technology is extensively utilized to support reflection practice. We aim to better to facilitate students' reflection on design impact through developing tools. The results were based on exploratory studies which were primarily conducted by qualitative research methods like interviews and workshops. The design requirements are still theoretical proposition which could only be used as reference. There is space for modification and improvement. We believe that in-deep observation and long-time-tracking of their reflection practice in different design projects could bring us more insights.

Besides the purpose of learning by engagement of design reflection, designers can also benefit to get better sense of their design work [57] for other purposes like communication. Narratives and story constructions which are effective means of reflection are also highly recommended for the sense-making for the design work. Both the literature and propositions of developing storytelling tools for design reflection from the workshops informed us a specific direction for our future work.

6   Conclusion

In this paper, we presented two studies about exploring design tools for reflection on design impact. We particularly focused on reflection on design impact in order to enhance the awareness of design impact in the context of designing for experience. And proposed the design requirements for tools in support of reflection on design impact. Reflection is a crucial part of the creative design, and we believe that appropriate tools can facilitate design students' reflection practice and promote the awareness of performing reflection frequently with the support of the excellent tools. The proposed design requirements could be regarded as a starting point for future work and invite interested researcher to join in this work.

Acknowledgements. This research is part of the PhD research. It was also supported by the funding WLWH17-23 and 2016ZO36. Appreciations for all the participants for interviews and workshops.

References

1. Dorst, K., Cross, N.: Creativity in the design process: co-evolution of problem–solution. Des. Stud. **22**(5), 425–437 (2001)
2. English, S.G.: Enhancing the Reflective Capabilities of Professional Design Practitioners (2009)
3. Schon, D.A.: Designing as reflective conversation with the materials of a design situation. Res. Eng. Design **3**(3), 131–147 (1992)
4. Luppicini, R.: Reflective Action Instructional Design (RAID): a designer's aid. Int. J. Technol. Des. Educ. **13**(1), 75–82 (2003)
5. Baumer, E.P., Khovanskaya, V., Matthews, M., Reynolds, L., Schwanda Sosik, V., Gay, G.: Reviewing reflection: on the use of reflection in interactive system design. In: Proceedings of the 2014 Conference on Designing Interactive Systems, pp. 93–102 (2014)
6. Ylirisku, S., Halttunen, V., Nuojua, J., Juustila, A.: Framing design in the third paradigm. In: Proceedings of the SIGCHI Conference on Human Factors in Computing Systems, New York, pp. 1131–1140 (2009)
7. Brown, T., Katz, B.: Change by design. J. Prod. Innov. Manag. **28**(3), 381–383 (2011)
8. Camacho, M.: David Kelley: From design to design thinking at Stanford and IDEO. She Ji J. Des. Econ. Innov. **2**(1), 88 (2016)
9. Improving design processes through structrued reflection
10. Reymen, I.M.M.J.: Research on design reflection: overview and directions. In: DS 31: Proceedings of ICED 2003, the 14th International Conference on Engineering Design, Stockholm (2003)
11. Schon, D.A., DeSanctis, V.: The Reflective Practitioner: How Professionals Think in Action. Taylor & Francis (1986)
12. Prior, J., Ferguson, S., Leaney, J.: Reflection is hard: teaching and learning reflective practice in a software studio. In: Proceedings of the Australasian Computer Science Week Multiconference, New York, pp. 7:1–7:8 (2016)
13. Kori, K., Pedaste, M., Leijen, Ä., Mäeots, M.: Supporting reflection in technology-enhanced learning. Educ. Res. Rev. **11**, 45–55 (2014)
14. Sas, C., Dix, A.: Designing for reflection on experience. In: CHI 2009 Extended Abstracts on Human Factors in Computing Systems, New York, pp. 4741–4744 (2009)
15. Fleck, R., Fitzpatrick, G.: Reflecting on reflection: framing a design landscape. In: Proceedings of the 22nd Conference of the Computer-Human Interaction Special Interest Group of Australia on Computer-Human Interaction, pp. 216–223 (2010)
16. Baumer, E.P.S.: Reflective informatics: conceptual dimensions for designing technologies of reflection. In: Proceedings of the 33rd Annual ACM Conference on Human Factors in Computing Systems, New York, pp. 585–594 (2015)
17. Fleck, R.: Designing for Reflection, Sustainability and Simplicity, p. 4

18. Li, I., Dey, A., Forlizzi, J.: A stage-based model of personal informatics systems. In: Proceedings of the SIGCHI Conference on Human Factors in Computing Systems, pp. 557–566 (2010)
19. Slovák, P., Frauenberger, C., Fitzpatrick, G.: Reflective practicum: a framework of sensitising concepts to design for transformative reflection. In: Proceedings of the 2017 CHI Conference on Human Factors in Computing Systems, New York, pp. 2696–2707 (2017)
20. Dewey, J.: How We Think. Courier Corporation (1997)
21. Moon, J.A.: Reflection in Learning and Professional Development: Theory and Practice. Routledge, New York (2013)
22. Hatton, N., Smith, D.: Reflection in teacher education: towards definition and implementation. Teach. Teach. Educ. 11(1), 33–49 (1995)
23. Davis, E.A.: Characterizing productive reflection among preservice elementary teachers: seeing what matters. Teach. Teach. Educ. 22(3), 281–301 (2006)
24. Procee, H.: Reflection in education: a Kantian epistemology. Educ. Theor. 56(3), 237–253 (2006)
25. Quinton, S., Smallbone, T.: Feeding forward: using feedback to promote student reflection and learning–a teaching model. Innov. Educ. Teach. Int. 47(1), 125–135 (2010)
26. Clarà, M.: What is reflection? Looking for clarity in an ambiguous notion. J. Teach. Educ. 66(3), 261–271 (2015)
27. Renner, B., Prilla, M., Cress, U., Kimmerle, J.: Effects of prompting in reflective learning tools: findings from experimental field, lab, and online studies. Front. Psychol. 7, 820 (2016)
28. Sengers, P., Boehner, K., David, S., "Jofish" Kaye, J.: Reflective design. Presented at the proceedings of the 4th decennial conference on critical computing: between sense and sensibility, pp. 49–58 (2005)
29. McDonnell, J., Lloyd, P., Valkenburg, R.C.: Developing design expertise through the construction of video stories. Des. Stud. 25(5), 509–525 (2004)
30. Lauche, K.: Heedful action, reflection, and transfer in the design process, pp. 267–274. WDK Publications (2001)
31. Badke-Schaub, P., Wallmeier, S., Dörner, D.: Training for designers: a way to reflect design processes and cope with critical situations in order to increase efficiency. In: International Conference on Engineering Design, pp. 24–26, August 1999
32. Valkenburg, R., Dorst, K.: The reflective practice of design teams. Des. Stud. 19(3), 249–271 (1998)
33. Lauche, K.: Facilitating creativity and shared understanding in design teams. In: DS 30: Proceedings of DESIGN 2002, the 7th International Design Conference, Dubrovnik (2002)
34. Atasoy, Berke, Martens, J.-B.: STORYPLY: designing for user experiences using storycraft. In: Markopoulos, Panos, Martens, J.-B., Malins, Julian, Coninx, Karin, Liapis, Aggelos (eds.) Collaboration in Creative Design, pp. 181–210. Springer, Cham (2016). https://doi.org/10.1007/978-3-319-29155-0_9
35. Friedman, B.: Value-sensitive design and information systems. Interactions 3(6), 16–23 (1996)
36. Strauss, C.F., Fuad-Luke, A.: The slow design principles, p. 14
37. Reymen, I.: Improving design processes through structured reflection: a domain-independent approach. Technische Universiteit Eindhoven (2001)
38. Dalsgaard, P., Halskov, K., Nielsen, R.: Maps for design reflection. Artifact 2(3–4), 176–189 (2008)
39. Lin, J., Newman, M.W., Hong, J.I., Landay, J.A.: DENIM: finding a tighter fit between tools and practice for Web site design. In: Proceedings of the SIGCHI Conference on Human Factors in Computing Systems, pp. 510–517 (2000)

40. Mendels, P., Frens, J., Overbeeke, K.: Freed: a system for creating multiple views of a digital collection during the design process. In: Proceedings of the SIGCHI Conference on Human Factors in Computing Systems, New York, pp. 1481–1490 (2011)

41. Sharmin, M., Bailey, B.P.: ReflectionSpace: an interactive visualization tool for supporting reflection-on-action in design. In: Proceedings of the 9th ACM Conference on Creativity & Cognition - C&C 2013, Sydney, p. 83 (2013)

42. Hook, J., Hjermitslev, T., Iversen, O.S., Olivier, P.: The ReflecTable: bridging the gap between theory and practice in design education. In: Kotzé, Paula, Marsden, Gary, Lindgaard, Gitte, Wesson, Janet, Winckler, Marco (eds.) INTERACT 2013. LNCS, vol. 8118, pp. 624–641. Springer, Heidelberg (2013). https://doi.org/10.1007/978-3-642-40480-1_44

43. Nakakoji, K., Yamamoto, Y., Takada, S., Reeves, B.N.: Two-dimensional spatial positioning as a means for reflection in design. In: Proceedings of the 3rd Conference on Designing Interactive Systems: Processes, Practices, Methods, and Techniques, pp. 145–154 (2000)

44. Ju, W., Ionescu, A., Neeley, L., Winograd, T.: Where the wild things work: capturing shared physical design workspaces. In: Proceedings of the 2004 ACM Conference on Computer Supported Cooperative Work, pp. 533–541 (2004)

45. Klemmer, S.R., Thomsen, M., Phelps-Goodman, E., Lee, R., Landay, J.A.: Where do web sites come from? Capturing and interacting with design history. In: Proceedings of the SIGCHI Conference on Human Factors in Computing Systems, pp. 1–8 (2002)

46. Nielsen, J., Christiansen, N.: Mindtape: a tool for reflection in participatory design. In: PDC 2000, pp. 309–313 (2000)

47. van Dijk, J., van der Roest, J., van der Lugt, R., Overbeeke, K.C.: NOOT: a tool for sharing moments of reflection during creative meetings. In: Proceedings of the 8th ACM Conference on Creativity and Cognition, pp. 157–164 (2011)

48. Garrett, J.J.: Elements of User Experience, the: User-Centered Design for the Web and Beyond. Pearson Education, Upper Saddle River (2010)

49. Hassenzahl, M.: User experience and experience design. In: The Encyclopedia of Human-Computer Interaction, vol. 2 (2013)

50. Blaiklock, K.: Te Whāriki, the New Zealand early childhood curriculum: is it effective? Int. J. Early Years Educ. 18(3), 201–212 (2010)

51. Seibert, K.W.: Reflection-in-action: Tools for cultivating on-the-job learning conditions. Org. Dyn. 27(3), 54–65 (1999)

52. Cake, S.A., Solomon, L., McLay, G., O'Sullivan, K., Schumacher, C.R.: Narrative as a tool for critical reflective practice in the creative industries. Reflective Pract. 16(4), 472–486 (2015)

53. Johns, C.: Engaging Reflection in Practice: A Narrative Approach. Wiley-Blackwell, London (2006)

54. Bolton, G.: Reflective Practice: Writing and Professional Development. Sage Publiccations, London (2010)

55. Daudelin, M.W.: Learning from experience through reflection. Org. Dyn. 24(3), 36–48 (1996)

56. Yukawa, J.: Co-reflection in online learning: collaborative critical thinking as narrative. Int. J. Comput. Support. Collaborative Learn. 1(2), 203–228 (2006)

57. Sharmin, M., Bailey, B.P.: "I Reflect to Improve My Design": investigating the role and process of reflection in creative design. In: Proceedings of the 8th ACM Conference on Creativity and Cognition, New York, pp. 389–390 (2011)

Designer Led Computational Approach to Generate Mappings for Devices with Low Gestural Resolution

Roberto Montano-Murillo[1(✉)], Teng Han[2(✉)], Pourang Irani[2(✉)], Diego Martinez-Plasencia[1(✉)], and Sriram Subramanian[1(✉)]

[1] Department of Informatics/Interact Lab, University of Sussex, Brighton, UK
{R.Montano-Murillo, D.Martinez-Plasencia, Sriram}@sussex.ac.uk
[2] Department of Computer Science, University of Manitoba, Winnipeg, MB, Canada
{hanteng, Pourang.Irani}@cs.umanitoba.ca

Abstract. We present an approach for the semi-automatic generation of gesture mappings for devices with low gestural resolution such as the Myo Armband, an off-the-shelf EMG capture device. As an exemplar interactive task, we use text-entry: a pervasive and highly complex interaction. We quantify data related to interaction combining systematic studies (i.e., error, speed, accuracy) and semi-structured workshops with experts (e.g., cognitive load, heuristics). We then formalize these factors in a mathematical model and use optimization algorithms (i.e. simulated annealing) to find an optimum gesture mapping. We demonstrated our method in a text-entry application (i.e., complex interactive dialogue) comparing our approach with other computationally determined mappings using naive cost functions. Our results showed that the designers mapping (with all factors weighted by designers) presented a good balance on performance in all factors involved (speed, accuracy, comfort, memorability, etc.), consistently performing better than purely computational mappings. The results indicate that our hybrid approach can yield better results than either pure user-driven methodologies or pure data-driven approaches, for our application context featuring a large solution space and complex high-level factors.

Keywords: Gestural interaction · Semi-automated interaction design · Optimization · Computational approaches

1 Introduction

Gestures play an inherent role in our everyday communication, to the extent that we make use of them even when our interlocutor is not present, such as when speaking on the phone [26]. Gestures can be used to communicate meaningful information

Electronic supplementary material The online version of this chapter (https://doi.org/10.1007/978-3-030-29381-9_38) contains supplementary material, which is available to authorized users.

(*semiotic*), manipulate the physical world (*ergotic*) or even to learn through tactile exploration (*epistemic*) [4]. *Semiotic* gestures have been of particular interest to the HCI community as a powerful way to communicate with computers [23, 27].

The creation of interfaces involving gestural interaction remains a challenge. On one hand, advances in hardware have been remarkable. Gestural interaction is no longer restricted to data-gloves [7, 16, 34], and there is an increasing range of potential devices, allowing gesture tracking on un-instrumented hands or even in mobile formats. On the other hand, the methods and approaches to design these experiences have followed a much slower progression, not copying with the increasing number of devices available, and still relying on iterative methods and designers' expertise [9, 30].

As a result, interaction designers are faced with a very challenging task, with many factors involved in the creation of the gestural interface. While some factors will be easy to assess (e.g., device's comfort, accuracy, speed), others will be more complex (e.g., social acceptability and cognitive load). Particularly challenging is the elicitation of the most appropriate gestures and their mapping to tasks, which can easily lead to a combinatorial explosion. For instance, our example case study (text entry) offers more than 35K ways to map gestures to input commands and more than 12K ways to map these to actual letters. While iterative methodologies, designers' intuition and heuristics might help, it will be costly to navigate this vast solution space and identify the optimum interactive dialogue. In contrast, computational approaches might struggle to capture the complex subjective factors (i.e. social acceptability or cognitive load).

Unlike previous methods, we propose a hybrid approach, merging designer-led methods and computational approaches for the generation of robust gestural mappings under such challenging conditions (i.e. large solution space involving complex high-level factors). More specifically, we present an expert-guided, semi-automated design of interactive dialogues for low gestural resolution devices. Our approach consists of four steps: **(i)** *quantify low-level factors* (gesture error rates, speed or accuracy); **(ii)** *semi-structured workshops with designers* (identify *higher-level* factors, such as cognitive load and experts' heuristics); **(iii)** *formalization & optimization* (using objective and designers' knowledge to produce a mathematical model, and compute an optimum mapping); and **(iv)** *comparative evaluations* (to guide the iterative interface design, in a cost-effective manner).

We demonstrate this approach applying it to the design of a text entry technique using a Myo device. Figure 1(g) shows the result – a multi-level mapping between the input gestures and characters for text entry. To assess the value of our approach, we compared the mapping produced from our hybrid approach (incorporating designers' *high-level* factors) to several purely computational, naïve mappings. Particularly, we defined 6 alternative cost functions (i.e. models to assess the quality of a mapping) optimizing for time and accuracy, and explored up to 2.7 billion possible mappings, finding the optimum mapping for each of the 6 naïve cost functions.

Figure 1 shows histograms for all these mappings according to: the naïve computational metrics (a–f) and our approach (g). The optimum mappings computed are also highlighted within each histogram (bars). These show that, while naïve functions are highly ranked according to the designers-led metric (i.e. low scores, in Fig. 1g), the designers-led mapping ranked relatively poorly according to each of the 6 naïve cost functions used (red bar showing high values in Fig. 1(a–f)). This could either point

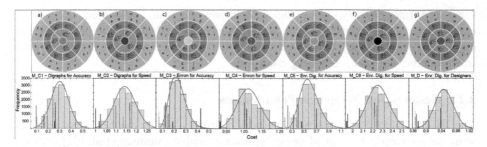

Fig. 1. From left to right (Top), the resulting mappings from the full optimization using different training database and cost function's factors. Below each layout, its histogram is shown. The cost per layout is represented along all histograms using color code (M_C1 = green, M_C2 = blue, M_C3 = yellow, M_C4 = magenta, M_C5 = cyan, M_C6 = black and M_D = red). (Color figure online)

towards designers' insight being irrelevant (or even harmful) or to computational methods failing to capture the complexity of the task. The results from our study show that the designers-led mapping actually showed a good balance on performance in all factors involved (speed, accuracy, comfort, memorability, etc.), consistently performing better than purely computational mappings. This reveals an untapped power in the designers' ability to identify a good cost function, with our approach helping to produce a suitable formalization to exploit the exploratory potential of computational approaches.

We finish the paper reflecting on these results and on how they should open a discussion on the added value of designers' intuition and heuristics when exploring gestural interfaces, and the need to make these an integral part of current design methodologies, for large solution spaces.

2 Related Work

2.1 Gestural Input Devices: A Growing Landscape

An increasing number of device options are available to support gestural interaction. Early instances included data gloves and tracking systems, mostly used for Virtual Reality [34] and multimodal interaction. These provide high gestural resolution (i.e. high number of distinct gestures), but require user instrumentation, hindering their applicability (i.e. users cannot simply walk-up and use them, wires limit mobility, etc). Wireless tracking systems (e.g., Leap Motion, Kinect, Project Soli) can improve applicability [6, 33] but their sensors are typically fixed, constraining the user to specific working spaces.

Mobile solutions have also been proposed. Kim et al. [17], presented a wrist-mounted optical system, allowing for hand gestural interaction. Myo armbands use Electromyography (EMG) to record and analyse electrical activity, allowing light-weight mobile gestural input, without hindering the use of our hands and avoiding self-occlusion problems. EMPress [22], combines EMG and pressure sensors, providing the same affordances of Myo bands, but with improved gestural resolution. Solutions to extend smartwatch interaction with around device gestural interaction have also been explored [20], but they either provide limited gestural resolution [15] or involve instrumenting the user's gesturing hand [36].

2.2 Gestures and Mappings: Point Studies

The HCI literature has produced a plethora of studies, which can help designers deal with the increasing number of device options available. Sturman et al. [31] explored and provided guidelines to improve gestural interaction in VR. Studies from Rekimoto [25], Wu and Balakrishnan [35] provide insight in the context of interactive surfaces, and Grossman et al. [12] explored the topic in the context of 3D volumetric displays, just to mention some. However, these illustrate how information related to gestural interaction is scattered across individual point studies, focused on specific tasks and contexts.

A more general approach to designing gestural interaction has been to formalize user elicitations [10, 14]. Designers seek end-user input on mapping gestures to tasks, classifying gestures into *high-level* groupings based on salient properties (e.g., the direction of movement, finger poses, etc). Elicitation studies have been successfully used in a number of contexts, but have also been criticized for biasing results by basing them on input from populations unfamiliar with the task or capabilities of a device [5, 10].

Alternatively, designers can gain insight about the mapping between gestures and tasks from related literature. Focusing on text entry (closest to our case study), the QWERTY keyboard serves as a preeminent example of discrete mapping, enforcing a 1:1 mapping between each key (gesture) and a letter (task). It also illustrates a mapping designed around the mechanical limitations of past typing machines, rather than its appropriateness for human input.

Computational approaches have proved to be valid tools to identify better mappings. Zhai et al. showed clear improvements for clarity (avoid gesture ambiguity) and typing speed for the most common digraphs in English [2] by simply swapping two keys (I and J). Bi et al. [1] explored alternative mappings by swapping a few neighbouring keys, to get a layout with better performance on speed, while retaining QWERTY similarity. Smith et al. showed a similar approach, improving clarity, speed and QWERTY similarity for 2D gesture typing. Alternatives for situations where 1:1 mappings are not available (e.g., mobile phones) have also been tackled using computational approaches, mostly through predictive text entry models [11, 24]. Other works have focused on exploring the extent of human hand's dexterity, creating mappings that benefit from all its bandwidth. Oulasvirta et al. [29] explored the biomechanical features of the hand (flexion levels, inter-digit dependencies), while PianoText [8] leverages users' musical skills, using a piano keyboard and chords to create an ultrafast text-entry system. In all cases, the benefits of computational approaches are limited by the use of low-level, quantifiable factors.

This situation motivates our approach. Interface designers might rely on methods that introduce biases into the process and will struggle to iteratively explore large solution spaces. Alternatively, computational approaches have great exploratory power, but they might fail to capture *higher-level* aspects of such complex tasks as they tend to bias/limit their results towards quantifiable factors that are easy to assess. Our approach intends to bridge this gap, being the first one to put together the benefits of both approaches (designers-led vs computational solutions), by blending designers' methods/insight and computational approaches.

3   Our Approach: Semi-automatic Mappings for Low Input Resolution

Our method aims to bridge the differences between designer-led and computational solutions, capturing designers' tacit knowledge of the domain, and formalizing it to be exploited by computational approaches. We thus combine *quantitative parameterization of relevant factors* with *domain expert knowledge elicitation*, into a structured approach. We refine these into a *formal model* quantifying the quality of each mapping and using a *global optimization algorithm* to explore the solution space, finding (potentially) the best solution. Our approach is compatible with iterative methodologies and can be seen as the tasks required for one iteration cycle. The outline of our approach can be divided into four stages:

(i) Quantification of Low-level Factors and Constraints

This stage involves the experiments and in-lab tests required to measure and quantify *low-level factors* and *constraints*. *Low-level factors* are simple parameters (e.g., time, errors) associated with the device or modality that might influence the design of the mapping and are easily quantifiable. *Low-level constraints* represent limitations within the device or the way it is used. Using our case study as an example, *factors* can include time to perform each Myo gesture, while excluding the double tap gesture due to its low accuracy can be an example of a *constraint*.

These quantified values will be used in the two following stages: First, they will inform designers, to help produce mappings and formulate heuristics; Second, they provide quantifiable data, used by our optimization methods.

(ii) Domain Expert Knowledge Elicitation

We use small teams of experts as a way to elicit the relevant factors that need consideration to design the interactive dialogue. Different methodologies can be used (e.g., workshops, elicitation studies, prototypes), which help on addressing a broad spectrum of aspects that cannot be covered by computational approaches alone (e.g., interface design, feedback elements, definition of the interactive dialogue, etc.).

However, while designers must consider the mapping of gestures to tasks, the ultimate intent of this process is *not* the specific mapping they create (computational searches will help make this specific choice). Instead, we focus on the designers' rationale that they use to determine what might be a good choice of gestures and mapping.

We reflect this rationale as *constraints* (i.e. conditions that must be obeyed) and *high-level factors* (i.e. non-obvious aspects or heuristics affecting interaction, such as social acceptance). These will help our following formalization process and the weighting of the relative importance of each of these factors.

(iii) Formalization & Optimization

In order to optimize our mappings, we first need to provide a metric for the quality of any given mapping. We formalize the quality of a mapping M as a cost function C computed as a weighted average of the factors identified by the experts, with lower values identifying better mapping:

$$C(M) = \sum k_i \cdot Factor_i(M) \tag{1}$$

The different factors are all normalized to a homogeneous range $[0, 1)$, according to the maximum and minimum values observed from the quantification. The value for k_i (influence of a given $Factor_i$ in the mapping M) needs to be estimated from the experts' impressions and analysis (further details follow). This assures that the contribution of each factor to the quality of M is the result of the designer's insight, and not the result of the factors' relative orders of magnitude. In our example, the sum of factor weights (Σk_i) equals one (factor as a ratio), but any other weight distribution reflecting the expert's impressions can be used. We then use a global optimization method to explore the solution space, converging towards an optimized solution given the factors and weighing values identified. Although our case study used Simulated Annealing [18], other optimization approaches can also be used.

(iv) Comparative-Summative Evaluation

While the normalization of the factors identified follows quantitative criteria, the estimation of the weight distribution (k_i) does not, and it relies on the subjective assessment of domain experts. Different weight distributions might reveal different ways of thinking about the solution (e.g., how more relevant is minimizing time over cognitive load?). Computing optimized mappings, according to different weight distributions, and comparing them through summative evaluations can allow for the best mapping to be identified. This reduces the exploration of the solution space to a few candidates (each resulting from a different weighting strategy), and integrates easily with iterative methodologies for gestural interaction, such as [9].

4   Case Study with Myo: Compute vs Design

We tested our approach using a Myo device (i.e. very low gestural resolution) for a text-entry task, both as a worst-case scenario and as an obvious match to Foley's analogy between natural language and a general interactive dialogue. The in-built IMU was not used and only the muscle activation was considered. This reduces our gestural resolution even further (more challenging solution space) but it also lends itself to interesting application scenarios. IMU-based gestures are defined relative to the body, and might be restricted during our daily life (i.e. while sitting in a bus, walking or inside a busy elevator). In contrast, our gestures remain relative to the hand, being still available in any situation where the wrist can be moved.

Finally, we also wanted to assess the added value of our designers' guided approach when compared to unconstrained computational approaches, based on observable and quantifiable factors alone. We replace the last stage of the method **(iv)**, by a description of the naïve computational mappings used, and a comparison against the results provided by these alternative approaches.

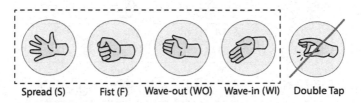

Spread (S)   Fist (F)   Wave-out (WO)   Wave-in (WI)   Double Tap

Fig. 2. Gestures possible with a Myo armband. We used the enclosed gestures in this work.

4.1 Problem Delimitation

Although Myo supports up to five gestures, at the time when this work was carried out "Double tap" was a recent addition with known inconsistencies in its detection [32]. Also, any fast and consecutive pair of gestures was detected as "Double tap" (i.e. false positives), conflicting with the use of other potential gesture chains For that reason, only the four remaining gestures were used (see spread (S), fist (F), wave-out (WO) and wave-in (WI), in Fig. 2). We quantified the performance of 16 possible 2-step chain gestures (consecution of two gestures, as in Fig. 3). Such 2-step chains require an intermediate relax action (i.e. hand returning to a neutral status between gestures) to be recognized by the system.

We asked our designers to categorize the 2-step chain gestures and they identified three different groups: *opposite*, *orthogonal* and *repeat*. *Opposite* chains combine gestures that activate opposing muscles. *Orthogonal* chains invoke orthogonal muscle groups; and *Repetitive* chains contain two instances of the same gesture (see Fig. 3). For example, WI+WI is a *Repeat*, WI+WO is of type *Opposite*, and WI+F is of type *Orthogonal*. We will borrow this for the analysis in this section (even if the distinction only appeared during the later workshops), as its analysis allows us to assess to what extent designers' insight reflects trends in data, or if some aspects pointed by designers would be likely to be included or ignored by alternative purely computational approaches. Finally, we also conducted a similar study for 3-step chain gestures. However, designers soon disregarded these chains during the later workshop (only use 2-chain gestures – **C1**), so our results for 3-step chains are omitted here for brevity.

(i) Quantification of Relevant Factors. We conducted a quantitative study, where participants performed a series of 2-step chain gestures under different input speeds to evaluate potentially relevant factors (i.e. errors, ergonomics, and preferred 2-step chain gestures). We calibrated the Myo for each individual participant and allowed them to become familiar with the 4 Myo gestures (Fig. 2) and our 2-step chain gestures (Fig. 3). They were then asked to perform the 2-step chain gestures shown on a display, which changed at regular speeds (i.e. each single gesture shown during 0.6 s, 0.8 s, 1.0 s or 1.2 s). Participants were asked to complete the gestures accurately and within the length of the prompts, which helped us identify the appropriate "typing speed".

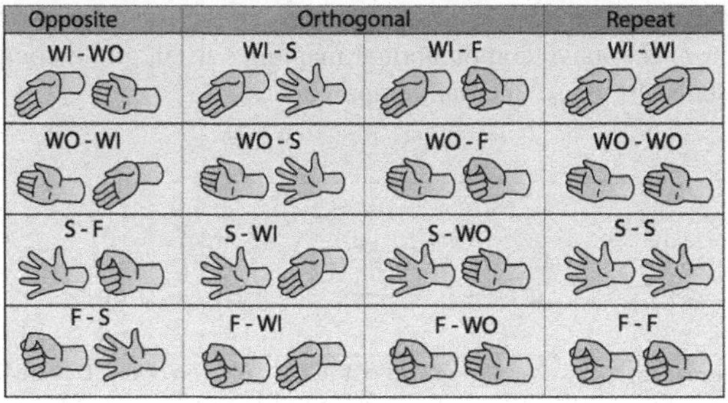

Fig. 3. Two-step chain gestures under designers' categories.

The experiment consisted of 4 blocks (one block for each input speed) including three repetitions of each of the sixteen 2-step chains gesture, resulting in 192 trials per participant. To avoid participants fatigue given this number of trials, each block was designed to be completed in about 4 min giving participants a 3 min break between blocks. Due to fatigue could potentially affect participants' performance, we ensured that each block duration was short with enough time to rest. The full experiment duration was then about 30 min, including calibration, training and breaks between blocks.

We counterbalanced the order of the input ratios using a Latin Square design, but gesture order was randomly selected. Time per gesture chain and accuracy (whether the gesture was recognized by Myo or not) were recorded. After each block (i.e. input speed), participants also filled in a Borg CR10 Scale [3] questionnaire (i.e. specially designed to quantify perceived exertion and fatigue [3, 28]) for each of the 16 2-step chain gestures. The experiment was performed by twelve participants (4 females), with an average age of 23.53 (21 to 30) SD = 2.98, with the study being approved by the local ethics board. The recruitment criteria were: (i) all participants right-handed; (ii) normal or correct-to-normal vision; (iii) no affections/injuries on their hands and wrists; and (iv) no prior experience with hand gesture interaction. Outliers were removed from the data (i.e. mean ± 2 standard deviation), filtering out 129 trials (5.59% of samples). We then conducted factorial repeated measures ANOVA ($p = 0.05$ to determine significance) on the factors measured, which we report in the following subsections.

Time Per Gesture **(F1).** Figure 4(a) shows the results of time for each 2-step chain. This analysis revealed significant effects of gesture type on time performance ($p < 0.001$), justifying its later inclusion as a factor (**F1**), even for a purely computational approach. Post-hoc tests with Bonferroni corrections show significant differences between certain gestures (e.g., WI+WO vs F+WO, $p = 0.03$; WI+WI vs F+F, $p < 0.001$), but the high number of pairs to compare (120), made such analysis poorly informative. Therefore, we did analyse time performance based on the categories proposed by the designers (*Repeat*, *Orthogonal* and *Opposite*). *Opposite* gestures performed best (M = 1.965 s; SD = 0.229 s), with significant differences ($p < 0.001$)

between the duration of *Opposite* and *Repeat* gestures (M = 2.022 s; SD = 0.255 s) and also between *Opposite* and *Orthogonal* gestures (M = 2.028 s; SD = 0.240 s; p = 0.001). On the other hand, clustering techniques (for time, accuracy or comfort) did not lead to identifying these categories. Thus, this is considered designers' tacit knowledge and would not be captured by purely computational approaches.

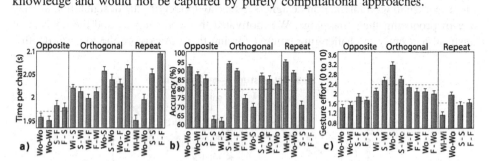

Fig. 4. (a) Time per chain gestures for Opposite, Orthogonal and Repeat categories (Mean in seconds); (b) Accuracy per chain gestures (Mean in %); (c) Effort results per chain gesture.

Accuracy Per Gesture (F2). Figure 4(b) shows our results for accuracy, revealing overall accuracy is low (70%–90%). An ANOVA analysis revealed an effect of gesture on accuracy (used as factor **F2**). Again, significant differences were found between specific pairs of gestures, but we focus the analysis on designers' categories. We only found significant differences between Repeat (M = 86.8%; SD = 21.57%) and Orthogonal categories (M = 81.28%; SD = 24.45%; p = 0.032), but with reduced effect size. Also, no clear patterns could be observed by looking at the categories (values well above and below the mean are present in all categories, in Fig. 4(b).

Gesture Comfort (F3). Comfort was rated by participants using a Borg CR10 Scale [3] questionnaire (Fig. 4(c) shows the average of participants' effort per gesture). According to their answers, we found *Repeat* gestures as the most comfortable (M = 1.5, SD = 0.33) followed by *opposite* gestures (M = 1.66 BCR10 and SD = 0.2) and the most uncomfortable reported were *orthogonal* gestures (M = 2.35 BCR10, SD = 0.38). It is worth mentioning that due to the number of trials (192) during the experiment, fatigue could potentially affect participants' performance. However, as shown in Fig. 4(c), the maximum score of effort was about 3.2 (in a scale from 0 to 10) suggesting that although we could observe differences in effort (e.g. *orthogonal* gestures were more uncomfortable), participants gave generally low scores in effort and therefore we considered unlikely that these low scores represent a negative effect on participants' performance during the experiment.

Typing Speed of 1 s (C2). The effects of typing speed on gesture time (Fig. 5(a)) and accuracy (Fig. 5(b)) were also analyzed. This revealed the first gesture (M = 0.783 s; SD = 0.119 s) is significantly shorter than the second one (M = 0.843 s; SD = 0.109 s), and also more accurate (p = 0.012). Using an input speed of 0.8 s users barely could keep up with the input speed (first gesture > 0.8 s, accuracy significantly smaller than input at 1.2 s (p < 0.001)). It is interesting how users (even if allowed more time) did not take more than 0.97 s to perform each gesture. No significant differences were found for typing speeds of 1 s or 1.2 s. Thus, we included typing speed of 1 s (**C2**) as a *low-level constraint* (i.e. fastest speed allowing sustained typing).

(ii) Designer's Workshop. After obtaining the relevant low-level factors, we carried out a workshop with interaction designers, as a way to identify the design rationale they use in producing their mappings. We motivated the workshop around the concept of gestural text-entry, a challenging context forcing them to explore the topic in depth.

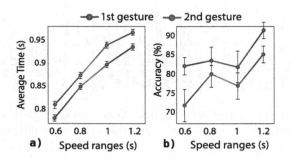

Fig. 5. (a) Average time for the first and second gesture; (b) Average accuracy for the first and second gesture. Error bars represent standard error.

We recruited four UX designers (no specific expertise on text-entry) from Anonymous University HCI group (other than where the main study was conducted), to produce a design scheme for the system. The workshop session lasted four hours. To encourage a broad perspective towards the design of an effective interactive dialogue, designers were encouraged to think about these four questions: *How to map gestures with letters? What is a good interface layout? What feedback elements are required? Is the operation easy to remember?* The workshop was kept open-ended to encourage creative thinking, but one researcher stayed in the room, to answer designers' questions. It must be noted that the quantitative results from **(i)** (e.g., speed, accuracy) were only provided if and when specifically requested by designers, to not bias their thoughts.

At the beginning of the workshop, designers considered using chained gestures right away. Three-chain gestures were soon discarded by designers, due to their high cognitive load (too many potential gestures to remember) and discomfort (orthogonal and opposite gestures). Thus, they limited their search to 2 step-chain gestures (**C1**) and a predictive text entry. This used 8 categories, mapping 4 letters to each gesture/category and addressing 32 characters: the 26 letters from the English alphabet and the 6 most common punctuation characters (space, period, comma, question mark, exclamation mark and hyphen). They also felt inclined to explore alternatives beyond the constraints defined (such as using both hands or using continuous gestures, using the duration of the gesture as a variable). At the end of the workshop, designers were asked to present their interface layout and to reflect on it, as a way to verbalize their rationale. In the next subsection, we report these observations as *high-level factors* and *constraints*.

From Designers' Rationale to Factors and Constraints. Designers soon got interested in the time (**F1**) and accuracy (**F2**) of each gesture and experimented the level of
comfort (**F3**) afforded by each gesture by performing them casually. They considered
the *WI* gesture to be the most 'natural' gesture, and *WO* as the least comfortable. They
also found the *F* and *S* gestures hard to perform. Designers also became interested in
the frequency of using each letter, using the ENRON corpus [19] to inform this aspect.

At the end of the workshop, they presented their proposed interface design (see
Fig. 6(a)), reflecting both the appropriate interface design and the way the interactive
dialogue should work. The UI layout consisted of several concentric circles, working as
a decision tree with choices at each node. Users would identify the target letter in the
external level/ring and then follow the path through the ring from the inside out,
performing the gestures to reach the chosen letter. The interface should highlight the
rings, as gestures are recognized, e.g., Figure 6(b), shows Fist + Spread gestures used
to type '*q*', and feedback displayed.

The final scheme presented reflected aspects of their rationale (*high-level factors*),
highly relevant for our approach. For instance, they attempted to maximize the usage of
WI (**F4**), while avoiding *WO* (**F5**) and *S* gestures (**F6**). They also found the use of
orthogonal gestures very uncomfortable and suggested avoiding them (**C3**).

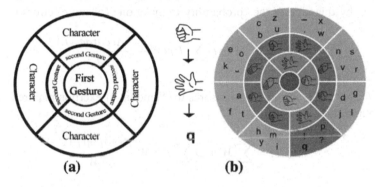

(a)   **(b)**

Fig. 6. (a) Interface layout proposed by designers; (b) Final design using their factors and our
search method. Typing a "q" requires to perform the chain gesture fist (F) - spread (S).

As a second major concern, designers also attempted to reduce the cognitive load of
the mapping, by applying several heuristics. For instance, they suggested keeping all
vowels clustered together (in two categories only) (**F7**). They also placed alphabetically
adjacent letters in the same categories (e.g., "abcd"), which was considered as a relevant factor (**F8**). These techniques were meant to facilitate users' ability to remember
the layout.

Designers also tried to assign the comfortable and fast gestures to the most frequent
characters. They attempted to build a mapping solving the problem in an optimal way,
and including all identified factors. However, they failed to find a clear candidate
mapping, illustrating the challenge designers face when addressing large solution
spaces.

(iii) Formalization & Optimization. We used the *constraints* (C1–C3) and *factors* (F1–F8) identified in the previous stages to refine our definition of the problem and to formalize the description of our candidate mappings. Due to our constraints, we limited our search to 2-step chain gestures (C1), with typing speed 1 s (C2) and used only *"opposite"* and *"repeated"* gestures (C3), resulting in only 8 possible gesture chains (see Fig. 3).

Each factor was formalized (quantified), with the common criteria that lower values represent a better mapping. Let D be our dictionary (we use the ENRON database [19], with duplicates to represent word frequency). Let W be a word and L a letter. Let *Time (L)*, *Accuracy (L)* and *Exertion (L)* be the mean time, accuracy and effort (i.e. the inverse of comfort) of the gesture associated with letter L, as measured from our quantitative studies from **(i)**.

Time Factor (F1). This factor favours fast typing speeds, by quantifying the "average time to input a letter according to our dictionary".

$$F1(M) = \sum_{W \, in \, D} \sum_{L \, in \, W} \frac{Time}{|D||W|} \qquad (2)$$

Accuracy Factor (F2). This factor enforces mappings with gestures of high accuracy recognition, by quantifying the "probability to make one (or more) errors in a word".

$$F2(M) = \sum_{W \, in \, D} \sum_{L \, in \, W} \frac{1 - Accuracy(L)}{|D|} \qquad (3)$$

Comfort Factor (F3). This factor measures the "amount of exertion required to input a letter", to minimize effort.

$$F3(M) = \sum_{W \, in \, D} \sum_{L \, in \, W} \frac{Exertion(L)}{|D||W|} \qquad (4)$$

Wave-in Factor (F4). This factor encourages the use of *WI* gesture, considered comfortable by designers. This factor computes "the average density of non-*WI* gestures per letter".

$$F4(M) = \sum_{W \, in \, D} \sum_{L \, in \, W} \frac{isNot \, Wi(L)}{|D||W|} \qquad (5)$$

Wave-out Factor (F5). This factor discourages the use of *WO* gesture, as it was considered less comfortable. Particularly, it quantifies "average density of *WO* gestures per letter".

$$F5(M) = \sum_{W \, in \, D} \sum_{L \, in \, W} \frac{is \, Wo(L)}{|D||W|} \qquad (6)$$

Spread Factor (F6). This factor penalizes the use of S gestures, as they were considered less comfortable. This factor computes the "average density of S gestures per letter".

$$F6(M) = \sum W \, in \, D \sum L \, in \, W \frac{is \, S(L)}{|D||W|} \tag{7}$$

Vowels Factor (F7). This factor counts the "number of categories containing vowels", to favour vowels are grouped in a few categories.

$$F7(M) = \max(|V|), \, V \subset C / \forall c \in V, \, \{a,e,i,o,u\} \cap c \neq \varnothing \tag{8}$$

Consecution Factor (F8). This factor benefits mappings where letters are assigned to categories in consecutive order. Thus, it measures the "number of non-consecutive (NC) letter per category (C)".

$$F8(M) = \frac{NC(C[0], C[1]) + NC(C[1], C[2]) + NC(C[2], C[3])}{3} \tag{9}$$

Determining the Weight of Each Factor and Optimization. Each factor was normalized to a *[0, 1)* range, as in Table 1. This allows the relevance of each factor to be assessed in terms of weight alone (and not according to the factor's scale). Constants s_w and l_w represent the length of the shortest and longest words in D, respectively; m_t and M_t stand for the minimum and maximum gesture times, and m_a and M_a stand for the minimum and maximum gesture accuracy respectively. Weights were then determined based on the designers' insight. It must be noted that this was the interpretation of the research team (i.e. two transcribing and cross-validating notes from the experiment, and two translating them into the weights described in Table 1), as we had no further access to the designers involved in **(ii)**.

Table 1. Factors used use for MDes (our proposed mapping), ranges and weights (ki).

	F1	F2	F3	F4	F5	F6	F7	F8
Min	$|s_w| \cdot m_t$	$|s_w| \cdot (1 - m_a)$	0.125	0	0	0	2	0
Max	$|l_w| \cdot M_t$	$|1w| \cdot (M_a)$	1.75	1	1	1	5	1
Ki	0.35	0.20	0.1	0.05	0.05	0.05	0.1	0.1

We used these weights (cost function as described by Eq. (1)) and simulated annealing (SA) [18] to find the optimum mapping. Initially, letters were randomly assigned to the 8 categories (only *"opposite"* and *"repeated"* gestures, see Fig. 3) and neighbour states were computed by permutation of single letters between two random categories (diameter = 32). Transition acceptance between states follows the traditional method by Kirkpatrick [18]. The cooling schedule was empirically tuned with $N_s = 20$

step adjustments per temperature step, $N_t = 7$ temperatures steps per temperature change, $R_t = 0.85$ (Cooling factor). The initial temperature was set in $T(0) = 180$. The final mapping is shown in Figs. 7(b) and (c).

Given the designers' constraints (no *Orthogonal* gestures), the solution space was limited to $\binom{32}{4} = 35960$ mappings and a full search would have been feasible. However, this was not feasible for the pure computational solutions we compared against (larger solution space), and we used the same schedule to aid fairness in comparison.

(iv) Computing Alternative Approaches. Some of the factors and observations made by designers were hard to justify purely looking at the data. The categories identified (*Repeat, Opposite* and *Orthogonal*) show weak differences and, given any performance metric, all of them have gestures both well above and below the sample mean. Even in the case of time per gesture (clearer distinctive behaviour for *Opposite*), the use of clustering techniques would not result in the categories identified.

Picking specific data could seem to back up the designers' insight. For instance, *WI+WI* was the most comfortable gesture (M = 1.15 Borg CR10 Scale –BCR10) and *WO+S* as the least comfortable (M = 3.15 BCR10), followed by *S+WO* (M = 2.6 BCR10). While *WO+WI* resulted the fastest 2-step chain gesture (M = 1.947 s, SD = 0.228), *WI+WI* was second fastest (M = 1.949 s, SD = 0.242), the most accurate (M = 95.13%, SD = 13.73) and the most comfortable gesture performed (M = 1.15 BCR10), whilst *WO+S* the least comfortable (M = 3.15 BCR10).

These point observations could support designers' factors **F3** and **F4**, but observational bias and the limited size of the sample would make for weak evidence. This was found worrying, as it could point towards a weak ability of the designers to analyse the complexity of the problem. On the other hand, factors could also reflect designers' *tacit knowledge*, that is, understanding of complex mechanics of the task which were difficult to articulate, but still relevant. Thus, we decided to compare the designer's guided solution against six naïve computational solutions, not considering designers' *high-level factors* and *constraints* (e.g., 8 categories used to allow comparison, but not constrained to *Repeat* and *Opposite* gestures alone). These naïve solutions will both help us assess the added value introduced by feeding the designers' insight into the optimization method; and also challenge their decisions/constraints.

These six solutions were generated as a combination of two elements: **(a)** the training dataset: the Enron (E) dataset [19]; the most common Digraphs (D) in English language [21], and a combination of both (E+D); and **(b)** the cost functions: two were defined, one assessing time per gesture (factor **F1**) and another one assessing accuracy (**F2**). e.g., **M_C1** represents the mapping obtained with the best *Accuracy* assessed by Digraphs dataset. For each of the six combinations, we generated all the possible subsets of 8 gestures (from the 16 different 2-step gestures possible) and used Simulated Annealing to compute the best letter combinations. We explored $\binom{16}{8} \cdot \binom{32}{4} \cdot 6 = \sim 2.8$ *billion* possible mappings, with Fig. 1 showing the best mapping for each of the 6 naïve cost functions.

Table 2. The percentile per mapping (0 to 100) across the seven cost functions (CF) used in the optimization process. On the right columns, AVG and SD for the data per CF condition are shown. The best mappings for speed (M_C4) and accuracy (M_C5) are highlighted in green while our proposed mapping (M_Des) is highlighted in blue.

Cost/Mapping	M_C1	M_C2	M_C3	M_C4	M_C5	M_C6	M_Des	Average	SD
C1-A$_{Acc}$	0	33	5	3	1	31	33	0.304	0.077
C2-A$_{Sp}$	21	0	65	1	45	1	67	1.147	0.052
C3-E$_{Acc}$	4	100	0	11	1	29	5	0.238	0.066
C4-E$_{Sp}$	81	50	45	0	60	1	40	1.077	0.064
C5-D+E$_{Acc}$	1	80	1	3	0	20	10	0.587	0.014
C6-D+E$_{Sp}$	49	4	42	1	40	0	41	2.258	0.110
D-D+E$_{Mix}$	10	40	1	1	1	1	0	0.949	0.025

5 Analytical and Summative Evaluation

Figure 1 shows histograms for all possible mappings according to our seven metrics (the naïve computational metrics (a–f) and designer-led (g)). The best mappings per metric are also highlighted (as colour bars) in the remaining histograms, for comparison. Table 2, shows this information in a numerical format. The best results for Accuracy mappings (i.e. M_{C1}, M_{C3} and M_{C5}) was M_{C5} (best average percentile across the 6 naïve functions, within its category), while the selected mapping for Speed (i.e. M_{C2}, M_{C4} and M_{C6}) was M_{C4}. For clarity, during the comparative evaluation, we will refer to these as time (M_{Ti}), and accuracy mappings (M_{Acc}), instead of (M_{C4} and M_{C5}).

It was also interesting to see how the designers-led layout (M_{Des}), rated against the other mappings. While computational mappings consistently scored well using the designers' cost function (see the last row), the designers mapping scored much more mediocre results (see column M_{Des}), being usually in fourth or fifth position (or even last) among the mappings considered. We then carried out a user study to evaluate the performance of the generated mappings: M_{Ti}, M_{Acc} and M_{Des}. We added one additional mapping for text-entry i.e. a simple alphabetical distribution (M_{Abc}) shown in Fig. 7(d), as a baseline comparison (minimum cognitive load, not optimized).

5.1 Experiment Setup

At the beginning of the session, we calibrated the Myo for each individual participant. Subsequently, each mapping was shown on the screen with its different layout and letter distribution (see Fig. 7). Participants were then instructed to "type" a sentence shown above the circle by performing the specific chain of gestures (i.e. identifying the two gestures they need to perform to select a given letter). The system included feedback cues i.e. visual highlights in the category selected at each step (see Fig. 6(b)), and auditory effects.

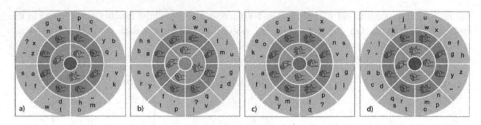

Fig. 7. (a) Gesture mappings of time factor (M_{Ti}), (b) accuracy factor (M_{Acc}), (c) mixed mapping according to designers' factors (M_{Des}) and (d) alphabetical gesture mapping (M_{Abc}).

Participants were allowed to practice the chain gestures in a training stage to complete 4 sentences before each block, in order to get familiar with the layouts. Participants performed 4 blocks of 3 sentences each, completing 28 sentences in total (700 letters/gesture chains). The sentences in the blocks had from 4 to 6 words, and 4 to 6 letters per word, being selected by using the Levenshtein algorithm [13] to compute representative sets of sentences from our dictionary. The full experiment duration was 45 min. Similarly, as described in the first study, each block was designed to be completed in about 8 min giving participants a 3 min break between blocks to avoid fatigue. Moreover, since *orthogonal* gestures (the most uncomfortable gestures found in the first study and rated on average ~3.2 in a scale from 0 to 10) were not employed in this study, we considered unlikely that fatigue negatively affects participants' performance during the experiment. We counterbalanced the order of the sets (i.e. sentences) and mappings using a 4×4 Latin Square design. Figure 8 shows our experimental setup.

The system collected the time per letter and error rate automatically. User–satisfaction questionnaires after each block (mapping), collected information about typing comfort and how easy each it was to remember each mapping. Finally, at the end of the experiment, participants also chose their favourite mapping according to 4 aspects (easy to type, comfort, speed and easy to remember). Sixteen right-handed participants took part in the experiment (4 Females, average age of 29.33, SD = 3.86), which was approved by the local ethics board. The recruitment criteria were the same as in the first experiment.

Fig. 8. Experimental setup for the typing task.

An a priori statistical power analysis was performed for sample size estimation in G*Power. Running a power analysis on a repeated measures ANOVA between mapping conditions (i.e., M_{Ti}, M_{Acc}, M_{Des} and M_{Abc}), repeated 28 times corresponding to the 28 sentences on the experiment, a power of 0.95, an alpha level of 0.05, and a medium effect size (f = 0.196, ηp^2 = 0.037, critical F = 1.1), required a sample size of approximately 8 participants. Thus, our proposed sample of 12 participants was adequate for the purposes of this study.

5.2   Analysis of Results

A Repeated Measure ANOVA was conducted to compare the effect of the four types of mappings (M_{Ti} vs M_{Acc} vs M_{Des} vs M_{Abc}) on the time of chain of gestures. Results revealed a significant effect on the average time, $F_{(3,45)} = 25.82$, $p < .001$ depending on the type of mapping, with the designers' mapping providing best results. Post-hoc comparisons using Bonferroni correction showed statistically significant differences in time, specifically between M_{Des} ($M = 1.577$ s, $SD = 0.622$ s) compared to M_{Abc} ($M = 1.785$ s, $SD = 0.674$ s; $p < 0.001$), but also M_{Des} and M_{Ti} ($M = 1.782$ s, $SD = 0.653$ s; $p < 0.001$). No such difference was found compared to M_{Acc} ($M = 1.64$ s, $SD = 0.71$ s), $p = 0.279$. Surprisingly, M_{Ti} did not provide the best results for time, which seems to indicate it failed to capture the complexity of the typing task.

The average error per mapping was small for all conditions. As expected, M_{Acc} got the lowest error score as it was computed to minimize errors. Repeated Measure ANOVA showed a significant effect of the type of mapping (M_{Ti} vs M_{Acc} vs M_{Des} vs M_{Abc}) on the number of errors $F_{(3,45)} = 7.71$, $p < .001$($\eta_p^2 = 0.009$ small effect). Post-hoc comparisons showed statistically significant differences for errors, specifically between M_{Acc}($M = 0.072$errors, $SD = 0.293$errors) compared to M_{Des} ($M = 0.139$errors, $SD = 0.444$errors), $p = 0.001$ and M_{Abc} ($M = 0.149$errors, $SD = 0.520$errors), $p = 0.001$; but no such difference was found compared to M_{Ti} ($M = 0.087$errors, $SD = 0.369$errors), $p = 1$. Additionally, we found a significant difference in M_{Ti} compared to M_{Des}, and M_{Abc}, p <= 0.035. These results suggest that M_{Acc} and M_{Ti} produced the lowest number of errors when participants performed the gesture chains to "type" the sentences.

Figure 11 shows the score given by participants after each block in relation to memorability (left) and comfort (right). In both cases, participants gave higher scores to

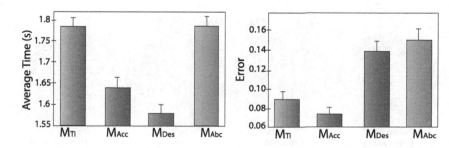

Fig. 9. Scatter plot of average gesture time (left) and errors (right) per mapping. Bars represent standard error of mean.

M_{Acc} and M_{Des}, with worse results for M_{Ti}. These results align with the user's final appreciations at the end of the experiment, in which participants compared among all mappings (see Fig. 10). In this case, most of the participants reported M_{Des} as the most comfortable (50%) and easiest to type mapping (44%), followed by M_{Acc} (31% and 25%, respectively). Although M_{Des} allowed for faster typing (Fig. 9, left), M_{Acc} was perceived as faster by participants. As expected, participants also reported M_{Abc}, as the easiest to remember (44%), followed by M_{Des} (31%).

6   Discussions

Our results seem to indicate the designer-led semi-automatic mapping M_{Des} provided better results in terms of time, comfort and users' preference when compared to the remaining mappings. It consistently appeared as the best or second-best option, only performing worse in terms of accuracy, where very small differences (effect size) were present among mappings. This suggests that users preferred the mappings created by the combinations of experts' knowledge (proposed weights for M_{Des}) and the computational optimization. This might reflect the difficulty to model all aspects related to interaction using only low-level factors, and how these might be misleading when the complexity of the task increases. Even for our naïve cost functions, M_{Ti} did not actually lead to faster typing speeds; and they also failed to predict the performance of M_{Des} (expected to be poor, as shown in Table 2), even for the specific factors (i.e. time) they measured. The results also highlight the value of designers' higher-level insight, even if it cannot be directly justified from data. For instance, the categories identified (*Orthogonal*, *Repeat*, *Opposite*) guided constraint **C3**, but they could not be identified from clustering techniques. During the workshop, we pointed out that the *high-level factors* **F4**, **F5** and **F6** were already covered by *low-level* ones, but designers still decided to keep them. We understand these reflect *tacit knowledge* which, even if hard to verbalize/rationalize, was still relevant to the task. The results obtained by the designers' mapping should highlight the relevance of such designers' insight (i.e. high-level factors identified), but it also illustrates the value of our hybrid approach, exploiting computational methods to keep this human knowledge in the optimization loop.

The resources required for both the designers' workshops and the brute-force exploration of alternative mappings must also be considered. The full search to create

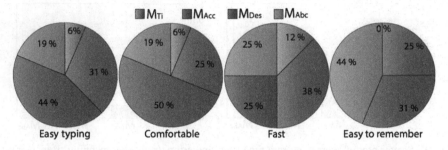

Fig. 10. Participants' preference per mapping (M_{Ti}, M_{Acc}, M_{Des} and M_{Abc}) regarding their task experience (ease typing, comfort, speed and ease to remember).

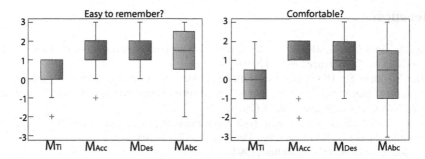

Fig. 11. Box plots for memorability (left) and comfort (right) per mapping. Horizontal red bars and boxes represent medians and IQRs. Whiskers stretch to points within median ± 1.5 IQR. Outliers shown as single red crosses. (Color figure online)

our alternative mappings (2.7 billion combinations explored, for the 6 alternatives) required 5 standard desktop machines running over 5 days (development costs for software not considered). In comparison, the designers' feedback was gathered during a single workshop of 4 h and still managed to identify relevant *high-level factors*, *constraints*, and provided good results for the final mapping. This seems to indicate designers' involvement can be easily justified, producing relevant input to underlying computational approaches and potentially reducing development costs.

Finally, our use-case must be considered as an illustrative example of our approach, rather than an exemplar text-entry system. Text entry systems can leverage extensive task-specific knowledge (e.g., digraph transitions, predictive models, etc.), which can allow defining effective mappings even from low-level factors. Instead, our case study provides an example that is generalizable to a broader spectrum of applications using gestural interaction; illustrates the challenges related to creating complex interactive dialogues from low-level factors; and highlights the benefits related to designers' insight into the process.

7 Conclusion

We presented an approach for semi-automatic generation of gesture mappings for devices with low gestural resolution. Our approach consists of quantifying observable *low-level factors* such as individual gesture error rates, speed and accuracy; identifying how designers weigh different factors to create a weighted cost function, which is then fed into a computational approach to find the optimum gesture set and its mapping to tasks. Comparing the results of our mapping with the mappings obtained from other naïvely constructed cost functions shows that overall users perform consistently well with our mapping in terms of speed, comfort and memorability. These results highlight the value of our approach, as a tool to guide the designer-led computational approach to generate complex mappings. This approach should not stand as a replacement for traditional HCI methods, but as a tool to help such iterative processes to converge faster towards satisfying solutions, particularly within complex application domains featuring large solution spaces and complex/subjective factors influencing interaction.

References

1. Bi, X., Smith, B.A., Zhai, S.: Quasi-qwerty soft keyboard optimization. In: Proceedings of the SIGCHI Conference. ACM (2010)
2. Bi, X., Zhai, S.: IJQwerty: what difference does one key change make? gesture typing keyboard optimization bounded by one key position change from qwerty. In: Proceedings of the 2016 CHI Conference. ACM (2016)
3. Borg, G.: Psychophysical scaling with applications in physical work and the perception of exertion. Scand. J. Work Environ. Health 1, 55–58 (1990)
4. Cadoz, C.: Les réalités virtuelles (1994)
5. Davey, B., Parker, K.R.: Requirements elicitation problems: a literature analysis. Issues Inform. Sci. Inf. Technol. 12, 71–82 (2015)
6. Dutta, T.: Evaluation of the Kinect™ sensor for 3-D kinematic measurement in the workplace. Appl. Ergon. 43(4), 645–649 (2012)
7. Fabiani, L., Burdea, G.C., Langrana, N.A., Gomez, D.: Human interface using the Rutgers Master II force feedback interface. In: VRAIS (1996)
8. Feit, A.M., Oulasvirta, A.: Pianotext: redesigning the piano keyboard for text entry. In: Proceedings of the 2014 Conference DIS. ACM (2014)
9. Gabbard, J.L., Hix, D., Swan, J.E.: User-centered design and evaluation of virtual environments. IEEE Comput. Graph. Appl. 19(6), 51–59 (1999)
10. Gelain, M., Pini, M.S., Rossi, F., Venable, K.B., Walsh, T.: Elicitation strategies for soft constraint problems with missing preferences: properties, algorithms and experimental studies. Artif. Intell. 174(3), 270–294 (2010)
11. Gong, J., Haggerty, B., Tarasewich, P.: An enhanced multitap text entry method with predictive next-letter highlighting. In: CHI 2005. ACM (2005)
12. Grossman, T., Wigdor, D., Balakrishnan, R.: Multi-finger gestural interaction with 3D volumetric displays. In: Proceedings of the 17th Annual ACM UIST. ACM (2004)
13. Haldar, R., Mukhopadhyay, D.: Levenshtein distance technique in dictionary lookup methods: an improved approach. arXiv e-print (arXiv:1101.1232) (2011)
14. Kammer, D., Wojdziak, J., Keck, M., Groh, R., Taranko, S.: Towards a formalization of multi-touch gestures. In: ACM ISS, pp. 49–58. ACM (2010)
15. Kerber, F., Lessel, P., Krüger, A.: Same-side hand interactions with arm-placed devices using EMG. In: Proceedings of the ACM CHI, pp. 1367–1372. ACM, Seoul (2015)
16. Kessler, G.D., Hodges, L.F., Walker, N.: Evaluation of the CyberGlove as a whole-hand input device. ACM TOCHI 2(4), 263–283 (1995)
17. Kim, D., et al.: Digits: freehand 3D interactions anywhere using a wrist-worn gloveless sensor. In: Proceedings of ACM UIST. ACM (2012)
18. Kirkpatrick, S., Gelatt, C.D., Vecchi, M.P.: Optimization by simulated annealing. Science 220(4598), 671–680 (1983)
19. Klimt, B., Yang, Y.: The enron corpus: a new dataset for email classification research. In: Boulicaut, J.-F., Esposito, F., Giannotti, F., Pedreschi, D. (eds.) ECML 2004. LNCS (LNAI), vol. 3201, pp. 217–226. Springer, Heidelberg (2004). https://doi.org/10.1007/978-3-540-30115-8_22
20. Knibbe, J., et al.: Extending interaction for smart watches: enabling bimanual around device control. In: CHI 2014. ACM (2014)
21. Lyons, J.: A branch of both mathematics and computer science, cryptography is the study and practice of obscuring information. http://practicalcryptography.com/
22. McIntosh, J., et al.: EMPress: practical hand gesture classification with wrist-mounted EMG and pressure sensing. In: Proceedings of the 2016 CHI Conference. ACM (2016)

23. McNeill, D.: Hand and Mind: What Gestures Reveal About Thought. University of Chicago Press, Chicago (1992)
24. Pavlovych, A., Stuerzlinger, W.: Model for non-expert text entry speed on 12-button phone keypads. In: Proceedings of the SIGCHI Conference. ACM (2004)
25. Rekimoto, J.: SmartSkin: an infrastructure for freehand manipulation on interactive surfaces. In: Proceedings of the SIGCHI Conference. ACM (2002)
26. Rimé, B.: The elimination of visible behaviour from social interactions: effects on verbal, nonverbal and interpersonal variables. Eur. J. Soc. Psychol. **12**(2), 113–129 (1982)
27. Rimé, B., Schiaratura, L.: Gesture and Speech (1991)
28. Robertson, R.J., et al.: Concurrent validation of the OMNI perceived exertion scale for resistance exercise. Med. Sci. Sports Exerc. **35**(2), 333–341 (2003)
29. Sridhar, S., Feit, A.M., Theobalt, C., Oulasvirta, A.: Investigating the dexterity of multi-finger input for mid-air text entry. In: Proceedings of ACM CHI Conference (2015)
30. Sturman, D.J., Zeltzer, D.: A design method for "whole-hand" human-computer interaction. ACM Trans. Inf. Syst. (TOIS). **11**(3), 219–238 (1993)
31. Sturman, D.J., Zeltzer, D., Pieper, S.: Hands-on interaction with virtual environments. In: Proceedings of the 2nd Annual ACM SIGGRAPH UIST. ACM (1989)
32. Thalmic-Labs. https://support.getmyo.com/hc/en-us/articles/205180865-Double-Tap-gesture-is-not-recognized
33. Weichert, F., Bachmann, D., Rudak, B., Fisseler, D.: Analysis of the accuracy and robustness of the leap motion controller. Sensors **13**(5), 6380–6393 (2013)
34. Weissmann, J., Salomon, R.: Gesture recognition for virtual reality applications using data gloves and neural networks. In: International Joint Conference on Neural Networks, 1999. IJCNN 1999. IEEE (1999)
35. Wu, M., Balakrishnan, R.: Multi-finger and whole hand gestural interaction techniques for multi-user tabletop displays. In: Proceedings of ACM UIST. ACM (2003)
36. Zhang, Y., Zhou, J., Laput, G., Harrison, C.: SkinTrack: Using the body as an electrical waveguide for continuous finger tracking on the skin. In: Proceedings of the 2016 CHI Conference. ACM (2016)

Ensuring the Consistency Between User Requirements and GUI Prototypes: A Behavior-Based Automated Approach

Thiago Rocha Silva[1](✉) [iD], Marco Winckler[2] [iD], and Hallvard Trætteberg[1]

[1] Department of Computer Science,
Norwegian University of Science and Technology (NTNU), Trondheim, Norway
{thiago.silva,hal}@ntnu.no
[2] SPARKS-i3S, Université Nice Sophia Antipolis (Polytech),
Sophia Antipolis, France
winckler@unice.fr

Abstract. In a user-centered design process, graphical user interface (GUI) prototypes may be seen as an important early artifact to design and validate user requirements before making strong commitments with a full-fledged version of the user interface. Ensuring the consistency of GUI prototypes with other representations of the user requirements is then a critical aspect of the design process. This paper presents an approach which extends Behavior-Driven Development (BDD) by employing an ontology in order to provide automated assessment for GUI prototypes as design artifacts. The approach has been evaluated by exploiting user requirements described by a group of experts in the flight tickets e-commerce domain. Such requirements gave rise to a set of User Stories that have been used to automatically check the consistency of Balsamiq prototypes which were reengineered from an existing web system for booking business trips. The results have shown our approach was able to identify different types of inconsistencies in the set of analyzed artifacts, allowing to build an effective correspondence between user requirements and their representation in GUI prototypes.

Keywords: Behavior-Driven Development (BDD) · User Stories · GUI Prototypes · User Requirements Assessment

1 Introduction

In iterative processes, the design of graphical user interfaces (GUIs) can evolve all along the software development process as a result of requirements evolution and change, or the need of understanding and validating a given interpretation of requirements [1]. While the beginning of the project usually requires a low-level of formality with GUI prototypes being hand-sketched to explore design solutions and clarify user requirements, the development phase requires more refined versions

© IFIP International Federation for Information Processing 2019
Published by Springer Nature Switzerland AG 2019
D. Lamas et al. (Eds.): INTERACT 2019, LNCS 11746, pp. 644–665, 2019.
https://doi.org/10.1007/978-3-030-29381-9_39

frequently describing presentation and dialog aspects of interaction. Full-fledged versions of user interfaces are generally produced only later in the design process, and frequently corresponds to how the user "see" the system. In the users' point of view, if some feature is not available through the presentation of a user interface, this feature does not exist for them.

Behavior-Driven Development (BDD) [2] has stood out in the software engineering community as an effective approach to provide automated acceptance testing by specifying natural language user requirements and their tests in a single textual artifact. BDD benefits from a requirements specification based on User Stories [3] which are easily understandable for both technical and non-technical stakeholders. In addition, User Stories allow specifying "executable requirements", i.e. requirements that can be directly tested from their textual specification. Despite its benefits providing automated testing of user requirements, BDD and other testing approaches focus essentially on assessing interactive artifacts that are produced late in the design process, such as full-fledged versions of user interfaces. As far as early artifacts such as rough GUI prototypes are a concern, current approaches offer no support for automated assessment.

Motivated by such a gap, this paper presents an approach based on BDD and User Stories to support the specification and the automated assessment of user requirements on low-fidelity web GUI prototypes designed along the development cycle of interactive systems. The approach helps to align methods for GUI design and assessment with methods for engineering interactive systems. On one hand, our method proposes to engineer GUIs by guiding the development team (especially designers) to avoid design solutions that conflict with the user requirements. On the other hand, the method also helps to pinpoint eventual violations of user requirements at the user interface level, helping designers to have a better understanding of where and when violations of user requirements occur.

The common-ground of concepts for describing the prototypes as well as the set of user-system interactive behaviors is provided by means of an ontology [4, 5]. Requirements in BDD stories can be formulated and tested at two levels: the domain level and the interaction level. Our approach targets requirements at the interaction level, and this paper shows how the ontology can support test automation of requirements at this level without manually coding the tests. The following sections present the related works and foundations, the proposed approach with its technical implementation, and the results we got by assessing the reengineered GUI prototypes from an existing web system to book business trips.

2 Related Works

Artifacts other than final versions of user interfaces are not commonly tested. A common argument is that they cannot be "executed" in order to be tested. Since long time ago, the design aspect of early representations of user interfaces is usually only inspected manually in an attempt to verify its adequacy [6]. Inspections can be of different types including formal technical reviews, walkthroughs, peer desk check, informal ad-hoc feedback, and so on [7]. When evaluation of the user requirements representation on such artifacts is considered, requirements traceability techniques are employed as a way to trace such requirements along their multiple versions (horizontal traceability) or along their representation in another artifacts (vertical traceability) [8].

Some approaches concentrated efforts in providing automated tools to keep compatibility between requirements and their own artifacts. Luna et al. [9], for example, propose WebSpec which is a requirement artifact that can be used in conjunction with mockups to provide UI simulations, allowing some level of requirements validation, but not for out-of-approach UI prototypes like Balsamiq. Buchmann and Karagiannis [10] presents a modeling method for the elicitation of requirements for mobile apps that enables semantic traceability for the requirements representation. The method however is not focused on UI prototypes and can only validate requirements modeled within the approach. As far as a common vocabulary for the dialog aspect of a UI is at a concern, SWC [11] and SXCML [12] offer a language based on the state machine concepts. PANDA [13] is a tool which exploits the aforementioned ontology [4, 5] to design medium-to-high fidelity executable prototypes allowing the use of interactive behaviors semantically meaningful to the user interface elements. However, PANDA does not support the design and assessment of low-fidelity wireframes and sketches. Other solutions focused on generating UIs from other software models, which in theory would keep them consistent, is also a topic that has received attention for long time [14–17].

When considering user requirements specified through BDD to evaluate software models, studies have been conducted to explore its use within user-centered [18] and agile [19] approaches to support enterprise modeling, when analyzing automated acceptance testing to support BDD traceability [20], as well as its compatibility with business modeling [21, 22] and BPMN [23].

There is also an intrinsic relationship between user interface design and task modeling, when considered in a user requirements perspective. Some authors have even tried to establish linguistic task modeling for designing user interfaces [24] where a notation enables identification of task input elements based on the task state diagram and dynamic tasks. Martinie et al. [25], followed by Campos et al. [26], propose a tool-supported framework and a model-based testing approach to support linking task models to an existing, executable, and interactive application, defining a systematic correspondence between the user interface elements and user tasks. The problem with this approach is that it only covers the interaction of task models with a concrete fully-functional user interfaces, not covering user interface prototypes.

Finally, previous studies [27, 28] which analyzed the current state-of-the-art prototyping tools have concluded that features to support (at some level) the assessment of prototypes and scenario-based specifications have been covered by less than 10% of the tools analyzed.

3 Foundations

3.1 Behavior-Driven Development and User Stories

Behavior-Driven Development (BDD) is a specialization of Test-Driven Development (TDD) [29, 30], and is intended to make the practice of writing automated testing more accessible and intuitive to newcomers and experts alike. It shifts the vocabulary from being test-based to behavior-based. It positions itself as a development paradigm, emphasizing communication and automation as equal goals. In BDD, the behaviors represent both the requirements specification and the test cases.

BDD drives development teams to a requirements specification based on User Stories in an understandable natural language format. User Stories were firstly proposed by Cohn [3] and provide in the same artifact a narrative, briefly describing a feature in the business point of view, and a set of scenarios to give details about business rules and to be used as acceptance criteria, giving concrete examples about what should be tested to consider a given feature as done. Cohn and North [3, 31] propose a useful template for that:

```
Title (one line describing the story)
Narrative: As a [role], I want [feature], So that [benefit]
Scenario 1: Title
Given [context], When [event], Then [outcome]
```

This structure is largely used in BDD and has been named by North [31] as a "BDD story". According to this template, a User Story is described with a *title*, a *narrative* and a set of *scenarios* representing acceptance criteria. The title provides a general description of the story, referring to a feature this story represents. The narrative describes the referred feature in terms of role that will benefit from the feature, the feature itself, and the benefit it will bring to the business. The acceptance criteria are defined through a set of scenarios, each one with a title and three main clauses: *"Given"* to provide the context in which the scenario will be actioned, *"When"* to describe events that will trigger the scenario and *"Then"* to present outcomes that might be checked to verify the proper behavior of the system. Each one of these clauses can include an *"And"* statement to provide multiple contexts, events and/or outcomes. Each statement in this representation is called *step*.

This format allows specifying executable requirements by means of a Domain-Specific Language (DSL) provided by Gherkin [32]. Gherkin is a DSL that has been developed for BDD to let users and developers describe software behavior without detailing how that behavior is implemented. By using this language, requirements specifications can be used to implement automated tests, which can conduct to living documentation, making easier for clients and other stakeholders to set their final acceptance tests. The drawback of using plain-vanilla Gherkin to specify requirements at the domain level, as proposed in [31], is to require that a developer manually implements the tests corresponding to each individual step of the scenarios.

3.2   Ontological Support for GUI Automated Testing

A GUI prototype is an early representation of a graphical user interface for an interactive system. In a software development perspective, GUI prototypes can be seen as concrete and tangible design artifacts [33]. By running simulations on prototypes, we can also determine potential scenarios that users can perform in the system and relate them to the requirements. When such requirements are specified through User Stories, a recurrent problem is that they often contain semantic inconsistencies. For example, it is not rare to find scenarios that specify an action such as a selection to be made in a widget such as a *Text Field* that does not support that action. To tackle this problem, previous works explored the use of an ontology describing common behaviors with a standard vocabulary for writing User Stories as scenario artifacts [4, 5]. The main benefit of this strategy is that User Stories using this common vocabulary can support specification and execution of automated test scenarios on GUI prototypes. The ontology covers concepts related to presentation and behavior of interactive components used in web and mobile applications. It also models concepts describing the structure of User Stories, tasks, scenarios and prototypes.

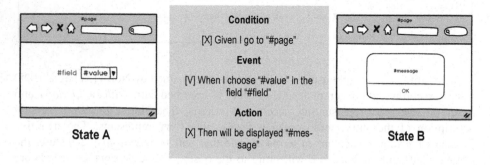

Fig. 1. Representation of a User Story scenario using the state machine concepts.

The dialog part of a GUI, as illustrated by Fig. 1, is described in the ontology by means of concepts borrowed from abstract state machines. The User Story *scenario* meant to be run in a given GUI is represented as a *transition*. *States* are used to represent the original and resulting GUIs after a transition occur (states A and B in Fig. 1). Scenarios in the transition state always have at least one or more *conditions* (represented in scenarios by the "*Given*" clause), one or more *events* (represented in scenarios by the "*When*" clause), and one or more *actions* (represented in scenarios by the "*Then*" clause). The presentation part of a GUI is described in the ontology through *interaction elements* which represent an abstraction of the different widgets commonly used in web and mobile user interfaces.

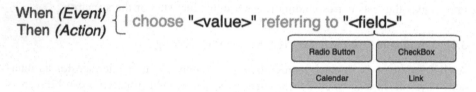

Fig. 2. Structure of a behavior as specified in the ontology.

The common behaviors in the ontology describe textually how users could interact with the system whilst manipulating graphical elements of the user interface. An example of behavior specification is illustrated by Fig. 2. The specification of behaviors encompasses when the interaction can be performed (using *"Given"*, *"When"* and/or *"Then"* clauses), and which graphical elements (i.e. *CheckBoxes, TextFields, Buttons*, etc.) can be affected. Altogether, behaviors and interaction elements are used to implement the test of expected system behavior. In the example of Fig. 2, the behavior *"I choose '<value>' referring to '<field>'"* has two parameters: *"<value>"* and *"<field>"*. The first parameter is associated to data, whilst the second parameter refers to the interaction element supported by this behavior: *"Radio Button"*, *"CheckBox"*, *"Calendar"* and *"Link"*.

The ontological model describes only behaviors that report steps performing actions directly on the user interface through interaction elements, i.e. behaviors referring to the interaction level in the user requirements description. This is a powerful resource because it allows keeping the ontological model domain-free, which means it is not subject to particular business characteristics in the User Stories, promoting the reuse of steps in multiple scenarios. Thus, steps can be easily reused to build different behaviors for different scenarios in different business domains.

Table 1. Example of interactive behaviors described in the ontology. *Transition: (C)ontext, (E)vent, (A)ction.*

Behavior	Transition C	E	A	Interaction Elements
choose ≡ select			▓	Calendar, Checkbox, Radio Button, and Link
chooseByIndexInTheField			▓	Dropdown List
chooseReferringTo			▓	Calendar, Checkbox, Radio Button, and Link
chooseTheOptionOfValueInTheField			▓	Dropdown List
clickOn			▓	Menu, Menu Item, Button, and Link
clickOnReferringTo			▓	Menu, Menu Item, Button, and Link
doNotTypeAnyValueToTheField ≡ resetTheValueOfTheField	=		▓	Text Field
goTo			▓	Browser Window
isDisplayed			▓	Browser Window
setInTheField ≡ tryToSetInTheField			▓	Dropdown List, Text Field, Autocomplete, and Calendar
typeAndChooseInTheField ≡ informAndChooseInTheField	=		▓	Autocomplete
willBeDisplayed			▓	Text

When representing the various interaction elements that can attend a given behavior, the ontology also allows extending multiple design solutions for the UI while still keeping the consistency of the interaction. For example, even if a *Dropdown List* has been chosen to attend, for example, a behavior *setInTheField* in a first version of a prototype, an *Auto Complete* field could be chosen to attend this behavior on a next version, once both UI elements share the same ontological property for this behavior. This kind of flexibility keeps the consistency of the interaction, leaving the designer free for choosing the best solutions in a given time of the project, without modifying the behavior specified for the system. The current version of the ontology covers more than 60 interactive behaviors and almost 40 interaction elements for both web and mobile user interfaces. Table 1 exemplifies some of these interactive behaviors, the transition component during which they can be triggered and the set of corresponding interaction elements.

4   The Proposed Approach for Automated Assessment

There are multiple notations and tools with different implementations for designing and modeling GUI prototypes [27]. Among these, we have chosen to implement a proof of concept of our approach with the wireframe sketching tool Balsamiq[1] in its current version (2.2.28), since it is a wide-spread and highly-regarded prototyping tool and uses a documented XML format for persisting the prototypes. Nonetheless, we have designed a flexible and open architecture where other notations and tools could benefit from our approach by just implementing new classes in accordance with their own patterns to implement and model prototypes.

```
<control  controlID="15"  controlTypeID="__group__"  x="588"
y="403"  w="96"  h="117"  measuredW="96"  measuredH="117"  zOr-
der="6" locked="false" isInGroup="-1">
    <groupChildrenDescriptors>
        <control controlID="0" controlTypeID="com.balsamiq.mock-
ups::Label"  x="0"  y="0"  w="-1"  h="-1"  measuredW="92"  mea-
suredH="21" zOrder="0" locked="false" isInGroup="15">
            <controlProperties>
                <text>Departure%20Date</text>
            </controlProperties>
        </control>
        <control controlID="1" controlTypeID="com.balsamiq.mock-
ups::Calendar" x="0" y="21" w="96" h="96" measuredW="96" mea-
suredH="96" zOrder="1" locked="false" isInGroup="15"/>
    </groupChildrenDescriptors>
</control>
```

Fig. 3.   Grouped field "Departure Date" and its XML source file.

```
<control  controlID="14"   controlTypeID="com.balsamiq.mock-
ups::Button" x="1051" y="459" w="-1" h="-1" measuredW="63" mea-
suredH="27" zOrder="8" locked="false" isInGroup="-1">
    <controlProperties>
        <text>Search</text>
    </controlProperties>
</control>
```

Fig. 4.   Button "Search" and its XML source file.

The assessment of GUI prototypes in our approach is an automated process. Our strategy for testing Balsamiq prototypes is parsing their XML source files and

---

[1] balsamiq.com.

identifying UI elements that match the ontology description for each behavior. The first step for assessing such prototypes is therefore getting from the ontology the list of UI elements which support the behavior under testing. Taking a step *"And I set 'Valid Departure Date' in the field 'Departure Date'"* as an example, according to the ontology, the associated interactive behavior *"setInTheField"* is supported by the UI elements *"Dropdown List"*, *"Text Field"*, *"Autocomplete"* and *"Calendar"*, when performing an action (*Then*) or an event (*When*) in a state machine transition.

After getting such a list of supported UI elements, we analyze the Balsamiq XML file to identify firstly if a field named "Departure Date" exists (Fig. 3). This is made by reading the tag *"<text>"* identified in the parent tag *"<controlProperties>"* for a given *"<control>"* element. If such a field exists, i.e. there is a tag *"<text>"* carrying its name (case insensitive), so we retrieve which interaction element is associated with it. At this point, we implemented a reference file containing the mapping between the abstracted interaction elements in the ontology and the Balsamiq concrete implementation of such elements.

Notice at the left side of Fig. 3 that the field "Departure Date" has been modeled with a *"Calendar"*, i.e. the UI designer has chosen the UI element *"Calendar"* to design the field "Departure Date". Thus, by checking the list of supported UI elements in the ontology, we find that the behavior *"setInTheField"*, addressed by the field "Departure Date", is supported by a *"Calendar"* element, so the test passes. If other elements than *"Dropdown List"*, *"Text Field"*, or *"Autocomplete"* had been chosen, the test would fail.

```
foreach step from US Scenarios do
    supportedUIElements <- correspondent UI Elements from the ontology
    fieldName <- name of the UI Element from the step
    foreach UI Element from the Balsamiq prototype do
        if the attribute text is equal to fieldName && is not in group then
            if the attribute controlTypeID is equal to one of the
                supportedUIElements then
                    numElements++
            endif
        else if the attribute text is equal to fieldName && is in group then
            if the attribute controlTypeID of some member of the group is
                equal to one of the supportedUIElements then
                    numElements++
            endif
        endif
    endforeach
endforeach

if numElements == 1 show Success
else show Fail
```

Fig. 5. Testing algorithm for assessing Balsamiq prototypes.

Our algorithm (see Fig. 5) must take into account that Balsamiq has two methods for representing UI elements on its XML source files. They can be directly assigned with a unique *"controlID"* (Fig. 4) or be part of a group that encompasses a *label* and the UI element itself (Fig. 3). In the first case, the *label* "Search" in Fig. 4 is directly associated with the element *"Button"* itself (*com.balsamiq.mockups::Button*). In the second case, we can notice the *label* for "Departure Date" in Fig. 3 is part of a group (*isInGroup='15'*). In the same group, but with other *"controlID"*, we find the element

"*Calendar*" itself (*com.balsamiq.mockups::Calendar*). When looking for matching elements, the algorithm identifies which Balsamiq method has been used to design the element. If the parent tag is a *label*, it means that the element is part of a group that contains the element itself in a sibling tag. This sibling tag is then identified by reading the attribute "*isInGroup*". If the parent tag is not a *label*, so it is already the element itself. After identifying it, the algorithm checks if some of the UI elements received from the ontology matches with the element from the prototype that is being investigated. If so, the variable "*numTasks*" is increased by one. After investigating the whole set of tags, the value of this variable is returned and must be equal to "1", which means only one UI element for representing the "*fieldname*" has been found. If this value is equal to "0", it means that no UI element has been found in the prototype with that "*fieldname*", while if it is greater than "1", it means that more than one UI element has been found with the same "*fieldname*". In both cases, the algorithm identifies the failure and the test does not pass. This process is conducted for each step of the scenario.

Notice that for GUI prototypes at this level of refinement, we only assess the presentation aspect of the prototype. We are not considering for testing at this level the dialog aspect and the consequent dynamic aspect of the interaction. It means that to check the consistency of the UI elements modeled in the prototype, we only consider the presence (or the absence) of the right kind of interaction elements on the GUI prototype where the interaction is supposed to occur. Behaviors that perform a state transition (e.g. navigating from one screen to another or getting mock values from the fields as a result of an interaction) are not being taken into account in the results.

4.1 Tool Support

The algorithm presented in the previous section has been implemented in Java as an open source project and integrates different frameworks such as JUnit and JDOM. Figure 6 represents the flow of calls we have designed for running tests on Balsamiq prototypes. The flow starts with the class "*MyTest.java*" that is a JUnit class in charge of triggering the battery of tests (its content is illustrated in Fig. 7). This class indicates which files will be used for testing (flow 1). These files are distributed in two packages. The first one contains the User Story files ("*.story*" files where the scenarios for testing are), and the second one contains the Balsamiq files (which are the BMML source files of Balsamiq prototypes). Both the User Story and the Balsamiq files remain separate files in each package and are tested individually. In the example provided in Fig. 7, it has been indicated for testing the User Story "*Flight Ticket Search.story*" on the Balsamiq prototype "*Book Flights.bmml*".

Each one of the steps in the User Story under testing makes calls to the class "*MySteps.java*" (flow 2) that knows which behaviors are supported. Based on the behavior referenced by the step, this class makes a call to the class "*Balsamiq.java*" to get the list of Balsamiq interaction elements that supports such a behavior (flow 3). The class "*Balsamiq.java*" in its turn makes a call to the class "*MyOntology.java*" (flow 4) in charge of reading the OWL file of the ontology and recovering the list of abstract interaction elements supported by a given behavior. Such a list is then returned to the class "*Balsamiq.java*" (flow 5) that checks, for each abstract element returned by the ontology, which are the corresponding concrete interaction elements in Balsamiq in charge of implementing the mentioned behavior (flow 6). This mapping is recovered from the file "*Balsamiq.mapping*" (flow 7).

Afterward, the class "*Balsamiq.java*" returns such a list with the concrete Balsamiq elements to the class "*MySteps.java*" (flow 8) that originally made the call. With the list of supported Balsamiq elements for the step under testing, the class "*MySteps.java*" calls to the class "*MyXML.java*" (flow 9) in charge of parsing the Balsamiq "*.bmml*" file (flow 10). This parsing aims to check if the prototype carries the interaction element mentioned in the step under testing, and if so, if such an element supports the behavior mentioned in the step. The result of this parsing is then returned to the class "*MySteps.java*" (flow 11). At this point, based on the algorithm presented in the previous section, we verify how many instances have been found for the searched element. Finally, the class "*MySteps.java*" asserts the value and returns the result to the class "*MyTest.java*" (flow 12) that indicates if the test has failed or not.

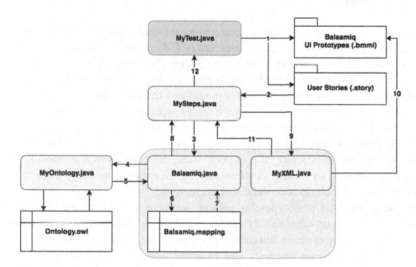

Fig. 6. Flow of calls for running tests on Balsamiq prototypes. (Color figure online)

```
@Test
public void testAllStories() throws Throwable {
    eng.addSteps(new MySteps("src/test/resources/lfprototypes/Book Flights.bmml"));
    eng.addStories("/stories/Flight Tickets Search.story");
    eng.run();
}
```

Fig. 7. "*MyTest.java*": class for running tests on Balsamiq prototypes.

Notice the independence of the components assigned at the core of the structure represented in Fig. 6 (highlighted in yellow). Those components are related to the particularities of test implementation for Balsamiq prototypes. "*Balsamiq.java*" treats the demands for getting the correspondent abstract interaction elements from the ontology and translates them to the concrete interaction elements implemented by Balsamiq. "*Balsamiq.mapping*" provides such a translation. Finally, "*MyXML.java*" is in charge of parsing the BMML files of Balsamiq, searching for the element under testing. By this way, we deliver a flexible architecture allowing, in the future, that UI prototypes modeled by other prototyping tools could also be tested by just implementing new interfaces for this core.

In summary, considering the presented architecture, to setup and run a battery of tests, we must: (*i*) place the set of BMML files that will be tested in the package "Balsamiq UI Prototypes", (*ii*) place the set of User Stories files ("*.story*") that will be tested in the package "User Stories", (*iii*) indicate in the "*MyTest*" class which prototype will be tested with which User Story (only a prototype with a User Story at a time), and (*iv*) run the "*MyTest*" class as a JUnit test.

5   Case Study

To evaluate our approach, we have conducted a case study with an existing web system for booking business trips. In a previous study [34], domain experts were invited to produce some User Stories to describe a feature they considered important to that system. This previous study aimed at analyzing how the experts write User Stories (and the difficulties they have) whilst using a predefined template. In the present study, the gathered User Stories were refined to get a representative set of user requirements to be assessed on the GUI prototypes of the existing system, showing how we can automate the test of Balsamiq prototypes. This refinement was only necessary because, in the context of the previous study, the experts were deliberately not trained to use the ontology vocabulary, so we had to refine the User Stories produced by them to use this vocabulary and to include additional test scenarios.

To obtain the GUI prototypes for testing, we have studied the current implementation of the existing system, and by applying reverse engineering [35], we redesigned the targeted GUI prototypes in Balsamiq. The aim of this software reengineering was to have such artifacts to run our tests and examine which types of inconsistencies our approach would be able to identify.

5.1   Methodology

To conduct the case study, we first set up an initial version of the User Stories and their test scenarios. We then reengineered initial versions of Balsamiq prototypes from the existing web system. Following this step, we ran the initial version of User Stories to initial versions of the prototypes designed with Balsamiq.

The strategy we follow for running tests on the prototypes parses each step of the scenario at a time, so if an error is found out, the test stops until the error is fixed. That requires to run several batteries of tests until having the entire scenario tested. It leads us to fix all the inconsistencies step-by-step, and consequently to get fully consistent scenarios at the end of running. However, when analyzing the reason related with each inconsistency, we can eventually conclude that the origin of the inconsistency is actually in the specification of the step in the User Story scenario, and not in the artifact itself. As a result, to fix such an inconsistency, steps of User Story scenarios may also be modified along the battery of tests to comply with a consistent specification of the user requirements. An immediate consequence of this fact is that the steps used to test a given version of an artifact can be different than that ones used to test another artifact previously. It means that regression tests are crucial to ensure that a given modification in the set of User Stories scenarios did not break some previous test in other artifacts and made some artifact (that so far was consistent with the requirements) inconsistent again.

5.2 Results

In total, we set up for assessment 3 User Stories with 15 different scenarios and reengineered 11 Balsamiq prototypes. The sequence of prototypes (*a–h*) in Fig. 8 shows the different states and designs of some of the developed prototypes. The prototype (*a*) presents our first design for a UI prototype to search flights. The figure represents a UI for searching flights based on a round trip (and (*b*) based on a one-way/multidestination trip). The prototype (*c*) presents the next UI in sequence, showing the list of flights matching the selection criteria. When the user selects one of the available flights, then the system turns out to the state shown in (*d*). The user, at this state, can confirm his/her selection or change the fare profile of his/her flight.

The prototype (*e*) finally shows the UI of confirmation of a flight selection. The user can accept the general terms and conditions and confirm the booking or withdraw the trip. In the latter case, the system asks the user to confirm the choice (*g*), and if confirmed, cancels the trip (*h*). If the user does not confirm the withdrawing or opt to confirm the trip at the first stage, then the system shows a message confirming the booking (*f*). To discuss the results that we got by testing different versions of Balsamiq prototypes, we present in Table 2 results of several batteries of testing in each version of the prototypes developed to perform a successful roundtrip booking (one of the possible full scenarios). We present sequentially each step of the target scenario, the corresponding elements in the Balsamiq source files, errors that have been found in a given battery, and finally the subsequent battery of tests following the fixes. Once the goal is to assess the most possible number of interaction elements in the prototype, we have chosen to run our tests presented below on the full versions of the scenarios, i.e. in those ones interacting with all the optional fields.

We notice that the first battery of tests found an error already in the first step (*"Given I go to 'Book Flights'"*). It was expected a correspondent element "*BrowserWindow*" associated to the name "Book Flights" in the prototype, but the element found was a "*SubTitle*". The "*BrowserWindow*" was named "Travel Planet", the name of the system under testing. As the behavior "*goTo*" is supposed to be performed only in a window (and its variants), such a step could not be performed in a field describing a "*SubTitle*", which is a semantically inconsistent field for that behavior. At the end, the window ended up being named "Flight Search" and both the scenario and the prototype have been updated accordingly.

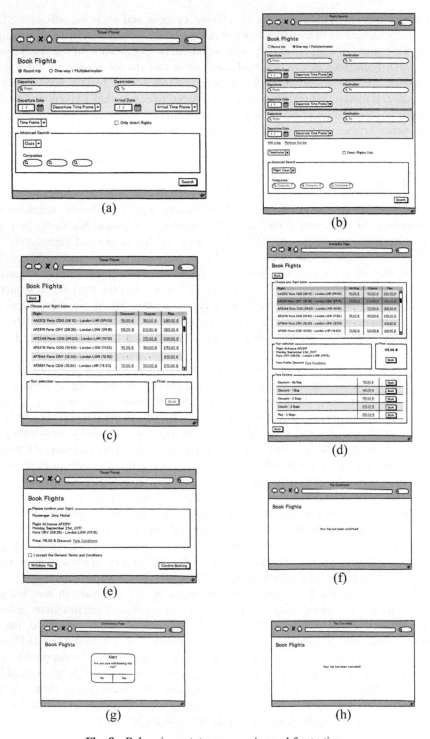

Fig. 8. Balsamiq prototypes reengineered for testing.

Table 2. Test results in Balsamiq prototypes.

Battery	Step	Balsamiq source file	Error
	Scenario: *Successful Roundtrip Tickets Search With Full Options*		
1	1 - *Given I go to "Book Flights"* (**FAILED**, assertion error: expected <1> but was <0>).	Element: *SubTitle* Name: **Book Flights**	Expected "*BrowserWindow*", but the element was "*SubTitle*".
2	2 - *When I inform "Toulouse" and choose "Toulouse, Blagnac (TLS)" in the field "Departure"*		-
	3 - *And I inform "Paris" and choose "Paris, Charles-de-Gaulle (CDG)" in the field "Destination"*		-
	4 - *When I set "Sam, Déc 1, 2018" in the field "Departure Date"* (**FAILED**, assertion error: expected <1> but was <0>).	Element: *Label*, Group: **0** Name: **Departure Date** Element: *DateChooser*, Group: **22**	The label "Departure Date" and the element "*DataChooser*" are in different groups.
3	5 - *And I set "08:00" in the field "Departure Time Frame"*		-
	6 - *When I choose "Round Trip"*		-
	7 - *And I set "Lun, Déc 10, 2018" in the field "Arrival Date"* (**FAILED**, assertion error: expected <1> but was <0>).	Element: *Label*, Group: **0** Name: **Arrival Date** Element: *DateChooser*, Group: **23**	The label "Arrival Date" and the element "*DataChooser*" are in different groups.
4	8 - *When I set "10:00" in the field "Arrival Time Frame"*		-
	9 - *And I choose the option of value "2" in the field "Number of Passengers"* (**FAILED**, assertion error: expected <1> but was <0>).	?	The field "Number of Passengers" does not exist.
5	10 - *When I set "6" in the field "Timeframe"* (**FAILED**, assertion error: expected <1> but was <0>).	Element: *ComboBox* Name: **Time Frame**	Expected field "Timeframe" but was "Time Frame".
6	11 - *And I select "Direct Flights Only"* (**FAILED**, assertion error: expected <1> but was <0>).	Element: *CheckBox* Name: **Only direct flights**	Expected field "Direct Flights Only" but was "Only direct flights".
7	12 - *When I choose the option of value "Economique" in the field "Flight Class"* (**FAILED**, assertion error: expected <1> but was <0>).	Element: *ComboBox* Name: **Class**	Expected field "Flights Class" but was "Class".
8	13 - *And I set "Air France" in the field "Companies"* (**FAILED**, assertion error: expected <1> but was <3>).	Element: *Label*, Group: **27** Name: **Companies** Element: *SearchBox*, Group: **27** Element: *SearchBox*, Group: **27** Element: *SearchBox*, Group: **27**	Three elements "*SearchBox*" to address the same field "Companies".
9	14 - *When I submit "Search"*		-
	15 - *Then will be displayed "2. Sélectionner un voyage"* (**FAILED**, assertion error: expected <1> but was <0>).	-	Dynamic behavior between screens. Untraceable interaction.
	Scenario: *Select a Return Flight Searched With Full Options*		
Battery	**Step**	**Balsamiq source file**	**Error**
1	16 - *Given "Availability Page" is displayed* (**FAILED**, assertion error: expected <1> but was <0>).	?	"Availability Page" does not exist.
2	17 - *When I click on "No Bag" referring to "Air France 7519"* (**FAILED**, assertion error: expected <1> but was <0>).	Element: *DataGrid* Name: Flight, **Discount**, Classic, Flex	Expected field "No Bag" but was "Discount".
	18 - *And I click on "No Bag" referring to "Air France 7522"*		-
3	19 - *When I click on "Book"*		-
	20 - *Then will be displayed "J'accepte les Conditions d'achat concernant le(s) tarif(s) aérien(s)."* (**FAILED**, assertion error: expected <1> but was <0>).	-	Dynamic behavior between screens. Untraceable interaction.

(continued)

Table 2. (*continued*)

Battery	Step	Balsamiq source file	Error
	Scenario: *Confirm a Flight Selection (Full Version)*		
1	21 - *Given "Confirmation Page" is displayed* (**FAILED**, assertion error: expected <1> but was <0>).	?	"Confirmation Page" does not exist.
2	22 - *When I choose "J'accepte les Conditions d'achat concernant le(s) tarif(s) aérien(s)."*		-
	23 - *And I click on* **"Finalize the trip"** (**FAILED**, assertion error: expected <1> but was <0>).	Element: **Button** Name: **Confirm Booking**	Expected field "Finalize the trip" but was "Confirm Booking".
3	24 - *Then will be displayed "Votre voyage a été confirmé!"* (**FAILED**, assertion error: expected <1> but was <0>).	-	Dynamic behavior between screens. Untraceable interaction.

During the second battery of tests, the steps 1, 2 and 3 passed, and an error was found at the step 4 (*"When I set 'Sam, Déc 1, 2018' in the field 'Departure Date'"*). This error refers to the label "Departure Date" that has been found in a different group than the element *"DataChooser"* which was used to model it. As detailed in Sect. 3, Balsamiq implements UI elements either as independent instances (i.e. with the name and the interaction element defined in the same tag), or as part of a group (i.e. defining the name in the tag "label" and the interaction element itself in another tag). In the second case, the group must be modeled as a single unit, with a unique identifier. The label "Departure Date" was found in a given group and its interaction element *"DataChooser"* in another one, so they could not be recognized as a single unit. To fix the error, they were regrouped.

During the third battery of tests, the steps 4, 5 and 6 passed, and the same error was found at the step 7 ("And I set 'Lun, Déc 10, 2018' in the field 'Arrival Date'"). The label "Arrival Date" and its correspondent element "DataChooser" were found in different groups. The same solution to fix it was applied. During the fourth battery of tests, the steps 7 and 8 passed, and an error was found at the step 9 ("And I choose the option of value '2' in the field 'Number of Passengers'"). The field "Number of Passengers" was not found in the prototype. It was added to fix the error.

During the fifth battery of tests, the step 9 passed, and an error was found at the step 10 ("When I set '6' in the field 'Timeframe'"). The field "Timeframe" was named as "Time Frame". The field was renamed in the prototype to fix the inconsistency. The same occurred during the sixth and seventh battery of tests, respectively with the fields "Direct Flights Only" (step 11) and "Flight Class" (step 12). They were named as "Only direct flights" and "Class" respectively. They were also renamed, so the test passed.

During the eighth battery of tests, an error was found at the step 13 (*"And I set 'Air France' in the field 'Companies'"*). Three elements *"SearchBox"* were found to address the same field named only as "Companies". The solution was to identify uniquely each one of the fields *"SearchBox"*, once each one of them is able to receive different values during the interaction. If we redesign the step to call specifically one of the fields (e.g. Company 1) the test passes, as we are interacting with just a unique and determined field. If otherwise we call the group Companies as a whole, we do not know with which field we should interact. The three fields were named respectively as "Company 1", "Company 2" and "Company 3", leaving the name "Companies" to reference only the group as a whole. Once again, both the scenario and the prototype have been updated.

During the ninth battery of tests, the steps 13 and 14 passed. For the step 15, at the end of the first scenario, the message referenced by the last step is supposed to be displayed in another screen as a result of the interaction. As stated in Sect. 3, tests on prototypes at this level of refinement do not consider the dynamic aspect of the interaction, so tests like this, involving navigation between screens, will always fail.

Following the booking process, the second scenario (*"Select a Return Flight Searched With Full Options"*) ran only 3 batteries of tests before getting a consistent prototype. The first battery found an error in the element "Availability Page" that is missing in the prototype. During the second battery, the field "No Bag" was named as "Discount" in the grid. Finally, the third battery fell in the case mentioned previously, which consists in checking a message that is supposed to be displayed in the next screen as a result of the interaction.

The third and last scenario to conclude the booking (*"Confirm a Flight Selection Full Version"*), also ran only 3 batteries of tests before getting a consistent prototype. The first one found the same error related to the name of the page. In the second one, the button "Finalize the trip" was named as "Confirm Booking", and the third and last battery felt in the case of dynamic behavior between screens. Notice that, for testing purposes, the message *"I accept the General Terms and Conditions"* in English was considered equivalent to the message *"J'accepte les Conditions d'achat concernant le (s) tarif(s) aérien(s)."* in French.

In our further test batteries with other scenarios, we got errors when testing steps such as *"And I choose 'One-way Trip'"* and *"When I choose 'Multidestination Trip'"* because these options do not exist in the UI prototypes for searching flights. In fact, the corresponding option was named *"One-way/Multidestination"* (Fig. 8, (a)). Here we get an important inconsistency related with the design options. During the specification of scenarios, we can notice that three options were planned to select the trip type: one-way, roundtrip, or multidestination. However, in this version of the prototype, it has been modeled only two options: one for choosing a roundtrip, and another for choosing a one-way/multidestination trip. This option has been made for the prototype because, in terms of interaction, the action required for providing data for multidestination flights is actually the same as the one for providing data for a set of one-way flights. In terms of user requirements, this is a conflicting specification, so such an inconsistency needs to be identified and fixed. Thus, either the prototype should follow what has been specified in the scenarios, or the scenarios should be fixed to comply with the inter-action supported by the prototype.

In a scenario for describing a successful multi-destination ticket search, our algo-rithm has identified, as expected, three fields named "Departure" and "Destination" (see Fig. 8, (b)). For each element, the results returned the count of 3, when it was expected to be 1. When designing such a UI, as the three fields have been just replicated (copied and pasted) with the same name, with the purpose of illustrating the change on the UI when the "One-way/Multidestination" option is selected, the group to which such fields belonged has been maintained, so this set up the inconsistency. Otherwise, if the fields had the same name, but belonged to different groups, an inconsistency would not be signalized as it would indicate that the fields were intentionally modeled as different objects.

Finally, for the step *"And I set 'Sam, Déc 1, 2018' in the field 'Departure Date'"* in the same scenario, the field "Departure Date" was also replicated, but the pair of elements (labels and actual fields) has not been associated to a group, i.e. each element (label and field) has been found belonging to distinct groups in each instance of the field "Departure Date". The inconsistency was also detected and signalized.

5.3   Discussion and Limitations

By summarizing the results presented above, below we can categorize the types of inconsistencies found by our testing approach when assessing the Balsamiq prototypes as follows:

- Conflict between expected and actual elements
- Element and label in different groups
- Missing elements
- Element semantically inconsistent
- More than one element to represent the same field
- Untraceable interaction between screens

As presented above, we identified 6 different types in the tested scenarios. *"Conflict between expected and actual elements"* was the most frequent type and refers to elements that are specified with different names in the step and in the prototype. *"Missing elements"* and *"untraceable interaction between screens"* comes next and refer respectively to the real absence in the prototypes of elements that are specified in the step, and to the cases where the interaction changes the state of the interface (e.g. transitioning between screens or making appear a given value in a field). *"Untraceable interaction between screens"* is a particular type of inconsistency due to the level of refinement we are considering for prototypes. Balsamiq is a prototype tool that actually supports a basic dialog description, using links between prototypes and simulating a real navigation on user interfaces. However, we have chosen to not cover such a feature for now, since the ontology we use can already support more robust interactions in other levels of prototype refinements, such as the one that has been implemented by PANDA [13].

"Elements and labels in different groups" is the next type in line and refers to one of the mechanisms of modeling used by Balsamiq when there is an absence of group links between labels and the actual interaction element in the prototype. When a given UI element is composed by a label name and the interaction element itself, this encompassed structure is modeled by an entity named "group". Thus, to be considered as a unique and single element, both the label and the interaction element itself must be

placed at the same group. If it is not the case, we are not able to reach the element and then an inconsistency is detected. This inconsistency leads to a misidentification of elements in Balsamiq but could eventually not be an issue in other prototyping tools.

"More than one element to represent the same field" is a type of inconsistency caused when there are at least two elements (or more) in the prototype which are of the same type and are placed in the same group (or have the same name) of the searched field. Finally, the type of inconsistency named *"elements semantically inconsistent"* refers to the core problem we address with the ontology, i.e. the use of interaction elements in the prototype that are semantically inconsistent with the behavior they are supposed to model. This kind of inconsistency is detected when we get the list of supported interaction elements from the ontology and check if the interaction element used in the prototype is equivalent to one of them.

The types of inconsistencies identified by our approach are useful to provide information about the consistency between user requirements and GUI prototypes at any stage of a user-centered design process. Especially at the early stages, where user requirements still have a high level of uncertainty, the identification of these inconsistencies is an important resource to both designers and domain experts to validate a given understanding of the requirements and to ensure that the multiple proposed design options still remain consistent with the requirements. A conducive factor to that is our strategy based on a static analysis for implementing the assessment of GUI prototypes. When opting for a static analysis of Balsamiq source files, we gain in performance and availability of tests. Unlike approaches implementing co-execution, and specially in environments requiring a high-availability of tests to be executed continuously along multiple iterations, static approaches benefit from an instantaneous consistency checking by analyzing in seconds several hundreds of source files at the same time.

As limitations, we point out that this study has been conducted performing a manual reverse engineering of the existing system currently in production to obtain the respective prototypes for testing. Therefore, as a manual process, it was expected that inconsistencies would be naturally introduced during the modeling. Indeed, these inconsistencies were identified and that allowed us to evaluate our approach. Nonetheless, if an automated approach of reverse engineering had been used instead, such inconsistencies would probably not have taken place. Future studies should confirm this hypothesis. Since both the conduction of the study and the interpretation and analysis of the results have initially been made by the authors, a possible bias should be considered as a threat to validity. To mitigate that, the results were cross-checked by independent reviewers, experts in software engineering and modeling. They examined both the reengineered GUI prototypes and the testing results, then they performed a qualitative analysis of the types of inconsistencies identified. The results presented in this paper are thus a consolidated and revised version of the testing outcomes.

5.4   Conclusion

In this paper, we describe a novel approach for assessing low-fidelity wireframes and sketches developed by commercial prototyping tools like Balsamiq. Our approach has the main advantage of ensuring a reliable correspondence between the different interaction elements modeled in GUI prototypes and the user requirements specified by stakeholders. By using a supporting ontology, the approach provides automated testing for Balsamiq prototypes, implementing an open and flexible architecture which allows other GUI prototyping tools fitting in the future. For that, it is enough to implement a new core interface for describing the way such tools deal with their interaction elements and how they can be identified in their source files.

This approach has also been extended and adapted to assess other early artifacts such as task models, as well as late artifacts such as final UIs [36–40]. As an integrated approach, User Stories can also be assigned to automatically assess both task models, UI prototypes in different levels of abstraction, and final UIs, ensuring a consistent verification, validation and testing (VV&T) approach for interactive systems with high-availability of tests and immediate feedback about the consistency of artifacts and user requirements since the early stages of development.

Next steps on this research include evaluating the impact of maintaining and successively evolving UI prototypes throughout a real software development process. Future studies should also explore the assessment of GUI prototypes using new interaction techniques, which has the potential to bring new challenges. Concerning the tools, the development of an Eclipse plugin to suggest and autocomplete steps of the User Stories scenarios based on the interactive behaviors of the ontology is also envisioned. It would allow experts and other stakeholders to directly create their own User Stories by following the proposed vocabulary.

References

1. Wood, D.P., Kang, K.C.: A Classification and Bibliography of Software Prototyping. Pittsburgh, Pennsylvania (1992)
2. Chelimsky, D., Astels, D., Helmkamp, B., North, D., Dennis, Z., Hellesoy, A.: The RSpec Book: Behaviour Driven Development with RSpec, Cucumber, and Friends. Pragmatic Bookshelf, New York (2010)
3. Cohn, M.: User Stories Applied for Agile Software Development. Addison-Wesley, Boston (2004)
4. Silva, T.R., Hak, J.-L., Winckler, M.: A behavior-based ontology for supporting automated assessment of interactive systems. In: Proceedings of the 11th IEEE International Conference on Semantic Computing (ICSC 2017), pp. 250–257 (2017). https://doi.org/10.1109/ICSC.2017.73
5. Silva, T.R., Hak, J.-L., Winckler, M.: A formal ontology for describing interactive behaviors and supporting automated testing on user interfaces. Int. J. Semant. Comput. **11**(04), 513–539 (2017). https://doi.org/10.1142/S1793351X17400219

6. Jeffries, R., Miller, J.R., Wharton, C., Uyeda, K.: User interface evaluation in the real world: a comparison of four techniques. In: Proceedings of CHI 1991 Proceedings of the SIGCHI Conference on Human Factors in Computing Systems, pp. 119–124 (1991). https://doi.org/10.1145/108844.108862
7. Tian, J.: Software inspection. In: Jeff, T. (ed.) Software Quality Engineering: Testing, Quality Assurance, and Quantifiable Improvement, pp. 237–250. John Wiley & Sons, Inc., New York (2005). https://doi.org/10.1002/0471722324.ch14
8. Ebert, C.: Global Software and IT: A Guide to Distributed Development, Projects, and Outsourcing. Wiley, Hoboken (2011)
9. Luna, E.R., Garrigós, I., Grigera, J., Winckler, M.: Capture and evolution of web requirements using webspec. In: Benatallah, B., Casati, F., Kappel, G., Rossi, G. (eds.) ICWE 2010. LNCS, vol. 6189, pp. 173–188. Springer, Heidelberg (2010). https://doi.org/10.1007/978-3-642-13911-6_12
10. Buchmann, R.A., Karagiannis, D.: Modelling mobile app requirements for semantic traceability. Requir. Eng. 22(1), 41–75 (2017). https://doi.org/10.1007/s00766-015-0235-1
11. Winckler, M., Palanque, P.: StateWebCharts: a formal description technique dedicated to navigation modelling of web applications. In: Jorge, J.A., Jardim Nunes, N., Falcão e Cunha, J. (eds.) DSV-IS 2003. LNCS, vol. 2844, pp. 61–76. Springer, Heidelberg (2003). https://doi.org/10.1007/978-3-540-39929-2_5
12. Barnett, J.: State Chart XML (SCXML): State Machine Notation for Control Abstraction. W3C (2017). http://www.w3.org/TR/scxml/
13. Hak, J., Winckler, M., Navarre, D.: PANDA: prototyping using annotation and decision analysis. In: Proceedings of the 8th ACM SIGCHI Symposium on Engineering Interactive Computing Systems, pp. 171–176 (2016). https://doi.org/10.1145/2933242.2935873
14. Elkoutbi, M., Khriss, I., Keller, R.K.: Generating user interface prototypes from scenarios. In: Proceedings of the IEEE International Symposium on Requirements Engineering (Cat. No. PR00188), pp. 150–158 (1999). https://doi.org/10.1109/ISRE.1999.777995
15. Han, L., Yang, J., Zhao, W., Sheng, Q.Z.: User interface derivation for business processes. IEEE Trans. Knowl. Data Eng. (2019). https://doi.org/10.1109/TKDE.2019.2891655
16. Schlungbaum, E., Elwert, T.: Automatic user interface generation from declarative models. Comput. Aided Des. User Interfaces (CADUI) 5, 3–18 (1996)
17. Wolff, A., Forbrig, P., Dittmar, A., Reichart, D.: Linking GUI elements to tasks – supporting an evolutionary design process. In: Proceedings of the 4th International Workshop on Task Models and Diagrams, pp. 27–34 (2005). https://doi.org/10.1145/1122935.1122941
18. Valente, P., Silva, T.R., Winckler, M., Nunes, N.J.: The goals approach: enterprise model-driven agile human-centered software engineering. In: Bogdan, C., et al. (eds.) HCSE/HESSD-2016. LNCS, vol. 9856, pp. 261–280. Springer, Cham (2016). https://doi.org/10.1007/978-3-319-44902-9_17
19. Valente, P., Silva, T., Winckler, M., Nunes, N.: The goals approach: agile enterprise driven software development. In: Gołuchowski, J., Pańkowska, M., Linger, H., Barry, C., Lang, M., Schneider, C. (eds.) Complexity in Information Systems Development. LNISO, vol. 22, pp. 201–219. Springer, Cham (2017). https://doi.org/10.1007/978-3-319-52593-8_13
20. Lucassen, G., Dalpiaz, F., Van Der Werf, J.M.E.M., Brinkkemper, S., Zowghi, D.: Behavior-driven requirements traceability via automated acceptance tests. In: Proceedings - 2017 IEEE 25th International Requirements Engineering Conference Workshops, REW 2017, pp. 431–434 (2017). https://doi.org/10.1109/REW.2017.84

21. de Carvalho, R.A., Manhães, R.S., de Carvalho e Silva, F.L.: Filling the gap between business process modeling and behavior driven development (2010). arXiv: https://arxiv.org/abs/1005.4975

22. de Carvalho, R.A., de Carvalho e Silva, F.L., Manhaes, R.S.: Mapping business process modeling constructs to behavior driven development ubiquitous language (2010). arXiv: https://arxiv.org/abs/1006.4892

23. Lübke, D., Van Lessen, T.: Modeling test cases in BPMN for behavior- driven development. IEEE Softw. **33**, 15–21 (2016). https://doi.org/10.1109/MS.2016.117

24. Khaddam, I., Mezhoudi, N., Vanderdonckt, J.: Towards task-based linguistic modeling for designing GUIs. In: 27th Conference on l'Interaction Homme-Machine (2015). https://doi.org/10.1145/2820619.2820636

25. Palanque, P., Martinie, C., Winckler, M.: Designing and assessing interactive systems using task models. In: Bernhaupt, R., Dalvi, G., Joshi, A., KB, D., O'Neill, J., Winckler, M. (eds.) INTERACT 2017. LNCS, vol. 10516, pp. 383–386. Springer, Cham (2017). https://doi.org/10.1007/978-3-319-68059-0_35

26. Campos, J.C., Fayollas, C., Martinie, C., Navarre, D., Palanque, P., Pinto, M.: Systematic automation of scenario-based testing of user interfaces. In: Proceedings of the 8th ACM SIGCHI Symposium on Engineering Interactive Computing Systems - EICS 2016, pp. 138–148 (2016). https://doi.org/10.1145/2933242.2948735

27. Silva, T.R., Hak, J.-L., Winckler, M., Nicolas, O.: A comparative study of milestones for featuring GUI prototyping tools. J. Softw. Eng. Appl. **10**(06), 564–589 (2017). https://doi.org/10.4236/jsea.2017.106031

28. Silva, T.R., Hak, J.-L., Winckler, M.A.: A review of milestones in the history of GUI prototyping tools. In: IFIP TC.13 International Conference on Human-Computer Interaction – INTERACT 2015 Adjunct Proceedings, pp. 267–279 (2015)

29. Beck, K.: Test Driven Development: By Example, 1st edn. Addison-Wesley Professional, Boston (2002)

30. Astels, D.: Test-Driven Development: A Practical Guide, 1st edn. Prentice Hall, Upper Saddle River (2003)

31. North, D.: What's in a Story? (2019). https://dannorth.net/whats-in-a-story/. Accessed 01 Jan 2019

32. Gherkin. Gherkin Reference. https://cucumber.io/docs/gherkin/reference/

33. Beaudouin-Lafon, M., Mackay, W.E.: Prototyping tools and techniques. In: Prototype Development and Tools, pp. 1–41 (2000)

34. Silva, T.R., Winckler, M., Bach, C.: Evaluating the usage of predefined interactive behaviors for writing user stories: an empirical study with potential product owners. Cognit. Technol. Work, 1–21 (2019). https://doi.org/10.1007/s10111-019-00566-3

35. Chikofsky, E.J., Cross II, J.H.: Reverse engineering and design recovery: a taxonomy. IEEE Softw. **7**, 13–17 (1990). https://doi.org/10.1109/52.43044

36. Silva, T.R., Winckler, M.A.A.: Towards automated requirements checking throughout development processes of interactive systems. In: 2nd Workshop on Continuous Requirements Engineering (CRE), REFSQ 2016, pp. 1–2 (2016)

37. Silva, T.R.: Definition of a behavior-driven model for requirements specification and testing of interactive systems. In: Proceedings of the 24th International Requirements Engineering Conference (RE 2016), pp. 444–449 (2016). https://doi.org/10.1109/RE.2016.12

38. Silva, T.R., Hak, J.-L., Winckler, M.: Testing prototypes and final user interfaces through an ontological perspective for behavior-driven development. In: Bogdan, C., et al. (eds.) HCSE/HESSD -2016. LNCS, vol. 9856, pp. 86–107. Springer, Cham (2016). https://doi.org/10.1007/978-3-319-44902-9_7

39. Silva, T.R., Hak, J.-L., Winckler, M.: An approach for multi-artifact testing through an ontological perspective for behavior-driven development. Complex Syst. Inform. Model. Q. **7**, 81–107 (2016). https://doi.org/10.7250/csimq.2016-7.05
40. Silva, T.R., Winckler, M.: A scenario-based approach for checking consistency in user interface design artifacts. In: Proceedings of the 16th Brazilian Symposium on Human Factors in Computing Systems (IHC 2017), vol. 1, pp. 21–30 (2017). https://doi.org/10.1145/3160504.3160506

Integrating Personas and Use Case Models

Anke Dittmar$^{(\boxtimes)}$ and Peter Forbrig

University of Rostock, Rostock, Germany
{anke.dittmar,peter.forbrig}@uni-rostock.de

Abstract. Multidisciplinary design is characterized by phases of distributed work and co-design activities. An effective sharing and integration of design representations that are created by sub-teams from different disciplines is still often challenging and typically requires the reconciliation of diverging design perspectives. This paper investigates an integrated use of personas and use cases - two popular types of design representations among interaction designers and software engineers respectively. The proposed integration is particularly suitable for role-based interactive systems and differs from existing integration approaches in that it is based on a critical examination of the prevalent understandings of the goal concept in persona and use case approaches. In the paper we suggest distinguishing between organizational and user goals (while at the same time acknowledging their interplay). Corresponding adaptations to use case notations and personas are introduced and discussed. These remove the tight coupling between goals and tasks and allow integration of organizational and different persona-specific design perspectives within one use case specification and at the interaction level. As a result, interactive systems can be specified by a more compact sets of use cases. This is illustrated by an example in the context of course management systems in higher education.

Keywords: User-centred design · Personas · Use cases · Design representations

1 Introduction

External design representations such as scenarios, prototypes, and formal models are ubiquitous in interaction design [17]. According to Visser [42], the interactive system under design emerges from the creation, transformation and evaluation of design representations about the what, how and why of this system. This paper will particularly look at personas and use cases: two types of design representations which have been developed (together with corresponding methods) in relative isolation from each other in the context of human-computer interaction and software engineering respectively. Personas mainly contribute to the description of the why and use cases more to the description of the what of

© IFIP International Federation for Information Processing 2019
Published by Springer Nature Switzerland AG 2019
D. Lamas et al. (Eds.): INTERACT 2019, LNCS 11746, pp. 666–686, 2019.
https://doi.org/10.1007/978-3-030-29381-9_40

an interactive system. Multidisciplinary design is established as a basic principle of user-centred design [24, 25]. It is generally assumed that multidisciplinary design teams are more likely capture the multiple viewpoints which need to be considered to achieve product quality. For instance, Mackay [32] points out that science, design and engineering disciplines offer valuable skills and perspectives, but each discipline also "has the potential to miss important aspects of the design problem". Multidisciplinary teams need to acknowledge both distributed work by specialized sub-teams and discussions and sharing in heterogeneous teams [2]. Design representations created and used by specialists are shaped by the notations, techniques and methods they are used to in their professional practices to accomplish specific design tasks. External representations in heterogeneous teams must facilitate a flexible interpretation by collaborators from different disciplines. Team members couple and transform initially provided design representations in order to reveal and employ differences in existing design perspectives. However, even if an integration of these perspectives and a shared design understanding is achieved (and this may require the rethinking of assumptions and concepts of the collaborators' respective design approaches), it only becomes effective if it is documented in ways that fit again into subsequent specialized design activities.

This paper investigates how interaction designers, requirements engineers, and other stakeholders can be supported in sharing and integrating their viewpoints by using personas and use cases. Personas are user representations which are widely employed in user-centred design approaches to establish the interaction designers' empathy and understanding of the users of the system under consideration [11, 22, 37]. Use cases capture high-level functional requirements of systems from a usage perspective. They were adopted as a part of the Unified Modeling Language (UML)[1], the de-facto standard language for object-oriented software engineering. Use case diagrams are among the most widely used parts of the UML [27]. Both personas and use cases are 'simple' representations in the way that they can be easily understood and modified by stakeholders with different backgrounds. They thus support collaboration in heterogeneous teams. They also both embody the perspective of users, but do so with different understandings and objectives which therefore requires reconciliation. Use cases focus on functionality and are based on rather abstract models of users. Personas bring more emphasis to the diversity of users and contexts of use but are less detailed in their description of the interaction between user and system.

Use cases and personas are partly based on similar concepts and vocabulary, which is deceptive as there is not always the same underlying understanding. Existing integration approaches of personas and use cases such as [8, 39] do not pay sufficient attention to the different uses of the goal concept. They map one or more personas to an actor of a use case at the goal level, but do not integrate the personas' perspectives at the use case specification level (the interaction level). As a consequence, the set of use cases describing the system under consideration becomes difficult to manage and easily leads to incoherent designs.

---

[1] https://www.omg.org/.

This paper suggests an approach to reconcile the different understandings of goals. Based on a review of personas, use cases, and existing integration approaches (Sect. 2), more precise understandings of the concepts of user, goal and task are developed by distinguishing between organizational and user goals (Sect. 3.1). Basically, organizational goals and related tasks are understood in the context of work systems and are assigned to roles (described by actors in use cases). The concept of user refers to individuals acting in those roles. It is assumed that they generally share the goals established by the work system they are involved in but that they also have their specific backgrounds and personal goals. A single use case model has to specify both the similarities and the differences of the users' diverse ways to achieve the (organizational) goal of that use case.

A main contribution of the paper is the introduction and discussion of different adaptations to use case notations and personas to support an integration according to the above ideas (Sect. 3.3). Adaptations include persona-specific goals and actions in use cases, the ⟨⟨automate⟩⟩-stereotype in use case diagrams, and task-related user goals for personas. They preserve the essential character of persona and use case descriptions, but also facilitate the enhancement of use cases by ideas derived from personas, and thus, the described functionality not only covers the perspective of the considered work system but also the perspectives of diverse users. The suggested approach is particularly suitable for analyzing and designing role-based systems. The proposed notations are applied to an illustrative example which is introduced in Sect. 3.2. The paper closes with a discussion, some conclusions and future work (Sect. 4).

2   Background and Related Work

This section gives a short background to use cases and personas. In the context of this paper, readers are assumed to be less familiar with use cases. Therefore, Sect. 2.1 provides an introduction to these. Subsection 2.2 provides an overview about persona approaches. We then review existing approaches for integrating personas into requirements engineering approaches.

2.1   Use Cases in Software Engineering

Use cases were introduced into object-oriented software development by Jacobsen et al. [26] in the early 1990ies, but it is not an inherently object-oriented modeling technique. The approach aims at supporting 'user-centric solutions' [30]. Use cases describe systems as they appear to outside users. They "represent the things of value that the system performs for its actors" [4], and according to Kulak and Guiney, "[a]ll requirements that drive the development of use cases come from actual business needs of the users" [30]. In the use case approach, *users* are represented by *actors* but the terms should not be used interchangeably. Cockburn [10] defines an actor as a role outside the system that can be played by people, organizations, or technical systems and further distinguishes

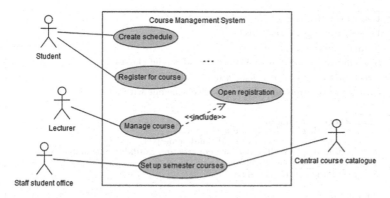

Fig. 1. Part of a use case diagram for a course management system with three primary actors and one secondary actor.

between primary actors and secondary actors. While the former interact with the system to achieve certain goals the latter are used by the system to provide services to primary actors [10]. Hence, Kulak and Guiney refer to primary actors in their definition of a use case as "a collection of possible sequences of interactions between the system under discussion and its Users (Actors), relating to a particular goal" [30].

Generally, a use case model consists of a use case diagram and a set of use case specifications. Use case diagrams are part of the UML[2] and can be understood as contextual descriptions. Systems and their environment are depicted by the names of use cases (indicating the actors' goals), the actors, and their relationships [31]. The diagram in Fig. 1 shows, for example, that students want to use the system under consideration to achieve two goals (create schedule and register for course). The central course catalogue is a secondary actor that is used by the system to support staff members in setting up semester courses. The real work, though, is in the creation of the use case specifications with details about the interaction between primary actors and the system. There is no standardized format but the most common are semi-formal textual specifications. Cockburn's [10] template (or variations) is widely used and it is also the basis for the adaptations to use cases which are suggested in this paper. The template recommends including the following points in a use case description.

- Name of the use case and context of use,
- Scope (enterprise/system/subsystem scope) and corresponding level of description (complex/task/function level),
- Primary actor and (other) stakeholders with their interests,
- Preconditions and trigger to run the use case,
- Success end condition and minimal guarantees,
- Main success scenario (basic course),

---

[2] The graphical notation for use case diagrams is defined in the UML specification (see https://www.omg.org/spec/UML/).

Use Case: *Create schedule*

Description level: Task level

Primary actor: Student

Stakeholders: Lecturer - students should attend classes,...

Precondition: Student is logged in

Success end condition: Recommended schedule without conflicts

...

Main success scenario:
1. System displays list of courses of study
2. Student selects course of study and semester
3. System displays all obligatory courses and available optional courses
4. UC: Select optional courses
5. System generates schedule

...

Extensions:
5a. Time conflict between two courses:
    5a.1. System displays conflicting courses
    5a.2 Student removes one course
    Rejoin at 4

...

Fig. 2. Part of the use case description *Create schedule* according to the template in [10].

- Extensions (alternative courses and their conditions),
- Variations of interactions,
- Other relevant information.

As mentioned previously, a use case specifies a set of sequences of actions or scenarios. The set contains at least the main success scenario which is the basic course of actions starting with the trigger and stopping with the success end condition and goal achievement. Cockburn [10] points out that steps or actions in the scenarios can be of three types: (1) an interaction between actor and system, (2) a validation by the system, and (3) an internal state change of the system. Scenarios should not only describe how primary actors achieve their goals but they should also make visible additional actions that are needed to consider other stakeholders' interests (e.g., validation steps). Figure 2 partly depicts the detailed description of one of the use cases in Fig. 1. The main success scenario is complemented by scenarios with additional actions (alternative courses) to deal with time conflicts (extension part). The example also illustrates that use cases can be included in or extend other use cases to obtain more succinct descriptions. For instance, sub-use case *Select optional courses* is 'folded' into a single action (step 4) in the main success scenario. The use case in Fig. 2 will be revisited later in this paper to illustrate the proposed integration approach.

Use cases can be used for both analyzing and designing systems but currently they are mainly employed for the latter purpose to capture functional requirements from the perspective of utility. Ideally, use cases should be used throughout the whole development process, but Jacobsen et al. [27] show at the example of use case slices for agile development that adaptations are needed to meet the requirements of specific development practices. It is generally not easy to keep the set of use case specifications of a system small and to create and maintain manageable use case models of high quality. Cockburn [10] states in this context: "I often refer to the set of use cases as an ever-unfolding story. It is our job to write this story in such a way that the reader can move around it comfortably". Recommendation and methodological guidance are given, e.g., in [10, 30].

2.2 Personas in Interaction Design

The persona concept was introduced into interaction design by Cooper [11] in the late 1990ies. "A persona is an archetype of a user that is given a name and a face, and it is carefully described in terms of needs, goals and tasks" [5]. It represents a whole user group, but according to authors such as Cooper [11] and Grudin [22], interaction designers engage better with personas than with abstract information about user groups. Personas work as design representations due to the human ability to make predictions about a person's behavior based on a precise description of their backgrounds and goals [23]. Typically, a small set of personas is identified for a system under consideration[3]. Designers then use the set as a communication tool to identify the functionality of the system, to support design decisions, to develop plausible usage scenarios or to evaluate whether a user interface covers the users' needs. The persona set helps them to discuss the system from the perspective of different user groups, and at the same time they are prevented from designing systems "that supposedly fit everyone but in the end fit no one" [18].

However, personas are not a panacea to ensure a user-centred design perspective and Floyd et al. [20] argue that there is no single persona approach which is applicable in every context. The authors identify different persona types (e.g., initial and final personas [11], ad-hoc personas [38]) and discuss their benefits and limitations. In [16], six dimensions concerning the user representation and the practical implementation of the persona method are identified along which persona usage can vary. For example, there are differences in the identification of user groups and the empirical basis upon which personas are constructed [9]. Another dimension concerns the presentation of a persona that can range from simple bullet-point lists to narrative descriptions (enriched with visual material). A persona becomes useless if it describes almost everyone ('elastic persona' [29]) or if it excludes users from the represented user group by giving too many details of the fictive person [9]. Nielsen [35] distinguishes between 'flat' characters as used, e.g., in goal-directed design [11], and 'rounded' descriptions that include "both personal (inner) and inter-personal (social, public, and professional) elements" [36]. She points out that it is a rounded depiction that evokes the designers' empathy.

There are other aspects that influence the effectiveness of personas. Although personas are considered to be 'simple' design representations, designers must

---

[3] There can be a further distinction between primary, secondary and anti-personas to express priorities between the needs of different user groups [12].

be skilled to identify with personas that are different from themselves [37] or to recognize bad quality descriptions such as elastic personas or 'my mother' personas [29]. Blomquist and Arvola [5] suggest that personas are more likely be used when they are created in the design team itself. Persona approaches must be related to other design approaches but an appropriate combination is mostly discussed within the user-centred design community and less across disciplinary boundaries with software engineers (see next subsection). For instance, Grudin states that "[p]ersonas come first and drive the construction of scenarios around them" [22] and all participants in the empirical study in [37] understood personas and scenarios as a combined method. Bødker et al. [6] point out that personas should not replace the active involvement of users and other stakeholders and studies such as [43] illustrate how personas can support participatory design processes.

2.3   Existing Integration Approaches

Various authors recognize the potential of persona methods to particularly enrich requirements engineering practices. Acuña et al. [1] state that "[p]ersonas provide an understanding of the user, often overlooked in SE [software engineering] developments". Schneidewind et al. [40] characterize challenges in requirements engineering as follows: (1) requirements of the users are often neglected, (2) insufficient communication about future users, and (3) users, tasks and context of use are not thoroughly connected to the requirements of a system. The authors suggest employing personas to better prioritize and illustrate use cases, and to identify and specify nonfunctional requirements. However, their approach is not further elaborated. Similarly, Francescomarino et al. [21] and Faily [19] call for integrating of concepts and analysis techniques of different approaches such as user-centred design and goal-oriented requirements engineering to better represent user needs in "user-intensive" systems [21] but do not discuss in detail the indicated relationships between personas, scenarios and use cases.

Acuña and colleagues [1,8] assume that persona methods can only be successfully built into the requirements stage of regular software engineering developments if they come with a detailed definition of activities and products. The authors developed PersonaSE, a persona method that consists of eleven activities which are mapped to four common requirements engineering activities (elicitation, analysis, specification, and validation of requirements). Each activity is defined by a name, objectives, techniques and expected outcomes or products. In the context of this paper, activity 10 ("build use cases") is of particular interest. Here, Acuña et al. [1] suggest to map a set of primary and secondary personas to each use case and to create separate use case descriptions for each persona (see Fig. 3(b)). However, this would lead to a large number of use case specifications for a system. Inconsistencies between single specifications are more likely. In our approach, we are less interested in normative process models for integrating persona and use case methods. We rather focus on adapting existing use case notations to enrich single specifications but keep the overall set of use case specifications minimal and manageable.

The case study in [39] investigates an integrated use of personas and use cases in the context of a small information system for tracking training of employees in a community hospital. Randolph [39] points out that personas better aid the designing of user interaction that meets a user's needs and goals, and use cases give more details about the specifics of users' task requirements. In the case study, personas are mapped in a one-to-one way to actors in use case models suggesting that a persona is a representation of role (see Fig. 3(a)). A more differentiated view is proposed in [34]. Miller and Williams argue that use cases only support a role-based requirements engineering and that the integration of the persona perspective allows "to examine the different types of people who could play a role" [34]. Similarly to [1], the authors suggest to develop separate use case descriptions for each persona. A slightly different approach is taken in [41]. Sim and Brouse also start with the identification of roles and corresponding use cases. Personas are used through a process of role refinement to construct viewpoints which form the basis for later conceptual modeling. One or more viewpoints can be defined for each persona. A viewpoint is described in terms of goals, concerns, scenarios, tasks, functional and non-functional requirements. However, the relationship between these concepts is not clarified.

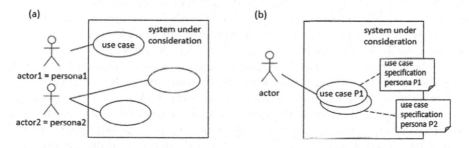

Fig. 3. (a) 1:1-mapping between primary actors and personas in [39], (b) separate use case specifications for personas in the role of the primary actor in [1,34].

3   The Integration Approach

In the previous section, we have seen that personas as well as use cases aim at understanding an interactive system from the perspective of its users. Existing integration approaches stress that use cases reduce the description of users to abstract roles and refer to the potential of personas to provide a richer picture. However, they stop at the level of use case diagrams and separate specifications are developed for each persona assigned to a use case. The underlying assumption, although not stated explicitly, seems to be that there are no similarities at all in the personas' ways to achieve the goal of the use case. As a consequence, the number of use case specifications for a system 'explodes' and use case models become less useful for subsequent design activities. In our approach, we aim at providing means to produce smaller, more manageable sets of specifications leading to more coherent designs. This requires a better clarification of concepts shared by persona and use case approaches. Based on the revision of goals and tasks in the next subsection, adaptations of the use case notations introduced above are developed which allow the unification of perspectives of different user groups within single use case specifications. The suggested adaptations are applicable to role-based interactive systems as will be illustrated by an example introduced in Subsect. 3.2.

3.1   Conceptual Understandings

Personas were originally intended to support a goal-directed design [11]. In this context, goals are mainly considered to be individuals' goals ('user goals') with some of them originating from a group an individual is involved in (e.g., a corporation, an institution). In [12], three types of user goals are distinguished: experience goals ("how someone wants to feel while using a product"), end goals ("motivation for performing the tasks associated with using a specific product"), and life goals ("long-term desires, motivations, and self-image attributes, which cause a persona to connect with the product"). User goals are complemented in [12] by customer goals, corporate goals, and technical goals. However, Cooper and Reimann [12] emphasize the role of end goals in driving the design of the interactive artifact. Cooper's personas were later criticized for their strong focus on goals easily leading to the description of 'flat' characters [35] which fail to evoke the designer's empathy. Still, goals in most persona approaches are mainly described as goals 'owned' by individuals. In contrast, goals in use cases have rather to be understood in an organizational context. Actors specify roles with "certain operational responsibilities imposed by the business processes and business rules of the business domain" [33]. Hence, their goals are 'organizational' goals that are established in an organization in order to consider (at least to a certain degree) the interests of involved stakeholders.

Goals in use case approaches and personas' end goals are seen as end conditions which can be achieved by accomplishing tasks. Use case specifications at the task level are restricted to goals that actors achieve through interactions with the system under consideration and show some similarities to task models commonly used in human-computer interaction [13]. In particular, nested goal structures are assumed which are tightly related to corresponding task hierarchies. This is graphically depicted in Fig. 4(a) where some of the actions of use case UC are 'folded' use cases. The goal of UC can be accomplished either by performing the actions or steps of the basic course (forming the main success scenario) or by 'departures' to those alternative courses which still guarantee the success end condition. On the one hand, these sequences of actions specify a task structure. On the other hand, actions can be use cases themselves and thus represent goals. Goal unfolding results in interaction or task refinement [33]. Figure 4 shows four sub-use cases or sub-goals, two of them are included in the basic course of UC (UC1, UC2) and two are steps in alternative courses (UC3, UC4) which is also indicated by the include- and extend-relationships in the corresponding use case

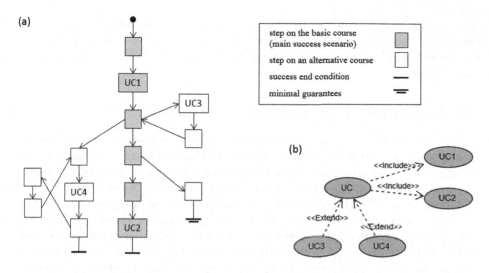

Fig. 4. A schematic use case UC: (a) Visualization of the specified action sequences (adapted from [33]). Sub-use cases UC1..UC4 are 'folded' to actions. (b) The corresponding part of the use case diagram depicts the nested goal structure more explicitly.

diagram. In the context of task analysis for human-computer interaction, Diaper and Stanton [13] criticize the broad, often vague use of the term goal and the extreme linking of goals and tasks described above. The authors point out that people rarely do anything for just one reason and that their multiple goals interact in complex ways [13,15]. Diaper [14] also mentions problems of generalization and notes that "...almost all task analysis methods claim to be able to combine descriptions of a task performed by different people in different ways. Quite a few methods are able to combine different tasks into a single task representation". This critique equally applies to use case specifications where even a main success scenario is assumed suggesting that there is 'one best way' to achieve a goal.

In our approach, we restrict ourselves to role-based interactive systems; that is, to software systems which are applied in work systems where roles guide the distribution of work. We distinguish between *organizational goals* as intended states or conditions of the work system and individual or *user goals* which express intentions and preferences of the people who are part of the work system and actually use the interactive system under consideration to fulfill their responsibilities (referred to simply as the users). We assume an interaction between organizational goals and individual goals. Users internalize or appropriate organizational goals by relating them to their own values, attitudes, and goals. Such appropriation processes are unique to every person, and at the same time shaped by procedures (task structures) that exist in the work system. Users externalize their individual goals in their particular ways to perform tasks in the work system (and this can, in turn, shape organizational goals). Based on these assumptions, we suggest complementing goal descriptions of use cases by task-related goals of personas. Before we consider the implications of such different goal sets in more detail and develop corresponding adaptations to use case specifications, we briefly introduce the example that will be used to illustrate the proposed adaptations.

3.2   Introduction to the Illustrative Example

The example considers a use case of a course management system called *StudOrg*. Course management systems have become standard components in higher education and their features can be leveraged for a variety of academic purposes (e.g., management and retrieval of course material) [28]. Some typical roles of such systems are already shown in Fig. 1. We focus here on use case *Create schedule* with role *Student* as primary actor. Two personas are developed to give a richer and more differentiated picture of students (following recommendations in [35,36]). Figures 5 and 6 show those parts of the narrative descriptions of *Adrian* and *Stephanie* which are relevant for the use case, together with photos depicting them in action. The next subsection presents two alternative adaptations to use case specifications. The general ideas are illustrated and explained in more detail by extended versions of *Create schedule* in Fig. 2. Both versions integrate the perspectives of Stephanie and Adrian within a single specification.

Adrian grew up in a small village near Rotown and completed a vocational diploma in crop farming. His parents wanted him to go to university but he decided to work in a local farming company. Although he liked the work as such he soon realized that he really has few development options without further qualification. Now, Adrian is in his third semester. His girlfriend Iris already studied in Rotown and so it was no big decision to study agricultural science there.

For Adrian, much of what they learn is too theoretical. He focuses on what he likes to do such as practical projects and he is happy about his voluntary work in the "Intercultural Garden". In their last soil measurement project he got a really good grade and could even help other students with the analysis tool. But he let other things slide and he sometimes forgets to go to classes. In one case, he now has to repeat the whole course. He had a fight with Iris about it. She said that he should have a printout of his schedule in their kitchen and that it is easy to create with StudOrg...

https://www.pexels.com

Fig. 5. Fragment of persona *Adrian* (25 years old).

3.3   Adaptations to Use Case Models

Similarly to [1,34], we consider different types of users who could play a role in a work system (see Subsect. 2.3). But due to the interplay between organizational and user goals described above, we assume both differences and similarities in the ways different user groups achieve a goal. In our integration approach, use

Stephanie had applied to Bellcity University. She knew that they always have many applicants and was not too disappointed about the rejection. So, she started studying communication and media studies in her hometown, but definitely wants to get a Master degree at Bellcity University. Last summer, she used the time between high school and university to go to Bellcity for an internship in a PR agency.

Stephanie manages the Facebook page of her volleyball club. She likes to post pictures from her iPhone, a Christmas present of her grandmother who is Stephanie's most faithful 'follower'. They try to meet regularly though they both need their calendars to find a date. Stephanie thought the first semesters would be more difficult but she could manage the workload well. Now she would like to attend additional courses, especially the one on creative writing. She wonders whether she can arrange it with her regular semester schedule...

Fig. 6. Fragment of persona *Stephanie* (20 years old).

cases represent organizational goals, primary actors represent roles, and personas represent user groups acting in the different roles of an organization. The persona descriptions especially provide insights into the users' specific appropriation of organizational goals. They allow implications to be drawn about the way tasks are performed in order to satisfy both the organizational goals and the users' goals and preferences. Personas also enable general implications for the user interface design which can be summarized in a table similar to the one recommended in [39]. Table 1 shows persona-specific implications in the running example. The explicit consideration of organizational and user goals leads to modifications in the use case specifications. Goal descriptions and end conditions need to be extended to include persona-specific aspects; implications for the user interface can be inserted. This is indicated below with Cockburn's template [10].

Use Case: ⟨name of the use case⟩
Description level: task level
Primary actor: ⟨name of the role⟩
    with personas *Persona 1, Persona 2,...*
Goal: ⟨description of organizational goal⟩
    Persona 1: ⟨description of task-related user goals⟩
    Persona 2: ...
Success end condition: ⟨the state of the world upon successful task completion⟩
    Persona 1: ⟨persona-specific state⟩
    Persona 2: ...
Implications for user interface:
    Persona 1: ⟨persona-specific implications⟩
    Persona 2: ...

Use cases describe now a set of *persona-specific goal sets* which have the overall organizational goal in common. The resulting question is: how should

Table 1. Persona-specific implications in the example.

	Adrian	*Stephanie*
Description	Infrequent user of StudOrg via laptop at home, familiar with Word, Excel, domain-specific analysis programs; digital technology has low priority	Frequent user of StudOrg; enjoys using technology and social media (iPhone, iPad and Mac)
Interface implications	StudOrg should be easy to use; show only most necessary features	Flexible interface with additional features
Create schedule - task-related user goals	Printout of the schedule with a clear layout; registered for all courses in the schedule	Efficient but flexible composition of the schedule; transfer to iCloud Calendar

action sequences (scenarios) be specified to make visible the differences and similarities in the personas' task structures. Two alternative ideas are sketched in Fig. 7.

– *Adaptation 1:* The constraint of having only one basic course (the main success scenario) is relaxed. There are overlapping persona-specific basic courses as

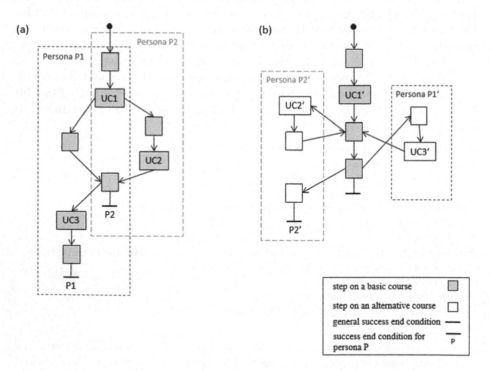

Fig. 7. (a) Adaptation 1: overlapping persona-specific main success scenarios, (b) Adaptation 2: one common main-success scenario with persona-specific extensions.

indicated for two personas in Fig. 7(a). The figure abstracts from alternative courses and variations which can additionally be defined for personas.
- *Adaptation 2:* As usual, one basic course is defined (possibly with persona-specific variations). Persona-specific interactions with the system are modeled exclusively by alternative courses and extension points. Figure 7(b) depicts this in a schematic way for two personas.

Figure 8 applies adaptation 1 to the use case *Create schedule* in Fig. 2 to better consider the specific perspectives of the two personas in the example. Two basic courses are specified: steps 1, 2, 3, 4, 5, A-6, A-7, A-8, 11, 12 form the main success scenario of *Adrian* and steps 1, 2, 3, 4, 5, S-6, S-7, S-8, S-9, S-10, 11, 12 form that of *Stephanie*. The achievement of the main goal - a schedule that is consistent with recommendations and without conflicts - is ensured by the shared parts in the scenarios (steps 1..5, 11, 12). It is an organizational goal that serves the interests of various stakeholders (e.g. lecturers, see Fig. 2). Additionally, *Adrian* is supported by an automatic course registration (steps A-6..A-8) and *Stephanie* can use an extended editing mode to add other than recommended courses to her schedule (steps S-6..S-10). The variations in step 12 handle the different preferences of *Adrian* and *Stephanie* concerning the form of the generated calendar. Extensions to the main success scenarios are only indicated in Fig. 8. The textual representation of the two basic courses in the example is similar to the graphical visualization in Fig. 7(a).

An example for adaptation 2 can be seen in Fig. 9. There is one main success scenario which guarantees the success end condition for the organizational goal. Persona-specific interactions are expressed by alternative courses in the extension part. According to [33], alternative courses are a guarded variation of a part of another course (in particular, of the basic course) and can describe optional parts of behavior, alternative interaction parts, business error recovery or fault handling. Figure 9 indicates two persona-specific alternative courses (one for *Adrian* and one for *Stephanie*, each starting at step 6 of the basic course). The corresponding guards 6a-A and 6b-S are persona-specific goals and preferences.

Annotated Use Case Diagrams and the $\langle\langle automate \rangle\rangle$-relationship: Figure 10 gives an overview of the similarities and differences in the personas' interaction with the considered system. The annotated use case diagram shows mappings between personas and use cases which result from the example specification in Fig. 8 (adaptation 1). Annotated $\langle\langle include \rangle\rangle$-relationships exist between use case *Create schedule* and those sub-use cases which are steps in the personas' basic courses. In contrast, the description of persona-specific behavior in adaptation 2 is exclusively based on $\langle\langle extend \rangle\rangle$-relationships (annotated by the personas' names).

$\langle\langle Include \rangle\rangle$- and $\langle\langle extend \rangle\rangle$-relationships are predefined stereotypes in the UML and describe required and optional subgoals respectively. We introduce another type - the $\langle\langle automate \rangle\rangle$-relationship - to describe different degrees of automation for different personas. In the example, *Adrian* prefers automatic course registration within the use case *Create Schedule* (see Figs. 8 and 9) while

Use Case: *Create schedule*

Description level: Task level

Primary actor: Student, with personas *Adrian* (A) and *Stephanie* (S)

Goal: Student wants to compose the schedule for the next semester.

Adrian: Wants to follow recommendations and automatic registration for all selected courses.

Stephanie: Composed schedule contains, in addition to recommended courses, other courses she is interested in.

Implications for user interface:

Adrian: Simple and consistent interface, only basic features visible.

Stephanie: Interface with additional features, can be customized.

Precondition: Student is logged in

Success end condition: Schedule which is consistent with recommendations and without conflicts.

Adrian: Printout of schedule, confirmation of course registrations.

Stephanie: Schedule is integrated in personal digital calendar.
...

Main success scenario:

1. System displays list of courses of study
2. Student selects course of study and semester
3. System displays all obligatory courses and available optional courses
4. UC: Select optional courses
5. System generates and displays schedule

A-6. Adrian confirms and activates automatic registration	S-6. Stephanie activates the extended editing mode
A-7. System saves schedule and registers Adrian for each course in the schedule	S-7. System changes to extended editing mode
A-8. System sends confirmation message for registrations	S-8. UC: Add additional course
	S-9. UC: Remove additional course
	S-10. UC: Select optional courses
	(repeat steps S-8..S-10 in any order)

11. Student chooses format of schedule

12. System provides schedule in chosen format

Extensions:

5a. Time conflict between two courses: ...

A-7a. A course is fully booked: ... | S-8a. Time conflict: ...
...

Variations:

12. Schedule as printout (*Adrian*) or calendar export (*Stephanie*)

Fig. 8. Adaptation 1 applied to use case *Create schedule* in the example.

Use Case: *Create schedule*
Description level: Task level
Primary actor: Student, with personas *Adrian* (A) and *Stephanie* (S)
...

Main success scenario:
1. System displays list of courses of study
2. Student selects course of study and semester
3. System displays all obligatory courses and available optional courses
4. UC: <u>Select optional courses</u>
5. System generates and displays schedule
6. Student confirms schedule
7. System saves schedule
8. Student chooses format of schedule
9. System provides schedule in chosen format

Extensions:
5a. Time conflict between two courses: ...

6a-A. Adrian additionally wants to be registered automatically:
    1.   Adrian activates automatic registration
    2.   ...
6b-S. Stephanie wants to add other courses:
    1.   Stephanie activates the extended editing mode
    2.   ...
...

Fig. 9. Adaptation 2 applied to use case *Create schedule* in the example. (Descriptions of goals, end conditions etc. are the same as in Fig. 8.)

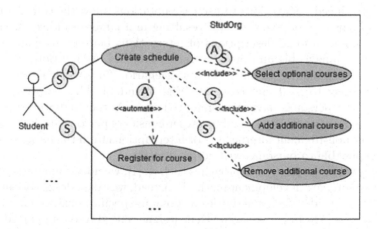

Fig. 10. Adaptation 1: use case diagram in the example, annotated by personas *Adrian* (A) and *Stephanie* (S) acting in role *Student*.

Stephanie interacts with the system to register for single courses. Hence, the diagram in Fig. 10 depicts *Stephanie* (but not *Adrian*) as primary actor of use case *Register for course* and there is a corresponding ⟨⟨automate⟩⟩-relationship annotated by *Adrian* (A).

4   Discussion

"Interaction design requires input from science, engineering and design disciplines" [32]. Authors such as Mackay discard the idea that interaction designers should develop expertise in all of the component disciplines but emphasize that multidisciplinary teamwork requires from participants an increased understanding and appreciation for other disciplines. Design activities have to be created "in which all members of the design team, including users, can participate equally" [32]. The suggested coupling of personas and use cases, in the context of role-based interactive systems, supports a shared discussion and refinement of design ideas across sub-disciplines.

Bellotti et al. [3] point out that for an effective collaboration in multidisciplinary teams, a revision of each others' assumptions can be necessary. Existing integration approaches of personas and use cases do not reflect sufficiently on the different understanding of the goal concept. This paper shows that the tight coupling of tasks and goals as is common in use case specifications should be considered critical. The suggested distinction and interplay between organizational and user goals acknowledges differences and similarities in the ways tasks are performed by the different people in a work system. It is a valuable conceptual contribution that can also be applied to hierarchical task modeling approaches in human-computer interaction [13].

The introduced adaptations to use case notations allow the consideration of persona-specific sets of goals without resulting in a large set of use case specifications with overlapping descriptions of interactions between user and system, which is less manageable and prone to inconsistencies. Adaptation 1 rejects the idea of one basic course or main success scenario. The persona-specific basic courses are easy to read and compare (Figs. 7 and 8). This notation is to be preferred if the personas have the same priority as Adrian and Stephanie in the example. Adaptation 2 (Figs. 7 and 9) rather considers persona-specific goals and behaviors as non-frequent alternatives or interruptions from the basic course and is more applicable to personas with lower priority.

In contrast to integration approaches such as [1], we do not aim at adapting a prescriptive software development method. Instead, we take a design-oriented perspective and consider design activities as domain-specific construction of design representations [42]. In [7], we argue that designers need to be supported in generating ideas, but also in comparing different design representations and in understanding how they are related and whether or not they satisfy some initial or evolving design specifications and constraints. Generally, it is still challenging to effectively couple different design representations in interaction design [7]. The proposed stronger interweaving of personas and use case models supports their co-development and the integration of different design perspectives. Use case models and personas change their character with the suggested adaptations. For instance, implications from single personas can be traced in the models and the proposed ⟨⟨automate⟩⟩-relationship facilitates thinking about automation and interaction. However, the changes are not radical ones and it can be assumed that they help to 'bridge' practices of interaction designers and software engineers.

Personas help to view interactive systems from an individual's perspective, although one should keep in mind that they are abstractions from user groups themselves which can complement or support, but not replace, an active involvement of users and other stakeholders into the design process. The success of the suggested integration depends to a great extent on the description of the personas' appropriation of organizational goals. 'Flat' descriptions (see [35]) where personas do not reflect on their roles and responsibilities do not encourage more discussion among the design team members nor do they make abstract roles and corresponding actors in use case models 'more alive'.

The suggested concepts and notations for an integrated use of personas and use cases were successfully used in teaching. Empirical evidence of the benefits to software development practice still needs to be shown. In [24], an action research approach was applied to investigate how changes in the development process aimed at improving user involvement and usability influenced the outcome of the process. A similar approach could be taken here.

5   Conclusions and Future Work

With personas and use cases, two types of design representations have been investigated that are popular and commonly used in the disciplines of interaction design and software engineering respectively. An integration of these representations has been proposed which preserves their essential character, but at the same time supports creative collaboration of interaction designers, software engineers and other stakeholders in capturing requirements for role-based interactive systems from an organizational perspective as well as from the users' perspectives. The adaptations are based on a revised conceptual understanding of goals and task-goal relationships and include task-related user goals for personas, persona-specific goals and actions in use cases, and the ⟨⟨automate⟩⟩-stereotype in use case diagrams. A carefully worked out example serves as an initial validation of the integration approach, but future empirical studies are needed to examine its effectiveness. At the conceptual level, we want to investigate in future work how to better relate the adapted use case models to other design representations from interaction design such as 'rich' scenarios and user interface models.

Acknowledgements. We thank Louisa Jochum for the discussions and her help.

References

1. Acuña, S.T., Castro, J.W., Juzgado, N.J.: A HCI technique for improving requirements elicitation. Inf. Soft. Technol. **54**(12), 1357–1375 (2012)
2. Baker, M., Détienne, F., Burkhardt, J.M.: Quality of collaboration in design: articulating multiple dimensions and viewpoints. In: 1st Interdisciplinary Innovation Conference, Paris, France (2013)
3. Bellotti, V., Shum, S., MacLean, A., Hammond, N.: Multidisciplinary modelling in HCI design in theory and in practice. In: SIGCHI Conference on Human Factors in Computing Systems, CHI 1995, pp. 146–153. ACM (1995)
4. Bittner, K., Spence, I.: Use Case Modeling. Addison-Wesley, Boston (2002)
5. Blomquist, A., Arvola, M.: Personas in action: ethnography in an interaction design team. In: Proceedings of NordiCHI 2002, pp. 197–200. ACM (2002)
6. Bødker, S., Christiansen, E., Nyvang, T., Zander, P.O.: Personas, people and participation: challenges from the trenches of local government. In: Proceedings of PDC 2012, pp. 91–100. ACM (2012)
7. Bowen, J., Dittmar, A.: Coping with design complexity: a conceptual framework for design alternatives and variants. In: Bernhaupt, R., Dalvi, G., Joshi, A., Balkrishan, D.K., O'Neill, J., Winckler, M. (eds.) INTERACT 2017. LNCS, vol. 10513, pp. 483–502. Springer, Cham (2017). https://doi.org/10.1007/978-3-319-67744-6_30
8. Castro, J.W., Acuña, S.T., Juzgado, N.J.: Enriching requirements analysis with the personas technique. In: I-USED. CEUR Workshop Proceedings, vol. 407. CEUR-WS.org (2008)
9. Chapman, C.N., Milham, R.P.: The personas' new clothes: methodological and practical arguments against a popular method. In: The Human Factors and Ergonomics Society Annual Meeting, pp. 634–636. SAGE Publications (2006)
10. Cockburn, A.: Writing Effective Use Cases. Addison-Wesley, Boston (2000)
11. Cooper, A.: The Inmates are Running the Asylum. Macmillan Publishing Co., Inc., Indianapolis (1999)
12. Cooper, A., Reimann, R.: About Face 3.0: The Essentials of Interaction Design, 3rd revised edn. Wiley, Hoboken (2007)
13. Diaper, D., Stanton, N.: The Handbook of Task Analysis for Human-Computer Interaction. L. Erlbaum Associates Inc., Hillsdale (2004)
14. Diaper, D.: Understanding task analysis for human-computer interaction. In: Diaper, D., Stanton, N. (eds.) The Handbook of Task Analysis for Human-Computer Interaction. L. Erlbaum Associates Inc., Hillsdale (2004)
15. Diaper, D., Sanger, C.: Tasks for and tasks in human-computer interaction. Interact. Comput. **18**(1), 117–138 (2006)
16. Dittmar, A., Hensch, M.: Two-level personas for nested design spaces. In: Proceedings of CHI 2015, pp. 3265–3274 (2015)
17. Dix, A., Gongora, L.: Externalisation and design. In: Second Conference on Creativity and Innovation in Design, pp. 31–42. ACM (2011)
18. Eriksson, E., Artman, H., Swartling, A.: The secret life of a persona: when the personal becomes private. In: Proceedings of CHI 2013, pp. 2677–2686. ACM (2013)
19. Faily, S.: Bridging user-centered design and requirements engineering with GRL and persona cases. In: de Castro, J.B., Franch, X., Mylopoulos, J., Yu, E.S.K. (eds.) Proceedings of the 5th International i* Workshop 2011. CEUR Workshop Proceedings, vol. 766, pp. 114–119. CEUR-WS.org (2011)
20. Floyd, I.R., Jones, M.C., Twidale, M.B.: Resolving incommensurable debates: a preliminary identification of persona kinds, attributes, and properties. Artifact J. Virtual Des. **2**(1), 12–26 (2008)

21. Francescomarino, C.D., et al.: A bit of "persona", a bit of "goal", a bit of "process" ... a recipe for analyzing user intensive software systems. In: iStar. CEUR Workshop Proceedings, vol. 586, pp. 36–40. CEUR-WS.org (2010)
22. Grudin, J.: Why personas work: the psychological evidence. In: Pruitt, J., Adlin, T. (eds.) The Persona Lifecycle: Keeping People in Mind Throughout Product Design. Morgan Kaufmann Publishers Inc., San Francisco (2005)
23. Grudin, J., Pruitt, J.: Personas, participatory design and product development: an infrastructure for engagement. In: Proceedings of PDC 2002, pp. 144–161 (2002)
24. Gulliksen, J., Göransson, B., Boivie, I., Blomkvist, S., Cajander, Å.: Key principles for user centred systems design. Behav. Inf. Technol. **22**(6), 397–409 (2003)
25. ISO: ISO 9241-210:2010 - Ergonomics of human-system interaction - Part 210: Human-centred design for interactive systems (2010). http://www.iso.org/iso/iso_catalogue/catalogue_ics/catalogue_detail_ics.htm?csnumber=52075
26. Jacobson, I., Christerson, M., Jonsson, P., Övergaard, G.: Object-Oriented Software Engineering: A Use Case Driven Approach. Addison-Wesley, Boston (1992)
27. Jacobson, I., Spence, I., Kerr, B.: Use-case 2.0. Commun. ACM **59**(5), 61–69 (2016)
28. Jarrahi, M.H.: A structurational analysis of how course management systems are used in practice. Behav. Inf. Technol. **29**(3), 257–275 (2010)
29. Jones, M.C., Floyd, I.R., Twidale, M.B.: Teaching design with personas. In: Proceedings of HCIEd (2008)
30. Kulak, D., Guiney, E.: Use Cases: Requirements in Context. Addison-Wesley, Boston (2000)
31. Larman, C.: Applying UML and Patterns: An Introduction to Object-Oriented Analysis and Design and Iterative Development, 3rd edn. Prentice Hall, Upper Saddle River (2004)
32. Mackay, W.E.: Educating multi-disciplinary design teams. In: Proceedings of Tales of the Disappearing Computer, Santorini. ACM Press (2003)
33. Metz, P., O'Brien, J., Weber, W.: Specifying use case interaction: types of alternative courses. J. Object Technol. **2**(2), 111–131 (2003)
34. Miller, G., Williams, L.: Personas: moving beyond role-based requirements engineering. Technical report, North Carolina State University. Department of Computer Science (2006)
35. Nielsen, L.: From user to character: an investigation into user-descriptions in scenarios. In: Proceedings of DIS 2002, pp. 99–104. ACM (2002)
36. Nielsen, L.: Personas In "The Encyclopedia of Human-Computer Interaction, 2nd edn." (2013). http://www.interaction-design.org/encyclopedia/personas.html
37. Nielsen, L., Hansen, K.S.: Personas is applicable: a study on the use of personas in Denmark. In: CHI, pp. 1665–1674 (2014)
38. Norman, D.: Ad-hoc personas & empathetic focus. In: Pruitt, J., Adlin, T. (eds.) The Persona Lifecycle: Keeping People in Mind Throughout Product Design. Morgan Kaufmann Publishers Inc., San Francisco (2005)
39. Randolph, G.: Use-cases and personas: a case study in light-weight user interaction design for small development projects. Informing Sci. Int. J. Emerg. Transdiscipline **7**, 105–116 (2004)
40. Schneidewind, L., Hörold, S., Mayas, C., Krömker, H., Falke, S., Pucklitsch, T.: How personas support requirements engineering. In: Proceedings of the First International Workshop on Usability and Accessibility Focused Requirements Engineering, UsARE 2012, pp. 1–5. IEEE Press (2012)
41. Sim, W.W., Brouse, P.S.: Empowering requirements engineering activities with personas. Procedia Comput. Sci. **28**, 237–246 (2014)

42. Visser, W.: Designing as construction of representations: a dynamic viewpoint in cognitive design research. Hum.-Comput. Interact. **21**(1), 103–152 (2006)
43. Wärnestål, P., Svedberg, P., Nygren, J.: Co-constructing child personas for health-promoting services with vulnerable children. In: Proceedings of CHI 2014, pp. 3767–3776 (2014)

Smart Interactive Packaging as a Cyber-Physical Agent in the Interaction Design Theory: A Novel User Interface

Justina Lydekaityte[✉]

Aarhus University, Birk Centerpark 15, 7400 Herning, Denmark
justina@btech.au.dk

Abstract. The emerging infrastructure of cyber-physical systems consisting of everyday items, as product's packaging, and advanced digital communication devices opens a new digital dimension for interaction and user experience. Consequently, the concept of human-packaging interaction goes beyond the pragmatic aspects of physical packaging attributes, and, in turn, embraces the potentials of ICT systems. Due to the new forms of human-packaging interactive systems, designers have to address the relevancy of the interaction design and the complexity in the relationship between consumer behavior and interactive system design, i.e. digitally-enhanced packaging. Therefore this research aims to describe the digitally-enhanced packaging as a digital interactive system in regards to the theories of human-computer interaction, interaction design, and user-centered design. In this paper, the critical elements of the interactive packaging design are described. This study concludes that for the interactive systems to be effective and used, designers have to build not only a reward-based, intuitive and simple interaction design that would persuade users to take actions, but also they have to think of other mediate interactions, internal and external resources that are significant to reach the final aim.

Keywords: Human-packaging interaction · Smart interactive packaging · Interaction design · Cyber-technical systems

1 Introduction

Within the exponential growth in the application of computer systems, a wide range of all sorts of artifacts and interfaces have arisen ranging from mobile devices and domestic appliances to vehicles and whole houses [1]. The given access to these gadgets by information and communication technology (ICT) made communication more advanced and diverse. Today the consumer market brings into play many miscellaneous digital interfaces to create the interaction between consumers, products and brands to deliver unexpected and unique experiences [1]. Product packaging also became one of such digital interfaces.

Out of the many roles packaging has to perform, the user interaction is likely to have a profound effect on packaging innovation [2]. Packaging, also referred as 'communication surface', 'an extended user interface', 'communication medium', 'contact point', or 'silent salesman' encounters consumers daily through various visual and tactile

© IFIP International Federation for Information Processing 2019
Published by Springer Nature Switzerland AG 2019
D. Lamas et al. (Eds.): INTERACT 2019, LNCS 11746, pp. 687–695, 2019.
https://doi.org/10.1007/978-3-030-29381-9_41

interplays [3]. The communication between the user and packaging occurs in every step of the supply chain, including producer, distributor, retailer and end consumer [4]. The current research on human-packaging interaction (HPI) [5, 6], also called as user-packaging interaction [4] or consumer-packaging interaction [3], investigates either the ergonomic- or marketing-concerning factors. The former is related to the handling and usability of packaging and the utilization of the packed product [6], whereas the latter is associated with the visual appearance of the packaging [4] in terms of physical attributes as color, shape, material or typography. However, the emerging infrastructure of cyber-physical systems, induced by advanced wireless communication devices and IoT, opens a new digital dimension for interaction and user experience [7] and goes beyond the pragmatic aspects of HPI. Consequently, traditional passive packaging is able to embrace the digital transformation and become network-connected [8] due to applied a wide range of mobile, digital and wireless communication technologies. As these technologies improve, the new forms of human-packaging interactive systems appear, and thereby designers have to address the relevancy of the interaction design in relation to the complex relationship between the consumer behavior and interactive system design, i.e. digitally-enhanced packaging [9]. Therefore this research aims to (i) describe the digitally-enhanced packaging as a digital interactive system in relation to the theories of human-computer interaction, interaction design, and user-centered design, and, in turn, (ii) investigate what are the key elements of designing an effective interactive packaging design.

This research presents the work in progress and it is based on literature review focused on articles related to human-packaging interaction, HCI, interaction design, and user-centered design. This study creates a link between the everyday item, as product's packaging, and interaction design of HCI systems.

2   Theory

2.1   Smart Interactive Packaging

Generally, product packaging can be perceived as: "a socio-scientific discipline which operates in society to ensure the delivery of goods to the ultimate consumer" [5]. It is also defined as a combination of product, package, and distribution which is intended to provide the functions of protection, convenience, containment, and communication [4, 10]. However, the importance of the packaging role and the improvement of its functionalities have increased over the years due to changes in market globalization, demographics, lifestyles and consumer preferences [11]. Having in mind that packaging already served as an effective means of communication medium [10], recent advances in printed electronics, conductive printed materials, and wireless communication devices improved the communication function even more. This transformation allowed packaging to enter digital innovation and become network-connected [8]. As a result, smart interactive packaging goes beyond the traditional one-way informational flow and triggers the unique interaction capability between the package and consumer. Reference [12] contributes and states that integrated printable circuits onto consumer packaging would add to products such features as brand protection, customer feedback and visual product enhancement. Connected packaging ability to collect and analyze data empowers brands to understand the effectiveness of the packaging/product and consumers' engagement better, and dynamically adapt to emerging needs by improving their services and products. Therefore, the design of smart interactive packaging, as an interactive system, has to take into account both the insights of the interactive design and user experience.

2.2   Interaction Design of Digitally Enhanced Packaging

With the increasing use of the Internet, home and leisure computing, and digital interactive consumer products, the two disciplines of engineering and design merged due to a common goal to amplify discretionary use and user experience [13]. The perspective of the user and the context of use went beyond the traditional computer and mechanical systems and started to penetrate into products and environments people interact with in daily life [5]. Consequently, the user-centered design has broadened to other cultures that gave new opportunities for consumer industry and brand owners.

The popularization of consumer-oriented ICT systems lets designers create special moments and environments giving brands the opportunity to have in-depth communication with their consumers filled with emotional and sensorial facets. As a result, it forms an exceptional link between customers and manufacturers [1]. However, the success of creating this bond depends on whether the designed artefacts and environments can offer a pleasing interface with the user [1]. Therefore, the main aim of interaction design is to: "create interactive products and systems which are usable – easy to learn, effective and pleasant to use" [1]. Reference [14] concurs and states that interaction design has been aroused by increasing industry's demand for intuitive, effortless and enjoyable computing systems. User-centered design is intended to transfer user needs into products specifications to ensure the satisfaction aspect [5]. Generally, the interaction design combines elements of HCI and user experience design to build overall essence and structure of interactive systems that support and facilitate user's goals for helpful and engaging product interfaces [1, 14]. In other words, interaction design concentrates on constructing the ways users interact with products and systems.

The design of digitally-enhanced packaging, as a digital interactive system, has to follow the principles of interaction design, if the functional and pleasing user experience is the main goal to accomplish [5]. There are four critical elements for enhanced packaging design that is based on principles of user-centered design, consumer experience, HCI, and usability theory presented by [15]: consumer, task, package and context.

Understanding the Consumer

Since consumer experience plays a central role in the interactive packaging design, the investigation of (i) the characteristics of the person including physical and cognitive capabilities, beliefs, habits and previous experience, as well as (ii) the way people respond to a stimulus is needed [5, 15]. Also, it is relevant to understand the user's needs and desires in a thorough manner to design interactive solutions that address these needs precisely [16]. Furthermore, the user's perception is built during the interaction with packaging [4]. Once an interactive system is able to find the best way to engage with its user, stronger emotional and memorable reactions are provoked that might result in higher efficiency and recurrent use of the interactive system [17].

The Task

Interactive packaging design has to consider the series of actions and goals to be performed and accomplished by the user that interacts with the package [15]. In regards to HCI, these tasks go further from conventional actions carried out with packaging as opening, handling, reading instructions, disposing [4], and involve a new set of interactive activities related to ICT systems, where users, for example, have to bring their mobile devices to scan the package, download an app, enabling specific communication settings to enable the consumer-packaging interaction [18].

The Package

Digitally enhanced packaging can be embodied with various digital communication electronics, thus the design and integration of these objects of interaction should also be taken into account. Reference [7] refers to such packaging as a hybrid digital physical object consisting of Cyber-Physical Systems, Cloud Computing and IoT. Cyber-Physical Systems, like microprocessors, sensors and actuators can be embedded into objects, like product's packaging, and the interaction will happen not directly with the digital device, but with ordinary everyday objects with concealed digital technology [7].

The Context

Another critical element of HPI is the identification of specific stages, context or touch-points, where users interact with packaging in order to support designers and manufacturers and help them understand the elements necessary at each stage of interaction to evaluate, modify or develop packages that would achieve targeted goals [4]. The first stage of the interaction occurs in the distribution system, including warehousing, transportation, and stacking. Due to ICT, packaging with integrated RFID tags can improve real-time location tracking and, in turn, ease logistics operations, whereas packaging with smart temperature, pressure, or shock sensors can register accidents during distribution and handling allowing users to re-evaluate the most efficient means of transportation and the best conditions for it [8]. The second stage takes place at the point of purchase, where packaging reaches the retailer and thereby it has to fulfill a set of new communication activities to draw attention, convince or persuade consumers to purchase the product [2]. At this stage, for instance, light emitting devices or capacitive touch sensors added to the package's exterior design provide distinctive characters as flashy and multisensory effects that may add value to the product and trigger momentary and instantaneous desire to purchase it due to peculiar visual appearance [17, 18]. Finally, once the packaging is bought, it lives at consumer's home and becomes a part of their life, therefore more tactile-based in-depth interaction happens during consumption and utilization of the packed product [3]. Contrary to visual awareness, usage after purchase might give an impulse to the emotional and physical connections to the product and the brand [17]. Sensory, emotional and social sensations induced by IoT-enhanced packaging providing insights of user consumption behavior to improve his/her health condition can be the building blocks for better engagement and entertainment. As a result, this research put emphasis on the last two stages of consumer-packaging interaction, in-store and at-home, due to their particular importance for user-centered design, user experience and interactive activities.

3   Cases of Smart Interactive Packaging

In this section three conceptual cases of digitally enhanced packaging will be described including emphasizing the perspective of user-centered design, instead of technological capabilities of the interactive system. The described cases will be used for more in-depth assessment in regards to the HCI and interaction design in the discussion. Furthermore, each case is summarized in Table 1 according to the four-elements-based framework of user-centered and HCI-supporting packaging design presented in the theory section.

3.1   Olive Oil Package with Attached NFC Tag

The credibility of the source the product was obtained from could have a higher impact on persuading the consumers to purchase a product [18]. Therefore the interactive visual demonstration of the origin of the food product, as olive oil, as well as the conditions and the environment of the plants and harvest might trigger instant decision to buy the product. Cyber-Physical Systems can bring the consumers during their grocery shopping closer to the olive tree plants in sunny southern Italy. The olive oil packaging with incorporated NFC tag can redirect the shopper to a website of the olive oil producer filled with photos and videos of the farming site by a single scan on the package with a mobile device.

3.2   Cereal Package with Integrated NFC Tag

Although marketing is considered as a secondary function of packaging, in the retail environment it plays a significant role in convincing shoppers to take the item out of the shelf and place it in their shopping bag [4]. One of the highly persuading marketing techniques is the coupon, voucher or discount system. A cereal package with an advert "tap me with your phone and get 10% to milk", for instance, in exchange of the email address, would give higher changes that the products will be bought since cereals and milk are usually consumed together. Likewise, by tapping on a NFC tag attached to cereal packaging, users can download a discount code or voucher valid for a particular period.

3.3   Mouthwash Bottle with Smart Sensors

As mentioned earlier, at the stage of product usage it is more likely to make strong emotional, sensory and social connections to the product and brand. However, more pretentious aims require higher consumer interaction resulting in continuous and long-lasting activities/tasks. Likewise, the more time the activities take, the more sophisticated ICT systems are enrolled in the overall interactive system design. In this case, Cyber-Physical Systems, as smart capacity sensors, Cloud Computing and IoT cooperate for better engagement [7]. A smart capacity sensor incorporated in the mouthwash lid can estimate how much of the product is left, then collect, transmit and analyze the data to build a personal profile for a user to track his/her usage history and dental hygiene habits. The interactive system can contribute to the user's well-being and encourage healthier behavior in a form of reminders.

Table 1. The summary of each packaging case

Package	Users	Tasks (few examples)	Context
Olive oil package with attached NFC tag	Grocery shoppers Olive oil users	Enable NFC settings Download the app (iOS) Find symbol and scan/tap	In-store
Cereal package with attached NFC tag	Grocery shoppers Cereals users		In-store
Mouthwash bottle with smart sensors in the lid	Dental hygiene supporters	Download the app Consume the product Track personal profile React to reminders	At-home

4   Discussion and Conclusion

The aim of this section is twofold. The first part will describe and illustrate how digitally enhanced packaging as a digital interactive system fits the overall HCI and interaction design theory. The second part will present the five steps approach that should be considered when designing a successful interaction packaging design.

4.1   The Design of Digitally Enhanced Packaging

In relation to the interaction design theory presented by [19], the design of smart interactive packaging usually encompasses (i) the human agent, i.e. the consumer of the product, (ii) the computational agent, i.e. the mobile device, and (iii) the cyber-physical agent consisting of a physical product packaging and digital communication devices (Fig. 1). In this model of interaction, the computational agent is an intermediate part between the human agent and cyber-physical agent. In other words, the interaction between the human agent and the cyber-physical agent can only be granted by the computational agent. For instance, in the presented case of olive oil packaging, the shopper first has to interact with the mobile device (to download the app, enable settings, unlock the screen, and other), and only then tap with the device of the package.

On the other hand, this sequence of interactions and the involvement of different agents highly depends on the ICT system incorporated into packaging design and could be done the other way around, i.e. human agent-package-mobile device. For example, packaging with printed capacitive touch buttons will induce direct human agent-packaging interaction, and a mobile device could be used to display the digital content aroused by this interaction.

Human Agent   Computational Agent   Cyber-Physical Agent

Fig. 1. The interacting agents in the interaction design of digitally-enhanced packaging

4.2 The Five Step Approach for Interactive Packaging Design

There are five critical concerns that should be addressed when designing a successful interaction packaging design:

1. *Why the user should take action or perform a task?*

First designers should think carefully how to encourage consumers to use technologies [18]. Because it is a consumer that chooses to download or open a mobile application or not in order to obtain digital packaging experience [18]. In this stage, according to [18]: "marketers must first convince the consumer to use their application before convincing them to buy their product". Therefore, in order to take action, consumers should get a stimulus from the environment [1], an implied benefit upon completion [19] in the form of a particular reward. Consequently, if the user is satisfied with the reward, it can contribute to continued and enhanced usage of the interactive system [9].

2. *Is the overall design intuitive and simple to use?*

For successful implementation and acceptance of a system, users have to be consciously aware what actions to take [19, 20]. For instance, the graphic design of the interactive system must clearly state where to scan or tap with the phone, which mobile application to download and etc. Also, actions have to be simple and intuitive, because the design of any interaction has to consider the human agent's inherent capacity to accomplish this task [19]. As a result, the designers have to build simple, fast and intuitive actions that could be carried out without mastering any extra skills [20].

3. *What other interaction might appear in the process of accomplishing the main interaction?*

The modelling of the interaction space that surrounds the new interaction designers wish to create is significant and consists of the two main steps [19]. First, other agents that will be local to the new interaction have to be indicated, and then their likely effects on the new interaction have to be examined [19]. The comprehensive analysis of other mediated interactions enhances the chance for the main interaction to succeed [19]. In the context of the interactive packaging system, the main interaction is between the consumer and product packaging. However, other forms of mediate interactions, such as user-phone or phone-packaging, have to be taken into account in order not to subvert the main interaction. As a result, it is crucial to keep the user motivated during all steps of interaction to reach the final aim [19].

4. *What other internal and external resources are needed for accomplishing the interaction?*

Designers have to take into account and build all internal and external ICT systems that support and are directly related to the core interaction. In terms of smart interactive packaging, the internal resource could be a mobile phone that enables the user to perform a task, i.e. tap on the package and read the NFC tag. Whereas, the external resource could be a QR code printed on the package to download the app for NFC tag reading. Also, one should consider that such internal or external agents have their own tasks, cost, benefit, and limitations [19]. Therefore, the implied benefit upon the completion has to be greater than the cost of resources in order to induce the human agent that all actions are worth doing [19].

5. *What other attitudes, intentions and motivations of user have to be incorporated into overall design?*

The design of information and communication system has to consider the people who will use them [19]. User-centered design demonstrates a great importance in the design process, thus designers have to investigate their potential users attitudes, intentions, motivations, and inspirations [19]. According to the author, the user research with the aim to ascertain their goals has to be carried out before creating interactions.

Based on the findings, it is apparent that for the interactive systems to be effective and used, designers have to build not only a reward-based, intuitive and simple interaction design that would persuade users to take actions, but also they have to think of other mediate interactions, internal and external resources that are significant to reach the final aim. New insights of consumer packaging as a digital interactive system are expected to have significant practical implications for brand owners and retailers that aim to improve their consumer engagement and make memorable, long-lasting connections. Especially, in these days, when people are always connected to the Internet, new forms of interaction with purchased goods via ICT technologies might turn into unique business models to improve consumer satisfaction, perception, and loyalty.

References

1. Bezerra, P.F., Arruda, A., Araujo, K.: Experience design as a tool to promote interaction among users in the beverage market: proposal for a new emotional approach in usability. Procedia Manufact. **3**, 6028–6035 (2015)
2. Wever, R.: Touching tubs and grabbing gable-tops: an editorial to the special issue on human-packaging interaction. Packag. Technol. Sci. **29**(12), 603–606 (2016)
3. Ryynänen, T., Rusko, E.: Professionals' view of consumers' packaging interactions–a narrative analysis. Packag. Technol. Sci. **28**(4), 341–355 (2015)

4. Mumani, A., Stone, R.: State of the art of user packaging interaction (UPI). Packag. Technol. Sci. **31**(6), 401–419 (2018)
5. Carli Lorenzini, G., Olsson, A.: Towards patient-centered packaging design: an industry perspective on processes, functions, and constraints. Packag. Technol. Sci. **32**(2), 59–73 (2019)
6. Joutsela, M., Latvala, T., Roto, V.: Influence of packaging interaction experience on willingness to pay. Packag. Technol. Sci. **30**(8), 505–523 (2017)
7. Petrelli, D.: Industry 4.0: Is it time for interaction design craftsmanship? Des. J. **20**(sup1), S2735–S2745 (2017)
8. Nilsson, H.E., et al.: System integration of electronic functions in smart packaging applications. IEEE Trans. Compon. Packag. Manuf. Technol. **2**(10), 1723–1734 (2012)
9. Candy, L., Costello, B.: Interaction design and creative practice. Des. Stud. **6**(29), 521–524 (2008)
10. Schaefer, D., Cheung, W.M.: Smart packaging: opportunities and challenges. Procedia CIRP **72**, 1022–1027 (2018)
11. Azzi, A., Battini, D., Persona, A., Sgarbossa, F.: Packaging design: general framework and research agenda. Packag. Technol. Sci. **25**(8), 435–456 (2012)
12. Tudor Gethin, D., Huw Jewell, E., Charles Claypole, T.: Printed silver circuits for FMCG packaging. Circuit World **39**(4), 188–194 (2013)
13. Lowgren, J.: The Encyclopedia of Human-Computer Interaction. https://www.interaction-design.org/literature/book/the-encyclopedia-of-human-computer-interaction-2nd-ed/interaction-design-brief-intro. Accessed 27 May 2019
14. Wray, T.B., Kahler, C.W., Simpanen, E.M., Operario, D.: User-centered, interaction design research approaches to inform the development of health risk behavior intervention technologies. Internet interv. **15**, 1–9 (2018)
15. de la Fuente, J., Bix, L.: A tool for designing and evaluating packaging for healthcare products. Patient Compliance **1**, 48–52 (2011)
16. Stolterman, E., Wiberg, M.: Concept-driven interaction design research. Hum.-Comput. Interact. **25**(2), 95–118 (2010)
17. Tafesse, W.: An experiential model of consumer engagement in social media. J. Product Brand Manag **25**(5), 424–434 (2016)
18. Petit, O., Velasco, C., Spence, C.: Multisensory consumer-packaging interaction (CPI): the role of new technologies. In: Velasco, C., Spence, C. (eds.) Multisensory Packaging, pp. 349–374. Palgrave Macmillan, Cham (2019)
19. Coiera, E.: Interaction design theory. Int. J. Med. Inform. **69**(2–3), 205–222 (2003)
20. Maguire, M.: Socio-technical systems and interaction design–21st century relevance. Appl. Ergon. **45**(2), 162–170 (2014)

Design Principles for Safety/Critical Systems

Deep System Knowledge Required: Revisiting UCD Contribution in the Design of Complex Command and Control Systems

Elodie Bouzekri[1], Alexandre Canny[1], Célia Martinie[1(✉)],
Philippe Palanque[1,2], and Christine Gris[3]

[1] ICS-IRIT, University of Toulouse 3, Toulouse, France
{martinie,palanque}@irit.fr
[2] Department of Industrial Design, Technical University Eindhoven,
Eindhoven, The Netherlands
[3] Airbus Operations SAS, Blagnac, France

Abstract. Command and control systems centralize information from multiple underlying systems to support operators in the performance of their mission. Beyond the mission itself (that may be complex), operators must also ensure the correct functioning of these systems (often called platform). Platform systems (e.g. engines or electric system) may be very different from each other and exhibit a large number of functional states. When applied to the design of command control systems, User Centered Design methods support understanding and capturing operators' needs to perform the mission, as well as to propose solutions to design usable mission-related user interfaces. However, user interfaces for platform management need to present and organize information about the underlying complex systems. Understanding those systems and abstracting away information about their behavior (so that operators can manage them) requires deep knowledge beyond UI/UX designers and UCD methods experts. In this paper, we propose a system-centered process that would complement UCD approaches for the design of command and control systems. That process takes as input the detailed functioning of underlying systems and provides abstract and structured information to inform UCD methods. Beyond supporting usability property, the integrated process supports reliability and safety properties that UCD approaches usually overlook. We present how the proposed process has been applied for the design of a large civil commercial aircraft warning system and show generalizability to other domains.

Keywords: Command and control systems · Development process · UCD · Models · Architectures

1 Introduction

User Centered Design processes [26] target the design of usable interactive systems and promote the inclusion of real users in various development phases from early needs identification and design until evaluation and deployment. Recent contributions have tried to classify and structure the various concepts underlying UCD and interaction design [28] as well as associating success criteria. For instance, *interaction as transmission* focusses on the information passing between the user and the system and a success criterion is the maximum efficiency for reaching a goal. Another example is *interaction as experience* which focusses on the user feelings and on subjective qualities perceived while interacting with the systems. While *interaction as transmission* could be associated to early work in Human Factors [49] (and is referred to as *classical approach* [42]), *interaction as experience* has received a lot of focus in recent HCI research building on the seminal work from Hassenzahl [25] (and is referred to as *contemporary approach*). While the classical approach was focusing on supporting users' work and avoiding the negative (such as user errors), the contemporary one mainly targets at entertainment and leisure and focusses on the positive (such as enjoyment and fun [7]). However, usability is still not trivial to reach for complex command and control systems.

This evolution might be seen as migrating from a solved problem to a new difficult problem missing clear understanding and solutions. UCD approaches are flexible but are still far from being adequate for the design and evaluation of command and control systems in general, and critical ones in particular. For instance, cockpit design by aircraft manufacturers and suppliers is performed jointly with Human Factors experts (with a deep knowledge about operators' tasks and environmental conditions) and test pilots (with a deep knowledge about missions and platform systems) [45]. This is required as command and control systems centralize information from multiple underlying systems to support operators in the performance of their mission. Beyond the mission itself (that may be complex), operators must also ensure the correct functioning of these systems (often called platform). This does not mean engaging repair activities but shutting down a faulty system or starting a redundant one [46]. The systems gathered in the platform such as a cooling system, solar panels or engines might be very different from each other an exhibit a large number of functional states very specific to each system. When applied to the design of command and control systems, User Centered Design methods support understanding and capturing operators' needs, their goals and tasks [18] in order to perform their mission. In addition, UCD approaches propose solutions to design usable user interfaces. However, when dealing with command and control that supports activities dedicated to the management of the platform, those user interfaces need to present and organize information from the underlying complex systems. Understanding those systems and abstracting away information about their behavior in order to allow operators to manage them, requires deep system knowledge beyond UI/UX designers and UCD methods experts' knowledge. Beyond, the complexity of those systems require knowledge that cannot be acquired by those UCD experts within the lifespan of the project.

As UCD approaches do not provide explicit support for building an abstract view on the system and its services, we propose a system-centered process (that would complement UCD approaches) dedicated to the design of command and control systems. That process takes as input the detailed functioning of underlying systems and provides abstract and structured information to inform the UCD of command and control systems. As UCD approaches target at improved usability, our integrated process targets at feasibility as relevant additional and required property. That process is also positioned with respect to regulations in command and control systems that target at dependability and safety. Regulatory authorities build their certification processes on top of standards that vary significantly from one domain to another. For instance, ECSS target at space systems [15], ESARR at Air Traffic Control [19] and DO-178-C at Aeronautical systems [12]. Their integration within the design processes is mandatory for critical systems and their explicit connection with UCD is thus required when building dependable, safe and usable systems [29].

The paper is organized as follows. Section 2 details the limitations of UCD approaches for command and control systems and motivations for extending UCD them with deep knowledge about underlying systems. Section 3 presents a high-level view of the proposed approach while Sect. 4 presents the foundations of the proposed process. The main steps of the System Centered Design process are presented in Sect. 5. Section 6 presents how the process has been applied for the design of a commercial aircraft warning system and Sect. 7 concludes the paper.

2 Motivations: Why UCD Is Not Enough to Design C&C Systems

The design of command and control systems requires information that is not provided by UCD (e.g. all the possible states for each device). This section highlights the actual conflicts between several principles of the UCD and the specificities of C&C systems.

2.1 Specificities of C&C Systems

The users who interact with C&C systems, named operators, interact according to predetermined procedures, predetermined tasks and predetermined behaviors [47]. Their abstract workflow [47] is to understand the system state, to compare it with the desired system state and to apply the relevant procedure and tasks to achieve the target system state. The number of possible states for devices and of information presented to the user depend on the system and devices that compose the whole system. C&C systems aim at managing large amount of system and devices, which leads to a huge number of possible operational states to deal with. It is not possible for the users know all of these possible states. In addition, the user will not be able to interact with all of the possible systems' behaviors during the whole time s/he operates the system. For example, in the case of a commercial aircraft, a fire engine may happen one time out of one billion flight hours. Most of the commercial airlines pilots' will (fortunately) never have to interact with the cockpit C&C interface to recover from an engine fire. The design and development of C&C systems are thus driven by safety and dependability objectives:

- Manufacturers of C&C systems have to set safety and dependability objectives for their systems and have to demonstrate that the delivered systems match these objectives [14]. Depending on the application domain and on the level of assurance required for a function, regulation specifications let the manufacturer proves that the targeted objective is reached using methods and techniques of its choice or indicates prescriptive means of compliance to the requirements [14]. For high assurance levels, structured development processes and model-based approaches are means of compliance to the requirements.

- Manufacturers of C&C systems have to ensure that the C&C functions and interfaces match the users' tasks [17]. For these purposes, Human factors experts identify, gather and record exhaustively and precisely the users' tasks [16, 47].
- The design of functions and presentations for C&C tasks is performed jointly with Human Factors experts (with a deep knowledge about operators' tasks and environmental conditions) and test pilots (with a deep knowledge about missions and extant systems) [45]. The produced design documents are shared amongst the different stakeholders.

2.2   Main Principles of UCD and Their Limitations

User Centered Design is "a general term for a philosophy and methods which focus on designing for and involving users in the design of computerized systems" [1] and has the following main principles:

- Focus (early) on the user [22, 23], involve actively the user [11, 23, 31]: the user and associated characteristics, tasks and context drive the design.
  The operators have cumulative experience about the C&C systems they have been operating, and about the systems' behavior they have been interacting with. As far as they know neither all the possible system's states and all the systems' characteristics nor this information for the future systems, they do not have enough knowledge to propose design solutions that contain relevant abstraction level and relevant information. As UCD methods and techniques have historically been proposed to deal with simple in home entertainment computers [5], it may be a reason why this aspect is missing in UCD.
  Moreover, focus (early) on the systems is required too. Exhaustive and detailed information about each system is required before the design of the C&C interface. For example, in the commercial aircrafts application domain, engines are specified before the start of the cockpit design.
- Apply an iterative design process [11, 22, 31], apply an iterative and incremental system development process [23]: the design process alternates the production of multiple design solutions (evolvable prototypes) and their evaluation with users in order to accommodate requirements changes and integrate new parts of the system. An iterative and incremental process does not provide support to have a generic architectural view on the system and of its various components [48]. Consequently, it also makes very difficult to demonstrate that the system reach objectives in terms of levels of safety and dependability [48].
- Produce simple design representations [23]: The design solutions are represented in a way that can be easily understood by all stakeholders.
  The representations that provide support to C&C tasks have to contain the relevant information concerning the systems' characteristics and states. According to the complexity of C&C systems as well as the amount of information dealt with [47], the design representations cannot be as simple as mass-market systems design representations.

- Perform empirical measurement [22], evaluate use in context [23]: User evaluations are conducted throughout the iterative design process.
  The recruitment of operators for user evaluation as well as the preparation and implementation of the test sessions is constrained [41]. It is not possible to cover all the operators' tasks and procedures and several types of users must be involved at the same time during the test sessions.
- Multi-disciplinary design teams [23, 31].
  Several types of expertise are required (engineering, physics, human factors, software, hardware...). Stakeholders bring their expertise. The produced design and development artefacts are shared amongst the stakeholders.

2.3 Existing Approaches for Integrating UCD in System Development Processes

The fact that UCD do not explicitly address the whole development process for an interactive system has been acknowledged since decades [23, 33, 35]. From a system and software engineering perspective, development processes such as the waterfall process [43] and the V cycle process [36] have proven useful to reach safety and dependability objectives (i.e. "to build the system right") [8] but they fail in taking into account the usability property (i.e. "to build the right system") [8]. The Spiral [8] and Agile processes [44], even if they are iterative, do not explicitly take into account user needs and tasks [30]. To overcome these issues, Goränsson et al. [23] proposed a design process centered on usability. Larusdottir et al. [30] proposed an approach to integrate UX design activities in Agile development processes. Gross [24] proposes a generic process based on the high level UCD phases and complemented with system development phases in order to encourage system designers and developers with no HCI background to apply UCD techniques. Martinie et al. [33] proposed a development process for safety-critical interactive systems, taking into account the development of the training program.

These existing approaches do not provide explicit guidance and support on how to use systems design artefacts within UCD phases, although system design artefacts provide the information required to identify what should be presented to the users and to take into account the feasibility of the interface and interactions design solutions. The existing approaches fail in taking into account the properties required for C&C systems: feasibility, usability, dependability and safety.

3 Holistic View on Command and Control System Development

Figure 1 presents a generic approach for taking into account the properties required for C&C systems: feasibility, usability, dependability and safety. This generic approach was designed and developed in collaboration with cockpit experts and engineers in the aeronautics domain during a four-year project on aircraft operational systems' states. This approach, named the clover process covers these properties thanks to three different sub-processes: The System Centered Design (SCD) process, the User Centered Design (UCD) process and the Regulator Centered Design (RCD) process.

The SCD process identifies all the feasible command and control system functions. Experts for each type of system should participate in this process. The aim of this process is to provide information about the available command and control devices, services and associated states by the mean of structuration and abstraction. This information is composed of data, architecture, behavioral models and sample presentation layout for the command and control system. This information thus feeds the design and the evaluation phases in the UCD process. The foundations for the information produced by the SCD process as well as the detailed phase by phase view on the process (with the documents and information that flow between the phases) is described in the next two sections of this paper.

The UCD process aims to ensure the usability property of the command and control system and should then be conducted by usability experts. HCI main principles and techniques can be applied but, as these activities require deep knowledge about the command and control system, the UCD process has to take as an input the output of the SCD process (data, models and sample presentation layouts of the systems, services and associated states). For example, the task modeling activity requires the exhaustive list of system functions, services and presentation information. If an important usability issue that is due to the C&C system is identified, the design of the C&C system must be amended (red dotted arrow from UCD to SCD in Fig. 1). In the same way, the outputs of the UCD process can be regulated during the RCD process that may output proposals for modifications (red dotted arrow from RCD to UCD in Fig. 1). System devices or services can also be adapted by SCD (green arrows propagating modifications from one process to another.

The RCD process aims to set dependability and safety properties and to verify them. It should thus be conducted by safety experts. In the aircraft domain, the DO-178C [12] standard defines development assurance level for systems of aircraft systems and associated recommendations. In addition, the CS-25 [17] defines certifications specifications and associated means of compliances for aircraft systems. Following these means of compliances, manufacturers show to the certification authorities that they developed and deployed systems that conform to these specifications and standard. A non-compliance leads to a new iteration of the UCD process or of the SCD process, and then to a new iteration of the RCD process in order to verify that the compliance issue is solved. For example, the CS-25 specifies that aircraft systems have "to be designed so that qualified flight-crew members trained in its use can safely perform their tasks associated with its intended function" [17]. Then, in order to be accepted during the RCD process, each identified user tasks (identified during the UCD process) must match a system function (defined during the SCD process with architecture and data models) for the command and control system design. This highlights the impact of dependability on usability [20].

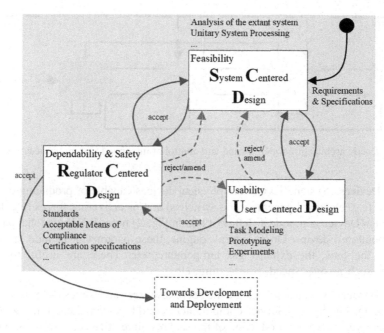

Fig. 1. The clover process for the design and development of command and control systems (Color figure online)

4   Foundations for "Systems Centered Design" for Command and Control Systems

The SCD outputs data about systems devices, services and their associated states. For example, in a commercial aircraft, the "FUEL" service is associated to the aircraft fuel systems (fuel tank, pump, cross-feed valves, etc.). In order to provide support for covering all the possible devices, services and their associated states in the design solutions for the C&C interfaces and interactions, we present: (1) an architecture built upon the concept of abstraction hierarchy framework [6], and (2) a generic and abstract state description applicable to the all of the architecture components (devices, services).

4.1   Handling Complexity with a Generic Architecture for the Command and Control of Integrated System Services and Devices

DSCU (Device, System service, Compound service and User Service) is a generic architecture designed around four types of components, each representing different level of system abstraction for command and control. Figure 2 introduces the architecture. From left to right, it goes from physical implementation of the system (devices) to services that are of interest for the end-user, named "User Service". This decomposition is close to the one proposed in the abstraction hierarchy framework [6] and thus allow to reason on the entire system.

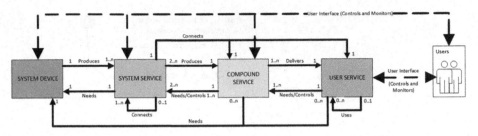

Fig. 2. Generic architecture for command and control of integrated system services and devices.

System Devices. System devices are physical devices capable of producing or routing resources (e.g. electrical generator and switches) and/or delivering forces (e.g. torque). The System Device component (leftmost box in Fig. 2) holds the operational parameter of the monitored device. On an aircraft engine, these parameters include the rotation speed of the fans, the exhaust gas temperature, etc. These are useful to identify problems such as over speed, overheating, etc.

System Service. System services are the set of resources and forces a device is capable of producing. The System Service component (second box from the left in Fig. 2) holds information regarding the production of the said resource or force, named "Service" for generalization purpose. The System Services produced by an aircraft engine are, for example, "Thrust" or "AC Electricity". The System Service "Engine 1 AC Electricity" holds information related to the monitoring of the Engine 1 generator such as output Voltage or Current.

Devices dedicated to routing (e.g. electrical switches, fuel valves) enable system services such as "Electricity routing" or "Fuel routing".

Compound Service. A Compound Service is a system-wide resource made available to devices and other services after aggregation from multiple producers. For example, on a twin-engine aircraft, the "AC Electricity" compound service is the result of the compounding of "Engine 1 AC Electricity", "Engine 2 AC Electricity", "Auxiliary Power Unit AC Electricity" and "AC Electricity Routing". "Compound Service" (third box for the left in Fig. 2) are particular as their operational parameters may be nominal even though some system services used to produce it are faulty. Indeed, in complex systems, redundancy is an example of safety mechanism designed to prevent complete loss of compound services. This means that even though a system service is not working anymore (e.g. "Engine 1 AC Electricity"), the compound service to which it participates (i.e. "AC Electricity") may still be properly made available. The role of the "Compound Service" is to allow for the identification of such combination and their proper monitoring.

User Service. A User Service (fourth box from the left in Fig. 2) is a service that is of interest for the user, or in other word directly associated to his/her goal. It needs and controls one or multiple "Compound Services" in order to be delivered. For example, on an aircraft preparing for takeoff at night, the flight crew needs to dim the cabin light in order to comply with safety procedure. In this case, "Cabin Light" is a user service that principally relies on the "AC Electricity" compound service in order to be delivered.

4.2 Handling State Explosion with a Generic and Abstract Systems and Services States Description

OQCR is a generic state based framework designed to allow the description of the status of devices and systems according to 4 variables. These variables were identified by analyzing the existing synoptic pages and alerts on command and control systems. The variables used in OQCR are:

- **Operational State**: Is the device/service on, off, powering on, etc.?
- **Qualitative State**: Is the device/service working properly? (e.g. is a battery delivering sufficient or insufficient voltage? Is it dead?)
- **Contextual Attribute**: Is the device/service in a suitable environment for operating properly? (e.g. is it within operating temperature range? Is it plugged to a suitable electrical network (voltage, frequency)?
- **Restrictive Attribute**: Is it allowed to use the device/service?

The values these variables may receive are either boolean (for the attributes) or extracted from a set of component-dependent values (for the states). The second line of Table 1 details the size of each set of values the OQCR variables (first line in Table 1) may receive. This section presents (i) the sets of OQCR states and (ii) the sets of OQCR attributes.

Table 1. Structure of an OQCR state/attributes description.

Operational state	Qualitative state	Contextual attribute	Restrictive attribute
1 value out of 4	1 value out 3	1 out of 2	1 out of 2

Operational and Qualitative States. In OQCR, the Operational and Qualitative states are meant to provide real-time and predictive information regarding the behavior of the devices and services. To do so, they indicate whether the device/service is in operation (Operational state) and to which extant it is operating/it can operate properly (Qualitative State). Since DSCU covers a variety of components, slight variations in the wording of the state values help to reflect the role of each component. Table 2 presents the Operational states of OQCR.

Table 2. OQCR Operational states for components of the DSCU architecture

Device	System service	Compound service	User service
NOT RUNNING	NOT PRODUCING	NOT DELIVERING	
STARTING	RAMPING UP		
RUNNING	PRODUCING	DELIVERING	
SHUTING DOWN	RAMPING DOWN		

The values for the qualitative attributes are presented in Table 3. While the Operational state is a real-time value only, we observe that the Qualitative state owns a predictive value when a device/service is not running/producing/delivering. Indeed, it may indicates that attempting the use the device/service will lead to either (1) the expected behavior, (2) an unexpected behavior or (3) a failure to start due to a previously identified loss of the device/service.

Table 3. OQCR Qualitative states for components of the DSCU architecture

Device	Services	Definition
FUNCTIONAL		The device can run or run properly. The service is (or can be) produced/delivered as required
DEGRADED		The device is not capable of running properly and suffers performance penalty. The service cannot be produced or delivered as required
OUT OF ORDER	OUT OF SERVICE	The device is not capable to run. The service cannot be produced or delivered

Contextual and Restrictive Attributes. The OQCR Contextual and Restrictive attributes are meant to provide information regarding the environment the device/service evolves in (Contextual attribute) and how safe it is to use it (Restrictive attribute). Table 4 presents and define the Contextual and the Restrictive attributes for DSCU components. It is important to note that multiple factors such as resource availability (e.g. low fuel pressure for an engine) or environment-related ranges (e.g. temperature range, altitude range) impact the contextual attribute. The restrictive attribute is the result of the computation of other system state that may forbid the usage of a given device/service under some circumstances. (e.g. if a ventilation system is **out of service**, it is **not allowed** to use the device it is meant to cool).

Table 4. OQCR attributes for components of the DSCU architecture.

Attribute	Value	Definition
Contextual	WITHIN CONTEXT	The device/service is in its nominal context of use
	OUT OF CONTEXT	The device/service is not in its nominal context of use
Restrictive	ALLOWED	The device/service can be use
	NOT ALLOWED	The device or service must not be in use

5 A Detailed Process for "System Centered Design" of Command and Control Systems

The SCD process aims at structuring and abstracting the C&C systems' descriptions and states. This process uses the DSCU architecture to describe each system in a structured way and the OQCR states abstraction for each component of the systems described with the DSCU architecture. The outputs of this process are an integrated architecture of the systems, the behavioral models of the C&C system and sample presentation layouts of devices and services states. HCI designers can use these artefacts during the UCD process to propose design solutions for the C&C user interface. Figure 3 presents the System Centered Design process of C&C systems. The process takes as input all the systems being under supervision of the extant command and control system. The process steps are applied for each system one by one and the last step consists in integrating the information produced for each system.

5.1 Data Collection

This step consists in collecting the extant information concerning the selected system. Each system must have a well-specified documentation including specification of alarms, services, and operation and training manuals.

5.2 DSCU Generic Architecture and OCQR States Instantiation

During the second step, system designers analyze the selected system according to the DSCU architecture. The designers have to identify the devices, the routing devices, the system services, the compound services and the user services composing the selected system. The specification documentation on the services of the system and the operation and training manuals are used during this step.

This steps aims at identifying if a service is useful to enable another service or system, and if a service is directly useful to reach a user goal. For example, in the case of a commercial aircraft cockpit, if the pilot needs to perform a "climb" at the beginning of the flight, then the service "climb" is a User Service. The operation and training manual are helpful to understand the services utility for users' tasks. The result of this analysis is an instantiated DSCU architecture. The OQCR states provide an abstraction of all the possible values of devices or services parameters (e.g. value of speed or quantity) for this architecture. However, in some particular domain, specific parameters may be important to abstract the device or service state. During this step, the OQCR states (presented from Sect. 4.2) can thus be customized for a particular device or service if needed for the application domain (an example of such customization is presented in Sect. 6.1).

5.3 Unitary System Processing

The aim of this step is to detail the behaviour of each component of the instantiated DSCU architecture. The description of the devices and services behaviour will be useful during the UCD process to understand which events trigger a state change. In order to achieve this, the designer must follow three sub steps described hereinafter.

Unitary Alarms Identification. This sub step aims to assign each alarms of the system to the DSCU components.

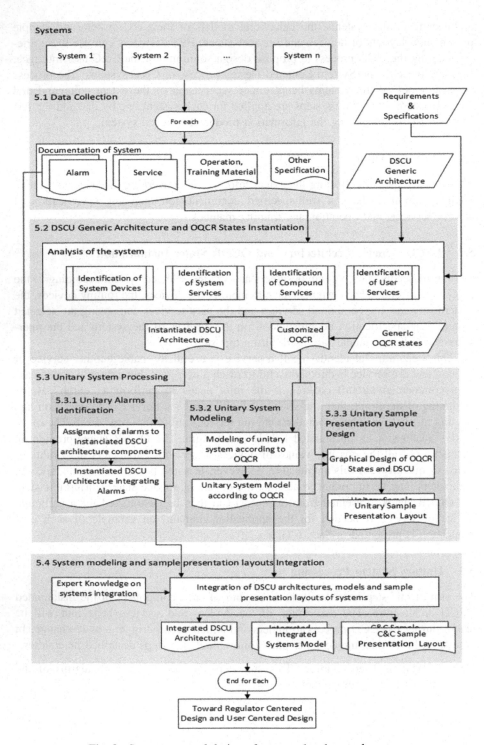

Fig. 3. System centered design of command and control systems

This assignment is the answer to the question "is the alarm affecting the system device, routing device (or service), system service, compound service or user service?" This step of alarm assignation is useful to determine in which conditions the device or service under consideration is "DEGRADED", "OUT OF ORDER/SERVICE", "OUT OF CONTEXT" or "NOT ALLOWED".

Unitary System Modeling. This step consists in producing a description of the behavior of the system following the DSCU instantiated architecture with alarms and OQCR states in this sub step. The behavior of the device or service can be described thank to various languages and notations like automata, Petri nets, or flow-based notation. This model describes in which conditions and after which events the device or service under consideration changes state.

Unitary Sample Presentation Layout Design. This step consists in producing sample presentation layouts to help to understand the available services of the system and the behavior of the system according to the alarms and user tasks. The sample layouts must make visible all that is feasible with the system under consideration, as well as all the possible states for the presented system components. Several different sample presentation layouts of the C&C interface for the system are produced in accordance with operational scenarios. These different sample presentations will then be easier to use during the UCD process as they are explicitly bound to scenarios. The operations and training manuals contain procedures for nominal and abnormal situations taking into account the system context. This is why they are useful resources for this sub step.

5.4 System Modeling and Sample Presentation Layouts Integration

The C&C interface must provide an integrated vision of the systems' characteristics and states. The last step of the SCD process is thus to integrate the outcome of the previous steps for each processed system. The integration of the information about the different systems can reveal new services or some introduced errors during the structuration and abstraction process. Then, the expertise of the C&C systems' experts is needed to correctly identify the final services of the integrated systems. This integration step produces the final integrated DSCU architecture, the final integrated systems models and the finals systems sample presentation layouts when every system of the whole command and control system were processed.

6 Application of the System Centered Design Process to an Interactive Cockpit Application

In this section, we present a summary of the result we obtained applying the SCD process to the design of a future crew alerting system for large civil aircrafts. This work was performed in collaboration with Airbus Operation SAS in a project called "Integration of the Cockpit and its Systems". This project involved, at various level, additional stakeholders such as Airbus Helicopters, Dassault Aviation and Thales Avionics.

The commercial aircraft Airbus A350-900 is the system selected for the case study. The following set of materials and documentation were used for the application of the process:

- **User-related materials** such as the aircraft Flight Deck Briefing for Pilots and its Flight Crew Operation Manual (FCOM);
- **Training materials** such as the Flight Crew Training Manual (FCTM);
- **Specifications of aircrafts systems** such as logical datasheets for the Warning System, system specifications, system requirements, etc.;
- **Regulatory documentation** including standard for software development in aeronautics [12], design assurance guidance for airborne systems [13] and Certification Specification and Acceptable Means of Compliance for large aeroplanes [10].

During the first quarter of the project, weekly meetings with a Cockpit Display expert, and a Flight Warning Engineer were dedicated to the analysis of the input materials and documentations. The Flight Warning System (FWS) aggregates data from most aircraft systems, hence its development in close cooperation with experts of aircraft systems providing input to the FWS. The next two months focused on a subset of the aircraft systems: Auxiliary Power Unit (APU), Bleed, Electricity, Fire Protection System (FPS) and Fuel. For each of these systems, we collected data from the documentation (5.1) and used this data to derive an architecture from DSCU (5.2). At this point, we realized that the wording of OQCR states and attributes could be refined for each components of the architecture (5.2). A Flight Warning System expert then joined the project to help us with step 5.3. The Flight Warning System expert contributed largely to the integration step (5.4). We had several meetings with various stakeholders to validate the outcome of each step. After each review, we recorded a list of modifications and amendments of the architectures, models and presentation layouts. We then validated the new versions of the architectures, the models and the presentation layouts with engineers and experts before pursuing the project at a larger scale. This section presents an extract of the application of the SCD process to the aircraft system: Engines.

6.1   Example of the Application of the SCD Process to the Aircraft Engines

Data Collection (step 5.1 in the Fig. 3). The documents gathered to understand the functioning and the use of aircraft engines are:

- the specification of the engines (sections concerning the behaviour, envelope, services and needed resources) in the FCOM (Flight Crew Operation Manual) [2],
- the list of possible alarms for the engines and their associated recovery procedures (FCOM too),
- the usage instructions with associated C&C interfaces screenshots in the FCOM and the FCTM (Flight Crew Training Manual).

A screenshot of a possible state of the extant Command and Control (C&C) interface for engines in an A350-900 cockpit is presented in Fig. 4. The information presented is related to "ALL ENG FLAME OUT" (both engines stopped running) alarm. This status of the engines can be derived from the display as:

1. the engines are indicated as failed (represented with the amber attention getting boxes in left-hand side of Fig. 4) and
2. the vibrations of rotors are not updated anymore (represented with the "XX" amber indications for the vibrations of rotors).

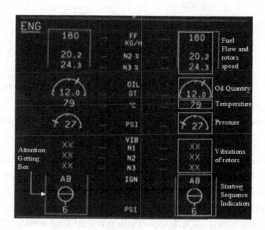

Fig. 4. Current ENGines System Display page after "ALL ENG FLAME OUT" alarm triggered

DSCU Generic Architecture and OQCR States Instantiation. (step 5.2 in Fig. 3)

DSCU Instantiated Architecture for Engines. Figure 5 presents the DSCU architecture instantiated for the two engines of the Airbus A350-900. It includes two ENGines System Devices (blue components of Fig. 5 labelled "ENG 1" and "ENG 2"). From the specification of the engines, we know that both engines produce HYDRaulic, BLEED, ELECtricity and THRUST (i.e. force pushing forward) services. Then, both ENGines produce a System Service for each of these services (green components connected to ENG 1 and ENG 2 in Fig. 5 labelled "ENG 1 HYDR", "ENG 1 BLEED"...). Combined, ENG 1 and ENG 2 produce services corresponding to the merging of the services of each Engine. These Compound Services (yellow components connected to engines System Services in Fig. 5) include "THRUST" from "ENG 1 THRUST" and "ENG 2 THRUST", BLEED ... Each service requires a routing device and a routing service to be transported. In consequence, the DSCU architecture of the engines includes a routing System Service for each Compound Services (components labelled routing and network System Service components of Fig. 5: "ELEC NETWORK", "BLEED ROUTING"...).

In addition, the engines need a FUEL service for their operation. Then, the DSCU architecture of engines includes a FUEL Compound Service as a resource for ENG to function (FUEL Compound Service yellow component on the left-hand side of Fig. 5).

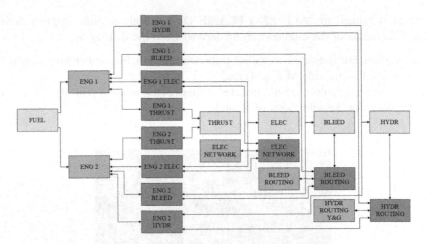

Fig. 5. Instantiated DSCU architecture for engines (Color figure online)

OQCR States Customization. During the analysis process, we found that the engines may be in an unknown state when they have not been turned on yet. Indeed, we cannot know its quality of operation state. In the same way, in case of a data update failure from the systems to the C&C interface, the whole state of the system is unknown. In consequence, we customized OQCR description by adding a value "UNKNOWN" that applies to each OQCR state descriptor (O and Q) and each attribute (C and R).

Unitary System Processing. (step 5.3 in Fig. 3)

Unitary Alarms Identification. The ENGines documentation contains all the alarms that may occur with this system. The FCOM indicates 60 possible alarms for the engines [2]. We present here two examples assignment of alarms to the components of the DSCU architecture: the caution alarm "THRUST LOCKED" and the warning alarm "ALL ENG FLAME OUT". The "THRUST LOCKED" alarm indicates that the THRUST is frozen for one or both ENGines. The concerned components in DSCU are ENGines THRUSTs (green ENG 1 TRHUST and ENG 2 THRUST System Services components in Fig. 5). The "ALL ENG FLAME OUT" alarm indicates that both engines are shutdown during the flight, represented in DSCU by ENGines devices (blue ENG 1 and ENG 2 System Devices components in Fig. 5).

Unitary System Modeling. We used ICO Petri nets [39] to describe the behaviour of the engines. One of the reasons we choose ICO notation is its ability to scale that is needed for the integration step. Beyond, this notation has been widely used in multiple domain for describing interactive systems behaviours for cockpits [9] or Air Traffic Control Workstations [40]. As it is grounded on Petri nets theory, this notation is also able to deal with concurrency and large number of states, beyond what State machines can represent.

Unitary Sample Presentation Layout Design. To produce sample presentation layout of engines states, we used the recommended recovery actions (for abnormal situations) and normal checklists (for nominal situation) described in the FCOM [2].

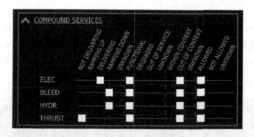

Fig. 6. A sample presentation layout of DSCU structuration and the OQCR states of the engines Compound Services in case of ALL ENG FLAME OUT.

Figure 6 presents one mockup of a presentation layout. It depicts the states of every Compound Services of the engines when a "ALL ENG FLAME OUT" warning alarm occurs. The mockup shows that, after the occurrence of that alarm, the ENGines System Devices are in the operational state "NOT RUNNING". All the Compound Services are "OUT OF CONTEXT" (abnormal lack of resources). In addition, BLEED and HYDraulic Compound Services are "RAMPING DOWN" as the ENGines stop producing this services. The user service THRUST is "NOT DELIVERING" and the engines are "NOT RUNNING". The ELECtricity Compound Service is still "DELI-VERING" thanks to an automatically turned on backup system for ELECtricity. Finally, all the Compound Services are still "FUNCTIONAL" and have the restrictive attribute "ALLOWED" because the warning concerns the ENGines System Devices and that there are no restriction of usage in this context for these Compound Services.

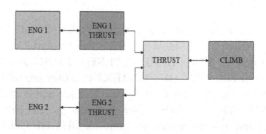

Fig. 7. Integration of CLIMB user service in the DSCU architecture of engines

System Modeling and Integrated Presentation Layouts. (step 5.4 in the Fig. 3)

Integrated DSCU Architecture. Together with the experts, we identified that THRUST Compound Service produces the CLIMB User Service (used by the pilots during takeoff for example). We thus integrated CLIMB User Service into the DSCU archi-tecture as shown in Fig. 7.

Integrated Systems Models. During this sub step, we connected the model of the behavior of the THRUST Compound Service to the model of the behavior of CLIMB User Service. These behavioral models are not presented here due to space constraints. The interested reader can find similar models (covering nominal and abnormal situations in [21]).

C&C Sample Presentation Layout. Figure 8 presents a mockup of presentation layouts produced for the "ALL ENGs FLAME OUT" alarm. In this layout, the ENG 1 and ENG 2 System Devices are in the qualitative state DEGRADED because of the alarm.

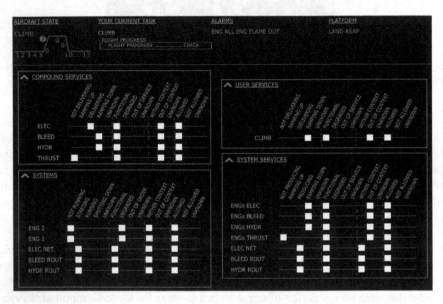

Fig. 8. A layout of the presentation for the system under design (following DSCU and OCQR).

In addition, they are in the operational state NOT RUNNING because the warning alarm indicates that they are shutdown. All of the System Services related to the ENGines ("ENGs ELEC", "ENGs BLEED", "ENGs HYDR" and "ENGs THRUST") have the contextual attribute OUT OF CONTEXT and they are in the operational state RAMPING DOWN, except the THRUST System Service that is in the operational state NOT PRODUCING. The CLIMB User Service is in the operational state RAMPING DOWN and has the contextual attribute OUT OF CONTEXT. Indeed, the THRUST resource is no longer produced and the plane will slowly start to glide. Routing System Services are still PRODUCING (operational state) –FUNCTIONAL (qualitative state) -WITHIN CONTEXT (contextual attribute) –ALLOWED (restrictive attribute).

6.2 Towards UCD of the Crew Alerting System

Each artefact produced during the application of the SCD process can be exploited by most UCD techniques and methods. The set of DSCU architectures and the OQCR (states and attributes) provides the exhaustive list of devices, services and their associated states and attributes. This information provides support for designing mock-up and prototypes of the interface of the C&C interactive systems. They also provide support to crosscheck the prototypes and the task models, in order to determine whether all the devices are bound to at least one user task. They also can be of great help provide support to observation and interview activities as they help understanding which services and devices are required for each user service (e.g. the connection between the engines and climb in DSCU architecture represents explicitly the fact that engines have to be functional to perform CLIMB). The system components behavioral models provide additional support to define the behavior of mockups and prototypes beyond their layouts. In the same ways, the coverage of both nominal and abnormal situations provide support to produce prototypes that cover all the cases but also helps identifying in an exhaustive way operators' tasks [37] identifying corner cases to be addressed in interviews and observations preparation. Furthermore, the system components behavioral models provide support to the application of dependable computing techniques [38], that provides means of compliance for the application of the RCD process.

7 Conclusion and Perspectives

While UCD approaches focus on the usability of the interactive system under design, constraints beyond users' needs that have to be taken into account when designing complex command and control systems. For instance, feasibility is a first class citizen but it is not addressed by UCD approaches. For instance, without a deep understanding of aircrafts physics, it is not possible to design a cockpit that will meet feasibility. Beyond, this paper has demonstrated that without a deep understanding of aircraft systems, cockpit design is a task doomed to fail, especially when interfaces for system management are concerned. However, it is not possible for designers to learn all this information for every type of command and control system they are likely to design. This paper tackles that specific problem by providing a generic design process for gathering the information of underlying systems when designing a command and control system. This process makes explicit use of available documentation (both technical and operational) and provides stepwise progress towards User Centered Design.

In this paper, the proposed approach is applied to the design of user interfaces for aircraft cockpits. However, the approach is generic enough and applicable to other command and control systems. For example, in the space domain, the satellite platforms and the missions they support are firstly designed for feasibility. The design of ground segment applications to monitor and control the various sets of devices of the satellites and of the ground communications systems also requires knowledge beyond the UI/UX designers and UCD experts' knowledge [32]. The paper has also emphasized the importance of standards and certification activities in the design of these systems. Indeed, even automotive systems rely on existing standards such as AUTOSAR [4] and ISO 26262 [27] that provide regulatory framework for autonomous cars design and development. We believe that this paper can provide support to designers involved in design tasks of C&C systems that have been so far not supported by UCD processes leaving, very unfortunately, Command and Control interactive systems design incapable to benefit from UCD benefits. Such approach requires techniques to trace and analyze the coverage of regulatory requirements, feasibility requirements and design options [34].

References

1. Abras, C., Maloney-Krichmar, D., Preece, J.: User-centered design. In: Bainbridge, W. (ed.) Encyclopedia of Human-Computer Interaction. Sage Publications, Thousand Oaks (2004)
2. Airbus A350 Flight Crew Operating Manual, 5T1 A350 FLEET FCOM. Technical Report. Airbus
3. APA 2017: Publication Manual of the American Psychological Association, 6th edn
4. AUTOSAR AUTomotive Open System ARchitecture development: "Foundation". www.autosar.org. Accessed 14 May 2018
5. Beaudouin-Lafon, M.: Designing interaction not interfaces. In: Proceedings of AVI, pp. 15–22. ACM (2004)
6. Bisantz, A.M., Vicente, K.J.: Making the abstraction hierarchy concrete. Int. J. Hum Comput Stud. **40**, 83–117 (1994)
7. Blythe, M., Monk, A. (eds.): Funology 2. HIS. Springer, Cham (2018). https://doi.org/10.1007/978-3-319-68213-6
8. Boehm, B.: A spiral model of software development and enhancement. ACM SIGSOFT Softw. Eng. Notes **11**(4), 14–24 (1986)
9. Bouzekri, E., et al.: Engineering issues related to the development of a recommender system in a critical context: application to interactive cockpits. Int. J. Hum Comput Stud. **121**, 122–141 (2019)
10. CS-25 – Amendment 17 - Certification Specifications and Acceptable Means of Compliance for Large Aeroplanes. EASA (2015)
11. Dix, A., Finlay, J., Abowd, G., Beale, R.: Human-Computer Interaction, 3rd edn. (2004)
12. DO-178C/ED-12C: Software Considerations in Airborne Systems and Equipment Certification. RTCA and EUROCAE (2012)
13. DO-254/ED-80: Design Assurance Guidance for Airborne Electronic Hardware, published by RTCA and EUROCAE (2000)
14. Dodd, I., Habli, I.: Safety certification of airborne software: an empirical study. Reliab. Eng. Syst. Saf. **98**(1), 7–23 (2012)
15. ECSS-Q-ST-40C Safety, March 6, 2009, Safety Standards for Space Systems, European Space Agency. European Cooperation for Space Standardization
16. Endsley, M.R.: Designing for Situation Awareness: An Approach to User-Centered Design, 2nd edn. CRC Press Inc., Boca Raton (2011)
17. European Aviation Safety Agency: CS-25 – Certification Specifications and Acceptable Means of Compliance for Large Aeroplanes (2017)
18. Eurocontrol Model for Task and Job Descriptions of Air Traffic Controllers, HUM.ET1.ST01.1000-REP-01. EATCHIP Reference Material (1996)
19. ESARR 4 - Risk Assessment and Mitigation in ATM & Acceptable Means of Compliance with ESARR 4, Oct 2009, Eurocontrol

20. Fayollas, C., Martinie, C., Palanque, P., Deleris, Y., Fabre, J.-C., Navarre, D.: An approach for assessing the impact of dependability on usability: application to interactive cockpits. In: EDCC 2014, Newcastle, pp. 198–209 (2014)

21. Fayollas, C., Palanque, P., Fabre, J.-C., Martinie, C., Déléris, Y.: Dealing with faults during operations: beyond classical use of formal methods. In: Weyers, B., Bowen, J., Dix, A., Palanque, P. (eds.) The Handbook of Formal Methods in Human-Computer Interaction. HIS, pp. 549–575. Springer, Cham (2017). https://doi.org/10.1007/978-3-319-51838-1_20

22. Gould, I.D., Lewis, C.: Designing for usability: key principles and what designers think. Commun. ACM **28**(3), 300–311 (1985)

23. Göransson, B., Gulliksen, J., Boivie, I.: The usability design process – integrating user-centered systems design in the software development process. In: Software Process Improvement and Practice, vol. 8, no. 2, pp. 111–131. Wiley (2003)

24. Gross, T.: *UCProMo*—towards a user-centred process model. In: Bogdan, C., et al. (eds.) HCSE/HESSD -2016. LNCS, vol. 9856, pp. 301–313. Springer, Cham (2016). https://doi.org/10.1007/978-3-319-44902-9_19

25. Hassenzahl, M., Platz, A., Burmester, M., Lehner, K.: Hedonic and ergonomic quality aspects determine a software's appeal. In: ACM CHI Conference, pp. 201–208 (2000)

26. ISO 9241-210: Ergonomics of human-system interaction – Part 210: Human-centred design for interactive systems, Geneva

27. ISO 26262, Road vehicles – Functional safety (2011)

28. Hornbæk, K., Oulasvirta, A.: What is interaction? In: Proceedings of the CHI Conference on Human Factors in Computing Systems, pp. 5040–5052 (2017)

29. Ladry, J.-F., Navarre, D., Palanque, P.: Formal description techniques to support the design, construction and evaluation of fusion engines for sure (safe, usable, reliable and evolvable) multimodal interfaces. In: ACM International Conference on Multimodal Interaction, pp. 185–192 (2009)

30. Larusdottir, M., Gulliksen, J., Cajander, A.: A license to kill – improving UCSD in Agile development. J. Syst. Softw. **123**, 214–222 (2017)

31. Maguire, M.: Methods to support human-centred design. Int. J. Hum Comput Stud. **55**(4), 587–634 (2001)

32. Martinie, C., Palanque, P., Fahssi, R., Blanquart, J.-P., Fayollas, C., Seguin, C.: Task model-based systematic analysis of both system failures and human errors. IEEE Trans. Hum. Mach. Syst. **46**(2), 243–254 (2016)

33. Martinie, C., Palanque, P., Navarre, D., Barboni, E.: A development process for usable large scale interactive critical systems: application to satellite ground segments. In: Winckler, M., Forbrig, P., Bernhaupt, R. (eds.) HCSE 2012. LNCS, vol. 7623, pp. 72–93. Springer, Heidelberg (2012). https://doi.org/10.1007/978-3-642-34347-6_5

34. Martinie, C., Palanque, P., Winckler, M., Conversy, S.: DREAMER: a design rationale environment for argumentation, modeling and engineering requirements. In: Proceedings of the 28th ACM International Conference on SIGDOC, pp. 73–80. ACM, New York (2010)

35. Mayhew, D.J.: The Usability Engineering Lifecycle: A Practitioner's Handbook for User Interface Design, 1st edn. Morgan Kaufmann Publishers Inc., San Francisco (1999)

36. McDermid, J., Ripken, K.: Life cycle support in the Ada environment. SIGAda Letters (1983)

37. Martinie, C., et al.: Formal tasks and systems models as a tool for specifying and assessing automation designs. In: Proceedings of the International Conference on ATACCS, Toulouse, pp. 50–59 (2011)

38. Navarre, D., Palanque, P., Basnyat, S.: A formal approach for user interaction reconfiguration of safety critical interactive systems. In: Harrison, M.D., Sujan, M.-A. (eds.) SAFECOMP 2008. LNCS, vol. 5219, pp. 373–386. Springer, Heidelberg (2008). https://doi.org/10.1007/978-3-540-87698-4_31
39. Navarre, D., Palanque, P., Ladry, J.-F., Barboni, E.: ICOs: a model-based user interface description technique dedicated to interactive systems addressing usability, reliability and scalability. ACM Trans. Comput.-Hum. Interact. **16**, 18:1–18:56 (2009)
40. Navarre, D., Palanque, P., Bastide, R.: A tool-supported design framework for safety critical interactive systems. Interact. Comput. **15**(3), 309–328 (2003)
41. Reuzeau, F.: Finding the best users to involve in design: a rational approach. Le travail humain **64**(3), 223–245 (2001)
42. Rogers, Y.: HCI theory: classical, modern, and contemporary. Synth. Lect. Hum.-Centered Inform. **5**(2), 1–129 (2012)
43. Royce, W.: Managing the Development of Large Software Systems, pp. 1–9. IEEE Wescon (1970)
44. Schwaber, K.: Agile Project Management with Scrum. Microsoft Press (2004)
45. Singer, G.: Minimizing pilot-error by design: are test pilot doing a good enough job? Hum. Factors Aerosp. Saf. **1**(4), 301–321 (2001)
46. Singer, G., Dekker, S.: Pilot performance during multiple failures: an empirical study of different warning systems. Transp. Hum. Factors **2**(1), 63–76 (2000)
47. Stanton, N., et al.: Development of a generic activities model of command and control. Cog., Tech. & Work (2008)
48. Turk, D., France, R., Rumpe, B.: Limitations of agile software processes. In: Proceedings of the International Conference on eXtreme Programming and Agile Processes in Software Engineering, Italy (2002)
49. Vicente, K.: Cognitive Work Analysis: Toward Safe, Productive, and Healthy Computer-Based Work, 417 p. Lawrence Erlbaum Associates (1999)

Detecting and Influencing Driver Emotions Using Psycho-Physiological Sensors and Ambient Light

Mariam Hassib[1], Michael Braun[1,2]($\boxtimes$), Bastian Pfleging[1,3], and Florian Alt[1,4]

[1] LMU Munich, Munich, Germany
mariam.hassib@ifi.lmu.de
[2] BMW Group Research, New Technologies, Innovations, Munich, Germany
michael.bf.braun@bmw.de
[3] Universiteit Eindhoven, Eindhoven, The Netherlands
b.pfleging@tue.nl
[4] Bundeswehr University, Munich, Germany
florian.alt@unibw.de

Abstract. Driving is a sensitive task that is strongly affected by the driver's emotions. Negative emotions, such as anger, can evidently lead to more driving errors. In this work, we introduce a concept of detecting and influencing driver emotions using psycho-physiological sensing for emotion classification and ambient light for feedback. We detect arousal and valence of emotional responses from wearable bio-electric sensors, namely brain-computer interfaces and heart rate sensors. We evaluated our concept in a static driving simulator with a fully equipped car with 12 participants. Before the rides, we elicit negative emotions and evaluate driving performance and physiological data while driving under stressful conditions. We use three ambient lighting conditions (no light, blue, orange). Using a subject-dependent random forests classifier with 40 features collected from physiological data we achieve an average accuracy of 78.9% for classifying valence and 68.7% for arousal. Driving performance was enhanced in conditions where ambient lighting was introduced. Both blue and orange light helped drivers to improve lane keeping. We discuss insights from our study and provide design recommendations for designing emotion sensing and feedback systems in the car.

Keywords: Affective computing · Automotive UI · EEG · Ambient light

1 Introduction

Driving is a sensitive task, deeply embedded in our everyday lives. While modern cars are designed to reduce the driver's physical effort through assistive systems and features, the demand on focus and cognitive abilities is still high. Even as

© IFIP International Federation for Information Processing 2019
Published by Springer Nature Switzerland AG 2019
D. Lamas et al. (Eds.): INTERACT 2019, LNCS 11746, pp. 721–742, 2019.
https://doi.org/10.1007/978-3-030-29381-9_43

we move towards the era of (semi-) automated driving, we expect that drivers will still need to maneuver in various situations and take over control. Hence, it is important to understand and react to the driver's state [40,56].

The driver's state does not only comprise cognitive abilities or how sleepy or focused they are, but also includes their emotional state. Prior research shows that emotions have a strong impact on driving performance and capabilities, and negative emotions while driving (e.g., sadness, anger) can lead to undesired consequences and driving errors [15]. Extreme positive emotions like overexcitement, where the driver's arousal (i.e., activation) state is very high, can also have negative effects on driving [16,27,61,65]. Hence, monitoring and reacting to driver emotion is an important rising area of automotive HCI research.

With wearable sensors and sensing capabilities embedded in modern cars we are a step closer to realizing the vision of having a ubiquitous sensing environment inside the car. Using sensors, researchers can detect driver drowsiness through camera-based methods and physiological sensing [28,62], driver stress through GPS traces [59], or the driver's cognitive load and interruptibility using physiological sensors [31,56]. While the importance of maintaining balanced emotional states while driving has been recognized, there is little work on closing the loop by not only sensing emotions, but also providing feedback [25,41,65].

We introduce the concept of a full sensing and feedback loop in automotive contexts using wearable physiological sensors and ambient light. We look into the use of light-weight psycho-physiological sensors as an implicit emotion detection method: Consumer-level bio-electric signals such as electroencephalography/electromyography (EEG/EMG) and heart rate (HR) sensors to detect emotional arousal and valence. These sensors have proven their ability to detect emotional and cognitive states with acceptable accuracies [4,17,23,56]. On the feedback side, we explore the use of ambient light as an emotional feedback modality. Light was shown to have an effect on moods and emotions, e.g., by influencing the circadian system [10]. Ambient lighting in the car has been explored as a means of providing a more comfortable interior, through warning signals of upcoming traffic or to calm down the driver [35]. Combining input and output modalities we aim to assess the complete concept.

We investigate the effects of easy and stressful driving scenarios under elicited negative emotions on driver performance. In an experiment ($N = 12$), we explore two different ambient light colors (blue and orange) and their effects on the driving performance, physiological data, and self-reported emotional state. Results show that ambient lighting feedback can positively impact driving performance and lead to more focus or relaxed states. We envision a future where the car becomes an emotional feedback companion for the driver which attempts to support them by reacting to their emotional state.

Contribution Statement. This paper makes the following contributions: First, we introduce our concept and vision of the car as an emotional sensor and feedback companion. We then present an evaluation of the concept in a static driving simulator with a real car, to investigate the influence of (a) negative emotions during easy and stressful rides and (b) ambient lighting on driving performance, physiological data, and self-reported emotional state. Third, we provide recommendations for designers of emotional feedback systems in cars.

2   Background and Related Work

When considering emotions in the car, we see three related research aspects, namely: the effect of emotions in driving scenarios, the detection of emotions using psycho-physiological sensors, and finally, in-car responses to regulate and influence driver emotions. We therefore divide prior work that influenced our research into these three main groups.

2.1   Emotion in Driving Scenarios

The emotional state of drivers has a strong impact on their driving performance [15,20,21,29]. Prior work identified emotional states which influence driving and relate to driving safety [9,27]. These include aggressiveness, happiness, anger, fatigue, stress, sadness, confusion, urgency, and boredom.

When driving a car, the driver's tasks are typically divided into three classes [9]: (1) *Primary driving tasks* include all necessary tasks in order to keep the vehicle on track such as steering, lane selection, accelerating, braking, and stabilizing, (2) *Secondary tasks* comprise activities to improve driving performance or safety (e.g., blinking, or activating wipers and headlights), and (3) *Tertiary tasks* consist of all other tasks that are performed while driving including changing temperature, adjusting radio settings, interacting with a cellphone or talking to other passengers. The aforementioned emotions differently impact the driver's tasks: Primary tasks are strongly related to safe driving and are usually compromised by negative emotions. Secondary and tertiary tasks affect the driver's comfort more than ensuring safe driving [9]. However, these factors often lead to a change in emotion or a shift in attention that endangers safe driving.

According to Russell's model of affect [52], emotions can be defined on two axes, valence and arousal: Valence refers to whether the emotion is more positive or negative, and arousal refers to the amount of activation in the emotion [52]. Using this model, research found positive emotions (i.e., a more positive valence) to result in a better driving performance and happy drivers to produce fewer accidents [20,21,29]. However, extremely positive emotions (having a very high level of arousal/activation) can also negatively effect safe driving [3,21]. Yerkes and Dodson [63] found in an experiment that the best human performance values are measured with a medium level of arousal (activation), keeping in mind that the optimal level depends on task difficulty. Coughlin et al. [12] applied this model to the automotive domain.

Looking at negative emotions, prior work determined that aggressiveness and anger (i.e., low valence, high arousal) as well as sadness (i.e., low valence, low arousal) all negatively impact driving behavior and are shown to increase the risk of causing an accident [13,61]. Sadness usually is accompanied by resignation and passiveness, resulting in longer reaction times not just in critical situations, but also by reducing the driver's attention [13]. The low arousal state may also result in fatigue or sleepiness, which is a very dangerous precondition since it negatively affects all abilities that are necessary for safe driving [28,62].

As for all other tasks that require cerebral capacity, stress is very likely to occur while driving. The primary driving task itself is often a stressful task. Moreover, drivers often experience a higher workload due to additional tasks beyond driving: additional factors or tasks such as following a car, making faster progress (changing lanes during rush-hour traffic), receiving phone calls, the need to arrive on time, or communicating with passengers, increase the mental workload [56]. High mental workload comes with high arousal, which reduces driver performance [39,46,56,59].

2.2 Driver Emotion Detection

The steady development of accurate emotion recognition techniques allows its application in different contexts, including driving. Eyben et al. [15] state four major modalities for emotion recognition in automotive contexts: audio (i.e. speech), video, driving style, and physiological measurements. However, not every measurement technique is suitable to detect every emotion. Prior work investigated the use of *audio* recording to detect anger and nervousness by employing speech features such as volume and pitch [14,15,41]. A disadvantage of speech in the car is the necessity for drivers to constantly speak or express themselves in an audible way. Emotion recognition from *driving style* was explored by different researchers to detect states of stress, high cognitive workload, interruptibility, and drowsiness [31,59,62]. High arousal states were found to result in more actions, such as frequent lane changes or having a large longitudinal variance, whereas low arousal states usually result in less active driving. Riener et al. [48] recognized nervousness from posture and motion in the seat. Their hypothesis was that nervous drivers move more than relaxed ones.

The emotional and cognitive states of humans is reflected through physiological signals which can be detected using, for example, body-worn sensors providing fine-grained feedback. Implicit emotion recognition while driving using *psycho-physiological sensors* was investigated by several researchers [47,55]. For example, heart rate gives an indication of the driver's state of arousal [30,56]. Lower heart rates indicate a more relaxed state, whereas higher heart rates occur during high driver activation. Respiration rate is also connected to arousal states, slower and shallower breathing indicates a relaxed state whereas alerted or active states result faster breathing and indicate emotional excitement [15]. Skin conductance levels (SCL) are associated with measures of emotion, arousal, and attention [25,56]. EEG signals measured from the top of the scalp give information about the cognitive and emotional state of the user [8,23,49].

Katsis et al. [30] used EMG, HR, respiration, and SCL to classify stress, euphoria, and disappointment in car-racing drivers. De Waard et al. [60] conducted a field study to investigate the effect of driving on different types of roads on the heart rate variability (HRV) and consequently the mental demand of drivers. Solovey et al. used machine learning classifiers with features from HR, SCL, and driving performance to detect the driver's mental workload [56]. Healey et al. [24] classified stress levels using HR, EMG, SCL, and respiration during driving on highways and urban roads. Jahn et al. [26] conducted a large-scale study and concluded that heart rate changes reflect emotional strain. Collet et al. [11] collected heart rate and skin resistance data during driving on a closed track and concluded that both physiological measures increased when performing additional tasks such as phone conversations. EEG sensing was used to detect drowsiness while driving [8] and to detect cognitive states in simulated virtual reality driving [34]. Schneegass et al. [54] presented a real-world driving study in which ECG, SCL, and skin temperature data was collected while participants drive in differing road environments. They found that SCL varied significantly across road types [54].

2.3   In-Car Responses to Regulate and Influence Emotions

While the larger body of automotive affective computing research is concerned with reliably detecting emotions, reflecting and regulating emotions once detected remains a challenge. Research introduced multiple mitigation strategies to either increase the driver's awareness of their emotional state [25] or introduced design suggestions to help shifting the driver's state to a more desirable one [65]. Zhu et al. [65] and Fakhrhosseini et al. [16] investigated the use of music to relieve anger situations while driving. Braun et al. explored the viability of ambient light, visual feedback, voice interaction, and an empathic voice assistant as strategies to regulate sadness and anger while driving [6]. Nass et al. investigated mirroring voice with driver emotions and found that when drivers' emotions matched the car's voice emotion, they had fewer accidents, focused more on the road and spoke more to the car [41]. Harris and Nass researched behavioral and attitudinal effects of cognitively re-framing frustrating events using voice prompts [22]. They found that voice prompts telling drivers that the actions of others on the road were unintentional reduced driver frustration and negative emotions [22]. Roberts et al. [50] studied the differences between warning users through visual and auditory alerts in real-time or post-hoc. They found drivers to be more receptive to post-hoc critic [50]. Hernandez et al. envision a concept of a reflective dashboard, making drivers aware of their stress levels measured through skin conductance sensors by showing red or green light. They showed that people slow down upon red light [25].

2.4   Summary

Related work shows that negative emotions impact driving performance. Researchers investigated the use of physiological sensors to gain insight into driver emotions, and, more recently, started to explore different design opportunities to reflect, relieve, or mitigate negative emotions. In our work, we present a concept which combines emotion detection and reflection in the car. We investigate the feasibility of using lightweight EEG and heart rate sensors to detect negative valence while driving, and the effects of using dashboard ambient lighting to reflect and influence emotions.

3 Concept and Vision

We envision the car as a companion which senses, reflects, and communicates feedback to the driver in a subtle and seamless manner. Our concept uses psycho-physiological sensors for continuously detecting the driver's emotional state without jeopardizing drivers' attention by asking repeatedly for subjective feedback (e.g., by using questionnaires). To provide emotional feedback to the driver we use ambient lighting on the dashboard through LEDs to provide subtle, yet perceivable feedback. The intention is that this light shifts the driver's emotions towards a desirable state through emotional awareness and regulation. Below we discuss both input and output modalities used in our concept.

3.1 Emotion Detection: Psycho-Physiological Sensing

Researchers explored different psycho-physiological correlates that enable emotion recognition [4]. Signals captured from the human body reveal a plethora of information about users' current emotional, physical and cognitive states. In our concept we rely on EEG/EMG and heart rate sensing wearables. The proliferation of consumer-level wearable sensors into the market in suitable form factors allowed researchers to further explore their use in HCI [23].

In our concept, we use both consumer-level EEG and heart rate sensors for emotion detection. Whereas heart rate has been successful in detecting arousal rates [17], EEG has been successful in detecting emotional valence [4,34]. Physiological sensors in general allow for collecting fine-grained unbiased emotional information, without adding further workload on users which is critical when driving a car. In addition, compared to camera-based techniques, using physiological sensors is not sensitive to light conditions or occlusions. On the other hand, physiological sensing, is person-dependent and prone to be influenced by muscle and movement artifacts [57].

3.2 Emotion Feedback: In-Car Ambient Light

For the output modality, we chose ambient lighting as a subtle way to visualize feedback in the car. Using different lighting techniques in the car is not a new concept in itself. Many modern cars include ambient lighting to provide a feedback about different states (e.g. doors open, car locked), or as reading lights (for example, BMW Moodlight[1]). Outside the car, ambient lighting is also used in other road environments such as tunnels[2]. This familiarity makes it a useful and

---

[1] https://legacy.bmw.com/com/en/newvehicles/x/x6/2014/showroom/design/ambiente_light.html, accessed February 2018.

[2] http://www.thornlighting.com/download/TunnelINT.pdf, accessed September 2018.

Fig. 1. A driver in our simulator study to evaluate our concept, wearing the EEG and heart rate sensors during the blue (left) and orange (right) ambient lighting conditions. The sensors were used to detect the driver's emotions while the ambient light was used to influence driving behavior. Both light colors improved driving performance compared to a baseline ride due to their warning (orange) and calming (blue) effects. (Color figure online)

suitable modality to augment the car's interior with further information that can easily be perceived by the driver.

Prior work investigated using ambient lighting in the car for signaling, for increasing awareness [36], enhancing night vision [51], or signaling upcoming road conditions [33]. Löcken et al. present a survey on in-car ambient lighting [35]. However, ambient lighting in the car has rarely been used to reflect and influence the driver's emotional state.

In our concept we chose two ambient lighting colors, a cool color (blue) and a warm color (orange): Blue ambient lighting is related to vitality, energy, and power. Additionally, it is perceived as a calming and pleasant color but barely arousing emotions [37]. Red and orange are associated with a higher arousal level [35]. To differentiate the warm color stimulus from a warning signal (e.g. such as traffic lights), we chose orange instead of red to increase arousal. To evaluate our concept, we conducted a simulator study that integrates different emotion evoking rides and uses psycho-physiological sensors for emotion detection and ambient light conditions for regulation and reflection.

4   Simulator Study: Emotional Driving

To evaluate our concept, we conducted a driving simulator study equipped with a real car. In the study we tested the effect of driving performance under negative elicited emotions during easy and stressful rides, and different ambient lighting conditions. Our main goals were: (1) to analyze psycho-physiological responses during actual driving context and the feasibility to classify emotions in this setup using light-weight wearable sensors; (2) to analyze the effect of negative emotions while driving easy and hard rides; and (3) to investigate the effect of ambient lighting on driving performance and emotional arousal and valence.

4.1   Apparatus

Emotion Elicitation. In this study we focused on driving starting in a negative emotional state. As we have presented in the related work section, negative emotions such as sadness have a negative effect on driving performance.

To ensure that drivers were in a negative state before the start of the driving tasks, we used the DEAP database [32] which consists of 120 excerpts of music videos from different music genres that are rated according to valence and arousal on the SAM scale [5]. This database was already used and evaluated with medical grade EEG data collection and promising results were found: In a lab study, Koelstra et al. extracted 40 videos from the database which showed the strength of elicited emotions [32]. For our study, we chose four videos from the dataset that were ranked lowest. These videos (#23, #24, #28, and #30) were all rated in the low arousal and low valence quadrant [32].

Driving Simulator and Ride Description. Our static driving simulator consisted of a fully equipped stationary car (BMW i3), a projector, and speakers. The projector showed the driving scenario on a 5 m × 3 m wall. We used four drives in our study: one easy baseline drive where the driver had a car-following task on an almost empty highway, and three stressful car-following drives where the driver was on a busy highway and faced several annoying driving maneuvers from other drivers. Each drive was six minutes long.

Baseline drive: The simulation was modeled according to SAE J2944 standard criteria [19]. The driver follows another vehicle in the center of the lane, with constant speed and headway, without lane changes, on a straight highway.

Stressful drives: This concept was adapted from Schmidt et al. [53] who designed a number of traffic scenarios to induce negative emotional states. The rides contain multiple lane changes and various stressful events, such as a close encounter with trucks or a construction site with narrowed lanes. Participants were also instructed to follow a designated vehicle in the center of the lane and keep a constant and safe distance.

Data Collection. During the study we collected physiological data, driving performance, and emotional ratings. To collect and record EEG/EMG signals, we used a Muse brain-sensing headband[3]. This headband uses four electrodes placed on the frontal and parietal lobes according to the 10–20 positioning system, namely: AF7, AF8, TP9, and TP10. The device provides access to raw EEG and relative EEG frequency bands, blinks, and jaw clenches. The data is sent to a computer via Bluetooth. To measure participants' heart rate, we used a Polar H7 chest strap sensor[4]. The sensor sends HR information via Bluetooth

---

[3] https://www.choosemuse.com/.

[4] https://www.polar.com/us-en/products/accessories/H7_heart_rate_sensor.

Fig. 2. Three images showing the simulator study setup: (A) The projected driving scenario during an overtake. The distance to the followed vehicle is shown in yellow (B) The dashboard of the car showing the ambient lighting LEDs around the wheel and along the passenger side. On the right, the tablet is shown depicting the continuous ASAM scale. (C) The driving simulator showing the stationary car and the projected driving scenario. (Color figure online)

low energy at a rate of 1 Hz. All data streams and task triggers were combined in an experimenter interface, where consistent timestamps were assigned.

To collect ground truth data about driver emotions in a driving context, we used the automotive self-assessment method (ASAM) [7]. Using a 9-point SAM would have been quite intrusive during the rides. In this case, users would need to choose a SAM rating from radio buttons during driving. On the other hand, asking users to verbally indicate their emotional ratings whilst driving can lead to biased results due to the experimenter being there to collect the answers.

Hence, we fitted a tablet to the right of the driver with two continuous scales which can easily be reached and clicked by the driver with the right hand. Figure 2(B) shows the interior of the car, depicting the tablet, the scales, and a smiley face in the middle. The top scale, arousal, is reflected in the eyes of the smiley face in the middle which goes from a sleepy face to an awake face. The bottom scale depicts the valence and it adjusts the mouth of the smiley going from negative to positive. The scales are from 1–100. We adjusted the sensitivity of the scales so that the driver can click anywhere over or under the top or bottom of the scale and it would adjust accordingly. The tablet was always within arm's reach. Finally, we collected driving data through the driving simulator. This included speed and acceleration, distance to followed car, lane variations, and crashes.

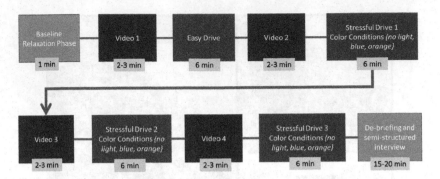

Fig. 3. Study procedure block diagram showing each step with durations. The baseline relaxation phase and easy drive were always fixed in the beginning. The order of the color conditions during the stressful drives was counter balanced between participants. In the end a debriefing session and semi-structured interview were conducted.

Dashboard Ambient Light. We used Philips Hue[5] LED light stripes with 1,600 lumen to create ambient light insight the car. Connected over the Philips Hue bridge, we selected the colors of the light strips with the corresponding mobile app. We used a 2 m strip of the Hue LEDs which were fixed around the dashboard as shown in Figs. 1 and 2(B). As explained in the concept section, we evaluated the effect of two colors, blue and orange.

4.2   Study Design

We used a repeated measures design with two independent variables, namely, driving scenario (4 levels) and light color condition with three levels (*no light, blue light, orange light*). As explained previously, we had four main drives – one baselines drive and three stressful drives. The duration of all drives was six minutes. During the baseline drive, no ambient light was triggered. One stressful drive was in the *no light* condition, where no light was triggered, one was in the *blue light* condition, and one in the *orange light* condition.

Figure 3 illustrates a block diagram of the procedure of the whole study with durations. The light was triggered in fixed intervals of one minutes and lasting for 30 s each time. ASAM ratings were triggered at 1.5 min intervals constituting four ASAM ratings per drive. The order of the rides was counterbalanced to reduce learning effects. Figure 4 depicts the process of triggering light and ASAM experience sampling questions during the stressful drives, with (a) showing the light conditions and (b) the no light condition.

---

[5] https://www.meethue.com/, last access: 2018-09-19.

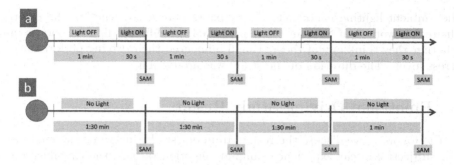

Fig. 4. The procedure of one run from the stressful drives which included the color condition (no light, blue, orange). (a) depicts timings for the blue and orange light conditions, and (b) depicts timings for the no light condition. The timing of the ASAM triggers was exactly the same as for the blue/orange/no light as the figure shows. (Color figure online)

4.3 Participants and Procedure

Twelve participants took part in our study (4 females, 21–61 years, $M = 31, SD = 11.4$). Participants were mostly engineers or students, all had driving licenses.

After our participants arrived at the lab we explained that the purpose of the study was to collect physiological data while driving in different scenarios and showed them the sensors. We introduced how we collect the subjective ASAM feedback on the mounted tablet during the ride and explained that the participant's input will be triggered several times during each ride with a short beep sound. Participants did not know a priori about the use of the installed ambient light. Before the study, the participants signed a consent form.

We first asked the participants to put on the sensors and ensured good contact. Next, participants adjusted the car seat and started a short test drive to get used to the car and simulation. The scenario used for this ride was an empty highway. A test ASAM question was then triggered on the tablet with a short beep and participants were requested to answered it while driving. When participants stated to be comfortable with driving, we terminated the test drive and started the study.

The first part of the study included a one minute relaxation task to collect baseline EEG and HR measurements. Afterwards, participants watched the first music video on the projection wall while they were seated in the car and received an ASAM prompt at the end of the video clip. The first ride was then the baseline ride for six minutes. We reminded the participants that they should keep a distance between 50 to 70 m to the car lead vehicle. After the end of this ride, the participants continued with the three other video-ride combinations with the different color conditions. The order of the videos and the ambient light conditions were randomized. After the study we conducted a short semistructured interview to gather feedback about their perceptions of the rides and the ambient lighting conditions. Participants were asked whether the emotion elicitation worked, if and how they perceived the different lighting modes, and whether they think any of these stimuli influenced their driving performance or stress levels. The duration of the study was around 1 h.

5   Emotional Driving Study Results

In the following we discuss the results from our study, including the analysis of the subjective in-car experience sampling emotion ratings, the classification of physiological data, and finally the driving performance analysis.

5.1   Emotional Ratings

We collected 480 ratings from the twelve participants, 240 for each arousal and valence. Four ratings per drive and one rating per music video making up 20 ratings for each arousal and valence from each participant. We calculated the mean and standard deviations of the arousal and valence scores from the continuous 1–100 ASAM ratings. Our results show that, first, the music videos were indeed successful in putting participants in a negative valence before each ride, with a mean rating of 48.5 ($SD = 23.0$) for arousal and 40.25 ($SD = 18.04$) for valence. Participants rated the easy baseline rides with a mean of 57.3 ($SD = 18.34$) for arousal and 52.5 ($SD = 16.5$) for valence. They rated stressful drives with no ambient lighting almost the same on the arousal scale ($M = 57.9$, $SD = 20.16$) but lower on the valence scale ($M = 48.2, SD = 15.24$), indicating that they were in a more negative mood during the stressful rides.

Looking at the ambient lighting conditions, we found that participants rated both arousal and valence higher than for the no ambient lighting condition for both the orange and the blue lights. The mean arousal for blue light was 61.5 ($SD = 18.34$), and the mean valence was rated 53.4 ($SD = 17.38$). For the orange ambient lighting condition the mean arousal was 61.04 ($SD = 16.5$), and the mean valence was rated 52.04 ($SD = 16.8$).

Since the scales for arousal and valence are nonparametric, we used nonparametric tests to test for significance (Friedman and Wilcoxon tests). Wilcoxon sign-rank test for pairwise comparisons yielded no significant results except for valence between videos and the blue light condition ($p = 0.003$), and valence of light and no-light condition ($p = 0.02$). The results overall show an increase in valence in the ambient lighting conditions compared to the no light condition under the same stressful driving scenario.

5.2   EEG and HR Classification

For the analysis of the heart rate we used the data collected via the Polar chest strap. The data from three participants was removed due to hardware issues. We averaged the heart rate from the last minute for each drive per person to get insights into the overall change in heart rate depending on the drive type [53].

The mean baseline heart rate was 67.4 bpm ($SD = 8.4$). For the easy drives, the mean heart rate was 69.6 bpm ($SD = 7.4$). The stressful drives all increase the heart rate means from the baseline and easy drives with the stressful drive in the *no light* condition having the highest average of 71.8 bpm ($SD = 7.7$). The stressful drive under the *blue light* condition had a mean of 70.2 bpm ($SD = 6.6$) and finally the stressful drive with *orange light* achieving a mean of 71.4 bpm ($SD = 5.4$).

Although the data from only nine participants was considered in the analysis, we see that heart rates increased for the stressful drives compared to the baseline and easy drives. Additionally, the blue light condition achieved lower heart rates than both the orange and the no light conditions.

For drives in the ambient lighting conditions, we analyzed the 30 s segments which had blue or orange light compared to the 30 s segments before or after. A Wilcoxen sign-rank test found significant effects on the heart rate between the 30 s before the orange segment and the 30 s during the orange segment ($Z = -1.955, p = 0.05$). Whereas we did not find significant differences for the blue segments and the segments before them, we found significant differences when comparing the blue segments to the segments after them ($Z = -2.037, p = 0.038$). This shows that the blue and orange ambient lighting had indeed an effect on heart rate. Overall, heart rate decreased in the stressful rides with ambient lighting compared to the no light stressful ride.

For the analysis of the EEG data, we first extracted the EEG frequency band powers provided by the Muse headband, which were common average referenced and band-passed between 0.1 Hz and 30 Hz and notch-filtered at 50 Hz. We first epoched the EEG data into 2.5-s windows. We calculated the 2.5-s mean of the spectral powers for each electrode and frequency resulting in 20 features. We calculated 20 more features from asymmetry differences and asymmetry ratios that were successful in prior work [64]. The asymmetry differences for each frequency band on each electrode pair (TP and AF) were calculated as follows: $AsymD_f = f_{Right} - f_{Left}$ where $AsymD$ represents the asymmetry difference and f are the left (AF7, TP9) and right side (AF8, TP10) mean spectral powers. Calculating all asymmetry values for all frequency bands produces another 10 features. We calculated the asymmetry ratios of the frequency bands according to the formula $AsymR_f = f_{Right}/f_{Left}$, where $AsymR$ is the ratio between two frequency bands and f are the left (AF7, TP9) and right side (AF8, TP10) mean spectral powers resulting in 10 more features (40 features in total).

We labelled the data according to the aggregated ASAM scores collected from the digitized ASAM ratings presented on the tablet to obtain a score between 1 (low arousal/valence) to 4 (high arousal/valence). We chose a random forest classifier and classified the data using Weka[6]. This particular classification algorithm was chosen due to its success application in other EEG classification tasks [23,64]. We performed a person-dependent classification with a 10-fold cross validation.

---

[6] http://www.cs.waikato.ac.nz/ml/weka/.

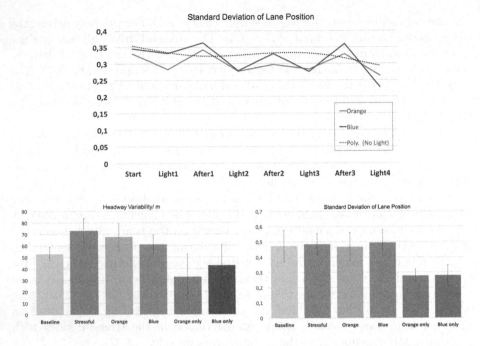

Fig. 5. Results from the driving performance analysis. *Top:* The overall SDLP during the orange and blue light conditions showing the variations between light on and light off segments. *Bottom:* The mean and SD of headway variability (left) and SDLP (right) for each of the rides. The two right most bars show lower values during the segments with the orange or blue lights on. (Color figure online)

The results are promising for classifying 4-class arousal and valence ratings. For arousal, all four classes were represented through our participants' ASAM ratings. F1 scores have an average of 68.7% over all four classes. For the valence classification, F1 scores have an overall average of 78.9% for all four classes, albeit the absence of two of the classes (classes 1 and 4) completely from three participants and the representation of only one class for one participant (P10).

5.3 Driving Performance Analysis

We calculated mean headway variability as well as standard deviation of lane position (SDLP) for each tested concept and ride. Headway variability is influenced by the behavior of preceding traffic, like lane changes, and provides a value of how well a driver is following the car in front [1]. We observed a mean headway variability of 52.98 m ($SD = 5.63$ m) for the baseline ride and a significantly higher value of 73.00 m ($SD = 10.56$ m) for the stressful ride without lights ($F = 14.65, p < 0.001$). Orange and blue lights during the ride did not lead to significant differences to either baseline or no-light condition with 67.49 m ($SD = 11.69$ m) and 61.00 m ($SD = 8.14$ m), respectively. If we look at the subsections of each ride where light was displayed, we can, however, see significant differences to all rides (Fig. 5, left). Orange light led to a headway variability of 32.82 m $(SD = 19.79\,\mathrm{m})$ and blue light to 42.74 m $(SD = 17,59\,\mathrm{m})$. This is a substantial decrease in headway variability when lights are displayed.

The standard deviation of lane position (SDLP) is a measure of lateral movement during the ride which is considered a core metric for assessing driving performance in simulations and provides high test-retest reliability [42,58]. We report insignificant differences between the four rides with SDLPs from 0.47 m to 0.49 m as shown in Fig. 5 (middle). Here again, the segments of the ride where light was shown improved the driving performance significantly $(F = 19.38, p < 0.001)$. When orange light was displayed, a SDLP of 0.28 m $(SD = 0.04\,\mathrm{m})$ was measured and blue light performed comparably with 0.28 m $(SD = 0.07\,\mathrm{m})$.

At first glance, we suspected the data was influenced by sequence effects as the lights were always shown during the ride and not at the very start. We could, however, verify the effect by visualizing the ride progress and associated SDLP values. Figure 5 (right) shows the values for sequences with and without light compared to the polynomial trend of the stressful ride without lights. We can clearly see here that SDLP is lower when the lights are turned on and higher if they are off.

5.4   Qualitative Feedback

We collected feedback through semi-structured interviews after the study. All participants stated that the drives were quite stressful, due to all the overtaking and catching up, and following the car. This indicates that the rides were successful in putting participants in a challenging situation.

When we asked participants how they perceived the different ambient lighting conditions, we got varying opinions. Several participants stated that they surely perceived the lights but did not think it had any relation or effect on their driving performance or mood (P1, P2, P4, P5). Two participants stated that they felt the lights were alerting them to be more focused on the road and avoid getting bored, distracted, or sleepy, regardless of the color of the light (P3, P7). One participant stated that the effect of the driving scenario on him is greater than the effect of any ambient lighting regardless of the color (P11). Two participants indicated that the orange light made them more alarmed, since it uses the same color metaphor as alerts (P9, P4). One participant stated that the orange color made him more 'critical' of his driving, thinking back at what he did wrong and what he can do better in the following phase (P9). Two participants stated that the blue light made them feel more relaxed, comfortable yet focused. However they were not sure if that really had an effect on their driving (P8, P10).

Most participants perceived blue light as relaxing and providing a nice feel to the interior of the car, whereas orange was perceived as an alarming, undesirable light, except for short periods of time to make users focus more on the road.

5.5   Limitations and Lessons Learned

We explored the feasibility of using psycho-physiological sensors and ambient lighting in a real vehicle. For this, we utilized light-weight wearable sensors for emotion recognition. We acknowledge that this setup could have introduced more artefacts in the measured physiological data than a controlled context. We used a machine learning approach with signal filtering algorithms to pre-process the data aiming to reduce artefacts. However, more complex signal processing approaches for more rigorous artefact filtering would be required in a scenario, e.g., with a moving car), to compensate for movement artefacts.

For three participants, heart rate was not recorded properly. Hence, we decide to exclude this feature from classification. We acknowledge that using features from heart rate information such as heart rate variability (HRV) could further enhance the classifier model [56].

We used videos to elicit emotions at the beginning of each ride to have consistent emotional baselines across all participants. We only elicited negative emotions on the low arousal and low valence level as a starting point before the beginning of each drive. In a real scenario the emotional states of the user may be more diverse, for example, highly excited or very angry. To keep our study consistent and confined in timing, we deliberately focused on certain combinations of arousal and valence. Future work could look at more combinations.

Finally, eliciting emotions for studies is a challenging task. Future work could look at using other methods for doing so.

6   Discussion and Design Recommendations

We discuss our findings and provide recommendations to designers of emotional feedback in the car. We provide insights regarding implicit emotion sensing and privacy, the use of ambient lighting as emotional awareness or influencing modality. Finally, we suggest how the findings from our studies can be used in ubiquitous road environments and for semi-autonomous driving scenarios.

6.1   Emotion Sensing: Privacy Considerations

The use of physiological sensing to detect emotions has been subject to recent research. It is no longer confined to laboratory settings and experiments but slowly finds it way into day-to-day life contexts. This creates the need for several privacy considerations. Emotions, naturally, are very private [44]. People have the freedom to hide their emotions by not talking about them or keeping a neutral facial expression purposefully.

However, overriding or faking emotions that are collected through physiological sensing is quite difficult [2,38,44]. Does this mean that future affective systems diminish the choice of self-expression and desired state of self presentation (cf. Goffman's work on self representation [18])?

In our first investigation of the concept, we did not consider the car a social setting shared with other people. Albeit that, we got feedback from our semi-structured interviews that tapped into this area. One participant even mentioned that he was feeling watched, although he knew that no one is currently looking at his sensed data and neither is it shared with anyone. Multiple other participants stated that they felt as if the car is warning them about themselves or criticizing their driving (mostly in the orange light condition). Note, that in our study, the drivers were the only people in the simulator and no other drivers or passengers were in the car. This means, the emotional feedback was limited to the driver. This suggests that, counter-intuitively, situations were the user is driving alone should be subject to investigation, looking into how emotional states can be presented in a privacy-preserving manner [45]. In addition, this is also relevant in situations were other passengers are present.

We encourage designers of emotional feedback systems to alter the feedback depending on the context. For example, when using ambient lighting, designers can limit the location of the feedback light to the front of the driver only when multiple passengers are in the car. This however, may affect how the light affects the driving performance. Future work should further investigate scenarios with passengers, considering in particular their relationship to the driver.

6.2 Ambient Lighting: Awareness or Influence

Our drivers did not know a priori what the ambient lighting meant. Qualitative feedback showed that multiple participants thought that the light was triggered in reaction to either their sensed physiological data or their subjective emotional feedback. Multiple participants stated that the orange light, owing to its close-ness to red, indicated that something was wrong, and raised their *awareness*. They stated that they definitely focused and drove better afterwards. This was also reflected in the driving performance analysis where the lowest variability in headway and in lane positions was achieved during period of orange light. In contrast, participants stated that the blue light was there to *influence* their emotional state and driving performance making them more relaxed.

Through our study we cannot determine if one type of feedback, *awareness or influence*, worked better. While our participants drove better under the *orange* condition, which multiple participants felt was an *awareness* cue, several participants stated that they did not find the orange light very comfortable. On the other hand, the blue drives were also successful in reducing driving errors, and also in reducing the heart rate. This shows that it indeed had a calming effect on the drivers. This is in line with findings from prior work. For example, Nass et al.'s work on mirroring in-car voice to current emotions [41] which proved to work better using a contrasting tone to the current emotion.

Designing emotional feedback, be it ambient lighting or a different form, can fall into either category. While we only evaluated the use of two colors during emotional driving scenarios, it was clear that there is indeed an effect based on the choices of colors. Future work should investigate the mental models associated with the different forms of feedback, or variations in one form (e.g. colors in ambient lighting scenarios) as well as personally customized color choices. Designers of emotional feedback systems should ensure that users have the correct mental model of the system.

6.3 Ambient Lighting in the Wild

Through our studies, participants repeatedly mentioned their familiarity with ambient lighting as a modality, from its recent integration in home and car environments. We see this as an opportunity for providing and influencing emotional states on the road. Several participants mentioned that night lights on the streets and in particular in tunnels can use this concept. A possible idea would be to use blue lighting in tunnels, e.g., to calm drivers down, especially those not comfortable with driving in narrow and dark places.

Another suggestion is to use car-to-car communication systems to trigger lighting in or outside of the car, depending on the traffic state. For example, when there is traffic congestions or an accident, the predicted emotional state of the drivers arising from these traffic situations could be considered. Extending this concept to other types of vehicles, such as buses and trains, by equipping the vehicle with LED lights can not only influence the driver, but also other passengers whose wellbeing influences driving performance through decreasing distractions [43]. In the aviation industry, ambient light similarly supports the flight experience and helps to arrive relaxed and with less jetlag[7].

7 Conclusion and Future Work

In this work we explored the concept of using physiological sensing, namely EEG and HR, as emotion sensing during driving scenarios, and ambient lighting as emotional feedback. In a simulator study with a real car we investigated (1) the feasibility of classifying emotions based on physiological data collected in context, and (2) the effect of different ambient lighting conditions on the emotional state and driving performance during stressful driving scenarios. Our findings show that it is possible to use light-weight sensors to classify emotional arousal and valence in a driving context with an acceptable accuracy. We also found that using ambient lighting in the car enhances driving performance. Participants found that blue light relaxed them and that orange light made them more critical of their performance.

Future work could explore the design of different ambient lighting colors and locations. We intend to explore scenarios with multiple passengers in the car. In addition, we are interested in exploring the use of physiological sensors and ambient lighting in a real road driving scenario. Also, embedding more sensing technologies (e.g., measuring the skin conductance level, SCL) may allow higher classification accuracies and more fine grained information to be achieved.

---

[7] http://www.a350xwb.com/cabin/, last access: 2018-09-20.

References

1. AAM Driver Focus-Telematics Working Group: Statement of Principles, Criteria and Verification Procedures on Driver Interactions with Advanced In-Vehicle Information and Communication Systems. AAM, Washington, DC (2006)
2. Arapakis, I., Konstas, I., Jose, J.M.: Using facial expressions and peripheral physiological signals as implicit indicators of topical relevance. In: Proceedings of the MM 2009, pp. 461–470. ACM, New York (2009). https://doi.org/10.1145/1631272.1631336
3. Arnett, J.J.: Developmental sources of crash risk in young drivers. Inj. Prev. **8**(suppl 2), ii17–ii23 (2002). https://doi.org/10.1136/ip.8.suppl_2.ii17
4. Bos, D.O.: EEG-based emotion recognition the influence of visual and auditory stimuli (2007)
5. Bradley, M.M., Lang, P.J.: Measuring emotion: the self-assessment manikin and the semantic differential. J. Behav. Ther. Exp. Psychiatry **25**(1), 49–59 (1994)
6. Braun, M., Schubert, J., Pfleging, B., Alt, F.: Improving driver emotions with affective strategies. Multi. Technol. Interact. **3**(1), 21 (2019)
7. Braun, M., Serres, K.: ASAM: an emotion sampling method for the automotive industry. In: Adjunct Proceedings of the AutoUI 2017, pp. 230–232. ACM (2017)
8. Brown, T., Johnson, R., Milavetz, G.: Identifying periods of drowsy driving using EEG. Ann. Adv. Automot. Med. **57**, 99 (2013)
9. Bubb, H.: Fahrerassistenz - primär ein beitrag zum komfort oder für die sicherheit? In: Der Fahrer im 21. Jahrhundert, pp. 25–44. VDI-Berichte 1768. VDI-Verlag, Düsseldorf (2003)
10. Canazei, M., Weiss, E.: The influence of light on mood and emotion, vol. 1, pp. 297–306, October 2013
11. Collet, C., Clarion, A., Morel, M., Chapon, A., Petit, C.: Physiological and behavioural changes associated to the management of secondary tasks while driving. Appl. Ergon. **40**(6), 1041–1046 (2009). https://doi.org/10.1016/j.apergo.2009.01.007. Psychophysiology in Ergonomics
12. Coughlin, J.F., Reimer, B., Mehler, B.: Monitoring, managing, and motivating driver safety and well-being. IEEE Pervasive Comput. **10**(3), 14–21 (2011). https://doi.org/10.1109/MPRV.2011.54
13. Dula, C.S., Geller, E.: Risky, aggressive, or emotional driving: addressing the need for consistent communication in research. J. Saf. Res. **34**(5), 559–566 (2003). https://doi.org/10.1016/j.jsr.2003.03.004
14. Eyben, F., Wöllmer, M., Graves, A., Schuller, B., Douglas-Cowie, E., Cowie, R.: On-line emotion recognition in a 3-D activation-valence-time continuum using acoustic and linguistic cues. J. Multimodal User Interfaces **3**(1), 7–19 (2010). https://doi.org/10.1007/s12193-009-0032-6
15. Eyben, F., et al.: Emotion on the road—necessity, acceptance, and feasibility of affective computing in the car. Adv. Hum.-Comput. Interact. **2010** (2010). https://doi.org/10.1155/2010/263593
16. Fakhrhosseini, S.M., Landry, S., Tan, Y.Y., Bhattarai, S., Jeon, M.: If you're angry, turn the music on: music can mitigate anger effects on driving performance. In: Proceedings of the AutoUI 2014, pp. 18:1–18:7. ACM, New York (2014). https://doi.org/10.1145/2667317.2667410
17. Gable, T.M., Kun, A.L., Walker, B.N., Winton, R.J.: Comparing heart rate and pupil size as objective measures of workload in the driving context: initial look. In: Adjunct Proceedings of the AutoeUI 2015, pp. 20–25. ACM, New York (2015). https://doi.org/10.1145/2809730.2809745

18. Goffman, E.: The presentation of self. In: Brissett, D., Edgley, C. (eds.) A Dramaturgical Sourcebook: Life as Theater. Transaction Publishers, New Brunswick (2006)

19. Green, P.: Standard definitions for driving measures and statistics: overview and status of recommended practice j2944. In: Proceedings of the AutoUI 2013, pp. 184–191. ACM, New York (2013). https://doi.org/10.1145/2516540.2516542

20. Grimm, M., et al.: On the necessity and feasibility of detecting a driver's emotional state while driving. In: Paiva, A.C.R., Prada, R., Picard, R.W. (eds.) ACII 2007. LNCS, vol. 4738, pp. 126–138. Springer, Heidelberg (2007). https://doi.org/10.1007/978-3-540-74889-2_12

21. Groeger, J.A.: Understanding Driving: Applying Cognitive Psychology to a Complex Everyday Task. Psychology Press, New York (2000)

22. Harris, H., Nass, C.: Emotion regulation for frustrating driving contexts. In: Proceedings of the CHI 2011. ACM, New York (2011). https://doi.org/10.1145/1978942.1979050

23. Hassib, M., Pfeiffer, M., Schneegass, S., Rohs, M., Alt, F.: Emotion actuator: embodied emotional feedback through EEG and EMS. In: Proceedings of the CHI 2017, pp. 6133–6146. ACM, New York (2017). https://doi.org/10.1145/3025453.3025953

24. Healey, J.A., Picard, R.W.: Detecting stress during real-world driving tasks using physiological sensors. IEEE Transact. ITS 6(2), 156–166 (2005). https://doi.org/10.1109/TITS.2005.848368

25. Hernandez, J., McDuff, D., Benavides, X., Amores, J., Maes, P., Picard, R.: AutoEmotive: bringing empathy to the driving experience to manage stress. In: Proceedings of the DIS Companion 2014, pp. 53–56. ACM, New York (2014). https://doi.org/10.1145/2598784.2602780

26. Jahn, G., Oehme, A., Krems, J.F., Gelau, C.: Peripheral detection as a workload measure in driving: effects of traffic complexity and route guidance system use in a driving study. Trans. F 8(3) (2005). https://doi.org/10.1016/j.trf.2005.04.009

27. Jeon, M., Walker, B.N.: What to detect? Proc. Hum. Factors Ergon. Soc. Ann. Meet. 55(1), 1889–1893 (2011). https://doi.org/10.1177/1071181311551393

28. Ji, Q., Yang, X.: Real-time eye, gaze, and face pose tracking for monitoring driver vigilance. Real-Time Imaging 8(5), 357–377 (2002). https://doi.org/10.1006/rtim.2002.0279

29. Jones, C.M., Jonsson, I.M.: Automatic recognition of affective cues in the speech of car drivers to allow appropriate responses. In: Proceedings of the OZCHI 2005, pp. 1–10. CHISIG, Narrabundah, Australia (2005). https://doi.org/1108368.1108397

30. Katsis, C., Ntouvas, N., Bafas, C., Fotiadis, D.: Assessment of muscle fatigue during driving using surface EMG. In: Proceedings of the IASTED BioEng 2004, vol. 262 (2004)

31. Kim, S., Chun, J., Dey, A.K.: Sensors know when to interrupt you in the car: detecting driver interruptibility through monitoring of peripheral interactions. In: Proceedings of the CHI 2015, pp. 487–496. ACM, New York (2015). https://doi.org/10.1145/2702123.2702409

32. Koelstra, S., et al.: DEAP: a database for emotion analysis; using physiological signals. IEEE Trans. Affect. Comput. 3(1), 18–31 (2012). https://doi.org/10.1109/T-AFFC.2011.15

33. Laquai, F., Chowanetz, F., Rigoll, G.: A large-scale LED array to support anticipatory driving. In: Proceedings of the SMC 2011, pp. 2087–2092, October 2011. https://doi.org/10.1109/ICSMC.2011.6083980

34. Lin, C.T., Lin, K.L., Ko, L.W., Liang, S.F., Kuo, B.C., Chung, I.F.: Nonparametric single-trial EEG feature extraction and classification of driver's cognitive responses. EURASIP J. Adv. Signal Process. **2008**(1), 849040 (2008)
35. Löcken, A., Heuten, W., Boll, S.: Enlightening drivers: a survey on in-vehicle light displays. In: Proceedings of the AutoUI 2016, pp. 97–104. ACM, New York (2016). https://doi.org/10.1145/3003715.3005416
36. Löcken, A., Müller, H., Heuten, W., Boll, S.: "Should I stay or should I go?": different designs to support drivers' decision making. In: Proceedings of the NordiCHI 2014, pp. 1031–1034. ACM, New York (2014). https://doi.org/10.1145/2639189.2670268
37. Loehmann, S., Landau, M., Koerber, M., Butz, A.: Heartbeat: experience the pulse of an electric vehicle. In: Proceedings of the AutoUI 2014, pp. 19:1–19:10. ACM, New York (2014). https://doi.org/10.1145/2667317.2667331
38. Lopatovska, I., Arapakis, I.: Theories, methods and current research on emotions in library and information science, information retrieval and human-computer interaction. Inf. Process. Manage. **47**(4), 575–592 (2011). https://doi.org/10.1016/j.ipm.2010.09.001
39. Matthews, G., Dorn, L., Hoyes, T.W., Davies, D.R., Glendon, A.I., Taylor, R.G.: Driver stress and performance on a driving simulator. Hum. Factors **40**(1), 136–149 (1998). https://doi.org/10.1518/001872098779480569. PMID: 9579108
40. Miller, D., et al.: Distraction becomes engagement in automated driving. Proc. HFE Ann. Meet. **59**(1), 1676–1680 (2015). https://doi.org/10.1177/1541931215591362
41. Nass, C., et al.: Improving automotive safety by pairing driver emotion and car voice emotion. In: CHI 2005 EA, pp. 1973–1976. ACM, New York (2005). https://doi.org/10.1145/1056808.1057070
42. National Highway Traffic Safety Administration: Visual-manual NHTSA driver distraction guidelines for in-vehicle electronic devices. National Highway Traffic Safety Administration (NHTSA), Department of Transportation (DOT), Washington, DC (2012). https://www.nhtsa.gov/staticfiles/rulemaking/pdf/Distraction_NPFG-02162012.pdf
43. Neyens, D.M., Boyle, L.N.: The influence of driver distraction on the severity of injuries sustained by teenage drivers and their passengers. Accid. Anal. Prev. **40**(1), 254–259 (2008)
44. Picard, R.W.: Affective computing: challenges. Int. J. Hum.-Comput. Stud. **59**(1), 55–64 (2003). https://doi.org/10.1016/S1071-5819(03)00052-1. Applications of Affective Computing in Human-Computer Interaction
45. Picard, R.W., Healey, J.: Affective wearables. In: First International Symposium on Wearable Computers, Digest of Papers, pp. 90–97. IEEE (1997)
46. Rakauskas, M.E., Gugerty, L.J., Ward, N.J.: Effects of naturalistic cell phone conversations on driving performance. J. Saf. Res. **35**(4), 453–464 (2004). https://doi.org/10.1016/j.jsr.2004.06.003
47. Rebolledo-Mendez, G., Reyes, A., Paszkowicz, S., Domingo, M.C., Skrypchuk, L.: Developing a body sensor network to detect emotions during driving. IEEE Transact. ITS **15**(4), 1850–1854 (2014). https://doi.org/10.1109/TITS.2014.2335151
48. Riener, A., Ferscha, A.: Driver activity recognition from sitting postures. In: Mensch & Computer Workshopband, pp. 55–62 (2007)
49. Riener, A., Jeon, M., Alvarez, I., Frison, A.K.: Driver in the loop: best practices in automotive sensing and feedback mechanisms. In: Meixner, G., Müller, C. (eds.) Automotive User Interfaces. HIS, pp. 295–323. Springer, Cham (2017). https://doi.org/10.1007/978-3-319-49448-7_11

50. Roberts, S.C., Ghazizadeh, M., Lee, J.D.: Warn me now or inform me later: drivers' acceptance of real-time and post-drive distraction mitigation systems. Int. J. Hum. Comput. Stud. **70**(12), 967–979 (2012). https://doi.org/10.1016/j.ijhcs.2012.08.002

51. Rösler, D., Krems, J.F., Mahlke, S., Thüring, M., Seifert, K.: Evaluation of night vision enhancement systems: driver needs and acceptance. Fahrerass.-syst. (2006)

52. Russell, J.: A circumplex model of affect. J. Pers. Soc. Psychol. **39**(6), 1161–1178 (1980)

53. Schmidt, E., Decke, R., Rasshofer, R.H.: Correlation between subjective driver state measures and psychophysiological and vehicular data in simulated driving. In: IEEE IV 2016, pp. 1380–1385 (2016). https://doi.org/10.1109/IVS.2016.7535570

54. Schneegass, S., Pfleging, B., Broy, N., Heinrich, F., Schmidt, A.: A data set of real world driving to assess driver workload. In: Proceedings of the AutoUI 2013, pp. 150–157. ACM, New York (2013). https://doi.org/10.1145/2516540.2516561

55. Singh, R.R., Conjeti, S., Banerjee, R.: A comparative evaluation of neural network classifiers for stress level analysis of automotive drivers using physiological signals. Biomed. Signal Process. Control **8**(6), 740–754 (2013). https://doi.org/10.1016/j.bspc.2013.06.014

56. Solovey, E.T., Zec, M., Garcia Perez, E.A., Reimer, B., Mehler, B.: Classifying driver workload using physiological and driving performance data: two field studies. In: Proceedings of the CHI 2014, pp. 4057–4066. ACM, New York (2014). https://doi.org/10.1145/2556288.2557068

57. Tan, D., Nijholt, A.: Brain-computer interfaces and human-computer interaction. In: Tan, D., Nijholt, A. (eds.) Brain-Computer Interfaces. HCIS, pp. 3–19. Springer, London (2010). https://doi.org/10.1007/978-1-84996-272-8_1

58. Verster, J.C., Roth, T.: Standard operation procedures for conducting the on-the-road driving test, and measurement of the standard deviation of lateral position (SDLP). Int. J. Gen. Med. 359 (2011). https://doi.org/10.2147/ijgm.s19639

59. Vhaduri, S., Ali, A., Sharmin, M., Hovsepian, K., Kumar, S.: Estimating drivers' stress from GPS traces. In: Proceedings of the AutoUI 2014, pp. 20:1–20:8. ACM, New York (2014). https://doi.org/10.1145/2667317.2667335

60. Waard, D.D., Jesserun, M., Steyvers, F.J.J.M., Regatt, P.T., Brookhuis, K.A.: Effect of road layout and road environment on driving performance, drivers' physiology and road appreciation. Ergonomics **38**(7), 1395–1407 (1995). https://doi.org/10.1080/00140139508925197. PMID: 7635129

61. Wells-Parker, E., et al.: An exploratory study of the relationship between road rage and crash experience in a representative sample of us drivers. AAP **34**(3) (2002). https://doi.org/10.1016/S0001-4575(01)00021-5

62. Yang, J.H., Jeong, H.B.: Validity analysis of vehicle and physiological data for detecting driver drowsiness, distraction, and workload. In: Proceedings of the SMC 2015, pp. 1238–1243, October 2015. https://doi.org/10.1109/SMC.2015.221

63. Yerkes, R.M., Dodson, J.D.: The relation of strength of stimulus to rapidity of habit-formation. J. Comp. Neurol. Psychol. **18**(5), 459–482 (1908). https://doi.org/10.1002/cne.920180503

64. Zheng, W.L., Zhu, J.Y., Lu, B.L.: Identifying stable patterns over time for emotion recognition from EEG. IEEE Trans. Affect. Comput. **PP**(99), 1 (2017). https://doi.org/10.1109/TAFFC.2017.2712143

65. Zhu, Y., Wang, Y., Li, G., Guo, X.: Recognizing and releasing drivers' negative emotions by using music: evidence from driver anger. In: Adjunct Proceedings of the AutoUI 2016, pp. 173–178. ACM, New York (2016). https://doi.org/10.1145/3004323.3004344

Evaluating Mixed Reality Notifications to Support Excavator Operator Awareness

Markus Wallmyr[1,2(✉)], Taufik Akbar Sitompul[1,2], Tobias Holstein[1,3], and Rikard Lindell[1]

[1] School of Innovation, Design and Engineering, Mälardalen University, Västerås, Sweden
markus.wallmyr@gmail.com, {taufik.akbar.sitompul, tobias.holstein, rikard.lindell}@mdh.se
[2] Department of Product Management, CrossControl AB, Västerås, Sweden
[3] Hochschule Darmstadt, Darmstadt, Germany

Abstract. Operating heavy vehicles, for instance an excavator, requires a high level of attention to the operation done using the vehicle and awareness of the surroundings. Digital transformation in heavy vehicles aims to improve productivity and user experience, but it can also increase the operators mental load because of a higher demand of attention to instrumentation and controls, subsequently leading to reduced situation awareness. One way to mitigate this, is to display information within the operators' field of view, which enhances information detectability through quick glances, using mixed reality interfaces. This work explores two types of mixed reality visualizations and compares them to a traditional display setup in a simulated excavator environment. We have utilized eye-tracking glasses to study users' attention to the task, surrounding awareness, and interfaces, followed by a NASA-RTLX questionnaire to evaluate the users' reported mental workload. The results indicate benefits for the mixed reality approaches, with lower workload ratings together with an improved rate in detection of presented information.

Keywords: Mixed reality · Human-vehicle interaction ·
Situational awareness · Head-up display · Excavator · Heavy-vehicles

1 Introduction

Many industrial sectors, such as agriculture, construction, material handling, forestry, mining, and transportation, rely on mobile machines to support their work, which generally referred to as heavy vehicles. Operating these vehicles can be a complex and demanding task. The operator may be required to drive the vehicle while performing a task that requires additional attention and control, for example lifting an object. Completing the task can also require a high level of precision and be performed in co-operation with other workers, where un-safe operation causes unnecessary risk to the health of nearby people. To assist the operator, modern heavy vehicles are increasingly being equipped with information systems and assistive systems, where the interaction is done via a visual user interface. A result of this transformation is that many heavy

© IFIP International Federation for Information Processing 2019
Published by Springer Nature Switzerland AG 2019
D. Lamas et al. (Eds.): INTERACT 2019, LNCS 11746, pp. 743–762, 2019.
https://doi.org/10.1007/978-3-030-29381-9_44

vehicles are now equipped with multiple displays inside the cabin, including displays from both the original manufacturer and third-party equipment suppliers. It is not uncommon for an operator to have more than five displays: one main instrument cluster, one secondary vehicle display, a navigation system display, one or more displays for add-on equipment, and finally, one or two camera monitors. With more and more information displayed visually to the operator, the cognitive load on the operator is becoming untenable leading to increased mental fatigue. The current state of affairs prompted Sanches et al. [1] to state that "the need for research that informs the design of effective, intuitive, and efficient displays is a pressing one".

Moreover, operators often spend a large portion of their working days operating the machine and they are required to be both efficient and safe while carrying out their tasks. Reports of past accidents show that the human factor has a big impact on accidents. For example, a recent study on earth moving equipment show that 46% of the cases involved misjudgment of the hazardous situation by the operator [2]. In addition, an analysis of wheel loader accidents shows that incidents where mining and non-mining personnel were hit, struck or run over by the wheel loader are the most common wheel loader-related accident, which represent 41% of the total fatalities [3]. Assisting operators' awareness could thus help improve the safety and wellbeing of operators, surrounding workers, and pedestrians.

While the intent of an increase in-vehicle information systems is to aid the operators performing their tasks and allow them to be more informed about the operation, one possible drawback of these additions is that the operators will spend more time focusing on displays and digital information, resulting in reduced attention to the surrounding environment and potentially leading to an increase of hazardous situations [4]. Alternatively, the operators might miss vital information that is displayed, either due to a high mental workload or that the information is presented outside of their main field of view [5]. These drawbacks could result in a lack of situational awareness [6], when the operator is missing critical elements needed for a full comprehension of what is happening and anticipation of what will happen. A lack of situation awareness has been listed as one of the bigger causes of accidents in safety-critical situations [7]. Studies on how to support operators' awareness show that safety-enhancing systems, for example collision avoidance systems, can assist operators while carrying out their tasks [8, 9]. However, having to look away in order to obtain the information can result in an increased risk of incidents. A notable example of this situation is the Llanbadarn Automatic Barrier incident report, where a train passed a crossing with the bars raised. The immediate cause of this incident was that the operator of the train was occupied with the machine interface and therefore failed to check the crossing indicator [4].

One way to improve the operator's situation awareness is to study various approaches in which the information can be communicated more naturally integrated into their normal workflow. For example using mixed reality interaction technologies such as head-up displays where information can be presented within the operator's line-of-sight through the windscreen [10, 11]. This might help the operator to effectively detect and obtain the presented information, thus potentially reducing the risk of missing any vital information. Another approach is to use other senses, but these senses are also already in use in this context. For audio, there are existing audio alerts, the communication between co-workers, and noise pollution from machines and the surrounding area. Some operators that we interviewed also describe how they use hearing already, for example through the different sounds that an excavator's bucket makes when touching various materials. This audible feedback can reveal if the operator is digging gravel, hitting a rock, or colliding with a buried pipe. The tactile channel is also affected by existing vibrations from the engine and hydraulics of a heavy vehicle and through the movement in the terrain during groundworks. Moreover, there are prior studies [12–14] that indicate a strong user preference for the visual channel, compared to other senses, which can then be used to improve performance further.

In this paper, we evaluate how visual cues deployed through mixed reality displays might affect information processing and situational awareness of heavy vehicles' operators. More specifically, by comparing the performance of test subjects using a traditional head down display against two types of mixed reality interfaces when displaying navigational information, as well as warning messages for obstacles in an excavator, which is a common type of heavy vehicle. The excavator is a versatile machine that can be used for many purposes, such as digging, material handling, demolition and groundworks. Operating an excavator puts a significant mental workload on the operator [15]. While performing the tasks at hand, the operator controls the boom and the attachment along all 3 axes, often with high accuracy requirements. Additionally, the operators also have to pay attention to their immediate surroundings, in order to prevent accidents involving people or objects.

The paper will first cover related work, followed by an overview and explanation of the visual information presented to the operator. It will then present how the user evaluation in a simulated environment was performed, followed by its results, including both quantitative and qualitative findings. After a summarizing discussion on the results we wrap up this paper with limitations of the study and outlines for future work, as well as the conclusion.

2   Related Work

Research on the use of mixed reality displays to aid users with their task completion stems as long back as the 1940s, where head-up displays were used to aid pilots of military aircraft and has since been explored in many domains [16, 17]. Mixed reality displays have also shown potential in the automotive vehicle sector for their possibilities to increase safety and aid user experience [18–20], to reduce workload and increase driver comfort [21]. For example, a head-up display speedometer produces improved performance and shortened response time to hazardous situations [22] as well as better speed control [11].

While the vast body of work around mixed reality displays for vehicles is related to on-road vehicles, there is also a potential use for heavy vehicles [23]. One related application area, that has been both researched in academia and used in industry, is the use of virtual and augmented reality for operator training and simulation. These studies suggest that VR and AR-based training can improve the quality of training for becoming operators [24, 25].

One example of evaluation in heavy vehicles, is in the forest harvester, where Englund et al. [26] investigated the result of moving the graphical interface from a traditional display to a head-up display. They found that the operators were positive about seeing system information closer to the area of operation. This work was however limited to a productivity perspective, where production data that was normally presented on a head-down display was moved to a head-up display.

Using mixed reality displays has also shown potential to improve the ergonomic situation, both in terms of comfort and fatigue [27]. This is an area of note, as one of the major reasons for work-related injuries in heavy vehicles, is awkward postures of the operators [28]. Furthermore, Akyeampong et al. [15] evaluated two different interface designs to improve usability and ergonomics while controlling an excavator. Their design was based on an augmented interaction style and their setup used a Virtual Reality (VR) simulation using VR headsets for visualization. They concluded that "the major strength in both HMIs designs was the heads-up display concept".

Taking prior research into account, there is still work needed to be done to understand how mixed reality displays and augmented interaction can be used in heavy vehicles, both in terms of the implementation of the technology and interaction design. For example, on the use of mixed reality displays to improve excavator operators comfort and safe operation, by presenting warnings and navigational cues closer to the operators line of sight.

3   Conceptualization

Heavy vehicles generally have a cabin with large windscreens to enable the operator to view the surroundings around the machine (see examples in Fig. 1). This is important for both the general operation, as well as to be able to see obstacles and hazards around the machine. Moreover, displays in the cabin are normally placed quite low, as to not obstruct the operator's field of view. This low placement puts the displays outside the operators' area of attention with the apparent risk of the operators missing key

Fig. 1. To the left, a cabin with large windscreens for good visibility. To the right, an example of a cabin with four displays covering the windscreen, including one display which is not visible.

information. The size of the display is often limited due to space or cost, thus restricting the amount of information that can be comfortably displayed and reducing the size of presented information. Modern vehicle displays commonly range from 3 to 15-in. displays, with some niche examples of both smaller and larger displays. With more information being presented, additional screens might be needed to fit the new data. Due to space limitations, these displays might be placed more in-line-of-sight. However, this placement causes additional drawbacks, since the displays are now hindering the operator's ability to monitor the surrounding area. We asked ourselves, what if we could use the windscreen as the display to keep the operator notified in terms of navigation and the presence of potential obstacles, without obscuring visibility of the surrounding area.

3.1 Using the Simulator to Create Situations for Ideations

The approach of this experiment was to perform the evaluation in a simulated scenario to understand how the information that is presented within line of sight of the operator would be used. Prior observations in the simulator have shown difficulties in obstacle detection and difficulties to know the position of the bucket in relation to other objects. We thus sought to support the operator to be aware of obstacles while progressing through the track, as well as to support the navigation of the excavator and its boom. For further insights, we drove the excavator through the simulation to detect challenging areas, as well as recording them through screenshots. Examples of the

Fig. 2. Example of pencil sketches of navigational support as well as warning notification for the operators.

challenges are the course presented included tight paths where the user will be close to obstacles, as well as human avatars positioned where the machine structure hindered visibility. We then used these screenshots as the base for sketching. This enabled us to ideate based on the environment in which the users were operating.

From these screenshots, several designs were made and discussed internally. Figure 2 shows some examples of the sketches that we made, where the upper figures show images of how to provide graphical aid to help the operator to navigate. The lower images show examples pictographic icons for obstacle notifications.

3.2   Operator Support and Virtual Scenario

A visual warning system was designed based on the sketches. The aim was to aid the user to perform the assigned task in the track as well as to support the user in detecting hazards. This system consisted of simple graphical figures shown on a display. The selected design of the symbols aimed to be naturally recognizable by the user, by using familiar polygonal shapes resembling traffic signs, see Fig. 3. Whether this assumption was successful in this context is however not verified, as the aim of the study was to evaluate the different placement of information rather than the information design as such.

Fig. 3. The notification symbols used to notify the operator in the simulated environment. From left: human warning (shown with stop or warning), stop, warning, navigation direction.

When an obstacle was close to the excavator, a warning triangle was shown together with a numeric value indicating the distance to the obstacle. When the excavator was in imminent danger to collide with an object, a hexagon-shaped stop sign was shown in place of the warning icon. When an avatar, representing a virtual human, was close to the excavator, an additional circular warning sign was shown besides the other warnings. The user was free to look around and operate the machine within the open 3D environment. For direction guidance there was an arrow, pointing from the excavator's bucket towards the next pillar in the scenario, similar to the arrow icon commonly used in automotive and mobile navigation systems.

Figure 4 shows a schematic illustration of the scenario used. The purpose was to represent a varied set of operator challenges, as will be further described in the qualitative results. The path was made with inspiration from field observations, for example where an operator had to move through a narrow passage, as well as to be guided in a precision bucket operation task. We selected to not involve a digging task, as this would have resulted in a static scenario with machine rotations. The main task in the scenario was to demolish three pillars, comprised of stacked cubes placed on top of each other and located to the side of the machines proscribed path. The first pillar was placed in the beginning of the track and the two last pillars at the end of the track. The pillars were of different heights and their top two cubes were colored orange. The user was supposed to use the excavator's bucket to tip the pillars by knocking the orange cubes placed on their top. Getting to the pillar, the user had to navigate along a track with some narrow passages restricted by cones, a pile of sand with a curved path, and other vehicles in the area. Also, there were two human avatars along the track, one standing next to the path and another one constantly walking back and forth over the path.

The purpose of the creation of this scenario was to provide the user with several observable challenges and to force the user's attention into several different fields of focus. To complete the task successfully, the user needed to remain aware of the surrounding area and monitor several directions, such as the path forward, the ground surrounding the machine and the rotation of the excavator track, the bucket, as well as looking up when approaching the pillars.

Fig. 4. Left: A bird view of the virtual scenario.

4 Evaluation

To evaluate the use of mixed reality displays for presenting information and the use of symbolic notifications during operation, a study was performed with fifteen users. In this study the users completed a scenario with the help of the visual support system, using two types of mixed reality displays, as well as a reference in the form of a head-down display that represents the traditional monitor used in today's excavator cabins. Each of them displayed the same kind of information, which are the directional arrow and the obstacle detection presented above.

One of the mixed reality displays was a head-up display, in the form of a physical representation of a head-up display in the cabin's windscreen. The other mixed reality display was a projected display inside the virtual world, placed further away in front of the excavator. The head-down display was also placed on the operators' side, similar to the actual placement in existing cabins. The mixed reality displays are subsequently more in line of sight, while the head-down display requires the user to look away from the primary working area to look at what is presented on the display.

4.1 Simulator Overview

The simulation was performed in a CAVE-like room. When compared to full-scale industrial vehicle simulators, it offers a cost-effective solution that can be easily reconfigured for prototyping. It has also been evaluated in favor of a traditional monitor-based simulation because the user can look around and is immersed within the virtual world [29]. Compared to VR-based simulations, it also enables the mixing of real and virtual content to test various forms of user interfaces.

The user sits on a chair, whose left armrest is equipped with a head-down display and a keyboard to control the excavator's movement. The excavator's boom and bucket were controlled using a traditional joystick interface, placed on the user's right armrest. In front of the user there was a prototype head-up display made by using a transparent film, acting as a combiner, attached to a metal frame (0.6 × 0.9 m). The image created was full color and was generated from a projector, placed directly under the display. The virtual world was projected by a head-worn laser projector onto the reflective wall material, giving a wide field of view of 83,6° × 47,5°. This creates an undistorted image, centered in front of where the user was looking.

Fig. 5. To the left, a schematic picture of the CAVE simulation room and its primary components. To the right, a photo that shows all three display solutions at once (the simulation only showed one at a time).

The mix of different sources of image generation and traditional displays deployed in this particular setup works in this arrangement due to the specific combination of projectors and reflective materials. The image on the head-up display was designed to be clearly visible and achieved due to the bright projector, rated at 1200 lumens. The head-worn projector, with a value of just 15 lumens, emits a light level low enough not to create interference with the head-up display, even when faced directly. But its image was still clearly visible on the highly reflective material used for the CAVE walls.

The virtual environment and all visualizations are modeled and run using Unity [30], where a mobile phone attached to the head-worn projector hosts the virtual world. The head-down display computer hosts the visualization for the head-up display and the head-down display. Figure 5 shows all the displays together, including the virtual content projected on the CAVE wall.

4.2 Interacting in the Simulation

The excavator simulator allows the user to drive a virtual excavator and operate its boom and bucket. The body of the excavator is rotated through the joystick's horizontal axis. The lower excavator's boom is moved up and down through the joystick's vertical axis, while the upper boom is extended and retracted by twisting or turning the joystick around the Z axis. Finally, two buttons on the top of the joystick control the bucket movement of the excavator. The user can drive the excavator by pressing the keys on the numerical keyboard. One can argue that a keyboard is not a natural interaction device in an excavator, but the use of a keyboard made it natural and easy to understand the navigation of the excavator, especially for those who have experienced computer gaming. Performing the evaluation with professional drivers would probably have benefited from a joystick also for navigation of the excavator.

4.3 Additional Evaluation Apparatus

The user was recorded both using a side video camera and an eye-tracker. The digital video camera was placed facing the user within the simulator to obtain verbal comments as well as reactions while performing the scenario. The eye-tracking equipment was based on a pair of eye-tracking glasses from Pupil labs [31, 32], giving a recording of where the user is looking while performing the evaluation.

The equipment was calibrated for each user, using the software on-screen display calibration, before starting each test run. The accuracy of the gaze tracking is $0,6°$ and the gaze precision is $0,08°$. The quality was adequate for detecting what part of the environment, or display, that the user is paying attention to. A more detailed study on exact areas of attention would require a more exact calibration.

Each user was also asked to fill in a NASA Raw Task Load Index (NASA-RTLX) form after completing the evaluation [33].

4.4 Users

The evaluations were conducted with fifteen users based on the guideline that already 10–12 users would suffice to provide a significant result [34]. Twelve of the participants were male and three were female. The eye-tracking result from three users had to be left out, due to the inability to capture their eye gazes. For the remaining users, two users had prior experiences of operating a real excavator, seven users had prior experiences of industrial vehicles or industrial simulators, and six users had prior experiences of a virtual reality headset or head-worn projection systems. The age distribution was defined in intervals, with no one under 25, eight users reported an age between 26–35 years, and four users being 35 or older.

4.5 Method

Before the tests started, users were informed about the purpose of the study and introduced to the equipment, the controls, as well as the task to perform in the scenario. The users were evaluated one at a time. Each user was first equipped with the head-worn projection system as well as the eye-tracking equipment. The eye-tracking equipment was calibrated using the on-screen based calibration in the software. The recordings were started after the user was informed about the purpose of the recordings, how we would use them, and that they had given informed consent for participating in the experiment. Each user was also informed that he or she could discontinue the study at any time.

The user was then asked to complete the given scenario. When the scenario was completed, it was restarted, and the user was asked to do it with the next type of displays. Thus, each user performed the scenario for each of the display types. The order was randomized to avoid familiarity bias. Completing all three runs in the scenario took around 15 min, with some minor variation between each of the participants. Each run was generally completed faster than the user's prior run.

After completion of the test runs, the users were asked to fill a questionnaire to document their experiences with the prototype. The questionnaire was divided into two sections. The first part contains general questions about age and earlier experiences. This was followed by a NASA-RTLX questionnaire [33], which is used to rate the workload differences between the type of displays [35].

After finishing the evaluation, two approaches were applied to the results: collecting quantitative results and seeking for qualitative findings. The questionnaires were compiled into a spread sheet and the eye-tracking videos were manually examined where all gazes at the different displays were recorded, including information in which section of the track they occurred. From this data box plots were generated, as presented in the result's section. ANOVA evaluations were also performed, from where the significant results are presented. When visible in the recording, the occasions whether the presented information was overlooked, were also listed. Additionally, other observations detected during the eye-tracking review, i.e. the first-person perspective of the user evaluations, were also noted and compiled together. Finally, the verbal comments by the users were transcribed into text.

5 Results

The following section presents the quantitatively measured results followed by more qualitative findings. As a baseline, the two mixed reality displays are compared to the head-down display and we will later look at the differences between each version of the mixed reality displays.

5.1 Quantitative Results Evaluation

The NASA Raw Task Load Index (NASA-RTLX) evaluation was used to get a measurement of the workload related to the different display types [36]. NASA-RTLX is a version of NASA-TLX that is simpler to fill in by the participants, while still providing similar quality of result [35, 37]. The pen-and-paper version of the questionnaire was used [33] and the questions were filled in for each set-up after all 3 test runs were completed. The NASA-RTLX consists of six workload categories: mental demand, physical demand, temporal demand, performance, effort, and frustration level. Each score is rated subjectively by the user on a 20-step scale (-10 to $+10$). The overall score for each type of displays was obtained by dividing the sum of the workload scores by seven, presented in Fig. 6.

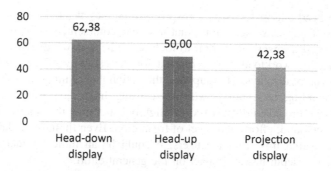

Fig. 6. Overall NASA-RTLX workload ratings for each display type.

The results show that the users rated the head-down display, placed at the left side of the armrest, with a higher workload rating than both mixed reality displays. An Annova test between the head-down display and each of the mixed reality displays shows a sigificant difference between the head-down display and the projection display $(F(1,24) = 6,545, p = 0,017)$.

Looking at the sub-scale categories, mental demand, physical demand, effort, and frustration show the largest differences, which are presented as average values with standard deviations in parentheses in Table 1, as well as box plots in Fig. 7. It can be seen that the mixed reality displays showed better results in all categories when compared directly with the head-down display, with a statisticaly significant difference between the head-down display and the projection display specifically for physical demand $(F(1,24) = 4,747, p = 0,039)$, effort $(F(1,24) = 8,653, p = 0,007)$, and frustration $(F(1,24) = 5,061, p = 0,034)$. The largest difference in the workload categories was for the physical demand, where the head-down display scored twice as high as both mixed reality displays. This result is probably due to the user being required to

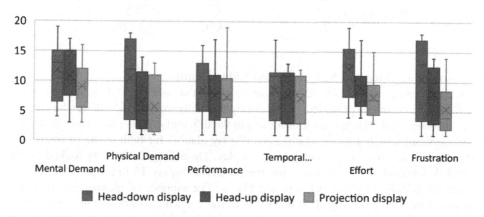

Fig. 7. NASA-RTLX subscale result for each type of displays represented with box plots. X represents the mean and the median is marked with a line separating the 2nd and 3rd quartile. The whiskers mark the largest or smallest data item not being an outlier.

move his/her head and re-focus the eyes every time they wanted to look at the head-down display. This is also something that has been commented by some of the users, where they stated a lower motivation to look at the head-down display.

The subjective workload scored highest for the category of mental demand and effort for all type of displays. This supports the notion that running the excavator was a mentally demanding task, but it was not causing frustration to the same degree. Additionally, the projected display scored slightly better than the head-up display with lower mental demand, effort, and level of frustration. Even though we did not get any comments regarding this from the users, it could be an indicator that the effort of moving the focal depth has an impact on the general effort.

In conclusion, the NASA-RTLX ratings indicate that mixed reality displays could be favourable for both information assimiliation and for the operator's physical well-being, but only the projection display showed a statistically significant difference. A larger and more diverse sample set would be beneficial for firm conclusions, as is also related to in the future work section.

Table 1. NASA-RTLX's average scores per category with standard deviation in parentheses.

Subscale	Head-down display	Head-up display	Projected display
Effort	12,2 (4,6)	9,00 (3,8)	7,5 (3,5)
Frustration	10,5 (6,8)	8,0 (5,0)	5,5 (4,4)
Mental demand	12,6 (4,4)	10,9 (4,4)	9,1 (4,1)
Performance	8,6 (4,5)	7,8 (4,8)	7,4 (4,9)
Physical demand	9,4 (6,7)	6,5 (4,9)	5,8 (4,6)
Temporal demand	8,7 (5,4)	7,9 (4,7)	7,2 (4,2)

Eye-tracking Data and Side Recorded Video Results

Each recording was analyzed to observe when the user looked at the presented information on the display. This was done by manually logging the glances for each of the displays used. While each user looked at the different displays to a varying degree, all users had a higher count of observed display glances for both of the mixed reality displays, in relation to the head-down display. On average, the users looked at the head-down display six times per run, the projected display 13 times per run, and the head-up display 12 times per run, see Fig. 8. The number of glances points to the assistive information being observed and used more when the information was closer to the users' line of sight. Taking away the outlier data from the sample set we get an ANOVA set of results between the head-down display and the head-up display at $(F(1,18) = 8,880, p = 0,008)$ and the projection display at $(F(1,18) = 16,419, p = 0,001)$.

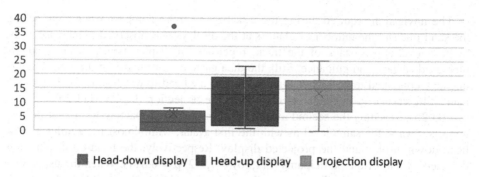

Fig. 8. The amount of display glances for each evaluated display type. The points outside the whiskers are considered as outliers.

Studying the different sections of the track shows a different usage for each display type, depending on the type of situation, seen in Fig. 9 and Table 2. The first part, when the user tips the first pile, highlights an example of how the users generally used the supportive system; when unsure of what to do and when in need of additional information to be able to proceed. Here one user had issues in the beginning and thus used the display a lot more than the other users.

The next measured sequence was the avatar standing partly hidden next to the excavator path. The average gaze results show a higher detection rate of its warning symbol and its presence for the mixed reality displays, but not a significant difference according to the ANOVA analysis. The next measure shows the rest of the gazes detected while passing through the alley, where the ANOVA analysis of the data shows a significant deviation value for the projection display ($F(1,20) = 4,377$, $p = 0,049$) (Fig. 9) (Table 2).

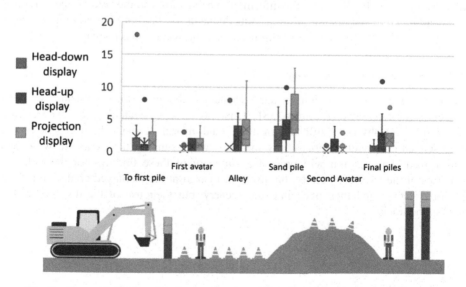

Fig. 9. Summed display glances for all users, divided in different parts of the track.

The navigation required during the task became more complex when approaching the sand pile and the number of glances at the displays was observed to increase to the highest level at any stage of the track, regardless of display types, as users sought increased support and guidance. Still, the data gathered for the use of the mixed reality displays continued to be higher than the use of the head-down display, with a significant difference in a higher level of use for the projection display ($F(1,20) = 5,880$, $p = 0,025$). Reaching the second avatar, the users were not reacting to the notification being shown in the same level as with the first avatar, with almost no readings on the head-down display and the projected display. Respectively, the head-up display was detected by half of the participants ($F(1,20) = 7,912$, $p = 0,011$). When the users were trying to tip the last two pillars to complete the assigned task, they had to look upwards towards the top of the pile.

Table 2. Average glances for the different display types.

	First pile	First avatar	Alley	Sand Pile	Second avatar	Final piles
Head-down display	2,3 (5,4)	0,4 (0,9)	0,7 (2,4)	2,1 (2,7)	0,1 (0,3)	0,5 (0,8)
Head-up display	1,2 (2,4)	0,7 (0,9)	2,1 (2,2)	4,0 (3)	1,2 (1,3)	2,6 (3,3)
Projection display	1,3 (1,8)	1,0 (1,3)	3,5 (3,6)	5,5 (3,8)	0,4 (0,9)	1,9 (2)

Here both versions of the mixed reality displays show more use over the head down display, with ANOVA analysis for the head-up display being ($F(1,20) = 4,246$, $p = 0,052$) and ($F(1,20) = 4,482$, $p = 0,047$) for the projection display. This high discrepancy is probably due to the information being closer to the area of operation and the head-down display being quite far outside the users' field of view forcing the users to significantly alter their head position to view the head-down display.

5.2   Qualitative Observations

To complement the quantitative data, especially the gaze measurements, we also searched for qualitative findings [38]. This was done by watching the eye-tracking recordings and observing information that could inform us about the user's behavior. The spoken comments expressed by the users while running the excavator were also transcribed. This section will present a summary of these findings for the different sections of the track. Generally, the users just gazed at the displayed content for short periods of time and then back into the scenery, but their use of the displays varied across the track.

First Part, Tipping the First Pillar

In the initial phase, the user mainly got acquainted with the current display type. The users could also navigate to the first pillar quite easily, without any obstacles in their path. As noted in the data above, a user drove past the first pillar and was able to see this in the navigation display.

Past the First Avatar and Through the Alley

After tipping the first pillar, many users glanced at the arrow and from there started to drive in the designated direction. They then drove to the narrowing alley of cones. In the beginning of this alley, they passed the first avatar, which was on the right side of the machine and as such in a blind spot behind the excavator's arm.

At the same time, the natural focus of the user was straight ahead, where he/she was going to go to a path between an alley of cones to get towards the next objective. As such, the user was mostly looking at the ground or straight ahead. It seemed that the head-up display and the projected display made it easier for the user to give the display a glance to see whether any warnings were present. Still, some users did not react to the avatar warning symbols, nor the warning of close obstacles. The users that reacted often rechecked the warnings, for example to see if the human warning was still active.

The Sand Pile

Following the alley section of the track, the users approached the sand pile. Here the user was supposed to go up and down the path, a passage that also required a bit of machine rotation. This was a more difficult passage to navigate and the users switched from being mostly reactive to the displayed content, to also actively searching for more visual support. The use between the head-up display and the projected display also differed at this stage. The head-up display was mainly used to check the direction of the arrow, while the projected display got the most glances for the warning and stop symbols. One possible reason for this is that the projected display was presented slightly lower and thus appeared to be on the ground, where the user was looking when driving the excavator.

The second avatar

Coming to the end of the sand pile, the user had to pass another avatar, this time walking back and forth over the track, to reduce the effect of the user knowing where the avatar was and thus neglecting it. However, even though the avatar was moving, there are almost no readings on the head-down display and the projected display, as the attention was already drawn more upwards, towards the final pillars. The head-up display is practically the only display where the human warning is detected. Possibly due to the head-up display being placed a bit more straight ahead in the line of sight for the user, and thus more visible.

The Last Set of Box Piles

The user was now approaching the end of the path. At this stage, the user was about to move into the designated place and also working with the bucket of the excavator at an extended height. At this stage, the usage seems to rely more on an individual operation style chosen by the user. Some users used the display support and did it for several display types, while other users simply focused at tipping the piles, without using the displays for visual support.

Operating the vehicle and performing the task was a demanding assignment. Not only did the user have to drive the excavator on the simulation track, the user also had to operate its boom to perform the tasks. This required a certain level of control and some users expressed this by deeply exhaling after finishing the course. Some users also commented that "it's not easy. Very tiring also!". Still, everyone seemed to enjoy the experience, with users giving comments like "The experience was great. I was engaged in the test simulation as it is my role to drive the excavator".

6   Discussion

The user observation and the quantitative data together show that the user benefited from the mixed reality displays while operating the vehicle, both in terms of lower effort and increased glances to the presented content. This result shows a coherence between heavy vehicles and related domains such as the automotive domain, where the use of head up displays shows better detection performance and faster reaction time [22, 39, 40]. It also aligns with other studies showing information more in line of sight can increase both the safety and experience of the vehicle operator [19], as well as lower mental load in the task operation [15].

Moreover, moving the information into the line of sight did not result in it being always detected. The general pattern of use was instead that the information intake was dependent on the need for support as well as the current workload. For example, the first part of the track was relatively simple to complete and during that part the users were more reactive to items popping up on both types of the mixed reality displays, while the head-down display messages were only detected by a few users. When they approached the more complicated part of the rack, i.e. the sand pile, they had to observe the surroundings around the machine more. At this stage, they also used the displays differently. Some users consciously monitored the display as they progressed. Other users checked it more in the process of their eyes scanning the surroundings and checking the display as their eyes naturally passed it. In this situation, they were more prone to miss key warnings. However, having the information presented within the line of sight aided for both taking glances while passing the display, as well as detecting and reacting to information.

The head-down display got some criticism for being out of sight for the users and that they were less motivated to use it. The users also reported higher physical demands (see Fig. 7), which align with simulated evaluations of operators' posture in excavators, that shows higher discomfort when having too look down rather looking at a head-up display [27]. One user also expressed that the projected display was preferred over the head-up display, for example, "for me the first one (the projected display) was more, what do we say, user friendly". This was followed by the comment that "I could recognize the things, objects near to me and how I should go. But in the next one (the head-down display) I was just confused. I couldn't recognize, I couldn't concentrate where should I look." One hypothesis for this is that the information is presented in between modalities in the head-up display, for example, not directly connected to the virtual environment and not on a specific surface. This might appear more confusing for the users than the projected display, where the information is more incorporated in the visual field. Some users also noted that the projected display looked like it was projected on the ground in front of the machine, a type of visual approach that has been investigated in the automotive domain for augmented navigation [20, 41].

Prior studies on the use of mixed reality show higher performance and reduced effort for processing the presented information [15, 42]. However, what is interesting is that our test subjects used the task-assistive information (the arrow that guides the boom) to a rather low degree. From early evaluations, we had noticed that the users had difficulties finding the correct depth between the bucket and the object. The arrow was thus designed to show the direction between the excavator's bucket and the top of the pillars. Even though we informed the users about this functionality, none of the users used the arrow for detailed bucket operation. Instead, the users were focusing on the task at hand and not paying attention to other things that were happening. This would be interesting to further evaluate, for example, if there is a difference between task information that is really needed by operator to perform the work and information that is more assistive.

In summary, we conclude that the results of the data analysis of this experiment point towards a recommendation of moving critical information into the operators' field of view. This information does not seem to create additional effort to the user, instead, our test subjects preferred the head-up displays and it improved information intake under complicated situations. Given the benefits observed of the projection display used in this experiment, we would also recommend the use of displays that can provide an extended focal depth, as it shows more significant results in reduced effort and physical demand on the user. We would however recommend further evaluations to involve a larger sample size to confirm these indications.

7   Limitations and Further Work

This study has used a rapid prototyping environment and a simplistic user interface, which is meant to evaluate the potential for mixed reality displays in heavy vehicles. Further evaluation of its potential benefits would gain from a higher fidelity simulation and a larger number of users, with different diversity and practical real-life experience of operating excavators.

The symbolic language itself can also be refined and evaluated, including additional types of information. The use of more human senses, for example, audio cues together with visual presentation, could further enhance detection and intake of vital information.

8   Conclusion

Advancements in digital transformation for industrial vehicles enable improved productivity, comfort, and safety. A well-designed interaction is vital to fully exploit this, and to avoid information loss and ergonomic strain. Furthermore, the design needs to avoid unsafe situations resulting from operators' decreased situation awareness because of their attention may be drawn from their task, or missing supportive information from the vehicle system. We have investigated and proposed the use of transparent interfaces based on mixed reality as an approach to facilitate the display of key information to the operators. To improve detectability, our designs display information close to the operators' focus area of attention. We have evaluated two mixed reality visualization approaches: a head-up display and a display projected in the virtual environment, and compared these designs with a head-down display. The designs presented an arrow, used for navigational guidance, and warnings symbols, used to inform the user about obstacles near the machine. The users were both more reactive and more seeking out information on the mixed reality displays. The eye-tracking measurement shows that the users used the mixed reality displays to a significantly higher level, on average twice as often than the head-down display. Moreover, the NASA-RTLX results indicate that the users had lower workload using the mixed reality interfaces, where the mixed reality displays scored better in each category.

Acknowledgements. This research has received funding from CrossControl AB, the Swedish Knowledge Foundation (KK-stiftelsen) through the ITS-EASY program, and the European Union's Horizon 2020 research and innovation programme under the Marie Skłodowska-Curie grant agreement number 764951.

References

1. Sanchez, J., Duncan, J.R.: Operator-automation interaction in agricultural vehicles. Ergon. Design Q. Hum. Factors Appl. **17**, 14–19 (2009)
2. Kazan, E.E.: Analysis Of Fatal And Nonfatal Accidents Involving Earthmoving Equipment Operators And On-Foot Workers (2013). https://digitalcommons.wayne.edu/oa_dissertations/731/
3. Kecojevic, V., Radomsky, M.: The causes and control of loader- and truck-related fatalities in surface mining operations. Int. J. Injury Control Saf. Promot. **11**, 239–251 (2004)
4. Department for Transport: Incident at Llanbadarn Automatic Barrier Crossing (Locally Monitored), near Aberystwyth, 19 June 2011 (2012)
5. Wallmyr, M.: Seeing through the eyes of heavy vehicle operators. In: Bernhaupt, R., Dalvi, G., Joshi, A., Balkrishan, D.K., O'Neill, J., Winckler, M. (eds.) INTERACT 2017. LNCS, vol. 10514, pp. 263–282. Springer, Cham (2017). https://doi.org/10.1007/978-3-319-67684-5_16
6. Endsley, M.R.: Toward a theory of situation awareness in dynamic systems. Hum. Factors J. Hum. Factors Ergon. Soc. **37**, 32–64 (1995)
7. Patrick, J., Morgan, P.L.: Approaches to understanding, analysing and developing situation awareness. Theoret. Issues Ergon. Sci. **11**, 41–57 (2010)
8. Ruff, T.M., Holden, T.P.: Preventing collisions involving surface mining equipment: a GPS-based approach. J. Saf. Res. **34**, 175–181 (2003)
9. Jo, B.W., Lee, Y.S., Kim, J.H., Kim, D.K., Choi, P.H.: Proximity warning and excavator control system for prevention of collision accidents. Sustainability **9**(8), 1488 (2017)
10. Lagnel, O., Engstr, J.: Better work environment with Head Up Display, JTI report - Agriculture and Industry, no 440 (2015)
11. Doshi, A., Cheng, S.Y., Trivedi, M.M.: A novel active heads-up display for driver assistance. IEEE Trans. Syst. Man Cybern. Part B **39**, 85–93 (2009)

12. Schwarz, F., Fastenmeier, W.: Augmented reality warnings in vehicles: effects of modality and specificity on effectiveness. Accid. Anal. Prev. **101**, 55–66 (2017)
13. Webb, A.K., Vincent, E.C., Patnaik, P., Schwartz, J.L.: A Systems Approach for Augmented Reality Design. In: Schmorrow, D.D.D., Fidopiastis, C.M.M. (eds.) AC 2016. LNCS (LNAI), vol. 9744, pp. 382–389. Springer, Cham (2016). https://doi.org/10.1007/978-3-319-39952-2_37
14. Vasilijevic, A., Miskovic, N., Vukic, Z.: Comparative assessment of human machine interfaces for ROV guidance with different levels of secondary visual workload. In: 2013 21st Mediterranean Conference on Control and Automation, MED 2013 - Conference Proceedings, pp. 1292–1297. IEEE, Chania (2013)
15. Akyeampong, J., Udoka, S., Caruso, G., Bordegoni, M.: Evaluation of hydraulic excavator human-machine interface concepts using NASA TLX. Int. J. Ind. Ergon. **44**, 374–382 (2014)
16. Freeman, M.H.: Head-up displays—a review. Opt. Technol. **1**, 63–70 (1969)
17. Van Krevelen, R., Poelman, R.: A survey of augmented reality technologies, applications and limitations. Int. J. Virtual Reality **9**, 1–20 (2010)
18. Kun, A.L., Tscheligi, M., Riener, A., van der Meulen, H.: ARV 2017: workshop on augmented reality for intelligent vehicles. In: 9th International Conference on Automotive User Interfaces and Interactive Vehicular Applications (AutomotiveUI 2017) Adjunct, pp. 47–51 (2017)
19. Gabbard, J.L., Fitch, G.M., Kim, H.: Behind the glass: driver challenges and opportunities for AR automotive applications. Proc. IEEE **102**, 124–136 (2014)
20. Kim, K., Wohn, K.: Effects on productivity and safety of map and augmented reality. IEICE Trans. Inf. Syst. **E94–D**, 1051–1061 (2011)
21. AblaBmeier, M., Poitschke, T., Bengler, F.W.K., Rigoll, G.: Eye gaze studies comparing head-up and head-down displays in vehicles. In: 2007 IEEE International Conference on Multimedia and Expo, pp. 2250–2252. IEEE, Beijing (2007)
22. Sojourner, R.J., Antin, J.F.: The effects of a simulated head-up display speedometer on perceptual task performance. Hum. Factors **32**, 329–339 (1990)
23. Wallmyr, M.: Reflections on augmented reality for heavy machinery- practical usage and challenges. In: Adjunct workshop on Augmented Reality for Intelligent Vehicles, at Automotive User Interfaces and Interactive Vehicular Applications Adjunct - AutomotiveUI 2017, pp. 47–51. ACM Press, New York (2017)
24. Akyeampong, J., Udoka, S.J., Park, E.H., Carolina, N.: A hydraulic excavator augmented reality simulator for operator training. In: Conference on Industrial Engineering and Operations Management, pp. 1511–1518 (2012)
25. Wang, X., Dunston, P.S.: Design, strategies, and issues towards an augmented reality-based construction training platform. Electron. J. Inf. Technol. Constr. **12**, 363–380 (2007)
26. Englund, M., Lundström, H., Bruneberg, T., Löfgren, B.: Evaluation of head-up display showing bucking information in final felling, SkogForsk Report, no 869 (2015)
27. Akyeampong, J., Nevins, L., Udoka, S., Carolina, N.: Using digital human modeling to enhance work visibility for excavator. In: Proceedings of the 2013 Industrial and Systems Engineering Research Conference, pp. 1909–1919. ProQuest (2013)
28. Kittusamy, N.K., Buchholz, B.: Whole-body vibration and postural stress among operators of construction equipment: a literature review. J. Saf. Res. **35**, 255–261 (2004)
29. Wallmyr, M., Kade, D., Holstein, T.: 360 degree mixed reality environment to evaluate interaction design for industrial vehicles including head-up and head-down displays. In: Virtual, Augmented and Mixed Reality: Applications in Health, Cultural Heritage, and Industry, VAMR 2018, pp. 377–391 (2018)
30. Unity. http://www.unity.com
31. Pupil labs. https://pupil-labs.com/

32. Kassner, M., Patera, W., Bulling, A.: Pupil: an open source platform for pervasive eye tracking and mobile gaze-based interaction. In: Proceedings of the 2014 ACM International Joint Conference on Pervasive and Ubiquitous Computing: Adjunct Publication, pp. 1151–1160 (2014)
33. NASA TLX Paper and Pencil Version. NASA Ames Research Center (2016)
34. Macefield, R.: How to specify the participant group size for usability studies: a practitioner's guide. J. Usability Stud. **5**, 34–45 (2009)
35. Hart, S.G.: Nasa-Task Load Index (NASA-TLX); 20 Years Later. Proc. Hum. Factors Ergon. Soc. Annu. Meet. **50**, 904–908 (2006)
36. Hart, S.G., Staveland, L.E.: Development of NASA-TLX (Task Load Index): results of empirical and theoretical research. Adv. Psychol. **52**, 139–183 (1988)
37. Byers, J.C.: Traditional and raw task load index (TLX) correlations: are paired comparisons necessary? In: Advances in industrial ergonomics and safety, pp. 481–485 (1989)
38. Schreier, M.: Qualitative content analysis. In: Flick, U. (ed.) The SAGE Handbook of Qualitative Data Analysis, pp. 170–183. SAGE Publications Ltd, Thousand Oaks (2013)
39. Wittmann, M., et al.: Effects of display position of a visual in-vehicle task on simulated driving. Appl. Ergon. **37**, 187–199 (2006)
40. Liu, Y.C., Wen, M.H.: Comparison of head-up display (HUD) vs. head-down display (HDD): driving performance of commercial vehicle operators in Taiwan. Int. J. Hum. Comput. Stud. **61**, 679–697 (2004)
41. Ng-Thow-Hing, V., Bark, K., Beckwith, L., Tran, C., Bhandari, R., Sridhar, S.: User-centered perspectives for automotive augmented reality. In: 2013 IEEE International Symposium on Mixed and Augmented Reality, pp. 13–22. IEEE (2013)
42. Yang, J.: Visual Support System for Remote- Control Construction Machine Based on Autonomous Cameras (2015)

Exploring the Effects of Replicating Shape, Weight and Recoil Effects on VR Shooting Controllers

Jose Luis Berna-Moya[✉] and Diego Martinez-Plasencia

Department of Informatics/Interact Lab, University of Sussex, Brighton, UK
{J.Berna, D.Martinez-Plasencia}@sussex.ac.uk

Abstract. Commercial Virtual Reality (VR) controllers with *realistic* force feedback are becoming available, to increase the realism and immersion of first-person shooting (FPS) games in VR. These controllers attempt to mimic not only the shape and weight of real guns but also their recoil effects (linear force feedback parallel to the barrel, when the gun is shot). As these controllers become more popular and affordable, this paper investigates the actual effects that these properties (shape, weight, and especially directional force feedback) have on performance for general VR users (e.g. users with no marksmanship experience), drawing conclusions for both consumers and device manufacturers.

We created a prototype replicating the properties exploited by commercial VR controllers (i.e. shape, weight and adjustable force feedback) and used it to assess the effect of these parameters in user performance, across a series of user studies. We first analysed the benefits on user performance of adding weight and shape vs a conventional controller (e.g. Vive controller). We then explore the implications of adding linear force feedback (LFF), as well as replicating the shape and weight. Our studies show negligible effects on the immediate shooting performance with some improvements in subjective appreciation, which are already present with low levels of LFF. While higher levels of LFF do not increase subjective appreciations any further, they lead users to reach their maximum distance skillset more quickly. This indicates that while adding low levels of LFF can be enough to influence user's immersion/engagement for gaming contexts, controllers with higher levels of LFF might be better suited for training environments and/or when dealing with particularly demanding aiming tasks.

Keywords: Virtual reality · First person shooters · Force feedback

1 Introduction

Current VR controllers are moving away from vibrotactile feedback, and controllers with more realistic force feedback are becoming available. Custom design controllers for FPS games like Strike VR [1], MAG P90 [2], Delta Six [3] or Haptec recoil systems [4] are available, which mimic the shape, weight and recoil of real guns. All aim to increase realism, immersion and sense of presence in VR environments. However, the effects of replicating these parameters (shape, weight and recoil feedback) on users' performance are unclear. In spite of their higher price tag, their benefits when compared

© IFIP International Federation for Information Processing 2019
Published by Springer Nature Switzerland AG 2019
D. Lamas et al. (Eds.): INTERACT 2019, LNCS 11746, pp. 763–782, 2019.
https://doi.org/10.1007/978-3-030-29381-9_45

to cheaper alternatives (e.g. passive controllers such as the PlayStation VR aim [5], Wii gun [6] or NES Zapper [7]) remain unclear.

On one hand, the use of more realistic controllers (e.g. those that replicate shape/weight) can improve learning time [8–10], presence [11] and involvement [12]. Including force feedback has been shown to improve hand-eye coordination [13], performance and potentially reduce learning time [14]. On the other hand, a strong recoil is also known to have negative effects (i.e. reducing aim accuracy [15, 16], causing exhaustion and injuries [17]). Tactile augmentation (replicating shape) [18] has proved to enhance presence in VEs, but its effects on aiming performance

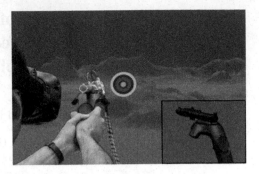

Fig. 1. Force feedback device and the environment used to test the effects of recoil on shooting performance. Right button corner, in-game visual representation of the controller, replicating the shape of the physical prototype.

are unclear. Besides unclear/conflicting factors, works exploring performance using LFF [14, 19] are not consistent, not reporting or using different levels of LFF in each study. There is a lack of standardisation in characterising/reporting LFF levels in the literature, and commercially available gun controllers do not report their feedback levels either.

We first describe an experimental setup to deliver LFF (a pneumatic attachment for the HTC controller), and we characterise three levels of LFF (i.e. allowing for reproducibility of results) that are later used on our user studies. We describe a replicable testbed to measure LFF on FPS game controllers, based on standards for ballistic research. This provides an objective characterisation of the LFF levels used in our studies, allowing for reusability of our results and, more importantly, providing a replicable setup for future comparisons with this/other LFF controllers.

Our first study explores the shooting performance of a conventional VR controller (i.e. HTC Vive) with that of a passive prop controller. That is, a controller replicating the shape and weight of a commercial gun controller (i.e. as in a Nintendo Zapper [7] or Wii gun [6]), but not including actual force feedback, arguably the main factor driving up the costs of controllers such as StrikeVR. Our study revealed that, despite its weight (~ 1 kg), the performance was not decreased, and participants had a better subjective appreciation for a controller matching the gun's shape and weight.

Our second Study then explores the benefits of adding LFF to a gun-shaped controller with realistic weight, mimicking the cues provided by current VR FPS controllers (e.g. Strike VR [1], MAG P90 [2]) and testing three different levels of LFF. No further effects on performance could be observed due to the inclusion of LFF, but participants' subjective impressions improved, even for the lowest level of LFF.

The third study explores the effects of LFF on participants' learning curve, showing that higher levels of LFF improved skill acquisition, allowing participants to reach maximum aiming distance within fewer shots. We finish the paper by discussing the implications of our results for the future design and usage of LFF controllers for VR FPS.

2 Related Word

We focused the related work in three main areas: general approaches for haptic VR controllers; studies on the effects of force feedback in 3D pointing/shooting; and military literature describing recoil properties and measurement techniques.

2.1 Haptic VR Controllers

Tethered force feedback devices [20–22] (i.e. not portable/wearable) offer high accuracy and precision. These devices have been extensively used in VR training for tasks that require LFF, replicating needle insertion [23], surgery training [24] or teleoperation [25]. Although very precise, these devices are normally expensive and better suited for research/industrial applications.

Untethered interfaces trade accuracy or haptic fidelity for a portable setup. Exoglove designs like Dexmo [26] provide active forces on the movement of users' fingers. Asymmetric vibration, such as in Waves [27] or Traxion [28], has proved to be a feasible approach to deliver distinguishable/perceivable cues that help users navigate a space with push/pull effects. However, the magnitude of the force delivered is weak and therefore not suitable to replicate recoil effects. Electric Muscle Stimulation (EMS) has been used to deliver strong force feedback (e.g. punches [29]) by contracting the user's muscles. However, this technique cannot yet deliver precise and controlled LFF (i.e. vector direction defined by user's joints) and is not applicable to small muscle groups (i.e. individual fingers or wrist, which are greatly affected by recoil).

A series of task-specific controllers that enhance VR experiences have been published over the last couple of years. NormalTouch [30] recreates low definition shapes while HapticRevolver [31] provides a palette of textures (i.e. to match the surface properties of objects in the VE or rotating buttons). Claw [32] (among other features) provided vibrotactile feedback on the fingertip and force feedback on the trigger finger. Researchers highlighted how the users enjoyed the gun operation mode. Although these solutions deliver high-quality haptic feedback, none of them assessed the effects of the feedback/recoil on user performance.

Following the popularity of VR headsets (HTC & Oculus), several companies have commercialised controllers that replicate the shape, weight, and recoil effects of real guns. Strike VR [1] provides advanced controllers with LFF available for multiplayer and arena games. Other companies like MAG P90 [2] or Delta Six [3] offer comparable solutions. Similarly, Haptec [4] develops electromagnetic recoil simulators that cover from small guns to heavy weapons with a focus on training applications. Most of these controllers are aimed at improving users' immersion. However, no information is available on the specific levels of LFF used by these controllers or on their influence on the user's aiming performance.

2.2 Linear Force Feedback, Shape and Weight Aid for Aiming/Shooting

Pointing tasks within 2D Graphical User Interfaces (GUIs) have been studied extensively (e.g. Fitts' law [33]), even in combination with LFF. In a study comparing linear force, audio and visual feedback, the haptic condition yielded quicker motor response

[34]. Later work used a multimodal mouse design with LFF (using a solenoid to stimulate the tip of the finger) and drag force control [35]. Their results showed that LFF reduced stop-time and the time to select a target after the cursor has stopped. Further research by Cockburn et al. corroborates that tactile feedback could reduce mean target acquisition time [36]. Although positive, these studies only explored 2D interfaces and, unlike recoil, the feedback was always delivered before the user action (feedforward).

Understanding of pointing techniques in 3D and in combination with feedback techniques is not as mature. Modified models have been proposed for 3D pointing [21–23] that complement the original Fitts model, but they are not so broadly accepted. Moreover, other aspects, such as the role that supporting cues/modalities play is still unclear. For instance, Krol et al. [14] used a wireless controller (uWand) modified with a solenoid to provide LFF, reporting that 3D selection using LFF was faster than using visual or audio cues [14]. However, later work [19] using a similar system (Wii remote) found that haptic technology provided a more discrete improvement on performance than previously reported. Beyond using different hardware, studies fail to report the levels of LFF used, limiting their replicability and the scope where their results apply.

Studies using VR for military training are available [37–39] which, even if focussed on real guns and experienced shooters (instead of gamers), stand against the decision of using high levels of LFF for VR controllers. Recoil at the level of real military weapons is detrimental to aim [15] and can even lead to the development of injuries [40]. Research in self-transformation devices [38] also challenges the choice of commercial VR controllers to recreate the actual gun's shape and weight, suggesting that the controller's weight distribution is much more important to recreate a realistic device [41, 42]. Precision in shooting is also affected by two main components; visual (i.e. aiming) and proprioception (i.e. gun-holding & posture). Several studies [43–46] have shown how knowledge of performance (KP - i.e. shooting accuracy) or knowledge of result (KR - stability, pose or balance) are both directly affected by the ergonomics of the gun and can improve user performance. This is particularly relevant for FPS VR games, where the camera view (i.e. head) is decoupled from the controller (i.e. hand) [47].

2.3   Recoil Properties and Measuring Techniques

One of the reasons behind the mixed results about the influence of force feedback on 3D pointing could come from the level of force feedback/recoil used in each study. Commercially available gun controllers do not report their feedback levels, and there is also a lack of standard in reporting this in the literature, where the magnitude of the feedback is usually not characterized [7, 20].

To inform the levels of force feedback used in the user study (i.e. asses safety ranges and allow replicability), we looked at existing approaches to measure LFF. Two main approaches are more commonly used for ballistic measurements, reading impulse with load cells (N/s) or displacement using accelerometers (m/s^2). While acceleration is greatly affected by the user's grip on the controller, impulse provides a robust metric comparable across LLF devices, and the design os measuring setups can be adopted from equivalent rigs for real guns [48–50]. Other researchers have identified peak force as a more representative parameter to describe recoil felt by the user [50], and our setup and experiments will allow us to measure and report both impulses and peak forces.

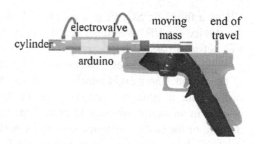

Fig. 2. Overview of the LFFa. Enclosure is omitted to show the internal parts.

Although rare, there have been cases where vibrations of game controllers have been related to injuries, such as the hand-arm vibration syndrome [51], making it advisable to characterise and limit the LFF to safe levels. Although these effects are dependent on the physiology of the person [17], some guidelines exist. Spine et al. recommends limiting recoil to a maximum of ~ 13.33 N/s to avoid injuries for real weapons [15], while the H&S Executive body in the UK sets limitations of vibration exposure to a maximum of 2.5 m/s^2 daily. We considered these restrictions within the design and implementation of our attachment, as described in Sect. 3.2.

3   Experimental Setup

Commercial recoil controllers use tracking systems based on existing VR solutions (e.g. HTC or Oculus systems) to maximise compatibility. We built a linear force feedback attachment (LFFa) for the handheld controllers of an HTC Vive as a replica of existing recoil controllers. The LFFa aimed to provide weight, shape and LFF comparable to existing VR gun controllers. The device was designed to reproduce a range of LFF level, tested during our studies. The following subsection will describe the design and operation of our LFFa when mounted on the controller and the LFF levels produced.

We also describe a reproducible testbench implemented to characterise the impulses and peak forces of the LFFa, as these parameters are related to the perceived intensity of recoil. We then, describe the design of a hand dynamometer used to measure the handgrip strength and identify users' hand fatigue. This will allow us to put our results in perspective according to objective parameters. Furthermore, details of the design allow for replicability of the setup and testbed, providing a set of tools for future studies on the use of linear force feedback.

3.1   Haptic Feedback Attachment

We used the HTC Vive controller as the foundation for our recoil controller. The controller ergonomics have a similar design to that of a pistol grip (Fig. 2), with the top ring serving as an attachment feature. Using the controller's in-built tracking system also rendered equivalent accuracy to commercial recoil controllers.

We aimed to reproduce the external shape of a futuristic gun as can be seen in some commercial controllers [1]. However, the extra footprint of this enclosure occluded IR receivers on the HTC VR controller and affected tracking performance. As a result, we settled for a minimum enclosure (Aluminium tube) and motivated the visual design in

VR as a futuristic SCI-FI gun (see Fig. 1 and Fig. 3 left). The visual representation of the device (in VR) was designed to match its physical shape closely, so that it could still act as a passive haptic prop.

The attachment uses a pneumatic cylinder to displace a weight attached to the end of the piston. The weight attached is added to increase the kinetic energy of the moving piston and, in turn, the perceived recoil force. The moving piston and weight were housed in an aluminium tube to protect the user from finger entrapment. A metal cap at the end of the enclosure transferred the kinetic energy upon impact. The total weight of the final device was 950 g (controller $\sim$470 g; recoil FA $\sim$ 400 g), closely matching the weight of an example MAG P90 VR Gun controller ($\sim$500 g + controller).

The pneumatic piston used was an SMC Double Action Roundline Cylinder, CD85N20-125-B, connected to a 5/2 electrovalve (VUVG-BK10-B52) and powered by a 24 V 0.2 A power supply. Pneumatic components were modified by increasing the inside diameter to 3.8 mm as this reduced airflow constraints. An air compressor (Bambi models 150/500) supplied up to 8 bars of pressure to the system. We used 4 mm outside diameter pipes to connect the compressor to the electrovalve and 2 mm pipes to connect the electrovalve to the piston. A microcontroller (Arduino Nano) and TIP120 circuit were used to control the electrovalve. Communication with Unity was done via Serial COM at 2,000,000 baud speed.

3.2   Characterising LFF Feedback: Impulse and Peak Force Testbench

The design of our measuring testbench is based on ballistic research [49] and the principles described by Spine et al. [15]. This design was chosen as it is the most effective method to measure the impulse forces component on the horizontal axis. The logged data allowed us to compare the LFF with existing data [52] and to assess LFF effects against related guidelines. Furthermore, readings with this measuring are independent of the user's pose or grip.

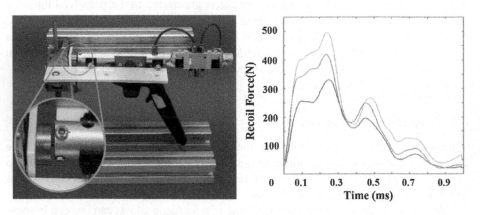

Fig. 3. Left – image of the recoil testbed with the LFFa and controller, detail image shows the load cell and end of travel cap. Right – Reading of the 3 different levels of LFF at 2, 3 and 8 bars of pressure.

To build the testbench frame (Fig. 3 left) we used V-slot linear aluminium rails (40 × 40 mm) where the device rested. U-shape clamps with bearings fitted on the barrel minimised friction on the travel axis.

The end of travel cap of our LFFa rested against a Phidget load cell (0/200 kg), which was used to convert the mechanical impact to an electric signal. To filter and amplify the signal, we used an INA125 IC circuit and logged the data using a Pico-scope 2204A. After assembly, the load cell was calibrated using a series of known weights following a standardised process. The testbench was used to select the ideal moving mass of our LFFa. We measured the impulse response using various weight attached to the piston (60 g, 120 g, 180 g, 240 g and 300 g). The heaviest weight tested (300 g) increased the overall device weight above the 1 kg mark and produced no significant increment on the max impulse response (weight decreased acceleration on the moving mass). A weight of 240 g proved to be the optimal weight - delivering the highest impulse recoil forces while retaining the overall weight of the LFFa bellow 500 gr.

We conducted a short pilot-study to determine the minimum pressure of the pneumatic system that produced a realistic recoil. Below 2 bars of pressure, the piston acceleration was too slow to recreate an impact. With the 240 g weight, the 2 bar setting delivered a peak of 337.5 N and lasted for approximately 1 ms. The maximum pressure of the compressor used (8 bars) delivered a maximum peak force of $\sim$500 N, lasting also $\sim$1 ms. We then defined a middle LFF setting (3 bars), resulting in a peak force of 412 N (midpoint from the 2 other settings). We used the data collected to calculate the impulse of each of the conditions: 2 bar delivers a 0.028 N/s, 3 bar = 0.035 N/s and 8 bar = 0.042 N/s, and we will refer to them as LOW, MED and HIGH levels in the rest of the paper.

The final impulse response from these three LFF levels is shown in Fig. 3 right. It must be noted that the short duration of the response is due to the inelastic impact measured (load cell, end cap and moving mass are steel). A real user holding the device will result in a much more elastic response, although the final impulse (i.e. summation of force over time) will still be the same.

To measure hand fatigue during our user studies and to avoid any potential ill effects, we measured each participant's hand grip force before and after each condition trial. Grip strength is directly related to the fatigue on hand and forearm muscles, and a decline in strength acts as an indicator of fatigue [53]. We build a precision digital hand dynamometer (Fig. 4), designed using CAD software and printed using a MakerBot 3D printer. We measured the grip force using a load cell Phidget 0/50 kg and similar amplifier (INA125 IC) and calibration procedure used for the recoil testbench. Reading values were logged using a Pico-scope 2204A and data processed using R. Grip force measurements followed the standardized protocol described in [54], measuring grip forces across 3 repetitions.

Fig. 4. Hand dynamometer used to measure hand grip strength.

4 User Studies

4.1 User Study 1: Effects of Shape and Weight

This first study was aimed to assess the performance of a VR FPS controller reproducing the shape and weight of a gun (i.e. similar to passive props such as Wii gun) when compared to a conventional VR controller. Prior literature has shown that tactile augmentation (i.e. recreation of shape and weight) can increase immersion. However, most commercial recoil controllers are above 1 kg, and such extra weight could hinder the experience and performance due to fatigue or momentum when moving the controller.

Experimental Setup
The experimental setup was designed using Unity 2017.3.1f1 and a HTC Vive headset. The VE consisted of an open field with no clear points of reference within the scene (Fig. 1 and Fig. 5 left), to avoid muscle memory of the position of the target and therefore carryover effects. The user was located on an elevated platform to allow shooting at targets above and below head level. A cross on the floor marked the centre of the platform as a reference for the user to remain at the same position. During the user study, a series of targets were successively presented in front of the user. Targets were arranged, on 4 planes at different distances (25, 35, 45 and 55 m from the user's initial position) according to a 3 × 3 layout. The central target was rendered at the user's eye level (measured at the beginning of the experiment), and the remaining ones were presented at 2.5 m around the central target (i.e. leaving a space of 0.5 m between adjacent targets). During the trial condition, each target was displayed twice, adding to a total of 72 tasks per condition (4 distances × 9 targets × 2 repetitions). An initial countdown of 5 s was presented at the beginning of the task (i.e. prepare the user for the task), and an in-game questionnaire (answers selected via touching, not shooting) was used at the end of each of the 72 trials. The shooting in the VE was implemented using a ray-casting technique. Gravity, wind or any other environmental conditions were not considered, not affecting the linear trajectory of the shots.

Participants
A total of 14 participants (9 male and 5 female) of ages 18 to 46, average age 32.2 years (SD = 7.19) took part in the experiment. All participants were right-handed and had a normal or corrected-to-normal vision and were screened prior to the user study to ensure no hand injuries. Half of the participants were experienced in a similar task (FPS games). The study was approved by the local Ethics Committee.

A priori statistical power analysis was performed for sample size estimation in G*Power. Running a power analysis on a repeated measures ANOVA with two feedbacks, a power of 0.95, an alpha level of 0.05, and a medium effect size (f = 0.25, $\eta p^2 = 0.06$, critical F = 1.30) [55, 56], suggested a sample size of 8 participants. Given the high response of participants, we incremented the number of participants to 14.

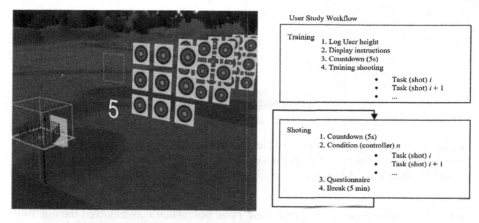

Fig. 5. Left – Overview of the virtual environment, from left to right in the image; user platform, questionnaire, countdown, and all targets rendered simultaneously. Right – User study workflow, subdivided into training and $n = 2$ trials based on the number of controllers tested.

Method

In this initial user study, we compared the user's performance looking at two conditions: a controller with our LFFa as a passive prop (no LFF due to pneumatic activation) and a conventional HTC controller. We used a within-subjects design, counterbalancing the order of the two conditions. A schematic of the user study workflow is shown in Fig. 5 right. Each user study session started with participants filling in a background questionnaire (i.e. demographics, previous experience with related activities like paintball/clay shooting/FPS gaming), followed by a brief introduction to the VR system and the controller. Here, participants were explained their goal (hit as many targets in the centre as possible); they were shown a two-handed pose to hold the controller (i.e. weaver stance) and were shown how to use the sights to aim at targets. Users were instructed to shoot as soon as they were ready and informed that they had only one shot per target. The user study started with a training task with $i = 36$ targets at the closest distance (25 m) followed by the two test conditions ($n = 2$): passive LFFa and HTC controller. Participants had to take a 5 min break between tasks without the headset.

During each condition, participants shot targets as they appeared one at a time (with randomised position and distance). In each trial, a single target was rendered for 3 s, with a delay of 1.5 s between consecutive targets. If the target was hit the user received audio feedback and a red sphere was displayed showing the ray/target collision point.

Dependent variable indicators of performance in FPS games [57] were automatically logged. Time per shoot (*TPS*) measured the time elapsed since the target was rendered until the participant pressed the trigger; *Hit* registered a bool variable with true if the target was hit, while hit distance (*HD*) measured the distance between the hit point and the centre of the target in meters.

After each task, participants answered 4 questions using a 7-point Likert scale. These questions aimed to measure; enjoyment of the experience (Q1 – "*How much did you enjoy the experience?*"), perceived arm/hand fatigue (Q2 – "*I felt that the condition*

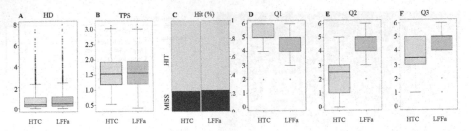

Fig. 6. From left to right Distribution of Hit Distance results in metres to the centre of the target. Time per shot in seconds, % of hit and miss per condition. Right boxplot shows result from Q1, Q2 and Q3 from a 0–7 Likert scale.

that I used makes my arm/hand feel tired") and how much they believed the controller affected/aided their aiming (Q3. *"I found the feedback useful to aid aiming within the gaming experience"*). Finally, a forced choice question asked participants their preferred condition (Q4 – *"What controller would you prefer using?"*).

Results

Significance was tested for p < 0.05. We used Levene and Shapiro tests as well as QQ plots to test for ANOVA assumptions, and we will only refer to the required corrections used wherever they were necessary. Also, where mean or standard deviations need to be mentioned in the text, these will be noted as M and SD respectively. We analysed the questionnaire results using Wilcoxon signed-rank test as the distribution of the residual were not normal.

Accuracy results (see HD in Fig. 6A) were similar between the HTC controller (M = 0.851, SD = 1.118) and the controller with passive attachment (M = 0.92, SD = 1.196), with no significant differences between conditions (F (1,13) = 1.161, p > 0.1).

Performance results (TPS, in Fig. 6B) were similar, with mean time values for HTC controller (M = 1.584, SD = 0.530) and passive controller (M = 1.577, SD = 0.517). Once again, no significant difference were found between conditions (F (1,13) = 0.016, p > 0.1). Differences could not be found in terms of Hit rate either (Fig. 6C). Analysis of performance according to user experience did not show any additional differences.

Q1 (enjoyment – Fig. 6D) and Q3 (effect on aim - Fig. 6F) analysis showed no significant difference between the conditions. Q2 (perceive fatigue – Fig. 6E) showed a significant difference between the HTC controller (M = 2.36, SD = 1.60) and the passive prop controller (M = 4.5, SD = 1.34), (Z = −1.882, p < 0.05). This suggests that participants using LFF had the perception of feeling more tired after the experiment. Finally, Q4 rated controller preference, with a total of 10 out of the 14 participants (71.4%) indicating a preference for the modified passive LFFa controller.

Participants answers to Q2 suggested a perceived increase in fatigue following the use of the LFFa. However, aim performance did not degrade over time and no significant difference was found on hand grip strength. A higher number of users showed a preference for the passive prop on Q4. This is in line with previous work that suggests that tactile augmentation increases enjoyment and immersion [18], but it could, however, be influenced by novelty effects. We found that providing tactile augmentation did not improve performance with our replica during the user study. As the passive LFFa did not influence performance we proceeded to assess if the addition of LFF could introduce any additional benefits.

4.2   User Study 2: Effects of LFF on VR Controllers

In this experiment, we investigate the effect on user performance when adding actual LFF on a controller that already replicates the shape and weight of the gun. This is included as a way to assess the extra benefits from a current commercial VR PFS controller (e.g. StrikeVR, MAG P90) when compared to cheaper alternatives using only a passive prop with the shape of the gun.

Method
Experimental setup and VE remained unchanged, but this user study tested four different conditions (n = 4): passive LFFa and LFFa with LOW, MED and HIGH levels of recoil (see Sect. 3.2). As in Study 1, each condition included i = 72 trials, and the same variables (TPS, Hit) were recorded. As a difference, we measured error angle (EA) instead of distance to the centre as a more consistent measurement over different distances to target [58]. Reduce Latin square counterbalancing was used across conditions.

Introduction and training remained unchanged from Study 1. However, the questions focused on the effects of the addition of LFF, versus the passive attachment: Q5 – *"The haptic feedback matched the action in the demo"*; Q6 – *"I enjoyed the use of the controller in the demo"*; Q7 – *"The feedback made the controller feel more realistic"*, while Q8 remained as a forced choice, identifying their favourite condition. Hand grip force was measured before and after each condition (8 times in total), with no ill effects being detected for any participant or condition.

Participants
Twelve participants were recruited (8 male and 4 female) of ages 18 to 46. The average age was 28.6 years (SD = 4.2). All participants were right-handed had normal or corrected-to-normal vision and were pre-screened prior to the experiment. Some participants had played video games before (n = 6), and a smaller group had played FPS games (N = 3), some participants had previous experience with VR headsets (N = 5). We ran an estimation in G*Power, resulting in a required sample size of 8 participants.

Results
Data collected was analysed for significant effects using one-way repeated measures ANOVA and Friedman's test with Holm corrections [59] for the questionnaires. Results obtained for this study were in line with Study 1, showing no significant effects on users' aim performance, but with subjective differences in the questionnaire responses.

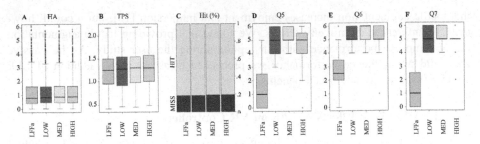

Fig. 7. From left to right, distribution of Error Angle (EA), Time per shot (TPS) and Hit rates for study 2. Right, boxplot showing the result obtained from questions 5, 6 & 7.

The differences on the EA were low (Fig. 7A), with a greatest mean difference between conditions of $\sim 0.07°$ (LFFa - M = 1.30, SD = 1.39), (LOW - M = 1.30, SD = 1.33), (MED - M = 1.34, SD = 1.34), (HIGH - M = 1.37, SD = 1.44) and no significant differences across conditions (F $(3,13) = 1.01$, p > 0.1). Similarly, TPS (Fig. 7B) and Hit rate (Fig. 7C) were very similar across conditions, showing no significant differences with only a small trend in TPS between LFFa (M = 1.238, SD = 0.383 s) and HIGH (M = 1.281 s, SD = 0.377 s), suggesting that increasing impulse could also result in a slight increase in TPS (i.e. slowing down the shooting).

Analysis of the questionnaires revealed significant differences (p < 0.005) between conditions for Q5 (Fig. 7D), (LFFa - M = 1.44, SD = 1.59), (LOW - M = 4.94, SD = 1.06), (MED - M = 5.19, SD = 0.75), (HIGH - M = 4.50, SD = 1.63), with paired analysis showing differences between any of the 3 LFF conditions and the passive LFFa condition. This indicates that delays between the trigger being pressed and the recoil were low enough as not to affect participant's sense of agency [60, 61], and that the force feedback had a positive impact for the representation of the shooting action. The fact that the specific LFF level (LOW, MED or HIGH) did not influence participants' impressions suggests that while some amount of LFF can improve this perception of action/consequence matching, we cannot justify the need of higher LFF levels for these tasks.

A similar result was obtained from the analysis of Q7 – enjoyment (see Fig. 7E: LFFa - M = 2.69, SD = 1.70; LOW - M = 5.31, SD = 0.70; MED - M = 5.50, SD = 0.63; and HIGH - M = 5.00, SD = 1.26), and Q8 – realism (see Fig. 7F: LFFa - M = 1.44, SD = 1.55; LOW - M = 4.93, SD = 0.85; MED - M = 5.25, SD = 0.68 and HIGH - M = 4.94, SD = 0.93). Statistical differences could be found in all cases (p < 0.01), and paired analysis showed that both Q6 and Q7 were rated higher when using LFF. The results from our forced-choice question (Q8) also seemed to match the idea that a high amount of LFF is not required. From twelve participants 6 preferred the LOW condition, 3 participants MED and 2 preferred passive LFFa. All these results make it hard to justify the need for high levels of LFF for commercial VR FPS controllers (i.e. no gains in terms of performance, similar or lower levels of subjective appreciation).

4.3   User Study 3: Effect of LFF on the Learning Curve

Our previous studies showed no effects on users' performance, and only improvements on participants' subjective assessment due to feedback cues (shape, weight and LFF). This study analysed the effect of these feedback cues over time. That is, even if the feedback is delivered after the shot, forces could engage with the user's proprioceptive system, alleviating registration (i.e. a mismatch between the real position of the gun and where it is seen in VR) and perceptual errors (e.g. depth compression introduced by VR headsets). Better loops with the users' proprioceptive system could thus reinforce eye-hand coordination, which is key for shooting/pointing tasks.

To assess such carryover effects (i.e. learning curve) we modified the user study, gradually increasing task difficulty according to the participant's performance until a maximum shooting distance was achieved for each condition. The VE and hardware remained unchanged and only the experimental method was modified.

Methods

The experimental procedure remained unchanged from the previous study. Although the position of the target within its 3×3 layout remained randomized, the distance between the user and the target varied incrementally, following a staircase design (i.e. instead of random positions and distances, as in Study 2). Targets started at an initial distance of 25 m from the participant, and moved in steps of ± 4 m, using a 'three up - one down' design. That is, participants had to hit 3 targets in a row for the task to increase in complexity (i.e. move target 4 m away) and a single missed shot reduced the distance. The initial distance of the target was based on users' hit rate from Study 1 (96% hit rate at 25 m), being suited for participants of any aiming skillset level. A minimum set distance of 8 m from the user was used (but no upper limit). A counter of number of targets hit was shown on the top right of the virtual environment to motivate the user to perform well [62]. The step distance (± 4 m) was selected from a pilot study with 4 participants, settling in for a value that felt moderately incremental at each step but that still resulted in challenging distances within the duration of each test, even for skilled participants.

As in Study 2, we tested four conditions (LFFa, LOW, MED, HIGH) with 72 trials per condition, producing a final set of 72 distances ($d_1 - d_{72}$). We performed an introduction at the start of the user study and measured the hand grip before and after each condition as previously. No questionnaires were used and handgrip tests corroborated no ill effects on participants' grip and no relevant differences across conditions.

Participants

We recruited 16 participants for a within-subject user study (11 male and 5 female), of ages 18 to 46. The average age was 32.3 years (SD = 5.5). All participants were right-handed had a normal or corrected-to-normal vision and were pre-screened prior to the user study to make sure they did not have any hand injuries. Some participants had played video games before (N = 11), fewer had previous experience with VR headsets (N = 6). With a sample size estimation in G*Power for a power of 0.95, an alpha level of 0.05, and a medium effect size (f = 0.25, ηp^2 = 0.06, critical F = 1.34) required a sample size of 8 participants.

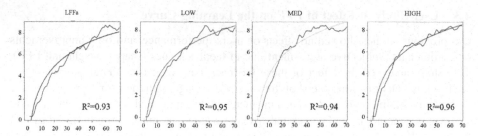

Fig. 8. Linear model regression for the 4 conditions and r-square value, showing the models obtained and the fitting model for each. The Y axis represents the normalised distance from 0 to 10 while the X axis represents the number of shots taken.

Results

We analysed the data using repeated measures ANOVA on the different conditions. Given the different aiming skillset of participants, we first normalised DT values [63] for each participant. This allowed us to combine users' curves, computing the mean normalised distance per trial and obtaining a single characteristic curve

Table 1. Intercept and log coefficient of the fitting models.

Model	Coefficients
LFFa	$-0.288 + \log_{0.26}(x)$
LOW	$-0.287 + \log_{0.267}(x)$
MED	$-0.253 + \log_{0.265}(x)$
HIGH	$-0.221 + \log_{0.252}(x)$

of performance per condition. Using the data taken from all the participants we calculated the mean average curve per condition and performed a linear model fitting per condition [64]. We compared the result models using Friedman's test with Holm-Bonferroni corrections.

A log model provided the best fitting results, using the form; $f(x) = a + \log_b (x)$. Parameter a determines the starting offset value on the slope, while b determines the slope of the curve (lower values of b indicate a steeper slope on the log plot, associated with fewer shots required to reach maximum distance skillset and, hence, higher learning speed).

All the curves showed a good fitting coefficient $R^2 > 0.93$ (see Fig. 8). The coefficients of the models per curve are shown in Table 1. HIGH shows the lowest value on b, indicating that participants reach their maximum skillset at a faster rate than using the other conditions. To compare the effect of the LFF on individual conditions (normalised $d_1 - d_{72}$), instead of on the mean fitting curve, we used Friedman's test. Significant differences were found between passive LFFa & LOW/MED ($p < 0.05$) and passive LFFa & HIGH ($p < 0.001$).

The analysis suggests that LFF does help to reach users' maximum skillset faster than with the other conditions on our experimental setup. All the participants achieved similar results on the max distance value at the end of each condition, hence the improvement from condition HIGH is not the result of the degradation of a participant's max distance. Following the previous hand measure results, we did not find any indicator of fatigue. We suspected a decline in aim accuracy after a given amount of time due to fatigue (each condition trial lasted ~ 12 min where the participant held the controller with extended arms). However, although subjective fatigue was present, at no point on the condition trial did participants' maximum distance decline, suggesting our controller did not affect performance negatively.

5 Discussion

This paper explored the effects that a controller replicating the cues of current commercial VR FPS controller (i.e. shape, weight and recoil) has on aiming performance.

The results also indicate that, when performance is considered (hit rates, accuracy, shooting time), the addition of these feedback cues did not alter immediate aim. As such, consumers of existing recoil VR FPS controllers should not expect an immediate improvement on performance when using this type of controllers.

These feedback cues did provide improvements in users' subjective appreciation. While the inclusion of LFF (i.e. recoil) did improve appreciation over a passive prop (shape and weigh alone) or a conventional controller, higher LFF levels did not necessarily translate on better subjective assessments of immersion, engagement and realism. From our discussions with participants, they highlighted how a low LFF was enough to recreate the action, and higher levels did not increase the reality or involvement, which matched our observations from the questionnaire responses and forced choice questions on their preferred feedback configuration.

Hence, device manufacturers could consider using lower LFF levels, as our results suggest that this would not lead to any significant loss in subjective appreciation. At the same time, lower levels of LFF could help reduce the costs of the hardware (e.g. impulse levels do not increase linearly with pressure, as illustrated by the three levels LFF we used), which would allow them to reduce their price tag and reach a broader audience. Similarly, lower LFF levels cause less interference with tracking system components (i.e. a strong recoil can disrupt readings from the accelerometers used by tracking systems, such as HTC Vive), reducing technical challenges related to isolating tracking from recoil feedback in their devices, and also contributing to reduced costs.

Also, the fact that impulse responses and peak forces did not affect (increase) aiming performance could be informative for eGame competitions, who could consider allowing participants to use them during their competitions.

Our studies also revealed that the inclusion of LFF resulted in an increase in the learning curve slope, which did increase for higher levels of LFF. Thus, the inclusion of such higher levels of LFF would still remain relevant for devices intended for professional or training environments, which could find the related increases in cost justified in exchange for improved skillset acquisition.

Readings from handgrip strength tests showed no significant differences across any of the conditions, suggesting the LFF levels used were not enough to induce significant fatigue, even for the relatively long duration of our studies ($\sim$1 h). However, it is worth noting that, even if physiological effects (i.e. handgrip) remained safe and accuracy was not decreased over time (e.g. towards the end of the trials in Study 3), participants did report increased levels of perceived fatigue, which should be carefully considered particularly when applied to entertainment applications.

It must be noted that our results and recommendations should be considered within the context of devices and parameters tested (weight, impulse response and peak forces), as characterised by our proposed testbed measuring setup. Other factors, such as weight distribution, trigger quality, materials and grip shape will also influence the appreciation and success of such controllers. Similarly, more advanced techniques for feedback control (e.g. based on voice coils), can result into more sophisticated haptic patterns (i.e. compared to our testing device) which could offer other improvements and/or support the action of the game beyond simple recoil effects.

Even in this case, the parameters explored here (shape, weight and LFF) remain key for this kind of systems, and the recoil measuring testbed and experimental setups presented in the paper will provide a valuable means to create replicable and reusable LFF levels and experiences, as well as providing a way to interpret and compare results and findings from future studies in terms of quantifiable metrics, such as impulse and peak force.

6 Conclusions

This paper has presented an exploration of the effects of shape, weight and LFF on 3D shooting/pointing task motivated by the recent commercialisation of gun-shaped VR controllers. Our results reveal that these types of controllers provide improvements for user immersion and learning time. We also found that tactile augmentation of controllers using LFF did not significantly affect users' immediate performance. Our findings suggest that FPS controllers do not require high levels of recoil to increase objective appreciation when used by people with little or no experience of real guns.

Following previous research on LFF, we encountered that different approaches to the implementation of LFF and modelling do not follow a particularly methodical system. The lack of reporting on force magnitude or on the controller properties could be the potential reasons for the previous contradictory results. Through our study we have illustrated in detail a simple approach to characterise these effects, allowing for reusability of results and replication of our findings. Any future work on linear force feedback could benefit from using similar techniques to model and report their applications and results in a standardised and comparable manner.

Acknowledgements. This work is supported by the Engineering and Physical Sciences Research Council (EPSRC). We would like to thank Dr Emanuela Maggioni and Dr Rod Bond for their advice on the user study design and data analysis. Also, we would like to thank Prof. Sriram Subramanian for the feedback on the user study.

References

1. The Arena Infinity, Product, Striker VR. https://www.strikervr.com/arena-infinity
2. MAG P90 Gun Controller VR Rifle Xbox One, PS4PRO, HTC Vive, Oculus, Windows Mixed Reality, BeswinVR. https://www.magp90.com/

3. VR Gun Controller: Buy The Best - The Delta Six. https://www.avengercontroller.com/vr-gun-controller/
4. haptech, Products. https://www.haptech.co/products
5. PlayStation VR Aim Controller – PlayStation VR Accessories. https://www.playstation.com/en-us/explore/accessories/playstation-vr-aim-controller/
6. This Wii Gun Collection Will Give You Hours of Fun with Your Shooting Games! https://www.nintendo-wii-explained.com/wii-gun.html
7. Nintendo NES Zapper - Computing History. http://www.computinghistory.org.uk/det/37107/Nintendo-NES-Zapper/
8. Tamborini, R., Bowman, N.D.: Presence in video games. In: Immersed in Media: Telepresence in Everyday Life, pp. 87–109 (2010)
9. Cooper, N., Milella, F., Cant, I., Pinto, C., White, M., Meyer, G.: Augmented cues facilitate learning transfer from virtual to real environments. In: 2016 IEEE International Symposium on Mixed and Augmented Reality (ISMAR-Adjunct), pp. 194–198. IEEE (2016)
10. Huizenga, J., Admiraal, W., Akkerman, S., ten Dam, G.: Mobile game-based learning in secondary education: engagement, motivation and learning in a mobile city game. J. Comput. Assist. Learn. **25**, 332–344 (2009)
11. Meehan, M., Insko, B., Whitton, M., Brooks, F.P.: Physiological measures of presence in virtual environments. In: Proceedings of 4th International Workshop on Presence, pp. 21–23 (2001)
12. Tamborini, R., Skalski, P.: The role of presence in the experience of electronic games. In: Playing Video Games: Motives, Responses, and Consequences, pp. 225–240 (2006)
13. Arsenault, R., Ware, C.: Eye-hand co-ordination with force feedback. In: Proceedings of the SIGCHI Conference on Human Factors in Computing Systems, pp. 408–414. ACM, New York (2000). https://doi.org/10.1145/332040.332466
14. Krol, L.R., Aliakseyeu, D., Subramanian, S.: Haptic feedback in remote pointing. In: CHI 2009 Extended Abstracts on Human Factors in Computing Systems, pp. 3763–3768. ACM (2009)
15. Spine, R.J.: Recoil in Shoulder Fired Weapons: A Review of the Literature. US Army Human Eng. Laboratory (HEL), US Army Armament Res. Develop. Command (ARDEC), Dover, NJ, USA, Technical report 296 (1982)
16. Morelli, F., et al.: Shooter-system performance variability as a function of recoil dynamics. Hum. Factors **59**, 973–985 (2017). https://doi.org/10.1177/0018720817700537
17. Blankenship, K., Evans, R., Allison, S., Murphy, M., Isome, H.: Shoulder-fired weapons with high recoil energy: quantifying injury and shooting performance (2004)
18. Hoffman, H.G., Hollander, A., Schroder, K., Rousseau, S., Furness, T.: Physically touching and tasting virtual objects enhances the realism of virtual experiences. Virtual Real. **3**, 226–234 (1998). https://doi.org/10.1007/BF01408703
19. Bateman, S., Mandryk, R.L., Gutwin, C., Xiao, R.: Analysis and comparison of target assistance techniques for relative ray-cast pointing. Int. J. Hum. Comput. Stud. **71**, 511–532 (2013). https://doi.org/10.1016/j.ijhcs.2012.12.006
20. 3D Systems Phantom Premium. https://uk.3dsystems.com/haptics-devices/3d-systems-phantom-premium
21. Force Dimension - products - omega.6 - overview. http://www.forcedimension.com/products/omega-6/overview
22. HAPTION SA - Virtuose™ 6D TAO. https://www.haption.com/en/products-en/virtuose-6d-tao-en.html
23. Mastmeyer, A., Hecht, T., Fortmeier, D., Handels, H.: Ray-casting based evaluation framework for haptic force feedback during percutaneous transhepatic catheter drainage punctures. Int. J. CARS **9**, 421–431 (2014). https://doi.org/10.1007/s11548-013-0959-7

24. Trier, P., Noe, K., Sørensen, M.S., Mosegaard, J.: The visible ear surgery simulator. Stud. Health Technol. Inform. **132**, 523–525 (2008)

25. Preusche, C., Ortmaier, T., Hirzinger, G.: Teleoperation concepts in minimal invasive surgery. Control Eng. Pract. **10**, 1245–1250 (2002). https://doi.org/10.1016/S0967-0661(02)00084-9

26. Gu, X., Zhang, Y., Sun, W., Bian, Y., Zhou, D., Kristensson, P.O.: Dexmo: an inexpensive and lightweight mechanical exoskeleton for motion capture and force feedback in VR. In: Proceedings of the 2016 CHI Conference on Human Factors in Computing Systems, pp. 1991–1995. ACM (2016)

27. Culbertson, H., Walker, J.M., Raitor, M., Okamura, A.M.: WAVES: a wearable asymmetric vibration excitation system for presenting three-dimensional translation and rotation cues (2017). https://doi.org/10.1145/3025453.3025741

28. Rekimoto, J.: Traxion: a tactile interaction device with virtual force sensation. In: Proceedings of the 26th Annual ACM Symposium on User Interface Software and Technology, pp. 427–432. ACM, New York (2013). https://doi.org/10.1145/2501988.2502044

29. Lopes, P., Ion, A., Baudisch, P.: Impacto: simulating physical impact by combining tactile stimulation with electrical muscle stimulation. In: Proceedings of the 28th Annual ACM Symposium on User Interface Software & Technology, pp. 11–19. ACM, New York (2015). https://doi.org/10.1145/2807442.2807443

30. Benko, H., Holz, C., Sinclair, M., Ofek, E.: NormalTouch and TextureTouch: high-fidelity 3D haptic shape rendering on handheld virtual reality controllers. In: Proceedings of the 29th Annual Symposium on User Interface Software and Technology, pp. 717–728. ACM, New York (2016). https://doi.org/10.1145/2984511.2984526

31. Whitmire, E., Benko, H., Holz, C., Ofek, E., Sinclair, M.: Haptic revolver: touch, shear, texture, and shape rendering on a reconfigurable virtual reality controller (2018). https://doi.org/10.1145/3173574.3173660

32. Choi, I., Ofek, E., Benko, H., Sinclair, M., Holz, C.: CLAW: a multifunctional handheld haptic controller for grasping, touching, and triggering in virtual reality (2018). https://doi.org/10.1145/3173574.3174228

33. Fitts, P.M.: The information capacity of the human motor system in controlling the amplitude of movement. J. Exp. Psychol. **47**, 381–391 (1954)

34. Akamatsu, M., MacKenzie, I.S., Hasbroucq, T.: A comparison of tactile, auditory, and visual feedback in a pointing task using a mouse-type device. Ergonomics **38**, 816–827 (1995)

35. Akamatsu, M., MacKenzie, I.S.: Movement characteristics using a mouse with tactile and force feedback. Int. J. Hum. Comput. Stud. **45**, 483–493 (1996). https://doi.org/10.1006/ijhc.1996.0063

36. Cockburn, A., Brewster, S.: Multimodal feedback for the acquisition of small targets. Ergonomics **48**, 1129–1150 (2005)

37. Bhagat, K.K., Liou, W.-K., Chang, C.-Y.: A cost-effective interactive 3D virtual reality system applied to military live firing training. Virtual Real. **20**, 127–140 (2016). https://doi.org/10.1007/s10055-016-0284-x

38. Williamson, B., Wingrave, C., LaViola, J.J., Roberts, T., Garrity, P.: Natural full body interaction for navigation in dismounted soldier training. In: The Interservice/Industry Training, Simulation & Education Conference (I/ITSEC) (2011)

39. Witmer, B.C., Bailey, J.H., Knerr, B.W.: Training dismounted soldiers in virtual environments: route learning and transfer. Army Research Inst for the Behavioral and Social Sciences, Orlando, FL Orlando Field Unit (1995)

40. Harper, W.H., Ellis, P.H., Hanlon, W.E., Merkey, R.P.: The Effects of Recoil on Shooter Performance. Army Research Lab Aberdeen Proving Ground, MD (1996)

41. Shigeyama, J., et al.: Transcalibur: weight moving VR controller for dynamic rendering of 2D shape using haptic shape illusion. In: ACM SIGGRAPH 2018 Emerging Technologies, pp. 19:1–19:2. ACM, New York (2018). https://doi.org/10.1145/3214907.3214923
42. Kajiyama, H., Inoue, A., Hoshi, T.: SHAPIO: Shape I/O controller for video games. In: Proceedings of the 2015 Annual Symposium on Computer-Human Interaction in Play, pp. 565–570. ACM, New York (2015). https://doi.org/10.1145/2793107.2810318
43. Mononen, K.: The effects of augmented feedback on motor skill learning in shooting: a feedback training intervention among inexperienced rifle shooters. University of Jyväskylä (2007)
44. Rao, H.M., et al.: Sensorimotor Learning during a Marksmanship Task in Immersive Virtual Reality. Front Psychol. **9** (2018). https://doi.org/10.3389/fpsyg.2018.00058
45. Sharma, D.A., Chevidikunnan, M.F., Khan, F.R., Gaowgzeh, R.A.: Effectiveness of knowledge of result and knowledge of performance in the learning of a skilled motor activity by healthy young adults. J. Phys. Ther. Sci. **28**, 1482–1486 (2016). https://doi.org/10.1589/jpts.28.1482
46. Viitasalo, J.T., Era, P., Konttinen, N., Mononen, H., Mononen, K., Norvapalo, K.: Effects of 12-week shooting training and mode of feedback on shooting scores among novice shooters. Scand. J. Med. Sci. Sport **11**, 362–368 (2001)
47. Martel, E., Muldner, K.: Controlling VR games: control schemes and the player experience. Entertain. Comput. **21**, 19–31 (2017). https://doi.org/10.1016/j.entcom.2017.04.004
48. Koptyug, A., Ainegren, M.: Experimental measurement of rifle dynamics during the range shooting of Biathlon weapons. Procedia Eng. **112**, 349–354 (2015). https://doi.org/10.1016/j.proeng.2015.07.261
49. Hall, M.J.: Measuring felt recoil of sporting arms. Int. J. Impact Eng. **35**, 540–548 (2008). https://doi.org/10.1016/j.ijimpeng.2007.03.007
50. Canfield-Hershkowitz, B., Foster, T., Meijer, W.: Rifle and shotgun recoil test system, p. 79
51. Cleary, A.G., McKendrick, H., Sills, J.A.: Hand-arm vibration syndrome may be associated with prolonged use of vibrating computer games. BMJ **324**, 301 (2002). https://doi.org/10.1136/bmj.324.7332.301a
52. Measuring the Recoil Force from a Gun. http://www.loadstarsensors.com/blog/recoil-force-from-a-gunshot.html
53. Mathiowetz, V., Weber, K., Volland, G., Kashman, N.: Reliability and validity of grip and pinch strength evaluations. J. Hand Surg. **9**, 222–226 (1984)
54. Ahmed, T.: The effect of upper extremity fatigue on grip strength and passing accuracy in junior basketball players. J. Hum. Kinet. **37**, 71–79 (2013). https://doi.org/10.2478/hukin-2013-0027
55. Lakens, D.: Calculating and reporting effect sizes to facilitate cumulative science: a practical primer for t-tests and ANOVAs. Front. Psychol. **4** (2013). https://doi.org/10.3389/fpsyg.2013.00863
56. Faul, F., Erdfelder, E., Lang, A.-G., Buchner, A.: G*Power 3: a flexible statistical power analysis program for the social, behavioral, and biomedical sciences. Behav. Res. Methods **39**, 175–191 (2007). https://doi.org/10.3758/BF03193146
57. Vicencio-Moreira, R., Mandryk, R.L., Gutwin, C., Bateman, S.: The effectiveness (or lack thereof) of aim-assist techniques in first-person shooter games (2014). https://doi.org/10.1145/2556288.2557308
58. Kopper, R., Bowman, D.A., Silva, M.G., McMahan, R.P.: A human motor behavior model for distal pointing tasks. Int. J. Hum. Comput. Stud. **68**, 603–615 (2010). https://doi.org/10.1016/j.ijhcs.2010.05.001
59. Conover, W.J., Conover, W.J.: Practical nonparametric statistics (1980)

60. Eagleman, D.M., Holcombe, A.O.: Causality and the perception of time. Trends Cogn. Sci. **6**, 323–325 (2002). https://doi.org/10.1016/S1364-6613(02)01945-9
61. Buehner, M.J.: Contiguity and covariation in human causal inference. Learn. Behav. **33**, 230–238 (2005). https://doi.org/10.3758/BF03196065
62. Mekler, E.D., Brühlmann, F., Opwis, K., Tuch, A.N.: Disassembling gamification: the effects of points and meaning on user motivation and performance. In: CHI 2013 Extended Abstracts on Human Factors in Computing Systems, pp. 1137–1142. ACM, New York (2013). https://doi.org/10.1145/2468356.2468559
63. Jones, L.A., Tan, H.Z.: Application of psychophysical techniques to haptic research. IEEE Trans. Haptics **6**, 268–284 (2013). https://doi.org/10.1109/TOH.2012.74
64. Han, S.H., Song, M., Kwahk, J.: A systematic method for analyzing magnitude estimation data. Int. J. Ind. Ergon. **23**, 513–524 (1999). https://doi.org/10.1016/S0169-8141(98)00017-1

On the Reliability and Factorial Validity of the Assessment Scale for Creative Collaboration

Aekaterini Mavri[1]([⊠]) [iD], Andri Ioannou[2] [iD],
and Fernando Loizides[3] [iD]

[1] Cyprus Interaction Lab, Department of Multimedia and Graphic Arts,
Cyprus University of Technology, 30 Archbishop Kyprianou Street,
3036 Limassol, Cyprus
`aekaterini.mavri@gmail.com`
[2] Research Centre on Interactive Media,
Smart Systems and Emerging Technologies (RISE),
Julia House, 3 Themistokli Dervi Street, 1066 Nicosia, Cyprus
[3] School of Computer Sciences and Informatics,
Cardiff University, Cardiff CF24 3AA, UK

Abstract. Creativity, a primary objective across academic disciplines, has received considerable attention over the past few decades. While much focus has been put on the measurement of individual creativity, a notable research gap remains regarding social collaborative creativity that occurs in blended learning settings. This work offers an initial validation of the psychometric properties of a self-reported instrument, the Assessment Scale for Creative Collaboration (ASCC) that can measure learner perceptions of creative collaboration in a team within a computer-supported collaborative learning (CSCL) context. In this study, 236 undergraduate and graduate students rated the key variables of creative collaboration. Exploratory factor analysis resulted in a three-factor scale (21 items) measuring 'Synergistic Social Collaboration', 'Distributed Creativity' and 'Learning Regulation and Achievement'.. Cronbach's alphas indicated good internal consistency for the subscales. An instrument with psychometric properties for the assessment of creative collaboration is much-needed for the growing community of researchers and practitioners looking into creativity in education. It is also critical in advanced technical subjects, such as Design, HCI and Engineering, where collaboration is essential in developing innovative products.

Keywords: Creative Collaboration · Blended learning · Psychometric measure

1 Introduction and Theoretical Background

Recent decades have seen the rise of creativity as a critical element in higher education (HE). Creativity can provide a competitive advantage for today's young graduates and enhance their employment prospects as they transition into innovation-oriented digital industries [33]. Yet, the field appears significantly under-researched [5]. The bulk of present research has largely focused on organizational settings, while creativity in education, particularly in the areas of Design, HCI, and Engineering, has not been the

© IFIP International Federation for Information Processing 2019
Published by Springer Nature Switzerland AG 2019
D. Lamas et al. (Eds.): INTERACT 2019, LNCS 11746, pp. 783–792, 2019.
https://doi.org/10.1007/978-3-030-29381-9_46

focus of targeted investigation. Furthermore, collective, versus individual, creativity has yet to be robustly investigated, despite the expanding practice of sociocultural learning approaches in HE [29].

A multi-dimensional construct, creativity has always been challenging, especially in investigations seeking to identify the elements required for its effective practice and evaluation, as well as its technology-supported configurations. Research has provided a number of frameworks and models that attempt to theorize about creativity. These primarily focus on personality characteristics [41] and outcomes [15]. Various methodologies, such as the observatory [20], self-reported [27], evaluative [2, 15] and neurobiological [5] aim to capture different perspectives of the construct. Some of the assessment strategies for creativity include protocol analysis [12], purpose-specific coding for content analysis, behavior and activity-based testing [32], interaction analysis [29] and external evaluation of creative products [2, 15]. Lastly, the majority of psychometric measures, such as the 'Torrance Test of Creative Thinking' (TTCT) [30] and the 'Kaufman Domains of Creativity Scale' (K-Docs) [12], focus on individual dimensions of creativity. For collaborative endeavors, the assessment of creativity remains largely under-explored. A few studies have qualitatively observed brainstorming teams in an attempt to document collaborative creativity [23]. Others reported on distributed creativity through a computer-mediated discourse analysis approach [30]. What remains missing from the literature is an instrument aimed at the assessment of *social* creativity in education.

This work focuses on the creative collaborative processes of students in blended HE settings – especially those in highly technical fields, such as Design, HCI and Engineering, which require high levels of collaboration to develop innovative products.

As such, this study seeks to derive a psychometrically valid measure for the evaluation of participant perceptions of such group processes using an existing instrument, the Assessment Scale for Creative Collaboration (ASCC), as the main deliverable of the European-funded CoCreat Lifelong Learning Project [36]. The reliability measure for the 25 items of the instrument was reported at an earlier stage of the project; its psychometric properties had yet to be assessed.

The scale measures the principal variables of creative collaboration as perceived by team members in blended learning settings, based on underlying CSCL and creativity theories [7, 9, 10, 17]. The term refers to the collaboration processes between people across creative and other disciplines. The initial 25 items of the scale measure the creative processes that stem from ill-defined problems, which initiate cycles of imagination, divergent thinking and problem-solving that are driven by learners' interest and engagement in a task. Learners draw from prior subject-level knowledge and withstand time pressures to develop novel and appropriate outcomes.

The purpose of this study is to extend these findings by:

1. Determining the factors of ASCC and presenting its subscales' reliability.
2. Interpreting and analyzing the conceptual relationships of subscale variables, guided by background work.

In short, an instrument with psychometric properties for the assessment of creative collaboration—so as to be able to research creativity in HE—is both needed and not yet in place. The process for its development is described in the following sections.

2 Methodology

2.1 Instrumentation

The ASCC questionnaire uses a 7-point Likert scale and aims to elicit information about key concepts of creative collaboration in CSCL settings. It employs the term 'creative collaboration' based on multiple CSCL theories. The 25 questionnaire items prompt for divergent thinking, domain-level knowledge, critical thinking, response to real-life problems, social aspects of co-present and distant collaboration, conceptual factors of interest and engagement in collaboration, individual and joint time-management, learning regulation and time pressure.

2.2 Participants

The ASCC was completed by a total of 236 international undergraduate and graduate students who had prior experience of collaborative projects. The sample falls within the fair-to-good range of roughly 10 observations per item [24]. Students were asked to complete the questionnaire based on their most recent collaborative project experience.

2.3 Parallel Analysis (PA)

To define the statistically significant factors (eigenvalues) to be extracted, we first conducted Parallel Analysis (PA). Both PA and scree plot suggested a three-factor structure for the 25 items of the ASCC, which also matched the eigenvalue of >1 criterion.

2.4 Exploratory Factor Analysis (EFA)

Descriptive statistics presented an average range of item means of 4,26–5,92 (M = 5,29) and adequate diversity in opinions (SD = 1,46). EFA was conducted, using the Principal Axis Factor (PAF) extraction method as well as an Oblimin Oblique rotation method (delta = 0) on the ASCC's variables, which were expected to be correlated - a typical phenomenon in social studies. The Kaiser-Meyer-Olkin measure of sampling adequacy was found to be of an optimal value of ,913. The Bartlett's test of sphericity, reporting on the homogeneity of the correlation matrix [30], was found to be significant (χ^2 (300) = 3117,52 p < .001). The three factors obtained accounted for 47,28% of the total variance in the ASCC variables. Extracted factor eigenvalues and respective total variance percentages were as follows: Factor 1 = 9,084 and 36,33%, Factor 2 = 1,672 and 6,68%, Factor 3 = 1,065 and 4,26%.

A within variables approach indicated that the variables have a moderate to high level of common variance based on the extracted communality values: >.5 accounted for the 48%, >.4 accounted for the 40% and the rest for values of <4. The rotated pattern matrix (pattern coefficients) results indicated an initial set of eleven variables for Factor 1, seven variables for Factor 2, and seven variables for Factor 3. We retained variables with the following criteria: (a) a pattern coefficient of 0,4 and above and (b) significant differences in cross-loading values (approximately ≥ 0,20) [21].

Table 1. Scale dimensions, descriptions and individual items

Dimension 1	Synergistic social collaboration	Theoretical origin
A 9-item subscale that assesses social collaborative learning and the conceptual variables of interest and emotional factors such as belonging, mutuality and trust		
Group interest in the task	1. Everyone in our group was interested in the task	Interest
Trust between participants	2. Classmates/colleagues in my group trust each other	Social collaborative learning
Orientation towards the task	3. Everyone in my group wanted to make a successful product	Interest
Safe atmosphere	4. We had a feeling of belonging together	Social collaborative learning
Communication	5. We were all able to express our ideas, even controversial ones, freely	Creativity
Discussion of ideas	6. We were able to share and discuss our ideas with each other	Creative collaboration
Level of collaboration	7. We understood each other's viewpoints at the start of the project	Social collaborative learning
Adequate knowledge base	8. Our group had the necessary knowledge to be able to complete our task	Social collaborative learning
Shared knowledge and goals	9. I had a good idea of what the others in my group knew that is relevant to this activity	Interest
Dimension 2	Distributed creativity	Theoretical origin
A 7-item subscale that assesses collective divergent thinking and externalization, the degree of tension and perceived co-presence in distant teams		
Problem boundaries stretched or broken	10. We weren't always certain about how to carry out the task which led us to explore different possibilities	Creativity
A degree of disagreement or tension	11. We sometimes disagreed, but we discussed our different points of view	Creativity
Group-based time pressure	12. My group was pressured to complete in time	Time pressure
Degree of co-presence (formally - text based)	13. We were able to share information between group members e.g. via a wiki or shared document	Interest
Possibilities for externalizing representations	14. We could see or find out what other people knew or were thinking about. For example, we could draw, write or build things on the computer that the other group members could see and/or read	Creativity
Degree of co-presence (informally - SN)	15. We were able to chat informally with the other group members via text or social networking	Interest
Level of divergent thinking	16. My group generated diverse and novel ideas in response to the task	Creativity
Dimension 3	Time regulation and achievement	Theoretical origin
A 5-item subscale assesses the degree of individual and collective time-management as components of learning regulation and achievement		
Stretching boundaries	17. We went beyond the set task.	Creativity
Group-level time management	18. Our group organized our time for learning well	Time management
Individual time management	19. I organized my time for learning well	Time management
Emotional expression	20. The set task/activity enabled us to express our emotions.	Social Collaborative achievement
Level of imagination	21. Between us we used a lot of imagination	Creativity

Qualitative judgements about the retention of variables were made during post-PAF-processing. With the exception of items 2, 4 and 7 in Factor 1, the rest cross-loaded on other factors, but were maintained due to their compliance with retention criterion (b). Factor 2 loaded with a total of seven items. Item 16 failed the retention criteria, but was retained due to its critical conceptual significance related to divergent thinking. Factor 3 loaded with a total of seven items, out of which two did not match retention criteria and were thus dropped from the instrument. Factor 3 resulted in a total of five variables (see Table 1).

2.5   Reliability Analysis

Following FA, we proceeded to investigate the three subscales' internal consistency reliability and expected the following: (a) a Cronbach's alpha coefficient minimum of $\alpha = 0,70$ for the subscales [6] (the minimum value of 0,7 is acceptable for newly developed scales [16]), (b) Inter-item correlations ranges of 0,3 and 0,7 to indicate homogeneity but no redundancy [25], (c) small inter-item correlations standard deviation, preferably $\leq.1$ [25] and finally, (d) a minimum value of 0,4–0,75 for corrected item-to-totals as indicated in the item-total statistics results [21]. These are presented in Table 2, while individual reliability results for each sub-scale are outlined in the following three sections.

Table 2. Initial Reliability Statistics for the ASCC Subscales (N = 236)

	Cronbach's alpha	Mean inter-item correlations	SD of inter-item correlations	No. of items
Factor 1	,924	,695	0,01	11
Updated*	,893*	,654*	0,00*	9*
Factor 2	,778	,505	0,01	7
Factor 3	,758	,529	0,01	5

Subscale 1. This subscale presented an optimal level of internal consistency at $\alpha = ,92$ [6]. Most items fell within the inter-item-correlation ranges, apart from three items, which were above the value of 0,7. A closer examination in conjunction with the item-to-total correlation results, indicated that two out of three were far higher than the recommended upper limit and were therefore deleted. Item 1 was retained as a key conceptual variable of 'interest' within the subscale. A second reliability analysis, resulted in a lower (updated*), but still high, Cronbach's value of $\alpha = ,89$ (see Table 2).

Subscale 2. Reliability analysis of its seven items concluded an acceptable value of Cronbach's $\alpha = ,77$ (see Table 2). This subscale presented an item (12) that failed to meet the minimum criteria, in a few of the inter-item-correlation ranges. Based on the fact that it measures 'time pressure', a key conceptual element inherently linked to creativity and collaboration, the variable was retained.

Subscale 3. Reliability analysis of the subscale's five items concluded an acceptable Cronbach's value of $\alpha = ,76$ (see Table 2). Item 20 scored just below the minimum value of 0,3 in the inter-item-correlation matrix (0,29). It was nevertheless retained in the subscale due to its critical theoretical significance (see Table 1). As all subscale coefficients resulted in high alpha values ($\alpha \geq ,70$), the scale presents high internal consistency.

3   Discussion

This work undertook an initial validation of ASCC in response to an increasing need for instruments to assess collaborative creativity in HE team-work settings. EFA resulted in a three-factor scale, with a total of 21 items measuring 'Synergistic Social Collaboration', 'Distributed Creativity' and 'Time Regulation and Achievement'.

3.1   Subscale 1: Synergistic Social Collaboration

The choice of term for this subscale relies on the role of synergy amongst collaborative team members in the production of greater results than the sum of separate individual parts. It comprises concepts related to both co-present computer-supported, as well as distant collaborative learning (CSCL) [11, 22]. The first subscale includes 11 items and addresses all co-present, physical, computer supported and distant collaborative learning (CSCL). It includes a number of affective variables, such as the sense of belonging, mutuality and trust between participants, as well as cognitive variables such as the ability to develop a shared understanding of individual viewpoints within a group (see Table 1).

The persistent recurrence of interest as an intrinsic motivational variable is anticipated, as it appears strongly intertwined with literature on collaborative learning and creativity. With both affective as well as cognitive traits, the construct of interest and engagement is linked to conceptualizations about one's self as well as the social, physical, and conceptual environment (i.e. 'Shared knowledge and goals') [34]. It is an intrinsic component of task-value derived from the Expectancy-Value theory. It also acts as a motivation for, and expectation of, success in performing a task i.e. 'Orientation towards task success' [35]. This is supported by the high correlation value between the two variables, 'Group engagement' and 'Task Success' (r = ,664).

Further theoretical associations confirm the structure of this subscale. For example, as interest and engagement grow, learners and collaborators in a field become naturally more inquisitive and explorative ('Discussion of early ideas') leading to further generation and analysis of ideas. The 'Discussion of early ideas' is evidently a significant stage in both collaborative and creative learning processes and it is also highly correlated to 'Group Engagement' (r = ,558) in the subscale. The ASCC report posits that this variable, typically related to brainstorming activities, is explicitly linked to Collaborative creativity literature [19]. Similarly, 'Adequate knowledge base' is regularly encountered across theoretical domains. Sufficient level of domain knowledge is projected by Amabile [2] in her componential theory of creativity and is also a primary variable in social constructivism as a precursor to higher-level cognitive functions in collaborative learning. Prior knowledge is also strongly connected to interest and engagement in this subscale (r = ,550) and across the literature [18].

3.2   Subscale 2: Distributed Creativity

Drawing from Sawyer's and DeZutter's [29] definition, this seven-item subscale is labeled 'Distributed Creativity', as the majority of its variables relate to this concept. Creativity is presented in the form of original ideas or products of the team-driven 'Level of divergent thinking', which are deemed suitable for a purpose (i.e. 'My group generated different and novel ideas in response to the task'). This type of collective creativity is heightened in response to ill-defined problems that lack explicit directions ('Problem boundaries stretched or broken'). Furthermore, a moderate 'Degree of disagreement and tension' within a respectful and trusting context is a positive precursor to collective novelty in ideas. This is supported in the correlation value between these two variables (r = ,452). A 'Degree of disagreement or tension' in the form of argumentative exchange can also enforce reflective reasoning during a collective creative task [36]. Tension in itself denotes evidence of engagement and interest, which is also found in the form of 'Degree of co-presence' (formal/informal and offline/online) in the subscale.

Another point of interest is the positive relationship between time pressure, and creativity, which is evident in the subscale. This relationship appears to work in opposite ways in the literature. Studies have shown that working under pressure impedes creativity by leading participants to choose safer options, rather than the more exploratory or time-consuming [1]. That said, working with mild-to-moderate time pressure, as a "challenge stressor" [28] can be beneficial, reportedly triggering creative effort and motivation. Apart from the high inter-item correlations in 'Degree of co-presence' (r = ,544), these variables correlate with 'Externalizing representations' (r = ,473), the latter of which is also highly correlated with 'Level of divergent thinking' (r = ,476), presenting the second-highest correlation in the sub-scale. The link between creativity and externalization in social collaboration is key, particularly in the domains of Design and Engineering.

The process of using physical or digital artefacts such as paper sketches, texts or 3D-prototypes to portray thoughts on to tangible objects is used for communicative, coordinative, explorative and reflective creative activity [38]. These require a high degree of co-presence amongst team members, which is made evident through the subscale's high inter-item correlation structure between the two variables.

Finally, 'Group-based time pressure' and 'Stretching problem boundaries' present high inter-item correlations (r = ,463). The latter correlates well with the 'Degree of disagreement or tension' (r = ,443). We note that 'Stretching problem boundaries' refers to the exploration of different possibilities, as opposed to 'Stretching boundaries' in subscale 3, which suggests going beyond or improving upon the expected quality of the assigned deliverable.

3.3 Subscale 3: Time Regulation and Achievement

This factor's name draws from the inherent interaction between learning regulation (encompassing time regulation) and achievement, based on relevant literature [26]. It consists of five items. 'Individual' and 'Group-level time management' carry—as expected—high inter-item correlation (r = ,636) in the subscale. The literature indicates that time-management is a primary component of learning regulation [26, 31] and reports on its three components, namely, self-regulation, co-regulation (pairs) and "socially shared regulation" [13] (teams). Shared learning regulation, in terms of time and effort, concerns tactics that are implemented according to a plan, so as to increase learning gains (self) or attain a collective target.

Additionally, the relationship between self/collective regulation ('Group time-management'), efficacy and creative achievement ('Stretching boundaries') is well documented in behavioral studies [26]. Bandura [4] states that an understanding of one's abilities, as well as "being purposive" towards an end goal is what leads to drafting and following a systematic learning action plan to the point of completing or going beyond the end goal ('We went beyond the task'). These two variables bear positive inter-correlations in the subscale (r = ,463). Imagination, a factor synonymous with divergent thinking, is also highly correlated with 'Stretching boundaries' and 'Group time management' (r = ,435). The literature denotes that creative individuals consciously seek to regulate their practices to produce novel outcomes [37].

'Emotional expression' also relates to conceptions of regulated learning as a means of commitment and orientation towards an end goal. The term has a positive correlation with achievement ('Boundaries stretched') in the subscale (r = ,334). It is also supported by the literature [28], which widely agrees that collaboration built on socio-emotional spaces that foster inter-connectedness amongst participants enhances creativity. Conversely, negative emotional load stemming from a distrustful or restrictive atmosphere hinders expression and generates poor creative outcomes.

4 Conclusion

An instrument with psychometric properties that can assess creative collaboration is much-needed in the growing community of researchers focusing on creativity in higher education. This is especially important in the educational areas of Design, HCI and Engineering, where collaboration is key to produce innovative outcomes. The ASCC, a self-reported questionnaire, is designed to measure the perceived creative collaboration amongst teams working in blended learning settings. The objective of this study was to examine the ASCC's psychometric properties by (i) determining its subscales and presenting their reliability value and (ii) interpreting and analyzing the relationships of the subscale variables, guided by conceptual groundings from earlier work. Factor analysis resulted in a three-factor structure (21 items), namely, 'Synergistic Social Collaboration' (9 items), 'Distributed Creativity' (7 items), and 'Time Regulation and Achievement' (5 items), all bearing good reliability values. Future improvements could focus on using a Confirmatory Factor Analysis to provide additional validity for the ASCC instrument.

References

1. Amabile, T.M., et al.: Creativity under the gun. Harvard Bus. Rev. **80**, 52–63 (2002)
2. Amabile, T.M.: Social psychology of creativity: a consensual assessment technique. J. Pers. Soc. Psychol. **43**(5), 997 (1982)
3. Amabile, T.M., Pillemer, J.: Perspectives on the social psychology of creativity. J. Creative Behav. **46**(1), 3–15 (2012)
4. Bandura, A.: Social cognitive theory of self-regulation. Organ. Behav. Hum. Decis. Process. **50**(2), 248–287 (1991)
5. Batey, M.: The measurement of creativity: from definitional consensus to the introduction of a new heuristic framework. Creativity Res. J. **24**(1), 55–65 (2012)
6. Cronbach, L.J.: Coefficient alpha and the internal structure of tests. Psychometrika **16**(3), 297–334 (1951)
7. Dillenbourg, P., et al.: The evolution of research on computer-supported collaborative learning. In: Balacheff, N., Ludvigsen, S., de Jong, T., Lazonder, A., Barnes, S. (eds.) Technology-Enhanced Learning, pp. 3–19. Springer, Dordrecht (2009). https://doi.org/10.1007/978-1-4020-9827-7_1
8. Eccles, J.: Expectancies, values and academic behaviors. In: Presented at the Achievement and Achievement Motives: Psychological and Sociological Approaches, San Francisco (1983)
9. Ferrari, A., et al.: 23. ICT as a driver for creative learning and innovative teaching. In: Measuring Creativity, p. 345 (2009)
10. Fischer, G., Shipman, F.: Collaborative design rationale and social creativity in cultures of participation. In: Carroll, J. (ed.) Creativity and Rationale, pp. 423–447. Springer, London (2013). https://doi.org/10.1007/978-1-4471-4111-2_20
11. Gaggioli, A., et al.: The creative link: investigating the relationship between social network indices, creative performance and flow in blended teams. Comput. Hum. Behav. **42**, 157–166 (2015)
12. Gero, J., Kan, J.: Empirical results from measuring design creativity: use of an augmented coding scheme in protocol analysis. In: DS86: Proceedings of the Fourth International Conference on Design Creativity. Georgia Institute of Technology, Atlanta (2016)
13. Hadwin, D.H., et al.: Handbook of Self-regulation of Learning and Performance. Taylor & Francis, New York (2011)
14. Hirst, G., et al.: A cross-level perspective on employee creativity: goal orientation, team learning behavior, and individual creativity. Acad. Manag. J. **52**(2), 280–293 (2009)
15. Horn, D., Salvendy, G.: Product creativity: conceptual model, measurement and characteristics. Theor. Issues Ergon. Sci. **7**(4), 395–412 (2006)
16. Lance, C.E., et al.: The sources of four commonly reported cutoff criteria: what did they really say? Organ. Res. Methods **9**(2), 202–220 (2006). https://doi.org/10.1177/1094428105284919
17. Lew, K.H., et al.: The relationship among creativity thinking ability, creative personality and creative product. Adv. Sci. Technol. Lett. **36**, 58–62 (2013)
18. Linnenbrink-Garcia, L., et al.: Developing conceptual understanding of natural selection: the role of interest, efficacy, and basic prior knowledge. J. Exp. Educ. **80**(1), 45–68 (2012)
19. Mamykina, L., et al.: Collaborative creativity. Commun. ACM **45**(10), 96–99 (2002)
20. Meneely, J., Portillo, M.: The adaptable mind in design: relating personality, cognitive style, and creative performance. Creativity Res. J. **17**(2–3), 155–166 (2005)
21. Netemeyer, R.G., et al.: Scaling Procedures: Issues and Applications. Sage Publications, Thousand Oaks (2003)

22. Paulus, P.B., et al.: Collaborative creativity—group creativity and team innovation. In: Handbook of Organizational Creativity, pp. 327–357. Elsevier (2012)
23. Paulus, P.B., Nijstad, B.A.: Group Creativity: Innovation Through Collaboration. Oxford University Press, New York (2003)
24. Pearson, R.H., Mundform, D.J.: Recommended sample size for conducting exploratory factor analysis on dichotomous data. J. Modern Appl. Stat. Methods **9**(2), 359–368 (2010). https://doi.org/10.22237/jmasm/1288584240
25. Pett, M.A., et al.: Making Sense of Factor Analysis: the Use of Factor Analysis for Instrument Development in Health Care Research. Sage, Thousand Oaks (2003)
26. Pintrich, P.R.: A conceptual framework for assessing motivation and self-regulated learning in college students. Educ. Psychol. Rev. **16**(4), 385–407 (2004). https://doi.org/10.1007/s10648-004-0006-x
27. Plucker, J.A., Renzulli, J.S.: Psychometric approaches to the study of human creativity. In: Handbook of Creativity, pp. 35–61 (1999)
28. Prem, R., et al.: Thriving on challenge stressors? Exploring time pressure and learning demands as antecedents of thriving at work. J. Organ. Behav. **38**(1), 108–123 (2017). https://doi.org/10.1002/job.2115
29. Sawyer, R.K., DeZutter, S.: Distributed creativity: how collective creations emerge from collaboration. Psychol. Aesthetics Creativity Arts. **3**(2), 81 (2009)
30. Scott, T.J.: Distributed affect as a framework for understanding creative collaboration. In: Proceedings of the 2015 ACM SIGCHI Conference on Creativity and Cognition, pp. 335–336 ACM, New York (2015). https://doi.org/10.1145/2757226.2764768
31. Stoeger, H., Ziegler, A.: Evaluation of a classroom based training to improve self-regulation in time management tasks during homework activities with fourth graders. Metacognit. Learn. **3**(3), 207–230 (2008). https://doi.org/10.1007/s11409-008-9027-z
32. Torrance, E.P.: Torrance tests of creative thinking: norms-technical manual research edition. In: Verbal Tests, Forms A and B: Figural Tests, Forms A and B. Flere materialer. Personell Press (1966)
33. Turbot, S.: Is higher education equipping young people for the jobs market? https://www.weforum.org/agenda/2015/06/is-higher-education-equipping-young-people-for-the-jobs-market/
34. Wentzel, K.R., Miele, D.B.: Handbook of Motivation at School. Routledge, London (2009)
35. Wigfield, A., Eccles, J.S.: Expectancy–value theory of achievement motivation. Contemp. Educ. Psychol. **25**(1), 68–81 (2000)
36. Wishart, J., et al.: CoCreat Research Plan. Internal report of the CoCreat project (2011)
37. Zampetakis, L.A., et al.: On the relationship between individual creativity and time management. Thinking Skills Creativity **5**(1), 23–32 (2010). https://doi.org/10.1016/j.tsc.2009.12.001
38. Zurita, G., et al.: Introducing a collaborative tool supporting a learning activity involving creativity with rotation of group members. J. UCS **22**(10), 1360–1379 (2016)

Author Index

Printed in the United States
By Bookmasters